Vermont

Vermont

Christina Tree and Diane E. Foulds

The Countryman Press * Woodstock, Vermont

ELEVENTH EDITION

DEDICATION

In memory of Peter Jennison, Vermonter extraordinaire, founder of
The Countryman Press, and longtime coauthor of this book.

In memory of Ray Foulds.

We welcome your comments and suggestions. Please contact Explorer's Guide
Editor, The Countryman Press, P.O. Box 748, Woodstock, Vermont 05091, or
e-mail countrymanpress@wwnorton.com.

ISBN-10: 0-88150-711-3
ISBN-13: 978-0-88150-711-9
ISSN 1523-9462

Maps by Moore Creative Design, © 2006 The Countryman Press
Cover and interior design by Bodenweber Design
Text composition by PerfecType, Nashville, TN
Cover photograph of Jenne Farm near Reading © James Randklev

Published by The Countryman Press, P.O. Box 748, Woodstock, Vermont 05091

Distributed by W. W. Norton & Company, Inc., 500 Fifth Avenue, New York,
NY 10110

Printed in the United States of America

10 9 8 7 6 5 4 3 2 1

EXPLORE WITH US!

We have been fine-tuning *Vermont: An Explorer's Guide* for the past 23 years, a period in which lodging, dining, and shopping opportunities have more than quadrupled in the state. As we have expanded our guide, we have also been increasingly selective, making recommendations based on years of conscientious research and personal experience. What makes us unique is that we describe the state by locally defined regions, giving you Vermont's communities, not simply its most popular destinations. With this guide you'll feel confident to venture beyond the tourist towns, along roads less traveled, to places of special hospitality and charm.

WHAT'S WHERE

In the beginning of the book you'll find an alphabetical listing of special highlights, with important information and advice on everything from antiques to weather reports.

LODGING

Prices. Please don't hold us or the respective innkeepers responsible for the rates listed as of press time in 2006. Some changes are inevitable. **We do not include the 9 percent state room and meals tax in rates unless stated.** Many lodging establishments also add a gratuity to their listed rate, something we try to note but do not always catch. It's best to check ahead of time.

    Smoking. State law bars smoking in all places of public accommodation in Vermont, including restaurants and bars.

RESTAURANTS

Note the distinction between *Dining Out* and *Eating Out*. By their nature, restaurants listed in the *Eating Out* group are generally inexpensive.

KEY TO SYMBOLS

- ∞ **Weddings**. The wedding-ring symbol appears beside establishments that frequently serve as venues for weddings and civil unions.
- ✿ **Special value**. The special-value symbol appears next to lodging and restaurants that combine high quality and moderate prices.
- 🐾 **Pets**. The dog-paw symbol appears next to lodgings that accept pets (usually with a reservation and deposit) as of press time.
- ✐ **Child-friendly**. The kids-alert symbol appears next to lodging, restaurants, activities, and shops of special appeal to youngsters.
- ♿ **Handicapped access**. The wheelchair symbol appears next to lodging, restaurants, and attractions that are partially or fully handicapped accessible.

We would appreciate your comments and corrections about places you visit or know well in the state. Please e-mail Chris: ctree@traveltree.net.

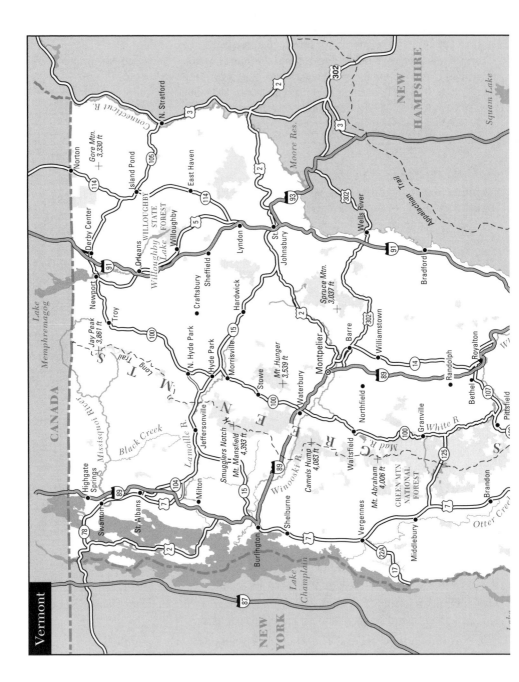

Vermont

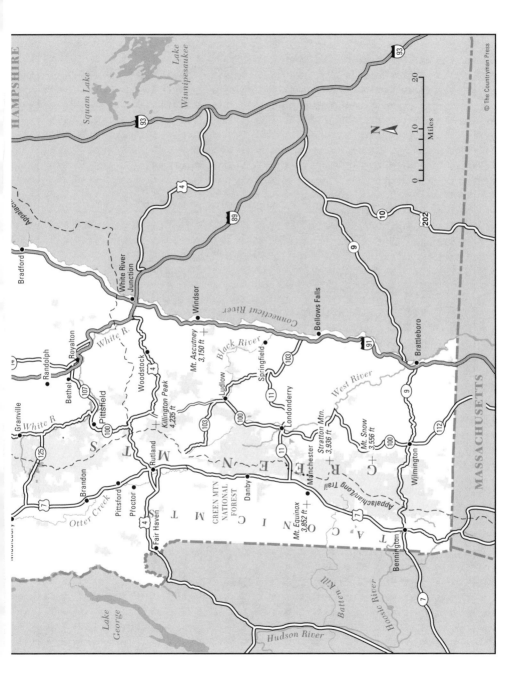

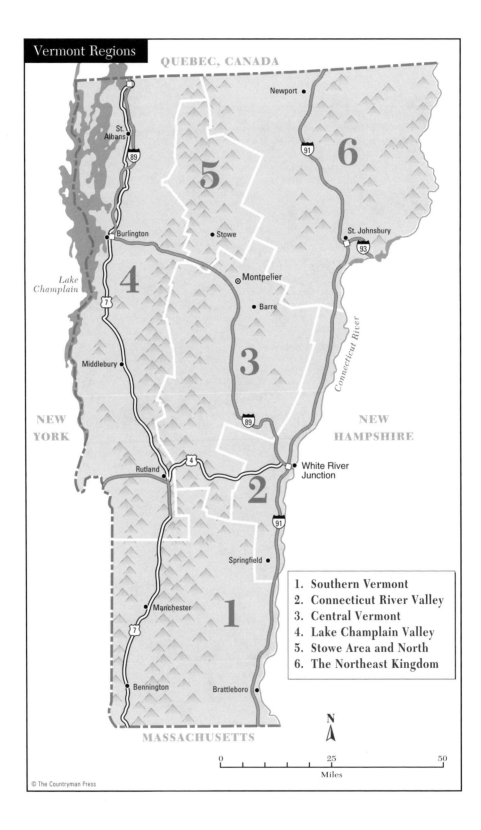

Vermont Regions

QUEBEC, CANADA

Newport

St. Albans

89

Burlington

Lake Champlain

7

4

Middlebury

NEW YORK

Rutland

4

Manchester

7

Bennington

5

Stowe

Montpelier

Barre

3

89

White River Junction

2

91

Springfield

1

Brattleboro

MASSACHUSETTS

91

St. Johnsbury

93

6

Connecticut River

NEW HAMPSHIRE

1. Southern Vermont
2. Connecticut River Valley
3. Central Vermont
4. Lake Champlain Valley
5. Stowe Area and North
6. The Northeast Kingdom

N

0   25   50
Miles

© The Countryman Press

CONTENTS

INTRODUCTION

Welcome to the Green Mountain State and this 11th edition of the most comprehensive guide to its distinctive landscape, character, and places to see and stay. No other portrait of Vermont gathers so much practical information between two covers—so much that even Vermonters find it useful.

We have divided the guide into generally accepted regions. Each section begins with a verbal snapshot of the area against a historical background, and includes descriptions of just about every legal form of recreation, from skiing and swimming to llama trekking and whitewater rafting.

We describe roughly two-thirds of Vermont's inns, B&Bs, farm stays, and family-owned (but not chain) motels. We are candid about what we like and don't like. We visit regularly and we describe many reasonably priced gems found in no other book.

We critique upscale restaurants (*Dining Out*) and everyday options (*Eating Out*), plus good delis, bakeries, and coffeehouses. Local entertainment, interesting shops, and special events round out coverage of virtually every city and town, and most villages.

In winter visitors converge at alpine resorts and areas known for cross-country skiing. On fall foliage weekends the traffic quadruples, and visitors without reservations are lucky if they can find a spare bedroom. At that time of year it's best to come midweek—preferably with reservations, and this book. Vermont invented "foliage season," and it has been promoting this drive-through spectacle ever since. In the process it has developed more facilities (see *Foliage* in "What's Where") for lodging "leaf-peepers" at peak periods than have other New England states.

Ironically, Vermont's fame as an autumn and winter destination has upstaged its original tourist season. Vermont's summer is soft, still, and deep, almost secretive. While traffic jams New England's coastal resorts, Vermont's roads and widely scattered lodgings remain blissfully quiet. Wooded paths and swimming holes are never far but rarely obvious.

Whatever the season, this book is about exploring beyond highways and tourist routes. Mud season aside, Vermont is best viewed from its vast network of unpaved roads. Whether it's a cross-country ski network or crafts studio, a farm or B&B, a waterfall, covered bridge, or corn maze, our intent is to lure you into as well as around the state.

A NOTE ON LODGING LISTINGS

We do not charge innkeepers to be included in this book. It's worth noting that some guides do impose a "processing fee" in order to be included. Within this edition we supply hundreds of web sites, but we feel strongly that the Internet has increased rather than obviated the need for an honest, opinionated guidebook based on actual snooping around rather than virtual research. This is the best search engine to visiting Vermont, but it's also much more: a combination of critical, current sleuthing and a sense of how to convey what's out there, based on decades of exploring and describing the Green Mountain State.

Contrary to its image, Vermont's landscape varies substantially from north to south and even more from east to west. Rather than following the main tourist routes (east–west Rts. 9 and 4 and north–south Rt. 100), we suggest that (weather permitting) you drive the dramatic but well-paved "gap" roads (see *Gaps, Gulfs, and Gorges* in "What's Where") east or west across the state's relatively narrow width, bundling very different landscapes—mountain valleys and the broad sweep of farmland along Lake Champlain—into a few hours' drive.

While focusing on all the state's regions through the same lens (our format), we fervently hope that this book conveys the full spectrum of Vermont's beauty: the river roads of the Upper Valley, the high rolling farmland around Tunbridge and Chelsea, the glacially carved, haunting hills of the Northeast Kingdom, and the limestone farmsteads of Isle La Motte. Villages range from the elegant, gentrified resorts such as Stowe, Woodstock, and Manchester, to the equally proud but far less traveled villages of Craftsbury Common, Grafton, and Newfane, and the Victorian brick streetscapes of Brattleboro and Burlington.

Despite the inevitable inroads of today's shopping-center culture, Vermont has mostly preserved the genuine rural character for which countless urbanites and suburbanites hunger. Currently, for every acre of open land paved for a parking lot, at least 10 acres are added to the holdings of the Vermont Land Trust, therefore shielded from development. The administrators of Act 250, the state's pioneering land-use program, also still exercise sensible controls over new commercial development, defeating sporadic efforts to dilute the act's provisions. Vermonters, prudently and in a spirit of thrift, have been loath to tear down the past. Abandoned farmhouses have been restored, and in a score of towns adaptive preservation techniques have been thoughtfully applied.

Vermont has never been a "rich" state. Except for machine tools, the industrial revolution passed it by; as one political scientist noted, Vermonters leaped from "cow chips to microchips." Nevertheless, at least a few 19th-century families made their fortunes from lumber, wool, marble, and railroads. The 14 years that it existed as a sovereign nation (between 1777 and 1791) stamped Vermont with a certain contrariness. Many examples of its free spirit animate its subsequent history, from the years when Ethan Allen's Rabelaisian Green Mountain Boys wrested independence from the grip of Hampshiremen, 'Yorkers, and "The

TOURISM IN VERMONT

Contrary to common belief, tourism (for lack of a better word to describe the phenomenon of visitors "from away") is an integral part of Vermont's history, one that has affected its landscape—not just since the '50s but for 150 years.

Before the Civil War, southerners patronized mineral spas in every part of the Green Mountain State, from Brattleboro to Brunswick Springs. You can still see glimpses of these antique establishments in such off-the-beaten-track places as Clarendon Springs. After the war, Vermont's burgeoning railroads teamed up with the state's Board of Agriculture to promote farm vacations. Railroad guides also promoted Newport, with its elegant four-story Lake Memphremagog House ("one of the largest and finest hotels in New England"), and Lake Willoughby ("one of the most remarkable places in the continent"). Carriage roads were built to the top of Jay Peak, Mount Mansfield, and Mount Equinox, and of course there was a summit hotel atop Mount Mansfield (the highest peak in the state) as well as a large hotel beside the Green Mountain Inn in Stowe Village.

In the 1850s the Equinox House was recognized as one of New England's leading hotels. By 1862 the *Manchester Journal* could report that the previous summer, "Every house in the village was as full as a 'Third Avenue car,' almost entirely New Yorkers." Woodstock was equally well known in the right Manhattan circles by the 1890s.

All 19th- and early-20th-century visitors arrived by train (the exception being those who crossed Lake Champlain by ferry), and Vermont was slower than many other states to provide roads suitable to touring. The flood of 1927 washed out a number of major highways and bridges. In 1936 a proposal for building a federally funded, 260-mile Green Mountain Parkway the length of the state—passing just below the crests of Pico, Killington, and several other peaks—was roundly defeated in a public referendum.

After World War II, however, Vermont launched what may be the world's first and most successful campaign to turn off-season into peak season.

"If you can pick and choose, there is no better time for a motor trip through Vermont than in autumn," Abner W. Coleman wrote in the first issue of *Vermont Life*, a state publication. The autumn 1946 article continued: "To the color photographer, Vermont during the autumn months offers delights indescribable. Should film become more plentiful this year, hundreds of cam-

Cruel Minestereal Tools of George ye 3d" to their quashing of British attempts to retake the Champlain Corridor. This autonomous spirit was later responsible for the abolitionist fervor that swept the state in the years before the Civil War and impelled Vermonters to enlist in record numbers when President Lincoln appealed for troops. Vermonters voted their consciences with much the same

era enthusiasts will be roaming around these hills, knocking themselves out in a happy frenzy of artistic endeavor. For the autumn woods run the entire spectrum's course, from the blazing reds of the maple through the pale yellows of beech and birch to the violet of far-off mountain walls." The story was illustrated with the first of many vividly hued photos for which *Vermont Life* remains famous.

While Vermonters can't claim to have invented skiing, the state does boast America's oldest ski resorts. In the 1930s skiers began riding rope tows up slopes in Woodstock, at Pico, and on Mount Mansfield; after World War II Stowe became "Ski Capital of the East." Patrons at Mad River Glen built the country's first slope-side lodging, and in the early '60s nearby Sugarbush opened with the East's first bottom-of-the-lifts village. In ensuing decades more than a dozen Vermont ski areas have evolved into year-round resorts, several (Stowe, Sugarbush, and Killington) spawning full-fledged communities. Stowe and Warren were towns before they were resorts.

Vermont's ski communities mirror (in reverse) the story of its mill towns. Whereas mills were positioned on waterfalls—and no longer need the water to generate power—ski resorts have grown around mountains chosen for their good terrain and "dependable" snowfall. Only in recent years has it become apparent that access to enough water—to make snow—is crucial.

The question of whether skiing or any other manifestation of "tourism" (again that inadequate term) contributes to the preservation or destruction of the Vermont character and landscape can be argued interminably. But the fact is that it has been here for 150 years. Today Vermont inns and B&Bs outnumber farms, and Vermont visitors outnumber cows.

Today's visitor is more likely than not to be welcomed by ex-visitors: More than 40 percent of the state's population of 619,107 has come "from away," a post–World War II phenomenon that has profoundly affected the cultural and political landscapes.

Much has been made of the proverbial "Vermont mystique," that indefinable quality of life and character. It is, we are happy to report, alive and well, especially along the back roads and in villages and hamlets where "neighboring" still reigns. While the portrait of the legendary Vermont Yankee—frugal, wary, taciturn, sardonic—has faded somewhat in today's homogenized culture, independent-minded Vermonters (many of them ex-"tourists") take care of each other, tolerate eccentricities, and regard the world with a healthy skepticism.

zeal when, in both world wars, the legislature declared war on Germany, in effect, before the United States did. More recently Vermont was the first state to legalize civil unions between same-sex couples. It boasts one of the nation's highest percentages of women in the legislature and a strict environmental policy, and is always prepared—if push comes to shove—to secede.

The Authors

A flatland author, born in Hawaii, raised in New York City, and living near Boston, Chris Tree claims to be a professional Vermont visitor. Her infatuation with the state began in college.

"The college was in Massachusetts, but one of my classmates was a native Vermonter whose father ran a general store and whose mother knows the name of every flower, bird, and mushroom. I jumped at her invitations to come 'home' or to 'camp' and have since spent far more time in Vermont than has my friend. As a travel writer for the *Boston Globe*, I have spent more than 35 years writing newspaper stories about Vermont towns, inns, ski areas, and people. I interviewed John Kenneth Galbraith about Newfane, Pearl Buck about Danby. I rode the Vermont Bicentennial Train, froze a toe on one of the first inn-to-inn ski treks, camped on the Long Trail and in state parks, paddled a canoe down the Connecticut, slid over Lake Champlain on an iceboat as well as paddling it in a kayak, soared over the Mad River Valley in a glider, and hovered above the Upper Valley in a hot-air balloon. I have also tramped through the woods collecting sap, ridden many miles with Vermont Transit, led a foliage tour, collided with a tractor, and broken down in a variety of places."

Research for this edition represents the 11th time that Chris has combed regions around the Green Mountain State, traveling back roads to check out B&Bs, craftspeople, cheesemakers, and (yes!) swimming holes. It all seems to take longer than it once did, perhaps because there's more to talk about along the way. Vermont is as much about people as landscape, and both welcome an old friend.

Diane Foulds is an eighth-generation Vermonter. Her father was a forester whose frequent travels took her to some of the state's remotest corners. She remembers gazing unseeing from the backseat of the family car, absorbed in childhood fantasies, barely aware of the scenery whizzing by.

After graduating from the University of Vermont with degrees in Russian studies and French, she left for Europe, a hiatus that lasted 20 years. She spent the time interpreting, guiding tours, and working with refugees. In Vienna she took up writing, first for the BBC World Service and then for United Press International and the *Washington Post*. She covered the Middle East for Germany's largest news service and finally spent 3 years in Prague, where she published a book on Bohemian glass. But "home" was always Vermont.

In 1994 she returned to her native Burlington, more flatlander now than Vermonter, and coauthored *Curious New England*, a guide to eccentric destinations in the Northeast. She also started exploring the state to research stories for the *Boston Globe*.

"It was like seeing Vermont for the first time. It all seemed new."

Working on this edition of *Vermont: An Explorer's Guide* allowed her to revisit some of those off-the-beaten-track places to which her father had taken her decades before, this time with eyes wide open. It's to his memory that she has dedicated this book.

"I had no idea," she said, "that there was so much beauty and variety in this one little state."

Chris and Diane are deeply indebted to Peter Jennison, a sixth-generation Vermonter, who was born on a dairy farm in Swanton, attended one-room schoolhouses, and graduated from Middlebury College. After 25 years in the publishing business in New York City, he became a "born-again" Vermonter, returning to his native heath in 1972 and founding The Countryman Press. Peter coauthored this book during its first eight editions, and many of the best words in it remain his. He passed on in December 2004 and is sorely missed.

Chris wishes to thank Laura Howe of East Jamaica, William Hays in Brattleboro, Judy Hayward of South Royalton and Windsor, Thom and Joan Gorman and Susan Roy in the Mad River Valley, Beth Kennett of Rochester, Jane Doerfer of Brookfield, Carol and Michael Calotta of North Shrewsbury, Julie Pierce of Chester, Margaret Ramsdell of Craftsbury, Molly Newell of North Danville, Deb and Bob Winder of Montgomery, Jim and Mary O'Reilly of Lyndonville, Joan Du Moulin of Morgan, and Joanie Binns of Quimby Country. Thanks too to those chamber of commerce directors who helped beyond the call of duty: Annette Compton of the Woodstock, Ed Egan of the Okemo Valley, and Darcie McCann of the Northeast Kingdom chambers were extremely helpful. Thanks also to Pat Fowler of Bellows Falls for her input, and to husband Bill Davis, long-suffering companion during much of this research.

Diane would like to thank Jason Aldous of the Vermont Department of Tourism and Marketing, John Dumville of the Vermont Division for Historic Preservation, Barbara Thomke of Smugglers' Notch, Pam Knights of Northfield, Diane Dickerman of the Mountain Top Inn and Resort, Lauren Jarvi and Len Gerardi of St. Johnsbury, William Jenney of Plymouth Notch, Rux Martin of Vergennes, David Fairbanks Ford of White River Junction, Steve and Marge Bissette of Marlboro, and the many staffers at local organizations and chamber of commerce offices for their generous assistance.

Both authors are grateful to Kermit Hummel for launching this update and to Jennifer Thompson for shepherding it to fruition with the help of our ever-speedy and supportive copy editor, Laura Jorstad.

Christina Tree (ctree@traveltree.net)

Diane Foulds (czechrep@together.net)

WHAT'S WHERE IN VERMONT

AREA CODE The area code for all of Vermont is **802**.

AGRICULTURAL FACTS AND FAIRS
Some 1.25 million acres of the state's total of 6 million acres are devoted to agriculture. The farmhouse and barn are still a symbol of Vermont, and a Vermont vacation should include a farm visit, whether to buy syrup, cheese, wool, or wine, maybe to pick apples or berries, tour the dairy operation, or to stay for a night or a week. Finding farms can be an excuse to explore unexpectedly beautiful back-country.

Of course a "farm" isn't what it used to be. Fewer than 1,300 of Vermont's 6,400 farms are now dairy, compared with 10,000 dairy farms 40 years ago. Even so, the average size of dairy herds has increased: With just 15 percent as many dairy farms, the state produces more than twice as much milk as it did 45 years ago. Vermont farms today are more likely to raise goats or llamas, beef cattle, or minia-ture donkeys, not to mention Christ-mas trees and flowers, vegetables, fruit, or trout. Bear in mind that before cows, there were sheep. In the 1830s and '40s, meadowland was far more extensive, and was populated by millions of merino sheep. When the Civil War ended, so did the demand for wool blankets, and a significant number of sheep farms went under. Luckily, railroads were expanding to every corner of the state by the 1870s, and railroad companies teamed up with state agriculture departments to promote farms to "summer boarders."

Now farmers are once again look-ing to visitors as well as to new forms of agriculture to maintain their farms. Within "What's Where" we suggest

Robert Eddy

how to find a variety of agricultural products, from apples to wine. Request a packet of brochures from the Vermont Agency of Agriculture (802-828-2416; 116 State St., Drawer 20, Montpelier 05620-2901; www.vermont agriculture.com) or contact the Vermont Farms! Association (1-866-348-FARM; www.vermontfarms.org).

The **Champlain Valley Exposition** (www.cvfair.com) in Essex (lasting an entire week around Labor Day) is by far the state's largest agricultural fair. **Addison County Fair and Field Days** in early Aug. in New Haven, as well as the **Orleans County Fair** in Barton (www.orleanscounty fair.com, 5 days in mid-Aug.) and the **Caledonia County Fair** (802-626-5917; www.vtfair.com) always the following weekend in nearby Lyndonville, all feature ox, pony, and horse pulling as well as a midway, live entertainment, and plenty to please all ages. The **Bondville Fair** (2 days in late Aug.) in southern Vermont is also the genuine thing, the **Vermont State Fair** (802-775-5200; www .vermontstatefair.net) in Rutland (9 days in early Sep.) is big, and the **Tunbridge World's Fair** (4 days in mid-Sep.) is the oldest and most colorful of them all (1-802-889-5555; www.tunbridgefair.com). See also in this chapter *Apples, Cheese, Christmas Trees, Farmer's Markets, Farms Open to the Public, Farm Stays, Gardens, Maple Sugaring, Pick Your Own, Sheep and Wool*, and *Wine*.

AIR SERVICE **Burlington International Airport** (802-863-1889; www .burlingtonintlairport.com) currently offers most of the scheduled (largely commuter) service in Vermont. Carriers include: **Delta** (1-800-221-1212), **Continental** (1-800-525-0280), **Northwest** (1-800-225-2525), **JetBlue** (1-800-538-2583) with reasonable fares to New York's JFK International Airport, **United Airlines** (1-800-241-6522), connecting with most U.S. points via Chicago, and **US Airways Express** (1-800-428-4322), which also serves **Rutland State Airport** and **Lebanon Municipal Airport** (603-298-8878), in N.H. just across the river from White River Junction. **Bradley International Airport** in Windsor Locks, Ct., is served by major carriers and handy to much of central and southern Vermont (www.bradleyairport.com), while busy **Albany Airport** (www .albanyairport.com) in New York is convenient for much of the western part of the state. **Manchester (N.H.) Airport** (www.flymanchester.com) is the largest airport in northern New England, with many domestic and some international flights.

AIRPORTS Click on www.vermont airports.com for details about Vermont's 17 airports, just 2 (see above) with scheduled flights, but all accessible to private and some to charter planes. Request a copy of the *Vermont Airport Directory* from the Vermont Agency of Transportation (802-828-2587).

AMTRAK Amtrak service (1-800-USA-RAIL; www.amtrak.com) has improved in recent years. Amtrak's **Vermonter** runs from Washington to St. Albans with stops (at decent hours both north- and southbound) in Brattleboro, Bellows Falls, Claremont (N.H.), Windsor, White River Junction, Randolph, Montpelier, Waterbury, and Burlington. From St. Albans, a connecting bus continues north to Montreal. The **Adirondack** runs up the western shore of Lake Champlain en route from Manhattan to Montreal and stops at Port Kent, N.Y., accessible to Burlington by ferry. The **Ethan Allen Express** connects Rutland with New York City (with special weekend ski-season runs and bus shuttles to Killington and Okemo) and Albany. All Vermont trains accept skis (but not bicycles) as baggage.

Christina Tree

HARLOW FARMSTAND IN PUTNEY

ANTIQUARIAN BOOKSELLERS The **Vermont Antiquarian Booksellers Association** (VABA; http://members .valley.net/~vaba) publishes a pamphlet listing its more than 60 member dealers, available online or in the stores.

ANTIQUING The pamphlet *Antiquing in Vermont*, listing more than 80 members of the Vermont Antiques Dealers' Association (www.vermont ada.com), is available by sending a double-stamped, self-addressed, business-sized envelope to Elizabeth Harley—VADA, 88 Reading Farms Rd., Reading 05062. The association sponsors an **annual antiques show** in Sep. Major concentrations of dealers can be found in Bennington, Burlington, Dorset, Manchester, Middlebury, Woodstock, and along Rt. 30 in the West River Valley. The **Weston Antiques Show** (802-824-5307; www.westonantiquesshow.org), usually the first weekend in Oct., is the state's oldest and still one of its best. Vermont's largest group dealerships are in Quechee (Quechee Gorge Village, Rt. 4 west off I-89, Exit 1; 1-800-438-5565) and East Barre (the East Barre Antique Mall, junction of Rts. 302 and 110; 802-479-5190).

APPLES During fall harvest season the demand is not only for bushel baskets already filled with apples but also for an empty basket and the chance to climb a ladder and pick the many varieties grown in Vermont—primarily in the Champlain Islands, the Champlain Valley around Shoreham, and the Lower Connecticut River Valley between Springfield and Brattleboro. Listings of orchards and apple festivals can be found under descriptions of these areas in this book and by requesting a map/guide to farms from the Vermont Apple Marketing Board (www.vermontapples.org) through the Agency of Agriculture (802-828-2416; 116 State St., Drawer 20, Montpelier 05620-2901). From the earliest days of settlement through the mid-1800s, more apples, it's said, were used for making hard cider and brandy than for eating and cooking. In 1810 some 125 distilleries were producing more than 173,000 gallons of apple brandy annually. Today wineries and cideries are once more making apple wines (see *Wine*).

ART GALLERIES Vermont's principal collections of art (painting, sculpture, and decorative arts) are found at the **Bennington Museum** (works by

Grandma Moses); the **Robert Hull Fleming Museum** at the University of Vermont, Burlington; the **Firehouse Gallery at the Firehouse Center for the Visual Arts** in Burlington; the **Middlebury College Museum of Art**; the **St. Johnsbury Athenaeum and Art Gallery**; the **Shelburne Museum** in Shelburne; the **Chaffee Art Gallery**, Rutland; the **Southern Vermont Arts Center** in Manchester; the **Thomas Waterman Wood Art Gallery**, Montpelier; the **Helen Day Art Center** in Stowe; the **Chester Art Guild** in Chester; and the **Chandler Gallery** in Randolph. Brattleboro, Manchester, Woodstock, Brandon, and Bellows Falls offer the greatest number of private galleries. Burlington and Brattleboro hold open gallery tours the first Friday of every month (for maps of Burlington studios, go to www.burlingtoncityarts.com); Bellows Falls, on the third Friday of every month. For more information, see the Vermont Museum & Gallery Alliance's excellent web site, www.vmga.org.

ARTS COUNCILS Vermont's local arts councils organize films, festivals, and concerts throughout the year. Those listed here are the largest organizers of cultural happenings in their areas: **Rockingham Arts & Museum Project (RAMP)** in Bellows Falls (802-463-3252; www.ramp-vt.org); **Vermont Arts Exchange** in Bennington (802-442-5549; www.creativecommunitiesonline.org/site_20.html); **Arts Council of Windham County**, Brattleboro (802-257-1881); **Northeast Kingdom Arts Council** in Hardwick (802-572-8800; www.nekarts.org/townhouse.htm); **Art Resource Association**, Montpelier (802-485-8428); **River**

Arts in Morrisville (802-888-1261; www.riverartsvt.org); **Crossroads Arts Council**, Rutland (www.crossroadsarts.com; 802-775-5413); **Catamount Film & Arts Center** (802-748-2600; www.catamountarts.com) in St. Johnsbury; and **Pentangle Council on the Arts**, Woodstock (802-457-3981; www.pentanglearts.org). The overall information source is the **Vermont Arts Council** (802-828-3291; 136 State St., Drawer 33, Montpelier 05633-6001; www.vermontartscouncil.org).

AUCTIONS Most major upcoming auctions are announced in the Thursday edition of Vermont newspapers, with a listing of items that will be up for bid. Auctions may be scheduled at any time, however, during summer months, advertised primarily on local bulletin boards and in shop windows. Among well-known auctioneers and auction houses: **Thomas Hirchak**, Morrisville; **Duane Merrill**, Burlington; **Bob Arbuckle**, Chester; **Robert Prozzo**, Rutland; **C. W. Gray** of East Thetford (farm and construction equipment); **Mary Anne Lukas** of the Southern Vermont Auction Gallery in Danby; and **Chuck Eaton**, in Fairlee.

BALLOONING Year-round flights are offered by **Balloons of Vermont** (802-291-4887; www.balloonsofvermont.com), based in Quechee; inquire, too, at the **Stoweflake Resort** in Stowe (802-253-7355). Ascents are also offered by **Brian Boland** at Post Mills Airport (802-333-9254), who will show you the 100-odd balloons he's collected in the hot-air **Balloon Museum** in a nearby barn. Lastly, **Above Reality** (802-899-4007; 1-877-386-7473;

www.balloonvermont.com) lifts you over northern Lake Champlain and the Champlain Valley, while **Balloons Over New England** (1-800-788-5562; www.balloonsovernewengland.com) operates in Quechee, Maine, and Massachusetts. The **Annual Balloon Festival** in Quechee is held in June during Father's Day weekend.

BARNS Many barns along the highways and byways have distinctive touches, such as ornate Victorian cupolas, and still more are connected to farmhouses in the connected architectural style that served as shelter for the farmers' trips before dawn in deep snow. Just 13 round barns survive in Vermont, all built between 1899 and World War I. The concept of the round barn is thought to have originated with the Shakers in Hancock, Ma., where the original stone barn, built in 1824, is now the centerpiece of a museum. The Vermont survivors include: the **Moore barn** in East Barnet; the **Hastings barn** in Waterford; the **Metcalf barn** (Robillard Flats) in Irasburg; the **Parker barn** in Grand Isle, converted into a housing center for the elderly; two barns in Coventry; the **Powers barn** in Lowell; the **Parker barn** in North Troy; one in Enosburg Falls; and **Southwick's** in East Calais. In Waitsfield the **Joslin round barn** is now a cultural center with a swimming pool in its bowels, attached to the **Inn at Round Barn Farm**; in Strafford the **Round Barn Farm**, a 350-acre working dairy farm, takes guests. The **Welch Barn** on Rt. 12 in Morristown just north of Lake Elmore rises into view as you drive the beautiful stretch north from Montpelier.

Round-barn addicts should check at local general stores for exact location and to secure permission to photograph the structures. Among other Vermont barns open to the public are those at Shelburne Farms, including the vast, five-story, 416-foot-long, Norman-style **Farm Barn**, the acre-large **Breeding Barn**, and the handsome **Coach Barn** in Shelburne. The round barn once in Passumpsic has been moved to the Shelburne Museum. Two lively, illustrated guides are *A Field Guide to New England Barns and Farm Buildings* by Thomas Visser and *Big House, Little House, Back House, Barn: The Connected Farm Buildings of New England* by Thomas Hubka (both from the University Press of New England).

BED & BREAKFASTS The hundreds of B&Bs we have personally inspected are listed under their respective locations in this book; they range from working farms to historic mansions, $55–2,700 per room.

BICYCLE TOURING In Vermont the distance via back roads from swimming hole to antiques shop to the next inn is never far. John Freidin, author of *Backroad Bicycling in Vermont* (The Countryman Press), introduced the whole notion of guided bike tours for adults back in 1972. Woodstock-based **Bike Vermont** (1-800-257-2226; www.bikevt.com) is now by far the state's largest, most respected inn-to-inn tour outfitter, providing a "sag wagon" (a support vehicle with spare parts and snacks), renting 27-gear hybrid bikes, specializing in small (under 20) groups, and a wide variety of Vermont and foreign destinations. Guided camping tours (with a sag wagon) are offered by **POMG (Peace of Mind Guaranteed) Bike Tours of Vermont**

Bike Vermont

(1-888-635-2453; www.pomgbike
.com). **Vermont Bicycle Touring**
(1-800-245-3868; www.vbt.com) offers
inn-to-inn biking tours to several destinations. **Vermont Inn-to-Inn
Walking** (802-228-8799 or 802-875-
3658; www.vermontinntoinnwalking
.com; Box 243, Ludlow 05149) is an
association of innkeepers whose
establishments are a comfortable bike
ride (or hike) from each other. Participants are largely on their own, but
rental equipment is available and baggage is transferred from inn to inn.

Bicycle paths continue to grow and
multiply in Vermont. Stowe's **"Rec"
Path** (5.3 miles) and easy rentals
make it an ideal place to sample the
sport. The **Burlington Bike Path**
(802-864-0123; www.enjoyburlington
.com/bikepath) follows the shore of
Lake Champlain for 8 miles (rentals
available); from South Burlington
there's another 15 miles. The 26-mile
Missisquoi Rail Trail follows an old
railbed from St. Albans to Richford;
the **Bennington Historic Bike
Route** leads bikers around local
sights; and the 34-mile **D&H Recre-**

ation Trail follows an abandoned
railroad bed almost 20 miles from
Castleton to West Rupert, with the
remainder in New York State. Within
each chapter we have described
sources for local bike rentals. Note
that many inns and outfitters offer
shuttle service from Amtrak stops.
See also *Mountain Biking*.

BIRDING While the hermit thrush,
the state bird, is reclusive and not too
easy to spot, Vermont offers ample
opportunities for observing herons
and ducks, as well as raptors like owls,
hawks, falcons, ospreys, even bald
eagles. It's home to more than 240
species of birds. Outstanding birding
areas include the **Missisquoi National Wildlife Refuge** (802-868-4781;
http://missisquoi.fws.gov) in Swanton,
the **Dead Creek Wildlife Refuge**
(802-759-2398) in Vergennes, and the
4,970-acre **Victory Basin** east of St.
Johnsbury. The 255-acre **Green
Mountain Audubon Nature Center** in Huntington (802-434-3068;
www.vt.audubon.org/centers.html) is
open year-round; inquire about guided walks and special programs. The
neighboring **Birds of Vermont
Museum** (802-434-2167; www.birds
ofvermont.org) in Huntington is well
worth checking out; an exceptionally
well-mounted display (in their natural
habitats) of lifelike carvings of over
200 species, showing both male and
female plumage, all the work of master carver Bob Spear of Colchester.
The **Vermont Institute of Natural
Science (VINS)** has a new nature
center beside Quechee Gorge (802-
457-2779; www.vinsweb.org) that's
open year-round, with owls, hawks,
eagles, and other raptors in residence
and a full program of naturalist walks
and demonstrations.

BOAT EXCURSIONS If you don't own a yacht, there are still plenty of ways to get onto Vermont rivers and lakes. Possible excursions include the *Belle of Brattleboro* (802-254-1263; www .belleofbrattleboro.com), which plies the Connecticut from Brattleboro; the *Spirit of Ethan Allen II* (802-862-8300; www.soea.com), an excursion vessel based in Burlington; the **M/V Carillon** (802-897-5331; www.paxp .com/carillon), which offers narrated cruises from Larrabee's Point in Shoreham up and down Lake Champlain near Fort Ticonderoga; and the **M/V Mountain Mills** (802-464-2975; www.greenmountainflagship.com), which sails on Harriman Reservoir near Whitingham. For details, check under respective locations in this book. See also *Ferries*.

BOATING A booklet, *Laws and Regulations Governing the Use and Registration of Motorboats*, is available from the Vermont State Police, Marine Division, in Williston (802-878-7111). Click onto www.boatsafe .com/vermont. (See also *Canoeing and Kayaking, Connecticut River*, and *Whitewater*.)

BOOKS In addition to the books we mention in specific fields or on particular subjects, here are some of the most useful current titles: *Vermont Atlas and Gazetteer* (DeLorme) and *Vermont Place Names: Footprints in History*, by Esther Swift (Vermont Historical Society). *The Roadside History of Vermont*, by Peter Jennison (Mountain Press), is an informal narrative of what happened where and when along main travel routes. *Hands on the Land: A History of the Vermont Landscape*, by Jan Albers, published by the MIT Press for The

Orton Family Foundation, is also essential reading for anyone truly interested in understanding why Vermont looks the way it does. Lovers of natural history should seek out *The Nature of Vermont*, by Charles Johnson (University Press of New England). For children, *Vermont: The State with the Storybook Past*, by Cora Cheney (New England Press), is the best. Basic reference directories include *The Vermont Yearbook*, published by the National Survey in Chester, and the *Vermont Encyclopedia* (University Press of New England). Civil War buffs will be rewarded by Howard Coffin's *Full Duty: Vermonters in the Civil War*; *Nine Months to Gettysburg: Stannard's Vermonters and the Repulse of Pickett's Charge*; and *The Battered Stars: One State's Civil War Ordeal During Grant's Overland Campaign* (all The Countryman Press).

Our favorite current Vermont fiction writer is unquestionably Howard Frank Mosher of Irasburg, whose evocative novels include *Disappearances, Northern Borders, Where the Rivers Flow North*, and *A Stranger in the Kingdom*; the last two are also films. Joseph Citro is the author of several books about occult occurrences and folk legends in the state, including *Green Mountains, Dark Tales* (University Press of New England), and *Ghosts, Ghouls, and Unsolved Mysteries* (Houghton Mifflin). The Brattleboro-based mysteries of Archer Mayor, including *Open Season* and other titles in his Joe Gunther police-procedural series, are gaining momentum. And look for the charming little *Art of the State: Vermont* by Suzanne Mantell (Abrams). For a narrative guide to some off-the-beaten-path attractions, seek out *Off the*

Leash: Subversive Journeys around Vermont by Helen Husher (The Countryman Press). *Northeastern Wilds* (AMC Books), by Stephen Gorman, features stunning photography and includes informative text about Vermont's stretch of the northern forest.

BREWERIES Civil War–era Vermont was New England's leading hops-producing state; in the United States only New York surpassed its output. In the late 19th century, however, temperance movements and other factors virtually eliminated its beer and wine industries. But Vermont brewing is back. Check out www .vermontbrewers.com. **Magic Hat Brewing Co.** (802-658-2739) in South Burlington, **Harpoon Brewery** (802-674-5491) in Windsor, and **Otter Creek Brewing** (802-388-0727) in Middlebury offer tours and tastings, while **Bobcat Café & Brewery** (802-453-3311) in Bristol, **Long Trail Brewing** (802-672-5011) in West Bridgewater, **Maple Leaf Malt & Brewing** (802-464-9900) in Wilmington, **Jasper Murdock's Alehouse** at the Norwich Inn (802-649-1143), **The Shed** (802-253-4364) in Stowe, **McNeil's Brewery** (802-254-2553) in Brattleboro, and **Trout River Brewing Co.** (802-626-9396) in Lyndonville all serve their own brews. **Rock Art Brewery** (802-635-9758) in Johnson welcomes visitors by appointment.

BUS SERVICE **Vermont Transit**. For a current timetable, contact Vermont Transit Co., Inc. (1-800-552-8737; 345 Pine St., Burlington 05401), or go to www.vermonttransit.com. Outside New England contact Greyhound (1-800-231-2222). The company has made major routing cuts in recent years, but still travels to Vermont's major towns from Boston and New York City. The main routes are (1) from Hartford, Ct., north through Brattleboro, Bellows Falls, White River Junction, Montpelier, and Burlington up to Montreal, and (2) from Boston via White River Junction and Montpelier to Burlington and Montreal. Inquire about service to and from the Manchester (N.H.) Airport. Children 2–11 travel at nearly half price; and those under 2 can travel for free as long as they stay on an adult's lap. The 345 Pine St. terminal in Burlington offers ample parking but is several blocks from downtown. At this writing the Montpelier terminal is a battered trailer off State St. *Note:* A passport is required to cross into Canada by bus.

CAMPS, FOR CHILDREN For information about more than 50 Vermont summer camps for boys and girls, contact the **Vermont Camping Association** (1-888-VT-CAMPS; www.vermontcamps.org).

CAMPGROUNDS Vermont has over 77 privately owned campgrounds, 40 state campgrounds, and seven camping areas within its sole national park, the Green Mountain National Forest. A detailed annual publication,

Kim Grant

Vermont Campground Guide, is published by the Vermont Campground Association and is available online (www.campvermont.com), at the welcome centers on Vermont's interstates, and from the Vermont Department of Tourism (1-800-VERMONT). The private campgrounds have the advantage of extra comforts that the state and national parks lack, such as snack bars, stores, playgrounds, electricity, cable TV, even Internet hookups. For those same reasons, the state parks are often quieter.

A list of Vermont's state parks is available from Vermont State Parks (802-241-3655), 103 S. Main St., Waterbury 05671-0601. Their web site (www.vtstateparks.com) is excellent, describing each park in detail with maps of the camping areas. State facilities include whole furnished cottages, unfurnished cabins, lean-tos, and tent and trailer sites. Fees vary with the class of the area; in 2005 the range was $14–25, with cottages available on a weekly basis. Reservations can be made up to 11 months in advance online anytime at www.vt stateparks.com or by phone at 1-888-409-7579 weekdays 9–4. Within this book each park is described as it appears geographically. Trees separate most Vermont state park campsites from neighboring sites, and they are well maintained. Many offer organized programs such as hikes, campfire sings, films, and lectures. Most parks are relatively uncrowded, especially midweek; the most popular are Branbury, Stillwater, Groton Forest, Grand Isle, and Lake St. Catherine.

There are seven designated camping areas within the 300,000-acre **Green Mountain National Forest**, three in the north, four in the south. Sites are available on a first-come, first-served basis for a maximum 14-day period for about $13 a night. These areas are **Hapgood Pond Recreational Area** near Peru, **Red Mill Brook Campground** near Woodford, **Grout Pond Recreational Area** near Stratton, **Greendale Campground** north of Weston, **Silver Lake** and **Moosalamoo** near Goshen, and **Chittenden Brook Campground** near Brandon. Camping is also permitted in the wilds without fee or prior permission, but before you pitch your tent, visit one of the district ranger offices; see *Green Mountain National Forest*. The U.S. Army Corps of Engineers, New England District, also maintains 75 campsites close to flush toilets, showers, and swimming at the **Winhall Brook Camping Area** at Ball Mountain Lake in Jamaica. Fees are $16–20 per night. For details click on www.nae .usace.army.mil. To reserve sites at any of these campgrounds, phone the National Recreation Reservation Service at 1-877-444-6777 or go to www .reserveusa.com. *Note:* In 2005 the U.S. Army Corps of Engineers began charging noncampers (over 12) entering the camping areas $1 per person, with a maximum of $4 per vehicle.

CANOEING AND KAYAKING Organized canoe and kayaking trips have increased in recent years. **BattenKill Canoe** (1-800-421-5268; www.batten kill.com) in Arlington offers day trips and inn-to-inn tours throughout the state; **Clearwater Sports** (802-496-2708; www.clearwatersports.com) in Waitsfield offers guided tours, instruction, and special expeditions, as does **Umiak Outdoor Outfitters** (802-253-2317; www.umiak.com) in Stowe. **Vermont Canoe Touring Center** (802-257-5008) in Brattleboro offers canoe rentals, shuttle service, and river camping on the Connecticut, just as **North Star Canoe Livery** (603-542-6929; www.kayak-canoe .com), based in Cornish, N.H. (with a branch in White River Junction), offers rentals and shuttles for the scenic reach between White River Junction and the Cornish–Windsor bridge, one particularly rich in camping spots (see "Upper Valley River Towns"). **Wilderness Trails** (802-295-7620) in Quechee offers similar trips on the neighboring stretch of the river, also on nearby ponds and on the White River. The stretch of the Lamoille River around Jeffersonville is served both by **Smugglers' Notch Canoe Touring** (802-644-8189; www.smugglersnotchcanoetouring.com) and by **Green River Canoe** (802-644-8336). For the upper reaches of the Connecticut check out **Hemlock Pete's Canoes & Kayaks** (603-667-5112) in North Haverhill, N.H.; in the Connecticut Lakes area **Pathfinder Tours** (603-538-6651) offers guided tours on both the lakes and the Connecticut River.

Fish Vermont, a map/guide free from the Vermont Fish and Wildlife Department (802-241-3700; 1-800-837-6668; 103 S. Main St., in the 10 South building, Waterbury 05671-0501; www.vtfishandwildlife.com), notes ponds, lakes, and put-in places. A *Winooski River Canoe Guide* is $3.95 if you pick it up; $4.95 by mail from the Winooski Valley Park District, Ethan Allen Homestead, Burlington 05401. Recommended books: Roioli Schweiker's third edition of *Canoe Camping Vermont and New Hampshire Rivers* (The Countryman Press) is a handy guide, and the *AMC River Guide: Vermont/New Hampshire* (AMC Books) is good for detailed in-

formation on canoeable rivers. (See also *Connecticut River* and *Whitewater*.)

CATAMOUNT TRAIL (www.catamount trail.org) You may not want to ski the 300 miles from Massachusetts to Canada, but it's nice to know you can—along the longest cross-country ski trail in this country. Since 1984, when three young skiers bushwhacked their way the length of Vermont, the Catamount Trail has been evolving. The nonprofit Catamount Trail Association (CTA) now has over 1,800 members. Over the years countless permits and dozens of easements have secured use of private and public lands. Bridges have been built, trailhead parking created, and a newly updated 8th edition of *The Catamount Trail Guidebook* ($18.95) maps and describes each of the trail's 31 segments. The excellent web site includes a "trip planning" section with suggested places to stay along the way. Contact the CTA at 802-864-5794; 1 Main St., Suite 308A, Burlington 05401. Members receive a regular newsletter and discounts at participating touring centers. Also see *Skiing, Cross-Country*.

CHEESE In recent years Vermont's production of cheese has increased to more than 100 million pounds annually and has become more varied, with sheep and goat as well as cow cheeses winning top national and international honors. Check out the following producers among the 34 **Vermont Cheese Council** members currently listed at **www.vtcheese.com**. Print out the Vermont Cheese Trail map on this site and use it to tour and taste.

Of course a century ago most Vermont towns had a cheesemaker to

CROWLEY CHEESE FACTORY

which farmers brought the day's surplus milk. **Crowley Cheese** (1-800-683-2602; www.crowleycheese-vermont.com), established in 1882 and billed as "the oldest continuously operated cheese factory in the U.S.," is the only survivor of this era, and welcomes visitors to its wooden factory just west of Ludlow on Rt. 103 in Healdville (open weekdays 8–4; store open daily). This distinctive cheese is creamier than cheddar and still made the traditional way. **Cabot Creamery** (802-563-2231; www.cabotcreamery.com) in Cabot is the state's largest, most famous producer, a farmer-owned cooperative since 1919 with a modern plant turning out 12 million pounds of cheese a year. Its visitors center is open daily, year-round, and offers plant tours (call ahead for cheesemaking days); its annex in Waterbury Center south of Stowe sells a variety of the dairy products and cheeses that have made market inroads nationwide.

Award-winning **Vermont Shepherd Cheese** (802-387-4473), a rich, tangy sheep's-milk cheese from Westminster, opens its "cave" to visitors at certain times (call); the nearby **Westminster Dairy** at Livewater Farm (a variety of delicious hard and soft cow

cheeses) is open daily 7–7. **Grafton Village Cheese Company** (1-800-472-3866) in Grafton had its beginnings around 1890 and was resurrected by the Windham Foundation in 1966; visitors view the cheesemaking from outside, through a picture window. The **Plymouth Cheese Company** (802-672-3650) was founded in 1890 by Colonel John Coolidge, father of President Coolidge, and is now producing and selling the same old-fashioned granular curd cheese that he did, using the name **Frog City Cheese** (802-672-3650). The **Taylor Farm** (802-824-5690) in Londonderry (southern Vermont) is making a reputation with its Gouda, and **Woodcock Farm** in Weston has won top national honors for its European-style sheep cheese. Also in southern Vermont, **Peaked Hill Farm** in Townshend welcomes visitors at convenient times. In Randolph Center, minutes off I-89, Exit 4, at **Neighborly Farms** (802-728-4700), you can walk down a hallway and view cows on one side and cheesemaking on the other (open Mon.–Sat. 10–5). **Vermont Butter & Cheese Company** in Websterville (800-884-6287) makes a wide variety of tantalizing goat cheeses, and **Blythedale Farm** (802-439-6575) in Corinth produces multiple soft cheeses (a fine Vermont Brie, a Camembert, a Green Mountain Gruyère, and Jersey Blue), but neither is open to visitors. **Sugarbush Farm** (802-457-1757), set high on a hill in Woodstock, smokes and packages several varieties of cheddar cheese and welcomes visitors.

At **Shelburne Farms** (802-985-8686; open daily, year-round), in Shelburne near Burlington, prizewinning cheddar is made from the milk of a single herd of Brown Swiss cows. In New Haven, **Orb Weaver Farm** (802-877-3755) produces a creamy, aged, Colby-type cheese, made in small batches entirely by hand (available in 2-pound wheels and 1-pound waxed wedges). In the northwest corner of the state goat cheese is made at **Willow Hill Farm** (802-893-2963) in Milton and at **Lakes End Cheeses** (802-796-3730) in Alburg. In nearby Highgate Center visitors are welcome at **Green Mountain Blue Cheese** (802-868-4193). The Northeast Kingdom also has its share of cheesemakers. **Bonnie View Farm** in Craftsbury makes a superb sheep's-milk cheese, and **Jasper Hill Farm** in Greensboro is known for its Bayley-Hazen Blue cheese. Also see *The Cheeses of Vermont: A Gourmet Guide to Vermont's Artisanal Cheesemakers*, by Henry Tewksbury (The Countryman Press), which includes a map of cheesemakers that welcome visitors.

CHILDREN, ESPECIALLY FOR Look for the ✐ symbol throughout this book; it designates child-friendly attractions as well as lodging and dining. Alpine slides delight children of all ages at **Bromley's** summer **Thrill Zone** (where there are also DévalKart rides and **Pig Dog's Fun Park** for toddlers; www.bromley.com). There's another alpine slide at **Stowe** (www .stowe.com) and at Pico, part of the **Killington/Pico Adventure Center** (www.killington.com), which includes waterslides, a climbing wall, an in-line skate park, mountain biking, guided hikes, and more. Alpine lifts, which operate in summer, are also a way of hoisting small legs and feet to the top of some of Vermont's most spectacular summits. In Stowe, **Mount Mans-**

field, Vermont's highest peak, and **Killington Peak**, second highest in the state, are accessible via gondola on weekdays. **Jay Peak**, commanding as dramatic a view as the others, is accessible on aerial tram (www .jaypeakresort.com). In southern Vermont, **Stratton**'s gondola runs daily all summer and fall.

Santa's Land in Putney is the only commercial attraction geared specifically to children (open late May–mid-Dec.; 1-802-387-5550; www.santasland .com), but stuffed-animal lovers shouldn't miss the **Vermont Teddy Bear Factory** (1-800-829-BEAR; www.vermontteddybear.com) in Shelburne, where tours demonstrate how the toys are made.

The **Shelburne Museum** (www .shelburnemuseum.org) has many exhibits that please youngsters, as does the **Fairbanks Museum and Planetarium** (www.fairbanksmuseum .org), St. Johnsbury, which is filled with taxidermied animals, birds, and exhibits from near and far. The **Montshire Museum of Science** (www.montshire.org) in Norwich is a real standout, with hands-on exhibits explaining many basic scientific mysteries plus a 2-acre outdoor exhibit inviting plenty of water experiments (bring a towel) and a beautiful river-

FAIRBANKS MUSEUM IN ST. JOHNSBURY

Liam Davis

side walk. **ECHO at the Leahy Center for Lake Champlain** (www.echocenter.org) is a new science center and aquarium featuring 2,200 live fish, amphibians, and reptiles, with hands-on exhibits for kids 3–17. The **Billings Farm & Museum** (www.billingsfarm.org) and **Vermont Institute of Natural Science** (www.vinsweb.org), both in the Woodstock area, are child pleasers.

Over the past few years, as ski areas have come to compete for family business, resorts have developed special programs for children. **Smugglers' Notch** (www.smuggs.com) offers a full summer day camp for a wide range of ages. The **Tyler Place Family Resort** (802-868-4000) in Highgate Springs and the **Basin Harbor Club** (www.basinharbor.com) in Vergennes are family-geared resorts with teens' and children's programs. The **Wildflower Inn** in Lyndonville, **Highland Lake Lodge** in Greensboro, and Quimby Country in the northeasternmost corner of the state all offer summer half-day programs for children. (See also *Agricultural Facts and Fairs*, *Farms Open to the Public*, *Farm Stays*, *Boat Excursions*, and *Railroad Excursions*.)

CHRISTMAS TREES Christmas tree farms are plentiful throughout the state and most open after Thanksgiving, inviting customers to come tag the tree they want, leaving it until the last moment to cut. Check the Vermont Agency of Agriculture web site, www.vermontagriculture.com, or the Vermont Christmas Tree Growers Association, www.vermontchristmas trees.org, for a listing of growers, and www.vermontfarms.org for a list of the more imaginative marketers. These include **Redrock Farm** (1-866-685-

4343; www.christmastrees.net) in Chelsea and **Elysian Hills** (802-257-0233; www.elysianhillsfarm.com) in Dummerston, where you can pick out a tree in summer or fall and have it shipped to you at Christmas anywhere in the continental United States the day it's cut. (If you do this, judging from our own experience, schedule delivery for the beginning of the week and at least a week before Christmas.) In recent years bed & breakfasts and inns have teamed up with farms to offer preholiday lodging packages that include a fresh Christmas tree (contact the Vermont Chamber of Commerce: 802-223-3443; www.vtchamber .com). For a do-it-yourself experience, contact the Green Mountain National Forest Service in Rochester (802-767-4261) and inquire about tagged trees you can cut for a nominal fee.

CIVIL UNIONS In the first year (2001) that Vermont sanctioned civil unions between couples of the same sex, 2,479 such ceremonies were performed, with almost twice as many females as males taking vows. Only 479 couples were from Vermont. The post office in the Central Vermont village of Gaysville has become a favorite venue for wedding pictures. Throughout this guide, we indicate venues that specialize in weddings and civil unions with the wedding-ring symbol ∞.

COLLEGES For information about all the state's colleges and universities, contact the **Vermont Higher Education Council** (802-878-7466; P.O. Box 47, Essex Junction 05453-0047; www.vhec.info). Also check out the **Association of Vermont Independent Colleges** web site: www .vermont-icolleges.org.

CONNECTICUT RIVER New England's longest river rises near the Canadian–New Hampshire border and forms the boundary between that state and Vermont for some 255 miles. Not far below its source are a series of lakes: five in New Hampshire's North Country town of Pittsburg, and two—Moore and Comerford—near St. Johnsbury. The 145 miles between Barnet and Brattleboro are punctuated by four dams, each creating deeper pools that turn the river into a series of slow-moving, narrow lakes. But of the 275 miles the river runs from its source to the Massachusetts border, 134 miles are free flowing. The entire river is now the centerpiece of the 7.2-million-acre, four-state Silvio O. Conte National Fish and Wildlife Refuge (www.fws.gov/r5soc), and the Connecticut River National Scenic Byway. The Connecticut River Joint Commissions (603-826-4800; P.O. Box 1182, Charlestown, N.H. 03603), the nonprofit organization responsible for establishing bistate information centers in Bellows Falls, White River Junction, and St. Johnsbury, also in Lancaster and Colebrook, N.H., maintains two excellent web sites. Click onto www.crjc.org for a series of detailed boating maps (also for directions on ordering hard copies) and onto www.ctrivertravel.net for a historical and cultural guide. Note that we include information about river towns in both states in our Connecticut River Valley chapters.

COVERED BRIDGES The state's 99 surviving covered bridges are marked on the official state map and on our maps and are described in the appropriate chapters of this book under *To See*. Bridge buffs should get a copy of *Covered Bridges of Vermont* by Ed Barna (The Countryman Press). The new **Vermont Covered Bridge Museum** in Bennington features a theater production, dioramas, interactive exhibits, and a model railroad with covered railroad bridges (www.vermontcoveredbridgemuseum.org).

CRAFTS More than 1,500 Vermonters make their living from crafts. There are also more than 100 retail crafts venues in the state, ranging from local shops to fine galleries. The dazzling **Frog Hollow Vermont State Craft Center** in Middlebury has branch stores in Manchester and Burlington and educational programs in Manchester and Middlebury. The **Vermont State Craft Center** in Windsor is well worth checking out (802-674-6729; www.vmga.org/windsor/vsscwindsor.html), as are Montpelier's **Artisan's Hand** (802-229-9492; www.artisanshand.com) and Bristol's **Art on Main** (802-453-4032; www.artonmain.net). Artists also sell their work at events ranging from farmer's markets and church bazaars to juried shows and festivals. Within this book we have described outstanding local crafts studios, galleries, and shops as they appear geographically

COLUMBIA COVERED BRIDGE

Bill Davis

Ryan Wonderchuck

JOSH LETOURNEAU BLOWS GLASS IN
PUTNEY.

and have also included major crafts
fairs. Best of all is the **Open Studio
Weekend**, held annually Memorial
Day weekend, with more than 300
artisans in almost as many locations.
Request a copy of the *Vermont Crafts
Studio Tour Map*, available at information centers and on request from
the Vermont Crafts Council (802-223-
3380; P.O. Box 938, 104 Main St.,
Montpelier 05601-0938; www
.vermontcrafts.com).

CUSTOMS INFORMATION Vermont
shares a 90.3-mile border with the
Canadian province of Quebec. Since
the September 11 terrorist attacks, all
border crossings have become far
stricter. Even in Derby Line (Vermont), where it's tempting to walk the
few steps into Stanstead (Quebec) to
a restaurant, repercussions can be

serious. Travelers must present a picture ID (preferably a passport) and, if
they are not American or Canadian,
valid tourist visas. Pets are required to
have a veterinarian's certificate showing a recent vaccination against
rabies. For detailed information contact the U.S. Customs District Office
in St. Albans (802-524-6527), in Montreal (514-636-3875), or in Toronto
(416-676-2606).

DINERS Vermont will not disappoint
diner buffs. Hearty meals at reasonable prices can be found in Burlington at **Henry's Diner** and the **Oasis**,
both on Bank St. **Libby's Blue Line
Diner**, Rt. 7 (just off I-89, Exit 16),
Colchester, is busy and popular,
perched on a hill with a great view.
The **Parkway Diner** at 1696 Williston Rd., South Burlington, is known
for its Greek specialties, such as
homemade pastitsio. The **Miss Lyndonville Diner** on Bond St., Lyndonville, is admired for its pies (a
breakfast special) and has been augmented by the nearby **Miss Vermont**
(Rt. 5, St. Johnsbury Center), though
lines are still long on Sunday morning.
Anthony's Restaurant on Railroad
St. in St. Johnsbury has expanded and
is wheelchair accessible but still offers
great food at great prices.

GALLERY IN THE WOODS, BRATTLEBORO

Christina Tree

Just off 1-91 in Wells River, the **P&H Truck Stop** (open early and late but no longer 24 hours) is a trucker's paradise that serves large, reasonably priced meals and up to 23 flavors of pie. The **Wayside Restaurant and Bakery** (Exit 7; follow signs for Rt. 302 and it's on your left) south of Montpelier has expanded gradually over the years to become Vermont's ultimate family restaurant. **The Blue Benn Diner**, 102 Hunt St. in Bennington, serves imaginative vegetarian as well as standard diner fare. Add to these the **Farina Family Diner**, Rt. 4 in Quechee Gorge Village; the **Green Mountain Diner**, Main St. in Barre; and **Steve's Park Diner** in downtown Middlebury.

T. J. Buckley's in Brattleboro may look like the battered vintage Worcester diner it is, but inside oak paneling gleams and the fare (dinner only, and only by reservation) is recognized as some of the best in the state. West Brattleboro also offers the **Chelsea Royal Diner**, west on Rt. 9, which, while a bit heavy on diner decor, is still a great family bet (wheelchair accessible). In Chester there is the **Country Girl Diner** and its competition down the road, **City Slickers Diner**. **Miss Bellows Falls Diner** is on the National Register of Historic Places; the equally historic **Windsor Diner** has been nicely restored. The **Fairlee Diner** in Fairlee is the real thing, as is the **Polka Dot Diner** in White River Junction. The state's newest addition is the **Springfield Royal Diner and Precision Valley Corvette Museum**, a 1955 diner that stood in Kingston, N.Y., until the chrome classic was moved to Springfield in 2003 and a showroom filled with vintage Corvettes was tacked on. The food is great, and they've added a genuine 1950s-era ice cream soda fountain. Check these establishments out in their respective chapters. (Also see *Highway Road Food*.)

EMERGENCIES Try **911** first. This simple SOS has finally reached most corners of Vermont. For state police phone 802-878-7111, for poison 1-800-222-1222, and for help with dental emergencies 1-800-640-5099.

EQUESTRIAN SPORTS Horses are as much a part of the Vermont landscape as the famous black-and-white Holsteins. Vermont has three polo clubs: **Sugarbush Polo Club** (802-496-3581), based in the Mad River Valley and Middlebury; **Green Mountain Polo Club** near Manchester (802-375-9491; 802-442-8070; www.greenmountainpolo.com), which offers a polo school in summer; and **Quechee Polo Club** (802-775-5066.). All hold games on Saturday and Sunday during summer (usually at 1 PM); most games are free or inexpensive. The **Vermont Summer Horse Festival** (www.vt-summerfestival.com), the largest of several hunter-jumper shows around the state, takes place at the Harold Beebe Farm in East Dorset, mid-July–mid-Aug. The **Vermont Quarter Horse Association** (www.vtqha.com) hosts shows around the region in summer. The VQHA season begins the first weekend of June. The **Green Mountain Horse Association** in South Woodstock (802-457-1509; www.gmhainc.org) holds **Dressage Days** in mid-July; see www.gmhainc.org/acted/calendar.html for a complete list of dressage events. **Miniature horse and donkey farms** are proliferating around the state, and many show their animals by appointment (for a listing of farms, go to the American Miniature Horse Association, www.amha.com, or the National Miniature Donkey Association, www.nmdaasset.com). Driving is also gaining popularity, and pleasure-driving events can be fun to watch; the web site is www.american drivingsociety.org. Resorts offering horseback riding include the **Top-notch** in Stowe, the **Mountain Top** in Chittenden, and **Hawk Mountain** in Plymouth. Inn-to-inn treks are offered by **Vermont Icelandic Horse Farm** (www.icelandichorses .com) in Waitsfield and by **Kedron Valley Stables** (www.kedron.com) in South Woodstock, the state's out-standing place for beginners to learn and for experienced equestrians to ride. Other options for trail rides are listed in almost every chapter.

EVENTS Almost every day of the year some special event is happening somewhere in Vermont. Usually it's something relatively small and friend-ly like a church supper, contra dance, community theatrical production, concert, or crafts fair. We have worked up our own *Special Events* for each region, and listings can also be found in various ways on the state's travel web site, www.vermontvacation.com. Still, many of the best events are like fireflies, surfacing only on local bul-letin boards and in the Thursday edi-tions of local papers. In Burlington check out the free and information-rich *Seven Days*, a funky weekly list-ing of local arts and entertainment, available in shops and grocery stores all over town.

FACTORY OUTLETS Within the book we have mentioned only a small frac-tion of the factory outlets of which we are aware. Our bias has been to favor

distinctly made-in-Vermont products. Among our favorites: **Johnson Woolen Mills** (quality wool clothing for all ages) in Johnson; **Bennington Potters** (dinnerware, housewares, and more) in Bennington and Burlington; and **Vermont Marble** in Proctor. **Charles Shackleton and Miranda Thomas** produce outstand-ing furniture and ceramics in an old mill in Bridgewater. **Pompanoosuc Mills** in East Thetford and **Copeland Furniture** in Bradford are also top-notch, and sell seconds in their work-shops. Manchester is known for its concentration of brand-name outlet stores specializing in upscale clothing, and **Simon Pearce** in Quechee and Windsor sells seconds of his gorgeous glassware at affordable prices. The Outlet Center just off I-91, Exit 1, in **Brattleboro** harbors some genuine finds. **Manchester** merchants refuse to call the dozens of upscale stores clustered in their town "outlets," but the prices in stores like Giorgio Ar-mani, Baccarat, and Brooks Brothers are lower than retail; this is in fact the state's prime destination shopping center.

FARMER'S MARKETS Mid-June–early Oct., count on finding fresh vege-tables, fruit, honey, and much more at farm prices in commercial centers throughout the state. Click on **www .vermontagriculture.com** for a complete list. Major venues include Burlington, Enosburg, Morrisville, Newport, St. Johnsbury, Norwich, Fair Haven, Middlebury, Montpelier, Rutland, Brattleboro, Manchester, Waterbury, Windsor, and Woodstock.

FARMS OPEN TO THE PUBLIC For a list of farms open to the public for tours, to sell their products, or for farm stays, check out the Vermont Farms! Association web site, **www .vermontfarms.org**.

FARM STAYS A century ago hundreds of Vermont farms took in visitors for weeks at a time. "There is no crop more profitable than the crop from the city," an 1890s Vermont Board of Agriculture pamphlet proclaimed, a publication noted by Dona Brown in *Inventing New England* (Smithsonian, 1995). Articles advised farmers on how to decorate, what to serve, and generally how to please and what to expect from city guests—much as B&B literature does today. Our own family found a farm stay so enriching that we returned year after year and are happy to see that the phenomenon is on the increase again. Within the book we have listed those farms that we have personally visited. For a fuller listing you can click on the Vermont Farms! Association's web site, **www.vermontfarms.org**.

 Maple Crest Farm (802-492-3367) in Shrewsbury deserves special mention because it remains in the same family who have been taking in guests on this working farm since the 1860s. In Rochester, **Liberty Hill Farm** (802-767-3926) has pioneered the resurgence in farm stays by prov-

HARLOW FARMSTAND, WESTMINSTER

Christina Tree

ing how successful they can be. **Allenholm Farm** (802-372-5566) in South Hero offers a B&B in the midst of a major apple orchard. **Round-Robin Farm** (802-763-7025), way off Sharon's beaten track, and **Emergo Farm Bed and Breakfast** (1-888-383-1185), on the edge of Danville Village, are also genuine working farms. **Hollister Hill Farm** (802-454-7725) in Marshfield invites guests to participate in sugar making and take home the results of their labors, while **Rooster Ridge Farm** (802-472-8566) in Wolcott and **The Parent Farmhouse** (802-524-4201) in Milton are all working farms/B&Bs. At the other extreme is lakeside **Shelburne Farms**, the most beautiful farm in the state—with its most elegant inn, the **Inn at Shelburne Farms** (802-985-8686).

FERRIES A number of car-carrying ferries ply Lake Champlain between the Vermont and New York shores, offering splendid views of both the Green Mountains and the Adirondacks. The northernmost crosses to Plattsburgh, N.Y., from **Grand Isle**, on Rt. 314 (year-round; 12-minute passage). From **Burlington** they cross to Port Kent, N.Y. (1 hour), and the **Essex Ferry** travels between Charlotte and Essex, N.Y. (20 minutes). All three are operated by the **Lake Champlain Transportation Company** (802-864-9804; www.ferries .com), descendant of the line founded in 1828 claiming to be "the oldest steamboat company on earth." Near the southern end of the lake, the **Fort Ticonderoga Ferry** (802-897-7999; www.middlebury.net/tiferry) provides a scenic shortcut between Larrabee's Point and Ticonderoga, N.Y. This small, car-carrying ferry makes the

7-minute crossing continuously between 8 AM and 7:45 PM during the summer season, less frequently in spring and fall. Service runs May 1–late Oct. Officially, the Fort Ti Ferry has held the franchise from the New York and Vermont legislatures since about 1800.

FIDDLING Vermont is the fiddling capital of the East. Fiddlers include concert violinists, rural carpenters, farmers, and heavy-equipment operators who come from throughout the East to gather in beautiful natural settings. The newsletter of the **Northeast Fiddlers Association** (802-476-7798; www.nefiddlers.org) lists fiddling meets around the state, such as the **Northeast Regional Oldtime Fiddler's Contest and Festival** in Barre (usually the last weekend in Sep.). Other annual events include the **Cracker Barrel Bazaar & Fiddle Contest** in Newbury in July (802-866-5580) and the **Lake Champlain Bluegrass Festival** fiddle and banjo contest mid-Aug. in Alburg (802-482-8110; www.lakechamplain music.com). Fiddle festivals tend to start late morning and end around midnight.

FILM A number of Hollywood hits have been filmed in Vermont, including *The Cider House Rules*, *Forrest Gump*, *The Spitfire Grill*, and *What Lies Beneath*. But Vermont filmmakers have produced independent hits of their own in recent years. Jay Craven's dramatizations of Howard Frank Mosher's novels—*Where the Rivers Flow North*, *A Stranger in the Kingdom*, and *Disappearances*—evoke life as it was in the Northeast Kingdom not so long ago. Nora Jacobson's *My Mother's Early Lovers* and

Nothing Like Dreaming are absorbing narratives. By the same token, John O'Brien's film trilogy, *Vermont Is for Lovers*, *Man with a Plan*, and *Nosey Parker*, go right to Vermont's still very real rural core. *Man with a Plan* actually launched its hero's real-life political campaign in 1998: To the amazement of the country, retired Tunbridge dairy farmer Fred Tuttle not only defeated a wealthy carpetbagger for the Republican nomination but won a respectable percentage of the vote for a U.S. senatorial seat. Sadly, Tuttle died in 2003, but O'Brien continues to make films; *The Green Movie* was in production in 2005. For a complete listing of Vermont-made films, visit the Vermont Film Commission's excellent web site, www .vermontfilm.com.

FISHING Almost every Vermont river and pond, certainly any body of water serious enough to call itself a lake, is stocked with fish and has one or more access areas. Brook trout are the most widely distributed game fish. Visitors ages 15 and over must have a 5-day, a 14-day, or a nonresident license good for a year, available at any town clerk's office, from the local fish and game warden, or from assorted commercial outlets. Because these sources may be closed or time consuming to track down on weekends, it's wise to obtain the license in advance from the **Vermont Fish and Wildlife Department** (802-241-3700; www.vtfishand wildlife.com). Request an application form and ask for a copy of *Vermont Guide to Fishing*, which details every species of fish and where to find it on a map of the state's rivers and streams, ponds, and lakes. Boat access, fish hatcheries, and canoe routes are also noted.

Kim Grant

Orvis Company, which has been in the business of making fishing rods and selling them to city people for more than a century, also maintains an outstanding museum devoted to fly-fishing. Many inns, notably along Lake Champlain and in the Northeast Kingdom, offer tackle, boats, and advice on where to catch what.

Quimby Country (802-822-5533; www.quimbycountry.com), with a lodge and cabins on Forest and Great Averill Pond; **Seymour Lake Lodge** (802-895-2752; www.seymourlake lodge) in Morgan; and **Seyon Ranch** (802-584-3829) on Noyes Pond in Groton State Forest have all catered to serious fishermen since the 19th century. Landlocked salmon, rainbow trout, brown trout, brookies, and lake trout are all cold-water species plentiful in the Northeast Kingdom's 37,575 acres of public ponds and 3,840 miles of rivers and streams. For guiding services check in those chapters. Warm-water species found elsewhere in the state include smallmouth bass, walleye, northern pike, and yellow perch.

Federal fish hatcheries can be found in **Bethel** (802-234-5241) and **Pittsford** (802-483-6618), and state hatcheries are in **West Burke** (802-467-3660), **Bennington** (802-442-4556), **Grand Isle** (802-372-3171), **Roxbury** (802-485-7568), and **Salisbury** (802-352-4471). Ice anglers can legally take every species of fish (trout only in a limited number of designated waters) and can actually hook smelt and some varieties of whitefish that are hard to come by during warmer months; the **Great Benson Fishing Derby** held annually in mid-February on Lake Champlain draws thousands of contestants from throughout New England. The **Lake Champlain International Fishing Derby**, based in Burlington (call 802-862-7777 for details), is a big summer draw. Books to buy include the *Vermont Atlas and Gazetteer* (DeLorme), with details about fishing species and access; the *Atlas of Vermont Trout Ponds* and *Vermont Trout Streams*, both from Northern Cartographics Inc. (Box 133, Burlington 05402); and *Fishing Vermont's Streams and Lakes* by Peter F. Cammann (The Countryman Press). Within this book we have listed shops, outfitters, and guides as they appear within each region. **Vermont Outdoor Guide Association** (1-800-747-5905) represents qualified guides throughout the state; check out their informative web site, www.adventureguidesvt.com.

FOLIAGE Vermont is credited with inventing foliage season, first aggressively promoted just after World War II in the initial issues of *Vermont Life*. The Department of Tourism (see *Information*) maintains a foliage "hotline" and sends out weekly bulletins on color progress, which is always earlier than assumed by those of us who live south of Montpelier. Those in the know usually head for northern Vermont in late Sep. and the first week of Oct., a period that coincides with peak color in that area as well as with the **Northeast Kingdom Fall Foliage Festival**. By the following weekend Central Vermont is usually ablaze, but visitors should be sure to have a bed reserved long before coming, because organized bus tours converge on the state. By the Columbus Day weekend, when what seems like millions of families within driving distance make their annual leaf-peeping expedition, your odds of finding a bed are dim unless you take advantage of those chambers of commerce (notably Middlebury, Woodstock, Brattleboro, Manchester, Central Vermont, and St. Johnsbury) that pride themselves on finding refuge in private homes for all comers. During peak color, we recommend that you avoid Vermont's most congested tourist routes; there is plenty of room on the back roads, especially those unsuited to buses. We strongly suggest exploring the high roads through Vermont's "gaps" (see *Gaps, Gulfs, and Gorges*) during this time of year.

GAPS, GULFS, AND GORGES Vermont's mountains were much higher before they were pummeled some 100,000 years ago by a mile-high sheet of ice. Glacial forces contoured the landscape we recognize today, notching the mountains with a number of handy "gaps" through which humans eventually built roads to get from one side of the mountain to the other. Gaps frequently offer superb views and access to ridge trails. This is true of the **Appalachian**, **Lincoln**, **Middlebury**, and **Brandon Gaps**, all crossing the Long Trail and linking Rt. 100 with the Champlain Valley; and of the Roxbury Gap east of the Mad River Valley. Note, however, that the state's highest and most scenic gap

of all is called a *notch* (**Smugglers Notch** between Stowe and Jeffersonville), the New Hampshire name for mountain passes. Gaps at lower elevations are *gulfs*, scenic passes that make ideal picnic sites: Note **Granville Gulf** on Rt. 100, **Brookfield Gulf** on Rt. 12, **Proctorsville Gulf** on Rt. 103 between Proctorsville and Chester, and **Williamstown Gulf** on Rt. 14. The state's outstanding gorges include: 163-foot-deep **Quechee Gorge**, which can be viewed from Rt. 4 east of Woodstock; **Brockway Mills Gorge** in Rockingham (off Rt. 103); **Cavendish Gorge**, Springfield; **Clarendon Gorge**, Shrewsbury (traversed by the Long Trail via footbridge); **Brewster River Gorge**, south of Jeffersonville off Rt. 108; **Jay Branch Gorge** off Rt. 105; and (probably the most photographed of all) the **Brown River** churning through the gorge below the Old Red Mill in Jericho.

GARDENS Vermont's growing season is all the more intense for its shortness. Commercial herb and flower gardens are themselves the fastest-growing form of agriculture in the state, and many inns and B&Bs pride themselves on their gardens. Lodging places with especially noteworthy gardens include **Willow Pond Farm** in Shelburne, **Basin Harbor Club** in Vergennes, the **Inn at Shelburne Farms** in Shelburne, **Judith's Garden B&B** and **Blueberry Hill**, both in Goshen, the **Hidden Gardens B&B** in Hinesburg, **the West Hill House** in Warren, and the **Jackson House** in Woodstock. **Historic Hildene** in Manchester also features formal gardens with thousands of peonies, and the **Shelburne Museum** holds an annual Lilac Festival in mid- to late May. Within this book we describe our favorite commercial gardens in *Selective Shopping*. For a listing of commercial nurseries click onto www.vermontagriculture.com/links.

GENERAL STORES Still the hub of most small Vermont communities, general stores retain traces of their onetime status as the source of all staples and communication with the outside world. The most famous survivor is the **Vermont Country Store** in Weston and Rockingham, a genuine family business that has expanded into a Vermont version of L.L. Bean. Its thick catalog is still a source of long underwear and garter belts, Healthy Feet Cream, shoe trees, and gadgets like a kit that turns a plastic soda bottle into a bird feeder. "The General Store in Vermont," an oral history by Jane Beck, is available from the Vermont Folklife Center in Middlebury. Within this book we have described our favorite general stores as they appear geographically.

As we updated this 11th edition of our guide, we couldn't help noting how this genre is changing: We found the best of the old-timers in Stowe (where Shaw's is still the "real thing"), Barton, Greensboro Village, West Danville, Marshfield, Sharon, and Norwich (among many others), but new owners tend to add café tables, armchairs, fine wines, cappuccino, baked items, and specialty foods and products; a few now employ full-time chefs. For an overview check out the newly formed **Vermont Alliance of Independent Country Stores** at www.vaics.org.

GOLF More than 60 Vermont golf courses are open to the public, and more than half of these have 18 holes,

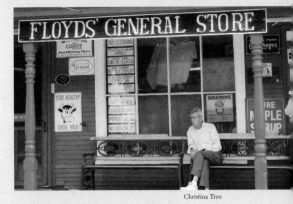

Christina Tree

FLOYD'S GENERAL STORE, RANDOLPH CENTER

half a dozen of them justly famed throughout the country. A full program of lodging, meals, and lessons is available at Mount Snow, Killington, Okemo, Stratton Mountain, Sugarbush, and Stowe. The Woodstock Inn, Lake Morey Inn, and others also offer golf packages. The Manchester area boasts the greatest concentration of courses. Sixty-seven courses are identified on the *Vermont Attractions Map*; for detailed descriptions and editorials see the glossy annual magazine *Vermont Golf* (1-800-639-1941; www.playnortheastgolf.com). Also see www.vermontvacation.com.

THE GREEN MOUNTAINS Running 160 miles up the spine of this narrow state, the Green Mountains themselves range in width from 20 to 36 miles, with peaks rising to more than 4,000 feet. A part of the Appalachian Mountain chain, which extends from Alabama to Canada's Gaspé Peninsula, they were once far higher. The Long Trail runs the length of the range, and Rt. 100 shadows its eastern base. Also see *Hiking and Walking* and *Gaps, Gulfs, and Gorges*.

GREEN MOUNTAIN CLUB See *Hiking and Walking*.

**GREEN MOUNTAIN NATIONAL FOR-
EST** The Green Mountain National
Forest encompasses 821,000 Vermont
acres managed by the USDA Forest
Service. It's traversed by 900 miles of
trails, including the **Appalachian
Trail** and the **Long Trail**, which follows the ridgeline of the main range
of the Green Mountains (see *Hiking
and Walking*). The forest harbors six
wilderness areas. Use of off-road
recreational vehicles is regulated.
Information—printed as well as verbal—about hiking, camping, skiing,
berry picking, and bird-watching is
available from the ranger stations in
Manchester Center (802-362-2307),
Middlebury (802-388-4362), and
Rochester (802-767-4261). Request a
free "mini map" from the **Green
Mountain National Forest** (802-
747-6700; 231 N. Main St., Rutland
05701). All four offices maintain visitors centers, open weekdays 8–4:30;
Rochester is open 8–4 except Sun.,
weekdays only off-season.

HANDICAPPED ACCESS The wheelchair symbol ♿ indicates lodging and
dining places that are handicapped
accessible.

HEALTH Almost every Vermont town
has a health clinic or local physician
(as of this writing, 93-year-old Dr.
Harry Rowe is still seeing patients
at the Wells River Clinic). But hospitals are not far away. The two largest
are in Burlington and just over the
border from White River Junction,
in Lebanon, N.H. The **Dartmouth-
Hitchcock Medical Center** (1 Medical Center Dr., Lebanon, NH 03756;
603-650-5000; www.dhmc.org) oversees children's, cancer, spine, and car-
diology centers, a medical school, and
a level one trauma center. A branch of

Dartmouth-Hitchcock is the 201-bed
**Veterans Affairs Regional Medical
and Office Center** (215 N. Main St.,
White River Junction 05009-0001; 1-
866-687-8387; www.visn1.med.va.gov/
wrj). **Fletcher Allen Health Care** in
Burlington (111 Colchester Ave.,
Burlington 05401; 802-847-0000;
www.fletcherallen.org), also a level
one trauma center and teaching hospital, has just doubled the size of its
emergency room as part of a major
expansion.

Other Vermont hospitals include
(from south to north) **Brattleboro
Memorial Hospital** in Brattleboro
(802-257-0341; www.bmhvt.org);
**Southwestern Vermont Health
Care** in Bennington (802-442-6361;
www.svhealthcare.org); **Grace Cottage Hospital** in Townshend (802-
365-7357; www.otishealthcarecenter
.org); **Springfield Hospital** in
Springfield (802-885-2151; www
.springfieldhospital.org); **Rutland
Regional Medical Center** in Rutland (802-775-7111; www.rrmc.org);
Porter Medical Center in Middlebury (802-388-4701; www.porter
medical.org); **Mt. Ascutney Hospital
and Health Center** in Windsor
(802-674-6711; www.mtascutneyhosp
.hitchcock.org); **Gifford Medical
Center** in Randolph (802-728-7000;
www.giffordmed.org); **Central Vermont Medical Center** in Barre
(802-371-4100; www.cvmc.hitchcock
.org); **Copley Hospital** in Morrisville
(802-888-4231; www.copleyhealth
systems.org); **Northwestern Medical Center** in St. Albans (802-524-
5911; www.northwesternmedical
center.org); **Northeastern Vermont
Regional Hospital** in St. Johnsbury
(802-748-8141; www.nvrh.org); and
North Country Hospital in Newport (802-334-7331; www.nchsi.org).

For more general information, contact the **Vermont Association of Hospitals and Health Systems** in Montpelier at (802-223-3461 or www.vahhs.org). As elsewhere in the country, when faced with a medical emergency, dial 911.

HIGH SEASON "High season" varies from Vermont community to community and even within a community such as Manchester (one side of town is nearer the ski resorts; the other is geared more to summer). While "foliage season" represents peak price as well as color everywhere, a ski condo can easily cost four times as much in February as it does in July. Meanwhile, a country inn may charge half its July price in February.

HIGHWAY ROAD FOOD As we have cruised Vermont's interstates over the years, we have developed patterns of exiting for food at places where (1) food is less than a mile from the exit, and (2) food is good, and we strongly favor diners and local eateries over fast-food chains. Needless to say, wherever there's food, there's gas (no pun intended). All the following restaurants are described in their respective chapters.

Along **I-91**, south to north: *Exit 2* is handy to the many choices in downtown Brattleboro and to the **Chelsea Royal Diner**, west on Rt. 9. *Exit 4:* The **Putney Inn** is good for all three meals; around the corner is **Curtis' Barbecue**, and just up Rt. 5 is the **Putney Diner**. *Exit 15:* The **Fairlee Diner** is just north. *Exit 16:* **The Hungry Bear** is just off I-91; the **Bradford Village Store** in the middle of the village serves hot soups and deli sandwiches (try for the window seat), while for dinner there's **Cola-**

tina **Exit** and **Perfect Pear Café**. *Exit 17:* **P&H Truck Stop** is worth a stop. *Exit 23:* Turn north onto Rt. 5 to find the **Miss Lyndonville Diner**.

Along **I-89**: *Exit 3:* **Eaton's Sugar House** is right off the exit. *Exit 7:* Follow signs to Rt. 302 and the **Wayside Restaurant and Bakery**, a real find, is on your left. *Exit 10:* Turn left, then left again, and you are in the middle of Waterbury at **Arvad's**. *Exit 14W:* Burlington is just down the hill, worth a detour. *Exit 14E:* Turn east onto Williston Rd. and head away from town to find **The Parkway Diner**. *Exit 16:* **Libby's Blue Line Diner** is right there on the hill, and great. Also see *Diners*.

HIGHWAY TRAVEL INFORMATION See *Information*.

HIKING AND WALKING More than 700 miles of hiking trails web Vermont—which is 162 miles long as the crow flies but 255 miles long as the hiker trudges, following the **Long Trail** up and down the spine of the Green Mountains. But few hikers are out to set distance records on the Long Trail. The path from Massachusetts to the Canadian border, which was completed in 1931, has a way of slowing people down. It opens up eyes and lungs and drains compulsiveness. Even die-hard backpackers tend to linger on rocky outcrops, looking down on farms and steeples. A total of 98 side trails (175 miles) meander off to wilderness ponds or abandoned villages; these trails are mostly maintained, along with the Long Trail, by the **Green Mountain Club** (802-244-7037; www.greenmountainclub.org), founded in 1910. The club also maintains about 66 shelters and 70 campsites, many of them staffed by caretakers during summer months. The club publishes the *Long Trail Guide*, which gives details on trails and shelters throughout the system, as well as the *Day Hiker's Guide to Vermont*. These and other guides are sold in the club's **Hiker's Center** (4711 Waterbury Rd., Waterbury Center 05677; open 9–5 daily, but closed on weekends in the off-season). The **Appalachian Trail Conservancy** (P.O. Box 807, Harpers Ferry, WV 25425; www.appalachiantrail.org) includes detailed information in its *Appalachian Trail Guide to Vermont and New Hampshire*, and a wide assortment of trails are nicely detailed in *50 Hikes in Vermont* (The Countryman Press).

Backpackers who are hesitant to set out on their own can take a wide variety of guided hikes and walks. **Adventure Guides of Vermont** (1-800-747-5905; www.adventure guidesvt.com) and **Vermont Outdoor Guide Association** (1-800-425-8747; www.voga.org) can put you in touch with guides and adventure-geared packages throughout the state. Organized tours are offered by **Umiak Outdoor Outfitters** (802-253-2317), based in Stowe. In the Ludlow area several inns also offer support services (route planning, baggage transfers) as well as meals and lodging; check out www .vermontinntoinnwalking.com. Within this book we suggest hiking trails as they appear geographically. Also note the recent proliferation of trail systems: In the Northeast Kingdom check out **Kingdom Trails** in East Burke, the **Vermont Leadership Center** near Island Pond, and the **Hazen's Notch Association Trails** (www.hazensnotch .org). We should also note that both Killington and Stowe offer ridge hiking from the top of their lifts. (See also *Birding, State Parks, Mountain Biking,* and *Nature Preserves*.)

HISTORY Vermont is a small state, but it has had a dramatic life. In essence, the whole state is a living history museum, even though most towns were settled after the Revolution. Many often overlapping land grants issued by the royal governors of both New Hampshire and New York were not truly sorted out until 1791, when Congress admitted Vermont as the 14th state, after 14 years as an independent republic.

The Abenaki presence in Vermont is far more pervasive than was acknowledged until very recently. Today's **St. Anne's Shrine on Isle La Motte** memorializes Samuel de Champlain's first landfall on the lake that bears his name; the site was certainly an Indian village and by 1666 a mission as well as a French fort. It was abandoned in 1679 but remains an evocative place. A colossal granite statue of Champlain depicts an unnamed Indian guide at his feet. Nearby in present-day Swanton, the Indian village of Missisquoi became a mission village, a way stop for Abenaki headed for Canada. Abenaki life is presented in an exhibit at the **Abenaki Tribal Museum and Cultural Center** (802-868-2559), 100 Grand Ave., Swanton; open Mon.–Fri. 9–4 (but call ahead). Abenaki settlements are also recorded at Otter Creek, and the 18th-century tavern at **Chimney Point State Historic Site** in Addison has a well-mounted display that explains the territory's Native American and French colonial heritage. In Newport the new lakeside state office building displays the **Memphremagog Historical Society**'s exhibit on northern Vermont Abenaki people, from Paleolithic through current times, and at the **Fort at Number 4** in Charlestown, N.H. (see "The Lower Connecticut River Valley"), a community in which settlers and Indians lived side by side, the reconstructed fort exhibits Native American artifacts from the Connecticut River Valley.

Bennington, chartered by the avaricious Governor Benning Wentworth in 1749, the first chartered town west of the Connecticut River in the New Hampshire Grants, became the tinderbox for settlers' resistance to New York's rival claims, confirmed by King George in 1764. The desperate grantees found a champion in the protean Ethan Allen from Connecticut. This frontier rebel—land speculator, firebrand, and philosopher—recruited the boisterous Green Mountain Boys militiamen, who talked rum and rebellion at the Catamount Tavern in **Old Bennington**, pledged defiance of the 'Yorkers, and then fought the British. Ethan's rambunctious life is reflected in the **Ethan Allen Homestead**, the farm north of Burlington where he died in 1789.

In Westminster, on the bank of the Connecticut River, the 1775 **"Massacre"** was thought, incorrectly, to have been the first armed engagement of the Revolution. But the death of William French, shot by a 'Yorker sheriff ("The Cruel Minestereal Tools of George ye 3d"), galvanized opposition to both New York and England, leading to a convention in Westminster in January 1777, where Vermonters declared their independence of everyone.

Formal independence was declared the following July, upriver in Windsor, where delegates gathered in Elijah West's tavern (now **The Old Constitution House**). They adopted a model constitution, the first to abolish slavery, before rushing off to attack the British, who had retaken Fort Ticonderoga. (While in Windsor, visit the **American Precision Museum**, a landmark showcasing early gun makers and the heyday of the machine tool industry.)

Since its discovery by Samuel de Champlain in 1609, Lake Champlain has been not only one of the nation's most historic waterways, but a strategic corridor in three wars. The French controlled the lake until 1759, when Lord Jeffery Amherst drove them out of Fort Carillon (now **Ticonderoga**) and then captured Montreal. In the American Revolution, the British used the lake as an invasion route to divide the colonies, but were thwarted when Ethan Allen's Green Mountain Boys captured Fort Ticonderoga in 1775.

Facing Ticonderoga across the lake's narrowest channel, the **Mount Independence State Historic Site** near Orwell dramatizes the struggle that ended with the decisive British defeat at Saratoga in 1777. The only battle of the Revolution to have been fought on Vermont soil is commemorated at the **Hubbardton Battlefield** near Castleton, where a small force of Green Mountain Boys under

Sandy Levesque for Vermont Historical Society

INFORMATION

The **Vermont Department of Tourism and Marketing** (1-800-VERMONT) offers vacation planning, information packets, seasonal conditions, and an excellent web site: www.vermontvacation.com. Their business office (802-828-3237) is at 6 Baldwin St., Montpelier 05633-1301. Request: (1) *Vermont's Official Attractions Map and Guide*, a road map with symbols locating attractions, covered bridges, golf courses, state parks and historic sites, ski areas, public boat and fishing access ramps, and more.

(2) *Vermont Travelers Guidebook* (spring–summer and fall) and *Vermont Winter Guide*, helpful and current magazine-format guides published by the **Vermont Chamber of Commerce** (802-223-3443), which maintains its own useful web site: www.vtchamber.com. You can also request the *Vermont Historic Sites Guide*, the *Vermont Farms* brochure, and the *Vermont Campground Guidebook*; from the chamber you can request a pamphlet guide to country inns and B&Bs. We have noted local chambers of commerce town by town in each chapter of this book under *Guidance*. In towns not served by a chamber, inquiries are welcomed by the town clerk. First-time visitors may be puzzled by Vermont's Travel Information System of directional signs, which replace billboards (banned since 1967, another Vermont first). Stylized symbols for lodging, food, recreation, antiques and crafts, and other services are sited at intersections off major highways.

Vermont's 20 interstate welcome and information centers with pay phones and bathroom facilities are generally open 7 AM–11 PM and marked on the state map. At the Massachusetts border, northbound at Guilford on I-91, the state's largest and most complete **Welcome Center** (802-254-4593; open 24 hours) displays Vermont products and exhibits. Other I-91 welcome centers, open daily, are northbound at **Bradford** (802-222-9369), southbound

WAYPOINT VISITORS CENTER, BELLOWS FALLS

Christina Tree

GUILFORD INFORMATION CENTER

Christina Tree

at **Lyndon** (802-626-9669), and at **Derby Line** (802-873-3311). At the junction of I-91 and I-89 (in downtown White River Junction) the **White River Junction Welcome Center** (802-281-5050), housed in the Amtrak station, is open varying hours. Along I-89 welcome centers are found at **Sharon**, north- and southbound; at **Randolph**, northbound (802-524-0015) and southbound (802-524-0018); at **Williston** southbound (802-879-2360); and north of Burlington both north- and southbound in **Georgia**. At the Canadian border you'll find a major welcome center at **Highgate** (802-868-3244, 7 AM–11 PM). There's also an inviting welcome center just over the state line on I-93 at **Waterford** (802-748-9368, 7 AM–11 PM), as well as visitors centers at the New York–Canadian border on Rt. 2 in **Alburg** (802-796-3980, open 10–6) and on the New York border on Rt. 4A in **Fair Haven** (802-265-4763, open 7 AM–9 PM). In **Montpelier** the **Capital Region Visitors Center**, 134 State St. (802-828-5981, open 9–5 daily), is the source of statewide information. **AAA Emergency Road Service**: 1-800-222-4357.

For road conditions dial 511 or click on www.511vt.com. Also see *Highway Road Food* and *Weather Reports*.

Steve Cook

Colonel Seth Warner stopped a far larger British contingent as Burgoyne's British troops marched south. The invaders were soon repulsed again in the battle of Bennington—actually fought in New York—marked by the **Bennington Battle Monument** and by exhibits in the **Bennington Museum**.

The lake also figured in naval warfare when Benedict Arnold and a quickly assembled American flotilla engaged a heavier British squadron off Plattsburgh, N.Y., in the battle of Valcour Island in October 1776. One of Arnold's small gunboats, the *Philadelphia*, sunk by the British, was salvaged in 1935 and reposes in the Smithsonian. An exact replica is moored at the **Lake Champlain Maritime Museum** at Basin Harbor near Vergennes. A number of ships and other artifacts of that battle have been found buried in the mud on the lake bottom in recent years. In 1814 the British again tried to use Lake Champlain as an invasion route. Thomas McDonough moved his headquarters from Burlington to Vergennes and a shipyard at the mouth of Otter Creek. His small fleet barely managed to defeat British ships at Plattsburgh Bay, a bloody engagement that helped end the War of 1812.

With Vermont in the vanguard of the antislavery movement of the 1840s, the Underground Railroad flourished, notably at **Rokeby**, the home of the Robinson family in Ferrisburgh, now a museum. Evidence of the state's extraordinary record in the Civil War and its greater-than-average number of per capita casualties may be seen in the memorials that dot most town and village greens. How Vermonters turned the tide of the battle at Cedar Creek is portrayed in Julian Scott's huge and newly restored painting that hangs in the **State House** in Montpelier. The anniversary of the October 1864 **St. Albans Raid**, the northernmost engagement of the Civil War, is observed annually.

There are few 18th-century structures in the state, but the settlers who poured in after 1791 (the population nearly tripled, from 85,000 to 235,000 in 1820) built sophisticated dwellings and churches. **Dorset**, **Castleton**, **Chester** (Old Stone Village), **Middlebury**, **Brandon**, **Woodstock**, and **Norwich** are architectural showcases of Federal-style houses. Several historic, outstandingly splendid mansions built by 19th-century moguls are open to the public: the **Park-McCullough House**, North Bennington; the **Wilburton Inn** and **Hildene**, Manchester; **The Castle Inn**, Proctorsville; **Wilson Castle**, West Rutland; the **Marsh-Billings-Rockefeller National Historical Park**, Woodstock; and **The Inn at Shelburne Farms** (built by Lila Vanderbilt Webb and William Seward Webb), Shelburne.

Vermont's congressional delegations, especially in the 19th century, always had more influence in Washington than the state's size might suggest. For example, the **Justin Morrill Homestead** in Strafford, a spacious Gothic Revival house, reminds us of the distinguished career of the originator of the Land Grant Colleges Act, who served in Congress from 1855 to 1898.

State and local historical societies have faithfully preserved the cultural evidence. The **Vermont Historical Society Museum** (www.vermont history.org), which reopened after a complete makeover and expansion in 2004, is housed in a replica of the

Pavilion Hotel that stands beside the Vermont State House in Montpelier. The society also maintains a research library in Barre with changing special exhibits. Arts, crafts, architecture, and transportation are featured in the **Shelburne Museum** in Shelburne. In Woodstock the **Billings Farm & Museum** re-creates a model 1890s stock farm and dairy and the **Marsh-Billings-Rockefeller National Historical Park** traces the state's environmental history. Outstanding collections of the ways people lived and worked can be found in town historical societies, notably the **Farrar Mansur House** in Weston, the **Sheldon Museum** in Middlebury, and the **Dana House** in Woodstock. For a lively, popular story of the state from its origins to the present, read Peter Jennison's *Roadside History of Vermont* (Mountain Press). A pamphlet guide to Vermont state historic sites, operated by the Division for Historic Preservation, is available at information centers throughout the state, and the sites are also profiled, along with events and historic roadside markers, at www.historicvermont.org. See also *Historical Societies*.

HISTORICAL SOCIETIES The attics of every town, historical societies are frequently worth seeking out, but because most are staffed by volunteers, they tend to be open just a few hours a week, usually in summer. Of Vermont's 251 towns, 184 have historical societies; we have tried to give accurate, current information on them within each chapter. The Vermont Historical Society publishes a free booklet, *Passport to Vermont History*, listing hours and contact phones for more than 170. Another information source is www.vermont history.org. The most outstanding local historical societies are in **Brattleboro**, **Brownington**, **Newfane**, and **Middlebury**. *Note:* On the last weekend of June the Vermont Historical Society sponsors the **Vermont History Expo**. Held at the fairgrounds in Tunbridge, it is billed as "a celebration of Vermont's Story as Told by the Keepers of Its Treasures and Traditions" and includes a full schedule of folk songs, lectures, demonstrations, displays, and live entertainment.

HUNTING The *Vermont Digest of Hunting, Fishing and Trapping Laws* and a useful *State of Vermont Hunting Map* are available from the Vermont Fish and Wildlife Department (802-241-3700; 103 S. Main St., in the 10 South building, Waterbury 05671-0501; www.vtfishandwildlife.com). Of special interest to nonresidents: a reasonably priced, 5-day small-game license. The ruffed grouse or "partridge" is the state's most abundant game bird, while woodcocks, or "timberdoodles," are found throughout the state. The wild turkey is considered "big game"—as hunters will understand when they try to bag them (in-season in Oct. and May). October is bow-and-arrow season for white-tailed deer, and Nov. is buck season. Black bear and moose populations are both healthy, but hunting regulations vary with the year.

ICE CREAM Vermont's quality milk is used to produce some outstanding ice cream as well as cheese. The big name is, of course, **Ben & Jerry's**, proud producers of what *Time* has billed "the best ice cream in the world." Their plant on Rt. 100 in Waterbury (featuring factory tours, free samples, real cows, and a gift shop full of reproductions in every conceivable shape) has quickly become one of the state's most popular tourist attractions. Other good Vermont ice creams include **Seward's** in Rutland, **Wilcox Brothers** in Manchester, **Ellsworth Ice Cream** in North Springfield, the **Strafford Organic Creamery** in Strafford, the **Mountain Creamery** in Woodstock, and **Green Mountain Gelato** in Barre.

INNS It's safe to say that we have visited more Vermont inns, more frequently, than anyone else living today. We do not charge for inclusion in this book, and we attempt to give as accurate and detailed a picture as space permits. We quote 2005–06 rates—which are, of course, subject to change. Summer rates are generally lower than winter (except, of course, at lake resorts); weekly or ski-week rates run 10–20 percent less than the per diem price quoted. Many inns insist on MAP (Modified American Plan—breakfast and dinner) in winter but not in summer. Some resorts have AP (American Plan—three meals), and we have shown EP (European Plan—no meals) where applicable. We have attempted to note when 15 percent service is added, but you should always ask if it has been included in a quoted rate and whether an additional local tax is added. Always add the 9 percent state tax on rooms and meals. It's prudent to check which, if any, credit cards are accepted. Many lodging places now insist on minimum 2- or 3-day stays during busy seasons. Within the text, special icons highlight lodging places offering exceptional value ❦, those that appeal to families ✧, those that are handicapped accessible ✧, those that

accept pets ❧, and those that specialize in weddings and civil unions ∞.

LAKES The state famed for green mountains and white villages also harbors more than 400 relatively blue lakes: big lakes like **Champlain** (150 miles long) and **Memphremagog** (boasting 88 miles of coastline, but most of it in Canada), smaller lakes like **Morey**, **Dunmore**, **Willoughby**, **Bomoseen**, and **Seymour**. Lakes are particularly plentiful and people sparse in Vermont's Northeast Kingdom. A century ago there were many more lakeside hotels; today just a handful of these classic summer resorts survive: **Quimby Country** in Averill, **Highland Lodge** in Greensboro, the **Tyler Place** in Highgate Springs, the **Basin Harbor Club** near Vergennes, and the **Lake Morey Inn Resort** in Fairlee. There are half a dozen smaller, informal inns on scattered lakes, but that's about it. Still, you can bed down very reasonably within sound and sight of Vermont waters either by renting a cottage (more than half of those listed in *Four Season Vacation Rentals*, available from the Vermont Department of Tourism and Marketing, are on lakes) or by taking advantage of state park campsites on **Groton**

LAKE MEMPHREMAGOG

Christina Tree

Lake, Emerald Lake, Island Pond, Maidstone Lake, Lake Bomoseen, Lake Carmi, Lake Elmore, Lake St. Catherine, and Silver Lake (in Barnard). On Lake Champlain, there are a number of state campgrounds, including those on Grand Isle (accessible by car) and Burton Island (accessible by public launch from St. Albans Bay). See *Campgrounds* for details about these and the free campsites on Ball Mountain Lake, maintained by the Army Corps of Engineers. There is public boat access to virtually every Vermont pond and lake of any size. Boat launches are listed on the state map.

LIBRARIES The small village of Brookfield boasts the state's oldest continuously operating public library, established in 1791. Most libraries that we mention here date, however, from that late-19th-century philanthropic era when wealthy native sons were moved to donate splendidly ornate libraries to their hometowns. Notable examples are to be found in Barre, Chester, Ludlow, Wilmington, Rutland, Newport, Woodstock, St. Johnsbury, and Brattleboro. For research, the Vermont Historical Society Library in Barre is a treasure trove of Vermontiana and genealogical resources, as is the Wilbur Collection of the Bailey-Howe Library at the University of Vermont and the Russell Collection in Arlington. Three of the Vermont state colleges—Castleton, Johnson, and Lyndon—have collections of Vermontiana in the Vermont Rooms of their libraries.

LLAMA TREKKING Check out Applecheek Farm in Hyde Park (802-888-4482); Northern Vermont Llama Co. (802-644-2257) in Waterville; the Stowe Llama Ranch (802-253-5118); Cold Hollow Llamas (802-644-5846) in Belvidere; On the Loose Expeditions (1-800-688-1481) in Huntington; Maple Leaf Llamas (802-586-2873) in Craftsbury Common; and Dream Come True Farm in Hartland (802-295-1573).

MAGAZINES *Vermont Life* (802-828-3241; www.vtlife.com), the popular and colorful quarterly published by the Agency of Development and Community Affairs and edited by Tom Slayton, is an outstanding chronicle of Vermont's people and places, featuring distinguished photographers. *Vermont Magazine* (802-388-8480; www.vermontmagazine.com), the upbeat, statewide bimonthly launched in 1989, covers major issues, townscapes, products, and personalities, and reviews inns and restaurants. The new (since 2004) bimonthly *Livin' the Vermont Way* (802-879-2013; www.livinmagazine), aimed instate instead of out, covers issues of local concern such as the environment, industry, and politics, with smaller features on folklore, food, and recreation. *Seven Days* (802-864-5684; www.sevendaysvt.com), Burlington's free weekly tabloid of area arts and entertainment, is far more than a calendar of events.

MAPLE SUGARING Vermont produces some 400,000 gallons of maple syrup each year, over a third of the national supply and more than any other state. Approximately 2,000 maple growers tap an average of 1,000 trees each. About a quart of syrup is made per tap; it takes 30 to 40 gallons of sap to make each gallon of syrup. The process of tapping trees and boiling sap is stubbornly known as *sugaring*, rather than *syruping*, because the end product for early settlers was sugar. Syrup was first made in the early 19th century, but production flagged when imported cane sugar became more accessible. The Civil War revived the maple sugar industry: Union supporters were urged to consume sugar made by free men and to plant more and more maples.

We urge visitors to buy syrup direct from the producer, any time of year (finding the farm is half the fun), but also to seriously consider making a special trip to a sugarhouse during sugaring season in March and April. It's then (not in autumn) that sugar maples really perform, and it's a show that can't be seen through a windshield. Sugaring season begins quietly in February as thousands of Vermonters wade, snowshoe, and snowmobile into their woods and begin "tapping," a ritual that has changed since plastic tubing replaced buckets. But the timing is the same. Traditionally, sugaring itself begins on Town Meeting Day (the first Tuesday in March). But sap runs only on those days when temperatures rise to 40 and 50 degrees during the day and drop into the 20s at night. When the sap does run, it must be boiled down quickly. What you want to see is the boiling process: sap churning madly through the large, flat evaporating pan, darkening as you watch. You are enveloped in fragrant steam, listening to the rush of the sap, sampling the end result on snow or in tiny paper cups. Sugaring is Vermont's rite of spring. Don't miss a sugar-on-snow party: plates of snow dribbled with viscous hot syrup, accompanied by doughnuts and dill pickles.

A *Vermont Maple Syrup Map*, available by phoning 1-800-VER-MONT, lists and pinpoints producers who open their doors to the public on **Maple Open House Weekend** in mid-March. See www.vermont.com/maple or www.vermontmaple.org for similar information and a list of producers who ship. The **Vermont Maple Festival**, held in late April in St. Albans, is a 3-day event that includes tours through the local sugarbush (802-524-5800; www.vtmaple festival.org). At **Maple Grove Farm** of Vermont, "the world's largest maple candy factory" in St. Johnsbury, factory tours are offered Mon.–Fri. year-round, and there is a maple museum and gift shop. Videos on maple are also shown in the **New England Maple Museum** in Pittsford and in the maple museum at **Sugarmill Farm** in Barton. Within this book we list maple producers in the areas in which they are most heavily concentrated. There are many more than found on any formal lists. Ask locally.

MAPS *Vermont's Official Attractions Map and Guide* (see *Information*) is free and extremely helpful for general motoring but will not suffice

Kim Grant

for finding your way around the webs of dirt roads that connect some of the most beautiful corners of the state. Among our favorite areas where you will need more detail: the high farming country between Albany, Craftsbury, and West Glover; similar country between Chelsea and Williamstown; south from Plainfield to Orange; and between Plymouth and Healdville. We strongly suggest securing a copy of the *Vermont Atlas and Gazetteer* (DeLorme) if you want to do any serious back-road exploring, or the *Vermont Road Atlas and Guide* (Northern Cartographics); both are widely available at bookstores, gas stations, and general stores. Among the best regional maps for anyone planning to do much hiking or biking are those published by Map Adventures (www.map adventures.com). Also see *Hiking and Walking*.

MONEY Don't leave home without MasterCard or Visa, the two credit cards that are far more readily accepted in Vermont than American Express or personal checks. Each inn has its own policy about credit cards and checks.

MOUNTAIN BIKING Several ski areas offer lift-assisted mountain biking. The **Mount Snow Mountain Bike School** (802-464-4040) was the first, offering 45 miles of trails, some served by lifts. **Stratton Sports** (802-297-4230; 1-800-STRATTON), at Stratton Mountain, rents mountain bikes and offers a variety of terrain. In the Burlington area, **Bolton Valley** (802-434-3444) and the **Catamount Family Center** (802-879-6001) both offer extensive cross-country trail networks and rentals. **Killington** (www .killington.com) and **Jay Peak Resort**

(www.jaypeakresort.com) also permit mountain biking on ski trails, accessible via lifts.

In recent years, however, Vermont mountain biking options have dramatically broadened beyond the state's ski mountains as the potential for its hundreds of miles of dirt and Class 4 roads as well as cross-county trail systems has been recognized. The **Craftsbury Outdoor Center** (www .craftsbury.com) up in the Northeast Kingdom was the first place to rent mountain bikes and offer guided tours over dirt and abandoned logging roads. A former prep school now devoted to running and rowing as well as biking in summer and cross-country skiing in winter, it's set in high, rolling farm country with mountain views. There's another magnificent trail system in the Burke Mountain area: **Kingdom Trails**, a 100-mile mix of trails maintained by a nonprofit organization. Pick up a map and day pass at **East Burke Sports** (802-626-3215), or visit www.kingdomtrails.org. In Randolph you can arrive with your bike via Amtrak and take advantage of the **Three Stallion Inn**'s network of trails. In southeastern Vermont the **West Hill Shop** (802-387-5718) publishes its own map to an extensive network of singletrack trails and forgotten roads.

We describe inns and bike shops that offer bike rentals in almost every chapter, but here we should mention **Blueberry Hill Inn** (1-800-448-0707), set high in Goshen with easy access to trails in the Moosalamoo region of the Green Mountain National Forest and to Silver Lake. The nominally priced *Topographic Maps & Guides* produced by Map Adventures (www.mapadventures .com), are useful map/guides outlining rides in various parts of Vermont: the Burlington and Stowe areas, the White River Valley, the Upper Valley, and Southern Vermont, among others. **Adventure Guides of Vermont** (1-800-747-5905) supplies every imaginable guide and maintains an excellent web site, www.adventureguides vt.com. See also *Bicycle Touring*.

MOUNTAINTOPS While Vermont can boast only seven peaks above 4,000 feet, there are 80 mountains that rise more than 3,000 feet and any number of spectacular views, several of them accessible in summer and foliage season to those who prefer riding to walking up mountains. **Mount Mansfield**, which at 4,393 feet is the state's highest summit, can be reached via the Toll Road and a gondola. The mid-19th-century road brings you to the small Summit Station at 4,062 feet, from which the 0.5-mile Tundra Trail brings you to the actual summit. The Mount Mansfield gondola, an eight-passenger, enclosed lift, hoists you from the main base area up to the Cliff House Restaurant (802-253-3500), from which a trail also heads up to the Chin. **Killington Peak**, Vermont's second highest peak at 4,241 feet, can be reached via a 1.2-mile ride on a gondola that takes you to a summit restaurant and a nature trail that even small children can negotiate. **Jay Peak**, a 3,861-foot summit towering like a lone sentinel near the Canadian border, is accessible via a 60-passenger tram (daily July–Labor Day, and again mid-Sep.–Columbus Day), and a "four-state view" from the top of **Stratton Mountain** is accessible via the ski resort's six-passenger gondola, Starship XII (daily in summer and fall). Other toll roads include the Auto

Road to the 3,267-foot **Burke Mountain** in East Burke, the Toll Road to the 3,144-foot summit of **Mount Ascutney** in Ascutney State Park, and the Skyline Drive to the top of **Mount Equinox** in Sunderland. There are also chairlift rides to the tops of **Bromley** (you don't have to take the alpine slide down) and **Mount Snow**.

MUD SEASON The period from snowmelt (around the middle of March) through early May (it varies each year) is known throughout the state as mud season for reasons that few visitors want to explore too deeply. It's worth mentioning that dirt roads can turn quickly into boggy quagmires, and travel off the main roads in this season can be challenging.

MUSEUMS Vermont museums vary from the immense **Shelburne Museum**—with its 39 buildings, many housing priceless collections of art and Americana, plus assorted exhibits such as a completely restored lake steamer and lighthouse—to the **American Precision Museum** in Windsor, an 1846 brick mill that once produced rifles. They include a number of outstanding historical museums (our favorites are the **Bennington Museum** in Bennington, the **Sheldon Museum** in Middlebury, the **Old Stone House Museum** in Brownington, and the **Dana House** in Woodstock) and some collections that go beyond the purely historical: The **Bennington Museum** is famed for its collection of Grandma Moses paintings as well as early American glass and relics from the Revolution, and the **Fairbanks Museum and Planetarium** in St. Johnsbury has vaulted wooden halls filled with taxidermied birds and animals. The

BRATTLEBORO MUSEUM & ART CENTER

Billings Farm & Museum in Wood-stock shows off its blue-ribbon dairy and has a fascinating, beautifully mounted display of 19th-century farm life and tools. The **Vermont Museum & Gallery Alliance** lists them all on its web site, www.vmga.org. Within this book, we have listed museums in their geographic areas.

MUSIC The Green Mountains are filled with the sounds of music each summer, beginning with the **Discover Jazz Festival** (www.discoverjazz .com), more than 100 concerts held over a week around Burlington in early June. In Putney a late-June-through-July series of three evening chamber music concerts each week is presented in the **Yellow Barn Festival** (1-800-639-3619; www.yellowbarn .org). In July and Aug. options include the internationally famous **Marlboro Music Festival** (802-254-2394; www .marlboromusic.org) at Marlboro College, presenting chamber music on weekends, and the **Vermont Mozart Festival** (802-862-7352; www.vt mozart.com), a series of 20 concerts performed at a variety of sites ranging from beautiful barns at the University of Vermont and Shelburne Farms to a

Lake Champlain ferry and including some striking classic and modern churches and a ski area base lodge. The **Killington Music Festival** (802-773-4003; www.killingtonmusicfestival .org) is a series of Sunday concerts at Rams Head Lodge from late June to early Aug., and the **Manchester Music Festival** (802-362-1956; 1-800-639-5868; www.mmfvt.org) brings leading performers to various venues around Manchester. Also well worth noting: the **Central Vermont Chamber Music Festival** (802-728-9133; www.centralvtchambermusicfest.org) at the Chandler Music Hall in Randolph in mid- to late Aug., the **Summer Music School** in Adamant (802-229-9297; www.adamant.org/summer .htm), concerts at the Town House in Hardwick by the **Craftsbury Chamber Players** (1-800-639-3443; www .craftsburychamberplayers.org), and in Stowe, for a week in late July, at the **Performing Arts Festival** (802-253-7792; www.stowearts.com).

Other concert series are performed at the **Southern Vermont Arts Center** (Thu., and Sun., 802-362-1405; www.svac.org); at the **Fine Arts Center**, Castleton State College (802-468-1119); at the **Dibden Center for the Arts**, Johnson State College (802-635-1388); and at **Middlebury College Center for the Arts** (802-443-3174). The **Vermont Symphony Orchestra** (802-864-5741; 1-800-VSO-9293; www.vso.org), the oldest of the state symphonies, figures in a number of the series noted above and also performs at a variety of locations, ranging from Brattleboro's Living Memorial Park and the State House lawn to Wilson Castle, throughout summer. In Weston the **Kinhaven Music School** (802-824-4332; www .kinhaven.org) offers free concerts on summer weekends, and in Brattleboro the **Brattleboro Music Center** (802-257-4523; www.bmcvt.org) brings in world-renowned classical groups for its year-round Chamber Music Series. See also *Fiddling*.

NATURE PRESERVES The **Vermont Land Trust** (www.vlt.org), founded in 1977, is dedicated to preserving Vermont's traditional landscape of farms as well as forest (it has helped protect more than 400 operating farms), and many local land trusts have acquired numerous parcels of land throughout the state. Many of the most visitor-friendly preserves are owned by **The Nature Conservancy** (802-229-4425; http://nature.org), a national nonprofit that has preserved close to 7 million acres throughout the United States since its founding in 1951. Its Vermont branch is at 27 State St., Montpelier 05602.

OPERA HOUSES Northern New England opera houses are a turn-of-the-20th-century phenomenon: theaters built as cultural centers for the surrounding area, stages on which lecturers, musicians, and vaudeville acts as well as opera singers performed. Many of these buildings have long since disappeared, but those that survive are worth noting. The **Hyde Park Opera House**, built in 1910, has been restored by the Lamoille County Players, who stage four annual shows—one play, two musicals, and an annual foliage-season run of *The Sound of Music*. The **Barre Opera House**, built in 1899, is an elegant, acoustically outstanding, second-floor theater, home of the Barre Players; productions are staged here year-round. In Derby Line, in the second-floor **Opera House** (a neoclassical struc-

ture that also houses the Haskell Free Library), the audience sits in Vermont watching a stage that is in Canada. Tom Thumb and Houdini performed at Rutland's 1914 **Paramount Theater**, which was restored in 2000 and now offers a full repertory from cabaret to jazz, comedy, and musicals. The theater company **Northern Stage** has taken up residence at White River Junction's **Briggs Opera House**, offering year-round performances and courses for children and young adults in summer months. The **Chandler Center for the Arts** in Randolph and the opera houses in **Vergennes** and **Enosburg Falls** have been restored for cultural events.

PETS We note lodging places that accommodate pets with the symbol ☻. We should note that while traveling with a dog or cat generally tends to rule out the possibility of staying in inns or B&Bs, some of Vermont's most elegant inns do permit them, most for a small additional fee: the **Inn on the Common** in Craftsbury, **Topnotch** in Stowe, the **Basin Harbor Club** in Vergennes, the **Woodstock Inn and Resort** in Woodstock, the **Mountain Top Inn and Resort** in Chittenden, and the **Waybury Inn** in East Middlebury. At least one inn, **The Paw House Inn** in West Rutland, actually caters to guests with dogs: supplying dog-sitters and off-leash areas, as well as equipping each room with dog bowls, beds, biscuits, and a can opener.

PICK YOUR OWN Strawberry season is mid- to late June. Cherries, plums, raspberries, and blueberries can be picked in July and Aug. Apples ripen by mid-Sep. and can be picked through foliage season. For specifics on where, see *Apples* and *Farms Open to the Public*.

QUILTS A revival of interest in this craft is especially strong in Vermont, where quilting supply and made-to-order stores salt the state. The **Vermont Quilt Festival** (www.vqf.org) is held for 3 days in late June in Essex Junction, including exhibits of antique quilts, classes and lectures, vendors, and appraisals. **Shelburne Museum** has an outstanding quilt collection, and the **Billings Farm & Museum** holds an annual show.

RAILROAD EXCURSIONS The **Green Mountain Railroad** (802-463-3069; 1-800-707-3530; www.rails-vt.com) runs a number of excursion trains around the state. The Green Mountain Flyer, named for the fastest train on the old Rutland Railroad, runs between Bellows Falls on the Connecticut River and Chester (13 miles), with special foliage runs for another 14 miles to Ludlow and seasonal Santa Claus runs before Christmas.

RENTAL COTTAGES AND CONDOMINIUMS *Four Season Vacation Rentals*, an annual booklet available from state information centers (vermont@cyberrentals.com), lists upward of 200 properties, most of them either lakeside cottages or condominiums near ski areas but also including a variety of other housing, ranging from wooded summer camps by streams to aristocratic brick mansions with priceless views. Another source is the web site www.vermont property.com.

RESTAURANTS Culinary standards are rising every day: You can lunch simply and inexpensively nearly

everywhere and dine superbly in a score of places. Further boosting culinary standards is Vermont Fresh Network, a nonprofit organization that partners local farmers with aspiring chefs. Fixed price menus (prix fixe) have been so noted. We were tempted to try to list our favorites here, but the roster would be too long. Restaurants that appeal to us appear in the text in their respective areas. Note that we divide restaurants in each chapter into *Dining Out* (serious dining experiences) and *Eating Out* (everyday places). See also *Highway Road Food*.

ROCKHOUNDING The most obvious sites are the **Rock of Ages Quarry and Visitors' Center** in Barre and the **Vermont Marble Museum** in Proctor, both with interactive exhibits. Vermont fossils, minerals, and rocks (including dinosaur footprints) may be viewed at the **Perkins Museum of Geology** at the University of Vermont, Burlington, (www.uvm.edu/perkins/visitor.htm); and the **Fairbanks Museum** in St. Johnsbury. The 480-million-year-old coral reef at Fisk Quarry on Isle La Motte is

Christina Tree

another must-see. And an annual **Rock Swap and Mineral Show** is held in early Aug., sponsored by the Burlington Gem and Mineral Club (www.burlingtongemandmineralclub .org). Gold, incidentally, can be panned in a number of rivers, notably Broad Brook in Plymouth; the Rock River in Newfane and Dover; the Williams River in Ludlow; the Ottauquechee River in Bridgewater; the White River in Stockbridge and Rochester; the Mad River in Warren, Waitsfield, and Moretown; the Little River in Stowe and Waterbury; and the Missisquoi in Lowell and Troy.

SHEEP AND WOOL Specialty sheep and alpaca farms are multiplying quickly in Vermont. A number of farmers specialize in processing wool and fiber. Check www.vermontsheep .org and www.vtllama.com. The annual **Vermont Sheep and Wool Festival**, featuring sheepshearing, spinning, weaving, and plenty of critters, is held in early Oct.

SHIPWRECKS Well-preserved 19th-century shipwrecks are open to the public (licensed divers) at any of nine underwater historical preserves in Lake Champlain near Burlington. Check with the **Lake Champlain Maritime Museum** (802-475-2022, ext. 102; www.lcmm.org) in Vergennes, which is charting underwater remains. Nondivers can explore the lake's shipwrecks at the museum's Nautical Archaeology Center, which has interactive exhibits, a touch-screen "Virtual Diver," and archaeologists on site.

SKIING, CROSS-COUNTRY The **Vermont Ski Areas Association** lists 31 cross-country centers in their *Vermont Winter Guide*. For descriptions

and conditions click on www.ski vermont.com. Within this book we have described each commercial touring center as it appears geographically. Given the dearth of natural snow in recent years, it's more important than ever to check conditions before you jump in the car. Vermont's most dependable snow can be found on high-elevation trails in **Stowe**, at **Craftsbury Outdoor Center** in Craftsbury Common, **Hazen's Notch** in Montgomery Center, **Bolton Valley Resort** (between Burlington and Stowe), **Burke Mountain Cross-Country** in East Burke, and **Blueberry Hill** in Goshen. **Mountain Top Inn** in Chittenden, **Mountain Meadows** in Killington, and **Grafton Ponds** in Grafton offer some snowmaking. All the cross-country ski centers mentioned above are located on the 300-mile **Catamount Trail**, a marked ski trail that runs the length of the state (see *Catamount Trail*). Inn-to-inn tours are possible between **Craftsbury Outdoor Center** and the **Highland Lodge and Ski Touring Center** in Greensboro; **Trapp Family Lodge** and **Edson Hill Manor** in Stowe; **Chipman House** in Ripton and **Churchill House Inn** in Brandon; and between the **Landgrove Inn** and **Londonderry Inn**. **Mad River Glen** and **Bolton Valley** are two alpine resorts that specialize in telemarking. The Vermont Chamber of Commerce and the Vermont Department of Tourism and Marketing publish a glossy *Vermont Winter Vacation Guide* (available free at www .vtchamber.com). Also see *State Parks* and *Green Mountain National Forest*.

SKIING, DOWNHILL Since the 1930s, when America's commercial skiing began with a Model-T Ford engine pulling skiers up a hill in Woodstock, skiing has been a Vermont specialty. Sixteen ski areas are members of the Vermont Ski Areas Association and accessible with daily updated snow conditions and weather on the web site www.skivermont.com. The Vermont Chamber of Commerce publishes a glossy *Vermont Winter Guide* (available free at www.vtchamber .com). Daily lift tickets are, of course, not the cheapest way to ski; all resorts deeply discount multiday lifts and lodging packages, and there are discounts for ordering ahead online. **Killington/Pico**, the largest ski resort in the East, and **Mount Snow**, Vermont's second largest area, are owned by the American Skiing Company; lift tickets and passes at one are honored at the others, and at ASC resorts in New Hampshire and Maine. **Sugarbush**, which was an ASC property, has been returned to local ownership. A number of long-established Vermont ski areas have become self-contained resorts. Both **Bolton Valley** and **Smugglers' Notch** cater to families; **Okemo**, **Stratton**, and **Sugarbush** offer varied skiing and facilities, appealing to a full range of patrons. Though no longer Vermont's biggest, **Stowe** remains the Ski Capital of the East when it comes to the quantity and quality of inns, restaurants, and shops. We have described each ski area as it appears geographically. A 24-hour snow-condition report for the state is available by calling the **Ski Vermont Information line**, 802-229-0531; or, again, you can check www.skivermont.com.

SLEIGH RIDES Sleigh rides are listed under *To Do* as they appear geographically in the book.

SNOWBOARDING An international sport first popularized by Burton Snowboards (born in Manchester, long since moved to Burlington, where we list details about its factory store). Snowboarding lessons, rentals, and special terrain parks are offered at every major Vermont ski area except Mad River Glen (the only holdout in the East).

SNOWMOBILING Vermont's 5,000 miles of well-marked, groomed trails are laced in a system maintained by the **Vermont Association of Snow Travelers (VAST)**. VAST's corridor trails are up to 8 feet wide and are maintained by 140 local snowmobile clubs; for detailed maps and suggestions for routes, activities, and guided tours, contact the group at 802-229-0005; 41 Granger Rd., Barre 05641; www.vtvast.org. Also check www .snowmobilevt.com. Due to insurance laws, snowmobile rentals and tours are relatively few. The Northeast Kingdom in general and Island Pond in particular are best geared to snowmobiling, with storage facilities and a wide choice of lodging handy to trails. The Northeast Kingdom Chamber of Commerce (802-748-3678; 1-800-639-6379; www.nekchamber.com) publishes a snowmobiling map/guide to the area.

SNOWSHOEING Snowshoeing is experiencing a rebirth in Vermont, thanks to the new lightweight equipment available from sources like Tubbs Snowshoes in Stowe. Virtually all ski-touring centers now offer snowshoe rentals, and many inns stock a few pairs for guests.

SOARING **Sugarbush Soaring** (802-496-2290; www.sugarbush.org; at Sugarbush Airport, Warren), in the

Mad River Valley, is known as one of the prime spots in the East for riding thermal and ridge waves. The Sugarbush Airport is a well-established place to take glider lessons or rides or simply to watch the planes come and go. The **Fall Wave Soaring Encampment** held in early Oct. (weather permitting) draws glider pilots from throughout the country. Gliders and airplane rides are also available at the **Stowe-Morrisville Airport** (802-888-5150) and **Post Mills Aviation** in Post Mills (802-333-9254), where soaring lessons are also a specialty, along with simply seeing the Connecticut Valley from the air.

SPAS Vermont is home to the lion's share of New England's resort spas. In Stowe both **Topnotch Resort and Spa** (www.topnotchresort.com) and **Stoweflake Mountain Resort & Spa** (www.stoweflake.com) can claim to be the region's biggest and best. The recently expanded and rebuilt **Avanyu Spa at The Equinox** (www.equinox.rockresorts.com) in Manchester Center is also a magnificent full-service spa, as is the smaller but beautiful **Castle Hill Spa** in Cavendish, near Okemo (www.castlehillspa.com). In 2007 major new spas are also planned for the **Woodstock Inn & Resort** (www.woodstockinn.com) and for **Spruce Peak** at Stowe (www.stowe.com).

SPIRITUAL CENTERS/RETREATS
Karmê Chöling Shambhala Meditation Center (802-633-2384; www.karmecholing.org) is a long-established retreat in Barnet with many special programs. **Yoga Vermont** in Burlington (802-660-9718; www.yogavermont.com) draws Ashtanga yoga practitioners from throughout the country. The **Green Mountain Dharma Center and Maple Forest Monastery** in Hartland is the scene of a major retreat (families welcome) in July and throughout winter (802-436-1103; www.greenmountaincenter.org), and the **Weston Priory** (802-824-5409; www.westonpriory.org) in Weston is a longtime Benedictine monastery known for its music, offering unstructured retreats.

STATE PARKS Vermont's more than 50 exceptionally well-groomed state parks include camping and/or day-use facilities, and are so diverse an assortment of properties that no one characterization applies. Within this book we attempt to describe each as it appears geographically. Vermont state parks are also detailed in an exceptional web site (**www.vtstateparks.com**) and are part of the **Department of Forests, Parks and Recreation** (802-241-3655; 103 S. Main St., Waterbury 05671-0601; www.vtfpr.org), which manages more than 157,000 acres of state land, offering opportunities for hunting, fishing, cross-country skiing, mountain biking,

SNOWSHOEING AT MAD RIVER GLENN

snowmobiling, and primitive as well as supervised camping. Also see *Campgrounds*.

SUMMER SELF-IMPROVEMENT PRO-GRAMS Whether it's improving your game of tennis or golf, learning to take pictures or to weave, cook, identify mushrooms, fish, or bike, or simply to lose weight, there is a summer program for you somewhere in Vermont. See *Tennis*, *Golf*, *Canoeing and Kayaking*, and *Fishing* for lodging and lesson packages. Intensive language programs are offered at **Middlebury College** (among the offerings are Arabic and Japanese, as well as more standard ones; www.middlebury.edu), and a writers' conference is held at its Bread Loaf summer campus. Senior citizens can take advantage of some outstanding courses offered at bargain prices (which include lodging) as part of the **Elderhostel** program. For details, contact Elderhostel, 11 Avenue de Lafayette, Boston, MA 02111-1746; 1-877-426-8056; www.elder hostel.org. The state's oldest, most respected crafts program is offered by the **Fletcher Farm School for the Arts and Crafts** (802-228-8770; 611 Rt. 103 South, Ludlow 05149; www .fletcherfarm.com): off-loom weaving, wooden-spoon carving, quilting, pottery, bookbinding, gourd or birch-bark vessel design, virtually every craft imaginable, including meals and lodging (minimum age 18, except for Young Artists programs). The non-profit **Shelburne Art Center** (802 985-3648; www.shelburneartcenter .org) offers similar courses though on a smaller scale, and the **Vermont Studio Center** in Johnson (802-635-2727; www.vermontstudiocenter.org) has a national reputation. Working visual artists and writers come to re-new their creative wellsprings or to explore completely new directions during intensive sessions that feature guidance and criticism by some of the country's premier artists. **Craftsbury Outdoor Center** in Craftsbury (802-586-7767; 535 Lost Nation Rd.; www.craftsbury.com) has summer programs for all ages in running and sculling.

SWIMMING On the *Official Vermont Attractions Map*, you can pick out the 36 day-use areas that offer swimming, most with changing facilities, maintained by the Vermont State Department of Forests, Parks and Recreation (www.vtstateparks.com). Similar facilities are provided by the Green Mountain National Forest at Hapgood Pond in Peru, and the U.S. Army Corps of Engineers has tidied corners of its dam projects for public use in Townshend and North Springfield. There are also public beaches on roughly one-third of Vermont's 400 lakes and ponds (but note that swimming is prohibited at designated "Fishing Access Areas") and plenty on Lake Champlain (in Burlington, Charlotte, Colchester, Georgia, and Swanton). Add to these all the town recreation areas and myriad pools available to visitors and you still haven't gone swimming Vermont-style until you've sampled a Vermont swimming hole. These range from deep spots in the state's ubiquitous streams to 100-foot-deep quarries (**Dorset Quarry** near Manchester and **Chapman Quarry** in West Rutland are famous) and freezing pools between waterfalls (see "Sugarbush/Mad River Valley"). We have included some of our favorite swimming holes under *Swimming* in each section but could not bring ourselves to share them all. Look for cars along the road on a hot day and ask in local general stores. You won't be disappointed.

TENNIS Vermont claims as many tennis courts per capita as any other state in the Union. These include town recreation facilities and sports centers as well as private facilities. Summer tennis programs, combining lessons, lodging, and meals, are offered at **Ascutney**, **Bolton Valley**, **Killington**, the **Village at Smugglers' Notch**, **Stratton**, **Topnotch Resort** in Stowe, and at **Sugarbush**'s Health and Racquet Club. Check *Tennis* in each area.

THEATER Vermont's two long-established summer theaters are both in the Manchester area: the **Dorset Playhouse** and the **Weston Playhouse**. Other summer theater can be found in Castleton, in Saxtons River, in Waitsfield (the **Valley Players**), in Warren (**Phantom Theater**), in Stowe (the **Stowe Playhouse** and the **Lamoille County Players** in Hyde Park), and **Northern Stage** at the Briggs Opera House in White River Junction. There's also the **Lost Nation Theater** in Montpelier, and in Brattleboro there is the **New England Youth Theatre** and the **Vermont Theatre Company.** The **Flynn Theater** in Burlington and the **Paramount Theater** in Rutland are the scene of year-round film as well as live entertainment.

TRAINS See *Amtrak* and *Railroad Excursions*.

VERMONT PUBLIC RADIO Stations for those addicted to National Public Radio can be found throughout the state on the FM dial (click onto www

.vpr.net). In the Burlington area, tune in to WVPS (107.9), in the Windsor area to WVPR (89.5), in the Rutland area to WRVT (88.7); WVPA (88.5) is in St. Johnsbury; and WBTN (94.3), in Bennington.

WATERFALLS Those most accessible and worth seeing include (north to south): the falls at **Brewster River Gorge**, Rt. 108 in Jeffersonville and, farther south off Rt. 108 (the Mountain Road) in Stowe, **Bingham Falls** (an unmarked pull-off on the north side of the road); a trail leads downhill to the falls and gorge, recently conserved and deeded to the state. In Stowe also look for **Moss Glen Falls**, a 125-foot drop off Rt. 100. (About 3 miles north of the village, turn right onto Randolph Rd., then right again on Moss Glen Falls Rd.; park at the area on the left just before a 90-degree turn across from a narrow bridge and look for the well-worn trail.) Beware **Big Falls** in Troy (directions are in our Jay Peak chapter): The top of this series of drops and cascades is a dramatic but rather scary spot; they represent the largest undammed waterfall on any major Vermont river (the Missisquoi). Also in northern Vermont: the **Great Falls of the Clyde River** in Charleston; **Duck Brook Cascades** in Bolton; **Little Otter Creek Falls** in Ferrisburgh; the seven falls on the **Huntington River** in Hanksville; **Shelburne Falls** in Shelburne; and **Cadys Falls** in Morrisville.

On the east–west roads linking the Champlain Valley with Rt. 100 (see *Gaps, Gulfs, and Gorges*), several falls are worth noting. On Rt. 17 look for the parking area, picnic table, and a short trail leading to the 45-foot **Bartlett Falls** in Bristol Memorial Park.

VDT

On Rt. 125 check out **Middlebury Gorge** in East Middlebury; off Dugway Road note the scenic **Huntington Gorge** in Huntington (responsible for at least 20 drowning deaths); and in Hancock don't miss 35-foot **Texas Falls**, well marked and a great picnic spot. North on Rt. 100 from Hancock also look for 45-foot **Moss Glen Falls** in Granville Gulf; here a boardwalk leads back to the falls, passing **Little Moss Glen Falls**. In the Upper Valley of the Connecticut River look for **Cow Meadows Ledges** in Newbury, the falls on the **Waits River** by Rt. 5 in the village of Bradford, and **Glen Falls**, a 75-foot drop in Fairlee almost opposite the fishing access on Lake Morey Rd.

In southern Vermont look for **Buttermilk Falls** (a popular swimming hole) in Ludlow; **Old City Falls** in Strafford off Old City Falls Rd.; the **East Putney Falls** and **Pot Holes**; and, our favorite of all, 125-foot **Hamilton Falls** in Jamaica, cascading down a schist wall with pools (responsible for more than one death over the years). Ask locally for directions to 160-foot **Lye Brook Falls** in Manchester. It's best accessed via a trail

from Jamaica State Park off Rt. 30/ 100. Most of these sites can be located on the invaluable *Vermont Atlas and Gazetteer* (DeLorme); also check Dean Goss's fact-filled www.northeast waterfalls.com and the colorful www.newenglandwaterfalls.com.

WEATHER REPORTS For serious weather travel information in Vermont, check with the Vermont Agency of Transportation's weather line: Dial 511 or 1-800-ICY-ROAD, or go to www.511vt.com. Listen to *An Eye on the Sky* on Vermont Public Radio (see *Vermont Public Radio* for stations; www.fairbanksmuseum.org). In the show, produced by the Fairbanks Museum and Planetarium, Mark Breen and Steve Maleski make their reports on life's most constant variable both entertaining and informative. The Vermont Chamber of Commerce web site (www.vermont vacation.com) also carries current weather information.

WEB PAGES In this edition we list hundreds of web sites within each region. Among the most helpful statewide sites are the following: **www.vermontvacation.com** is maintained by the Vermont Department of Tourism and Marketing. The Vermont Outdoor Guide Association, **www .voga.org**, maintains the best overall site for activities of every kind in the state; **www.vtstateparks.com** includes locator maps and special programs related to state parks; while independently published **www.scenes ofvermont.com** and **www.vermont .com** are mines of general information and links. The Vermont Chamber of Commerce is at **www.vtchamber .com**, and the Vermont Lodging and Restaurant Association maintains

Marilyn Pastore

THE INN AT MOUNTAIN VIEW FARM

www.visitvt.com. This guide is probably the single best directory to Vermont web sites, listing them by subject in each chapter and as they appear geographically throughout the book.

WEDDINGS Destination weddings have become big business in Vermont, so big and so ubiquitous that we use the wedding-ring symbol ∞ to designate establishments that specialize in them. Contact www.vermont weddingguide.com or www.wedding events.com to request a free copy of the promotional *Vermont Wedding Guide* (remember, it's all advertising). One great wedding site that doesn't make these listings is the elegant **Grand Isle Lake House** (802-865-2522; www.grandislelakehouse.com) in the Champlain Islands, a turn-of-the-20th-century summer hotel maintained by the Preservation Trust of Vermont. Also see *Civil Unions*.

WHITEWATER During whitewater season beginning in mid-April, experienced canoeists and kayakers take advantage of stretches on the **White**, the **Lamoille**, and the **West Rivers**, among others. **Whitewater rafting** is also available on the **West River** during spring dam releases.

WINE Vermont has traditionally made apple and other fruit wines, but recently two wineries in the very northern reaches of the state have begun planting, harvesting, and fermenting grapes, with respectable results. These are **Boyden Valley Winery** (802-644-8151; www.boyden valley.com)—also good for premium apple wines—in Cambridge, and **Snow Farm Vineyard and Winery** (802-372-9463; www.snowfarm.com) in South Hero. **North River Winery** (802-368-7557; www.northriverwinery .com), Vermont's long-established vintner, produces fruit wine, and the associated **Ottauquechee Valley Winery** (802-295-9463) in Quechee, **Flag Hill Farm** (802-685-7724; www .flaghillfarm.com) in Vershire, **Grand View Winery** (802-456-7012; www .grandviewwinery.com) in East Calais, and **Putney Mountain Winery** (802-387-4610) in Dummerston all make cider and apple wine and brandy. The newest addition is **Shelburne Vineyard** (802-734-1386; www.shelburne vineyard.com), which leases land from Shelburne Farms but operates as a separate enterprise.

Southern Vermont

Diane E. Foulds

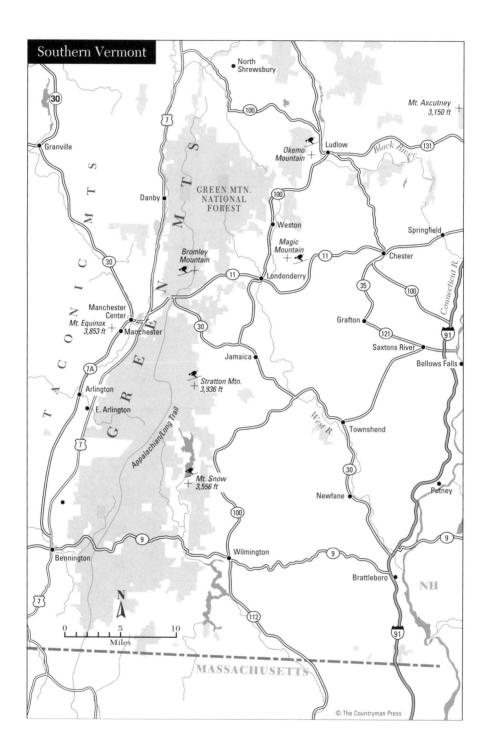

Southern Vermont

BRATTLEBORO, PUTNEY, AND THE WEST RIVER VALLEY

Wedged between the Green Mountains and the Connecticut River, Vermont's southeastern corner is the obvious gateway to the state from points south, and many visitors (a number of them now residents) get no farther. Brattleboro, the area's commercial and cultural hub, contrasts with the classic white-clapboarded, green-shuttered towns of Newfane, Townshend, and Jamaica, which are strung like pearls along the West River, and with equally rural Putney, half a dozen miles north on the Connecticut.

Brattleboro is a vibrant artistic and an activist community in which the spirit of the '60s continues to build. The supermarket is a co-op showcasing Vermont cheeses, the movie house is a restored art deco theater, and several buildings are honeycombed with artists' studios. Downtown Victorian-era blocks are a rich mix of traditional stores and an ever-increasing number of galleries, restaurants, and cafés, not to mention owner-operated bookstores, boutiques, and counter-counterculture shops. The first Friday of every month is Gallery Walk, incorporating more than 40 venues.

Despite its accessibility, this is far from the most touristed corner of Vermont. The confluence of the Connecticut and West Rivers at Brattleboro is itself a beautiful, placid place to paddle. Beyond the widely scattered country inns, antiques dealers, and crafts studios and shops lie swimming holes, and hiking trails that lead to unexpected vistas. Back roads web the area, connecting villages in sometimes heart-stoppingly beautiful ways.

GUIDANCE Brattleboro Area Chamber of Commerce (802-254-4565; www.brattleborochamber.org), 180 Main St., Brattleboro 05301, is good for walk-in information (open year-round, Mon.–Fri. 8–5, Sat. 10–2). It maintains seasonal information booths staffed by knowledgeable senior citizens on Rt. 5 at the common, just north of the junction with Rt. 30. Public **restrooms** are in the Robert H. Gibson Garden building on Main St. at the light, across from High St. (Rt. 9). Also see www.brattleboro.com.

The **Southern Vermont Regional Market Organization** (1-877-887-2378; www.southernvermont.com) maintains a good web site for the entire region and sends out printed material.

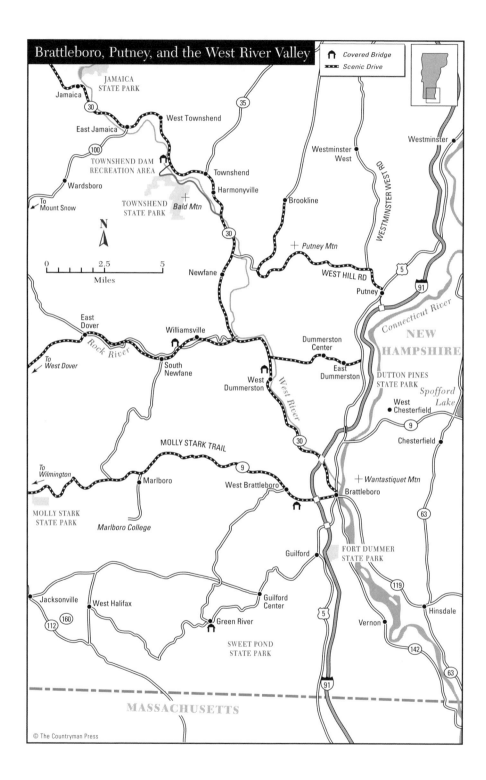

Brattleboro, Putney, and the West River Valley

Covered Bridge
Scenic Drive

JAMAICA STATE PARK
Jamaica
30
West Townshend
35
East Jamaica
100
Westminster West
Westminster
WESTMINSTER WEST RD
TOWNSHEND DAM RECREATION AREA
Townshend
Wardsboro
Harmonyville
To Mount Snow
TOWNSHEND STATE PARK
Bald Mtn
Brookline
N
30
Putney Mtn
0   2.5   5
Miles
Newfane
WEST HILL RD
5
Putney
91
East Dover
Williamsville
Dummerston Center
Connecticut River
NEW HAMPSHIRE
To West Dover
Rock River
South Newfane
East Dummerston
DUTTON PINES STATE PARK
Spofford Lake
West Dummerston
West River
West Chesterfield
9
MOLLY STARK TRAIL
30
Chesterfield
To Wilmington
Marlboro
9
West Brattleboro
Wantastiquet Mtn
Brattleboro
MOLLY STARK STATE PARK
Marlboro College
63
Guilford
FORT DUMMER STATE PARK
Jacksonville
West Halifax
Guilford Center
119
Hinsdale
112
160
Green River
5
Vernon
SWEET POND STATE PARK
142
63
91
MASSACHUSETTS

© The Countryman Press

The Southeast Vermont Welcome Center, I-91 in Guilford (open daily 7 AM–1 AM), is the state's most elaborate visitors center, with displays on all parts of the state, featuring local attractions and events. **Restrooms** open 24 hours.

Newspapers: The *Brattleboro Reformer* (802-254-2311; www.reformer.com) publishes a special Thursday calendar that's the best source of current arts and entertainment. Also check out *The Observer* (802-874-4360), a weekly.

GETTING THERE *By bus:* **Greyhound/Vermont Transit** (800-552-8737; www.vermonttransit.com) offers service from New York and Connecticut, also from Boston via Springfield. The bus stop is north of town on Rt. 5 at its junction with Rt. 9 west.

By train: **Amtrak** (1-800-USA-RAIL; www.amtrak.com) trains from Washington, DC, and New York City stop twice daily at Brattleboro's vintage railroad station, now a museum.

By air: **Bradley International Airport** (www.bradleyairport.com) in Connecticut offers connections with all parts of the county.

GETTING AROUND **Brattleboro Taxi** (802-254-6446) will meet trains, buses, and airports.

Parking: Main St. has metered parking; side streets are possible. A large parking area (Harmony Place) in the rear of the Brooks House is close to shops on High, Elliot, and Main Sts.; access is from High St. (Rt. 9). Brattleboro's Transportation Center offers multilevel parking with access from Elliot or Flat Sts. Another large lot runs between High and Grove Sts.

WHEN TO GO In winter skiers tend to speed through up Rt. 30 to Stratton or across Rt. 9 to Mount Snow, but in summer this is a favorite area both for day-tripping (from Boston, western Massachusetts, and Connecticut) and for longer stays in the many gracious inns and B&Bs. The annual Strolling of the Heifers through downtown Brattleboro the first week in June is a big draw, and "Marlboro Season" (early July through early August) brings chamber music lovers. Foliage brings more day-trippers, and it's wise to avoid Rt. 9. Luckily, there are many options (see *Scenic Drives*). Thanksgiving weekend draws canny shoppers for the Putney Craft Tour.

MEDICAL EMERGENCY Emergency service is available by calling **911**.

Brattleboro Memorial Hospital (802-257-0341), 17 Belmont Ave., Brattleboro. **Grace Cottage Hospital** (802-365-7357), Rt. 35, Townshend.

✳ Towns and Villages

Brattleboro. This largely 1870s brick and cast-iron town is the commercial

BROOKS HOUSE

William Hays

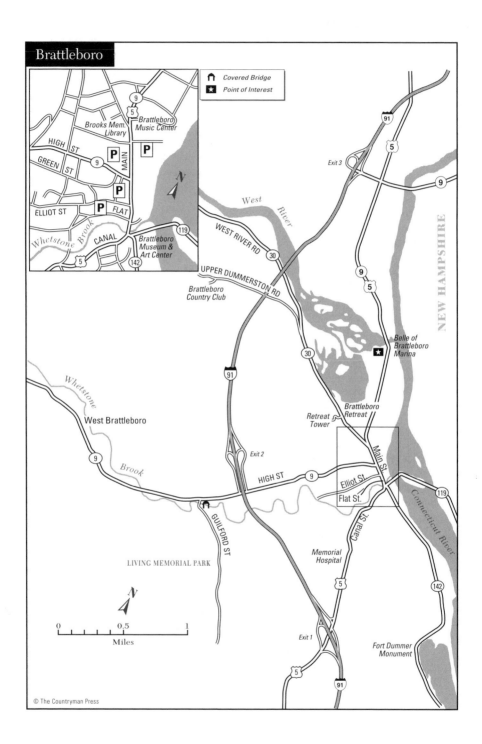

Brattleboro

Covered Bridge
Point of Interest

Brooks Mem. Library
Brattleboro Music Center
HIGH ST
GREEN ST
MAIN
FLAT
ELLIOT ST
Whetstone Brook
CANAL
Brattleboro Museum & Art Center

West River

Exit 3

NEW HAMPSHIRE

WEST RIVER RD

UPPER DUMMERSTON RD

Brattleboro Country Club

Belle of Brattleboro Marina

Whetstone

West Brattleboro

Brook

Retreat Tower

Brattleboro Retreat

Exit 2

HIGH ST

Elliot St.

Flat St.

Main St.

Connecticut River

GUILFORD ST

LIVING MEMORIAL PARK

Memorial Hospital

Canal St.

N

0   0.5   1
Miles

Exit 1

Fort Dummer Monument

© The Countryman Press

hub for rural corners of three states. (Population swells from 12,000 at night to 20,000 by day.) The particular mix of native Vermonters and flatlanders here was seeded in the 1970s by former members of the commune that flourished in this area in the '60s. Artists, musicians, and social activists continue to be drawn by local educational institutions, which include the burgeoning Brattleboro Music Center as well as Marlboro College and World Learning in neighboring Dummerston (begun in 1932 and best known for its School for International Training). Galleries, bookstores, boutiques, alternative shops, and restaurants now outnumber traditional stores. Sam's Outdoor Outfitters, Brown & Roberts Hardware, and Miller Brothers–Newton continue to thrive, but antiques and crafts stores have replaced former downtown anchors. On the first Friday of every month dozens of galleries and studios now host a Gallery Walk (www.gallerywalk.org).

During its long history, this town has shed many skins. The site of Fort Dummer, built in 1724 just south of town, has been obliterated by the Vernon Dam. Gone, too, is the early-19th-century trading and resort town; no trace remains of the handsome, Federal-style commercial buildings or the two elaborate hotels that attracted trainloads of customers who came to take their water cures. The gingerbread wooden casino in Island Park and the fine brick town hall, with its gilded opera house, are gone, but the great slate-sided sheds in which hundreds of thousands of Estey organs were made are slowly being restored—one houses the new Estey Organ Museum.

A motorist bogged down in the perpetual Main Street bottleneck notices Brooks House, built splendidly in 1872 as an 80-room hotel, once frequented by Rudyard Kipling, now converted to housing, offices, and shops. A couple of blocks down the 1930s art deco Latchis Hotel and Theater have been restored inside as well as out.

Brattleboro is full of pleasant surprises. The former railroad station is now the lively Brattleboro Museum and Art Center. The Connecticut River is accessible by both excursion boat and rental canoe and can be viewed from a hidden downtown park and from the Robert H. Gibson River Garden, a weatherproofed public space (with public restrooms). Live theater, music, and dance are presented without hoopla. The fanfare seems to be reserved for the annual winter carnival, begun eons ago by Fred Harris, who also founded the Dartmouth Winter Carnival and the U.S. Eastern Amateur Ski Association, and for the Strolling of the Heifers down Main Street, the first Saturday in June.

Along Rt. 30 in the West River Valley
Newfane (www.newfanevermontusa.com). A columned courthouse, matching Congregational church, and town hall—all grouped on a handsome green—are framed by dignified, white-clapboard houses, including two elegant inns. When Windham County's court sessions began meeting in Newfane in 1787, the village was about the same size it is now: 20 houses and two hotels. But in 1787, the village was 2 miles up on Newfane Hill. Beams were unpegged and homes moved to the more protected valley by ox-drawn sleighs in the winter of 1824.

Newfane inns have been famous for more than a century, at first because the whitewashed jail accommodated 25 paying guests, feeding them (as an 1848 poem says) "good pies and oyster soup" in the same rooms with inmates. By the time this facility closed (in the 1950s), the Old Newfane Inn—which incorporates much of its original hilltop structure—was beginning to acquire a reputation for gourmet fare. Economist John Kenneth Galbraith, a summer resident in the area since 1947, helped publicize the charms of both the village and the inn—whose onetime chef eventually opened the Four Columns Inn at the rear of the green. Newfane Village is more than a place to dine, sleep, and stroll. It is the site of one of the state's oldest and biggest Sunday flea markets, and the immediate area offers an unusual number of antiques shops. Beyond the stores and the remnants of the railway station (which served the narrow-gauge Brattleboro–Londonderry line from 1880 to 1936) is a fine old cemetery.

Newfane has bred as well as fed famous people. You'll learn about some of them in the exceptional **Historical Society of Windham County** (802-365-4148), Rt. 30, south of the common (open Memorial Day–mid-Oct., Wed.–Sun. noon–5, and for special events). It looks like a brick post office, but exhibits fill both the main floor and second-floor gallery; in addition to changing shows, there are permanent displays on the West River Railroad, which operated between Brattleboro and Jamaica (1880s–1927) and is remembered as "36 miles of trouble"; on Porter Thayer's photographs of local turn-of-the-20th-century scenes; and on the saga of John Wilson (see Brookline, below).

Brookline. Half as wide as it is long, Brookline is sequestered in a narrow valley bounded by steep hills and the West River. (Turn off Rt. 30 at the Newfane Flea Market.) Its population of 410 is four times what it was 50 years ago but a small fraction of what it was in the 1820s and '30s, when it supported three stores, three schools, two hotels, and a doctor. Those were the decades in which its two landmark brick buildings were constructed. One is a church, but the more famous is a round schoolhouse, said to be the only one in the country—and also probably the only school designed by a crook.

John Wilson never seems to have mentioned his past career as Thunderbolt, an infamous Scottish highwayman. In 1820 the obviously well-educated newcomer designed the circular schoolhouse. He gave it six large windows, the better (it was later noted) to allow him to see whoever approached from any side. Wilson taught for only a term before moving to the neighboring (and more remote) town of Dummerston, just about the time that an Irish felon, "Lightfoot" Martin, was hanged in Cambridge, Massachusetts. In his confession (reprints are sold at the historical society), Martin fingered Wilson as his old accomplice, but with no obvious effect. Not long thereafter, Wilson added "Dr." to his name and practiced medicine in Newfane, then in Brattleboro, where he married, fathering a son before his wife divorced him "because of certain facts she learned." When he died in 1847, scars on Wilson's ankles and neck

NEWFANE VILLAGE

Kim Grant

suggested chains and a rope. Today
several of Thunderbolt's pistols are
preserved by the HSWC Museum
(see Newfane, above) and in Brattleboro's Brooks Library.

Unfortunately, the round schoolhouse
is now virtually never open. In 1928
the town's first eight grades moved
down the road to the current wooden
schoolhouse. As the population
dwindled through the '30s, '40s, and
'50s, the building was used for town
meeting, but that assemblage is now

Kim Grant

TOWNSHEND GREEN

held in the vestry of the Baptist church, Brookline's second landmark. Built in
1836, the church has been beautifully restored, thanks to fund-raising efforts like
the annual Musicale Sunday, usually held late in July, sponsored by the Ladies
Benevolent Society.

Townshend (population: 1133). The next village green north on Rt. 30 is a full 2
acres, complete with Victorian-style gazebo. It's bordered on one side by a classic
white 1790 Congregational church flanked by lovely clapboard houses, on others
by a columned and tower-topped stucco town hall of the Leland and Gray Union
High School (founded as a Baptist seminary in 1834), and by a clapboard commercial block. On the first Saturday in August the common fills with booths and
games to benefit Grace Cottage Hospital, which has grown out of the back of a
rambling old village home. (Known for the quality of its service, this is Vermont's
first hospital to have installed a birthing bed.) West Townshend, farther along
Rt. 30, is a three-corners with a photogenic church and post office. The town
also harbors a state park, a public swimming area, Vermont's largest single-span
covered bridge, 15 cemeteries, and several good places to stay and to eat.

Jamaica (www.jamaicavt.com). The village—center for a town of 935—clusters
around its white Congregational church (1808) on Rt. 30. Jamaica is the kind of
place you can drive through in 2 minutes, or stay a week. The village buildings
are few but proud, and there is swimming and plenty of hiking as well as camping in **Jamaica State Park**. The village, which lies within the bailiwick of Stratton Mountain's resort community, also offers some surprisingly good shopping.

North along Route 5

Putney (www.putney.net and www.iputney.com). This town's riverside fields
have been heavily farmed since the mid–18th century, and its hillsides produce
more than one-tenth of all the state's apples. Putney is an unusually fertile place
for progressive thinking, too. Back in the 1840s it spawned a group who practiced Bible Communism, the sharing of all property, work, and wives. John
Humphrey Noyes, the group's leader, was charged with adultery in 1847 and fled
with his flock to Oneida, New York, where they founded the famous silverplate
company. Known today for experimental education rather than religion, Putney
is the home of the Putney School, a coed, college preparatory school founded in

Estey Organ Museum (802-258-2363; www.esteyorganmuseum.org), 108 Birge St. (rear), Brattleboro (turn off Canal St. at the Sunoco station). Open June–Columbus Day, Sat. 10–5, Sun. 1–5. Admission $2. For many years Brattleboro's largest employer, the Estey Organ Co. produced thousands of organs each year between 1846 and its demise in 1960. This fledgling museum, founded in 2002, is housed in a former engine house, a large, airy, well-lit space in which exhibits trace the history of organs in general and of Estey organs in particular. There are examples of reed organs from the 1860s and the ornately carved parlor organs found in countless Victorian homes. There are also the pipe organs Estey made for small churches throughout the county, and finally there are electronic organs, highly innovative when they first appeared. Eventually the museum will include sound as well as visuals and several more buildings. Inquire about frequent special events.

ORGANISTS IN THE ESTEY ORGAN MUSEUM   Christina Tree

ESTEY ORGAN WORKS

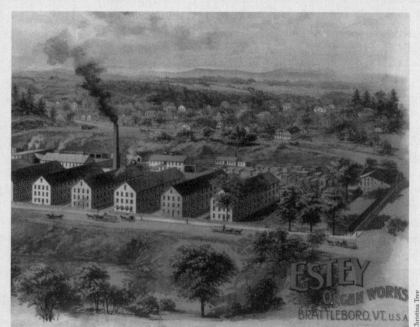

Christina Tree

1935, with a regimen that entails helping with chores, including raising animals. Landmark College is the country's only fully accredited college specifically for dyslexic students and those with other learning disabilities. In July the **Yellow Barn Music School and Festival** is housed in a barn behind the library; concerts are staged there and at other local venues throughout the month. The **Sandglass Theater** (serious puppetry) is also based in Putney Village, which offers interesting shopping, augmented by exceptional artisans who welcome visitors. During the 3 days following Thanksgiving some two dozen local studios are open for the **Putney Artisans Craft Tour** (www.putneycrafts.com). Putney's scenic roads are also well known to serious bicyclists, and Putney Mountain (see *Hiking*) is beloved by both hikers and mountain bikers.

Putney's native sons include the late George Aiken, who served as governor before going on to Washington as a senator in 1941, a post he held until his retirement in 1975. Frank Wilson, a genuine Yankee trader who was one of the first merchants to enter Red China, built the first of his **Basketvilles**, "The World's Largest Basket Stores," in the village. The **Putney Historical Society** (802-387-5862; www.putneyhistory.org) is housed in the town hall, open when it's open.

South on Route 5
Guilford. Backroaded by I-91 (which has no exit between Brattleboro and Bernardston, Ma.), this old agricultural town rewards with quiet rural scenery anyone who drives or pedals its roads. Check out **Sweet Pond State Park**, a former 125-acre estate with a large pond, good for swimming and boating, and circled by a nature path. Labor Day weekend is big here, the time for the old-fashioned **Guilford Fair** and for the annual 2-day, free concerts sponsored by Friends of Music at Guilford (802-257-1961) in and around the **Organ Barn**. The **Guilford Historical Society**, open Memorial Day–Columbus Day, Tue. and Sat. 10–2 and by appointment (call Addie Minott at 802-254-5910), maintains exhibits in the 1822 town hall, in the 1837 meetinghouse, and in the 1797 one-room brick schoolhouse.

✳ To See
MUSEUMS

PUTNEY GENERAL STORE

Kim Grant

&. **Brattleboro Museum & Art Center** (802-257-0124; www.brattleboromuseum.org), 10 Vernon St. (corner of Canal and Rt. 119), Brattleboro. Open except Mar., daily except Tue., 11–5. $4 adults, $3 seniors, $2 students. The town's 1915 rail station makes a handsome home for increasingly compelling changing exhibits with an emphasis on local and contemporary art. Inquire about frequent lectures related to the exhibits, family workshops, and concerts.

The **Brattleboro Historical Society** (802-258-4957; www.bratttleborohistorical society.org) maintains a "history room" (a restored 1800s classroom) and more than 7,000 photographs dating from the mid-1800s. It's on the third floor of the Municipal Center (230 Main St.; open mid-July–late Oct., weekends 1:30–4:30).

Brooks Memorial Library (802-254-5290), 224 Main St. (open daily except Sun.), mounts changing exhibits of regional art and has a fine collection of 19th-century paintings and sculpture, including works by Larkin G. Mead, the Brattleboro boy who first won recognition by sculpting an 8-foot-high angel from snow one night and placing it at the junction of Rts. 30 and 5.

Also see the **Historical Society of Windham County** in Newfane under *Towns and Villages*.

COVERED BRIDGES In Brattleboro the reconstructed **Creamery Bridge** forms the entrance to Living Memorial Park on Rt. 9. North on Rt. 30 in West Dummerston, a Town lattice bridge across the West River is the longest still-used covered bridge in the state (for the best view, jump into the cool waters on either side; this is a popular swimming hole on a hot summer day). The **Scott Bridge**, Vermont's longest single-span bridge, stands by Rt. 30 in West Townshend just below the Townshend Dam, but it's closed to traffic. The region's oldest covered bridge spans the Rock River between Williamsville and South Newfane. The Green River in Guilford also boasts a covered bridge.

FOR FAMILIES ✿ **Retreat Farm** (802-257-2240), 350 Linden St., Rt. 30 just north of Brattleboro. Open Memorial Day–Oct., Wed.–Sat. 10–4, Sun. noon–4, also holiday Mondays. $5 ages 12 and over, $4 under 12. Brattleboro Retreat's working dairy farm, now owned by the Grafton-based Windham Foundation, also includes llamas, pigs, emus, lambs, sheep, goats, oxen, donkeys, horses, chickens, kittens, shaggy Highland cattle, and a cow that visitors are invited to milk. A gift shop features farm-related toys and Grafton Village Cheese.

✿ **Santa's Land** (802-387-5550; www.santasland.com), Rt. 5, 4 miles north of Putney. Hours 10–5. Open Memorial Day–July 1, Fri.–Sun.; July 2–Labor Day, Thu.–Sun., then weekends, weather permitting, through mid-Dec. $15 adults, $13 children over age 2, $10 seniors. Designed for children ages 2–8, this Christmas theme village includes Christmas shops, Santa's home, reindeer, kiddie rides, a barnyard and unusual animals, a kiddy train, and, of course, Santa.

Also see the **Southern Vermont Natural History Museum** at Hogback Mountain (west of Brattleboro) in "Mount Snow/Wilmington Area" and the **Nature Museum** of Grafton in "The Lower Connecticut River Valley."

SCENIC DRIVES The hilly, heavily wooded country between the West and Connecticut River Valleys is webbed with roads, most of them dirt. Our favorites include:

Putney Mountain Road to Brookline. At the Putney General Store on Rt. 5, turn left onto Westminster West Rd. and left again about a mile up the hill onto West Hill Rd. Not far above the Putney School, look for a dirt road on your right. It forks immediately; bear right to Putney Mountain. Trees thicken and sunlight dapples through in a way that it never seems to do on paved roads. Chipmunks scurry ahead on the hard-packed dirt. The few drivers you pass will wave. The road curves up and up—and up—cresting after 2.1 miles. Note the unmarked parking area on your right (see Putney Mountain under *Hiking*). The road then snakes down the other side into Brookline.

The **Molly Stark Trail**—Rt. 9 between Brattleboro and Bennington—is dedicated to the wife of General John Stark, hero of the battle of Bennington. The 17-mile stretch west from Brattleboro passes by Marlboro, climbing high over Hogback Mountain before winding down into Wilmington. Very scenic but heavily trafficked during foliage season.

West Dummerston to West Dover. Beautiful in a car or on a bike, the 13 miles between Rt. 30 and Rt. 100 form a shortcut from Newfane to Mount Snow. Turn west off Rt. 30, 2 miles north of the covered bridge. Follow the Rock River (in summer, clumps of cars suggest swimming holes) west from West Dummerston and Williamsville, on through the picturesque village of South Newfane (the general store is a source of picnic fare); detour 0.5 mile into the old hill village of Dover, very different from West Dover down on busy Rt. 100.

Route 30 from Brattleboro to Jamaica (you can loop back on Rt. 100 and take either of the two routes sketched above) shadows the West River, passing two covered bridges and going through the exceptionally picturesque villages of Newfane and Townshend, as well as by the Townshend Dam (good for swimming). Both villages offer first-rate crafts and antiques.

East Dummerston to West Dummerston. A handy shortcut from Rt. 5 to Rt. 30 (or vice versa), just 2 miles up one side of a hill to picturesque Dummerston Center and 2 miles down the other. This was long known in our family as the Gnome Road because of the way it winds through the woods to Vermont's longest (recently refitted) traffic-bearing covered bridge. It's generally known as the East/West Rd.

Brattleboro to Guilford Center to Halifax and back. This can be a 46-mile loop to Wilmington and back; ask locally for shortcuts back up to Rt. 9. Take Rt. 5 south from Brattleboro to the Guilford Country Store (selling sandwiches), then right into Guilford Center. Continue for 0.5 mile and bear right on Stage Rd. to Green River with its covered bridge, church, and recently restored crib dam. Bear right at the church (before the bridge) and then left at the Y; follow Green River Rd. (along the river) and then Hatch School Rd. into Jacksonville. To complete the loop, see *Scenic Drives* in "Mount Snow/Wilmington Area."

✳ To Do

BICYCLING Some 200 miles of dirt and abandoned roads, along with miles of off-road trails, add up to a well-established mecca for bicyclists. While Amtrak no longer permits you to carry your own bike, it does still stop in Brattleboro where you can rent a hybrid at the **Brattleboro Bicycle Shop** (802-254-8644; 1-800-BRAT-BIKE; www.bratbike.com), 178 Main St., and pick up plenty of advice about where to use it. In Putney the **West Hill Shop** (802-387-5718;

www.westhillshop.com), open daily, just off I-91, Exit 4, is under new ownership but still offering mountain and road bike rentals. It's also still home to the **Putney Bicycle Club**, which organizes races and (hard-core) tours. The **Ranney-Crawford House** in Putney (see *Lodging*) is geared to cyclists.

BOATING **Vermont Canoe Touring Center** (802-257-5008; vtcanoe@sover
.net), 451 Putney Rd., Brattleboro. Located on the West River at the cove at Veterans Memorial Bridge, Rt. 5, just north of the junction with Rt. 30. Open daily Memorial Day weekend–Labor Day weekend 9–dusk, weekends to Columbus Day, weather permitting. John Knickerbocker rents canoes and kayaks, and offers shuttle service, guided trips, and camping on the river. The 32 miles from Bellows Falls to the Vernon Dam is slow-moving water, as is the 6-mile stretch from below the dam to the Massachusetts border.

Connecticut River Tours (802-254-1263; www.belleofbrattleboro.com), Putney Rd., Brattleboro. The 49-passenger, mahogany-trimmed *Belle of Brattleboro* offers cruises Wed.–Sun. and holidays, Memorial Day–Columbus Day. Bring your own food and drink.

Whitewater on the West River. Twice a year, once in spring and again in September, the Army Corps of Engineers releases water from the Ball Mountain Dam (802-874-4881) in Jamaica, creating whitewater fit for national kayak championships. The races are no longer run here, but commercial whitewater rafters as well as whitewater kayakers and canoeists take advantage of the flow, especially in fall, when many of the region's other whitewater courses are dry.

FISHING In the **Connecticut River** you can catch bass, trout, pike, pickerel, and yellow perch. There is an access on Old Ferry Rd., 2 miles north of Brattleboro on Rt. 5; another is from River Rd. on the New Hampshire shore in Westmoreland (Rt. 9 east, then north on Rt. 63). For fishing boat rentals contact the **Marina Restaurant** (802-257-7563).

The **West River** is a source of trout and smallmouth bass; access is from any number of places along Rt. 30. In Vernon there is a boat access on **Lily Pond**; in Guilford on **Weatherhead Hollow Pond** (see the DeLorme *Vermont Atlas and Gazetteer*).

GOLF **Brattleboro Country Club** (802-257-7380), Upper Dummerston Rd., offers 18 holes and includes a full driving range, practice areas, and instructional range. The **Tater Hill Golf Club** (802-875-2517), Popple Dungeon Rd. in North Windham, recently acquired and redesigned by Okemo, also offers 18 holes. Also see **Mount Snow** and **Stratton** ski resorts under *Downhill Skiing*; both offer golf schools and 27 holes.

HIKING In **Brattleboro** a pleasant path up to the Retreat Tower, a 19th-century overlook, begins beside Linden Lodge on Rt. 30. Another trail follows the West River along the abandoned **West River railroad bed**. Access is off Rt. 5 north of town; take the second left turn after crossing the bridge. **Wantastiquet Mountain**, overlooking Brattleboro from across the Connecticut River in New

Hampshire, is a good 1½-hour hike from downtown, great for picnics and views of southeast Vermont. See also Fort Dummer State Park under *Green Space* for a wooded trail south of town overlooking the Connecticut, and Townshend State Forest for a steep trek up Bald Mountain.

Putney Mountain between Putney and Brookline, off Putney Mountain Rd. (see *Scenic Drives*), is one of the most rewarding 1-mile round-trip hikes anywhere. A sign nailed to a tree in the unmarked parking area assures you that this is indeed Putney Mountain. Follow the trail that heads gently uphill through birches and maples, then continues through firs and vegetation that change remarkably quickly to the stunted growth usually found only at higher elevations. Suddenly you emerge on the mountain's broad crown, circled by a deep-down satisfying panorama. The view to the east is of Mount Monadnock, rising in lonely magnificence above the roll of southern New Hampshire, but more spectacular is the spread of Green Mountain peaks to the west. You can pick out the ski trails on Haystack, Mount Snow, and Stratton.

Jamaica State Park offers a choice of three interesting trails. The most intriguing and theoretically the shortest is to Hamilton Falls, a 125-foot cascade through a series of wondrous potholes. It's an obvious mile (30-minute) hike up, but the return can be confusing. Beware straying onto Turkey Mountain Rd.

Black Mountain Natural Area, maintained by The Nature Conservancy of Vermont (802-229-4425). Cross the covered bridge on Rt. 30 in West Dummerston and turn south on Quarry Rd. for 1.4 miles. The road changes to Rice Farm Rd.; go another 0.5 mile to a pull-off on the right. The marked trail begins across the road and rises abruptly 1,280 feet to a ridge, traversing it before dropping back down, passing a beaver dam on the way back to the river. The loop is best done clockwise. Beautiful in laurel season.

HORSEBACK RIDING **Green Mountain Horse Ranch** (802-387-2511; www. greenmountainhorseranch.com), 601 Bellows Falls Rd. (Rt. 5), Putney. Open mid-May–Jan., 9:30–5:30. One- and 2-hour trail rides ($35/$60) by reservation; also pony rides ($5) and wagon rides (reservation only: $8). Inquire about sleigh rides and snowshoeing. Also see **Sun Bowl Ranch** (at Statton Mountain) under *Horseback Riding* in "Manchester and the Mountains."

RAILROAD EXCURSION The **Green Mountain Flyer** (802-463-3069; www .rails-vt.com), based just north of this area in Bellows Falls, offers a 26-mile run in-season. (See "The Lower Connecticut River Valley.")

SWIMMING ♂ **Living Memorial Park**, west of downtown Brattleboro on Rt. 9, offers a public pool (mid-June–Labor Day). In the West River Valley at the **Townshend Lake Recreation Area** (802-874-4881) off Rt. 30 in West Townshend you drive across the top of the massive dam, completed in 1961 as a major flood-prevention measure for the southern Connecticut River Valley. Swimming is in the reservoir behind the dam, with a human-made beach and gradual drop-off, good for children. Changing facilities provided; small fee. The **West River** itself offers a few swimming holes, notably under the West Dummerston covered bridge on Rt. 30 and at Salmon Hole in Jamaica State Park. **Hamilton Falls**, accessible from the park, and **Pikes Falls**, also in Jamaica (ask directions locally), are favorite swimming holes, but not advised for children. Just off Rt. 30, a mile or so up (on South Newfane Rd.), the **Rock River** swirls through a series of shallow swimming spots; look for cars. In Guilford there is swimming at **Sweet Pond State Park** (802-257-7406), a former 125-acre estate with a large pond circled by a nature path. Also handy to Brattleboro, **Wares Grove** is across the Connecticut River in Chesterfield, N.H. (9 miles east on Rt. 9, the next left after the junction with Rt. 63). This pleasant beach on Spofford Lake is good for children; you'll find a snack bar and makeshift changing facilities.

✳ Winter Sports

CROSS-COUNTRY SKIING **Brattleboro Outing Club Ski Hut** (802-254-4081), Upper Dummerston Rd., Brattleboro. Trails through woods and a golf course, 16 km machine tracked, rentals, instruction. In **Living Memorial Park** (802-254-4081), Brattleboro, a 6 km trail through the woods is not only set but also lighted for night skiing. **West Hill Shop** (802-387-5718), just off I-91, Exit 4, is the source of cross-country information for the Putney area. **Townshend Outdoors** (802-365-7309), Rt. 30 south of Townshend Village, rents cross-country skis and snowshoes. **Jamaica State Park** in Jamaica (see *Green Space*) offers marked trails.

See also **Grafton Ponds Recreation Center** in "The Lower Connecticut River Valley."

DOWNHILL SKIING The big ski areas are a short drive west into the Green Mountains, either to **Mount Snow** (Rt. 9 from Brattleboro and then up Rt. 100 to West Dover—see "Mount Snow/Wilmington Area") or up Rt. 30 to **Stratton** (see "Manchester and the Mountains").

SLEIGH RIDES **Fair Winds Farm** (802-254-9067), Upper Dummerston Rd.; the **Robb Family Farm** (802-254-7664; 1-888-318-9087), 827 Ames Hill Rd.; and **Green Mountain Horse Ranch** (see *Horseback Riding*) in Putney all offer sleigh rides.

SNOWMOBILING See **Mount Snow** (in "Mount Snow/Wilmington Area") and **Stratton** (see "Manchester and the Mountains") ski resorts for tours and rentals. The VAST (Vermont Area Snow Travelers; www.vtast.org) trail system can be accessed in West Brattleboro.

✳ Green Space

Fort Dummer State Park (802-254-2610), Guilford. Located 2 miles south of Brattleboro (follow S. Main St. to the end). Surrounded by a 217-acre forest, overlooking the site of its namesake fort, built in 1724 to protect settlements along the Connecticut River. It was flooded by the Vernon Dam in 1908. There are 51 tent/trailer sites and 10 lean-tos, hot showers, and a dump station but no hookups. There are also hiking trails and a playing field.

Townshend State Park (802-365-7500), Townshend, marked from Rt. 30 south of town. Open early May–Columbus Day. Up a back road, an attractive, classic '30s Civilian Conservation Corps (CCC) stone-and-wood complex with a picnic pavilion. This is really an 856-acre state forest with 41 acres reserved for the park. The camping area (30 tent/trailer campsites, four lean-tos) is near the start of the 2.7-mile (steep) climb to the summit of Bald Mountain; trail maps are available at the park office.

✔ **Jamaica State Park** (802-874-4600), Jamaica. This 758-acre wooded area offers riverside camping, swimming in a great swimming hole, a picnic area, and an organized program of guided hikes. An old railroad bed along the river serves as a 3-mile trail to the Ball Mountain Dam, and an offshoot mile-long trail leads to Hamilton Falls. A weekend in spring and again in fall is set aside for white-water canoe races. There are 61 tent/trailer sites and 18 lean-tos. A large picnic shelter is handy to the swimming hole; a playground includes swings, a teeter-totter, and slides.

Ball Mountain Lake (802-874-4881), Jamaica. This 85-acre lake, created and maintained by the U.S. Army Corps of Engineers, is a dramatic sight among the wooded, steep mountains, conveniently viewed from the access road off Rt. 30. Over 100 campsites are available on Winhall Brook at the other end of the reservoir, open mid-May–Columbus Day; it's accessible off Rt. 100 in South Londonderry. For reservations phone 1-877-444-6777. A controlled release from this flood dam provides outstanding canoeing on the West River below Jamaica each spring and fall (see *Boating*).

✔ **Living Memorial Park**, just west of Brattleboro on Rt. 9. This is an unusual facility for any community. It includes a swimming pool (mid-June–Labor Day), ice-skating rink (early Dec.–mid-Mar.), tennis courts, a playground, camping sites, lawn games, a nine-hole golf course, and a ski hill serviced by a T-bar.

Dutton Pines State Park (802-254-2277), Brattleboro. On Rt. 5, 5 miles north of town, this is a picnic area with a shelter

See also *Hiking* and *Swimming*.

✳ Lodging

COUNTRY INNS 🐾 ♿ **Four Columns Inn** (802-365-7713; 1-800-787-6633; www.fourcolumnsinn.com), Newfane 05345. This Greek Revival mansion, built in 1830 by General Pardon Kimball to remind his southern wife of her girlhood home, fronts on Newfane's classic green. Innkeepers Bruce and Debbie Pfander offer 15 guest rooms, varying from merely country elegant, to deluxe (with gas fireplace), to extravagant suites (two-person whirlpool or soaking tub, typically with a view of the gas fireplace). The very best suite fills the space above the four columns, formerly a porch, with a Jacuzzi overlooking the green. While it's set in a splendid village, the inn backs onto 150 steep and wooded acres, good for walking or snowshoeing. Dining is a big attraction (see *Dining Out*), and facilities include a seasonal swimming pool. $160–315 per night midweek, $185–365 weekends, $195–390 holidays and foliage season. Breakfast included. $25 extra for pets.

Windham Hill Inn (802-874-4080; 1-800-944-4080; www.windhamhill .com), West Townshend 05359. High above the West River Valley, this 1825 brick farmhouse, presently owned by Joe and Marina Coneeny, is a luxurious retreat. Several of the 21 guest rooms have soaking tub, private deck, Jacuzzi, fireplace, or gas stove, and all have private bath and phone. All are furnished with antiques and interesting art. Eight are in the White Barn Annex, some with a large deck looking down the valley. Common space in the inn itself includes a music room with grand piano and an airy sunporch with wicker. Two sitting rooms are country elegant with wood-burning fireplace, Oriental carpets, and wing chairs, and the dining room also has a fireplace, a formal dining table, and tables for two (see *Dining Out*). A nicely landscaped pool overlooks the mountains and tennis court. The 160-acre property also includes an extensive network of hiking paths, groomed as cross-country trails in winter (when the frog pond freezes for skating). Inquire about weddings, both inside (there's a small conference center in the barn) and outside (for up to 75 guests). $195–380 per couple B&B plus $50 in foliage season.

∞ ♥ **Three Mountain Inn** (802-874-4140; 1-800-532-9399; www.three mountaininn.com), Rt. 30, Jamaica 05343. This 1790s inn in the middle of a classic Vermont village is now owned by Ed and Jennifer Dorta-Duque. There are 7 upstairs rooms and 7 in neighboring Robinson House, all newly decorated, several with whirlpool tub and 10 with gas or wood fireplace or stove. Sage Cottage in the garden features a Jacuzzi tub, gas fireplace, two skylights and a stained-glass

window, surround sound, and, of course, a TV/DVD. Common space includes the old tavern room with its large hearth and a corner bar. There are two small but elegant dining rooms (see *Dining Out*) and a new private gallery/dining room featuring a new artist every 6 weeks. Jamaica State Park and its trails are a short walk, and Stratton Mountain, with its 27-hole golf course, is a short drive. From $145 for a small room in the inn to $295 for the ground-floor two-room Jamaica Suite with French doors in the bedroom and sitting rooms opening onto the patio; $325 for the cottage; a three-course breakfast is included. Add $20 during foliage season and holidays. $15 less for solo travelers.

🍴 🐾 ✿ ♿ **The Putney Inn** (802-387-5517; 1-800-653-5517; www.putney inn.com), P.O. Box 181, Putney 05346; just off I-91, Exit 4. The inn's centerpiece is an 18th-century red-clapboard farmhouse. In the early 1960s, when the land was divided for construction of I-91, it was sold to local residents, who renovated the farmhouse without disturbing the posts and beams or the central open hearth. Plants and antiques add to the pleasant setting of the entry and large dining rooms. Twenty-five air-conditioned guest rooms occupy a motel-like wing, each with Queen Anne reproductions, bath, color TV, and phone. Pets are permitted but "must be smaller than a cow and not left alone in the rooms." The complex is set in 13 acres, with views of the river valley and mountains. Under longtime ownership by the Ziter family. Staff are helpful and the restaurant features first-rate New England fare made with local products (see *Dining Out*). At $98–158 per couple (children free under age 14) with a "farmer's breakfast," this is one of the best values around. $10 pet fee.

Chesterfield Inn (603-256-3211; 1-800-365-5515; www.chesterfieldinn .com), P.O. Box 155, Chesterfield, N.H. 03443. On Rt. 9, 2 miles east of Brattleboro. The original house served as a tavern from 1798 to 1811 but the present facility is contemporary, with a large attractive dining room, spacious parlor, and 13 guest rooms and two suites divided between the main house and the Guest House. All rooms have sitting area, phone, controlled heat and air-conditioning, optional TV, and wet bar, and some have a working fireplace or Jacuzzi. Innkeepers Phil and Judy Hueber have created a popular dining room and a comfortable, romantic getaway spot that's well positioned for exploring southern Vermont as well as New Hampshire's Monadnock region. $150–295 in low season, $175–320 in high, includes a full breakfast.

BED & BREAKFASTS

In Brattleboro
The Artist's Loft B&B and Gallery (802-257-5181 phone/fax; www.the artistsloft.com), 103 Main St., Brattleboro 05301. Artist William Hays and his wife, Patricia Long, offer a third-floor middle-of-town two-room suite that's spacious and colorful, with a private entrance, queen-sized bed, and river view (private bath). This is a great spot if you want to plug into all that Brattleboro offers in the way of art, music, dining, and shopping; Patricia and William delight in sharing their knowledge about their adopted town. Their web site features an extensive area guide. $118–158 includes continental breakfast.

Meadowlark Inn (802-257-4582; 1-800-616-6359; www.meadowlarkinn vt.com), Orchard St., P.O. Box 2048, Brattleboro 05301. The town of Brattleboro includes some surprisingly rural corners, like this maple-walled ridge road. The large farmhouse, set in lawns with vista views, has been renovated by innkeepers Lucia Osiecki and Deborah Jones. Common space includes a wraparound screened porch as well as a large living room. The yard offers a shady garden with Adirondack chairs, a hammock, and several tables with umbrellas. Rooms are divided between the main house and an 1870s coach barn with its own central area warmed by a hearth and decorated by a rural mural. All rooms have private bath and phone. In the Main House, the Pine Room has a king bed, fireplace, TV, and views all around; in the coach house, two have Jacuzzi and views of the woodland garden. The coach house also has two more luxurious rooms with king bed, views, and refrigerator. The innkeepers are culinary school graduates who enjoy creating a fresh and bountiful breakfast with a choice of hot entrées and freshly baked goods. Guests may want to take advantage of the 3-mile loop walk beginning at the front door, and cross-country ski trails at the nearby Brattleboro Country Club. $110–180.

☀ ✄ **Forty Putney Road** (802-254-6268; 1-800-941-2413; frtyptny@sover .net), 40 Putney Rd., Brattleboro 05301. Just north of the town common and within walking distance of downtown shops and restaurants, this house with steeply pitched, gabled roof is said to be patterned on a French château. It was built in 1930 for the director of the neighboring

Brattleboro Retreat. Lowell and Lindsay Hanson are avid gardeners and can frequently be found tending the landscaped grounds. Five tastefully furnished guest rooms, each with phone, TV, and private bath, include a two-room suite and a two-room cottage with a gas fireplace and full kitchen. There's a cozy bar serving guests a wide selection of beer and wine. We would request one of the rear two rooms overlooking the gardens, away from Rt. 5 (Putney Rd.), but front rooms are air-conditioned so noise is muted. Common space is plentiful and attractive, and landscaped grounds with working fountains border the West River. The $120–180 double rates include a full breakfast served, weather permitting, on the garden patio. The fireplace suite is $210 and the cottage, $250 double. Dogs and children welcome.

In Putney

&. **Hickory Ridge House** (802-387-5709; 1-800-380-9218; www.hickory ridgehouse.com), 53 Hickory Ridge Rd. south, Putney 05346. An 1808 brick mansion, complete with Palladian window, set on 12 acres with walking/cross-country ski trails. Miriam and Cory Greenspan offer six softly, authentically colored guest rooms in the inn and a two-bedroom cottage (two baths and full kitchen facilities, a wood-burning fireplace in the sitting room). Inn rooms come with and without wood-burning or gas fireplaces, but all have private bath, phone, and (hidden) TV/VCR. The original Federal-era bedrooms are large, with Rumford fireplaces, and there's an upstairs sitting room. A first-floor room is handicapped accessible. The cottage can be rented as whole or as separate rooms. A swimming hole lies within walking distance, and cross-country touring trails are out the back door. $145–195 per couple includes a full breakfast, perhaps orange French toast.

Ranney-Crawford House (802-387-4150; 1-800-731-5502; www.ranney -crawford.com), 1097 Westminster West Rd., Putney 05346. Another handsome brick Federal (1810) homestead on a quiet country road, surrounded by fields. Innkeeper Arnie Glim is an enthusiastic bicyclist who knows all the local possibilities for both touring and mountain biking. Four attractive guest rooms—two spacious front rooms with hearths, along with two smaller back rooms, all with private bath—are $135–160, including a three-course breakfast served in the formal dining room.

In the West River Valley

❧ **Boardman House** (802-365-4086; 1-888-366-7182), village green, Townshend 05353. We like the friendly feel of this 1840s Greek Revival house tucked into a quiet (away from Rt. 30 traffic) corner of one of Vermont's standout commons. Sarah and Paul Messenger offer five attractive guest rooms (one can be a suite) with private bath. There's also a two-bedroom suite, a parlor, and an airy, old-fashioned kitchen. Breakfast usually includes fresh fruit compote and oven-warm muffins with a creative main dish. $80 for rooms, $110–120 for a suite.

❧ **Ranney Brook Farm** (802-874-4589; www.ranneybrookfarm.com), P.O. Box 1108, West Townshend 05359. Set back from Rt. 30 in wooded grounds, this comfortable old red farmhouse is just up the road from boating and swimming at Townshend Dam. It's an informal, relaxing place with a piano in the den, a "great room" in the rear (a former 1790s barn), and a cheerful dining room in which a full breakfast is served family-style. Residents include a dog, two cats, and a parrot. The four rooms are upstairs; two have private bath. Diana Wichland is innkeeper; her husband, John, owns Miller Brothers–Newton, a long-established clothier in Brattleboro. $70–80 (no surcharge for foliage season).

🍁 Rock River Bed & Breakfast

(802-348-6301; www.rockriverbb .com), 408 Dover Rd., South New-fane 05301. Off the beaten path, between the West River and Mount Snow Valleys and on the edge of a small village, Chris and Nissa Petrak share their 1795 house with guests lucky enough to find them. Two guest rooms are upstairs under the eaves, and the prize room is downstairs off the dining room, overlooking the gardens and Rock River. All rooms are furnished with family antiques and original art; the reasonable rates ($65–95 in low season, $75–110 in high) include a full breakfast.

In Guilford

Green River Bridge House (802-257-5771; 1-800-528-1861; www .greenriverbridgehouse.com), 2435 Stage Rd., Green River, Guilford 05301. Joan Seymour has totally rehabbed a vintage-1791 house next to the covered bridge in this classic back-roads village. It's full of whimsical touches, like a former confessional as the reception window and specially designed ceilings to display her collection of crystal chandeliers. Amenities range from Jacuzzis to hair dryers. There are three guest rooms with private bath. Gardens and lawn stretch back along the river, with a

"meditation garden," a venue for weddings. $165–235 per couple includes a full breakfast, organic by prearrangement. Inquire about renting the whole house. Appropriate for children over 14 years.

OTHER LODGING 🍁 **Latchis Hotel** (802-254-6300; www.latchis.com), 50 Main St., Brattleboro 05301. This downtown, art-deco-style hotel first opened in 1939 and was resurrected after a thorough restoration. It remained in the Latchis family until 2003, when it was acquired by the Brattleboro Arts Initiative (BAI), a local group dedicated to turning the hotel's magnificent theater into a performance center. Push open the door into the small but spiffy lobby, with its highly polished terrazzo marble floors. Surprises in the rooms include WiFi, restored 1930s furniture, air-conditioning, and soundproof windows (a real blessing). Rooms are cheerful, brightly decorated, all with private bath, phone, fridge, and coffeemaker. The 27 rooms and 3 two-room suites are accessible by elevator. The rooms to request are on the second and third floors, with views down Main St. and across to Wantastiquet Mountain. The hotel is so solidly built that you don't hear the traffic below. For more about the theater see *Entertainment*. Rates are from $65 single, $75 double to $150–180 for suites, including continental breakfast.

The Sugar House (802-365-7573), P.O. Box 480, 47 Radway Hill Rd., Newfane 05345. Beside but entirely separate and private from Lenore and Dennis Sazman's home, this former 18th-century sugarhouse has been nicely converted into a cozy guest house with a queen bed facing a

RUDYARD KIPLING AND NAULAKHA

Rudyard Kipling first visited Brattleboro in the winter of 1892 and determined to build himself a house high on a hill in Dummerston (just north of the Brattleboro line), on property owned by his wife's family. The young couple then headed for Samoa to see Robert Louis Stevenson but got no farther than Yokohama; at that point their bank failed, taking virtually all their money. Returning to Vermont, they rented a cottage while building Naulakha; the name is a Hindi word meaning "great jewel." The shingled house is 90 feet long but only 22 feet wide, designed to resemble a ship riding the hillside like a wave. Its many windows face east, across the Valley to the New Hampshire hills with a glimpse of the summit of Mount Monadnock. Just 26 years old, Kipling was already one of the world's best-known writers, and the two following years here were among the happiest in his life. Here he wrote the *Jungle Books*. Here the local doctor, James Conland, a former fisherman, inspired him to write *Captains Courageous* and also delivered his two daughters. Kipling's guests included Sir Arthur Conan Doyle, who brought with him a pair of Nordic skis, said to be the first in Vermont. Unfortunately, in 1896 a highly publicized falling-out with his dissolute brother-in-law drove the family back to England. They took relatively few belongings from Naulakha, and neither did the property's two subsequent owners, who used it as a summer home. Happily, in 1992 it was acquired by The Landmark Trust USA, which rewired, repaired, and replumbed it (a new septic system was required) but otherwise preserved every detail of the home as Rudyard and Carrie Kipling knew it. Though the house is not available for functions and rarely for tours, it can be rented for $1,150–3,000 per week and, depending on the season, for a few days at a time ($250–335 per day, 3-night minimum). There are

RUDYARD KIPLING IN HIS STUDY AT NAULAKHA, CIRCA 1895

Landmark Trust USA

Landmark Trust USA

FROM THE ORIGINAL ARCHITECTURAL DRAWING OF NAULAKHA, WHERE RUDYARD KIPLING LIVED FROM 1893 TO 1896

four bedrooms (three baths). Some 60 percent of the present furnishings are original, including a third-floor pool table. A game of tennis, anyone, on the Kipling court? Or how about curling up with the *Jungle Books* on a sofa by the fire, only a few feet from where they were written? Or steeping in Kipling's own deep tub? For details about renting Naulakha, contact The Landmark Trust USA (802-254-6868; www.landmarktrust.usa), c/o 707 Kipling Rd., Dummerston 05301. *Rudyard Kipling in Vermont: Birthplace of the Jungle Books* by Stuart Murray (Images from the Past) offers an excellent description of Kipling's relation to and portrayal of the area.

Landmark Trust USA has restored two more historic buildings at neighboring 571-acre Scott Farm. **The Sugarhouse**, a classic century-old sugarhouse, has been fitted with radiant floor heating and a gas log stove, a bedroom (sleeping two), and a fully equipped kitchen with a dishwasher and linens ($500 per week, $125–160 per night, 3-night minimum). The eight-room **Dutton Farmhouse** is an 1837 Greek Revival white-clapboard homestead set near the highest point of the farm with 30-mile views over the Connecticut River Valley to Mount Monadnock. There are four bedrooms—two doubles and two with twins—two and a half baths, a full kitchen, a living room with gas log fireplace, a dining room, and a fully equipped kitchen ($900–1,400 per week, $225–275 per night, 3-night minimum). Both properties offer access to hiking trails on the farm and to the tennis courts at Naulakha.

working hearth and twins in a loft above. The fridge is stocked with milk, juice, fruit, and cheese. Fresh muffins arrive in the morning. $200 per night.

CAMPGROUNDS See *Green Space* for information on camping in Fort Dummer State Park, Townshend State Park, Jamaica State Park, and Ball Mountain Lake.

✳ Where to Eat

DINING OUT

In Brattleboro

T. J. Buckley's (802-257-4922), 132 Elliot St. Open Thu.–Sun. 6–9. Reservations suggested. From the outside this small (eight tables) but classic red-and-black 1920s Worcester diner looks unpromising, even battered. Inside, fresh flowers and mismatched settings (gathered from yard sales) brighten the tables, walls are oak paneled, and chef-owner Michael Fuller prepares the night's fish, chicken, and beef (vegetarian is also possible) in the open kitchen behind the counter. Fuller buys all produce locally, and what's offered depends on what's available: On a July day the menu included bluefin tuna with roast lobster stock, carrots, celery, and fresh horseradish root, served with a risotto with a ginger-pheasant stock; and a chicken breast with white truffle and goat Fontina, served with flageolet beans (white) with fresh artichoke and julienned Romano beans. The $35 entrée includes salad; appetizer and dessert are extra. The wine list ranges $20–85. No credit cards, but personal checks are accepted.

Peter Havens (802-257-3333), 32 Elliot St. Open from 6 PM Tue.–Sat. Just 10 tables in this nifty restaurant

decorated with splashy artwork, and with an inspired menu to match. Chef owned for more than 17 years and a universal favorite. The evening's entrées might include pasta del mar (a nest of linguine with a creamy pesto sauce topped with shrimp, scallops, and artichoke hearts), tenderloin with blue cheese and walnut butter, tortellini with Andalusian sausage, and always fresh seafood. Entrées $28–38, including salad. Credit cards accepted.

Max's (802-254-7747; www.maxs restaurant.com), 1052 Western Ave., West Brattleboro. Open for dinner Wed.–Sun. from 5:30. When Max's changed hands in fall 2003, former sous-chef Adam Silverman became chef, perpetuating the menu and ambience that have won this attractive restaurant an enthusiastic following. The à la carte menu is large, with many appetizer and pasta choices that change frequently. Specialties that tend to stick include the grilled filet mignon with roasted shallots, a Gorgonzola mashed potato brick, shiitake mushrooms, and grain mustard, finished with a red wine reduction. Pastas $16–28, nonpasta entrées $20–26. The wine list is large and reasonable.

Capers Restaurant (802-251-0151), 51 Main St. Open Wed.–Sat. for lunch and dinner, Sunday brunch. A new venture by two locally proven chefs, a storefront bistro with simply but deftly prepared dishes. Dinner entrées from $15 for savory vegetable potpie to $19 for seared sea scallops with onion grass.

Thirty9 Main (802-254-3999), 39 Main St. Open Thu.–Mon. from 5:30 PM. Chef-owner Matthew Miner offers a zany decor and eclectic dishes. Entrées include tapas-style "small plates" like a three-cheese tart with fig salsa ($7–8), "bigger plates" from $13 for baked tofu with roasted tomatoes, artichokes, and olives, and $16 for venison chop with cider glaze.

✦ ⚄ **Riverview Café** (802-254-9841; www.riverviewcafe.com), 36 Bridge St. Open daily for lunch and dinner. The big news here is the (seasonal) rooftop seating with the best dining view of the Connecticut River along its 410-mile length; there's also a downstairs deck and, of course, windowside dining. Chef-owner Tristan Toleno has transformed this old standby into an informal but sophisticated restaurant with a mainstream menu, including fish-and-chips, steak, and applewood-smoked spicy pork spareribs. Full liquor license and regional microbrews on tap. Entrées $7–19.95.

Along Rt. 30

The Four Columns Inn (802-365-7713; www.fourcolumnsinn.com), Rt. 30, Newfane. Serving 5:30–9 nightly except Tue.; reservations suggested. Chef Greg Parks has earned top ratings for his efforts, served in a converted barn with a large brick fireplace as its centerpiece. The emphasis is on herbs (homegrown), stocks made from scratch, and locally raised lamb. While the menu changes frequently, it might include a whole Vermont squab with cider reduction, huckleberries, and raspberries, and roast pork loin stuffed with artichoke, spinach, and mushrooms, served with red currants and smoked bacon vinaigrette. Entrées $22–33.

Old Newfane Inn (802-365-4427), Rt. 30, Newfane Village. Open for dinner nightly except Mon. Reservations requested. The low-beamed old dining room is country formal. Chef-owner Eric Weindl is widely known for his Swiss-accented Continental menu with entrée choices like roast duckling au Cointreau à l'orange or rack of lamb for one ($19–32).

Windham Hill Inn (802-874-4080; 1-800-944-4080; www.windhamhill.com), West Townshend. The exceptionally attractive, candlelit dining room, overlooking a pond, is open to the public for dinner (6–8:30) by reservation. You could opt for the four-course prix fixe dinner for $50 or order à la carte from a menu that might include homemade morel ravioli as an appetizer, grilled halibut fillet with white lentils, citrus salad, a fresh ruby grapefruit buerre blanc, and a roasted eggplant tart filled with Vermont chèvre and tomatoes, served with wilted spinach and roasted summer vegetables. Entrées $27–31.

Three Mountain Inn (802-874-4140), Rt. 30, Jamaica. Dinner reservations recommended. While enjoying a candlelit dinner in front of the fireplaces in the two small dining rooms of this 18th-century village house, it's easy to imagine that you're in a colonial tavern. Chef Timothy Richen changes the menu weekly. Signature dishes include cocoa-dusted scallops and lobster strudel, also an apple tart. There's a $55 prix fixe, but items can be ordered à la carte. Entrées $24–36.

🦐 **Asta's Swiss Restaurant** (802-874-8000), 3894 Main St. (Rt. 30), Jamaica. Open for dinner 5–10 except Wed.; also for Sun. brunch noon–3. Chef-owner Michel de Preux hails from the Swiss canton of Valais and has a sure touch with everything he prepares, from turkey breast snitzel (topped with lemon, caper, and anchovies) and roast half duckling à l'orange (finished with an orange green peppercorn sauce) to filet mignon café de Paris (topped with mustard, herbs, and spice butter, and served with rösti potatoes). There are options for vegetarians, such as falafel with garlic tahini, cucumber salad, hummus, and pita chips; also look for Swiss specialties like fondue and raclette (both cheese and meat) and choucroute garnie. Sunday brunch offers plenty of egg dishes plus pastas, salads, even grinders. All entrées come with bread and salad. The ambience is warm. $15.95–26.50. Wine and beer.

Elsewhere

❦ ✿ **The Putney Inn** (802-387-5517; 1-800-653-5517; www.putneyinn.com), just off I-91, Exit 4, in Putney. Open for all three meals. The area's oldest 18th-century homestead retains its open hearth and is now an attractive restaurant as well as centerpiece for an inn. The dinner menu features classic but classy New England comfort food with an emphasis on local ingredients. Lunch choices might include macaroni and cheese Vermont-style (with Grafton Village extra-sharp cheddar) and roasted (local) turkey potpie. Dinner choices might include roasted Vermont lamb with sausage risotto cake, and maple Dijon horseradish glazed prime rib with Vermont cheddar mashed potatoes. Entrées $18.50–28 (for butter-poached half lobster and potato-crusted scallops).

EATING OUT

In Brattleboro

✿ **The Marina Restaurant** (802-257-7563; www.vermontmarina.com), Rt. 5 just north of the West River bridge. Open daily Apr.–mid-Oct., less frequently off-season. Situated at the confluence of the West and Connecticut Rivers, this place has a great view and maximizes it, with a screened porch and patio as well as a dockside deck; in winter there's fireside dining. The reasonably priced menu includes plenty of seafood and vegetarian choices at both lunch and dinner, but also burgers. Full liquor license. A great place to enjoy a margarita while watching the sunset.

Shin La Restaurant (802-257-5226), 57–61 Main St. Open 11–9, closed Sun. Yl'soon Kim is the dynamo behind this attractive Korean restaurant, really a standout that has evolved over its years at this storefront. It's known for homemade soups, dumplings, and other Korean fare and includes a sushi bar.

Amy's Bakery Arts Café (802-251-1071), 113 Main St. A good lunch spot. There are river views from tables in the back of this attractive storefront café, and the food is appealing, too: spinach and cheese croissants, salads, and sandwiches, some with meat but plenty without.

Back Side Cafe (802-257-5056), Green St. Extension. Open weekdays for breakfast and lunch, dinner Thu.–Sat. nights; Sunday brunch. A great place for breakfast if you like an omelet with lots of fresh garlic or homemade salsa. Lunch features homemade soups, salads, deli sandwiches, and bagels; dinner runs from burgers to roast chicken, with a full bar featuring Vermont beers. Brunch both Sat. and Sun.

Brattleboro Food Co-op (802-257-0236), 2 Main St., Brookside Plaza. Open Mon.–Sat. 8–9, Sun. 9–9. An outstanding natural food market and deli worth checking out for its stellar choice of Vermont cheese—but while you're there, take advantage of the Café and Juice Bar featuring creative smoothies, first-rate sandwiches, and salads.

India Palace Restaurant, 69 Elliot St. Open daily for lunch and dinner, both reasonably priced for authentic Indian curries, tandoori, and biryani dishes. The list of Indian breads alone is long, and the menu is immense. Dinner specials include multicourse meals.

Sarkis Market DeliCafe (802-258-4906), 50 Elliot St. Open for lunch and dinner (until 8), for take-out and eat-in. A great source of stuffed grape leaves, spinach pies, lamb stew, home-made baklava, and falafel pockets.

Thai Garden (802-251-1010), 7 High St. Open daily for lunch (11:30–3) and dinner (5–10). Sign of the times! For many years this was the site of Dunkin' Donuts, since replaced by this representative of a small, regional chain. Dishes typically feature Thai basil and crisp vegetables. Try the Goi See Mee, fried crispy yellow noodles with chicken and shrimp, onions, carrots, mushrooms, and bamboo shoots. Wine and beer are served.

Mole's Eye Café (802-257-0771; www.moleseyecafe.net), corner of Main and High Sts. Open Mon.–Thu. 4–midnight, Fri.–Sat. 11:30–1 AM. No food after 9 PM. A popular local gathering place serving soups, chili, and sandwiches, with a full bar and frequent live and lively music until 1 AM.

✍ **Brattleboro Farmer's Market**. If you happen into town around noon on a sunny Saturday or Wednesday, head for the farmer's market. Saturday is the big day (early May–Oct., 9–2) just west of town by the Creamery Bridge. A live band and crafts, as well as produce vendors, are usually on hand. On Wed. (mid-June–Sep., 10–2) it's downtown off Main St. by the Merchants Bank Building (look for the parking lot right there), with food

vendors next to a small park overlooking the river.

Along Putney Rd. and in Putney

🐾 ✍ **Top of the Hill Grill** (802-258-9178), 632 Putney Rd. Open mid-Apr.–Oct., 11–9. You have to be looking for this unusual BBQ place. It comes up fast after the bridge, heading north on Rt. 5 out of town. You order, get a card, take in the view of the river and "Retreat Meadows," and sit at a picnic table or in the screened deckhouse (muffling traffic noise, including restrooms) until your card is called (could be the Queen of Hearts). Indiana-born Julian Johnson hickory smokes his brisket and pork ribs, and apple smokes his turkey. He also makes corn bread and coleslaw from scratch. You can also get a tempeh burger, Cajun dishes, a salad, or a hot dog. Sides include red beans and rice, garden greens, and garlic-rosemary potatoes.

✍ **Curtis' Barbeque** (802-387-5474). Summer through fall, Tue.–Sun. 10–dusk. Follow your nose to the blue school bus parked behind the Mobil station on Rt. 5 in Putney, just off I-91, Exit 4. Curtis Tuff cooks up pork ribs and chicken, seasoned with his secret barbecue sauce, also foil-wrapped potatoes, grilled corn, and beans flavored with Vermont maple syrup. There are picnic tables and a weather-proofed pavilion.

Front Porch Café (802-387-2200), 133 Main St. Open for breakfast, lunch, and Sunday brunch. The rambling old white tavern on Putney's green is once more the village gathering place, thanks to Jeremy Burrell and Steven Griffiths, former owners of the Saxtons River Inn. Fresh-baked muffins, scrambled egg wraps, soups, sandwiches, and daily specials along with coffees and teas are ordered and served up in a small corner space adjoining the informal café space with a hearth (also adjoining Heartstone Books). The $14.95 Sunday brunch is a sellout.

✦ ♪ Putney Diner (802-387-5433), Main St. Open 6 AM–8 PM daily. Another pleasant option in the middle of Putney Village, open for all three meals. Good for Belgian waffles, Philly cheese steak, and homemade vegetable lasagna, super sandwich plates, salads, chicken-fried steak, grilled liver and onions, even burritos and tacos. Pastries made daily. Children's menu.

Putney Food Co-op (802-387-5866), Rt. 5 just south of the village. Open for lunch at 11. This is a great, quick lunch stop at a supermarket-sized cooperative with a pleasant café area: daily soups, salads, and deli.

Putney Village Pizza (802-387-2203), 84 Main St. John and Nancy Papadopoulos offer classic (Greek) pies with all the toppings; also subs, salads, and pastas.

Putney General Store (802-387-5842), Main St. Open 6–6 daily. Despite other options within steps of one another, the deli-café at the rear of this classic general store remains a local favorite. There's a genuine soda fountain and booths, and you can lunch on a veggie deluxe as well as a BLT.

Along Rt. 30

Williamsville General Store (802-348-7300), 26 Dover Rd., Williamsville. Open 6 AM–7 PM weekdays, Sat. from 8, Sun. noon–5, 2 miles west of Rt. 30. The deli display, wine selection, and gourmet items could be in upscale Manhattan, but prices are reasonable and breads are freshly made. Friday is pizza night. Obviously catering is a sideline. Pick up a sandwich or salad and picnic by the nearby covered bridge or swimming hole.

Rick's Tavern (802-365-4310), just south of Newfane Village. Open daily for lunch and dinner, live jazz Thursday, and acoustic music Saturday night. The bar was built around 1890 in Bismark, North Dakota, but the draft beers are Vermont microbrews. Daily blackboard specials, pizza, homemade desserts.

Townshend Pizza (802-365-4800), junction of Rts. 30 and 35, Townshend green. Open 11–9. In 2005 John and Nancy Papadopoulos, owners of Putney Village Pizza, opened this attractive eatery featuring their already proven pizza plus calzones, subs, gyros, salads, and pastas. Beer and wine are served.

✦ ♪ The Townshend Dam Diner (802-874-4107), Rt. 30, 2 miles north of the Townshend Dam. Open daily 5 AM–8 PM. Breakfast all day. There's a big U-shaped counter and plenty of table seating, the greenery is genuine, and the waitresses are friendly. Specialties include homemade French toast, home fries, muffins and biscuits, the "best dam chili," soups, and bison burgers (from the nearby East Hill Bison Farm). Dinner staples include roast turkey, spaghetti, and garlic bread, daily specials. Peanut butter and jelly with chips and pickle is still $1.75.

Along Rt. 9 west

♪ Chelsea Royal Diner (802-254-8399; www.chelsearoyaldiner.com), Rt. 9, West Brattleboro. Open 6 AM–9 PM. A genuine '30s diner that's been moved a few miles west of its original

site (it's a mile west of I-91, Exit 2).
Plenty of parking and diner decor.
Serving breakfast all day as part of a
big menu that includes pizza, burgers,
platters, and daily blue plate specials.

**WINE AND BREWS McNeill's Brew-
ery** (802-254-2553), 90 Elliot St.,
Brattleboro. Open at 4 Mon.–Thu.
and at 2 Fri. and Sat. This brewery
was once the town firehouse/offices/
police station and jail. Ray McNeill
was working on a graduate degree in
music when he decided to focus
instead on his second passion. This
mecca for beer and ale lovers has
medals to show for its variety of 35
brews, including lagers, traditional
cask-conditioned real ales, and barley
wines. A dozen are usually on tap. The
rustic bar features communal tables, a
horseshoe bar, a dartboard, and enchanting (local) art. Occasionally you
will find McNeill playing his cello.

Flat Street Brew Pub (802-257-
1911), 6 Flat St. Open 4–1 weekdays,
from noon on weekends. The hot
spot in town, opened in 2005 in the
Latchis complex. There are 20 microbrews on tap, including 10 from the
Berkshire Brewing Company based in
South Deerfield, Ma., not far down
the Connecticut Valley. Food ranges
from Thai lettuce wraps to the stuffed
spud du jour; seating includes couches and armchairs as well as bar stools
and tables.

Mocha Joe's (802-257-7794), 82
Main St., Brattleboro. Coffee is taken
seriously here, roasted as well as
brewed. Live music on weekends.

Twilight Tea Lounge (802-254-8887),
under 51 Main St., Brattleboro. Open
Wed.–Sun., noon to varying hours. A
barbershop for 75 years, this pleasant

space is filled with mismatched tables
and chairs and the aroma of rare teas.
A cooperative, the venue for Thursday-
night poetry and music.

Putney Mountain Winery (802-387-
5925). Music professor and composer
Charles Dodge has established a reputation for the quality of his sparkling
apple wines. Tastings are offered on
weekends at Basketville in Putney.

✳ Entertainment

The Latchis Theater (802-254-
6300; www.latchis.com), 50 Main St.,
Brattleboro, shows first-run and art
films, also live performances. For film
buffs, this 900-seat art deco movie
house with three screens is itself a
destination. Apollo still drives his
chariot through the firmament on the
ceiling; walls are graced with Doric
columns, and the lobby floor bears
the zodiac signs in multicolored terrazzo. Along with the Latchis Hotel in
which it's housed, the theater is
owned by the Brattleboro Arts Initiative; there's also an art gallery.

New England Youth Theatre (802-
246-1479; http://neyt.org). Year-round
productions of children's and all-time
classics in the New England Youth
Theatre, part of the Latchis complex
(see above).

Sandglass Theater (802-387-4051;
www.sandglasstheater.org), Kimball
Hill, Putney. A resident theater
company performs original work
combining live theater with puppetry
performances. When not on tour they
perform in a 60-seat renovated barn
theater in Putney Village.

**Sanctuary: Hooker-Dunham
Theater** (802-254-9276; www.
hookerdunham.org), 139 Main St.,

Brattleboro. Check out what's going on at this middle-of-town venue: theater, music, classic films, and lectures.

Whittemore Theater at Marlboro College (802-257-4333), Marlboro, is the setting for frequent presentations.

Kipling Cinemas (at Fairfield Plaza, Rt. 5 north of Brattleboro), a multiplex, also shows first-run films.

MUSIC Yellow Barn Music Festival (802-387-6637; 1-800-639-3819; www .yellowbarn.org), Putney. Begun in 1969, this is a series of chamber music concerts in July and early August, staged both in a 150-seat barn in Putney Village and at Amherst College in Amherst, Ma. Artists include both well-known professionals and 40 students chosen each summer from leading conservatories.

Brattleboro Music Center (802-257-4523; www.bmcvt.org), 38 Walnut St., Brattleboro. Housed in a former convent, this burgeoning music school sponsors a wide variety of local musical events and festivals as well as a fall-through-spring Chamber Music Series.

Vermont Jazz Center (802-254-9088; www.vtjazz.org), 72 Cotton Mill Hill, Studio 222, S. Main St., Brattleboro, stages frequent musical, vocal, and jazz happenings.

Friends of Music at Guilford (802-257-1961; 802-257-1028), Guilford. A series of concerts throughout the year at various locations. Note the free Labor Day weekend concerts under *Special Events.*

Also see the **Marlboro Music Festival** in "Mount Snow/Wilmington Area," and under *Eating Out* see the **Mole's Eye Café** and **Rick's Tavern**.

✳ Selective Shopping

ANTIQUES

In Brattleboro

Twice Upon a Time (802-254-2261; www.twicetime.com), 63 Main St. Open Mon.–Wed. 10–6, Thu.–Sat. until 8, Sun. noon–5. Auctions are held 6 PM Wed. at the Roller Dome, north of the bridge on Rt. 5. "I always wanted a consignment shop that would be able to display anything that anyone wanted to give me," says Randi Crouse, proprietor of this truly amazing shop that now fills the entire three-level space created in 1906 for the E. J. Fenton Department Store. In the '50s it was chopped into smaller storefronts, but the two-story-high Corinthian columns, bubble glass, and wooden gallery are back, a setting for clothing, antique furniture, and furnishings. The markdown schedule is patterned on that of Filene's Basement. More than 100 dealers and a total of 3,000 consignors are represented. If there's something special you're looking for, chances are Crouse can find it.

Along Rt. 30

More than two dozen dealers are found along this route. Pick up a copy of their pamphlet guide at the first place you stop. They include:

Newfane Flea Market (802-365-4000), just north of Newfane Village. Sundays, May–Oct. Billed as the largest open-air market in the state; usually 100 tables with assorted junk and treasure.

Jack Winner Antiques (802-365-7215; www.winnerantiques.com), Rt. 30, Newfane. Open Thu.–Mon. 10–5. Specializing for over 30 years in 18th- and 19th-century formal and country furniture, equestrian antiques, Spode china, brass, and hunting prints.

Auntie M's Attic (802-365-9796), Rt. 30, south of Newfane Village. Open May–Oct., Thu.–Mon. A nice selection of antique china, furniture, glass, lamps, linens, and prints.

NU-tique (802-365-7677), Newfane Village. Open May–Oct., Sat.–Wed. 10:30–4:30 and by appointment. Books, including New England histories, poetry, military, children's; also old lamps, glass, sheet music, records.

Riverdale Antiques (802-365-4616), Rt. 30, Harmonyville (between Newfane and Townshend). Open year-round, daily 10–5. More than 70 dealers selling quality antiques and collectibles.

Townshend Auction Gallery (802-365-4388), Rt. 30, Townshend. Over 30 years Kit Martin and Art Monette have established a solid reputation for their frequent auctions.

Also see **Old Corkers Emporium** in Jamaica under "Art and Crafts Galleries."

Sprague Auctions (802-254-8969), Rt. 5, Dummerston. Specializing in estates. Auctions every Wed. evening.

ART AND CRAFTS GALLERIES *Note:* The first Friday of each month is Gallery Walk in Brattleboro: open house with refreshments and music at dozens of downtown businesses that hang works by local artists and at studios as well as at formal galleries, usually 5:30–8:30; a special brochure is prepared for each walk. Check out www.gallerywalk.org.

Windham Art Gallery (802-257-1881; www.windhamartgallery.com), 69 Main St., Brattleboro. Open Wed.– Sun. noon–5, weekends until 7:30. Exhibits by members of an outstanding artists' cooperative, also source of the Arts Council of Windham County quarterly publication *Arts in the Season*, which lists current theater, poetry readings, and gallery shows throughout southeastern Vermont.

Artist's Loft Gallery (802-257-5181 phone/fax; www.theartistsloft.com), 103 Main St., Brattleboro. Realistic landscapes as well as portraits and other worth-checking oils by William Hays.

Vermont Artisan Designs (802-257-7044), 106 Main St., Brattleboro. Open daily. Ever-expanding to fill three floors of a former department store, an outstanding contemporary crafts gallery displays the work of 300 artisans; check out changing art exhibits in Gallery 2 upstairs.

Gallery in the Woods (802-257-4777; www.galleryinthewoods), 143 Main St., Brattleboro. For decades Dante and Suzanne Corsano's gallery has been a standout, featuring folk art, finely crafted furniture, and known painters and artists in a variety of media from throughout the world. Don't miss the changing exhibits on the basement level.

Catherine Dianich Gallery (802-254-9076; www.catherinedianich gallery.com), 139 Main St., Brattleboro. On the ground floor of the Hooker-Dunham Building, a former shoe factory that now houses many artists' studios. This sleek studio offers changing exhibits in varied media.

Borter's Jewelry Studio (802-254-3452; www.bortersjewelry.com), 103 Main St., Brattleboro. Gemstones; silver and gold jewelry handcrafted into stunning settings on the premises.

The Art Building, 127 Main St., Brattleboro, houses a dozen studios, open irregularly and for Gallery Walk. Visitors are welcome to stroll up any day and see whose door is open. The **River Gallery School** (802-257-1577) offers frequent classes and workshops here.

In Putney

Note: **The Putney Craft Tour** (www.putneycrafts.com), held for more than 27 years for 3 days after Thanksgiving, showcases the work of two dozen craftspeople working within a dozen miles of Putney. The quality and scenery are exceptional, drawing many repeat visitors every year.

At www.putney.net more than 60 artists and craftspeople are listed, but most do not maintain shops or open studios. The exceptions are:

Penelope Wurr Glass (802-387-5607; www.penelopewirr.com), 12 Kimball Hill. Open Fri. noon–6, Sat. 11–6, Sun. and holidays 11–5. Trained as a printmaker, this English-born designer who has operated studios in London and SoHo (NYC) has been living and working in Putney for more than a decade. She recently opened a shop to showcase her amazing glass, distinctive for the way it's patterned, suggesting textiles more than art glass—which it is.

Edel Byrne Stained Glass (802-387-2115), 88 Main St. Closed Jan.; open the rest of the year by chance or appointment. Dublin-born Byrne specializes in "lace leadwork," creating medieval-inspired geometric patterns in windows and lamps.

Brandywine Glassworks (802-387-4032; www.robertburchglass.com), Fort Hill Rd. (off Rt. 5 north). Robert Burch, a pioneer in art glass, hand-

blows his signature cobalt perfume bottles and vases, veiled with delicate silver bubbles, and amber and ruby swirling paperweights in a 200-year-old barn beside his home. He supplies some 200 shops and galleries across the country and is also a respected teacher of his craft, drawing students regularly from Boston. Phone before you stop by. Seconds are available.

Lilli Pottery Gallery (802-387-2222), 2888 Westminster West Rd. Open Mon.–Fri. 10–4, weekends noon–5. Lilli Crites Flesher crafts wheel-thrown, functional, but decorative and brilliantly glazed pottery.

Richard Bissell Fine Woodworking (802-387-4416), Signal Pine Rd. Open Mon.–Fri. 8–4. Exceptional Shaker-inspired furniture, cabinetry, Windsor chairs.

Kenneth Pick (802-387-5995), 187 Westminster West Rd. Call ahead. Ken Pick creates functional and sculptural pottery in a vintage tobacco barn, surrounded by colorful and dynamic ceramic sculptures and flower gardens, just uphill from the village. He's best known for his award-winning, massive wall platters and lusciously glazed vases, teapots, casseroles, and more.

Green Mountain Spinnery (802-387-4528; 1-800-321-9665; www.spinnery.com), just off I-91, Exit 4. Open Mon.–Fri. 9–5:30, Sat. 10–5:30; Labor Day–Thanksgiving, also Sun. noon–4. Founded as a cooperative more than 25 years ago, this is a real spinning mill in which undyed, unbleached fibers—alpaca, mohair, wool, and organic cotton—are carded, spun, skeined, and labeled. You can buy the resulting yarn in various plies in natural and 55 dyed colors. More than 40 original patterns are shown in the cat-

Christina Tree

GREEN MOUNTAIN SPINNERY

alog. The store also carries buttons, and knitting and spinning supplies.

Along Rt. 30
Newfane Country Store (802-365-7916; www.newfanecountrystore.com), Newfane. Open daily, year-round. Owner Marilyn Distelberg is herself a quilter—and quilts, many locally handmade as well as Amish and imported, are the big reason to stop.

Taft Hill (802-865-4200), Harmonyville (Townshend). Open daily 11–5. Gifts and furnishings, featuring fine hand-painted glass and china created here at Crest Studio.

Dunberry Hill Designs (802-874-7288; www.dunberryhilldesigns.com). Studio usually open but call. Just off Rt. 30 near Townshend Dam, Cameron Howard creates durable and distinctive cotton canvas floorcloths with geometric and folk art designs.

Jennie Blue (802-874-4222; www.vermontpottery.net), Jamaica Village. Open 9:30–5 daily except Tue. Local potter Susan Leader's bright, irresistible plates, vases, and pots with

cheerful designs and Jennie's personalized wedding and other special-occasion plates and bowls are the specialties here.

Margie's Muse Handweaving & Gallery (802-874-7201; www.margiesmuse.com), Rt. 30, Jamaica Village. Open Thu.–Mon. Handwoven wool blankets, chenille throws and scarves, hand-dyed and -spun natural yarns, changing artwork and local crafts.

Elaine Beckwith Gallery (802-874-7234), Rt. 30/100, Jamaica Village. Open daily except Tue. 10–5:30. This is a long-established, standout gallery featuring work by artist-printmaker Joel Beckwith but also representing some 30 artists in a variety of styles.

Old Corkers Emporium (802-874-4172; www.oldcorkersantiques.com), Rt. 30, Jamaica. Open year-round. Summer and fall, Wed.–Mon. 10–5; off-season weekends 10–5. Skip and Maureen Woodruff began by selling Adirondack lodge camp furniture and furnishings; Skip now handcrafts a line of his own: tables, servers, mirrors, frames, and more. They still also collect and sell the antiques. A great stop!

Nancy Price Gallery (802-374-4489), Main St. Open Wed.–Sun. 10–6. Photography by Robert Reichart and others.

BOOKSTORES The Book Cellar (802-254-6026; www.vtbookcellar.com), 120 Main St., Brattleboro. An outstanding, long-established, full-service bookstore, particularly strong on Vermont and New England titles.

Everyone's Books (802-254-8160; www.everyonesbks.com), 25 Elliot St., Brattleboro. This is an earnest and interesting alternative bookstore, specializing in women's books; also a great selection of children's and multi-cultural titles.

Old & New England Books (802-365-7074), 47 West St., Newfane. Open May–Oct., Thu.–Mon. 10:30–6. A delightful browsing place with an interesting stock of books old and new.

Heartstone Books (802-387-2100; www.heartstonebooks.com), at the junction of Rt. 5 and West Hill Rd. in Putney. Open daily 10–6. Housed in the restored old tavern at the center of Putney Village, a full-service bookstore that also carries used books, cards, and toys and invites browsing, with a frequently working hearth in the adjacent Front Porch Café.

Brattleboro Books (802-257-0777), 34 Elliot St., Brattleboro. Open 10–6 daily except Sun. An extensive selection of used and out-of-print books; over 70,000 titles fill two storefronts and the basement. Browsing strongly encouraged.

Basket's Paperback Palace Book Store (802-258-4980), 48 Harmony Place, Brattleboro. A trove of used paperbacks.

SPECIAL SHOPS

In Brattleboro

Delectable Mountain (802-257-4456), 125 Main St. Fine-fabric lovers make pilgrimages to Jan Norris's store, widely known for its selection of fine silks, all-natural imported laces, velvets, cottons, and upholstery jacquards. It also offers a wide selection of unusual buttons.

Brattleboro Food Co-op (802-257-0236), 2 Main St., Brookside Plaza. Open Mon.–Sat. 8–9, Sun. 9–9; deli and fresh-baked products. The cheese counter could just be the best show-case for Vermont cheese in the state; cheeses from around the world are also knowledgeably selected and presented (note the "cheese of the week"), and there's local produce, grains, wines, and a café.

Adavasi Imports (802-258-2231), 8 Flat St. Shram and Elissa Bhanti keep prices low because they are also wholesalers, traveling to northwest India to buy their fabrics: linens and clothing hand blocked with natural vegetable dyes; silk saris for $25; cotton rugs; and a wide variety of crafted items and jewelry. It's an exotic, fragrant emporium that keeps expanding.

Tom & Sally's Handmade Chocolates (802-254-4200), Rt. 30. Locally made and worth a taste.

Sam's Outdoor Outfitters (802-254-2933; www.samsoutfitters.com), 74 Main St. Open 8–6, until 9 on Fri., closed Sun. The business that Sam Borofsky started in 1934 now fills two floors of two buildings with a full stock of hunting, camping, and sports equipment. Prices are reasonable, but people don't shop here for bargains. The big thing is the service—skilled help in selecting the right fishing rod, tennis racket, or gun. There are also name-brand sports clothes and standard army and navy gear. On the first day of deer hunting season (early Nov.), the store opens at dawn and serves a hunter's breakfast at I-91, Exit 1 (it also sells licenses). *Tip:* There's free popcorn every day, all day.

A Candle in the Night (802-257-0471), 181 Main St. Donna and Larry Simons have built up a vast knowledge as well as inventory of Oriental and other handcrafted rugs over the decades.

Save the Corporations from Themselves (802-254-4847; www .savethecorporations.com), 169 Main St. Hemp clothing is the specialty here, but don't miss the "activists' attic."

Beadnicks (802-257-5114), 115 Main St. Beads, baubles, and whimsical wonders.

In Putney

Basketville (802-387-5509; www .basketville.com), Rt. 5. Open daily 8 AM–9 PM in busy seasons, 8–5 in slack seasons. The first of "The World's Largest Basket Stores" now scattered along the East Coast, it's also one of the oldest crafts producers in the state. Founded by Frank Wilson, an enterprising Yankee trader in the real sense, this is a family-run business. The vast store features woodenware, wicker furniture (filling the entire upstairs), wooden toys, and exquisite artificial flowers as well as traditional baskets and myriad other things, large and small. *Note:* Check out the Columbus Day weekend Basketville Seconds Sale.

Silver Forest of Vermont (802-387-4149), 14 Kimball Hill (middle of the village). A must-stop: clothing and accessories, also housewares and locally made silver jewelry, filling two floors, worth checking.

BEADNIKS IN BRATTLEBORO

William Hays

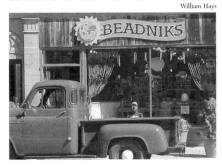

Offerings (802-387-4566; www .offeringsjewelry.com), middle of the village. Featuring handmade silver jewelry with semiprecious stones, unusual gold jewelry, watches, and cards.

Along Rt. 30

Lawrence's Smoke House (802-365-7751), Newfane. Corncob-smoked hams, bacon, poultry, fish, meats, and cheese are the specialties of the house. Catalog and mail order.

Jamaica Country Store (802-874-9151), Jamaica Village. Just a real country store, selling cheese, syrup, and souvenirs along with everything else. Note the freezer full of discounted Ben & Jerry's seconds.

FARMS TO VISIT One of the state's concentrations of farms and orchards is here in the Lower Connecticut River Valley, some offering "pick your own," others welcoming visitors to their farm stands, sugaring houses, or barns. Call before coming.

Note: Also see **Brattleboro Farmer's Market** under "Eating Out" and www .vtfarms.org for details and directions for many of the following.

Cheese

Vermont Shepherd (802-387-4473; www.vermontshepherd.com), Patch Rd., Westminster West. Vermont Shepherd holds one of the country's top awards for its distinctive, hand-pressed, sweet creamy sheep's-milk cheese. It's made Apr.–Oct., then aged 4 to 8 months and available mid-Aug. until the year's supply runs out in spring. Call for appropriate visiting times. A self-serve shop is open daily.

Peaked Mountain Farm (802-365-4502), 1541 Peaked Mountain Rd., Townshend. Call first. In an idyllic locale high above the West River Valley, Ann and Bob Works make sheep's-milk cheese, combination sheep/cow's-milk "Ewe Jersey," and a sheep/goat cheese.

Other

Robb Family Farm (802-254-7664; 1-888-318-9087; www.robbfamilyfarm .com), 827 Ames Hill Rd., Brattleboro. This 420-acre dairy farm has been in the same family since 1907, and visitors are welcomed here in a number of ways and in all seasons. In spring the sugarhouse is a fragrant, steamy place; year-round it's also the Country Shop (open Mon.–Sat. 10–5, Sun. 1–5, closed Wed.), stocked with maple products and floral items. Visitors are also welcome in the barn, moved here from Halifax in 1912 (50 of the 100-head herd are presently milked). Inquire about a Day on the Farm, beginning with breakfast, also about hayrides, sleigh rides, hiking, and the Apple Fritter Fest in October.

Olallie Daylily Gardens (802-348-6614; www.daylilygarden.com), 129 Augur Hole Rd., South Newfane. Open early May–Labor Day weekend, daily 10–5 except Tue. No charge for self-guided tours, but a 2-hour guided tour is $5. Pink irises in mid-June; daylilies June, July, and Aug.–Sep. PYO organic blueberries in July and Aug. Garden shop and potted plant nursery. Inquire about the Daylily Festival.

Dutton Berry Farm and Stand (802-365-4168), farm stand on Rt. 30, Newfane. Open year-round. This is a large, varied stand featuring varied fruit and other produce from Paul and Wendy Dutton's family farm, Christmas trees, much more.

Hickin's Mountain Mowings Farm (802-254-2146), 1999 Black Mountain Rd., Dummerston. Retail shop open Apr.–Dec. Selling raspberries July–Oct., other farm-fresh fruit in-season, also jams, jellies, and preserves, maple pickles, fruitcake, syrup, cheese, and honey. Marked off the East/West Rd. between Putney and Rt. 30 (see *Scenic Drives*).

Dwight Miller & Son Orchards (802-254-9158), 581 Miller Rd., East Dummerston. Open daily year-round. One of Vermont's oldest family farms. A retail stand with the farm's own organic fruit and vegetables, preserves, pickles, and syrup; seasonal pick-your-own apples and varied fruit in-season.

Elysian Hills Tree Farm (802-257-0233; www.elysianhillsfarm.com), 209 Knapp Rd., Dummerston. Bill and Mary Lou Schmidt maintain this 100-acre tree farm. Trees are available for tagging from July on, but the traditional "Tag Days" are Columbus Day weekend and the two following weekends: wagon rides, pumpkins, and marked hiking trails. Tagged trees, wreaths, and other decorations are also shipped UPS and FedEx in Dec.

∞ Green Mountain Orchards (802-387-5851; www.greenmountain orchards.com), 130 West Hill Rd., Putney. Open daily in-season. Pick-your-own apples and blueberries; cider available in-season. Christmas trees, local crafts, and produce also sold, gift shop, horse-drawn wagon rides on weekends, also wedding sites.

The Scott Farm (802-254-6868; www.landmarktrustusa.org), 707 Kipling Rd., Dummerston. Turn off busy Putney Rd. (Rt. 5) at the sign for WORLD LEARNING AND SCHOOL FOR INTERNATIONAL TRAINING and follow it up beyond the hardtop to this historic gentleman's farm currently under restoration by the Landmark Trust USA (see *Lodging*). The farm stand carries its peaches, pears, cherries, grapes, berries, and quince, but heirloom apples are the specialty, with more than 70 varieties.

Walker Farm (802-254-2051; www .walkerfarm.com), Rt. 5, Dummerston. A 200-year-old farm and garden center (open Apr. 15–fall, 10–6), specializing in hard-to-find annuals and perennials and garden books by local authors. A destination for serious gardeners who can choose from 30 kinds of heirloom peppers and 50 kinds of tomatoes as well as a peerless choice of flowers (30 varieties of pansies and 1,200 other annuals and perennials started from seed, plus 700 other plants nurtured in 17 greenhouses) and full line of produce June–Thanksgiving, featuring their own organic vegetables and local fruit. Display gardens, and calves for petting.

Harlow's Sugar House (802-387-5852; www.harlowssugarhouse.com), Rt. 5 north of Putney Village. Open Mar.–late Dec., Harlow's is one of the most visitor-oriented operations. The Sugar House lets you watch maple production in-season, and there's a film and maple museum; the big store sells their own syrup and honey and offers pick-your-own apples, blueberries, and strawberries. The produce stand features a wide variety of apples in-season.

FACTORY OUTLETS **Big Black Bear Shop at Mary Meyer** (802-365-4160; 1-888-758-BEAR; www.big blackbear.com), Rt. 30, Townshend, west of the village. Open daily. The original location of Vermont's oldest stuffed-toy company. More than 500 designs, 20–70 percent off.

The Outlet Center (802-254-4594; 1-800-459-4594; www.vermontoutlets .com), Canal St., Brattleboro; Exit 1 off I-91. Open daily 9:30–8 except Sun. 10–6. This former factory building that once produced handbags is an old-fashioned factory outlet center with 15 varied stores, worth checking, one being **Winterset Designs** (802-246-1471), which features locally made laundry bag holders (ingenious but difficult to describe), solidly built furniture, Lamson & Goodnow cutlery, and Bennington Pottery.

✳ Special Events

Note: **Gallery Walk** (www.gallery walk.org) in Brattleboro is the first Friday of every month.

February: **Brattleboro Winter Carnival**, with many events in Living Memorial Park—a full week of celebrations, climaxed by the Washington's birthday cross-country ski race.

May–October: The **Brattleboro Area Farmer's Market**, Sat. on Rt. 9 at the Creamery Covered Bridge and Wed. downtown.

Memorial Day: **Dawn Dance**, 8 PM–7 AM in Brattleboro.

First Saturday of June: **Strolling of the Heifers** down Main St., Brattleboro, along with a Dairy Fest and marketplace, Heifer Ball.

Late June: Dummerston Center **Annual Strawberry Supper**, Grange Hall, Dummerston.

July–August: **Yellow Barn Music Festival** in Putney (see *Entertainment*).

July 4: A big **parade** winds through Brattleboro at 10 AM; games, exhibits,

THE WINDHAM GALLERY DURING BRATTLE-
BORO'S ANNUAL GALLERY WALK

refreshments in Living Memorial Park; **fireworks** at 9 PM.

Last Saturday of July: Annual **sale and supper** sponsored by the Ladies Benevolent Society of Brookline; an old-fashioned affair with quality crafts.

Last weekend of July: Events in Brattleboro both days climaxed by the **Riff Raff Regatta** Sunday, a raft competition off the Marina Restaurant at the confluence of the West and Connecticut Rivers.

First Saturday of August: **Grace Cottage Hospital Fair Day**—exhibits, booths, games, rides on the green in Townshend. Free concert series on Newfane common.

September: **Labor Day Dawn Dance**, 8 PM–7 AM, Brattleboro. Labor Day weekend in Guilford is observed both with the old-style

Guilford Fair and with the annual 2-day music festival in **Guilford's Organ Barn** (802-257-1961). Concerts are free. **Whitewater on the West River**, Jamaica State Park; see *Boating*. **Heritage Festival Benefit** in Newfane, sponsored by the Newfane Congregational Church. **Putney Artisans Festival**, Putney Town Hall. **Apple Days** (*last weekend*) in downtown Brattleboro.

October: **Newfane Heritage Fair** on Columbus Day—crafts, dancing, raffle, sponsored by the Newfane Congregational Church.

Mid-October: The **Apple Pie Festival** in Dummerston features hundreds of Dummerston's famous apple pies, also crafts, at the Dummerston Center Congregational Church and Grange. **New England Bach Festival**, a series of major concerts in area churches sponsored by the Brattleboro Music Center (802-257-4523; see *Entertainment*). The annual **Pumpkin Festival** on Townshend common features biggest-pumpkin and best-pumpkin-pie contests, plenty of vendors, food.

Weekend after Thanksgiving: **Putney Craft Tour**—some two dozen local studios open to the public.

Early December: **Christmas Bazaar** on the common, Newfane.

December 31: **Last Night Celebrations**, Brattleboro. Fun family day and night with fireworks at the Retreat Meadows about 9 PM.

MOUNT SNOW/WILMINGTON AREA

Mount Snow made its splashy debut as a ski destination in 1954. Reuben Snow's farm was transformed by ski lifts and trails, lodges, a skating rink, and an immense, floodlit geyser. Ski lodges mushroomed for miles around, varying in style from Tyrolean to 1950s futuristic. By the early '70s bust had followed boom, and the ski area was absorbed by one company after another. Acquired in 1994 by the American Ski Company, Mount Snow incorporated Haystack a few miles down the valley. But in 2005 Haystack split off, and the two are once again independently owned. Both have standout golf courses.

West Dover is a picturesque lineup of church, inn, and town offices, and much of the 9 miles of Rt. 100 between Wilmington and Mount Snow is a visual reflection of the well-being that has flowed in from the ski industry since the late '50s, despite frequent ups and downs. Perhaps because the valley's visitors come largely from urban areas, a number of inns and restaurants are several cuts above average. Beyond this narrow corridor, mountains rise on all sides. The village of Dover is a knot of white-clapboard buildings on the crest of a hill, a few miles east but palpably farther away. Forest surrounds Rt. 100 north to the classic village of Wardsboro, south to the delightfully backroaded towns of Jacksonville and Whitingham, and east to the college town of Marlboro, site of the world-class Marlboro Music Festival in July and August.

Although the surrounding hills were once lumbered extensively, they are now dotted with handsome second homes. Two former logging villages actually lie at the bottom of the sizable Harriman and Somerset Reservoirs, which have transformed the Deerfield Valley into one of the most watery parts of Vermont, good for fishing, photo taking, boating, and swimming.

GUIDANCE **Southern Vermont Regional Marketing Organization** (1-877-887-2378; www.southernvermont.com) maintains a good web site and is a source of printed area information.

Mount Snow Valley Chamber of Commerce (802-464-8092; 1-877-887-6884; www.visitvermont.com) maintains a major Vermont Information Center on 21 W. Main St. in Wilmington (Rt. 9 west, seven doors from the junction of Rts. 9 and 100). Pick up the useful *Mount Snow Valley Visitor's Guide* and the more

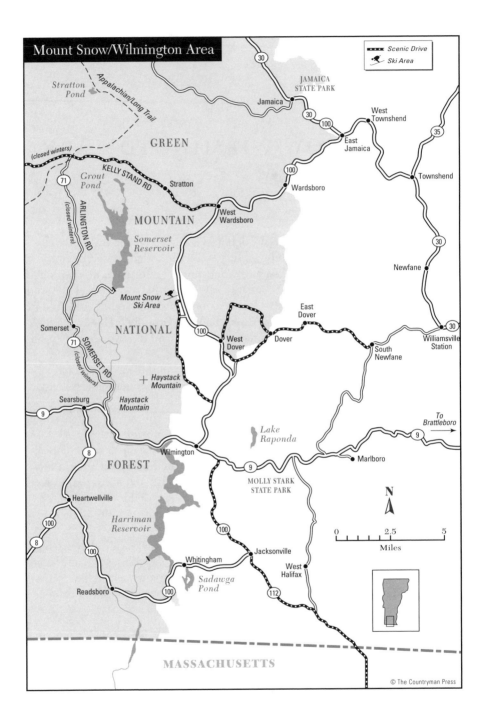

Mount Snow/Wilmington Area

Scenic Drive
Ski Area

Stratton Pond
Appalachian/Long Trail

JAMAICA STATE PARK
Jamaica
West Townshend
East Jamaica
Townshend

GREEN

(closed winters)
KELLY STAND RD
Stratton
Grout Pond
Wardsboro

MOUNTAIN
West Wardsboro
Somerset Reservoir
Newfane

Mount Snow Ski Area
East Dover
Dover
Williamsville Station

NATIONAL
West Dover
South Newfane

Somerset
SOMERSET RD (closed winters)
Haystack Mountain
Haystack Mountain

Searsburg
Lake Raponda
To Brattleboro

Wilmington
Marlboro

FOREST
MOLLY STARK STATE PARK

Heartwellville
N

Harriman Reservoir
0   2.5   5
Miles

Whitingham
Jacksonville
West Halifax

Readsboro
Sadawga Pond

MASSACHUSETTS

© The Countryman Press

comprehensive *Southern Vermont Adventure* magazine, both of which are free.
The *Deerfield Valley News*, the local weekly, is also a good source for current
events.

GETTING THERE The obvious route to Mount Snow from points south and east
is I-91 to Brattleboro, then Rt. 9 to Wilmington. There are also two scenic shortcuts: (1) Rt. 30 north from Brattleboro 11.1 miles to the marked turnoff for
Dover; follow the road through the covered bridge in South Newfane past
Dover to West Dover; (2) turn off I-91 onto Rt. 2 in Greenfield, Massachusetts;
follow Rt. 2 for 3.6 miles to Colrain Rd. (turn at Strawberryfields) and proceed
17.3 miles to Jacksonville, where you pick up Rt. 100 into Wilmington.

From New York City: **Adventure Northeast Bus Service** (718-601-4707; www
.adventurenortheast.com) goes in both directions daily during ski season, typically Thanksgiving weekend–April. Call for reservations.

GETTING AROUND The **MOO-ver** (802-464-5457; www.moover.com) is a free
community bus service operated by the Deerfield Valley Transit Association
(DVTA). It connects points of interest in the valley, along Rt. 100 from the
Deerfield Valley Health Center in Wilmington, picking up passengers at DVTA
stops 7 AM–10 PM. Look for its Holstein cow logo.

WHEN TO GO High season is Christmas through February; in March snow is less
dependable here than in other parts of the state. Golfers arrive in June, and in
July and August both Art on the Mountain at Haystack and the Marlboro Music
Festival draw a cultured crowd. Summer is, however, very low-key. Foliage usually fills every inn and restaurant during October's first three weekends.

MEDICAL EMERGENCY Emergency service is available by calling **911**.

✳ To See

SCENIC DRIVES **East along the Molly Stark Trail**. Wilmington is midway
between Bennington (21 miles) and Brattleboro (20 miles) on Rt. 9, which is
dedicated to the wife of General John Stark, hero of the battle of Bennington.
Five miles east of Wilmington you come to Hogback Mountain. Formerly a ski
area, this is now a major overlook, said to offer a 100-mile view (weather dependent) facing south. This is also the site of the **Southern Vermont Natural History Museum** (802-464-0048; www.vermontmuseum.org; open daily Memorial
Day–late Oct., 10–5, Nov.–May most weekends, but call to be sure). Larger than
it looks from the outside, it displays mounted specimens of more than 500 New
England birds and mammals in 80 dioramas, the collection of taxidermist Luman
R. Nelson. When we visited, live exhibits included two hawks and four hoot
owls, plus an intriguing collection of small (taxidermied) albino animals.

Marlboro. Continue along the Molly Stark Trail east some 5 miles to the turnoff
to Marlboro Village, home of Marlboro College. From mid-July until mid-August
its campus is the venue for the **Marlboro Music Festival** (802-254-2394;
www.marlboromusic.org). The **Marlboro Historical Society** (802-464-0329),

with its collection of pictures, old farm tools, and antique furniture, is housed in the Newton House and the 1813 one-room schoolhouse on Main St. and is open in July and Aug., Sat. 2–5 or by appointment. See *Selective Shopping* for the studios of notable Marlboro craftspeople. Continue into Brattleboro and return via the Dover Hill Rd. or follow the road past the college to the T, turn right, and you are soon in Jacksonville. See the following tours.

Jacksonville and Whitingham. From Wilmington follow Rt. 100 south 6 miles, past Flames Stable and the turnoff for Ward's Cove, to the village of Jacksonville. Near the junction of Rt. 100 and Rt. 112 stop by **Stone Soldier Pottery** (802-368-7077; www.stonesoldierpottery.com), open daily, known for its distinctive contemporary designs. Just down Rt. 112 is the **North River Winery** (802-368-7557; www.northriverwinery.com; open daily 10–5 except major holidays), dedicated to producing fruit wines. We can speak for the full-bodied apple-blueberry, neither too dry nor too sweet. Green Mountain apple, cranberry-apple, and a number of other blends are offered (free samples come with the tour). Follow Rt. 100 another 1.5 miles south and turn left onto Town Hill Rd. (marked for the Brigham Young Monument) into Whitingham. At the top of Town Hill a monument commemorates the Mormon prophet who led his people into Utah and is hailed as the founder of Salt Lake City. He was born on a hill farm here, the son of a poor basket maker. The view takes in surrounding hills; there are picnic benches, grills, a playground, and a parking area. Continue down the hill to Brown's General Store and turn right onto Stimpson Hill. Look on the right-hand side of the road near the top of this hill for a small marker that proclaims this to be the homestead site of Brigham Young: BORN ON THIS SPOT 1801 . . . A MAN OF MUCH COURAGE AND SUPERB EQUIPMENT. (BRIGHAM YOUNG FATHERED 56 CHILDREN BY 17 OF HIS 52 WIVES.) Before leaving the village, note the 25-acre "floating island" in the middle of Sadawga Pond. Whitingham was once a busy resort, thanks to a mineral spring and its accessibility via the Hoosic Tunnel and Wilmington Railroad. The old railroad bed is now a 12-mile walking trail along this remote shore of Lake Whitingham. (Continue 1 mile south on Rt. 100 beyond the store, and take a right onto Dam Rd.; park and walk across the dam. Note the "Glory Hole," a large concrete overflow funnel that empties into the Deerfield River.)

GREEN MOUNTAIN HALL IN WHITINGHAM
Christina Tree

Dover Hill Road, accessible from Rt. 100 via either Dorr Fitch Rd. in the village of West Dover or East Dover Rd. farther south (just below Sitzmark). The road climbs steeply past the tiny village center of Dover.

Here you could detour onto Cooper Hill Rd. for a few miles to take in the panorama of mountains. On an ordinary day, you can pick out Mount Monadnock in New Hampshire beyond Keene. You can either loop back down to Rt. 100 via Valley View Rd., or continue down the other side of the hill through East Dover to the general store, covered bridge, and picturesque village center in South Newfane, following Augerhole Rd. back to Rt. 9—or, if you're out for a real ride, continuing to Rt. 30, then south to Brattleboro and back to Wilmington on Rt. 9.

Handle Road runs south from Mount Snow, paralleling Rt. 100, turning into Cold Brook Rd. when it crosses the Wilmington line. The old farmhouses along this high, wooded road were bought up by city people to form a summer colony in the late 1880s. It's still a beautiful road, retaining some of the old houses and views.

Arlington–Kelley Stand Road heads west from West Wardsboro through the tiny village of Stratton. At 6.3 miles the Grout Pond turnoff is clearly marked and leads 1.3 miles to the pond. Hiking trails loop around the pond, through the woods, and continue to Somerset Reservoir. Beyond this turnoff is the monument to Daniel Webster, who spoke here to 1,600 people at an 1840 Whig rally. The hiking trail to Stratton Pond that begins just west of the monument is the most heavily hiked section of the Long Trail. It's possible (your vehicle and conditions permitting) to return to Rt. 9 through the Green Mountain Forest via the Arlington–Somerset Rd. (closed in winter). Roughly halfway down you pass the turnoff for Somerset Reservoir.

✳ To Do

AIRPLANE RIDES **Mount Snow Airport** (802-464-2196), off Country Club Rd., West Dover, offers scenic air rides.

BOATING **Green Mountain Flagship Co.** (802-464-2975; www.greenmountain flagship.com), 389 Rt. 9 west from Wilmington. Richard Joyce offers seasonal excursions on the Harriman Reservoir (also known as Lake Whitingham) aboard the M/V *Mt. Mills*, a twin-stacked pontoon vessel accommodating 65. Joyce caters to bus groups, but there are usually at least half a dozen seats left over. His narration of the logging history of the area is often accompanied by live music. Canoes, sailboats, and kayaks can be rented, too.

High Country (802-464-2108; 1-800-627-7533; www.high-country-tours.com), 2 miles west of Wilmington Center on Rt. 9, on Lake Harriman, rents fishing boats, pontoon boats, tracker boats, and Waverunners.

Zoar Outdoor (1-800-532-7483; www.zoaroutdoor.com), Charlemont, MA. The Deerfield River flows south into Massachusetts, where a regular dam releases power whitewater rafting that's exciting enough to satisfy most jocks but still doable for children. This long-established outfitter also rents kayaks and sit-on-top canoes for lower stretches of the river. Charlemont is about 40 minutes south of Wilmington via Rt. 8A.

Equipe Sport (802-464-2222; www.equipesport.com), on the Mount Snow Access Rd. in West Dover, rents canoes and kayaks.

BOWLING **North Star Bowl and Mini Golf** (802-464-5148), Rt. 100, Wilming-ton, open daily 11:30 AM–10 PM for candlepin bowling; also videos and pool tables, with ice cream and pizza parlor.

CHAIRLIFT **Mount Snow** (1-800-245-SNOW). The lift operates on weekends in summer and daily throughout foliage season.

DAY CAMPS ❧ **Mount Snow Day Camps** (802-464-3333), Mount Snow. Mini Camp (ages 6 weeks–12 months), Kids Camp (ages 5–8), and Sports Camp (ages 9–12) run during summer, Mon.–Fri. 9–4. Activities include swimming, chairlift rides, arts and crafts, nature hikes, field trips, and more.

FISHING The **Deerfield River** is known for rainbow and brook trout (the season is the second Saturday in April through October). The remote Harriman Bypass Reach, a 4.5-mile stretch of the river between the dam in Whitingham and Readsboro, is a good bet. Fly-anglers can readily find guides: Note **Taddingers/ Orvis Fly Fishing School and Guiding Service** (802-464-6263; www.taddingers .com), Rt. 100 north, Wilmington, and **Hookenum Fishing Tours**, 2 W. Main St., Wilmington (802-368-2945). **Harriman Reservoir** is stocked with trout, bass, perch, and salmon; a boat launch is located off Fairview Ave.

Somerset Reservoir, 6.5 miles west of Wilmington then 10 miles north on Somerset Rd., offers bass, trout, and pike. There is a boat launch at the foot of the 9-mile-long lake. Smaller **Sadawga Pond** in Whitingham and **Lake Raponda** in Wilmington are also good for bass, trout, perch, salmon, pickerel, northern pike, and smelt; there is a boat launch on the former.

Fishing licenses ($7) are available at Bill's Bait Shop, Whitingham; from the Wilmington town clerk; and at the Orvis dealership at Taddingers, Wilmington.

GOLF **Mount Snow Country Club** (802-464-4254; www.thegolfschool.com), Country Club Rd., West Dover. Billing itself as "The Original Golf School," this program has been evolving since 1978. Weekend and 2- to 5-day midweek golf school packages are offered May–Sep.; the 18-hole, Cornish-designed champi-onship golf course is also open on a daily basis.

Haystack (802-464-8301; www.haystackgolf.com), Mann Rd., off Cold Brook Rd., Wilmington. Eighteen holes designed by Desmond Muirhead with a club-house and full pro shop; recently upgraded with rave reviews.

Sitzmark Golf & Tennis Club (802-464-3384), 54 E. Dover Rd., Wilmington; 18 holes, club and cart rentals. No tee times.

HIKING Along with the trails in **Molly Stark State Park** (see *Green Space*) and a short, self-guided trail atop Mount Snow, there are a number of overgrown roads leading to ghost towns. The Long Trail passes through the former logging town of Glastenbury (261 residents in 1880), and a former colonial highway in **Woodford State Park** (see "Bennington Area") leads to a burying ground and 18th-century homesites. Somerset is another ghost town. The Hogback Mountain Overlook on Rt. 9 is the starting point for a hike up the old ski area access road to the Mount Olga fire tower. Inquire at the Mount Snow Valley Chamber of Commerce about accessing the 12-mile trail along the undeveloped shore of **Lake Whitingham**. Also see Grout Pond Recreation Area under *Green Space*.

Forest Care Nature Walks (802-254-4717; www.heartwoodpress.com). Consulting forester Lynn Levine leads popular nature and animal tracking walks in summer and fall, discussing area ecology and wildlife. Reserve a week ahead.

HORSEBACK RIDING ✔ **Flames Stables** (802-464-8329), Rt. 100 south, Wilmington. Western saddle trail rides, half-hour horse-drawn wagon rides, pony rides for young children.

Mountain View Stables (802-464-2462), Higley Hill Rd., Wilmington. One-hour guided trail rides, English and Western saddles.

Whitingham Farm (802-368-2620; 1-800-310-2010) offers wagon rides using their Percheron/Morgan team, Blitz and Blaze, on an antique bobsled.

✔ **Brookside Stables** (802-464-0267; www.brooksidestables.com), Rt. 100 north of Wilmington. Pony rides for the kids.

MOUNTAIN BIKING **Mount Snow Sports** adjacent to the Grand Summit Hotel at Mount Snow (802-464-4040; 1-800-245-SNOW) offers bike lessons, rentals, and repairs on its 45 miles of trails, with lifts servicing a portion in the summer months. Inquire about lodging/biking packages, clinics, and guided tours.

Alpine Trader (802-464-7101; www.alpinetrader.com), 316 Rt. 100, West Dover. Call for opening hours in summer; open 8–6 in winter. Sales and rentals of Jamis mountain bikes.

Equipe Sport (802-464-2222; www.equipesport.com), on Mount Snow Access Rd. in West Dover, rents cross-country bikes and helmets.

PAINTING WORKSHOPS Wilmington landscape artist Karen Baker offers seasonal workshops in pastels, oils, and watercolor as part of the **Vermont School of Art & Creativity**. Among them are 3-day courses held at the Hermitage Inn. For details call 727-366-6477 or go to www.kbakerstudios.com.

SWIMMING There are several beaches on 11-mile-long Harriman Reservoir, also known as Whitingham Lake. **Mountain Mills Beach** is 1 mile from Wilmington Village, posted from Castle Hill Rd. **Ward's Cove Beach** is on Rt. 100 south of Wilmington—turn right at Flames Stables and follow signs. Inquire locally about less publicized places.

Sitzmark Lodge (802-464-3384), north of Wilmington on Rt. 100, has a pool that's open daily to the public 11–6 ($2 adults, $1 children). Snacks and a bar are available poolside.

TENNIS The two municipal courts at **Baker Field** off School St. in Wilmington are open to the public; also eight courts at Sitzmark (see above).

✳ Winter Sports

CROSS-COUNTRY SKIING White House Winter Activity Center (802-464-2135; www.whitehouseinn.com), Wilmington. A total of 25 km of tracked trails meander through the woods at elevations of 1,573–2,036 feet. Snowshoes are also available, and there's snow tubing down the hill the inn stands on. Rentals, lodging, ski weeks.

Timber Creek Cross Country Ski Area (802-464-0999; www.timbercreekxc .com), West Dover. Just across Rt. 100 from the entrance to Mount Snow, a high-elevation, 14 km wooded system of mostly easy trails that hold their snow cover; ski and snowshoe rentals, instruction available, plus sauna and Jacuzzis on site. Open daily 9–4:30. Full- and half-day trail fees and special packages.

Prospect Mountain Cross Country Touring Center (802-442-2575), Rt. 9, Woodford, features 35 km of groomed trails with special trails for snowshoeing and a comfortable base lodge with a fireplace, home-cooked food, and baked goods. Trail fees are $15 adults, $12 juniors and seniors. Rentals. Because of its elevation, Prospect Mountain often has snow when other areas are bare.

DOWNHILL SKIING/SNOWBOARDING ⚓ Mount Snow (802-464-3333 information; 802-464-2151 snow report; 1-800-245-SNOW reservations; www.mount snow.com), West Dover. Owned by the American Skiing Company, this 598-acre area is one of the oldest in the state. Since its beginnings half a century ago, a community of inns, restaurants, chalets, and shops has sprung up in the vicinity to cater to the thousands who converge each year on what is now the Northeast's second largest ski destination (after Killington). Crowning the resort is the sprawling Grand Summit Hotel, a modern, self-contained city of 196 rooms plus shops and services. Farther down by a small lake is the more modest Snow Lake Lodge, popular with college students and young families for its inexpensive (though basic) rooms ($49 for a double, $189 for a lake and ski-slope view in peak season). But the vast majority of the area's 2,100 "on-mountain" beds are rentals and condos in the boxy residential communities spread out around the foot of the mountain. As for skiing, there are four distinct areas: the Main Mountain, the expert North Face, and the Sunbrook and Carinthia slopes; each has its own web of trails. (The Haystack Mountain area, which split off in 2005, is closed while finalizing major renovation plans.) Mount Snow's vertical drop is 1,700 feet. The area also features one super-pipe, one tubing park, and four terrain parks. Base area facilities include three lodges, rental/repair shops, retail, and restaurants, plus the Perfect Turn Discovery Center, an instruction area with a learning slope and special lifts where beginners can get their feet wet. See the chapter introduction for the resort's history.

Lifts: 19 chairlifts—3 high-speed and 1 fixed quad, 7 triples, 4 doubles. There is also one surface lift and three Magic Carpets.

Ski/snowboard trails: 104, including 33 "easier," 66 "more difficult," 26 "advanced," and 2 "double black diamonds." You'll also find 139 acres of hand-cleared "Tree Terrain."

Snowmaking: 76 percent of the mountain.

Facilities: Four base lodges, an upper lodge near the summit, the Snow Barn (nightclub with entertainment, dancing), and the Grand Summit Resort spa.

Ski school: Over 200 instructors and dozens of clinics.

For children: Perfect Kids; Mountain Camp (ages 7–12); Mountain Riders (7–12); Snow Camp (4–6); Cub Camp (3-year-olds); Child Care (6 weeks–5 years).

Rates: Midweek adults $61 (weekends $69), young adults (ages 13–18) $51 (weekends $59), juniors (6–12) and seniors (ages 65 and over) $41 (weekends $47). Kids 5 and under ski free. See www.mountsnow.com for a full schedule of events.

DOGSLEDDING Snowdoggin' Inc. (802-380-2200), P.O. Box 151, East Dover, offers dogsled rides through the Green Mountains.

SLEIGH RIDES Sleigh rides are offered at **Adams Farm** (802-464-3762), Wilmington, with a refreshment stop at a cabin in the woods. They are also offered at **Flames Stables** (802-464-8329) on Rt. 100, south of Wilmington, and at **Whitingham Farm** (802-368-2620) in Whitingham.

SNOWMOBILING High Country Snowmobile Tours (802-464-2108; 1-800-627-SLED) in Wilmington and **Twin Brooks Snowmobile Tours** (802-442-4054; 1-888-616-4054) in Woodford, both on Rt. 9 west, offer rentals and guided tours. **Sitzmark** (802-464-5498) on Rt. 100 north in Wilmington is now a snowmobile touring center.

✳ Green Space

Molly Stark State Park (802-464-5460), Rt. 9 east of Wilmington Village. This 158-acre preserve features a hiking trail through the forest to the Mount Olga fire tower, at 2,415 feet, from which there is a panoramic view. The 34 campsites include 11 lean-tos. Open May 26–Oct. 15. See *Campgrounds* in "What's Where" for state park fees and reservations.

Grout Pond Recreation Area (802-362-2307), west of West Wardsboro, off the Arlington (aka Kelley Stand) Rd. A 1,600-acre piece of the Green Mountain National Forest designated for hiking, picnicking, fishing, boating, and camping. In summer a ranger resides at the Grout Pond Cabin, and campsites are available on a first-come, first-served basis (6 vehicle sites, 11 walk-in campsites, and 4 sites accessible by canoe). Twelve miles of trails, which circle the pond and connect with Somerset Reservoir, are open in winter for skiing (they are not groomed). At the north end of the pond there are five picnic sites.

✳ Farms to Visit

✍ **Adams Farm** (802-464-3762; www.adamsfamilyfarm.com), 15 Higley Hill Rd., off Rt. 100, Wilmington. Open 10–5, closed Mon. and Tue. Admission. A sixth-generation, exceptionally visitor-friendly farm. The livestock barn holds a variety of animals to pet and feed, including kittens, calves, horses, goats, sheep, donkeys, llamas, alpacas, chickens, pigs, and rabbits (Nov.–June, Wed.–Sun. 10–5), as well as humorous talks and demonstrations (like how to milk a goat). Visitors can ride a wagon around the farm in summer, see a bear cave, and eat s'mores by a huge bonfire. In winter there are sleigh rides to a cabin for hot chocolate. Kids can ride a tractor or pony, walk a llama, bottle-feed a lamb, gather eggs, or just romp in the hay. Special events include spinning bees, moonlight sleigh rides for two, guided snowshoe tours, and fiber arts retreats in fall and winter. The **Farm Store** and **Quilt & Fiber Arts Loft** feature homespun yarns and locally crafted gifts.

Wheeler Farm (802-464-5225), Rt. 100 north of Wilmington Village. A third-generation working farm with Jersey and Dutch belted cows, part of the co-operative that produces Cabot Cheese. Maple syrup is produced and sold, along with maple cream and sugar.

Boyd Family Farm (802-464-5618; www.boydfamilyfarm.com), 125 E. Dover Rd., Wilmington. A working hillside farm, with pick-your-own flowers and blueberries June–Sep., then pumpkins, gourds, and Christmas wreaths.

North River Winery. See Jacksonville and Whitingham in *Scenic Drives*.

Ridgeway Red Deer Farm (802-368-2556; www.ridgewayreddeerfarm.com), 157 Plumb Rd., Whitingham. Pet, feed, and learn about red deer from this working deer farm. Hour-long tours available Tue.–Sat. 10–5, Sun. 1–5. $5 adults, $3 children.

❋ Lodging

This area can sleep more than 10,000 visitors on any one night in its plethora of mountainside inns, condominiums, and ski lodges. The **Mount Snow Valley Chamber of Commerce** maintains a reservation line that includes inns as well as B&Bs, or you can reserve online (1-877-887-6884; www.visitvermont.com); the **SnowResorts at Mount Snow** (1-800-451-6876; www.mountsnow-vt .com) offers one- to four-bedroom condos to rent for short- or long-term stays. Our listings focus on the inns and B&Bs.

RESORT ⚓ **The Grand Summit Resort Hotel at Mount Snow** (802-464-6600; 1-800-498-0479; www .mountsnow.com/summer/grand summit.html), 89 Mountain Rd., Mount Snow 05356. At the base of the ski lifts, this 196-room, ski-in, ski-out condo hotel and conference center, built in 1998 to look something like an Austrian chalet, features one- to three-bedroom suites (many with kitchen) as well as the usual hotel rooms. Amenities include a year-round heated outdoor pool and hot tubs, child care and arcade, spa and fitness center, and, of course, ski lifts. In summer there are golf and mountain biking programs and schools. Moderately priced **Harriman's Restaurant** is open for breakfast and dinner; the **Grand Country Deli & Convenience Store** offers take-out. Rates vary seasonally as well as for midweek and weekend stays: Rooms can be anything from a basic two-person studio to a two-bedroom deluxe suite. The ritziest option is the three-bedroom, three-bath penthouse on the top floor. This two-level, 2,000-square-foot suite sleeps 12 and has a full kitchen, a fireplace, and a bird's-eye view of the mountain ($312 in low season, $1,149 in high). The standard rooms and the one-bedroom suites (consisting of a bedroom, bath, living room, and galley kitchen) range $70–943, including continental breakfast. Valet parking (more or less obligatory if you come by car) is $15 per night.

INNS

In Wilmington 05363

& **The White House of Wilmington** (802-464-2135; 1-800-541-2135; www.whitehouseinn.com), 178 Route 9 East. Built in 1915 on a knoll overlooking Rt. 9 as a summer residence for Martin Brown, founder of Brown Paper Company, the interior of this gorgeous Colonial Revival mansion lives up to its elegant facade. Bob Grinold, who purchased the property in 1978 and has restored it over the years, has now passed its management over to his son, Adam, who has given it a casual ambience. Common rooms are huge, light, and atmospheric, but also stay warm in winter—with the help of 14 yawning hearths. At the front is a sunken bar, an intriguing anachronism in an otherwise Old World decor of French wallpaper, hand-carved mahogany mantelpieces, and marble-topped antiques. A total of 25 rooms, including 3 suites, are divided among the main house, the guest house, and the cottage. Two rooms have a balcony with fireplace and two-person whirlpool tub; two have a terrace with fireplace and whirlpool tub. There's a 60-foot outdoor pool next to a formal garden, and a small, cozy indoor pool on the lower level with a sauna and steam

bath. There are views from every window and, in winter, 43 km of cross-country trails just outside the door. A filling breakfast (and Sunday brunch) awaits guests in the parlor downstairs (ask to see the secret staircase); dinner (see *Dining Out*) is served in a romantic candlelit dining room by a roaring fire. From $98–208 per room in low season to $160–285 in high. Discounts on nonholiday midweek stays in all facilities.

✧ & **Misty Mountain Lodge** (802-464-3961; www.misty-mountain-lodge.com), 326 Stowe Hill Rd. This old Vermont farmhouse perched on a hillside 1.5 miles north of Wilmington has been remodeled by its new owners, Mike Sanchez and Brad York, and now has greater common areas for guests to lounge in. Set on 12 acres, the windows look out over Mount Snow and Haystack Mountain, and hiking trails crisscross the property. There are six rooms, four with private bath, two with shared; one with a jetted whirlpool bath, two with gas fireplace. One is handicapped approved. All are lavished with designer fabrics with plush down bedding, featherbeds, and heavy bathrobes. Breakfast might be an omelet with portobello mushrooms, feta cheese, tomatoes,

THE WHITE HOUSE OF WILMINGTON

Joe Citro

and fresh herbs over maple-smoked bacon and fresh fruit. A family-friendly place. Guests can walk, cross-country ski, or relax by one of the gardens on the property, or settle down with a book by the fieldstone fireplace in the living room. $100–200 per room, double occupancy; no pets. Children 5 and under free.

Nutmeg Inn (802-464-7400; 1-800-277-5402; www.nutmeginn.com), P.O. Box 1899. This delightful 1777 roadside farmhouse on Rt. 9 west is a restaurant and bakery as well as a B&B. Situated on the western edge of Wilmington, it offers 14 guest rooms, 6 with fireplace. Of the four spacious suites, two have queen-sized beds, two king, and all have hourglass-shaped two-person whirlpool and wood-burning fireplace. The Grand Deluxe King Suite features a private balcony, cathedral ceilings, and a marble bath with skylights. All rooms have central air-conditioning and private bath; they're decorated with quilts, botanical prints, and braided rugs. There is a cozy antiques-filled living room, library, and BYOB bar, plus three intimate dining rooms for full gourmet breakfasts that might include caramelized pear stuffed French toast topped with a caramel pear syrup and bacon sausage. Fresh pastries are legion. Summer $99–215 double; fall $139–299; winter $109–234.

☙ **The Hermitage Inn** (802-464-3511; www.hermitageinn.com), 21 Handle Rd., West Dover. *Seclusion* is the operative word in this inn, a lovely white 1790s farmhouse set back on 24 private acres in the Mount Snow Valley. It rests above sloping lawns and an apple orchard and sugarhouse, yet innkeeper Winter Knight has given the interior such a vibrant new look

that guests feel anything but alone. The intimate, fireplace-warmed bar, where tapas are served on Sunday and Monday nights, is bright red with white accents. A classy, spacious dining room looks out over extensive gardens and features a gourmet menu and live piano on Saturday nights in winter (see *Dining Out*). The 15 rooms include 5 with king-sized bed, 2 with queen, and 7 with paired doubles, each done in stunning antiques, four-posters, and canopies. Four are in the main house, 7 in the attached Wine House, and 4 in the Carriage House, which is a short walk down the hill by the pond. All rooms boast fireplaces (for which firewood is provided) and comfortable private bath. Rates vary seasonally, $125–185. Dogs are $15 extra in the Carriage House rooms. The inn, bar, and restaurant are closed Tuesday.

The Red Shutter Inn (802-464-3768; 1-800-845-7548; www.red shutterinn.com), Rt. 9. Lucylee and Gerard Gingras, a professional chef, preside over this big, gracious, 1894 house on the edge of the village within walking distance of shops and restaurants. The nine nicely furnished guest rooms include two suites with fireplace in the attached Carriage House to the rear. The quiet Molly Stark Suite has a queen-sized bed and a two-person whirlpool tub under skylights, while the Apple Hill is good for families with its two doubles, sitting room, and large bath. The dining room, furnished with an assortment of old oak tables and antique tools, has a good reputation and is open to the public (see *Dining Out*). From $110 for a cozy room in the carriage house to $280 for the spacious two-room Courtemanche Suite in the main house; country breakfast included. No pets; children by mutual arrangement.

In West Dover 05356

The Inn at Sawmill Farm (802-464-8131; 1-800-493-1133; www.theinnat sawmillfarm.com), on Crosstown Rd. just off Rt. 100. Closed early Apr.–mid-May. This world-class inn was the creation of Rod Williams, an Atlantic City architect, and his wife, Ione, an interior designer, who discovered the old farm during a ski vacation and bought it on a whim. Over the years they have turned it into a vision of country luxury: rough wooden beams over plush furniture, Oriental carpets and old brick, fresh bouquets and antique portraits. The side of a barn and hayloft form a wall of the posh library. Management has now passed to the Williams's children. Brill, their son, has won awards for his superlative cuisine (see *Dining Out*). Each of the 20 guest rooms is different, most with king-sized bed. Our room had white marble bath surfaces, a double sink, a Jacuzzi, and an interior-lit shower big enough for two. Eleven rooms have wood-burning fireplace; the secluded Carriage House overlooks one of the two trout-stocked ponds and lawns that slope to the edge of a pine forest. There is a tennis court, an indoor heated pool, a workout room, and wide floorboards that creak underfoot. The multicourse breakfasts include fresh-squeezed juices, white truffle butter, and attentive, black-tie service. $375–900 per room MAP.

&. **Deerhill Inn** (802-464-3100; 1-800-993-3379; www.deerhill.com), 14 Valley View Rd. Chef-owner Michael Allen has won raves for his dining room (see *Dining Out*) as well as for his 14 luxurious rooms and suites, some in the old farmhouse, others in a newer wing. Three of the rooms have fireplace, a Jacuzzi, and French doors that open onto a deck overlooking the backyard gardens. From the newer wing—especially on the galleried second floor—you enjoy a smashing view of Haystack and Mount Snow. One comfortable sitting room adjoins the tiny bar and two spacious dining rooms, walled with the work of local artists; upstairs is another big lounge for guests, plus a library nook. In summer, flowers abound inside and out and around the patio of the new swimming pool. A lot happens here, too, especially during the valley's pre-Christmas festivities. $122–335, including a full served breakfast; MAP rates (an additional $90) are available except on holidays or in foliage season. Children over 12; no pets.

Doveberry Inn (802-464-5652; 1-800-722-3204; www.doveberryinn .com), Rt. 100. A spacious, well-built inn on Rt. 100 near the Mount Snow access. There's a comfortable, large living room with fireplace and wine bar. Upstairs, each of the eight rooms is immaculate and bright, with private bath and full vanities (some of them copper), also with cable TV and video player, one with a fireplace and balcony. Request a back room overlooking the woods. Innkeepers Michael and Christine Fayette are culinary school graduates and prepare all the northern Italian cuisine (see *Dining Out*). $105–195 per room with full breakfast in fall, $115–125 in winter, and $78–135 in summer. MAP is available on request.

West Dover Inn (802-464-5207; www.westdoverinn.com), P.O. Box 1208, 108 Rt. 100. Built in 1846 as the village inn and now on the National Register of Historic Places, Phil and Kathy Gilpin's handsome inn includes modern amenities and country-style appointments in each of its 12 guest rooms, 5 of which are fireplace suites with whirlpool tub. All rooms have doubles or queen (four with brass bed, four with four-poster), private bath, and cable TV. Guests enjoy a homey common room with a fireplace, as well as a cocktail lounge and casual restaurant (see *Dining Out*). B&B rates: $125–195 per room in summer and late fall; $158–278 in foliage and ski season. Some minimum stays required during holidays. Children welcome (pets not).

In East Dover 05431

∞ ♪ **Cooper Hill Inn** (802-348-6333; 1-800-783-3229; www.cooper hillinn.com), P.O. Box 146, Cooper Hill Rd. High on a hilltop on a quiet country road with one of the most spectacular mountain panoramas in New England, this sprawling 1797 white farmhouse-turned-inn has 10 guest rooms, all with private bath, including two-room family suites with fireplace and Jacuzzi. Innkeepers Charles and Lee Wheeler lived 12

years in Singapore, which explains the collection of Asian antiques. It's a good place for active groups, and can house a total of 24. The living room has a fireplace and piano, and the dining room, game room, deck, and covered porch are all spacious, with fields for softball, tag, and long walks. You can watch the sun rise on one side of the house and see it set on the other. B&B $100–190 per room in summer, $100–200 in winter.

BED & BREAKFASTS ♿ **The Four Seasons Inn** (802-464-8303; 1-877-531-4500; www.thefourseasonsinn .com), 145 Rt. 100, West Dover 05356. English innkeepers Ann and Barry Poulter have renovated this historic roadside inn, adding four-poster beds with lace canopies and velvet down-filled comforters, two-person Jacuzzis, and French doors that lead to private balconies overlooking the river. Many of the 16 rooms have fireplace, and all have private bath and air-conditioning. Full breakfast (including an authentic British version for $3 more) is served riverside on the deck in summer, as is English afternoon tea on weekends, including fresh scones and clotted cream that the Poulters import from Britain in tiny glass jars. $130–245 in low season, $140–375 in high, including breakfast.

🐾 **Austin Hill Inn** (802-464-5281; 1-800-332-7352; www.austinhillinn .com), Box 859, Rt. 100, West Dover 05356. Up a short dirt drive from Rt. 100, hosts John and Debbie Bailey offer 11 rooms in this contemporary chalet, each with private bath, some with balcony, fireplace, and hand stenciling. Three are large enough to accommodate more than two. Their

THE WEST DOVER INN IN WILMINGTON
Joe Citro

specialties are fall and winter Murder Mystery Weekend packages. $95–165 in summer and winter, $115–175 during fall foliage, includes breakfast and afternoon refreshments.

Trail's End, A Country Inn (802-464-2727; 1-800-859-2585; www.trailsendvt.com), 5 Trail's End Lane, Wilmington 05363, off East Dover Rd. Unusual spaces in this ski lodge include a library and game room, a large living room with a two-story, fieldstone fireplace, and a dining space with large, round, hand-carved pine tables. The 15 rooms all have private bath, and 4 have a wood-burning fireplace; the two fireplace suites also have canopy bed, refrigerator, microwave, and Jacuzzi, but no air-conditioning. Facilities include a clay tennis court, a nicely landscaped heated pool, and paths leading out into the gardens and up the hill to the pond. Guests have access to their own fridge, a plus in summer when no one wants to stray too far from the pool. $110–160 low season, $130–200 high season, includes breakfast.

☼ ⚘ **The Inn at Quail Run** (802-464-3362; 1-800-34-ESCAPE; www.theinnatquailrun.com), 106 Smith Rd., Wilmington 05363. Nicely positioned above the valley, this ski lodge/inn with 11 rooms is known for its breakfasts. Served in a flagstone-floored sunporch with mountain views, the morning menu might include a lobster-and-Boursin omelet, crème brûlée French toast, or pumpkin pancakes with ginger butter (the public is welcome for a prix fixe of $12.95, children $6.95). Common space is ample and includes a large living room with a piano and fireplace, as well as a small, inviting bar. Amenities include a heated pool and

nine-person Jacuzzi. Children and pets are welcome on the lower level of the inn (the coolest in summer). Summer $100–180; fall $115–210; ski season $115–198.

☙ **Whetstone Inn** (802-254-2500; www.whetstoneinn.com), 5550 South Rd., Marlboro 05344. Handy to the Marlboro Music Festival, this is a 1786 tavern with a Palladian window, part of the cluster of white-clapboard buildings—including the church and post office—that form the village core. Innkeepers Jean and Harry Boardman have been here more than 20 years, and there's a casually comfortable feel to the place. Most guests have been here before and have their own favorite rooms, of which there are 12, 7 with private bath and 3 with kitchen. Singles with private bath run $50–80; doubles, $80–90. Breakfast, served daily, is extra, as is dinner, which is served on weekends and selected weekdays. There's swimming in a spring-fed pond.

❀ **Shearer Hill Farm** (802-464-3253; 1-800-437-3104; www.shearerhillfarm.com), 297 Shearer Hill Rd. P.O. Box 1453, Wilmington 05363. Off Rt. 9, 5 miles southeast of the village in Halifax. Keep going on this back road, bearing left at the fork, to Bill and Patti Pusey's simple, restored 200-year-old farmhouse a stone's throw from the Massachusetts border. Three rooms in the main house have private bath; there is an annex with a ground-floor room and kitchenette, plus two bedrooms and a sitting room upstairs, all with private bath. The pleasant large living room in the farmhouse has a VCR library. $95–105 double, $70 single with continental breakfast buffet. Cross-country skiing on the grounds, and maple sugaring in spring.

& **The Candlelight Bed & Breakfast** (802-368-2004; 1-866-429-1702; www.candlelightbandb.com), 3358 Rt. 100, Jacksonville 05342. Fran and Peter Madden run this attractive three-room B&B set above a rural stretch of Rt. 100; two guest rooms feature fireplace. $100–150 per couple includes breakfast.

& **Gray Ghost Inn** (802-464-2474; 1-800-745-3615; www.grayghost inn.com), 290 Rt. 100 north, West Dover 05356. Closed Apr. Swedish-born Carina and Magnus Thorsson run this family-friendly '50s-era ski lodge with its large basement game room, hot tub, play area, and outdoor pool. Both breakfast and dinner (entrées $8–15) are served in a red-walled dining room with red-checkered tablecloths; children's menu. Dogs are welcome in summer and fall (there are two in residence). Each of the 26 rooms has private bath; one is a three-room suite. The third floor is has rustic pine interiors and terrific views.

Old Red Mill Inn (802-464-3700; 1-877-733-6455; www.oldredmill.com), Rt. 100 north on the edge of Wilmington. Jerry Osler has owned this converted 1828 sawmill for 34 years. The 26 rooms are small but clean with a queen-sized bed or two singles, each with private bath, individually controlled heat, air conditioners, and cable TV. Downstairs is a round fireplace, restaurant, tavern, and fascinating antique fixtures dating to the mill's early days. In summer lunch is served on an open riverside deck. $75–81. Ask about special packages.

CONDOS AND LODGES Mount Snow Condominiums (802-464-7768; 1-800-451-4211; www.mountsnow.com/

lodging.html). A general reservation service that includes condos at the base of the mountain from studios to three-bedroom units with full kitchens and access to pools, saunas, and fitness rooms.

Mountain Resort Rentals (802-464-1445; 1-888-336-1445, www.mountain resortrentals.com). Rentals ranging from the humble to the sublime; for short- or long-term stays. Open daily, year-round.

CAMPGROUNDS See Molly Stark State Park and Grout Pond Recreation Area in *Green Space*.

OTHER The Amos Brown House, the oldest house in the back-road town of Whitingham, has been meticulously restored by the nonprofit Landmark Trust USA. The brick Cape-style farmhouse, built around 1800 with connected barn and sheds, is set in 30 acres of meadow on a quiet dirt road and features a pantry and modern amenities as well as an old wooden four-holer privy in the adjacent barn For details about renting the house, contact Landmark at 802-254-6868 (www.landmarktrustusa.org).

✳ Where to Eat

DINING OUT The Inn at Sawmill Farm (802-464-8131), Rt. 100, West Dover. Open for dinner only, 6–9:30. The main dining room is the interior of a former barn, with lush chintz and 18th-century oil portraits. The linen-covered tables are set with sterling and fresh flowers; there is also a smaller, sun- and plant-filled dining room. The 34,000-bottle wine cellar has earned the Grand Award from *Wine Spectator*. Specialties include potato-encrusted striped sea bass with beurre blanc, seared moulard duck breast with spaetzle and bordelaise sauce, and Indonesian curried chicken with caramelized banana, toasted coconut, and chutney. Numerous appetizers, irresistible desserts. Casual business attire required (no jeans). À la carte entrées $29–36, four-course prix fixe menu $44.

Deerhill Inn (802-464-3100) 14 Valley View Rd. (off Rt. 100), West Dover. Michael Allen presides over the kitchen of this luxurious establishment. You might begin with handmade sage tagliatelle with smoked chicken in a cream and white wine sauce, then continue with Zinfandel-braised pheasant served with poached plums in a black currant sauce, or with wild Pacific salmon topped with a shallot and cream reduction sauce. All breads, pastas, pâtés, and ice creams are made from scratch, and the desserts are sublime. Entrées $26–35.

The Hermitage Inn (802-464-3511), 21 Handle Rd., Wilmington. A popular, highly regarded restaurant with two dining rooms, fine art on the walls, and a casual yet classy feel. You might begin dinner with crispy artichoke hearts topped with a lemon-garlic butter and baked under a blanket of cheeses, proceeding to rack of lamb with rosemary-garlic rub, boneless duck breast in a port cherry sauce, or venison tournedos with a chanterelle mushroom peppercorn sauce. Desserts are just as appealing, and the tapas menu is long. Entrées $18–39.

Ravello (802-464-8437), on Rt. 100 north of Wilmington. Open 5:30 till closing, Fri.–Mon. The former Le Petit Chef is now a fine Italian trattoria in four rooms of this 250-year-old white-clapboard farmhouse. Chef-owners Douglas and Carolyn Sanzone offer a palette of Italian classics, making their pastas, breads, sorbets, and gelati from scratch. The signature dishes are osso buco and the constantly changing pastas, which you can order in half portions or whole. There are multiple coffees and desserts (like warm chocolate soup with whipped cream), and a three-page list of Italian wines, 17 available by the glass. Entrées $18–28. Reservations suggested.

Doveberry Inn (802-464-5652), Rt. 100, West Dover. Closed Tue. This elegant inn is chef owned, and the accent is authentic northern Italian. The à la carte menu might include stuffed zucchini blossoms with red pepper drizzle, and rack of venison with Chianti demiglaze. Extensive wine list. Entrées $23–36.

West Dover Inn (802-464-7264), Rt. 100, West Dover. The dining room at the West Dover Inn is low-lit and romantic with a fireplace and seasonally changing menu that usually includes crabcakes and jumbo shrimp cocktail among starters, plus the popular applewood-smoked pork tenderloin with aged balsamic syrup, toasted pistachio nuts, and fruit chutney. Entrées $20–32.

Two Tannery Road (802-464-2707), 2 Tannery Rd., Rt. 100, West Dover. Open Tue.–Sun. The building itself is said to date in part from the late 1700s, when it stood in Marlboro, Ma., and has moved several times within this valley, serving for a while as a summer home for Theodore Roosevelt's son. The bar began service in the original Waldorf-Astoria (present site of the Empire State Building). The food is highly rated, with a large à la carte menu that might include

Tannery country pâté, pecan-stuffed shrimp, or the Nutty Vermonter, a ham-and-cheese-stuffed chicken breast with an almond crust. Entrées $24–32. Nightly specials and fresh fish.

The Red Shutter Inn (802-464-3768), Rt. 9, Wilmington. Closed Mon. The candlelit dining room is romantic with its wide stone hearth and antique tools. Owner Gerard Gingras, who cooked the food for Steven Spielberg's film *Amistad*, works fresh Vermont ingredients into the menu. Appetizers usually include escargots with wild mushrooms or lobster ravioli with pesto sauce, and entrées range from fresh Long Island duckling with raspberry sauce to rack of lamb with sesame crust served with red currant port wine sauce. In summer you can dine on the awning-covered porch. (Breakfast is available to the public on Sat. and Sun., 9:30–11.) Entrées $19.50–31.50.

The White House of Wilmington (802-464-2135), Rt. 9 east, Wilmington. The elegant wood-paneled dining room is warmed by a glowing hearth in this mansion atop a hill, and the gourmet menu is extensive and skillfully prepared. You might find Parmesan-encrusted sea scallops on the menu, along with filet mignon or semi-boneless stuffed duck with mandarin orange and wild blueberry melba. $19–31.

EATING OUT The Vermont House (802-464-9360; www.thevermont house.com), 15 W. Main St., Wilmington. Brenda and Charley Waldron, who also own the bakery (802-464-9600) down the street, offer a menu varied both in price and quantity, from breaded artichoke hearts with

garlic butter sauce to steaks, meat loaf, burgers, and Yankee pot roast. This is where the locals go. There is a bar in the next room, and 10 tastefully decorated rooms upstairs in this 1850 stagecoach stop. Entrées $8–16.

✍ **Poncho's Wreck** (802-464-9320; www.ponchoswreck.com), 10 S. Main St., Wilmington. Open nightly for dinner; lunch and brunch Sat. and Sun. Early-bird menu ($11.95–12.95) daily 4–6. A cozy, nautical atmosphere that specializes in steaks, Mexican fare, and year-round fresh lobsters and steamers, helped by the fact that they own the fish market next door. Frozen drinks and a wide selection of beer. Try Poncho's Combo. Frequent live entertainment. Entrées $14.95–22.95.

🍴 ✍ **Dot's Restaurant** (802-464-7284; 802-464-6476), Wilmington, is open 5:30 AM–8 PM, until 9 PM Fri. and Sat. This cheerful, pine-sided diner is a local institution and the most popular breakfast place in town. There's a long Formica counter as well as tables, a fireplace in back, and wine by the glass. Stop by for a bowl of Jailhouse Chili, the hottest in New England. The soup and muffins are homemade, and the Reubens are first-rate. Dinners $11.95–15.95.

🍴 **Anchor Seafood House & Grille** (802-464-2112; www.anchorseafood .com), 8 S. Main St., Wilmington. Daily lunch and dinner, Sunday brunch. An intimate, upscale spot with a marble and oak bar. Daily specials like Parmesan baked tilapia, fresh Maine lobsters, and horseradish-encrusted salmon. Lunch $6–15, dinner $14–20.

The Roadhouse Restaurant (802-464-5017), Rt. 100, Wilmington. Open for dinner daily 6–10. Considered one of the better deals in the valley because all dinners ($20–27) come with soup, homemade bread, salad, and dessert, and the food is good. Entrées might include sautéed pork tenderloin, roast duckling with orange sauce, fresh Boston scrod, and pasta dishes. Those who don't wish bread, salad, and dessert can go without and subtract $6 from the price.

✿ **Rhythm & Bean** (802-464-2922), 20 W. Main St., Wilmington. Open daily 11–11. Wilmington's only Japanese restaurant doubles as a coffeehouse. Owner Sean Conroy serves pasta and sandwiches for lunch. Dinner might be Japanese pancakes and ginger pork with mirin, ginger, and garlic, or sushi at prices that hover around $10. Live music Wed.–Sat. nights. The entrance is on the side.

♪ **Alonzo's Pasta and Grille** (802-464-0123), at the Crafts Inn, W. Main St., Wilmington. Open daily 5–10 PM. An affordable, chef-owned place specializing in homemade pastas and slow-roasted grilled ribs. $3.99 kid's menu and traditional homemade desserts. Entrées $9.99–21.95. Tuesday is Italian night, when a dish of pasta and a large salad go for $9.99.

Mildred's Fine Foods Deli (802-464-1224), Rt. 9, Wilmington Village. Open 11–5. A source of standout deli sandwiches and wraps; eat in or take on a picnic.

BREWS **Bean Heads Cafe** (802-464-1208), Main and River Sts., Wilmington. Espresso, cappuccino, bagelry, soup, and sandwiches. Open daily 6–4.

Maple Leaf Malt & Brewing (802-464-9900), 3 N. Main St., Wilmington. Open for lunch and dinner, full bar. The local microbrew is a cozy space with a full bar and weekly entertainment. Open daily noon–closing.

✳ Entertainment

Memorial Hall Center for the Arts (802-464-8411; www.memhall.org), lodged in the McKim, Mead & White–designed theater next door to the historic Crafts Inn, Wilmington. This nonprofit center hosts community theater productions as well as films, a range of live musical performances, and community events.

Mountain Park Cinema (802-464-6447), Mountain Park Plaza, Rt. 100, about 5 miles north of Wilmington in West Dover, has three movie theaters for first-run films; matinees on rainy weekends.

APRÈS-SKI During ski season the following places feature live entertainment or DJs on most nights; in summer they come to life on weekends: In the center of Wilmington, **Rhythm & Bean** (802-464-2922) features live music most nights of the week. On Rt. 100, between Wilmington and Mount Snow, look for **Deacon's Den** (802-464-9361), and **Snow Barn Entertainment Center** (the old Rubin's Barn at Mount Snow). The **Billiard Sanctuary Bar** (802-464-9975; www.billiardsanctuary .com), 183 Rt. 100, has six professional pool tables, five televisions, and live music every Fri. and Sat. **Mo Jazz** (802-464-2280; www.mojazzcafe.com), under the Village Pub on S. Main St. on the corner of Rts. 9 and 100 in Wilmington, has music on Fri. and Sat. 9–midnight.

✳ Selective Shopping

ANTIQUES **Wilmington Antique & Flea Market** (802-464-3345), junction of Rts. 9 and 100. Open May–Oct., Sat. and Sun. Bills itself as southern Vermont's largest outdoor flea market.

Left Bank Antiques (802-464-3224), Rts. 9 and 100, Wilmington. Country furniture, old paintings, and prints.

ARTISANS AND CRAFTS **Quaigh Designs** (802-464-2780), Main St., Wilmington. This is a long-established showcase for top Vermont crafts; imported Scottish woolens are also a specialty. Lilias MacBean Hart, the owner, has produced a Vermont tartan. There's also lots of Vermont painted-woodcut artist Mary Azarian's work. The art gallery is on the second floor.

The Vermont Bowl Company (802-464-8175; www.vermontbowl.com), 103 W. Main St., Rt. 9, Wilmington. Adjacent to the John McLeod Ltd. Store and factory. A Scottish engineer, McLeod fell in love with the state and decided to settle here and make a living from woodturning. Hardwood bowls, clocks, mirrors, cutting boards, and furniture on the western edge of the village; open daily.

Young & Constantin Gallery (802-464-2515; www.ycgallery.com), 10 S. Main St., Wilmington. Chinese antique furniture, fine art, and a superb collection of art glass in what used to be the town's Unitarian church, with its stained-glass windows compounding the shimmering effect. Open daily 10–5.

Gallery Wright Sticks & Stones Studio (802-464-9922; www.gallery wright.com), 7 N. Main St., Wilmington. Area's finest selection of fine art, including landscapes, figures, and still lifes in oil, pastels, and prints. The artisan jewelry of gallery director Mary Therese Wright is also featured. In summer open daily 11–6; in winter Tue. and Wed. or by appointment.

Turnpike Road Pottery (802-254-2168; www.theturnpikeroad.com), Marlboro. Call for directions and hours. Malcolm Wright and Hanako Nakazato produce Japanese-inspired wood-fired pottery.

Applewoods (802-254-2908), 8 miles east of Wilmington on Rt. 9, in Marlboro. Open in summer Thu.–Mon. 10–4, or by appointment. David and Michelle Holzapfel create amazing tables, benches, and vessels from burls and other wood forms.

SUMMER MUSIC FESTIVAL

Marlboro Music Festival, Persons Auditorium, Marlboro College. (For advance tickets write to Marlboro Music Festival, 135 S. 18th St., Philadelphia, PA 19103; 215-569-4690; after June 6 contact the Marlboro box office, 802-254-2394; www.marlboromusic.org.) Concerts, primarily chamber music, are offered Fri.–Sun., early July–mid-Aug. This unusual "festival" is a 7-week gathering of 70 or so world-class musicians who come to work together. It is held on this rural campus because Rudolf Serkin, one of its founders, owned a nearby farm. Pablo Casals came every year from 1960 to 1973. Some concerts are sold out in advance, but you can frequently find good seats before the performance (chairs are metal, and regulars bring cushions). There are (almost) always bargain-priced seats in the tent just outside the auditorium's sliding glass doors.

Gallery in the Woods and Dante's Infurniture (802-464-5793; www .galleryinthewoods.com), 1825 Butterfield Rd. (off Rt. 9), Marlboro. Dante Corsano makes widely respected tables, dressers, armoires—whatever you need. The lines are simple, and the craftsmanship is so exceptional that the pieces are striking. His wife, Suzanne, crafts equally striking pottery lamps in a range of soft hues. Jewelry, glass, sculpture, and painting by other artists. There's a new gallery in downtown Brattleboro.

Craft Haus (802-464-2164), Top of the Hill Rd., Wilmington. Set high on a hillside, this is a gallery with gardens and a covered bridge. The big attractions are works by folk artist Will Moses and Ursula's cloisonné and enamel-plated jewelry, which sells for far higher prices in urban stores. Open late May–mid-Nov., Thu.–Mon. 10–5 or by appointment.

Jen Violette Designs (802-464-5206; www.jenviolette.com), 12 New England Power Rd., Wilmington.

More galleries: Pick up an *Art Galleries* map/guide to the burgeoning number of galleries.

BOOKSTORES **Bartleby's Books and Music** (802-464-5425; www.bartlebys vt.com), N. Main St., Wilmington, an independent bookstore offering new books (mostly paperbacks), greeting cards, cassettes, art supplies, stationery, games, and music.

Austin's Antiquarian Books (802-464-8438; 1-800-556-3727; www .austinsbooks.com), 123 W. Main St. on Rt. 9, 0.5 mile west of downtown Wilmington. Open daily 10–6. Maps, prints, and 15,000 used, rare, and out-of-print books, many with leather bindings.

R&S Kurland Fine Books (802-464-9670), 59 Davis Dr., Wilmington. Mid-May–mid-Oct. Used and antiquarian books. First editions, New Englandiana, Americana, Civil War. Call before coming.

SPECIAL SHOPS **Taddingers** (802-464-6263; 1-800-528-3961; www .taddingers.com), Rt. 100, Wilmington. Seven specialty shops under one roof: antiques and fine prints, exclusive decorative accessories, Christmas Room, Nature Room, Vermont Country Food Store, and an Orvis dealership, with gear for fly-fishing, fly-tying, and shooting, plus sponsorship of 1- and 2-day fly-fishing schools.

Manyu's Boutique (802-464-8880), 4 N. Main St., Wilmington, has casual, contemporary clothes and accessories for women. Open daily 10–6, Sun. 10–5.

Down in the Valley (802-464-2211), 7 W. Main St., Wilmington. A long-established, genuinely discount ski- and sportswear shop, featuring fleece outerwear.

Hundredth Monkey (802-464-4640), Rt. 9 W., 17 W. Main St., Wilmington. A holistic health food store offering vitamins, supplements, homeopathic remedies, organic foods, an array of books, organic bulk herbs and spices, and fair-trade food, clothing, and gifts. Upstairs there are yoga classes, holistic workshops, plus reflexology, massage therapy, and nutritional coaching.

1836 Country Store Village (802-464-5102), W. Main St., Wilmington, has an eclectic stock of decorative brasses, pierced-tin lanterns, toys and games, Vermont specialty foods, and the usual souvenirs. Note the amazing old floors.

Norton House (802-464-7213; www
.norquilt.com) adjacent to the 1836
Country Store at 30 W. Main St.,
Wilmington, was pulled here by oxen
in the 1830s and dates from 1760,
making it Wilmington's oldest structure. A quilter's paradise with over
3,000 fabrics and every quilting acces-
sory. Note the yawning brick hearth
and the historical objects upstairs in
the windowed closet.

Pickwell's Barn (802-464-3198; www
.pickwellsbarn.com), 22 W. Main St.,
Wilmington, has pottery, clocks,
prints, colorful glassware, Vermont
wines, and specialty foods.

SweDenNor Ltd. (802-464-2788),
Rt. 100, West Dover. Established in
1972, this store features a wide selection of country and casual furniture;
also lamps, paintings, and gifts.

✴ Special Events

Late January: **Harriman Ice Fishing Derby** on Lake Whitingham
(802-368-2773).

Easter weekend: Nondenominational
sunrise service on Mount Snow's
summit with continental breakfast.
Eggs hidden all over the mountain,
good for prizes.

Memorial Day: **The Great Duck
Race**—over 1,500 rubber ducks are
released at noon at Wilmington's
bridge. BBQ, games, prizes, duck
quacking contest.

July 4 weekend: A very big celebration in these parts with fireworks,
parades, et cetera.

Late July–mid-August: **Marlboro
Music Festival** (802-254-2394; see
Entertainment).

Art on the Mountain (802-423-7535;
www.artonthemountain.org). One
of southern Vermont's largest and
best nonprofit exhibits of Northeast
artists and craftspeople and their
work, held at the Mount Snow
Resort's Sundance Upper Base
Lodge. Open late July–early Aug.,
daily 10–5 (call for exact dates and
admission fees).

August: **Deerfield Valley Farmers
Day** (802-464-8092), Wilmington—an
old-fashioned agricultural fair with
midway, livestock exhibits.

Mid-August: **Dover Free Library's
Annual Garden Tour** (802-348-
7488), a self-guided glimpse of the
town's private and public gardens,
9–4. Admission.

First weekend in September: **Southern Vermont Garlic and Herb
Festival**. Food, horticulture, and 50
vendors at Beaver Brook Field at the
junction of Rts. 9 and 100, Wilmington, 10–5. Small admission. **Annual
Brewers' Festival at Mount Snow**
(802-464-4191)—food, microbrews,
and live music.

Mid-October: **Gilfeather Turnip
Festival**—savor turnip delicacies,
plus farmer's market and crafts fair,
noon–4 at the Wardsboro Town Hall
in Wardsboro.

November 25–December 25: **"Nights
Before Christmas"** celebration—
wreath sales, fashion shows, concerts,
Festival of Lights, holiday tour of
country inns, Living Nativity, and other
events in the Mount Snow Valley.

BENNINGTON AREA

Vermont's southwest corner is dominated by Bennington, the state's fifth largest town and one of its most historic. Named for the avaricious Governor Benning Wentworth, it was the first town settled west of the Connecticut River in the 1749 New Hampshire Grants. The settlement became a hotbed of sedition when the "Bennington Mob," or Green Mountain Boys, formed in 1770 at Fay's Catamount Tavern under the leadership of Seth Warner and Ethan Allen to expel both the 'Yorkers (who claimed the territory) and, later, the British.

The battle of Bennington (more precisely, the battle for Bennington) on August 16, 1777, deflected General Burgoyne's occupation of the colonies when New Hampshire general John Stark's hastily mobilized militiamen beat the tar out of Colonel Baum's overdressed Hessians on high ground near the Walloomsac River, across the New York border.

Today Bennington is nationally known as the home of distinguished Bennington College, established in the early 1930s, as well as Southern Vermont College, headquartered in the splendid Everett Mansion. It is also remembered fondly by collectors of Bennington Pottery.

GUIDANCE A good visitors guide to Bennington County is provided by the **Bennington Area Chamber of Commerce** (802-447-3311; 1-800-229-0252; www .bennington.com), 100 Veterans Memorial Dr., Bennington 05201, which also has a well-supplied information center.

GETTING THERE *By car:* Bennington lies at the convergence of Rts. 7, 7A, 9, 67, and 67A. Going north can be confusing; watch the signs carefully to choose between the limited-access Rt. 7 to Manchester and the more interesting but slower Historic Rt. 7A to Shaftsbury and Arlington.

MEDICAL EMERGENCY Emergency service is available by calling **911**.

Southwestern Vermont Medical Center (802-442-6361; www.svhealthcare .org), 100 Hospital Dr., Bennington.

✳ To See

Historic Bennington Walking Tours, self-guided with a keyed map/brochure from the chamber of commerce—also available at www.bennington.com—that

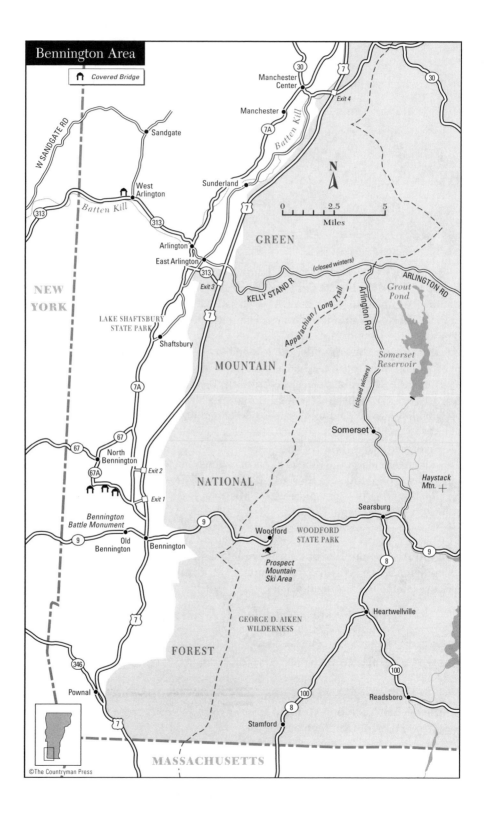

Bennington Area

Covered Bridge

W SANDGATE RD

Sandgate

West
Arlington

Batten Kill

313

313

Arlington

East Arlington

313

Exit 3

7

NEW
YORK

LAKE SHAFTSBURY
STATE PARK

Shaftsbury

7A

67

67

North
Bennington

67A

Exit 2

NATIONAL

Exit 1

Bennington
Battle Monument

9

Old
Bennington

Bennington

9

7

346

Pownal

7

Manchester
Center

30

7

Exit 4

Manchester

7A

Batten Kill

30

Sunderland

7

GREEN

N

0   2.5   5
Miles

MOUNTAIN

KELLY STAND R

(closed winters)

ARLINGTON RD

Appalachian / Long Trail

Arlington Rd

Grout
Pond

Somerset
Reservoir

(closed winters)

Somerset

Haystack
Mtn.

Searsburg

9

Woodford

WOODFORD
STATE PARK

9

8

Prospect
Mountain
Ski Area

GEORGE D. AIKEN
WILDERNESS

8

Heartwellville

100

FOREST

100

8

Stamford

Readsboro

MASSACHUSETTS

©The Countryman Press

describes Old Bennington, including the 306-foot, blue limestone shaft of the
Bennington Battle Monument, dedicated in 1891; all the fine early houses along
Monument Ave.; the Old Academy; Old First Church; the Burying Ground,
where five Vermont governors and Robert Frost repose; and the venerable Walloomsac Inn, now a private home. A second walking tour of the downtown area
includes the 1898 railroad depot (now a restaurant), constructed of blue marble
cut to resemble granite; old mills; and Victorian homes.

Bennington Battle Monument (802-447-0550), Old Bennington. Open mid-
Apr.–Oct., daily 9–5, this Sandy Hill dolomite limestone shaft commemorates
General John Stark's defeat of General Burgoyne's invading British and Hessian
forces at Walloomsac Heights, 5 miles to the northwest, on August 16, 1777.

MUSEUMS & **Bennington Museum** (802-447-1571; www.benningtonmuseum
.org), 75 Main St., Rt. 9, Bennington. Open daily except Wed. and holidays, 9–5.
This top-notch collection features memorabilia from the battle of Bennington,
including one of the oldest American Revolutionary flags in existence, plus early
American furniture, dolls, tools, a spectacular two-room collection of American
glass (including iridescent Tiffany and Loetz pieces), and historic Bennington
Pottery, notably an extraordinary 10-foot ceramic piece created for the 1853 Crystal Palace Exhibition in London. In a separate room is a luxury 1925 Wasp touring car, the only surviving model of the rare automobiles made by Karl Martin in
Bennington. The one-room schoolhouse that Grandma Moses (Anna Mary
Robertson, 1860–1961) attended as a child now houses the country's largest collection of her paintings, along with some of her personal possessions. There's a
gift shop, café, genealogical library, and changing exhibitions. Give yourself a few
hours to absorb it all. $8 adults, $7 students/seniors, under 12 free. Family $19.

The Park-McCullough House (802-442-5441), near Rt. 67A in North Bennington. Open for tours late May–Oct. and Dec., daily 10–4. Last tour at 3 PM.
$8 adults, $7 seniors, $5 students. A splendid 35-room Victorian mansion built in
1865 by Trenor W. Park, a forty-niner who struck it rich as a lawyer in California
and later as a railroader. He built the house on part of the farm owned by his
father-in-law, Hiland Hall, a representative to Congress and governor of Vermont. Park's son-in-law, John G. McCullough, became governor of Vermont in
1902 and raised his family in this capacious house. It has been open to the public
since 1965 and is on the National Register of Historic Places, functioning as a
community arts center. There's an appealing children's playhouse replica of the
mansion and a stable full of carriages; also a gift shop. Afternoon tea on the side
veranda by reservation.

Bennington Center for the Arts
(802-442-7158; www.bennington
centerforthearts.org), Rt. 9 at Gypsy
Lane, houses four fine art galleries,
including Native American arts and
fine art bird carvings, and a performance area for the Oldcastle Theatre
Company, whose season runs
May–mid-Oct. Open May–Christmas,

THE BENNINGTON MUSEUM

Diane E. Foulds

Diane E. Foulds

PARK-McCULLOUGH HOUSE AND DOLL-
HOUSE IN NORTH BENNINGTON

Tue.–Sun. 10–5; weekends only in winter. Adults $8, seniors/students $7, families $20, children under 12 free.

The Shaftsbury Historical Society, Rt. 7A, is gradually developing a cluster of historic buildings, including two schools and an 1846 Baptist meetinghouse. Open June–mid-Oct, Mon–Sat. 2–4 PM. Free.

Hemmings Old-Fashioned Filling Station (802-442-3101; www.hemmings .com), 216 Main St., Bennington. Open daily 7 AM–8 PM. A full-service classic Sunoco filling station and convenience store with vintage vehicle displays (including a 1937 Hudson and a 1910 Buick) and a quasi-museum selling auto-related memorabilia. Open seasonally or by appointment.

Robert Frost Stone House Museum (802-447-6200; www.frostfriends.org), 121 Rt. 7A, Shaftsbury. Open May–Dec., Tue.–Sun. 10–5. $5 adults, $2.50 ages 18 and under; 6 and under free. The poet lived and worked for a time in this stone-house-turned-museum; it was here that he wrote "Stopping by Woods on a Snowy Evening." From the windows you can still see the apple trees, stone walls, and country lanes that inspired him. Biographical exhibits and a few of his personal belongings are on display.

Vermont Covered Bridge Museum (802-442-7158; www.vermontcovered bridgemuseum.org), at the corner of Rt. 9 (West Rd.) and Gypsy Lane, Bennington. A wide-ranging, well-produced presentation of Vermont's covered-bridge lore delivered through videos, dioramas, and interactive exhibits, part of the Bennington Center for the Arts. Open May–Christmas, Tue.–Sun. 10–5; weekends only in winter. $8 adults, $7 seniors/students, $20 families; under 12 free.

WINERY North River Winery outlet (802-442-9463; www.northriverwinery .com), Rt. 9, Bennington, in Camelot Village, is open daily 10–5. The winery itself (in Jacksonville) offers daily tours May–Dec., 10–5, where it sells its fruit-based wines a few dollars cheaper per bottle than at its outlets.

THE OLD FIRST CHURCH IN OLD BENNINGTON

Kim Grant

COVERED BRIDGES Three stand just off Rt. 67A in North Bennington: **Silk Road**, **Paper Mill Village**, and the **Burt Henry**. There are two more in Arlington, and a self-guided driving tour map of all five is available through the chamber.

✴ To Do

CANOEING BattenKill Canoe Ltd. (802-362-2800; 1-800-421-5268; www

.battenkill.com), River Rd., off Rt. 7A, Arlington, is the center for day trips—with van service—canoe camping, instruction, rentals, and equipment. Customized inn-to-inn tours arranged.

FARMS TO VISIT Shaftsbury Alpacas (802-447-3992; www.shaftsburyalpacas .com), 12 S. Stateline Rd., Shaftsbury. Sandy and Johan Harder invite you to spend a day as an alpaca farmer—or just to shop in the Alpaca Shack for throws, slippers, outerwear, and more.

The Apple Barn and Country Bake Shop (802-447-7780; 1-888-8APPLES; www.theapplebarn.com). Open daily 8:30–6. Up to 30 varieties of apples to pick, a corn maze for the kids, and plenty of candy, cheese, pies, and food specialties in the farm store.

GOLF AND TENNIS Mount Anthony Country Club (802-447-2617), 180 Country Club Dr. (just below the Battle Monument): 18-hole golf course, tennis and paddle courts, pool, lunch and dinner.

HORSEBACK RIDING Kimberly Farms Riding Stables (802-442-5454; www .kimberlyfarms.org), 1214 Cross Hill Rd., Shaftsbury, offers trail rides, lessons, and an overnight horse camp on its 60-acre farm.

✍ **Miles to Go Farm** (802-442-4354;; www.milestogofarm.com), 1524 Myers Rd., Shaftsbury. Julia and Richard Hine offer trail rides, lessons, and other horsey activities.

Lively's Livery (802-447-7612; 802-379-1299; www.livelyslivery.com), 193 Crossover Rd., Bennington. Horse-drawn carriage service, wagon rides, sleigh rides, bridge tours.

SKIING ✍ Prospect Mountain (802-442-2575; www.prospectmountain.com), Rt. 9 east of Bennington. An intimate, friendly, family ski area, with cross-country (25 km), downhill, and telemark facilities, ski school, rentals and repairs, learn-to-ski packages, group rates, cafeteria, and bar. Open daily 9–5, as long as there's snow. Moderate prices for all.

SNOWMOBILING Twinbrooks Tours (802-442-4054; 1-888-616-4054; www .twinbrookstours.com) in nearby Woodford (about 10 miles east of Bennington). Offers snowmobile rentals, trail maps, and guided tours.

✳ Green Space

✍ **Lake Shaftsbury State Park** (802-375-9978; www.vtstateparks.com/htm/ shaftsbury.cfm), 10.5 miles north on Rt. 7A, has swimming, picnicking, boating, and a nature trail on an 84-acre area surrounding Lake Shaftsbury. Open May 26–Sep. 5.

✍ **Woodford State Park** (802-447-7169; www.vtstateparks.com/htm/woodford .cfm), Rt. 9 east of Bennington. This 400-acre heavily wooded area includes 103 camping sites, 20 with lean-tos, swimming in Adams Reservoir from a small beach, a children's playground, picnic spots, canoe and rowboat rentals.

✻ Lodging

INNS The Four Chimneys Inn
(802-447-3500; www.fourchimneys
.com), 21 West Rd. (Rt. 9), Old Bennington 05201. This stately, 1910
Colonial Revival home, once the
estate of Phillip Jennings, offers 11
luxurious rooms, all spacious with private bath, TV, and phone, most with
fireplace and Jacuzzi, and two with
glassed-in porch. Firewood provided.
The owners, Peter and Lynn Green,
keep the grounds beautifully landscaped. Two are appropriate for families of four, but the inn is not suited
to pets or children under age 12.
Rates $110–230 per room, including
full breakfast. (See also *Dining Out*.)

**BED & BREAKFASTS South Shire
Inn** (802-447-3839; www.southshire
.com), 124 Elm St., Bennington
05201. This turn-of-the-20th-century
Victorian mansion is a most attractive
guest house, featuring 10-foot ceilings
with plaster moldings, a library with a
massive mahogany fireplace, an Italianate formal dining room, and comfortable bedrooms furnished with
antiques. Three of the five guest
rooms have a fireplace, and all have a
private bath; two can be joined as a
suite. Four newer rooms have been
added in the old carriage house, each
with whirlpool tub, fireplace, and TV.
Tea is served 4–6 PM. $89–200 with
breakfast; children 12 and older.

♧ **Molly Stark Inn** (802-442-9631;
1-800-356-3076; www.mollystarkinn
.com), 1067 E. Main St., Bennington
05201. Reed and Erin Fendler offer
nine cozy bedrooms in this 1890
home, all with private bath, some with
Jacuzzi and/or woodstove. Each room
is decorated with Americana, antiques,
and quilts, and there are wicker chairs

on the wraparound porch. The three
spacious guest cottages in the back
come with Jacuzzi and fireplace.
$80–150 includes an ample breakfast
served on Bennington Pottery. Children over 10.

♧ **Alexandra B&B** (802-442-5619;
1-888-207-9386; www.alexandrainn
.com), Historic Rt. 7A south at
Orchard Rd., Bennington 05201.
Daniel and Amanda Tarquino offer
12 spacious rooms in this newly refurbished 1859 farmhouse, each with private bath, king or queen four-poster
bed, fireplace, and fine linens. The six
newest rooms in the attached addition
have sitting area and water jets in the
tub. Guests can linger downstairs in
the sunroom or sitting room, sit out
on the terrace, or wander the garden
with its view of the Bennington Monument. Breakfast is a gourmet affair,
and the Tarquinos now offer nightly
dinner for guests and their friends
(sign up before 4 PM) at a prix fixe rate
that ranges $25–35. Room rates, de-
pending on season, are $89–159,
including breakfast. Two-night mini-
mums on most weekends and holidays.

♧ **The Henry House** (802-442-7045;
1-888-442-7045; www.henryhouseinn
.com), 1338 Murphy Rd., North Bennington 05257. Don and Judy Cole
have six beautiful guest rooms, four
with private bath, in this restored historic place, built in 1769 on 25 acres,
complemented by four common
rooms. Among the guest rooms, the
Ballroom, with its vaulted 14-foot
ceiling, four-poster canopy bed, and a
sitting area with working fireplace, is
the most notable ($135). The others
are also distinctive: $85–135 year-
round, including breakfast. Pets may
be kept in the garage or crated. Children over 12 are welcome.

Samuel Safford Inne (802-442-5934; www.samuelsaffordinne.com), 722 Main St., Bennington 05201. Sandy Redding runs her B&B out of the oldest house in Bennington Village, built by Lieutenant Colonel Samuel John Safford; it was restored during the Victorian period. She has five guest rooms, three with private bath, and serves a full breakfast. $78–135.

HoneyBee B&B (802-447-2941), 103 Church St., Shaftsbury 05262. A beautiful 1840 Victorian home with a large front porch, five comfortable bedrooms, and three working fireplaces. Full breakfast included. $70–125.

MOTELS **Vermonter Motor Lodge** (802-442-2529; www.thevermonter motorlodge.com), Rt. 9 (2968 West Rd.), Bennington 05201. This motel, 2 miles west of Old Bennington, is an attractive mini resort with nicely decorated rooms and cabins, cable TV, room phone, swimming, boating, bass pond, **Sugar Maple Inne Restaurant**; $55–129 per room.

Paradise Motor Inn (802-442-8351; www.theparadisemotorinn.com), 141 W. Main St., Bennington 05201, close to the Bennington Museum, has 79 air-conditioned rooms, a pool, a tennis court, and a Chinese restaurant, **The Panda Garden**, on the premises. $65–220 includes continental breakfast.

❄ **Knotty Pine Motel** (802-442-5487; www.knottypinemotel.com), 130 Northside Dr. (Rt. 7A), Bennington 05201. The locals use this motel to put up their guests, which is always a good sign. There's a pool and an adjacent diner, and pets are welcome as long as they are not left alone. The clean, well-kept rooms range $63–77 in summer, $79–95 in fall.

Kirkside Motor Lodge (802-447-7596; www.kirksidemotorlodge.com), 250 W. Main St. (Rt. 9 west), Bennington 05201. The Kirkside offers 25 pleasant, individually decorated guest rooms (and morning coffee) in a downtown setting. $59–119.

Catamount Motel (802-442-5977; 1-800-213-3608), 500 South St., Bennington 05201. This downtown motel has 17 comfortable rooms, each with two double beds and an in-room fridge. Summer guests can use the outdoor pool. $49–110.

❄ **Harwood Hill Motel** (802-442-6278; 1-877-442-6200; www.harwood hillmotel.com), 864 Harwood Hill Rd., Bennington 05201. Perched on a hilltop north of Bennington, this motel "with the million dollar view" offers eight deluxe rooms, three cottages, and three economy units, all with air-conditioning, refrigerator, and cable TV. The deluxe rooms have microwave and phone; **Hunter's American Grill** is within walking distance. $51–80; pets (with restrictions) $8 per night.

OTHER LODGING ✿ **Greenwood Lodge & Campsites** (802-442-2547; www.campvermont.com/greenwood), P.O. Box 246, Bennington 05201, 8 miles east of town on Rt. 9. Open mid-May–late Oct. A rustic lodge-hostel and 40 campsites on 120 acres in Woodford, adjacent to the Prospect Mountain ski area. There are dorms for American Youth Hostel members and private rooms; bring your own linen or sleeping bags. Three ponds for swimming, boating, and fishing, and hiking trails nearby. Inexpensive.

✿ **Camping on the Battenkill** (802-375-6663; 1-800-830-6663; www .campvermont.com/battenkill), 48 Camping on the Battenkill, Arlington

05250. This quiet family-owned campground on the Battenkill River has more than 100 campsites spread out in woods, fields, and along the river. Suitable for tents or RVs; some have complete hookups, electric, and water, some don't. The two bathhouses feature toilets, sinks, and hot showers.

✳ Where to Eat

DINING OUT Pangaea (802-442-7171; 802-442-4466 lounge; www.vermontfinedining.com), 1 Prospect St., North Bennington. Open Tue.–Sun. 5–10. This chef-owned eatery in the center of tiny North Bennington is southern Vermont's culinary star. Owner William Scully aims to draw the best from every continent, and it shows in his menu. His wine cellar has won *Wine Spectator* awards, and his gourmet beers come from as far away as India and the Czech Republic. Appetizers have included Vermont chèvre and cardamom strudel with a Riesling glaze and champagne grapes; pheasant confit tossed with hazelnut demiglaze and served in a scallion tuile with chive oil; and butternut squash brûlée with hints of citrus and curry, a sherry and roasted chestnut purée, and a pickled Chiogga beet. A typical entrée might be something Asian, like a stir-fry of soba noodles, honshimeji mushrooms, and snow peas served on red cabbage with Chinese long beans and green curry peanut sauce. Some of the dishes are true indulgences, like the filet mignon alla Rossini, which comes with a foie gras/black truffle pâté de campagne, pancetta, and Gruyère, all rinsed with parsley vinaigrette. Simpler (and less pricey) fare is served in the lounge, and in summer the seating extends to an outdoor terrace overlooking the river. Entrées $33–38 in the dining room, $9–22 in the lounge.

The Four Chimneys Inn (802-447-3500), 21 West Rd. (Rt. 9), Old Bennington. Open Wed.–Sun. for dinner in a gracious, casual dining room and an enclosed porch. Dinner could begin with coconut Thai shrimp in a red curry sauce ($12) or goat cheese blini ($8) and continue with roast free-range quail stuffed with apricots and baked couscous in a Madeira veal sauce ($22), or grilled filet mignon with morel mushrooms and a Madeira demiglaze and garlic mashed potatoes with shaved truffles ($36). Full bar, fresh flowers, white linen. Entrées $22–36.

Bennington Station (802-447-1080), 150 Depot St., Bennington. Open daily for lunch and dinner. Train buffs love this converted Romanesque railroad station built in 1897 of rough-hewn blue marble for the Bennington & Rutland Railroad, with historic photos on the walls. For lunch you can have the Club Car, the Rail Splitter, or the Depot (railroad-worker-sized sandwiches). The dinner menu includes such things as pistachio-encrusted baked scrod ($17), wild grilled salmon with a citron cream sauce ($18), and ginger-infused tuna steak with peanut soba noodles ($20).

☺ **Mount Anthony Country Club** (802-442-2617; www.golfingvermont.com), 180 Country Club Dr. The original clubhouse once housed a military boarding school that burned in 1957. Golf or no golf, you can now enjoy lunch or dinner in this scenic setting just below the Bennington Battle Monument. For lunch try the chicken Caesar wrap ($7.95), the citrus-poached salmon ($10.95), or the Mt. Anthony burger with horseradish and blue cheese ($7.95). For dinner chef Jerry St. Pierre does a nice job with roast duck with raspberry-orange sauce ($21.95), seafood linguine in a (creamless) white sauce ($19.95), and grilled filet mignon with mushrooms and green peppercorn sauce ($22.95). A good spot for banquets.

EATING OUT **Izabella's Eatery** (802-447-4949), 351 W. Main St., Bennington, open for breakfast and lunch Tue.–Fri. 8:30–4, Sat. 9–4. Order at the counter from the overhead menu, then take a seat and people-watch. This new (2005) Italian-themed downtown spot is wildly popular for its creative sandwiches made from fresh, organic ingredients. A panini might combine goat cheese, avocado, tempeh, artichokes, ginger chutney, and free-range chicken; in summer you can eat outside (if you can snag a seat at all).

✿ **Blue Benn Diner** (802-442-5140), Rt. 7, near Deer Park, Bennington, open daily from 6 AM for breakfast, lunch, and dinner. This Worcester-style diner combines "road fare" with more esoteric items like eggs Benedict, tabouli, falafel, and herb teas. A 10-minute wait for a seat is not uncommon.

Alldays & Onions (802-447-0043), 519 Main St., Bennington. Open every day for breakfast, lunch, and dinner. The range of choices runs from bakery items and full breakfasts to gourmet pastas, deli sandwiches, and dinner entrées. There's outdoor seating in warm weather and live weekly entertainment.

Kevin's at Mikes Place III (802-442-0122), 27 Main St., North Bennington. With soup, salads, burgers, steaks, and lots of hot snacks, this is

everything a sports bar should be— and there's a full dinner menu. Open daily 11 AM–midnight.

✿ **Carmody's Restaurant** (802-447-5748), 421 Main St., Bennington. Open daily, 11 AM–10 PM, the bar later. An Irish pub with family dining and take-out. A wide variety of sandwiches, pastas, chicken, seafood, and nightly specials.

Rattlesnake Cafe (802-447-7018; www.rattlesnakecafe.com), 230 North St., Bennington. Open Tue.–Sun., 4:30–9. Choose your margarita, pardner. You can have a Cadillac, a Snake Bite, a Gold, a Bennington Blue, a Frozen Raspberry, or an Over the Top. Also lots of beer and Mexican food, including plenty of nachos to accompany the liquid refreshment. Entrées $7.95–15.95.

✳ Entertainment

Oldcastle Theatre Company (802-447-0564; www.oldcastle.org), Box 1555, Bennington. This accomplished theater company offers a full summer season of performances in the Bennington Center for the Arts. Comedy, drama, and musicals, early June–mid-Oct.

✳ Selective Shopping

Camelot Village (www.theshopsat camelotvillage.com), located in a string of renovated 18th-century barns just west of the Old First Church on Rt. 9 in Bennington, can keep a shopper happy for a long time. Its two largest shops are the **Antique Center** (802-447-0039; www.antiquesat camelot.com), displaying antiques and collectibles from more than 140 dealers, and the **Craft Center** (802-447-0228; www.camelotcraftcenter.com), representing the work of over 200 regional artisans. **The Country Store and Wine Shop** (802-442-3997; www .vermontfudge.com) sells Vermont cheese, specialty foods, maple products, and its own homemade fudge, **John McLeod Ltd.** produces fine woodware, and **Occasional Flowers** (802-442-61291) specializes in folk art and home decor. Other shops include **Granite Lake Pottery**, **Magic Sleigh**, **North River Winery**, and **Vermont Soap & Candle**. There's even food, so you can browse at leisure.

BOOKSTORES Bennington Bookshop (802-442-5059), 467 Main St., Bennington This independent bookstore specializes in Vermont books, adult and children's titles, and greeting cards. Open daily 9–5:30, Fri. till 9 PM, Sun. noon–4.

Now and Then Books (802-442-5566; www.nowandthenbooksvt.com), 439 Main St., 2nd floor, Bennington. Open Sun. and Mon. noon–5:30, Wed.–Sat. 11:30–5:30. Closed Tue. The oldest used- and collectible-book shop in the area, with an emphasis on fiction, cookbooks, and Vermont. Nearly 50,000 tomes.

CRAFTS SHOPS Hawkins House (802-447-0488; www.hawkinshouse .net), 262 North St. (Rt. 7), Bennington, is a crafts market complex for the work of some 400 artisans in silver and gold, unusual textiles, handblown glass, pottery, quilts, cards, books, music, prints and woodcuts, stained glass, candles, and more. Open daily except Christmas and New Year's.

Mahican Moccasin Factory (802-823-5294; www.sover.net/~moc), 2970 Rt. 7 in Pownal, 6 miles south of Ben-

nington on the right. Open Memorial Day–Christmas, daily (except Wed.) 9:30–4:30; in winter, Fri.–Mon. 10–4. Closed Mar. Charles Gray crafts handmade footwear from deerskin, elk, cow, and buffalo hide.

Bennington Potters Yard (802-447-7531; www.benningtonpotters.com), 324 County St., Bennington. Open year-round, Mon.–Sat. 9:30–6, Sun. 10–5. The factory store where Bennington Pottery is made also stocks specialty foods, housewares, and gifts and offers tours. The simple, tasteful bakeware and tableware has been made here for the past half century.

Fiddlehead at Four Corners (802-447-1000), 338 Main St, Bennington. Open 10–5, Sun. 11–3. Closed Wed. A downtown gallery featuring fine art and contemporary crafts housed in a former bank with marble walls, high ceilings, and brass chandeliers. Former teacher Joel Lentzner and his wife, Nina, themselves produce one-of-a-kind hand-painted furniture. Dr. Seuss art, glass, sculpture, jewelry, ceramics, Judaica.

GALLERIES Images from the Past (802-442-3204), W. Main St., Bennington. Open daily Apr.–Dec., winter weekends. Fascinating ephemera: postcards, prints, holograms, historic house boxes.

Bennington Center for the Arts. See *Museums*.

SPECIAL SHOPS ✍ The Chocolate Barn (802-375-6928), 5055 Historic Rt. 7A north in North Shaftsbury, is an unusual combination: two floors of antiques, plus fudge, 65 varieties of hand-dipped chocolates, and special orders from over 800 antique candy molds. Open daily 9:30–5:30.

🍎 **Apple Barn & Country Bake Shop** (802-447-7780). Near Bennington, there are cornfield mazes starting in Sep. and haunted mazes for Halloween. Watch out for the pumpkin-eating dinosaur.

International Herbs (802-442-7870; www.internationalherbs.com), 2068 Rt. 7 south, Bennington, is one of the most complete culinary, medicinal, and botanical herbal shops in the East, a health store without the food. Open 9:30–5:30 Mon.–Sat.

✳ Special Events

May 1: **Annual Bennington Road Race**—the local marathon, at the Park McCullough House, North Bennington.

Late May: **Bennington Mayfest**—a 10–5 street festival downtown with crafts and entertainment.

May–October: **Funky Friday**. The second Friday of each month, galleries all over the area are open 5–8 PM with receptions, special sales, and an opportunity to meet the artists.

June weekends: **Bennington JuneARTS**—art, music, dance, and street performances downtown on the first 3 weekends in June.

July 4: **Annual 4th of July Celebration** with evening fireworks, Willow Park.

July: **Annual Bennington Museum Antique Show** (see *Museums*). **Pownal Valley Fair** (802-823-5683)— exhibits, antique tractor pull, bingo, music, fireworks, petting zoo, and more.

Mid-July–mid-August: **Summer in the Park**—free concerts 7–9 PM at the corner of North and Pleasant Sts., downtown Bennington.

Mid-August: **Bennington Battle Day Week of Celebrations**, with the annual Fire Department's Sunday parade. Battle reenactments, special museum events, family activities.

September 7: **Grandma Moses Birthday Party** at the Bennington Museum (802-447-1571).

September 11: **Annual Wine, Cheese & Southern Vermont Food Festival**, noon–4 at the Apple Barn, Rt. 7 south, Bennington (802-442-2845; www.theapplebarn.com). Proceeds benefit the local animal shelter.

Mid-September: **Annual Bennington-Hemmings Car Show & Swap Meet** at Green Mountain Racetrack, Pownal (802-447-3311, ext. 14). Crafts fair, flea market, tractor pull, motorcycle show, food, and entertainment. **Annual Bennington Quilt Fest** (www.benningtonquiltfest .com)—an exhibit of statewide quilts, plus lectures and demonstrations.

Late September: **Casino at the Castle** at the Edward Everett Mansion, Southern Vermont College (802-442-6323). Blackjack, roulette, bingo, craps, slot machines, a chocolate fountain, and fireworks. Admission $25.

Late November–mid-December: **Festival of the Trees**, Bennington Museum. Silent auction, food, and tour of decorated trees and wreaths throughout the museum's galleries (802-447-1571).

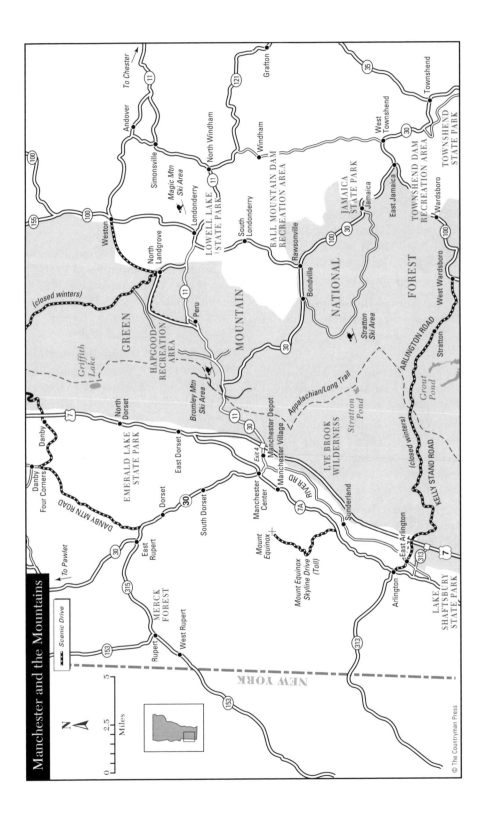

Manchester and the Mountains

© The Countryman Press

Scenic Drive

Miles
0   2.5   5

NEW YORK

To Pawlet

Rupert
West Rupert
MERCK FOREST

East Rupert

Danby Four Corners
Danby
DANBY MTN ROAD
North Dorset
EMERALD LAKE STATE PARK
East Dorset
Dorset
South Dorset

Mount Equinox
Mount Equinox Skyline Drive (Toll)

Manchester Center
Manchester Village
Exit 4
Manchester Depot
RIVER RD
Sunderland
1A

Arlington
East Arlington
LAKE SHAFTSBURY STATE PARK

Bromley Mtn Ski Area

GREEN
Griffith Lake
(closed winters)
HAPGOOD RECREATION AREA
North Landgrove
Weston

To Chester
Andover
Simonsville
Magic Mtn Ski Area
Londonderry
Peru

MOUNTAIN

LYE BROOK WILDERNESS
Appalachian/Long Trail
Stratton Pond

NATIONAL

FOREST

Stratton Ski Area
ARLINGTON ROAD
(closed winters)
KELLY STAND ROAD
Grout Pond
Stratton
West Wardsboro

North Windham
South Londonderry
Rawsonville
Bondville

LOWELL LAKE STATE PARK
BALL MOUNTAIN DAM RECREATION AREA
Windham
Grafton
Townshend

JAMAICA STATE PARK
Jamaica
East Jamaica
West Townshend
Wardsboro
TOWNSHEND DAM RECREATION AREA
TOWNSHEND STATE PARK

MANCHESTER AND THE MOUNTAINS

INCLUDING ARLINGTON, DORSET, DANBY, LANDGROVE, LONDONDERRY, PAWLET, AND PERU

No Vermont community has changed more dramatically in recent decades than Manchester. A summer resort since the Civil War, Manchester has also long been a place to stay while skiing at nearby Stratton and Bromley, and on southern Vermont's most dependably snowy cross-country trails.

What's new is the breadth and depth of shopping in this proud old town: upward of 50 top-brand outlet stores and another 50 or so specialty shops and galleries. Manchester is also home to some of Vermont's best inns and restaurants, including one of its grandest resorts. Furthermore, the town is positioning itself as a cultural center for the state with the spectacular Southern Vermont Arts Center, the Riley Rink at Hunter Park with its lengthy list of summer concerts, and two of the state's premier summer theaters, the Dorset Playhouse and the Weston Playhouse.

The white-columned, tower-topped, 183-room Equinox is as much a part of Manchester's current appeal as it was in the 1850s, the era in which the town's status as a resort was firmly established. Mrs. Abraham Lincoln and her two sons spent the summers of 1863 and '64 at the Equinox, booked again for the summer of '65, and reserved a space for the entire family the following season. The president, unfortunately, never made it.

Other presidents—Taft, Grant, Theodore Roosevelt, and Benjamin Harrison—came to stay at the Equinox, but it was Lincoln's family who adopted the village. Robert Todd Lincoln, who served as secretary of war under President Garfield, minister to Britain under Harrison, then president of the Pullman Palace Car Company, selected Manchester Village as his summer home, building Hildene, the lavish mansion that's now such an interesting place to visit. Other opulent "summer cottages" are sequestered off River Road and nearby country lanes.

Manchester Center and Village are both down in the wide Valley of Vermont, but Mount Equinox, a stray peak from New York's Taconic Range, thrusts up a full 3,800 feet from the village, rising dramatically behind its namesake hotel.

Luckily the 1930s Work Progress Administration plan to carve ski trails on Mount Equinox never panned out, and Manchester Village retains its serene, white-clapboard good looks, at least for the time being. The hotel faces the Congregational church and gold-domed Bennington Courthouse, and the few tasteful stores include a branch of Frog Hollow, Vermont's premier crafts shop. Public buildings trail off into a line of historic mansions spaced behind marble sidewalks.

Discount shopping begins 0.25 mile north in Manchester Center, a village with a different zip code and zoning. The center was "Factory Point" in the 19th century, when sawmills, marble works, and a tannery were powered by the Batten Kill's flow.

Fears that the former Factory Point might become Vermont's future factory outlet capital began in the mid-1980s, with the opening of a trendy wood-and-glass shopping complex at the traffic heart of town, the junction of Rts. 7A and 11/30—known locally as "Malfunction Junction."

The strip malls, however, haven't materialized. Instead, outlets along Rt. 7A fill old homes and house-sized compounds, blending nicely with shopping landmarks like the Orvis Retail Store, a spacious new building done in the style of a country lodge, which has been supplying the needs of fishermen and other sporting folk since 1856.

The Green Mountains rise even within Manchester town limits to 3,100 feet on the east, then roll off into heavily forested uplands punctuated by picturesque villages like Peru, Landgrove, Weston, and Londonderry, all noteworthy for cross-country skiing and equally appealing in summer. Dorset and Danby are also well worth a visit.

GUIDANCE Manchester and the Mountains Regional Chamber (802-362-2100; 1-800-362-4144; www.manchestervermont.com), 5046 Main St., Manchester Center. This white-clapboard chamber of commerce information booth is walled with pamphlets, good for general walk-in information. The chamber does not make reservations but does keep a running tally on space in member lodging places and on short-term condo and cottage rentals.

Stratton Mountain maintains a reservation and information service (in-state: 802-297-4000; 1-800-STRATTON; 1-800-787-2886; www.stratton.com) and serves over 20 lodges, condo clusters, and inns on and around Stratton.

In winter the **Bromley Village Lodging Service** (1-800-824-5522; www.bromley.com) also makes reservations for condominiums.

The Arlington Chamber of Commerce has merged with the Manchester Chamber, but it maintains a self-serve information booth on Rt. 7A open May–Oct.

Dorset Chamber of Commerce (802-867-2450; www.dorsetvt.com), P.O. Box 121, Dorset 05251.

Londonderry Chamber of Commerce (802-824-8178) maintains an information booth and office in the Mountain Marketplace (the Londonderry shopping center) at the junction of Rts. 11 and 100.

GETTING THERE *By car:* From Bennington, US 7 to Manchester is a limited-access highway that's speedy but dull, except for viewing Mount Equinox. You get a more interesting taste of the area, especially around Arlington, by clinging to Historic Rt. 7A. From the southeast, the obvious access is I-91 to Brattleboro, then Rt. 30 north. And from the Albany–Troy area, take US 7 heading east into Vermont, where it becomes VT 9 east. In the center of Bennington, take VT 7 north to Exit 4, or follow Historic Rt. 7A.

MEDICAL EMERGENCY Emergency service is available by calling **911**.

Northshire Medical Center (802-362-4440), Manchester Center. **Manchester Medical Center** (802-362-1263), Rt. 7A, Manchester. **Mountain Valley Medical Clinic** (802-824-6901), Rt. 11, opposite the Flood Brook School, 2 miles west of Londonderry, 3 miles east of Peru. **Carlos Otis Clinic** (802-297-2300), at Stratton Mountain. **Tri Mountain Rescue Squad** (802-824-3166) serves Bondville, Landgrove, Peru, and Stratton.

✳ Villages

In addition to Manchester, the area's picturesque places include Arlington, 7 miles south along Rt. 7A; Weston, 15 miles to the northeast; Dorset, 8 miles to the northwest; Pawlet, another 7 miles to the north on Rt. 30; and Danby, 8 miles north of Dorset and 10 miles east of Pawlet.

Although never formally the capital of Vermont, **Arlington**, on Rt. 7A, was the de facto seat of government during most of the Revolutionary period. Fearing British attacks in the north, Vermont's first governor, Thomas Chittenden, moved south from Williston, liberated a Tory property in Arlington (the area known as Tory Hollow), and conducted affairs of state from there, making it one of Vermont's most historic villages.

Many older visitors to Arlington fondly remember Dorothy Canfield Fisher, the author of 50 immensely popular, warmhearted novels and a Book-of-the-Month Club judge for 25 years. Another famous resident was artist Norman Rockwell, who lived in West Arlington from 1939 to 1953 and incorporated local scenes into his paintings of small-town Americana. Each year in May there's a reunion of Arlington individuals who posed as his models.

Dorset. This pristine village is visible evidence that it takes money to "prevent the future." A fashionable summer refuge for years, few signs of commerce mar its state of carefully manicured nature. Today's tranquility, making it a haven for artists, writers, and the affluent, contrasts sharply with the hotheaded days of its youth. In 1776 the Green Mountain Boys gathered in Cephas Kent's tavern and issued their first declaration of independence from the New Hampshire

MOUNT EQUINOX BEHIND MANCHESTER VILLAGE

Joe Citro

Grants, signed by Thomas Chittenden, Ira Allen, Matthew Lyon, Seth Warner, and other Founding Fathers of Vermont. Today the Dorset Inn, said to be the state's oldest continuously operating hostelry, is the village focal point, along with the Dorset Playhouse, one of New England's most venerable summer theaters. The first marble to be quarried in North America came from Dorset, and one quarry—now a popular swimming hole—supplied the marble for New York City's Public Library. The private Dorset Field Club, a nine-hole golf course, is billed as the state's oldest, and there are several fine inns.

Pawlet. Not far north of Dorset, this hamlet on Rt. 30 is an unexpected delight, with a mix of architectural styles in buildings that cling to the rather steep slopes leading up from Flower Brook, over which Johnny Mach's General Store extends. Gib Mach harnessed the rushing brook to a turbine that generated his electricity and built a glass-topped counter at the end of a store aisle through which you can still peer down at the water surging through the narrow gorge below. Next door, a former railroad station is now the Station Restaurant and Ice Cream Parlor; a clutch of nearby shops is worth investigating.

Danby. A bypassed hamlet on Rt. 7 between Dorset and Wallingford, Danby is an antique village known for its marble quarries and as home base for Silas Griffith, an 1850s lumber baron who was Vermont's first millionaire. In the 1960s, novelist Pearl Buck bought seven local buildings and began to renovate them; since her death, some inns, restaurants, and intriguing shops have opened here.

Weston. A mountain crossroads that's a logical hub for exploring all of southern Vermont, this village of just 630 souls looms large on tourist maps. It's the home of one of the country's oldest and best summer theaters and the Vermont Country Store, New England's number one nostalgia outlet. The oval common is shaded with majestic maples, and a band plays regularly in the bandstand. Free summer concerts are presented by the Kinhaven Music School high on a back road; visitors are also welcome at Weston Priory, a small community of Benedictine monks, nationally known for the music sung and played at Sunday liturgies. Weston was actually one of the first villages in Vermont to be consciously preserved. The theater, the unusually fine historical collection in the Farrar Mansur House, and (indirectly) the Vermont Country Store all date from the "Weston Revival" of the 1930s. Today it offers exceptional lodging and dining as well as theater and shopping.

✳ To See

MUSEUMS & **Southern Vermont Arts Center** (802-362-1405; www.svac.org), West Rd., 1 mile north of the Equinox, Manchester Center. Open all year, Tue.–Sat. 10–5, Sun. noon–5. $6 nonmembers, $3 students; free for members and children under 13. The Elizabeth de C. Wilson Museum, which opened in July 2000, is a work of art in itself with its soaring, light-filled galleries that house some first-class touring shows of paintings, sculpture, prints, and photography. Concerts and lectures are held in the adjacent, 430-seat Arkell Pavilion; there are other special events throughout the year. Light lunches are served in the Garden Café (see *Eating Out*), and there are extensive trails through the woods, among them a botany trail (past outdoor sculpture) featuring rock formations, 67 varieties of wildflowers, and birches. Limited handicapped accessibility.

The American Museum of Fly Fishing (802-362-3300; www.amff.com), next to Orvis on Rt. 7A, Manchester Village. Open daily 10–4 (closed major holidays); $5 adults, $3 ages 6–14; free for students and children under 6. The museum displays the beautiful flies of Mary Orvis Marbury as well as hundreds of rods and reels made by famous rod builders and owned by such luminaries as Daniel Webster, Bing Crosby, Ernest Hemingway, and Presidents Hoover and Eisenhower. The private research library upstairs (admission $20) is open by appointment.

Norman Rockwell Exhibition (802-375-6423), Rt. 7A, Arlington. Open May–Oct. 9–5, otherwise 10–4. Admission. Housed in a Hudson River Gothic church are some 500 of the artist's *Saturday Evening Post* cover illustrations and prints. There's a 20-minute film, and a gift shop. Rockwell's former home is now a bed & breakfast (see *Lodging*).

The **Dr. George A. Russell Collection of Vermontiana** (802-375-6153) believed to be the third largest such collection, is housed upstairs over the Martha Canfield Library in Arlington. Although not a museum (there are no displays), the collection is open to the public on Tue. 9–5, or by appointment (802-375-9296 or 802-375-6974). Dr. Russell, the country doctor immortalized in the Rockwell print that hangs in thousands of doctors' offices, collected Vermontiana for most of his long life and left his collection to this private, nonprofit library. It includes Dorothy Canfield Fisher materials, a limited selection of Norman Rockwell's work, many photographs from the period 1860–90, an extensive number of town histories, and a wealth of genealogical materials (deeds, letters, wills, account books, and diaries) pertaining to Arlington and nearby communities.

The Martha Canfield Memorial Free Library (802-375-6153), 528 East Arlington Rd., Arlington (named for Dorothy Canfield Fisher's aunt). Mid-June–Columbus Day weekend, the library holds a weekend book sale in the Arlington Community House on Route 7A in the town center Fri. and Sat. 9–5, Sun. 1–5, and Mon. 9–5 (when it's a holiday). Books can be snagged for 25¢ to $2, and records, glossy coffee-table books, and jigsaw puzzles can be had for a song. The library hours are Tue.–Thu. 9–5, Fri. 2–5, Sat. 10–3, and Tue. and Thu. evenings 6:30–8. Closed Sun. and Mon.

Northshire Museum & History Center (802-362-5777), Historic Rt. 7A (in back of Ye Olde Tavern restaurant), Manchester. This bright red, exquisitely restored 17th-century saltbox built by Oliver Rice was moved here recently from its Bennington location to house the Manchester Historical Society. A vintage gristmill is next door; their interiors are still in development, but check for upcoming exhibits.

HISTORIC HOMES & **Historic Hildene** (802-362-1788; www.hildene.org), Rt. 7A, Manchester Village. Mid-May–Oct., 9:30–4:30. $10 adults, $4 ages 6–14. Members and children under 6, free. Limited handicapped accessibility. A standout among the village's historic houses, this 24-room Georgian Revival manor is set on 412 acres, including formal gardens and an observatory to the

Kim Grant

HISTORIC HILDENE, ROBERT TODD
LINCOLN'S SUMMER HOME

side that overlooks spectacular mountain views. Bring a picnic lunch and plan to stay half the day. The 90-minute tour begins at the Carriage Barn, now a sophisticated visitors center with a film about Robert Todd Lincoln. You learn that he first came to the village as a boy with his mother for a stay at the Equinox House; his father was assassinated before the family could return, as they had intended, the following summer. It was Todd's law partner who later persuaded him to build this summer home adjacent to his own mansion. Todd died here in 1926, and members of the family lived here until 1975. Guides are familiar with at least one Lincoln and with the true character of the authentically furnished house. Tours include the restored formal gardens, changing upstairs exhibits, one of Abraham Lincoln's rare stovepipe hats, and a brief (taped) concert by the 1,000-pipe organ, which was once playable both manually and with one of 240 player rolls. Picnic tables outside command a view of the valley below, and there are numerous trails to stroll or—in winter, when the Carriage Barn becomes a warming hut—to explore on skis. In summer, Sunday-afternoon polo matches are a popular spectator sport. Inquire about organ concerts and other special events.

&. **Farrar Mansur House** (802-824-5294; 802-824-6624), village green, Weston. Open Sat. 10–5 and Wed. and Sun. afternoons 1–5 in July and Aug.; Sat. 10–5 only in Sep.; Sat. 10–5 and Fri. and Sun. 1–5 during the first 2 weeks of Oct. Limited handicapped accessibility. Even if you have never set foot inside a historic house, make an exception for this one, built in 1797 as a tavern with a classic old taproom. Thanks to 1930s Work Progress Administration (WPA) artists, murals of Weston in its prime cover the living room walls, and a number of primitive portraits hang in the adjacent rooms over period furniture and furnishings donated by Weston families. The upstairs ballroom has recently been redone in magnificent 1820s color and stenciling. In the attic, a rendition of townspeople dancing—each face is painted to resemble a specific resident—conjures the spirit of a town that knew how to have fun.

Weston Mill Museum (802-824-5294), adjacent to the Farrar Mansur House. Open for guided tours Fri. noon–4, Sat. 10–4, and Sun. noon–4 in July, Aug., and the first 2 weeks in Oct. See the waterwheel, turbines, and dam in this reproduction of a 1780 gristmill, plus the work of David Claggett, a skilled tinsmith who uses 18th-century methods to create exceptional chandeliers, lanterns, sconces, and folk art.

SCENIC DRIVES **Mount Equinox** (802-362-1114; www.equinoxmountain.com). The summit of Mount Equinox is 3,825 feet high. Most of the mountain is owned by the Carthusian monks who occupy the monastery, which you can see from the top. A toll road (open May–Oct., 9 AM–dusk; $7 per car and driver; $2 per passenger) climbs more than 5 miles from Rt. 7 to the top. This can be a spectacular ride on a clear day, even more dramatic if the mountain is in the clouds and the road keeps disappearing in front of you. Be sure to drive back down in low gear and in total sobriety. There are also trails to the top.

Green Mountain National Forest Road Number 10, Danby to Landgrove. Closed in winter. The longest (14 miles) and most isolated of these byways, the road (beginning in Danby) climbs through the White Rocks Recreation Area, crossing a number of tempting hiking paths as well as the Long Trail. There are some fine views as you continue along, and you might want to picnic somewhere in the middle of the forest, as we did by a beaver pond. The road follows Tabor Brook down into Landgrove, itself a tiny, picturesque village.

Peru to Weston. From the village of Peru, an enticing, wooded road is paved as far as Hapgood Pond, then continues smoothly through Landgrove, a minuscule village with an outstanding inn (open to the public for dinner) set in rolling fields. The way to Weston is clearly marked.

East Rupert to Danby. Danby Mountain Road is the logical shortcut from Dorset to Danby, and it's quite beautiful, winding up and over a saddle between Woodlawn Mountain and Dorset Peak. Well-surfaced dirt, with long views in places. If you're coming from East Rupert, be sure to turn right at Danby Four Corners and follow Mill Brook into Danby.

Kelley Stand Road. From Rt. 7A, follow the East Arlington Road past Candle Mill Village and continue until you cross a one-lane bridge. Turn right onto Kelley Stand Rd., which is a great foliage-viewing trip all the way to Stratton. Closed in winter.

✷ To Do

BICYCLING In Manchester, mountain bike, hybrid bike, and touring bike rentals and touring information are available from **Battenkill Sports Cycle Shop** (802-362-2734; 1-800-340-2734; www.battenkillbicycle.com), open daily 9:30–5:30, at 1240 Depot St., in the Stone House at the junction of Rts. 7 and 11/30.

First Run Ski Shop (802-297-4321) at Stratton Mountain rents mountain bikes and offers off-mountain guided tours (with 5 days' prearrangement). Open Mon.–Fri. 9–5, Memorial Day weekend–July 4; then daily 9–5. In winter open 8–6.

Equipe Sport and Mountain Riders (802-297-2847; www.equipesport.com), junction of Rts. 30 and 100 in Rawsonville; also on Mount Snow Access Rd. in West Dover (802-464-2222) and in the Village Square at Stratton Mountain (802-297-3460).

CAMPING **Green Mountain National Forest** (802-362-2307; www.fs.fed.us/r9/gmfl), District Ranger Office, Manchester. A public information office serving the southern half of the 400,000-acre Green Mountain National Forest is located on Rt. 30/11 east of Manchester at 2538 Depot St.; open year-round, Mon.–Fri. 8–4:30. Maps and details are available about where to fish, hike, cross-country ski, and camp. All national forest campsites are available on a first-come, first-served basis.

Emerald Lake State Park (802-362-1655; www.vtstateparks.com/htm/emerald), 65 Emerald Lake Lane, East Dorset. Just off Rt. 7, this scenic area offers 105 campsites, including 36 lean-tos; also hiking and nature trails, among them a 3.4-mile round-trip trek to a natural bridge.

& **Hapgood Pond Recreation Area**, Peru. Acquired in 1931, this was the beginning of the Green Mountain National Forest. There is swimming, fishing, and limited (but wheelchair-accessible) boating on the 7-acre pond. Removed from the picnic ground and beach are 28 campsites (first come, first served). A pleasant 8-mile forest trail threads through the woods.

Greendale Campground, 2 miles north of Weston on Rt. 100. This small, remote spot runs along Greendale Brook and includes a 4.5-mile hiking loop. There are 11 sites in a wooded setting. Check water availability before leaving home.

Camping on the Batten Kill. See "Bennington Area."

🐾 **Dorset RV Park** (802-867-5754), Rt. 30, Dorset. Open May–Nov. A family-run area offering 13 sites with hot showers, flush toilets, rec room and outdoor games, electric and water hookups, laundry, and camp store. Dogs must be leashed.

See also "Brattleboro, Putney, and the West River Valley" for details about Jamaica State Park.

CANOEING The **Batten Kill** makes for satisfying canoeing in spring; the Manchester-to-Arlington section is relatively flat water, but it gets difficult a mile above Arlington.

BattenKill Canoe Ltd. (802-362-2800), Rt. 7A in Arlington. An outfitter offering inn-to-inn canoe trips throughout the state and as far afield as Costa Rica and England, also rents canoes and offers shuttle service on the Batten Kill.

First Run Ski Shop (802-297-4321), on Stratton Mountain. Canoe and kayak tours, rentals, and sales. Weekend tours begin at 9:30 and 1:30, weekdays at 10:30.

DRIVING TOURS **Off-road School at the Equinox Resort** (802-362-4700; www.equinoxresort.com), Manchester Village, at the Equinox. The Country Pursuits Centre has merged with the Equinox Resort to provide courses in archery and British falconry, plus year-round off-road Land Rover driving courses, with junior off-road for the 5 to 12 age set (summer months only). Expert instructors offer tips at the school's 80-acre course. Extra passengers are welcome; drivers must have a valid license. The junior course, in the woods behind the hotel, features mini Landrovers the size of go-karts which have a brake and gas pedal and max out at about 5 mph.

Backroad Discovery Tours (802-362-4997; www.backroaddiscovery.com). Sharon O'Connor drives six to eight guests in her special touring vehicles through the back roads and byways of southern Vermont, stopping along the way to give you a taste of local history. She also knows the best places to watch sunsets and view fall foliage. Daily, June–Oct.

FISHING Fly-fishing has been serious business in the Batten Kill since the mid–19th century. The Orvis Company began manufacturing bamboo rods in Manchester Village near the spot where they are still produced.

The **Batten Kill** is generally recognized as Vermont's best wild trout stream; access is available at a number of places off Rt. 7A. Brown trout can also be found in **Gale Meadows Pond**, accessible via gravel road from Rt. 30 at Bondville. **Emerald Lake** in North Dorset is stocked with pike, bass, and perch; rental boats are available at the state park facility.

Orvis Fishing Schools (1-800-235-9763; www.orvis.com), *the* name in fly-fishing instruction as well as equipment; 2-day courses are offered two to three times weekly, Apr.–Oct. There are six other schools around the country and others in foreign locales.

Chuck Kashner's Guide Service (1-800-682-0103; www.vermontfishingtrips .com). Chuck will take care of the tackle, rods, flies, bait, and gear and will provide a hot meal on full-day trips. Four-hour, 6-hour, or full-day (8-hour) trips available, fly- or spin fishing.

Battenkill Anglers (802-379-1444) is a Thomas & Thomas–sponsored fly-fishing school and outfitter.

Peter Basta (802-867-4103), P.O. Box 540, Dorset 05251, offers guide service and on-stream instruction.

Marty Oakland (802-375-6339) guides and teaches fly-fishing in addition to running **Quill Gordon**, a small Arlington B&B that caters especially to fisherpersons.

GOLF The 18-hole **Gleneagles Golf Course** at the Equinox Country Club (802-362-3223), Manchester Center, which was established in the 1920s for guests of the Equinox House, has in more modern times undergone a $3 million renovation and is open to the public. The **Dormy Grill** at the Gleneagles Clubhouse (see *Eating Out*) offers pleasant noontime dining with a beautiful view of the course.

The Stratton Golf School (802-297-2200; 1-800-843-6867) offers weekend and midweek sessions, including professional instruction, use of the 27-hole course at the Stratton Mountain Country Club, and a special 22-acre "training site." A good and reasonably priced seasonal lunch is available at the club.

Tater Hill Golf Club (802-875-2517; www.taterhillgolfclub.com), Popple Dungeon Rd., Windham. An 18-hole course, built on the site of one of New England's largest and oldest potato farms. Facilities include a pro shop, carts, and dressing rooms. The **Clubhouse** serves brunch on Sunday and lunch (daily) including salads, sandwiches, and burgers.

The Practice Tee (802-362-3100), Rt. 7A, Manchester Center. A 335-yard driving range offering group and individual lessons. Open in-season, weather permitting, weekdays 9–7, weekends and holidays 8–7.

HIKING From the Green Mountain National Forest District Office (802-362-2307, request hiking maps for **Lye Brook Wilderness**, a 14,600-acre preserve south of Manchester with a 2.3-mile trail to the Lye Brook Waterfalls and the **Long Trail**. This Massachusetts-to-Quebec path doubles as the Appalachian Trail throughout the area; portions of the trail make good day hikes, either north over Bromley Mountain or south over Spruce Peak from Rt. 11/30. Another popular route is the Stratton Pond Trail, which starts at Kelley Stand Rd. and stretches to Stratton Pond; there is one shelter in the immediate area, and swimming is permitted. **Griffith Lake**, accessible from Peru and Danby, is a less crowded swimming and camping site on the trail. For details, consult the Green Mountain Club's *Long Trail Guide*.

Mount Equinox. Details about the rewarding, 6-mile Burr and Burton Trail from Manchester Village to the summit are available in *Day Hiker's Guide to Vermont* (Green Mountain Club). At 3,825 feet, this is the highest mountain in the state that is not traversed by the Long Trail. See also *Green Space*.

Tracks of Vermont (802-824-9642; www.explorevt.com), P.O. Box 252, Weston 05161. Organized day trips and longer outings, specifically for women.

HORSEBACK RIDING, ETC. ✎ **Horses for Hire** (802-297-1468; www.horsesfor hire.net), Rt. 30, Bondville. Deb Hodis and Ron Amedon offer 1- and 2-hour and half-day trail rides, sleigh rides, and riding lessons for individuals and groups, even in winter, weather permitting.

Karl Pfister Farm (802-824-4663; 802-824-6320; www.sover.net/~npfister/), Landgrove. Fall foliage carriage and wagon rides available by reservation.

✎ **Sun Bowl Ranch** (802-297-9210; www.sunbowlranch.com), on Mountain Rd. at Stratton Mountain Resort, offers trail rides, donkey rides, sleigh rides, lessons, junior riding camps, and overnight rides in summer and winter. Letitia and John Sisters also operate **Mountain View Ranch** (802-293-5837) at 502 Easy St. in Danby.

✎ **Chipman Stables** (802-293-5242; www.chipmanstables.com), at the Equinox in Manchester, and at Danby Four Corners. Year-round horse and pony rides, hayrides, and kids' camp by the day or week, Western-style. Trail rides are $30 per person (discounts for groups larger than four).

HUNTING **Orvis Manchester Shooting School** (802-362-3622; 1-800-548-9548) of Manchester offers 1-day ($495) and 2-day wingshooting courses ($990) July–Oct. Tuition includes guns, ammo, and lunch, but not lodging.

The **British School of Falconry** (802-362-4780) at the Equinox hotel, Manchester Village, offers introductory lessons, hawk walks, and pheasant hunting with hawks and falcons.

MOUNTAIN RIDES ✎ **Bromley Mountain** (802-824-5522; www.bromley.com), Rt. 11, Peru (6 miles east of Manchester). This 3,284-foot-high mountain offers excellent views of Stratton and Equinox Mountains. It's traversed by the Long Trail and also accessible by hiking the ski trails from the midpoint exit on the chairlift. This lift, serving the alpine slide, is open Memorial Day–mid-Oct., weather permitting, on weekends 10–5 and daily July–Labor Day 9:30–6 (fee).

The Bromley Alpine Slide, the longest in this country, is a great ride with fabulous views whatever your age. The DévalKarts, the Condor Cable Coaster, and the Bromley Thrill Sleds (similar to a winter luge) are big draws for the teen set. You'll also find miniature golf, a 24-foot climbing wall, space bikes, the Big Splash, a parabounce, the "trampoline things," and an extreme zipline. Lunch, snacks, and drinks are available at the base lodge.

Bromley Mountain

THE ALPINE SLIDE AT BROMLEY MOUNTAIN

 Stratton Mountain (802-297-2200; 1-800-STRATTON; www.stratton .com) offers a four-state view from its summit, accessible by gondola from the ski resort (Rt. 30, Bondville). The gondolas run 10–5, Sep. 23–Oct. 10. And there's lots of summer action in its Adventure Zone—a skate park, a climbing wall, boulders, and a cave.

NATURE WALKS AND WORKSHOPS **Vermont Institute of Natural Science** (VINS), in partnership with the Equinox Preservation Trust (802-362-4374), offers natural history walks and programs for adults, families, and children. The fee-based programs run year-round, geared to the season.

SWIMMING **Dana L. Thompson Recreation Area** (802-362-1439), Rt. 30 north, 340 Recreation Park Rd., Manchester Center, is open daily in summer, but hours for general swimming are limited; nominal fee.

 Dorset Quarry, aka Norcross-West Quarry, off Rt. 30 on Kelly Rd. between Manchester and Dorset (turn at the historic marker), is a deep, satisfying pool but lacks easy access, making it unsafe for small children. Though the land is private property, the owners allow access by members of the public who treat it respectfully.

 Hapgood Pond in Peru, with its sand and calm, shallow drop-off, is favored by families with young children.

 Emerald Lake State Park (802-362-1655), Rt. 7, North Dorset, offers clear lake swimming.

See also *Green Space*.

TENNIS **Gunterman Tennis Schools at Stratton Mountain** (802-297-4230; 1-800-787-2886; www.great tennis.com) Tennis pro Kelly Gunterman offers instruction for adults both mid-week and on weekends on 15

THE DORSET QUARRY

Kim Grant

outdoor and 4 indoor courts. (*Note:* Stratton Mountain offers free "KidsKamp" supervision for two children ages 4–12 whose parents are enrolled in the golf and tennis programs, late June–early Sep. The Junior Tennis Day Camp runs weekdays for children 6–15.

Dana L. Thompson Recreation Area, Manchester. Public courts are available with weekly memberships or on a per-hour basis.

Equinox Hotel Tennis (802-362-4700), Rt. 7A, Manchester Village. Three Har-Tru courts are open to the public for an hourly fee.

Dorset Tennis Club (802-362-2236), Rt. 7A, 4 miles north of Manchester. Indoor court; lessons.

✳ Winter Sports

✐ CROSS-COUNTRY SKIING **Viking Nordic Centre** (802-824-3933; 802-824-5602; www.vikingnordic.com), 615 Little Pond Rd., Londonderry. Trail fee. The Viking trail system now includes 35 km of groomed trails, 3 km lighted for night skiing on Sat. and holidays, and dedicated snowshoe trails. You'll also find instruction, rentals, a retail shop, on-snow kid-sitters (by reservation), and a café serving drinks, light breakfasts, and lunches. The **Viking Nordic House** is a beautiful post-and-beam home with a library, hearth, and four bedrooms that sleeps 10. Winter, $800 per weekend (2 nights), $1,200 for a nonholiday week ($800 in summer), including ski passes. Call for details.

Wild Wings Ski Touring Center (802-824-3933; www.wildwingsski.com), North Rd., Peru. Tracy and Chuck Black run a family-oriented touring center located within the Green Mountain National Forest, 2.5 miles north of Peru. Trails are narrow, geared to beginning and intermediate skiers. This area tends to get a heavier snowfall than other local touring centers; the 28 km of groomed one-way trails are at elevations between 1,650 and 2,040 feet. Instruction and rentals; no skate skiing or dogs.

Stratton Mountain Nordic Center (802-297-2200), Stratton Mountain. Based at the Sun Bowl, a 30 km series of groomed loops plus adjoining backcountry trails. Guided backcountry tours as well as a variety of other tours are offered. Hot lunch and snacks available at the Sun Bowl Base Lodge.

Hildene Ski Touring Center (802-362-1788; www.hildene.org), Manchester. The Lincoln Carriage Barn serves as a warming hut for this system of 12 km of groomed and mapped trails on the estate built by Robert Todd Lincoln. Trails meander through woods and fields on a promontory overlooking the Batten Kill Valley between Mount Equinox and Lye Brook Wilderness. Lessons and equipment available.

Equinox Ski Touring Center (802-362-3223) has 35 km of groomed trails and tracked terrain, snowshoeing, instruction, a lounge, tours, vacation camps, and rentals. This network includes trails on the golf course, up through the forests of the Equinox Preservation Trust, and around Equinox Pond.

DOWNHILL SKIING ✿ **Bromley** (802-824-5522), 3984 Rt. 11 in Peru, 6 miles east of Manchester. Founded in 1936 by Fred Pabst of the Milwaukee brewing family, this is among the oldest ski areas in the country. It was also one of the first to develop snowmaking, a slope-side nursery, chairlifts, and condominiums. Pabst set up a rope tow in what is now the parking lot. Later he invented the J-bar, which allowed skiers to be pulled up the mountain rather than having to clutch a rope. Fred sold the area to Stig Albertsson in 1971, but remained president until his death in 1977. Albertsson brought the first alpine slide to North America, helping Bromley develop into more than just a winter destination. Today the resort is owned by Boston-based Joe O'Donnell, who made extensive renovations in 1999, adding a snowboarding park and half-pipe, a high-speed quad chairlift that gets skiers from base to summit in 6 minutes, and a new lodge. The Halo Terrain Park is wired for sound and has its own T-bar, half-pipe, tabletops, glades, spines, quarter-pipes, and dedicated groomer. Most of the trails are suited to beginners and intermediates, but there are a number of challenging runs on the mountain's east side, particularly Stargazer, Blue Ribbon, Avalanche, Havoc, and Pabst Peril.

Lifts: 10: 1 high-speed detachable quad, 1 fixed-grip quad, 4 doubles, 1 T-bar, 2 Mighty-Mites, and Magic Carpet.

Trails: 43 trails—35 percent intermediate, 34 percent beginner, 31 percent expert.

Vertical drop: 1,334 feet.

Snowmaking: 80 percent of terrain from base to summit.

Facilities: The base lodge offers two cafeterias as well as more formal areas. Skiers unload right at the base lodge; the driver then parks in an area across Rt. 11 and rides back on a shuttle bus. Valet parking is another option.

Ski school: Ski and snowboard school.

For children: The Bromley Thrill Zone is one of the largest summer amusement parks in the state, with the 700-foot Condor Cable Coaster zipline, an 18-hole mini golf course, a 0.7-mile triple-track alpine slide, DévalKarts (gravity-driven mountain go-carts), a 24-foot climbing wall, and a variety of spinning, splashing rides. For the youngest set there's PigDog's Fun Park, with a 24-foot inflated slide, Bounce House, and bumper boats. Adults can settle in with a snack at the Sun Café and enjoy the view.

✿ **Stratton** (1-800-STRATTON; 802-297-4211 ski report). Located atop a 4-mile access road from Rt. 30 in Bondville, Stratton is a popular, well-groomed mountain. It was here that Jake Burton invented the snowboard, an event the mountain has made the most of with weekly races, not to mention the hosting of the U.S. Open Snowboarding Championships. Stratton keeps a loyal following by harvesting a steady crop of snow for what are predominantly intermediate-level runs, but there are also plenty of opportunities for advanced skiers along its 90 trails, including some good moguls and long top-to-bottom runs of 2,000 vertical feet. As one of Vermont's youngest ski areas (it was established in 1961, a year after Killington and five after Mount Snow), it is among the most modern, with a vibrant après-ski scene in winter and a well-known golf and tennis school. During the off-season, the slope-side population shrinks to 150 (although in 1960, its residents numbered a mere 24). Acquired by the Canadian resort company Intrawest in 1994, Stratton is respected statewide for its environmental policies; it has relinquished development rights on nearly a third of its acreage to protect bear, deer, and thrush habitat.

The mountain itself rises to 3,936 feet, with two separate areas: the original North Face, otherwise known as Stratton Village, and the distinctly sunnier Sun Bowl, the newer of the two. Thanks to the quantity of lifts, skiers are generally dispersed over the trail network. Stratton Village, a complex that includes a variety of shops, a dozen restaurants, a 91-room condo hotel, a 750-car garage, and 170 condominiums, dwarfs the base facility. A sports center includes a 25-yard-long pool, whirlpool, indoor tennis courts, racquetball courts, exercise equipment, and a lounge.

A lot happens here in summer, too. There's a 27-hole golf course, hiking, mountain biking, paintball, fishing, kayaking, scenic gondola rides, and tennis and golf schools. Sun Bowl Ranch offers a variety of horseback-riding opportunities; there's a hockey and dance camp, and kids ages 6 weeks–12 years can attend KidsKamp for half or full days, late June–early Sep.

Lifts: 16: a 12-passenger gondola, four 6-passenger high-speed detachable, four quads, one triple, one double chair, two surface lifts, and three Magic Carpets.

Trails and slopes: 90.

Terrain parks: Four, including the pro Power Park and Power Superpipe, designed and built with the stamp of approval from Stratton snowboarder and Olympic medalist Ross Powers. The superpipe is 420 feet long, with walls of 17–22 feet. Skiers and riders must earn access to Stratton's biggest park by completing a safety awareness session.

Vertical drop: 2,003 feet.

Snowmaking: 90 percent.

Facilities: Restaurant and cafeteria in the base lodge, also cafeterias midmountain and in Sun Bowl Ranch. Chapel of the Snows at the parking lot, a little Bavarian-style church, has frequent nondenominational and Roman Catholic services. A shuttle bus brings skiers from inns on the mountain to the base lodge. Also a clinic, sports center, and shops and restaurants in the base area Village Square.

Ski school: Ski and snowboard lessons.

For children: Childcare Center for ages 6 weeks–3 years; Mountain Riders 5–8 and 9–18. A separate base lodge and new slope-side meeting place for KidsKamp; combined ski and play programs are offered—Little Cubs (ages 4–6), Big Cubs (7–12), Junior Newcomers (7–12).

Rates: $59 per adult midweek, $72 weekends and holidays; $52 midweek and $60 weekends for young adults and seniors. Many special multiday packages.

❦ ✐ **Magic Mountain Ski Area** (802-824-5645; www.magicmtn.com), south of Londonderry off Rt. 11, 18 miles east of Manchester. The smallest of southern Vermont's ski areas, Magic Mountain may also be its most challenging. Its 34 trails are twisty and narrow, and almost half of its 1,600 vertical feet are steep drops. The 108-acre area was developed in 1960 by Swiss ski instructor Hans Thorner, who hoped to re-create the atmosphere of a Swiss alpine village. He chose this mountain for the sheer drama of its terrain. The company foreclosed in 1989, and though it reopened in 1997, Magic Mountain remains relatively overlooked, making it a perfect destination for those out to escape the crowds (and expense) of the larger resorts. Though the advanced trails are the real draw here, there is still plenty of good, well-groomed terrain for beginners and intermediates. The two chairlifts, the red double and the black triple, are long and comparatively slow, reminding you of what it was like to ski before high-speed detachable chairs were invented.

Beginners should turn left at the top and follow the Magic Carpet trail a third of the way down, then choose a blue or green route to the bottom. Intermediate-level skiers and riders should take the red double lift to Whiteout or Betwixt. Advanced skiers will want to go straight down Redline and turn a little right from the red chair to try Twilight Zone and Goniff Glade, which are steep and dotted with numerous surprises, among them trees, rocks, bushes, and other natural obstacles. Magic Mountain is good for families, as the central base lodge is easy to find yet spacious enough to spread out in. Though it lacks the indulgences and amenities of the larger resorts, the commercial hype and sprawling condos are refreshingly absent. Kids will enjoy the Ala Kazaam Tubing Park, which is illuminated Sat. and holiday nights until 8; it's the only tubing park in the region with its own tow. Summer activities are gearing up at Magic Mountain, with a mountain biking program and a skateboard ramp in the base lodge.

Lifts: 4: 1 triple chair, 1 double, and 2 surface.

Trails and slopes: 34.

Vertical drop: 1,600 feet.

Facilities: Cafeteria in the base lodge.

Ski school: Ski and snowboard lessons. Ask about special events and lift packages.

ICE SKATING **Riley Rink at Hunter Park** (802-362-0150; 1-866-866-2086; www.rileyrink.com), a paradise for music lovers in summer and sports enthusiasts in spring, is transformed into an Olympic-sized ice-skating rink in winter. Public skating hours (starting mid-Oct.) are Mon.–Fri. 10–12:45, Fri. evenings 7:30–9:30, Sat. 1:30–3:30 and 8–10 PM, Sun. 2–4. Adults $5 weekdays, $7 weekends; ages 12 and under and 55 and over $3 weekdays, $5 weekends.

SLEIGH RIDES **Karl Pfister Farm** (802-824-6320; www.sover.net/~npfister) in Landgrove offers the most remote, romantic sleigh rides around.

Other options include **Sun Bowl Ranch** (802-297-9210) at Stratton Mountain Resort, the **Equinox** hotel (802-362-4700), **Merck Forest and Farmland Center** (802-394-7836), and the **Taylor Farm** (802-824-5690), box-style sleighs pulled by Belgian draft horses courtesy of cheesemakers Jon and Kate Wright, on Rt. 11 in Londonderry. (The benefit here is that you can buy some of their wonderful cheese at the same time.)

SNOWMOBILING A *Winter Recreation Map*, available free from the Green Mountain National Forest District Ranger Office (802-362-2307), Manchester, shows trails presently maintained in this area by the Vermont Association of Snow Travelers.

Equinox Snowmobile Tours (802-824-6628), Rt. 11/30 just west of Bromley Mountain, offers guided snowmobile tours on state-of-the-art vehicles. Helmets are provided; boots and clothing can be rented.

Twin Brooks Tours (802-442-4054; 1-888-616-4054; www.twinbrookstours .com) in nearby Woodford has guided tours by the hour, half day, or full day.

✳ Green Space

✔ **Equinox Preservation Trust** (802-362-4374), Manchester Village. A not-for-profit organization created in 1993 by Equinox Resort Associates and administered through the Vermont Land Trust and The Nature Conservancy. Some 855 acres on Mount Equinox are now a user-friendly preserve. Secure a map/guide to the trail system (a portion is open to cross-country skiers) and inquire about the nature walks and seminars offered year-round, some geared to children, in conjunction with the Vermont Institute of Natural Science. Horseback riding and mountain biking are also permitted on the ski trails in summer and fall. Be sure at least to walk the 1.2-mile loop through the hardwoods around Equinox Pond. *Note:* All parking for access to the trust property is at the parking lot of the Equinox hotel.

✔ **Merck Forest and Farmland Center** (802-394-7836; www.merckforest .org), P.O. Box 86, 3270 Rt. 315, Rupert 05768. Open year-round, dawn to dusk; free. This 3,150-acre forest and farming area, set aside in the 1950s to serve as a model for conservation and sustainable land use, is a nonprofit environmental education organization reliant solely on donations. Workshops and nature programs are offered year-round, and there is an organic farm, an organic sugarbush, and Friends of the Forest, a gift shop selling farm products. The forest contains 28 miles of trails for walking, hiking, skiing, snowshoeing, and horseback riding, and a spring-fed swimming pond at the end of a 2-mile hike. Six rustic but fully enclosed cabins accommodating anywhere from 6 to 15 campers are available year-round (by reservation) for a modest fee, each with a woodburning stove, wooden bunks, and a nearby outhouse. Shelters and tent sites are also available. The **Stewardship Field Program** offers educational day programs and camping trips for children ages 4–20. Open year-round.

Grout Pond Recreation Area (802-362-2307), west of the village of Stratton, marked from Kelley Stand Rd. Deep in the Green Mountain National Forest, this remote, forest-encircled lake is a great spot to bird-watch or picnic, complete with grills and a small beach. Tables and fireplaces overlook the shore, and there is a launch for canoes. Short hikes lead around the pond, and one of them wanders 2 miles through the Green Mountain National Forest, emerging at the Somerset Reservoir. Campsites available on a first-come, first-served basis.

See also *To Do—Camping.*

✳ Lodging

RESORT **The Equinox Resort & Spa** (802-362-4700; 802-362-1595; 1-800-362-4747; www.equinoxresort.com), Rt. 7A, Manchester Village 05254. This historic white-columned inn has become one of Vermont's most prestigious destinations, and though already sizable, it continues to grow. In the mid-1980s it was renovated from the foundations up, an unavoidable process that left it sound but, many said, soulless. Thanks to a 1990s capital infusion, the 136 rooms and 47 suites, most of them spacious, have acquired modern plumbing, new pine furniture, and a bright, contemporary feel. Common rooms include a paneled bar, billiards room, and meeting rooms with a country-club atmosphere. The Equinox's public spaces and conference areas are roomy and chandeliered, reminiscent of a fine urban hotel. Meals are excellent and on the formal side (see *Dining Out*). Facilities include the recently improved 18-hole golf course, a spa and fitness center with outdoor and indoor pool, touring bikes, a 14-acre stocked trout pond, tennis courts, a cross-country ski network, snowmobiling, an archery and falconry school, and learning to drive Land Rovers and Hummers off-road.

THE EQUINOX RESORT & SPA

Diane E. Foulds

The **Charles Orvis Inn** next door is even classier, though from the outside it looks like a traditional Vermont home. In fact, this was the 19th-century residence of the founder of the Orvis fly-fishing empire. In its current incarnation, each of its nine one- and two-bedroom suites comes with all the bells and whistles: a cherry-paneled kitchen, marble bath, oak floors, gas fireplace, living room, and other perks. There is also a new row of town houses.

Room rates at the Equinox range $189–639, at the Charles Orvis Inn $629–929; a daily $19 resort fee is tacked on. Inquire about midweek discounts and MAP packages.

INNS AND BED & BREAKFASTS

In Manchester

& **The Inn at Ormsby Hill** (802-362-1163; 1-800-670-2841; www.ormsbyhill.com), 1842 Main St., Manchester Center 05255. The inn is 2 miles southwest of Manchester Village on Rt. 7A, set in 2.5 acres of rolling lawns with spectacular mountain views. This gracious, elegant manor was the home of Edward Isham—Robert Todd Lincoln's law partner—and his family's home for 100 years. Its connection to Hildene is strong, spiritually and aesthetically. Innkeepers Chris and Ted Sprague have 10 guest rooms and obviously enjoyed distinctively decorating some in Waverly prints, all with exceptional antiques. Each has a fireplace and two-person Jacuzzi; some come with two-person steam sauna. The spacious Taft Room, with its wood-burning fireplace and huge four-poster, is the unofficial honeymoon suite, but every one of the rooms is romantic enough to qualify. The downstairs Library

Suite is handicapped accessible. Common space includes a formal parlor and an inviting library lined with bookshelves that hold many of Isham's personal volumes. The huge, many-windowed dining room with ornately carved hearth is the scene of bountiful breakfasts featuring Chris's famous breakfast dessert, a specialty of the house. Ask to see the prison cell in the basement; it may be Manchester's earliest jail. Room rates ($170–270 midweek, $265–330 weekends, more on holidays) include breakfast.

The Inn at Manchester (802-362-1793; 1-800-273-1793; www.innat manchester.com), 3967 Main St., Rt. 7A, Box 41, Manchester Village, 05254. A gracious old home set back from Main Street with an expansive front porch, big windows, gables, and three floors. Frank and Julie Hanes acquired the inn in 2005 and have upgraded its 18 rooms, which include 5 suites (4 rooms are in the restored, vintage-1867 carriage house out back). All have full private bath and central air-conditioning, and four have working fireplace. The dining room and parlors are imaginatively and comfortably furnished with a mix of modern and 19th-century art under high ceilings. The tapestries and Oriental carpets give the common areas a worldly, sophisticated feel. In the back is a beer and wine bar and game room warmed by an antique wood-stove. Summer brings use of the secluded pool in the back meadow and plenty of rocking chairs on the flowery porch. Breakfasts are full and hearty, including homemade breads and such treats as cottage cakes—a cottage cheese concoction served with hot apricot sauce. The rooms have no phones (and there's only one TV downstairs), but those who need to plug in can access the computer in the hall or tune their laptops in to the wireless Internet connection available throughout the house. Children over 8 are welcome. Rates are $135–295 per room, including a full breakfast and afternoon tea.

✑ **Manchester Highlands Inn** (802-362-4565; 1-800-743-4565; www .highlandsinn.com), P.O. Box 1754, 216 Highland Ave., Manchester Center 05255. Inkeepers Diana and Didier Cazaudumec call this spacious Victorian inn "Manchester's best-kept secret." Recently repainted a Victorian blue with cream and beige accents, it's on a quiet side street, a short walk from all the shops and restaurants but with an away-from-it-all feel, especially on the back porch and lawn (with its pool), both of which command an expansive view of Mount Equinox. The 16 guest rooms, all but one with private bath, are nicely decorated with family antiques and personal touches, many with canopy beds. Common space includes a comfortable living room, a wicker-filled sunroom, and a TV room (with a library of movies to feed the VCR). In winter the loss of the pool and porch is assuaged by a game room in the basement. A very full breakfast featuring morning glory muffins, maybe lemon soufflé pancakes and cheddar soufflés, is served, plus home-baked afternoon snacks and tea. $135–225 per room; $25 more in foliage and holiday weeks.

♿ **1811 House** (802-362-1811; 1-800-432-1811; www.1811house.com), P.O. Box 39, 3654 Main St., Manchester Village 05254. This magnificent building was erected during the American Revolution and has been an inn since 1811, except for the few years when it was owned by President Lincoln's granddaughter, Mary Lincoln Isham. The public rooms are as elegant as they are historic, and the 13 guest rooms each come with private bath, 7 with wood-burning fireplace. One, the Jeremiah French Suite, is wheelchair accessible. Innkeepers Bruce and Marnie Duff and Cathy and Jorge Veleta dispel any stuffiness in this rarefied world. The cozy pub, replete with dartboards and a wide selection of single-malt scotches, is open to the public 5:30–8. An expansive lawn and newly redesigned English-style gardens overlook the Gleneagles Golf Course. A wonderful full breakfast is included in the room rate, from $140 per person for a cozy double to $280 per person for a suite with a king-sized four-poster canopy bed, fireplace, and sitting room. Rates include gratuity. Children over 16 are welcome. Off-season rates available.

∞ **Reluctant Panther Inn & Restaurant** (802-362-2568; 1-800-822-2331; www.reluctantpanther .com), 17–39 West Rd., Manchester 05254. This gray, purple-shuttered home, a village landmark, burned to the ground in September 2005, only a month after it changed hands. New innkeepers Liz and Jerry Lavalley and their son Matt are rebuilding, adding a restaurant and wine cellar and improving the 20 guest rooms while retaining some of the inn's historic look. The suites in the adjacent Porter House, which the fire missed, have been redecorated with fine linens and antiques. Several rooms and all the suites have fireplace. Many suites feature two wood-burning fireplaces— one in front of the two-person whirlpool bath and a second in the bedroom. All have private bath, room phone, and cable TV, and starting in the fall of 2006, two rooms will be wheelchair accessible; breakfast will be served in-house to guests only, but the sophisticated dining room, the tavern, and a more casual bottle-lined eatery, The Wine Cellar, will be accessible to all. Open year-round; $179–459 per room includes breakfast.

∞ ✹ ♪ **The Village Country Inn** (802-362-1792; 1-800-370-0300; 802-362-7238 fax; www.villagecountryinn .com), Box 408, Rt. 7A, Manchester 05254. This century-old, three-story Main Street inn has a long piazza lined with wicker and rockers. There are 32 guest rooms (18 suites and luxury rooms), 1 with Jacuzzi, some with gas fireplace, all with private bath, and many recently refurbished in lace, antiques, and chintz. Outside is a formal garden and gazebo, swimming pool, and patio; inside, an informal tavern and separately owned restaurant. Rates, including breakfast, are $129–345 double occupancy.

∞ ♪ ♿ **Wilburton Inn** (802-362-2500; 1-800-648-4944; www.wilburton .com), River Rd., Manchester 05254. This is a baronial brick turn-of-the-20th-century mansion set up a hill and well off the main road on 20 acres of manicured, sculpture-covered gardens with long views of the Batten Kill Valley. It was originally built for Albert Gilbert, a wealthy Chicago businessman, who wanted a country estate adjacent to the mansion of his friend, Robert Todd Lincoln. Common rooms are richly paneled and the living room is immense, complete with piano, comfortable window seats and couches, and Oriental rugs. The house itself offers four suites and five bedrooms; there are also 25 rooms in the outlying cottages (the Curry House sleeps 14; the Ortlieb House, 6). These are better suited to families due to their privacy and direct access to the seemingly limitless lawn—which harbors a pool and tennis courts. All rooms have private bath. Breakfast is served at wrought-iron, glass-topped tables in the Terrace Room, and dinner, in the Billiard Room, is reminiscent of an exclusive men's club, with a leather bar and a huge tiled fireplace. The views are exquisite. Albert Levis, the inn's owner since 1987, has opened a holistic center, Teleion Holon, in the cottage that was built as a wedding gift for the daughter of the mansion's original owner, and offers massage, clinics, and workshops on mind–body harmony. The inn is open year-round. $115–315 per couple (plus a 10 percent service charge) includes a full breakfast and afternoon tea. Weddings are a specialty here.

The Inn at Willow Pond (802-362-4733; 1-800-533-3533 outside Vermont; www.innatwillowpond.com), Box 1429, Manchester Center 05255. Located 2.3 miles north on Rt. 7A and owned by the Bauer family, this inn offers 40 spacious guest rooms and suites in three separate, contemporary, Colonial-style buildings on a hillside overlooking the Manchester Country Club's golf course. The 18th-century Meeting House reception building contains the lofty main lounge, conference facilities, a fitness center with exercise equipment, two saunas, and a library. There's also an outdoor lap pool and a restaurant (northern Italian cuisine) in a renovated 1770 house (see *Dining Out*). The suites feature a living room with a wood-burning fireplace. From $178

for a standard room, to $228 for a one-bedroom fireplace suite, to $388 for a two-bedroom fireplace suite. Full breakfast is served in the restaurant on weekends and holidays. Midweek and other packages available.

🦋 ✎ **Seth Warner Inn** (802-362-3830; www.sethwarnerinn.com), P.O. Box 281, 2353 Main St., Manchester Center 05255. This imposing vintage-1800 house is set back from Rt. 7A southwest of Manchester Village, and it's a beauty—carefully restored by Stasia and Richard Carter. Ask to see the thank-you note that Robert Todd Lincoln wrote after staying here in 1911. Rooms with open beams and stenciling are furnished in antiques and curtained in lace. Five bright guest rooms have country quilts, queen canopy bed, and private bath. Common space includes a gracious living room, a small library, and the dining room, in which guests gather for a full breakfast. There is also a deck outside overlooking the brook-fed duck pond. $125–135 per room includes breakfast. Children 12 and over.

♿ **The Battenkill Inn** (802-362-4213; 1-800-441-1628; www.battenkillinn .com), P.O. Box 1245, Manchester 05254. This 1840 Victorian farmhouse sits at the foot of the Mount Equinox Skyline Dr. and backs onto meadows that stretch down to the Batten Kill. The 10 guest rooms all have private bath and are furnished with antiques, and the common rooms include two sitting rooms and two small dining rooms—plenty of space to relax in. One room with a double bed and fireplace is fully handicapped accessible. Your hosts are Alan and Judy Edmunds. $130–190 per couple includes a full breakfast and complimentary hors d'oeuvres. Springtime midweek specials are available. Children 6 and over welcome.

In Arlington 05250

∞ **The Arlington Inn** (802-375-6532; 1-800-443-9442; www.arlington inn.com), 3904 Rt. 7A in the center of Arlington, occupies the stunning 1848 Greek Revival mansion built by Martin Chester Deming, a Vermont railroad magnate, and has been used as an inn off and on since 1889. Owners Eric and Elizabeth Berger offer 18 rooms: 6 suites in the main house, 6 in the carriage house, and 6 in the adjacent 1830 parsonage. Most are spacious and furnished with Victorian antiques, and there's a formal parlor. Sylvester's Study on the ground floor of the main building is particularly impressive. The units in the parsonage have Drexel cherry four-posters and sleigh beds, TV, and air-conditioning. The inn is also a popular spot for dinner (see *Dining Out*), and the gardens make this a great spot for weddings or civil unions. Rates per room are $125–315, including a full breakfast. MAP also available. Open all year.

✿ ♿ **West Mountain Inn** (802-375-6516; www.westmountaininn.com), on Rt. 313 west of Arlington. Open year-round. A large, rambling former summer home with splendid views of the mountains and valley, converted and expanded into an inn. The 22 attractive rooms, 9 of which are suites, are named for famous people associated with Arlington, and a copy of Dorothy Canfield Fisher's *Vermont Tradition* is in every room. Breakfast and dinner are served daily; Sunday brunch seasonally (see *Dining Out*). The inn's property includes more than 5 miles of walking and snowshoeing trails, gardens, and llamas in residence. A num-

ber of special events are featured, such as a St. Lucia Festival of Lights in early December, Maple Weekend in early May, and Ethan Allen Days over Father's Day weekend. Amie Emmons is the innkeeper. $149–300 B&B for two, $224–379 MAP. There are also three town houses at the Historic Mill on the property.

∞ ✿ ♿ **Hill Farm Inn** (802-375-2269; 1-800-882-2545; www.hillfarm inn.com), 458 Hill Farm Rd. Located off Rt. 7A north of the village, this historic farmstead, owned and managed by Al and Lisa Gray, is set on 50 acres of land bordering the Batten Kill. The 1830 main building, 1790 guest house, and four seasonal cabins hold a total of 15 rooms, some of them suites or cottages, all with private bath. Licensed for beer and wine. Double rooms are $80–195, including full country breakfast. Children are welcome at special rates.

∞ 🐾 ✿ **The Inn on Covered Bridge Green** (802-375-9489; 1-800-726-9480; www.coveredbridgegreen .com), 3587 River Rd. Fans of Norman Rockwell can now actually stay in his former home, a pretty white 1792 Colonial across from a red covered bridge and the village green where Ethan Allen mustered his Green Mountain Boys. The inn offers nine guest rooms, all with private bath (four have two-person spa tubs), fireplace, and air-conditioning. Pets are accepted in the two cottages, one of which was the studio where Rockwell painted. There's swimming, canoeing, and fly-fishing in the Batten Kill just a few hundred feet from the inn, and the setting is quintessentially Vermont. The full country breakfasts are events, served on bone china by candlelight. $130–225.

Country Willows B&B (802-375-0019; 1-800-796-2585; www.country willows.com), 332 East Arlington Rd. Anne and Ron Weber run this tidy, 1850s village historic landmark with five spacious guest rooms with private bath (two with claw-foot tubs), decorated in Victoriana. The West Mountain Room has a fine view, a fireplace, and a sitting area. The Dorset Suite is a two-bedroom, one-bath suite that can accommodate parents with school-aged children. There is a wraparound porch and a hammock for two. (The Webers also offer a two-bedroom, self-catered Manchester cottage.) Rates of $138–232 per double include full country breakfast, possibly Anne's French toast served with Ron's secret-recipe apple compote.

🎣 **Ira Allen House** (802-362-2284; 1-877-362-2284; www.iraallenhouse .com), Box 251, Rt. 7A. Ray and Sandy Walters run this smartly renovated old roadside home that Ira and Ethan Allen built. The inn has nine guest rooms, some set up for families. The property across Rt. 7A fronts the Batten Kill, good for trout fishing and, for the warm-blooded, a dip in a 10-foot-deep swimming hole. $125–275 per room with full breakfast.

🎣 **Green River Inn** (802-375-2272; 1-888-648-2212; www.greenriverinn .com), 3402 Sandgate Rd., Sandgate 05250 (off Rt. 313, 4 miles west from Rt. 7A, Arlington), has 16 renovated guest rooms, all with private bath, some with whirlpool bath, balcony, and fireplace. There are quilts, down comforters, Waverly prints, and antiques, and the rooms have river or mountain views. Guests are also welcome in the sunroom, on the outdoor deck, and in the special children's room. Bob and Carol Potozney, who

took over in 2004, have a lot of ideas about what to do outdoors on their 450 secluded acres. $100–205 with breakfast, plus 15 percent gratuity.

In Danby 05739

The Quail's Nest (802-293-5099; 1-800-599-6444; www.quailsnestbandb .com), 81 S. Main St., is a homey, pleasant B&B in an 1835 house. The six guest rooms, all with private bath, are furnished with antiques and country quilts. Four have king-sized beds. There's a comfy living room with a wood-burning fireplace, hardwood floors, and a library where guests can browse the titles or choose a movie to play on the VCR. In summer months breakfast is served on a back deck with views of the Green Mountains. Children 16 and over welcome. Reservations essential. $88 includes a full breakfast.

In Dorset 05251

∞ ♿ **The Dorset Inn** (802-867-5500; 1-877-367-7389; www.dorsetinn .com), 8 Church St. A national historic site and the state's most venerable hostelry (in continuous operation since 1796) faces Dorset's pristine town green. It has been stylishly renovated in country antiques by owner Sissy Hicks, who doubles as the inn's chef. Known for its excellent cuisine (see *Dining Out*) and relaxing atmosphere, the inn has 30 guest rooms, all with air-conditioning and private bath. It's within walking distance of antiques shops and the theater and offers a cozy fireplace in the parlor as well as a lineup of front-porch rockers from which you might not want to stir. $100–225 includes breakfast; $195–330 MAP. Dogs in residence.

🐾 ♿ **The Barrows House** (802-867-4455; 1-800-639-1620; www.barrows

house.com), 3156 Main St., Box 98. This exceptional mini resort on Rt. 30, now owned by Linda and Jim McGinnis, features attractive, flexibly arranged accommodations (18 rooms, 10 suites) in the main house and 8 rooms in adjacent buildings. The 1796 house, Dorset's first parsonage, is a short walk from the center of this historic village, but there is an out-in-the-country feel to the 12-acre grounds, which include organic gardens, a gazebo, a heated outdoor swimming pool, sauna, and two tennis courts. In summer, bikes are available; golf and hiking are nearby. In winter, cross-country ski equipment is available. There are comfortable sitting rooms in the main house and the larger cottages, where large families or groups can be lodged. A convivial bar is wall-papered to resemble a private library. Dogs are welcome in two separate accommodations. The dining room and a guest room in one of the outer buildings are wheelchair accessible. The dining room is outstanding (see *Dining Out*). $230–340 per couple, including breakfast and dinner; B&B rates also available.

∞ ♂ ♿ **Inn at West View Farm** (802-867-5715; 1-800-769-4903; www .innatwestviewfarm.com), Rt. 30, just south of Dorset, is a small, well-groomed lodge with an appealing personality, once the focus of a 200-acre farm, now known especially for its exceptional cuisine. (Under the direction of chef Raymond Chen, the dining room—see *Dining Out*—remains the focal point of the inn.) Christal Siewertsen is the innkeeper. The inn has a large, cozy living room with a wood-burning fireplace; common space also includes an inviting, wicker-filled sunporch. One downstairs room

has been fitted for handicapped access, and the 10 upstairs rooms are all furnished comfortably with cheerful paper, private bath, and bright, crisp fabrics; all rooms are air-conditioned. Rates are $110–200, including full breakfast. Children over 12.

♣ ♂ **Marble West Inn** (802-867-4155; 1-800-453-7629; www.marble westinn.com), out Dorset West Rd. This Greek Revival house has seven marble columns on its marble front porches, and there are marble walkways and three marble fireplaces. It offers eight well-decorated guest rooms (one a two-room suite with fireplace), an inviting living room, and a music room. The stencil work in the entrance hallway and on stairway walls is exceptional, and the high ceilings and bull's-eye moldings are pleasant reminders of an earlier era, as is the gracious hospitality of owners Pamela and Paul Quinn. Guests mingle in the library for drinks and conversation. Rates are $109–209 per couple, including a candlelit, gourmet breakfast and afternoon tea. Pets by pre-arrangement.

Dovetail Inn (802-867-5747; 1-800-4-DOVETAIL; www.dovetailinn .com), Rt. 30. An 1800s inn facing one end of Dorset's green with 11 bedrooms (all with private bath), run by Jean and Jim Kingston. Breakfast is served in the Keeping Room or in guest rooms. $105 for the smallest double room in low season; $250 for a two-room suite with a fireplace and TV, sleeping up to four. Ask about midweek rates.

In Weston 05161
∞ ♦ ♣ ♂ ♿ **Colonial House Inn & Motel** (802-824-6286; 1-800-639-5033; www.cohoinn.com), 287 Rt. 100. A rare and delightful combination of

nine motel units and six traditional inn rooms (shared baths), connected by a very pleasant dining room, a comfortable, sunken sitting room with dried flowers hanging from the rafters, and a solarium overlooking the lawn; there's also a fully equipped game room. Innkeepers Kim and Jeff Seymour (Kim is the daughter of former owners John and Betty Nunnikhoven) make all ages feel welcome, and most guests are repeats. Rates include memorable, multicourse breakfasts. Dinners are served family-style ($19.95). The inn is 2 miles south of the village, with lawn chairs facing a classic farmscape across the road; most guest rooms overlook a meadow. Rooms are $60–118 double occupancy (B&B); extra charges for children, singles, and service. Ramp available for wheelchairs.

☀ ♫ **The Darling Family Inn** (802-824-3223; www.thedarlingfamilyinn .com), 815 Rt. 100. An 1830s house, exquisitely furnished with family antiques by Joan and Chapin Darling. The five guest rooms have private bath, canopy bed, fine quilts, and artistic touches. There are wide-plank floors throughout, and Joan has expertly painted the walls. Full country breakfasts, by candlelight, are included in the rates. In summer the pool adds a nice touch. $85–145 per couple, including breakfast, except for guests in the two attractive (and fully equipped) cottages up on the hill (where kids and pets are welcome). Cash or checks (no credit cards); discounts on stays of 5 nights or more.

Inn at Weston (802-824-6789; www .innweston.com), P.O. Box 66, Rt. 100. Bob and Linda Aldrich own this 13-room establishment that offers lodging in the main inn, the Coleman House, or the Carriage House. There's a gourmet dining room (see *Dining Out*) with live music, a full bar, a library, a deck, an orchid greenhouse, fine furniture, and a terrific eat-in gazebo out back with lovely views. $195–215 in the main inn and the Coleman House, $315 in the Carriage House. Add $50 per room on holidays.

In Peru 05152

∞ ☀ ♫ **Johnny Seesaw's** (802-824-5533; 1-800-424-CSAW; www.johnny seesaw.com), 3574 Rt. 11. Built as a dance hall in 1920 and converted into one of Vermont's first ski lodges, this is a wonderfully weathered, comfortable place. Within walking distance of the slopes in winter, it offers tennis and an Olympic-sized pool in summer. There are 25 air-conditioned rooms—doubles, master bedrooms with fireplace in the main house, and family suites—also four cottages with fireplace, good for large families and small groups. There is a licensed pub (see *Dining Out*); "Yankee cuisine" dinners are à la carte and have a French accent. The living room boasts Vermont's first circular fireplace. Rates are $80–140 per room in the lodge, cottages $110–360, including a full breakfast. Add 15 percent service charge, and $5–6, depending on season, for children staying in a room with parent. $10 nightly for pets.

∞ ♫ **The Wiley Inn** (802-824-6600; 1-888-843-6600; www.wileyinn.com), P.O. Box 7, 2759 Rt. 11, just 1 mile from Bromley. Its core is an 1835 farmhouse containing a delightful living room with fireplace, library, and dining room. A six-room motel-like wing, now refurbished, includes one room with a fireplace and a two-person whirlpool tub. A room with the same amenities is available in the main house. Jerry and Judy Goodman extend a special welcome to families with the configuration of a number of rooms, as well as a game room with a TV, videos, a piano, and toys. Couples, on the other hand, may prefer the suitably quiet and romantic rooms in the original part of this rambling inn, with its total of 14 rooms and 3 two-bedroom suites, all with private bath. Summer facilities include a backyard heated pool and play area; there's also a hot tub in the woods that holds eight. The inn's relatively small and attractive dining room is currently the **Bromley Beach**, an Italian bistro open weekends and holidays. Rooms for two, including breakfast, are $95–225 in summer and fall; suites range $185–265 in winter. All children stay free in parent's room.

In Landgrove 05148

⊚ 🦞 🐾 ✍ ♿ **The Landgrove Inn** (802-824-6673; 1-800-669-8466; www .landgroveinn.com), 132 Landgrove Rd. Innkeepers Tom and Maureen Checchia have improved this red-clapboard building that rambles back and around, beginning with the 1820 house, ending an acre or two away. The "Vermont continuous architecture" draws guests through a handsome lobby, past 18 air-conditioned rooms (16 with private bath) that meander off in all directions, through the inviting Rafter Room Lounge (huge, filled with games and books), to the attractive dining room in the original house. Its serene location and multiple wings make it an ideal place for a writing workshop or retreat. Our favorite rooms are tucked up under the eaves in the oldest part of the inn, papered in floral prints and furnished with carefully chosen antiques but with new baths. Many rooms are well suited

to families, who also will appreciate the heated pool, the stocked trout pond (catch and release), lawn games, and the two tennis courts. In winter you can take a sleigh ride or step out onto the 15-mile cross-country trail system that leads through the picturesque village of Landgrove (just a church, a former school, and a salting of homes cupped in a hollow), on into the surrounding Green Mountain National Forest. Bromley Ski Area is just 6 miles away, and Stratton is a 20-minute drive. Breakfast is an event here, served on oak tables in the wood-beamed dining room with a many-windowed wall overlooking the garden. The dining room is open to the public 5 nights a week. Dining is by candlelight, with a choice of entrées prepared by a well-respected local chef (see *Dining Out*). $80–225 per couple with full breakfast, pets $10.

The Macartney House (802-824-6444; www.macartneyhouse.com), 24 Vermont Rt. 11. James and Elaine Nelson-Parker's forested retreat, formerly the Meadowbrook Inn, has seven guest rooms, all with private bath, some with fireplace and/or two-person whirlpool tub, plus comfortable robes and a fully licensed pub. Their 20 km trail system is available to guests in all seasons for hiking, biking, nature walks, and cross-country skiing. $175–295, with a gourmet breakfast included. Children over 16.

In and around Londonderry

Frog's Leap Inn (802-824-3019; 1-887-FROGSLEAP; www.frogsleapinn .com), 7455 Rt. 100, Londonderry 05148. One of the oldest inns in the area, this is a classic Colonial, built in 1842 and set well back from the road above a sloping lawn. The estatelike place has an excellent dining room,

32 acres of pasture and forests with 2 miles of hiking and cross-country trails, an outdoor heated swimming pool, and a tennis court. There are eight rooms with private bath in the main house, and four suites with private bath in the annex, plus the Tad Pool House, an air-conditioned second-floor apartment with two bedrooms, a kitchen, a living room, and a deck overlooking the pool. B&B rates ($89–114 per room for two) include a full breakfast. Rates for the Tad Pool House and the Forest Glen House are $260 without housekeeping.

🌸 ✒ ♿ **The Londonderry Inn** (802-824-5226; 1-800-644-5226; www .londonderryinn.com), 8 Melendy Hill Rd., South Londonderry 05155. On a knoll overlooking the West River, this large historic home has been a country inn since 1940. The 21 guest rooms are decorated with folk-art-painted furniture and walls and patchwork quilts; with teddy bears on every bed. Room 6 (on the third floor) sleeps eight. The bright common rooms include a huge stone fireplace, tropical bird aviary, billiards room, movie room, and Maya's antique bell collection. Fresh-baked cookies are available every afternoon. Full hot organic vegetarian buffet breakfast and afternoon tea are included. Chrisman and Maya Kearn have won state recognition for running an environmentally conscious inn. Children will enjoy the resident dogs and cats, thriving gardens, spring-fed outdoor swimming pool, and the many nooks to explore. Gift shop on premises. Room rates run $136–336 including breakfast, plus 15 percent heating oil surcharge. Being a "guest participation" inn, the Kearns ask that those staying more than 1 night make their own beds each morning.

MOTELS ⏥ ✒ ♿ **Palmer House Resort** (802-362-3600; 1-800-917-6245; www.palmerhouse.com), P.O. Box 1964, Manchester Center 05255. A family-owned luxury motel with 50 rooms/suites with fireplace and Jacuzzi, all with cable TV, refrigerator, in-room coffee, phone, indoor/outdoor pool, exercise room, stocked trout pond, tennis, and nine-hole golf course, all on 22 acres adjacent to the Green Mountain National Forest. The venerable **Ye Olde Tavern** restaurant (see *Dining Out*) is right next door. Rooms $75–175, suites $160–280, depending on season. Children 12 and over.

✒ ♿ **The Manchester View** (802-362-2739; 1-800-548-4141; www .manchesterview.com), P.O. Box 1268, Rt. 7A, Manchester Center 05255. Tom and Pat Barnett own this place just north of town with marvelous views. Thirty-five rooms with fridge, cable TV, VCR, and wireless Internet, plus 3 two-bedroom suites and 7 one-bedroom suites (most with fireplace, living room, and two-person Jacuzzi); also handicapped-accessible units. Facilities include a heated outdoor pool in summer. Golf and tennis available at nearby Manchester Country Club. Rates are $85–275 double occupancy, $185–275 for suites.

🌸 ✒ **Swiss Inn** (802-824-3442; 1-800-847-9477; www.swissinn.com), 249 Rt. 11, Londonderry 05148. From its exterior this looks like a standard motel, but step inside for a pleasant surprise. Joe and Pat Donahue feature Swiss dishes in their dining room (see *Dining Out*). Nineteen rooms, all with private bath, are large enough to accommodate families, and public space includes a library as well as a sitting room and bar. There's also an outdoor pool. $60–150 per room includes a full breakfast.

⚤ ♪ The Barnstead Inn (802-362-1619; 1-800-331-1619; www.barnsteadinn.com), Box 998, 349 Bonnet St., Manchester Center 05255. Just up Bonnet St. (Rt. 30), two blocks from the amenities of town, this is a genuine former hay barn converted into 14 attractive motel units, all with private bath. It's all been done with consummate grace and charm, with many small touches like braided rugs and exposed old beams. There is also an outdoor pool and hot tub. $99–229. Child-friendly; no pets, no meals.

♪ The Weathervane Motel (802-362-2444; 1-800-262-1317; www.weathervanemotel.com), Rt. 7A, 2212 Main St., Manchester 05254. Set back from the road with two picture windows in each of its 22 large units, this is a motel with class. Each air-conditioned room has TV, free coffee, and full or queen-sized beds, many with linens as fine as any upscale inn. Some of the rooms connect. There is a common area with Oriental carpets, antiques, and an outdoor deck. Out back you'll find a volleyball court, a trampoline, and a heated pool. Kids are welcome, pets not. $65–150 includes breakfast in summer.

CONDOMINIUMS AND SKI LODGES

Stratton Mountain Inn (1-800-STRATTON; www.stratton.com), 61 Middle Ridge Rd., Stratton Mountain 05155, with over 125 rooms and suites, is the largest lodging facility on the mountain. Rooms have private bath, phone, and TV, and facilities include a large dining room, saunas, and whirlpools. On winter weekends room rates start at $83–333 per night.

The on-site **Stone Chimney Grill** offers breakfast and candlelit dining.

Stratton Condominiums (1-800-STRATTON), Stratton Mountain 05155. Roughly 250 of the resort's privately owned condominium units are in the rental pool at any given time, in a range of sizes and shapes; they run $130–264 per room per day. All resort guests have access to the sports center and its indoor pool, exercise machines, and racquetball and tennis courts (a fee is charged).

Liftline Lodge (1-800-STRATTON), Stratton Mountain 05155. This older, Austrian-style 70-room lodge is close to Stratton's lifts and village shops and restaurants. Two restaurants. Lodging $59 per person midweek. Weekends from $83 per room.

Long Trail House (1-800-STRATTON), Stratton Mountain 05155. The newest Stratton property has a heated pool, hot tub, and sauna. Weekend and holiday rates start at $259 per night, plus a 20 percent tax and service charge.

⚤ ♪ Bromley Village (802-824-5458; 1-800-865-4786; www.bromley.com), P.O. Box 1130, Manchester Center 05255, is a complex of 50 attractive one- to four-bedroom condo units adjacent to the ski area. Summer facilities include a pool and tennis courts. In winter you can walk to the trails; there is also a shuttle bus. Call for rates.

CAMPGROUNDS See *To Do* for campground options in the area.

✳ Where to Eat

DINING OUT **Chantecleer** (802-362-1616), Rt. 7A, East Dorset. Open daily except Tue. (Mon. and Tue. in winter, except on holidays) 6–closing. Long regarded as one of Vermont's top restaurants, Swiss chef Michael Baumann's establishment is known for nightly game specials, whole Dover sole Chantecleer ($36), and Australian roast rack of lamb ($38). Leave room for profiterole de maison or coupe Matterhorn. The setting is an elegantly remodeled old dairy barn with a massive fieldstone fireplace. There is an extensive wine list. Reservations essential.

Forty nine forty main street (802-362-9839), 4940 Main St., Manchester. Lunch and dinner daily noon–closing. Entrées range from a Black Angus burger for $8.95 to seafood stew for $19.

Inn at Weston (802-824-6789; www .innweston.com), Rt. 100, Weston. Executive chef James Bennett has made this a favorite. You might begin with grilled black tiger shrimp bruschetta or Florida mango soup, then move on to coarse sea salt and black pepper rubbed filet mignon, or Long Island duckling with cognac-peach flambé. Seatings begin at 6; reservations essential. Entrées $26–34.

Wilburton Inn (802-362-2500; 1-800-648-4944; www.wilburton.com), River Rd., Manchester Village. Dinner in the mansion's baronial Billiard Room is an event. You might start with stuffed baby artichokes with Boursin and roasted garlic spinach, and move on to baby rack of lamb with pomegranate glaze, garlic whipped potatoes, and cumin-rubbed eggplant napoleon, or pan-roasted filet mignon with a stuffed mushroom in bordelaise sauce and asparagus au gratin. The inn holds a series of special dinners on the terrace, and an annual Mediterranean Romance evening with live music and Greek dancing. Entrées $26–32.

Three Clock Inn (802-824-6327; www.threeclockinn.com), Middletown Rd., South Londonderry. Dinner daily except Mon. Reserve and request directions. Owner Serge Roche works magic in a rustic dining space with low beams and glowing hearths on a back street in this little-visited hamlet. The à la carte menu changes frequently but might include grilled clams baked with peppers, olives, and savory herbs, foie gras with Black Mission figs in a port marinade, hanger steak with shiitake butter, or a venison chop with poached pear. $60 prix fixe, $36 à la carte. There is an extensive wine cellar.

Mistral's at Toll Gate (802-362-1779), off Rt. 11/30, 5 miles east of Manchester. Open for dinner daily except Wed. Reservations recommended. Chef Dana Markey and his wife, Cheryl, run this longtime dining landmark located in the old tollhouse once serving the Boston-to-Saratoga road. During warm-weather months a brook rushes along just under the windows. The menu might include tournedos of veal morel, salmon cannelloni, or rack of lamb. All are accompanied by a *Wine Spectator*–recognized wine list. Entrées $27–36. Seatings start at 6 PM.

The Barrows House (802-867-4455), Rt. 30, Dorset. Open for dinner nightly from 5:30. The Dorset Room, a spacious, somewhat formal country dining room, is walled with primitive murals showing how this village looked in the 19th century. In an adjacent room you can watch the snow fall from behind glass walls. On the wall beside the full bar is an autograph collection discovered in an old shoe box; signatures include U.S. presidents and such personalities as P. T. Barnum, Brigham Young, and Jefferson Davis. Diners can select from an à la carte menu that changes seasonally; nightly specials are also offered. Phyllo-wrapped leek, asparagus, and Stilton strudel or seared Maine crabcake might be followed by pan-roasted veal Sinatra or hazelnut-crusted pork tenderloin with peach mostarda sauce. Entrées $18–32.

Inn at West View Farm (802-867-5715; 1-800-769-4903), 2928 Rt. 30, Dorset. Open for dinner Thu.–Mon. The main dining room is exceptionally attractive, and the food is dependably good. Chef Raymond Chen's entrées range $26–32 and might include braised short ribs, paupiette of halibut, or coriander-crusted venison. Asian-inspired "little dishes" ($4–12) are served in the tavern.

The Black Swan (802-362-3807), Rt. 7A, Manchester Village (next to the Jelly Mill). Open for dinner daily except Wed. The food in this crisply decorated and managed old brick Colonial house is a treat for the senses. A representative dinner might begin with chilled calamari salad or broiled green lip mussels topped with garlic butter, and proceed to Nana's fried chicken with pan gravy ($16.25) or almond-crusted flounder ($18.50). Lighter fare is served in the **Mucky Duck Bistro**.

Reluctant Panther (802-362-2568; www.reluctantpanther.com), 39 West Rd., Rt. 7A, Manchester Village. Open for dinner starting in the fall of 2006. The relatively formal (jacket required for men) dining room of this popular inn, newly rebuilt following a 2005 blaze, looks out onto picturesque Mount Equinox and a relandscaped backyard featuring a pond, gardens, and a gazebo. The cuisine is "Northeast regional" with an ever-changing menu, and the wine list is extensive. Sit in the intimate tavern with its full bar, or try the **Wine Cellar**, a smaller and more casual eatery downstairs (dinners include lighter fare and are priced lower). Entrées range $28–32.

The Perfect Wife (802-362-2817; www.perfectwife.com), Rt. 11/30, 1 mile east of the Rt. 7 overpass. Open Tue.–Sun. 5–10 for dinner. Amy Chamberlain features locally raised chicken with mascarpone and eggplant, sesame-crusted tuna, or the Howling Wolf vegetarian special. There's live music in the tavern every weekend. Entrées $6.95–28.

The Dorset Inn (802-867-5500; 1-877-367-7389), 8 Church St., Dorset. Open daily for breakfast, lunch, and dinner. Chef Sissy Hicks can be relied on for outstanding New England fare. Dinner entrées include duck confit with wild rice and plum chutney ($22.75), or eggplant crêpes rolled with spinach and ricotta ($14.75). Entrées $13–26.

The Marsh Tavern at the Equinox Resort & Spa (802-362-4700), Rt. 7A, Manchester Village. A prix fixe Sunday brunch is a tradition for residents and visitors in the vaulted Colonnade dining room. The atmospheric Marsh Tavern is open for breakfast, lunch, and dinner daily, serving hearty soups, salads, pastas, and such specials as cornmeal-crusted trout, squash, and portobello mushroom strudel, and shrimp and saffron pasta. Entrées $24–30.

Bistro Henry (802-362-4982), 1942 Rt. 11/30, Manchester. Open for dinner daily except Mon. Dina and Henry

Bronson run this Mediterranean-style dining room with a casual atmosphere, a full bar, and a *Wine Spectator* Award of Excellence. You might begin with a vegetable and Vermont goat cheese tart, then dine on the risotto of the day or quail stuffed with foie gras. Entrées $16–30.

The Restaurant at Willow Pond (802-362-4733), Rt. 7 north of Manchester Center. A restaurant in a restored 1770s farmhouse. Dinner every night (but check in the off-seasons). The menu is "authentic" northern Italian. You might begin with a spinach salad, or grilled eggplant with a three-cheese-and-spinach stuffing and a fresh diced tomato and porcini mushroom sauce. Entrées include linguine alla pesto ($12.95) and veal Piccata ($19.95).

Swiss Inn (802-824-3442), Rt. 11, Londonderry. Open to the public for dinner daily except Wed., the Swiss Inn has a strong local following. While ownership is no longer Swiss, the current owner-chef seems to have the right touch with such dishes as Geschnetzeltes (veal à la Swiss), beef fondue, and chicken Lugano (chicken breast dipped in a Gruyère cheese batter); also Continental dishes like shrimp à la Marseilles and veal Marsala. Fondues are a specialty. Entrées run $13–23.

❧ **Johnny Seesaw's** (802-824-5533; 1-800-424-CSAW; www.johnny seesaw.com), 3574 Rt. 11, Peru. A Prohibition-era dance hall, then one of New England's first ski lodges, this atmospheric inn with its central round fireplace is well worth a dinnertime visit even if you don't happen to be staying there. The extensive French-influenced menu usually includes a choice of veal and seafood dishes and pork chops Vermont-style, but huge prime rib of beef is the house special (children can always get hamburgers or pasta as well as half-sized portions). Adult entrées $19–34. Soft music played live on weekends.

❧ **The Landgrove Inn** (802-824-6673), 132 Landgrove Rd., Landgrove. Dinner by reservation Wed.–Sun. This fine old inn is off by itself up dirt roads at the edge of a tiny village. Meals are by candlelight in a delightful old dining room with windows overlooking the garden. You might begin with a delectable carrot vichyssoise, then dine on roast duck or rack of lamb. Entrées $18–28. Children's portions and delicious homemade desserts. Three-course prix fixe "Vermont night" dinners offered year-round on Wed. and Sun. (nonholiday periods) for $23.

❧ **Ye Olde Tavern** (802-362-0611), 214 N. Main St., Manchester Center. Open daily from 11:30 for lunch and 5 for dinner. A 1790 tavern theoretically specializing in "authentic American" dinner dishes like roast tom turkey and pot roast, but seafood fettuccine is also on the menu, and the Tavern Seafood Stew is laced with vermouth, tomato, and fennel ($19). The several veal specialties all are priced at $21–24, and there's lots of prime rib ($22). One of the better values in town.

The Arlington Inn (802-375-6532), Rt. 7A, Arlington. There's a mauve-walled formal dining room, or you can dine in the more casual **Deming Tavern**. The two share the same menu; you might choose artichoke and mushroom ragout with Marsala cream in a puff pastry shell as an appetizer, and continue to Arlington Inn mixed grill or baked salmon with a grapefruit beurre blanc. Entrées $22–32.

West Mountain Inn (802-375-6516), River Rd., Arlington. Chef Jeff Scott's dining room is open daily by reservation 6–8:30 PM, featuring a $42 prix fixe menu that might include pan-seared Chilean sea bass, spinach and roasted red pepper ravioli, or a Black Angus filet mignon.

See also the "Brattleboro, Putney and the West River Valley" for **Three Mountain Inn** in Jamaica.

EATING OUT

In and around Manchester

The Dormy Grill (802-362-4700, ext. 833), at the Gleneagles Golf Course clubhouse on Union St., serves lunch outside daily mid-May–mid-Oct., 11:30–4, on the back deck. Never mind the food; feast your eyes on the spectacular mountain vistas here at one of the best views in town. Tasty soups, salads, burgers, and wraps, $5–14. Dinners till Labor Day weekend, Thu.–Sun. 5:30–8. Reservations are wise, as the best seats fill up fast.

Garden Café at the Southern Vermont Arts Center (802-366-8298), West Rd., Manchester Village. Open for lunch May–mid-Oct., Tue.–Sat. 11:30–2:30, Sun. noon–2. The food is fine and the setting is superb: a pleasant indoor room or the outside terrace, both with views over the sculpture garden and down the mountain to Manchester Village.

Al Ducci's Italian Pantry (802-362-4449; 1-800-579-4449), Elm St., one block up Highland Ave. from Rt. 11/30, Manchester Center. An authentic Italian deli, eat in or take out. Daily specials, plus the best supply of specialty cheeses and artisan breads in the region. Open daily except Tue. till 6 PM.

&. **Little Rooster Cafe** (802-362-3496), Rt. 7A south, 4645 Main St., Manchester Center. Breakfast and lunch 7:30–2:30; closed Wed. This cheerful midtown café is probably the hottest lunch spot in town. If you come at noon, be prepared to wait. Sandwiches $6–9. No credit cards.

&. **Laney's Restaurant** (802-362-4456; www.laneysrestaurant.com), Rt. 11/30, Manchester Center. Open from 5 PM, this is a festive, kid-friendly spot, specializing in exotic pizzas from a wood-fired brick oven, Adam's Ribs (baby back pork ribs), Gone with the Wind (pork and beef ribs), and Oliver Twist (pasta primavera); draft beer in frosted mugs.

&. **Maxwell's Flat Road Grill** (802-362-3721), Rt. 11/30, 575 Depot St., Manchester Center, across from r. k. Miles. Diner food done well, everything from popcorn chicken and quesadillas to chili and big burgers. For dinner you might try crabcakes or horseradish-crusted salmon. All entrées are less than $15, some considerably less. Kids' menu.

&. **Sherrie's Cafe** (802-362-3468), Rt. 11/30, 709A Depot St., Manchester. Open 8–3, this café serves great

THE DORMY GRILL AT THE EQUINOX RESORT & SPA

Diane E. Foulds

breakfasts, homemade soups, sandwiches, salads, and desserts. Outdoor seating.

✧ **Bob's Diner** (802-362-8171), Rt. 11/30, 2279 Depot St., Manchester Depot. Open daily for breakfast, lunch, and dinner. A shining chrome diner with very good food (the milk shakes are literally the best) at good prices in this upscale part of the world. Give it a try, especially with kids.

Gourmet Café and Deli, Rt. 7A, Manchester Center. Open daily 7:30–5. Tucked back into Manchester Center's Green Mountain Village shopping center, this café offers great salads and sandwiches, plus a pleasant terrace to eat on in warm weather.

Candeleros (802-362-0836), Main St., Manchester Center, is a Mexican cantina open daily for lunch and dinner; there's a pleasant outdoor patio in summer, and margaritas are half price on Thu.

Up for Breakfast (802-362-4204), 4235 Main St., Manchester. Breakfast Mon.–Fri. 7–noon, weekends 7–1. Bright, art-decked space with tables and a counter, an open kitchen, and blackboard menu specials—maybe a sausage, apple, and cheddar omelet, trout with eggs and hash browns, or wild turkey hash. Worth climbing the stairs.

Mika's (802-362-8100), Avalanche Motor Lodge, Rt. 11/30, Manchester. Open daily for lunch and dinner until 10 PM for fans of traditional Chinese and Japanese cuisines; the full-service sushi bar has a local following.

For pizza: **Christo's** (802-362-2408), 4931 Main St., and the **Manchester Pizza House** (802-362-3338) in the Manchester Shopping Center on Rt. 11/30, both offer high-quality pizza as well as salads, subs, grinders, and Italian lunches and dinners. Both serve beer and wine and will deliver locally.

Elsewhere

Gatewood's (802-293-5755; www.gatewoods.net), 52 S. Main St., Danby. Open daily except Tue., 3–6 PM for drinks and tapas on the back patio (weather permitting), 6–9 for dinner. Chef-owner Jon Gatewood's weekly changing menu includes duck raised on local farms, nightly seafood specials, and homemade breads and desserts in a historic Cape with saffron-colored walls and a pressed-tin ceiling. Next to the town library. Entrées $18–30.

Jonathon's Table (802-375-1021), Rt. 7A, Arlington. Open May–Dec. Keep your eyes peeled for the sign; the place is worth your trouble. Cheerful and done in lots of natural wood, Jonathon's Table is attracting both a local and a tourist crowd. Jonathon serves Veal Jonathon with a sherry and mushroom sauce and Vermont rainbow trout as well as steak, ribs, and pasta. The prices are moderate, and the food is good.

White Dog Tavern (802-293-5477), Rt. 7 north of Danby. Open for dinner at 5, Wed.–Sun. This is an 1812 farmhouse with a central chimney and three fireplaces, each serving as the focal point of a dining room. There's a cheery bar, and an outdoor deck in summer. The blackboard menu includes clams, shrimp, and the house special—chicken breasts à la Tom, served up with herbs, garlic, and melted cheese over spaghetti. Options might include blackened catfish and clams zuppa ($16–18).

Café at the Falls (802-824-5288), Weston Playhouse, on the green in Weston. Open for dinner on theater nights beginning at 5:30; 5 on Sun. A pleasant dining room by the falls, good, and then you're there. Reserve. (See also *Entertainment*.)

♦ ♪ **The Barn Restaurant and Tavern** (802-325-3088), Rt. 30, Pawlet. Open daily for dinner June–Oct. This is a genuine old barn with a huge fireplace and a view of the Mettawee River. A large menu offers something for everybody, but it's best known for seafood, steaks, and burgers in the tavern. There's also a salad bar and children's menu. Entrées $16–22.

Jake's Marketplace Café (802-824-6614), Mountain Marketplace at the junction of Rts. 100 and 11, Londonderry. Open daily for lunch and dinner (lunch on weekends only in winter). A local institution with a lively sports lounge, a lunch counter, and a pleasant pink dining room. Overstuffed sandwiches, salads, homemade soups, burgers. Pasta, steak, fish, and personal pizzas ($11–21) are the dinner offerings.

Gran'ma Frisby's (802-824-5931), Rt. 11 east of Londonderry. Open daily except Tue. for lunch and dinner. When Magic Mountain Ski Area is open, you're lucky to get in the door of this wonderfully pubby place. Known for its fries and fresh-dough pizza, this is a friendly, reasonably priced find any time of year.

The Station Restaurant and Ice Cream Parlor (802-325-3041), School St., Pawlet. Open 7 AM–2:30 PM. Closed Wed. in summer, Tue. and Wed. in winter. If you think about it, railroad depots make perfect diners—with the counter and a row of stools down the length of the building

and tables along the sides. This classic 1905 depot was moved here from another town and positioned above a babbling brook. It's a particularly pleasant place. Coffee cups bearing regulars' names hang by the door.

♪ **Mulligans** (802-297-9293) at Stratton Mountain also has a Manchester Village locale (802-362-3663). This spacious restaurant is open daily for lunch and dinner; good for burgers, sandwiches, salads, and dinner options. Children's specials include a Ninja Turtle Burger and Gorilla Cheese. There's a baked stuffed lobster special on Mon. and Tue. No plate sharing.

Out Back at Winhall River (802-297-FOOD), Rt. 30, Bondville, serves dinner daily from 5 PM, with lunch on weekends. Eight beers on tap, a lengthy wine list, a children's menu, pool table, and game room. Entrées $13–29.

The Bryant House (802-824-6287), Rt. 100, Weston. Now owned by the neighboring Vermont Country Store, this fine old house belonged to one family—the Bryants—from the time it was built in 1827 until the family line petered out. Upstairs, a special room is set aside to look as it did in the 1890s. There are plenty of salads, sandwiches, and Vermont-style chicken pie. Lunch served 11:30–3, $8–10. Closed Sun.

Village Pantry du Logis (802-824-9800; 1-800-404-7587; www.villagepantry.net), 1 Main St., South Londonderry. Open daily, 7 AM–8 PM. This superb French deli camouflaged as a Vermont country store is a culinary gem, with a smorgasbord of entrées and salads, cheeses, wines, and fresh-baked desserts. Owner Serge Roche owns the Three Clock restaurant just up the hill.

ICE CREAM AND SNACKS Wilcox Brothers Dairy (802-362-1223), Rt. 7A south, Manchester. Some of the creamiest, most delectable flavors in Vermont are made in this family-owned and -run dairy, available at the grocery store and in a variety of local restaurants. The ice cream stand, open only in summer, is 7 miles south of the blinking light in Manchester on the west side of the road.

Mother Myrick's Confectionary (802-362-1560; 1-888-669-7425; www.mothermyricks.com), Rt. 7A, 4367 Main St., Manchester Center. Sumptuous baked goods, handmade chocolates, and fudge.

✴ Entertainment

MUSIC Vermont Symphony Orchestra (1-800-VSO-9293; www.vso.org). When it's not on tour, especially around the Fourth of July weekend, the symphony's concerts in the arena are major events. Concerts often held at the Hildene Meadowlands. Bring a picnic at 6 PM; concerts at 7:30.

Kinhaven Music School (802-824-4332; 610-868-9200; www.kinhaven .org), Lawrence Hill Rd., Weston, a nationally recognized summer camp for musicians ages 10–19, presents free concerts by students in July, usu-

THE WESTON PLAYHOUSE

Joe Citro

ally Fri. at 4 and Sun. at 2:30. Faculty perform Sat. at 8 PM. Performances are in the Concert Hall, high in the meadow of the school's 31-acre campus. It still looks more like a farm than a school. Picnics are encouraged.

Strattonfest (802-297-0100), Stratton Mountain, July and Aug. This series usually includes folk, jazz, classical, and country-western music on successive weeks.

Manchester Music Festival (802-362-1956; 1-800-639-5868; www .manchestermusicfestival.org), early July–mid-Aug. at the Arkell Pavilion at the Southern Vermont Arts Center, and mid-July–mid-Aug. at the Riley Center for the Performing Arts, Burr and Burton Academy. A 7-week series of evening chamber music concerts. Also fall and winter performances in Manchester and Dorset.

THEATER Dorset Playhouse (802-867-5777; 802-867-2223; www.dorset theatrefestival.com), P.O. Box 510, Cheney Rd., Dorset 05251. The Dorset Players, a community theater group formed in 1927, actually owns the beautiful playhouse in the center of Dorset and produces winter performances there. In summer the Dorset Theatre Festival stages new plays as well as classics, performed by a resident professional group 6 days a week June–early Sep.

Weston Playhouse (802-824-5288; westonplayhouse.org), 703 Main St., Weston. Not long after the Civil War, townspeople built a second floor in their oldest church on the green and turned the lower level into a theater, producing ambitious plays such as Richard Sheridan's *The Rivals*. Theatrics remained a part of community life, and in the 1930s a summer resident financed the remodeling of the defunct church into a real theater. Now billed as "the oldest professional theater in Vermont," the Weston Playhouse has a company composed largely of professional Equity actors and routinely draws rave reviews. Quality aside, Weston couldn't be more off-Broadway. The pillared theater (the facade is that of the old church) fronts on a classic village common and backs on the West River, complete with a waterfall and Holsteins grazing in the meadow beyond. Many patrons come early to dine at Café at the Falls and linger after the show to join cast members at the Cabaret (reservations often necessary). Performances are every night except Mon. (plus Wed. and Sat. matinees), late June–Labor Day weekend, plus a fall production. Tickets run $27–46. A second, smaller stage, **Other Stages**, offers more avant-garde productions.

FILM **Village Picture Shows** (802-362-4771; www.villagepictureshows .com), 263 Depot St., Rt. 30/11, Manchester Center.

✳ Selective Shopping

ANTIQUES SHOPS See *Special Events* for area antiques shows and festivals.

Gristmill Antiques/Hayloft Collectibles (802-375-2500), 316 Old Mill Rd., East Arlington, in Candle Mill Village. Ethan Allen's cousin, Remember Baker, built a gristmill on Peter's Brook in 1764. Two hundred years later it became a candle factory. Now the building is an inviting shop representing several area dealers with an emphasis on 1800s and early-1900s period antiques. **Hayloft Collectibles**

is just next door. Open July–mid-Oct, daily 10:30–5.

The Farm Antiques (802-375-6302), on Rt. 313 west of Rt. 7A in Arlington. Seventeenth-, 18th-, and 19th-century country furniture and decorative and folk arts. Open year-round by appointment.

Danby Antiques Center (802-293-5990), 82 S. Main St., Danby. Open year-round, daily 10–5. American country and formal furniture and accessories from 24 dealers in 11 rooms and the barn. Call ahead for Tue. and Wed. hours Jan.–Mar.

Antiques Fine & Funky (802/293-2154), 134 Depot St., one block west of Rt. 7, Danby. Early American and European furniture, decorative arts, rugs, chinoiserie, Kashmirs, paisleys, and more.

Equinox Antiques and Fine Art (802-362-3540; www.equinox antiques.com), 5063 Main St., Manchester. Open daily 10–5. Fine 18th- and 19th-century furniture and art.

Judy Pascal Antiques (802-362-2004), 145 Elm St., Manchester Center. Antique clothing, fabrics, linens, architectural salvage, painted and garden furniture, ironstone, quilts, hooked and rag rugs, American and English silver, tableware, mirrors, and garden ornaments. Open year-round.

Peg & Judd Gregory (802-325-2400; www.gregoryantiques.com), 2 miles from Dorset Village at the junction of Dorset West Rd. (Rt. 315) and Rt. 30. Quality 17th-, 18th-, and early-19th-century furniture, paintings, folk art, and decorative arts. Call ahead.

Geranium (802-867-5588) in Dorset. Early American and English ceramics, 17th- and 18th-century Dutch and English Delft. By appointment only.

Marie Miller Antique Quilts (802-867-5969; www.antiquequilts.com), 1489 Rt. 30, Dorset. Over 200 antique quilts, all in superb condition, plus hooked rugs, Quimper, and other faience. Open 10–5.

East Arlington Antiques Center (802-375-6144), just off Rt. 7A on East Arlington Rd. Open daily 10–5. Some 70 dealers selling everything from linens to silver, furniture, and art in an old movie theater.

Comollo Antiques (802-362-7188; www.vtantiques.com), 4686 Main St., Manchester Center. Open daily (except Wed.) 10–5. Furniture, paintings, and accessories.

ART GALLERIES **Artists Guild of Manchester** (802-362-4450; www.artistsguildgallery.com), 1011 Depot St. (Rt. 11/30), at the Farmhouse at Manchester Marketplace, Manchester Center. Open daily 9–6, 10–5 on Sun. A gallery of over 40 regional artists, running the gamut from furniture makers to photographers and every kind of craft.

Southern Vermont Arts Center (see *Museums*). In addition to solo shows held throughout the year, the SVAC hosts a Members' Show in early summer and a National Fall Exhibition. There are also outdoor sculpture shows May–Oct., and other special exhibits in winter.

The Norman Rockwell Exhibit (802-375-6423), Rt. 7A, Arlington. Open daily, 9–5; closed Jan. An exhibit of the artist's *Saturday Evening Post* magazine covers; Rockwell lived in this town 1939–1953. Housed in an old church, staffed by locals who knew the artist. Rockwell prints available in gift shop.

Gallery North Star (802-362-4541), 3962 Rt. 7A, Manchester Village. Open daily 11–5. Closed in spring months and Nov. Showcases Vermont-based artists.

Tilting at Windmills Gallery (802-362-3022; www.tilting.com), 24 Highland Ave., Rt. 11/30, Manchester Center. Open daily 10–5, Sun. 10–4. An unusually large gallery with national and international works in oils and egg tempera, mostly realism and impressionism.

Todd Gallery (802-824-5606; www.toddgallery.com), southern edge of the village at 614 Main St. in Weston. Open 10–5, closed Tue.–Wed. Housed in an 1840s carriage barn, this attractive gallery displays owner Robert Todd's representational watercolors of Vermont and Ireland. Also whimsical photography, original sculpture, and unusual pieces crafted by Vermont artists.

BOOKSTORES ✍ **The Northshire Bookstore** (802-362-2200; 1-800-437-3700; www.northshirebookstore.com), 4869 Main St., Manchester Center. Open Tue.–Sat. 10–9, Sun. and Mon. 10–7. One of Vermont's most browse-worthy bookstores. The Morrows have stocked the venerable Colburn House with a wide range of volumes, including used and antiquarian. A broad selection of adult titles, children's books, and records, along with current hits and classics. They schedule frequent author lectures, book signings, and co-sponsored events, and offer breakfast, lunch, and snacks in their **Spiral Press Café** (802-362-9944), open 8 AM–9 PM, until 7 PM Sun. and Mon.

Meander Bookshop (802-362-0700), Elm St., Manchester Center. Open

Sat. and Sun. 11–6. Nice selection of used and rare books.

CRAFTS SHOPS **The Porter House of Fine Crafts** (802-362-4789), Green Mountain Village Shops, Manchester Center. Open daily 10–6. Unusual jewelry and handcrafts, clothing, toys, fabric art, kitchenware, alternative music.

Flower Brook Pottery (802-867-2409), 3210 Rt. 30, Dorset. Open in summer, daily 10–5; in winter, closed Sun. A showroom for Vitriesse Glass, hand-painted pottery, baby clothes, candles, cards, whimsical slippers, and more.

D. Lasser Ceramics (802-824-6183; 1-888-824-6183; www.lasserceramics .com), 6405 Rt. 100, Londonderry. Open daily 9–6. A studio showroom with potters doing their thing, and shelves—inside and out—filled with bright pitchers and platters, bowls and vases, mugs and plates, all highly original and affordable. We're delighted with the multicolored "stix" we bought that hold either candles or flowers.

Vitriesse Glass Studio (802-645-9800), 1258 Bett's Bridge Rd. West Pawlet; call for appointment. Lucy Bergamini's Venetian-inspired glass-bead jewelry is very special. The gallery also carries her blown-glass vessels, goblets, and perfume bottles in richly woven latticino colors.

Danby Marble Company (802-293-5425), 279 Rt. 7 in Danby Village, open 9–5 Sat., 10–5 Sun., closed Nov.–May. At first glance this is just another array of marble bookends, lamps, chessboards, candleholders, trivets, and vases. Look more closely, though, and you'll realize that this is a showcase for marble from throughout the East. (Danby itself is the site of what's billed as "the largest underground marble quarry in the world.") Owner Tom Martin cuts marble to whatever size and shape you want.

Susan Sargent Designs (802-366-8017; www.susansargent.com), at the intersection of Rts. 7A and 11/30, Manchester Village. Open daily 10–6. The store features Sargent's striking designs woven into rugs, pillows, and throws. Other household goods, as well.

FACTORY OUTLETS This contemporary cluster of designer discount stores in Manchester Center evokes mixed feelings from Vermonters. Some chafe at what they consider corporate intrusion into a once quiet village. Others welcome the increased exposure, not to mention the acres of quality goods. In general, the prices are not rock bottom, but better than you'd find in the city. Most are open 10–6 daily, later in summer.

Manchester Designer Outlets (1-800-955-SHOP; www.manchester designeroutlets.com). The glass-and-wood anchor complex at and near the junction of Rts. 7A and 11/30 in Manchester Center presently houses Giorgio Armani, J. Crew, Baccarat, Brooks Brothers, Coach, Anichini, Crabtree & Evelyn, Adrienne Vittadini, Movado, Polo/Ralph Lauren, Reed & Barton, Timberland, and many others.

Battenkill and Highridge Outlet Centers (914-949-5030; www.outlet find.com) houses Tommy Hilfiger, Bose, Dana Buchman, Liz Claiborne, Ellen Tracy, Van Heusen, Natori, DF&C Co., Lancome, Jockey, PacSun, Farberware, Nine West, and more.

Equinox Square (Rt. 11/30) includes Coldwater Creek, Burberry's, Garnet Hill, Carter's, et cetera.

Manchester Marketplace Outlet Shops (next to the Super Shoes Factory Store) harbors more shops.

J. K. Adams Co. and **The Kitchen Store**, Rt. 30. Open daily 9–5:30. A three-floor cornucopia of top-quality kitchen gear, from butcher blocks to knife racks, tableware, and cookbooks, with an observation deck over the woodworking factory. Everything a foodie could want.

GENERAL STORES The Vermont Country Store (802-824-3184), Rt. 100, Weston Village. Open year-round, Mon.–Sat. 9–6. Established by Vrest Orton in 1946 and billed as America's first restored country store, this pioneer nostalgia venture included one of the country's first mail-order catalogs. The original store (actually an old Masonic temple) has since quintupled in size and spilled into four adjacent buildings. The specialty of both the catalog (which accounts for 75 percent of the company's business) and the store is the functional item that makes life easy, especially anything that's difficult to find nowadays—jumbo metal hairpins, hardwood coat hangers, slippery-elm throat lozenges, garter belts. Lyman, the present Orton-in-charge, has a penchant for newfangled gadgets,

THE VERMONT COUNTRY STORE IN WESTON

Diane E. Foulds

such as a plastic frame to hold baseball caps in dishwashers. He's a zealot when it comes to basics that seem to have disappeared, and he frequently finds someone to replicate them, as in the case of the perfect potato masher. The store's own line of edibles features the Vermont Common Cracker, unchanged since 1812, still stamped out in a patented 19th-century machine.

The Weston Village Store (802-824-5477; www.westonvillagestore .com), Rt. 100, Weston. Open daily. A country emporium catering to visitors, boasting the state's largest collection of weather vanes.

J. J. Hapgood Store (802-824-5911), off Rt. 11, Peru. Daily 8–8. Nancy and Frank Kirkpatrick's genuine general store has a potbellied stove, old-fashioned counters covered with food, and some clothing staples; geared to locals as well as tourists.

H. N. Williams General Store (802-867-5353), 2691 Rt. 30, about 2 miles south of Dorset. Open daily. A large white barn of a store housed in what started out as an 1840 harness shop. You can still see the steep staircase to the second floor, where the help lived in the old days. In the same family for six generations, the store sells everything from yard equipment to clothing, fertilizer, tools, and furniture.

Peltier's General Merchandise (802-867-4400), Dorset Village, opposite the Dorset Inn. Daily 7–8. A village landmark since 1816: staples and then some, including gourmet dinners to go, baking to order, Vermont products, wines, and gourmet items like hearts of palm and Tiptree jams. Because there are few lunch or snack shops in Dorset, this also serves the purpose; good for picnic fare.

Mach's General Store (802-325-3405), Rt. 30, Pawlet Village. Daily 6 AM–8 PM. The focal point of this genuine old emporium is described under Pawlet (see *Villages*), but the charm of this family-run place goes beyond its water view. Built as a hotel, it's filled with a wide variety of locally useful merchandise.

SPECIAL SHOPS **Orvis Retail Store** (802-362-3750; www.orvis.com), 4200 Rt. 7A, Manchester Center, supplying the needs of anglers and other sportsmen since 1856. Known widely for its mail-order catalog, Orvis recently opened a luxurious retail store done in the style of a country lodge but still specializing in the fishing rods made in the factory out back. There's also fishing tackle and gear, country clothes, and other small luxury items—from silk underwear to welcome mats—that make the difference in country, or would-be country, living.

Herdsmen Leathers (802-362-2751), Manchester Center. Open daily, year-round, calling itself "New England's finest leather shop": coats, boots, shoes, and accessories; watch for sales.

Two Sisters (802-362-5112; 1-877-362-5112), 4676 Main St., Manchester. Home furnishings including desks, lamps, dressers, furniture, slipcovers, and just about anything else you could think of for your home.

Jelly Mill Marketplace (802-362-3494; www.jellymill.com), Rt. 7A, Manchester Center. Open daily. The Marketplace includes the Jelly Mill Shop, the House Works, the Jewel of the Mill, and the Toy Shoppe.

Equinox Village Shops. This cluster of historic buildings opposite the Equinox hotel in Manchester Village includes gift, clothing, and housewares shops.

Equinox Nursery (802-362-2610; www.equinoxvalleynursery.com), Rt. 7A, south of Manchester. Open daily 8–5, Sun. 9–4. An outstanding farm stand and nursery managed by three generations of the Preuss family; good for picking vegetables, berries in-season. Especially famous in fall for the 100,000 pounds of pumpkins it produces, also for its display of scarecrows and pumpkin faces. Sells pumpkin bread, pie, ice cream, and marmalade, along with other farm stand staples, annuals, perennials, and shrubs. In Jan. and Feb. the family cultivates a tropical conservatory with birds and indoor flowering plants.

East Arlington is a charming hamlet of specialty shops across the street from **Candle Mill Village Antiques**. There's the **Village Peddler** and the **Bearatorium**, a teddy bear shop, and another antiques center around the corner.

Basketville (802-362-1609), on Rt. 7A near Equinox Skyline Dr., offers a plethora of baskets of every size and shape, plus wicker furniture and gifts. Open daily 9–6.

Vermont Country Bird Houses (802-293-5991), 12 N. Main St., Danby. Imaginatively handcrafted birdhouses in various architectural styles, with steeples, cupolas, bell towers, and the like, by Jim Kardas. Open daily 9–4:30.

Bob Gasperetti (802-293-5195; www.gasperetti.com), **Dan Mosheim** (802-867-5541; www.dorsetcustom furniture.com), **Bill Laberge** (802-325-2117; www.williamlaberge.com), **David Spero** (802-824-4550; www .vermontwindsorchairs.com), and **Joe**

Breznik (802-824-3263; www.fine woodenfurniture.com) produce hand-made, heirloom-quality furniture in the Dorset area, and welcome visitors to their showrooms.

✳ Special Events

March: Spring skiing, sugaring.

April: Trout season opens; Easter parades and egg hunts at ski areas. Whitewater canoeing on the West River.

May: **Vermont Symphony Orchestra** performs at Hunter Park; Hildene opens.

June: **Strawberry festivals** in Dorset; the annual **Antique and Classic Car Show** at Hildene (800-362-4144) and **vintage sports car climb** to Equinox Summit; **Hildene Peony Festival**, and the annual **Stratton Quilt Festival**.

July: Manchester and Dorset host an **old-fashioned Fourth**, a daylong celebration that culminates in fireworks. The **Vermont Summer Festival Horse Show** comes to Manchester for 3 weeks.

July–mid-August: **Kinhaven Music School** concert series; **Dorset Playhouse** and **Weston Playhouse** open; a **major antiques show** is held at Hildene Meadows in even years, at Dorset in odd ones. **Manchester Music Festival** breaks out with a series of concerts from early July to mid-August. The **Vermont Symphony Orchestra** takes up residence at Hunter Park. **Strattonfest** at Stratton Mountain Resort, and the **Green Mountain Jazz Festival** at the Southern Vermont Arts Center (802-362-1405).

August: **Southern Vermont Crafts Fair**—juried exhibitors, entertainment, food, and music at Hildene. **Wine & Food Festival** (*second week*) at Stratton Mountain Resort. **Norman's Attic** in Arlington is a townwide tag sale, and the **Manchester Sidewalk Sale** is a garage sale of designer goods.

September: The month is chock-full of antiques shows around the area; the biggest is the annual **Vermont Antiques Dealers Association Show** at Riley Rink in Hunter Park, but there's also one at Hildene. **Peru Fair**—just 1 day (*fourth Saturday*), considered one of Vermont's most colorful (and crowded), it includes a pig roast, crafts, food, and entertainment, followed by the **Bromley Country Fair** (802-824-5522) later in the month.

October: **Hildene Foliage Art & Craft Festival** (*first week*) at Hildene Meadows. **Weston Antiques Show** (*first weekend*), one of the state's oldest and most respected, staged in the Weston Playhouse. The **Weston Crafts Fair** follows during the second week of October.

November: Harvest dinners and wild game suppers abound; check local papers and bulletin boards.

December: A **tour of the historic inns** of Manchester Village takes place the first two Saturdays of December. **Christmas Prelude** (*first three weekends*)—weekend events in Manchester including Vermont's largest potluck dinner. There's a **Winter Solstice Walk** at Merck Forest in Rupert. **Candlelight Tours of Hildene** (*between Christmas and New Year's*)—sleigh rides, refreshments in the barn, music on the organ.

OKEMO VALLEY REGION
INCLUDING LUDLOW, CHESTER, TYSON, AND SHREWSBURY

Okemo is the name of a mountain, not a valley, but it's a major ski mountain and in this era of "branding" the label applies to a large and varied region. Okemo towers 3,300 feet above Ludlow, a lively village on the eastern edge of the Green Mountains. It is, in fact, in the valley named for the Black River, which rises in the chain of ponds and lakes north of town and there joins Jewell Brook, forming the power source for the 19th-century mills around which the town was built. North of Ludlow, Rt. 100 threads the series of lakes in a steep-sided valley while Rt. 103 angles off to climb west through Mount Holly to Belmont, Hortonville, and Shrewsbury—beautiful high country. East of town Rt. 103/131 follow the Black River through the smaller mill villages of Proctorsville and Cavendish. Rt. 103 branches south, following the Williams River to Chester, a handsome old crossroads community with lodging places, restaurants, and shops gathered around its green.

GUIDANCE **Okemo Valley Regional Chamber of Commerce** (802-228-5830; 1-866-216-8722; www.okemovalleyvt.org), P.O. Box 333, Ludlow 05149. This walk-in information office in the Marketplace, across from Okemo Mountain Access Rd. on Rt. 103 (look for the clock tower), has menus, events listings, and lodging brochures. Open except Sunday during summer, fall, and ski season, closed Saturdays too in off-seasons. The chamber maintain information for towns throughout this area and a seasonal information booth on the green in Chester (802-875-2939). Restrooms both places. Request the current issue of the *Okemo Valley Regional Guide*. For lodging in the Chester area, also check out www .chesterlodging.com; for other area lodging, www.okemo.com.

GETTING THERE *By train:* See "Rutland and the Lower Champlain River Valley" for Amtrak express service from New York City to Rutland (25 miles away).

By air: The Albany, Hartford, and Burlington airports are all a 2-hour drive.

By car: From points south, take I-91 to Vermont Exit 6 to Rt. 103 north, which leads you to Chester and on to Ludlow. The area can also be accessed from I-91, Exits 7 and 8.

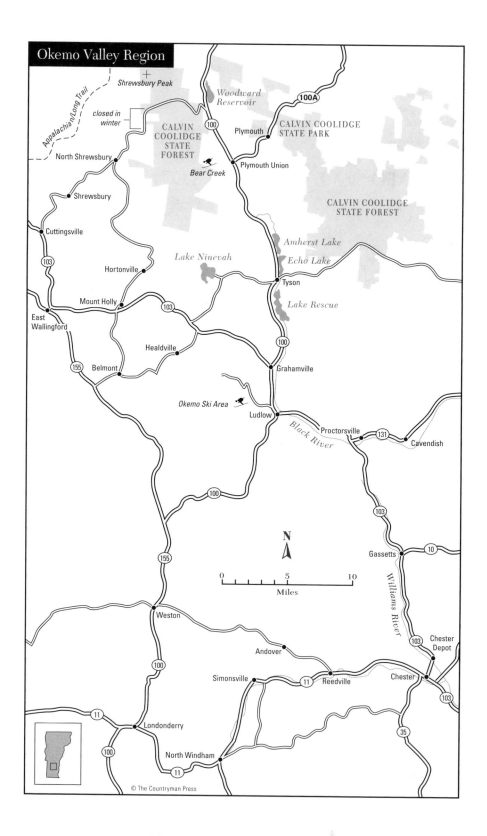

Okemo Valley Region

Shrewsbury Peak

Appalachian/Long Trail

closed in winter

Woodward Reservoir

100A

CALVIN COOLIDGE STATE PARK

North Shrewsbury

100

Plymouth

CALVIN COOLIDGE STATE FOREST

Bear Creek

Plymouth Union

Shrewsbury

CALVIN COOLIDGE STATE FOREST

Cuttingsville

103

Amherst Lake

Echo Lake

Hortonville

Lake Ninevah

Tyson

Mount Holly

103

Lake Rescue

East Wallingford

Healdville

100

155

Belmont

Grahamville

Okemo Ski Area

Ludlow

Proctorsville

131

Cavendish

Black River

100

103

10

N

Gassetts

0   5   10

Miles

Williams River

155

Weston

Chester Depot

100

Andover

103

Simonsville

11

Reedville

Chester

Londonderry

103

11

North Windham

35

100

11

© The Countryman Press

GETTING AROUND **George's Shuttle Service** (1-800-208-3933), based in Weathersfield, provides transport by reservation to and from the railroad stations in Bellows Falls and Rutland, as well as airports throughout New England.

Okemo Mountain Resort (802-228-4041) offers a free shuttle to the village during peak times in ski season.

Ludlow Transport is a free shuttle service that runs several routes throughout Ludlow and the surrounding area. The service operates Mon.–Fri. Pick up the schedule at the chamber of commerce.

WHEN TO GO Nearby lakes make Ludlow as much of a summer destination as Chester and the hill towns. In winter, Okemo is the big draw; cross-country skiers also head for Andover and Shrewsbury. Snowmobile trails crisscross the region.

MEDICAL EMERGENCY Service is available by calling **911**.

✳ Towns and Villages

Ludlow (population: 2,640) boomed with the production of "shoddy" (fabric made from reworked wool) after the Civil War, a period frozen in the red brick of its commercial block, Victorian mansions, magnificent library, and academy (now the Black River Museum). In the wake of the wool boom, the General Electric Company moved into the picturesque mill at the heart of town and kept people employed making small-aircraft engine parts until 1977. Okemo opened in 1956, but for years it was a sleeper—a big mountain with antiquated lifts on the edge of a former mill town. Ski clubs nested in the Victorian homes, and just a few inns catered to serious skiers. Tim and Diane Mueller bought the ski area in 1982, and it has been evolving ever since as one of New England's most popular ski resorts, known for the quality of its snowmaking, grooming, and on-mountain lodging and other facilities. A major golf course has recently been added that doubles as a full-service cross-country ski center.

The effect on Ludlow has been dramatic. The old General Electric plant has been turned into condominiums. Other lodging options as well as restaurants have multiplied. For a sense of Ludlow B.O. (Before Okemo) visit the **Fletcher Library** (802-228-8921), Main St. Open Mon.–Fri. 10–5:30, Sat. 10–1 and 6:30–8:30, it offers reading rooms with fireplaces; old-style, green-shaded lights; and 19th-century paintings of local landscapes. The **Black River Academy Historical Museum** (802-228-5050), 14 High St., is open June–Labor Day, Mon.–Sat. noon–4, then through mid-Oct. just Fri. and Sat., same hours. $2 adults, free under age 12. Built in 1889, the academy's reputation drew students from throughout New England. President Calvin Coolidge was a member of the class of

BLACK RIVER ACADEMY HISTORICAL MUSEUM IN LUDLOW

Christina Tree

CHESTER ART GUILD

Christina Tree

1890. Exhibits about "Main Street" circa 1900 and the third-floor classroom offer a sense of what it meant (and still means) to live in the Black River Valley.

North of town off Rt. 100, rental cottages can be found on all four lakes, as well as on Lake Ninevah in nearby Mount Holly. Given its central location and lodging both on and off the mountain, Ludlow is a good base from which to explore much of southern and central Vermont.

Chester (population: 3,044) encompasses three distinct villages within a few miles, each of them worth noting. The village of Chester itself is a beauty, sited at the confluence of three branches of the Williams River and of five major roads. Its stringbean-shaped village green is lined with shops, restaurants, and lodging places, including the double-porched old Fullerton Inn. Across the street (Rt. 11) is the fine old 19th-century Academy, its ground floor now occupied by the **Chester Art Guild**. Upstairs the **Chester Historical Society** (open June–Oct., Sat.–Sun. 2–5) presents the town's colorful history, including the story of Clarence Adams, a prominent citizen who broke into more than 50 businesses and homes between 1886 and 1902 before being apprehended.

Don't miss Chester's **Stone Village** up on North St. (Rt. 103): a double line of 30 buildings faced in gneiss, a rough-hewn, gleaming mica schist quarried from nearby Flamstead Mountain. Cool in summer, warm in winter, stone houses are a rarity in New England. All of these are said to have been built by two brothers in the pre–Civil War decade, with hiding spaces enough to make them a significant stop on the Underground Railroad.

Midway between Main and North Sts. is **Chester Depot**, a pleasant old traffic center that resembles neither of these places. The well-kept Victorian depot serves as the northern terminus for the **Green Mountain Flyer**, spilling more than 100 passengers at a time to browse and stroll.

SCENIC DRIVES **Okemo Mountain Road** in downtown Ludlow (off Rt. 100/103) follows the Okemo Mountain Access Road beyond the base lodge (stay left). This is a ski trail in winter but in summer and fall offers a hard-topped 2.5-mile route to the summit. There's a small parking lot and a 0.5-mile trail through the woods to a former fire tower that boasts (on a clear day) 360-degree views.

Shrewsbury Loop. From Ludlow head north 2 miles on Rt. 100, then northwest on 103 for 5 miles to Healdville and the sign for the **Crowley Cheese Factory**. In the 1880s every Vermont town had its cheese factory to process surplus milk, but Crowley Cheese, which the family had begun making in the 1820s, was distributed up and down the East Coast. The three-story wooden building, built in 1882 by Winfield Crowley, is now billed as America's oldest cheese factory. It's a 2-mile detour down a side road but well worth the effort.

EXTERIOR OF CROWLEY CHEESE FACTORY
IN HEALDVILLE

Christina Tree

Visitors are welcome weekdays 8–4, but cheese is actually made Tue.– Fri., and the best time to come is around 1 PM when the cheese is being "drained." The shower-capped employees also hand cut and rake the curd, rinsing it with springwater, draining 75 percent of the whey. This is a Colby cheese, which is moister and ages more quickly than cheddar. It takes 5,000 pounds of fresh milk to make 500 pounds of Crowley Cheese. Needless to say, you can pick up samples and reasonably priced "ends." Rt. 103 climbs on to **Mount Holly**, then continues another 5 miles to Cuttingsville. Turn up the road ("Town Hill") posted for Shrewsbury, and right again at the T. **Shrewsbury Center** is marked by a white wooden church set back on a knoll beside two face-to-face taverns, now both B&Bs. One of these, **Maple Crest Farm**, remains in the same family that built it in 1808 and has been taking in guests since the 1860s. Although the dairy herd is gone, this is still a working farm with more than 30 head of beef cattle and some 300 acres in hay. Stop and take in the view and the quiet and long vistas. In **North Shrewsbury**, 2 more miles up the hill, is the **W. E. Pierce General Store** (owned by the Vermont Preservation Society, presently closed), with a '50s gas pump out front. Check out the signs tacked to the a big old fir tree nearby. They point west to Rutland and east to Plymouth Union, confirming the impression that you are standing on the peaked roof of this entire region. Fasten your seat belt and (conditions permitting) plunge east downs the vintage-1930s **CCC Road**, one of Vermont's steepest and most scenic routes. It's 6 miles seemingly straight down—with superlative mountain and valley views—to Rt. 100 in Plymouth. Note the pullout for **Shrewsbury Peak**, trailhead for a steep 1.2-mile path connecting with the Long Trail here. Remarkably enough, this was the site of Vermont's second rope tow, installed in 1935 by the Rutland Ski Club. According to the write-up, some 2,400 spectators came up this road (brand new then, it's closed now in snow season) to watch the skiers come down.

Continue down to Rt. 100A to **Plymouth Union**, perhaps the first rural Vermont village to appear in publications throughout the world—on August 2, 1923, the day Calvin Coolidge was sworn into office here as the 30th U.S. president. It's now the **Calvin Coolidge Historic Site** (for a full description, see "Killington/ Plymouth Area"). Make your way back to Rt. 100; from Plymouth it's a scenic 9-mile ride south past a chain of lakes to Ludlow.

CHEESEMAKERS AT CROWLEY CHEESE FACTORY

Christina Tree

✳ To Do

ADVENTURE SPORTS Extreme Adventures of Vermont (802-875-4451; www
.extremeadventuresvt.com). This Andover-based outfitter offers year-round guided tours: rock climbing, whitewater rafting, kayaking, mountain biking, hiking,
and orienteering in summer and fall; ice climbing, winter caving, mountaineering, snowshoeing, and cross-country skiing in winter.

ARTS AND CRAFTS Fletcher Farm School for the Arts and Crafts (802-
228-8770; www.fletcherfarm.org), Rt. 103 east, Ludlow. Operated since 1947 by
the Society of Vermont Craftsmen, headquartered in an old farmstead on the
eastern edge of town. More than 200 courses in a wide variety of crafts are
offered in summer and more than 100 in winter in traditional crafts, contemporary crafts, and fine art. In summer lodging and meals are available on campus;
fall through spring, multiday workshops are offered at area inns. Crafts include
fiber arts, basketry, theorem painting, glass, weaving, woodcarving, quilting, oil
and watercolor painting, spinning, rug hooking and braiding, and more. Many
classes are also offered fall–spring at Fletcher Farm.

BIKING Mountain Cycology (802-228-2722), 5 Lamere Square, Ludlow. No
rentals but equipment, repair, guidebooks, and local advice as well as sales.
Rentals are available from **Joe Jones Sports** (802-228-5440), 57 Pond St., Ludlow. **Bike Vermont** (1-800-257-2226; www.bikevermont.com) offers a choice of
inn-to-inn tours in this area.

BOATING Echo Lake Inn (802-228-8602), Rt. 100, Tyson, rents canoes and
other boats to guests only. **Camp Plymouth State Park** (802-228-2025) off
Rt. 100 in Tyson also offers seasonal canoe, kayak, and rowboat rentals (see
Swimming for directions). Nearby **Lake Ninevah** (turn off Rt. 103 just past
Harry's Café onto Shunpike Rd., then right again onto Ninevah Rd.) is quieter,
with some beautiful marshes and woods. **Hawk Inn and Mountain Resort**
(802-672-3811) in Plymouth also rents boats. For paddling sites see www.okemo
valleyvt.org/activities/paddle.html.

FISHING Public access has been provided to Lake Rescue, Echo Lake, Lake
Ninevah, Woodward Reservoir, and Amherst Lake. Fishing licenses are required
except under age 16. The catch includes rainbow trout, bass, and pickerel. There
is also fly-fishing in the Black River along Rt. 131 in Cavendish, and the 6-mile
stretch from the covered bridge in Downers down to a second covered bridge is
stocked and maintained as a trophy trout section, stocked each spring with 1.5-
pound brown trout and 18-inch rainbows.

GOLF The **Okemo Valley Golf Club** (802-228-1396; www.golf.okemo.com),
Fox Lane, Ludlow. An 18-hole championship "heathland-style" course featuring
wide fairways with dips, ripples, rolls, and hollows said to suggest Scottish links.
The **Okemo Valley Golf Academy** also utilizes an 18-acre outdoor Golf Learning Center with a 370-yard-long driving range, four practice greens, a 6,000-
square-foot indoor practice area, a computerized virtual golf program, class-

rooms, and changing rooms with showers. The Club House includes a fully stocked Pro Shop and Willie Dunne's Grille (see *Eating Out*).

Tater Hill Golf Club (802-875-2517), 6802 Popple Dungeon Rd., North Windham (off Rt. 11, not far from Chester). A recently renovated 18-hole course with a pro shop and practice range, now owned by Okemo.

HORSEBACK RIDING AND HORSE-DRAWN RIDES **Cavendish Trail /Horse Rides** (802-226-7821), Twenty Mile Stream Rd., Proctorsville, offers guided tours and pony and wagon rides through fields and hills.

Hawk Inn and Mountain Resort on Rt. 100 in Plymouth (see "Killington/ Plymouth Area") also offers trail rides.

SPA **Castle Hill Spa** (802-226-7419; www.castlehillresortandspa.com), junction of Rts. 103 and 131, Cavendish. An aesthetically pleasing center set apart from the inn and open to the public. The outdoor pool and whirlpool are heated for year-round use, the workout room offers aerobics classes as well as Nautilus equipment ,and the Aveda spa offers a variety of wraps and massages; there's also a salon and Har-Tru tennis courts.

SWIMMING ✓ **West Hill Recreation Area** (802-228-2849), West Hill off Rt. 103 in Ludlow, includes a beach (with lifeguard) on a small, spring-fed reservoir; also a snack bar and playground/picnic area. Fee charged.

Buttermilk Falls, near the junction of Rts. 100 and 103. This is a swimming hole and a series of small but beautiful falls (turn at the VFW post just west of the intersection).

✓ **Camp Plymouth State Park** (802-228-2025). Turn east over the bridge off Rt. 100 across from the Echo Lake Inn at Tyson. Continue 1 mile to the crossroads, then turn left onto Boy Scout Camp Rd. There's a sandy beach on Echo Lake, picnic area, boat rentals, volleyball, horseshoes, and playground. Try panning for gold in Buffalo Brook. **Star Lake** in the village of Belmont in Mount Holly is also a great place for a swim.

WALKING **Vermont Inn to Inn Walking, Hiking & Biking** (1-800-728-0842; www.vermontinntoinnwalking.com). Four-night, inn-to-inn walking tours (3 to 10 miles per day) are offered among four area inns (Rowell's Inn, the Combes Family Inn, the Inn Victoria, and Old Town Farm). Luggage is transported for you, and a trail snack is provided. $499 per person includes lodging, breakfast, and dinner.

✳ Winter Sports

CROSS-COUNTRY SKIING AND SNOWSHOEING **Okemo Valley Nordic Center** (802-228-1396; www.okemo.com), junction of Rts. 100 and 103, Ludlow. A café and a rental shop are surrounded by the open roll of the golf course; there are also wooded and mountain trails adding up to 26 km (including 20 km of skating lanes), plus 10 km of dedicated snowshoe trails. The clubhouse offers a

DOWNHILL SKIING

🎿 **Okemo** (802-228-4041 information; 802-228-5222 snow report; 1-800-78-OKEMO reservations; www.okemo.com). A big mountain with southern Vermont's highest vertical drop, Okemo is a destination ski and snowboard resort with a small-resort, family feel. This is a ski area of many parts—in fact five distinct areas: Jackson Gore Peak, Solitude Peak, South Face, Glades Peak, and South Ridge. Recent addition Jackson Gore is still big news in 2006, adding a second entrance (on Rt. 103) and base area infrastructure, including the Jackson Gore Inn with its own fitness center and restaurants.

Family owned and operated since 1982 by Tim and Diane Mueller, Okemo is far larger than it looks from its base. Surprises begin at the top of the initial chairlifts, where you meet a wall of three-story condominiums and find your way down to the spacious Sugar House base lodge—from which the true size of the mountain becomes apparent. From the summit, beginners can actually run a full 4.5 miles to the base; there are also a number of wide, central fall-line runs down the face of Okemo. World Cup is a long and steep but forgiving run with sweeping views down the Black River Valley to the Connecticut River.

Lifts: 18: 9 quad chairs (including 5 high-speed quads), 3 triple chairs, and 6 surface lifts.

Trails and slopes: 117 slopes trails and glades—32 percent novice, 38 percent intermediate, 30 percent advanced expert.

Vertical drop: 2,200 feet (highest in southern Vermont).

Snowmaking: Covers 95 percent of trails (589 acres).

Facilities: Base lodge with cafeteria; midmountain Sugar House base lodge with café, Smokey Jo's BBQ, Ozone Pizza Pub, deli; Summit Lodge with café, Sky Bar, Jumps (Asian specialties); Solitude Day Lodge with

fireplace, restaurant and lounge, changing rooms, rentals, and showers. $20 adult, $15 for a half day.

Also see **Grafton Ponds Recreation Center** in Grafton (in "Lower Connecticut River Valley") and **Viking Nordic Centre** in Londonderry (in "Manchester and the Mountains").

SNOWMOBILE RIDES **Okemo Snowmobile Tours** (802-422-2121; 1-800-FAT-TRAK; www.snowmobilevermont.com) at Okemo Mountain Resort. The "Mountain Tour" is a 1-hour tour through the woods, while the "Back Country Tour" is a 25-mile ride into the Calvin Coolidge State Forest for beginner through expert. From $39 for a passenger with guide for the 1-hour tour to $164 for two riders and guide.

DOWNHILL SKIING AT OKEMO
Okemo Mountain

Gables restaurant, snack bar, and outdoor BBQ (open 11–3). At Jackson Gore you'll find the Roundhouse, Vermont Pizza Co., and Coleman Brook Tavern (see *Dining Out*); Waffle House is at the bottom of the Black Ridge Triple.

Ski school: Okemo's Cutting Edge Learning Center is staffed by 250 instructors. Children's programs include Snow Star Skiers (ages 4–7), Young Mountain Explorers (7–12), and Get Altitude (3–16). Children's snowboard programs are Snow Star Riders (5–7) and Young Riders (7–12). Ski and snowboard programs include Women's Alpine Adventures (2- to 5-day intensive programs) and Adult Snowboard Camps. Senior discounts are available on group lessons; an Adaptive Program includes discounted ski and snowboard lessons (reservations required) and tickets. The state-approved Penguin Day Care Center serves children 6 months–6 years and offers supervised indoor and outdoor activities. A Mini Stars ski program is also available for ages 3–4. Inquire about Kids' Night Out programs, available 6–10 PM in-season.

Lift tickets: Adult $63 midweek, $69 weekend and holiday; ages 13–18 and 70+, $53 midweek, $59 weekend; 7–12, $41 and $45. Kids 6 and under ski free. Savings on multiday tickets are substantial.

☀ Lodging

RESORTS Okemo Mountain Resort (802-228-5571; 1-800-78-OKEMO; www.okemo.com), Ludlow 05149. Open year-round, featuring winter skiing and summer golf, with lodging options that include nearly 700 condominium units, along with **Jackson Gore Inn**, a 123-room condo-style lodge at the Jackson Gore Base Area with restaurants, a reception area, health club, and underground parking; and **Okemo Mountain Lodge**, a three-story hotel at the entrance to the resort that's really a cluster of 55 one-bedroom condos, each with a sleeping couch in the living room. There's a compact kitchen with eating counter and a fireplace; enough space for a couple and two children. **Kettle Brook** has one-, two-, and three-bedroom units, all nicely built, salted along trails. **Winterplace**, set high on a mountain shelf, consists of

17 buildings with a total of 250 units ranging in size from two bedrooms to three bedrooms plus a loft. Residents have access to a fitness center with indoor pool. **Solitude Village** is a ski-in/ski-out complex of one- to five-unit condos and town houses plus a lodge with indoor/outdoor heated pool and a service area with a restaurant, ski shop, and children's learning center. **Ledgewood Condominiums** are three- and four-bedroom units with garages accessed by their own trail. Rentals also are available through **Strictly Rentals** (1-800-776-5149; www.strictlyrentals.com) in downtown Ludlow. See *Condominiums* (below) and *Downhill Skiing* (above).

Also see **Hawk Inn and Mountain Resort** in Plymouth, described in "Killington/Plymouth Area."

INNS The Governor's Inn (802-228-8830; 1-800-GOVERNOR; www .thegovernorsinn.com), 86 Main St., Ludlow 05149. Open year-round except Dec. 23–26. William Wallace Stickney, governor of Vermont 1900–1902, built this Victorian house with its ornate slate, hand-painted fireplaces. Now it's owned by Jim and Cathy Kubec. The eight upstairs guest rooms are furnished with antiques, and an inviting suite in the rear of the house features a whirlpool bath and sitting area. Jessica's Room has a jetted tub for two; six rooms have gas fireplace. The living room is small but elegant. Full bar service is offered to guests in the den. Dinner, prepared by Cathy, is an elegant, six-course event that might begin with artichoke hearts in puff pasty pockets with a Vermont cheese custard, feature crispy duckling, and end with Kentucky bourbon pecan pie. It's offered Saturday and on

special occasions, for guests only. A three-course breakfast is in a cheery back room, warmed by the sun and a woodstove. A serious tea is served in the front parlor. Cathy also does picnic baskets with a little prior notice, and she runs very popular cooking weekends. $165–315 B&B double in fall and winter, $129–249 in regular season, $164–319 during foliage and ski seasons; add $90 per couple MAP plus 18 percent dinner gratuity.

⊙ **The Castle** (802-226-7361; 1-800-438-7908; www.thecastle-vt.com), P.O. Box 525, Proctorsville 05149. Quarry and timber baron Allen Fletcher, elected governor of Vermont in 1913, built this imposing neo-Jacobean stone manor on a knoll, importing European artisans in 1901 for the oak and mahogany woodwork and detailed cast-plaster ceilings. The 10 rooms are regal, 6 with gas or wood-burning fireplace and 4 with whirlpool bath. Rates $149–300; ask about spa, ski, and a variety of other packages. The Castle owners have acquired the neighboring Clarion Hotel at Cavendish Pointe (see *Motels*) on Rt. 103, which currently serves as their check-in desk. Also inquire about lodging in "resort homes" currently under development on the inn's property. See the day spa under *To Do* and the well-respected restaurant under *Dining Out*. Weddings and civil union celebrations for up to 200 are also a specialty, with facilities to accommodate many guests.

The Andrie Rose Inn (802-228-4846; 1-800-223-4846; www.andrie roseinn.com), 13 Pleasant St., Ludlow 05149. Michael and Irene Maston preside over this complex on a quiet back street with unexpectedly luxurious rooms and suites and a reputation for fine dining. The inn itself is a turn-of-the-20th-century house in which the old detailing has been carefully preserved, but the feel—thanks to skillful decor and skylights—is light-filled and cheerful. Five of the nine upstairs guest rooms have whirlpool tub, and all are furnished with antiques and designer linens. Summit View features a skylight framing the summit of the mountain. Next door the Federal-style Guesthouse contains townhouse suites geared to families (each with kitchen facility and washer/dryer) as well as suites for two; also next door is Solitude, an 1840s Greek Revival building with seven luxury suites featuring bedside whirlpool tub for two facing a gas fireplace. See *Dining Out* for details about dinner. Guests in the main house breakfast in the dining room, while those without kitchen facilities in the neighboring buildings receive breakfast in a basket. Amenities include shuttle service to and from Okemo. Rates are $90–350 in low season, $120–725 in high season.

ⓂⓈ **Echo Lake Inn** (802-228-8602; 1-800-356-6844; www.echolakeinn .com), Rt. 100 in Tyson, but the mailing address is P.O. Box 154, Ludlow 05149. One of the few survivors of the many nineteenth-century summer hotels that once graced Vermont lakes, this is a gem, a white-clapboard, four-story inn, rambling on from its 1820 core, through the 1840s, finishing with Victorian-style dormers and a long porch, lined in summer with pink geraniums and vintage red rockers. Now winterized, it offers 23 rooms, all with private bath, and seven condo units in the adjacent Cheese Factory and Carriage House. With good taste and carpentry skills innkeepers Laurence Jeffery and Peter Modisette

have brought it back up a notch or two. The living room with its hearth and richly upholstered couches is once more elegant as well as comfortable, and there's an inviting pub as well as a low-beamed dining room that's been recognized as outstanding (see *Dining Out*). Guest rooms vary far more widely than in most inns, from country traditional (iron bedstead, small-print wallpaper, and genuine 19th-century cottage furnishings), to romantic come-ons with king-sized beds and jetted tubs in the room, to spacious family suites with several beds. Amenities include a spa room, tennis courts, an outdoor pool, and a dock on Echo Lake across the road, with rowboats and canoes. Rates also vary widely: $99–209 per couple in summer, $149–219 in fall, from $109 in winter and from $79 in "value season," full breakfast included. Inquire about MAP rates and special packages.

Ⓜ **The Inn at Water's Edge** (802-228-8143; 1-800-706-9736; www.inn atwatersedge.com), 45 Kingdom Rd., Ludlow 05149. The aforementioned water is Echo Lake, and Bruce and Tina Verdrager have taken full advantage of the location, offering canoeing and fly-fishing as well as bicycles for guests. The expansive,

ECHO LAKE INN

Christina Tree

150-year old home has 11 smallish but well-appointed rooms and suites, 10 with Jacuzzi and many with gas fireplace. Doc's English Pub is a good spot for lounging, and guests sit down to a four-course candlelit dinner. Rates are $200–300 plus 15 percent gratuity, including breakfast and dinner; inquire about B&B rates and midweek summer specials.

∞ **Cavendish Inn** (802-226-7080; www.cavendishinnvt.com), 1589 Main St., Cavendish 05142. A Gothic mansion built splendidly and romantically of local stone (it was named Glimmerstone) for the local mill owner, completed (it took 5 years) in 1845. Brothers Tim and Pete Jefferson, both with a (California) background in food and hospitality, seem the right people to open its nine charming rooms (we prefer the six in the inn to the three in the carriage house) to guests and its many-windowed dining room to patrons. With the barn and back terrace as additional dining and dancing space, this is now also a standout venue for weddings. Rooms are $99–199. Also see *Dining Out.*

The Fullerton Inn (802-875-2444; 1-866-884-8578; www.fullertoninn .com), 40 The Common, P.O. Box 968, Chester 05143. Bret and Nancy Rugg now own this big, old-fashioned, 1920s-style inn on the Chester green. It's so much the heart of town that we are sad to see it locked during the middle of the day, a sign of our paranoid times. The Ruggs have renovated many of the 21 guest rooms (private baths), adding crisp paper and fabrics, sitting rooms, and ceiling fans. Common space includes the immense old lobby, a huge stone fireplace, informal as well as formal dining (see *Dining Out*), and a sunny breakfast room. No

children under age 13. $99–179 for rooms and suites, $109–189 during foliage and ski seasons.

BED & BREAKFASTS

In the Ludlow area

❦ **The Okemo Inn** (802-228-8834; 1-800-328-8834 out of state; www.okemo inn.com), junction of Rts. 100 north and 103, Ludlow 05149. Open year-round except for 2 weeks in Apr. and Nov. Ron Parry has been the innkeeper here since 1972, and his 1810 home has the feeling of a well-kept lodge, effortlessly welcoming. There are 11 nicely furnished guest rooms, 2 on the ground level, most with kings and queens, all with private bath. In the living room a table in front of the hearth is made from old bellows, and the dining room has low, notched beams; there's also a TV room, a sauna, and in summertime a pool. $110–175 per day B&B per couple includes a full breakfast. Inquire about ski, golf, and crafts packages.

♿ **Golden Stage Inn** (802-226-7744; 1-800-253-8226; www.goldenstage inn.com), P.O. Box 218, 399 Depot St., Proctorsville 05153. Sandy and Peter Gregg are at the helm of this handsome, historic house. An inn in the 18th century, it belonged to the Skinner family for 100 years, beginning in 1830. There are two suites and eight guest rooms, one named for the writer and performer Cornelia Otis Skinner. Dining areas include the solarium, the inn's greenhouse. The inn is centrally air-conditioned and wheelchair accessible; a swimming pool is set in gardens. Ski packages $79–300 B&B, MAP available.

❀ ✐ **The Combes Family Inn** (802-228-8799; 1-800-822-8799), 953 East Lake Rd., Ludlow 05149. Ruth and

Bill Combes have celebrated their 28th anniversary as innkeepers, welcoming families to their peaceful 1891 former dairy farm home. There are 11 guest rooms, all with private bath—6 in the farmhouse and 5 in an attached unit (where pets are allowed). B&B double rates are $75 spring, $96 summer, $114–165 winter. Ruth's delicious Vermont-country dinners are available nightly by reservation at $16 per adult and $8 for kids.

Whitney Brook (802-226-7460; www.whitneybrook.com), 2423 Twenty Mile Stream Rd., Proctorsville 05153. Jim and Ellen Parrish welcome guests to their pretty 1870 farmhouse on a quiet road. There are four guest rooms, three with queen beds and one with a double and a single. Two rooms have private bath, two share. Guests enjoy a private living room downstairs and a sitting room upstairs. $70–115 per room includes full breakfast.

In Chester (www.chesterlodging.com)

♿ **Inn Victoria** (802-875-4288; 1-800-732-4288; www.innvictoria.com), 321 Main St., Chester 05143. Yellow brick with purple shutters, a mansard roof, and columned porch, this showy Victorian on the Chester green has seven antiques-furnished guest rooms and a suite. All rooms have queen-sized bed, three have Jacuzzi, and the first-floor garden room is handicapped accessible. Innkeepers Jon and Julie Pierce hail from Cambridge, England, and their Vermont connection is unusual—a story you should get them to tell. They are enthusiastic and thoughtful hosts (there's a stocked guest fridge), serving a full breakfast at the dining room table. No children under 15, please. Request a room with access to hot tub on the back deck. From $120

for a small room to $215 for a suite, breakfast included.

Henry Farm Inn (802-875-2674; 1-800-723-8213; www.henryfarminn.com), 2206 Green Mountain Turnpike, Chester 05143. There's a nice out-in-the-country feel to this old tavern, set in 56 rolling acres. Larger than other farmhouses of the period, it was built in 1760 as a stagecoach stop on the Green Mountain Turnpike (now a quiet dirt road but minutes from the edge of Chester village green). It retains its pine floors, beehive oven, and sense of pleasant, uncluttered simplicity. The nine rooms are large, all with small bathroom. Two of the rooms are suites with kitchen, accommodating three or four. What you notice are the quilts and the views. A path leads to the spring-fed pond up the hill, and a swimming hole in the Williams River is just across the road. Inquire about frequent quilting workshop weekends. Your hosts are Patricia and Paul Dexter and their enterprising son Joseph. Children welcome. $90–135 for rooms, $110–155 for suites includes a country breakfast.

Stone Cottage Collectables (802-875-6211; www.stonecottagebb.net), 196 North St., Chester 05143. Chris and Ann Curran are your hosts at this 1840 stone house in Chester's Stone Village historic district. Three sitting rooms are furnished with antiques and collectibles; you'll also find a pleasant patio, deck, and garden. There are two guest rooms with private bath, but the find here is a glorious queen-bedded room with fireplace created by the late owner, best-selling author Olivia Goldsmith (*The First Wives Club*). Room rates, including full breakfast, are $95–125. The Currans also operate a shop here, featuring radios and tubes, cameras, and stamps as well as antiques.

Chester House Inn (802-875-2205; 1-888-875-2205; www.chesterhouse inn.com), 266 Main St., on the green, Chester 05143. Common space includes a keeping room with fireplace (beer and wine are served). Paul Lantieri and Bill Lundy offer seven rooms in all. Room 1 has a queen bed and a whirlpool bath; Room 2, queen bed plus steam bath and sitting area; Room 4, queen bed, sitting area, and whirlpool. All have telephone and air-conditioning. $95–195 B&B. Inquire about ski packages.

✍ **Hugging Bear Inn & Shoppe** (802-875-2412; 1-800-325-0519; www .huggingbear.com), 244 Main St., Chester 05143. A teddy bear lover's haven with bears on the beds of six guest rooms (private bath). The place teems with them: teddy bear wallpaper, teddy bear sheets and shower curtains, and more than 6,000 stuffed bears in the shop behind the kitchen. Georgette Thomas believes that people don't hug enough. Everyone is invited to hug any bear in the house, and the atmosphere here is contagiously friendly. Rates are $65–95 single, $90–155 double; the higher rates are for a suite. Full breakfast is included.

Park Light Inn (802-875-4417; 1-888-875-4417; www.parklightinn .com), 232 Depot St., Chester 05143. New owners Jack and Jo-Ann Silver came from Staten Island to renovate this old inn with five guest rooms (private bath) plus two suites with sitting room (one with a Jacuzzi). $95–243 in high season, $85–215 in low.

Night With A Native Bed & Breakfast (802-875-2616; www .nightwithanative.com), P.O. Box 327,

266 Depot St., Chester 05143. Doris Hastings is a sixth-generation Vermonter who obviously enjoys accommodating guests in a house that conveys a lively interest in many things. The two small, antiques-decorated bedrooms have private bath. Breakfast is included. $75–95 per couple. Children 12 and over.

Up in the hills west of Ludlow

ಞ **Crisanver House** (802-492-3589; 1-800-492-8089; www.crisanver.com), 1434 Crown Point Rd., Shrewsbury 05738. Set high on 120 acres of woods and meadows, with panoramic views, this is a find—but it's booked many weekends for weddings. The totally renovated 1802 portion of the house offers eight attractive guest rooms, all with down comforters and pillows, exposed beams, original art, robes, and individual heat control. The casually elegant living room has a fireplace and grand piano, and a downstairs game room has table tennis and a pool table. The building was a summer inn, the Tip Top House, when Carol and Michael Calotta bought it in 1971, along with friends who were looking for a ski house. The following winter, however, they discovered the chill meaning of "unwinterized." It's since been totally renovated, also deftly restored. We prefer the upstairs front rooms with a view off across Lake Champlain to the Adirondacks, but the most luxurious are two mini suites with Jacuzzi and heated towel rack in the bathroom. A barn has been designed to accommodate 120 people for weddings and parties. In summer there's a heated pool and an all-weather tennis court; in winter, cross-country skiing and snowshoeing; Okemo and Killington are also within striking distance. A five-course dinner

Maple Crest Farm (802-492-3367), 2512 Lincoln Hill Rd., Shrewsbury 05738. Open year-round except Jan. This handsome, white-brick farmhouse sits high on a ridge in the old hilltop center of Shrewsbury. It was built in 1808 as Gleason's Tavern and is still in the same family—they began taking in guests in the 1860s and have done so off and on ever since. The Smiths offer three antiques-filled rooms (the front ground-floor room with a half bath is our favorite) sharing two baths, and two charming apartments that can accommodate small families. "Every piece of furniture has a story," says Donna Smith—and she knows each one. Ask about a rocking chair or spool bed, and you'll begin to sense who has lived in this unusual house down through the years. Books and magazines are everywhere, focusing on local and Vermont tales and history. The Smiths raise beef cattle and hay, and are noted for the quality of their maple syrup, produced in the sugar-house at the peak of the hill; the same sweeping view can be enjoyed in winter on cross-country skis. You can walk off in any number of directions. $60–100 per room. Breakfast is included. Inquire about theorem painting workshops. No credit cards.

MAPLE CREST FARM

Christina Tree

can be arranged (BYOB) at $37.50 per person. Rates, including a full breakfast, tea, and transfers to bus, train, and airport, are $150–170 for rooms, $110–225 with private bath, $205–265 for suites, less midweek and single. Minimum 2-night stay on weekends.

Balm of Gilead B&B (802-492-7010), 774 CCC Rd., Shrewsbury 05738. A new but traditionally and beautifully designed home high on the steep dirt road (see *Scenic Drives*) between Shrewsbury and Plymouth. Sarah Schiermeyer offers the Pink Suite, the Blue Suite, and the Green Room for $200–350, depending on the season, including breakfast and supper. The great room has a Steinway grand piano and a billiards table. The views out the windows are of mountains, mountains, and more mountains.

The Buckmaster Inn (802-492-3720; www.buckmasterinn.com), 20 Lottery Rd., Shrewsbury 05738. Built as the three-story Buckmaster Tavern beside the Shrewsbury church in 1801, the house is owned by Richard and Elizabeth Davis, who have lightened and brightened its decor. Eight to 10 guests can be accommodated in four rooms (private bath). There is a spacious living room, a library with fireplace and TV/DVD player, and a long, screened-in porch that's especially inviting in summer and fall. The Davises are enthusiastic hosts who can tell you what to see and do. $105–125 double includes a full breakfast featuring home-baked goodies.

CuttingsGate (1-800-667-0208; www.cuttingsgate.com), 24 Spring Lake Rd., Shrewsbury 05738. Set back from Rt. 103 a mile or so west of Cuttingsville, this is a striking old farmstead that Susan and Jim Reid have renovated nicely. They offer four guest rooms in the house ($60–180) as well as a cottage suite ($120–180). The 25-acre property includes a pond and walking/snowshoe paths.

Out in the country

Rowell's Inn (802-875-3658; 1-800-728-0842; www.rowellsinn.com), 1834 Simonsville Rd. (Rt. 11), Andover 05143. Open year-round. This distinctive, double-porched, brick stage stop has been serving the public off and on since 1820. Its most colorful era, according to innkeeper Michael Brengolini, was that of early auto touring, which happened to overlap with Prohibition. Photos show patrons of the day arriving with their chauffeurs, and Rowell's looms large on an "Ideal Tour" map, with few other stops in Vermont. Located midway among Londonderry, Weston, and Chester, the inn is off by itself with some fine walks and cross-country skiing out the back door. Mike and wife Susan McNulty (who offers acupuncture and Reiki) have seven comfortable guest rooms with private bath, one with a working fireplace. Two roomy spaces on the third floor have been carved from the old ballroom, furnished grandly with antiques and Oriental rugs. Ample common space includes an English-style pub. Mike, the former owner of a San Francisco restaurant, offers a single-entrée dinner Friday and Saturday nights (24-hour reservations required) and during the week by reservation to groups of six or more. A $25 four-course meal might begin with cheese pie, featuring cognac-glazed Cornish hens as the entrée. Inquire about "Mad Mike's Hot Sauce." $85–150 per couple includes a full country breakfast.

The Inn at High View (802-875-2724; www.innathighview.com), 753 East Hill Rd., Andover 05143. This is certainly "up in the hills but in a different direction" (southeast of Ludlow) than the B&Bs mentioned above. It's an attractive inn set high on 72 acres of East Hill. A portion of the house dates from the 18th century, but it's been a ski lodge for decades, one of the first to cater to cross-country skiers. In summer a pool and Jacuzzi are set in the rock gardens. Massage, Reiki, and spa treatments are offered. $135–185 includes breakfast.

Popple Fields (802-875-4219; www.popplefields.com), P.O. Box 636, 1300 Popple Dungeon Rd., Chester 05143. It took Conrad Delia 10 years (1989–1999) to build this amazing reproduction 18th-century house, and it's a beauty, remarkable for its detailing, right down to a Colonial-style bar. It's on a back road, set in 18 rolling acres. There are four guest rooms, two with private bath, and Conrad has made much of the furniture, too (he operates a Windsor chair and cabinet shop on the premises). Marylin Delia serves a full buffet breakfast in the large country kitchen. No children under 15, please. $100–160. Inquire about the property's two-bedroom cottage, a real gem.

⊕ ☜ ☙ ✍ **Old Town Farm Inn** (802-875-2346; 1-888-232-1089; www .otfi.com), 665 Rt. 10, Chester 05143. This former "Town Farm" is in Gassetts, a village midway between Chester and Ludlow. Long known to families as a reasonably priced ski lodge, the old place with its wideboard floors has been nicely rehabbed by Michiko and Alex Hunter. There are now seven comfortable guest rooms, all with private bath. It's set in 11 acres with a pond. $79–99 per couple in summer/fall and $119–139 in ski season with breakfast; $10 per extra person. This is also now a popular place to dine on sushi (see *Dining Out*). The pond is becoming a popular place for weddings and reunions (with a pondside BBQ).

Also see **The Inn at Cranberry Farm** in the "Lower Connecticut River Valley" chapter. It's in physically in Rockingham, equally distant from Chester, Grafton, and Bellows Falls.

MOTELS ✍ **Clarion Hotel at Cavendish Pointe** (802-226-7688; 1-800-438-7908; www.cavendishpointe .com), Rt. 103, Cavendish 05142. A contemporary motor inn with 70 fairly large rooms equipped with cable TV, speakerphone, fridge, and coffeemaker. Facilities include an indoor pool, hot tub/spa room, business center, and game room; a restaurant/bar is open only during ski season. Breakfast year-round. $109–159 in summer, $119–219 in winter.

☙ ✍ **Timber Inn Motel** (802-228-8666; www.timberinn.com), 112 Rt. 103, Ludlow 05149. This 17-room

cedar and knotty-pine motel on the Black River is on the eastern fringe of town with surprisingly good views, a winter shuttle-bus stop for Okemo. Hot tub and sauna in winter, heated outdoor pool in summer, rooms with phone, AC, and cable TV; there are some two-bedroom, two-bath units, as well as a two-bedroom apartment with full kitchen (winter season). Dogs are accepted by reservation ($10 per night). $69–199 includes morning coffee and teas.

✻ Where to Eat

DINING OUT **Echo Lake Inn** (802-228-8602; 1-800-356-6844; www.echo lakeinn.com), Rt. 100 north in Tyson. Open to the public for dinner. The dining room, with print wallpaper and shades of mauve, is attractive. Chef Kevin Barnes has established an enviable reputation over the past 17 years. The à la carte menu offers genuine choice and usually includes a freshly made vegetarian pasta dish, such as grilled asparagus and smoked mozzarella ravioli; and a local game dish, maybe medallions of Vermont venison wrapped in maple-smoked bacon or a roast country duckling served with the day's sauce. Entrées $18–25.

The Castle Resort and Spa (802-226-7361), intersection of Rts. 131 and 103, Proctorsville. Open for dinner Thu.–Sat. The interior of this stone mansion is a rich blend of American oak, Mexican mahogany, and French marble. The à la carte menu ranges from vegetable cassoulet to baked Atlantic salmon Wellington (with crabmeat, spinach, and shallots in a puff pastry) and broiled Black Angus sirloin. Entrées $20–27.

The Andrie Rose Inn (802-228-4846; www.andrieroseinn.com). Open to the public by reservation (before 3 PM) Fri.–Sat. with a set, four-course dinner at $46 per person (three-course, $40). Chef-owner Irene Maston's menu on a fall Friday included a choice of Cavendish Farm quail with apricot glaze and rosemary demiglaze, and prosciutto-wrapped scallops with roasted red pepper sauce.

Coleman Brook Tavern (802-228-1435), Jackson Gore Inn, Rt. 103, Ludlow. This is the signature restaurant in Okemo's new base complex and it's sleekly comfortable, with sofas, wing chairs, and dim lighting to mitigate its size. The cherrywood-paneled Wine Room is the most intimate setting. The menu ranges from vegetarian strudel to steak, pan-seared with a green peppercorn sauce. Entrées $15–22. A Wednesday "Lobster Fest" with steamers, mussels, and all the fixings is $14.95.

Tokai-Tei Japanese Restaurant at the Old Town Farm Inn (802-875-2346; 1-888-232-1089), 665 Vermont Rt. 10, Chester. Open Thu.–Sun. 5–9 by reservation. Halfway between

NORTH SHREWSBURY ROAD SIGN

Christina Tree

Chester and Ludlow isn't exactly where you expect to find a first-rate Japanese restaurant, but that's where Michiko Hunter presides over the kitchen of this old family-geared lodge, turning out tantalizing and reasonably priced sushi. Entrées include *gyu-aspara maki* (beef asparagus roll) and *buta niku no shoga yaki* (gingered pork). It's BYOB, and desserts include green tea or red bean ice cream and Japanese snow white jelly, all made at the inn. Entrées $16–24, including miso soup and garden salad.

Cavendish Inn (802-226-7080), 1589 Main St. (Rt. 103), Cavendish. Open weekends for dinner by reservation, also for special functions. The dining rooms in the historic Glimmerstone stone mansion are now an elegant dining option. Executive chef Tim Jefferson blends Californian and French dishes with local produce. In fall the four-course $46 prix fixe menu might begin with fig and chèvre crostini or poached salmon tartlet; offer a choice of Provençal chicken, beef tenderloin, and butternut ravioli, with harvest baked apples (stuffed with dried fruit, nuts, and Vermont cheddar) or pumpkin custard for dessert. Fully licensed.

Fullerton Inn (802-875-2444), 40 The Common, Chester. Open nightly except Sunday. This pleasant dining room is surprisingly casual with a varied menu ranging from pizza to schnitzel Fullerton (breaded veal sautéed with mushrooms and Dijon cream sauce) and pan-roasted New Zealand venison. Inquire about live music. Entrées $10–23.

Also see **The Inn at Weathersfield** ("The Lower Connecticut River Valley") and **The River Tavern** at Hawk Inn and Mountain Resort in Plymouth ("Killington/Plymouth Area").

Also see **Rowell's Inn** under *Lodging*. Open to the public by reservation with 24 hours' notice.

EATING OUT

In Chester

Raspberries and Tyme (802-875-4486), on the green. Open Wed.–Sat. 8–4, and Fri.–Sat. for dinner 5–9. Great salads, simmering soups, and a wide choice of sandwiches are named for a variety of village establishments.

Baba-A-Louis Bakery (802-875-4666), Rt. 11 west. Closed Apr. and the first part of Nov., as well as Sun. and Mon., but otherwise open 7 AM–6 PM. A long-established bakery with an open kitchen and self-serve lunch fare that includes soups and a salad bar as well as quiche and panini. Breakfast options include sticky buns and cinnamon twists, and no one leaves without a loaf of this top-drawer bakery's specialty breads.

Moon Dog Café (802-875-4966), on the green. Open 10–8 daily. A newly expanded café and health food market now fill the town's biggest old storefront. Great soups and salads.

Country Girl Diner (802-875-2650), junction of Rts. 11 and 103. An authentic Silk City diner made in Paterson, New Jersey, in the early '40s. It's a homey, popular spot open Mon.–Sat. 6 AM–8 PM, Sun. 7 AM–8 PM. Classic diner with classic diner fare.

Rose Arbour Tea Room (802-875-4767), 55 School St., just off the green. Hours vary with the season: Open 11–5, but closed Tue. only at busy times, Thu.–Sun. at quiet times. A combination gift store and tearoom. Specializing in two-course high teas but also good for salads, sandwiches, and quiche. Chef-owner Suzanne

Nielson is known for her scones and pastries.

Heritage Deli & Bakery (802-875-3550), Rt. 103 south of the green. Open daily 7–5. A café/gourmet food and wine shop with baked breakfast goods, a big sandwich board, also soups and salads, box lunches, wine and beer served.

In and around Ludlow

✔ **Harry's Cafe** (802-259-2996), Rt. 103, Mount Holly. Open daily 5–10. Trip Pierce took the funky old Backside Restaurant and turned it into the nicest kind of a light, airy space with a bar, tables and booths, good art, and a woodstove. Best of all is the food: Begin with a salad Niçoise or corn and shrimp bisque with fresh dill. It's a big menu ranging from hot smoked salmon with ginger sauce, to Jamaican jerk pork, to roast half duck with all the trimmings. You can also get fish-and-chips or pizza; "For Kids," there's also plenty of choice and curly fries. Every Thursday a three-course Thai meal is featured.

Sam's Steakhouse (802-228-2087), 91 Rt. 103, just east of downtown Ludlow. Open for dinner nightly from 5 with midweek specials. Known for filet mignon you can cut with a butter knife, excellent seafood, a good salad bar, and sinful desserts.

Willie Dunne's Grille (802-228-1387), at the Okemo Valley Golf Club & Nordic Center, Rt. 100. Open year-round for lunch and dinner, serving surprisingly affordable and good food. Two windowed walls are open to views of the pond and the 18th green. All entrées are served with greens.

DJ's Restaurant (802-228-5374), 146 Main St., Ludlow. Open from 4:30 for dinner. A downtown eatery that's been

191

OKEMO VALLEY REGION

upscaled, best known for its broiled scallops and shrimp, extensive salad bar, and nightly specials.

Cappuccino's Cafe (802-228-7566), 41 Depot St., Ludlow, serves dinner Wed.–Sun.; reservations suggested. Chef-owner Steve Degnan and his wife, Dawna, have created a pleasant ambience and a varied menu of pasta, seafood, beef, chicken, and nightly specials; full bar.

✍ **Pot Belly Restaurant and Pub** (802-228-8989), 130 Main St., Ludlow. Open for dinner nightly and lunch most days. Since 1974, a pleasant atmosphere with live music (swing and blues bands, jug band music, and rock and roll) on weekends. At lunch try a Belly Burger or the Cajun chicken sandwich. The dinner menu ranges from comfort food like turkey and meat loaf to seafood diablo: scallops, calamari, mussels, and shrimp in a spicy marinara sauce.

Java Baba's Slow Food Café (802-228-4131), at the base of the Okemo Access Rd., features overstuffed chairs and couches, serves fresh-baked muffins and pastries, homemade soups, sandwiches, salads, desserts, and a variety of coffee drinks. WiFi.

Crows Bakery and Opera House Café (802-226-7007), 73 Depot St., Proctorsville. Off Rt. 103. Open Tue.–Fri. 6–2, weekends 7–2. An attractive café serving full breakfasts and exotic wraps such as Veggie Wrapsody and Tuna Kahuna, plus a choice of veggie sandwiches as well as ham and Swiss. The bakery is open until 6 most nights, known for its from-scratch pastries and breads.

Over Easy Restaurant (802-492-3435), Rt. 102, Cuttingsville. Open daily 6:30–2. Regulars (like U.S. senator Jim Jeffords) group around the horseshoe-shaped counter, but there are tables too in this sunny, pine-vaulted restaurant next to the post office in the town's former railroad station. Omelets are a specialty.

✳ Selective Shopping

ANTIQUES SHOPS

In Chester

Stone House Antiques (802-875-4477), Rt. 103 south, is an antiques mall with 250 dealers and a touristy collection of country crafts. Open daily 10–5. See also **Stone Cottage Collectables** under *Bed & Breakfasts*.

William Austin's Antiques (802-875-3032; www.wmaustin.con), 42 Maple St., Chester. A full line (more than 500 pieces) of antique country furniture and collectibles.

ART GALLERIES Chester Art Guild Gallery on the Green (802-875-4373), Rt. 11, Chester. Open late May–mid-Oct., Fri.–Sun. 2–5. Housed in the venerable brick Academy Building at the heart of town, this is a lively local art center offering open studios (Tue. and Sat. mornings 9–noon) as well as ongoing exhibits and sales.

Crow Hill Gallery (802-875-3763), Flamstead Rd., Chester. This is a great excuse to ride up Crow Hill; the contemporary gallery shows the work of Jeanne Carbonetti and other local artists. Open Wed.–Sat. 10–5, Sun. by appointment.

Reed Gallery (802-875-6225), on the green, Chester. Open Thu.–Sun. 10–5. Featuring local artwork and offering workshops and demonstrations, the gallery is owned and operated by Bob and (watercolorist) Elaine Reed.

BOOKS AND MAPS Misty Valley Books (802-875-3400; www.mvbooks.com), on the green, Chester. Open daily. Lynne and Bill Reed maintain an unusually friendly, well-stocked bookshop; browsing is encouraged and author readings are frequent, making it a lively cultural center.

Over Andover Used Books (802-876-4348; call for directions), Andover. Open July, Aug., Oct., Thu.–Mon. 11–5, and Fri.–Mon. year-round. A barn full of over 20,000 rare and unusual used books (specialties include King Arthur, C. S. Lewis, gardening, Vermont and Vermont authors).

CRAFTS Craft Shop at Fletcher Farm (802-228-4348), 611 Rt. 103, east of Ludlow. Open late June–mid-Sep., 9:30–5, and weekends from Memorial Day. Work by members of the Society of Vermont Craftsmen.

The Silver Spoon (802-228-4753), 44 Depot St., Ludlow. Steve Manning fashions an amazing variety of things—from bracelets (including watches) to decorative trees and fish. Local artists and sculptors are also featured.

Underandover Weavers (802-226-7331), 74 Quarry Rd. (off Twenty Mile Stream Rd.), Proctorsville. Open weekends and by appointment. A weavers' studio and gallery featuring blankets, linens, rugs, and wall hangings. Wendy Regier and Susan Lawler use natural fibers and hand-dyed yarns to create one-of-a-kind pieces.

Bonnie's Bundles (802-875-2114; www.bonniesboundlesdolls.com), Stone Village, Rt. 103, Chester. Open weekends and by appointment. Housed in an 1814 stone house, a doll lover's find. Bonnie Waters hand-crafts wonderfully original dolls.

SPECIAL SHOPS Vermont Industries Factory Store (802-492-3451; 1-800-826-4766), Rt. 103 in Cuttingsville, open daily 10–5:30. A big barn full of hand-forged, wrought-iron products—freestanding sundials, sconces, candleholders, hanging planters, chandeliers, and a wide range of fireplace accessories. The distinctive floor lamps sell for substantially more in stores throughout New England.

Clear Lake Furniture (802-228-8395; www.clearlakevt.com), 322 Rt. 100 north, Ludlow. The workshop and showroom for elegantly simple custom-made pieces in cherry, curly maple, oak, and walnut by Brent Karner and Frank Procopio. Open Mon.–Sat. 9–6, Sun. noon–5.

Conrad Delia, Windsor Chair Maker (802-875-4219), Popple Dungeon Rd., Chester. After a long career as a home builder on Long Island, Conrad Delia studied with several New England chair makers before opening his own shop. Call to schedule a visit.

Hugging Bear Shoppe (802-875-2412; 1-800-325-0519; www.huggingbear.com), 244 Main St., Chester. Georgette Thomas has filled four rooms at the rear of her middle-of-town Victorian house with more than 10,000 teddy bears, plus plush animals and collectibles. It's a phenomenon.

Inn Victoria Teapot Shop (802-875-4288), 321 Main St., Chester. Teapots in all shapes and sizes and tea accessories.

Forlie-Ballou (802-875-2090), off Main St., Chester Village. Worth checking. Suzy Forlie and Mary Ballou carry a fine selection of women's clothing and accessories.

FOOD **Crowley Cheese Factory and Shop** (1-800-683-2606; www.crowleycheesevermont.com), Rt. 103, 5 miles northwest of Ludlow. See *Scenic Drive* for the history of this exceptional cheese, which is sharper and creamier than cheddar. The factory (802-259-2340) is open Mon.–Fri. 8–4 and the shop (802-259-2210) on Rt. 103, which carries other Vermont products as well, is open daily 10–5:30 but closed mid-Jan.–Memorial Day weekend Tue.–Wed.

Green Mountain Sugar House (802-228-7151), Rt. 100, 4 miles north of Ludlow. You can watch syrup being produced in March and April; maple candy is made throughout the year on a weekly basis. This is also a place to find freshly pressed cider in September. The gift and produce shop is open daily 9–6 "most of the time."

Black River Produce (802-226-7484), Rt. 103 in Proctorsville. The purveyor of fruits and vegetables to the area's best restaurants, an exceptional source of fruit, vegetables, fresh breads, cheese, seafood, and flowers, excellent prepared foods, lobsters steamed to go, chowder and fish-and-chips on Friday.

Singleton's Store (802-226-7666), downtown Proctorsville. A long-established family-run grocery store just east of Rt. 103 on Rt. 131 in the middle of Proctorsville has kept abreast of the demands of the area's condo owners while continuing to cover the basics: a Vermont liquor store, fishing and hunting licenses, rods and reels, guns and ammo, sporting goods, outdoor wear and boots, plus fine wines, choice meats, a standout deli, and a gun shop; the specialty of the house is smoked and marinated meat (an average of 350 pounds of meat sold per day).

Belmont General Store, across the street from Star Lake in Belmont Village. Former Nikki's Restaurant chef Chris Kelly and his wife, Louisa, have turned this general store into a source of homemade bread and pastries, lunch and dinner menus to go, as well as local eggs and other produce.

Also see the **Vermont Country Store** in Weston and Rockingham.

✳ Special Events

February–March: **Okemo Winter-Fest** includes "the Ludlow Olympics" —tobogganing, snow sculpture contest, fireworks, ski races, and torchlight parade. Call 802-228-4041 or 802-228-6110 for details.

Memorial Day weekend: Townwide tag sale and Open Studio tour.

July 1: **Fletcher Farm Arts and Crafts Fair**, Rt. 103, Ludlow; **St. Joseph's Carnival; horse show and community picnic**, Chester.

July 4: Fireworks, West Hill Park, Ludlow.

Late July–August: **Okemo Valley Music Festival**—free concerts in Ludlow (Tue.), Cavendish (Wed.), and Chester (Thu.).

August: **Chester Outdoor Art Show. Vermont State Zucchini Festival**, Ludlow—4 days of "zucchini madness" include a costume parade, Z-buck auction, and other events. **Thursday-evening concerts** on the Chester green all month.

Last weekend of September: **Fall Crafts Fair**, Chester.

October: **Historical Society Halloween Cemetery Tour**.

December: **Overture to Christmas** (usually the second Saturday), Chester. Tree lighting and a candlelight caroling procession from church to church.

The Connecticut River Valley

Christina Tree

INTRODUCTION

The Connecticut River flows 410 miles from its high source on the New Hampshire–Quebec border to Long Island Sound in the state of Connecticut. What concerns us here are its 270 miles as a boundary—and bond—between the states of New Hampshire and Vermont. Defying state lines, it forms one of New England's most beautiful and distinctive regions, shaped by a shared history.

Judging from 138 archaeological sites along this stretch of the river, its banks have been peopled for many thousands of years. Evidence of sizable Western Abenaki villages have been found at Newbury, at Claremont (N.H.), and at the Great Falls at present-day Bellows Falls. Unfortunately, these tribes, along with those throughout the "New World," were decimated by disease contracted from English traders.

By the late 17th century English settlements had spread from the mouth of the Connecticut up to Deerfield, Ma., just below the present N.H.–Vt. border. In 1704 Deerfield was attacked by French and Indians, who killed 40 villagers and carried off more than 100 as captives to St. Francis, a full 300 miles to the northwest. This was one in a series of bloody incidents drily dismissed in elementary schools as "the French and Indian Wars."

Recent and ongoing scholarship is deepening our sense of relationships among Frenchmen, Western Abenaki tribespeople, and Englishmen during the first half of the 18th century. By 1700 many settlers had adopted the canoe as a standard mode of travel and, according to Dartmouth professor Colin G. Calloway in *Dawnland Encounters*, in 1704 New Hampshire passed a law requiring all householders to keep "one good pair of snow shoes and moqueshens [moccasins]." Settlers and Abenaki traded with each other. Beaver remained the prime source of revenue for the settlers, and the Indians were becoming increasingly dependent on manufactured goods and alcohol. Both at Fort Dummer—built in 1724 in what, at the time, was Massachusetts (now Vernon, Vt.)—and at the Fort at No. 4, built 50 miles upriver in 1743 in present Charlestown, N.H., settlers and Indians lived side by side.

Unfortunately, during this period former friends and neighbors also frequently faced each other in battles to the death. At the reconstructed Fort at No. 4 you learn that five adults and three children were abducted by a band of Abenaki in 1754 (all survived), and that in 1759 Major Robert Rodgers and his Rangers retaliated for the many raids from the Indian village of St. Francis (near Montreal) by killing many more than 100 residents, including many women and children. The suffering of "Rodgers' Rangers" on their winter return home is legendary. A historic marker on Rt. 10 in Haverhill (N.H.) offers a sobering description.

After the 1763 Peace of Paris, France withdrew its claims to New France and English settlers surged up the Connecticut River, naming their new communities for their old towns in Connecticut and Massachusetts: Walpole, Plainfield, Lebanon, Haverhill, Windsor, Norwich, and more.

This was, however, no-man's-land.

In 1749 New Hampshire governor Benning Wenworth had begun granting land on both sides of the river (present-day Vermont was known as "The New Hampshire Grants"), a policy that New York's Governor George Clinton refused to recognize. In 1777, when Vermont declared itself a republic, 16 towns on the New Hampshire side opted to join it. In December 1778, at a meeting in Cornish, N.H., towns from both sides of the river voted to form their own state of "New Connecticut," but neither burgeoning state was about to lose so rich a region. In 1779 New Hampshire claimed all Vermont.

In 1781 delegates from both sides of the river met in Charlestown (N.H.) and agreed to stick together. Vermont's Governor Chittendon wrote to General Washington asking to be admitted to the Union, incorporating towns contested both by New Hampshire and New York. Washington replied: Yes, but without the contested baggage.

In 1782 New Hampshire sent 1,000 soldiers to enforce their jurisdiction. Not long thereafter Washington asked Vermont to give in—and it did. Needless to say, the river towns were unhappy about this verdict.

The Valley itself prospered in the late 18th and early 19th centuries, as evidenced by the exquisite Federal-era (1790s–1830s) meetinghouses and mansions still to be seen in river towns. With New Hampshire's Dartmouth College (established 1769) at its heart and rich floodplain farmland stretching its length, this valley differed far more dramatically than today from the unsettled mountainous regions walling it in on either side.

The river remained the Valley's highway in the early 19th century. A transportation canal was built to circumvent the Great Falls at present-day Bellows Falls, and Samuel Morey of Orford (N.H.) built a steamboat in 1793. Unfortunately Robert Fulton scooped his invention, but the upshot was increased river transport—at least until the 1840s, when railroads changed everything.

"It is an extraordinary era in which we live," Daniel Webster remarked in 1847, watching the first train roll into Lebanon, N.H., the first rail link between the Connecticut River and the Atlantic. "It is altogether new," he continued. "The world has seen nothing like it before."

In this "anything's possible" era, the Valley boomed. At the Robbins, Kendall & Lawrence Armory in Windsor gun makers developed machines to do the repetitive tasks required to produce each part of a gun. This meant that for the first time an army could buy a shipment of guns and know that if one was damaged, it could be repaired with similar parts. In the vintage-1846 armory, now the American Precision Museum, you learn that this novel production of "interchangeable parts" became known as the "American System" of precision manufacturing.

Springfield too became known for precision tool making. This area is still known as Precision Valley.

In places the railroad totally transformed the landscape, creating towns where there had been none, shifting populations from high old town centers like Rockingham and Walpole (N.H.) to the riverside. This shift was most dramatic in the town of Hartford, where White River Junction became the hub of north–south and east–west rail traffic.

The river itself was put to new uses. It became a sluiceway down which logs were floated from the northern forest to paper mills in Bellows Falls and farther downriver. Its falls had long powered small mills, but now a series of hydro dams were constructed, including the massive dam between Barnet, Vt., and Monroe, N.H., in 1930. This flooded several communities to create both Comerford Reservoi—and the visual illusion that the Connecticut River stops there. At present 16 dams stagger the river's flow between the Second Connecticut Lake above Pittsburg, N.H., and Enfield, Ct., harnessing the river to provide power for much of the Northeast. By the 1950s the river was compared to an open sewer and towns turned their backs to it, depositing refuse along its banks.

Still, beyond towns, the river slid by fields of corn and meadows filled with cows. In 1952 the nonprofit Connecticut River Watershed Council was founded to "promote and protect wise use of the Connecticut Valley's resources." Thanks to the 1970s Clean Water Act and to acquisitions, green-ups, and cleanups by numerous conservation groups, the river itself began to enjoy a genuine renewal. Visitors and residents alike discovered its beauty; campsites for canoeists were spaced along the shore. At present kayaks as well as canoes can be rented along several stretches.

The cultural fabric of towns on either side of the river has remained close knit and, although many bridges were destroyed by the hurricane of 1927, the 21 that survive include the longest covered bridge in the United States (connecting Windsor, Vt., and Cornish, N.H.). It's only because tourism promotional budgets are financed by individual state taxes that this stretch of the river valley itself has not, until recently, been recognized as a destination by either New Hampshire or Vermont.

Happily, a respected nonprofit, bistate group, the Connecticut River Joint Commissions—founded in 1989 to foster bistate cooperation and represent 53 riverfront towns—has stepped into this breach, with dramatic results. It has now spawned the Connecticut River Scenic Byway Council dedicated to, among other things, creating an infrastructure to identify appropriate places in which to promote tourism and the cultural heritage.

At this writing seven "waypoint" information centers are salted along the river. Those in Bellows Falls, White River Junction, Wells River, Haverhill (N.H.), Lancaster (N.H.), St. Johnsbury, and Colebrook (N.H.) are serving visitors well, and in the process reestablishing the Connecticut to its rightful place as the centerpiece of a genuine region. Similar centers in Claremont (N.H.) and Windsor are gearing up and another, in Brattleboro, awaits funds for remodeling. Their work has been enhanced by the federally funded Silvio O. Conte National Fish and Wildlife Refuge, which seeks to preserve the quality of the natural environment within the entire Connecticut River watershed. For a sense of wildlife and habitat in this area, stop by the Montshire Museum (the name melds both states) in Norwich, Vt.

In 2005 the Connecticut River corridor officially became "the Connecticut River National Scenic Byway." We are proud to note that for the past 20 years both our New Hampshire and Vermont Explorer's Guides have included an Upper Valley section describing both sides of the river. Our 2006 editions expand this coverage to include the Lower Connecticut Valley and the Lower Cohase region on the north. Just above this area the Valley widens and two dams have impounded Comerford Lake and the Moore Reservoir, breaking the continuity of the river. Here our "Connecticut River Valley" section ends, but we continue to describe the glorious landscape as the Valley once more narrows and the river is banked in meadows with views (best from the Vermont side) of the White Mountains towering in the east. This is one of the most beautiful stretches along the entire length of the river.

Visually visitors see a river, not state lines. Interstate 91 on the Vermont side has backroaded Rt. 5, as it has Rt. 10 on the New Hampshire side. Even more backroaded and beautiful are the roads marked from Rts. 10 and 12A along the New Hampshire bank. Access to the river via canoe and kayak has increased in recent years, thanks to both outfitters and conservation groups that maintain launch areas and campsites.

Within each chapter prime sights to see shift from one side of the river to the other; the same holds true for places to eat, stay, hike, and generally explore this very distinctive region. Of course in this book we focus in more detail on Vermont, while in the latest edition of *New Hampshire: An Explorer's Guide* the focus is more detailed on that state.

GUIDANCE **www.ctrivertravel.net**, an excellent, noncommercial web site covering the entire stretch of the Connecticut shared by Vermont and New Hampshire, is maintained by the **Connecticut River Scenic Byway Council**. Also look for "waypoint" information centers serving both sides of the river, described under *Guidance* in ensuing chapters.

Helpful pamphlet guides available from the Connecticut River Joint Commissions (603-826-4800; www.ctrivertravel.net) include:

Boating on the Connecticut River in Vermont and New Hampshire (a map/guide).

Explorations Along the Connecticut River Byway of New Hampshire and Vermont (a map/guide).

Connecticut River Heritage Trail (a 77-mile driving/biking tour for the historically and architecturally minded).

Connecticut River Birding Trail map/guides (two): *Northern Section* and *Upper Valley*.

RECOMMENDED READING *Proud to Live Here in the Connecticut River Valley of Vermont and New Hampshire* by Richard J. Ewald with Adair D. Mulligan, published by the Connecticut River Joint Commissions (www.crjc.org).

Confluence: A River, Politics, and the Fate of All Humanity by Nathaniel Tripp (Steerforth Press, Hanover, N.H.).

This American River: Five Centuries of Writing About the Connecticut by Walter Wetherell (University Press of New England, Hanover, N.H.).

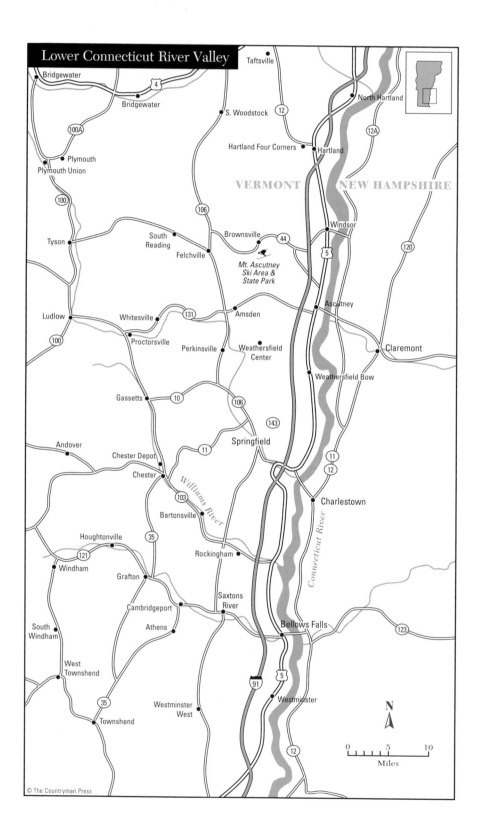

Lower Connecticut River Valley

Taftsville

Bridgewater

Bridgewater

North Hartland

S. Woodstock

100A

Plymouth

Plymouth Union

Hartland Four Corners · Hartland

VERMONT **NEW HAMPSHIRE**

100

106

Windsor

Tyson

South
Reading

Brownsville

44

120

Felchville

5

*Mt. Ascutney
Ski Area &
State Park*

Ludlow

Whitesville

131

Amsden

Ascutney

100

Proctorsville

Perkinsville

Weathersfield
Center

Claremont

Weathersfield Bow

Gassetts

10

106

143

Andover

11

Springfield

11

12

Chester Depot

Williams River

Charlestown

Chester

103

Bartonsville

Houghtonville

35

121

Rockingham

Connecticut River

Windham

Grafton

Cambridgeport

Saxtons
River

South
Windham

Athens

Bellows Falls

123

West
Townshend

35

Westminster
West

91

5

Westminster

Townshend

12

N

0   5   10
Miles

© The Countryman Press

THE LOWER CONNECTICUT RIVER VALLEY

INCLUDING BELLOWS FALLS, SAXTONS RIVER, GRAFTON, SPRINGFIELD, WEATHERSFIELD, AND WINDSOR

The story here is water, gravity and time.
—Richard Ewald

A superb multimedia introduction to this 40-mile stretch of the Connecticut River Valley is hidden away in the gallery of the waypoint visitors center near the Bellows Falls rail yards. The work of historian and preservationist Richard Ewald, it details the area's strikingly visible historic layerings. Within walking distance here you can inspect Indian petroglyphs, an 1802 canal, and a late-19th-century brick mill and railroad center.

Sited at one of the largest drops in the entire length of the river, Bellows Falls itself cascades down glacial terraces so steep that steps connect the brick downtown with Victorian homes above and with surviving riverside mill buildings. All this bustle contrasts with the haunting stillness of the town's original settlement, gathered around the exquisite 18th-century Rockingham Meeting House a few miles north.

In Windsor the layerings are even more compressed along a Main Street that includes the 18th-century "Constitution House" (the official birthplace of Vermont), a 1950s diner, and a white-pillared 1790s Asher Benjamin church. South of the covered bridge is an 1846 brick armory in which inventors are credited with introducing the concept of interchangeable parts, a process that revolutionized the gun and tool industry globally. Locally it spawned some significant tool companies, the reason this area is still known as the Precision Valley.

Water and gravity have combined along this stretch of the Connecticut River and its tributaries—the Saxtons, Williams, and Black Rivers in Vermont and the Sugar River in New Hampshire—to power a variety of 19th-century mills. Around these the communities of Bellows Falls, Springfield, Windsor, and Claremont, N.H., have all evolved.

In Vermont the mills remained human scaled. Even in Springfield, where now defunct tool companies line a strip of Rt. 11, the compact downtown is appealing. Downtown Bellows Falls is a lively arts center.

While waterfalls no longer power mills, gravity still plays a part in the local economy—on more than 50 ski trails on Mount Ascutney. A lone monadnock that looms 3,144 feet above the Connecticut River, Ascutney has evolved into a year-round, family-geared resort with a 215-room condo hotel and sports center. Like the mills before it, this ski area is not large enough to affect the quintessential back-roads Vermont feel of the surrounding area with its scattered inns and B&Bs.

We include Grafton in this chapter because it's most closely associated with Saxtons River and Bellows Falls (7 and 10 miles east, respectively.) A classic old crossroads community, Grafton is also handy to several other areas in southern Vermont. Restored and preserved by the Windham Foundation, this is a "village beautiful," complete with gracious inn, cheese-making factory, low-key museums, shops and galleries, and a vintage covered bridge.

New England's longest and most famous covered bridge links the communities of Windsor and Cornish, N.H., site of the 19th-century summer home of sculptor Augustus Saint-Gaudens. Now a national historic site, the estate evokes the era (1885–1935) in which prominent artists, with the help of pioneering landscape architects, transformed many of the Valley's oldest farms into summer homes. They commuted from New York on the train line that still (miraculously) stops in Windsor and Bellows Falls en route from Manhattan to Montreal.

Today I-91, with exits for Bellows Falls, Springfield, Ascutney, and Windsor, is the quick way up and down this "Precision Valley." It's a stretch of river well worth savoring as slowly as possible, preferably from a kayak or canoe in the center of the region's original highway.

GUIDANCE Great Falls Regional Chamber of Commerce (802-463-4280; www.gfrcc.org), housed in the handsome waypoint visitors center (restrooms) on Depot St. (near the Amtrak station), is open daily 10–4. It serves the Walpole (N.H.) and Bellows Falls area. Pick up pamphlet walking tours to local villages.

The **Springfield Area Chamber Commerce** (802-885-2779; www.springfieldvt .com) answers phone queries year-round (weekdays 8–5) and maintains the 18th-century Eureka Schoolhouse (Rt. 11, near I-91) as a seasonal information booth.

The **Windsor–Mount Ascutney Area Chamber of Commerce** (802-674-5910; www.windsorvt.com) also answers phone queries.

In Grafton the **Daniels House Gift Shop/Café** (802-843-2255; www.windham -foundation.org), behind the Old Tavern, is open daily, year-round except Mar. and Apr., and doubles as a town information center with public restrooms. Pick up a walking tour brochure.

GETTING THERE *By bus:* **Vermont Transit** (1-800-552-8737; www.vermont transit.com) buses from points in Connecticut and Massachusetts stop at Bellows Falls in the square.

By train: **Amtrak** (1-800-USA-RAIL; www.amtrak.com). The Vermonter stops at Bellows Falls, Claremont (N.H.), and Windsor en route from New York City and Washington to Essex Junction and St. Albans (with connecting bus service to Montreal).

MEDICAL EMERGENCY Call **911**.

✳ Villages and Towns

Bellows Falls (a village, population: 3,165 within the town of Rockingham, total population: 5,309). Geologists tell us that 400 to 600 million years ago two continents collided and separated at this site, one of the narrowest points with one of the greatest single drops in the entire length of the Connecticut River. This has long been a sacred place for Native Americans, as evidenced by petroglyphs visible from the Vilas Bridge: a series of round heads, said to date in age anywhere from 300 to 2,000 years. (Unfortunately they have been eroded by logging and railroad blasting, and years ago were painted bright yellow to make them easier to see.)

Viewed from above the dam here, the river resembles a glassy, narrow lake. The view from below the village, however, is very different. Instead of thundering falls, what you usually see is a power station between two narrow water channels and several bridges. The Bellows Falls Canal Co. was the first in the country to obtain a charter, and it was an amazing feat easing flatboats through a series of locks, substantially expanding navigation up the Connecticut. The creation of the canal also formed the island separating the village from the Connecticut River, which for much of the year is now reduced to a modest cascade, dropping through the 0.5-mile gorge beneath the dam. It's on the island that the 1920s railroad station stands, serving Amtrak and the Green Mountain Flyer.

In 1869 William Russell developed the novel idea of making paper from wood pulp, using logs floated down from both sides of the river. He went on to found International Paper. The canal was put to work powering mills, and it still powers turbines generating electricity.

Despite major fires, much of the village architecture dates from the 1890s, the period depicted in a building-sized mural just south of the square. Rockingham Town Hall, with its Florentine-style tower, includes a recently restored, town-owned 500-seat Opera House used for frequent live performances as well as films. The surrounding square is lined with a lively mix of shops and restaurants.

Bellows Falls is also known as the home of Hetty Green (1835–1916), who parlayed a substantial inheritance into a $100 million fortune; she was called the Witch of Wall Street, to which she traveled by day coach, looking like a bag lady in threadbare bombazine. The **Bellows Falls Historical Society** is housed in the vintage-1831 Adams Grist Mill; it's open June–Oct., Sat. and Sun. 1–4. The **Rockingham Free Library** (802-463-4270), 65 Westminster St. (open Mon.–Thu. 1–7, Fri. 10–4, Sat. 10–2) has archival photos, genealogical archives, and a history museum (open summer Fri. 2–4 or by appointment) that includes Hetty Green memorabilia. For galleries and current entertainment check www.rockbf .org and www.www.gfrcc.org.

A MURAL IN DOWNTOWN BELLOWS FALLS
Christina Tree

Walpole, N.H. (population: 3,594) Along the length of the Connecticut River, few communities are more closely historically and physically linked (by two bridges), yet more different, than Walpole and Bellows Falls. Walpole's village is a white wooden New England classic, set high above Rt. 12, graced by fine old churches and dozens of mansions, some dating from the late 18th century, more from the early and mid–19th century, when it was a popular summer haven with several large inns. Louisa May Alcott summered here; Emily Dickinson visited. In the 20th century James Michener came here to research the opening chapter of *Hawaii*—the one about the New England–born missionaries and their families. Current creative residents include filmmaker Ken Burns and chocolate maker Lawrence Burdick. The **Walpole Historical Society** (603-756-3308; open June–Sep., Wed. and Sat. 2–4) displays a significant collection of paintings, photographs, furniture, and other local memorabilia. It's housed on three floors of the tower-topped Academy Building in the middle of the village and includes a large research library. Walpole's big hotels have vanished, but a vintage golf course remains. The town is undergoing a renaissance with Burdick's Bistro and Café and the Walpole Inn now offering destination dining.

Saxtons River, like Bellows Falls, is a village in the town of Rockingham. Said to be named for a surveyor who fell into the river and drowned, it's best known as the home of the Vermont Academy (founded in 1876, a private prep school since 1932). This village of 541 souls is also not a bad place to stay, eat, and shop. The **Saxtons River Historical Museum** (802-869-2566; open summer Sundays 1–4:30) is housed in a former Congregational church built in 1836 at the western end of the village. Its collection includes art, tinware, toys, Civil War memorabilia, and a furnished Victorian parlor and kitchen.

Grafton (population: circa 600; www.graftonvermont.org). Prior to the Civil War, Grafton boasted more than 1,480 residents and 10,000 sheep. Wool was turned into 75,000 yards of Grafton cloth annually; soapstone from 13 local quarries left town in the shape of sinks, stoves, inkwells, and foot warmers. But then one in three of Grafton's men marched off to the Civil War, and few returned. Sheep farming, too, "went west." An 1869 flood destroyed the town's six dams and its road. The new highway bypassed Grafton. The town's tavern, however, built in 1801, entered a golden era. Innkeeper Marlan Phelps invested his entire California gold rush fortune in adding a third floor and double porches, and his brother Francis organized a still-extant cornet band. Guests included Emerson, Thoreau, and Kipling; later both Woodrow Wilson and Teddy Roosevelt visited. By 1940, however, the Tavern was sagging, and nearly all the 80-some houses in town were selling—with plenty of acreage—for just $3,000–5,000. It wasn't until 1963 that Matthew Hall, a summer resident descended from of the town's first

GRAFTON POST OFFICE

Christina Tree

pastor, hit on a suitable use for the fortune his aunt Pauline Fiske had left for a worthy cause. Incorporated in 1963, the resulting Windham Foundation first focused on the town's rotting core, restoring the store, a Blacksmith Shop (open, with demonstrations, June–Oct., Wed.–Sun.), and the Old Tavern, now one of Vermont's destination inns. It went on to revive the Grafton Village Cheese Company, to bury the village wiring, and eventually to acquire many buildings and 2,000 acres with marked footpaths on which visitors can walk or cross-country ski down past the pond, into the woods, and home again. In the Daniels House behind the Tavern, pick up a pamphlet *Walking Tour of Grafton*. The **Grafton History Museum** (802-843-1010; www.graftonhistory.org), 147 Main St., is open daily during foliage season, weekends and holidays Memorial Day–Columbus Day 10–noon and 2–4 (admission). The **Nature Museum** (802-843-2111; www.nature-museum.org), on Townshend Rd. just south of the village, is open weekends year-round 10–4. It focuses on local flora and fauna, with hands-on exhibits for children, including an underground tunnel; there are also trails to hike and extensive family programs.

Springfield (population: 3,938; www.springfieldvt.com). Sited near the confluence of the Connecticut and Black Rivers, Springfield boomed with Vermont's tool industry in the 19th and first half of the 20th centuries—and has suffered as that industry has atrophied. Beyond the defunct factories and the powerful falls, the town's compact downtown offers several places to eat and shop. Gracious 19th-century mansions in residential neighborhoods terraced above the historic district include the **Springfield Historical Society and Miller Art Center** at 9 Elm St. (802-885-2415; open May–Oct., Tue.–Fri. 10–4, Sat. 10–1), with collections of pewter, Bennington Pottery, toys and dolls, primitive paintings, and costumes as well as changing art exhibits. Straight uphill from the village square, Hartness House, the town's elegant inn, is well known to astronomers. An inventor (Hartness patented 120 machines), aviator (he held one of the first 100 pilot's licenses in the United States and built Vermont's first airport), president of Jones Lamson, the town's leading tool company, and Vermont governor (1920–22), Hartness was also an astronomer who installed one of the first tracking telescopes in the country (tours by reservation). It was designed by fellow Springfield native Russell W. Porter and sits at the end of an underground corridor connected to the mansion. Porter also organized the country's first group of amateur telescope makers, and his **Stellafane Observatory** on Breezy Hill is home base for an annual convention during the week of the July/August new moon. It routinely attracts 3,000 amateur astronomers (www.stellafane.com). On River St. (Rt. 11/106) beside the Springfield Royal Diner, be sure to check out the **Precision Valley Corvette Museum** (802-886-1400; www.vettepassion.com), open daily 11–7, featuring half a dozen and more 1950s–'90s models of America's classic sports car. See *Biking* for the Toonerville Trail along the Black River. The 18th-century Eureka School House on Rt. 11 exhibits vintage books and school materials, and serves as a seasonal information center.

Charlestown, N.H. (population: 4,929) was a stockaded outpost during the French and Indian Wars. Its Main Street was laid out in 1763, 200 feet wide and a mile long, with more than five dozen structures that now make up a National

Historic District; 10 buildings predate 1800. Note the 1840s Congregational church; the former Charlestown Inn (1817), now a commercial building; the vintage-1800 Stephen Hassam House, built by the great-grandfather of impressionist painter Childe Hassam; and the Foundation for Biblical Research, housed in a 1770s mansion. *Historic Charlestown Walkabout*, a nominally priced guide, is available in most town stores. Also see **The Fort at No. 4** under *To See*.

Claremont, N.H. (population: 13,344). Massive textile mills and machine shops line the Sugar River as it drops 300 feet from the city's compact core around Tremont Square. At this writing the mills are being rehabbed. Tremont Square retains some magnificent 1890s buildings, notably the massive Italian Renaissance Revival–style city hall with its magnificent and well-used second-floor Opera House, and the Moody Building, built originally as a hotel in 1892. Adjoining Pleasant Street is now lined with antiques shops. The mammoth brick Monadnock Mills on Water Street (off Broad and Main) on the Sugar River are among the best-preserved small 19th-century urban mills in New Hampshire; note the 1840s gambrel-roofed brick Sunapee Mill across the river and the small brick overseers' cottages (also 1840s) on Crescent Street. The railroad was an essential contributor to Claremont's industrial and cultural heyday. It remains an Amtrak stop. The **Claremont Historical Society** (603-543-1400), 26 Mulberry St., is open seasonally. A walking tour is available from the chamber of commerce. West Claremont (3 miles west on Rt. 103) is a vanished village graced by New Hampshire's oldest Episcopal and Catholic churches. It seems that the Catholic priest who founded St. Mary's parish in 1824 was the son of the Episcopal rector who built St. John's across the street. Both buildings are interesting architecturally. The only sign of the congregations that both men taught and served is the West Part Burying Ground adjoining the churches. Note the waypoint visitors center on Rt. 11/10. The **Greater Claremont Chamber of Commerce** (603-543-1296) maintains a walk-in office in the Moody Building, 24 Tremont Square.

Weathersfield Center. On a scenic old north–south road between Springfield and Rt. 131 stands this gem of a hamlet with its brick 1821 Meeting House and Civil War memorial, a particularly sobering reminder of how many young Vermonters served and died (12 boys from just this small village) in that war. The **Weathersfield Historical Society** (802-263-5230), housed in the Reverend Dan Foster House, 2656 Weathersfield Center Rd. (open May–early Oct., Thu.–Mon. 2–5), displays Civil War memorabilia, archival photos, an old forge, and the last wildcat killed in Weathersfield (1867). It was Weathersfield native William Jarvis who transformed the economy of Vermont—and the rest of northern New England—by smuggling 4,000 sheep out of Spain during his term as U.S. consul in Lisbon. That was in 1810. By 1840 there were upward of two million sheep in Vermont.

Windsor (population: 3,759; www.windsorvt.com). In *Roadside History of Vermont*, Peter Jennison notes that while it is known as the "Birthplace of Vermont," Windsor can also claim to be the midwife of the state's machine tool industry. Windsor resident Lemuel Hedge devised a machine for ruling paper in 1815 and dividing scales in 1827. Asahel Hubbard produced a revolving pump in 1828, and Niconar Kendall designed an "under hammer" rifle, the first use of interchangeable parts, in the 1830s in the picturesque old mill that's now the American Precision Museum. Windsor's mid-19th-century prosperity is reflected in the handsome lines of the columned Windsor House, once considered the best public house between Boston and Montreal. The Italianate building across the street was designed in 1850 by Ammi Young as a post office (the oldest federal post office in continuous use in the United States) with an upstairs courthouse that served as Woodrow Wilson's summer White House from 1913 to 1915; the president spent his summers in Cornish, just across the Windsor–Cornish Covered Bridge. Cornish was at the time an artists' and writers' colony that had evolved around sculptor Augustus Saint-Gaudens. The colony nurtured artist Maxfield Parrish; his painting *Templed Hills* hangs in the Vermont National Bank branch that is next to Windsor House (Parrish left it in perpetua to the bank's tellers for "keeping my account balanced"). It depicts a mountain that resembles Mount Ascutney, towering above water that resembles Lake Runnemede. The lake is now a town-owned conservation area, good for walking and bird-watching, that's sequestered behind the town's mansion row, just north of the bank. The **Cornish Colony Museum** (802-674-6008; www.cornishmuseum .com), housed in the old firehouse at 147 Main St. (open Memorial Day–Oct., daily except Mon; Fri.–Sun. year-round) showcases prints and original work by Maxfield Parrish and other members of the art colony that flourished in this area 1885–1935 (admission: $6 adults, $4 children) around sculptor Augustus Saint-Gaudens. Across Main Street. stands the 1798 Old South Congregational Church designed by Asher Benjamin. Also worth noting: the contemporary St. Francis of Assisi Roman Catholic Church and its panels depicting the *Seven Sacraments*, donated by noted American painter George Tooker. On the common (off Main St.), St. Paul's, built in 1832, is Vermont's oldest Episcopal church. Townsend Cottage, across the square, is a striking example of 1840s Carpenter Gothic style. North of town a riverside, visitor-geared industrial park features the Simon Pearce glass factory and Harpoon Brewery.

✳ To See

Listed from south to north.

⚓ **Fort at No. 4** (603-826-5700; www.fortat4.com), Rt. 11, 1 mile north of Charlestown Village. Open June–late Oct., 10–5. $8 adults, $6 seniors, $5 children. This living history museum, set in 20 acres on the Connecticut River, conjures an otherwise almost forgotten chapter in New England history. The stockaded village exactly replicates the way the settlement looked in the 1740s. It served first as a trading post in which Natives and newcomers lived together peaceably until the outbreak of the French and Indian Wars. A full 50 miles north of any other town on the Connecticut River, the original fort fell once but then withstood repeated attacks. The complex includes the Great Hall, cow barns, and furnished living quarters; there is also an audiovisual program, and costumed interpreters prepare meals, perform chores, and staff a blacksmith forge. Inquire about frequent battle reenactments and special programs for children throughout summer. A small museum displays authentic local Native American artifacts, and the gift store carries historical books for all ages.

Rockingham Meeting House. Vermont's oldest unchanged public building is off Rt. 103 between Chester and Bellows Falls, and open Memorial Day–Columbus Day, 10–4. Built as a combination church and town hall in 1787, this Federal-style structure stands quietly above its graveyard. It's striking inside and out. Inside, "pigpen"-style pews each accommodate 10 to 15 people, some with their backs to the minister. The old burying ground is filled with thin old markers bearing readable epitaphs. An annual pilgrimage is held the first Sunday in August, with a 3 PM historical program.

ROCKINGHAM MEETING HOUSE

Kim Grant

The American Precision Museum (802-674-5781; www.americanprecision.org), 196 S. Main St., Windsor. Open Memorial Day–Nov. 1, 10–5 daily; $6 adults, $4 seniors, $4 over 6; $18 per family. Billed as the largest collection of historically significant machine tools in the country, housed in the 1846 Robbins, Kendall & Lawrence Armory, itself a National Historic Landmark, said to be the "birthplace of this country's modern system of industrial design and production." At the 1851 Great Exposition in London the firm displayed the manner in which it used interchangeable parts to assemble rifles. The British army ordered 25,000 rifles on the spot and bought 138 gun-making machines. The idea of using interchangeable parts was a significant breakthrough and became known as "the American System." Special exhibits can be excellent.

THE AMERICAN PRECISION MUSEUM IN WINDSOR

Kim Grant

Old Constitution House (802-674-6628; www.historicvermont.org), N. Main St., Windsor. Open mid-May–mid-Oct., Wed.–Sun. 11–5. Nominal admission. This is Elijah West's tavern (but not in its original location), where delegates gathered on July 2, 1777, to adopt Vermont's constitution, America's first to prohibit slavery, establish universal voting rights for all males, and authorize a public school system. Excellent first-floor displays trace the history of the formation of the Republic of Vermont; upstairs is the town's collection of antiques, prints, documents, tools and cooking utensils, tableware, toys, and early fabrics. Special exhibits vary each year. A path out the back door leads to Lake Runnemede.

View from Mount Ascutney in Mount Ascutney State Park, Windsor. Open late May–mid-Oct.; $2.50 adults, $2 children park day-use fee. A 3.8-mile summit road from Rt. 44A (off Rt. 5) between Ascutney and Weathersfield winds steeply up through mixed hardwoods to a parking lot in the saddle between the mountain's south peak and summit. A 0.8-mile foot trail takes you the additional 344 vertical feet to the summit. It's well worth the effort for an overview of the Valley. A former fire tower has been shortened and transformed into an observation platform. Local history traces the road to a trail cleared in 1825 for the Marquis de Lafayette's visit—but the marquis was a day behind schedule and came no closer than a coffee shop on Main Street. The present road was built in the '30s by the CCC.

Also see **Grafton** under *Villages and Towns*.

COVERED BRIDGES At 460 feet the **Cornish–Windsor covered bridge**, linking Rt. 5, Windsor, and Rt. 12A, Cornish, is said to be the country's longest covered bridge and is certainly the most photographed in New England. A lattice truss design, built in 1866, it was rebuilt in 1989. There are three more covered bridges in Cornish, all dating from the early 1880s: Two span Mill Brook—one in Cornish City and the other in Cornish Mills between Rts. 12A and 120—and the third spans Blow-Me-Down Brook (off Rt. 12A).

Also look for two covered bridges in Bartonsville (one is 1.5 miles north of Rt. 103; the other, east off Rt. 103) north of Rockingham (not far from the Vermont Country Store), one in Grafton village, and one in Saxtons River off Rt. 121, noteworthy for its "flying buttresses" (replaced in 1982).

GREEN SPACE ✿ **Wilgus State Park** (802-674-5422; 802-773-2657), 1.5 miles south of I-91, Exit 8, Rt. 5, Windsor. Open Memorial Day–Columbus Day. This small, quiet campground on the Connecticut River is ideal for canoeists—the 17 tent sites, six lean-tos, and two cabins are on the riverbank. Car shuttle service available (see *Boating*); playground, picnic tables, hiking trails, also canoe, kayak, and rowboat rentals.

Ascutney State Park (802-674-2060). Open mid-May–mid-Oct., Windsor. Rising out of the Valley to an elevation of 3,144 feet, Mount Ascutney represents some 3,000 acres of woodland. The 3.8-mile paved Summit Road begins on Rt. 44A, off Rt. 5, between Ascutney and Windsor (see View from Mount Ascutney, above). Granite was quarried here as early as 1808. A total of 49 tent sites, trailer sites, and lean-tos can be reserved. The ski slopes and self-contained Ascutney Mountain Resort (not on state land) are accessed from Rt. 44 in Brownsville.

✳ **To Do**

BICYCLING **Grafton Ponds** (802-843-2400; www.graftonponds.com) in Grafton rents mountain bikes for use on dirt roads radiating from the village and on its cross-country trails.

Ascutney Mountain Resort (802-484-3511; www.asctuney.com) in Brownsville rents mountain bikes and offers 32 km of trails.

In Springfield the **Toonerville Trail**, a new 10-foot-wide, paved recreation path good for bicycling and walking, follows the Black River along an old trolley line from the trailhead on Rt. 11 (behind the Robert Jones Industrial Center) 3 miles to another parking area on Rt. 5, just north of the Cheshire Bridge across the Connecticut.

Road biking is popular in this area thanks to the many interlinking back roads and river roads.

BIRDING *Connecticut River Birding Trail* (www.birdtrail.org), a pamphlet map/guide highlighting 46 birding sites in the Connecticut River Valley (*Rock-*

The Saint-Gaudens National Historic Site (603-675-2175; www.nps.gov/ saga), Rt. 12A, Cornish, N.H. Grounds open daily, dawn–dusk. Buildings open 9–4:30 daily late May–Oct. $5 adults (good for a week); free under age 17. This glorious property with a view of Mount Ascutney includes the sculptor's summer home and studio, sculpture court, and formal gardens, which he developed and occupied between 1885 and his death in 1907. Augustus Saint-Gaudens (1848–1907) is remembered primarily for public pieces: the Shaw memorial on Boston Common, the statue of Admiral Farragut in New York's Madison Square, the equestrian statue of General William T. Sherman at the Fifth Avenue entrance to Central Park, and the *Standing Lincoln* in Chicago's Lincoln Park. He was also the first sculptor to design an American coin (the $10 and $20 gold pieces of 1907). His home, Aspet, is furnished much as it was when he lived there. A visitors center features a 28-minute film about the artist and his work. Augustus Saint-Gaudens loved the Ravine Trail, a 0.25-mile cart path to Blow-Me-Up Brook, now marked for visitors, and other walks laid out through the woodlands and wetlands of the Blow-Me-Down Natural Area. Saint-Gaudens was the center of the "Cornish Colony," a group of poets, artists, landscape artists, actors, architects, and writers who included Ethel Barrymore, Charles Dana Gibson, Finley Peter Dunne, and Maxfield Parrish; President Woodrow Wilson's wife was drawn into this circle, and the president summered at a nearby home from 1913 to 1915. *Note:* Bring a picnic lunch for Sunday-afternoon chamber music concerts, at 2 PM in July and August.

ingham and North) is free (although donations are appreciated) at Connecticut River waypoint centers and by mail. Please send a self-addressed, stamped (60¢) envelope to Bill Shepard, 104 Railroad Row, White River Junction 05001. Outstanding areas include town-owned Lake Runnemede, Paradise Park in Windsor, North Springfield Lake (thanks to the local Audubon chapter there are trails and an observatory at the northern end of the lake), Mount Ascutney (hawks in September), and Herricks Cove in Rockingham.

BOATING With its placid water and lovely scenery, the Connecticut River through much of the Lower Valley is ideal for easygoing canoeists. The **Connecticut River Joint Commissions** (603-826-4800; www.ctrivertravel.net) has published a useful *Boating on the Connecticut River* guide. Canoeing the Connecticut can, admittedly, be a bit of a slog. The headwind is as infamous as the lack of current. So what? Why does canoeing have to be about going great distances?

⚓ **North Star Livery** (603-542-6929; www.kayak-canoe.com), Rt. 12A in Cornish, will shuttle patrons to put-ins either 3 or 12 miles above the Cornish–Windsor covered bridge. Roughly half of North Star's patrons camp, either at Wilgus State Park (see *Green Space*) or on an island. North Star itself is New England's most picturesque canoe livery: The check-in desk is in the barn of a working farm, redolent of bales of hay; the canoes and kayaks are stacked behind the farmhouse. Six-person rafts are also available. Full-day, half-day, and multi-day trips are offered. With over 90 boats, including 30 kayaks, this is the largest, oldest, and best-loved commercial rental service on the Connecticut River.

Still River Outfitters, Inc., at Quinnehtukqut Outdoor Center (802-674-6767; www.stillriveroutfitters.com), 36 Park Rd., Windsor. A barnlike structure beside the Harpoon Brewery in Windsor's visitor-geared industrial park (Simon Pearce is the other major occupant) serves as a base for this seasonal kayaking outfit. Rentals, instruction, guided tours, and shuttle service.

Boat access to the Connecticut River

Herrick's Cove. Picnic area, boat landing, and bird sanctuary, a good picnic spot off Rt. 5 near I-91, Exit 6, in Rockingham, above Bellows Falls.

Hoyt's Landing. Off Rt. 11 and I-91, Exit 7, in Springfield, a recently upgraded put-in that's also good for fishing and picnicking.

Ashley Ferry Boat Landing. Off River Rd. (parallel to Rt. 11/12), about 2 miles south of Claremont, N.H. A boat landing and park at a bend in the river.

Also see "Upper Valley River Towns."

Other boat access

North Springfield Lake and **Stoughton Recreation Area**, Reservoir Rd. between Springfield and Weathersfield, are maintained by the U.S. Army Corps of Engineers and offer boat launches.

CAMPING See Wilgus and Mount Ascutney State Parks under *Green Space*. The Vermont State Parks reservation line operates weekdays: 1-888-409-7549.

CAR RACING **Claremont Speedway** (603-543-3160), Bowker St., 4 miles east of I-91, Claremont, N.H. May–Sep., racing Sat. 7:30 PM.

GOLF **Bellows Falls Country Club** (802-463-9809), Rt. 103, Rockingham. Scenic nine-hole course; clubhouse with bar and lunchroom.

Tater Hill Golf (802-875-2517), 6802 Popple Dungeon Rd., North Windham. Now owned by Okemo, newly renovated, 18 holes with a pro shop.

Crown Point Country Club (802-885-1010), Weathersfield Center Rd., Springfield. A gem of an 18-hole course with pro shop, golf lessons, driving range, restaurant, and banquet facilities.

Hooper Golf Club (603-756-4020) Prospect Hill, Walpole. A vintage course offers nine holes and a clubhouse serving lunch.

HANG GLIDING **Mount Ascutney State Park**, Rt. 44A off Rt. 5, Windsor. Brownsville Rock, less than a mile by trail northwest of the Mount Ascutney summit, is a popular launch site. Note that a paved summit road accesses the trail.

Morningside Recreation Area (603-542-4416; www.flymorningside.com), Rt. 12 in Claremont, N.H., is the site of events on weekends. Lessons in hang gliding and paragliding are offered along with a repair service, sales, swimming, and hiking.

HIKING **Mount Ascutney** offers the area's most dramatic hiking. Of the four trails to the summit, we recommend the 2.9-mile ascent from Weathersfield with an 84-foot waterfall about halfway (the trailhead is on Cascade Falls Rd., 3.5 miles north off Rt. 131). The 3.2-mile Brownsville Trail begins on Rt. 44 between Windsor and Brownsville; the 2.7-mile Windsor Trail starts on Rt. 44A in Windsor. The 4.4-mile Futures Trail begins in Windsor State Park and links up with the Windsor Trail.

RAILROAD EXCURSIONS ⚓ **Trains Around Vermont** (802-463-3069; 1-800-707-3530; www.rails-vt.com), 54 Depot St., Bellows Falls. Round-trips on the Green Mountain Flyer are available Tue.–Sun. in summer; daily during foliage season. This 13-mile (one-way) route follows the Connecticut River past covered bridges, then heads up the Williams River and through wooded rock cuts, which include the spectacular Brockway Mills gorge. Inquire about special runs.

SPECIAL PROGRAMS **Great River Arts** (802-463-3330; www.greatriverarts .org), 33 Bridge St., Bellows Falls. Founded in Walpole, N.H., but now headquartered in nearby Bellows Falls, Vt., this nonprofit institute offers a variety of first-class literary and visual arts workshops and programs in venues on both sides of the river.

The Preservation Education Institute (802-674-6752; www.preservation works.org) offers workshops in preservation building skills.

SWIMMING ⚓ **Grafton Swimming Pond**, Rt. 121, 1 mile west of the village, is an oasis for children. **Stoughton Pond Recreation Area** (802-886-2775),

Stoughton Pond Rd. off Rt. 106 in Weathersfield, offers pond swimming, and in the village of Perkinsville the **Black River** cascades into delicious pools at an old power site. **Kennedy Pond** (Rt. 44 west) in Windsor has a small beach, great for kids. Inquire locally about numerous other swimming holes in the Black and Williams Rivers and about Twenty-Foot Hole (a series of cataracts and pools in a wooded gorge) in Reading.

✳ Winter Sports

CROSS-COUNTRY SKIING AND SNOWSHOEING **Grafton Ponds Recreation Center** (802-843-2400; www.graftonponds.com), Townshend Rd., Grafton. Thirty km of trails groomed both for skating and classic strides, meandering off from a log cabin warming hut, over meadows, and into the woods on Bear Hill. Snow-making on 5 km, rentals, and instruction, plus ice skating, snow tubing, and trails specifically for snowshoeing.

Ascutney Mountain Resort (802-484-7771; 1-800-243-0011), Rt. 44, Browns-ville. A touring center with instruction, rentals, 30 km of trails in eight loops with three separate loops for snowshoers.

DOWNHILL SKIING AND SNOWBOARDING **Ascutney Mountain Resort** (802-484-7771; 1-800-243-0011; www.ascutney.com), Rt. 44, Brownsville (I-91, Exit 8 or 9). A family-geared, self-contained resort. Facilities include a 215-unit condo hotel, a sports center with an Olympic-sized pool, weight and racquetball rooms, a basketball court, a skating rink, a full restaurant, and a base lodge. Owners Steve and Susan Plausteiner have increased snowmaking and added the North Peak Area, substantially increasing expert trails, served by a new mile-long quad chair.

Trails: 56.

Lifts: 6.

Vertical drop: 1,800 feet.

Snowmaking: 95 percent.

For children: Nursery/child care from 6 weeks.

Features: Nine double-diamond advanced trails, expert tree skiing, a terrain park, a tubing slope, a separate lift-served Learning Park, and a strong children's program.

Rates: $56 adults weekend, $42 seniors/juniors; $54/$38 midweek. Half-day tick-ets and many special packages are offered.

✳ Lodging

RESORT ✿ **Ascutney Mountain Resort** (802-484-7711; 1-800-243-0011; www.ascutney.com), Rt. 44, Brownsville 05037. A contemporary, 215-unit wooden condo hotel and flanking condominiums at the base of Mount Ascutney. Accommodations range from standard hotel rooms to three-bedroom units with kitchen, fireplace, and deck, all nicely fur-nished with reproduction antiques. In winter there are both alpine and cross-country trails; facilities include indoor and outdoor pools and an extensive

MOUNTAIN BIKING AT ASCUTNEY MOUNTAIN RESORT

Ascutney Mountain Resort

summer adventure program for adults (horseback riding, mountain biking, road biking, and kayaking/canoeing) as well as kids. Rooms $119, condo units $179–259 in summer and fall, more in winter (but nobody pays the rack rate); 2-night rates from $109 per night. Inquire about package rates from $79 per person midweek, including lodging and skiing.

INNS

Listed from south to north.

◯◯ ♿ **The Old Tavern** (802-843-2231; 1-800-843-1801; www.old-tavern.com), Main St., Grafton 05146, where Rts. 35 and 121 intersect. The brick core of this splendid building dates from 1788, but the double-porched facade is mid–19th century. The stylish interior (vintage 1965) tastefully re-creates a formal early American setting. There are 11 rooms in the Tavern itself, 19 more divided between the Windham and Homestead cottages, a few of which can be rented so that the inn can accommodate (as it does for weddings) 130 guests.

Guest rooms have private bath, but no TV or air-conditioning. Common rooms are formal and elegant. The Phelps Barn has a fireplaced lounge. In summer there are nearby tennis courts, platform tennis courts, and a sand-bottomed swimming pond; in winter, cross-country skiing. Youngsters are welcome in some cottages. Pets are not permitted, but you can bring your horse (there's a stable). $135–245 per room, $195–390 per suite, depending on the room, day (weekends are more expensive than weekdays), and season. Inquire about houses ($750–900) sleeping eight or nine people.

Inn at Saxtons River (802-869-2110; www.innsaxtonsriver.com), Main St., Saxtons River 05154. This vintage-1903 inn with a distinctive square, five-story tower has an attractive streetside pub and a large dining room (see *Dining Out*). Innkeeper Stuart Pease offers 16 recently redecorated rooms (all with private bath). $135–175 per couple includes continental breakfast. Inquire about packages.

∞ **Hartness House** (802-885-2115; 1-800-732-4789; www.hartnesshouse .com), 30 Orchard St., Springfield 05156. In 1903 James Hartness built himself a stone-and-shingle mansion set in 32 acres on a parklike bluff. The inventor (Hartness patented 120 machines), aviator (he held one of the first 100 pilot's licenses in the United States and built Vermont's first airport), astronomer, and governor (1920–22) installed one of the first tracking telescopes in the country at the end of a 240-foot underground corridor connected to the mansion in 1910. It's still in use (inquire about tours), and since 1939 the mansion has been an inn. It now offers 45 guest rooms, 11 in the main house, the remainder in connecting tasteful motel-like annexes. All rooms have private bath, phone, and color TV/ DVD player. There's a formal feel to the large lobby, with its traditional check-in desk, and to the pub and dining room (see *Dining Out*). Facilities include a swimming pool and nature trails. $130–215 per couple in the main house, $99–135 in the annexes includes breakfast. Weddings are a specialty. Inquire about numerous package plans.

∞ 🐾 **The Inn at Weathersfield** (802-263-9217; www.weathersfield inn.com), 1342 Rt. 106, Weathersfield 05151. Set way back from quiet Rt. 106, just south of the village of Perkinsville, this handsome inn dates in part from 1792 but columns give it an antebellum facade. This is one of Vermont's most distinctive and romantic inns, as well as one of its best places for fine dining. Jane and David Sandelman seem to be doing everything right. Each of the nine guest rooms and three suites is different. All have phone and private bath (ranging from powerful showers to Jacuzzis) and amenities such as slippers and plush robes; seven have a fireplace (some gas, some wood burning). Some have TV and DVD. Wireless Internet access throughout. The setting is 21 wooded acres with hiking/snowshoeing trails and an amphitheater used as a wedding venue. Hiking and ski trails on Mount Ascutney, a web of back roads good for biking, and a glorious swimming hole are all handy. Guests enjoy their own common room in the opposite side of the inn from the long, tiered dining room and pub. See *Dining Out* for more about the inn's legendary dining, thanks to executive chef Jason Tostrup. $169–270 in high seasons, $129–240 in low, includes a full breakfast and afternoon refreshments. Inquire about special packages.

∞ **Juniper Hill Inn** (802-674-5273; 1-800-359-2541; www.juniperhillinn .com), off Rt. 5 on Juniper Hill Rd., Windsor 05089. Set high on a hill above its impressive drive, with a magnificent view of Mount Ascutney and the Connecticut River Valley, this splendid 28-room mansion, built by Maxwell Evarts in 1901, combines Edwardian grandeur with the informal

JUNIPER HILL INN IN WINDSOR

Christina Tree

hospitality of innkeepers Robert Dean and Ai Nikki. Relax by the hearth in the huge main hall, in a second living room (with TV), or in the library with its leather armchairs and unusual hearth. One of Vermont's most romantic getaways, the inn offers no fewer than 11 guest rooms with fireplace (all but 4 are wood burning). All 16 guest rooms have private bath and are furnished with flair and genuinely interesting antiques. Guests gather for meals in the dining room, with floor-to-ceiling fireplace. Reserve for candlelit dinners. We could easily spend a day by the pool or walking around Lake Runnemede, a hidden conservation area within walking distance that's great for birding. Rates $115–225 per room, full breakfast included; add $30 for an additional person.

Across the river

The Walpole Inn (603-756-3320; www.walpoleinn.com), RR 1, Box 762, 297 Main St., Walpole, N.H. 03608. Originally this distinguished Colonial was home to Colonel Benjamin Bellows, commander of a strategic garrison along the Connecticut River during the French and Indian Wars. Now, in another life, it offers a restaurant that's among the best in the area (see *Dining Out*) and eight quietly elegant guest rooms, each furnished in chic understatement with a pencil-post, queen-sized bed and simple, tailored linens. Four have walk-in shower; the others feature a luxurious soaking tub with shower. You can choose among chess in the paneled parlor, tennis on the grounds, or golf at the nearby Hooper Golf Course. A full breakfast comes with an artist's view of meadows and hills, and is included in the $135–165 rate.

BED & BREAKFASTS

Listed from south to north.

In Grafton

✤ The Inn at Woodchuck Hill Farm (802-843-2398; www.woodchuckhill.com), Middletown Rd., Grafton 05146. Open most of the year. This 1780s farmhouse sits high on a hill, on a back road above Grafton. The porch, well stocked with comfortable wicker, has a peaceful, top-of-the-world feel, and there are views from the elegant living room and dining room, too. Operated as an inn by the Gabriel family for more than 30 years, it offers six rooms, four of them corner rooms with private bath (one with a fireplace) in the main house. In the west wing, an upstairs studio has its own kitchen and glass doors that open onto a private deck with views of the woods. Downstairs is a spacious suite with a king-sized canopy bed and a fridge, microwave, and coffeemaker sequestered in a hand-carved armoire. By the pond, the old barn has been rejigged to offer some great spaces. You can have either a double room with fireplace, two rooms with fireplace, or the whole barn with a two-story living room, woodstove, kitchen, and view of the pond. Spruce Cottage offers privacy and seclusion. Furnished in antiques, it's fully equipped and sleeps up to seven people ($375 per day). There's a sauna in the woods next to the pond, which is good for swimming, fishing, and canoeing, and the 200 rolling acres are laced with walking trails. No smoking. $99–270 B&B.

By the River Bed & Breakfast (802-843-2886), 460 Rt. 121, Grafton 05146. Bill Brooks is a master cabinetmaker, and his wife, Elise, is a yoga instructor. Their (shoes off) home is comfortably, unstuffily elegant, with choice contemporary furnishings, hung with striking art and with windows overlooking the gardens and river. There are two guest rooms with private baths. We just stopped by but would have liked to linger by the fire. $125 per couple includes breakfast.

☀ ♪ **The Grafton Homestead** (802-843-1111; www.graftonhomestead .com), 499 Rt. 121 east, Grafton 05146. Informal, comfortable rooms and suites in this 1802 roadside house are a good bet for families and pets. All rooms have private bath, TV, AC, some kitchen facilities. $76–120 per room, $124–195 for a suite, includes self-serve continental breakfast.

In Bellows Falls/Saxtons River

♪ **River Mist B&B** (802-463-9023; 1-888-463-9023; www.river-mist.com), 7 Burt St., Bellows Falls 05101. On a quiet street, this 1895 "painted lady" is high Victorian inside and out, reflecting the way the town's onetime mill owners lived. Michael, Verone, and Roger offer four lacy guest rooms with private bath, plenty of personal attention, and a very full breakfast— perhaps quiche and baked apples or stuffed French toast. $100–150.

Horsefeathers (802-463-9776; 1-800-299-9776; www.horsefeathers inn.com), 16 Webb Terrace, Bellows Falls 05101. Len and Tracey Poirier are enthusiastic new owners of this Victorian house set high in 3 acres on a bluff overlooking the Connecticut River. The six rooms are country comfortable, air-conditioned, with private bath. A two-course breakfast is served in summer on the front porch with its amazing view. $110–150.

Moore's Inn (802-869-2020; www .mooresinn.com), P.O. Box 424, 57 Main St. (Rt. 121), Saxtons River

05154. Dave Moore is a sixth-generation Vermonter who grew up in this Victorian house with its fine woodwork and spacious veranda. It remains very much Dave and Carol's family home and a guest house (as opposed to B&B). The spacious guest rooms—six on the second floor and three on the third—are all self-contained, all with private bath, TV, fridge, coffeemaker, and breakfast cereals. The three third-floor guest rooms share a living room and can, of course, be rented as a whole. $89–109 based on a 2-night stay. $10 more for just one night. Several rooms easily accommodate three people. The 75-foot enclosed lap pool is open mid-Apr. into Oct. Bicyclists are especially welcome and will find maps and plenty of advice.

∞ **Inn at Cranberry Farm** (1-800-854-2208; www.cranberryfarminn .com), 61 Williams River Rd. (off Rt. 103), Chester 05143. Despite the postal address, this appealing inn is in the town of Rockingham not far from the Rockingham Meeting House, with property that extends to the Williams River. Built as an inn in the 1990s, it has been renovated by Carl Follo and Pam Beecher. There are 11 guest rooms and 3 two-room suites (with whirlpool tub and fireplace). The airy design of the inn, with its spacious common areas, lends itself to groups and weddings (there's a pond outside the door). $150–250.

☀ **The Pond House at Shattuck Hill Farm** (802-484-0011; www .pondhouseinn.com), P.O. Box 234, Brownsville 05037. This 1830s Cape sits beside its barn on a steeply rising back road near Mount Ascutney, with views across its pond and fields to mountains. There are three guest rooms, sparely, tastefully furnished, each with private bath. Gretel Schuck is an avid cook; breakfast might feature orange French toast, and dinner (selective nights) might include tuna with artichoke hearts or wild mushroom risotto. Guests dine together in the square dining room with its pumpkin pine floors and original six-over-six window. Gretel is also an avid cyclist and delights in tuning guests to local back roads, also good for horseback riding. Horses ($25) and polite dogs ($10) can be accommodated. $150 per couple includes breakfast; dinner $50 per couple. $300 for 2 nights includes a dinner. Beware the strict cancellation policy.

The Inn at Windsor (802-674-5670; 802-236-5561), 106 Apothecary Lane, Windsor 05089. Holly Taylor's vintage-1786 Green Mansion is set above Main Street in downtown Windsor, handy to paths around Lake Runnemede and to Mill Pond. Guests enter through a landscaped garden, are asked to remove their shoes, and are given freshly laundered slippers. Both guest rooms have antique woodstoves built into the hearth, and there is a working fireplace in the suite. All three rooms are interestingly, eclectically furnished, as is the gathering space around the original kitchen hearth and a contemporary breakfast room. The old buttery is now a guest pantry complete with fridge. $125–165 includes a four-course breakfast served when guests desire.

Also see **Bailey's Mills Bed & Breakfast** in Reading in the "Woodstock/ Quechee" chapter.

Across the river

❧ **The Inn at Valley Farms** (603-756-2855; 1-877-327-2855; www .innatvalleyfarms.com), 633 Wentworth Rd., Walpole, N.H. 03608. Set in 105 acres bordering an apple orchard, this circa-1774 house offers exceptionally handsome, antiques-filled guest rooms along with lovely common rooms, including a formal parlor and dining room, and a sunroom overlooking a lovely perennial garden. Upstairs in the main house there is a two-bedroom suite with bath, along with two other bedrooms, each with four-poster bed, private bath, phone, and dataport. Niceties include fresh flowers, plush robes, and Burdick chocolates. Families can choose one of two cottages, each with three bedrooms, kitchen, and living area. Innkeeper Jacqueline Caserta is a serious organic farmer/gardener; she uses fresh eggs as well as her organic vegetable harvest creatively to make a breakfast that's both good and good for you. Inn rates: $139–175 per couple with full breakfast. Cottages, which sleep six, are $175 for two, plus $15 per person under 12; $29 per person over 12. A basket of homemade breads and muffins is delivered each morning to the door.

Rochambeau Lodge at Alyson's Orchard (603-756-9800; 1-800-756-0549; www.alysonsorchard.com), P.O. Box 562, Wentworth Rd., Walpole, N.H. 03608. Geared to groups: a renovated barn, set amid acres of working apple orchard, offering eight bedrooms, a laundry, kitchen, living room, and a long dining table. The neighboring **Caleb Foster Farmhouse** adds three more bedrooms and additional kitchen and common areas. Along with pumpkin fields and 30,000 apple trees, the property features miles of trails for cross-country skiing or hiking, and there are several spring-fed ponds suitable for swimming, canoeing, and fishing. The Orchard Room across the road is available for wedding receptions and conferences. To rent the lodge for a minimum 2-night stay is $1,300; $1,800 per week. The house is $1,000 for 2 nights; $1,500 for a week. Meals, prepared by a prizewinning chef, can be provided with advance notice.

Dutch Treat (603-826-5565; www .thedutchtreat.com), P.O. Box 1004, Charlestown, N.H. 03603. Open year-round. Formerly Maple Hedge, this handsome, 1820s Main Street house has been completely refurbished by Dob and Eric Lutze, natives of Holland who have also lived in Canada, England, and Austria and speak French and German. There's a Dutch theme to guest rooms with names like the Tulip Suite (our favorite) and the Delft Room, both big, sunny guest rooms in the front of the house. Smaller rooms—the Lace Maker (honoring the Dutch painter Vermeer), the twin-bedded Tasman Room (named for a Dutch explorer who discovered New Zealand and Tasmania), and the Generals Room (with a picture of a forefather who fought under both Napoleon and Wellington)—are also inviting. The sunny, square dining room is elegant. There's a big comfortable parlor, wicker on the porch, and an outdoor hot tub. Dob and Eric are delighted to help guests explore the best of the area.

✴ Where to Eat

DINING OUT The Inn at Weathersfield (802-263-9217; www.weathersfieldinn.com), 1342 Rt. 106, just south of Perkinsville. Open for dinner except Mon. The dining room is a former carriage house, candlelit with windows overlooking the garden and a floor-to-ceiling hearth. Historically this is one of the best restaurants in Vermont, a tradition as alive as ever with executive chef Jason Tostrup, who has come to Weathersfield via NYC, Aspen, and Napa and works directly with local farmers and producers to shape a menu that changes weekly. On an early-December night you might begin with Valley Brook Farms autumn squash soup ($8), or a salad with Cider House herb vinaigrette and local goat cheese ($8). Entrées include a vegetarian dish, a duck confit, and herb-crusted New York strip steak ($27–29). For dessert: a cinnamon brioche bread pudding or dark chocolate ganache ($7). The chef's tasting menu ($57 per person) features crab and basil cannelloni, Champlain Valley rabbit risotto, and duck confit, with accompanying wines. A pub menu is also offered at Lucy's Tavern. Inquire about special events such as "foraging" or a local farms dinner; also about the prizewinning wine list.

Oona's (802-463-9830), 15 Rockingham St., Bellows Falls. Open Mon.–Sat. for lunch and dinner, tapas and music Wednesday, and more music on Saturday (no cover). Oona Madden's storefront restaurant is the heart of the new Bellows Falls. It's colorful and comfortable, with an eclectic menu that changes daily, moderate at lunch and upscale at dinner, which might include pan-seared lamb chops with an orange-brandy demiglaze, and a creamy barley risotto with shiitake and portobello mushrooms, sea scallops, cheddar, crisp bok choy, and beets. Dinner entrées $14.50–25.50. More music is now staged a couple of doors down at The Windham (a defunct hotel), for which Oona's offers a bar service and light fare. Call for a schedule of events and nightly specials.

The Old Tavern (802-843-2231), Main St., Grafton, serves breakfast and dinner daily in the formal dining rooms or in the more casual Pine and Garden Rooms. Reviews celebrate the food and wine to be sampled in this formal old dining room amid fine portraits and Chippendale chairs. A fall menu might begin with cream of French lentil soup and cave-aged Gruyère ($8), or balsamic roasted local quail ($10); entrée choices might include crispy veal, blackened New England blackfish, and sautéed South Texas antelope ($26–30). The wine list is an unusually good value.

Inn at Saxtons River (802-869-2110), Main St., Saxtons River. Open theoretically for lunch and dinner except Mon., Sun. brunch in summer, but check. The à la carte menu might include grilled salmon fillet topped with an orange fig glaze, and sirloin tips marinated in Worcestershire sauce, tomatoes, and herbs as well as Vermont cheddar and rotini. Entrées $10.95–23.95. An "everyday menu" featuring quesadillas and fish-and-chips is also offered. This is the obvious spot to dine before Main Street Arts productions.

✔ **Leslie's** (802-463-4929; www.leslies tavern.com), Rockingham, Rt. 5 just south of I-91, Exit 6. Open nightly except Tue. Reservations appreciated. John Marston opened his restaurant in a 1790s tavern back in 1985 and continues to create new and eclectic dishes, fusing many influences with experience and using as much home-grown produce as possible. Certified Black Angus beef and free-range chicken are served a variety of ways,

and there's always a vegetarian plate. Choose from "small plates"—maybe wild mushroom ravioli—or go for the venison au poivre or "pescatra," large shrimp and sea scallops sautéed with garlic, lemon, fresh tomatoes, basil, and lobster ravioli. Entrées $18–28.

Hartness House (802-885-2115), 30 Orchard St., Springfield. Closed Mon. Open for lunch and dinner weekdays, dinner only on weekends. The dining room in this venerable landmark is a popular special-occasion place for local residents and generally has a good reputation. The dinner menu might include apple fennel and pork sausage wrapped in puff pastry for an appetizer, and prime rib as a main course. A complete dinner with appetizer, entrée, dessert, and a glass of wine is $22.95.

✔ **Windsor Station Restaurant** (802-674-2052; www.windsorstation .com), Depot Ave., Windsor. Open for dinner 5:30–9 except Mon. Built as a passenger train station (it remains an Amtrak stop), now decorated in natural wood plus velvet and brass. It serves reasonably priced dinner with entrées from chicken Kiev or amandine and veal Madeira to the Station Master filet mignon topped with shrimp, asparagus, and hollandaise sauce. A children's menu is available. Inexpensive to moderate.

✔ **Penelope's** (802-885-9186), on the square, 30 Main St., Springfield. Open daily for dinner except Sun.; no lunch on Sat. Polished woods, stained glass, and greenery, an attractive setting for dining from a large menu. Choices range from beef fillet flambéed in brandy to Rosie's Scrod and baked lasagna. Children's menu. Dinner entrées $10.95–24.95.

Worth crossing the river for

& **The Walpole Inn** (603-756-3320; www.walpoleinn.com), 297 Main St., Walpole, N.H. Open Tue.–Sun. for dinner 5–9, until 9:30 on Fri. and Sat. Bar and lounge open from 4 PM. The menu changes weekly. The dining room, overlooking a painterly scene of rolling meadows, is simple but elegant with celery-toned paneling, exposed brick, white linen, and appealing art. Favorite menu items include pan-seared halibut with cucumber and heirloom tomato salad ($25), and a grilled Black Angus strip steak with caramelized onions, melted Gorgonzola cheese, and whipped red potatoes for the same price. Reservations recommended.

& **Burdick's Bistro and Café** (603-756-2882; www.burdickchocolate .com), 47 Main St. (next to the post office), Walpole, N.H. Open Tue.–Sat. 11:30–2:30 for lunch; 5:30–9 for dinner; Sun. brunch 10–2. Also open Tue.–Sat. 7 AM–9 PM and Sun. and Mon. until 6 PM for drinks and dessert. Chocolatier extraordinaire Larry Burdick and his friend, filmmaker Ken Burns, have transformed the town's former IGA into a chic dining spot. Like the decor, the menu, much of which changes daily, is understated but close to perfect. Lunch features soups, pâtés, gravlax, salads, and omelets. On a summer day we discovered how good a salad of goat cheese with red and orange beets, walnuts, and greens can be. It came with French bread and oil and a pot of tea with lemon. Dinner might be pan-roasted chicken garnished with lemon and olive oil and served with straw potatoes; or maybe a slow-roasted pork loin served with fennel over white beans. The bread is crusty; the wine list, top-notch; the

chocolate desserts, to die for. Dinner entrées are $10.50–24.50; for two, figure $50 with wine.

EATING OUT

Listed from south to north.

Café Loco at Harlow Farm Stand (802-722-3515), Rt. 4 north of I-91, Exit 5, Westminster. Open Mon.–Sat., 7–5, Sun. 8–4. The farm stand is a standout, but it's easy to miss this delightful café featuring fresh-made soups, sandwiches, homemade pies, and daily specials.

✍ **Father's Restaurant** (802-463-3909), Rt. 5, 1 mile south of Bellows Falls. Open Sun. 7–3, Mon. 6–3, Tue.–Thu. 6–9, Fri.–Sat. 6 AM–9 PM. An attractive family restaurant with a salad bar, kids' menu, prime rib for $11.95, wine and beer.

Miss Bellows Falls Diner (802-463-9800), 90 Rockingham St., Bellows Falls. Open daily from 6 AM through dinner. Inside and out this Worcester Diner (#771) is still pure, unhokey 1920s. New owners in late 2005.

Joy Wah (802-463-9761), Rockingham Rd. (Rt. 5), Bellows Falls. Full-service Chinese fare in a Victorian farmhouse perched on a knoll overlooking the Connecticut River; includes all the familiar dishes on its lengthy menu. Open daily for lunch and dinner. Sunday brunch is a local favorite.

Golden Egg (802-869-2300), 16 Main St., Saxtons River. Open Tue.–Sat. 7–2:30, dinner Fri. 5–8:30. In addition to the breakfast and lunch basics are plenty of Mexican offerings: breakfast burritos, huevos rancheros, tacos, quesadillas, and more. Great local rep.

Daniels House Café (802-843-2255), Townshend Rd., Grafton. Just behind the Old Tavern and attached to the village's information center/gift shop. Open 11–4 for lunch with soups, salads, and sandwiches.

☙ **Morning Star Café** (802-885-6987; www.morning-star-cafe.com), 56 Main St., Springfield. Open Mon.–Fri, 6–5:30. An airy storefront with high ceilings, widely spaced tables, periodicals, and the comfortable feel of a big living room; good espresso, chai, latte, and pastries, plus a full deli with freshly made soups, quiche, salads, grilled veggie and meat sandwiches, and wraps. The dinner menu changes daily; on our last visit it included chicken hibiscus and Cundy's Harbor scallops. There's a wine list.

☙ **McKinley's** (802-885-9186), on the square, Springfield. Same fern-bar atmosphere as Penelope's (see *Dining Out*) but a different menu. A good lunch stop: burgers, taco salad, sandwiches, pastas, and soups.

☙ **Springfield Royal Diner and Precision Valley Corvette Museum** (802-886-1400; www.springfieldroyal diner.com), 363 River St. (Rt. 106). Open Sun.–Thu. 6 AM–9 PM, weekends 6 AM–10 PM. A vintage-1955 diner that stood in Kingston, New York, this chrome classic was moved to its present spot and restored and expanded in 2003 as an adjunct to a showroom full of classic Corvettes, the collection of a local resident who periodically auctions one off to boost the local (depressed) economy. The diner's food is just fine, judging from a cup of potato ham soup and a BLT on wheat toast. Specials included homemade turkey stew and an open-faced roast pork sandwich. Service is fast, and patrons are "honey" and "dear." You don't have to eat to tour the museum, which is free.

☙ **Country Creemee Restaurant**, Downers Corner (junction of Rts. 131 and 106), Amsden. Seasonal. Locals will tell you that everything tastes good here; we always get the super-long hot dog to consume at a picnic table under the trees.

Brownsville General Store (802-484-7480), Rt. 44 just west of the entrance to Ascutney Mountain Resort. A regular general store with busy gas pumps but also with a big red Aga cookstove behind the lunch counter, a clue to the quality of soups and daily specials like chicken and biscuits. Bread is fresh baked, and there's a full deli.

☙ **Dan's Windsor Diner** (802-674-5555), 135 Main St., Windsor. Open daily 6 AM–8 PM. The owner is Fred Borcuk, and this spiffed-up 1952 classic Worcester diner (#835) retains its rep for good diner food: meat loaf, liver and onions, and macaroni and cheese, along with omelets, burger baskets, pies, and more.

Windsor Café in Windsor House, Main St., Windsor. Open weekdays, 9–2, for breakfast and lunch. Operated by the Brownsville General Store team; great sandwiches.

Christopher's Cakes and Pastries (802-674-6999) at the Firehouse, 147 Main St., Windsor. Open Tue.–Sun. 7–5. Primarily pastries but some stuffed croissants and plenty of space to relax with tea and coffee.

Worth crossing the river for **Stuart & John's Sugar House and Pancake Restaurant** (603-399-4486), junction of Rts. 12 and 63 (entrance is Rt. 63), Westmoreland Depot, N.H. Open weekends (7–3) in spring (Feb.–Apr.) and fall (Sep.–Nov.). Stuart Adams and John Matthews have

Christina Tree

FRED BORCUK OWNS DAN'S DINER IN WINDSOR.

been serving up pancakes and all the fixings in their Sugar House (it now seats 98) for more than 30 years. Plenty of people drive up from Boston to sample their four different kinds of pancakes and several grades of syrup. Belgian waffles are another specialty, and of course there's sausage and bacon—but no eggs. That's where Ellie (mother of Stuart), who orchestrates this venture, draws the line. This is also one of the area's few surviving dairy farms, and sugaring is a big part of what keeps it going. Some 7,000 taps yield an average of 2,000 gallons a year. The family farm spreads across a rise above the Connecticut River. Ellie sells syrup year-round from the house beside the sugarhouse.

Charlestown Heritage Diner (603-826-3110), 122 Main St., Charlestown, N.H. Open daily 6 AM–2 PM; Sunday, when it's 8–11:30 AM, features a buffet. Also Wed.–Sat. 4–8 PM for fresh seafood and beef specialties. This authentic 1920s Worcester diner is attached to an 1820s brick building that expands its space (there are two small dining rooms in the older building), offering a choice of atmospheres but the same blackboard menu. There's also a tavern upstairs—and the liquor license extends to the diner. The breakfast menu is huge, while "The Live Free or Die Burger" with multiple toppings is a lunch specialty.

Daddypops Tumble-Inn Diner (603-542-0074), Tremont Square next to the Moody Building, Claremont, N.H. Open 5:30 AM–2 PM. A genuine classic 1941 Worcester diner (#778), with blue tile, a counter, and booths, that has received a new lease on life from owner Debbie Carter. It's a local hangout: The bottomless cup of coffee is 75¢, and the menu includes scrapple and corned beef hash. Fries are homemade. Admittedly the "turkey soup" we had here on our last visit tasted more like corned beef, but it hit the spot and the coffee was good.

✳ Entertainment

Bellows Falls Opera House (802-463-4766), on the square in Bellows Falls, operated by the town of Rockingham. Formerly the New Falls Cinema, this vintage theater in the town hall has recently been refurbished with new seating, flooring, screen, and sound system. First-run and classic movies are shown Fri.–Tue. for $3.50 ($2 on Tue.). This fine old vaudeville house is also the venue for live performances.

Main Street Arts (802-869-2960; www.mainstreetarts.org), Main St., Saxtons River. Year-round art workshop as well as music and theater productions.

Springfield Theater (802-885-2929), 26 Main St., downtown Springfield. First-run films.

Flying under Radar Series (www .flyingunderradar.com), a series of mostly folk music concerts by nationally known and local artists, is held regularly in the Windham Hotel, 40 Village Square, Bellows Falls. Organizer Charlie Hunt is also an artist known for his evocative posters and paintings. Look for them, and for event tickets, at the Village Square Booksellers adjacent to the Windham.

Front Porch Series. A series of Sunday concerts/BBQs/block parties centered on Bellows Falls porches in July and August. For details check the Village Square Booksellers web site: www.villagesquarebooks.com.

The **Grafton Cornet Band** performs in either Grafton or Chester (sometimes in Townshend) on summer weekends.

ARTS **Main Street Arts** (802-869-2960), Main St., Saxtons River. This local arts council sponsors dance and musical performances, parades, cabarets, recitals, and a midwinter solstice celebration (The Revels) as well as art classes and the Jelly Bean crafts shop.

❊ Selective Shopping

ANTIQUES SHOPS **Grafton Gathering Places Antiques** (802-875-2309), 748 Eastman Rd., open year-round daily except Tue. A two-story country barn filled with early country and period furniture and accessories.

ART GALLERIES

In Bellows Falls

The third Friday of every month, year-round, Bellows Falls stages an **Art Gallery Walk** 5–8 PM. In addition to the galleries listed below, changing artwork is also displayed in Oona's Restaurant and Village Square Booksellers. Music and literary events are usually part of the happening.

Spheris Gallery of Fine Art (603-756-9617; www.spherisgallery.com), 59 The Square. Once a fixture in Walpole Village, this standout gallery has moved across the river but still fea-

tures local artists with big-time names. Owner Cynthia Reeves was instrumental in founding Great River Arts.

Three Rivers Gallery (802-463-1991), Canal St. in the Exner Block. A showcase for the best of local art, custom furniture, and decorative accessories.

The Richter Gallery Arts & Antiques (802-463-2049; www.richtergallery.com), 2 Village Square. Open daily. Stephen Zeigfinger has solved the perennial artist's problems—regular income and studio space. Allison Richter, a custom framer, maintains the handsome frame and print shop across the way.

The Framery of Vermont (802-463-3295; www.theframeryofvermont.com), 22 Bridge St. The particular focus here is the Connecticut River Valley, its landscape, flora, and fauna, featuring Sabra Fields and Will Moses prints.

Great River Arts Institute (802-463-3330; www.greatriverarts.org), 33 Bridge St. Workshops in writing and a variety of visual arts are offered. Check current calendar for lectures, special events. Changing art exhibits.

In Grafton

Gallery North Star (802-843-2465; www.gnsgrafton.com), 151 Townshend Rd. Open daily except Tue. Six rooms in this Grafton Village house are hung with landscapes and graphic prints, oils, watercolors, and sculpture.

Jud Hartmann Gallery (802-843-2018), by the Brick Church on Main St. Open 10–5 mid-Sep.–foliage season and again in Dec. for the holidays. Hartmann began his career as a sculptor in Grafton and has since won national acclaim for his bronze renditions of Native Americans and increasingly complex historical renditions. He divides his time among studios here, Maine, and the Virgin Islands.

Elsewhere

The Vault (802-885-7111; www.gallery atthevault.com), 65 Main St., Springfield. Located strategically next to the Morning Star Café, this quality crafts store is all about Visual Art Using Local Talent (hence its name) and is definitely worth checking out.

Cider Hill Farm (802-674-5293), Hunt Rd., 2.5 miles west of State St., Windsor. Sarah Milek's commercial display garden is the setting for Gary Milek's studio, displaying his striking Vermont landscapes done in egg tempera, botanically correct floral prints, and stunning cards made from them.

BOOKSTORES Village Square Booksellers and Wireless Café (802-463-9404; www.villagesquarebooks.com), 32 The Square, Bellows Falls. Open Mon.–Sat. 9–6, Fri. until 7, and Sun. 10–3. Patricia Fowler's independent, full-service bookstore is an inviting place to linger with coffee and your laptop. This is a local cultural center

BLACKSMITH IAN EDDY IN HIS SAXTONS RIVER FORGE

Christina Tree

with regular poetry and authors' readings and other special programs, and also features local photography by Alan Fowler and changing work by local artists. Specialties include local authors and books on barging in Europe (you can also book a barge).

Ray Boas, Bookseller (603-756-9900; www.rayboasbookseller.com), 44 Elm St., Walpole, N.H. Open most days but best to call ahead if you're traveling a distance. More than 13,000 titles with an emphasis on nonfiction in a lovely old Colonial home. Decorative arts and antiques a specialty.

CRAFTS Vermont State Craft Gallery (802-674-6729; www.vscg .org), 85 Main St., Windsor. Open daily 10–6, Sun. 11–5. A stunning retail showcase/gallery for Vermont craftspeople: glass, ceramics, furniture, jewelry, textiles, metal, paper, photography, fine arts, and cards with constantly changing special exhibits.

Jelly Bean Tree (802-869-2326), Main St., Saxtons River. Open May.–Dec., daily noon–5. A crafts cooperative run by local artisans and carrying the work of many more on consignment: pottery, macramé, leather, weaving, batik, and handsewn, -knit, and -crocheted items.

Ian Eddy Blacksmith Studio (802-869-228; www.ianeddyblacksmith .com), 14 Pleasant Valley Rd. (off Rt. 121), Saxtons River. A great selection of functional and decorative items include lighting, bathroom and kitchen accessories, fireplace tools, and door hardware. Eddy works in his forge (a former auto body shop) most days, but call ahead.

Coyote Moon Jewelry & Imports (802-463-9529), 11 Canal St., Bellows Falls. Open daily except Sun.

Intriguing gifts from throughout the world with an emphasis on Mexico, and sterling-silver jewelry.

Maple Wings Artisans (802-460-4161), 18 Village Square, Bellows Falls. Open Thu.–Mon. 10–6. Woodworking is featured, along with a variety of local craftspeople.

Rusty Moose Gallery (802-843-1151; www.junkerstudio.com), Pleasant St., Grafton Village. Payne and Elise Junker create metal art, also feature New England craftspeople: functional pottery, woven scarves, jewelry, and more.

FOOD, FLOWERS, AND FARM STANDS **The Grafton Village Cheese Company** (802-843-2221; www.graftonvillagecheese.com) on Townshend Rd. is open Mon.–Fri. 8:30–4, Sat. and Sun. 10–4; cheesemaking weekdays 8–11. To produce its Covered Bridge Cheddar, vats of fresh milk are heated and the curd is cut by hand, tested, drained, milled, salted, molded, and pressed before aging.

Boggy Meadow Farm (1-877-541-3953; www.boggymeadowfarm.com), 13 Boggy Meadow Lane, Walpole, N.H.; location marked from Rt. 12. The 620-acre Boggy Meadow Farm has been in the Cabot family since 1820. Powell Cabot produces Fanny Mason Farmstead Swiss Cheeses, all made with raw milk and vegetable rennet that pasteurizes naturally during the 60-day curing process. Call to make sure the retail shop and cheese plant are open. The drive along the river to the shop is a treat in itself.

Allen Brothers Farms & Orchards (802-722-3395), 6–23 Rt. 5, 2 miles south of Bellows Falls. Open year-round, daily, 6 AM–9 PM. Offers pick-your-own apples and potatoes in-

season, also sells vegetables, plants and seeds, honey, syrup, and Vermont gifts.

Alyson's Orchard (603-756-9800; 1-800-856-0549; www.alysonsorchard.com), Wentworth Rd., Walpole, N.H. Some 28,000 trees cover this beautiful hilltop overlooking the Connecticut River Valley. Heritage-variety apples, peaches, pears, blueberries, raspberries, hops.

Harlow Farmstand (802-722-3515), Route 4, less than a mile north of I-91, Exit 5. Open May–Dec., daily 9–6. Organic produce, bedding plants, flowers, and baked goods. Also see Café Loco under *Eating Out*.

Plummer's Sugarhouse (802-843-2207; www.plummerssugarhouse.com), 3 miles south of Grafton Village on Townshend Rd. Open all year. A third-generation maple producer, making pure syrup for more than 30 years; also maple candy, sugar and more. Will ship anywhere in the United States.

Morning Star Perennials (802-463-3433; www.morningstarflowers.com), 221 Darby Hill Rd., Rockingham (off Rt. 5). More than 300 varieties of organically grown perennials, including many rare ones.

Wellwood Orchards (802-263-5200), 529 Wellwood Orchard Rd., Springfield. Pick your own strawberries (June and July), then raspberries and blueberries (mid- to late July), and finally apples (mid-Aug.–Oct.).

North Country Smokehouse (603-543-3016; 1-800-258-4304; www.ncsmokehouse.com), Claremont, N.H. Follow signs for the airport; it's across the way on a site established by Mike Satzow's grandfather in 1917. Delis throughout the Northeast carry North Country meats: hams, turkey, bacon, smoked goose and Peking duck, sausages, and more. Inquire about the catalog.

Harpoon Brewery (1-888-HARPOON; www.harpoonbrewery.com), south of Exit 9, north of Windsor on Rt. 5. Open Tue.–Sat. 10–6; periodic tastings. Founded in Boston in 1986 and still Boston based, Harpoon purchased this, the former Catamount Brewery, in 2000. The "visitors center" here consists of a shop that doubles as a "beer garden," selling deli sandwiches and, well, beer. Check the web site for special events.

SPECIAL SHOPS **Vermont Country Store** (www.vermontcountrystore .com), Rt. 103, Rockingham Village. An offshoot of the famous Vermont Country Store in Weston, this is also owned by Lyman Orton and houses a Common Cracker machine, which visitors can watch as it stamps out the hard round biscuits. The store also sells whole-grain breads and cookies baked here, along with a line of calico material, soapstone griddles, woodenware gadgets, natural-fiber clothing, and much more. There's also an upstairs bargain room.

Sam's Outdoor Outfitters (802-463-3500; www.samsoutdoor.com), 78 The Square, Bellows Falls, bills itself as "the biggest little store in the world." A branch of the Brattleboro store but still big.

Simon Pearce Glass (802-674-6280; www.simonpearce.com), Rt. 5, north of Windsor. Open daily 9–5. Pearce operated his own glassworks in Ireland for a decade and moved here in 1981, acquiring the venerable Downer's Mill in Quechee and harnessing the dam's hydropower for the glass furnace (see "Woodstock/Quechee Area"). He sub-sequently built this additional, 32,000-square-foot facility down by the Connecticut River. Designed to be visitor-friendly, it includes a catwalk above the factory floor—a fascinating place from which you can watch glass blown and shaped. Of course there's a big showroom/shop featuring seconds as well as first-quality glass and pottery. The pottery shed next door is also open to visitors.

✳ **Special Events**

Note: Check www.bellowsfalls.org for current happenings, and see Art Gallery Walk under Art *Galleries*.

June: **Roots on the River** (www .flyingunderradar.com)—a 4-day folk/rock/country music festival that's gaining national recognition.

July–August: Sunday-afternoon (2 PM) **lawn concerts** at the Saint-Gaudens National Historic Site (603-675-2175) in Cornish, N.H.; free with admission to the grounds. Bring a picnic.

July: On Saturday night at the **Old Grange Hall** (historical society: 802-824-5294) in Brownsville (West Windsor), baked bean and salad suppers have been held since 1935.

July 4 weekend: A big **parade in Saxtons River** and fireworks. **Windsor Heritage Days** (weekend following July 4) celebrate Vermont's birthplace as a republic.

August: Rockingham **Old Home Days**, Bellows Falls. A full weekend of events—railroad excursions, live entertainment, art show, Rockingham Meeting House Pilgrimage, more fireworks supplied by the Lisai family. **Cornish Fair** (www.cornishfair.com), a 3-day old-fashioned fair with a midway, horse and tractor pulls, 4-H exhibits, sheep and goat shows, lawn games, more.

UPPER VALLEY RIVER TOWNS

The Upper Valley ignores state lines to form one of New England's most rewarding and distinctive regions.

Upper Valley is a name coined in the 1950s by a local daily, the *Valley News*, to define its two-state circulation area. The label has stuck, interestingly enough, to the group of towns that back in the 1770s tried to form the state of "New Connecticut." The Dartmouth-based, pro–New Connecticut party was, however, thwarted (see the introduction to "The Connecticut River Valley").

In 1769 Eleazar Wheelock had moved his Indian school—which had been funded through appeals made by Mohegan preacher Samson Occum in England and Scotland to "spread Christian knowledge among the Savages"—from Lebanon, Ct., to Hanover, N.H. Initially Dartmouth College recruited Indian students, many from St. Francis, but the school also served white students and the percentage of Indians quickly dwindled.

The Valley itself prospered in the late 18th and early 19th centuries, as evidenced by the exquisite Federal-era meetinghouses and mansions still salted throughout this area. The river was the area's only highway in the 18th and early 19th centuries and was still a popular steamboat route in the years before the Civil War.

The Upper Valley phone book includes towns on both sides of the river, and Hanover's Dresden School District reaches into Vermont (this was the first bistate school district in the United States). Several Independence Day parades start in one state and finish across the bridge in the other. The Montshire Museum, founded in Hanover, N.H., but now in Norwich, combines the two states in its very name.

Dartmouth College in Hanover, N.H., remains the cultural center of the Upper Valley. With the nearby Dartmouth-Hitchcock medical complex and West Lebanon shopping strip, this area forms the region's commercial hub, handy to the highways radiating, the way rail lines once did, from White River Junction.

The Connecticut and White Rivers converge at White River Junction, an obvious stop for the area's first travelers, who arrived by canoe, then by raft and steamboat. Like an evolving species, they continued on land with the advent of the railroad, which spawned a brick village. In the mid–19th century, some 100 steam locomotives chugged into this station each day, bringing railcars full of tired, hungry passengers.

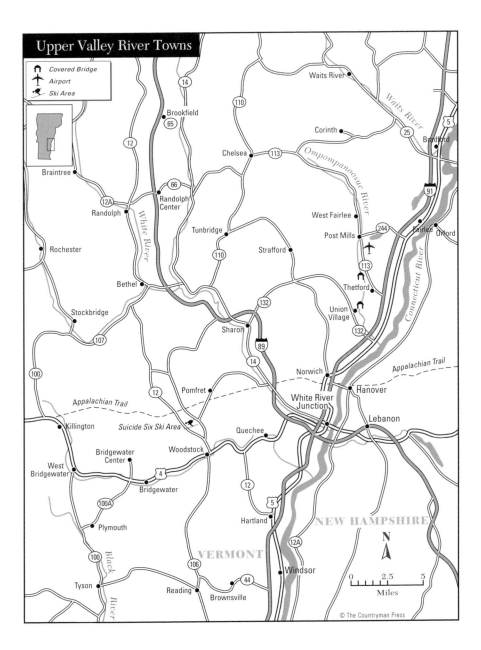

However, like a noose looping loosely around White River Junction, the inter-states (I-89 and I-91), have since channeled traffic away from this 19th-century village, slowly draining its lifeblood. Happily, the downtown commercial blocks here are presently evolving as an arts and dining center, still with the vintage rail depot—now a combination visitors center and transportation museum—at its core. Once more it even offers canoe access to the Connecticut River.

GUIDANCE White River Welcome Center (802-281-5050), 100 Railroad Row in the Amtrak station, White River Junction. Open daily 9–5, 9–4 in winter. This information-packed waypoint center is staffed by the state and offers friendly, knowledgeable advice, and restrooms; it adjoins an evolving New England Transportation Institute and Museum. Also see www.ctrivertravel.com

GETTING THERE *By car:* Interstates 91 and 89 intersect in the White River Junction (Vt.)–Lebanon (N.H.) area, where they also meet Rt. 5 north and south on the Vermont side; Rt. 4, the main east–west highway through central Vermont; and Rt. 10, the river road on the New Hampshire side.

By bus: White River Junction is a hub for **Vermont Transit** (1-800-552-8737; www.vermonttransit.com) with express service to Boston. **Dartmouth Coach** (1-800-637-0123; www.concordtrailways.com) offers aggressively competitive service from Boston and Logan Airport to Hanover, N.H.

By air: The **Lebanon Regional Airport** (603-298-8878), West Lebanon (marked from the junction of I-89 and Rt. 10), has frequent service to New York's LaGuardia Airport via US Airways Express, which also serves Philadelphia. Rental cars are available from Avis, Hertz, and Alamo; the airport is also served by **Big Yellow Taxi** (603-643-8294).

By train: **Amtrak** (1-800-872-7245) serves White River Junction, en route to and from New York/Washington and Essex Junction, Vt. Connecting bus service to Montreal.

MEDICAL EMERGENCY Dartmouth-Hitchcock Medical Center (603-650-5000), off Rt. 120 between Hanover and Lebanon, is generally considered the best hospital in northern New England.

Call **911**.

✳ Communities

Listed from south to north.

White River Junction (population: 2,500; www.whiteriverjct.com) is one of five villages within the town of Hartford. As noted in this chapter's introduction, downtown White River—which at its peak saw 100 steam locomotives chug into the station daily—is now a bit of cul-de-sac. Still, it's well worth finding. Stage North, a professional theater company, has fixed up the old Briggs Opera House and puts on performances year-round. There are printing and arts studios in the Tip Top building (a former commercial bakery), a natural food co-op, good restaurants, and the groundbreaking **Center for Cartoon Studies** (a 2-year program with a library endowed by Charles M. Schulz, creator of *Peanuts*). There are also several shops worth a detour in their own right. The **New England Transportation Institute and Museum** (603-252-9703; www.new englandtransportationmuseum.org) in the Amtrak station is volunteer operated ($2 per adult), theoretically open in summer Mon.–Fri. 9–5, Sat. 9–2; in winter Tue. and Fri. 9–4. Exhibits span the Valley's river and air history as well as rail.

The station itself is a seasonal departure point for the White River Flyer, an excursion train that runs along the river to the Montshire Museum. Follow the walkway along the tracks to the free **Main Street Museum** (802-356-2776; www.mainstreetmuseum .org), open Thu.–Sat. 1–6. Housed in a former firehouse, this "cabinet of curiosities" seems a parody of the museum genre. Owner David Fairbanks (as in St. Johnsbury's Fairbanks Museum) Ford's exhibits include Elvis Presley's gallstones and an eclectic range of stuffed and "found" objects. Check the web site for ongoing

Chris McKinley

AMTRAK'S VERMONTER PULLS INTO WHITE RIVER JUNCTION

events. At the center of the village is the Hotel Coolidge (see *Lodging*), one of the last of New England's railroad hotels. In its former incarnation as the Junction House, the hotel's clientele included Lillian Gish and President Calvin Coolidge, for whose father it is named. Ask to see the hand-painted murals in the Vermont Room, depicting the state's history from wilderness to the 1940s. Lovingly preserved by its present owners, the Coolidge is rich in character, something conspicuously absent from the interstate-geared, brand-name motels and fast-food stops along the village periphery. Horace Wells of White River Junction was, incidentally, the first person to use laughing gas as an anesthetic for pulling teeth. The other villages in the town of Hartford are Quechee (see the "Woodstock/Quechee" chapter), Hartford Village, Wilder, and West Hartford.

Norwich (population: 3,544), one of the prettiest towns in Vermont, was settled in 1761 by a group from Marshfield, Ct. It has always had close ties to Hanover (just across the bridge) and was itself the original home of Norwich University (founded 1819), which moved to Northfield after the Civil War. The village is an architectural showcase for fine brick and frame Federal homes. Note the Seven Nations House, built in 1832 as a commercial "tenement." Across the way is the Norwich Inn, dating back to 1797 and with a popular brewpub as well as dining room, the hospitable heart of town. Sequestered down by the river (east of I-91), the recently expanded **Montshire Museum** offers insights into ways the world and universe go 'round as well as into how the river shapes the immediate environment; it also offers trails through its 110 acres. **King Arthur Flour Company**'s flagship Baker's Store and Baking Education Center on Rt. 5, south of town, draws devotees from throughout the county.

Hanover, N.H., is synonymous with Ivy League **Dartmouth College** (www .dartmouth.edu), chartered in 1769 and one of the most prestigious colleges in the country. Dartmouth's student population averages 4,300 undergraduate men and women and 600 graduate students. Its handsome buildings frame three sides of an elm- and maple-lined green, and the fourth side includes a large inn, an arts center, and an outstanding art museum. The information booth on the green is the starting point for historical and architectural tours of the campus. **Baker Memorial Library**, a 1920s version of Philadelphia's Independence Hall, dominates the northern side of the green. Visitors are welcome to see a set of murals, *The Epic of American Civilization*, by José Clemente Orozco, painted between 1932 and 1934 while he was teaching at Dartmouth. (Some alumni once demanded these be removed or covered because of the Mexican artist's left-wing politics.) In the Treasure Room (near the western stair hall on the main floor), Daniel Webster's copies of the double elephant folio first edition of John Audubon's *Birds of America* are permanently displayed. The **Hopkins Center for the Arts** (603-646-2422) was designed by Wallace Harrison a few years before he designed New York's Lincoln Center (which it resembles). It contains three theaters, a recital hall, and art galleries for permanent and year-round programs of plays, concerts, and films. It's also home base for the Dartmouth Symphony Orchestra. **Dartmouth Row**, a file of four striking white Colonial buildings on the rise along the eastern side of the green, represents all there was to Dartmouth College until 1845. You might also want to find Webster Cottage, maintained as a museum by the Hanover Historical Society, and the vintage-1843 **Shattuck Observatory** (open weekdays 8:30–4:40, also Tue. and Thu. evenings by reservation: 603-646-2034). Also see the **Hood Museum of Art**, next page.

Lyme, N.H., is known for its splendid **Congregational church**, completed in 1812, a Federal-style meetinghouse complete with Palladian window, an unusual tower (three cubical stages and an octagonal dome), and no fewer than 27 numbered horse stalls. The gathering of buildings, including the inn, fine old houses, and general stores, is one of New Hampshire's most stately. Take **River Road** north by old farms and cemeteries, through an 1880s covered bridge.

Thetford has an unusual number of post offices per capita: There are six villages in all. Thetford Center has a friendly general store and handsome brick Methodist church. Thetford Hill is a beauty, the site of Thetford Academy, the Parish Players, and the **Thetford Historical Society** (open Aug., Sun. 2–5) and its **Historic Library** (open year-round, Mon. and Thu. 2–4 and Tue. 10–noon).

Fairlee Village, shelved between the Palisades and a bend in the Connecticut River, is a plain cousin to aristocratic Orford, N.H. (well known for its lineup of elegant Federal-era houses), just across the river. But we like it better. Check out Chapman's, a 19th-century pharmacy that has expanded in unusual directions. Summer camps and inns line nearby Lake Morey. Samuel Morey, a resident of Orford and a lumberman in Fairlee, was the inventor of the first steamboat: In 1793, 14 years before Fulton launched his *Clermont*, Morey was puffing up and down the river in a primitive craft barely big enough to hold him and his firewood. The remains of the little steamer are believed to lie at the bottom of Lake Morey, scuttled by its builder when the $100,000 in stock offered him by Robert Fulton turned out to be worthless. Morey also patented an internal combustion engine in 1825. Lake Fairlee, lined with children's camps and with a public swim beach, straddles the town line and is best accessed from Rt. 244 west of Ely.

Orford, N.H., is known for its **Ridge Houses**, a center-of-town lineup of seven houses so strikingly handsome that Charles Bulfinch has been (erroneously) credited as their architect. They were built instead by skilled local craftsmen

Hood Museum of Art (603-646-2808; www.hoodmuseum.dartmouth.edu), Dartmouth green, Hanover, N.H. Open Tue.–Sat. 10–5, until 9 on Wed.; Sun. noon–5. Free. An outstanding collection of world-class art from almost every geographic area of the world and historical period. Featuring ninth-century Assyrian reliefs from the Palace of Ashurnarsipal II at Nimrod (present-day Iraq); European Old Master prints and paintings; two centuries of American paintings, portraits, drawings, and watercolors; American decorative arts; ancient and Asian objects; traditional and contemporary African, Oceanic, and Native American collections; cutting-edge contemporary art; and a stunning set of murals by José Clemente Orozco. Two floors of galleries, permanent collections, traveling exhibitions. Explore on your own or arrange for a tour by calling (603) 646-1469. Hood Museum of Art Shop has something for all ages and budgets.

using designs from Connecticut Valley architect Asher Benjamin's do-it-yourself guide to Federal styles, *The Country Builder's Apprentice*. These houses testify to the prosperity of this valley in the post–Revolutionary War era. Each was built by an Orford resident—with money earned in Orford—between 1773 and 1839. The best remembered of the residents is Samuel Morey. While all his neighbors were in church one Sunday morning in 1793, Morey gave the country's first little steam-powered paddle-wheeler a successful test run on the river. Sam kept tinkering with the boat and in 1797 came up with a side-wheeler, but at this point Robert Fulton, who had encouraged Morey to talk freely with him and demonstrate the invention, went into the steamboating business, using a boat clearly patterned after Morey's. It's said that an embittered Morey sank his boat across the river in the Vermont lake that now bears his name. He also heated and lighted his house with gas, and in 1826 he patented a gas-powered internal combustion engine. The **Samuel Morey House** is the oldest of the seven, a centerpiece for the others.

✷ Must-See

The Vermont Institute of Natural Science/Vermont Raptor Center (802-FLY-5000; www.vinsweb.org), Rt. 4, Quechee. Open daily May–Oct., 10–5; Nov.–Apr., Wed.–Sun. 10–4.; also open holidays and school vacations. $8 adults, $7.20 seniors, $6.50 children. A beloved institution, VINS is a living museum devoted to birds of prey, located just west of Quechee Gorge. Resident raptors include bald eagles, peregrine falcons, snowy owls, and hawks that have been injured. They are displayed in large outdoor enclosures. There are outdoor interpretive exhibits, nature trails, and a nature shop. Inquire about naturalist walks and flight programs.

✷ To Do

AIR RIDES **Post Mills Airport** (802-333-9254), West Fairlee, Vt. Mid-May–mid-Nov., Brian Boland offers morning and sunset balloon rides (he spends the

✒ **Montshire Museum of Science** (802-649-2200; www.montshire.org), 1 Montshire Rd., Norwich. Open daily 10–5 except Thanksgiving, Christmas, and New Year's Day; $7.50 adults, $6.50 ages 3–17. Use of the trails is free. Few cities have a science museum of this quality. Happily this hands-on science center is on 110 trail-webbed acres beside the Connecticut River. The name derives from Ver*mont* and New Hamp*shire*, and the focus is on demystifying natural phenomena in the world in general and the Upper Valley in particular. River exhibits include an elaborate 2.5-acre Science Park: Water bubbles from a 7-foot Barre granite boulder, and from this "headwater" a 250-foot "rill" flows downhill, snaking over a series of terraces, inviting you to manipulate dams and sluices to change its flow and direction (visitors are advised to bring towels). You can also shape fountains, cast shadows to tell time, and push a button to identify the call of birds and insects within actual hearing. Note Ed Kahn's *Wind*

THE MONTSHIRE MUSEUM IN NORWICH

John Douglas

other 6 months in New Zealand). On the summer evening we tried it, the balloon hovered above hidden pockets in the hills, and we saw a herd of what looked like brown and white goats that, on closer inspection, proved to be deer (yes, some were white!). After an hour or so we settled down gently in a farmyard and broke out the champagne. Boland builds as well as flies hot-air balloons and maintains a private museum of balloons and airships. He also maintains rustic cabins on the premises for patrons ($50 per night) and offers packages in conjunction with nearby **Silver Maple Lodge** (1-800-666-1946; www.silver maplelodge.com), which includes the balloon rides on its web site.

Also see **Balloons of Vermont** and **Balloons over New England** in the "Woodstock/Quechee Area" chapter.

Wall, a billboard-sized sheet attached to the museum's tower, composed of thousands of silver flutter disks that shimmer in the breeze, resembling patterns on a pond riffled by wind.

Inside the museum a new, federally funded wing focuses on this stretch of the Silvio O. Conte National Fish and Wildlife Refuge; exhibits include a giant moose and tanks of gleaming local fish. Still, some of our favorite exhibits are in the original museum: the fog machine up in the tower, the see-through beehive, exhibits illustrating which vegetables and fruits float, and the physics of bubbles. There are also astounding displays on moths, insects, and birds. Most

Gilbert Fox

THE MONTSHIRE MUSEUM IN NORWICH HAS DOZENS OF FASCINATING EXHIBITS FOR CHILDREN

exhibits, even the boa constrictors (at designated times), are "hands-on." While there's a corner for toddlers, an outside playground, and many demonstrations geared to youngsters, this is as stimulating a place for adults as for their offspring. The gift shop alone is worth stopping for. Inquire about guided hikes, special events, and exhibits. In summer and fall the excursion train **White River Flyer** (1-800-707-3530) offers round-trip excursions from Union Depot in White River Junction up along the Connecticut River to the museum.

BICYCLING Given its unusually flat and scenic roads and well-spaced inns, this area is beloved by bicyclists. Search out the river roads: from Rt. 12A (just north of the Saint-Gaudens site) on through Plainfield, N.H., until it rejoins Rt. 12A; from Rt. 10 north of Hanover, N.H. (just north of the Chieftain Motel) through Lyme, N.H., rejoining Rt. 10 in Orford, N.H. A classic, 36-mile loop is Hanover to Orford on Rt. 10 and back on the river road. The loop to Lyme, N.H., and back is 22 miles. For inn-to-inn guided tours in this area, contact **Bike Vermont** (802-457-3553; 1-800-257-2226; www.bikevermont.com).

BOATING With its usually placid water and scenery, the Connecticut River through much of the Upper Valley is ideal for easygoing canoeists. The

Connecticut River Joint Commissions (603-826-4800; www.ctrivertravel.net) has published a useful *Boating on the Connecticut River* guide. Information on primitive campsites along this stretch of the river can be found on the web site maintained by the Upper Valley Land Trust (www.uvlt.org).

North Star Livery (603-542-6929; www.kayak-canoe.com), 58 Bridge St., White River Junction. Open seasonally, Thu.–Sun. This is a relatively new branch of the largest and oldest commercial rental service on the Connecticut River, offering shuttle service for self-guided paddles on the White River as well as down the Connecticut. Inquire about overnight camping trips and about running Class I and II rapids in spring and early summer. For more, see the description of its home base in Cornish ("The Lower Connecticut River Valley").

The Ledyard Canoe Club (603-643-6709), Hanover, N.H. Dartmouth's mellow, student-run canoeing and kayaking center with rentals but no shuttle service.

Fairlee Marine (802-333-9745), Rt. 5 in Fairlee, rents pontoons, canoes, rowboats, and small motors for use on the Connecticut and two local lakes.

Also see **Wilderness Trails** in the "Woodstock/Quechee Area" chapter.

Information on seven primitive campsites along this stretch of the Connecticut River can be found on the **Upper Valley Land Trust**'s web site: www.uvlt.org.

FISHING You can eat the fish you catch in the Connecticut River—it yields brown and rainbow trout above Orford. There's a boat launch on the Vermont side at the Wilder Dam, another just north of Hanover, N.H., and another across the river in North Thetford. Lake Mascoma (look for boat launches along Rt. 4A in Enfield, N.H.) and Post Pond in Lyme, N.H., are other popular angling spots.

Lyme Angler (603-643-6447; www.lymeangler.com), 8 S. Main St., Hanover, N.H. This is an Orvis outfitter and guide service offering a "Fly-Fishing School," guided trips, fly-tying classes, rental equipment, and a shop selling fishing clothing and gear.

GOLF Hanover Country Club (603-646-2000), Rope Ferry Rd., off Rt. 10, Hanover. Open May–Oct. Founded in 1899, an 18-hole facility with 4 practice holes, pro shop, PGA instructors. **Carter Golf Club** (603-448-4483), Rt. 4, Lebanon. Nine holes, par 36. **Lake Morey Country Club** (802-333-4800; 1-800-423-1211), Fairlee. Eighteen holes.

RAILROAD EXCURSION *Trains Around Vermont* (802-463-3069; 1-800-707-3530; www.rails-vt.com), Union Depot, 100 Railroad Row, White River Junction. Take a round-trip along the Connecticut River to the Montshire Museum and Thetford on the White River Flyer. Frequent round-trips mid-June–Labor Day and weekends in foliage season (mid-June–mid-Oct.) $10–14 adults, $7–10 children.

SWIMMING Ask locally about swimming holes in the Connecticut River.

Storrs Pond Recreation Area (603-643-2134), off Rt. 10 north of Hanover, N.H. (Reservoir Rd., then left). Open June–Labor Day, 10–8. Bathhouse with showers and lockers, lifeguards at both the (unheated) Olympic-sized pool and 15-acre pond. Fee for nonmembers.

🦆 𝄢 **Treasure Island** (802-333-9615), on Lake Fairlee, Thetford. This fabulous town swimming area is on Rt. 244 (follow Rt. 113 north of town). Open late June–Labor Day, 10–8 weekends, noon–8 weekdays. Sand beach, picnic tables, playground, tennis. Nominal admission.

Union Village Dam Recreation Area (802-649-1606), Thetford. Open Memorial Day–mid-Sep.; five swimming areas along the Ompompanoosuc River. Also has walking and cross-country skiing trails, picnic tables, and grills.

✳ Winter Sports

CROSS-COUNTRY SKIING AND SNOWSHOEING **Dartmouth Cross Country Ski Center** (603-643-6534), Rope Ferry Rd. (off Rt. 10 just before the country club), Hanover, N.H. Open in snow season Mon.–Fri. 9–7, weekends 9–5. $10 pass. Twenty-five km of varied trails, some geared to skating, through the Storrs Pond and Oak Hill areas; rental skis, skates, and snowshoes.

Lake Morey Inn Resort (802-333-4800; 1-800-423-1211), Fairlee. Turns the golf course into a touring center in winter; rentals, instruction.

Also see **Thetford Hill State Park** under *Green Space.*

DOWNHILL SKIING 𝄢 **Dartmouth Skiway** (603-795-2143; www.skiway.dart mouth.edu), Lyme Center, N.H., an amenity for families as well as the college, with a snazzy 16,000-square-foot timber base lodge. Open 9–4 daily; rentals and ski school. *Trails:* 32. *Lifts:* 1 quad chair, 1 double chair, a beginners' J-bar. *Vertical drop:* 968 feet. *Snowmaking:* 65 percent. *Rates:* $38 adults, $25 juniors on weekends; $26 and $18 weekdays; also half-day, senior, military, and more rates.

Whaleback 603-448-1489; www.whaleback.com), I-89, Exit 16, Enfield, N.H. Zero Gravity Skate Park open year-round, winter hours with skiing/snowboarding: noon–9 weekdays, 9 AM–9 PM Sat., 9–4:30 Sun. This beloved family mountain, just off I-89, is now an "action sports center." Reopened under new, local ownership in 2006, it offers 35 trails served by a double chair and 4 surface lifts (with 80 percent snowmaking) and night skiing. What's new: a renovated base lodge, indoor and outdoor skate parks, and seasonal mountain biking. Planned: a water ramp, BMX track, and paintball. Staff are headed by two-time Olympian Evan Dybvig, and it's all about teaching action sports. Weekday ski/snowboard rates: $25 adults, $20 night; skating $12.

Also see **Ascutney Mountain Resort** in the previous chapter.

✳ Green Space

Pine Park, just north of the Dartmouth campus between the Hanover Country Club and the Connecticut River, Hanover, N.H. Take N. Main St. to Rope Ferry Rd. Park at the trail sign above the clubhouse. These tall pines are one of the beauty spots of the Valley. The 125-year-old trees were saved from the Diamond Match Company in 1900 by a group of local citizens. The walk is 1.5 miles.

&. **Montshire Museum of Science Trails**, Norwich. The museum's 110 acres include a 12-acre promontory between the Connecticut River and the marshy bay at the mouth of Bloody Brook. The 0.25-mile trail leading down through tall white pines to the bay is quite magical. The 1.5-mile Hazen Trail runs all the way to Wilder Village. These trails are hard packed, accessible to strollers and wheelchairs.

Thetford Hill State Park (802-785-2266; www.vtstateparks.com), 622 Academy Rd., Thetford Center. Open Memorial Day–Labor Day. Developed by the Civilian Conservation Corps in the 1930s, 177 acres with a **campground** (14 tent/trailer sites, two lean-tos, hot showers), hiking and cross-country trails (maintained by Thetford Academy).

See also **Quechee Gorge State Park** in "Woodstock/Quechee Area."

✳ Lodging

HOTELS 🐾 ♂ &. **The Hanover Inn** (603-643-4300; 1-800-443-7024; www .hanoverinn.com), corner of Maine and South Wheelock Sts., Hanover, N.H. 03755. This is the Ritz of the North Country. A four-story, 92-room, neo-Georgian building owned and operated by Dartmouth College, the "inn" traces itself back to an 1780 tavern. It remains the heart of Hanover. In summer the front terrace is crowded with faculty, visitors, and residents enjoying a light lunch or beer. Both Zins Wine Bistro and the more formal Daniel Webster Room (see *Dining Out*) draw patrons from throughout the Upper Valley. Rates range from $260 for a standard room to $310 for a junior suite, no charge for children under age 12; senior citizens' discount; honeymoon, ski, golf, and seasonal packages. Handicapped accessible and pets accepted.

🦐 ♂ **The Hotel Coolidge** (802-295-3118; 1-800-622-1124; www.hotel coolidge.com), White River Junction 05001. Not luxurious but a beloved icon as New England's last railroad hotel. It's also comfortable, clean, and reasonably priced. All 30 elevator-served guest rooms have private bath, phone, and TV. Some back rooms are dark, but others are quite roomy and attractive, and the family suites (two rooms connected by a bath) are a good value. The hotel sits across from the Amtrak station, adjacent to the Briggs Opera House. Local buses to Hanover and Lebanon stop at the door, and rental cars can be arranged. Search out the splendid Peter Michael Gish murals in the Vermont Room, painted in 1949 in exchange for room and board while the artist was studying with Paul Sample at Dartmouth. Owner-manager David Briggs, a seventh-generation Vermonter, takes his role as innkeeper seriously and will arrange for special needs. $79–129 per room double. Under 17 free.

INNS

Listed from south to north.

∞ &. **Home Hill Country Inn** (603-675-6165; www.homehillinn.com), River Rd., Plainfield, N.H. 03781. Built in 1818, this is one of those magnificent, four-square mansions spaced along the Connecticut River. Innkeepers Victoria and Stephane de Roure have renovated the main house to offer three elegant guest rooms and a two-room suite; there are also six "country French" guest rooms in the Carriage House. A small cottage, La Piscine, with a bedroom and sitting room, is beside the pool. $195–425 per couple includes breakfast and afternoon refreshments. Add a 15 percent service fee. A 2-night package including two chef's tasting menus with pairings is $1,279–1,735. This inn is all about outstanding food; check *Dining Out*.

🍃 **Moose Mountain Lodge** (603-643-3529; www.themoosemountain lodge.com), P.O. Box 272, Moose Mountain Highway, Etna, N.H. 03750. Closed Mon. and Tue., also Nov.–Dec. 25 and late Mar.–mid-June. Just 7 miles from the Dart-mouth green, the feel is remote, and the view, spectacular. This is a classic "lodge," built from stones and logs cleared from these hills, walled in pine. The roomy porch (filled with flowers in summer) is like a balcony seat above the Valley, commanding a view of Vermont mountains from Ascutney to Sugarbush, with Killington center stage, beyond lower hills. This is also the view from the sitting room, with its window seats, baby grand piano, and massive stone fireplace. Upstairs the 12 rooms are small but inviting (with spruce log bedsteads made by innkeeper Kay Shumway); the 5 shared baths are immaculate. Kay is a cookbook author who continues to prepare feasts for hikers (the inn is just off the Appalachian Trail), bikers, and cross-country skiers. Innkeepers since 1975, Kay and Peter Shumway still welcome each new guest with enthusiasm and interest. The 350 acres include a deep pond, ample woods, meadows, and access to 50 miles of dependably snowy cross-country ski trails. $220 per couple in winter, $200 in summer includes breakfast and dinner; $55 under age 14. No smoking.

🍃 🏠 **Norwich Inn** (802-649-1143; www.norwichinn.com), 325 Main St., Norwich 05055. Just across the river from Hanover and less formal and expensive than the Hanover Inn, this is very much a gathering place for Dartmouth parents, faculty, and students. The present three-story, tower-topped inn dates from 1889 (when its predecessor burned). Since acquiring it in 1991, innkeepers Sally and Tim Wilson have steadily worked to restore its high-Victorian look inside and out. The 27 rooms are divided among the main building, the Vestry, and a backyard motel. All rooms have private bath, telephone, and cable TV. Sally has redecorated with a sure touch, adding Victorian antiques but not cluttering either the guest or public rooms. A brewpub, Jasper Murdock's Alehouse, features 15 varieties of inn-made brews (see *Eating Out*). The dining rooms are open for breakfast, lunch, and dinner. Rates run from $69 in the off-season in the motel and $109 in the inn to $149 for a two-bedroom suite in the Vestry. All three meals are served but not included.

THE NORWICH INN

Christina Tree

Dogs are permitted in one twin-bedded room in the motel.

Alden Country Inn (603-795-2222; 1-800-794-2296; www.aldencountryinn.com), On The Common, Lyme, N.H. 03768. Dating back to 1809, this substantial inn stands at the head of a classic common, offering three daily meals as well as 15 guest rooms (on the top two floors). All have private bath, phone, and air-conditioning. Frank and Darlene Godoy have renovated rooms; high-speed wireless access is available throughout. $130–195 in summer and fall, from $95 in winter, includes a full breakfast. Two-night stay required on weekends.

⚭ ✐ ♿ **Lake Morey Resort** (802-333-4311; 1-800-423-1211; www.lakemoreyresort.com), Club House Rd., Fairlee 05045. On the shore of Lake Morey, this sprawling, lakeside landmark best known for its golf course is also a winter getaway for cross-country skiers. In summer children's programs are offered. Given the grounds and reception areas, this is a wedding venue as well. The resort dates from the early 1900s and was owned by the Avery family for some 20 years beginning in the 1970s, then sold and reclaimed several years ago. It has since been completely renovated. There are 130 rooms and suites. The splendid lake view remains key, along with a player-friendly 18-hole golf course. Facilities include indoor and outdoor swimming pools, tennis and racquetball courts, a fitness center, cross-country ski and snowmobile trails. Grounds are nicely landscaped. All three meals are served. Winter $94–114 per room EP; MAP rates are offered. Summer and fall $110–242 per person, depending on season, day of the week, as well as accommodation. Inquire about golf and other packages.

BED & BREAKFASTS

Listed from south to north.

🐾 ✐ **Norwich Bed and Breakfast at Shear Luck Farm** (802-649-3800; www.norwichbnb.com), 229 Bradley Hill Rd., Norwich 05055. A newly renovated, 125-year old farmhouse on Bradley Hill offers two guest rooms, one of them a suite, both with king bed and private bath. Just 4 miles from Dartmouth College, this 20-acre farm offers sheep, chickens, and, mountain views. $100–180 includes breakfast; dinner on request.

White Goose Inn (603-353-4812; 1-800-358-4267; www.whitegooseinn.com), P.O. Box 17, Rt. 10, Orford, N.H. 03777. This is as an exceptionally handsome 1830s brick house—four chimneyed and green shuttered, with the original 1766 clapboard home now an el at the back. Marshall and Renee Ivey have lightened and brightened this inn, expanding the common spaces. There are eight antiques-furnished guest rooms with private bath and two that share. $89 (shared bath)–149 includes a full breakfast. Inquire about floorcloth workshops. Guests can take advantage of Peyton Place (see *Dining Out*), housed in the neighboring Federal-era tavern, one of the best places to dine in the Upper Valley.

🏵 🐾 ✐ ♿ **Silver Maple Lodge & Cottages** (802-333-4326; 1-800-666-1946; www.silvermaplelodge.com), 520 Rt. 5 south, Fairlee 05045. Situated just south of the village on Rt. 5, Silver Maple was built as a farmhouse in 1855 and has been welcoming travelers for more than 80 years. Now run by Scott and Sharon Wright, it has

Christina Tree

THE HOTEL COOLIDGE IN WHITE RIVER JUNCTION

seven nicely appointed guest rooms in the lodge and eight separate, pine-paneled, shaded cottages. The farmhouse has cheerful sitting rooms with exposed 200-year-old hand-hewn beams in the living room and dining room, where fresh breads appear with other continental breakfast goodies. The newest cottages with kitchenette and working fireplace are real beauties. Play horseshoes, croquet, badminton, or shuffleboard on the lawn, or rent a bike or canoe. Scott will also arrange a ride in a hot-air balloon for you at neighboring Post Mills Airport. Scott grew up on a Tunbridge farm and takes pride in introducing visitors to Vermont. $69–109 per couple. Pets are accepted in the cottages, one of which has wheelchair access.

HOSTEL 🐾 🖋 **The Hotel Coolidge** (802-295-3118). A wing of the Coolidge, described under *Hotels*, is a Hostelling International facility with dorm-style beds and access to a self-service kitchen and laundry. Private family rooms are also available by reservation. $19 for HI members, $29 for nonmembers.

✳ Where to Eat

DINING OUT 🖋 **Como Va** (802-280-1956; www.comovarestaurant.com), 1 S. Main St., White River Junction. Open Tue.–Sat. for lunch and dinner. Fine Mediterranean cuisine in this quiet corner restaurant with glass on two walls, the better to watch the comings and goings of trains and people in the center of the village. Chef-owner Howard Haywood is a graduate of the Culinary Institute of America (CIA). He makes inspired salads, pastas, and desserts in this bright place with its brick walls and Italian accents. You might begin with carpaccio, or mussels simmered with toasted garlic, fennel, sweet tomatoes, and vermouth; then proceed to "pasta your way," combining a choice of pastas with a choice of fillings and sauces ($13.95 adults, $7.95 children). The long list of entrées ranges from classic eggplant Parmesan to herb-roasted lamb chops and rosemary skewered Gulf shrimp. Entrées $13.95–28.95. Regional Italian wines are featured.

Carpenter and Main (802-649-2922; www.carpenterandmain.com), Main St., Norwich. Open for dinner except Tue. and Wed.; tavern 5:30–10, dining room 6–9; reservations suggested. Chef-owner Peter Ireland is known for vegetarian dishes complementing staples like bouillabaisse and roast pork loin. A fall trio of vegetables, all presented with their tops on, comprised baby pumpkin filled with sage cream and Gruyère, zucchini stuffed with creamy polenta, and sweet onion filled with barley. Try the house pâté for starters. Entrées $18–28; moderately priced tavern menu ($13 and below).

Norwich Inn (802-649-1143; www.norwichinn.com), 325 Main St., Norwich. Open for breakfast, lunch, and dinner, also Sun. brunch, but closed Mon. Across the river from Hanover, the dining room in this classic inn is popular with Dartmouth faculty and local residents, good for vegetarian as well as wide variety of entrées ($16.95–20.95). Jasper Murdock's Alehouse (see *Eating Out*), also on the premises, is beloved for its hand-crafted brews (sold only here) as well as for its atmosphere and pub food.

Simon Pearce (802-295-1470), The Mill, Quechee. Open daily for lunch and dinner (reserve). This is the one place no visitor wants to miss. It's frequently crowded and touristy, but a special place with delicious food. Housed in a mill that once formed the centerpiece for a village, with views of the waterfall. The tableware features handblown, hand-finished glass designed and blown in the mill and sold in the adjoining gift shop. At lunch try the shepherd's pie or coho salmon smoked here at the mill. Dinner entrées $20–38.

Across the river
Peyton Place (603-353-9100; www.peytonplacerestaurant.com), Rt. 10, Orford, N.H. Open for dinner Wed.–Sun. 5:30–10:30; in the off-season, Fri.–Sun. Reservations a must. Destination dining, this restaurant (named for owners Jim, Heidi, Sophie, and Shamus Peyton) is housed in a 1773 tavern with a genuine old pub room (and a genuinely interesting pub menu) as well as more formal dining rooms. Dinner entrées might range from house-made vegetarian ravioli, Asian shrimp stir-fry, and steak fritters to rack of lamb with wild mushrooms. Ice creams and sorbets are handmade as well. Wine and spirits are served. The pub menu might include house-made duck and chorizo dumplings, and quesadillas with tortillas made in-house. Dinner entrées $15.50–26.50. Inquire about cooking classes.

Home Hill Country Inn (603-675-6165), River Rd., Plainfield, N.H. Open for dinner Tue.–Sun. in summer and fall, Wed.–Sun. in winter. Reservations suggested. A four-square 1820s mansion by the river, this represents the Valley's priciest and most elegant dining. Guests tend to enjoy a drink in a plush armchair before sitting down to a linen-dressed table in one of the low-ceilinged dining rooms. Chef-owner Victoria de Roure trained at the Ritz Escoffier in Paris. Stephane de Roure, who is from the south of France, selects wine and oversees management of the restaurant. Dinner might begin with braised escargots or an asparagus-hazelnut tart with herbed goat cheese; you might then dine on roasted and braised milk-fed veal with morels, peas, and onions, followed by a frozen banana soufflé or tarte au chocolat with burnt orange ice cream. Appetizers $14–16; entrées $34–38; desserts $14. Prix fixe tasting menu $89, with wine parings $154. (Also see *Lodging*.)

Canoe Club Bistro and Music (603-643-9660; www.canoeclub.us), 27 S. Main St., Hanover, N.H. Open daily for lunch and dinner with light fare between meals (2–5) and late-night menus Thu.–Sat. Reservations suggested for dinner. Acoustic music nightly, also Sunday jazz brunch. "Sensational" is the way local residents describe this attractive addition to Hanover's dining options. The lunch may include wild mushroom stroganoff, pulled pork quesadilla, and warm smoked sausage with port-braised cabbage, a grilled baguette, and ale mustard. The dinner menu might include house-made ravioli (ingredients change daily) and Vermont lamb with Swiss chard, sun-dried tomato pesto, parsnips, sweet potatoes, and brussels sprout leaves. Dinner entrées $15–25.

EATING OUT

In Hartland Four Corners
Skunk Hollow Tavern (802-436-2139), Hartland Four Corners, off Rt. 12 south of Rt. 4, north of I-91, Exit 9. Dinner Wed.–Sun., more days during peak periods. Reservations suggested. Carlos Ocasio's split-personality restaurant, hidden away

in a small village, is a local favorite. Patrons gather downstairs in the pub to play darts and backgammon and to munch on fish-and-chips, mussels, or pizza; the more formal dining is upstairs in the inn's original parlor. The menu changes every few months, but staples include Chicken Carlos. Variables might be red pepper shrimp with Oriental pasta or shiitake chicken; always salad of the day and homemade soups. $8–24. Open-mike night Wed. and entertainment Fri. nights.

In White River Junction
The Tip Top Café (802-295-3312; www.tiptopcafevt.com), 85 N. Main St. Open Tue.–Sat. 11:30–2 and 5–9. Reserve on theater nights (see Northern Stage under *Entertainment*). Chef-owner Eric Harting (creator of the Perfect Pear) now presides in this glass-fronted bistro on the ground floor of a former commercial bakery. The decor incorporates industrial ducts, hanging lamps, and the polished cement floor. Walls are hung with big, splashy (changing) paintings, and tables are dressed with brown paper. Order from the blackboard menu at lunch; dinner is full service. Lunches include soups, salads, and

ERIC HARTING PRESIDES AT THE TIP TOP CAFÉ IN WHITE RIVER JUNCTION
Christina Tree

unusual sandwiches such as balsamic figs with spinach and Gorgonzola on rosemary focaccia. Dinner might begin with artichoke fritters with lemon jalapeño preserve; entrées might include sesame-crusted talapia with mango salsa and mixed greens. Lunch $6–10, dinner entrées $10–18.

The Polka Dot Restaurant (802-285-9722), 7 Main St. Open Tue.–Sun. 5 AM–7 PM. A classic diner, handy to the train station and more than a century old, looking better than ever after a fire a couple of years ago necessitated a total rehab. Proprietor Mary Shatney has a solid local following. The menu ranges from honeycomb tripe to prime rib, plenty of daily specials.

The Baker's Studio (802-296-7201), in the Hotel Coolidge. Open Mon. 7:30–2, Tue.–Fri. 7:30–5, Sat. 7:30–3. Artisan breads like olive parsley are the specialty, but there are also pizzas, quiches, New York–style bagels, breakfast muffins, cookies, coffee, and tables to linger at.

In Lebanon/West Lebanon, N.H.
Three Tomatoes Trattoria (603-448-1711), 1 Court St., Lebanon. Open for lunch Mon.–Fri. 11:30–2, and nightly for dinner. A trendy trattoria with a sleek decor, wood-fired oven and grill, and a reasonably priced menu: plenty of pasta creations like penne con carciofi—sautéed mushrooms, spinach, roasted garlic, and olive oil tossed with penne ziti regate. There are also grilled dishes like pollo cacciatora alla gorgolia—boneless chicken topped with tomato basil sauce, mozzarella, and Romano cheese, and served with linguine—and no less than 16 very different pizzas from the wood-fired oven. Wine and beer are served.

Gusanoz (603-448-1408; www.gusanoz.com), 410 Miracle Mile, Lebanon. Open Mon.–Sat. 11–9, Sun. 10–3. The Upper Valley's hottest Mexican restaurant is squirreled away in a Lebanon mini mall (off I-89, Exit 19; look for a movie theater and the DMV). Maria Limon and Nick Yager have already tripled their seating in answer to demand since their 2005 opening. Specialties include chicken mole, carnitas, tamales, and pork asado—staples of Limon's girlhood in Durango, Mexico. On Sunday it's a dazzling "all you can eat" brunch. The only problem still may be getting in.

❧ **Lui, Lui** (603-298-7070), Powerhouse Mall, West Lebanon. Open daily for lunch straight through dinner until 9:30. The former boiler house for the brick mill complex makes a multi-tiered, attractive setting for this popular, informal Italian restaurant. Pastas, salads, calzones, and specialty pizzas fill the bill of fare.

Yama Restaurant (603-298-5477), 96 Main St., West Lebanon. Open Tue.–Sat. (until 10 PM) for lunch and dinner; Sun. from 3 PM. The fare is essentially Korean and terrific, if you like a large choice of udon noodle, miso, seaweed, and spicy soups, as well as house specials like "Yukyejang," which turned out to be shredded beef and vegetables in a spicy broth with side dishes of pickled cucumber and sweet but firm baked beans. There are also donburi, tempura, and teriyaki dishes, and a reasonably priced sushi bar (served with miso soup). Wine and beer.

❧ **West Lebanon fast-food strip**. Rt. 12A just south of I-89, Exit 20, is lined with representatives of every major fast-food chain in New England—a godsend to families with cars full of kids.

In Norwich
Jasper Murdock's Alehouse in the Norwich Inn (802-649-1143), 225 Main St. Open 5:30–9. The house brew comes in many varieties. The Alehouse is a green-walled, comfortable pub; the bill of fare changes frequently but usually represents some of the best "bar food" in the Valley. The menu might include "Light Fare" like Maine crabcakes and Louisiana oyster po'boys (with homemade French bread), and moderately priced full-fare dishes such as pork schnitzel with apple sauerkraut and cider currant sauce, grilled flank steak with wheatberry and dried fruit sauté, and shepherd's pie.

Alléchante Patisserie and Cafe (802-649-2846), Main and Elm Sts. Open Mon.–Fri. 7:30–5:30; until 3 Sat. Formerly "Alice's," Nicky Barraclough's shop is in a small shopping complex, easy to miss but well known to local residents who drop by for a morning brioche and latte and to check the daily sandwich board. This might include freshly roasted beef with homemade horseradish cream on white sourdough, and imported fresh goat cheese with sliced tomatoes and green olive spread on a baguette. There are also daily baked artisan breads and pastries, plus a full deli with a weekly changing take-out dinner menu. It might include chicken potpies, roast skate with peas and mash and a variety of vegetables, plus a choice of meat and fish. This is also a place to pick up farmstead cheeses. The new name is French for "mouthwatering."

In Hanover, N.H.
Lou's Restaurant and Bakery (603-643-3321), 30 S. Main St. Open for breakfast weekdays from 6 AM, Sat. from 7, and Sun. from 8. Lunch Mon.–Sat. until 3 PM. Since 1947 this has been a student and local hangout and it's great: a long Formica counter, tables and booths, fast, friendly service, good soups, sandwiches, daily specials, and irresistible peanut butter cookies at the register.

Molly's (603-643-2570), 43 Main St. Open daily for lunch and dinner. The greenhouse up front shelters a big, inviting bar that encourages single dining. The menu is immense and reasonably priced: big salads, enchiladas, elaborate burgers at lunch, pasta to steak at dinner.

In Fairlee
The Third Rail (802-333-9126), Rt. 5, south of the bridge. Open for dinner except Sunday. A family find. Entrées might include roast salmon teriyaki and veal marinara but also a variety of burgers, fish-and-chips, and children's menu. Entrées $11.95–15.50.

Fairlee Diner (802-333-3569), Rt. 5. Closed Tue., otherwise 5:30 AM–2 PM; until 7 PM Thu. and 8 PM Fri. Turn left (north) on Rt. 5 if you are coming off I-91. This is a classic wooden diner built in the 1930s (across the road from where it stands), with wooden booths, worn-shiny wooden stool tops, and good food. The mashed potato doughnuts are special, and both the soup and the pie are dependably good. Daily specials.

Leda's Restaurant & Pizza (802-333-4773), Rt. 5. Open Wed.–Sun. for lunch and dinner. This is a friendly standby for Greek specialties like moussaka, gyros, and feta cheese pie along with burgers, pizza, and even rib-eye steak.

Note: See the **Fairlee Drive-In** under *Entertainment* for the best burgers in town.

✴ Entertainment

MUSIC AND THEATER Hopkins Center (603-646-2422 box office; www.hop.dartmouth.edu), on the Dartmouth green, Hanover, N.H. Sponsors some 150 musical and 20 theater productions per year, plus 200 films, all open to the public.

Lebanon Opera House (603-448-0400), town hall, Coburn Park, Lebanon, N.H. This 800-seat, turn-of-the-20th-century theater hosts frequent concerts, lectures, and performances by the North Country Community Players. Throughout the month of August **Opera North** (www.operanorth.org) stages excellent performances featuring soloists from major opera companies.

✿ **Northern Stage** (802-296-7000; www.northernstage.org), Briggs Opera House, White River Junction. Northern Stage is a professional nonprofit regional theater company that produces six mainstage shows Oct.–mid-Apr. in a 245-seat theater. These include dramas, comedies, musicals, as well as brilliant, lesser-known works and new plays fresh from Broadway and London's West End. Recent seasons have included *All My Sons*, *My Fair Lady*, *Private Lives*, *Proof*, and *Copenhagen*. It's a three-quarter-thrust theater with 245 seats. Prices range $16–43, depending on seat and day of the week.

The Parish Players (802-785-4344; www.parishplayers.org), based in the Eclipse Grange Hall on Thetford Hill, is the oldest community theater company in the Upper Valley; its Sep.–May repertoire includes classic pieces and original works; summer presentations vary.

FILM *✿* **Fairlee Drive-In** (802-333-9192), Rt. 5, Fairlee. Summer only; check local papers for listings. This is a beloved icon, the last of the Valley's seasonal drive-ins. It's attached to the Fairlee Motel and has a famously good snack bar featuring "thunderburgers," made from beef on the family's farm across the river in Piermont. The gates open at 7; films begin at dusk.

Dartmouth Film Society at the Hopkins Center (603-646-2576), Hanover, N.H. Frequent showings of classic, contemporary, and experimental films in two theaters.

Nugget Theaters (603-643-2769), S. Main St., Hanover, N.H. Four current films nightly, surround sound.

✴ Selective Shopping

ART GALLERIES AND CRAFTS CENTERS Simon Pearce Glass (802-674-6280), Quechee Village, off Rt. 4. Open daily 9–5. Pearce operated his own glassworks in Ireland before moving to Vermont in 1981. Here he acquired the venerable Downer's Mill in Quechee and harnessed the dam's hydropower for the glass furnace (see *Dining Out*). In 1993 he opened this new, visitor-friendly glass factory featuring a catwalk that overlooks the gallery where glass is blown and shaped. Of course, there's a big showroom/shop featuring seconds as well as first-quality glass and pottery.

Tip Top Media & Arts Building, 85 North St., White River Junction. A warren of studios and changing galleries, worth a look upstairs.

League of New Hampshire Craftsmen (603-643-5050), 13 Lebanon St., Hanover, N.H. Closed Sun. Next to Ben & Jerry's; a wide selection of local and regional crafts pieces. Classes offered.

Long River Studios (603-795-4909), 1 Main St., Lyme, N.H. Open Mon.–Sat. 10–5. A regional cooperative with a wide selection of art in many media, also cards, books, pottery, clothing, jewelry, and more.

SPECIAL SHOPS

In White River Junction

Lampscapes (802-295-8044; www.lampscapes.com), 77 Gates St. Open Tue.–Sat. 10–5. Kenneth Blaisdell is a former engineer and a serious landscape artist whose combination studio/shop is one of the more exciting shopping finds in Vermont. The metal lamps themselves are simple but artistic; the shades ($30–150) are definitely works of art, each one-of-a-kind and ranging from luminescent literal to semi-abstract, truly striking landscapes, priced within reasonable reach.

The Hundredth Monkey (802-295-9397), 79 Gates St. Open Tue.–Sat. 10–5 or by appointment. In this new, smaller location David Holtz has created a carefully selected mix of used and rare books with emphasis on photography, Americana, and children's books.

Revolution, Vintage & Urban Used Clothing (802-295-6487), 25 N. Main St. Kim Sousa offers an eclectic, funky selection of vintage, used, and handmade clothing plus jewelry and accessories.

Isobel Jones Luxury Wraps and Stoles (603-653-0111; www.isobel jones.com), 58 Bridge St. (in back). Open by chance or appointment. Jones designs lush stoles and wraps, using silks, wools, ostrich feathers, and other exotic materials. All colors, with lots of fringe.

In Norwich

King Arthur Flour Baker's Store (802-649-3361; 1-800-827-6836; www.kingarthurflour.com), 135 Rt. 5. Open Mon.–Sat. 8:30–6, Sun. until 4. Home as well as prime outlet for the country's oldest family-owned flour company (since 1790), this store draws serious bakers and would-be bakers from throughout several time zones. The vast store is a marvel, its shelves stocked with every conceivable kind of flour, baking ingredient, and a selection of equipment and cookbooks, not to mention bread and pastries made in the adjacent bakery (with a glass connector allowing visitors to watch the hands and skills of the bakers). Next door too is the **King Arthur Baking Education Center**, offering baking classes ranging from beginner to expert, from making

KENNETH BLAISDELL HARD AT WORK IN HIS LAMPSCAPES SHOP IN WHITE RIVER JUNCTION

Christina Tree

piecrust to braided breads and elegant pastries.

Dan & Whit's General Store (802-649-1602), Main St. The quintessential Vermont country store. Hardware, groceries, housewares, boots and clothing, farm and garden supplies, and a great community bulletin board: If they don't have it, you don't need it.

The Norwich Bookstore (802-649-1114), Main St., next to the post office. This is a light, airy store with well-selected titles and comfortable places to sit. The staff is very knowledgeable. Frequent readings, and a good children's section.

Points north
Pompanoosuc Mills (802-785-4851; www.pompy.com), Rt. 5, East Thetford. Dartmouth graduate Dwight Sargeant began building furniture in this riverside house, a cottage industry that has evolved into a riverside factory with showrooms throughout New England. Some seconds. Open daily until 6 PM, Sun. noon–5. Note the branch on Lebanon St. in Hanover, N.H.

Chapman's (802-333-9709), Fairlee. Open daily 8–6, until 5 on Sun. Since 1924 members of the Chapman family have expanded the stock of this old pharmacy to include 10,000 hand-tied flies, wines, Mexican silver and Indonesian jewelry, used books, and an unusual selection of toys—as well as nightcrawlers and manila envelopes. Check out the antiques in the barn. This time we bought a wooden puzzle and a stove mitt.

✳ Special Events

For details about any of these events, phone the town clerk, listed with information.

Mid-February: **Dartmouth Winter Carnival**, Hanover, N.H. Thu.–Sun. Ice sculptures, sports events, ski jumping.

Third weekend in June: **Quechee Balloon Festival and Crafts Fair** (802-295-7900), Quechee. Some 20 hot-air balloons gather, offering rides at dawn and dusk; barbecue, skydiving, crafts, food booths.

Fourth of July: **Independence Day Open Fields Circus**, Thetford. A takeoff on a real circus by the Parish Players. **Fourth of July celebration**, Plainfield, N.H. Community breakfast, footraces, parade, firemen's roast beef dinner. Lebanon, N.H., stages the largest fireworks display in the area.

Mid-July: **Norwich Fair**. Mix of old-time country fair and honky-tonk carnival. Lobster dinner, parade, ox pulling.

Early August: **North Haverhill Fair**, N.H. Horse show and pulling, evening live entertainment, midway. **Thetford Hill Fair**, Thetford Hill. Small but special: a rummage sale, food and plant booths, barbecue.

Late August: **Quechee Scottish Festival**, Quechee. Sheepdog trials, Highland dancing, piping, Highland "games," ladies' rolling-pin toss, more.

Saturday after Labor Day: **Railroad Days** in White River Junction (www.glorydaysoftherailroad.org): railroad excursions, music.

Saturday of Columbus Day weekend: **Horse Sheds Crafts Fair**, at the Lyme Congregational Church, Lyme, N.H. 10 AM–4 PM; also a **Fall Festival** lunch at the church.

Mid-December–Christmas: **Christmas Pageants** in Norwich and Lyme, N.H. **Revels North**, in the Hopkins Center, N.H. Song and dance.

WOODSTOCK/QUECHEE AREA

Cradled between Mount Peg and Mount Tom and moated by the Ottauquechee (pronounced *otto-KWEE-chee*) River, Woodstock is repeatedly named among the prettiest towns in America. The story behind its good looks, which include the surrounding landscape as well as historic buildings, is told at the Marsh-Billings-Rockefeller National Historical Park, the country's only national park to focus on the concept of conservation.

The Ottauquechee River flows east through Woodstock along Rt. 4 toward the Connecticut River, generating electricity as it tumbles over falls beneath the covered bridge at Taftsville and powering Simon Pearce's glass factory a few miles downstream in Quechee Village. Below Quechee the river has carved Vermont's "Grand Canyon," Quechee Gorge, spanned by Rt. 4 and by a high, spidery railroad bridge.

The Woodstock Railroad carried passengers and freight the 20 miles between Woodstock and White River Junction between 1875 and 1933. How to ease current traffic congestion, which includes 18-wheelers headed for Rutland as well as tour buses and tourists in summer and fall and skiers in winter, remains a very real challenge. Rt. 4 is the shortest way across "Vermont's waist," and an evergrowing stream of vehicles continues to wind up the valley, filing through the middle of Woodstock, around its exquisite green, and on through the village of West Woodstock, following the river west into Bridgewater.

Our advice: Walk. Park at the picnic area just beyond Quechee Gorge and savor the view of the river churning far below between 163-foot-high walls. Walk the path down to the water's edge or around VINS, the neighboring raptor and nature sanctuary. In Woodstock Village stroll the streets, then walk Mountain Avenue through Faulkner Park and on up to the top of Mount Tom then back down the Pogue Carriage Road to Billings Farm.

Like most of the world's famously beautiful and heavily touristed areas, especially those that are also home to sophisticated people who could live anywhere, the Ottauquechee River Valley offers visitors plenty to see and do superficially and still more, the more you explore.

GUIDANCE **The Woodstock Area Chamber of Commerce** (802-457-3555; 1-888-496-6378; www.woodstockvt.com), 18 Central St., Woodstock 05091, keeps

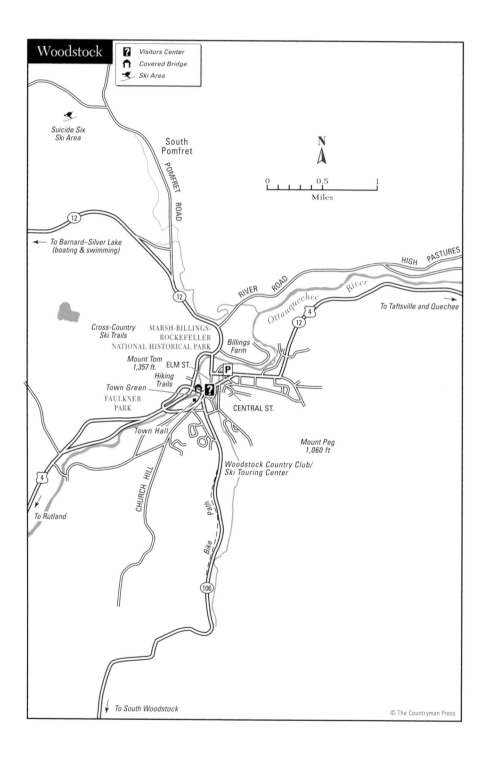

Woodstock

?	Visitors Center
∩	Covered Bridge
🎿	Ski Area

Suicide Six
Ski Area

South
Pomfret

POMFRET ROAD

N

0   0.5   1
Miles

12

← To Barnard–Silver Lake
(boating & swimming)

12

RIVER ROAD

HIGH PASTURES

Ottauquechee River

4
12

→ To Taftsville and Quechee

Cross-Country
Ski Trails

MARSH-BILLINGS-
ROCKEFELLER
NATIONAL HISTORICAL PARK

Billings
Farm

Mount Tom
1,357 ft.   ELM ST.

Hiking
Trails

Town Green

FAULKNER
PARK

P

CENTRAL ST.

Town Hall

Mount Peg
1,060 ft

Woodstock Country Club/
Ski Touring Center

4

CHURCH HILL

Bike Path

↓
To Rutland

106

↓ To South Woodstock

© The Countryman Press

publishes *Window on Woodstock*, a useful free pamphlet guide. Lodging places post available rooms on their web site, and sometimes during foliage season the chamber also finds beds in private homes for stranded leaf-peepers. Restrooms are available in the town hall, west of the green.

The Quechee Gorge Visitors Center (802-295-7900; 802-295-6852; 1-800-295-5451; www.quechee.com) is maintained by the Hartford Area Chamber of Commerce, Rt. 4 at Quechee Gorge. Open year-round, 9–5 Apr.–Oct.,10–4 off-season. New in 2006, this is a lovely, well-stocked center with helpful staff and restrooms.

GETTING THERE *By car:* Rt. 4 west from I-91 and I-89.

By train: **Amtrak** to White River Junction or to Rutland. **Woodstock Transportation** (802-770-0416) offers shuttle service from the train to Woodstock in a seven-person van by reservation.

By bus: **Vermont Transit** (1-800-552-8737) travels to White River Junction from Boston but no longer stops in Woodstock.

MEDICAL EMERGENCY Emergency service is available by calling **911**.

PARKING Two-hour meters on Central and Elm Sts. and 4-hour meters on Mechanic St. off Central are closely monitored 10–4, Mon.–Sat.: 25¢ per half hour; red drop boxes in front of the town's two pharmacies are provided to pay fines. There are free lots by the river on Pleasant St. and—on weekends only—at the elementary school on Rt. 106.

WHEN TO COME This area is as genuinely year-round as Vermont gets. Marsh-Billings-Rockefeller National Historical Park and the Billings Farm & Museum are open May through mid-October, but Woodstock's early-December Wassail Weekend is its most colorful happening, and January through March bring cross-country and alpine skiing. The Quechee Hot Air Balloon Festival is the area's most famous event.

✳ Villages

Woodstock. In the 1790s, when it became the shire town of Windsor County, Woodstock began attracting prosperous professionals, who, with local merchants and bankers, built the concentration of distinguished Federal houses that surround the elliptical green, forming an architectural showcase that has been meticulously preserved. In the 19th century it produced more than its share of celebrities, including Hiram Powers, the sculptor whose nude *Greek Slave* scandalized the nation in 1847, and Senator Jacob Collamer (1791–1865), President Lincoln's confidant, who declared, "The good people of Woodstock have less incentive than others to yearn for heaven."

Three eminent residents in particular—all of whom lived in the same house but in different eras—helped shape the current Woodstock (see the box on page 256).

Christina Tree

WOODSTOCK'S MAIN STREET

"Innkeeping has always been the backbone of Woodstock's economy, most importantly since 1892 when the town's business leaders and bankers decided to build a new hotel grand enough to rival the White Mountain resorts," Peter Jennison writes in *Woodstock's Heritage*. By the turn of the 20th century, in addition to several inns, Woodstock had an elaborate mineral water spa and golf links, and it had become Vermont's first winter resort, drawing guests from Boston and New York for snowshoeing and skating. In 1934 America's first rope tow was installed here, marking the real advent of downhill skiing.

By the early 1960s, however, the beloved Woodstock Inn was creaky, the town's ski areas had been upstaged, and the hills were sprouting condos. Laurance Rockefeller acquired the two ski areas (upgrading Suicide Six and closing Mount Tom) and had the 18-hole golf course redesigned by Robert Trent Jones Sr. In 1969 he replaced the old inn. Rockefeller also created the Woodstock Foundation, a nonprofit umbrella for such village projects as acquiring and restoring dozens of historic homes, burying power lines, and building a new covered bridge by the green. In 1992 it opened the Billings Farm & Museum. The Marsh-Billings-Rockefeller National Historical Park, which includes the neighboring Rockefeller mansion and the 550 surrounding forested acres on Mount Tom, opened in 1998.

Woodstock itself remains a real town with a lot going on. Events chalked on the "Town Crier" blackboard at the corner of Elm and Central Streets are likely to include a supper at one of the town's several churches (four boast Paul Revere bells), the current film at the theater in town hall, as well as events at the historical society and guided walks.

Note: The Woodstock Historical Society has published detailed pamphlets and guides available at Dana House (see *Also See*).

Quechee, on Rt. 4, some 6 miles east of Woodstock, is one of five villages in the township of Hartford. In the mid– and late 19th century life revolved around the J. C. Parker and Co. mill, which produced a soft baby flannel made from "shoddy" (reworked rags). A neighboring mill village surrounded the Deweys Mill, which made baseball uniforms for the Boston Red Sox and the New York Yankees. In the 1950s, however, both mills shut down. In the '60s the Deweys Mill virtually disappeared beneath a flood-control project (see North Hartland Lake under *Green Space*), and 6,000 acres straddling both villages was acquired by the Quechee Lakes Corporation, the largest second-home and condominium development in the state. Thanks in good part to Act 250, Vermont's land-use statute, the end result is unobtrusive. Most homes are sequestered in woods; open space includes two (private) 18-hole golf courses. In Quechee Village the mill is now Simon Pearce's famous glass factory and restaurant, and the former

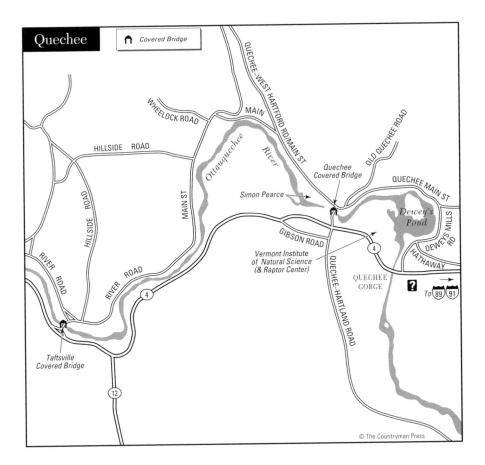

© The Countryman Press

millowner's mansion is the Parker House Inn. Dramatic Quechee Gorge is visible from Rt. 4 but is best appreciated if you follow the trail to the bottom. The VINS Quechee Nature Center is also here. Tourist-geared shops and eateries continue to proliferate along Rt. 4, but, along back roads, so does village conservation land.

✳ Must-See

East to west
Quechee Gorge, Rt. 4, is one of Vermont's natural wonders, a 3,000-foot-long, 163-foot-deep chasm sculpted 13,000 years ago. Visible from the highway, it is now encompassed by a state park that includes hiking trails along the rim and down into the gorge. See *Green Space*.

The Vermont Institute of Natural Science/Vermont Raptor Center (802-FLY-5000; www.vinsweb.org), Rt. 4, Quechee. Open daily May–Oct., 10–5; Nov.–Apr., Wed.–Sun. 10–4.; also open holidays and school vacations. $8 adults, $7.20 seniors, $6.50 children. A beloved institution devoted to rehabilitating birds of prey, VINS occupies 47 acres of rolling forestland just west of Quechee

VINS

A RED-TAILED HAWK MEETS THE PUBLIC
THANKS TO VINS

Gorge. Resident raptors include bald eagles, peregrine falcons, snowy owls, hawks, and other birds of prey that have been injured. They are displayed in huge outdoor flight enclosures. There are outdoor interpretive exhibits, nature trails, and a nature shop. Inquire about naturalist-led walks, and twice-daily flight programs.

Visitors Center for Billings Farm & Museum and the Marsh-Billings-Rockefeller National Historical Park, Rt. 12 north of Woodstock Village. Open May–Oct., daily 10–5. The parking lot and visitors center at Billings Farm serve both the farm and national park with displays on Marsh, Billings, and Rockefeller and a theater showing *A Place in the Land*, Charles Guggenheim's award-winning documentary dramatizing the story of all three men. (There's no admission fee for the restrooms and gift shop, but a nominal fee is charged to see the film if you aren't visiting the farm or museum.)

Note: A combination ticket to the Billings Farm & Museum and programs at Marsh-Billings-Rockefeller National Historical Park is offered: $13 adults, $10 seniors, $9 ages 13–17, $6.50 ages 5–12.

✍ ᴗ **Billings Farm & Museum** (802-457-2355; www.billingsfarm.org). Open May–Oct., daily 10–5, winter holiday weekends 10–4. $9.50 adults, $8.50 over 65, $7.50 ages 13–17, $5 ages 5–12, $2.50 ages 3–4. Exhibits demonstrate life on Frederick Billings's model "gentleman's" farm in the 1890s: plowing, seeding, cultivating, harvesting, and storing crops; making cheese and butter; woodcutting and sugaring. The 1890 farm manager's house has been restored. Visitors can also observe what happens on a modern dairy farm with a prizewinning Jersey herd. The farm's Percheron workhorses—Kate, Jim, Joe, Purse, and Daisy—welcome visitors. Almost every day activities are geared to kids, from toddlers on up. Cows are milked daily at 3 PM. Inquire about special events, like apple days and wool days in fall; Thanksgiving weekend and Christmas weekend celebrations; sleigh rally weekends in Jan. and Feb.; and periodic demonstrations and crafts exhibits.

PATIENT COWS AT BILLINGS FARM AND
MUSEUM IN WOODSTOCK

Billings Farm and Museum

Marsh-Billings-Rockefeller National Historical Park (802-457-3368; www.nps.gov/mabi), Rt. 12 north of Woodstock Village. Mount Tom carriage roads and forest trails (see *Green Space*) are open year-round, free in summer (for winter use see *Cross-Country Skiing*). The

Queen Anne mansion, the centerpiece of this estate, is notable for its antiques, Tiffany glass, and American art, and for a sense of the amazing individuals who lived there. Guided hour-plus tours, offered Memorial Day–Oct., are limited to a dozen visitors at a time; reservations are advised ($6 adults, $3 seniors and ages 6–15). These depart from the **Carriage Barn** (open late May–Oct., 10–5; free), an elegant space with dark bead board walls and the feel of a library, with exhibits that position Marsh, Billings, and Rockefeller within the time line of America's conservation history. A multimedia exhibit, *People Taking Care of Places*, profiles individuals practicing conservation around the world. Visitors are invited to record their own conservation stories on computers and to take advantage of the reading area with its conference-sized table (crafted from wood harvested on Mount Tom) and relevant books, including children's stories.

✳ Also See

The Dana House (home of the Woodstock Historical Society, 802-457-1822), 26 Elm St., Woodstock. Open May–Oct., Tue.–Sat. 10–4, and holiday weekend Sundays noon–4. Office and research library open year-round. Admission $5 (free under age 12); 40-minute tours on the hour. John Cotton Dana was an eminent early-20th-century librarian and museum director whose innovations made books and art more accessible to the public. Completed in 1807 and occupied for the next 140 years by the Dana family, this historic house has an interesting permanent exhibit portraying the town's economic heritage and an admirable collection of antiques, locally wrought coin silver, portraits, porcelains, fabrics, costumes, and toys. The John Cotton Dana Library is a research and reference center. There is also an exhibit gallery.

✐ **The Norman Williams Public Library** (802-457-2295), on the Woodstock green. Open daily except Sunday and holidays. A Romanesque gem, donated and endowed in 1883 by Dr. Edward H. Williams, general manager of the Pennsylvania Railroad and later head of Baldwin Locomotives. It offers children's story hours, poetry readings, and brown-bag summer concerts on the lawn; also Internet access for a small fee.

COVERED BRIDGES There are three in the town of Woodstock—the **Lincoln Bridge** (1865), Rt. 4, West Woodstock, Vermont's only Pratt-type truss; the **Middle Bridge**, in the center of the village, built in 1969 by Milton Graton, "last of the covered-bridge builders," in the Town lattice style (partially destroyed by vandalism and rebuilt); and the notable red **Taftsville Bridge** (1836), Rt. 4 east, utilizing multiple king- and queenposts and an unusual mongrel truss. This is the second oldest bridge in Vermont and overlooks a hydroelectric dam, still in use.

WOODSTOCK COVERED BRIDGE

Christina Tree

GEORGE PERKINS MARSH (1801–1882), FREDERICK BILLINGS (1823–1890), AND LAURANCE ROCKEFELLER (1910–2005)

Three men in particular have helped shape Woodstock's landscape. The first, George Perkins Marsh, born and raised here, had damaged his eyesight by age 7 by devouring encyclopedias and books on Greek and Latin. Sent outdoors, he studied the woods, fields, birds, and animals with equal intensity. As a man he noted the effects of logging on the landscape (60 percent of Vermont's virgin forest was harvested in the first half of the 19th century) and the resulting floods and destruction of fisheries. Later, traveling in the Middle East as the U.S. ambassador to Turkey, Marsh noted how once fertile land had become desert. He wrote: "I fear man has brought the face of the earth to a devastation almost as complete as that of the moon."

FREDERICK BILLINGS BY KURTZ, C. 1873

Courtesy Billings Farm Museum

Marsh wrote *Man and Nature* at age 63, while U.S. ambassador to Italy. Published in 1864, it is widely recognized as the first book to acknowledge civilization's effect on the environment, and the first to suggest solutions. In contrast with Henry David Thoreau (*Walden* appeared in 1854), Marsh doesn't idealize wilderness. Instead, he attempts to address the interdependence of the environment and society as a whole.

Man and Nature isn't an easy read, but it greatly influenced this country's nascent sciences of forestry and agriculture as well as many of the era's movers and shakers, among them Frederick Billings. Raised in Woodstock, Billings departed at age 25 for San Francisco. That city's first lawyer, he made a fortune registering land claims and speculating in land during the

SCENIC DRIVES The whole area offers delightful vistas; one of the most scenic shortcuts is North Rd., which leaves Rt. 12 next to Silver Lake in Barnard and leads to Bethel. Also be sure to drive Rt. 106 to South Woodstock.

✳ To Do

BALLOONING **Balloons of Vermont** (802-291-4887; www.balloonsofvermont), based in Quechee, operates year-round (the two-person basket has a seat) and

gold rush. As a returning son who had "made good," Billings spoke at the 1864 Windsor County Fair, remarking on the rawness of the local landscape, the hills denuded by logging and sheep grazing. In 1869 he bought the old Marsh farm and transformed the vintage-1805 house into a mansion. On Mount Tom he planted more than 100,000 trees, turned a bog into Pogue Pond, and created the carriage roads.

Billings's primary home was in New York, and as president of the Northern Pacific Railroad (the reason Billings, Montana, is named for him) he toured the country extensively. He continued, however, to retreat to Woodstock, creating a model dairy farm on his property, a project sustained after his death, through thick and thin, by his wife and two successive generations of Billings women.

Courtesy Billings Family Archives

GEORGE PERKINS MARSH BY G. P. A. HEALY, C. 1820

In 1934 Frederick Billings's granddaughter Mary French (1910–1997) married Laurance Rockefeller in Woodstock. John D. Rockefeller Jr. had been largely responsible for creating more than 20 state and national parks and historic sites; Laurance inherited his father's commitment to conservation and quickly became an effective advocate of ecotourism. In the 1950s Mary Rockefeller inherited the Billings estate in Woodstock and Laurance bought and replaced the old Woodstock Inn, incorporating the golf course and Suicide Six ski area into one resort. He also created the Woodstock Foundation, a nonprofit umbrella for numerous village projects (see *Villages*) and for collecting local antique farm tools and oral histories, opening the Billings Farm & Museum in 1983. In 1992 the Marsh-Billings-Rockefeller National Historical Park was created. It opened in 1998.

will launch from your home or inn (conditions permitting); **Balloons Over New England** (1-800-788-5562; www.balloonsovernewengland.com) operates seasonally from Quechee, which is also the scene of the **Quechee Hot Air Balloon Festival** on Father's Day weekend in June, New England's premier balloon festival, featuring rides as well as live entertainment and crafts (see *Special Events*).

BICYCLING **Bike Vermont** (802-457-3553; 1-800-257-2226; www.bikevt.com), Box 207, Woodstock. Vermont's most experienced, most personalized, and

Christina Tree

VIEW OF OTTAUQUECHEE VALLEY FROM
APPLEHILL INNE, TAFTSVILLE

altogether best inn-to-inn tour service, offering weekend, 5-, and 7-day
trips through much of Vermont.
Twenty-one-speed Trek and Cannon-
dale hybrids are available for rent.
Tours are also offered to Ireland.

**Biscuit Hill Bike and Outdoor
Shop** (802-457-3377), 490 Woodstock
Rd. (Rt. 4), West Woodstock. A source
of rentals and local bike maps (River
Rd. from Woodstock to Quechee Vil-
lage is a designated bike trail).

Wilderness Trails (802-295-7620),
Clubhouse Rd. at the Quechee Inn.
Bike rentals 1for the whole family,
plus maps.

Woodstock Sports (802-457-1568), 30 Central St., Woodstock, has mountain
and hybrid bike rentals, also offers repairs and clothing.

BOATING Wilderness Trails (802-295-7620), Clubhouse Rd. at the Quechee
Inn, offers guided canoe and kayak trips; also rentals and shuttle service on the
Connecticut, White, and Ottauquechee Rivers, as well as in the Deweys Mills
Waterfowl Sanctuary. Inquire about island camping.

Silver Lake State Park (802-234-9451) in Barnard rents rowboats, canoes, and
kayaks.

FISHING Vermont Fly Fishing School (802-295-7620), the Quechee Inn at
Marshland Farm. Marty Banak offers lessons as well as providing tackle and
guided fishing on Deweys Pond and the Connecticut, White, and Ottauquechee
Rivers.

GOLF AND TENNIS Woodstock Country Club (802-457-2114; www.woodstock
inn.com), part of the Woodstock Inn and Resort, offers one of Vermont's oldest
(1895) and most prestigious 18-hole golf courses, scenic and compact, redesigned
by Robert Trent Jones Sr. in 1961. Be warned that it crosses water 11 times. Tee
times can be made just 24 hours in advance of play. Facilities include a pro shop,
putting green and practice range, lessons, electric carts, restaurant, and lounge.
Resort facilities also include The Woodstock Health & Fitness Center with
10 outdoor courts (4 deco turf and 6 clay), which can be rented for 1½-hour
periods; also lessons and equipment rental.

↗ **Vail Field**, Woodstock. Two public tennis courts and a children's playground.

HEALTH AND FITNESS CENTER Woodstock Health & Fitness Center (802-
457-6656), part of the Woodstock Inn and Resort, Rt. 106, recently renovated
with indoor tennis and racquetball, lap pool, whirlpool, aerobic and state-of-the-
art fitness equipment; spa treatments, facials, massage, manicure and pedicure;
flexible memberships and day-use options; pro shop.

HORSEBACK RIDING Woodstock has been an equestrian center for generations, especially for the hardy Morgans, which are making a local comeback in South Woodstock.

Kedron Valley Stables (802-457-1480), Rt. 106, South Woodstock. Generally recognized as one of the best places to ride horseback—if you know how but don't happen to own a horse—in New England. Learn to ride or spiff up your skills in the ring, or take a guided trail ride, a weekend vacation, a 6-day riding clinic (with accommodations at Kendall Homestead), or a 4-day inn-to-inn tour that averages 20 miles a day, 5 hours in the saddle. Over the years Paul and Barbara Kendall have pieced together a network of paths to link appealing inns. They lead riders over hiking and recreation trails, dirt roads, and meadows. Inquire about carriage, wagon, and sleigh rides.

The Green Mountain Horse Association (802-457-1509; www.gmhinc.org), Rt. 106, South Woodstock. Sponsor of the original 100-mile ride, an annual event around Labor Day that draws entrants from all over. Visitors are welcome at shows and precision riding and driving events.

LLAMA TREKKING **Woodstock Llama Trekking** (802-457-3722; 802-457-5117; www.woodstockllamatreks.com), The Red Cupboard, Rt. 4, West Woodstock. Mid-May–Oct., Brian Powell leads patrons on trails up through the woods to a scenic picnic spot.

POLO **Quechee Polo Club**. Matches are held most Saturdays at 2 PM in July and August on the field near Quechee Gorge.

ROCK CLIMBING ♪ **The Wall** (802-457-2221; www.vermontrocks.com), just east of the intersection of Rts. 4 and 12, Quechee. Call for hours and rates. This indoor rock-climbing gym and bouldering cave draws serious local climbers year-round. Equipment rentals and instruction for adults and children; birthday parties a specialty. Also includes an outdoor driving range.

SWIMMING **Silver Lake State Park** (802-234-9451; 802-773-2657), 10 miles north on Rt. 12 in Barnard, has a nice beach, and there's another smaller one right next to the general store.

♪ **The Woodstock Recreation Center** (802-457-1502), 54 River St., has two public pools, mostly for youngsters.

Also see *Health and Fitness Center* for an indoor pool.

✳ Winter Sports

CROSS-COUNTRY SKIING AND SNOWSHOEING **Woodstock Ski Touring Center** (802-457-6674; www.woodstockinn.com) utilizes the 30 km trail system on **Mount Tom**, which ranks with some of the best groomed trails in New England. It's composed largely of 1880s carriage roads climbing gently from the valley floor (700 feet) to the summit (1,250 feet), skirting a pond, and finally commanding a view of the village below and down the Ottauquechee Valley. The system offers vistas in many directions and a log cabin heated with a woodstove.

The center itself, source of tickets, a map, ski (skating and classic stride) and snowshoe rentals (also poles), lockers and lessons, is at the Woodstock Country Club, Rt. 106 south of the village, part of the Woodstock Inn and Resort, with 10 km of gentle, meadow skiing out the door on the golf course, connecting with another 20 km of woodland trails on Mount Peg as well as 10 km of snowshoe trails. Group and individual lessons; rentals; salesroom; lockers; soup and sandwiches; $14 per adult all day, $10 half day; $10 full and $7 half day for juniors and seniors; skiers pay half price at the Woodstock Health & Fitness Center.

Wilderness Trails (802-295-7620; www.quecheeinn.com), Clubhouse Rd. at the Quechee Inn, has 18 km of track-set trails, including easy loops through the woods and meadows around Quechee Gorge, offering fine views of its waterfalls, also harder trails down into the gorge. Snowshoe rentals are also offered. $8 adults, $6 juniors.

DOWNHILL SKIING ✍ **Suicide Six Ski Area** (802-457-6661; www.woodstockinn .com), South Pomfret, 5 miles north of Woodstock on Pomfret Rd. Heir to the first ski tow in the United States, which was cranked up in 1934 but on the other side of this hill. Suicide Six is now part of the Woodstock Inn and Resort complex and has a base lodge finished with native woodwork. Its beginners' area has a J-bar; two double chairlifts climb 655 vertical feet to reach 23 trails ranging from easy to The Show Off and Pomfret Plunge, plus a half-pipe for snowboarders. Lessons, rentals, restaurant. Weekend/holiday lift rates are $52 for adults and $38 for seniors and children; weekdays (with just the big chair running) it's $30 adults, $25 seniors and children. Half-day and single-ride rates; free lifts and rentals midweek (nonholiday) to Woodstock Inn guests.

ICE SKATING **Silver Lake**, by the general store in Barnard. **Union Area**, at Woodstock Union High School, Rt. 4 west, occasionally has night skating for families. **Woodstock Sports** (802-457-1568), 30 Central St., Woodstock, offers skate and ski rentals. **Wilderness Trails** (see *Cross-Country Skiing*) in Quechee also rents skates and clears the pond on its property and across the road.

SLEIGH RIDES **Kedron Valley Stables** (802-457-1480; www.kedron.com), Rt. 106, South Woodstock. Weather permitting, sleigh rides are offered daily. **Three Bothers Farm** (802-457-4934). Peter and Beth Mantello offer sleigh rides, tours, and carriage rides.

✳ Green Space

Mount Tom's 1,250-foot summit towers above the village of Woodstock. It's one of Vermont's most walked and walkable mountains. From Mountain Ave. in the village itself **Faulkner Park** (donated by Mrs. Edward Faulkner, one of Woodstock's most thoughtful philanthropists) features a trail patterned on Baden-Baden's "cardiac" walks. A marked, 1.6-mile path zigzags up to the summit (bring a picnic; a bench overlooks the village). The **Marsh-Billings-Rockefeller National Historical Park** encompasses more than 500 acres on the back side of Mount Tom, with 30 miles of footpaths that were originally carriage roads, including a trail to Pogue Pond. Enter on Rt. 12 at the park (follow signs) or at the trailhead on Prosper Rd., just off Rt. 12. Inquire about frequent seasonal programs offered by the national park (802-457-3368). Also see *Cross-Country Skiing* for winter use.

Mount Peg Trails begin on Golf Ave. behind the Woodstock Inn. Open May–Oct. One is roughly 5 miles round-trip, a peaceful walk up along easy switchbacks beneath pines with a picnic bench at the summit, with views west down the valley to Killington.

Quechee Gorge State Park (802-295-2990; www.vtstateparks.com), off Rt. 4, Quechee. This 611-acre preserve encompasses the gorge (see *Must-See*), and trails from the rim lead gently down (south of Rt. 4) into the gorge, which should be approached carefully. On a hot day it's tempting to wade into the shallow water at the south end of the gorge—but beware sudden water releases that have been known to sweep swimmers away. Ditto for the rockbound swimming hole at the north end of the gorge under the spillway. Look for picnic tables under the pines on Deweys Mills Rd. The campground (open mid-May–Oct. 15) offers 47 tent/trailer sites, seven lean-tos, and a dump station. This property belonged to a local woolen mill until the 1950s when it was acquired by the U.S. Army Corps of Engineers as part of the Hartland Dam flood-control project.

North Hartland Lake Recreation Area (802-295-2855) is a 1,711-acre preserve created by the U.S. Army Corps of Engineers to control the confluence of the Ottauquechee and Connecticut Rivers. It offers a sandy beach, wooded picnic area with grills, and nature trail. Access is poorly marked, so ask directions at the Quechee information booth.

Silver Lake State Park (802-234-9451; Jan.–May: 1-800-299-3071; www.vt stateparks), Rt. 12, Barnard. Campground open mid-May–Labor Day. On Silver Lake, good for fishing, swimming, and boating (rentals available). The park offers a snack bar and wooded campground with 40 tent/trailer sites and seven lean-tos. Hot showers.

Teagle Landing is Woodstock's vest-pocket park, a magical oasis below the bridge in the middle of town (Central St.). Landscaping and benches invite sitting a spell by the river, a tribute to Frank Teagle (1945–1997), one of Woodstock's most dedicated residents.

Dewey Pond Wildlife Sanctuary, Deweys Mills Rd., Quechee. Originally a millpond, this is a beautiful spot with nature trails and a boat launch, good for bird-watching and fishing.

Hurricane Forest, Rt. 5, White River Junction. This 500-acre town forest harbors a pond and many miles of trails. Ask directions at the Quechee information booth.

Eshqua Bog, off Hartland Hill Rd., Woodstock. A 40-acre sanctuary managed by the New England Wild Flower Society and The Nature Conservancy with a white-blazed loop trail circling through 8 acres of wetlands, with orchids blooming in summer. Ask directions locally.

Also see **Vermont Institute of Natural Science** under *Must-See*.

✳ Lodging

RESORTS ✎ The Woodstock Inn and Resort (802-457-1100; 1-800-448-7900; www.woodstockinn.com), on the green, Woodstock 05091, is the lineal descendant of the 18th-century Eagle Tavern and the famous "old" Woodstock Inn that flourished between 1893 and 1969, putting the town on the year-round resort map. Today's 142-room, air-conditioned, Colonial-style 1970s edition was created by Laurance S. Rockefeller and has been regularly remodeled and tastefully expanded in recent decades to include a townhouse wing. The comfortably furnished main lobby is dominated by a huge stone fireplace where 5-foot birch logs blaze late fall through spring, the glowing heart of this sociable town.

The main dining room offers fine dining, while the bright, attractive Eagle Café serves all three meals and the appealing Richardson's Tavern is another less formal dining alternative. Common space also includes a library with games and a computer; the grounds feature a landscaped swimming pool. Guests have access to the scenic 18-hole Woodstock Country Club for golf and tennis (it's a cross-country ski center in winter) and to the splendid Health & Fitness Center, plus downhill skiing at the historic Suicide Six area. The creature comforts of these pearly precincts, beautifully appointed and managed in most respects, make this one of Vermont's premier places to stay and play. Current regular-season rates are $240–654 ($137–460 in spring and Nov. "Value Seasons"); spacious porch and/or fireplace suites in the Tavern Wing represent the high end. There is also a separate cottage, the Justin Morgan House, which has a full kitchen. Children under 14 free when staying in the same room with an adult. MAP available. Check out ski and golf packages.

Twin Farms (802-234-9999; 1-800-894-6327; 802-234-9990 fax; www.twinfarms.com), Barnard 05031. Ironically, the shades of Sinclair Lewis, whose novels satirized the materialism of American life in the '20s, and Dorothy Thompson, the acerbic foreign correspondent, hover over this 300-acre, luxurious Shangri-la that used to be their country home. Here and now, an exclusive group of corporate CEOs, heads of government, royalty, and celebrities are welcome to unwind, frolic, and be rich together in sybaritic privacy. Of the four stylish rooms in the main house, Red's is only $1,050 a day; Dorothy's, $1,200. The 16 cottages range from $1,200 to $2,700, all including Lucullan meals at any hour, open bars, and the use of all recreational amenities, including the former Sonnenberg ski lift, a fully equipped fitness center, Japanese furo, croquet court, pond, and mountain bikes. The common rooms and guest quarters display an extraordinary collection of modern art by David Hockney, Frank Stella, and Roy Lichtenstein, among others. There's a 2-night minimum on weekends, 3 nights over holidays, and a 15 percent service charge. The entire enclave can be yours for $24,000 a day.

☙ ✎ The Quechee Inn at Marshland Farm (802-295-3133; 1-800-235-3133; www.quecheeinn.com), P.O. Box 747, Quechee Main St., Quechee 05059. Off by itself on a quiet side road east of Quechee Village, just up from Deweys Mills Pond and Quechee Gorge, this historic farm is a comfortable and attractive inn with 25 guest rooms. Look closely in the oldest rooms and you'll see the rough-hewn beams of the original Georgian-style house built here by Colonel Joseph Marsh in 1793. With successive centuries and owners it expanded to include a distinctive, two-story, double-porched ell. In 1954 it was actually forced to move to higher ground to escape the rising waters caused by the Hartland Dam. In 1968 it became the first headquarters and accommodations for the Quechee Lakes Corporation; a decade later it was acquired by an energetic couple who established its present looks and reputation, which subsequent owners have preserved.

Rooms vary in size and feel. Three are suites; all have private bath and phone and are furnished with antiques. The brick-floored, raftered lounge with its piano, books, and games opens onto a big, sunny dining room in which breakfast and dinner (see *Dining Out*) are served. The inn is home to the Vermont Fly Fishing School and also offers canoeing and kayaking tours on the Connecticut, White, and Ottauquechee Rivers, along with mountain bike rentals. In winter it maintains 18 km of groomed cross-country ski trails. Guests also enjoy privileges at the nearby Quechee Club with its 18-hole golf course, tennis courts, health center, and pools. Rates range $90–245, depending on room and season. Inquire about packages.

INNS **The Jackson House Inn** (802-457-2065; 1-800-448-1890; www .jacksonhouse.com), 37 Old Rt. 4, West Woodstock 05091. This luxuriously appointed and equipped 1890

farmhouse has been expanded to include nine air-conditioned rooms and six single-room suites furnished in period antiques (from several different periods). It's all set amid 5 acres of manicured grounds and gardens, with a spring-fed pond. Rates begin at $195 in low season for the Josephine Bonaparte room on the ground floor, furnished in the French Empire style, and at $340 for one of the four new mini suites, three of which have a thermal massage tub for two. One mini suite, the Christine Jackson on the first floor, has a Brazilian mahogany four-poster queen bed, a gas fireplace, and French doors to the brick patio and garden. Rates include a memorable breakfast and a predinner glass of wine and hors d'oeuvres. Your hosts are Carl and Linda Delnegro. Also see *Dining Out*.

♾ 🐾 ✎ **The Kedron Valley Inn** (802-457-1473; 1-800-836-1193; www .kedronvalleyinn.com), P.O. Box 145, Rt. 106, South Woodstock 05071. The mellow brick inn has been welcoming visitors since 1828 and served as a stop on the Underground Railroad. The complex now includes the neighboring Tavern Building (built in 1822 as the village store) and a Vermont log motel unit, which sits beside an acre-plus swimming pond with sandy beach. The Kedron Valley Stables are just up the road. The 28 nicely decorated guest rooms, all recently renovated and all with private bath, include 5 suites with Jacuzzi and private deck. While rooms vary, all have canopy or antique oak beds and many have a fireplace or Franklin stove. New owners Jack and Nicole Maiden have cleverly fitted rooms in the log annex with Adirondack-style furnishings; those with fireplace are now some of the most attractive rooms of all. They have also gingered up the Tavern area with comfortable seating, expanded the Tavern menu, and extended summer service to the expansive, columned front porch. Room rates are $133–299 double for rooms, $250 for suites, B&B. Discounts are available for May–June and for midweek, off-peak periods year-round. The inn can host a reception for up to 200 and organizes weddings, using the village church and a horse-drawn carriage or sleigh. Also see *Dining Out*.

⊙ ☘ **Parker House Inn** (802-295-6077; www.theparkerhouseinn.com), 1792 Main St., Quechee 05059. A red-brick mansion built in 1857 by Vermont senator Joseph Parker beside his flannel mill on the Ottauquechee River, this inn is best known for food (see *Dining Out*) but is also a comfortable place to stay. Since acquiring it, Chef Alexandra Adler and husband Adam have installed eight new baths and totally revamped the rooms. The downstairs parlors are now dining rooms, but there is a small second-floor sitting room with a TV, a sunny downstairs reading nook, a breakfast room, and a riverside deck. $135–165 includes a full breakfast. Add 15 percent for service. Dogs are $30. Guests have access to Quechee Club facilities.

BED & BREAKFASTS

In Woodstock 05091
Note: Parking can be tough, hence the advantage of the many in-town B&Bs described below. All face major thoroughfares, however; you might want to request back- or side-facing rooms.

The Charleston House (802-457-3843; 1-888-475-3800; www.charlestonhouse.com), 21 Pleasant St. This luxu-rious, recently expanded Federal brick town house (vintage 1835) in the middle of the village is especially appealing, with period furniture in nine guest rooms, all with private bath and air-conditioning, several with fireplace and Jacuzzi. Rates are $135–240 (higher during foliage season) and include full breakfast in the dining room or continental breakfast bedside. Your genial hosts are Willa and Dixi Nohl (Dixi for many years managed Burke Mountain ski area in the Northeast Kingdom).

Canterbury House (802-457-3077; 1-800-390-3077; www.thecanterbury house.com), 43 Pleasant St. Bob and Sue Frost's village Victorian has seven air-conditioned rooms with private bath (our favorites are the original second-floor bedrooms in the front) and air-conditioning. Guests meet around the hearth in the large, gracious living room. From $150 for a back room overlooking the parking lot to $185 for the Monk's Tale, which has a fireplace and cable TV ($115–165 in low seasons). Full breakfast.

Ardmore Inn (802-457-3887; 1-800-497-9652; www.ardmoreinn.com), 23 Pleasant St. A meticulously restored 1867 Greek Revival that offers five spacious rooms, each with private marble bath. The room we like best here is Tully, with its tall four-poster, eyebrow windows, and marble bathroom. Guests breakfast around the antique Nantucket dining room table and relax in the attractive library or on the large, screened veranda overlooking the back garden. $135–195, less off-season, includes a three-course breakfast (at 8:30 sharp) and afternoon refreshments. Innkeepers Cary and Charlotte Hollingsworth are from Pasadena.

The 1830 Shire Town Inn (802-457-1830; 1-866-286-1830; www.1830shiretowninn.com), 31 South St. Arlene Gibson is a natural host, and her 1830 home, within walking distance of the green. has three comfortable rooms with private bath. Our favorite is the downstairs, very private Woodstock Room, set into the rocks with a leafy view. The common rooms feature wide-pine floors, hand-hewn beams, a fireplace, and good art. $85–135 includes a hearty country breakfast.

The Woodstocker (802-457-3896; 1-866-662-1439; www.woodstockervt.com), 61 River St. (corner of Rt. 4). While this 1830s Cape-style house fronts on busy Rt. 4, rooms ramble away to the leafy back area. The original house offers comfortable living and dining rooms; in the newer wing there are seven individually furnished, spacious guest rooms with queen beds, private bath, most with air-conditioning. At the very back are two attractive two-room suites. Rooms $165–195, suites $145–250 double with a full breakfast. Innkeepers Dora Foschi and David Lively moved here from London in 2005.

The Village Inn of Woodstock (802-457-1255; 1-800-722-4571; www.villageinnofwoodstock.com), 41 Pleasant St., is a romantic pink Victorian manse with fireplaces, oak wainscoting, and pressed-tin ceilings. David and Evelyn Brey offer seven comfortable rooms with private bath. $130–240 in high season, $100–190 in low with full breakfast.

Out of town

♣ ♪ **Deer Brook Inn** (802-672-3713; www.deerbrookinn.com), 535 Woodstock Rd. (Rt. 4), Woodstock 05091. Five miles west of Woodstock and 10 miles east of Killington's Skyeship Gondola, George DeFina and David Kanal have added some great decorating touches to this restored 1820 farmhouse, set back in fields across the road from the Ottauquechee River. The floors are wide honey-colored pine, and each of the five rooms has a full bath and climate-controlled heat and air-conditioning. A ground-floor two-room suite with a sitting room is a delight and good for families. Our favorite of the four second-floor rooms is Room 1, with its skylight above the bed and in the bathroom. $105–165 includes a full breakfast served either at a common or an individual table in the light-filled dining room.

∞ **Applehill Inne** (802-457-9135; www.applehillinn.com), P.O. Box 24, 2301 Hartwood Way, Taftsville 05091. Beverly and Andrew Cook welcomed visitors to the Applebutter Inn (see below) for 15 years before building this dream house atop the hill behind. It's designed to maximize the spectacular 30-mile view of the Ottauquechee and surrounding hills, which can be enjoyed from the big country kitchen, from the spacious common rooms and deck, and from two of the three guest rooms (one with a private entrance and kitchenette). Eighteenth-century antiques and Oriental rugs add a richness to light-filled spaces, as do the surrounding fruit and vegetable gardens. An avid (organic-geared) cook and baker, Bev caters receptions and wedding receptions in the glorious inside/outside "tea room." There's also a wedding barn. $135–195; $20 per extra person includes a full, healthy breakfast.

Applebutter Inn (802-457-4158; 1-800-486-1734; www.applebutterinn.com), P.O. Box 395, Happy Valley Rd.,

Taftsville 05073. This is a graceful 1850s Federal with wide-pine floors and a bright, spacious dining area/library and an elegantly comfortable living room with a fireplace. The seven guest rooms, each named for a different variety of apple, have private bath, AC, and wireless; five have working wood fireplace or stove. Your hosts are Barbara Berry and Michael Pacht. $100–215 per couple (from $80 off-season) includes a full breakfast and afternoon tea.

Shepherd's Hill Farm (802-457-3087; www.shepherdshillfarm.com), P.O. Box 34, 25 Hartwood Way, Taftsville 05073. High on the hill above the Taftsville General Store, Ellen Terie raises Polypay sheep, a breed developed in Idaho in 1976 and good for both wool and high-quality meat. This new, well-designed house features an open kitchen and two-story living room, furnished in antiques and wonderful "stuff" collected over many years and many interests. It overlooks the Ottauquechee Valley and its hemming hills. Ellen, an artist and psychotherapist, has covered the walls with varied art. The two guest rooms are on their own second-floor wing and share a bath and well-appointed sitting room. $125–150 (less for longer "farm-stays" in which guests are invited to share in chores) includes a full breakfast. Dinner can be arranged. Inquire about the self-contained efficiency suite, good for families.

🐑 ⚘ **Top Acres Farm** (802-457-2135; topacresfarm@aol.com), 3615 Fletcher Hill Rd., South Woodstock 05071. This is a fabulous find for families. Milton and Pat Fullerton's 1850s gabled white-clapboard, hilltop farmhouse has been in the family—and known for the quality of its maple syrup—for four generations. There is an upstairs apartment with a fully equipped kitchen, three bedrooms, a large living and dining room, laundry facilities, TV, and VCR, and also a separate, single room with bath. Fridges are stocked for your first morning's breakfast. $150 for the upstairs apartment and $80 for the room ($200 for both).

⚘ **Inn at Chelsea Farm** (802-234-9888; www.innatchelseafarm.com), P.O. Box 127, Rt. 12, Barnard 05031. Some places just click the moment you walk in, and for us this classic white Cape, set back from Rt. 12 and surrounded by gardens, was one of those places. Inside spaces flow from the living room with its fireplace and are filled with quiet light and nicely decorated with original art. The three guest rooms, each named for a season (there's no "winter"), are also bright and comfortable without being fussy, and fitted with fine linens and down comforters. A large ground-floor suite has a cherry four-poster, a sofa, armchairs, a coffee table, and TV if requested. Host Emmy Fox spent much of her life managing a prestigious Bermuda inn, and hospitality comes naturally. Children are welcome; there are pet sheep in the field.

TOP ACRES FARM B&B IN SOUTH WOODSTOCK

Christina Tree

Inquire about fly-fishing. Silver Lake State Park and its beach are just up the road. $120–160 per couple includes a full breakfast.

The Fan House (802-234-9096; www.thefanhouse.com), P.O. Box 294, Rt. 12 north, Barnard 05031. This distinguished, 1840s clapboard house is filled with light, decorated with heirloom tapestries and antique furnishings to create the feel of an Italian farmhouse. The three artfully furnished guest rooms have private bath and are appointed with high-thread-count linens and Turkish bath sheets. Silver Lake and the Barnard General Store are within walking distance. $120–200 includes a full breakfast.

❦ **Bailey's Mills Bed & Breakfast** (802-484-7809; 1-800-639-3437; www.baileysmills.com), 1347 Bailey's Mills Rd., Reading 05062. As happens so often in Vermont, surprises lurk at the end of a back road, especially in the case of this venerable guest house, a few miles west of Rt. 106. With a two-story porch and fluted columns, Bailey's Mills resembles a southern antebellum mansion. The 17-room brick home includes 11 fireplaces, two beehive ovens, a dance hall, and an 1829 general store, all part of an ambitious manufacturing complex established by Levi Bailey (1766–1850) and operated by his family for a century. Today Barbara Thaeder offers several comfortable rooms, two with working fireplace, each with a cozy sitting area and private bath, tastefully furnished with antiques. A spacious solarium makes the Honeymoon Suite especially appealing. The library with its Rumford fireplace has a large collection of fascinating books and is furnished, as is the dining room, with family

antiques and "old stuff." Paths lead off across the meadows into the woods and to a swim pond. Barbara is an avid conservationist, a member of Green Hotels of Vermont. $100–170 with breakfast. (Ask about the adjacent Spite Cemetery.) Justly popular Keepers Cafe (see *Dining Out*) is minutes away.

♿ **Maple Leaf Inn** (802-234-5342; 1-800-516-2753; www.mapleleafinn.com), P.O. Box 273, 5890 Rt. 12, Barnard 05031. Gary and Janet Robison opened up this sparkling new place in a faithfully reproduced turn-of-the-20th-century Victorian farmhouse, designed specifically as a B&B. Stenciling, stitchery, and Janet's handmade quilts decorate the seven air-conditioned guest rooms, each with a capacious private bath, king-sized bed, sitting area, telephone, and TV/VCR. Most guest rooms have wood-burning fireplace and whirlpool bath. The parlor, library, and dining room are bright and inviting. Rates are $190–260 in high seasons, $130–200 in low, with full breakfast. The Country Garden Room on the main floor has easy access for anyone who needs special assistance, and a whirlpool bath.

MOTELS ❦ ✐ **Pond Ridge** (802-457-1667; www.pondridgemotel.com), 506 Rt. 4, West Woodstock 05091. Set way back from Rt. 4, 1.5 miles west of Woodstock Village, in 6 landscaped acres with a picnic/barbecue area bordering the Ottauquechee River (swimming, fishing), this family-run motel is a real find. The 14 units are fitted with two double beds or one queen as well as air-conditioning, cable TV, and coffee machines. There are also six apartments with full kitchens, great for families. Rooms from $79 in midseason (from $110 in foliage); a two-bedroom apartment is $195. Value-season rates: $59–178. Children 6 and under are free.

♂ ♿ **Shire Riverview Motel** (802-457-2211; www.shiremotel.com), 46 Pleasant St., Woodstock 05091. Location, location. This two-story, independently owned 42-unit motel is within walking distance of downtown, and while it fronts on Pleasant St. (Rt. 4), it backs on the river and many rooms have river views and deck access. A separate new building with six upscale suites is also in back; another recently refurbished building houses three more high-end rooms. All rooms are comfortable with phone and computer hookup, furnished with two queens, two doubles, or a king. Most have a fridge, and some have gas fireplace and Jacuzzi. From as low as $138–148 for a standard river view room in midseason to $218 for a luxury room and $300 for a suite.

Also see **Farmbrook Motel** in "Killington/Plymouth Area."

OTHER LODGING ♂ At **Quechee Lakes Resort** (www.quecheelakes .com) rental units range from small condos to six-bedroom houses, all with access to resort facilities, which include the golf courses and clubhouse with its indoor pool and squash courts. These can be rented through local Realtors, such as **Quechee Lakes Rentals** (802-295-1970; 1-800-745-0042; www.quecheelakesrentals .com) and **Care-free Quechee** (802-295-9500; 1-800-537-3962; www.care freequecheevacations.com).

Note: For camping at the area's two state parks, see *Green Space.*

✳ Where to Eat

DINING OUT **The Prince and the Pauper** (802-457-1818; www.prince andpauper.com), 24 Elm St., Woodstock. Open daily for dinner (reservations advised). One of the state's best; "worth every calorie and dollar," we said in the first edition of this book, and we have had no reason to change our minds. For more than 25 years, owner-chef Chris Balcer's genuinely Continental cuisine has been consistently superior. Given the number of regular patrons, the $43 prix fixe changes nightly, but there are always half a dozen appetizers and entrées from which to choose. The house pâté of pork, veal, and chicken livers with sun-dried cherries and pistachios is a fixture; boneless rack of lamb in puff pastry is also always on the menu. The dining room is candlelit, elegantly rustic. In the more casual wine bar a bistro menu ($13–20) usually includes Maine crabcakes and hearth-baked pizzas.

Parker House Inn (802-295-6077; www.theparkerhouseinn.com), 1792 Main St., Quechee. Open for dinner daily; reservations, please, also for lunch summer weekends. Chef Alexandra Adler has brought a new look and menu to the dining rooms in this classic brick Victorian mill owner's mansion. Lace has been replaced by elegant bistro colors and napery; the taste is French. You might begin with a warm duck confit crêpe or a warm goat cheese tart, followed by sea bass Provençal or rack of lamb with sweet pea risotto. The specialty is bouillabaisse. Entrées $17–28. Light fare and cocktails are served in the riverside back bar. Lunch, when served, is on the riverside deck.

Simon Pearce Restaurant (802-295-1470; www.simonpearce.com), The Mill, Quechee. Open for lunch (11:30–2:45) and dinner (6–9; reservations advised) daily. This is a cheerful, upbeat, contemporary place for consistently superior food, served on its own pottery and glass, overlooking the waterfall. Despite its high profile as a tourist stop (with a store that remains open through the dinner hours), it gets raves from locals for the wine list and service as well as the food. The patio is open in summer, and the Ballymaloe brown bread alone is worth a visit. Lunch entrées could be spinach and endive salad with cheddar and apple fritters, spiced nuts, and apple vinaigrette, or beef and Guinness stew; at dinner you might begin with a Sullivan Harbor smoked trio of salmon, trout, and char, followed by crisp roast duckling served with vegetable fried rice and mango chutney. Dinner entrées range from $20 for ravioli to $38 for grilled filet mignon.

The Jackson House Restaurant (802-457-2065), Rt. 4 west, Woodstock. Open Wed.–Mon. Highly rated and priced. A sleekly contemporary dining room with a floor-to-ceiling double hearth and windows opening on gardens is the setting for cuisine that reflects the style of the current chef. Presently Jason Merrill's menu might include pan-seared scallops with mango and cucumber, and crispy skin wild salmon as appetizers; ginger steamed halibut, and roulade of rabbit and foie gras with pistachios and papaya as entrées; and steamed lemon pudding as a dessert. Choose from a 3-course prix fixe menu ($55), 4-course ($70), or 10-course "Chef's Degustation"—which, along with a similar vegetarian menu, runs $95.

The Meadows at the Quechee Inn at Marshland Farm (802-295-3133; 1-800-235-3133; www.quecheeinn .com), Clubhouse Rd., Quechee. Open nightly, this country-elegant dining room is just enough off the beaten track to be a discovery, the quiet setting for dependably good food. You might dine on crispy Long Island duck with a passionfruit apricot demiglaze, or on roast rack of lamb. Entrées $22–28; a "supper menu" features lighter dishes ranging from classic bouillabaisse to wine and shallot marinated beef tips served with a Boursin potato pancake ($12–17).

The Barnard Inn (802-234-9961; www.barnardrestaurant.com), 10 miles north of Woodstock on Rt. 12, Barnard. Open Tue.–Sat. from 5, dinner 6–9. Reservations advised. Chef-owners Ruth Schimmelpfennig and Will Dodson operate this 1796 brick house with its nicely appointed formal rooms. A three-course $55 prix fixe menu includes a choice of soups, salads, and appetizers such as mussels steamed in saffron and orange white

THE DINING ROOM AT SIMON PEARCE OVERLOOKS THE OTTAUQUECHEE RIVER.

Kim Grant

wine fumé, or applewood-smoked salmon with horseradish crème fraîche. Entrées might include roast lamb with wild mushrooms and rosemary-roasted potatoes, or pork loin with roasted garlic mashed potatoes and apple-pear chutney. Desserts are $8 extra and usually include Ruth's crème brûlée. In the less formal Max's Tavern, the menu might range from pasta primavera with prosciutto to roast lamb top round with "fixin's." A large selection of wines and beers is available by the glass.

The Woodstock Inn and Resort (802-457-1100; www.woodstockinn .com), on the green, Woodstock. Open for dinner and Sunday brunch. The large, cheerfully contemporary main dining room, with its alcoves and semicircular bay, is an especially attractive setting for the sumptuous Sunday brunch buffet ($24.95) and executive chef Daniel Jackson's truly superior dinners. Entrées might include a bouillabaisse of sea scallops, mussels, and Gulf shrimp in saffron-tomato broth, or pine nut crusted rack of lamb with truffled white beans, slow-roasted tomatoes, and toasted cumin jus. Entrées $22–42. Lighter fare and breakfast and lunch are served in the less expensive Eagle Café and in the richly paneled Richardson's Tavern, where there's live music Friday and Saturday evenings.

✎ **The Kedron Valley Inn** (802-457-1473; www.kedronvalleyinn), Rt. 106, 5 miles south of Woodstock. Open for dinner nightly in high season, otherwise Thu.–Mon. The large, low-beamed dining room is country elegant. Entrées might include grilled venison loin with herb spaetzle, huckleberry compote, and juniper sauce; or sesame-crusted Atlantic salmon with creamed leeks, shiitake mushrooms, and lobster sauce. $24–30. The informal Tavern offers a pub menu.

Mangowood Cafe (802-457-3312), 530 Woodstock Rd. (Rt. 4), West Woodstock. Open Tue.–Sat. 6–9:30. Chef-owner Teresa Tan grew up in Malaysia and is a graduate of the Cordon Bleu. Be prepared for new taste combinations such as braised duck with bok choy or a crispy whole fish with udon noodles and ginger scallion sauce. Don't pass up the maple ginger crème brûlée. Entrées $19–32. Full liquor license.

Osteria Pane e Salute (802-457-4882; www.osteriapaneesalute.com), 61 Central St. (upstairs), Woodstock. Closed Nov. and Apr.; otherwise, open for dinner Thu.–Mon. (reservations recommended). Deidre Heekin and Caleb Barber have acquired a passionate following for their authentically Italian fare, expanding in 2006 from a small street-level café to a full dining room upstairs. Entrées might include veal cutlets in lemon sauce; whole roast chicken with rosemary, lemon, and garlic; and halibut with salsa verde. A prix fixe four-course menu is $36.50, but courses are also available à la carte (main courses for $18). Tuscan pizza is $9–12; there's a wine bar. The wine list numbers 100 labels, all Italian.

✎ **Keepers Cafe** (802-484-9090), Rt. 106 at Baileys Mill Rd., Reading. Open Tue.–Sat. 5–9, until 9:30 Fri. and Sat. The former Hammondsville Store is now one of the most popular restaurants around. Totally rebuilt, its three connecting rooms are a warm green, with finished wood floors, good-sized pedestal tables, and hardy wooden office chairs. The feel is

Shaker and the food is fresh, simply presented on white ironstone, and outstanding. Choose from several salads as well as starters, then dine on the likes of herb-rubbed half chicken with mashed potatoes, Swiss chard, and a sherry-caper sauce; or grilled marinated sirloin in a green peppercorn demiglaze. Desserts might include ginger crème brûlée and an old-fashioned Bavarian layer cake. Entrées $14–21, but there's also always a "Stump's burger" ($9). The downside: No reservations for fewer than six people.

Also see **Norwich Inn**, **Carpenter and Main**, and **Skunk Hollow Tavern** in "Upper Valley River Towns," and **The Corners Inn and Restaurant** in "Killington/Plymouth Area."

EATING OUT **Bentley's Restaurant** (802-457-3232), Elm St., Woodstock. Open daily for lunch and dinner. The original restaurant here, an oasis of Victoriana and plants, has been expanded to include a café/ice cream parlor. A lifesaver in the middle of town, good for everything from brawny hamburgers and croissant sandwiches to veal Marsala and Jack Daniels steak. Frequent live entertainment.

*✔ **FireStones** (802-295-1600), Rt. 4, Waterman Place, Quechee. Open daily for lunch and dinner and Sunday brunch. Live piano music Friday and Saturday evenings; open mike Thursday. The proprietors of Bentley's (see above), also help operate this rustic, lodgelike restaurant, with a big wood-fired oven as its centerpiece, featuring made-to-order flatbreads, fire-roasted shrimp marinated in Long Trail Ale, fire-roasted chicken, and steaks. You'll also find pastas, soups, sandwiches, and salads; BBQ baby back ribs and

good daily specials; and a friendly barman. Children's menu; outdoor rooftop deck.

*✔ **EastEnder Restaurant** (802-457-9800), 442 Woodstock Rd. (Rt. 4), Woodstock. Open for dinner Tue.–Sat. from 5. Pleasant, casual atmosphere with a menu that changes seasonally but usually includes flank steak and spinach salad, and New York sirloin. Entrées $14–24, but also lighter-fare options.

*✔ **Off the Green** (802-457-4435; www.offthegreentavern.com), 71 Central St., Woodstock. A welcome addition to sit-down lunch options in Woodstock Village, this sleek new upstairs restaurant is great for a fried calamari salad with field greens and dipping sauce, or a club sandwich. Dinner options have yet to establish a following (entrées $13–22), but there is a children's menu.

Woodstock Country Club (802-457-6672), Rt. 106 south, Woodstock. Open in summer for lunch 11:30–3. This is a Woodstock insider's meeting spot for lunch but open to the public, especially appealing on sunny days when you can dine on the deck. Designer sandwiches and salads, burgers, a good grilled Reuben. During ski season hot chili and snacks are available for cross-country skiers.

Woodstock Coffee & Tea (802-457-9268), 43 Central St., Woodstock. Open Mon.–Sat. 7–6, Sun. 9–5. Judging from its popularity, this comfortably furnished café is a village gathering center. A variety of free-trade and organic coffee roasts as well as an extensive selection of teas and fruit smoothies are offered. Breakfast sandwiches and exceptional corn muffins, also locally made pastries, and "quick bites" for lunch.

Dana's By the Gorge (802-295-6066), Rt.4, Quechee. Open May–Nov., daily 7–11:15 and 11:45–2:45. This down-home, family-owned and -geared eatery sits smack dab in the area's single most touristed spot. Try Vermont rarebit for breakfast (an open-faced English muffin topped with Canadian bacon, Vermont cheddar, and sliced fresh tomatoes). The lunch menu features a wide selection of salads and sandwiches.

✑ **Mountain Creamery** (802-457-1715), Central St., Woodstock, serves breakfast daily 7–11:30, lunch until 3, pastry and espresso until 6. This is the local meeting place but less friendly to visitors than it used to be. Soups, sandwiches, salads, daily specials, and their own handmade ice cream as well as apple pie. Pies and cakes are also for sale.

Ott Dog Snack Bar (802-295-1088), Rt. 4, Quechee Gorge. Open mid-May–mid-Oct. Family owned with the motto "Not fast food. Good food fast." Fresh soups and five different kinds of hot dogs are the specialties.

Barnard General Store (234-9688), Rt. 12, Barnard Village. A classic general store (established 1832) but with

BARNARD GENERAL STORE

Kim Grant

a 1950s lunch counter serving stand-out breakfasts, ice cream, soups, and sandwiches as well as pizza all day. Handy to Silver Lake.

South Woodstock Country Store (802-457-3050), Rt. 106, South Woodstock. Open Mon.–Fri. 6–6, Sat. 7–6, Sun. 8–5. The only general store we know that has its own chef. Under new owner Dan Noble, the store stacks staples and local specialties like the fabulous Woodstock Water Buffalo yogurt made in South Woodstock (the water buffalo are around the corner up on Churchill Rd.). Stop by for homemade muffins, omelets, or breakfast sandwiches; soups, sandwiches, and pizzas at lunch. Check the menu for dinner take-homes like eggplant parmigiana.

Umpleby's, "makers of fine baked goods" (802-672-1300), The Mill, Rt. 4, Bridgewater. Open 7:30–5:30; closing 3 PM Sun. Tucked away in a corner of this former 1840s woolen mill, Charles Umpleby bakes breads (try the Crazy Wheat) but also genuine European-style croissants and raspberry brioche for breakfast, delectable leek and onion tarts, sausage rolls, and individual quiches to go with homemade soups. If it's not mealtime, there's espresso and homemade ice cream. In summer, tables on a balcony overlooking the river supplement the few inside.

PICNICS On a beautiful summer or fall day the best place to lunch is outside. In Woodstock itself there's Teagle's Landing, right on Central St. by the river, and Faulkner Park on Monument Ave. See *Green Space* for other ideas.

The Village Butcher (802-457-2756), 18 Elm St., Woodstock, a superb butcher and a deli with sandwiches, soups, and specials to go, along with its top-flight meats, wines, and baked goods, plus homemade fudge.

Woodstock Farmers' Market (802-457-3658), Rt. 4 west, has a thoughtful deli case, plus soups and an outstanding selection of sandwiches, fresh fish, free-range chicken, local produce, meals to go, and Baba à Louis bread and cookies.

✳ Entertainment

Pentangle Council on the Arts (802-457-3981; www.pentanglearts .org), Town Hall Theater, 31 The Green, Woodstock. First-run films are shown Fri.–Mon. evenings at 7:30 in the Town Hall Theater. Live presentations at town hall and at the Woodstock Union High School include a variety of musical and other live entertainment. Check the Town Crier blackboard at the corner of Elm and Central Streets for current happenings. Also inquire about the Woodstock Film Society.

✳ Selective Shopping

ANTIQUES SHOPS The Woodstock area is mecca for antiques buffs. There are two big group galleries. **Quechee Gorge Village Antique Mall** (802-295-1550), Rt. 4, east of Quechee Gorge, open daily, is one of New England's largest antiques collectives, with some 450 dealers represented. The **Antiques Collaborative** (802-296-5858), Waterman Place, Rt. 4 at the blinking light in Quechee, is also open daily (10–5) and shows representative stock from some 150 upscale dealers: period furniture usually in good condition, silver, Oriental rugs, and more.

Among the more than dozen individual dealers: **Wigren & Barlow** (802-457-2453; www.wigrenandbarlow.com), 29 Pleasant St., is Woodstock's most elegant antiques shop, with a large selection of fine country and formal furniture, decorative accessories, and garden appointments (open daily 10–5); **Pleasant Street Books** (802-457-4050), 48 Pleasant St., Woodstock, carries 10,000 selected titles in all fields (open daily 11–5 in summer and fall, by appointment off-season); **Fraser's Antiques** (802-457-3437), Happy Valley Rd., just off Rt. 4 in Taftsville, has a good stock of early American furniture and accessories; **Mill Brook Antiques** (802-484-5942), Rt. 106, Reading (11 miles south of Woodstock), has a shop and barn full of early American furniture, primitives, stoneware, china, quilts, and more (open year-round, but call ahead).

ART GALLERIES

In Woodstock

V Gallery: Vermont Arts & Lifestyles (www.vgalleryarts.com; 802-457-9292), 102 Pomfret Rd., and (802-457-2200), 6 Central St. Open 11–5 except Tue. Visit the main gallery, 1 mile north of the village at the junction (a "V") with Pomfret Rd. The in-town branch features contemporary realist paintings; the larger, original gallery, home to the Guild of Vermont Furnituremakers, showcases woodworkers as well as a variety of contemporary artists. **Woodstock Folk Art, Prints & Antiques** (802-457-2012), 8 Elm St., specializes in contemporary carvings, prints, and antiquities. **Stephen Huneck Studio** (802-457-3206), 49 Central St., offers the celebrated St. Johnsbury woodcarver's fanciful animals of all kinds

MILLS

The Bridgewater Mill, also known as "The Old Inn Marketplace" and "The Mill," Rt. 4, Bridgewater. The core of this vast, yellow wooden mill dates back to the 1820s, when it worked cotton, switching to wool in the 1840s, supplying uniforms and blankets for the troops in several wars. In the 1970s when it closed, the building was saved by a local bootstrap effort and became a hive of small shops. It has had its ups

Charles Shackleton Furniture/Miranda Thomas Pottery

CHARLES SHACKLETON FURNITURE AND MIRANDA THOMAS POTTERY ARE BASED AT THE MILL AT BRIDGEWATER CORNERS.

and downs since, but current occupants are a rich mix. By far the most famous are **Charles Shackleton Furniture** and **Miranda Thomas Pottery** (see *Artisans*), whose shop and workspace are accessible from the west entrance. Exhibit space has recently expanded, with furniture and pottery complemented by fine **InnerSanctuary** rugs. **David Crandall** (802-672-5475) makes custom-styled 18-karat gold jewelry. He began on The Mill's second floor but has since moved to prime first-floor space beside Shackleton/Thomas at the west entrance. The Mill's upper floors are partially filled with offices and artists' studios, launching pads for enterprises like InnerSanctuary (802-672-1621; www.innerasiarugs .com), which retains most of its stock on the third floor. On the second floor check out **Whisper Hill**, fine handmade soaps (www.whisperhillsoaps.com).

The central, oldest part of The Mill is a wonderfully mixed bag. Down in the basement the **Hillbilly Flea Market** (802-672-1331; open Thu.–Sun. 10–5),

adorning furniture, wall reliefs, jewelry, and other witty, uncommon pieces. **Gallery on the Green** (802-457-4956), corner of Elm St., features original art, limited-edition prints, photography, and occasionally sculpture, from New England artists. **Polonaise Art Gallery** (802-457-5180), 15 Central St., features contemporary and traditional styles in paintings and sculpture. **Robert O. Caulfield Art Gallery** (802-457-1472), 11 The Green, is the artist's

studio; realistic oil and watercolor landscapes and street scenes.

ARTISANS **Charles Shackleton Furniture** and **Miranda Thomas Pottery** (802-672-5175; 1-800-245-9901; www.shackletonthomas.com), The Mill, Rt. 4, Bridgewater, and at 23 Elm St., Woodstock. Open daily 10–5:30 at both places; inquire about mill tours. This couple met at art school in England and again at Simon Pearce Glass. Charles was an appren-

based on the "one man's junk is another man's treasure" theory, has upscaled a couple of notches in as many years and now specializes in very usable furniture. On the first floor, beyond the village post office, is the **Sun of the Heart Bookstore** (802-672-5151, open daily 10–6). The mill's oldest tenant, it's a genuinely bright spot at its heart, an independent shop reflecting owner Akanakha Perkins's interest in many New Age subjects. Also well worth checking is **Northern Ski Works Outlet** (802-672-3636; www.northernski.com), an outlet for retail shops by that name in Ludlow and Killington. The aromas of baking, suffusing much of the first floor, emanate from **Umpleby's** (802-672-1300), a small café tucked in a back corner overlooking the Ottauquechee River (see *Eating Out*).

Simon Pearce Glass (802-295-2711; www.simonpearce.com), The Mill, 1760 Main St., Quechee. The brick mill by the falls in the Ottauquechee was the 19th-century home of J. C. Parker and Co., producing "shoddy": wool reworked from soft rags. Parker was known for fine baby flannel. It closed for a spell, then served as offices for Quechee Lakes Resort. In 1981 Simon Pearce opened it as a glass factory, harnessing the dam's hydropower for his glass furnace. Pearce had already been making his original glass for a decade in Ireland, and here he quickly established a reputation for his distinctive production pieces: tableware, vases, lamps, candlesticks, and more. Visitors can watch glass being blown and can shop for individual pieces from the retail shop, along with Simon Pearce pottery. The shop (802-295-2711) is open 9–9 daily; pottery throwing can be viewed daily 9–4, glassblowing 9–9. The **Simon Pearce Restaurant** (see *Dining Out*), overlooking the falls, is justifiably one of Vermont's most popular. Simon Pearce now also operates a large, visitor-friendly glass and pottery factory in nearby Windsor (see "Upper Valley River Towns") as well as in Maryland and Pennsylvania. His glass and pottery are sold in over 300 stores throughout the country.

tice glassblower before he switched to furniture making; Miranda founded the pottery studio there, and the showroom carried both their work. But no longer. They have since acquired much of the Bridgewater Mill, and Charles works with more than two dozen fellow crafters to produce exquisite furniture. It's made to order, but models are displayed (along with seconds at the mill), complemented by Miranda's distinctive pottery, hand thrown and carved with traditional designs, such as rabbits, fish, and trees. Her pottery is housed in a former worker's cottage in the mill's parking lot.

Clear Lake Furniture Gallery (802-457-2822; www.clearlakefurniture .com), 24 Elm St., Woodstock. Open Mon.–Sat. 10–5; Sun. hours vary. Handcrafted in a workshop in Ludlow, this line of furnishings is well worth checking out—but don't expect to walk way with a table or dresser.

Rather, it will be specially designed for you in your choice of woods.

FossilGlass (802-457-4102), 75 Central St., Woodstock. Christina Salusti's distinctive glassware is sold in top shops around the country, but Woodstock is home. This new store showcases the full spectrum of her work and serves as an outlet. Hand-spun plates, bowls, and platters are unusually shaped and frequently partially colored; the surfaces suggest fossil imprints.

Woodstock Potters (802-457-1298), Mechanic St., Woodstock, has a studio/workshop for stoneware and hand-painted porcelains, plus gold and silver jewelry.

D. Lasser Ceramics (802-824-6182; www.lasserceramics.com), 23 Central St., Woodstock. Open daily. Many years have passed since dozens of tall purple and blue crooked pottery candlesticks in a roadside field brought us to a screeching stop. Turns out they are hollow and can double as bud vases. We still love them and are delighted to find this Vermont company's colorful plates, casserole dishes, goblets, and more part of Woodstock's chic shopping drag.

Anderson Furniture & Design/ Miss Jane's (802-457-1922), 73 Central St., Woodstock. Custom furniture made on the premises, home furnishings.

Mark Lackley Furniture Maker (802-457-9286; www.lackley.com), Rt. 4., Quechee. Lackley designs and builds everything in his workshop/ showroom.

BOOKSTORES The Yankee Bookshop (802-457-2411), Central St., Woodstock, carries an unusually large stock of hardbound and paperback books for adults and children, plus cards; it features the work of local authors and publishers. **Shiretown Books** (802-457-2996; www.shiretown books.com), 9 Central St., Woodstock, is an intimate, very personalized shop that has a carefully selected stock of books for adults and children. Also see **Sun of the Heart Bookstore** in the "Mills" box.

SPECIAL SHOPS

In Woodstock Village
F. H. Gillingham & Sons (802-457-2100; 1-800-344-6668), Elm St., owned and run by the same family since 1886, is something of an institution, retaining a lot of its old-fashioned general store flavor. You'll find plain and fancy groceries, wine, housewares, and hardware for home, garden, and farm. Mail-order catalog.

✍ **Woodstock Pharmacy** (802-457-1306), Central St. Open daily 8–6, Sun. until 1 PM. Another Woodstock institution that has branched out well beyond the basics, especially good for stationery and (downstairs) for children's toys and books.

Unicorn (802-457-2480), 15 Central St., is a treasure trove of unusual gifts, cards, games, toys, and unclassifiable finds.

Arjuna (802-457-3350), 20 Central St., is a small cornucopia of unusual collectibles and items from around the world, plus funky jewelry.

Who Is Sylvia? (802-457-1110), 26 Central St., in the old village firehouse, houses two floors of great vintage clothing and accessories for men as well as women.

Red Wagon Toy Company (802-457-9300), 41 Central St., specializes in creative toys and children's clothing, from infant to preteen.

The Whipple Tree (802-457-1325), 7 Central St., has yarns, knitting, sewing, and art supplies (and Vermont Transit bus tickets).

Also see **FossilGlass** under *Artisans*, and check out *Antiques Shops*.

In and near Quechee

F. H. Clothing Co. (802-296-6646; www.fathat.com), corner of Rt. 4 and Clubhouse Rd., Quechee. A business that has evolved over more than 25 years from making floppy "fat hats" to a variety of comfortable, colorful clothing.

New England Specialties Shoppe (802-295-6163), Rt. 4, Quechee. The Laros's store, east of the gorge, has an especially large and carefully selected stock of Vermont products, from cheese, syrup, and preserves to sweatshirts and toys. In the same complex look for **Ottauquechee Valley Winery** (802-295-9463), sequestered behind the Mesa Home Factory Store. It's a relatively new offshoot of North River Winery in Jacksonville, producing half a dozen fruit wines from pears and apples, rhubarb, and a blend of blueberries and apples.

✍ **Quechee Gorge Village** (802-295-1550; 1-800-438-5565; www.quecheegorge.com), Rt. 4 at Quechee Gorge. The most elaborate of several Rt. 4 shopping complexes, it includes the Antique Center (see *Antiques Shops*) and Farina Family Diner (see *Eating Out*), also an arts and crafts center, general store, and Christmas Loft.

Vermont Toy & Train Museum and Gift Shop at Quechee Gorge (802-295-1550; 1-800-438-5565; www.quecheegorge.com), Rt. 4, 1 mile

east of Quechee Gorge. Open year-round, an antique merry-go-round, a 2-foot-gauge railroad, interactive games, and a gift shop.

Taftsville Country Store (802-457-1135; www.taftsville.com), Rt. 4 east, Taftsville. Refurbished and restocked, this 1840 landmark is also still the post office and carries carefully chosen Vermont gifts as well as a good selection of cheeses, maple products, jams, jellies, smoked ham, and bacon, plus staples, wine, and books. Mail-order catalog.

Scotland by the Yard (802-295-5351), Rt. 4, 3 miles east of Woodstock, imports tartans and tweeds, kilts, capes, coats, sweaters, skirts, canes, books, records, oatcakes, and shortbreads.

The Fool on the Hill (802-457-3641; www.thefoolonthehill.com), Rt. 4 west of Quechee Gorge. Open daily 9–5, later in fall. Closed Jan.– mud season. Ed and Debbie Kerwin's unabashed tourist trap sells pottery, gifts, and Vermont specialty foods. Memorial Day–Oct., it features corn roasting on an open flame.

FARMS Sugarbush Farm (802-457-1757; 1-800-281-1757; www.sugar bushfarm.com), RR 1, Box 568, Woodstock, but located in Pomfret: Take Rt. 4 to Taftsville, cross the covered bridge, go up the hill, turn left onto Hillside Rd., then follow signs. *Warning:* It's steep. Beware in mud season, but it's well worth the effort: Sample seven Vermont cheeses, all packaged here along with gift boxes, geared to sending products to far corners of the world. In-season you can watch maple sugaring, walk the maple and nature trail, or visit with their farm animals.

Woodstock Water Buffalo Company (802-457-4540; www.woodstock waterbuffalo.com), 2749–01 Church Hill Rd. (off Rt. 106), South Woodstock. Visiting hours on weekdays, 10–2. David Muller has introduced this country to yogurt and mozzarella made from water buffalo milk. Both products are available at the South Woodstock Country Store—and they're delicious. The buffalo are fun to watch, but for health reasons visitors are not allowed in the barns. The creamery is designed with an observation window through which you can observe cheese and yogurt preparation.

Talbot's Herb & Perennial Farm (802-436-2085; www.talbotsfarm .com), Hartland–Quechee Rd., 3 miles south of the Rt. 4 blinker. Open mid-Apr.–Oct., daily 9–5 except Mon. Patty and David Talbot have been a popular source of local herbs, perennials, and annuals since 1971. Inquire about gardening courses.

✳ Special Events

Note: Check the **Town Crier blackboard** on Elm St. for Woodstock weekly happenings.

Washington's birthday: **Winter Carnival** events sponsored by the Woodstock Recreation Center (802-457-1502).

March: **Home Grown Vermont**— sugaring and festival of Vermont foods.

May: **Plowing Match** (*first weekend*) among dozens of teamsters and draft horses and oxen at Billings Farm & Museum, also the scene of **Sheep Shearing**. In downtown Woodstock the **Memorial Day Parade** is worth a trip to see.

First Sunday of June: **Covered Bridge Quechee/Woodstock Half Marathon**.

Father's Day weekend: **Quechee Hot Air Balloon Festival** (802-295-7900)—a gathering of more than two dozen balloons with ascensions, flights, races, crafts show, entertainment.

July 4: **An Old Fashioned 4th** at Billings Farm & Museum includes a noon reading of the Declaration of Independence, 19th-century-style debates, games, and wagon rides.

August: **Quechee Scottish Festival** (*third Saturday*)—pipe bands, sheepdog trials, Highland dancing, more than 50 clans. **Billings Farm Quilt Show** (*all month*). Also at the farm: **Antique Tractor Parade** (*first Sunday*) and **Children's Day** (*last Saturday*).

Mid-October: Quechee **antiques and crafts festivals**. **Apple & Crafts Fair** (*Columbus Day weekend*), Woodstock—more than 100 juried craftspeople and specialty food producers.

Second weekend of December: **Christmas Wassail Weekend** includes a grand parade of carriages around the Woodstock green, Yule log lighting, concerts.

LOWER COHASE

*C*ohase is an Abenaki word meaning "wide valley." That's according to the chamber of commerce by that name that now embraces this gloriously little-touristed 15-mile stretch of the Connecticut River north of the Upper Valley.

Its southernmost towns are sleepy Piermont, N.H., and (relatively) bustling Bradford, built on terraced land at the confluence of the Waits River and the Connecticut. Bradford is a 19th-century mill village producing plows, paper, and James Wilson, an ingenious farmer who made America's first geographic globes. Handsome Low's Grist Mill survives across from the falls, now housing a popular restaurant, and a golf course spreads below the business block across the floodplain. From Bradford the view across the river encompasses Mount Moosilauke, easternmost of the White Mountains.

Moving upriver, Haverhill, N.H., and Newbury, two of northern New England's most handsome and historic towns, face each other across the river.

Haverhill is immense, comprising seven very distinct villages, including classic examples of both Federal-era and railroad villages. Thanks to a fertile floodplain, this is an old and prosperous farming community, even now. Haverhill Corner, N.H., was founded in 1763 at the western terminus of the Coos Turnpike that wound its way up the Baker Valley and over the mountains from Plymouth. It became the Grafton County seat in 1773; a graceful 19th-century courthouse has recently been restored as a performance and information center. The village itself is a gem: a grouping of Federal-era and Greek Revival homes and public buildings around a double, white-fenced common.

Just north of Haverhill Corner (but south of the junction of Rts. 10 and 25) a sign points the way down through a cornfield and along the river to the site of the Bedell Bridge. Built in 1866, this was one of the largest surviving examples of a two-span covered bridge, until it was destroyed by a violent September windstorm in 1979. The site is still worth finding because it's a peaceful riverside spot, ideal for a picnic.

In North Haverhill, N.H., you come unexpectedly to a lineup of modern county buildings—the courthouse, a county home, and a jail—and then you are in downtown Woodsville, N.H., a 19th-century rail hub with an ornate 1890s brick Opera Block and three-story, mustard-colored railroad station. The

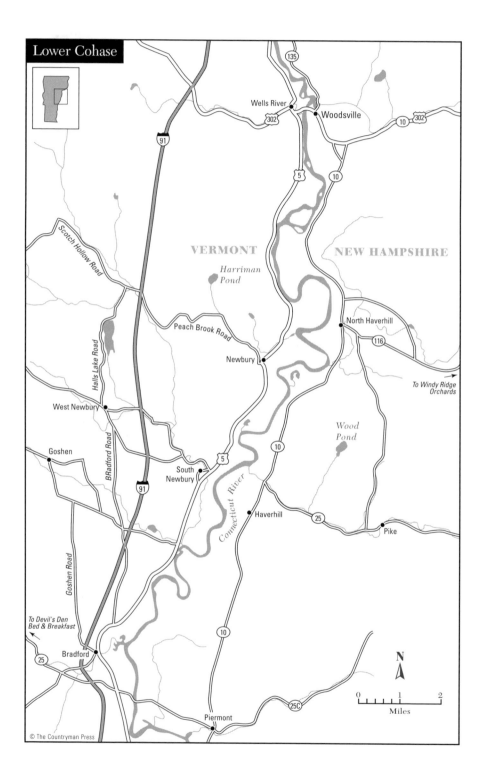

Lower Cohase

Haverhill–Bath covered bridge, built in 1829 and billed as the oldest covered bridge in New England, is just beyond the railroad underpass (Rt. 135 north).

Newbury is one of Vermont's oldest towns, founded in 1761 by Jacob Bailey, a Revolutionary War general still remembered as the force behind the Bayley-Hazen Road, conceived as an invasion route northwest to Canada. It was abandoned two-thirds of the way along, but after the Revolution it served as a prime settlement route. A plaque at the northern end of the business block in Wells River (a village in Newbury) notes the beginning of the trail, while another in Hazen's Notch marks its terminus. Newbury was the site of a Native American village for many thousands of years, and its mineral springs drew travelers as early as 1800. Wells River marked the head of navigation on the Connecticut through the 1830s. In the 1840s river traffic was upstaged by the railroad, which transformed Woodsville.

GUIDANCE **Lower Cohase Regional Chamber of Commerce** (802-222-5631; 1-866-526-4273; www.cohase.org), P.O. Box 209, Bradford 05033, publishes a helpful map/guide and maintains a seasonal welcome center in Wells River, just west of the bridge on Rt. 302.

Alumni Hall (603-989-5500), Court St., Haverhill Corner, N.H. Open mid-June–mid-Oct., 10–4. Built gracefully in brick in 1846 as the Grafton County courthouse, later part of Haverhill Academy, and recently restored as a venue for performances, art shows, and the like and as a Connecticut River Scenic Byway interpretive center. Cultural map/guides and books published by the Joint River Commissions are featured, along with local information.

✳ To Do

BICYCLING Given the beauty of the landscape and the little-trafficked, level nature of Rt. 10 and of this stretch of Rt. 5, the appeal to bicyclists is obvious. Less obvious are the long-distance routes that draw serious cyclists up over the White Mountains on Rts. 116 and 25. At the **North Haverhill Inn and Bicycle Shop** (603-787-6480), 2531 Dartmouth College Hwy. (Rt. 10), N.H., Tom and Noreen Bourassa offer a full-service bike shop and four rooms ($77 with breakfast) catering to cyclists (noncyclists also welcome).

BOATING **Hemlock Pete's Canoes & Kayaks** (603-667-5112; www.hpcanoes .bizland.com), Rt. 10, North Haverhill, N.H. Scott Edwards teaches at the local high school and actually makes as well as rents canoes and kayaks; guided tours, too. His shop is the barn beside Union House B&B (stay 2 nights and get a free rental), across from the fairgrounds.

GOLF **Bradford Golf Club** (802-222-5207), Bradford. Nine holes down by the river. **Blackmount Country Club** (603-787-6564; www.blackmountcountry club.com), 400 Clark Rd., North Haverhill, N.H. Cart rentals, driving range, practice green. A par-36, nine-hole golf course.

SWIMMING **Lake Tarleton State Park**, Rt. 25C in Piermont, Warren, and Benton, N.H. More than 5,000 acres surrounding Lake Tarleton, smaller Lakes

Katherine and Constance, and much of Lake Armington are now public land divided between White Mountain National Forest conservation trusts and a state park featuring the sand beach on Lake Tarleton (part of a onetime resort). The property was slated for major development in 1994 when preservation forces, spearheaded by the Trust for Public Land, raised more than $7 million to preserve this magnificent woodland with its views of Mount Moosilauke. The lake is stocked with trout and also beautiful for canoeing and kayaking (public boat launch). Hiking trails are taking shape, including a connector to the Appalchian Trail, which passes through the property 0.5 mile from the lake.

✳ Lodging

🐾 ♿ **Piermont Inn** (603-272-4820), 1 Old Church St., Piermont, N.H. 03779. A 1790s stagecoach stop with six rooms, four in the adjacent carriage house (only the two in the inn are available year-round), all with private bath. The two in the main house are outstanding rooms, both carved from the tavern's original ballroom, high ceilinged and spacious, with writing desks and appropriate antiques. The carriage house rooms are simple but cheery; one is handicapped accessible. Common space includes a living room with a fireplace, TV, wing chairs, and a nifty grandfather clock. Charlie and Karen Brown are longtime Piermont residents who enjoy tuning guests in to the many ways of exploring this upper (less touristed) part of the Valley, especially canoeing the river. Rooms in the main house are $135, and in the carriage house $95, full breakfast included.

🐾 **The Gibson House** (603-989-3125; www.gibsonhousebb.com), RR 1, Box 193, Haverhill, N.H. 03765. Open June–Oct. New innkeepers Susie Klein and Marty Cohen have kept this amazing place exactly as artist Keita Colton restored it. One of the Valley's finest Greek Revival homes, it was built in 1850 on the green in Haverhill Corner and at one point was a stagecoach inn. The seven guest rooms, especially the four big second-floor rooms, are artistic creations, each very different from the next. Taj North is the most opulent and exotic with its faux balcony, rich colors, and glowing stained-glass moon. We enjoyed the golden, Asian-themed Bamboo Room, but our favorite is the Seashore Room, with its quilts and colors (twin beds), overlooking the garden. While the house fronts on Rt. 10, the 50-foot-long sunny back porch with wicker seats and swing takes full advantage of the splendid view west across the terraced garden and the Connecticut River. A full breakfast is served in the fanciful dining room or, weather permitting, on the first-floor screened porch. $125–175 includes a full breakfast.

🐾 **Peach Brook Inn** (802-866-3389), Doe Hill, off Rt. 5, South Newbury 05051. Joyce Emery has opened her spacious 1837 home with its splendid view of the Connecticut River. What a special place! Common space includes two nicely furnished parlors with exposed beams and a fireplace, an open kitchen, and a screened porch with a view of Mount Moosilauke across the river. The house is on a country lane in the almost vanished village of South Newbury, once connected to Haverhill, N.H., across the river by a long-gone covered bridge. Plenty of farm animals are within walking distance. There are three comfortable guest rooms; $65 with shared bath, $80 with private, including full breakfast. No smoking. No children under 10, please; under 18 are $10.

☘ Union House Bed & Breakfast (603-080-5931; www.unionhouse bandb.com), 1260 Dartmouth College Hwy. (Rt. 10), North Haverhill, N.H. 03774. Susan Brown welcomes guests to the oldest house in Haverhill, formerly a stagecoach stop and tavern. What's offered is the former Hired Man's Room with a separate entrance and full bath. It's an attarctive, air-conditioned room with a queen-sized bed. Guests are welcome to use the indoor Endless Pool. Brown is a long-time Valley resident and a font of advice on where to eat and what to see and do. $85 per night ($5 discount for cash).

The Hayloft Inn at Blackmount (603-787-2367; prfctlie@earthlink .net), 440 Clark Pond Rd., North Haverhill, N.H. 03774. The plain exterior of this house belies its airy, open post-and-beam interior. Innkeeper Joyce Read is a native of Plainfield, N.H., where her mother modeled a couple of times as a young girl for painter Maxfield Parrish. Read has been collecting the artist's distinctive prints all her life and displays them in a special gallery room. There are two bright, tastefully furnished guest rooms with private bath, as well as a two-room suite (one with two double beds and one with twins, sharing both a bath and sitting area). A hearty breakfast is served at 8 AM. The Blackmount Country Club is next door.

✳ Where to Eat

DINING OUT The Perfect Pear Café (802-222-5912; www.the perfectpearcafe.com), the Bradford Mill, Main St., Bradford. Open for lunch Tue.–Sat. 11:30–2, dinner 5–8:45. Jan.–Apr., closed for dinner Mon.–Wed. Dinner reservations recommended. Adam Coulter, formerly at the Norwich Inn, is now chef-owner. This remains a charming bistro, housed in a historic brick mill by a falls, especially appealing in summer when there's dining on the flower-decked patio overlooking the Waits River, churning along because the big falls are just across the road. Lunch is reasonably priced with choices like Gorgonzola and candied walnut salad with maple balsamic vinaigrette, and a lamb and rosemary sausage sandwich on whole grain with honey mustard. Dinner might begin with crispy pork dumplings and feature crabmeat-stuffed rainbow trout with a pesto cream, or pork tenderloin served with polenta, as well as vegetarian choices like truffled cannellini bean ravioli with a shiitake Marsala sauce and braised greens. Dinner entrées $12.95–18.95.

⚓ Warners Gallery Restaurant (802-429-2120), just off I-91, Exit 17, on Rt. 302, Wells River. Open Tue.–Thu. 5–8:30 PM, Fri. and Sat. 5–9, Sun. 11–8. A dependable (90 percent of the time) all-American family restaurant with some atmosphere. Entrées usually include twin stuffed lobster tails, a fisherman's platter, baked stuffed shrimp, and roast prime beef au jus. There's a children's menu, and Sunday brunch (11–2) is billed as "best in the Northeast." Dinner entrées $13–24. Full liquor license.

EATING OUT For lunch in Bradford/ Piermont check, **Perfect Pear** under *Dining Out*.

☞ **Colatina Exit** (802-222-9008), Main St., Bradford. Open daily 5– 9 PM, weekends until 10:30. Carol Meagher's Vermont trattoria has been here more than 30 years but recently doubled in size, added a wood-fired pizza oven, and expanded its to-go menu. We still like the original dining room best: candles in Chianti bottles, Italian scenes on the walls, checked (green in summer, red in winter) tablecloths, and a few tables in back with a view of the river. The big menu offers plenty of antipasto and insalata choices and traditional Italian dishes like "lasagna classico" and veal parmi- giano; also some nice surprises like grilled chicken portofino (with sautéed portobello mushrooms and fresh spinach in a red Marsala mari- nara sauce) and wood-roasted scallops carbonara (with spinach and smoked bacon). Plenty of pizza choices and calzones. There's also an upstairs pub with river views.

Bliss Village Store and Deli (802- 222-4617), Main St., Bradford. Housed in a former 19th-century hotel, this is a classic general store but with Crock- Pots full of soup, chili, or stew-fried chicken and a deli with daily specials;

NEWBURY VILLAGE STORE

Christina Tree

tables are in the back—including a booth with the best river view in town.

Newbury Village Store (802-866- 5681), 4991 Rt. 5, Newbury. Open 6 AM–8 PM weekdays, Sat. 7–8, Sun. 8–6. This is the new breed of nouvelle general store. Gary and Maggie Hatch have added comfortable seating near the periodicals and expanded the deli to feature sandwiches named for local landmarks like "The Oxbow" ("basil herb roasted turkey breast with Ver- mont cheddar, ripe tomatoes, leaf let- tuce and the house garlic cream cheese spread on multi grain bread"). There's also a hummus wrap and "The Flatlander" ("shaved black pastrami warmed and piled high on rye and pumpernickel swirl bread, topped with swiss cheese and deli mustard"). There are staple groceries, also a selection of wine and Vermont prod- ucts. Locals tells us these are the best sandwiches around. There are tables in the back, overlooking the river.

Happy Hours Restaurant (802-757- 3466), Rt. 5, Wells River. Open daily 11:30–8, later in summer. This large, pine-paneled family restaurant in the middle of town has been lightened and brightened in recent years and hums with a sense of friendly service and satisfied patrons. Most entrées include the salad bar—and servings are generous. We couldn't finish a tender sirloin topped with red wine mushroom sauce, with baked potato and good coleslaw (a $12.99 special). Dinner entrées $11.99–22.99.

Shiloh's (802-222-5666), 142 Main St., Bradford. Open 6–2. The usual sandwiches, soups, wraps, and burg- ers, but the beef and as many ingredi- ents as possible are local.

☞ **P&H Truck Stop** (802-429-2141), just off I-91, Exit 17, on Rt. 302, Wells

River. Now open just 6 AM–10 PM for hot meals but still 24 hours for to-go premade sandwiches, pies, and the like. Dozens of rigs are usually parked outside on one side, and the range of license plates on cars in the other lot is usually broad. This is a classic truck stop with speedy service, friendly waitresses, and heaping portions at amazing prices. Plus which the bread is homemade; ATM and phone are available (cell phones don't tend to work around here, and pay phones are scarce).

The Little Chef (603-747-8088), 19 Central St., Woodsville, N.H. Open Tue.–Sat. 8–8; Sun. 8–noon (breakfast only). A good breakfast and lunch stop with a big menu and reasonable prices. The dinner menu is basic and reasonably priced (meat loaf for $7.99, veal Parmesan for $11.99); no liquor license.

New Century (603-747-2368), 85 Central St., Woodsville, N.H. Open daily for lunch through dinner. Locals tell us that this Chinese (Mandarin, Szechuan, and Cantonese) restaurant is a standout. Service is fast, prices are reasonable, and we like the look of the menu.

ICE CREAM **Mountain Scoops**, Rt. 10, North Haverhill, N.H. Open Memorial Day–Columbus Day 11–9. This colorful stand in the middle of town is the source of Rhonda Abrams's homemade ice cream.

✳ Entertainment

Middle Earth Music Hall (802-222-4748; www.middle-earth-music.com), 134 Main St., Bradford. It's all about music, nightly. Check out the web site for current schedule: jazz, blues, honkytonk, open mike.

Old Church Community Theater (802-222-3322), 137 Main St., Bradford (call Paul Hunt: 802-222-4254).

Alumni Hall (603-989-5500), Court St., Haverhill Corner, N.H. Open mid-June–mid-Oct., 10–4. Built gracefully in brick in 1846 as the Grafton County courthouse, later part of Haverhill Academy and recently restored as a venue for concerts and other performances, art shows, and the like. Call for current schedule.

✳ Selective Shopping

Woodsville Bookstore (603-747-3811), 91 Central St., Woodsville, N.H. Dave Major's friendly, well-stocked bookstore is an unexpected find here, the best for many miles around. One room of new, one of used books.

Copeland Furniture (802-222-5300; www.copelandfurniture.com), 64 Main St., Bradford. Open Mon.–Fri. 10–6, Sat. 9–5. Contemporary, cleanly lined, locally made furniture in native hardwoods displayed in the handsome showroom in the converted 19th-century brick mill across from Bradford Falls. Seconds.

Farm-Way, Inc. (1-800-222-9316), Rt. 25, Bradford. One mile east of I-91, Exit 16. Open Mon.–Sat. until 8 PM. Billed as "complete outfitters for man and beast," this is a phenomenon: a family-run source of work boots and rugged clothing that now includes a stock of more than 2 million products spread over 5 acres: tack, furniture, pet supplies, syrup, whatever. Recently expanded: Shoes and boots remain a specialty, from size 4E to 16; 25,000 shoes, boots, clogs, sandals, and sneakers in stock; also kayaks, sporting equipment, furnishings, and gifts.

Bruce Murray: Potter (802-222-5798; www.brucemurraypotter.com), 3458 South Rd., Bradford. Open May–Oct., 10–5. A timber-frame barn surrounded by farm fields, this exceptional, long-established studio showcases a wide variety of handmade and hand-decorated stoneware, both functional and decorative.

Round Barn Shoppe (603-272-9026), 430 Rt. 10, Piermont, N.H. Open May 2–Christmas, Thu.–Mon. 9–5; Jan.–May 1, Fri.–Sun. This 1990s post-and-beam round barn replicates the authentic 1906 barn across the road. It houses a shop selling New England products ranging from baskets and dolls to local dairy milk and fresh pies. Some 300 New England craftsmen and 100 small manufacturers are represented.

4 Corners Farm (802-866-3342), just off Rt. 5, South Newbury. Bob and Kim Gray sell their own produce and flowers. An exceptionally pretty farm, just off but up above the highway, known for strawberries, PYO vegetables.

Windy Ridge Orchard (603-787-6377), Rt. 116, North Haverhill, N.H. Open daily Labor Day–Thanksgiving,

4 CORNERS FARM IN NEWBURY

Christina Tree

9–6; weekends Thanksgiving to Christmas, 9–4. Pick your own apples and pumpkins, farm animals, kids' corral playground, nature trails, picnic tables, Cider House Café, gift shop. Apple picking begins in mid-August and lasts through mid-October depending on the variety. There are 3,500 apple trees on 20 acres, overlooking the Valley and Green Mountains. There's also a Christmas tree plantation—and you can cut your own trees.

✳ Special Events

Note: Farmer's markets are held in Woodsville on Wednesdays.

July: **4th of July Parade and celebration in Woodsville and Wells River**: marching bands, floats, horses, chicken barbecue, dancing, fireworks. **Connecticut Valley Fair** (*mid-month*), Bradford. Ox and horse pulling, sheep show, midway, demolition derby. **Cracker Barrel Bazaar** (*third or final weekend*), Newbury, includes fiddlers' contest, antiques show, quilt show, sheepdog trials, church suppers. The **North Haverhill (N.H.) Fair** (*last weekend*) is an old-style fair with ox and tractor pulls, pig races, and more.

September: **Whole Hog Blues & BBQ Festival** (*last weekend*). Blues music by leading bands, roast pig cook-off, arts and crafts.

October: **Vermont North by Hand** (*weekend before Columbus Day*)—25 crafts and art studios hold open house. Contact Bruce Murray: Potter (802-222-5798).

November: **Annual Wild Game Supper** (*Saturday before Thanksgiving*), Bradford (802-222-4721)—hungry visitors pour into the Congregational church for this feast.

Central Vermont

KILLINGTON/PLYMOUTH AREA

THE WHITE RIVER VALLEYS

SUGARBUSH/MAD RIVER VALLEY

BARRE/MONTPELIER AREA

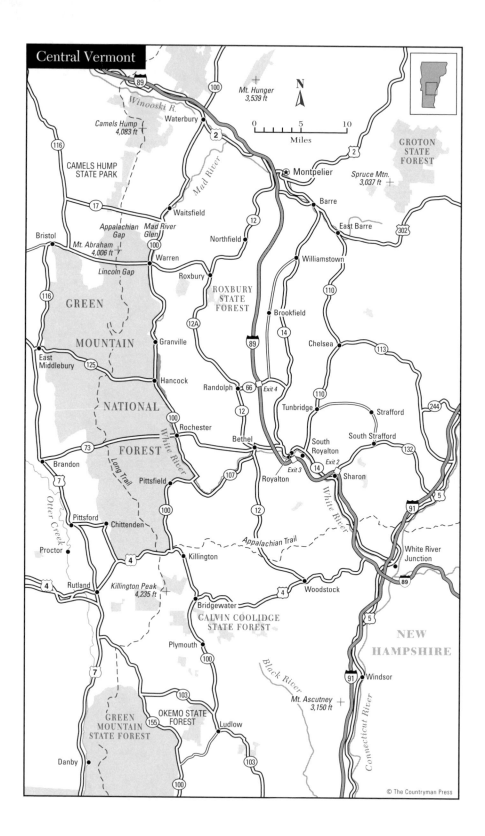

Central Vermont

KILLINGTON/PLYMOUTH AREA

K illington is the largest ski resort with the longest ski season in the East. It boasts seven mountains and the most extensive snowmaking system in the world. It's said that some 18,000 visitors can bed down within 20 miles.

Killington Peak, the second highest summit in the state, is flanked by four other mountains and faces another majestic range across Sherburne Pass. Although the road through this upland village has been heavily traveled since the settling of Rutland (11 miles to the west) and Woodstock (20 miles to the east), there was never much of anything here. In 1924 an elaborate, rustic-style inn was built at the junction of Rt. 4, the Appalachian Trail, and the new Long Trail. A winter annex across the road was added in 1938, when Pico (now part of Killington) installed one of the country's first T-bars. But the logging village of Sherburne Center (now the town of Killington) was practically a ghost town in 1957 when Killington began.

Condominiums cluster at higher elevations while lodges, inns, and motels are strung along the 5-mile length of Killington Rd. and west along Rt. 4 as it slopes ever downward through Mendon to Rutland. Ski lodges are also salted along Rt. 100 north to the pleasant old town of Pittsfield, and in the village of Chittenden, sequestered up a back road from Rt. 4, near a mountain-backed reservoir. In summer this is exceptional hiking and mountain biking country. The K1 Express Gondola, to the summit of Killington Peak, carries bikes. What Killington terms "Endless Adventures" include major golf and tennis programs and plenty of family-geared activities. Summer also brings theater and ballet, a series of musical, horsey, and other events, and—because this is still primarily a winter resort area—substantial savings on summer accommodations.

Southeast of Killington, down Rt. 100 and a few miles up Rt. 100A, stands the village of Plymouth Notch, looking much the way it did on August 3, 1923, when Calvin Coolidge was sworn in by his father as the 30th president of the United States in his kerosene-lit home. Now the President Calvin Coolidge State Historic Site, it's arguably the only Vermont village in which the story of its remarkable residents as well as its buildings has been preserved.

GUIDANCE **Killington Central Reservations** (1-800-621-6867), Rt. 4, located in the Shops at the Shack. Open mid-Nov.–May, daily 8 AM–9 PM, the bureau

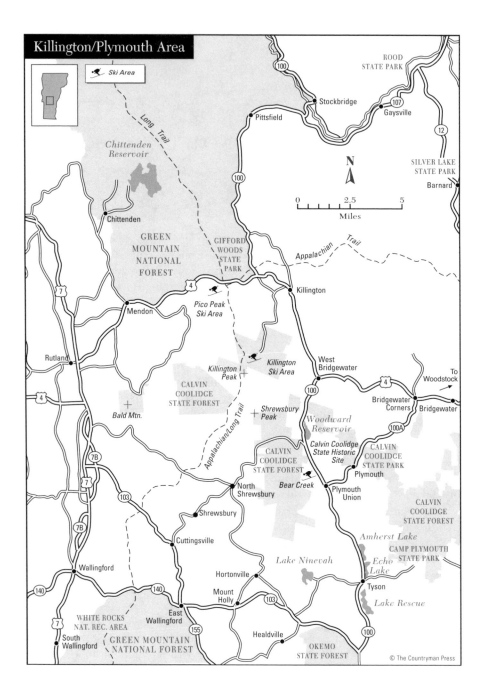

Killington/Plymouth Area

Ski Area

ROOD
STATE PARK

Stockbridge
Gaysville
107
100
Pittsfield
12

Chittenden
Reservoir

SILVER LAKE
STATE PARK
Barnard

N

0   2.5   5
Miles

Chittenden

GREEN
MOUNTAIN
NATIONAL
FOREST

GIFFORD
WOODS
STATE
PARK

Appalachian Trail

Killington

Mendon

Pico Peak
Ski Area

Rutland

Killington
Peak

Killington
Ski Area

West
Bridgewater

To
Woodstock

4

CALVIN
COOLIDGE
STATE FOREST

Shrewsbury
Peak

Woodward
Reservoir

Bridgewater
Corners   Bridgewater

100A

Bald Mtn.

Appalachian/Long Trail

100

Calvin Coolidge
State Historic
Site

CALVIN
COOLIDGE
STATE PARK

CALVIN
COOLIDGE
STATE FOREST

7B

CALVIN
COOLIDGE
STATE FOREST

North
Shrewsbury

Bear Creek

Plymouth

Plymouth
Union

103

7B

Shrewsbury

Amherst Lake

CALVIN
COOLIDGE
STATE FOREST

Cuttingsville

CAMP PLYMOUTH
STATE PARK

Wallingford

Lake Ninevah

Echo
Lake

140

Hortonville

Tyson

Lake Rescue

Mount
Holly

103

7

WHITE ROCKS
NAT. REC. AREA

East
Wallingford

140

155

Healdville

100

South
Wallingford

GREEN MOUNTAIN
NATIONAL FOREST

OKEMO
STATE FOREST

© The Countryman Press

keeps a tally on vacancies and makes reservations. A wide variety of 2- to 5-day ski packages is available; for summer packages, phone 1-877-4K-TIMES. The web site for all information related to the area is www.killington.com.

Killington Chamber of Commerce (802-773-4181; 1-800-337-1928; www .killingtonchamber.com) is a source of year-round information about the area.

GETTING THERE *By rail:* **Amtrak**'s Ethan Allen Express (1-800-USA-RAIL; www.amtrak.com) from New York City stops in Rutland.

By bus: **Vermont Transit** (1-800-552-8737; www.vermonttransit.com) stops in Rutland. Some inns will pick up guests.

By plane: Rutland Airport is served by **Commutair** (1-800-523-3273, Continental Connection), operated by Continental Airlines from Boston. For direct service from New York, see "Burlington Region."

GETTING AROUND **Gramps Shuttle** (802-558-1543; 802-236-6600; www .grampsshuttle.com). John King will shuttle you around the area year-round in passenger vans, a Lincoln Navigator, or a 14-person stretch limousine. Call for reservations.

The Bus (802-773-3244, ext. 1; www.thebus.com). The Marble Valley Regional Transit District operates winter shuttle buses that run from the Amtrak station in Rutland to several Killington points, from Pico Resort on Rt. 4 to the Skyship Base Station on Rt. 14 and up and down the length of Killington Rd. Hail a bus curbside. Tickets are $2 per ride (more for the Amtrak Connection), but much of Killington is a fare-free zone. Ask your inn for free bus passes.

WHEN TO GO In theory Killington's ski season begins mid-October and runs through May, but the full trail system rarely opens before Christmas, and by Easter it's pretty much all over with. Given its size and high profile, Killington attracts more ski-weekers than other New England areas, enough for a lively midweek atmosphere but still leaving ample room on the slopes (not always true during February weekends and school vacations). July through foliage season is pleasant: plenty to do and a wide choice of places to stay at off-season prices.

KILLINGTON PEAK

On a clear day the view from the summit of the state's second highest mountain (4,241 feet) encompasses five states. It sweeps northwest to the Adirondacks, east to the White Mountains, and north along the spine of the Green Mountains. It's the spot on which the Reverend Samuel Peters in 1763 is said to have christened all that he could see "Verd monts." The K1 Express Gondola (daily Memorial Day–Labor Day, then mid-Sep.–Columbus Day; 802-422-6200) hoists visitors up from the Killington Base Lodge to the Peak Restaurant (cafeteria lunch menu and special dinners in foliage season) just below the summit, and a nature trail leads to the peak. No matter how hot it is down on Rt. 4, chances are you will need a jacket on top. Bring a picnic and stay awhile. This is one of those special places.

MEDICAL EMERGENCY Emergency service is available by calling **911**.

Rutland Regional Medical Center (802-775-7111; www.rrmc.org), 160 Allen St., Rutland.

Killington Medical Clinic (802-422-6125; Killington Courtesy phone: ext. 6125), adjacent to Rams Head Lodge, provides emergency medical services to the resort area.

✳ To Do

AERIAL RIDES The **Killington K1 Express** runs from Killington Base Lodge to the top of Killington Peak (see the box on page 291). During foliage season (mid-Sep.–Columbus Day), the **Killington Skyeship Express**, a speedy, eight-passenger gondola, runs from Rt. 4 to an elevation of 3,800 feet. Both cost the same, and for both the phone is 802-422-6200.

BICYCLING Killington Mountain Bike Center (802-422-6232; 1-877-4K-TIMES). The Killington K1 Express Gondola operates Memorial Day–Columbus Day hoisting bicyclists and their bikes to Killington Peak, accessing 45 miles of marked trails; $32 for a mountain biking trail pass, $13 for a ride on the gondola. During foliage season the Skyeship (see above) is also available. Guided tours, instruction, bike rentals and packages.

True Wheels (802-422-3234; www.truewheels.com), top of the Killington Rd., also rents mountain bikes. The only place on the mountain for bike repair, and a great source of info for local trail and road riding.

Vermont Adventure Tours (802-773-3343; www.vermontadventuretours.com), 223 Woodstock Ave. (Rt. 4), offers gear, guides, and information on mountain biking, rock climbing, fly-fishing, mountaineering, foliage drives, paddling, and snowshoeing.

CAMPING See *Green Space*.

CANOEING AND KAYAKING Chittenden Reservoir is a sublime place to canoe or kayak, an expansive 674 acres backed by mountains. Boat access is at the end of Chittenden Dam Rd. **Woodford Reservoir** on Rt. 100 south is another beautiful spot to paddle.

Kayak King (802-746-7952; www.kayakking.8m.com) in Killington offers kayak rentals on Kent Pond.

FISHING Licenses are available from the Killington town clerk, River Rd., and also from sporting goods stores and state park rangers. Landlocked salmon and trout can be had in Chittenden Reservoir; trout are the catch in Mendon Brook. There also is fishing in Kent and Colton Ponds, and the White, Tweed, and Ottauquechee Rivers. Woodward Reservoir on Rt. 100 south and Echo Lake in Tyson (accessible from Plymouth Camp State Park) are also good fishing.

Stream & Brook Fly-Fishing (802-989-0398; www.streamandbrook.com) offers beginners programs and full- and half-day guided trips.

CALVIN COOLIDGE AND PLYMOUTH NOTCH

Calvin Coolidge (1872–1933) is best remembered for his dry wit and thrift, his integrity and common sense, all famously Vermont virtues. The village of Plymouth Notch—in which Coolidge was born, assumed the presidency, briefly governed the country (in the summer of 1924), and is buried—is said to be the best-preserved presidential birthplace in the nation. It may also be the best-preserved Vermont village, offering an in-depth sense of the people who lived there.

In the spirit of Coolidge himself, the village remains low-key: no 1920s costumed interpreters, no multimedia displays. The cheese factory built by the president's father, John Coolidge, showcases the history of Vermont cheesemaking and produces its own granular curd cheese. The square-steepled Union Christian Church, with its acoustically superb interior, is the setting for frequent concerts and lectures. The general store sells pickles, afghans, and some Vermont specialty foods like dilled carrots and Moxie—reportedly Coolidge's favorite drink (it was, after all, Prohibition).

"Colonel" John Coolidge became storekeeper here in 1868, and his son Calvin was born on the Fourth of July, 1872, in the modest attached house. The family moved across the street to the larger "Coolidge Homestead" when he was 4 years old, and it was there, because he happened to be home helping with the haying, that Vice President Calvin Coolidge learned of President Warren Harding's unexpected death. At 2:47 AM on August 3, 1923, he was sworn in, by his father, as 30th president of the United States.

THE CALVIN COOLIDGE STATE HISTORIC SITE

Diane E. Foulds

"I didn't know I couldn't" was the reply Coolidge Sr. gave when reporters asked how he knew he could administer the presidential oath of office. "Colonel John" was a former state senator, a notary public, and the village sheriff as well as shopkeeper. His terse response typifies the dry wit for which his son would later become known.

It should come as no surprise that in this classic Vermont village you encounter a classic Vermont family. The Coolidges were hardworking (up before dawn for chores), self-sufficient (you see an intricate quilt that was stitched by Cal at age 10 and a graceful carriage built by his father), and closely linked to the land. Coolidge is buried with seven generations of his family in the small graveyard across the road from the village. Village residents numbered 29 during Coolidge's presidency, and a high percentage of these formed the Old-Time Dance Orchestra, which played in the dance hall above the general store. This same room served as the office of the Summer White House for a dozen days in 1924. At the time Calvin and his wife, Grace, were grieving the death of their son Calvin Jr., a promising 16-year-old who had died due to a complication from an infected blister he acquired while playing tennis at the White House.

Plymouth resident Ruth ("Midge") Aldrich opened several tourist cabins (prefab jobs brought up from Boston) to accommodate the Secret Service and a Top of the Notch Tea Room to serve a steady stream of the Coolidge-curious. Plymouth Notch, however, never really hit the big time as a tourist attraction, perhaps because, while he continued to visit "The Notch," President Coolidge himself retired to private life not here but in his adopted home, Northampton, Massachusetts. After graduating from nearby Amherst College, Coolidge had opened a law practice in Northampton, and it was there that he met his wife (fellow Vermonter Grace Anna Goodhue, who was teaching there at the Clarke School for the Deaf) and served as mayor. He represented Northampton in the Massachusetts Legislature before becoming governor of the Bay State, and he died in Northampton.

It was Aurora Pierce, the family housekeeper, who fiercely

PRESIDENT CALVIN COOLIDGE

Vermont Division for Historic Preservation

preserved the Coolidge Homestead, adamantly opposing even minor changes, like plumbing and electricity. Not until Aurora's death in 1956 did Vermont's Historic Sites Commission assume management of the house and its contents (which Grace Coolidge had deeded to them). The state had already purchased the 1840s village tavern that had also been Calvin's mother's home, turning it into a lunchroom and information center.

The President Calvin Coolidge State Historic Site presently encompasses 25 buildings, the majority of the village. Twelve buildings, including the cheese factory, the 1840s church, the general store and its upstairs hall (restored to look just as it did as the office of the Summer White House), and the recently reconstructed Wilder Barn (housing farm implements, horse-drawn vehicles, and an enclosed picnic area), are open to the public. There is also a good restaurant (see *Eating Out*) and a visitors center (with changing exhibits). Power lines have been buried (electricity actually didn't reach Plymouth until after Calvin's death), and roads have been paved. Otherwise the village looks about as it did in the 1920s, sitting quietly at the foot of East Mountain. It's set in 560 acres presently owned by the Vermont Division for Historic Preservation, surrounded by the 500-acre Coolidge State Park, in turn abutting the 16,000-acre Calvin Coolidge State Forest. The President Coolidge State Historic Site (802-672-3773; www.historicvermont.org/coolidge) is open late May–mid-Oct., daily 9:30–5. $7.50 adults, $2 ages 6–14; 5 and under are free. During the off-season the Aldrich House, which doubles as an office and exhibit space, is open weekdays (no charge)—but call ahead.

THE VISITORS CENTER AT THE CALVIN COOLIDGE STATE HISTORIC SITE

Diane E. Foulds

Christina Tree

CHITTENDEN RESERVOIR

FITNESS CENTERS/SPAS **Cortina Health Club** (802-773-3333; www.cortina inn.com), Cortina Inn, Rt. 4, Killington. Heated indoor pool, whirlpool, exercise room, saunas, massage, facials, exercise classes.

Pico Sports Center (802-422-6200; 1-866-667-PICO; www.picomountain.com/ sportscenter.html), 4763 Killington Rd., Rt. 4, Killington. A 75-foot Olympic lap pool, aerobics area, fitness and cardiovascular room, Jacuzzi, saunas, tanning, massage, fitness evaluations.

The Spa at the Woods (802-422-3139; www.spaatthewoods.com), 53 Woods Lane, Killington. Built as the heart of a deluxe condo complex but open to drop-ins, an unusually attractive, full-service spa with pool, Jacuzzi, and a full massage and body treatment menu.

Mountain Green Health Club (802-422-3113; www.mtgreen.com), center of Killington Village at 133 East Mountain Rd. Located in the Mountain Green complex, a club with a 54-foot indoor lap pool, Jacuzzi, aerobics classes, steam rooms, sauna, facials, massage.

New Life Hiking Spa (1-800-228-4676; www.newlifehikingspa.com), based at the Inn of the Six Mountains. Mid-May–Sep. Since 1978 Jimmy LeSage has been refining and fine-tuning fitness programs (2 to 11 days and longer) that combine sensible eating and moderate exercise. The daily regimen begins with a pre-breakfast walk and includes body conditioning, yoga, and hiking (all levels). Meals are varied, and the focus is on increasing energy and stamina (a good solo vacation).

FOR FAMILIES ✔ **Killington/Pico Adventure Center** (802-422-6200; www .killington.com) is physically divided between the base areas of Pico, down on Rt. 4, and of Killington itself. Open Memorial Day through late June on week-ends, then daily through Labor Day, 10–5. An Adventure Center Pass covers everything; passes are also available for single activities.

❧ *At Pico:* **The Alpine Slide**. Patrons ride a triple chairlift up and then slide down a total of 3,410 feet; the slide begins halfway up the mountain with a sweeping view of the valley to the west. Lunch and snacks are served at a snack bar. "Endless Activities" here also include miniature golf (19 holes) and chairlift rides.

❧ *At Killington:* Waterslides, outdoor climbing wall, skateboard and in-line skate park, as well as mountain biking and a hiking center.

GOLF **Killington Resort** (802-422-6700; www.killington.com), Killington Rd., Killington, has its own 18-hole, 6,326-yard, par-72 course designed by Geoffrey Cornish. Weekend clinics and golf packages. PGA professional instruction, rental clubs. The **Mountain Golf School** (1-800-343-0762), at the Killington Resort, features 2-day weekend and 3-day midweek instructional programs.

Green Mountain National Golf Course (802-422-4653; www.gmngc.com), Barrows–Towne Rd. and Rt. 100, Killington. This highly rated 18-hole course opened in 1996 and includes a clubhouse, three practice teeing areas, four target greens, and an 8,000-square-foot putting green.

Also see White River Golf Club in The "White River Valleys"— affordable and good for families.

HIKING **Deer Leap Trail**, off Rt. 4 behind the Inn at Long Trail, is the most popular short hike: a 45-minute one-way trek up a winding, moderately steep path that yields a southerly panoramic view from the top of a tall cliff. For a whole-day hike, you can continue along the Long Trail to Chittenden Reservoir or branch east at the Maine Junction onto the Appalachian Trail. This trail also connects with Gifford Woods State Park. Plant a car at the other end and be sure to bring a hiking map.

Bald Mountain. This 3-mile, 3-hour round-trip hike is in Aiken State Forest, off Notch Rd. from Rt. 4 in Mendon. The blue-blazed circle trail begins just past the intersection with Wheelerville Rd.

Fox Creek Inn shuttles hikers to the Long Trail as part of the Country Inns Along the Trail program (802-326-2072; 1-800-838-330; www.inntoinn.com).

Killington Information Center (802-422-6200) at the base of Killington Rd. Pick up a hiking map to the mountain and its lifts at the Killington base lodge. Inquire about "Hike and Stay" packages.

HORSEBACK RIDING **Mountain Top Inn & Resort Equestrian Program** (802-483-2311; www.mountaintopinn.com) offers horseback riding geared to every level from beginner to experienced, both English and Western. Jumping, dressage, cross-country, and children's instruction are available, along with the basics of driving the two resident Percherons. Group and private instruction, sleigh rides.

Hawk Inn & Mountain Resort (802-672-3811; www.hawkresort.com), at Salt Ash, Rt. 100, in Plymouth. The Stables at Hawk offers lessons, trail rides for 10 and over, and pony rides. Open Memorial Day weekend–Labor Day.

ROCK CLIMBING **Green Mountain Rock Climbing Center** (802-773-3343; vermontclimbing.com). Based in Rutland at 223 Woodstock Ave. and at the Killington Snowshed Lodge, the center offers lessons and climbs for all abilities, from age 4 up. Inquire about winter ice climbing.

TENNIS **Killington School for Tennis at the Cortina Inn** (802-773-3331; 1-800-451-6108; www.killingtontennis.com), Rt. 4, Killington. Numerous options are available Memorial Day–early Sep. from half-day to weeklong sessions using eight outdoor courts and the Village at Killington. There's also a Junior Tennis Academy.

Summit Lodge (802-422-3535), Killington Rd., Killington. Two outdoor courts are available to the public if not in use by members. Public courts are also maintained by the towns of Chittenden and Killington.

✳ Winter Sports

CROSS-COUNTRY SKIING AND SNOWSHOEING 🐾 ✍ **Mountain Meadows Cross Country Ski and Snowshoe Center** (802-775-7077; www.xcskiing.net), 209 Thundering Brook Rd. off Rt. 4, Killington, 0.25 mile east of the main Killington access road. Open daily (conditions permitting) 9–5. One of Vermont's oldest and most serious touring centers, set on 50 km groomed trails for skating and classic stride, plus 500 acres of backcountry terrain. Some instruction, rentals, kids' programs, and simple, hot lunches. Call for telemark rentals and for Nordic and snowshoe tours of the backcountry. Dogs welcome after 2.

Mountain Travelers (802-775-0814; 1-800-339-0814; www.mtntravelers.com), 147 Rt. 4 east in Rutland, sells lightweight camping and hiking gear, kayaks, canoes and summer sportswear. They also have a branch at 937B Killington Rd. (802-422-8353). Open Mon.–Sat. 10–6, Sun noon–4.

Mountain Top Nordic Ski & Snowshoe Center (802-483-6089; www .mountaintopinn.com), Mountain Top Rd., Chittenden. Eighty kilometers of trails, 60 km of which are groomed, begin at the Nordic Center, the country's oldest commercial cross-country ski center and an ideal location at 1,495–2,165 feet, with sweeping views of the mountains and of Chittenden Reservoir; rentals, lessons, and snowmaking.

Hawk Inn & Mountain Resort (802-672-3811; www.hawkresort.com), Rt. 100 south, Plymouth, offers rentals, lessons, and groomed trails meandering along a brook.

Killington Snowshoe Tours (1-800-767-7031; www.killingtonsnowshoetours .com). Based at the Cortina Inn and Resort on Rt. 4 in Killington, Katy Landwehr offers daily guided tours that include snowshoes and snacks. Reservations essential.

DOWNHILL SKIING/SNOWBOARDING ✍ **Killington Resort** (1-800-621-MTNS; www.killington.com), 4763 Killington Rd., Killington. With seven parking lots, six base lodges, six interconnected mountains—plus Pico—and the longest snowboard terrain park in the East, Killington is just plain immense. When it was purchased by the American Skiing Company in 1996, it was dubbed Beast of the

East. Thanks to its four entry points and far-flung network of lifts and trails, the crowds are neatly dispersed throughout the area. In recent years the resort has upgraded its snowmaking system, already the world's most extensive, guaranteeing good conditions whatever the weather. While visitors sleep, its 18-vehicle grooming fleet goes to work manicuring anywhere from 50 to 80 percent of the terrain. Among recent changes are a spiffy food court and six terrain parks, including a 430-foot superpipe at Bear Mountain with its 18-foot walls, a challenge to even the most proficient snowboarder. With 1,215 acres of slopes, Killington has something to please everyone, including high-elevation views, trails that lead mountain to mountain, and 16 tree slopes. It boasts the tallest summit in the East accessible by lift: a heated express gondola that treks 4,215 feet to the summit of Killington, the highest of the seven peaks. A quarter of its 200 trails are easy; a third are moderate, and about 40 percent are difficult. The longest, the so-called Juggernaut, runs 6.2 miles. Killington's base lodges offer extensive services, plenty of food, and some of the best ski shops in New England. The virtually self-contained Rams Head is great for kids. Among its facilities are a family center for rentals, a skier development program, child care, a food court, and Snow Play Park. Killington Rd. itself is a glut of restaurants and shops from the modest to the sublime.

The resort calms somewhat in summer, when the focus turns to golf. Starting in May, Killington rolls out its 18-hole championship green (www.killingtongolf.com), and there are 20 others nearby. You can ride the chairlift to the top of the mountain and hike, mountain bike the 40 miles of designated trails, or cart your way down the alpine slide, with its 650-foot vertical drop. Kids enjoy the Killington/Pico Adventure Center, a play area with waterslides, a climbing wall, and special park for skateboards and in-line skates. Then there are special events. In May, Killington hosts a triathlon and a mountain-climbing contest known as the Killington Klimb. In July there are wine and Renaissance festivals. Classic motorcycles rally in September, and beer lovers gather for the Brewfest in October. Probably Vermont's most popular ski area, Killington continues to grow. A new resort village is slated to go up in 2006, and a stream of winter events is planned, from national freestyle championships to entertainment and on-snow parties.

Lifts: 33, including 12 quads (6 high-speed) plus the Skyeship and K1 Express Gondolas, 4 doubles, 6 triples, 8 surface lifts (carrying 43,446 riders per hour).

Trails and slopes: 200.

Vertical drop: 3,050 feet.

Snowmaking: 814 acres of terrain, with 1,850 snowguns.

Snowboarding: Superpipe with 18-foot walls, half-pipe with 12-foot walls, six terrain parks.

Facilities: Six cafeterias, five ski rental shops, one mountaintop restaurant, four lounges.

For children: Comprehensive Perfect Kids ski and snowboard coaching program based at the Family Center. Children 12 and under ski and ride free when accompanied by an adult with a 5-day pass; kids 5 and under ski free with an adult.

Special programs: School for Ski Professionals, for Snowboard Professionals, Women's Snowboard Clinics, early-December Ski Raceweek and Snowboard Freeriding and Carving Camp, Women's Turn, Mogul Clinic Weekends.

Rates: 1-day—$69 adults, $54 ages 13–18, $45 ages 6–12. Multiday rates and interchangeable tickets (with other ASC resorts) can bring adult tickets down to $52 per day, less if you buy online at least 14 days in advance or combine with lodging (inquire about packages).

Bear Creek Mountain Club (802-672-4242; www.bearcreekclub.com). The chairlift operates Thu.–Sun. and during holiday weeks in-season at the former Round Top ski area. A 1,300-foot vertical drop, a chairlift, 15 miles of trails on 51 acres, and a new clubhouse with a better than average restaurant (see *Dining Out*) are the draws here. An evolving semi-private resort, the slopes are uncrowded, as ticket sales are limited to 450 people a day. Nonmembers are welcome by reservation: $75 adults, $50 ages 17 and under, $35 on Sunday morning; kids 6 and under ski free with parent. Inquire about lifetime memberships.

DOGSLEDDING **Arctic Paws** (802-483-6089), at the Nordic Center of the Mountain Top Inn & Resort in Chittenden. Forty-five- to 60-minute guided mushing tours for individuals or groups (maximum eight people), daily 10–4.

SLEIGH RIDES **Cortina Inn** (802-773-3333), Rt. 4 east, Mendon. Wed., Sat., and some holidays. Sleigh rides are also offered at **Mountain Top Resort** (802-483-2311) and as part of ski weeks at Killington (802-422-6200).

Mountain Top Inn & Resort (802-483-2311; www.mountaintopinn.com).Thirty-minute horse-drawn sleigh rides daily (except holidays). $25 adults, $15 children under 14.

SNOWMOBILING **Killington Snowmobile Tours** (802-422-2121; 1-800-FAT-TRAK; www.snowmobilevermont.com), at the base of Killington Rd., next to Bill's Country Store. Watch for the sign. One- and 2-hour mountain and backcountry tours, plus snowcross track for kids ages 4–11. Rental helmets, clothing, and boots. This is also a source of info about local clubs.

✳ Green Space

Note: For more information about both of the following, see www.vtstateparks.com.

Calvin Coolidge State Forest. This 16,000-acre preserve, which actually includes Killington and Shrewsbury peaks, is scattered through seven local towns and divided by Rt. 100 into two districts. The recreational center is **Coolidge State Park** (802-672-3612), Rt. 100A east of Plymouth Notch. Open late May–mid-Oct., these 500 acres include a campground (60 campsites including 35 lean-tos, a dump station, picnic area, and restrooms with hot showers), picnic shelters (but no hookups), and hiking and snowmobile trails. In another part of the forest, **Camp Plymouth State Park**, off Rt. 100 in Tyson, served as a Civilian Conservation Corps (CCC) camp in 1933 and offers a beach on Echo Lake (picnic area, food concession). Inquire about gold panning and trails into the abandoned village of Plymouth Five Corners. North of the turnoff for Rt. 100A, the steep CCC Rd. (marked for Meadowsweet Farm) climbs away from Rt. 100 into the western swatch of the forest, with beautiful views back down the valley. It's unfortunate (but sensible) that this road is closed in winter, because it harbors some of the area's snowiest cross-country trails, accessible only by going the long way around through Shrewsbury (see *Scenic Drive* in "Okemo Valley Region").

Gifford Woods State Park (802-775-5354 summer), 0.5 mile north of Rt. 4 on Rt. 100, Killington. The campground (27 tent/trailer and 21 lean-to sites, restrooms, and hot showers) is patronized by hikers on the Appalachian Trail, which runs through the park. Across the road is the Gifford Woods Natural Area, a 7-acre stand of virgin hardwoods (sugar maple, yellow birch, basswood, white ash, and hemlock). Trails lead up to Deer Leap Mountain and to the lovely waterfalls where Kent Brook enters Kent Pond. In winter cross-country trails connect with Mountain Meadows.

✳ Lodging

Note: Killington's Skyeship Gondola on Rt. 4 also puts the inns of Plymouth to the southeast within easy reach, and lodging in both Woodstock (see "Woodstock/Quechee Area") and Ludlow (see "Okemo Valley Region") is within 14 miles. See *Guidance* for central reservations numbers.

RESORTS ✑ ♿ **The Killington Grand Resort Hotel & Conference Center** (1-888-64-GRAND; www.killingtonresortvillage.com), 228 East Mountain Rd., Killington 05751. At the base of the lifts, this 200-room, vintage-1997 facility offers standard hotel rooms, also studios and one-, two-, and three-bedroom suites (with kitchen). It's immense, with endless corridors and Vermont's biggest meeting space (the Grand Ballroom)—ergo conventions. The rooms are, however, irreproachably comfortable. Amenities include an outdoor heated pool, health club, on-site day care, Ovations Restaurant (see *Dining Out*), and a café. It's close not only to the base lodge, but in summer to the

golf course. $102–369. Better values year-round if combined with a sports package.

⊗ ♥ ✑ ♿ **Mountain Top Inn & Resort** (802-483-2311; 1-800-445-2100; www.mountaintopinn.com), 195 Mountain Top Rd., Chittenden 05737. Set high on a hill with a spectacular view of Chittenden Reservoir against a mountain backdrop, this self-contained resort has been operating as an inn since the 1940s. It hosted President Dwight Eisenhower and his entourage in 1955 when he arrived for a fishing expedition (he stayed in what is now called Ike's View, a corner room with a terrific view). Today it is one of the few Vermont resorts to offer both horseback riding and a cross-country skiing center (both open to the public). Each of the 33 rooms in the main inn has been redecorated; 7 on the lake side are luxuriously appointed with fabulous linens, TV hidden in armoires, and whirlpool bath or steam shower. Many have themes; Stags Run, for instance, features a huge rough-hewn log bed. Our favorite was the Angler's Retreat, whose balcony affords a bird's-eye view of the stunning Green Mountain National Forest below. There are also five cabins and several private "resort chalets" available for larger groups. In addition to riding, summer activities include swimming in both the lake and a heated pool, tennis, lawn games, canoeing and kayaking, claybird shooting, fly-fishing, and scenic pontoon boat rides on the lake, where moose sightings are not unusual. There's a horsemanship summer camp for kids, and any number of winter activities: 80 km of cross-country ski trails, snowshoeing, horse-drawn sleigh rides, dogsledding, ice skating, a billiards room, and spa services. Rooms in the inn are $175–485 including breakfast (add 15 percent service) during summer and winter seasons. Be sure to request a room with a lake view. Pets are $25 per night (they receive a dog bed, bowls, and a welcome treat) plus a $200 security deposit. Inquire about the many packages.

🐾 ✇ ♿ **Hawk Inn and Mountain Resort** (802-672-3811; 1-800-685-4295; www.hawkresort.com), Rt. 100, HCR 70, Box 64, Plymouth 05056. Set on 1,200 acres and owned by longtime residents Brenda and Jack Geishecker, this ranks among Vermont's most luxurious modern resorts. Lodging options include freestanding "mountain villas" salted away on hillsides with splendid views, as well as the townhouse-style Ledges Villas high above the Black River Valley and the 50-room Hawk Inn and River Tavern (see *Dining Out*). Situated halfway between Killington and Okemo (basically 10 minutes from each) and 3

miles from the trails at Bear Creek Mountain Club, the resort is well positioned for alpine skiers and offers its own extensive cross-country trail network as well as a heated outdoor pool, a spa, ice skating and sleigh rides, and its own 70-acre nature preserve. In summer there's tennis, horseback riding, swimming, mountain biking, and fly-fishing, as well as canoeing, kayaking, sailing, and rowing on Lake Amherst. The heart of the inn itself is a 19th-century farmhouse, and rooms are in modern wings. Each is decorated differently. Some have whirlpool bath; all are equipped with down comforter, feather bed, and large-screen TV. The spa has a large indoor/outdoor pool, massage and spa therapy services, and a salon. In winter rates are $325–690 per couple in the inn, $450–800 in the Ledges Villas, and $530–1,000 in the freestanding mountain villas; in summer/fall $295–685 in the inn, $350–650 in the Ledges Villas, and $450–850 in Mountain Villas. Inn rates (2-night minimum) include full breakfast. Lunch is served poolside during summer.

🐾 ✇ ♿ **Cortina Inn and Resort** (802-773-3333; 1-800-451-6108; www.cortinainn.com), Killington 05751. This contemporary luxury lodge at 103 Rt. 4 is designed to enable the average American family to pamper themselves. In summer there's serious tennis (www.killingtontennis.com) with pros using eight courts, also the Stream & Brook Fly-Fishing School (lessons and guide service) and golf programs utilizing six local 18-hole golf courses. The grounds include an extensive nature and a touring trail system connecting with both the Mountain Meadows and Mountain

Top trail networks in winter. Year-round there's the fitness center with whirlpools, saunas, exercise machines, and 42-foot indoor pool; massage and spa therapies are offered. Afternoon tea is served in the two-story lobby, which has a round hearth in the center and exhibit space for local sculpture and art in the gallery. There are 96 air-conditioned rooms, all individually decorated with private bath, and seven suites, some with fireplace and whirlpool bath (Room 215 is immense), some suites with lofts, and five rooms that are wheelchair accessible. Common space includes a children's game room, art gallery, reading room, and library. $109 per couple B&B low seasons; $189 B&B high seasons. Children 13 and under, $10 in the same room with parent (breakfast included). Pets find a pet treat waiting on arrival ($10 per night). The Cortina dining rooms are Zola's Grille and casual Theodore's Tavern (see *Dining Out* and *Eating Out*). Inquire about tennis, golf, and ski packages.

✄ ♿ **Mountain Meadows Lodge** (802-775-1010; 1-800-370-4567; www.mtmeadowslodge.com), Thundering Brook Rd., Killington 05751. The main building is an 1856 barn, nicely converted into a classic lodge with an informal dining room, a game room, a spacious sunken living room with a beautiful lake view, and tons of atmosphere. Michelle and Mark Werle gear the year-round inn to families, catering to people who like the outdoors in warm-weather months as well as in winter. This is a hospitable, thoroughly relaxing kind of lodge. There are 20 guest rooms, many of them great for families, all with private bath. A sauna and outdoor Jacuzzi are among the amenities. In summer there is a swimming pool and 100-acre Kent Lake, which abuts the property and is good for fishing and canoeing as well as swimming; the town tennis courts are just down the road. In winter this is a major ski-touring center; nearby dogsled mushing is also an option. Year-round residents include Alice, the miniature potbellied pig, a pony, sheep, chickens, and a rooster. The lake is stocked with trout and bass. Low seasons $85–100 per couple B&B; high season $100–300 for a family room.

INNS ⊙ ✿ ✄ **The October Country Inn** (802-672-3412; 1-800-648-8421; www.octobercountryinn.com), junction of Rts. 4 and 100A, Bridgewater Corners 05035. Handy to Killington and Woodstock (8 miles) as well as most of the things to do and see in this chapter, yet sequestered up a back road with hiking trails that lead past the swimming pool to the top of a hill for a sweeping, peaceful view. This old farmhouse has a large, comfortable living room with inviting places to sit around the hearth and at the big round table in the dining room—not to be confused with the other cheery dining room in which guests gather around long tables for memorable meals. Innkeepers Edie and Chuck Janisse offer gourmet candlelit dinners with wine and all-fresh local produce served family-style, prix fixe, for $21.50. Breakfasts are equally creative and ambitious, geared to fuel bikers in summer and skiers in winter. The 10 guest rooms (8 with private bath) vary in size; most have queen-sized beds, many with Edie's handmade quilts. $100–165 includes breakfast. Open most of the year.

⊗ 🐾 ✎ ♿ **Fox Creek Inn** (802-483-6213; 1-800-707-0017; www.foxcreek inn.com), 49 Chittenden Dam Rd., Chittenden 05737. This is backwoods luxury in a superb house owned at one time by the inventor William Barstow, who summered here after selling his various holdings for $40 million right before the 1929 stock market crash. Ann and Alex Volz offer nine carefully furnished guest rooms, all with private bath, most with Jacuzzi, and three with gas fireplace. The Honeymoon Suite, also good for a family of four, has two fireplaces and a two-person Jacuzzi, and (handicapped-accessible) Room 7 is a visual feast of designer fabrics in black -and-white filigree. Guests gather around the big stone fireplace in the paneled den, in the comfortable living room, and at the cozy bar. The four-course candle-light dinners are a point of pride. There is swimming, canoeing, and fishing in the Chittenden Reservoir just down the road, and in winter you can cross-country ski or just lounge around and pet Maggie, the resident golden retriever. The Volzes also shuttle guests to hiking trails. For reasons that we soon discovered, they get

FOX CREEK INN

Joe Citro

a lot of return visits. $160–295 B&B, $190–325 MAP ($249–410 during foliage season). Call ahead about pets.

🌿 ♿ **The Vermont Inn** (802-775-0708; 1-800-541-7795; www.vermont inn.com), Killington 05751. Set above Rt. 4 with a view of Killington and Pico, this 19th-century farmhouse has a homey feel to its public rooms—the living room with woodstove, the pub/lounge with fireplace, a game room, and an upstairs reading room, a sanctuary in the evening when the dining room is open to the public (see *Dining Out*). Summer facilities include a pool, a tennis court, and lawn games. The sauna and hot tub are available year-round. Innkeepers Megan and Greg Smith offer 18 guest rooms, ranging from smallish to spacious, all bright with brass and antique or canopy bedstead and private bath. Five have a fireplace, one with a Jacuzzi and one, wheelchair accessible. $115–155 per couple MAP in summer, $125–250 MAP in fall; 2-day winter weekends, $360–570 MAP. Less for midweek and longer stays. Inquire about golf, fishing, and other packages.

⊗ 🐾 ✎ ♿ **Red Clover Inn** (802-775-2290; 1-800-752-0571; www.red cloverinn.com), Box 7450, Woodward Rd., Mendon 05701. Tricia and Bill Pedersen have turned this 1840s farm-house complex at the end of a forested road into a top-notch inn and restaurant. Set on 13 secluded acres with a pond, each of its 14 air-conditioned rooms is different and each a delight, with beautiful linens, king or queen beds, and plenty of light. Our favorite is Country Crossing, a spacious suite in the back with a king-sized four-poster bed, polenta-colored walls, a fireplace, and a balcony with views of

Pico peak. In the main house, Tuscany features skylights, a rocker, a queen-sized bed, and a hand-painted mural of the Tuscan countryside (not to mention the soaking tub for two). There are unusual touches throughout (Maggie's Treasure Chest, for instance, has an octagonal window). The three luxury rooms come with king-sized bed, fireplace, a whirlpool bath for two, and sitting area with alpine views. Common space is ample in this Select Registry inn, as are the breakfasts, which in summer include fresh berries and just-baked pastries. The intimate restaurant serves first-rate cuisine and is open to the public (see *Dining Out*). Rooms $160–290 B&B, $60 per room higher in peak season. For MAP, add $87 per room. Children under 12 months and over 12 years welcome. Pets permitted in the carriage house at $20 extra per day. Check web site for specials.

⌒ ♂ **Casa Bella Inn & Restaurant** (802-746-8943; 1-877-746-8943; www .casabellainn.com), P.O. Box 685, Pittsfield 05762. Located 8 miles north of Killington in the center of the village on a handsome green, this double-porched old inn has been welcoming guests since 1835. Innkeeper Susan Cacozza is from Britain and her husband, Franco, is a chef from Tuscany. The restaurant is important here and open to the public (see *Dining Out*), but the feel is very much that of a village country inn in the center of this classic Vermont town that's removed from, but still handy to, Killington. The eight guest rooms, all with private bath, are $90–145, including a delicious breakfast. Children over 10 welcome.

🐾 ♂ **Salt Ash Inn** (802-672-3748; 1-800-SALT-ASH; www.saltashinn.com),

Rt. 100, Plymouth 05056. Built in the 1830s, this historic structure was a stagecoach stop when Salt Ash was the town's name (it was later changed to Plymouth). It also did a stint as a general store. A bar area retains the original grocery counter and the old post boxes where the Coolidge family fetched their mail. Owners Jonathan Petrie and Jordan Phillips have transformed the place into a trove of historic curiosities. Ingenious antiques cover the barnboard interiors; treasures lurk in every corner. A circular hearth serves the purpose of the old potbellied stove, exuding warmth and a cozy atmosphere. More a sanctuary than anything else, this is a place where you feel comfortable enough to waltz around in your pajamas (and many do). The 17 guest rooms are distributed among three buildings, all with private bath, TV, DSL, and wireless. Outdoors you'll find a heated pool, a hot tub, lush gardens, and plenty of lounge chairs. The entire place can be rented by groups of up to 50. $95–235 B&B, depending on the room (from economy to deluxe with fireplace), the season, and the day of the week; less for weekdays and longer stays; group discounts. Weekends are 2-day packages.

LODGES ⌒ ♞ ♂ **The Summit Lodge** (802-422-3535; 1-800-635-6343; www.summitlodgevermont .com), P.O. Box 119, Killington Rd., Killington 05751. This four-season hostelry at the top of Killington Rd. combines a classic mountain ski lodge with year-round amenities, plus a lovely white gazebo, an outdoor/indoor heated pool, four red-clay tennis courts (including instruction), and flower gardens. In winter ski trails can be glimpsed from every spot. The downhill slopes are minutes away, or you can hike, ski, or snowshoe the many trails right here; Summit Pond becomes a skating rink. Spa services include a sauna, Jacuzzi, facials, hot tub, and massage, and charter bus tours of the area are available. At night you can curl up by the massive fieldstone fireplace, sip a beer at the **Saint's Pub** with its big-screen TV (it's named for the lodge's two resident Saint Bernards; open Fri.–Sun. 5–9), munch bar fare, or dine at **Maxwell's Restaurant**. The common areas feature barnboard, hand-hewn exposed beams, stained-glass windows, and fireplaces. The 45 guest rooms are simple but comfortable, with private bath, cable TV, king and queen beds (the family rooms sleep up to six), and, most important, mountain views. From $66 in low season to $216 during foliage season, when there's a 3-night minimum stay.

∞ ♪ ⅙ **Inn of the Six Mountains** (802-422-4302; 1-800-228-4676; www.sixmountains.com), Killington Rd., Killington 05751. A 103-room, four-story, Adirondack-style hotel with gabled ceilings, skylights, balconies, and a two-story lobby with a fieldstone fireplace. Common spaces include a second-floor sitting room and a third-floor library. There is also a spa with lap pool, Jacuzzis, and exercise room, plus a dining room. In summer $79–159 per room, fall $199–249, winter $149–309, depending on the day and week, continental breakfast included. In winter check on the 2-day packages that include skiing, lodging, and breakfast. Children are free with two adults but $17 if over 12. Inquire about Jimmy LeSage's New Life Hiking Spa (www

.newlifehikingspa.com), a program based here early May–Oct.

🐾 **The Inn at Long Trail** (802-775-7181; 1-800-325-2540; www.innatlongtrail.com), Rt. 4, Killington 05751. Closed in shoulder seasons. This is the first building in New England specifically built to serve as a ski lodge. It began in 1938 as an annex to a splendid summer inn that has since burned. Designed to resemble the inside of the forest as much as possible, the interior incorporates parts of trees and boulders and is a casual place. The inn caters to through-hikers on the Appalachian and Long Trails and outdoors people of all sorts. The 22-foot-long bar is made from a single log, and a protruding toe of the backyard cliff can be seen in both the pub and the dining room. The 14 rooms are small but cheery (2 are family suites); there are 5 two-room suites with fireplace. The hot tub is used only in winter. Dinner is served varying nights in the restaurant, but you can usually count on McGrath's Irish Pub (see *Eating Out*). Summer $68–98 per room B&B, about $20 more during foliage; winter $95–125 B&B. Nonholiday weekends $360–470 per couple (more at peak times). Gratuity is 10 percent. Pets (by advance arrangement) $10 per night.

∞ 🐾 ⅙ **Cascades Lodge** (802-422-3731; 1-800-345-0113; www.cascadeslodge.com), 58 Old Mill Rd., Killington 05751. This neat, contemporary, 45-room hostelry is practically next to the Killington base lodge and on clear days has exceptional mountain views. Some rooms have balconies, and there's an indoor pool, sundeck, whirlpool, sauna, lounge, and highly rated restaurant (see *Dining Out*).

$99–139 in summer, $139–219 in fall and on winter weekends, less mid-week in winter, more for suites, 9 percent gratuity. Children stay free in summer and fall, and pets are welcome for a small fee.

🐾 🐾 ⚲ **Butternut on the Mountain** (802-422-2000; 1-800-524-7654; www .butternutlodge.com), Box 306, Killington Rd., Killington 05751. Open year-round except May and June. A family-owned motor lodge with 18 large standard rooms with color TV and phone. Facilities include an indoor heated pool, whirlpool, fireside library and lounge, game room, and laundry facilities. $58–200 per room with full breakfast (continental in summer), 15 percent service charge in winter; ski packages available. Pets accepted in summer and fall by previous arrangement.

MOTEL ⚲ ⚲ **Farmbrook Motel** (802-672-3621; www.farmbrookmotel .net), Rt. 100A, Plymouth 05056. Open last week of May–third week of Oct. An unusually attractive 12-unit motel with a babbling brook and working waterwheel. Two rooms come with kitchenette; many have balcony, and some sleep five. It's a mere 3 miles from Coolidge's birthplace and handy to Killington. The beautifully landscaped grounds have outdoor fireplaces and picnic tables for summer use. $55–110 per couple; children under 12, free.

CONDOMINIUMS **The Killington Lodging Bureau** (1-800-621-6867; 1-800-324-6819; www.killingtonresort village.com) serves hundreds of mountain properties, among them **Killington Resort Villages** (1-877-

458-4637)—700 condo units, including the Killington Grand—and **Sunrise Mountain Village**, high on the mountain. In summer Killington Resort Villages becomes a mini resort in its own right, nicely landscaped and filled with a mix of mountain bikers, families, golfers, retirees, and family reunions. Amenities include pools and whirlpools for each condo cluster. In winter you can walk to the lifts, and while some units are slope-side, other are a schlep from the shuttle to the base lodge. Still, you're right at the nerve center of Killington's vast lift and trail network. Winter package rates (with lift tickets) range upward from $59 per person per night for 5 nights. In summer packages start at $35 and in fall at $36 per person per day (book early). **Pico Resort Hotel** on Rt. 4 in Killington, which is owned by Killington Resort Village, abuts the Pico base lodge. The 152 units are basic: one-bedroom suites in the Village Square; two-, three-, and four-bedroom units in the village, with phone. The sports center here comes with a 75-foot indoor pool, Nautilus equipment, aerobics room, Jacuzzi, saunas, and lounge.

Also see **Tupper Farm Lodge** and **Hawk North** in "The White River Valleys."

CAMPGROUNDS See *Green Space* for information on camping in Calvin Coolidge and Gifford Woods State Parks.

✳ Where to Eat

DINING OUT **Hemingway's** (802-422-3886; www.hemingwaysrestaurant .com), 4988 Rt. 4, Sherburne Flats, east of Killington. Closed Mon. and

Tue. Between Linda's eye for detail in the decor and service and Ted's concern for freshness, preparation, and presentation, the Fondulas have created one of the most exceptional dining experiences in New England. Chandeliers, fresh flowers, and floor-length table linens grace the peach-colored, vaulted main room, while a less formal atmosphere prevails in the garden room and stone-walled wine cellar. It's billed as "regional, classic cuisine," but whatever name you give it, it's divine. You might begin with a risotto of exotic mushroom and truffle, or fallen soufflé of Vermont goat cheese, mâche, and endive; then dine on roasted day-boat cod with jasmine shrimp, artichoke, and confit of local tomatoes, topped off by Venetian chocolate cake with caramel sauce. The three-course prix fixe menu is $62, but inquire about midweek specials; a four-course vegetarian menu is available for $55, which can be made totally vegan with advance notice.

The Corners Inn and Restaurant (802-672-9968; www.cornersinn.com), Rt. 4, Bridgewater Corners. Open for dinner Wed.–Sun., daily during peak season. Reservations suggested. Known for the unusual ways he uses fresh, local ingredients, chef-owner Brad Pirkey has created an informal, standout small restaurant in an 1890 farmhouse. In winter request a table near the fireplace, and in summer on the terrace with its forested views. There's also a friendly bar. Specials on a summer night included beef Wellington and lobster spring rolls, and the menu ranged from home-made pastas with sweet Italian sausage, prosciutto, mushrooms, garlic, and roasted red peppers to veal with wild mushrooms and artichoke

hearts. All entrées ($15.95–21.95) come with daily homemade cheese spread and fresh-baked bread—and if nothing fills the bill, Brad will whip up whatever you want.

☯ **Red Clover Inn** (802-775-2290; 1-800-752-0571; www.redcloverinn .com), Box 7450, Woodward Rd., Mendon 05701. Open for dinner Thu.–Sun. at 6; nightly during holidays and foliage. New England Culinary Institute graduate Richard Serafin brings his love for Vermont cheeses, game, and wild edibles to this secluded restaurant east of Killington, and the results are memorable. A recent menu started with Vermont goat cheese en croute with a roasted pepper coulis and basil oil, or grilled prawns with passion fruit vinaigrette and watercress. Entrées included Long Island duck over grilled asparagus with a grape-cognac reduction, and roast venison with green beans, roasted shallots, and a preserved-lemon and plum sauce vinaigrette. Desserts might include chocolate truffle mousse and chocolate and Tahitian vanilla crème brûlée. The connected dining rooms have low ceilings and exposed beams, and you dine by candlelight on white tablecloths. Two of the rooms have open hearths with crackling fires in winter; the wine menu has won the *Wine Spectator* Award of Excellence yearly since 1996. Entrées $18–32. Ask about the special wine-paired dinners the third Tuesday of every month.

🍴 ✂ **The Countryman's Pleasure** (802-773-7141; www.countrymans pleasure.com), just off Rt. 4, Mendon. Open 5–9 daily. Chef-owner Hans Entinger, a native of Austria, is known for top-drawer Austrian-German specialties: veal schnitzel cordon bleu, sauerbraten, goulash, and so on. Seafood is also a specialty. The attractive dining rooms occupy the first floor of a charming house. There's a long wine list, and beers as well as international coffees and nonalcoholic wines and beers are served. The atmosphere is cozy and informal with an open fireplace. Early-bird specials (5–6 PM) are under $14. Otherwise entrées are $13.95–22.95. Senior and kids' menu.

☙ ✿ ⅋ **The Vermont Inn** (802-775-0708; 1-800-541-7795; www.vermont inn.com), HC 34, Box 37K, Rt. 4, Killington. Open for dinner nightly. Chef Stephen Hatch has captured first place three times in the Killington-Champagne Dine Around Contest. It's a pleasant inn dining room with a huge fieldstone fireplace and a varied menu that changes nightly. Entrées might range from eggplant Parmesan and Vermont roast turkey to rack of lamb roasted with parsley, rosemary, garlic, and black pepper. Entrées $12.95–22.50.

Bear Creek Mountain Club 802-672-4242; www.bearcreekclub.com), Plymouth. Late Dec.–early Apr., Wed.–Sun. noon–10; mid-May–mid-Dec., Wed.–Sat. 6–10. Executive chef Dan Croft serves everything from slow-roasted baby back ribs with homemade root vegetable chips at the pub to grilled ginger pork tenderloin with potato dumplings in the main dining room of this newly built mountainside clubhouse. Entrées $23–28.

✿ **Zola's Grille at the Cortina Inn** (802-773-3333), Rt. 4, Killington. Open daily for dinner, 5:30–9 (closed midweek in early Nov. and late Mar.). This is a spacious, nicely decorated dining room. You might begin with grilled shrimp wrapped in prosciutto,

then dine on scallops atop spinach and creamed oysters with buckwheat blinis. Entrées $10.95–23.95. The all-you-can-eat Sunday buffet brunch is a winner at $14.95.

⅋ **River Tavern** (802-672-3811; www .hawkresort.com/dining) at Hawk Inn and Resort, Rt. 100, Plymouth. Open daily for breakfast and dinner, Thu.–Sat. in low season, and for lunch in summer. Dinner reservations essential. The restaurant itself is country elegant, with windowed walls framing the landscape and a deck where you can sit out under the stars in warm weather. A summer à la carte menu might feature pan-seared rainbow trout or lobster ravioli steeped in brandy and tomato blush sauce. Dinner entrées $18–28.

☙ **Choices Restaurant** (802-422-4030), Glazebrook Center, 3 miles up Killington Rd., Killington. Open Dec.–Apr., daily at 5, Sunday brunch 11–2:30 (summer and spring hours vary). This combination bistro/brasserie/pub has a huge menu of savory appetizers, salads, soups, raw bar, sandwiches, and pastas, not to mention entrées ranging from curried vegetables with couscous to filet mignon with portobello mushrooms and double-cream blue cheese. Chef-owner Claude Blays is a 1975 graduate of the Culinary Institute of America. Dinner entrées $15.25–24.95.

Birch Ridge Inn (802-422-4293; 1-800-435-8566; www.birchridge .com), Killington Rd. and Butler Rd., Killington. Open for dinner at 6 PM Wed.–Sun. and nightly during holiday weeks. Hidden away up off Killington Rd., this oddly shaped inn (essentially two interconnected A-frames) features a dining room and lounge with ambience. The menu is ambitious, with dishes such as grilled medallions of beef tenderloin with Roquefort butter and shallot au jus or roast rack of lamb with a mint pesto crust, mushroom strudel, and Cabernet-thyme reduction. Entrées $21.50–31.50. Lounge and full liquor license.

∞ ✍ **The Highlands Dining Room** at the Mountain Top Inn and Resort (802-483-2311; www.mountaintopinn.com), 195 Mountain Top Rd., Chittenden. Open for dinner (and breakfast) by reservation to nonguests. The lower-level dining room is large and slightly formal with white tablecloths, a booming stone fireplace, and views of the lake and mountains. The à la carte menu includes such appetizers as sautéed wild mushrooms over greens drenched in sherry vinaigrette Parmesan, and avocado gazpacho. Entrées might feature sea bass wrapped in a tomato and mozzarella jacket over basil polenta and grilled asparagus; grilled lamb with shoestring potatoes and a cucumber-chickpea relish; or potato and truffle ravioli with forest mushrooms and wilted greens in a potato-leek broth. There's a choice of salads and desserts, an impressive wine list, and a kids' menu. Entrées $24–32. The adjacent **Highlands Tavern**, which is more casual, is open daily for lunch and dinner. The menu features pizzas, wraps, burgers, paninis, and a full bar, plus more elevated fare: cannellini and garlic stuffed ravioli with smoked tomato cream sauce, for example, or cedar-planked salmon, as well as veal osso buco. Dinner prices $8–26.

🍽 ✍ **Cascades Lodge Restaurant** (802-422-3731; 1-800-345-0113; www.cascadeslodge.com), Old Mill Rd., Killington. Open daily 8–10 for breakfast, 6–9 PM daily in-season for dinner.

Locally known for its bounteous breakfasts and as a good dinner bet, with plenty of choices and entrées ranging from eggplant marinara to roast duck with orange sauce; fabulous desserts. Kids' menu, nightly specials, and terrific mountain views. Entrées $7–25.

✍ ♿ **Ovations Restaurant at the Killington Grand Resort** (802-422-6111), 228 East Mountain Rd., Killington, is open nightly 5–9. This is a family-geared hotel dining room with soups and salads served all day and dinner selections ranging from burgers and pasta to fine steaks. Entrées $10–25.

Casa Bella Inn (802-746-8943; 1-877-746-8943; www.casabellainn.com), 3911 Main St., Rt. 100, Pittsfield. Franco Cacozza is the chef-owner of this pleasant restaurant in the former Pittsfield Inn, a classic old stage stop in the classic village 8 miles north of Killington. The menu is traditional, too, and authentic. Try the linguine *al pescatore* (sautéed with shrimp, squid, and clams in a light tomato sauce) or the *Ravioli al Funghi* (ravioli filled with wild mushrooms in a butter sage sauce). Superb selection of Italian wines and scrumptious homemade desserts. Entrées $13.50–20.

The Garlic (802-422-5055), 1724 Killington Rd. (midway up). Open nightly, with a broad range of tapas at the bar. A cozy, informal setting for hearty Italian fare, with a choice of pasta dishes and entrées featuring the namesake ingredient. From $15.50 for "The Puttanesca" (linguine with the house sauce) to $26.95 for garlic-marinated char-grilled rack of lamb.

Café Toast (802-422-5777; www.cafetoast.com), 2822 Killington Rd., at the Glazebrook Center, Killington. Open

Tue.–Sun. 4–10 PM. Chef-owner Taylor Glaze delivers European cuisine with over 200 international wines (she and husband Red own the adjacent wine-and-cheese shop). Try the 4–6 PM wine tasting, which offers four tapas plates with matching wines for $12. The decor includes a fireplace, copper bar, and copper ceiling; a typical entrée might be flounder Florentine with artichoke risotto, cioppino with pasta, or pork fillets with caper sauce and lemon orzo. There's a full palette of Italian coffees, panini sandwiches, and desserts. Entrées $18–24.

EATING OUT ✐ **Grist Mill** (802-422-3970; www.gristmillkillington.com), Killington Rd. on the Summit Lodge grounds. Open for lunch and dinner, Sunday brunch; also for breakfast on weekends and holidays. The building is designed to look like a gristmill that has always stood on Summit Pond (there's a 90-year-old waterwheel). The interior is airy and pleasing, dominated by a huge stone hearth. The dinner menu ranges from steaks and veal dishes through grilled swordfish to vegetable stir-fry. There's a children's menu and blackboard specials. Full liquor license. Entrées $12.95–18.95.

Wilder House Restaurant (802-234-5171), at the Calvin Coolidge State Historic Site at Plymouth Notch. Open late May–mid-Oct., daily 10–3 for breakfast and lunch. Nick and Heidi Nikolaidis, caterers who own the Black Forest Café in Bethel, also run this quaint, pine-walled café with exposed beams in what was once the home of Calvin Coolidge's mother. Daily specials might include German potato salad with bratwurst, Greek spinach pie, cheeseburgers, and mixed berry pie. Moderately priced.

McGrath's Irish Pub at the Inn at Long Trail (802-775-7181; www.inn atlongtrail.com), Rt. 4, at the Inn at Long Trail, Killington. Open nightly for dinner and drinks. The 22-foot-long bar is made from a single log, and a protruding toe of the backyard cliff can be seen in both the pub and the dining room. The first place to serve Guinness on tap in Vermont, the pub boasts the state's largest selection of Irish whiskey and features Irish country and folk music in the pub on weekends. The house specialties are Guinness stew and shepherd's pie. Chef Patrick Boandl, a graduate of the Culinary Institute of America, cooks up appetizers that might include baked artichokes or Irish bangers (each $5.95) and entrées such as swordfish steaks marinated in orange, lemon, and lime juice, grilled and topped with citrus butter ($18.95); or boneless duck breast with a sauce of warmed pears ($21.95).

✐ **Casey's Caboose** (802-422-3795), halfway up Killington Rd., Killington. Open nightly for dinner in-season. The building incorporates a circa-1900 snowplow car and a great caboose to house the coveted tables, but you really can't lose: The atmosphere throughout rates high on our short list of family dining spots. Pot stickers, fresh calamari, a great seafood selection, and free Buffalo wings 3–6 PM. Children's menu.

✐ **Peppers Bar & Grill** (802-422-3177), top of Killington Rd. in the mall, Killington, open daily 7 AM–10 PM weekends, till 9 weekdays, is a popular spot for breakfast, lunch, dinner, and take-out food. On a weekday in summer this was the only place open and it was great: a cool and colorful inside in a 1940s-inspired stainless-and-mahogany diner decor. At breakfast omelets are a specialty; there's always a homemade soup of the day plus vegetarian specials, wraps, and burgers at lunch. Dinner specialties include Tennessee whiskey steak, fresh fish, and pastas. Full liquor license. A great kids' menu.

Charity's 1887 Saloon-Restaurant (802-422-3800), midway up Killington Rd., Killington. Open daily in-season for lunch and dinner. Happy hour (free wings) 3–6. Tiffany shades, 1880s saloon decor, and wooden booths—this is the place for French onion soup, a Reuben, or a vegetarian casserole at lunch. Steak is a good dinner choice. Informal, satisfying.

Peppino's Ristorante Italiano (802-422-3293), 1 mile up Killington Rd., Killington. Open nightly 5–10 in summer and ski season. A traditional, reasonably priced Italian restaurant with predictable menu and decor; reliable.

Mountain Meadows Lodge (802-775-1010), Thundering Brook Rd., Killington. Open to the public by reservation on weekends during ski season. This pleasant, family-geared lodge offers reasonably priced buffets and entrées for children.

Back Behind Saloon (802-422-9907), junction of Rts. 4 and 100 south, West Bridgewater. Open from 4 in the tavern, at 5 for dinner nightly during ski season and summer, less in the off-season. A zany atmosphere (look for the red caboose and antique Mobil gas pump), barnboard, stained glass, a big hearth. Specialties like venison and saloon roast duck augment basic American fare: steaks and

chicken, generous portions. Entrées on the high side ($14.95–26). Children's menu.

Theodore's Tavern (802-773-3331), Cortina Inn, Rt. 4, Killington. Open daily 5:30–9:30. A good bet for casual dining and après-ski with its rathskeller-like ambience and Fri. and Sat. night all-you-can-eat pasta ($10.95). Regular entrées $7.95–19.95.

Sugar & Spice (802-773-7832), Rt. 4, Mendon. Open daily 7–2. A pancake restaurant housed in a large replica of a classic sugarhouse surrounded by a 50-acre sugarbush. Besides dining on a variety of pancake, egg, and omelet dishes, along with soups and sandwiches, you can watch both maple candy and cheese being made several days a week. Gift shop.

See also "Rutland and the Lower Champlain Valley." Rutland is a good "eating-out" town.

PIZZA **Outback Pizza** (802-422-9885), at the Nightspot on Killington Rd., Killington. Open from 3 in winter and spring, from 5 in summer and fall. Features wood-fired brick-oven pizza with outdoor patio seating and live music.

Pizza Jerks (802-422-4111; www .pizzajerks.com), 1307 Killington Rd., Killington Open daily from 11 AM. A local favorite, part of a virtual café with Internet access. Pizza, calzones, subs.

✳ Entertainment

MUSIC The **Killington Music Festival** (802-773-4003), a series of mostly chamber music concerts in Snowshed Lodge and at a scattering of other local sites; weekends in July and Aug.

APRÈS-SKI The Wobbly Barn Steakhouse (802-422-6171; www.wobblybarn.com), 2229 Killington Rd., Killington. A steak and BBQ house (with a children's menu) offering live music, dancing, blues, rock and roll. Ski season only.

The Nightspot (802-422-9885), Killington Rd., Killington. Open nightly, year-round, at 5; in winter there's nightly dancing to a DJ.

McGrath's Irish Pub at the Inn at Long Trail (802-775-7181), Rt. 4, Killington. Live Irish music on weekends to go with the Gaelic atmosphere and Guinness on tap. It's a great pub with a 22-foot-long bar made from a single log and a boulder protruding from the back wall.

Pickle Barrel (802-422-3035; www.picklebarrelnightclub.com), Killington Rd., Killington. "Some of the finest rock 'n' roll bands in the East." Purchase tickets online for the best prices.

✳ Selective Shopping

Bill's Country Store (802-773-9313; www.billscountrystore.com), at the junction of Rts. 4 and 100, Killington, stocks a broad spectrum of Vermont products, including cheese, maple goodies, deerskin gloves, and woodwork.

The Shops at the Shack and **The Ski Shack** (802-422-6800), Rt. 4 at Killington Rd., Killington. This place has just about everything in the way of sports clothes and equipment for adults and kids, much at discount prices; boutique name-brand shops include Nordica, The North Face, Children's Shop, and Nike.

Long Trail Brewing Company (802-672-5011; www.longtrail.com), Rt. 4 west at Bridgewater Corners (near Rt. 100A), produces Long Trail Ale as well as Hibernator, India Pale Ale, Hit the Trail, Blackberry, Wheat, and Harvest. Pub fare daily 11–5 with riverside seating (in summer); gift shop, taproom, and self-guided tours daily 10–6.

See also the box on pagess 274–275 for the Marketplace at **Bridgewater Mill**.

✳ Special Events

January–March: Frequent **alpine ski and snowboard events** at Killington and Pico.

Memorial Day weekend: **Rage Weekend** with **Killington Triathlon**—ski/snowboard, mountain bike, cross-country run.

July 4: **Calvin Coolidge Birthday Memorial**, Plymouth.

July–August: **Killington Music Festival** (802-773-4003). **Killington Mountain Wine Festival** (802-773-4181). **Killington Renaissance Festival**.

August: **Killington Classic Motorcycle Rally** (www.killingtonclassic.com).

Columbus Day weekend: **Sheep and Wool Festival. Brew Fest**, Killington.

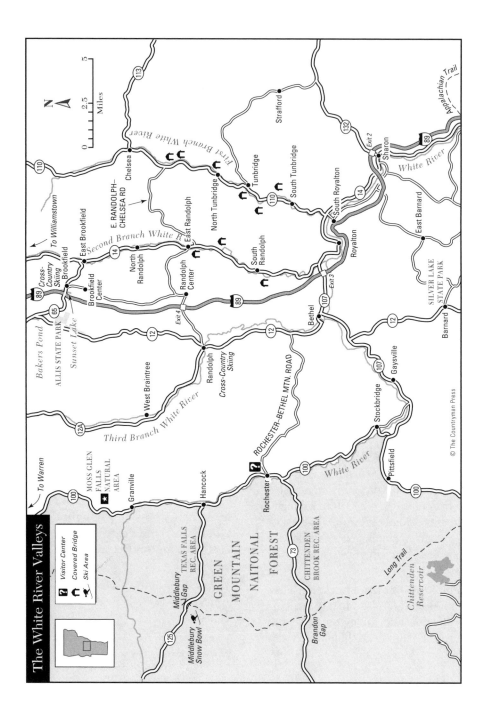

The White River Valleys

Legend:
- 🛈 Visitor Center
- ⌐ Covered Bridge
- ⛷ Ski Area

Scale: 0 — 2.5 — 5 Miles

© The Countryman Press

THE WHITE RIVER VALLEYS

V anishing Vermont" could be the subtitle for this chapter. As I-89 sweeps up through central Vermont in a grand 52-mile arc—from White River Junction to Montpelier—it yields a series of panoramas. Motorists see the high wall of the Green Mountains beyond the Braintree Range on the west and catch glimpses of an occasional valley village. What they don't see is one of Vermont's best-kept secrets: the classic old villages, abrupt valleys, and hill farms along the White River and its three branches.

The White River rises high in the Green Mountains above Granville Gulf and rushes down through Hancock, widening and slowing among farms in Rochester, keeping company with Rt. 100 until Stockbridge, where its course dictates a dog-leg in the highway. Turning sharply east and carving a narrow valley for Rt. 107 (the Gaysville reach is an especially challenging one for kayakers during spring freshets), the river reaches Bethel and begins to parallel Rt. 14 and I-89. As it courses through the Royaltons and Sharon, it's joined by the three northern branches; both tubing and fishing possibilities increase.

Each of these streams, rising some 20 miles north of the main stem of the river, has carved its own valley. The First Branch, shadowed by Rt. 110, threads six covered bridges, lush farmland, and the unself-consciously beautiful villages of Chelsea and Tunbridge. The Second Branch begins above the picturesque village of Brookfield, known for its floating bridge, and flows south along Rt. 14. The Third Branch rises in Roxbury, conveniently near a fish hatchery, and flows south through a lonely valley (along Rt. 12A) to Randolph, one of the area's few I-89 exits and an Amtrak stop as well as the only commercial center of any size in this entire area.

Beautiful as these valleys are, the high east–west roads that connect them, climbing up over the hills and down into the next valley, are more rewarding still. To begin exploring this backroaded and unresortified heart of Vermont, you might exit in Sharon and climb through the Straffords to Tunbridge and north to Chelsea, west to Brookfield, then south to Randolph, on down Rt. 12, and west over Rochester Mountain. See *Scenic Drives* for tours that can pleasantly fill many days.

GUIDANCE **Randolph Area Chamber of Commerce** (802-728-9027; 1-877-772-6365; www.randolphvt.com), 31 Rt. 66, Randolph 05060. Phone answered

CHELSEA VILLAGE

Christina Tree

and office open year-round, weekdays 8:30–4; information center maintained Memorial Day–mid-Oct. at State Plaza just off I-89, Exit 4 (next to the Mobil station).

& **Sharon Northbound Information Center and Vermont Vietnam Veterans' Memorial** (802-281-5216), I-89, Sharon. Open 7 AM–11 PM. Not what you expect to find at a roadside rest area. The 7,000 names on the memorial itself represent all the Vermonters who served in the Vietnam War, which is recalled through exhibits that include a time line and film clips. Also unexpected here: a "living greenhouse" filled with plants and descriptions of how they recycle waste. The center is staffed, a good source of local information. The restrooms, incidentally, are outstanding.

Green Mountain National Forest Ranger District Office and Visitors Center (802-767-4261), Rt. 100 in Rochester. Open 8–4 daily (except Sun.) Memorial Day–Columbus Day, weekdays off-season. A magnificent center (restrooms) with detailed information on hiking, biking, picnicking, bird-watching, camping, and other recreation in this part of the GMNF.

Eastern Vermont Gateway (1-888-848-4199), the state's marketing organization for this region, publishes a magazine and maintains a web site, www.eastern riververmont.com.

The *Herald of Randolph* (802-728-3232), Box 309, Randolph, a weekly published on Thursday, carries local news and events for Orange and northern Windsor Counties.

GETTING THERE *By train:* **Amtrak's** Vermonter (1-800-USA-RAIL; www.amtrak .com). Randolph and White River Junction (see "Upper Valley River Towns") are stops for trains from Washington, DC, and New York City via Springfield and Amherst, Ma.

By car: This area covers a wide, hilly swath of Vermont. I-89 runs diagonally across it but with only three exits (Sharon, Bethel/Royalton, and Randolph).

GETTING AROUND *By taxi:* **JT's Taxi & Courier** (802-728-6209) is based in Randolph.

By rental car: **Especially Imports** (802-728-4455), Rt. 66, Randolph, can arrange to meet you at the train.

WHEN TO GO Rochester offers winter cross-country skiing, and Tunbridge draws Vermonters for the Vermont History Expo in June and the World's Fair in September. March brings sugaring; in May there's kayaking and in summer, tubing along the lower reaches of the White River. In July there are old-fashioned Independence Day parades, the biggest one in Randolph. Labor Day weekend, that same town is the site of the New World Festival, with performances by more than 100 old-time northern New England and Canadian musicians. Given its scattering of appealing places to stay, its farms, and its back-roads scenery, this is a rewarding getaway area anytime except mud season (April and early May).

MEDICAL EMERGENCY Call **911** or **Gifford Medical Center** (802-728-4441), 44 S. Main St., Randolph.

✳ Villages

Sharon Village. An old commercial center at the junction of the river road (Rt. 14) and the high road (to Strafford), this remains a cluster of services just off I-89. The columned **Sharon Trading Post** is a classic general store with a serious meat department, also selling local maple products. The **Sharon Historical Society**, also at this crossroads, is open summer Sundays (1–3) and in early August on Old Home Day—a lively event at which guests over 70 can eat free at the chicken pie supper.

South Royalton Village. On a bend in the river and off Rt. 14, this classic railroad village frames an outsized green with two bandstands and a Civil War cannon. A granite arch recalls the 1780 raid on Royalton by more than 300 Native Americans commanded by an English lieutenant. The railroad hotel, an 1887 brick Queen Anne–style commercial block, the train depot, and many of the clapboard buildings within eyeshot have all received a new lease on life thanks to the presence of Vermont Law School. Founded in 1972 and headquartered in a tower-topped old school building (recently expanded, with new additions), this draws students from around the country. In the village of **Royalton**, north on Rt. 14, most buildings predate the Civil War.

Tunbridge. Some 20,000 people jam into this village of 400 for 4 days each September. They come for the **Tunbridge World's Fair**, first held in 1867. Sited in a grassy, natural bowl by a bend in the river, it has everything an agricultural fair should have: a midway, livestock displays and contests, a Floral Hall, collections of old-time relics, dancing, sulky racing, a fiddlers contest, horse pulls, a grandstand, and more. Known as the "Drunkards Reunion" during a prolonged era when it was claimed that anyone found sober after 3 PM was expelled as a nuisance, it's now a family event. In June the fairgrounds are also the site of the wonderfully colorful annual **Vermont History Expo**, showcasing Vermont historical societies from around the state with displays, reenactments, music, and much more. Tunbridge boasts four covered bridges (see our map), a fishing hole, and a photogenic brick Methodist church (in South Tunbridge).

Strafford. If it were any nearer a highway, this quietly spectacular village would be mobbed with tourists. Happily, it's 9 miles north of I-89, and not on the way to anywhere except Tunbridge. Coming *from* Tunbridge, the road climbs steeply through woods and fields, finally cresting and beginning its downhill run through beautifully restored farms with ponds out back (pools would be too garish), stables, and other signs of wealth not evident on the western side of the mountain. Aristocratic homes—which include the Gothic Revival **Justin Morrill Homestead** (see the box on page 320)—cluster near the common, at the head of which stands the churchlike white-clapboard Town House, built in 1799, so classic it's a staple of New England photo books.

Chelsea. A village with not just one but two picturesque commons and twin brick 1818 general stores (check out the ice cream at "Will's"). Noteworthy buildings also include a steepled church, the Orange County Courthouse, a brick library, a bank (since 1822), and many Federal-era homes. An amazing number of services—post office, restaurants, barber, and fish and wildlife office—are compressed into a small space.

Brookfield. "Pond Village," as it's known, easily ranks among the most picturesque four-corners in all New England. It boasts the state's oldest continuously operating library (established in 1791) and Sunset Lake, traversed by a floating bridge, buoyed by barrels (the lake is too deep to support a pillared span) but frequently sagging in the middle. During summer much of its traffic stops midway to fish, and on the last Saturday in January it's a coveted viewing point for one of New England's last ice-harvest festivals. At the center of the village are Green Trails Inn and Ariel's Restaurant, which draws diners from a 50-mile radius. **Allis State Park**, a few miles west, offers camping, picnicking, and a sweeping view. The **Marvin Newton House**, Ridge Rd. in Brookfield Center, is an eight-room home built in 1835, now housing local historical exhibits (open Sundays in July and August, 2–5; $2; 802-276-3959).

Bethel (population: 1,968). At the confluence of the White River and its Third Branch as well as of Rts. 107 and 12, this was once a major source of white granite used to face such buildings as Washington, DC's, Union Station. An eight-sided former school, now a community center, stands on Rt. 14 in West Bethel.

Randolph (population: 4,800). **Randolph Center** (east on Rt. 66 from I-89, Exit 4) is clearly the oldest of the five Randolphs. It's a lineup of brick and clapboard Federal-era mansions along a main street that was cut unusually wide with the idea that this might be the state capital. Instead it's now a quiet village in which life centers on **Floyd's General Store** and the nearby complex of Vermont Technical College, grown from the grammar school built here in 1806. According to a historical marker, musician and schoolmaster Justin Morgan brought a young stallion from Massachusetts to his home here in 1789 (Justin Morgan the man lies buried in the nearby cemetery; the grave of Justin Morgan the horse is marked by a simple stone off Rt. 110 in Chelsea). Randolph remains a horsey community, but with the arrival of the railroad in the mid–19th century, population shifted from the center down to the valley, 3 miles west (now the other side of I-89). It's here that Amtrak now stops, at the station on Main St.,

POND VILLAGE, BROOKFIELD

Christina Tree

steps from the **Chandler Center for the Arts**, a lively town-owned performance center. The **Randolph Historical Society Museum** (802-728-6677), upstairs in the police station, exhibits memorabilia, with the emphasis on railroading; three rooms are furnished in circa-1900 style. (Open third Sun. in May–Oct., 2–4; also July 4, noon–3.) Don't pass up the old-fashioned Ben Franklin's, recently rebuilt after a major fire and an exceptionally well-stocked representative of that vanishing breed. The **Independence Day parade** here is one of the biggest around.

Rochester (population: 1,171) straddles Rt. 100 in a quiet valley between the Green Mountains and the Braintree Range. It has a large village green, a reclusive summer population, and a surprising spread of lodging options, from luxurious hideaways to a working farm. The village itself is tiny but full of surprises, with some good shopping and a choice of places to eat. The approach over Rochester Mountain provides panoramic views and a delightful alternation of field and forest. North of the village on Rt. 100 the **Green Mountain National Forest Visitors Center** orients sportsmen, picnickers, and hikers to the largely uninhabited western portion of the town that lies within the GMNF. The Bingo area, in particular, offers swimming holes, abandoned town roads, cellar holes, and Civil War–era cemeteries. Rochester is also a center for mountain biking and for cross-country skiing. The **Rochester Historical Society** is upstairs in the library. Summer brings **Chamber Music Society** programs at the Federated Church and Sunday-evening concerts on the green.

✺ To See

Floating Bridge at Sunset Lake, Brookfield Village. First built in 1820 and replaced six times since, this is the only heavily used bridge of its kind in the country. It's quite picturesque. On our last visit it was sagging badly.

Joseph Smith Memorial and Birthplace (802-763-7742; www.placestovisit lds.org), Dairy Hill Rd., South Royalton. Open year-round during daylight hours; seasonal guided tours late May–mid-Oct., Wed.–Sun. 9–7; check for off-season hours. A marker on Rt. 14 (1 mile southeast of the village) points you up a steep, 2-mile hill to a complex maintained by the Church of Jesus Christ of the Latter-day Saints. The property itself begins with a steep hill of maples leading to a hilltop visitors center with paintings, sculpture, exhibits, and a film housed in two buildings. A 38.5-foot-high shaft, cut from Barre granite in 1908, marks the site of the farm on which the founder of the Church of Jesus Christ of Latter-day Saints was born in 1805 and lived until he was 10. Each foot on the shaft marks a year in the life of the prophet, who was murdered by a mob in Carthage, Illinois, in 1844. The 360 well-maintained acres include picnic tables.

THE JOSEPH SMITH MEMORIAL AND BIRTHPLACE, SOUTH ROYALTON

Christina Tree

Justin Morrill Homestead (802-828-3015; www.morrillhomestead.org), Rt. 132, Strafford Village. Open Memorial Day–Columbus Day, Wed.–Sun. 11–5; tours on the hour, $5. Justin Morrill never went to college but is remembered as the congressman who sponsored the Land Grant Colleges Acts (one in 1862 and another in 1890) that created more than 76 present institutions, currently enrolling some 2.9 million students. Many have evolved into state universities. The son of a Strafford blacksmith, Morrill made enough money as a country storekeeper (which he parlayed into a chain of stores) to retire at age 38 and enter politics on an antislavery and temperance platform. He served in Congress for 44 years (1855–98), never finding much time to spend in his striking, 17-room Gothic Revival mansion because he kept getting reelected. A man who was instrumental in the design and construction of the Washington Monument and the Library of Congress, Justin Morrill helped design his own house and (now restored) gardens and orchard. The icehouse and carriage barn are fitted with interpretive panels about Morrill and the many national events in which he played a role. Inside and out, this is a fascinating house, well maintained by the Vermont Division for Historic Preservation. Inquire about frequent events including the annual croquet tournament, the 19th-century apple festival, and Sunday-afternoon programs (2 PM) such as painting, landscape gardening, village walks, and more.

JUSTIN MORRILL HOMESTEAD IN STRAFFORD

COVERED BRIDGES There are five covered bridges in Tunbridge: the **Cilley Bridge**, south of the junction of Rt. 110 with Strafford Rd. and built in 1883; the **Howe Bridge** (1879), east off Rt. 110 in South Tunbridge; and in North Tunbridge, the 1845 **Flint Bridge** and 1902 **Larkin Bridge**, both east of Rt. 110. The **Mill Bridge** (1883), crushed by ice in the winter of 1999, has been rebuilt. In Randolph two multiple kingpost bridges, both built in 1904, are just off Rt. 14 between East Randolph and South Randolph. In Chelsea there is the **Moxley** or **Guy Bridge**, an 1886 queenpost, east off Rt. 110.

SCENIC DRIVES **The Quickie Tour**: Sharon to South Royalton via Strafford and Tunbridge (22 miles). Take I-89 to Exit 2, Sharon, and climb Rt. 132 to Strafford, site of the Justin Morrill Homestead and the Town House. Continue up and over the hills and down into Tunbridge. If time permits turn north on Rt. 110 for 5 miles and past three covered bridges (see above) to Chelsea. Otherwise turn south on Rt. 110 for the 5 scenic miles back (past one covered bridge) to Rt. 14 at South Royalton and pick up I-89 again at Exit 3 in Royalton, or turn back down Rt. 14 to Sharon. En route you pass the turnoff for the Joseph Smith Memorial.

Royalton to Randolph via Granville Gulf (117 miles). Take I-89 to Exit 3, just west of Eaton's Sugar House. The low road west (Rt. 107) follows the White River to Rt. 100, but the high road over **Rochester Mountain** saves 11 miles and is beautiful besides. At the junction in Bethel take Rt. 12 north a little more than 2 miles and turn left onto Camp Brook Rd. At the height-of-land the view is a panorama of the Green Mountains ahead. Keep to the main road (the one with the line down the middle) until a T, and turn left (it's marked) for the descent into Rochester. Turn north on Rt. 100 and, 4 miles up, note the Hancock Hotel and the turnoff for Middlebury Gap, Rt. 125 (see below). Continuing north on Rt. 100, the mountain walls close in as you near **Granville Gulf** and **Moss Glen Falls**. Turn off Rt. 100 into **Warren Village** (see "Sugarbush/Mad River Valley") and follow signs 2 miles to East Warren, where you turn onto the **Roxbury Gap Road**. Be sure to pull out near the top for a look back down the valley. It's a popular soaring center, and you may see a glider or hawks riding the thermal waves. Continue downhill to Rt. 12A and turn south, following the railroad tracks and the Third Branch of the White River past the turnoff for Braintree Hill to Randolph and back to I-89, Exit 4.

Randolph Center, **Brookfield**, **Chelsea** (27 miles). Take I-89 to Exit 4 and turn east into Randolph Center, then north along a glorious ridge road (marked TO BROOKFIELD) to Brookfield with its floating bridge across Sunset Lake, leading to Allis State Park. Addicted as we are to shortcuts, we still recommend passing up the gravel road from East Brookfield to Chelsea; go around through East Randolph (6 miles south on Rt. 14, then turn onto the road marked for Chelsea; it's 6 more miles). Return on Rt. 110 and Rt. 14 to I-89, passing six covered bridges.

Middlebury Gap. Robert Frost Memorial Drive is too glorious a stretch of road to pass by. From Rt. 100 in Hancock, turn onto Rt. 125 west and take the short detour into **Texas Falls** (see the box). Rt. 125 continues to climb through Middlebury Gap (the Long Trail crosses at an altitude of 2,149 feet). Then it's on through the Green Mountain National Forest until the rambling yellow Bread Loaf Inn and its annexes unexpectedly appear, banked in hydrangeas. Owned by Middlebury College, this 1860s hotel is nationally known for its summer literary programs. Just west, a dirt road leads to the Homer Noble farm; a short way past the farm is the **Robert Frost Cabin**, in which Frost spent 23 summers. Continue to the Robert Frost Wayside (see "Addison County and Environs"). Return the way you came or continue to Middlebury and return to Rt. 100 via Brandon Gap (Rt. 73), Appalachian Gap (Rt. 17), or Lincoln Gap (see "Sugarbush/Mad River Valley").

✳ To Do

BIKING In Randolph the **Three Stallion Inn** offers its own network of trails and rents bikes.

Green Mountain Bikes (802-767-4464; 1-800-767-7882; www.greenmountain bikes.com), Rt. 100 in Rochester Village. Doon Hinderyckx is a fount of information about local trails in and beyond the national forest. He offers guided tours and rents and sells mountain and cross bikes.

Also check with the **Green Mountain National Forest Visitors Center** (see *Guidance*), and see this chapter's *Scenic Drives*.

BOATING AND TUBING While most of the White River is navigable in high water (May–July), the 20-mile stretch from Rochester to Bethel is especially popular with canoeists, tubers, and kayakers. A good place to put in is at the cement bridge just south of Rochester. **Vermont River Adventures** (802-234-6361; www.tubevermont.com), based at White River Valley Camping, Rt. 107 in Gaysville, rents kayaks, tubes, and life jackets.

Tubing: Tubing on the White River is so popular that you can rent tubes at a number of places along the stretch from Gaysville to South Royalton. Try the **Gaysville Trading Company** (802-234-9118) on Rt. 107, and the **Stockbridge General Store** (802-234-9118).

FARMS TO VISIT ✄ **Neighborly Farms of Vermont** (802-728-4700; 1-888-212-6898; www.neighborlyfarms.com), North Randolph Rd., Randolph Center. Rob and Linda Dimmick and their three children run an organic dairy and make organic cheeses that they sell at the farm and through area stores. Visitors are welcome to see the cows and watch cheesemaking (call ahead).

Vermont Technical College maintains a demonstration farm in Randolph Center (802-728-3395). Visitors can tour the sugarhouse, apple orchard (pick your own in-season), and dairy barn.

Maple Ridge Sheep Farm (802-728-3081; www.mrsf.com) in Braintree, said to be the oldest and largest Shetland sheep farm in the country, produces fleece, machine-washable sheepskin, yarn, knit and woven items, meat. Call first.

✄ **Marge's B&B at Round Robin Farm** (802-763-7025), RR 1, Box 52, Fay Brook Rd., Strafford 05072. This is a 350-acre working dairy farm with one of Vermont's famous 10-sided round barns (built in 1917). It's been in the family for six generations. The 60 head of cows are milked between 5 and 7 PM; visitors welcome. There's also a sugarhouse and a B&B (see *Lodging*).

FISHING Trout abound at the junction of the Tweed and White Rivers, downstream of Bethel, above Randolph, and below Royalton. Fly-fishing enthusiasts find the Bethel area good for large rainbow and brown trout, while below Royalton there are bass, spring walleye, and trout.

Trout on the Fly (802-685-2100; www.troutonthefly.com). Brookfield-based husband-and-wife team Brad Yoder and Tamara Hutzler specialize in the White River and its tributaries, fly-fishing for all varieties of bass and trout. They offer lessons and float trips. Catch-and-release. Prices are high, but so is service—and guided trips include a gourmet streamside lunch.

Fishing licenses are available at **Tracy's Midway**, a convenience store and gas station on N. Main St. in Sharon.

Texas Falls, Hancock. On Rt. 125 west of Rt. 100, a sign points to the road to the falls. It's 0.25 mile. The falls are an exceptional series of shoots and pools, rimmed by interesting rock formations and spanned by footbridges. Swimming is not permitted, but a short, steep (be careful) trail leads down to the falls. A quarter mile farther up the road is a picnic area with grills and outhouses.

TEXAS FALLS

Kim Grant

Bakers Pond on Rt. 12 in Brookfield has a parking area and boat launch, good for trout fishing. There is a boat access on **Rood Pond** in Williamstown and a canoe access on **Sunset Lake** in Brookfield, also stocked with trout. The floating bridge is a popular fishing spot.

White River National Fish Hatchery, Gaysville (Bethel), Rts. 12/107 west of Bethel Village, raises imprint salmon for the Connecticut River restoration program.

Roxbury State Fish Hatchery, Rt. 12A in Roxbury, raises brookies and Atlantic salmon, over 350,000 fish per year. It abuts the Third Branch of the White River, and the fishing downstream can be amazing.

GOLF **Montague Golf Club** (802-728-3806), Randolph. One of the oldest courses in Vermont, 18 holes. The Second Branch of the White River winds through it. Light fare is served in the clubhouse; lessons offered. *Note:* A driving range maintained by the Three Stallion Inn is just west on Rt. 66.

The White River Golf Club (802-767-GOLF), Rt. 100, Rochester. Nine holes, clubhouse with a restaurant serving lunch (dinner by arrangement). Open May–Oct. Affordable, great for families, a historic and beautiful course. Next to it is a driving range (802-767-3211).

HIKING The **Green Mountain National Forest** (see *Guidance*) harbors numerous trails. On Rt. 100 itself in Granville Gulf there are two short nature trails. At Moss Glen Falls, the 0.5-mile loop on the west side of the road is more rugged than the 1-mile loop on the east side.

In **Allis State Park**, Brookfield (off Rt. 12; see *Green Space*), a 2.5-mile trail circles down through meadows and back up through woods. A trail leads from the picnic area to a fire tower with one of the best views in central Vermont (on a clear day, from Killington–Pico to Mount Mansfield to Ascutney). The Bear Hill Nature Trail is another reason for finding this special place.

LLAMA HIKING **Heart of Vermont Llama Hikes** (802-889-9611), Fernwood Llama Farm, Spring Rd., Tunbridge. Memorial Day–Columbus Day: Picnic hikes, moonrise hikes, half- and full-day hikes offered through the rural countryside. Fiber and fiber products also sold.

PICNICKING **Brookfield Gulf**, Rt. 12 west of Brookfield. Picnic facility, nature trail.

Braintree Hill, Braintree Hill Rd. (off Rt. 12A just west of downtown Randolph). A great picnic spot with an early cemetery and sweeping views to the White Mountains. The handsome Braintree Meeting House here is open by appointment and on Old Home Day (first Sun. in Aug.).

Bingo Brook in Rochester off Rt. 73 in the national forest. Picnic sites with grills by a mountain stream, good for fishing and swimming.

Also see Allis State Park in *Green Space*, Texas Falls in *To See*, and the Robert Frost Wayside in *Scenic Drives*.

SWIMMING Ask locally about various swimming holes in the First, Second, and Third Branches and the main stem of the White River. In Randolph Center there is a human-made beach, bathhouse, and picnic area. There is also a pool at the recreational park in Randolph.

✳ Winter Sports

CROSS-COUNTRY SKIING AND SNOWSHOEING **Green Mountain Ski Touring Club** (802-728-9122; 1-800-424-5575; www.3stallioninn.com), Three Stallion Inn, off Rt. 66, Randolph. Thirty-five km of groomed and tracked trails weave through woods and meadows; instruction and rentals available; marked from Rt. 66. Ski and snowshoe rentals; biweekly snowshoe tours.

Nordic Adventures (802-767-3272; www.vt-nordicadventures.com), Rt. 100, Rochester Village. Dean Mendell offers a full line of cross-country equipment and snowshoes, lessons, rentals and guided tours.

Green Mountain National Forest (see *Guidance*) maintains trails in Rochester on Liberty Hill and at Chittenden Brook.

Also see **Green Trails Inn** under *Lodging*.

✳ Green Space

Allis State Park (802-276-3175), Brookfield. Open May 30–Sep. 15. A camping area with 18 tent sites, 8 with lean-tos (no hookups), each on a wooded loop road separate from the picnic area, in which you can choose tables on a windy hilltop or under a pavilion. A hiking trail (see *To Do*) accesses a fire tower with an outstanding view.

Green Mountain National Forest (GMNF). Among the highlights of the Rochester district of the GMNF are the Long Trail and the Texas Falls Recreation Area. A good short hike is from Brandon Gap north 0.6 mile to the cliffs of Mount Horrid, where there are views to the east. Because of the abundance of other things to do in this area, be sure to drop in the new GMNF Visitors Center 2 miles north of the Rochester green on Rt. 100 (802-767-4261).

✳ Lodging

INNS ○○ **Three Stallion Inn** (802-728-5575; 1-800-424-5575; www.3stallioninn.com), Lower Stock Farm Rd., off Rt. 66, Randolph 05060. Geared to sports-minded guests, especially cross-country skiers, mountain bikers, and golfers. The inn is set on the 1,300-acre Green Mountain Stock Farm, a mix of pasture and woodland that's crisscrossed with some 35 miles of tracked trails. The lively Morgan's Pub (see *Eating Out*) and the inn's restaurant (see *Dining Out*) are set off from the rest of the inn. Facilities include a fitness room, a whirlpool and sauna, two tennis courts, and an outdoor lap pool. The adjoining Montague Golf Club is 18 holes, and the inn also maintains a driving range. There's swimming and fishing in the Third Branch of the White River, which runs through the property, and a trout pond invites catch-and-release. The 15 guest rooms include 3 family suites and range from $95 (shared bath) to $190 double for a room with private bath, continental breakfast included. Inquire about special packages.

🐾 ♪ **Tupper Farm Lodge** (802-767-4243; www.tupperfarmlodge.com), 4609 Rt. 100, Rochester 05767. An 1820s farmhouse on Rt. 100, known for its friendly atmosphere and good cooking. Roger and Ann Verme have been welcoming guests since 1971. They accommodate 30 in 10 rooms, most with private bath. They cater to skiers and bicyclists with bountiful breakfasts and candlelit dinners. The swimming hole is across the road in the White River. $50–60 per person (under age 12 $30–38) MAP; $75 per couple. Also group and ski-week rates. B&B available in summer only.

The Huntington House Inn (802-767-91400; huntingtonhouseinn.com), 19 Huntington Place, Rochester 05767. At the back of Rochester's large green, this small inn has been a dining destination for many years. It's presently owned by nonresident partners and was closed when we stopped by during foliage season. Rooms are tastefully furnished with private bath, air-conditioning, and TV. $125–175 in-season, $115–135 off-season includes breakfast. Also see *Dining Out*.

BED & BREAKFASTS

In Rochester
🐾 **Cooper-Webber House** (802-767-4742), Rt. 100 (Box 436), Rochester 05767. Ron and Sandy Brown have skillfully restored this magnificent vintage-1830s Federal house in the center of Rochester Village. Enter through the screened patio furnished with rocking chairs into a big country kitchen. Beyond: comfortable, uncluttered common spaces with fireplaces.

Three guest rooms are unfussily furnished with early-19th-century-style (but comfortable) four-poster beds and handmade quilts. One room with a private bath, two with shared. Also a suite. The upstairs library in the leafy back of the house has a woodstove and an irresistible stock of books. $70–75 year-round includes a full breakfast.

🐾 **The New Homestead** (802-767-4751; shaas@sover.net), Box 25, Rochester 05767. Don't be put off by the funky exterior of this old house in the village. Inside it's clean and comfortable, with an eclectic mix of art and attractive quilts: four rooms, three with private bath, one with shared. $55 per room, $50 single year-round, includes a sumptuous breakfast of home-laid eggs, jams, spuds, and homemade bread, maybe blintzes. Your hosts are country lawyer/state legislator Sandy Haas and David Marmor, who maintains that this is the most reasonably priced listing in this book. It's certainly a great value and a special place.

In Brookfield
Brookfield Guest House (802-276-3146; www.brookfieldbandb.com), Pond Village, Brookfield 05036. Former Bostonians George and Connie Karal offer a sophisticated B&B with a large veranda in the middle of this special village, steps from Sunset Lake and its floating bridge. The two suites are beauties, especially the ground-floor green room (sleeping three) with private bath and small kitchenette ($150). Upstairs, two rooms share a bath. $95–225 per couple includes a full breakfast. No children under 10, please.

Green Trails Inn (802-276-3412; www.greentrailsinn.com), P.O. Box 494, Brookfield 05036. This handsome house at the heart of Pond Village has welcomed visitors since Jessie Fiske, a Brookfield native who became one of the first women professors at Rutgers University, began renting rooms to her students and associates. Jane Doerfer, the present innkeeper, is an accomplished cook and cookbook author. She offers eight rooms, five with private bath. The beds have new, high-quality mattresses. A very full buffet-style breakfast is served in the big, sunny dining area with a stone hearth and view of the lake, where guests have access to a small beach on Sunset Lake. $95–145 depending on room, less off-season. Inquire about cooking classes, solo rates, and weekly rates for the whole house. Ariel's Restaurant (see *Dining Out*) is across the street.

Elsewhere

🍁 **Inn at Johnnycake Flats** (802-485-8961; www.johnnycakeflats.com), 47 Carrie Howe Rd., Roxbury (visible from Rt. 12A) 05669. Off the beaten track, but on the way (via Roxbury Gap) to Sugarbush, geared to guests with an interest in nature. Hosts Debra and Jim Rogler are widely traveled and enjoy tuning guests in to their surroundings, beginning with the 16 surrounding acres with sheep and two frog ponds. The house was an early-1800s stage stop, and the living room fireplace is made from handmade bricks. There are three guest rooms furnished with antiques and Debra's quilts. Choose from double, queen, or twin beds; a daybed room can work for children. $105–125 (for the room with private bath and a little library), a country breakfast included. Guests are welcome to use the innkeepers' snowshoes, cross-country skis, and bicycles.

Round Robin Farm (802-763-7025), RR 1, Box 52, Fay Brook Rd., Strafford 05072. This is a 350-acre working dairy farm with one of Vermont's famous 10-sided round barns (built in 1917). It's been in the family for six generations. What's offered is the homey, clean, and cheerful farmhouse with its Mission-style dining room and sitting room with a TV/VCR, or rooms therein (two rooms with double bed and two with twins, sharing one bath), plus a fridge with the fixings for making your own breakfast in the big country kitchen. Marge Robinson lives within call in the adjacent house. Cross-country ski or walk woods and meadows. No smoking and no pets, please. A double room is $40 per person per night. Inquire about the price for the whole house. Snowmobile trails run right through the property.

Four Springs Farm (802-763-7296; www.fourspringsfarm.com), 776 Gee Rd., Royalton 05068. Jinny Cleland raises organic vegetables, chickens, and flowers on her 70-acre farm and invites visitors to tag along on chores. Multiday participatory programs are also offered to the families and groups who stay here, either taking advantage

GREEN TRAILS INN

Christina Tree

🐄 ✆ **Liberty Hill Farm** (802-767-3926; www.libertyhillfarm.com), 511 Liberty Hill Rd., Rochester 05767. This is the real thing: a working, 150-head dairy farm set in a broad meadow, backed by mountains. Its 1890s red barn with cupola is one of the most photographed and painted in Vermont (Woody Jackson has printed it on silk screens that, we're told, sell by the thousands in Japan). There's a capacious white-clapboard 1825 farmhouse and, best of all, there is farmwife-host par excellence Beth Kennett. Beth's own family's farming history dates back to the 17th century in Maine, and "farmer" Bob Kennett's roots run deep into New Hampshire soil. Both families were horrified when Beth and Bob moved "west" to this 109-acre spread in this magnificent Vermont valley. Their own sons are now grown, but visitors of all ages are treated to a sense of how much fun (and work if they so desire) living on a farm can be.

Meals are served family-style, and Beth makes everything from scratch. The dinner we sampled on a summer evening at 6 (BYOB) was as delicious as it was prodigious: incredibly moist sliced turkey, a zucchini casserole, cucumber salad, a garden salad with tomatoes, pumpkin muffins, mashed potatoes, fresh-picked sweet corn, a choice of homemade dressings and stuffings—all set in the middle of a table seating eight adults and at least as many children. The kids disappeared after the main course, and adults lingered over blueberry pie with homemade (from the farm's own milk) raspberry ice cream.

LIBERTY HILL FARM

Christina Tree

There's plenty of common space, including a parlor with woodstove, but in summer adults seem to congregate on the porch. There are seven guest rooms (five with double beds, one with two single beds, and a room with five single beds) and four shared baths; families can spread into two rooms sharing a sitting room and bath. In summer you can hear the gurgle of the White River (good for trout fishing as well as swimming), and in winter you can ski or snowshoe up into the woods and off into the village across the meadows. $85 per adult, $40 per child under 12, MAP.

of eight secluded campsites ($20–25) or the four-bunk cabin with mountain views ($75). There's a central wash-house and a picnic pavilion.

SECOND HOMES AND COTTAGES ✍

Hawk North, Vermont's Mountain Hideaway (1-800-832-8007; www .vthideaway.com), Box 529, Rt. 100, Pittsfield 05762. Hawk homes are nice-ly designed vacation houses, hidden away in the woods on sites scattered around Rochester and Stockbridge. No longer related to Hawk Mountain Resort, Hawk North maintains a check-in office at the junction of Rts. 100 and 107. Each of the 10 homes is individu-ally owned, and decor varies, but all offer a spacious living/dining room and deck, full kitchen, and two to four bed-rooms. Some have sauna and/or hot tub. Rates fluctuate widely with the season: $240–475 per night for two to four bedrooms.

🐾 ✍ **Birch Meadow Farm** (802-276-3156; www.bbhost.com/birch meadow), 597 Birch Meadow Dr., Brookfield 05036 (East St. off Rt. 65 south). This is Mary and Matt Comer-ford's woodsy hideaway, with three modern, air-conditioned log cabins equipped for housekeeping. There are TVs and woodstoves, plus a B&B suite in the main house, which sits high on a hill with splendid views and a swim pond. $110–120 per couple, $15 each additional adult, $5 per child. Rates include the initial morn-ing's breakfast in the cabins.

Placidia Farm Bed & Breakfast (802-728-9883; www.placidia.com), 1470 Bent Hill Rd., Braintree 05060. This is an apartment in a hand-hewn log home (deck, kitchen, bedroom, and living room) on a large Christmas tree farm with its own pond. A full

breakfast in Viola Frost-Latinen's plant-filled sunporch is included. $125 per couple; $45 each additional person. Not appropriate for children under age 13.

CAMPGROUNDS **Lake Champagne Campground** (802-728-5298), P.O. Box C, Randolph 05061. Open Memorial Day weekend–mid-Oct. A 150-acre property with fields, a 3-acre swim lake, hot showers, mountain views, and facilities for tents through full-sized RVs.

Limehurst Lake Campground (802-433-6662), 4101 Rt. 14, Williamstown 05679. This family-geared campground offers 76 sites with full hookups for RVs, a separate area for lean-tos and tents, modern restrooms, hot showers, a waterslide, a sandy swim beach, boat rentals and fishing (no license required), and a game room.

Chittenden Brook Campground in the Green Mountain National Forest (802-767-4261), 5.3 miles west of Rochester on Rt. 73. The 17 campsites are fitted with picnic tables and grills; there are hand-operated water pumps and vault toilets. The surrounding forest provides good fish-ing, hiking, and birding. No trailers over 18 feet. No hookups or showers.

Note: Primitive camping is permitted almost everywhere in the Green Mountain National Forest.

Allis State Park (802-276-3175 sum-mer; 802-885-8891 winter; 1-800-299-3071 reservations). Open mid-May–Labor Day. Named for Wallace Allis, who deeded his Bear Mountain Farm to the state as a campground and recreational area. Sited on the summit of Bear Mountain, it includes a picnic area and trail to the fire tower, also 18 tent and 8 lean-to sites, each with a picnic table and fireplace. Hot showers but no hookups.

✳ Where to Eat

DINING OUT ✐ **Ariel's Restaurant & Pond Village Pub** (802-276-3939; arielsrestaurant.com), Brookfield. Reservations requested. Open Fri. and Sat. with a full menu; Wed., Thu., and Sun. with a pub menu. Closed Nov. and Apr. Reservations advised. Overlooking Sunset Lake in the middle of "Pond Village," this destination dining room is known as one of the best places to eat in Vermont. Lee Duberman and Richard Fink are longtime chef-owners who specialize in Mediterranean and Pacific Rim dishes, using local ingredients whenever possible. On an October day you might begin with a crabcake in Kataify pastry, then dine on grilled Cavendish Farm game hens with dried fruit sauce, topped off with a lemon napoleon with raspberry coulis. Entrées $21–27. Pub entrées range from hamburgers to pad Thai noodles with chicken and shrimp ($9–15). Children are welcome.

LEE DUBERMAN, CHEF AND CO-OWNER OF ARIEL'S IN BROOKFIELD

Christina Tree

Stone Soup Restaurant (802-765-4301), on the green, Strafford. Open for dinner Thu.–Sun. 6–9. Reservations strongly suggested. There is no sign for this elegantly rustic restaurant that has acquired a strong following over more than two decades. You step from Strafford's handsome green into a cheery tavern room with a large hearth. The candlelit, low-beamed dining rooms are beyond. On our last visit, the blackboard menu included Portuguese kale and fish stew, and veal with red pepper butter. Note the attractive herb garden. Personal checks, but no credit cards. Entrées $23.95–27.95.

♿ **Three Stallion Inn** (802-728-5575), off Rt. 66 (just off I-89), Randolph. Open for dinner Tue.–Sun., weekends in winter. This is a large, pleasant, informal dining room with a menu that might range from a garden burger, to grilled filet mignon, to naturally raised Vermont veal scaloppine with butternut squash risotto. Executive chef Bob Hildebrand and his sister Carol have coauthored two cookbooks, *500 Three Ingredient Recipes* and *500 Five Ingredient Desserts*. Entrées $8.50–18.95. Also see Morgan's Pub under *Eating Out*.

🦞 **Huntington House Inn Restaurant & Tavern** (802-767-9140), 16 Huntington Place, Rochester. Open Wed.–Sun. for dinner. This attractive dining room is dimly lit, the setting for meals that might begin with a savory Vermont cheese custard. The dinner menu we saw included yellowfin tuna, and risotto and veal chop Piccata with soft polenta. Entrées $21–28. The informal **Doc's Tavern** offers a selection of sandwiches and pizzas, also moderately priced steaks and Italian dishes.

EATING OUT Road food, listed geographically from south to north, off I-89.

I-89, Exit 2
Dixie's Country Kitchen (802-763-8721), Rt. 14 in Sharon on the way to South Royalton. Open for lunch and dinner. Good road food, seafood, steak, and $6.95 specials.

Chelsea Station (802-763-8685) on the green, South Royalton. Booths, a counter, breakfast from 6 AM, a friendly atmosphere, and a basic menu.

5 Olde, Tavern & Grill (802-763-8600), 192 Chelsea St., South Royalton. Open daily 11 AM–midnight. The original eatery by this name is at 5 Olde Nugget Alley (hence the name) in Hanover, N.H., and this too is a sleek, student-geared coffeehouse/pub with WiFi and a menu ranging from pizza and burgers, quesadillas and po'boys to reasonably priced dinner entrées such as veggie stir-fry and ribs.

South Royalton Market (802-763-2400; www.soromarket.com), on the village green, South Royalton. Open daily. This co-op style store, featuring local and organic produce, recently expanded to include Equal Grounds Café and access to neighboring Old Schoolhouse Books.

I-89, Exit 3
Eaton's Sugar House, Inc. (802-763-8809). Located at the junction of Rts. 14 and 107 in Royalton, just off I-89, Exit 3. Open daily 7–3. Under new ownership but still a good old-fashioned family restaurant featuring pancakes and local syrup, sandwiches, burgers, and reasonably priced daily specials. Try the turkey club made with fresh-carved turkey on homemade bread. Vermont maple syrup, cheese, and other products are also sold.

Route 110 in Chelsea
The Pines, Chelsea Village. Open from 3 PM. A friendly rural pub with a pool table, the local gathering spot and the food is fine.

Route 107
Tozier's Restaurant (802-234-9400), west of Bethel. Open May–Oct., in summer 11–8, limited hours in shoulder seasons. Under new ownership but still a classic road-food stop with pine paneling and a river view. Seafood (mostly fried, some broiled) is a dinner specialty, along with marinated steak tips and turkey dinner.

🍴 **Peavine Family Restaurant & Thirsty Bull Brew Pub** (802-234-9434), east of Stockbridge. In summer open nightly for dinner, also lunch Thu.–Sun. In winter only for dinner except Sun. This is a special place with a patio overlooking the river and a zany kid-geared decor with a train running around the open rafters. The name and train, along with photos and memorabilia, recall the 19-mile White River Valley Railroad (1900–33), known as the Peavine line because the narrow valleys forced it to thread along beside the winding White River, reminding some witty gardener of a peavine's wandering coils. The '27 flood pretty well crippled this railroad, as well as wiping out the woolen mills in the neighboring village of Gaysville. Lunch includes a wide choice of burgers, pasta, and pizza, also available at dinner along with apple brandy pork chops, sherry almond chicken, and beef with crabmeat and béarnaise sauce. Live dinner music Thu.–Sun. Kids' menu and a computer corner for their use.

Route 12 north of Bethel
Onion Flats (802-234-5169). Road food, good cones, and onion rings.

I-89, Exit 4, in Randolph

Three Bean Café (802-728-3533), 22 Pleasant St. Open 6:30–5. Closed Sun. The in gathering place for many miles around. Adjacent to the Randolph food co-op, it offers from-scratch croissants and baked goods, then nourishing soups and veggie sandwiches plus a variety of coffees and teas, the day's papers, and comfortable seating.

Patrick's Place (802-728-4405), 2 Merchants Row. Open for breakfast and lunch. Formerly Debbie's Corner Café, known for omelets and specialty sandwiches. Don't pass up the Mississippi Mud Pie.

Randolph Depot (728-3333), 2 Salisbury St. Open Mon.–Sat. 7–4. Housed in the town's Victorian-style brick train depot (Amtrak still stops), this attractive new restaurant features an unusual choice of salads as well as sandwiches and wraps.

Morgan's Pub at the Three Stallion Inn (800-424-5575), off Rt. 66 (just off I-89). This is a popular local gathering place with a tavern menu that usually includes char-grilled Black Angus burgers and grilled chicken sandwiches.

Randolph Village Pizza (802-728-9677), 1 S. Main St. Open daily 11–9, until 10 in summer and on weekends year-round. A wide variety of better-than-average pizzas and calzones; also salads, grinders, and pasta.

Along Route 100

Rochester Café & Country Store (802-767-4302), Rt. 100, Rochester Village. Breakfast 7–11:30, lunch until 4. Good fries and burgers.

Kristina's Kitchen (802-767-4258), 30 N. Main St. (Rt. 100), Rochester. Open Mon. and Thu. 8–5; Wed., Fri., and Sat. 8–8; Sun. 9–3. Closed Tue.

Just north of the general store and gas pumps, this 12-table café is part of the appealing complex that includes Seasoned Booksellers and a branch of Raiments & Adornments and features pottery by Judy Jensen (see *Selective Shopping* for all three) across the road. Good in the morning for espresso, fresh-made breads and muffins, and at lunch for soups, salads, and sandwiches. Dinner might feature pastas, fresh seafood, always vegetarian choices; beer and wine served.

Old Hancock Hotel (802-767-4976), Hancock, at Rt. 125. Open weekdays 7–9, until 8 in winter. A 19th-century village hotel known for its breads, muffins, and pies, good road food. Pick up a sandwich to take to nearby Texas Falls.

❋ Entertainment

The Playhouse Movie Theatre, Main St., Randolph, is the oldest movie house in the state. Shows first-run flicks.

Randall Drive-In Movie Theatre, Rt. 12 in Bethel, operates in summer only.

The White River Valley Players, (www.wrvp.org), a major community theater in Rochester, performs a spring musical and fall production in the high school.

❋ Selective Shopping

ART/CRAFT STUDIOS AND GALLERIES **Plush Quartz Art Glass** (802-767-4547), Rt. 100, Granville. Open Tue.–Sun. 9–5. Don't pass up this roadside studio and gallery. Vermont native Michael Egan shapes Venetian-style freehand blown glass into spectacular vases, pitchers, and a variety of housewares as well as art glass.

Judy Jensen Clay Studio (802-767-3271), Rt. 100 back behind the Rochester Café. Open daily. Jensen's pottery ranges from tiny vases to large urns, tile to chess sets, sculpture, handmade cards, and plenty of highly decorative functional ware. She also displays work in fiber, wood, glass, iron, and paper.

Big Town Gallery (802-767-9670; www.bigtowngallery.com), 99 N. Main St., Rochester Village. Open Wed.–Sat. 10–5, Sun. 11–4. Annie Mackay designs and makes wearable art but her studio showcases an eclectic mix of paintings, sculpture, and furniture as well as yarns and one-of-a-kind hats and scarves.

Nina Gaby Studio and Gallery (802-276-3726; www.ninagaby), Pond Village, Brookfield. Tucked up behind Green Trails Inn, this studio/gallery features changing shows, always including examples of Gaby's ceramic and clay work but also featuring other well-known artists in a variety of media. Generally open weekends but call. Check the web site and local calendars for openings.

SPECIAL STORES Porter Music Box Museum & Gift Shop (802-728-9694; 1-800-811-7087; www.portermusic box.com), Rt. 66 between I-89 and downtown Randolph. Open May–Dec. (call for hours). Small admission. The former home and office of Dwight and Mary Porter and the Porter Music Box Company. A large collection of music boxes is displayed, and both boxes and recordings are sold.

The Bowl Mill (802-767-4711; outside Vermont: 1-800-828-1005), Rt. 100, Granville. Open 9–5 daily, year-round. Tours offered 9–2:30 weekdays. Decorative wooden bowls

Kim Grant

MICHAEL EGAN AT WORK AT PLUSH QUARTZ ART GLASS

have been made here since 1857, with present machinery dating from the 1880s. Good for woodenware, toys, crafts, cards, books, baskets, maple products, specialty foods.

Raiments & Adornments (802-765-4335), Rt. 132, South Strafford Village. Open Thu.–Sat. 11–5, Sun. 1–5. This mix of top-quality designer and vintage clothing is well worth a stop. Check out the branch store at 30 Main St. in Rochester Village (open Sun.–Tue. 8–5, Wed.–Sat. 8–8).

Chandler Music Hall Chandler Center for the Arts (802-728-9133; www.chandlermusichall.org), 71–73 Main St., Randolph. A fine, acoustically outstanding music hall built in 1907 and restored to mint condition. It's now open year-round for musical and theatrical performances: chamber music, blues, jazz, opera, folksingers, the Vermont Symphony, and Mud Season Talent Show. The annual New World Festival on the Sunday of Labor Day weekend features 100 musicians performing northern New England and Canadian music here and in other local, weather-proofed venues.

Cover to Cover Books (802-728-5509), 27 N. Main St., Randolph. A friendly, full-service store, also cards, gifts. Inquire about author signings.

Old Schoolhouse Books (802-763-2434), 106 Chelsea St., on the green, South Royalton. An interesting selection of old and new books, now also with a café (see South Royalton Market under *Eating Out*).

Seasoned Booksellers (802-767-4258; www.seasonedbooks.com), 30 N. Main St., Rochester. Librarian Sandy Lincoln specializes in sustainable lifestyles, wilderness tales, and renewable energies.

The Brick Store and Specialty Shop (802-234-5378), Main St., Bethel. Clearly an old-time country store with a 1930s soda fountain, an outlet for locally made Vermont Castings stoves, also selling Vermont handcrafted items, souvenirs, cards, gifts, and more.

The Raptor Academy (802-767-3552), Rt. 100, Rochester. Noted bird carver Floyd Scholz operates a small store exhibiting his work and selling carving supplies. Inquire about the series of workshops that regularly draw students from around the country.

CHRISTMAS TREES **Redrock Farm** (802-685-2282; 1-866-685-4343; www.christmastrees.net), 2 Redrock Lane (off Jenkins Brook Rd., which is off Rt. 110), Chelsea. Call before coming, but you can pretty much drop by any day of the year and pick out a balsam fir or white spruce (up to 7 feet) and it will be FedExed to you—anywhere in the contiguous 48 states—at Christmas. Trees are $20–40 plus shipping; wreaths, too. Picking your tree is more difficult than you might think, given the thousands to choose from, but Richard and Stephanie Rockwood don't rush you. Once tagged with your name, your tree continues to stand during those 6 weeks in which most northern trees are making their way to market. Whether you live in California, Florida, or Boston, what you get is a freshly cut tree. You can order rather than select it, but that's missing half the fun. Fishermen are welcome to test their skills on the pond, and anyone can paddle the boat.

FARMS AND SUGARHOUSES *Note:* These maple producers sell syrup year-round and welcome visitors into their sugar shacks during the March production period.

Silloway Farms (802-728-5253; 802-728-5503), Boudro Rd., Randolph Center, welcomes up to 20 visitors at a time.

Vermont Technical College Farm (802-728-3395; 802-728-3391), Rt. 66 east off I-89, Randolph, invites visitors to tour sugaring operations.

North Hollow Farm (802-767-4255), Rt. 100, Rochester. Maple syrup, gift baskets.

BETHEL'S BRICK STORE

Christina Tree

Eaton's Sugar House, Inc. (802-763-8809), junction of Rts. 14 and 107, just off I-89, Exit 3. Open daily 7–3. An old-fashioned, family-run, maple-focused complex in which you can watch maple candies being made. See also *Eating Out*.

✴ Special Events

Last Saturday of January: **Brookfield Ice Harvest Festival**—ice cutting, ice sculpting, hot food, sledding, skating, skiing.

February: **Strafford Winter Carnival**.

March: **Open sugarhouses**. **Casino Night** at Vermont Technical College, Randolph Center, sponsored by the Randolph Area Chamber of Commerce in late March (802-728-9027).

Mid-June: **Vermont History Expo**, a 2-day gathering of Vermont historical societies from throughout the state, bringing their exhibits to fill the Tunbridge Fairgrounds—historic reenactments and demonstrations, music, grandstand, and many varied events.

July: **July 4 parades** in Strafford and Rochester, a bigger one in Randolph (usually over 5,000 spectators), with food and crafts. **Family Farm Festival**, Randolph Center. **Chandler Players** perform at Chandler Center for the Arts, Randolph. **Chelsea Flea Market**—150 dealers cover both greens. **Summer Night**, a community-wide celebration in Rochester.

July–August: **Randolph Gazebo Series** (802-728-3010)—Tuesday-evening music. **Summer music school**—workshops at the Mountain School, Vershire. **Huntington Farm Show**, Strafford. **Brookfield Blues Festival** (August), off Rt. 65 in

Christina Tree

WILL'S STORE IN CHELSEA

Brookfield. The **South Royalton Town Band**, in business for more than a century, gives free concerts on the green Thursday evenings. **Sharon Old Home Day**.

September: **New World Festival** (*Sunday before Labor Day*; www.new worldfestival.com) at the Chandler Music Hall in Randolph features northern New England and Celtic music, in addition to food and crafts. **White River Valley Festival**, Bethel. **Tunbridge World's Fair** (www.tunbridgefair.com), Tunbridge, 4 days midmonth, ongoing for more than 130 years in a superb setting, definitely one of the country's most colorful agricultural fairs with horse and oxen pulling, contra dancing, sheepdog trials, livestock and produce judging, horse racing, amusement rides, pig races, pony rides, and more. **Harvest Fair on the Park** in Rochester.

Columbus Day weekend: **Lord's Acre Supper**—sale and auction, Barrett Hall, Strafford.

November: **Annual Hunters' Supper**, Barrett Hall, Strafford.

SUGARBUSH/MAD RIVER VALLEY

There were farms and lumber mills in this magnificent valley before Mad River Glen began attracting skiers in 1948, but the unique look and lifestyle of this community have been shaped by three ski areas, just as truly as the earlier villages grew around mills and commons. Its present character has been evolving since the '60s, when Sugarbush and then Glen Ellen (the two have since merged) triggered an influx of ski-struck urbanites who formed polo and foxhunt groups, built an airport, and opened and patronized a gliding school, specialty shops, and fine restaurants. Young architects eager to test new theories of solar heating and cluster housing designed New England's first trailside homes, first bottom-of-the-lift village and condominiums. Most of these settling skiers have remained, their numbers now augmented by their grown children and second-home owners who have come to retire. It's a well-heeled, active, ecological- and community-minded group.

Physically just 4 miles apart, philosophically Sugarbush and Mad River Glen seemed at opposite poles of the ski world in the '90s. By then it was painfully clear that northern New England's natural snow is too fickle a base for the big business that skiing had become, and that to make snow you need water. The two ski areas faced this challenge in their own ways. Mad River Glen, the "ski it if you can" mountain, kept its demands modest, operating the nation's oldest lift, and becoming the country's first cooperatively owned ski area (divided among upward of 2,000 shareholders). It also remains the only area in the East that bars snowboarders, featuring telemarking and animal tracking instead.

Water for making snow was, however, essential for the survival of Sugarbush, a major ski resort and the Valley's workhorse. Luckily, in 1995 it was bought by the Maine-based American Ski Company (ASC) and acquired a 63-million-gallon snowmaking pond (to store water siphoned from the Mad River during peak flows) and other needed infrastructure improvements. ASC's proposal to build one of its signature "grand" hotels at the base of Lincoln Peak was, however, defeated, and the multiresort operator seemed to lose interest. Happily, this three-peak resort is now owned by a partnership composed of longtime residents and Valley skiers, who have been involved with both of its resorts and have an understanding of how the two complement each other. At this writing the big news in the Valley is the ongoing construction of a 140-unit condo hotel

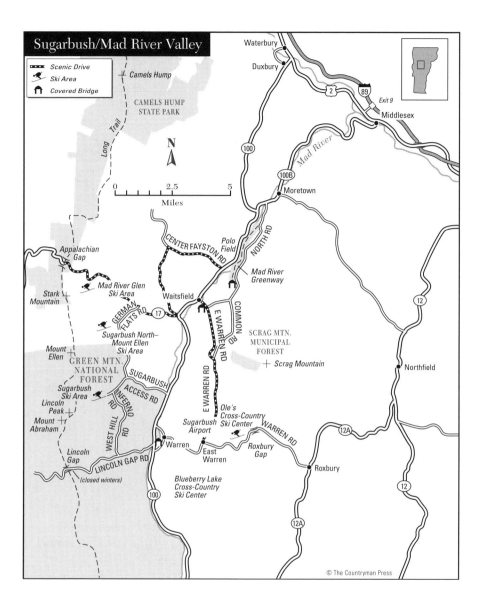

designed to complement the original 1960s ski village at the base of Lincoln Peak (centerpiece of Sugarbush Resort).

Not so long ago the very question of what to call this valley (Mad River? Sugarbush?) would have sparked a debate, but residents now agree: It's the Mad River Valley, named for the river down its center. Seven miles wide, it is magnificent, with meadows stretching to the Roxbury Range on the east. In summer and fall there is hiking on the Long Trail over some of the highest peaks in the Green Mountains, soaring in gliders above the Valley, mountain biking on ski trails and high woods roads, horseback riding, fishing and swimming in the Mad River itself, not to mention outstanding golf, tennis, and polo.

With direct links to the Champlain Valley via the scenic roads through Appalachian and Lincoln Gaps on the west, this is a logical lodging and dining hub from which to explore some of Vermont's most magnificent and varied landscapes, especially during foliage season. Dining and shopping are as good as you'll find at any resort area in the East. Several thousand visitors can bed down here on any given night, but it's far from obvious where.

Visitors tend to drive right through the Valley on Rt. 100, seeing nothing more than the clump of roadside shops in Waitsfield, missing Warren Village (6 miles south, just off Rt. 100) entirely. "The Valley" (as it's known locally) lacks the high-profile image enjoyed by rival Green Mountain resorts to north and south—which is fine by residents and regulars.

GUIDANCE **Mad River Valley Chamber of Commerce** (802-496-3409; 1-800-82-VISIT lodging; www.madrivervalley.com), Box 173, Waitsfield 05673. A walk-in visitors center in the General Wait House, Rt. 100, Waitsfield, is open year-round 9–5 weekdays, Sat. 9–1. During crunch times, vacancies are posted after 5 PM in the lobby by the courtesy phone (available 24 hours). Request the helpful, free guide.

Green Mountain National Forest Ranger District Office and Visitors Center (802-767-4261), Rt. 100 in Rochester. Open 8–4. While this magnificent information center is 25 miles south of Warren, it's worth knowing it's there (see "White River Valleys") as a resource for exploring much of the area immediately west and south of the Valley.

GETTING THERE *By bus and train:* Waterbury, 12 miles north of Waitsfield, is the nearest Vermont Transit and Amtrak stop.

By air: Burlington International Airport is 45 miles away; see "Burlington Region" for carriers.

By car: Valley residents will tell you that the quickest route from points south is I-89 to Randolph and 15 miles up Rt. 12A to Roxbury, then 8 miles over the Roxbury Gap to Warren. This is also the most scenic way (the valley view from the top of the gap is spectacular), but be forewarned that this high road can be treacherous in winter. In snow, play it safe and take I-89 to Middlesex, Exit 9, then Rt. 100B the 13 miles south to Waitsfield.

GETTING AROUND During ski season the **Mad Bus** fleet circles among condos at the top of the access road and restaurants and nightspots. These are free 26-passenger buses that link the Valley floor to all three mountain base areas, running daily and until 1:30 AM on Saturday night.

Mad Cab (802-793-2320), **C&L Taxi** (802-496-4056) and **Morf Transit** (802-864-5588; 1-800-696-7433) offer local and long-distance service.

Note: Waitsfield–Champlain Valley Telecom offers free local calls on some pay phones (but not all, so check) scattered around the Valley. Wireless Internet service is widely available in local lodgings.

WHEN TO GO Christmas week through February is high season, high volume, especially in a snowy season when Mad River Glen is wide open. Midweek during this same period is cheaper and far quieter. Ditto for March, when the human-made snow base at Sugarbush is deep and weekend crowds have eased. By mid-April it's all over. May and June appeal to birders (spring migration before trees are in full leaf). Warren's Fourth of July parade, small but famous, kicks off a series of summer events. As noted above, thanks to the gap roads (see *Scenic Drives*), this is an ideal hub for foliage. After the leaves fall it's dead until mid-December.

MEDICAL EMERGENCY Emergency service is available by calling **911**.

Ambulance (802-496-3600). **Mad River Valley Health Center** (802-496-3838), Rt. 100, Waitsfield. **Mad River Internal Medicine** (802-496-2202).

✳ Villages

The Mad River Valley includes Moretown (population: 1,653) to the north and Fayston (population: 1,140), an elusive town without a center that produced potatoes in the 1860s and was an important lumbering presence into the early 20th century. It's home to Mount Ellen and Mad River Glen ski areas and to inns along Rt. 17 and the German Flats Rd.

Warren Village. The village center of the long-established farm town of Warren (population: 1,700) is a compact clapboard cluster of town hall, steepled church, and bandstand, with a double-porched general store by a waterfall across from an inn. At first glance the village doesn't look much different from the way it did in the 1950s when Rt. 100 passed through its center, but the effect of Sugarbush, the ski resort that's way up an access road at the other end of town, has been total. The Pitcher Inn's self-consciously plain face masks an elegant restaurant and some of the most elaborate (and expensive) themed rooms in Vermont; the Warren Store (once a stagecoach inn itself) stocks a mix of gourmet food and upscale clothing and gifts. Arts, antiques, crafts, and a full-service spa are within an easy walk, and a covered bridge spans the Mad River. The village is the setting for one of Vermont's most colorful July 4 parades.

Waitsfield is the most populous (16,595) of the Valley's towns and its commercial center, with two small, tasteful shopping malls flanking Rt. 100 on land that was farmed until the 1960s. The old village center is 0.5 mile up Rt. 100, a gathering of 18th- and 19th-century buildings, including a library and steepled church, on and around Bridge Street (it's a covered bridge). Much larger and denser than

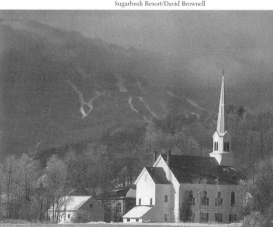

WARREN VILLAGE WITH SUGARBUSH SLOPES IN THE BACKGROUND.

Sugarbush Resort/David Brownell

it first looks, the village offers a sophisticated mix of boutiques and services and several first-rate restaurants. Changing historical exhibits are displayed in the General Wait House. Benjamin Wait, you learn, had been a member of Vermont's famed Rodgers' Rangers and weathered dozens of French and Indian Wars battles, as well as serving in the Revolution before founding the town at age 53 in 1789. He later was pitted against his fellow settlers on the question of where to put the common. He wanted it just about where the commercial center is today (the original common has been left high and dry out on Joslin Hill Rd.). Largely denuded of its woods during its era as a logging and sheep-farming community, the town is now mostly wooded and home to more people than ever.

✳ To Do

In winter the Valley's magnets are its alpine and cross-country ski areas, but in summer there are no chairlifts, no slides, no factory outlets, just an unusual number of activities to pursue. Check the following list!

BICYCLING The Valley's wide variety of terrain, from smooth dirt roads to technical singletrack, lends itself to mountain biking. For rentals and service, check **Clearwater Sports** (802-496-2708), **Inverness Ski Shop** (802-496-3343), and **Stark Mountain Bike Works** (802-496-4800), all on Rt. 100 in Waitsfield. The routes listed under *Scenic Drives* are also popular bike routes. Rentals and tours available.

Mad River Path. A 3-mile trail follows the Mad River from a parking area on Trembly Rd. (turn off Rt. 100 north of Waitsfield at the sign for the Mad River Inn).

CANOEING AND KAYAKING 🛶 **Clearwater Sports** (802-496-2708; www.clear watersports.com), Rt. 100, Waitsfield. Barry Bender offers learn-to-canoe and -kayak programs, full-moon canoe cruises on Waterbury Reservoir, camping excursions, also a children's day program (ages 9–13) and a 5-day wilderness camp program for 9- to 13-year-olds.

Vermont Pack & Paddle Outfitters (802-496-7225), Rt. 100, Waitsfield, offers kayaking and canoeing tours.

FARMS TO VISIT **Mountain Valley Farm** (802-496-9255; www.vermont experience.com), 1719 Common Rd., Waitsfield 05673. Set high on an open shoulder of the valley with a classic red cupolaed barn, the farm welcomes visitors for wagon and sleigh rides, weddings, birthday parties, or simply to meet the barnyard animals and walk or cross-country ski. Inquire about the guest suite.

FISHING Numerous streams offer good fly-fishing. The chamber of commerce (see *Guidance*) keeps a list of half a dozen guide services. Vermont fishing licenses are required and can be bought at Kenyon's Variety Store, Rt. 100, Waitsfield.

Fly Fish Vermont (802-253-3964). Rob Shannon offers 4-hour instructional stream tours.

FITNESS CENTERS **Sugarbush Health & Racquet Club** (802-583-6700; www
.sugarbush.com), Sugarbush Village, Warren. An outstanding complex with
indoor and outdoor pools, indoor and outdoor Jacuzzis, whirlpool, sauna, steam
room, exercise room, indoor squash, tennis and racquetball courts, massage
room, aerobics studio, 11-station Nautilus, and a full range of cardiovascular
equipment. The **Valley Rock Gym** (802-583-6754), part of this complex, features an indoor climbing wall, open 3–9 PM.

Bridges Family Resort and Tennis Club (802-583-2922; 1-800-453-2922;
www.bridgesresort.com), Sugarbush Access Rd., Warren. A year-round health
and tennis club with indoor and outdoor tennis, heated pools, fitness center, hot
tub, and sauna.

GOLF **Sugarbush Golf Course** (802-583-6725), Warren, at the Sugarbush Inn.
An 18-hole, Robert Trent Jones Sr. course, PGA rated 42, par 72; cart and club
rental, lessons, practice range, café. Inquire about golf/lodging packages.

HIKING *Trails, Paths & Long Trail Hikes Guide*, available at the chamber of
commerce (see *Guidance*), unlocks the area's many superb hiking secrets.

The **Long Trail** runs along the ridge of the Green Mountains here and is easily
accessible from three places: the two gap roads and the Sugarbush Bravo chairlift
(weekends only). From the Lincoln Gap Rd. (the gap itself is 4.7 miles west of
Rt. 100) you can hike a short way south to Sunset Ledge for a view of the Champlain Valley and Adirondacks. The more popular hike, however, is north from
the gap (be advised to start early; parking is limited) to the Battell Shelter and
on to Mount Abraham (5 miles round-trip), a 4,052-foot summit with spectacular
views west, south as far as Killington Peak, and north as far as Belvidere Mountain. From Mount Abraham north to Lincoln Peak (accessible by the Sugarbush
Resort chairlift) and on to Mount Ellen (4,135 feet) is largely above tree line;
3,600-foot General Stark Mountain to the north is best accessed (still a steep
2.6-mile hike) from Rt. 17 at Appalachian Gap. For details about the two shelters, contact the **Green Mountain Club** (802-244-7037; www.greenmountain
club.org). Mill Brook Inn's Joan Gorman also recommends beginning 2.1 miles
up Tucker Hill Rd. at the small parking area (on the left) at the CAMEL'S HUMP
STATE FOREST sign. Follow the blue blazes through the stand of pines known
as "the Enchanted Forest" to the top of Dana Hill Rd. (approximately 1 hour
round-trip, good for skiing and snowshoeing).

Mad River Glen (802-496-3551; www.madriverglen.com) offers a full schedule
of guided backcountry trips and bird-watching tours.

HORSEBACK RIDING **Vermont Icelandic Horse Farm** (802-496-7141; www
.icelandichorses.com), N. Fayston Rd., Waitsfield. Year-round. These strong,
pony-sized mounts were brought to Iceland by the Vikings, but are still relatively
rare. Karen Winhold uses her stable of around 20 mounts for 1- and 2-hour, half-
and full-day trail rides and (seasonal) inn-to-inn treks from her stable. The horses
have an unusually smooth gait (faster than a walk, gentler than a trot). Skijoring
is offered in winter.

Dana Hill Stable (802-496-6251), Rt. 17, Fayston. Clinics, extensive coaching weeks.

MINI GOLF ✎ **Lots-O-Balls** (802-244-5874), Rt. 100, in Duxbury, between Waitsfield and Waterbury. Open in-season from 11 AM, a great 19-hole miniature golf course.

POLO **Sugarbush Polo Club** (802-496-8938). The oldest and most active polo club in Vermont holds matches Thu., Sat., and Sun. during summer months and a USPA-sanctioned tournament on July 4. Lessons available. Polo fields are in Waitsfield Village near the Health Center and at the junction of the East Warren and Roxbury Gap Rds. Public welcome.

SCENIC DRIVES **East Warren Road**. If you miss this road, you miss the heart of the Valley. From Bridge St. in Waitsfield Village, cross the covered bridge, bear right onto East Warren Rd., and continue the 6 miles to East Warren. The views are of the Green Mountains set back across open farmland. For an overview of the Valley, take the Roxbury Gap Rd. up to the pullout (be careful, because there aren't many places to turn around). From East Warren, loop back the 2 miles through Warren Village to Rt. 100.

Bragg Hill Road. The views from this peerless old farm road are magnificent: down across pastures and the narrow valley cut by the Mill Brook to Mount Ellen. Begin at Bragg Hill Rd. (off Rt. 100 just north of the Rt. 17 junction) and drive uphill, continue as it turns to dirt, and follow it around (bearing left); it turns into Number 9 Rd. and rejoins Rt. 17.

> GAP DRIVES **Appalachian Gap**. Even if you aren't continuing down the other side, be sure to drive up Rt. 17 past the Mad River Glen base area to its high point (there's parking at the trailhead for the Long Trail) and look down across the Champlain Valley, across the lake, to the Adirondacks in the distance. This is a great sunset ride.
>
> **Lincoln Gap** is the steepest of Vermont's east–west gap roads (nothing allowed in tow, good brakes required, closed in winter), and the most spectacular. It begins on Rt. 100 just below Warren Village and climbs for 3 miles, seemingly straight up to the top of the 2,424-foot-high Lincoln Gap, where there's a pullout, a trailhead for the Long Trail. Next come magnificent vistas south, across farm fields (this stretch of road is unpaved in wide places and paved when it narrows). The village of Lincoln, clustered around a good general store, is about as quiet as Vermont gets. Continue through West Lincoln and down to Bartlett Falls in Rocky Dale (see "Addison County").
>
> For the **ultimate foliage loop** drive west over the Appalachian Gap (Rt. 17) 16 miles from Waitsfield to Rt. 116, then 2 miles south on Rt. 116 to the Lincoln Gap Rd. and head back east 14 miles to Warren.

Christina Tree

BRAGG HILL ROAD

Granville Gulf (see the map in "The White River Valleys"). Drive Rt. 100 south from Warren and the Valley quickly disappears, replaced by a dark, narrow, and twisty pass, part of the Granville Gulf State Reservation. At the height-of-land, the Mad River begins its north-flowing course toward the Gulf of St. Lawrence and the White River rises, flowing south to eventually empty into Long Island Sound. A few miles south **Moss Glen Falls** spills down a steep cliff by the road. To turn this 20-mile drive into a day trip, continue to Hancock and across the Middlebury Gap to Middlebury, back across Appalachian or Lincoln Gap (see the box) to the Mad River Valley.

SOARING **Sugarbush-Warren Airport** (802-496-2290; 1-800-881-SOAR), Warren. Open daily May–Oct. Respected as one of the East's prime spots for riding thermal and ridge waves. Solo and private glider lessons, rides, vacations available for all ages. Come just to see who's gliding in and out; lunch at the **Diner Soar Deli**.

SPAS **Alta Day Spa** (802-495-2582; www.altadayspa.com), 242 Main St., Warren Village. Adjacent to the Pitcher Inn, with which it shares ownership and patrons. A full menu of spa services is offered, from massage to aromatherapy to facials and salon services.

MadRiver Massage (802-496-5638; www.madrivermassage.com), Starch House overlooking the Mill Brook, Rt. 100, Waitsfield (just north of the Rt. 17 junction). Open daily 10–5, Sunday seasonally. A full range of massage, also shiatsu, reflexology, Reiki, and "stress-diffuser," plus body and bath products.

SUMMER DAY CAMPS *&* **Sugarbush Resort** (802-583-2381), the **Bridges Family Resort and Tennis Club** (802-583-2922; 1-800-453-2922) in Warren, and **Clearwater Sports** (802-496-2708) in Waitsfield all offer summer day camps. For ages 13 and up there's even a weeklong **Junior Soaring Camp** (802-492-2708) at the Sugarbush Airport (see *Soaring*). **Mad River Glen** also offers nature-geared day camps in summer.

SWIMMING South of Warren Village, the Mad River becomes a series of dramatic falls and whirlpools cascading through a gorge. The most secluded swimming hole is by the **Bobbin Mill** (the first right off Rt. 100 after Lincoln Gap Rd., heading south); park by the gravel pit and follow the path through the pines to a series of pools, all icy cold. Ask locally about **Warren Falls** and the best spot for skinny-dipping. The **Lareau Farm swimming hole** (now a town park) in the Mad River, south of Waitsfield on Rt. 100, is best for kids. **Blueberry Lake** in Warren is now owned by the Green Mountain National Forest; the **Ward Fishing Access area** on Rt. 100B in Moretown is another good bet.

Christina Tree

VERMONT ICELANDIC HORSE FARM, WAITSFIELD

Bristol Falls is just about 10 miles from Warren via the Lincoln Gap Rd. The **Sugarbush Sports Center** features a large, L-shaped outdoor pool with adjacent changing facilities, café, bar, and Jacuzzi; the **Bridges Family Resort and Tennis Club** offers indoor and outdoor pools and swimming lessons. Many inns also have outdoor pools. Inquire about the Punch Bowl (clothing optional).

TENNIS **The Bridges Family Resort and Tennis Club** (802-583-2922; 1-800-453-2922), Sugarbush Access Rd., Warren, offers indoor and outdoor courts and year-round tennis clinics for both adults and juniors.

WALKING AND RUNNING **The Mad River Path Association** (802-496-7284) maintains several evolving recreation paths in the Valley, namely: the **Warren Path**, beginning near Brooks Field at Warren Elementary School (Brook Rd., Warren); the **Millbrook Path** in Fayston, running along the hill through the woods (blue blazes) between Millbrook Inn and Tucker Hill Lodge, on up across German Flats Rd. to the Inn at Mad River Barn; the **Mad River Greenway** (see *Bicycling*); and the **Village Path**, which begins at Fiddlers' Green and heads south to the Irasville Cemetery and beyond. See also *Hiking* and *Scenic Drives*.

WEDDINGS Many inns and resorts throughout Vermont specialize in weddings—but those in the Valley were among the first to do so. Indeed, the area probably still represents the state's single largest concentration of venues and related services. Begin with the chamber—www.madrivervalley.com—and look for our weddings symbol ∞ throughout this chapter.

✳ Winter Sports

CROSS-COUNTRY, TELEMARK SKIING, AND SNOWSHOEING **Ole's Cross-Country Center** (802-496-3430; 1-877-863-3001; www.olesxc.com), at the airport, Warren. Fifty km of machine-tracked trails radiate out across the meadows and into the woods with elevations ranging from 1,120 to 1,640 feet. This is a hidden treasure at the heart of the valley—with views of the mountains on both sides. Rentals and instruction. Breakfast and lunch served weekends 10–3, otherwise soups and sandwiches 9–5 at the Diner Soar Deli.

🐾 **Blueberry Lake Cross-Country Ski Center** (802-496-6687), Plunkton Rd., Warren. On the scenic, east side of the Valley, a total of 60 km of secluded trails. Your dog is welcome here.

Clearwater Sports (802-496-2708), Rt. 100, Waitsfield, offers rentals, along with custom and group tours, backcountry skis, and "skins" for attempting local stretches of the Catamount Trail (below).

Local trails

Puddledock in Granville Gulf State Reservation on Rt. 100, south of Warren, has 3.5 miles of ungroomed trails marked with red metal triangles; a map is available at the registration box.

Check out the *Mad River Valley Snowshoe Trails* map/guide published by Map Adventures (www.mapadventures.com), detailing 15 tours and identifying local animal tracks.

Catamount Trail (www.catamounttrail.org). Check the guidebook (see "What's Where") and web site for stretches of the trail in the Valley. The most popular begins at the Battleground (see *Lodging*) on Rt. 17 and climbs steadily uphill to the Beaver Ponds in the Phenn Basin Wilderness area.

DOWNHILL SKIING ✍ **Sugarbush** (802-583-6300 information; 802-583-SNOW ski report; 1-800-53-SUGAR lodging reservations; www.sugarbush.com). Two separate trail systems on two major peaks—3,975-foot Lincoln Peak at Sugarbush South and 4,135-foot Mount Ellen at Sugarbush North—originally two different ski areas—were linked in 1995 by a 2-mile (9½-minute) quad chair

Stark Mountain by Snowshoe (Mad River Glen: 802-496-33551; www.mad riverglen.com), Warren. Half a dozen trails ranging in length from a short spur to 2.2 miles are marked, and Mad River's resident naturalist Sean Lawson offers a full program of guided **tracking treks**, including 2-hour **Nighttime Nature Rambles** every Friday and Saturday during ski season. An on-mountain nature center has been recently rehabbed and expanded. **Telemarking** is also a longtime specialty at **Mad River Glen**. Inquire about rentals, lesson and lift packages, and special events.

AN INTERPRETIVE TRIP UP STARK MOUNTAIN BY SNOWSHOE

Christina Tree

traversing the undeveloped Slide Brook Basin that separates them. Snowmaking coverage, long adequate at Mount Ellen, was also tripled to cover substantially more terrain at Lincoln Peak. Sugarbush skiers will tell you how fortunate their resort was to be sidelined during the era in which a large percentage of New England's best ski trails were smoothed, widened, and generally homogenized. In particular they are thankful that the Castle Rock trails, recognized throughout the country as some of the meanest, most natural, and most interesting expert terrain at any major American ski resort, survive.

Lifts: 17—7 quads, 3 triples, 4 doubles, and 3 surface. All operate 9–4, 8:30–4 weekends and holidays.

Trails: 111; 20 acres of patrolled tree skiing; 508 skiable acres.

Vertical drop: 2,650 feet.

Snowmaking: 285.5 acres overall.

Facilities: Cafeterias, lounges, ski shops, rentals, restaurants, sports center, condominiums.

Sugarbush Ski and Snowboarding School: Headed by Olympian Doug Lewis and extreme skier John Egan, the emphasis is on learning by doing. Clinics, special teen program; women's clinics, guided backcountry skiing are offered.

Snowboarding: Rentals, lessons, terrain parks.

For children: Nursery from infancy; special morning and afternoon programs for older kids.

Rates: In 2006, $52–67 adults, $44–62 ages13–17, $39–42 ages 7–12; cheaper day rates at Mount Ellen only, also savings with multiday rates, lodging packages, and the "Sugar Card"—good for savings of 18 to 30 percent, available online free. Skiers wear it like a season pass (you need a photo ID), also good for all on-mountain purchases.

✆ **Mad River Glen** (802-496-3551; 1-800-696-2001 in-state snow reports; outstanding web site: www.madriverglen.com). The ubiquitous red-and-white bumper sticker challenges MAD RIVER GLEN: SKI IT IF YOU CAN, but the mountain is one of the friendliest as well as the most challenging places to ski. It's also the only one in New England to prohibit snowboarding. One of the region's oldest major ski areas (the first to offer slope-side lodging), in 1995 it became the first to be owned cooperatively by its skiers, who are dedicated to preserving its narrow, continuously vertical trails, cut to the contours of the mountain. Access to the summit of Stark Mountain (3,637 feet) is via the vintage-1948 single chair (the only one left in the country, due for a $1.6 million "historic restoration"—but not replacement—in 2007). All trails funnel into the central base lodge area, the better for families, many of whom

VIEW OF SUGARBUSH'S LINCOLN PEAK AND MT. ELLEN TRAILS.

Courtesy Sugarbush Resort/Dennis Curran

Mad River Glen

MAD RIVER GLEN'S HISTORIC SINGLE
CHAIR

are now third-generation Mad River skiers. Another matter of Mad River fact: Some long-popular woods trails are off the ski map, a phenomenon that has since been aped by many other ski areas. This is also a favored place for telemarking and the only major ski mountain with a serious snowshoe trail system and full program of snowshoeing/nature treks. On a good snow day it's the region's best ski buy.

Lifts: 4 chairs, including the single, plus the Callie's Corner Handle Tow.

Trails and slopes: 21 expert, 8 intermediate, 16 novice, a total of 800 skiable acres.

Vertical drop: 2,037 feet.

Snowmaking: 15 percent, which includes top to bottom on the Practice Slope, also other high-volume, low-elevation areas.

Facilities: Base lodge, cafeteria, and pub; also the newly rehabbed Birdcage, halfway up the mountain, serving sandwiches, drinks; ski shop, rentals, ski school.

For children: Cricket Club Nursery for 6 weeks–6 years; programs for ages 3–17 include Junior Racing and Junior Mogul.

Rates: $50 adults, $37 juniors (14 and under) and seniors (65–69); $42/$29 half-day; multiday rates. Under 6 and over 70 ski free.

ICE SKATING **The Skatium** at Mad River Green Shopping Center in Waitsfield (lighted) offers rentals, also available from neighboring **Inverness Ski Shop** (802-496-3343); free day and night skating on the groomed hockey rink at Brooks Recreation Field off Brook Rd. in Warren.

SKIJORING Inquire about this sport (also about winter horseback riding) at **Vermont Icelandic Horse Farm** (802-496-7141) in Waitsfield (see *Horseback Riding*).

SLEIGH RIDES **Mountain Valley Farm** (802-496-9255) in Waitsfield offers sleigh rides.

SNOWMOBILING Eighty miles of local trails are maintained by the Mad River Ridge Runners; snowmobile registration can be purchased at **Kenyon's Store**, Rt. 100, Waitsfield. No rentals.

✳ Lodging

Note: The Sugarbush-based (1-800-53-SUGAR) reservation service is open 9–5 daily, 8–8 during high ski season, serving roughly half the Valley's condos and 21 inns and B&Bs.

Note also: Many lodging places in the Valley charge an extra 4 percent community fee, used to fund Valley-wide marketing and events, in addition to the usual 9 percent state tax. Most also request a 2-night minimum stay on winter and other popular weekends.

RESORTS Sugarbush Inn (802-583-6100; 1-800-537-8427; www.sugarbush.com), Warren 05674. The centerpiece of this complex is the fairly formal, 42-room Sugarbush Inn, owned by the same company that owns the mountain. There's a 24-hour front desk, room phones, air-conditioning, a library and sitting room, and an outdoor pool. $99–160 per couple, breakfast included, service extra.

⚓ The Bridges Family Resort and Tennis Club (802-583-2922; 1-800-453-2922), Sugarbush Access Rd., Warren 05674. A self-contained, family-geared resort just down the access road from the Sugarbush main lifts and base lodge. Tennis is the name of the game here. Facilities include indoor tennis and outdoor courts, squash, an indoor pool, saunas, Jacuzzi and exercise room, and 100 attractive condo-style units ranging from one to three bedrooms, each with fireplace, sundeck, TV, and phone, some with washer/dryer. $170 for a one-bedroom midweek to $955 for 2 nights (the minimum) for a three-bedroom on a weekend. Cheaper off-season and the longer you stay; inquire about ski and tennis packages.

INNS The inns listed below serve dinner as a matter of course; B&Bs may serve dinner on occasion.

Pitcher Inn (802-496-6350; 1-888-TO-PITCH; www.pitcherinn.com), Warren 05674. Designed by architect David Sellers to look like it's been sitting here in the middle of Warren Village for a century, the white-clapboard inn opened in the 1997–98 winter season, replacing a building that had burned. Inside, this luxurious inn, a member of Relais & Châteaux, offers some extraordinary spaces. We especially like the small library with books and a hearth, far from the large, elegant dining room (see *Dining Out*), and the downstairs pub. Each guest room was designed by a different architect to convey a different aspect of local history. The Lodge, for instance, suggests a Masonic lodge (once a major social force in the Valley), with a ceiling painted midnight blue and delicately studded with stars, and obelisk-shaped posts on the king-sized bed. From a bedside switch in the Mountain Room, you can make the sun rise and set over the mountains painted on the facing wall. Bathrooms are splendid. The Alta spa across the road, under the same ownership, offers massage, facials, and a variety of spa therapies. Two of the 11 rooms are suites. $350–600 for rooms, $700 for suites, includes breakfast in the inn. Add 10 percent service. Deduct $75 for single occupancy but add $75 per extra person.

♣ ☕ Millbrook Inn & Restaurant (802-496-2405; 1-800-477-2809; www.millbrookinn.com), Rt. 17, Waitsfield 05673. Open year-round except Apr., May, and mid-Oct.–mid-Dec. This 19th-century farmhouse is a gem. The two living rooms, one with a fireplace, invite you to sit down. The heart of the ground floor, however, is the dining room, well known locally as one of the best places to dine in the Valley (see *Dining Out*). Each of the seven guest rooms is different enough to deserve its own name, but all have stenciled walls, bureaus, antique beds with firm, queen- or king-sized mattresses, and private bath. Our favorite is the Wedding Ring Room with a wedding-ring-patterned quilt on the antique bed with its shell-shaped inlaid headboard and a picture of Thom's grandparents on the wall. A ski lodge since 1948, Millbrook has become a true country inn since Joan and Thom Gorman took over in 1979. They are constantly redecorating and landscaping the garden (breakfast is served on the patio, weather permitting), sustaining their enthusiasm with spectacularly adventurous, low-budget travels (Mount Kilimanjaro, South Africa, the Milford Track, Patagonia, and more) during the four months that they close. Guests can peruse the ever-growing stacks of photo albums chronicling these trips. They travel lightly and so there are remarkably few souvenirs, just new dishes on the menu and an ever-expanding wine list. In winter $130–150 per couple MAP; in summer $130 MAP, $90 B&B. The two-bedroom Octagon House on the wooded hillside across the brook rents for $300 a day in winter (minimum 3 days), less for a week, negotiable price in summer. Children ages 6 and older are welcome. Pets by prior approval. Wireless DSL access.

West Hill House (802-496-7162; 1-800-898-1427; www.westhillhouse .com), 1496 West Hill Rd., Warren 05674. A gabled farmhouse off in a far corner of the golf course but conven-

ient both to Sugarbush lifts and to the village of Warren. At this writing, just changing hands. It offers eight guest rooms, including two suites, all with private bath with either a Jacuzzi tub and shower or steam bath/tub/shower combo, and all with gas fireplace. The house offers an unusual amount of common space: a living room, library with fireplace, and sunroom with views to the mountains and spectacular gardens. Step out the front door to cross-country ski or play golf, out the back into 9 wooded acres. $135–180 per couple B&B midweek, $145–190 weekends with a 2-night minimum.

⊚ **1824 House Inn** (802-496-7555; 1-800-426-3986; www.1824house .com), 2150 Main St. (Rt. 100), Waitsfield 05673. North of the village, the gabled house is a beauty, decorated with an eye to room colors, Oriental rugs, and well-chosen antiques, in addition to comfort. The eight guest rooms vary, but all have private bath and feather bed. There are gracious drawing and dining rooms with fireplaces. The 15-acre property invites walking and cross-country skiing. There's also a good swimming hole in the Mad River just across the road, and the 1870s post-and-beam barn can shelter wedding receptions. The innkeepers are John Lumbra and Karl Lein. Lumbra, a professional chef, delights in whipping up four-course meals (see *Dining Out*). $163 per room includes a full breakfast and afternoon tea. Two-day minimum on weekends, 3 on winter holidays.

The Waitsfield Inn (1-800-758-2801; 1-800-758-3801; www.waitsfieldinn .com), P.O. Box 969, Rt. 100, Waitsfield 05673. Innkeepers Ronda and Mike Kelley seem equal to the task of managing this middle-of-the-village inn, an 1825 parsonage with a "great room"—offering plenty of space to relax in front of the hearth—in the (former) attached carriage and horse barn. The dining rooms (open to the public) are well away from the several comfortable spaces reserved for guests. The 14 guest rooms (all with private bath) vary from cozy doubles to family rooms with lofts. Appropriate for children ages 6 and older. $99–169 includes a full breakfast. Lunch and brunch are also served.

♣ ✂ **Inn at Mad River Barn** (802-496-3310; www.madriverbarn.com), 2849 Mill Brook Rd., Waitsfield 05673. Betsy Pratt, former owner of Mad River Glen Ski Area, preserves the special atmosphere of this classic 1940s ski lodge, with its massive stone fireplace and deep leather chairs, and a dining room filled with mismatched oak tables and original 1930s art. The food (breakfast only in summer, dinner too in winter) is fine, as are the pine-walled guest rooms, all with private bath (those in the annex come with small kitchenette). In summer there's a pool secluded in a grove of birches, while the deck overlooking landscaped gardens serves as a setting for weddings and receptions. In winter a trail connects with Mad River Glen. $75–110 per room includes breakfast. Dinner is $15 extra; special children's rates. Add 8 percent service charge in winter.

∞ **Tucker Hill Inn** (802-496-3983 phone/fax; 1-800-543-7841; www.tuckerhill.com), 65 Marble Hill Rd., Waitsfield 05673. A classic 1940s ski lodge with a fieldstone hearth in the pine-paneled living room. There are 18 recently renovated rooms and suites, all with private bath, phone, TV, and WiFi. Most rooms have queen or king bed and are accessed off one hall in the main house; five are in the newer Courtyard Building. The two-room Innkeeper's Suite on the lower level of the main house with a Jacuzzi, gas fireplace, and private entrance can accommodate a family (no children under 6, please). Innkeepers Phill and Alison Truckle include a full breakfast in $89–209 per double room, $149–239 per suite. Also see *Dining Out*.

Weathertop Lodge (802-496-4909; 1-800-800-3625; www.weathertop lodge.com), 755 Mill Brook Rd., Waitsfield 05673. Deceptively plain on the outside, inside Weathertop is filled with light—and also with Asian art, Persian carpets, and souvenirs from the several years innkeepers Lisa and Michael Lang spent traveling while based in Singapore. More surprises: In addition to a full breakfast they offer guests an optional full dinner menu with a dozen entrée choices ($10–16) such as spiced minced lamb with yogurt and mint sauce, or venison medallions in black pepper. Common space includes a large, comfortable living room with fieldstone fireplace and piano as well as TV with DVD/video player and a library of old movies. An exercise room and a game room with pool table are squirreled away on the top floor; down off the patio there's a hot tub and sauna. The eight air-conditioned rooms have either two quilt-covered double beds, a queen, or a king. All have fridge and full bath. $99–165 per room includes breakfast, from $79 off-season. Inquire about a slope-side condominium.

BED & BREAKFASTS ∞ **The Inn at Round Barn Farm** (802-496-2276; www.theroundbarn.com), East War-

Christina Tree

THE INN AT ROUND BARN FARM

ren Rd., Waitsfield 05673. Named for its remarkable round (12-sided) barn built in 1910 and now housing the Green Mountain Cultural Center (see *Entertainment*), with a lap pool and greenhouse on its ground floor, this old farmhouse is one of New England's most elegant bed & breakfasts. Innkeeper Anne Marie DeFreest offers 12 antiques-furnished rooms, 7 with gas fireplace, several with steam shower and/or Jacuzzi, all overlooking the meadows and mountains. Guests who come in winter are asked to leave their shoes at the door and don slippers to protect the hardwood floors. Common space includes a sun-filled breakfast room, a stone terrace, a book-lined library, and a lower-level game room with pool table, TV, VCR, and a fridge stocked with complimentary soda and juices. From $160 midweek for a double room with a regular shower to $315 on weekends in high season for a suite with marble fireplace, canopy king bed, Jacuzzi, and steam shower. Midweek packages start at $99 per room. Prices include gourmet breakfast and afternoon edibles.

Weddings are a specialty of the barn, which also serves as a venue for summer concerts (see *Entertainment*). In winter the inn maintains extensive snowshoe trails (snowshoes are complimentary to guests). Appropriate for children 15 and older. The inn hosts an Opera Festival in June, a photo exhibit in August, and a juried art show in foliage season.

∞ ♪ **The Lareau Farm Country Inn** (802-496-4949; 1-800-833-0766; www.lareaufarminn.com), Rt. 100, Waitsfield 05673. Guests feel right at home, checking in via the kitchen and settling in to the two sitting rooms (one with a fireplace). The broad, columned back porch overlooks an expansive spread of lawn that stretches down to a great (10-foot-deep) swimming hole and backs into a steep wooded hill. This is a 150-year-old farmhouse set in a wide meadow along the Mad River, a total of 67 acres with trails to walk or ski. Susan Easley, a warm host, offers 12 guest rooms and a suite with Jacuzzi, all nicely furnished with antique beds, quilts, and rockers. $90–135 for a double room with private bath, $80 with shared bath, includes a full breakfast (2-night minimum on weekends). $135–180 for the suite. Children are welcome "with well-behaved parents," and families occupy rooms along an ell off the main house. Weddings are a specialty; dinner on weekends is served in the American Flatbread Restaurant (see *Eating Out*) in the adjoining barn.

🐾 ✎ **Mountain View Inn** (802-496-2426; www.mountainview.com), 1912 Mill Brook Rd. (Rt. 17), Waitsfield 05673. This very Vermont house is bigger than it looks, with seven nicely decorated guest rooms (private baths). It's been geared to guests since it became one of the Valley's first ski lodges in 1948. Since 1978, under ownership by Fred and Susan Spencer, its year-round feel has been that of an unusually hospitable small country inn. Rooms are furnished with antiques (our favorite is the 1840s "rolling pin" tiger maple bed) and bright quilts. Guests gather around the wood-burning stove in the living room and at the long, three-centuries-old pumpkin pine harvest table for breakfast. Handy to Sugarbush, Mad River Glen, and the Mill Brook Path. $100–140 per couple B&B.

✎ **The Featherbed Inn** (802-496-7151; www.featherbedinn.com), 5864 Main St. (Rt. 100), Waitsfield 05673. Tom and Linda Gardner are the new innkeepers in this nicely restored 1806 inn, with exposed beams, pine floors and a formal living room as well as an informal "lodge room" with a fieldstone fireplace, games, and books. It's set far back from Rt. 100, overlooking flower gardens and fields. Ten guest rooms are divided between the main house, which includes two family-friendly suites, and a garden cottage with three more rooms, all with featherbed mattresses. $99–225 depending on room and season includes a full breakfast.

Deer Meadow Inn (802-496-2850; 1-888-459-9183; www.deermeadow inn.com), P.O. Box 242, Warren 05674. Ron and Randi Marjorell's gabled home is off by itself, set in 35 acres in the middle of the valley. In winter there are cross-country trails from the door, and Ole's Cross-Country Center is just up the road. In summer two spring-fed ponds are stocked with trout and bass, good for fishing. The graciously furnished house includes three guest rooms, all with private bath, phone, and TV. $140–160 includes a full breakfast.

Beaver Pond Farm (1-800-685-8285; beaverpondfarminn.com), 1225 Golf Course Rd., Warren 05674. There's a welcoming feel to Nancy and Bob Baron's beautifully renovated 1840s farmhouse, overlooking a beaver pond and set in the rolling expanse of the Sugarbush Golf Course. The five guest rooms all have private bath, fine linens, and down comforters, also spa robes to ease your way to the outside hot tub. Breakfast is an event, and the 24-hour wet bar includes complimentary coffee and tea, honor-system wine and beer. $119–169. Inquire about midweek winter ski packages.

✎ **The Mad River Inn** (802-496-7900; 1-800-832-8278; www.mad riverinn.com), P.O. Box 75, off Rt. 100, Waitsfield 05673. A house with turn-of-the-20th-century detailing, like fine woodwork and large picture windows with lace etchings in the living room. The seven guest rooms and one suite are furnished with an eye to Victorian fabric, color, and antiques.

The house overlooks a gazebo, meadow, and the Mad River, and it's handy to a good swimming hole. Facilities include an outdoor hot tub and a downstairs game room with a pool table. Rates from $100 for the smallest room with a private but hall bath, to $155 for the largest with private bath on a weekend; a three-course breakfast and afternoon tea are included. Children 5 years and older are welcome.

The Sugartree Inn (802-583-3211; 1-800-666-8907; www.sugartree.com), 2440 Sugarbush Access Rd., Warren 05674. This contemporary ski lodge, with a country inn interior, stands near the very top of the access road. When we stopped by, Graham Hewison and Maxine Longmuir were still fresh from London. They had immediately installed a hot tub in the gazebo and were promising further changes, including dinner, so check. The nine rooms have quilts, canopy and brass beds, also air-conditioning and private bath. A ground-floor suite with a gas fireplace can sleep a family of four. There's also a fireplace in the living room. In the dining room a two-course (sweet or savory) breakfast, with specials like stuffed pears and three-cheese soufflé, is included in $110–175 per couple; so is afternoon tea.

∞ **Caravan Bed & Breakfast** (802-496-7420; caravanbandb.com), 746 Rt. 100, Moretown 05660. This is an 1820s farmhouse that rambles back from the road, surrounded by 2 acres of gardens and fields beyond. Penny Percival and Jon Sutton offer five brightly decorated guest rooms and an attractive living room with a cheerful hearth and comfortable seating, good books, and games. Breakfast is full and healthy, using local ingredients as much as possible. Inquire about weddings, utilizing the 19th-century barn. $90–130 includes afternoon baked goods as well.

Yellow Farmhouse Inn (802-496-4263; 1-800-400-5169; www.yellow farmhouseinn.com), P.O. Box 345, 550 Old County Rd., Waitsfield 05673. This 1850s farmhouse sits off above meadows, minutes from the middle of Waitsfield. Minke and Sandi Ansatos have improved the decor and comfort of the seven guest rooms and a suite (all with private bath); several rooms have gas or electric Vermont Castings stove, some a whirlpool tub. $129–219 (the high end is for the two-room suite with Jacuzzi and kitchenette, sleeping four).

MOTEL ❀ ♪ **Wait Farm Motor Inn** (802-496-2033; 1-800-887-2828), Waitsfield 05673. Paul and Michelle Lavoie's eight motel units, four with kitchenette, as well as two double rooms in the main house, constitute this friendly family business. $60–95 per couple.

CONDOMINIUMS The Valley harbors more than 400 rental condominium units, many clustered around Sugarbush (Lincoln Peak), more scattered along the access road, and some squirreled away in the woods. No one reservation service represents them all.

Sugarbush Resort Condos (802-583-6100; 1-800-537-8427; www .sugarbush.com). The number of resort-managed units available varies and usually averages around 100—some slope-side, most walk-to-the-slopes—with health club access. From $99 for a one-bedroom to $750 for a four-bedroom. Prices vary with season. **Sugarbush Village Condominiums** (1-800-451-4326; www.sugarbushvillage.com) represents a similar range of condos and homes around Sugarbush. **Sugarbush Real Estate Rentals** (802-496-2591; www.sugarbushrentals.com) offers nightly, weekly, and monthly rentals in a variety of local condos and homes.

✍ **The Battleground** (802-496-2288; 1-800-248-2102; www.battleground condos.com), Rt. 17, Fayston 05673. An attractive cluster of town houses, each designed to face the brook or a piece of greenery, backing into each other and thus preserving most of the 60 acres for walking or ski touring (the area's 60 km network of trails is accessible). In summer there's a pool, tennis and paddle tennis courts, and a play area for children. Mad River Glen is just up Rt. 17. Rates (2-night minimum) for two-, three-, and four-bedroom units begin at $185.

♦ ☻ ✍ **PowderHound** (802-496-5100; 1-800-548-4022; www.powder houndinn.com), P.O. Box 135 (Rt. 100), Warren 05674. The old roadside farmstead now serves as reception and dining rooms—with a ski-season pub—for the 44 condo-style apartments clustered in back. Each of these consists of two rooms, one with two beds and another lounging/dining space with two more daybeds and a TV; token cooking facilities. It's all nicely designed and maintained, nothing fancy but a good deal for families and couples who like the privacy of their own space with an option to mix with fellow guests. Summer facilities include a swimming pool; there's a hot tub for year-round use, plus a winter shuttle to the mountain. $84–144 in winter, with many 2- and 3-day

(also midweek) ski packages; less off-season. Small charge for pets.

✳ Where to Eat

DINING OUT *Note:* The Valley restaurants are unusual in both quality and longevity. Most have been around for quite some time and, like most culinary landmarks, have their good and bad days.

Pitcher Inn (802-496-6350; www.pitcherinn.com), 275 Main St., Warren Village. Open for dinner. The elegant inn dining room features an à la carte menu orchestrated by chef Sue Schickler. You might begin with sorrel soup with smoked salmon crouton, then dine on grilled black bass with Thai green curry, coconut basmati rice, and green Romano beans, or a grilled vegetable napoleon with mozzarella, pesto, and browned butter vinaigrette. Entrées $24–34. The choice of wines by the glass is large, and the wine list itself is long and widely priced.

Chez Henri (802-583-2600), Sugarbush Village. Open only during ski season for lunch and dinner. (Check in the off-season.) A genuine bistro, opened in 1963 by Henri Borel, former food controller for Air France. It's a snug, inviting café with a fireplace, marble bar (imported from a Barre soda fountain), and terrace for dining out front in summer. Dinner entrées usually include roast duck with a fruit and pepper sauce and bouillabaisse, but items change frequently. Come early to get one of the coveted booths in the bar. Entrées $15–26.

♦ **Millbrook Inn & Restaurant** (802-496-2405; www.millbrookinn.com), Rt. 17, Waitsfield. Open for dinner except Apr., May, and late

PERIPATETIC CHEF THOM GORMAN AT THE MILLBROOK INN

Oct.–mid-Dec. For 25 years Thom Gorman has been the chef and Joan Gorman the pastry chef, hostess, and waitress in their attractive dining room, a double parlor with hearth and French doors opening onto a garden. This is, in fact, one of the most unusual and best-value restaurants in New England. Thom and Joan reenergize during the months they close by hiking, backpacking, kayaking, and camping in the world's far corners, bringing back new flavors (and wines) to share. They offer an eclectic, changing menu that might range from three-cheese fettuccine to five-peppercorn beef, but always includes a fish of the day and an "innkeeper's choice," along with a few Indian dishes, a legacy of Thom's Peace Corps days. We recommend the badami rogan josh, a wonderfully spiced (local) lamb dish. All dinners include Joan's anadama bread, as well as salad and starch—but save room for one of her freshly made pies, cakes, or ice creams. The wine list is varied and reasonably priced, especially interesting discoveries from small vineyards in Argentina, South Africa, and Australia. Beer is also served. Entrées $12.50–18.95.

The Spotted Cow (802-496-5151), Bridge St. Marketplace, Waitsfield. Open for dinner daily except Mon. Reservations suggested. Bermuda born and bred, Jay Young serves up authentic Bermuda fish chowder and conch fritters in his small, stylish restaurant, hidden down a lane near the covered bridge in Waitsfield Village. Fish is the specialty here, but entrées might also include grilled breast of duckling with forest mushrooms, dried cherries, port, applejack maple and pork sausage stuffing, saffron, basmati rice, and *haricots verts*. Entrées $18.95–26.95.

The Common Man Restaurant (802-583-2800; www.commonman restaurant.com), German Flats Rd., Warren. Dinner only, closed Mon. off-season. Reservations suggested. A mid-19th-century barn hung with chandeliers and warmed by an open hearth, this Vermont dining landmark recently acquired new owners for the first time since 1972. Keith and Julia Paxman have shifted to a more varied menu based on local produce. You might begin with a creamy butternut squash risotto, then feast on Cavendish pheasant, Weston farm rabbit, or a creamy New England fish stew. Desserts are tempting and the wine list, extensive. Four-course prix fixe $42; entrées $13.75–29.

☙ The Warren House Restaurant & Rupert's Bar (802-583-2421), 2585 Sugarbush Access Rd., Warren. Open for dinner daily from 5:30. Formerly Sam Rupert's, this attractive place still offers an inviting, low-key bar and "modern American cuisine"—entrées like herb-crusted pan-seared Atlantic salmon over a mustard-dill aioli, and balsamic-braised New Zealand lamb shank. Entrées $16.95–21.95.

1824 House Inn (802-496-7555; 1-800-426-3986; www.1824house.com), 2150 Main St. (Rt. 100), Waitsfield. Dinner by reservation Tue.–Sat. North of the village, a 19th-century farmhouse with elegant dining rooms is the setting for four-course dinners prepared by chef-owner John Lumbra. The several choices for each course might include fresh Maine crabcakes with a mango chile sauce, or baby mixed greens; filet mignon wrapped in bacon and topped with blue cheese, or veal Marsala; all topped off by crème brûlée. $44 prix fixe. The menu is also available à la carte; entrées $23–29.

Tucker Hill Inn (802-496-3983; www.tuckerhill.com), 65 Marble Hill Rd., Waitsfield. Open for dinner Tue.–Sat. year-round. Executive chef Eric Kiniburgh is so new at this writing that we have no feedback. The menu, however, looks promising, ranging from a daily vegetarian entrée to osso buco, Cajun grilled lamb, and mahimahi with roasted red pepper, ginger, coconut milk, basmati rice, and baby bok choy topped with fried leeks. Entrées $18.95–29.95.

EATING OUT 🍴 ✿ **Easy Street Café** (802-496-7234), Rt. 100, 0.5 mile south of the junction of Rts. 100 and 17 (next to the Catholic church). Open daily for breakfast and lunch 8–4; for dinner (except Mon.) 5:30–9:30. A winner! The kitchen is wide open, and the aromas are irresistible. On the damp day we visited, we had a choice of freshly made soups and chilis, sandwiches on freshly baked bread, and freshly made pastries, along with self-serve coffees and teas. The dinner menu is surprisingly varied: You might begin with roasted

littlenecks with cob-smoked bacon or vegetable tempura, then dine on vegetable timbales with grilled portobello mushrooms; shellfish in Thai-style curried broth with noodles, scallions, mushrooms, and sprouts; or rosemary-marinated rack of lamb. You could also simply have a crispy fish wrap with a mesclun, scallion, shredded lettuce, and tomato salad. Kids 12 and under can have a hamburger or grilled cheese with fries. This is also a source of take-out meals. The adjacent Purple Moon Pub (see *Après-Ski*) also features comfortable seating and good food as well as live music on weekends.

🍴 ✿ **The Den** (802-496-8880), just north of the junction of Rts. 100 and 17 in Waitsfield. Open daily for lunch and dinner until 10:30, sandwiches until 11. The cheerful, pubby heart of the Valley; booths, stained glass, a summer patio. The menu is large and always includes a homemade soup, a wide choice of burgers, and a salad bar; dinner entrées might include a grilled half duckling and jerk pork as well as house steak. A wide selection of beers.

American Flatbread Restaurant (802-496-8856), 40 Lareau Rd., Rt, 100, Waitsfield. Open Fri. and Sat. 5:30–9:30, year-round (more or less). George Schenk's distinctive pizza is baked in a primitive, wood-fired oven heated to 800 degrees; the results are distributed to stores from Florida to Chicago. On weekends the kitchen becomes an informal dining space featuring flatbread (toppings include cheese and herbs, sun-dried tomatoes, homemade sausage with mushrooms) and exceptional salads whose dressing boasts homemade fruit vinegar. Also specials such as grilled vegetables with garlic-herb sauce and oven-roasted chicken. Dine in or take out. Beer served. Each night Schenk writes a dedication, always food for thought.

Egan's Big World Pub and Grill (802-496-3033), junction of Rts. 100 and 17. Open nightly from 5; also Sunday brunch. Named for local extreme skier John Egan (who skis the world), this local gathering place has moved up in size and pricing from its old quarters down Rt. 100. Still the same chef. Brews and good hearty dishes like Hungarian goulash ($15.75) and New York sirloin ($18.25) are the specialty, but you can also dine on Chinese tofu, "mushroom love" (wild mushroom ravioli), or a burger.

🎿 **Jay's** (802-496-8282), Mad River Green Shopping Center, Rt. 100, Waitsfield. Open 8 AM–10 PM. A family restaurant, bright and spacious, with an immense menu. Dinner might be chicken pesto, pasta pillows filled with broccoli and Vermont cheddar in a curry cream sauce, or Jay's Giant Burger. Children's menu, pizzas; full liquor license.

🍷 🎿 **Hyde-Away Restaurant** (802-496-2322), Rt. 17, Open nightly 5:30–9:30 (9 midweek). An informal, affordable restaurant with plenty of appetizers and soups, sandwiches, and burgers. The dinner menu might include crabcakes served with homemade roasted red pepper aioli, Vermont maple chicken with garlic mashed potatoes, and vegetable pasta. All entrées come with salad and homemade bread. Seasonal outdoor deck dining. Children's menu and toy area.

🎿 **Michael's Good to Go** (802-496-3832), Village Square Shopping Center (a few doors down from Mehuron's Market), Waitsfield. Open Tue.–Fri.

for lunch, Thu.–Sat. 5–8 for dinner. Michael Flannagan, one of the Valley's favorite chefs, offers condo dwellers and local residents a great take-out menu ranging from Asian fusion to Vermont turkey potpie and Baja-style fish tacos plus the likes of a cheesy cheese pizza for kids.

Valley Pizzeria (802-496-9200), 4752 Main St. (Rt. 100), Waitsfield. Open 11–9:30, Sun. 4–9:30. New York–style pizza (not too thick or too thin) with a wide variety of toppings, hand tossed and baked in a stone oven. Eat in or take out; burgers and salads also served. Try the Greek pizza. No beer or wine.

Warren Store (802-496-3864), Warren Village. Open daily 8–7, Sun. until 6. Year-round the bakery produces French and health breads, plus croissants and great deli food and sandwiches; in summer a deck overlooks the small waterfall.

Three Mountain Cafe, Mad River Green Shopping Center, Waitsfield. The café and espresso bar features croissants, pastries, and chocolate truffles to go with Green Mountain Coffee.

Sweet Pea Natural Foods (802-496-7763), Village Square Shopping Center, Rt. 100, Waitsfield. Back behind Tempest Book Shop, a source of vegetarian soups and sandwiches as well as body care products, organic produce, healthy drinks, and more.

Village Grocery, Mobil & Deli (802-496-4477), 4348 Main St., Waitsfield. Pick up a really good, reasonably priced (they aren't called "designer") sandwich and head for the picnic tables a miles or so north under the pines (junction of Rt. 100 and Tremblay Rd.).

✳ Entertainment

Green Mountain Cultural Center (802-496-7722; www.theroundbarn.com/gmcc.htm) at the Joslyn Round Barn, East Warren Rd., Waitsfield. This concert and exhibit space in a classic round barn is the setting for a series of summer concerts, along with workshops and a major foliage-season art exhibit. The **Valley Players** (802-583-1674; www.valleyplayers.com), a community theater company, produces three or four plays a year in its own theater just north of Waitsfield Village, Rt. 100. The **Phantom Theater** (802-496-5997 in summer), a local group with New York City theater community members, presents original plays and improvisational performances for children and adults at Edgecomb Barn in Warren. Also note **Mad River Chorale** performances in June and December (check with the chamber of commerce: 802-496-7907).

APRÈS-SKI **The Blue Tooth** (802-583-2656), Sugarbush Access Rd., Warren. A ski-season "mountain saloon" open from 3 PM in ski season for après-ski snacks and drinks, moderately priced dinners, live entertainment, dancing. **The Hyde-Away** (802-496-2322) is the hot spot near Mad River Glen (Rt. 17). **The Purple Moon** (802-496-3400; www.purplemoonpub.com), Rt. 100 south of the Rt. 17 junction, features a fireplace, a mahogany bar, couches, and atypical late-night pub food like Vermont goat cheese fondue; live music Saturday nights.

✳ Selective Shopping

ANTIQUES **Warren Antiques** (802-496-4025), Warren Village. Open daily 10–5, May–Oct., then by appointment. Victoriana, furniture, ephemera.

ART GALLERIES **Artisans Gallery** (802-496-6256), Bridge St., Waitsfield. Open daily 10–5. A highly selective collection of furniture, baskets, canes, rugs, glass, decoys, ornaments, photography, and much more. The fine art and furniture galleries are in the rear.

The Bundy Fine Arts Center (802-496-5055), Bundy Rd. (off Rt. 100), Waitsfield. Phone to check hours. An interesting building that offers a mix of good art, in addition to a sculpture garden around and beyond a reflecting pond. A popular site for weddings.

Parade Gallery (802-496-5445) in Warren Village offers an affordable selection of prints and original art.

Bridge Street Bakery (802-496-0077), Bridge St., Waitsfield. Artist owned, a café most notable for its local paintings, prints, and photography (all for sale).

CRAFTS SHOPS AND GALLERIES **Cabin Fever Quilts** (802-496-2287; www.cabinfeverquiltsvt.com), the Old Church, Waitsfield. Closed Tue., otherwise open 10–5. Vee Lowell offers a selection of machine-sewn, hand-tied quilts in a range of sizes and patterns, priced $200–1,600; also 1,400 bolts of quilting fabrics plus pillows and gifts.

Waitsfield Pottery (802-496-7155; www.waitsfieldpottery.com), Rt. 100 across from Bridge St. Ulrike Tesmer makes functional, hand-thrown stoneware pieces, well worth a stop.

Warren Village Potter (802-496-4162), corner of Fuller Hill and Main St., Warren Village. Usually open daily 10–5. The functional stoneware is made on the premises; also a selection of crafts and candles.

Luminosity Stained Glass Studio (802-496-2231; www.luminositystudios.com), the Old Church, Rt. 100, Waitsfield. Open except Tue. This is a very special shop. Since 1975 this former church has served as the studio in which Barry Friedman fashions Tiffany lamp shades and a variety of designs in leaded and stained glass. Now he devotes most of his time to custom work but keeps a selection of opulent lighting, also showcases Arroyo craftsmen and mica lamps.

Mad River Glass Gallery (802-496-9388), 4237 Main St. (Rt. 100), Waitsfield Village. Melanie and Dave Leppia's handsome gallery is a must-stop. The glass is deeply colored, highly original, and created (blown and cast) on the premises.

Bradley House in Warren Village showcases work by an amazing variety of local craftspeople. It's a trove of hand-loomed rugs, woven baskets, quilts and pillows, wooden bowls, metalwork, furniture, fabric art, pottery, handblown glass, and more. Open daily.

Labyrinth Gifts (802-496-2259), Village Square Shopping Center, Waitsfield. Handcrafted jewelry, unusual pottery, blown glass, and fine prints—and now also kites, puzzles and wooden toys, shower clothes, and Vermont souvenirs.

The outstanding **Plush Quartz Art Glass** studio is in Granville, south of Warren on Rt. 100; see "The White River Valleys."

SPECIAL SHOPS Warren Store and More, Warren Village. Staples, wines, and the deli and bakery are down-stairs (see *Eating Out*); upstairs is one of Vermont's best-kept secrets, an eclectic selection of clothing, jewelry, and gifts. We treasure everything we have bought here, from earrings to a winter coat.

Schoolhouse Market (802-496-4559), 42 Roxbury Gap Rd., East Warren. Open year-round. Mon.–Thu. 11:30–6:30, Fri.–Sat. 8–8, Sun. 8–6:30. Closed Wed. The Faillace family make and sell several varieties of their own **Three Shepherds Cheese** (802-496-3998), along with local meats, Vermont wines and microbrews, and other Vermont artisanal cheeses and specialty foods.

All Things Bright and Beautiful (802-496-3397), Bridge St., Waitsfield. You'll find an incredible number of stuffed animals and unusual toys on two floors of this old village house.

The Store (802-496-4465), Rt. 100, Waitsfield. Since its 1965 opening, this exceptional shop has grown tenfold,

MAD RIVER GLASS

Christina Tree

now filling two floors of an 1834 former Methodist meetinghouse with superb early American, French, and English antiques, cookware, tabletop gifts, collectibles, lifestyle books, Vermont gourmet products, and children's toys and books from around the world.

Tempest Book Shop (802-496-2022), Village Square, Waitsfield. This family-run bookstore is a trove of titles in most categories, including children's books. We like their motto: "A house without books is like a room without windows" (Horace Mann). CDs, cassettes, posters.

Alpine Options (802-583-1763; 1-888-888-9131), with locations at Sugarbush (on the access road) and at Mad River Glen. Open daily, Fri. until 11 during ski season. Ski and snowboard rentals, demos and repair: the best-quality and all-around service according to the locals.

Country Crafts (802-496-2512), Rt. 100, Moretown. Open May–Dec., daily 10–6. Pauline LeBoeuf's small roadside shop is crammed with locally made crafts. Homemade pies, cookies, fudge, and produce also sold.

SUGARHOUSES **Eastman Long & Sons** (802-496-3448), Tucker Hill Rd., Waitsfield. "Sonny" Long sets 6,000 taps high on 100 wooded acres that have been in his family for generations. He maintains that the higher the elevation, the better the syrup, and he welcomes visitors to his roadside sugarhouse during sugaring season. On summer weekends, he sells from his van at the junction of Rts. 100 and 17.

Palmer's Maple Products (802-496-3696), East Warren Rd., Waitsfield. Delbert and Sharlia Palmer sell syrup from their farm on this scenic road.

✳ Special Events

Note: Check with the chamber of commerce (see *Guidance*) and its web site (www.madrivervalley.com) for weekly listings of special events.

March: **Annual New England Telemark Festival**, Mad River Glen.

April: **Vermont Adventure Games**, featuring the Sugarbush Triathlon—canoe, kayak, bicycle, cross-country ski races (more than 600 competitors), Sugarbush.

May–June: Paddling the Mad River; guided bird walks.

Mid-May–early October: **Farmer's Market**, Sat. 9–1 at Mad River Green, Rt. 100, Waitsfield (www.mrgfm.com).

July 4: Outstanding **parade**, Warren Village.

July–August: **Summer productions** by the Valley Players and by the Phantom Theater (see *Entertainment*). **Green Mountain Polo Tournament**, Warren.

August: **Vermont Festival of the Arts** throughout the Valley. **Mad River Valley Century Ride** (*third Saturday*; www.mrvcenturyride.com) —a 100-mile ride through central Vermont based at the Hyde-Away Inn/Restaurant.

August–October: **Farmer's Market**, Sat. 9:30–2 at the junction of Rts. 17 and 100. Crafts and food as well as produce.

Labor Day weekend: 2-day **crafts exhibits**. **Green Mountain Stage Race** (www.gmsr.org).

Early October: **Soaring Encampment** throughout the Valley. **Peak Foliage Celebration Day**, weekend chairlifts.

December: **Holiday events** throughout the Valley.

BARRE/MONTPELIER AREA

Any attempt to understand the character of Vermont entails a visit to the state capital, Montpelier, which has changed from a provincial backwater to a vibrant college town teeming with colorful shops, restaurants, and cultural activities. Don't miss a stroll through the Vermont Historical Society Museum and the ornate but informal State House, which is built of Vermont granite and marble and remains the only statehouse in the nation that is heated with wood. State and Main Streets are as charming as the Hollywood film they inspired (fittingly titled *State and Main*), and the back streets are a jumble of bridges, narrow lanes, and mansard roofs.

An exit on I-89, Montpelier is also at the hub of old roads radiating off into the hills, including Rt. 2, which runs all the way to Bangor, Maine, and Rt. 302 to Portland, which begins here as central Vermont's big commercial strip, "the Barre–Montpelier Road."

Billed as "the granite capital of the world," Barre (pronounced *Barry*) continues to quarry, cut, and sculpt its high-quality gray granite, now used primarily for memorial stones. The big attraction is the Rock of Ages Quarry in Graniteville, southeast of town, but Barre's Main Street has plenty to offer, and its two cemeteries showcase the work—ranging from quirky to spectacular—of generations of mostly Italian and Irish Barre sculptors. The newly opened Vermont History Center (headquarters of the Vermont Historical Society), the recently restored old Labor Hall, and the Barre Opera House, one of Vermont's most beautiful and active theaters, are all right downtown.

Southwest of Montpelier is the proud old town of Northfield, home of Norwich University and of no fewer than five covered bridges. East Barre and East Montpelier are both rural hamlets. Head either northeast on Rt. 2 or southeast or Rt. 302 to quickly find yourself in little-touristed farm country, much of which boils down to dense forest.

GUIDANCE **The Capital Region Visitor Center** (802-828-5981), 134 State St., Montpelier, is open 6:30–6 weekdays, 10–6 weekends. Housed in a redbrick house across the street from the capitol with a flag out front, it has knowledgeable, friendly staff and a restroom.

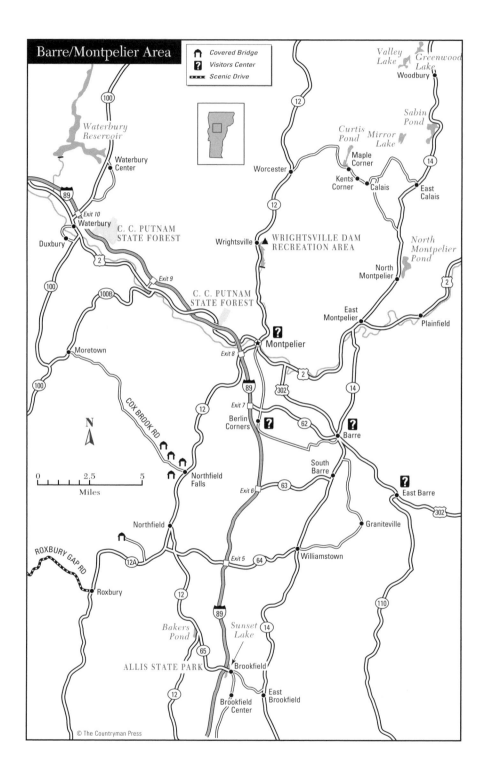

Barre/Montpelier Area

⌂	Covered Bridge
❓	Visitors Center
▪▪▪▪	Scenic Drive

Waterbury Reservoir

Valley Lake

Greenwood Lake

Woodbury

100

Waterbury Center

12

Sabin Pond

14

Curtis Pond

Mirror Lake

Worcester

Maple Corner

89

Exit 10
Waterbury

C. C. PUTNAM STATE FOREST

Kents Corner

Calais

East Calais

Duxbury

2

12

Wrightsville

▲ WRIGHTSVILLE DAM RECREATION AREA

North Montpelier Pond

100

Exit 9

100B

C. C. PUTNAM STATE FOREST

North Montpelier

2

East Montpelier

Plainfield

Moretown

❓ Montpelier

Exit 8

2

100

COX BROOK RD

89

302

14

N

12

Exit 7

Berlin Corners

❓

62

❓ Barre

0   2.5   5
Miles

⌂⌂⌂
⌂ Northfield Falls

Exit 6

63

South Barre

Graniteville

❓ East Barre

302

Northfield

⌂

Williamstown

ROXBURY GAP RD

12A

Exit 5

64

110

Roxbury

12

89

Bakers Pond

Sunset Lake

14

65

ALLIS STATE PARK

Brookfield

East Brookfield

12

89

Brookfield Center

In downtown **Barre** the Old Pinsly Depot, just off Main St., is now a combination welcome center and showcase for the evolving Granite Museum (802-476-4605; www.granitemuseum.com). Open Mon.–Fri. 8:30–4:30, most Saturdays 10–1. It offers restrooms, area information, and changing exhibits.

Central Vermont Chamber of Commerce (1-877-887-3678; www.central-vt .com) publishes a helpful booklet guide to the area and keeps track of vacancies in member inns during foliage season. Its walk-in info center is at 33 Stewart Rd., Berlin Corners. (Off I-89, Exit 7, take your first left; it's 0.5 mile on your left at the first four corners.) Open weekdays 9–5.

GETTING THERE *By bus:* **Vermont Transit** (802-229-9220; 1-800-451-3292) from Boston to Montreal, connecting with New York and Connecticut service, stops in Montpelier at a disgraceful trailer at 1 Taylor St., off State St.

By train: **Amtrak** (1-800-USA-RAIL; www.amtrak.com) stops in Montpelier Junction, a mile west of town on the other side of I-89.

By car: For **Montpelier** take I-89, Exit 8. At the second traffic light, make a left, crossing the river on Bailey Ave. At the light, turn right onto State St. The redbrick building that houses the information center is on your right, a good place to park. The capitol and Vermont Historical Society are a short way up across the street.

To reach **Barre** take I-89 to Exit 7 and follow signs for Rt. 62, a divided highway, to Main St.

WHEN TO GO This is a rare corner of Vermont that varies little from season to season. Come Jan.–Apr. to see the Vermont Legislature in action.

MEDICAL EMERGENCY Emergency service is available by calling **911**.

Central Vermont Medical Center (802-371-4100; www.cvmc.hitchcock.org) is in Berlin off Rt. 62; Exit 7 off I-89.

✳ Towns

Montpelier. The smallest and possibly the most livable of the nation's state capitals, Montpelier is a town of fewer than 9,000 people, with band concerts on summer Wednesdays, high school playing fields just a few blocks from the capitol. The gold dome of the State House itself is appropriately crowned by a green hill rising steeply behind it. A path leads right up that hill into **Hubbard Park**, 185 leafy acres with winding roads, good for biking and jogging. Stone Cutters Way down along the Winooski River is

IN MONTPELIER

Kim Grant

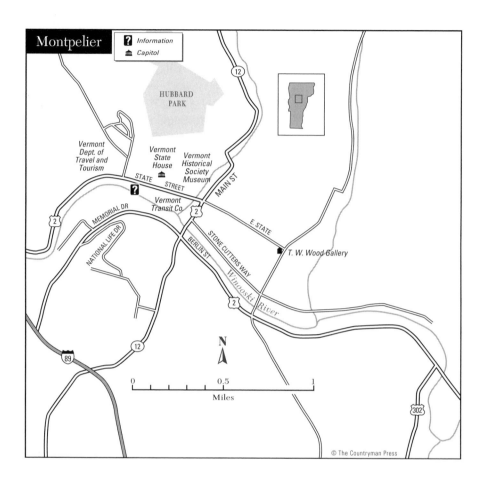

also a pleasant bike or jog. The State House, the Vermont Historical Society Museum, and the T. W. Wood Art Gallery are all must-see sights. Montpelier, moreover, is home base for the **New England Culinary Institute (NECI)**, currently enrolling some 600 students and staffing three of the town's outstanding restaurants.

Precisely why this narrow floodplain of the Winooski was selected as Vermont's statehouse site in 1805 is uncertain, as is why it was named for a small city in the Languedoc region of France. The fact is, however, that Vermont's first legislators picked a town noted for its unusual number of whiskey distilleries and named it for a town best known for its wine and brandy. It's also true that Montpelier is unusually accessible, by roads both old and new, from every corner of central and northern Vermont.

Barre. This is a city of 9,200 people, surrounded by a town of 7,600. Motorists caught in Main Street's perpetual traffic may ponder the facades of the commercial buildings. Most date from 1880–1910, during which the community's population jumped from 2,000 to 12,000, swollen by stonecutters and craftsmen from Scotland, Eastern Europe, Italy, and French Canada, not to mention England,

Scandinavia, Spain, Germany, and the Middle East. This volatile mix of largely underpaid workers who elected a socialist mayor were not afraid to strike for their rights or to shelter victims of strikes elsewhere. In the World War I era, many famous anarchists and socialists spoke here. The **Old Labor Hall** (vintage 1900) at 46 Granite St. (off N. Main), the focal point of this struggle, has been restored and can be rented or toured (phone: 802-476-0567 or 802-476-8777). The quarries continue to employ some 2,000 people to produce one-third of the country's memorial stones—for which **Hope Cemetery** and **Elmwood Cemetery** serve as museums of stonecarving virtuosity. A formal **Vermont Granite Museum** (www.granitemuseum.com) is taking shape in a former granite shed on the Barre–Montpelier Rd.; in the meantime there are exhibits to see in the downtown visitors center in the former depot.

The quarries themselves are southeast of town, primarily in Graniteville, where Millstone Hill has been chipped and chiseled since 1812, when the bedrock was turned into millstones, door stoops, and posts. In the 1830s huge slabs were hauled by oxen to build the State House, but it was only after the Civil War that the railway and a series of inventions enabled Barre to make its mark. The memorial stone business escalated after 1888, when the branch railroad finally linked the quarries to finishing sheds in the valley and to outlets beyond. All but one of the major quarries are now owned by Rock of Ages. This company has long made its operations a showcase for visitors, who can view the unforgettable, surrealistic landscape of the quarries themselves, hear the roar of the drills, and watch ant-sized men chip away at the giant pits.

Northfield (population: 5,791). This town's mid-19th-century commercial blocks suggest the prosperity that it enjoyed while native son Charles Paine served as governor. Paine actually railroaded the Vermont Central through his hometown instead of the more logical Barre. The old depot, now a bank, stands at one end of the handsome common. Today the town's pride is Norwich University, a private, coed college of 1,000 cadets, which bills itself as "the oldest private military college in the United States." In the Norwich University Museum in White Memorial Chapel, you learn that this institution sent more than 300 officers into the Civil War. It wasn't until 1867, however, that the college moved to Northfield from its original site in Norwich. More Northfield memorabilia as well as changing exhibits can be seen in the **Northfield Historical Society Museum** housed at 75 S. Main St. (open Sun. and Wed. 1–4, or by appointment, 802-485-6228 or 802-485-3110). Northfield also boasts six covered bridges, five of which are in publicly accessible areas.

✳ To See

In Montpelier
✍ ♿**The Vermont Historical Society Museum** (802-828-2291; www.vermont history.org), 109 State St., Montpelier. Open year-round, Tue.–Sat. 10–4; Sundays from May through October only, noon–4; closed Mon. $5 adults, $3 ages 6–17, students with ID cards, and seniors. This outstanding state museum, maintained by the Vermont Historical Society on the ground floor of the replica of the

Christina Tree

THE VERMONT HISTORICAL SOCIETY
MUSEUM IN MONTPELIER

Pavilion Hotel (which occupied this site between 1870 and 1966), has recently reopened after a total renovation. Freedom & Unity: One Ideal Many Stories, the new permanent exhibition, tells the story of Vermonters from the year 1600 to the present time. ("Freedom in Unity" is the state motto.) Beginning with Vermont's geological history, it then dramatizes Abenaki Indian life; draws visitors into Bennington's Catamount Tavern to explore the state's beginnings; and explores life in the 19th century through interactive exhibits and re-created buildings: a general store, creamery, marble shed, train station, and more. The story includes tourism (1900–1940s), World War II, the changing landscapes of the late 19th century, and a "hall of voices."

Camp Meade Victory Museum (802-223-5537; 802-476-7903; www.camp meade.com). Take Exit 9 off I-89 and follow the signs to Rt. 2 east. The museum is about 0.25 mile ahead on your right. Open Labor Day–Memorial Day and

Vermont State House (802-828-2228), State St., Montpelier. Open Mon.–Fri. 8–4, closed holidays. Friends of the Vermont State House offers free guided tours each half hour, Mon.–Fri. 10–3:30, Sat. 11–2:30, July–mid-Oct.; otherwise Mon.–Fri. 9–3. Groups should call in advance (802-828-1411). Visitors are welcome to watch the legislature in action, Jan.–mid-Apr.

Vermont's government was homeless from its founding in 1777 until 1805, when Montpelier was chosen as the "permanent seat of the legislature for holding all their sessions," on the condition that the town muster the land and get the capitol erected by 1808. The resulting three-story building was nine sided, with a single cupola, and warmed by a two-story stove. Legislators sat on plank seats at pine desks that were said to have been "whittled out of use" by the representatives' jackknives. The whole building had to be demolished in 1836 and was replaced by a granite Grecian temple designed by the Federal-era architect Ammi Young. After it was virtually destroyed by fire, it was rebuilt along the same but larger lines and completed in 1857.

While several chambers are quite opulent, there is noticeable informality in the way the 150 state representatives and senators talk with their constituents while standing in the Hall of Flags or seated on the black walnut

during foliage season, daily 9–4; closed Sun. and Mon. Free. This privately owned museum revisits the home front during the Great Depression and World War II in a former Civilian Conservation Corps camp. Vintage military vehicles are sprinkled over the grounds, including a 1944 Jeep, an F-86 bomber from the Korean War, and a Stuart tank. After watching a short film, visitors peruse several halls of 1930s and '40s Americana, listening to FDR's radio speeches and absorbing American life as it was during the war. There are wax replicas of Generals Eisenhower and MacArthur, painted panoramas of the Dust Bowl, and an intriguing collection of Japanese and swastika-covered mementos that the Gosselin family has amassed for over 20 years. The cabins become a motel in the summer (see *Lodging*), and breakfast and dinner are served at the on-site diner.

USS *Montpelier* Museum (802-223-9502; www.montpelier-vt.org), city hall, at 39 Main St. Tucked upstairs in a few back rooms of the city hall is this unexpected display of ship models, uniforms, medals, and diaries documenting the life of Admiral George Dewey, a native son who inspired the christening of at least three U.S. Navy ships after his hometown, the most recent a 1993 nuclear attack submarine. Open weekdays when city hall is, 8–4:30. Free.

T. W. Wood Art Gallery and Arts Center (802-828-8743; www.twwoodgallery .org) at Vermont College of Union Institute and University, 36 College St. (corner of E. State St.), Montpelier, open Tue.–Sun. noon–4. The gallery displays 19th-century art and mounts excellent shows featuring contemporary Vermont artists and craftspeople. Free.

sofas (which cost $60 apiece in 1859) at either end. The statue of Ethan Allen on the steps is Danby marble, and the handsome black-and-white floor of the lobby was quarried on Isle La Motte. The lobby is lined with portraits of Vermont-born heroes including Admiral George Dewey, Admiral Charles Clark (like Dewey, a hero of the Spanish-American War), and Calvin Coolidge, 30th president of the United States. Note especially the enormous oil painting by Julian Scott, *The Battle of Cedar Creek, 1864.* The cannon on the front steps was captured from the Hessians at the battle of Bennington in 1777. The Roman lady atop the gold-leafed dome is Ceres, goddess of agriculture.

Kim Grant

THE GOLD DOME OF THE VERMONT STATE HOUSE

Kellogg-Hubbard Library (802-223-3338; www.kellogghubbard.lib.vt.us), 135 Main St., Montpelier. Open weekdays 10–8, Fri. and Sat. till 5:30 (earlier in summer). This lovely Italianate structure is worth a visit for the architecture alone. Built in 1895 of rough granite blocks, it is as palatial inside as out. Behind its two-story columned entrance you'll find a second-floor balcony, ornate fireplaces, a fine oak-and-marble staircase, classical friezes, and a central skylight that fills the hall with light. A 1927 flood destroyed much of the original book collection, and a second in 1992 left structural damage, but a comprehensive makeover in 2001 has restored much of the building's original beauty. Ironically, this prominent landmark very nearly wasn't. Wealthy New York City real estate tycoon Martin Kellogg and his wife, Montpelier native Fanny Hubbard, each died in 1889, leaving their estate to the town for the construction of cemetery gates and a public library. But John E. Hubbard, Fanny's nephew, contested the will. The probate court ruled in his favor, and the town countersued in a battle that lasted three years and left Montpelier split in two. At the end of his wits, Hubbard offered a truce: He would build the promised library if the town would drop the dispute. He paid dearly in the end, as the structure finally cost him $30,000 more than the amount set aside in the will.

Ϡ **Hall of Fumes** (802-223-5141). One of Montpelier's more unusual distinctions is its annual International Rotten Sneaker Contest. The winning 21 (and counting) shoes are preserved at the Montpelier Recreation Department's 58 Barre St. headquarters inside a glass case, where they can be admired weekdays 9–4.

In Barre

Ϡ **Rock of Ages Visitors Center** (802-476-3119; www.rockofages.com), 560 Main St., Graniteville. The easiest way to get there, even from Montpelier, is via I-89, Exit 6, to Rt. 63. At the light go straight and follow signs. From the observation deck of the Manufacturing Division, you'll see the granite being polished and sculpted by master sculptors. The adjacent new visitors center is open May–Oct., Mon.–Sat. 8:30–5 and Sun. 10–5 (closed July 4), with many displays and interactive exhibits. June–mid-Oct. there's also a narrated shuttle tour to a working, 50-acre, 600-foot-deep quarry farther up the hill. Tours last 35 minutes, the first starting at 9:15, the last at 3:35. $4 adults, $3.50 ages 62 and over, $1.50 ages 6–12.

ROCK OF AGES QUARRY IN BARRE

Joe Citro

Vermont History Center (802-479-8500; www.vermonthistory.org), 60 Washington St., Barre. Open Mon.–Fri., 8–4:30 (closed state holidays). Housed in the splendid Spaulding School, designed in 1891 by Lambert Packard—the architect of St. Johnsbury's Fairbanks Museum—the Vermont Historical Society headquarters includes a gallery with changing exhibits.

Hope Cemetery, Rt. 14 just north of downtown Barre. If you're coming in off I-89 on Rt. 62, continue straight ahead up Maple St. (Rt. 14); if on N. Main St. (Rt. 302), turn up Maple. The impressive main gates are a ways up on your left; you can drive in. The 6,000 memorials here range from classic tableaux (a replica of Michelangelo's *Pietà*) to the more whimsical, including an armchair, a Civil Air Patrol plane, a half-scale racing car, a tractor-trailer truck, a perfectly executed cube resting on one corner, and a married couple in bed, holding hands. All were sculpted by stonecutters for themselves and their families, and they rank among the most elaborate to be found anywhere in the world. **Elmwood Cemetery**, at the opposite end of downtown (Rt. 302 turns into Washington St. as it heads east; take Hill St. at the first Y and it's right there), also has many striking memorials. Tours of Barre cemeteries can be arranged through the Old Labor Hall (802-476-0567).

COVERED BRIDGES

In Northfield
Off Rt. 12 in Northfield Falls (turn at the general store) stand three covered bridges: the **Station Bridge**, spanning 100 feet, and the **Newell Bridge** are within sight of each other; farther along Cox Brook Rd. is the **Upper Bridge**, with a span of 42 feet. Another bridge is just south off Rt. 12 on Slaughter House Rd.

SCENIC DRIVES **Roxbury to Warren**. The road through Roxbury Gap, while not recommended in winter, is spectacular in summer and fall, commanding a breathtaking view of the Green Mountains from the crest of the Roxbury Range. Do not resist the urge to stop, get out, and enjoy this panorama. Ask locally about the hiking trail that follows the ridgeline from the road's highest point.

Northfield to Moretown. Cox Brook Rd. (marked on our map) connects Northfield Falls with the village of Moretown. It's dirt part of the way, offering views in both directions near the crest and passing through three covered bridges at the Northfield Falls end. In Northfield, Turkey Hill Rd. begins across from Depot Square and climbs up to panoramic views.

✳ To Do

BIKING Check out the Central Vermont Chamber of Commerce web site (www .central-vt.com) for suggested routes through this area. **Onion River Sports** (802-229-9409; www.onionriver.com), 20 Langdon St., Montpelier, is the source of local bike maps and rentals (mountain bikes and hybrids).

A superb biking destination is the **Millstone Hill Bike Touring Center** at 422 Websterville Rd. in East Barre (802-479-1000; www.millstonehill.com), whose trails wind up and around one of the most granite- and quarry-rich areas of the state. Open 9–5 daily through Oct. Bike rentals and repair. You can also download free trail maps at the **Vermont Mountain Biking Association** web site (www.vmba.org), or the Central Vermont Chamber of Commerce: www.central -vt.com/visit/biketour/index.html.

BOATING AND FISHING Wrightsville Dam, just north of Montpelier; **North Montpelier Pond**, with a fishing access off Rt. 14; and **Curtis Pond** and **Mirror Lake** in Calais (pronounced *CAL-lus*). **Nelson Pond** and **Sabin Pond** in Woodbury are both accessible from Rt. 14, as are **Valley Lake** and **Greenwood Lake** (good for bass and pike). The **Stevens Branch** south of Barre and the Dog River in Northfield offer brook trout.

✔ **East Roxbury Fish Hatchery**, 2 miles south of Roxbury on Rt. 12A. This is a state hatchery in which salmon species are raised; children are allowed to feed the fish.

Brookies Guide Service (802-456-1399; www.vermontbrookies.com), 782 Number Ten Pond Rd., East Calais. George and Karen Clifford offer full- and half-day guided fly-fishing trips for every skill level, with meals, rentals, and instruction.

R&L Archery (802-479-9151; 1-800-269-9151; www.randlarchery.com), 70 Smith St., Barre. A well-stocked outfitter of fishing, bird-watching, archery, kayak, even gold prospecting gear that also issues hunting and fishing licenses. Open weekdays 10–8, Sat. 10–5, Sun. 11–4.

GOLF Montpelier Elks Country Club (802-223-7457), 1 Country Club Rd., Montpelier, nine holes. **Barre Country Club** (802-476-7658), 142 Drake Rd., Plainfield, 18 holes. **Northfield Country Club** (802-485-4515), 2066 Roxbury Rd., Northfield, nine holes.

HIKING/WALKING *Guidance:* **The Green Mountain Club** (802-244-7037; www.greenmountainclub.org), RR 1, Box 650, Rt. 100, Waterbury Center 05677. Encourages general inquiries and trail description updates (see *Hiking and Walking* in "What's Where").

Spruce Mountain, Plainfield. An unusually undeveloped state holding of 500 acres, rich in bird life. The trail begins in Jones State Forest, 4.2 miles south of the village; the 3-hour hike is described in *50 Hikes in Vermont* (The Countryman Press) and in *Day Hiker's Guide to Vermont* (Green Mountain Club).

Worcester Range, north of Montpelier. There are several popular hikes described in the books listed under Spruce Mountain (above), notably **Elmore Mountain** in Elmore State Park (a 3-mile trek yielding a panorama of lakes, farms, and rolling hills), **Mount Worcester** (approached from the village of Worcester), and **Mount Hunger**.

Groton State Forest, east of Montpelier. This 25,000-acre forest offers an extensive year-round trail system. See "St. Johnsbury, Craftsbury, and Burke Mountain."

Hubbard Park and **North Branch River Park** in Montpelier are both accessible from the Vermont Institute of Natural Science (VINS) North Branch Nature Center (802-229-6206; www.vinsweb.org), 713 Elm St. (Rt. 12 north). Hubbard Park, also accessible from the State House, is 200 acres webbed with trails and a stone observation tower; North Branch offers gentle trails along this fork of the Winooski as well as more challenging, higher-altitude trails. Both parks are used for cross-country skiing and snowshoeing. The nature center offers a year-round program of birding and other events.

HORSEBACK RIDING T-N-T Stables (802-476-3097; www.central-vt.com/web/tnt), 75 Pine Hill Rd., Barre. Tina and Tiffany Poulin offer hour-long trail rides, pony rides, and instruction for those 8 years and over. Helmets provided. Open weekdays 4:30–7, weekends 8–7 or until dark.

Pease Farm Stables (802-223-4828), 307 Culver Hill, Middlesex, 6 miles north of Montpelier, conducts riding lessons, summer day camps, and training on 200 rolling acres.

SWIMMING Wrightsville Dam Recreation Area, Rt. 12 north; also numerous swimming holes in the Kents Corner area.

CROSS-COUNTRY SKIING Morse Farm Ski Touring Center (802-223-2740; 1-800-242-2740; www.morsefarm.com), 1168 County Rd., Montpelier (3 miles north of downtown). Open 9–5 daily, 8:30–5 weekends and holidays. At an elevation of 1,200 feet, the farm offers a series of loops ranging from 0.7 to 3.9 km—over 15 km of trails in all. Rentals (on weekends and holidays), lessons, and a warming hut with snacks, soups, and hot drinks by the woodstove. Separate snowshoe trails. $10 adults, $8 ages 7–12 and seniors, $5 snowshoers.

Onion River Sports (802-229-9409; www.onionriver.com), 20 Langdon St., Montpelier, rents cross-country skis and snowshoes. Open daily, year-round, 9:30–6.

Millstone Hill (802-479-1000; www.millstonehill.com), 422 Websterville Rd., East Barre, has trails that weave around some 30 old quarries, many with spectacular long-distance views of the surrounding mountains. Stop for trail maps at the Bike Touring Center on the ground floor of the red barn, open 9–5 daily.

ICE SKATING The Central Vermont Civic Center (802-229-5900) at 268 Gallison Hill Rd. in Montpelier, open to the public Sat. 1:30–2:45 and Sun. 4–5:15.

Barre City B.O.R. Rink (802-476-0258; www.ci.barre.vt.us), 25 Auditorium Hill, Barre, open for public skating mid-Oct.–mid-Mar.

Note: For more on winter sports, see "Sugarbush/Mad River Valley."

✳ Lodging

In Montpelier 05602

⊙ 🥄 **The Inn at Montpelier** (802-223-2727; www.innatmontpelier.com), 147 Main St. Two of the town's most stately (adjacent) Federal-style manses, renovated and furnished with antiques, Oriental carpets, and fine linens. Both belonged to James Langdon, a prominent local businessman. A marvelous Greek Revival porch, added around 1900, wraps around the yellow-clapboard Lamb-Langdon house, its wicker chairs a perfect place to rest after an afternoon stroll. Of the 19 rooms, the 7 deluxe chambers (all but 1 with wood-burning fireplace) are the most handsome in town. Number 27 has a huge private deck; the smaller king-, queen-, and twin-bedded rooms are also lovely. Each comes with private bath and a breakfast of homemade cereals and jams, lemon curd, fresh-baked breads, and coffee or tea. Amenities include central air-conditioning, downstairs guest pantries for coffee and tea at any hour, in-room cable TV, phone, a sunroom on the second floor, and a beautifully appointed parlor and living room with period furnishings. Innkeepers Rita and Rick Rizza have hosted the likes of Laura Bush and Martha Stewart. $120–202. Children under 6, free.

Capitol Plaza (802-223-5252; 1-800-274-5252; www.capitolplaza.com), 100 State St. The former landmark tavern, a four-story downtown hotel with room service, a two-tiered café, and **J. Morgans**, a steak house featuring Sunday brunch, jazz nights, and weekend entertainment as well as conference and reception facilities. The 56 rooms vary from the standard two double and queen beds with comforters to individually decorated "colonial guest rooms" with bathrobes, eyelet sheets, and Ralph Lauren linens. There are three suites with jet tub, sofa, and refrigerator, and the Executive Suite opens into a large optional living room. All have air-conditioning, cable TV, and modem jack. From $104 for a standard double to $174 for a suite (higher in foliage season).

✂ **Betsy's Bed & Breakfast** (802-229-0466; www.betsysbnb.com), 74 E. State St. Betsy and Jon Anderson are warm, helpful hosts who offer 12 attractive rooms and suites in adjacent Queen Anne and Victorian houses and a carriage house in a quiet hillside neighborhood, a short walk from Vermont College and the middle of town. Rooms have private bath, cable TV, air-conditioning, and phone (with voice mail and dataports); eight rooms share full kitchen. $70–100 in low sea-

son, $80–110 in high ($10 more in foliage season), includes a generous breakfast. Discounts for 3 nights or more.

Comfort Inn at Maplewood (802-229-2222; 1-800-228-5150), RR 4, Box 2110 (take Exit 7 off I-89 for 0.2 mile). This handsome and relatively new two-story, 89-room motor inn has 18 two-room suites with kitchenette, and a VIP suite with kitchenette and whirlpool. Rates from $90 double, $130 for suites in summer (more during foliage season), with continental breakfast.

Beyond

🗑 ✂ **Maplecroft Bed & Breakfast** (802-476-0760; www.maplecroft vermont.com), 70 Washington St., Barre 05641. Convenient for anyone researching Vermont history or genealogy next door at the new Vermont History Center (originally a rather grand high school), this striking Victorian house is on Rt. 302 just above downtown and the small city park. Built by a granite sculptor in 1887, it is now home to local librarians Paul Heler, who also happens to be a magician, and Marianne Kotch. They offer four guest rooms, all with private bath and with beds featuring quilts made by Marianne (quilters, librarians, and magicians get a 10 percent discount). Needless to say there are plenty of good books around, as well as comfortable seating to read in the living room with its gas fireplace. $80 includes a continental breakfast with homemade jams and scones or popovers.

⊗ 🗑 ✂ **The Lodge at Millstone Hill** (802-479-1000; www.millstone hill.com), 59 Little John Rd., Websterville 05678. About 4 miles east of downtown Barre, this intriguing contemporary lodge is built inside a barn that was moved here from Warren. The interior is an architectural epiphany of open lofts, barnboard walls, exposed beams, and breathtaking views. The 5 guest rooms (3 with private bath, one with king-sized bed, two 2-room suites) include the delightful William Barkley Suite with its loftlike sitting room, granite-backed shower, and queen-sized bed, where you awaken to mountain views. Breakfast is served family-style at an oak table on plates bearing hunting themes. The common areas consist of multilevel living rooms and a secluded game room, all with Oriental carpets, mounted trophies, and leather armchairs. The whole house, which sleeps 10, can be rented for special events. Innkeeper Pierre Couture, who grew up right next door, is a walking encyclopedia when it comes to the 70 historic granite quarries that stretch from the one a few yards away to Lookout Hill a mile or so up above; about half of them dot the trails of the year-round recreation area he has developed nearby. $95–150 includes breakfast.

⊘ ✿ The Comstock House

(802-272-2693; 802-479-9898; www .comstockhousebb.com), 1620 Middle Rd., Plainfield 05667. A beautifully restored 1891 home on 175 acres with large-windowed, immaculate rooms, utter quiet, and spectacular mountain views on a dirt road 2 miles southwest of Plainfield. Innkeepers Warren Hathaway, a social worker, and journalist Ross Sneyd offer two comfortable rooms, one on the ground floor and a two-room suite upstairs, both with queen-sized bed, private bath, and radiant-heat flooring that visitors can adjust to keep toes warm. The

upstairs room has a gas fireplace and wide-pine floors and connects to a second room with a king or two single beds, ideal for groups or families (children 12 and over). There is an antiques-filled parlor where guests can mingle, and the dining room table overlooks a mountain panorama (and sunsets). Afternoon tea, full homemade breakfasts, outdoor patio in warmer months. No pets. $75–155.

⊘ ✿ ✿ The Northfield Inn (802-485-8558; www.thenorthfieldinn .com), 228 Highland Ave., Northfield 05663. Aglaia Stalb has renovated a grand old 1901 hillside mansion, nicely landscaped with a gazebo overlooking the town. Aglaia is a motherly, hospitable host who makes sure her guests are well fed and well oriented to her handsome town and its scenic surroundings (which include five covered bridges). There are 12 big, old-fashioned guest rooms, 9 with private bath (several combine into family suites), furnished with antiques, brass or carved-wood beds, and European feather bedding. It's delightfully easy to get lost in this rambling old house with its scattered common spaces, including a library, parlor, game room, and comfy third-floor TV room. $110–179, including a three-course breakfast, snacks throughout the day, and an evening nightcap. Well-behaved children welcome.

✿ ✿ ✿ ✿ The Autumn Harvest Inn & Restaurant (802-433-1355; www .autumnharvestinn.com), Clark Rd., Williamstown 05679, Rt. 64 east from Exit 5 off I-89. This century-old hilltop farm has splendid views and 46 acres with grazing horses; in winter trails are used by cross-country skiers and snowmobilers (they connect to VAST trails). Carolyn White offers 18

simple but bright and cheerful guest rooms with private bath and TV, including one that's handicapped equipped and two semi-suites, one with a fireplace. There's a big fireplace in the living room, and two dining rooms are open to the public (see *Dining Out*). Guests enjoy the swimming pond, two night-lit tennis courts, and sleigh rides. $99–159 in summer, $79–139 in winter (breakfast not included).

Marshfield Inn & Motel (802-426-3383; www.marshfieldinn.com), 5630 Rt. 2, Marshfield. Diana Batzel and Tracey Hambleton's big Victorian, flat-roofed farmhouse is set back and above Rt. 2 and forms the centerpiece of this friendly complex. Lodging is in the 10 neighboring motel units with queen or two double beds. A nominally priced breakfast (there's a full menu) is served in the main house 8–9 AM. Halfway between Montpelier and St. Johnsbury, it's a good hub from which to explore in many directions, and there's a riverside path through the extensive property. $65 double in summer, $90 in foliage season. Pets are welcome for an extra $10 per night.

Hollister Hill Farm B&B (802-454-7725; www.hollisterhillfarm.com), 2193 Hollister Hill Rd., Marshfield 05658. Technically in Marshfield but less than 2 miles uphill from Plainfield Village, this is a splendid 1825 farmhouse set in 204 acres with three guest rooms, all with private bath. Bob and Lee Light fled New Jersey for Vermont in 1972 and milked cows for 25 years, eventually replacing them with beefalo, pigs, chickens, and turkeys, all of which they sell from the farm store in the barn, along with honey from their

hives and their own maple syrup. One guest room has a red cedar sauna; the other two have fireplace (one can be a family suite by adding an adjoining room). In winter guests are invited to bring cross-country skis, and they will find snowshoes here; VAST trails also run through the property. $90–110 ($150–165 for the family suite) includes a full, homegrown and -hatched as well as homemade breakfast. Pets by prior arrangement.

Pie-in-the-Sky Farm Bed & Breakfast and Retreat (802-426-3777; www.pieinsky.com), Dwinell Rd., Marshfield 05658. This rambling Civil War–era farmhouse was home for a time to the Pie-in-Sky commune; it's since been a dairy farm and home for Jay Moore, Judy Sargent, and their two cats for many years. Three upstairs rooms can be rented as a suite, with or without living room and kitchen facilities, or as individual double and single rooms. There's common space, a guest kitchen with fridge and snacks, a sunroom with a large tiled hot tub, and 120 acres with a beaver pond and a barn (the cows are gone, and guest horses are welcome), as well as access to VAST trails on the property. Groton State Forest with hiking trails and swimming is nearby. From $85 (for a double) to $150 (for the full six-room apartment). Pets by prior arrangement.

Country Cottage B&B (802-426-3655), 3314 Rt. 232, Marshfield 05658. Dan and Judy Lloyd, who used to run the Creamery Inn in Cabot, now own and operate this establishment in Marshfield near Groton State Forest. They have two guest rooms with private bath. Children are welcome, but no pets, please. $75–85 includes full breakfast.

🌹 ♪ **Camp Meade** (802-223-5537; 802-476-7903; www.campmeade .com). The 20 vintage tourist cottages encircling this museum (see *To See*) are each named for a famous U.S. general. All have 1950s-style metal furniture, full bed (some have two), shower, cable TV, phone, heat, and air-conditioning; the family cabin ($83) has two rooms, one with a double bed, the other with two twins. Rates run $63–73, including continental breakfast, $5 more in foliage season. Full breakfast and dinner in the on-site diner, and guests get free run of the museum. The staff change the linens in a 1944 Jeep ambulance. Open Memorial Day weekend–late Oct.

✳ Where to Eat

DINING OUT **Chef's Table** (802-229-9202), 118 Main St., Montpelier. Open Mon.–Fri. for lunch, Sat. for dinner only. Reservations requested for dinner. This is the Montpelier-based New England Culinary Institute's upscale restaurant. Lunch on duck confit with handmade fettuccine, or a warm blue crab leek tartlet. The dinner menu might include starters like pistachio-dusted pork porterhouse and lemon thyme braised osso buco. Entrées $17–23.

🌹 **Sarducci's** (802-223-0229), 3 Main St., Montpelier. Open for lunch and dinner Mon.–Sat., 11:30 AM–midnight; Sun. 4:30–midnight. This spacious, yellow-walled restaurant with an open wood-fired oven is extremely popular, and because it takes no reservations, on weekends there's a line out the door. Come early and leave your name on the list, then stroll the downtown. Even if they've passed you on the list, you'll get the next free table. Many daily specials, plus antipasti,

customized pizzas, salads, and 18 pasta choices, such as shrimp with angelhair, tomatoes, and garlic. At dinner try the saltimbocca (sautéed veal with prosciutto and fresh sage in a portobello mushroom sauce, served with risotto). Entrées are surprisingly reasonable, given the quality and atmosphere: $10.95–15.95.

Conoscenti (802-262-3500), 52 State St., Montpelier. Open Mon.–Thu. 5–10, Fri. and Sat. until 11. Billed as creative cosmopolitan cuisine with Italian roots, chef-owner Dale Conoscenti's trendy trattoria features gleaming wood, white tablecloths, and family portraits on the walls. Everything is made from scratch (even the ice cream), and while the menu changes frequently, it might include hand-rolled gnocchi, timballo (Italian potpie), and lobster ravioli with layers of wilted spinach, lobster, squash puree, and a drizzle of truffle oil. Entrées $13.95 (for spaghetti and meatballs) to $22.95 for grilled Black Angus rib eye.

The Autumn Harvest Inn & Restaurant (802-433-1355; www .autumnharvestinn.com), Rt. 64, Clark Rd., Williamstown. Open Wed.–Sat. The superb views from the main dining room and wraparound porch complement the cuisine. You might begin with shrimp cocktail or crabcakes with honey mustard sauce, and follow with veal Marsala or chicken Parmesan. $10.95–18.

Sean and Nora's (802-476-7326; www.seanandnoras.com), 276 N. Main St., Barre. Mon.–Sat. 11:30–9, Fri. and Sat. till 10, and Sun. 4–8:30. This newcomer to Barre is about "food from America's neighborhoods," which includes staples like turkey, house-smoked Memphis ribs, North

End three-cheese manicotti, and mostaciolli with meatballs, but there's also filet mignon. In summer months you can dine outside on the patio. Dinner entrées $10.95–20.95.

Also see Ariel's Restaurant in Brookfield in "The White River Valleys."

EATING OUT

In Montpelier
The Main Street Bar and Grill (802-223-3188), 118 Main St. Open for breakfast, lunch, and dinner daily, as well as Sunday brunch. Montpelier-based New England Culinary Institute's signature eatery, a multilevel restaurant and pub with seasonal outdoor seating and a viewing window into the kitchen. Lunch on poached pear and Stilton salad with ginger bisque, or sausage and mussel stew. At dinner begin with a warm beef short rib terrine, and then choose between New England leg of venison and pan-seared rainbow trout. Entrées average $14.

The Black Door (802-223-7070; www.blackdoorvt.com), 44 Main St. Bar opens daily at 4, kitchen at 5. A romantic, dimly lit, upstairs hideaway with brick walls, art deco lamps, and an illuminated stained-glass bar in the space where Julio's got its start in 1981. Owner Phil Gentile, who sold the Mexican eatery in 2001, aims this time for a European feel. Chef David Nielsen serves creative, fresh entrées ($14–17) as well as bistro fare ($9–12) and several desserts. Appetizers might include salmon cakes or venison steamed dumplings with pomegranate soy reduction; for entrées you might have mustard seed crusted salmon or five-spice marinated chicken with a shiitake mushroom sauce and wasabi

mashed potatoes. Live music Thu.–Sat., daily drink specials.

✍ **Julio's** (802-229-9348), 54 State St. Open Mon.–Sat. for lunch and dinner, opening at 4 on Sun. A sophisticated Mexican restaurant that doesn't pretend to be the ultimate in authenticity but fills the bill as a pleasant downtown eatery, good for a grilled eggplant sandwich as well as a taco salad, for a hearty bowl of mussels or goat cheese enchiladas. There's a kids' menu and sidewalk dining, weather permitting. Fully licensed.

🐷 ✍ **Finkerman's Riverside BBQ** (802-229-2295), 186 River St. Open daily except Mon. for lunch and dinner, Sun. 11–9. Behind The Trading Post furniture shop (watch for the BBQ sign). This old barn with a pink pig tacked onto its front might look inauspicious, but inside it's a sunny, spacious, pine-paneled place with riverside seating, ceiling fans, and a cozy, full bar. Towels are used as napkins, and the portions are large; no New England grub here, though. This is southern cooking at its best. Heaps of pulled pork, BBQ meats, sweet potato fries, beef brisket, fresh-baked biscuits, hush puppies, and corn bread, not to mention bourbon pecan pie and weekly specials: Tue. for Mexican, Wed. for chicken potpie, Fri. for Vermont all-natural meat loaf. Entrées $8.50–14.95.

The Mountain Café (802-223-0888), 7 Langdon St. Open Tue.–Sat. for lunch 11–3, Sunday brunch 10–3. Tucked away at the end of Langdon (off Main), this Bohemian-looking café serves surprisingly good food. Don't be discouraged if you have to wait a few minutes in line to place your order. Grab a menu and study the many possibilities. An avocado salad with goat cheese, walnuts, ripe tomatoes, shredded red cabbage, carrots, and beef on greens, served with fabulous bread, was one of the best lunches we have had—a sentiment echoed by folks at the adjoining table who had ordered entirely different things, one a soba noodle dish and the other a fresh salmon panini. The most expensive lunch item is $7.50. Choose from many smoothies and teas.

Thrush Tavern (802-223-2030), 107 State St. Open weekdays for lunch and dinner 11–9, Sat. 4–9. Long a local hangout, this moderately priced spot serves basic, reliable fare in the 1826 brick Federal that was once the home of Silas French, who built the Pavilion Hotel next door (a replica of which is now the Vermont Historical Museum). One of its two rooms has a full bar, and there's outdoor seating in summer months.

La Brioche Bakery & Cafe (802-229-0443), 89 Main St. Open daily except Sun., 7 AM–5 PM. The source of pastries and bread for all New England Culinary Institute Montpelier restaurants. Order at the counter from among a delectable assortment of French-inspired pastries, freshly made salads, and made-to-order sandwiches. Eat in the dining room or on the patio or take out breakfast and sandwiches.

Coffee Corner, corner of Main and State. Open 6:30–3. A lively little chef-owned diner in the thick of things that's been here forever and specializes in fresh produce, fresh-baked bread, cozy booths, and fast, friendly service.

Hunger Mountain Food Co-op (802-223-8000; www.hungermountain .com), 623 Stone Cutters Way. Open

daily 8–8. Hidden away in a corner of this supermarket-style cooperative is an expanded deli with many vegetarian choices and a very attractive glass-sided café area overlooking the river.

Capitol Grounds (802-223-8411), 45 State St. Open Mon.–Thu. 6 AM–7 PM, Fri. and Sat. till 9, Sun. 8–5. An inviting self-service coffeehouse in a former bank, filled with the aroma of roasting brews and comfortable corners in which to sip them. Inquire about jazz, country, and blues nights.

Gesine's Confectionary (802-224-9930; www.gesine.com), 279 Elm St., Montpelier. Open Wed.–Fri. 8–5, Sat. and Sun. 9–4. Closed Mon. and Tue. This gourmet market and confectionary drew crowds at its 2005 opening when word got out that proprietor Gesine Prado's sister, actress Sandra Bullock, was working the counter. Though Bullock soon returned to Hollywood, Prado has stayed on, baking cookies, sticky buns, desserts, and her specialty macaroons for a growing clientele.

On the Barre–Montpelier Rd.
🍴 🍽 **Wayside Restaurant and Bakery** (802-223-6611), Barre–Montpelier Rd. (Rt. 302). Open daily 6:30 AM–9:30 PM. Vermont's ultimate family restaurant, featuring "home cooking away from home." Breakfast on corned beef hash and eggs (with home fries and toast), sausage gravy on a biscuit, or baked oatmeal. Lunch on the soup of the day and maple cream pie; dine on pork liver and bacon or rib-eye steak with fiddlehead ferns. The children's menu is $2.95. Brian and Karen Zecchinelli offer over 200 menu items to choose from plus at least four daily specials at country diner prices, and they're fully licensed.

In Barre

Hilltop House Restaurant (802-479-2129; www.central-vt.com/web/hilltop), Websterville, on Quarry Hill Rd., a mile from the Rock of Ages visitors center. Open daily for lunch and dinner, 11–1:30 and 5–9, Sun. 4:30–8. This classic eatery has been in John Reilly's family for two generations. The Rotary Club and Kiwanis hobnob here, along with almost everyone in town. Salad bar, children's menu, cocktails, and moderately priced fare.

Del's (802-476-6684), 248 N. Main St. Open Mon.–Sat. for lunch and dinner, Sun. from 4 PM. Sited across from the courthouse, this is a justly popular local gathering spot with a colorful decor and a suspiciously wide selection: pastas, Mexican dishes, pizza, subs. No complaints, however, about a great taco salad and fast service at lunch. Patrons vouch for the pasta. Pizza and subs are also available all evening.

All Fired Up (802-476-2036), 9 Depot Square. Just off Main St. Open daily 11–9 (Fri. and Sat. till 10). Not much atmosphere but good pizza, baked in an imported Italian wood oven. Also soups like Tuscan sausage and rice; "sandwich tarts" like sausage, caramelized onion, and mozzarella; and fresh ravioli.

In Plainfield

River Run Restaurant (802-454-1246), Main St. (off Rt. 2). Open Tue.–Sun. 7–2 and 5–9. Mississippi-born Jimmy Kennedy and his wife, Maya, dish up soul food to die for: biscuits and sausage, grits and jalapeños, as well as buttermilk pancakes for breakfast, fried catfish and BBQ ribs, pulled pork and grilled steak salad for lunch, and some BBQ at dinner along with "fancy southern"

items like roast duck, pork tenderloin, and pan-seared shrimp (entrées range $7.50–17.50). They've expanded into a new space with wood-paneled walls, a hodgepodge of wooden tables, and a wooden slab bar serving wine and beer. The menu is written out on blackboards, and there's a lounge area with toys for kids. The place can be packed at breakfast on weekends, so come early.

In Marshfield

Rainbow Sweets (802-426-3531), 1689 Rt. 2. Closed Tue., otherwise open weekdays 9–6, Fri. and Sat. 9–9, Sun. 9–3. Bill Tecosky and Patricia Halloran's colorful café has been a destination in its own right for going on 30 years. Stop by in the morning for empanadas and espresso or lunch a little later on a brioche filled with warm spinach and walnuts; dine on Moroccan-style shredded chicken in phyllo or real pizza. Come anytime for a St. Honore (a profiterole filled with custard, dipped in caramel with cream on puff pastry) or to pick up some butter cookies.

In Northfield

Depot Square Pizzeria (802-485-5500), Depot Square. Open Tue.–Thu. 11:30–8:30, Fri. and Sat. until 11. Sun. hours vary with the season. A pleasant little restaurant with bentwood chairs, flowers on the tables, and a menu that includes reasonably priced Italian specialties as well as pizza.

✳ Entertainment

THEATER Barre Opera House (802-476-8188; www.barreoperahouse.org), corner of Prospect and Main Sts., Barre. Built in 1899, after fire destroyed its predecessor, this elegant, acoustically outstanding, recently restored 650-seat theater occupies the second and third floors of the city hall. The Barre Players, a community theater, perform spring through fall, and this is also a venue for year-round music, dance, and other theater productions.

Lost Nation Theater Company (802-229-0492; www.lostnationtheater .org), Montpelier City Hall Arts Center, 128 Elm St., Montpelier. First-rate productions of contemporary plays, classics, and original works year-round by a professional troupe. The Summer Theater Series features five different shows, June–Oct., 5 nights a week.

Farmer's Night (802-828-2228; www .leg.state.vt.us/schedule/farmersnight .cfm). Free concerts given at the State House Jan.–Apr., when the legislature is in session. The series began in the 19th century for lawmakers who found themselves far from home with little to do in the evening after a day's session. At first the men performed for each other. Over the years the offerings have included everything from lectures to a high-wire act. Today it includes a variety of mostly musical performances.

FILM **The Savoy** (802-229-0598; 802-229-0509 or 1-800-676-0509 for a recording; www.savoytheater.com), 26 Main St., Montpelier, Vermont's premier theater for independent and international art films, with an impressive video shop underneath at **Downstairs Video** (802-223-0050, open Sat. 10–9, Sun.–Fri. noon–9). Two daily showings, occasional speakers, and special events.

The Capitol (802-229-0343), 93 State St., Montpelier, and **The Paramount** (802-479-9621), 241 N. Main

St., Barre, are both classic old movie houses showing first-run feature films.

✳ Selective Shopping

ART STUDIOS AND GALLERIES **The Artisans' Hand** (802-229-9492; www .artisanshand.com), 229 Main St. at City Center, Montpelier. Open Mon.–Sat. 10–6, Fri. until 8, Sun. noon–4. An exceptional variety of quality Vermont craftwork by a cooperative of some 125 artisans in many media.

River Street Potters (802-224-7000). Some 20 individual potters share this 141 River St. studio producing stoneware and porcelain, whimsical and functional.

Green Mountain Hooked Rugs (802-223-1333; www.greenmountain hookedrugs.com), 146 Main St., Montpelier. Open Wed.–Sat. noon–5. Stephanie Ashworth Krauss comes from four generations of rug hookers and sells colorful examples of the craft at this gallery. Inquire about June workshops at the Green Mountain Rug School, the nation's largest.

SPA (Studio Place Arts) (802-479-7069; www.studioplacearts.com), 201 N. Main St., Barre. This art center offering classes for both adults and children maintains the Studio Place Arts Gallery.

Thistle Hill Pottery (802-223-8926; www.thistlehillpottery.com), 95 Powder Horn Glen Rd., in the hills north of Montpelier. Jennifer Boyer sells her handmade functional stone pottery: dinnerware, vases, lamps, and more; bargains, seconds. Her studio is near Morse Farm.

Blackthorn Forge (802-426-3369), 3821 Rt. 2, Marshfield (between Plainfield and Marshfield). Working in a red barn, Steve Bronstein makes functional and sculptural ironwork.

Tait Studio Pottery (802-426-3153; www.taitstudio.com), Marshfield. Open by appointment. Trevor Tait's imaginative and colorful stoneware, sculpture, and stained glass can be viewed at his home studio on Johnson St., just off Rt. 2.

Also see **www.vermontcrafts.com.** This area is particularly rich in studios that open to visitors over the Memorial Day weekend and may or may not be accessible on a regular basis. Worth checking.

BOOKSTORES ✷ **Bear Pond Books** (802-229-0774), 77 Main St., Montpelier. Open Mon.–Thu. 9–6, until 9 on Fri. and Sat., Sun. 10–5. One of the state's best bookstores, heavy on literature, art, and children's books; author readings.

Rivendell Books (802-223-3928), 100 Main St., Montpelier. Open Mon.–Thu. 9–7, Fri. and Sat. till 8, Sun. 10–6. A delightful selection of primarily used but also new books, remainders, and bargain-priced best sellers.

Black Sheep Books (802-225-8906), 4 Langdon St., Montpelier. Open Tue.–Wed. 11–7, Thu.–Sat. 11–9, Sun. 11–6. A surprisingly good selection of scholarly used books run by an all-volunteer collective in a modest shop over the Langdon Street Café.

Barre Books (802-476-3114), 158 N. Main St., Barre. Open until 6, Fri. until 9, an array of general books with a good bargain section.

Capitol Stationers (802-223-2393), 54 Main St., Montpelier, includes new books, with a strong Vermont and New England section.

The Country Bookshop (802-454-0187; www.thecountrybookshop.com),

35 Mill St. (off Rt. 2 at the blinker), Plainfield. Open daily 10–5. Some 30,000 books, plus postcards and paper ephemera; Ben Koenig's specialties include folk music, folklore, and books on bells.

The Northfield Bookstore (802-485-4588), 67 Depot Square, Northfield. Open Tue.–Fri. 9–5:30, Sat. 9–3, Sun. 10–2. "Affable books and knowledgeable service" is the mission statement for this pleasant store stocking primarily used books with some best sellers, also cards, records, a children's section, and comfortable seating. Coffee, too.

FARMS ✷ **Morse Farm Maple Sugarworks** (802-223-2740; 1-800-242-2740; www.morsefarm.com), 1168 County Rd., Montpelier. (Go up Main St., turn right at the roundabout, continue up the hill 2.7 miles). Open year-round, daily except holidays. The farm has been in the same family for seven generations. The store features its own syrup and maple products, including a "maple creemee" cone, and Vermont crafts, a sugarhouse tour with tastings, exhibits, nature trails, and an outdoor Vermont farm life museum. Come watch sugaring off in March. Sugar-on-snow. Also see *Cross-Country Skiing.*

✷ **Bragg Farm Sugarhouse & Gift Shop** (802-223-5757; 1-800-376-5757; www.central-vt.com/web/bragg), Rt. 14 north, East Montpelier. Open daily, 8:30–8 (till 6 after Labor Day). This eighth-generation farm still collects sap the traditional way (in 2,500 buckets) and boils it over wood fires. The shop carries a variety of maple and other Vermont crafts and specialty foods and includes a museum and a maple ice cream parlor.

Grandview Winery (802-456-7012; www.grandviewwinery.com), East Calais. Open daily 11–5, closed Tue. Take Rt. 14 north 4 miles from East Montpelier, turn right onto Max Gray Rd., continue 2.3 miles. The tasting room at the farm is set in gardens amid works by Vermont artists. The wine selection is extensive, from rhubarb, dandelion, and blueberry to French grape blends; hard cider, too. There's also a tasting room at the Cold Hollow Cider Mill on Rt. 100 in Waterbury Center (open daily 11–5).

✔ **Knight's Spider Web Farm** (802-433-5568; www.spiderwebfarm.com), off Rt. 14 at 124 Spider Web Rd., at the south end of Williamstown Village. Open 9–6 daily June 15–Oct. 15, then weekends till Christmas; Jan.–Mar. by appointment. The weirdest farm you ever will see: Artists Will and Terry Knight grow and harvest spiderwebs in their own barn, then mount them onto wood. Will can tell you all about the little critters, and there's a gift store.

SPECIAL SHOPS **Zutano** (802-223-2229; www.zutano.com), 79 Main St., Montpelier. Open Mon.–Sat. 10–6, Sun. noon–4. With offices in nearby Cabot, Manhattan artists Uli and Michael Belenky, who didn't give a thought to baby clothes until their daughter Sophie arrived in 1989, produce a delightful collection of soft, whimsical baby clothes that defy the tired maxim that blue is for boys and pink for girls. Now known nationwide, this is the duo's flagship boutique.

Marshfield Village Store (802-426-3306; www.marshfieldvillagestore .com), 1425 Rt. 2, Marshfield. This classic, pillared, double-porched general store has formed the center of

Marshfield since 1852. It's presently run by three partners still dedicated to the "If we don't have it, you don't need it" credo; also sells Vermont products (will ship) and gives great directions.

Onion River Sports (802-229-9409), 20 Langdon St., Montpelier. An outstanding sporting goods store specializing in camping, cross-country, and biking gear, with cross-country and bike rentals.

ANTIQUES **East Barre Antique Mall** (802-479-5190), 133 Mill St., East Barre. Open daily 10–5. Closed Mon. and the third week in Oct. In the middle of this one-street village sandwiched between Rts. 302 and 110 is this sprawling former furniture store housing central Vermont's largest group shop: some 400 consignees and dealers on three floors with plenty of furniture, glass, and china and a whole room of kitchenware. Former innkeeper Bob Somaini prides himself on the cleanliness as well as the size and depth of the store. He also prides himself on the spread he puts out for customers during his huge Super Bowl Sale (Super Bowl weekend).

Woodbury Mountain Toys (802-223-4272), 24 State St., Montpelier. Open weekdays 10–5:30, Sat. 9–4:30, Sun. 11–4. This independent specialty toy store carries major lines and many locally made and hard-to-find items.

Buch Spieler Music (802-229-0449; www.bsmusic.com), 27 Langdon St., Montpelier. Open Mon.–Thu. 10–6, Fri. until 8, Sat. until 5, Sun. 11–4. An independent music store specializing in cards, novelties, and all kinds of music from around the world, since 1973.

✳ Special Events

Early March: **Rotten Sneaker Contest**, Montpelier Recreation Department (802-223-5141).

April: **Earth Day at the State House** with music, games, displays (802-229-1833).

Memorial Day weekend: **Open Studios weekend** throughout Vermont (www.vermontcrafts.com).

Early June: **Vermont Dairy Celebration**, State House lawn in Montpelier.

Late June: **Annual Vermont Composers Festival**, Montpelier (802-485-3972).

June–August: **Montpelier City Band Concerts**, State House lawn, Wednesdays at 4 PM.

July: **Montpelier's Independence Day Celebration**, sponsored by the Montpelier Downtown Community Association (802-223-9604; www.mdca.org)—pancake breakfast, games, performances, and a giant fireworks display July 3. **Barre Homecoming**

Days (*last weekend*)—music, fireworks, street dance, art exhibit.

Labor Day weekend: In Northfield, a pageant, parade of floats, and Norwich cadets.

September: **Old Time Fiddlers' Contest**, Barre Auditorium, one of New England's oldest contests. The **Barre Granite Festival** (weekend after Labor Day) at the evolving Granite Museum is the scene of rock splitting and cutting, a chicken barbecue, and more.

Early October: **Vermont Apple Celebration**, State House lawn, Montpelier.

Mid-October: **Cabot Apple Pie Festival**, Cabot.

Late October: **Festival of Vermont Crafts**, Montpelier High School (call Central Vermont Chamber of Commerce, 802-229-5711).

November: **Greater Barre Crafts Fair**.

December 31: **First Night** celebrations, Montpelier—music, readings, and performances.

Lake Champlain Valley

Christina Tree

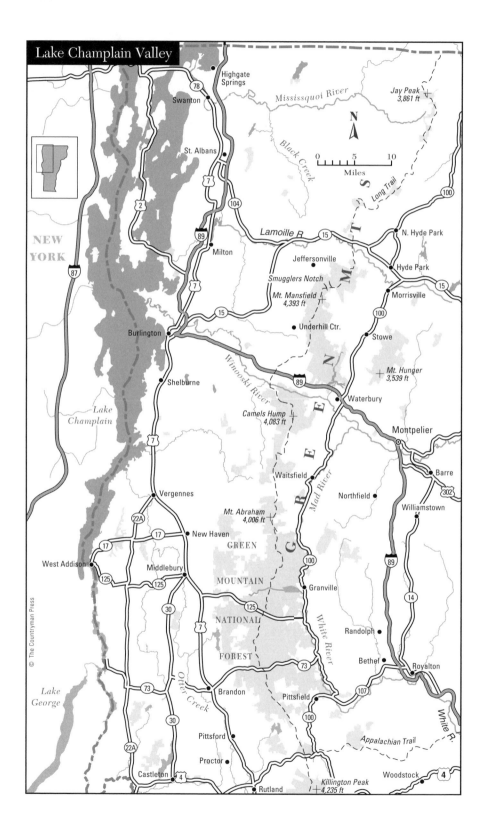

Lake Champlain Valley

NEW YORK

Highgate Springs
Swanton
St. Albans
Milton
Burlington
Shelburne
Vergennes
New Haven
West Addison
Middlebury

Lake Champlain

Lake George

Castleton
Proctor
Pittsford
Brandon

GREEN MOUNTAIN NATIONAL FOREST

Mississquoi River
Black Creek
Lamoille R.
Jeffersonville
Smugglers Notch
Mt. Mansfield 4,393 ft
Underhill Ctr.
Winooski River
Camels Hump 4,083 ft
Waitsfield
Mt. Abraham 4,006 ft
Granville
Pittsfield

Jay Peak 3,861 ft
Long Trail
N. Hyde Park
Hyde Park
Morrisville
Stowe
Mt. Hunger 3,539 ft
Waterbury
Montpelier
Barre
Northfield
Williamstown
Randolph
Bethel
Royalton
Woodstock

Mad River
White River
White R.
Otter Creek
Appalachian Trail

Killington Peak 4,235 ft
Rutland

0   5   10
Miles
N

78 89 7 104 2 87 15 100 7 22A 17 125 30 73 4 302 14 107 100 125

© The Countryman Press

RUTLAND AND THE LOWER CHAMPLAIN VALLEY

Rutland, Vermont's third largest city (after Burlington and Essex), is more than just a convenient stopover en route to the Killington-Pico ski resorts 15 miles east. Stolid, early-Victorian mansions and streets crisscrossed with railroad tracks testify to its 19th-century prosperity—when Rutland was known as "the marble city"—and it has retained its industrial base.

Today city fathers are working to preserve its historic core, which was buoyed in 1996 by the return of railroad passenger service. The daily *Rutland Herald*, the oldest newspaper in the state (founded 1794), continues to win journalism awards, including a Pulitzer Prize in 2001.

The long-established shops along Merchants Row and Center Sreet, one of the state's best-preserved commercial blocks, have held their own in recent years and number upward of 100, all concentrated within just a few square blocks. They include some genuinely interesting newcomers, among them some good restaurants.

The business and shopping center for the Lower Champlain Valley, Rutland occupies a broad, gently rolling corridor between New York State and the Green Mountains. In contrast with the rest of Vermont, this valley is actually broad enough to require two major north–south routes. Rt. 7 is the busier highway. It hugs the Green Mountains and, with the exception of the heavily trafficked strip around Rutland, is a scenic ride. Rt. 30 on the west is a far quieter ride through farm country and by two major lakes, Lake Bomoseen and Lake St. Catherine, both popular summer meccas.

Rt. 4 is the major east–west road, a mountain-rimmed four-lane highway from Fair Haven, at the New York line, to Rutland, where it angles north through the middle of town before turning east again, heading uphill to Killington. Rt. 140 from Wallingford to Poultney is the other old east–west road here, a quiet enough byway through Middletown Springs, where old mineral water springs form the core of a pleasant park.

GUIDANCE **The Rutland Region Chamber of Commerce** (802-773-2747; 1-800-756-8880; www.rutlandvermont.com), 256 N. Main St., Rutland 05701;

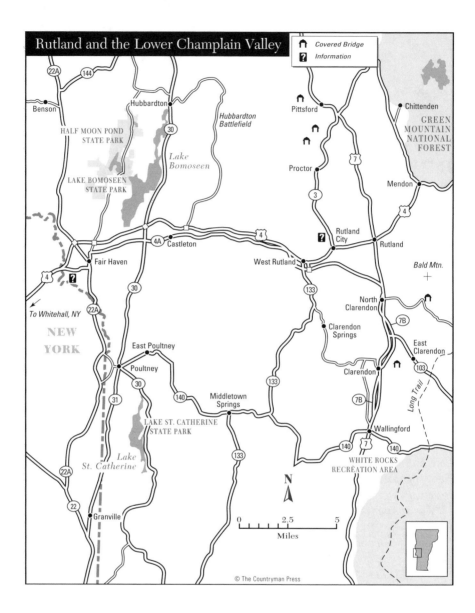

visitors center (802-775-0831) at the junction of Rts. 7 and 4, open late May–mid-Oct. The chamber supplies an illustrated *Visitor's Guide*.

The Fair Haven Welcome Center (802-265-4763) on Rt. 4 near the New York line is open every day 7 AM–9 PM.

Crossroads of Vermont (1-800-756-8880; www.vermontcrossroads.com) is the regional marketing organization.

Area chambers of commerce: **Poultney** (802-287-2010; www.poultneyvt.com); **Brandon** (802-247-6401; www.brandon.org); **Killington** (802-773-4181; www .killingtonchamber.com).

GETTING THERE *By train:* **Amtrak** (1-800-USA-RAIL). Daily service to and from New York City on the Ethan Allen Express.

By air: **US Airways Express/Colgan Air** (1-800-272-5488; www.colganair.com). US Airways Express small planes offer daily connecting service to Boston's Logan International Airport.

By car: Rts. 7 and 4; Rt. 103 from Bellows Falls.

GETTING AROUND *By bus:* **Marble Valley Regional Transit District** (802-773-3244), operator of "The Bus," connecting Killington, Castleton, the Rutland airport, and other points in the area.

MEDICAL EMERGENCY Emergency service is available by calling **911**.

Rutland Regional Medical Center Fast Track Emergency Service (802-747-3601), 160 Allen St.

✳ Villages

Fair Haven, located where Rts. 4, 4A, and 22A intersect, is at the core of Vermont's slate industry. One of its earliest developers in the 1780s was the controversial Matthew Lyon, who started an ironworks and published a newspaper called *The Scourge of Aristocracy*, in which he lambasted the Federalists. Elected to Congress in 1796, Lyon had scuffles on the floor of the House and criticized President Adams so vehemently that he was arrested and jailed under the Alien and Sedition Act. Lyon's case caused such a national uproar that this patently unconstitutional censorship law was soon rescinded. Lyon was reelected to Congress while still in jail and took his seat in time to cast the tie-breaking vote that made Thomas Jefferson president instead of Aaron Burr.

Around the spacious green are three Victorian mansions (two faced with marble) built by descendants of Ira Allen, founder of the University of Vermont.

Poultney, on Rt. 30, the home of Green Mountain College, also has significant journalistic associations: Horace Greeley, founder of the *New York Tribune*, lived at the venerable Eagle Tavern in East Poultney (now a private home) while he was learning the printing trade at the East Poultney *National Spectator* in the 1820s (and organizing a local temperance society). Working with him was George Jones, who helped found the *New York Times* in 1851. Attracted by the slate quarries, Vermont's first Jewish community settled here during the Civil War, and Welsh immigrants poured in to take up quarrymen jobs. Welsh was spoken here until the 1950s in what was one of the largest Welsh communities in the country. Poultney's Green Mountain College has an extensive Welsh archive, teaches Welsh heritage, and maintains the only choir in the country that sings Welsh songs at each of its performances.

East Poultney is a picturesque village worth detouring to see. The fine white Baptist church, built in 1805, is the centerpiece, standing on a small green surrounded by late-18th- and early-19th-century houses. The general store is also a classic and a source of good deli sandwiches. Its picnic benches are within earshot of the Poultney River, here a fast-flowing stream.

Castleton, at Rts. 4A and 30, has triple historical significance: Ethan Allen and Seth Warner planned the capture of Ticonderoga here. On a nearby hill in Hubbardton, Colonel Warner's scrubby militiamen made a valiant rear-guard stand while halting the British invasion force on July 7, 1777, the only Revolutionary War battle actually fought on Vermont soil. The town itself is a showcase of Greek Revival houses. One offshoot of the conspiratorial meeting in Remington's Tavern in 1775 was the exploit of the blacksmith Samuel Beach—Vermont's own Paul Revere—who reputedly ran some 60 miles in 24 hours to recruit more men from the countryside for the raid on Ticonderoga. After the Revolution, Castleton grew rapidly. Thomas Royal Dake, who arrived in about 1807, left his hallmark of design and workmanship on the pillared houses that line Main Street, including the **Ransom-Rehlen mansion**, with its 17 Ionic columns; and Dake's masterpiece, the Congregational Meeting House, now the **Federated Church**, with the lovely pulpit that Dake completed with his own funds. These heirloom houses are open for tours during Castleton's Colonial Days, usually held in late July. Between 1850 and 1870 the West Castleton Railroad and Slate Company was the largest marble plant in the country. The town is also the site of Castleton College, the oldest member of Vermont's state college system, and the state's first medical school, founded 1818.

Benson, west of Rt. 22A, 8 miles north of Fair Haven, is one of those tiny proverbial villages "that time forgot" except as a scenic photo op, but in recent years it has developed a creative personality with its artisans and special shops.

✳ To See

MUSEUMS **Chaffee Center for the Visual Arts** (802-775-0356; www.chaffee artcenter.org), 16 S. Main St., Rutland. Closed Tue., otherwise open 10–5, Sun. noon–4. One of the state's outstanding art galleries, representing 250 Vermont artists, in an 1896 Queen Anne Victorian listed on the National Register of Historic Places. Permanent and periodic exhibits and a youth gallery for school displays. Traditional and contemporary paintings, sculpture, crafts, graphics, and photography are included. Donation expected.

CENTER STREET IN DOWNTOWN RUTLAND
Kim Grant

Vermont Marble Exhibit (802-459-2300; 1-800-427-1396; www.vermont -marble.com), Rt. 3 from West Rutland, Proctor. Open mid-May–Oct., daily 9–5. Admission charge. The first commercial marble deposit was discovered and quarried in Vermont in 1784. The Vermont Marble Company, formed in 1870 when Redfield Proctor merged several quarries, has mined one of the state's principal resources. Marble from Proctor and Danby was used for the U.S. Supreme Court building, the Lincoln Memorial, and the Beinecke Library at Yale, among many other notable edifices. Proctor himself served as governor, U.S. senator, and secretary of war. Several other members of the Proctor family and chief executives of the company also filled the governor's chair, forming a political dynasty that lasted nearly a century. The company, run by the Swiss-based Pleuss-Staufer Industries after 1976, was closed down in 1991, but nearly 100,000 people still visit the marble exhibit every year, making it one of the biggest tourist attractions in New England. Featured are a special geological display, a film dramatizing the origins and uses of marble, a gallery of bas-reliefs of American presidents, a gift shop, **Dorothea's Cafe**, replicas of the *Pietà* and the *Last Supper*, a sculptor in residence, and a factory viewing site from which to watch the various stages of transformation from rough-cut blocks to polished slabs. The museum recently completed a walkway leading to the old Sutherland Falls Quarry.

Slate Valley Museum (518-642-1417; www.slatevalleymuseum.org), 17 Water St., Granville, NY 12832. Open year-round, Tue.–Fri. 1–5, Sat. 10–4. Admission $4 per person; children 12 and under are free. Just across the New York border in the heart of the slate industry's historic base, on a site where immigrant quarry workers once lived in tenements, this 19th-century Dutch barn reflects the many colors and shapes of slate. It includes a quarry shanty, tools, a mural, paintings, photographs, family artifacts, and a gift shop.

The New England Maple Museum (802-483-9414; www.maplemuseum.com), Rt. 7 north of Pittsford. Open June–Oct., daily 8:30–5:30, then 10–4 through Dec. and Mar. 17–May. $2.50 admission; group rates. The museum has an attractive display of the history, production, and consumption of maple syrup, once called "sweet water," and its by-products. You can view the Danforth Collection of antique equipment, murals, and a 10-minute slide show, and there is a tasting area and gift shop. Mail-order service.

Norman Rockwell Museum (802-773-6095; 1-877-773-6095; www.norman rockwellvt.com), Rt. 4 east, Rutland. Open June–Nov., daily 9–5. $4.50 adults, $4 seniors, $2.50 ages 5–15. The chronological displays of Rockwell's magazine covers, many ads, posters, portraits, and other published illustrations make this an interesting documentary of changing American culture and graphic styles. Audiovisual self-guided tour. Gift shop.

Rutland Historical Society (802-775-2006), 96 Center St., Rutland 05701. The distinctive 1860 Nickwackett Fire Station serves as the society's home, open for public use Mon. 6–9 PM, Sat. 1–4 PM, and by appointment.

The Carving Studio and Sculpture Center (802-438-2097; www.carving studio.org), P.O. Box 495, 636 Marble St., West Rutland 05777. Open Sat. and Sun. 1–4 PM or by appointment. The center offers 2-, 5-, and 7-day workshops in most sculpture disciplines. Participants and visitors alike are inspired by artists in residence, exhibitions, and the location among historic marble quarries in the Green Mountains. The Company Store offers gifts, tours, and refreshments.

HISTORIC SITES **The Hubbardton Battlefield** (802-273-2282; www.historic vermont.org/hubbardton) is on Monument Rd. in East Hubbardton, 7 miles north of the posted Rt. 4 exit. Battle buffs won't want to miss the diorama and narrated 3-D map of this 1777 Revolutionary War site, when Colonels Seth Warner, Ebenezer Francis, and Nathan Hale led Vermont, Massachusetts, and New Hampshire soldiers in a successful rear-guard action against British and German troops. They saved the main American army, which was retreating from Mount Independence and Fort Ticonderoga. Of all American battlefields, this one looks most the way it did on the day of the battle. Paths lead to signs describing the events that unfolded, and the views are spectacular, with sweeping vistas of the Taconic Mountains to the south, Pittsford Ridge to the east, and the Adirondacks to the west. A hilltop visitors center is open late May–Columbus Day, Wed.–Sun. 9:30–5. Admission $2.

Paul P. Harris Memorial, Rt. 7 south of Rutland, Wallingford. Paul Harris (1868–1947), who founded Rotary International while he was working in Chicago, went to school here in the small brick building on Main Street, where the local club still meets.

COVERED BRIDGES There are six in the area: the 1836 **Kingsley** or **Mill River Bridge**, East St., off Airport Rd., East Clarendon; the 1880 **Brown Bridge**, off Cold River Rd., Shrewsbury; the 1840 **Depot Bridge**, off Rt. 7 north, Pittsford; the 1849 **Cooley Bridge**, Elm St., Pittsford; the 1843 **Gorham** or **Goodnough Bridge**, Gorham Bridge Rd., off Rt. 3, Pittsford; and the 1830 **Twin Bridge**, East Pittsford Rd., off Rt. 7 north, Rutland.

Wilson Castle (802-773-3284; www.wilsoncastle.com), on W. Proctor Rd. leading from West Rutland to Proctor. This 19th-century turreted mansion overlooking 115 acres contains a priceless collection of decorative arts. Built in 1867 for the English bride of a Vermont physician, John Johnson, no expense was spared in its creation. Almost everything was imported, including the exterior brick. The opulent furnishings include Venetian tapestries, 400-year-old Chinese scrolls, a Louis XIV French onyx-covered table, and a gallery of classic sculpture, not to mention 84 stained-glass windows that light up like neon with rays of the sun. In the dining room are Polish chimes and a cabinet full of quartz crystal goblets; peacocks roamed the grounds. But the seclusion was too much for the aristocratic Mrs. Johnson; she returned to England 2 years later and the house was sold. It changed hands several times until 1939, when pioneering radio engineer Herbert Lee Wilson acquired it as a summer home and set about establishing AM radio towers around the world. In 1962 the Wilson family opened the castle to tours. Five generations of Wilsons have owned the property, part of which has come under a nonprofit foundation. Guided tours are available daily, late May–late Oct., 9–6. Special Saturday night murder mystery dinners, poker evenings, Halloween, and Christmas tours are also held. Admission.

FISH HATCHERY **Pittsford National Fish Hatchery** (802-483-6618; www.fws
.gov/r5pnfh), 4 Holden Rd., North Chittenden, VT 05763. Open 8–4 daily. The
Fish and Wildlife Service raises landlocked salmon and lake trout here.

✳ To Do

BIKING There's a lot of great bike riding in this area. The roads west and south
of Rutland are little traveled and very scenic. Also, there are snack bars sprinkled
throughout the area, which always helps. Rentals and route advice are available
from the **Great Outdoors Trading Company** (802-775-9989) at 219 Woodstock Ave. in Rutland, and from the **Sports Peddler** (802-775-0101) at 158
N. Main St., both in Rutland.

BOATING Boats can be rented from **Lake Bomoseen Marina** (802-273-2061;
802-265-4611; www.lakebomoseenmarina.com), **Duda Water Sports** (802-265-
3432), and **Woodard Marine, Inc.** (802-265-3690; www.woodardmarine.com),
all on Lake Bomoseen.

FISHING **Green Mountain Fishing Guide Service** (802-446-3375), 593
Rt. 140, Tinmouth. Fishing expeditions guided by Rod Start, a Vermonter with
over 25 years of fishing experience.

FITNESS CENTERS **The Gymnasium** (802-773-5333), 30 Merchants Row,
Rutland. A complete wellness and cardiovascular center, open Mon.–Fri. 6 AM–
9 PM, Sat. and Sun. 7–7.

Green Mountain Rock Climbing Center (802-773-3343; www.vermont
climbing.com), 223 Woodstock Ave., Rt. 4, Rutland. Open Mon.–Fri. noon–9,
Sat. 10–7, Sun. noon–5. $15 adults, $10 ages 6–12, $5 age 5 and under. Anybody
from age 2 on up can learn to rock climb on rock walls in this climate-controlled
indoor setting. Prices include equipment and all-day use of the center; first-time
belay lessons ($10) are available.

Vermont Sport & Fitness Center (802-775-9916), 40 Curtis Ave., Rutland.
Outdoor pool, indoor/outdoor tennis, racquetball, cardio equipment.

Better Bodies (802-775-6565), 32 Granger St., Rutland.

Vermont Martial Arts Academy (802-773-1373), 114 West St., Rutland.

Mountain Yoga (802-773-5045; www.mountainyoga.com), 135 Main St., Rutland.

Fair Haven Fitness (802-265-3470), 8 Main St., Fair Haven.

GOLF **The Rutland Country Club** (802-773-3254), a mile north of the business
section on N. Grove St., Rutland. An 18-hole golf course on rolling terrain;
restaurant.

Proctor-Pittsford Country Club (802-483-9379), Corn Hill Rd., Pittsford.
Eighteen holes, lounge, and restaurant.

Lake St. Catherine Country Club (802-287-9341), Rt. 30, south of Poultney.
Eighteen holes, lounge, and restaurant.

The Prospect Bay Country Club (802-468-5581) in Castleton offers nine holes.

Stonehedge Golf (802-773-2666), Rt. 103 west, North Clarendon, is a nine-hole, par-3 public course.

Also see "Killington/Plymouth Area."

HIKING **White Rocks Recreation Area**, Rt. 140 off Rt. 7 in Wallingford. Follow signs from the White Rocks Picnic Area. The big feature here is a 2,600-foot, conical white peak surrounded by quartzite boulders that retain ice and snow into summer. We advise picking up a hiking guidebook (see *Hiking and Walking* in "What's Where") before starting out.

Delaware Hudson Rail Trail, Poultney–Castleton. A rail-trail enjoyed by hikers, snowmobilers, walkers, bikers, equestrians, and cross-country skiers. A guide is available from the Department of Forest and Parks in Pittsford.

Helen W. Buckner Memorial Preserve (802-229-4425), West Haven. Hiking trails and nature exploration in this Nature Conservancy tract.

HORSEBACK RIDING ⚷ **Pond Hill Ranch** (802-468-2449; www.pondhillranch .com), 1683 Pond Hill Rd., Castleton, a 200-acre family-owned ranch offering trail rides, lessons, and pony rides for children.

Also see **Mountain Top Inn and Resort Equestrian Program** in "Killington/ Plymouth Area."

RODEOS **Pond Hill Ranch** (802-468-2449), Castleton. Saturday-night rodeos all summer long and into fall. Go into Castleton and follow the signs to Pond Hill.

SWIMMING **Elfin Lake Beach**, off Rt. 140 west, 2 miles southeast of Wallingford, and **Crystal Beach**, a municipally owned white sand beach on the eastern shore of Lake Bomoseen.

See also *Green Space.*

SKIING See "Killington/Plymouth Area."

SLEIGH RIDES **Cortina Inn** (802-773-3333; www.cortinainn.com), Rt. 4 east, Mendon. Wed., Sat., and some holidays.

Pond Hill Ranch (802-468-2449; www.pondhillranch.com), Castleton. One- to 3-hour rides.

✳ Green Space

Lake Bomoseen, just north of Castleton, is a popular local summer colony. The lake gained notoriety in the 1930s because of Alexander Woollcott's summer retreat on Neshobe Island. The portly "Town Crier" entertained such cronies as Harpo Marx, who was known to repel curious interlopers by capering along the shore naked and painted blue.

Lake Bomoseen State Park (802-265-4242; 802-786-0060), Rt. 4 west of Rutland, Exit 3, 5 miles north on Town Rd. Its 66 campsites, including 10 lean-tos, are set in a lovely wildlife refuge; beach, picnic area, nature program, trails, boat ramp, and rentals.

Half Moon State Park (802-273-2848; 802-786-0060), between Fair Haven and Rutland on Rt. 4; take Exit 4, go 6.5 miles north on Rt. 30, left on Hortonia Rd. and continue 2 miles, then go left on Black Pond Rd. for 2 miles. Wooded campsites (59 tent sites; 10 lean-tos) around a secluded pond; rental canoes; hikes to **High Pond**, a remote body of water in the hills.

Lake St. Catherine State Park (802-287-9158; 802-786-0060), 3 miles south of Poultney on Rt. 30. Fifty tent or trailer campsites and 11 lean-tos, plus sandy beaches, fishing, boat rentals, nature trails.

✳ Lodging

SUITES **The Victorian** (802-287-5505; www.victoriansuites.com), 2541 Vermont Rt. 31, Poultney 05764. Cathy and Bruce Ferguson have restored this 1890 Victorian and turned it into one- and two-bedroom rental suites, complete with equipped kitchen and sitting room. One-bedroom suites rent for $70 in midweek and $110 on weekends and holidays; two-bedroom suites go for $95 and $130, respectively. No credit cards.

RESORT ⊙ ⚤ ✍ **Edgewater Resort** (802 468-5251; 1-888-475-6664; www.edgewatervermont.com), 2551 Rt. 30, 2 miles north of Rt. 4, at Lake Bomoseen, 05732. This 9-mile lake was a celebrity playground in the big-band era; Benny Goodman and Glenn Miller played. Hollywood icons from Kitty Carlisle to Laurence Olivier and Vivien Leigh were regular guests. At one time there were five major hotels and a dance pavilion. Now all have vanished except this unsung resort, which the Poremski family nurtured from a cluster of cabins they bought in the 1950s to a summer-camp-like destination comprising the 150-year-old 9-room Edgewater Inn with its huge porch and pine paneling, an

8-room chalet, a 12-unit motel, 14 one- and two-bedroom condo apartments, 4 cottages, and 12 efficiencies. Though not luxurious, all are clean and moderately priced. Most have cooking facilities and lake views; some are right at the water's edge. The Trak-In Restaurant (see *Eating Out*) serves great breakfasts and dinners, and there is a beach, boating, fishing, an outdoor pool, an adjacent 9-hole golf course, a game room, a playground, and plenty to keep kids occupied on rainy afternoons. Most of the guests return year after year, and it's open year-round. No pets, please. MAP rates (double occupancy) range $95–120 per day, $600–750 per week. Rooms range only $55–80 per day, double occupancy, $350–500 per week; two-bedroom poolside condos $115 per night, $700 per week; two-bedroom cottage, $700 per week; three-bedroom lakeside cottages, $850–950 per week.

BED & BREAKFASTS **The Inn at Rutland** (802-773-0575; 1-800-808-0575; www.innatrutland.com), 70 N. Main St., Rutland 05071. This 1880s-era Victorian mansion with its oak detailing and high ceilings is on

Rt. 7 just north of the center of town. Innkeepers Leslie and Steven Brenner offer eight distinctive guest rooms on two upstairs floors, each with phone, private bath, antiques, and color TV. One includes a fireplace, two have private porch, and two have air-jetted tub. The woodwork in the dining room is exceptional, and the fire-placed living room is attractive. $100–220 includes a delicious three-course breakfast.

🐾 ⚘ **The Phelps House** (802-775-4480; 1-800-775-4620; www.the phelpshouse.com), 19 North St., Rutland 05071. An interesting home that offers a three-room suite with a queen-sized canopy bed and private bath, a two-room detached apartment that sleeps eight, and five rooms in the main house, all with shared baths. There's a grand piano, basement play-room, and tennis court. Betty Phelps's wonderfully primitive murals are worth the visit to what has been called "the first Frank Lloyd Wright house built in Vermont." $75–85.

🐾 **Chocolate Truffle** (802-747-5049; www.chocolatetruffle.info), 14 S. Main St. (at Rts. 7 and 4B), Rutland 05701. This 1895 white Victorian is within walking distance of the town's major attractions. The wrap-around porch is a great perch for summer evening concerts in the park, and the town's leading art center is right next door. Wendi Corbin and her two friendly dogs are your hosts, offering three rooms with queen-sized bed and private bath (one suitable for families), and a small room with shared bath. $89–169 rates include a full breakfast and one of Wendy's decadent chocolate desserts. Children over 14; no pets.

Baker's Bed & Breakfast (802-775-4835; 1-888-778-4835; http://members .aol.com/bakersbnb/), 80 Campbell Rd., Rutland 05071 (off Dorr Dr., south of the business district), is a spacious 1826 redbrick house with an inviting veranda and an outdoor swimming pool. Steve and Leslie Baker offer three large bedrooms with private bath. There's a living room, a library, and a dining room for brunchlike breakfasts, included in the $125 rate.

I. B. Munson House (802-446-2860; 1-888-519-3771; www.ibmunson.com), 37 S. Main St., Wallingford 05773, run by Lisa and Charles McClafferty, is fur-nished with classic Victorian antiques and period decor, including claw-foot bathtubs. There are six guest rooms, all with private bath, three with working fireplace. Rates range from $150–215 per room in high season to $140–165 in low, including full gourmet break-fast. No pets (two resident terriers); children over 12.

🐾 🐾 ⚘ **Maplewood Inn** (802-265-8039; 1-800-253-7729; www.maple woodinn.net), 1108 S. Main St., Rt. 22A south, Fair Haven 05743. Paul Stagg and Scott Rose's historic 1843 Greek Revival home (on the National Register of Historic Places) is decorated in period style with a stately dining room, a long lounging porch, a rear patio, and a parlor with a fireplace and complimentary cor-dials. The five air-conditioned rooms include two suites with fireplace and sitting area (one is suitable for fami-lies with both a queen and double). All have private bath, cable TV, and DVD player; guests can choose from a 1,400-title DVD library. Rates are $110–140 ($130–180 during foliage and holiday season), which includes a full made-to-order breakfast chosen from a frequently changing menu. Children and pets welcome.

Memory Lane (802-468-5394), 503 Main St., Castleton 05735. Antique furniture, toys, dolls, and china fill this Federal-style house, originally the home of the cofounder of the medical school at Castleton College. Now Barbara and Thomas Ettori offer two guest rooms with private bath, at $75–100.

The Haven Guest House Bed & Breakfast (802-265.8882; www.haven guesthousevt.com), 1 Fourth St. (near Rt. 4), Fair Haven 05743. Gisela and Werner Baumann are your hosts in this early-20th-century renovated Colonial with its wooden floors and expansive, curving porch. The four comfortable suites each have private bath, TV, and wireless access. The Apple Blossom Room has a king-sized bed, the Rosewood two twins, and there are queens in the other two. Guests can sit by a crackling fire in the living room, play chess at a dining room table, or sit in the parlor. There is a breakfast menu, and Gisela's hearty offerings include fresh breads and pastries. $99–129 includes breakfast. Children over 6; no pets.

Twin Mountains Farm (802-235-3700; www.twinmoutainsfarmbb .com), 549 Coy Hill Rd., Middletown Springs 05757. This 1830 farmhouse with modern comforts is secluded on a long dirt road about 2 miles south of the village on 150 acres stretching from the ridgeline of Coy Mountain on the north to Morgan Mountain on the south. Walt and Annie Pepperman's three air-conditioned guest rooms come with private bath and guest robes. The deluxe Deer Room has a queen-sized sleigh bed, a sofa, and a view of the swimming/skating pond. Each of the smaller Moose and Bear Rooms contains two twins. There's also a cottage with a queen-sized bed and rustic log furniture. Guests can lounge by the stone fireplace in the comfortable living room or relax on the screened-in porch. Cross-country skiing, snowshoeing,

LLAMA FARM IN MIDDLETOWN SPRINGS

Diane E. Foulds

and at least four good hiking trails are steps away (Walt, a retired lawyer, is a nature guide). A gourmet breakfast such as baked apples, pancakes with a maple-banana glaze, or eggs Benedict over fried tomatoes is served by a rumbling woodstove in winter, on the patio in summer. The stars pop out in the night sky, and the silence is deafening. $95–125 includes breakfast. Closed in Apr.

ⓒ ♪ **White Rocks Inn** (802-446-2077; www.whiterocksinn.com), 1774 Rt. 7 south, Wallingford 05773. Malcolm and Rita Swogger's elegantly furnished, antiques-filled farmhouse and its spectacular, landmark barn are on the National Register of Historic Places. The property includes a hilltop gazebo, a rose arbor, a pond with Adirondack chairs, and hiking paths that lead to glorious views of the Green Mountains and the White Rocks Recreation Area. It's a popular place to get married; the 15,000-square-foot Gothic-style barn, one of the largest in southern Vermont, is ideal for receptions, and guests can be chauffeured to dinner in Malcolm's vintage 1939 Cadillac limousine. (Ask him about the wedding and elopement packages.) The five guest rooms, each with private bath, have either king, queen, or double canopy beds and rent for $110–200 double occupancy, including full breakfast. The Milk House Cottage (with a whirlpool bath, living room, and full kitchen) is EP or B&B by the day ($200–250) or by the week, and the Nest Cottage (king canopy bed, air-jet tub, deck, loft with twin beds, farmhouse kitchen, fireplace) goes for $220–270, and by the week. Children over 12 are welcome in the house, of any age in the cottage. No pets.

See also Maple Crest Farm and Buckmaster Inn in "Okemo Valley Region."

MOTELS

In Rutland 05071

ⓒ ♣ ♪ **Mendon Mountain Orchards** (802-775-5477; www.mendonorchards.com), 16 Rt. 4, Mendon, isn't really a motel but rather a series of pleasant, old-fashioned cabins, surrounded by orchards, with a pool and a shop for homemade goodies, apples in-season, cider, and flowers. $47–60 for a double. **Holiday Inn Rutland/Killington** (802-775-1911; 1-800-462-4810), Rts. 7 and 4 south, includes **Paynter's Restaurant**, an indoor pool, sauna and exercise room, and **Centre Stage** lounge. The 151 rooms range $99–249 and come with coffee, refrigerator, and microwave. Rutland also has a **Best Western** (1-800-828-3334), a **Ramada Limited** (1-888-818-3297), a **Red Roof Inn** (802-775-4303), a **Travel Inn** (1-866-775-4348), a **Comfort Inn** (1-800-432-6788), and an **Econo Lodge** (802-773-2784).

CAMPGROUNDS See *Green Space* for information on campgrounds in Lake Bomoseen State Park, Half Moon Pond State Park, and Lake St. Catherine State Park.

✳ Where to Eat

DINING OUT See also "Killington/Plymouth Area."

Stanti's (802-775-0856), 37–41 N. Main St. (junction of Rts. 4 and 7), Rutland. Open daily 11–3 and 5–9:30, Sun. noon–9. The former Royal's 121 Hearthside is now Stanti's, owned by Swiss-born Konstantin Schonbachler and his wife, Soo, who run the popular Victorian Inn restaurant in nearby Wallingford. Stanti (Konstantin's nickname) strives to please a wide variety of tastes, offering steaks and seafood with stress on Italian. Appetizers include garlic soup, salmon carpaccio, and shrimp cocktail. Main courses might be jumbo crabcakes, ravioli with chicken and rosemary in a tomato and cream sauce, or grilled rib-eye steak au poivre. There's a lighter bar menu, a full line of beers and wines, and daily specials. Entrées $17–29.

Little Harry's (802-747-4848), 121 West St., Rutland. Open daily 5–10. This offspring of the popular Harry's Cafe in Mount Holly occupies the old space of 121 West. Owner Harrison Pearce calls his venture the "general store of ethnic eating." Besides pad Thai, a "signature" noodle dish, Little Harry's offers such fare as Jamaican jerk pork, shrimp sauté, New York sirloin, shrimp in crisp skins, and lively Spanish dishes plus burritos and steak sandwiches from what Pearce calls a "user-friendly" menu. Entrées $13.95–18.95.

The Victorian Inn at Wallingford (802-446-2099; www.thevictorianinn .com), 55 N. Main St., Rt. 7, Wallingford, serves dinner Tue.–Sat., and a gourmet Sunday brunch buffet 10–2 that involves parading through the kitchen past a multiplicity of cakes, cheeses, fruits, salads, and country breads. Swiss-born chef-owner Konstantin Schonbachler, formerly executive chef at the Kennedy Center in Washington, DC, brought his European culinary talents with him when he moved to this French Second Empire home in the center of Wallingford. Guests eat in one of three downstairs rooms in a casual, unpretentious ambience; this is very simply

the area's best restaurant. Dinner for two with wine comes to about $90. Closed in Nov. until Thanksgiving.

⊙ ⌒ **The Fair Haven Inn** (802-265-4907; 1-800-325-7074), 5 Adams St., Fair Haven. In a spacious, neo-Colonial setting, the Lemnotis family serves Greek American fare Mon.–Sat. for lunch 11:30–2 ($3.95–9.95). Dinner is served Mon.–Sat. 5–9 and Sun. noon–8, and includes veal Florentine ($16.95), moussaka ($10.95), and jumbo shrimp à la Grecque ($17.95). Other specials include spanakopita and seafood souvlakia. Early-bird special prices are available the first hour; a full Greek menu is offered on Sundays, from *tzatziki* and *skorthia* to baked lamb ($11.95–19.95).

EATING OUT **The Palms** (802-773-2367), 36 Strongs Ave., Rutland. Italian cooking is a specialty in Rutland because of all the Italians who came to work in the marble quarries. The Palms offers cooking by the fourth generation of the Sabatoso family, who prepare such specialties as baked lasagna, veal à la Palms, and steak Delmonico. Open 4:30–10 daily except Sunday.

South Station (802-775-1736), at the Trolley Barn, 170 S. Main St., Rutland. Open daily for lunch and dinner, specializing in prime rib of beef and such munchies as fried potato skins, stuffed mushrooms, chicken wings, hearty soups, salads, burgers, and teriyaki chicken. Dinner prices range from $8.95 for burgers to $24.95 for certain specials.

Three Tomatoes (802-747-7747), 88 Merchants Row, Rutland, has the same northern Italian flair as its siblings in Burlington and in Lebanon, N.H.—wood-fired pizzas and all.

Open for dinner nightly from 5. Shrimp sautéed with tomatoes, Greek olives, basil, garlic, crushed red chiles, and white wine, tossed with linguine, is but one sample dish. Entrées $10.95–16.95.

🍲 **Back Home Again** (802-775-9800), 23 Center St., Rutland, serves made-to-order sandwiches, salads, soups, and wraps, homemade breads, muffins, and wonderful juice drinks and desserts. They also prepare special smoothies, fancy coffees, and a tea-like drink called maté. The decor is low-lit and romantic with wood slab tables and intimate booths. Open Mon.–Thu. 8–9, Fri. 8–3, closed weekends.

✒ **The Sirloin Saloon** (802-773-7900), 200 S. Main St. (Rt. 7 south), Rutland. One in a Vermont mini chain (there are three), this colorful restaurant (lots of glasswork, art, and gleaming brass) is a good bet for family dinners. The menu runs from ground sirloin to prime rib to seafood cooked over the wood-fired grill. Entrées $11–19.

🍲 ✒ **The Weathervane** (802-773-0382; www.weathervaneseafoods .com), 124 Woodstock Ave., Rutland. One of an 18-restaurant chain of eateries whose proprietors, the Gagner family of Maine, own their own fishing fleet. Fresh daily offerings range from fish-and-chips for $6.95 to a variety of shrimp, lobster, and clam extravaganzas for $19.95. Chowders, steamers, and take-out, plus pasta, steak, and chicken.

Panda Pavilion (802-775-6682; 802-775-6794), Rt. 4 east, by Home Depot, Rutland. Open Mon.–Sat. 11:30–9:30, Sun. 1–10 for dinner only. Highly praised Szechuan-Hunan-Mandarin cuisine, like Double Happiness Chicken. Take-out service.

🍲 ✒ **Midway Diner & Steak House** (802-775-9901), 120 S. Main St., Rutland. Open daily, 6:30 AM–10:30 PM. Judging from its faded neon sign, you might dismiss this aptly named Rt. 7 eatery as just another truck stop. But the Midway is a friendly, air-conditioned community spot with good food, good prices, a broad menu, and decor that is pure Americana. Set back off Rt. 7 beside the municipal pool.

Birdseye Diner (802-468-5817), Main St., Castleton. This restored 1940s Silk City diner, open all day, is a justifiably popular spot for college students and local residents alike. Complete dinners begin at $8.

Lakehouse Pub & Grill (802-273-3000), 3569 Rt. 30 north, on Lake Bomoseen. Open May–Oct., daily for lunch and dinner. This popular place features a wooden hillside stairway leading down to umbrella-shaded waterside tables, spectacular sunset views from the air-conditioned indoor dining room, and an appealing menu with seafood specials and a full bar with live music on summer evenings. Freddie Field and Brad Burns have added panache to the menu. Light fare might include Thai sesame-tossed noodles; entrées range from fresh lobster to salmon poached in white wine with braised spinach, tomatoes, and artichoke hearts. Dinner entrées $15.50–22.95.

Trak-In Restaurant (802-468-3212), Rt. 30 on Lake Bomoseen. Open daily for breakfast and dinner Mother's Day–Oct. Red and Val Poremski have owned this lakeside resort for over 40 years, attracting a large following to their simple air-conditioned eatery by serving large portions of fresh, delicious food to the many guests staying at the adjacent Edgewater Inn and to those passersby lucky enough to find it. Entrées $14.95–18.95.

Wheel Inn (802-537-2755), Lake Rd. at Stage Rd., Benson. Open daily 6 AM–9 PM, this family-friendly place in a former carriage house has a loyal following largely because of its very reasonable prices. Menu offerings include chicken and biscuits on Wed. nights ($8.95) and fresh seafood on weekends, and nothing goes over $18.95, including salads and sides. Everything homemade but the hot dog buns.

Tokyo House (802-786-8080), 106 West St., Rutland. Open daily for lunch 11–3, dinner 4:30–10. Owner Ming Li is known for sushi, sashimi, and bento boxes. Eat in or take out; beer and wine.

Clem & Company (802-747-3340), 51 Wales St., Rutland. Breakfast is served all day, every day, 7 AM–closing at 1:30 PM. There are also great soups, salads, and sandwiches for lunch. A fast, friendly local eatery.

Seward Family Restaurant (802-773-2738), 224 N. Main St., Rt. 7, Rutland. Open daily 6:30 AM–10 PM. The Sewards have run a dairy business in the area since forever, and Seward's ice cream is among the best. Besides ice cream, the restaurant offers solid home cooking, a fresh salad bar, and a large gift shop of Vermont products.

Gill's Delicatessen (802-773-7414), 68 Strongs Ave., Rutland. Open daily except Sun., 8 AM–9 PM. Closed July 4 week. *Gill's* is short for "Gilligan's," and Kathy Gilligan Phillips is the second generation to run this peerless eat-in bakery-deli, the oldest in Rutland, whose hot Italian grinders are

hands down the best in Vermont. There are 10 tables, but most people grab and go. Grinders come in four sizes with innumerable fillings, including real Maine crabmeat.

Also see Costantino's Italian Imports in *Selective Shopping*.

COFFEEHOUSE/WINE BAR **Coffee Exchange** (802-775-3337), 101 Merchants Row, Rutland. Open weekdays from 7 AM, Sat. from 8; on Fri. the place doesn't close down until 10 PM. "Jazz, java, and jabber" is the theme of this upbeat coffee bar and sophisticated wine room at a key downtown intersection. Patrons sip and nosh on exotic beverages and pastries at outdoor tables in summer—perhaps fresh-roasted macadamia cream coffee and orange poppy seed scones. Salads, soups, and sandwiches at lunch.

✳ Entertainment

Paramount Theatre (802-775-0570; www.paramountvt.org), 30 Center St., Rutland. After years of a concerted community effort, this historic 1914 theater has been brought back to life with dance, music, drama, even magic and juggling acts. Call for tickets and schedules of events.

Crossroads Art Council (802-775-5413), 39 E. Center St., Rutland, sponsors a series of concerts, theater and ballet performances, and an arts education program.

See also Lakehouse Pub & Grill under *Eating Out*.

Movieplex 9 (802-775-5500), downtown Rutland Shopping Plaza, Merchants Row, and **Westway 1-2-3-4** (802-438-2888), Rt. 4A in West Rutland, show first-run flicks.

Tuttle Antiquarian Books (802-773-8229; www.tuttlebooks.com), 28 S. Main St., Rutland, facing the park (look for the life-sized wooden sculpture of a man reading). Open weekdays 9–5, Sat. 9–4; Jan.–Mar., open weekdays only. One of the largest stocks of used and rare books in New England in the house where Charles Tuttle was raised. The Tuttle family goes way back in Rutland's history. The family managed the *Rutland Herald* during the Civil War, when it reached the peak of its journalistic excellence. You'll notice the Tuttle Block downtown. Charles E. Tuttle began his publishing company in Tokyo right after World War II, building his book empire into the world's largest publisher of Japan titles written in English. When inventory outstripped storage space here, the Tuttles vacated and turned it into a warehouse. Eventually it became a bookstore. Today owners Jon Mayo and Jennifer Shannon stock 45,000 volumes on three floors, specializing in genealogy and New England history. There are foreign-language books in the basement, and an entire room devoted to miniature books, some no bigger than the head of a nail. The white-clapboard Colonial next door, a book warehouse built about 1794, is the oldest house in town.

✳ Selective Shopping

BOOKSTORES The Book King (802-773-9232), 94 Merchants Row, Rutland, is a bright, well-stocked store for new trade and children's books, paperbacks, cards, periodicals, and show tickets.

✎ **Annie's Book Stop** (802-775-6993), Trolley Square, 120 S. Main St., Rutland. Annie's has a large selection of new and used books; specializes in children's books and books on tape, plus educational puzzles and games.

The Book Shed (802-537-2010; www.bensonvermont.com), at the corner of Lake and Stage Rds., in what used to be the town clerk's office, is a used- and antiquarian-book store with 30,000 volumes just where you wouldn't expect to find it—in the tiny village of Benson. Open Wed.–Sun. 10–6; in winter, call ahead.

SPECIAL SHOPS The Great Outdoors Trading Center (802-775-9989; www.joejonessports.com), Woodstock Ave., Rutland, is a vast, complete sporting goods store, with a bike shop, gun shop, and fly-rod department, among others. Open daily 9–6, Sun. 10–5, till 8 PM Fri.

The Seward Vermont Dairy Deli Shop (802-773-2738), 224 N. Main St. (Rt. 7), Rutland. One corner of this vast restaurant (see *Eating Out*) showcases the cheddar cheeses produced by Cabot and Crowley (Seward family members no longer make their own cheese). One specialty is sharp cheddar, aged more than 9 months. Maple syrup and creamed honey are also available. The ice cream is the showstopper, however.

Costantino's Italian Imports (802-747-0777), 10 Terrill St., Rutland. Former antiques dealer Dan Costantino has renovated the former Bartlett's Studio building to create a shop that features shelves of imported Italian meats, cheeses, pasta, and olive oil. In the back a deli offers Italian sandwiches and pasta salads.

Vermont Canvas Products (802-773-7311), 259 Woodstock Ave., Rt. 4 East, Rutland, makes customized luggage and handbags. Open daily except Sun.

Truly Unique Gift Shop (802-773-7742), Rt. 4 east, Rutland, has an uncommon collection of country antiques, Vermont products, and gifts.

Rocking Horse Country Store (802-773-7882), Rt. 4 east, Rutland, combines Vermont food products (including its own homemade wine jelly), gifts, antiques, and collectibles.

Hand Made in Vermont (802-446-2400; www.handmadeinvermont .com), 205 S. Main St., Wallingford. Open June–Oct., Thu.–Mon. 11–6; Nov. 2–May, the store is open 11–6 on selected weekends only. Housed in America's first pitchfork mill, this old stone structure is now a gallery featuring the work of Vermont artists and craftspeople, including glass, pottery, furniture, and a huge selection of semi-precious jewelry.

Farrow Gallery & Studio (802-468-5683; www.vermontel.com/~farogal/), Old Yellow Church, 835 Main St., Castleton, shows Patrick Farrow's limited-edition, award-winning bronze sculptures, along with the work of other Vermont artists. Open daily except Tue. 10–5; in winter, call ahead.

Peter Huntoon Studio (802-235-2328; www.peterhuntoon.com), 17 Studio Lane, Middletown Springs, 05757. Open by appointment. Huntoon is one of Vermont's premier watercolorists, who also teaches and conducts workshops at his studio.

His work is available for viewing and for sale.

✳ Special Events

Late February: **Great Benson Fishing Derby**, sponsored by the Fair Haven Rotary Club—many prizes in several categories. Tickets for the derby: P.O. Box 131, Bomoseen 05732.

Early June: **Teenie's Fishing Derby** for seniors and the disabled at Teenie's Tiny Poultry Farm in Chittenden (802-773-2637).

June–August: Sunday-evening **concerts in the park**, 7:30 (802-773-1822).

Mid-July: **SolarFest** (802-235-2866; www.solarfest.org) has become an annual solar-powered music festival and sustainable future fair in Poultney.

Late July: **Ethnic Festival** and sidewalk sale, with dining, theater, and demonstrations (802-773-9380).

Early August: **Art in the Park Summer Arts Festival**, Rutland, sponsored by the Chaffee Center (802-775-0356), in Main Street Park, junction of Rts. 7 and 4 east.

August: **Castleton Colonial Days**, Castleton.

Early September: **Vermont State Fair** (802-775-5200)—midway, exhibits, races, demolition derby, and tractor pulls animate the old fairgrounds on Rt. 7 south, Rutland.

Mid-October: **Art in the Park Fall Foliage Festival**, Rutland, sponsored by the Chaffee Center (802-775-0356).

October 31: Rutland had one of the nation's first **Halloween parades**, and it's still one of the best.

December 31: Rutland's **First Night** celebration, 5 PM–midnight (802-773-9380).

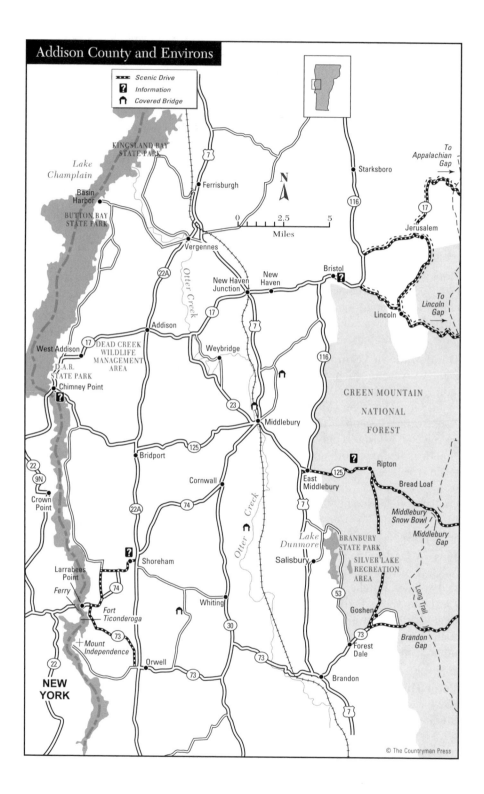

Addison County and Environs

Scenic Drive
Information
Covered Bridge

Lake Champlain

KINGSLAND BAY STATE PARK

Basin Harbor

BUTTON BAY STATE PARK

West Addison

D.A.R. STATE PARK

Chimney Point

Ferrisburgh

Vergennes

Otter Creek

Addison

DEAD CREEK WILDLIFE MANAGEMENT AREA

Weybridge

New Haven Junction

New Haven

Bristol

Starksboro

To Appalachian Gap

Jerusalem

To Lincoln Gap

Lincoln

GREEN MOUNTAIN NATIONAL FOREST

Middlebury

Bridport

Cornwall

East Middlebury

Ripton

Bread Loaf

Middlebury Snow Bowl

Middlebury Gap

Crown Point

BRANBURY STATE PARK

Lake Dunmore

Salisbury

SILVER LAKE RECREATION AREA

Long Trail

Larrabees Point

Ferry

Shoreham

Whiting

Goshen

Fort Ticonderoga

Mount Independence

Orwell

Forest Dale

Brandon Gap

Brandon

NEW YORK

Miles

N

© The Countryman Press

ADDISON COUNTY AND ENVIRONS

INCLUDING MIDDLEBURY, VERGENNES, BRANDON, AND BRISTOL

Addison County packs as much contrasting scenery within its borders as any county in the country. On the east rises the high wall of the Green Mountains laced with hiking trails and pierced by four of the state's highest, most dramatic "gaps" (passes). The mountains drop abruptly through widely scattered hill towns—Lincoln, Ripton, and Goshen—into a 30-mile-wide, farm-filled valley, a former ocean floor that now contains Vermont's largest concentration of dairy farms and orchards. Lake Champlain is far narrower here than up around Burlington, and the Adirondacks in New York seem higher and nearer, forming an improbable but spectacular backdrop to cows, water, red barns, and apple trees.

This stretch of the Champlain Valley is particularly popular with bicyclists, not only because it's the flattest piece of Vermont, but also because its quiet old farm roads wind through orchards to discoveries like the "Fort Ti Ferry" ("serving people and their vehicles since Mozart was three months old") and "the world's smallest bank" in Orwell.

Middlebury, the hub of Addison County, is among New England's most sophisticated towns, the home of one of its most prestigious private colleges and many interesting shops.

We hope that this book will lure visitors to explore the entire valley: the easily accessible scenery along Rt. 7 as well as the Lake Champlain shoreline, notched at regular intervals with quiet and accessible bays, and the Green Mountain forest roads, with their occasional but spectacular lake and valley views.

GUIDANCE **Addison County Chamber of Commerce** (802-388-7951; 1-800-SEE-VERMONT; www.midvermont.com), 2 Court St., Middlebury 05753, in the Painter House, offers information about every corner of its domain, from Vergennes and Bristol in the north to Orwell in the south. Open Mon. 10:30–5, Tue.–Fri. 9–5. This unusually large walk-in information center publishes a map/guide, stocks brochures, and refers visitors to a wide variety of lodgings, from inns and bed & breakfasts to seasonal cottages on Lake Dunmore. During foliage season it is unusually resourceful in finding lodging for all comers.

Vergennes Chamber of Commerce (802-388-7951), P.O. Box 335, Vergennes 05491, has an information booth on the common.

Brandon Area Chamber of Commerce (802-247-6401), P.O. Box 267, Brandon 05735; visitors booth on Park St. with brochures and information in front of the library across from the Brandon Inn. There's an informative self-guided walking tour guide to the town's rich architectural heritage.

Moosalamoo, from the Abenaki word possibly meaning "the moose departs" or "he trails the moose," is a dandy map and guide, with site signage, to the trails and other natural features of some 20,000 acres of Green Mountain National Forest, published and distributed by the Moosalamoo Partnership, available at chambers of commerce, the Catamount Trail Association, other outdoor recreation organizations, and several inns. Or call 802-247-6735; 1-800-448-0707.

GETTING THERE *By car:* The major north–south highway is Rt. 7, but we advise anyone from Boston to approach through the Middlebury Gap (see *Scenic Drives*). From the west you can take the toll bridge at Chimney Point year-round or the seasonal ferries described below.

By ferry: **Lake Champlain Ferry** (802-864-9804) from Essex, N.Y., to Charlotte operates spring through fall, takes 20 minutes, and puts you just above Vergennes.

Fort Ticonderoga Ferry (802-897-7999), Larrabees Point to Fort Ticonderoga. May–June, 8–5:45 daily; July–Labor Day 8–7:45, then 8–5:45 through the last Sun. in Oct. Cars $8 one-way, $12 round-trip.

MEDICAL EMERGENCY Emergency service is available by calling **911**.

✳ Villages

Middlebury (population: 8,517) is the county seat and hub of Addison County. It's also the home of prestigious Middlebury College and one of Vermont's most handsome, lively, and welcoming communities. Inns and restaurants serve visitors as well as potential students and their parents, and in recent years it has become a great place to shop. Middlebury College (founded in 1800 and now one of the nation's most sought-after private colleges) owes much to the energy and vision of Gamaliel Painter, a surveyor who settled here before the Revolution. Painter accompanied Ethan Allen on the Fort Ticonderoga raid and returned to Middlebury to become the town's principal landowner, sheriff, judge, and assemblyman. The fine mansion on Court Street, presently housing the information center, belonged to Painter. Another benefactor was Joseph Battell, who owned thousands of acres of forest and mountain land that he left to the college and the state when he died in 1915. He was the proprietor of the famous old summit house, the Bread Loaf Inn, now the nucleus of the summer Bread Loaf School of English and the Bread Loaf Writers Conference. Battell also owned a weekly newspaper in which he fulminated against the invasion of motorcars. Emma Hart Willard, who pioneered in the education of women, was another Middlebury luminary. The town's proudest buildings—the courthouse, the Middlebury Inn, the Battell House, and the fine Congregational church—are grouped, along with compact business blocks, around the common. It's a short walk down Main Street to the churning Otter Creek falls, a centerpiece for dozens of shops that have proliferated in the old mills and marbleworks on both banks of the river, connected by a footbridge. With the Vermont State Craft Center as its anchor store, this is now one of Vermont's most interesting places to shop. The college is worth a look, too, especially the lovely stone château housing the French Department.

Brandon is rich in historic architecture, from Federal style to Queen Anne; its entire center, some 230 homes, is on the National Register of Historic Places, which is unusual for a town of only 4,000 inhabitants. Luckily, several Brandon manses are open to the public as bed & breakfasts. Park Street, the town's classiest area, was built wide to accommodate military parades, and still bears marble hitching posts and curbside slabs where the ladies stepped down from their horse-drawn carriages. Sited in Rutland County (it's just over the southern border of Addison County) between Otter Creek and the Neshobe River, Brandon (and the adjacent town of Forest Dale) was the home of Thomas Davenport, who invented and patented an electric motor in 1838, and the birthplace of Stephen A. Douglas (1813–61), the "Little Giant" of the famous debates with Abraham Lincoln in 1858, when Douglas was a senator from Illinois. Brandon has blossomed in recent years with the addition of art galleries, antiques shops, bookstores, and some of the region's best dining.

Bristol. Billing itself as the "Gateway to the Green Mountains," Bristol is nestled at the foot of Lincoln Gap, at the junctions of north–south Rt. 116 (less heavily trafficked than Rt. 7) and east–west Rt. 17. Its broad Main Street is lined with a delightful mix of stores and restaurants, housed in a western-style 19th-century block that leads to a square green, complete with fountain, park benches, and a gazebo. Its pride is the elaborately hand-painted stagecoach in front of the historical society at 19 West St. and the **Lord's Prayer Rock** (on the south side of Rt. 17 entering Bristol from the east), which is inscribed with the Lord's Prayer. A physician named Joseph C. Greene commissioned the inscription in 1891, presumably because he was thankful for having reached this point safely when, as a youth, he was hauling logs over steep, slippery roads.

Vergennes, midway between Middlebury and Burlington, has long claimed to be the smallest city (2,700 residents) in the United States. Although 5 miles inland, its history and its present activities are linked closely to Lake Champlain. Otter Creek winds from the city to the lake, and the road leads to Basin Harbor, site of the area's premier resort and the Lake Champlain Maritime Museum. We recommend the lake road south from Basin Harbor, by Button Bay State Park and the D.A.R. State Park to Chimney Point. It passes some beautiful old stone houses; the ruins of the 18th-century fort at

SUDBURY MEETING HOUSE

Diane E. Foulds

Crown Point, N.Y., are just across the Lake Champlain Bridge. Vergennes's site on an impressive set of falls and its handsome, early-19th-century commercial buildings (especially the glass-domed library) suggest an unusual history. This is, in fact, one of the oldest, as well as the smallest, cities in the country. It was founded by Donald McIntosh in 1764 and later named by Ethan Allen for Charles Gravier, comte de Vergennes, the French minister of foreign affairs who was a strong supporter of the American Revolutionary cause. In 1811–12 Thomas Macdonough used the Otter Creek Basin just below the falls to build—in record time—three ships, including the 734-ton, 26-gun *Saratoga*. He also equipped nine gunboats, using them all to defeat the British fleet in Lake Champlain off Plattsburgh in 1814.

Shoreham is known for its many orchards. Shoreham Village is a beauty, with a classic Congregational church (1846), a Masonic temple (built in 1852 as the Universalist church), and the graceful St. Genevieve Catholic Church (1873), as well as the old inn and general store. Follow Rt. 74 southwest from the village through the orchards; or continue straight on Witherell Rd. where 74 jogs south, then turn south (left) onto Smith St. along the lake. Either way, you get to Larrabees Point, the site of Teachout's Store, built in 1836 from stones taken from Fort Ticonderoga just across the lake. The excursion boat M/V *Carillon* now departs from this spot; next door the small, car-carrying "Fort Ti" cable ferry makes the crossing to the fort itself in 6 minutes flat. It has held the franchise from the Vermont and New York Legislatures since 1799, but records indicate the service was initiated by Lord Jeffery Amherst in 1757 for use by his soldiers in the campaigns against the French. Continue south on Rt. 73 to the turnoff for Mount Independence.

Orwell. Best known for Mount Independence, the small village at the center of this orchard and dairying community circles a long, sloping green with a brick Congregational church (1843) on a rise by the white-clapboard town hall (built in 1810 as the Baptist church). It all overlooks a brief line of shops with the First National Bank of Orwell, billed as "the world's smallest bank," in the middle. Chartered in 1863 (but known as the Farmers Bank for many years, before Lincoln granted it the country's 212th official charter), the bank remains a real center of town, with notices of upcoming events tacked to the authentic old tellers' cages. The other village nerve center is **Buxton's General Store**, the genuine article.

✳ To See

MUSEUMS ♿ **Middlebury College Museum of Art** (802-443-3168; www .middlebury.edu/arts/museum), Rt. 30 South, Middlebury 05753. Open Mon.–Fri. noon–5, and select Saturdays noon–5. Free. The college's distinguished permanent collection ranges from the decorative arts through modern painting, with emphasis on photography, 19th-century European and American sculpture, and contemporary prints. Permanent and changing exhibits are displayed in galleries within the multi-tiered arts center, which also includes a café and several performance areas.

The Henry Sheldon Museum (802-388-2117; www.henrysheldonmuseum .org), 1 Park St., Middlebury. Open year-round, Mon.–Sat. 10–5. Guided and self-guided tours. $5 adults, $4.50 seniors, $3 ages 6–18. This 1829 marble merchant's house has no fewer than six black marble mantels and holds an intimate collection of furnishings, tools, household articles, clothes, books, games, and other artifacts portraying Vermont culture, all displayed in period rooms. A modern research ell has been added, with a gallery for changing exhibits. There are also frequent special events, all of which impart a sense of the history of the Champlain Valley. The gift shop is strong on Vermont books and early American reproductions.

The **Vermont Folklife Center** (802-388-4964; www.vermontfolklifecenter.org), 3 Court St., Middlebury (in the Masonic Hall). This growing organization (founded in 1984) collects and preserves the traditional arts and heritage of Vermont, primarily through taped interviews (its archive contains over 3,800). It mounts changing exhibits and sells its publications in its excellent on-site gift shop.

✍ **Lake Champlain Maritime Museum** (802-475-2022), 4472 Basin Harbor Rd., 7 miles west of Vergennes at the entrance to the Basin Harbor Club off Panton Rd. Open May 1–mid-Oct., daily 10–5; $9 adults, $8 seniors, $5 ages 6–17. This museum began with the gift of a local schoolhouse constructed from native limestone in 1808, moved stone by stone (2,000 of them) and reconstructed to house exhibits. The museum's 12 buildings, spread over 3 acres, now house nautical artifacts, a working blacksmith shop, and dozens of small craft built around the lake over a period of 150 years. Exhibits tell the story of the lake's past, including the hundreds of wrecks still beneath the surface. Attempts to raise them, you learn, began in the 1930s but have been abandoned because divers and historians have accepted the obvious: Wood that's been submerged in fresh water quickly disintegrates when exposed to air. Instead, the state of Vermont has created five underwater parks; inquire about guided scuba tours, lectures, boatbuilding and blacksmithing courses, field trips, and demonstrations. A working replica of Benedict Arnold's 1776 gunboat *Philadelphia II*, built on the spot, is open to visitors, and a full-sized replica of the 1862 canal schooner *Lois McClure* can be explored on the Burlington waterfront at Perkins Pier. The museum store carries maritime-related books, prints, gifts, and clothing.

Bixby Memorial Library (802-877-2211; www.vuhs.org/bixby), 258 Main St., Vergennes. Open Mon. and Fri. 12:30–8, Tue. and Thu. 12:30–5, Wed. 10–5, Sat. 10–2. Upstairs in this glass-domed neoclassical building is a vintage display of Plains Indian artifacts including baskets, clothing, and beadwork, along with mementoes from Vergennes's own past. The library also contains what might be the state's best archive of Vermontiana.

HISTORIC HOMES **Rokeby Museum** (802-877-3406), 3 miles north of Vergennes on Rt. 7 in Ferrisburgh. Open for guided tours mid-May–mid-Oct., Thu.–Sun. at 11, 12:30, and 2, and by appointment year-round. $6 adults, $4 students and seniors, $2 ages 12 and under. A period-furnished home and nine outbuildings evoke the lives of four generations of a Quaker abolitionist family

JOSEPH BATTELL BRIDGE

The bridge that Joseph Battell built in downtown Middlebury is but one element of an enormous and enduring legacy of mountaintops and mortar that this eccentric bachelor left to the state of Vermont as a whole and to Middlebury College in particular.

Battell was born in 1839 to a wealthy and influential Vermont family. He attended Middlebury College, but ill health kept him from finishing his degree. Instead, he went off to travel the world; upon his return he bought land in the mountain town of Ripton, where he ran an inn, mainly for his friends. Today that land and those buildings house two of the college's most highly regarded summer programs: the Bread Loaf School of English and the Bread Loaf Writers Conference. In addition to being publisher of the *Middlebury Register,* a local newspaper, Battell was also an author. One of his oddest efforts was a book titled *Ellen, or, The Whisperings of an Old Pine,* a dense tome that is seldom read but much wondered about.

Battell was a man who loved mountains and woods and hated cars, so much so that he refused to allow cars on the road that ran up to his Ripton inn. Yet it was because of Battell that the stone bridge spanning Otter Creek in downtown Middlebury is still, a century later, a key to the transportation infrastructure in Addison County. The original wooden bridge that carried traffic across the creek burned down a century ago. Middlebury's town fathers, in a fit of economy, decided to build an iron bridge on the site, but

whose members included pioneers, farmers, and Rowland E. Robinson, the 19th-century author, illustrator, and naturalist. Rokeby was one of several merino sheep farms that dotted the Vermont landscape in the early 19th century. More important, it was a destination for freedom-seeking slaves who took refuge here and worked in the open before the Civil War. The family occupied the property until 1961, when it became a museum. Frugal by nature, they kept every diary, receipt, and newspaper, which added up to an immense library (including 10,000 family letters), making this the best-documented Underground Railroad site in the country.

The John Strong D.A.R. Mansion (802-759-2309), 6656 Rt. 17W, West Addison, 05491, open Memorial Day–Labor Day, weekends 9–5. $3 per adult, $2 seniors and students. This is one of several historic structures built from stone taken from the ruins of Fort Crown Point and skidded across frozen Lake Champlain by oxen. General Strong, an early settler and Green Mountain Boy, built his (third) residence here in 1796 with brick from his own clay pits on the "Salt Lick" where he first hunted deer. Furnishings reflect five generations of the family.

Battell was opposed, arguing that a stone bridge would last significantly longer than an iron one. So determined was he that he is said to have paid the difference out of his own pocket.

A pioneering conservationist, Battell used to send his hired man into the woods, armed with blank deeds and instructions to buy as much acreage as he could from any farmer or logger he came across. Over time he acquired about 35,000 acres, including Camels Hump, which he donated to the state of Vermont for use as a state park. His landholdings also reached over Bread Loaf Mountain from East Middlebury to Hancock, Granville, and Rochester, along Rt. 100, and followed the spine of the Green Mountains from Mount Ellen south to Brandon Gap. When he died in 1915, most of this land was bequeathed to Middlebury College, which has sold off much of it over the years, keeping only a few hundred acres.

Battell is also the father of the University of Vermont's Morgan Horse Farm. He began breeding Morgans on his farm in the latter 1800s, an interest that would prove instrumental in saving America's first breed of horse from extinction. He hired architect Clinton Smith to build the beautiful white farm buildings that still stand in Weybridge. With typical Battell intensity, he spent years tracing out the pedigrees published in the first volume of the *Morgan Horse Register* in 1894. Then in 1906 he gave his farm and his Morgan horses to the U.S. government. It remains a working horse farm to this day, supplying stock to Morgan breeders across the country.

HISTORIC SITES ✍ ⅃ **Mount Independence State Historic Site** (802-948-2000; 802-759-2412; www.historicvermont.org/mountindependence), 497 Mount Independence Rd., on the shore of Lake Champlain, 7 miles west of the junction of Rts. 73 and 22A near Orwell. Grounds open year-round; museum open Memorial Day weekend–Columbus Day, daily 9:30–5:30. $5; ages 14 and under, free. This National Historic Landmark is one of America's best-preserved Revolutionary War sites. A state-of-the-art visitors center tells the story of the 12,000 men who built a massive fort here in 1776 to fend off the British, many of them freezing to death the following winter. An exhibit displays the musket balls, grenades, shovels, knives, forks, bottles, cuff links, dishes, even the fish bones they left behind on this rocky peninsula across the lake from Fort Ticonderoga. Six miles of marked hiking trails start at the visitors center—one of them handicapped accessible—weaving past the remains of the hospital, batteries, blockhouses, and barracks of this once bustling fort.

✍ **Fort Ticonderoga** (518-585-2821; www.fort-ticonderoga.org), Ticonderoga, N.Y. Open mid-May–late Oct., daily 9–5. $12 adults, $10.80 ages 65 and up, $6 ages 7–12. The 18th-century stone fort has been restored and includes a museum displaying weapons, uniforms, and historical artifacts. Built by the French (who named it Fort Carillon), it was captured by English general Jeffery Amherst and held by the British until 1775, when Ethan Allen and his Green Mountain Boys took the fort by surprise, capturing the guns that eventually helped free Boston. The fort is easily accessible from Larrabees Point on the Vermont shore. The **Log House** restaurant is open 9–5. No dogs.

Crown Point State Historic Site (518-597-4666, http://nysparks.state.ny .us/sites/info.asp?siteID=6), 739 Bridge Rd., Crown Point, NY 12928. Open May–Oct., Wed.–Mon. 9:30–5, or by appointment. $3 adults, $2 seniors (over 62) and students, $1 ages 6–12. Just across the Lake Champlain Bridge from Chimney Point, West Addison, Vt. Fifteen miles north of Fort Ticonderoga, Crown Point started out as the French-built "Fort St. Frederic." The British struggled to capture it and succeeded in 1759. But in 1775, on the eve of the Revolution, American colonists overtook it and hauled its cannons and heavy ordnance off to Boston for use in fighting the British. The complex includes 18th-century ruins and a visitors center with a museum.

& **Chimney Point State Historic Site** (802-759-2412; www.historicvermont .org/chimneypoint), at the Vermont end of the Lake Champlain Bridge, at the intersection of Rts. 125 and 17. Open Memorial Day–Columbus Day, Wed.–Sun. 9:30–5:30. A late-18th-century tavern, one of the state's oldest, houses an exhibit exploring three of Vermont's early cultures: the Abenaki, French, and early American. Each settled at this lakeside spot, recognizing its strategic importance. The area is still sparsely settled, making it easy to imagine what they experienced. Displays include Native American archaeological treasures, French colonial belongings, and an overview of 19th-century Abenaki weavings and basketry. A separate room houses changing exhibits of contemporary Abenaki crafts, illustrating the extent to which these skills have survived.

GARDENS **Pinewood Gardens** (802-247-3388; www.pinewoodgardencenter .com), 2473 Franklin St., Rt. 7 south, Brandon. Excellent perennials and annuals for sale, plus display gardens. Display gardens open daily May–Oct.

Rocky Dale Gardens (802-453-2782), 62 Rocky Dale Rd. (Rt. 116), Bristol. Open daily 9–6 except Tue. Extensive displays on 3 acres with dramatic rock outcroppings, plus a retail nursery.

Pine Tree Gardens (802-453-7555), 140 North St., Bristol. Apr.–July, open Mon.–Sat. 9–6, Sun. 10–4. Aug.–Oct., open Fri.–Mon. 10–6. Greenhouses, display gardens, and a retail nursery with fancy-leaved geraniums and other unusual plants.

FARMS ✍ **The UVM Morgan Horse Farm** (802-388-2011; www.uvm.edu/ morgan), 74 Battell Dr., Weybridge. Go through downtown Middlebury, heading west on Rt. 125, then turn right onto Rt. 23 (Weybridge St.) and follow signs. Open May–Oct., daily 9–4. $5 adults, $4 teens, $2 ages 5–12. The first "Morgan" was born in the late 1790s and is recognized as the sire of an entire breed of Vermont horse. Colonel Joseph Battell began breeding Morgans on this farm in the 1870s and is credited with saving the breed (America's first developed breed of horse) from extinction. The farm is now a breeding and training center operated by the University of Vermont. Guided tours of the stables and paddocks are available, along with an audiovisual presentation about the Morgan horse and farm.

Kim Grant

THE UVM MORGAN HORSE FARM IN WEYBRIDGE

🐑 **Wooly Hill Farm** (802-758-2284; www.woolyhill.com), 2695 Rattlin' Bridge Rd., Bridport. An organic sheep and alpaca farm with a yarn shop, spinning supplies, and gifts. Barn tours are offered Sat. 10–3, but call ahead. Also in Bridport is **Champlain Valley Alpacas** (802-758-3276; www.wcvt.com/~alpaca), 152 Merino Lane, a 200-acre alpaca ranch with a farm boutique that can be seen by appointment Mon.–Sat. 8–5 (buses welcome). Just south of Middlebury in Cornwall at 2170 Rt. 125 is **Moonlit Alpacas** (802-462-3510; www.moonlitalpacas.com) with a retail shop selling alpaca clothing, stuffed animals, and home accessories, open Wed.–Sun. 10–4. And in Brandon at 185 Adams Rd., Deb and Ed Bratton raise alpacas at **Maple View Farm** (802-247-5412; www.mapleview farmalpacas.com) and invite tourists to see their animals.

COVERED BRIDGES The **Pulp Mill Covered Bridge**, between Middlebury and Weybridge, spanning Otter Creek near the Morgan Horse Farm, is the oldest in the state (1808–20) and the last two-lane span still in use.

Halpin Bridge (1824), Middlebury, 2 miles east of Rt. 7, off Halpin Rd., is Vermont's highest bridge above the streambed.

Station (or Salisbury) Bridge, across Otter Creek in Cornwall (2 miles east of Rt. 30 on Swamp Rd.), is a 136-foot Town lattice bridge built in 1865.

Shoreham Covered Railroad Bridge, East Shoreham off the Whiting–Shoreham Rd. (turn south onto Shoreham Depot Rd.); the bridge is marked on area maps. A Howe bridge built in 1897 by the Rutland Railroad, spanning the Lemon Fair River, one of the few remaining railroad covered bridges left in Vermont. A designated state historic site.

Spade Farm Covered Bridge, located along Rt. 7 in Ferrisburgh, is now on the property of the Artisans Guild and Starry Night Café. It was built in 1824 and moved 3 miles to its present location in 1959.

SCENIC DRIVES **Middlebury Gap**. This is our favorite approach to Addison County from the southeast, and this stretch of Rt. 125 is more dramatic driving east to west. Begin in Hancock and stop at Texas Falls (see our map on page 402). The road quickly crests at its junction with the Long Trail, near the Middlebury Snow Bowl. Then it's all downhill through the woods until the huge, wooden Bread Loaf Inn (now part of Middlebury College) improbably appears. The Robert Frost Wayside Picnic Area and the Interpretive Trail are a short way beyond. We also like to stop in the small, 19th-century cemetery a bit farther down, where a wind chime strikes softly in a row of maples. The picturesque hill town of Ripton is just below, and as the road continues to plunge into the valley, you glimpse the Adirondacks in the distance.

Brandon Gap. Rt. 73 is a high road over Goshen Mountain and through Brandon Gap. At the height-of-land, several wooded hiking trails are posted, and a rest area has been sited to catch the full majesty of Mount Horrid's Great Cliff. The road then rushes downhill with Brandon Brook, joining Rt. 100 and the White River below Rochester.

Note: A well-surfaced woods road (Goshen Rd.) runs south from Ripton through the national forest, past the turnoffs for Silver Lake and past Blueberry Hill to Rt. 73 in the Brandon Gap.

Appalachian Gap. East from Bristol, Rt. 17 climbs steadily for 4 miles (past the Jerusalem General Store), eases off for a couple of miles, and then zigzags steeply to crest at more than 3,000 feet, yielding some spectacular views before dropping into the Mad River Valley. It's even more spectacular heading west.

Lincoln/Appalachian Gap Loop. From Bristol, follow Rt. 17/116 to the turnoff for Lincoln 2 miles east of Bristol, past Bartlett Falls (be sure to stop) to Lincoln and out Downingsville Rd. to Jerusalem, back down on Rt. 116 to Rt. 17.

Lincoln Gap. Follow Rt. 17/116 east from Bristol, as above, but from Lincoln continue on the narrow Gap Rd., unpaved in sections. Again there are beautiful views, and you are quickly down in Warren. *Note:* Unsuitable for trailers and RVs. Closed in winter.

Along Lake Champlain. See *Villages* for Shoreham and Orwell.

✳ To Do

APPLE PICKING ✍ September and early October is apple time in Addison County, where you are welcome to pick your own (PYO). The orchards are particularly thick in and around Shoreham: **Atwood Orchard** (802-897-5592) at 555 Barnum Hill, 0.5 mile from its stand on Rt. 22A (3 miles south of Shoreham Village), offers PYO apples and sells honey, syrup, and apple pies; also a picnic area and views of Lake Champlain. **Douglas Orchards** (802-897-5043), 1 mile west of the village at 1050 Rt. 74, has PYO apples, berries, cherries, and pumpkins mid-June through July and again Sept. till Thanksgiving, as well as a cider mill, a retail store, and hand-knit felt hats designed by Betty Douglas. **Champlain Orchards** (802-897-2777), farther west on Rt. 74, offers PYO fruits, cider-mill tours, hayrides, tastings, and weekend concerts in the hilltop orchard during apple season with beautiful lake views. Open daily in-season 8–6.

BICYCLING It's no coincidence that the country's first bicycle touring company was founded in this area. According to Bruce Burgess, a pioneer tour leader, there just isn't a more rewarding place to bike anywhere than this swath of the Champlain Valley, with its relatively flat terrain and mountain views, its wealth of back roads leading through covered bridges, connecting historic sites and comfortable inns with ample swimming holes, ice cream, and antiquing stops en route. Burgess shares a word of warning: Beware deceptively quiet but narrow, truck-trafficked roads like Rt. 22A and Rt. 30.

Bike Vermont (1-800-257-2226; www.bikevermont.com), based in Woodstock, gets good reviews for guided, small-group inn-to-inn tours in this area.

Vermont Bicycle Touring (VBT) (802-453-4811; www.vbt.com), 614 Monkton Rd., Bristol, the state's oldest bike tour company, offers guided group inn-to-inn tours.

The Bike Center (802-388-6666; www.bikecentermid.com), 74 Main St., Middlebury, is a source for a variety of rental bikes.

Country Inns Along the Trail (1-800-838-3301; www.inntoinn.com), P.O. Box 59, Montgomery 05470. Bike tours begin and end in Brandon, visiting a number of inns along the way. Bikes available for rent. Hiking and skiing tours available as well.

Mountain Biking at Blueberry Hill (802-247-6735), Goshen. An extensive network of ski trails and woods roads that is well suited to mountain biking; rentals, lessons.

BIRDING **Otter Creek**, near Lake Champlain in Vergennes, and the **Dead Creek Wildlife Management Area** in Addison (off Rt. 17) are particularly rich in bird life, especially during migration seasons in spring and fall. See also "What's Where."

BOATING *Carillon* **Cruises** (802-897-5331; www.paxp.com/carillon). A 60-foot, 49-passenger replica of a 1920s Thousand Islands luxury motor yacht operates daily Father's Day–Labor Day. Geared to groups in spring and fall but walk-ons accepted (call ahead), from Teachout's Lakehouse Store and Wharf at Larrabees Point. The 1½-hour cruise, beginning at 11 AM, and 1 and 3 PM, goes up to Hand's Cove, then across to Fort Ticonderoga (you can debark and catch a later boat), and on to Mount Independence and Mount Defiance, while the captain tells you what was happening along the route in the 1770s. Sat.–Tue. in July and Aug., weekends in Sep. and Oct.

Boat rentals are available from **Champlain Houseboat Charters** (802-948-2288; 802-948-2740; www.champlainhouseboatcharters.com), P.O. Box 62, Orwell 05760. **Waterhouse's** (802-352-4433; www.waterhouses.com), 937 West Shore Rd., Salisbury (Lake Dunmore), rents paddleboats, canoes, and motorboats; fuel station, fishing supplies, and a game room in the boathouse. **Champlain Bridge Marina** (802-759-2049; www.sayahoy.com), 7724 Rt. 17, West Addison. Boat access, pump-out station for boats less than 35 feet. **Chipman Point Marina & Campground** (802-948-2288), Rt. 73A, Orwell. Dockage for 60 boats, grocery store, pump-out station, game room, swimming, boat rentals. **Lake Dunmore Kampersville** (802-352-4501; www.kampersville.com), in Salisbury, also rents rowboats, canoes, sailboats, and paddleboats.

FACTORY TOURS **Otter Creek Brewing** (1-800-473-0727; www.ottercreek brewing.com), 793 Exchange St., Middlebury. Open year-round, daily except Sun., for free guided tours. Free samples, retail sales of its Otter Creek craft beers and Wolaver's organic ales.

Beau Ties Ltd. (802-388-0108; 1-800-488-8437; www.beautiesltd.com), 69 Industrial Ave., Middlebury. Tour the facility (call ahead for an appointment) to see handcrafters making bow ties from every fabric imaginable. The retail store features the current catalog choices plus vintage ties, accessories, and gifts. The store is open weekdays 8–4:30.

Vermont Soapworks (802-388-4302; 1-866-762-7482), 616 Exchange St., Middlebury. Open weekdays 9–5, Sat. 10–4, Sun. 11–4. See soap being made from a window onto the factory floor. There's a small soap museum in the factory store, and groups of 12 or more can schedule a factory tour (call in advance). Across from Otter Creek Brewing.

FISHING **Otter Creek** is a warm-water stream good for smallmouth bass and northern pike. The cooler **Neshobe River**, especially in Forest Dale, is better for trout, and rainbows can be found in the **Middlebury River** just below Ripton. The **New Haven River** between Lincoln and Bristol and south of New Haven Mills also offers good trout fishing.

GOLF **Ralph Myhre Golf Course** (802-443-5125), Rt. 30 just south of the Middlebury campus, is owned and operated by the college; 18 holes. Open mid-Apr.–Nov.

The Basin Harbor Club (802-475-2309), Vergennes, 18 holes. Open early May–mid-Oct.

Neshobe Golf Club (802-247-3611; www.neshobe.com), 224 Town Farm Rd. (just off Rt. 73), Brandon. Open Apr.–Oct. A full-service club; 18 holes.

HIKING **The Green Mountain National Forest District Office** (802-388-4362), 1007 Rt. 7 south, Middlebury 05753, offers a free pamphlet guide to 28 day hikes. Open year-round, weekdays 8–4:30.

Country Inns Along the Trail (802-326-2072; 1-800-838-3301; www.inntoinn .com). A dozen inns collaborate to provide lodging along an 80-mile stretch of the Long Trail and some of its side trails, including the section over Mount Mansfield.

Trail Around Middlebury (802-388-1007). The local Middlebury Area Land Trust has created this remarkable 18-mile loop that circles the town and strings together two parks and half a dozen woodland paths. The most scenic segment is the Otter Creek Gorge Trail, which runs riverside and traverses meadows, forests, and wilderness areas. The Land Trust publishes *The Trail Around Middlebury* (*TAM*), a free map/guide (P.O. Box 804, Middlebury 05753; 802-388-1007), and organizes monthly hikes May–Oct.

Snake Mountain, Bridport. From Rt. 22A, take Rt. 17 east; turn right after a mile onto Mountain Rd. Park about 2 miles up on your right in the designated area. The trail begins on Mountain Rd., about 300 feet south. The first half of this popular hike is easy, but it gets steeper and rockier as you reach the summit. The reward is the stunning lake and Adirondack view. A great afternoon hike.

Mount Abraham (802-388-4362), Lincoln. At over 4,000 feet above sea level, this is Vermont's fifth highest peak, its summit above the tree line, so the open views are magnificent. There are two trails, both strenuous. From the top of Lincoln Gap, you can park at the TV tower and follow the Long Trail (plan 3 ½ hours round-trip, and remember that the Lincoln Gap is not plowed in winter). You can also take the Battell Trail, a 5.8-mile loop that takes about 4 hours total. For this route, go to Lincoln Village and turn north onto Quaker St.; after 0.7 mile turn right onto Elder Hill Rd. The parking area is 2 miles ahead. Bring water, a detailed map, a sweater, and insect repellent.

Moosalamoo, an Abenaki word meaning "he trails the moose" or "the moose departs," is a 22,000-acre tract within the Green Mountain National Forest that is prime moose habitat. It is also crisscrossed with hiking routes and a 10-mile spur of the Long Trail, which begins at the parking area atop Brandon Gap on Rt. 73 and threads north for a steep 0.1 mile to a trail to Mount Horrid Cliffs, a rocky outcropping with memorable Adirondack views. The Long Trail stretch ends at a parking area on Rt. 125. Free trail guies are available from the conservation-minded Moosalamoo Association (1-800-448-0707; www.moosalamoo.org), P.O. Box 108, Forest Dale 05745-0108.

HORSEBACK RIDING **Mazza Horse Service** (802-758-9240), Hemenway Rd., Bridport. Trail riding, lessons.

♫ **Deerfield Farm Icelandics** (802-453-3247; www.deerfieldfarmvt.com), 542 Geary Rd. north, Lincoln. One-hour to half-day treks over 85 pristine acres. Lessons, summer camp, weekend horseback-riding treks from inn to inn.

SWIMMING **Middlebury Gorge**, East Middlebury, off Rt. 125 just above the Waybury Inn, where the road suddenly steepens beyond the bridge. Paths lead down to the river.

Dog Team Tavern Hole, 3.1 miles north of Middlebury, off Dog Team Tavern Rd. Park by the restaurant and walk along the riverbank until you find an appealing spot in the bends of the New Haven River. Small beach area, gentle current.

Lake Pleiad, behind the Middlebury College Snow Bowl about 8 miles from Middlebury on Rt. 125 east. Park in the lot past the entrance near the Long Trail and walk it south 0.5 mile, turning right on Lake Pleiad Trail. A truly idyllic setting, perfect for swimming and picnics. The large rocks on the western end provide a perfect perch from which to take in the pristine surroundings.

Bartlett Falls, Bristol. Near the beginning of Lincoln Gap Rd. (off Rt. 116 in Rocky Dale) there's a pull-off for this popular swimming hole with its 20-foot cliffs. A bronze plaque explains that the land is a gift from Irving Wesley Sr., in memory of his son who died at 19 fighting a 1943 forest fire in British Columbia. It's a beautiful spot by a stream with shallow falls dropping into pools. Swimming shoes are a good idea.

♫ **Lake Dunmore** (see *Green Space*), a scenic lake with a firm, sandy bottom and extensive sand beach, with plenty of space for running, game playing, and picnics.

See also *Green Space*.

✳ Winter Sports

CROSS-COUNTRY SKIING **Carroll and Jane Rikert Ski Touring Center** at the Bread Loaf Campus of Middlebury College (802-443-2744), Rt. 125, Ripton, 12 miles from the main campus, is owned and operated by Middlebury College. It has 42 km of groomed trails in the area of the Robert Frost Farm and the college ski bowl. Elevations range from 975 to 1,500 feet. Rentals, accessories, lessons, and repairs.

Blueberry Hill Inn (802-247-6735), 1307 Goshen–Ripton Rd, Goshen, has 50 km of tracked and groomed trails plus another 20 km of outlying trails on elevations of 1,400–3,100 feet. This is a surefire cross-country mecca during even marginal seasons. The ski center has retail and rental equipment, waxing, and repairs; a pass gets you free soup noon–2.

DOWNHILL SKIING **Middlebury College Snow Bowl** (802-388-4356; www .middlebury.edu), 15 miles east of Middlebury on Rt. 125, at Bread Loaf. A throwback to a less commercial era of skiing: well-maintained, winding trails with a library in the base lodge! Two double chairs, one triple, a total of 15 trails, two glades, and a large terrain park; 40 percent covered by snowmaking. It also offers a ski school, rentals, cafeteria. Closed Dec. 25. Adults $37 weekends, $30 weekdays.

FITNESS CENTERS **Vermont Sun** (802-388-6888; www.vermontsun.com), 812 Exchange St., Middlebury, is a spacious indoor sports and fitness center with training equipment, an Olympic-sized pool, and racquetball courts. Open daily for members; guests by the day or week.

Middlebury Fitness (802-388-3744; www.middleburyfitness.com), Wilson Rd. off Rt. 7 south, Middlebury, features state-of-the-art equipment. Guests by the day or by the week.

✳ Green Space

Note: Public preserves are clustered on the eastern and western fringes of the valley.

On or near Lake Champlain
Button Bay State Park (802-475-2377; 802-241-3655; www.vtstateparks.com), 5 Button Bay State Park Rd., off Panton Rd. just below Basin Harbor. Open late May–mid-Oct. Named for the unusual, buttonlike clay formations found along its shore, this 253-acre area overlooks splendid scenery of the lake and Adirondacks; 73 campsites (including 13 lean-tos), picnic areas, swimming, fishing, nature museum, and trails. Rocky Point juts into Lake Champlain like the prow of a ship.

Kingsland Bay State Park (802-877-3445; 1-888-409-7579; www.vtstateparks .com), 787 Kingsland Bay State Park Rd., Ferrisburgh. Marked from Rt. 7. Facilities include a picnic area on Lake Champlain, tennis courts, and hiking trails. This is a particularly lovely overlook of Kingsland Bay with lawns that roll down to the lakeside shaded by old maples. Weddings and summer get-togethers are very popular here.

Dead Creek Wildlife Management Area (802-759-2397; www.vtfishand wildlife.com), 1 mile west of Rt. 22A on Rt. 17, is a 2,800-acre, semi-wilderness tract with a parking area and posted visitors information about the many species of birds that congregate here, including herds of snow and Canada geese that can number up to 20,000 during spring and fall migrations.

D.A.R. State Park (802-759-2354; www.vtstateparks.com), 6750 Rt. 17 west, 8 miles west of Addison, a 95-acre park comprising the 1765 stone foundations of the area's first colonial structures (in the picnic area). A grassy field contains 70 campsites, including 24 lean-tos; flush toilets and hot showers. Steps lead down to a smooth shale beach for swimming.

In or near the Green Mountain National Forest

✿ **Lake Dunmore**, in Salisbury between Brandon and Middlebury on Rt. 53 off Rt. 7, is a tranquil, 1,000-acre lake that has licked its once infamous mosquito problem. It is lined with summer cottages at the foot of Mount Moosalamoo and along its hiking trails. On the east shore road is **Branbury State Park** (802-247-5925; www.vtstateparks.com), with a natural sandy beach, vast grassy areas, 39 tent sites, 6 lean-tos, boating, snack bar, picnic grove, museum nature trail, and hiking to the Falls of Lana. The trail begins just south of the Branbury Park entrance, and it's just 0.5 mile to the picnic area and falls. From Rt. 53 it's 1.6 miles past these falls up to secluded **Silver Lake**, once the site of religious camp meetings in the 1880s; a large hotel (actually constructed as a seminary) occupied the spot of the present picnic area and stood until around 1940, when it was destroyed by fire. About 1 mile long, it is now part of the Green Mountain National Forest, accessible only by foot and mountain bike (0.6 mile via the Goshen Trail from the second parking lot on Forest Rd. 27, off Goshen Rd.). There are 31 primitive campsites and a nature trail around the lake; swimming is permitted.

"Robert Frost Country" in the Green Mountain National Forest is a title officially bestowed in 1983 on a wooded piece of the town of Ripton because it was here, in a log cabin, that the poet summered for 39 years. This section of Rt. 125, between the old Bread Loaf Inn (part of the Middlebury College campus) and the village, has been designated the Robert Frost Memorial Highway; there is also a Robert Frost Interpretive Trail and a Robert Frost Wayside picnic area near the road leading to the farm and cabin. The picnic area has grills and drinking water, and it's shaded by red pines that were pruned by Frost himself. Just east of the wayside, a dirt road leads to the Homer Noble Farm, which Frost bought in 1939. Park in the lot provided and walk past the farm to Frost's cabin (it's not open to the public). The Robert Frost Interpretive Trail, a bit west on the opposite side of Rt. 125, is an easy walk, just 0.75 mile. It begins with a bridge across Beaver Pond (we actually saw a beaver here once) and winds through woods and meadow, past seven Frost poems mounted along the way. This trail is also popular with cross-country skiers and snowshoers, and with July and August blueberry pickers.

Texas Falls, in Hancock, is easily accessible from the marked road, 3 miles east of the Middlebury Gap. It's a short drive to the parking area, and the succession of falls is just across the road, visible from a series of paths and bridges. There's also a picnic area.

☀ Lodging

Mid VT for All Seasons Area Guide, Mid VT Map (1-800-733-8376; www.midvermont.com). This comprehensive guide to area lodging is available by calling the 800 number or visiting the web site.

INNS ∞ ❦ ♂ ⛬ **Swift House Inn** (802-388-9925; 802-388-9927; 1-866-388-9925; www.swifthouseinn.com), 25 Stewart Lane, Middlebury 05753. Formerly the family estate of the legendary philanthropist Jessica Stewart Swift, who lived to be over 100, the Swift House is now under the ownership of Dan and Michele Brown. Antiques, elaborately carved marble fireplaces, formal gardens, and extravagant wallpaper and upholstery add to the charm of this 1814 mansion. (Ask to see the vintage elevator.) Common space in the inn itself includes a cozy bar as well as two attractive living rooms. Meals (and full breakfasts) are served in the cherry-paneled main dining room, the library, or on the window-ringed sunporch. There are nine guest rooms in the main house, five in the Victorian gatehouse on Rt. 7, and six contemporary-styled ones in the renovated 1886 carriage house. One room is wheelchair accessible, as is the dining room. Some suites have fireplace, sitting area, whirlpool tub, and cable TV. $100–275 in high season, $90–225 in low. The dining room serves some of the best food in town (see *Dining Out*). Pets housed for $25 per day.

∞ ❦ ⛬ **Lilac Inn** (802-247-5463; 1-800-221-0720; www.lilacinn.com), 53 Park St. (Rt. 73 east), Brandon 05733. One of New England's most romantic inns, this grand old mansion has been totally restored. Built with an imposing five-arched facade in 1909 by a Brandon-born financier, and currently owned by Shelly and Doug Sawyer, it has some splendid common spaces (a glassed-in ballroom with its crystal chandelier is the scene of chamber concerts and wedding receptions), glorious antiques, and a wide entrance hallway with a grand staircase. There is also a formal garden with a gazebo and cobbled patio, a small living room with a fireplace and floor-to-ceiling bookcases, and a copper-topped bar with comfortable seating. The nine ample guest rooms all have luxurious bathrooms with deep, claw-foot tubs; each is furnished in antiques and has a hidden TV. The bridal suite (the original master bedroom) has a pewter canopy bed, whirlpool bath, fireplace, and dressing area. There is one handicapped-accessible room. Weddings are a specialty. Rates include a three-course breakfast served in the sun-filled garden room; dinner can be arranged. $175–295 in high season, otherwise $145–250. Inquire about MAP, winter weekends featuring music or dramatic readings, and the cottage for four. Children must be over 12, and pets require prior approval.

∞ ♞ ❦ ♂ ⛬ **Blueberry Hill Inn** (802-247-6735; 802-247-6535; 1-800-448-0707; www.blueberryhillinn.com), Goshen 05733, on Forest Rd. 32 in Ripton. Over the past three decades Tony Clark has turned this blue 1813 farmhouse on a high, remote back road into one of New England's most famous country inns. The lures are gourmet cuisine, peace and quiet, hiking and mountain biking, and, in winter, cross-country skiing. But there is more to it: a sure touch. The 12 rooms—some with loft, all with full bath—have antiques, handmade

RESORT ☀ ✍ ♿ **Basin Harbor Club** (802-475-2311; 1-800-622-4000;
www.basinharbor.com), Box 7, Vergennes 05491, located on Lake Champlain
5 miles west of town, off Panton Rd. Open mid-May–mid-Oct. This is Vermont's premier lakeside resort. The 700-acre retreat offers 136 rooms in the
main lodge, two guest houses, and cottages scattered along the shore.
Since 1886, when they first began taking in summer boarders, members of
the Beach family have assiduously kept up with the times. Over the years a
large swimming pool, an 18-hole golf course, and even an airstrip have been
added. Still, the handsome old farmhouse has been preserved. In summer
Dutchman's-pipe climbs as it always has around the porch pillars, and three
grand old maples shade the lawn, which slopes to fabulous flower gardens
and the round harbor beyond. There are 18 rooms in the inn, 13 more in the
attractive stone Harbor Homestead. The 77 cottages, geared to families (and
well-behaved pets), vary in rate depending on size and location. All have
phone, fridge, and wet bar; many have fireplace. Eight cottages are handicapped accessible, with ramps and bathrooms, as are all public areas. The
lakeside units are worth the little extra, with views of the lake and the
Adirondacks so extraordinary that it's difficult to tear yourself away from the
window or deck, especially at sunset.

Basin Harbor manages to please both children and elderly couples.
Youngsters can take advantage of the beach, elaborate playground, and lively, supervised (complimentary) children's program available 9:30 AM–1:30 PM
for ages 3–15, and younger children can also dine together and play until
9 PM. For those 10–15, there are golf and tennis clinics, movies, mixers, and
video games in the Red Mill, the resort's informal restaurant off by the airstrip. Those who like to dress for dinner have ample opportunity; at the main
restaurant, men and boys over 12 must wear jackets and ties. The food is
fine (see *Dining Out*). Daily rates per couple $120–350 B&B; with a full Ameri-
can plan (the only plan available June 13–Sep. 1), $216–447 per couple; add
15 percent gratuity. Daily rate extra for children 3 and older, depending on
age. There are also golf, tennis, and fall foliage packages; inquire about
kayaking, horticultural workshops, and birding and nature treks.

botanicals, and fine decor, and the common areas are cozy and inviting, with roses and geraniums blooming in the indoor greenhouse off the kitchen, and a stone fireplace in the dining room. Guests tend to mingle, from morning coffee to evening hors d'oeuvres and dinner, served family-style at long wooden tables. This inn has long been known for its extraordi-nary food, and British-born chef Tim Cheevers more than deserves the rep-utation, producing elaborate, creative dinners featuring fresh ingredients,

Diane E. Foulds

BLUEBERRY HILL INN

many of them straight from the garden. The cross-country ski center, with 50 km of tracked and groomed trails in the Moosalamoo region of the Green Mountain National Forest, tends to be snowy, thanks to its elevation. In midsummer the blueberry crop ripens and you can graze at leisure, provided half your take makes it to the kitchen. There's swimming in the pristine reflecting pond out back, gorgeous gardens, and a sauna. MAP $125–160 per person, service charges extra. Four rooms can accommodate a family group, with special rates for children 12 and under in room with parent. BYOB.

⌒ ✿ **The Middlebury Inn** (802-388-4961; 1-800-842-4666; www .middleburyinn.com), 14 Courthouse Square, Middlebury 05753, has been the town's imposing chief hostelry since 1827. The Emanuel family has completely renovated the 75 guest and public rooms spread out among four buildings. Rooms in the main house are on two floors (there's a 1926 Otis elevator) and are furnished in reproduction antiques. They have private bath, cable TV, air conditioner/heater, and direct-dial phone. There are also 20 motel units with inn-style furnishings, and the adjacent 1816 Porter Mansion, full of handsome architectural details and a lovely curved staircase, has 10 Victorian rooms. The common rooms include a vast, comfortable lobby with a formal check-in desk and portraits of the Battell family and Robert Frost. Elegant afternoon tea and light dinners are available in the pubby Morgan Tavern; buffet breakfast in the pillared, Wedgwood-blue, formal Founder's Room. Lunch is served in the Open Book Café (see *Eating Out*) and on the front porch in summer and early fall. Thoughtful touches include readable books on shelves near guest rooms and umbrellas next to the door for guests to use. Continental breakfast is included in rates that run $88–375 double, including afternoon tea. Inquire about packages. Pets are welcome in the motel units for a small daily fee, and arrangements for babysitting can be made.

☉ 🐾 🐾 ♪ **The Shoreham Inn** (802-897-5081; 1-800-255-5081 from out of state; www.shorehaminn.com), Rt. 74 west, Shoreham 05770. Closed in Nov. This friendly, comfortable place is old-time Vermont with an English touch. The 10 air-conditioned guest rooms are whimsically decorated, most with king-sized beds and some with daybeds for the many families and bicyclists who pass through this old stagecoach stop. Seven come with in-room bath, while three have a private bath in the hall. The age of this 1790 structure is felt in the floorboards, exposed beams, and steep, creaking stairs. At the center of a quaint village surrounded by apple country, it is not far from Lake Champlain and the college town of Middlebury. The common rooms have plenty of sofas and easy chairs, along with chess and backgammon boards, a wood-burning fireplace, British antiques, and, frequently, the aroma of coffee or some other culinary temptation emanating from the kitchen (see *Eating Out*). Rates range from $85 for a single in low season to $150 for a double, and include a full hot breakfast. Pets accepted with conditions.

Churchill House Inn (802-247-3078; 1-877-248-7444; www.churchill houseinn.com), 3128 Forest Dale Rd. (Rt. 73), Brandon 05733. Located west of the Brandon Gap on Rt. 73, this old farmhouse, run by Seth and Olya Hopkins, has nine guest rooms furnished in 19th-century style, some with whirlpool or Jacuzzi tubs. There are hiking, biking, and cross-country ski trails nearby. Breakfasts are big, and four-course dinners ($30 per per-

son plus service charges) can be arranged with advance notice. B&B rates are $125–175 per room, double occupancy; add $50 for a third adult, $25 for each child 5–12 sharing room with parent. No children under 5.

🐾 **Waybury Inn** (802-388-4015; 1-800-348-1810; www.wayburyinn.com), Rt. 125, East Middlebury 05740. A historic former stagecoach stop that exudes character in each of the 14 imaginatively furnished rooms on its two upper floors. Our favorites are the Nautical Room with its maritime theme, and the Pineapple Room with its unusual plaid walls. The grandest is the Robert Frost Room, with red walls and a king-sized bed. The Waybury was indeed a favorite of Robert Frost's when he lived up the hill in Ripton, and its exterior was used in Bob Newhart's 1982–90 TV series *Newhart* to represent the quintessential New England inn. There are two dining rooms, and you can dine on the porch in summer; a swimmin' hole under the nearby bridge can be used to cool off. In winter you can warm up by the fire in the pub downstairs. Dinner and Sunday brunch are served year-round. $110–250 double occupancy includes a full hot breakfast. Two-night minimum stay on busy weekends and holidays.

☉ **Chipman Inn** (802-388-2390; 1-800-890-2390; www.chipmaninn .com), P.O. Box 115, Rt. 125, Ripton 05766. On the way to or from Bread Loaf and the Middlebury College Snow Bowl, this 1828 inn sits in the center of the tiny village of Ripton, which consists of a schoolhouse, community meetinghouse, church, and general store. It's also within striking distance of Robert Frost's house and cabin and the Robert Frost Trail. The house has eight guest rooms of varying sizes, all with private bath. Guests can gather in the bar, around a very large old hearth, in the sunny sitting room near the woodstove, and elsewhere in this roomy house. There's no TV, but plenty of books to peruse. Innkeepers Joyce Henderson and Bill Pierce serve breakfast at large tables in the dining room. $115–170, depending on season, includes full breakfast. Two cats in residence. Children 12 and older; no pets.

⚲ ⚲ **The Inn at Baldwin Creek** (802-453-2432; 1-888-424-2432; www.innatbaldwincreek.com), 1868 N. Rt. 116, Bristol 05443. Open year-round. A classic 1797 Vermont farmhouse inn set on 25 acres including a perennial garden with paths down to Baldwin Creek. Mary's Restaurant, attached to the inn, is a favorite regional dining spot (see *Dining Out*). Five guest rooms with private bath include a couple of two-room suites, which work well for families. Weddings and catered events for up to 200 people. Heated outdoor swimming pool. Innkeeper Linda Harmon and chef Doug Mack are founding members of Vermont Fresh Network; in summer they host special farmhouse dinners featuring local farmers, cooking classes, and music and theater performances in their barn. $115–195 per room in summer, $85–145 in winter, including a three-course breakfast and afternoon refreshments.

⚲ ⚲ **The Brandon Inn** (802-247-5766; www.historicbrandoninn.com), 20 Park St., Brandon 05733. A large brick landmark overlooking the village green, this inn dates from 1892 and is on the National Register of Historic Places. Innkeepers Sarah and Louis Pattis have scaled down the number

of guest rooms from 46 to 40, refurbishing them nicely. Number 316, the honeymoon suite, has a marble Jacuzzi. There are TV rooms upstairs as well as large living rooms downstairs, and some of the 19th-century furniture and a good deal of the atmosphere survive. The inn's 5 landscaped acres include a swimming pool (with Jacuzzi) and a stretch of the Neshobe River, good for trout fishing. An 18-hole golf course is just up the way. Buses from New York, Boston, and Montreal still stop, as stages once did, at the front door. Low-season B&B rates are $95–215 per room; high season, $115–295. Children under 12, $20.

BED & BREAKFASTS

In and around Middlebury 05753

⚲ ⚲ **The Inn on the Green** (802-388-7512; 1-888-244-7512; www.innonthegreen.com), 71 S. Pleasant St. A welcome addition to the downtown hospitality scene, this attractive 1803 Federal town house has two impressive, colorfully decorated suites in the main house, plus eight other spacious rooms, each with private bath, phone, cable TV, and high-speed Internet access. There's also a more contemporary carriage house, same amenities. $98–275, breakfast included.

⚲ ⚲ **Fairhill** (802-388-3044), 724 E. Munger St., 4 miles east of Middlebury, on 75 acres of woodland, marsh, and meadows. Russell and Fleur Laslocky's 1825 center-chimney Cape has three guest rooms, one with an antique four-poster double bed and private bath; the other two share a bath. The breakfast area is in an 18th-century granary. Rates $85–110.

In and around East Middlebury 05740

By the Way B&B (802-388-6291), 407 E. Main St. Barbara Simoes, who has taken over from her mother, Nancy, provides two spacious guest rooms with private bath and air-conditioning, as well as a guest house available for long-term rental. The wraparound veranda is appealing, and an in-ground swimming pool is set in the orchard. $95–190 per room with breakfast; Children 8 and older; no credit cards.

Wild Wind B&B (802-453-7557; www.wildwindvermont.com), 430 Orchard Rd., Lincoln 05443. A huge shingle-style home on 130 acres at the base of Mount Abraham, Wild Wind offers truly remarkable panoramic views of surrounding mountains and valleys. The two rooms—French and Victorian—are done in full style. Open Memorial Day–Oct., 2-night minimum stays, no children under 15, no pets. $250, double occupancy.

In and around Vergennes 05491

🐾 🎗 **Whitford House** (802-758-2704; 1-800-746-2704; www.whitfordhouse inn.com), 912 Grandey Rd., Addison 05491. Between Nortontown and Townline Rds. off Rt. 22A. Situated east of the lake on rich farmland, this idyllic 1790 farmhouse is set among flower gardens on acres of fields and grazing sheep, with gorgeous views of the Adirondacks. Tranquility and warm hospitality are the hallmarks of Bruce and Barbara Carson's exceptional inn, which they share with a cat and two beagles. The two cozy upstairs rooms have king or twin beds, and a first-floor room comes with a four-poster double bed. There's also a cottage ($225–250 per couple) with a king-sized bed, a sitting room with

sofa bed, and a full bath (with radiant-heated floor) that can accommodate a family of four. All have private bath. The great room, with its wood-burning fireplace made from local Panton stone, is a wonderful place to unwind. There's a book-lined library, plenty of art and antiques, wide-plank floors, and exposed beams. Rates run $110–225, $25 more in high season, and include afternoon refreshments, a superb candlelit breakfast, and loan of the Carsons' canoe and bicycles. Pets upon prior arrangement ($10 per night).

🎗 ♿ **The Strong House Inn** (802-877-3337; www.stronghouseinn.com), 94 W. Main St. (Rt. 22A). Built in the 1830s by Samuel Paddock Strong in the graceful Federal style, this roomy old house features fine detailing, such as curly maple railings on the free-standing main staircase. Mary and Hugh Bargiel offer 14 guest rooms, all with private bath, cable TV, and telephone. The rooms are in the main house as well as in Rabbit Ridge Country House, a newer building in back. Rates of $90–275 (more during peak season), include full breakfast and afternoon refreshments. Inquire about quilting, crafting, and other special weekends. Children 8 and over; no pets.

🎗 **Emerson Guest House** (802-877-3293; http://emersonhouse.com), 82 Main St. There are six bright and airy guest rooms in this 1850 French Second Empire mansion once owned by a prominent local judge, two with king-sized bed and private bath, two with queen (one with half-bath), and two with twins. The Willard Suite has a cherry sleigh bed (king), Oriental carpets, and an adjoining sitting room with a trundle bed that opens into two singles. Susan and Bill Walsh serve delicious breakfasts in a beautiful downstairs nook bordered by stained glass that looks over four trail-covered acres. Quilts, antiques, a children's pool in summer, and hardwood floors. $55–145 with full breakfast.

Barsen House Inn (802-759-2646; 1-888-819-6103; www.barsenhouse inn.com), 53 TriTown Rd., Addison 05491. Innkeeper Peter Jensen, a skilled woodworker, built this house and most of its furniture. He and his wife, Daphne, host guests in three rooms with private bath, one with a king-sized bed and two with queen. Two of them form a suite with a sitting room, TV, and private bath. Kids will find plenty to do here: gathering eggs, picking berries, catching frogs, or roasting marshmallows in the fire pit. There's also swimming and boating at a 3-acre beach nearby. $105–190 includes light breakfast. No pets.

South and west of Middlebury

Cornwall Orchards (802-462-2272; www.cornwallorchards.com), 1364 Rt. 30, Cornwall 05753, about 2 miles south of the Middlebury golf course. English-born Juliet Gerlin and her husband Bob, a recovering lawyer, have turned this 1784 Cape into an airy, comfortable place with hardwood floors, antique linens, Oriental carpets, and a spacious living room with a wood-burning fireplace. There's an antique cast-iron cookstove in the open kitchen and a cozy sitting nook that overlooks an outdoor deck and lovely orchard views. Of the five guest rooms, four have queen-sized bed, and one has two twins tucked under the eaves; all have private bath. The ground-floor Governor Room is wheelchair accessible, and the cozy Turner Room upstairs has a skylight

and a trapezoid-shaped bathroom door. $110–125 includes a fresh, full breakfast served family-style in the light-drenched dining room. Two-day minimum during foliage season and on summer and holiday weekends. No pets.

Fairy Tale Farm (802-758-3065; www.fairytalefarmvt.com), 1183 Rt. 125, Bridport 05734. Nancy and Tom Maxwell fled TV careers in Los Angeles for this 1804 farmhouse with its 115 acres, barn, cows, two mammoth donkeys, and mountain views. Guests are greeted with refreshments in the sofa-filled great room with its wood-burning fireplace. The two guest rooms are both on the ground floor and have king-sized bed. One is wheelchair accessible and features a private deck and sitting area; the other has a large claw-foot bathtub in a window-edged nook, the perfect place to soak as the sun sets. $120 includes a full breakfast that usually features eggs freshly laid by the resident chickens. Inquire about pets and children.

Quiet Valley Bed & Breakfast (802-897-7887), 1467 Quiet Valley Rd., Shoreham 05770. A new house whose stressed-pine floors make it feel old, this Cape is hidden off a dirt road on 48 acres of hay fields along the Lemon Fair River. The living room includes a shallow, Rumford-style fireplace, and interesting antiques abound. Two of the four guest rooms have four-poster double bed, woodstove, and private bath. Another two have twin singles and share a bath. Bruce and Jane Lustgarten serve up fortifying breakfasts at a table overlooking inspiring mountain views. Guests are welcome to hike the trails or take the canoe for a run up the river. B&B $105–125.

Inn at Lover's Lane (802-758-2185; www.bbonline.com/vt/loverslane), Rt. 125 west, Bridport 05753. A two-dog welcoming committee meets guests in the driveway of this 1835 Greek Revival. The two rooms downstairs are a good place to lounge, but the three guest rooms are the chief attraction with their beautiful pine floors, air-conditioning, and private baths. One has its own sitting room with a sofa that folds out into a double bed. John and Pam Freilich make substantial breakfasts, served on the outside deck in summer months. Snowmobile trails nearby. $85–145. Children 9 and older; no pets.

☀ ☾ **Buckswood Bed & Breakfast** (802-948-2054), 633 Rt. 73, P.O. Box 9, Orwell 05760. Open year-round. Linda and Bob Martin offer two guest rooms (private baths) and ample common space in their 1814 home, located in a pleasant country setting just east of Orwell Village. Dinner by reservation. $65–75 per couple includes breakfast. Polite pets accepted.

In and around Brandon 05733
The Inn on Park Street (802-247-3843; 1-800-394-7239; www.theinn onparkstreet.com), 69 Park St. Park Street is Brandon's Park Avenue: it is lined with the town's finest homes, most of them on the National Historic Register. Judy Bunde, a professional pastry chef, offers six guest rooms in this delightful Queen Anne Victorian, five with private bath and the sixth part of a two-room suite. The Theresa Room comes with cable TV, a choice of videos, double sinks, and a two-person Jacuzzi on a marble floor. The bedding is down-filled and hand-pressed, rooms come with robes and fine toiletries, and in the morning fresh coffee appears outside the door.

In winter months a fire crackles in the tastefully furnished parlor with its baby grand piano; in summer you can dine on the spacious porch. A masterful dessert buffet is prepared each evening, and Bunde's breakfasts are scrumptious: fruits, juices, and fresh-baked breads, plus a choice of dishes that might include pecan-maple waffles or omelets with squash and tomatoes. Ask about the weekend cooking packages with visiting chefs. $115–185.

Old Mill Inn (802-247-8002; 1-800-599-0341; www.oldmillbb.com), 79 Stone Mill Dam Rd. (Rt. 73 east). This attractive 1786 farmhouse set above the Neshobe River adjoins the 18-hole Neshobe Golf Club. Innkeepers Roger and Patt Cavanagh Kowalsky offer four antiques-filled guest rooms with private bath, some with air-conditioning. A multicourse, mostly organic breakfast is served in the sunny breakfast room. Guests can lounge in the two art-filled living rooms or relax on the wicker porch chairs in warm weather. The neighboring river contains a good swimming hole. $95–125 per couple includes breakfast. Children over 10; no pets.

Rosebelle's Victorian Inn (802-247-0098; 1-888-767-3235; www.rose belles.com), 31 Franklin St., P.O. Box 370, Rt. 7. This nicely restored, mansard-roofed house has a high-ceilinged living room with fireplace and TV and a large dining room—the setting for afternoon tea and full breakfasts. Guests with small musical instruments are especially welcome. Hostess Ginette Milot speaks French. All but one of the five guest rooms have private bath, and two rooms can be joined to form a suite for four. $110–125 per double in high season,

$95–110 in low. Children over 10 must have a separate room. Two-night minimum stays are required on holiday weekends and during foliage season.

*The Gazebo Inn** (802-247-3235; 1-888-858-3235; www.vermontgazebo inn.com), 25 Grove St. (Rt. 7). This is another in-town, circa-1865 house with a wood-burning stove in the sitting room. It's decorated with folk art and antiques and has four comfortable guest rooms with private bath. Families welcome. Rates include a full breakfast. $95–140 per couple.

Judith's Garden (802-247-4707; www.judithsgarden.com), 423 Goshen–Ripton Rd., Goshen. Exquisite perennial gardens in a secluded mountain setting, with easy trail access for hikers, walkers, and cross-country skiers who want to explore the vast Moosalamoo forest. The gazebo in the garden is a particularly pleasant spot in summer. The restored 1830s farmhouse has three appealing bedrooms with private bath; $95–125 per room includes breakfast, and dinner is available upon prearrangement for an added $25 per person. Proprietors Dick Conrad and Judith Irven, a professional landscape designer, serve breakfasts of fruit, scones, and roasted garlic and potato frittata with locally made goat cheese, among other things; they are good cooks.

High Meadow (802-247-3820; www.highmeadowbb.com), 1742 Goshen–Ripton Rd., Goshen. A secluded country haven with mountain views and bright, sunny common rooms. Innkeeper Patrice Lopatin, a world-traveled chef and artist, has three guest rooms, one with its own bath, the other two sharing a bath. From the southwest room you can watch the sun set through a classic Vermont slanted window. Breakfasts are often organic with home-baked breads and fresh eggs from the inn's own chickens. Guests have access to kitchen facilities, but lunch and dinner can be arranged with advance notice. Child and pet care available for an extra fee (must be arranged before arrival). $85–95 per couple.

Salisbury Village Bed & Breakfast (802-352-6006), 2165 Westshore Rd., P.O. Box 214, Salisbury 05769. Not far from Lake Dunmore, this restored farmhouse has four guest rooms with double beds, two with private and two with shared bath ($65–75), and welcomes polite pets at $10 per night—even providing day care for them.

Other choices in the Brandon area include **12 Franklin St. B&B** (802-247-6672; www.12franklinstreet.com) and the **Wyndmere House B&B** (802-247-5006).

In and around Bristol 05443
Russell Young Farm (1-877-896-7026; www.russellyoungfarm.com), 861 Russell Young Rd., Jerusalem, is a beautifully restored yellow farmhouse at the end of a climbing dirt road with utterly spectacular mountain views from nearly every window (not to mention the chairs on the front porch). The ground floor is entirely wheelchair accessible, including the Shalmansir guest room with its quilts and Shaker-style furniture. The two upstairs rooms adjoin a delightful sunroom, and all are bright and airy with private bath, queen-sized bed, towel warmer, hair dryer, Internet hookup, and TV/VCR. The TV-free common areas include the Great Room with its 5-foot stone fireplace and a self-serve bar in the dining area. Amenities

include a video library, hot tub, swimming pond, and free snowshoe use. Innkeepers Carol and Dennis Hysko serve full breakfasts using homemade maple syrup and eggs fresh from their own chickens. $125 per couple. Two-night minimum during foliage season, 3-night Columbus Day weekend.

✿ **Crystal Palace Victorian B&B** (802-453-7609; 1-888-674-4131; www .crystalpalacebb.com), 48 North St. Stephen and Stacie Ayotte are the hosts at this impressive 1897 turreted mansion. There are 11 stained-glass windows, along with a grand staircase and vintage woodwork throughout. The three guest rooms all come with air-conditioning and private bath. One has its own dressing room, another a whirlpool bath; $90–135 with full breakfast. No pets; children by prior arrangement.

Bristol Coach House B&B (802-453-2236), 23 West St. Patricia Highley's home from the early 1800s overlooks the village green. The three rooms have shared bath and rent for $85, including continental breakfast.

COTTAGES **Lake Dunmore**. Some cottagers hope that the lake will remain off the beaten track; however, it's being "discovered." Here are some good bets:

✿ **Lake Dunmore's Sunset Lodge** (802-352-4290; 515-249-5888 off-season; www.sunsetlodgevermont.com), 425 West Shore Rd., Salisbury 05769. Nineteen housekeeping cottages with easy access to swimming, fishing, and boating. $500–700 weekly, May–Oct.

✿ **North Cove Cottages** (802-352-4236 in summer; 617-354-0124 in winter; www.northcovecottages.com), P.O. Box 76, Salisbury 05769. Nine housekeeping cottages, all with bath

and fully equipped kitchen. Sandy beach, free rowboats. $53–89 per night (2-night minimum), $350–545 per week, also in winter. Pets sometimes welcome; ask about fees.

Note: The Addison County Chamber of Commerce (802-388-7951) has a list of rental cottages on both Lake Dunmore and Lake Champlain.

MOTELS **Courtyard by Marriott** (1-800-388-7775; www.middleburycourt yard.com), 309 Court St. (Rt. 7 south), Middlebury 05753. A brand-new Courtyard just south of Middlebury Village is done in New England style with a wraparound porch. There are 89 rooms with all the amenities (including high-speed Internet access), suites with whirlpool tub and fireplace, a hot breakfast buffet, an indoor pool, and an exercise room. $89–275.

✿ ✿ ✿ **Maple Grove Dining Room and Cottages** (802-247-6644; 1-800-568-5971; www.maplegrovecottages .com), 1246 Franklin St. (Rt. 7 south), Brandon 05733. Open year-round. Located on Rt. 7, 1 mile south of Brandon, this is a shady campus of 20 cozy one- and two-room cottages of the kind so familiar in premotel motoring days. Most of the cottages have fireplace and cable TV, and there's a stocked trout pond, swimming pool, miniature golf across the highway, and a restaurant next door (see *Eating Out*). $69–129 includes continental breakfast. $10 charge for pets.

CAMPGROUNDS See *Green Space*.

✳ Where to Eat

DINING OUT *✿* **Starry Night Café** (802-877-6316; www.starrynightcafe .com), 5371 Rt. 7, North Ferrisburgh.

Open Wed.–Sun. 5:30–9 (reserve). Chef-owner David Huge, a Culinary Institute of America grad, is gaining kudos for his imaginative flavor combinations at this former cider mill with its art-covered walls and outdoor deck overlooking a pond. Appetizers might include warmed pink peppercorn encrusted goat cheese with snow peas; shiitake mushrooms, grilled onion, and mixed greens drenched in citrus vinaigrette; or cornmeal-encrusted calamari with yellow curry and coconut dipping sauce. Entrées (anything from pork to steaks and vegetarian dishes) come with brown bread and plum or rhubarb butter, smoked tomato beurre blanc, or maybe roasted figs. The menu constantly evolves based on what produce is locally available. Dinner for two $60–100.

Café Provence (802-247-9993; http: //cafeprovencevt.com), 11 Center St., Brandon. Open daily for breakfast, lunch, and dinner; Sunday brunch. Hidden above a shop in the center of downtown Brandon, this celebrated eatery doubles as pizza parlor and French country bistro. Chef-owner Robert Barral earned his stripes cooking for the Four Seasons restaurant chain, subsequently teaching for several years at Vermont's New England Culinary Institute. The dining room is small but tasteful, the open kitchen gleaming with polished chrome and hanging pans. What emerges is worth traveling long distances for: lobster consommé en croute, by way of example, or pan-seared scallops wrapped in smoked salmon on a bed of wilted spinach and warm tomato salad. Enjoy the outdoor terrace in summer. Entrées $10–22.

Christophe's on the Green (802-877-3413; www.christophesonthe green.com), 5 N. Green St., Vergennes. Open for dinner Tue.–Sat. 5:30-9:30, Thu.–Sat. in winter. Closed Nov. and Jan. Reservations suggested. A friendly yet first-class French restaurant housed in the Stevens House, a former hotel, on the town green. French-born chef and owner Christophe Lissarague pulls out all the stops with a dazzling menu and impressive wine list. You might begin with quail eggs, then dine on vol-au-vent of veal sweetbreads and cremini mushrooms served with sautéed spinach, finishing with apricot crème soufflé served with mascarpone mousse, or a plate of Pyrenees cheeses. All appetizers are $9.50 entrées $25.50, desserts $7.50. Ask about prix fixe dinners.

Black Sheep Bistro (802-877-9991), 253 Main St., Vergennes. Open daily 5–9:30 PM, this intimate place has been wildly popular ever since chef Michel Mahé started serving his innovative French-inspired dishes. You feel as if you're on a side street in Paris, except that the service is first-rate. A specialty is garlic mashed potatoes on the plate, plus French fries delivered in paper cones and served with ketchup and two flavored dips. All appetizers $7, large plates $17, salads and desserts $5; it simplifies the math. Terrace seating in summer months. Reservations essential.

The Storm Café (802-388-1063), 3 Mill St., Middlebury. This intimate, casual spot overlooking the river from an old stone mill building is considered by many to serve the most imaginative food in town. Lunch 11:30–2:30 (sandwiches $8–9) and dinner 5–9 Tue.–Sat. Entrées ($14.95–25.95) include grilled beef tenderloin, seafood stew, and a fish special of the day.

Swift House Inn (802-388-9925), 25 Stewart Lane, Middlebury. Dinner at this very popular downtown inn is served Thu.–Mon. 6–9 in three atmospheric rooms: a dining area with a working fireplace, a book-filled library, and a converted porch. Among the specialties are the Vermont chèvre and caramelized mushroom ravioli, the artichoke fritters, and crispy duck confit. Appetizers are all $6, entrées $17, and desserts $6. Also grilled steaks, salads, and burgers, plus pub snacks at the bar. Gluten-free and vegan dishes available with prior notice.

Fire & Ice Restaurant (802-388-7166; 1-800-367-7166; www.fireand icerestaurant.com), 26 Seymour St., Middlebury. Open weekdays at 4:30, Fri. and Sat. at noon, Sun. at 1. This is not so much a restaurant as a dine-in museum, with its stained-glass and mahogany nooks, its library, and a 1921 Hackercraft motorboat that serves as a salad bar. A local favorite since 1974, specializing in steaks ($14.95–20.95), prime rib ($14.95–19.95), and chicken dishes like a fresh boneless breast sautéed in a champagne and mushroom cream sauce ($14.95). The name was inspired by a Robert Frost poem.

Roland's Place (802-453-6309), 3629 Rt. 7, New Haven. A grand old cupola-topped mansion, this eatery (also known as the 1796 House) is the setting for dinner and Sunday brunch year-round, lunches for groups of 10 or more by reservation. Owner-chef Roland Gaujac has a Provençal background but specializes in foods fresh off nearby farms. His menu often includes local trout, venison, or emu

as well as more conventional fare, all very well prepared. (There are also three air-conditioned **guest rooms** upstairs that go for $75–105.) For a special treat, Roland will serve dinner for a foursome in the rooftop cupola, where the 360-degree views guarantee memorable sunset viewing. $50 per person.

Basin Harbor Club (802-475-2311), Basin Harbor, off Panton Rd., 5 miles west of Vergennes. If you don't stay at Basin Harbor, there's all the more reason to drive out for lunch or dinner, to see the lakeside setting and savor the atmosphere. The food is fine, too. The dining room is large and the menu changes frequently, but at dinner (reserve) you might begin with Green Mountain smoked trout, then enjoy seared breast of ginger soy marinated duck. The prix fixe is $36 plus 15 percent service charge. The wine list is extensive and excellent. Jacket and tie required. More casual dining is available near the resort's entrance at the **Red Mill Restaurant** (802-475-2317), a former sawmill with a rough-hewn interior and antique farm equipment on the walls. Open lunch and dinner; children's menu.

Tully and Marie's (802-388-4182; tullyandmaries.com), 5 Bakery Lane, Middlebury, open daily 11:30 AM–11 PM; Sunday brunch 10:30–3. You have the sense of being wined and dined on a small, three-decker art deco ship beached on the bank of Otter Creek. You can watch the water flow at every level as you await your meal, which might be a salad of Vermont organic baby greens with fresh strawberries, chèvre, toasted almonds, and black raspberry vinaigrette; shrimp with basil, coconut milk, lemongrass, and mango; or lamb brochettes with mashed chèvre potatoes and crabcakes with orange-ginger sauce. Desserts are delectable, and there's a full bar. Entrées run in the $10–15 range.

The Waybury Inn (802-388-4015; www.wayburyinn.com), Rt. 125, East Middlebury. Open daily for dinner. The center of action in tiny East Middlebury is the Waybury Inn, where moderately priced ($9.95–14.50) steaks and seafood are served on the lower level in a warm, trophy-mounted pub. Finer dining happens upstairs in the Coach Room, where garlic sautéed shrimp might be featured along with tenderloin of venison in mushroom and lingonberry-brandy sauce, or filet mignon served with a sherry-lobster sauce and crispy shiitake mushrooms. Entrées $19.50–29.50.

Mary's Restaurant at Baldwin Creek (802-453-2432; 1-888-424-2432), at the junction of Rts. 116 and 17, Bristol. Open Wed.–Sun. 5:30–9:30. Chef Doug Mack has made a name for this three-room restaurant on the banks of Baldwin Creek by serving a variety of seasonal and local specialties, including local rabbit, venison, and free-range chicken, forest mushroom pie, a vegetarian Angel on Earth, and the ever-wonderful cream of garlic soup. There are also a number of special Farmhouse Dinners with local producers, and cooking classes. Entrées $19–25; the bistro menu runs $8–12.

🍴 **The Dog Team Tavern** (802-388-7651; 1-800-232-7651; www.dogteam tavern.com), a jog off Rt. 7, 4 miles north of Middlebury. Open for dinner daily. Gift shop. Opened in the 1930s by Sir Wilfred Grenfell (1865–1940), a British medical missionary who established hospitals, orphanages, schools, and cooperative stores in Labrador and near the Arctic Circle. Traditional New England fare (sticky buns, relish trays, et al.). Fried chicken dinners are $13.95, ham steak with fritters $15.95, and prime rib is $21.95. The Dog Team has had the same menu for years now, and it keeps people coming back for more.

The Brandon Inn (802-247-5766), 20 Park St., Brandon. Open when serving booked groups (call ahead). Austrian-trained owner-chef Louis Pattis makes dinner something of an event; entrée choices are limited to just a few, but might include appetizers like crabcakes with a mango-habanero fruit sauce, and entrées such as roast duck served with wild blueberry ginger sauce. About $25 per person.

Bobcat Café (802-453-3311), 5 Main St., Bristol. A friendly local eatery where the food is substantial and well prepared, with small plates and large plates ranging $8–30. The Black Angus burgers are excellent, as is the highly popular Misty Knoll chicken dish. The enormous wooden bar was scavenged from a warehouse across the lake, and there aren't many empty bar stools. Open daily from 5 PM.

EATING OUT 🍴 **The Shoreham Inn** (802-897-5081; 1-800-255-5081; www.shorehaminn.com). Dominic and Molly Francis have transformed the downstairs of this old Vermont hostelry into a British-style "gastropub" serving such English standards as bangers and mash with a pint of Guinness. They installed a copper-topped bar and a mantel mirror from Greenwich, England, and serve excellent informal dinners on long wooden tables. Served Thu., Fri., Sat., and Mon. starting at 5, the menu might include boeuf au poivre, grilled salmon, or penne with Gorgonzola sauce. Entrées $7–18. Closed Nov.

Mister Up's (802-388-6724), 25 Bakery Lane, Middlebury, open daily lunch–midnight; Sunday brunch buffet 11–2. Dine outdoors on the riverside deck or in the brick-walled, stained-glass, oak-and-greenery setting inside. The menu is equally colorful, ranging from the Ultimate Salad Bar and Bread Board to grilled steaks, seafood, and pasta dishes: $11–20.

🦞 **The Bridge** (802-759-2152), 17 Rt. 17 west, Addison. A delightful country diner with fresh-baked pies (try the Vermont maple cream), huge portions, gentle prices, and doting waitresses. Open daily (except Tue.) at 6:30 for steaming breakfasts, plus lunch and dinner till 9 PM (8 in winter).

🦪 **Rosie's Restaurant** (802-388-7052), 1 mile south of Middlebury on Rt. 7, is open daily (6 AM–9 PM in winter, until 10 May–Nov.) and serves a lot of good, inexpensive food. This family mecca expands every 8 months or so to accommodate its fans. There's a friendly counter and three large, cheerful dining rooms. We lunched on a superb beef and barley soup and turkey salad on wheat. Dinner choices run from fish-and-chips to Smitty's top sirloin, and there are always stir-fries.

The Middlebury Inn (802-388-4961; 802-388-4666), 14 Courthouse Square, Middlebury. Breakfast, light lunches, and tea are served in the pleasant **Open Book Café**, an antiques-filled place resembling a library. Seating is on the front porch overlooking the town green in summer and early fall. Dinner is served in the wood-lined Morgan Tavern, Sunday brunch in the Founder's Room. A popular appetizer here is grilled

portobello mushrooms with goat cheese, watercress, cherry tomatoes, and balsamic reduction. The moderately priced menu includes fresh seafood, steaks, and a rotating market special each evening. $25 prix fixe menu Mon.–Thu., with a $19.95 filet mignon special on Friday evenings.

Noonie's Deli (802-388-0014), 2 Maple St. (in the Marble Works), Middlebury. Open Mon.–Sat. 8–8, Sun. 11–7. Good soups, the best sandwiches in Addison County (a half sandwich is plenty)—on homemade bread, you design it. Eat in or take out.

Patricia's Restaurant (aka **Sally's Place**) (802-247-3223), Center St., Brandon. Open daily from 11 for lunch and dinner; 1–8 Sun., when there's a senior citizen discount on complete dinners. Traditional fare like grilled pork chops, fried haddock, and Italian dishes ranging from cheese ravioli to spaghetti with hot sausage.

🦞 🦪 **Cattails** (802-247-9300), 2146 Grove St. (Rt. 7, just north of Brandon). Open Tue.–Sun. 11–9, Fri. and Sat. till 10 PM. Closed Mon. Lance and Stephanie Chicoine run a great, child-friendly eatery with large portions of southern comfort food, friendly service, and attractive prices. The lunch menu ($5.75–9.95) is varied and tasty, especially the applewood-smoked pulled pork. Dinners are surprisingly good, with such things as tenderloin au poivre in brandy cream sauce ($14.95). BBQ specials every Thursday night in summer for $13.95. Children's menu.

The Commodore Grill (802-877-2200), 165 Main St., Vergennes. Open daily for breakfast, lunch, and possibly dinner. Right downtown overlooking the park, this reasonably priced lunch spot commemorates Commodore

McDonough, whose fleet battled the British at Plattsburgh in 1814. An old print depicting the battle takes up one whole wall.

Café 206 (802-877-3004), 206 Main St., Vergennes. Open daily 6:30 AM–7 PM, later on weekends. This new addition to the expanding Vergennes culinary scene is a prime spot for a quick lunch or midafternoon snack. Jim Stone serves soups, salads, coffees, pies, pastries, and ice cream in a yellow-and-orange decor.

Snap's (802-453-2525), 24 Main St., Bristol. Open daily 6 AM–9 PM, Sun. 7–3. A cheery pine-walled café with booths, family-sized tables, and a fine pressed-tin ceiling; serving breakfast all day plus lunch, dinner, and Sunday brunch. Daily fresh soups, sandwiches, wraps, and salads. Lunches $6–9, dinners $7.95–13.95. Special menu selections for kids and seniors.

Bristol Bakery & Café (802-453-3280), 16 Main St., Bristol. Open daily from 5 AM, except Sun. when it opens at 6. This inviting storefront is filled with the aroma of coffee and breads. Design your own sandwich or stop for a muffin and espresso and take home a loaf of sourdough bread; there are also blackboard luncheon specials.

Eat Good Food (802-877-2772; www.eatgoodfoodvt.com), 221 Main St., Vergennes. A popular meeting place in the center of Vergennes, this gourmet café and take-out prepares terrific sandwiches and pastries, has a case full of gourmet cheeses and unusual drinks, and offers a selection of gourmet foods in the back. The decor is splashed with bright colors, there's outdoor seating in summer, and it's open daily. A good choice for lunch, early dinners, or picnics.

American Flatbread (802-388-3300; www.americanflatbread.com), 137 Maple St., at the Marble Works, Middlebury. The company started in the Mad River Valley but has spread like a well-turned pizza crust. The all-natural pizza is made with organic flour and toppings and baked in a wood-fired oven. Serving Fri. and Sat. evenings 5–9:30 year-round, with outdoor seating when possible. They'll do take-out, but only if they're not too busy, so call ahead.

Maple Grove Dining Room (802-247-6644; 1-800-568-5971; www.maplegrovecottages.com), 1246 Franklin St. (Rt. 7 south), 1 mile south of Brandon. Real mashed potatoes, homemade bread, and desserts like cappuccino crème brûlée set this little eatery apart. Entrées include rosemary and lemon chicken breast, Caribbean crabcakes, and prime rib of beef (the house special on Fri. and Sat. nights) roasted with garlic, Dijon mustard, and horseradish, served with horseradish cream sauce. Entrées $12.95–19.95. Open all year at 5 (closed Mon. and Tue.).

A & W Drive-in (802-388-2876), Rt. 7 south, a few miles from Middlebury. Vermont's last surviving carhop, open in summer months. The 1960s roadside spot still dispenses its root beer the old-fashioned way, in frosted mugs by girls on in-line skates. The usual burgers and fries. Flash your headlights for service.

MICROBREWERY Otter Creek Brewing (1-800-473-0727), 793 Exchange St., Middlebury. Open Mon.–Sat. 10–6. Free guided tours at 1, 3, and 5 PM. Ales and other beers can be sampled in the Tasting Room.

BARS/COFFEE SHOPS Carol's Hungry Mind Café (802-388-0101), 24 Merchants Row, Middlebury. Open Mon.–Sat. 7 AM–11 PM, Sun. 8 AM–4. A riverside coffeehouse with yellow- and merlot-colored walls that offers soft music, art, pastries, and plenty of spots to settle into with a book. Live music on weekends.

Antidote (802-877-2555), 3 N. Green St., Vergennes, in the Stevens House over Christophe's. Open 3 PM–1 AM. Harper Michael and Michel Mahé's solution to the Monday blues is this lounge with its artistically illuminated back bar and high-definition TV. In warm weather you can sit outside on the balcony overlooking the park. Full bar menu with tapas, cheeses, wines, and imported beers.

Mountain Greens Market & Deli (802-453-8538), 25 Mountain View St., Bristol. Open daily 9 AM–7 PM. A delightful small-town deli with organic foods, fair-trade fruits, wines, delicious coffee, and tasty take-out. A great place to browse.

✳ Entertainment

Middlebury College Center for the Arts (802-443-3168; box office 802-443-6433 weekdays noon–5; www.middlebury.edu/cfa). The stunning 370-seat concert hall in this dramatic new building on the southern edge of the college campus (Rt. 30 south) offers a full series of concerts, recitals, plays, dance performances, and film series.

Town Hall Theater (802-388-1436, box office 802-382-9222; www.townhalltheater.org), 52 Main St., Middlebury. Open May–Oct. Box office open weekdays noon–5 and an hour before performances. In 1997 a community group bought this 1884 town hall on the green and began restoring its stage. Now it once again offers music, dramatic performances, and children's events.

After Dark Music Series (802-388-0216; www.afterdarkmusicseries.com). A variety of musical offerings performed at the United Methodist Church, on Rt. 7 and Seminary St. in Middlebury. Come an hour early for a light meal and homemade dessert.

Vergennes Opera House (802-877-6737; www.vergennesoperahouse.org), 120 Main St., Vergennes. A renovated, century-old theater that once rang with the sounds of vaudeville now offers a spicy variety of music and theater in addition to "Friday Flicks"—silent movies on the first Friday of each month.

✳ Selective Shopping

ART GALLERIES Woody Jackson's Holy Cow (802-388-6737), 44 Main St., Middlebury. Woody himself, a Middlebury graduate whose Holstein products have become almost more of a symbol of Vermont than the maple tree, is usually on the premises. His black-and-white Holstein cows, immortalized on Ben & Jerry's ice cream cartons, decorate T-shirts, aprons, coffee mugs, boxer shorts, and more.

✎ **Norton's Gallery** (802-948-2552; www.nortonsgallery.com), in Shoreham. The small red gallery overlooking Lake Champlain houses an amazing menagerie of dogs, cats, rabbits, birds, and fish, along with flowers and vegetables—all the work of nature lover Norton Latourelle, sculpted from wood in unexpected sizes, unquestionably works of art and a visual delight for children and adults alike. Four miles west of Rt. 22A and 1 mile south of the Fort Ticonderoga Ferry on Rt. 73.

Prescott Galleries (802-453-4776), 47 E. River Rd., Lincoln. Open May–Dec., Tue., Fri., and Sat. 10–5 or by appointment. Reed Prescott III exhibits his oil paintings, many of which feature the Addison County landscape, as well as prints, books, and notecards.

Lapham and Dibble Gallery (802-897-5331), 410 Main St. Shoreham 05770. Open Tue.–Fri. 9–4. The gallery in this pristine red barn set over fields and mountains sells 19th- and early-20th-century paintings and prints, plus the work of Vermont artists and custom framing.

ANTIQUES SHOPS **Middlebury Antique Center** (802-388-6229; 1-800-339-6229 in Vermont), Rt. 7 at the junction of Rt. 116 in East Middlebury. Daily 9–6. A fascinating variety of furniture and furnishings representing 50 dealers. Air-conditioned.

Tom's Treasures (802-483-2334) 3295 Rt. 7, in the center of Pittsford. Open daily. Tom and Kathy Brown's collection fills three adjacent buildings, two houses, and a recently vacated Methodist church, and every kind of antique is represented, from linens to Oriental carpets, old birdcages to Bohemian glass.

Stone Block Antiques (802-877-6668; 802-989-1158; 802-877-3359), midtown Vergennes. Open Fri. 9–9, or by appointment. Greg Hamilton's impressive collection of fine glass, furniture, porcelain, old prints, and more.

Little Red Schoolhouse Antiques (802-388-7770), 1663 Rt. 7 south. Open most days. This one-room

schoolhouse dating from 1818 is packed with early corner cupboards, mirrors, paintings, glass, Shaker boxes, and more.

Antiques by the Falls (802-247-6600), 22 Park St., Brandon, next to the Brandon Inn. Open 10–9 summer and fall. A combination antiques shop and vintage-1950s soda fountain, serving Vermont's own Wilcox Ice Cream from an old marble counter and marble-topped tables.

Juniper Hill Antiques (802-623-8550), Rt. 73, Sudbury, 4.5 miles east of Brandon. Open most days 9–6. Cliff Alexander has a fascinating collection of early American furniture, decorative arts, and curiosities, including Civil War militaria and fishing tackle.

BOOKSTORES **Vermont Book Shop** (802-388-2061), 38 Main St., Middlebury, was opened in 1947 by Robert Dike Blair, who retired several years ago as one of New England's best-known booksellers and the publisher of Vermont Books, an imprint for the poems of Walter Hard. Robert Frost was a frequent customer for more than two decades, and the store has sold many autographed Frost poetry collections. It has a special section set aside for Vermont authors, right up front.

Briggs Carriage Bookstore (802-247-0050; www.briggscarriage.com), 16 Park St., Brandon. Open daily 9–6, later on weekends. A surprisingly well-stocked bookstore in the heart of town, with an upstairs café, **Ball and Chain**, and frequent evening events.

Seasoned Books (802-247-4700; www.seasonedbooks.com), on Rt. 7 just north of Brandon. Open daily except Mon. 10–6, Sun. 11–4. One of two stores (the other is in Rochester) selling new, used, and collectible books with emphasis on gardening, the environment, cooking, and living off the land.

Deerleap Books (802-453-4062; www.deerleap.com), Main St., Bristol. Open daily except Mon. A small, friendly, and carefully stocked bookstore that entices you to browse and to buy. Author readings are held.

Otter Creek Used Books (802-388-3241), Main St., Middlebury, is a book browser's delight: 25,000 very general titles.

✎ Monroe Street Books (802-388-1622; www.monroestreetbooks.com), 1485 Rt. 7, 2 miles north of downtown Middlebury. Open 10–5 daily, except in March, but it's a good idea to call. Dick and Flanzy Chodkowski have some 20,000 titles; specialties include children's books and cartoon, comic, and graphic art.

Bulwagga Books & Gallery (802-623-6800; 1-877-206-1357; www .bulwaggabooks.com), 3 S. Main St., Whiting, at the Whiting Post Office. Open Tue.–Sat. 10–6, Sun. and Mon. by appointment. More than 10,000 titles plus an art gallery, handcrafted furniture, and a reading room with mountain views and coffee.

In the Alley Books (802-388-2743), in the alley across from the Frog Hollow Craft Center, Middlebury. Open Mon.–Sat. 10–5, but call to be sure. Specialties are naturalist writings, poetry, peace studies, leftist U.S. history, feminist writings, Eastern religions, Native Americans, homesteading, and natural food cookbooks. Also used CDs and vintage vinyl LPs.

CRAFTS SHOPS **The Vermont State Craft Center at Frog Hollow** (802-388-3177; www.froghollow.org),

Middlebury. Open spring–fall, Mon.–Sat. 9:30–5, as well as Sun. afternoon. This not-for-profit gallery combines the natural beauty of Otter Creek falls, just outside its windows, with the best art and crafts in Vermont. More than 200 artisans are represented; you can come away with anything from a 50¢ postcard to a magnificent $14,000 harpsichord. A feast for the eyes, it's also a serious shopping source with outstanding selections of glass, pottery, woven clothing, wall hangings, jewelry, and woodwork, to name just a few.

Sweet Cecily (802-388-3353; www .sweetcecily.com), Main St., Middlebury. Nancie Dunn, former Frog Hollow gallery director, has assembled her own selection of ceramics, folk art, hooked rugs, and other items from numerous craftspeople, including Mexican and Amish artisans.

Vermont Folk Life Center Heritage Shop (802-388-4964; www .vermontfolklifecenter.org), 3 Court St. (by the Middlebury Inn), Middlebury. Open Tue.–Sat. 11–4. One-of-a-kind, handmade crafts and traditional art from Vermont and the world, including baskets, hand-hooked rugs, art photography, hearth brooms, wooden rakes, apple-head dolls, and whirligigs, plus books and recordings.

Danforth Pewterers (802-388-0098; www.danforthpewter.com), 211 Maple St., Middlebury. Open Mon.–Sat. 10–5 (Sun. 11–4 June–Dec.). Best known for its distinctive pewter oil lamps. Fred and Judi Danforth established Danforth Pewterers in 1975 with Thomas Danforth II of Middletown, CT, and his sons. They also make an extensive line of pewter jewelry, home accessories, and baby gifts. Call the retail store in the Marble Works for pewter-making demonstration times.

Diane E. Foulds

GOURMET PROVENCE IN BRANDON

Art on Main (802-453-4032; www
.artonmain.net/gallery), Artists' Alley,
25C Main St., Bristol. Open daily
10–6, Sun. noon–5. A nonprofit community art and crafts center and
gallery recently opened by the grassroots Bristol Friends of the Arts, displaying a changing exhibit of weavings,
jewelry, glass, ceramics, kaleidoscopes,
leather, and more.

Robert Compton Pottery (802-453-
3778; www.robertcomptonpottery
.com), 2662 N. Rt. 116, just north of
Bristol. A complex of kilns, studios,
and gallery space has evolved out of a
former farmhouse and now contains
the work space of this seasoned potter, who uses salt glazes and Japanese
wood-firing techniques to produce
everything from water fountains to
crockery to sinks. Compton throws his
pots in winter, and glazes them outdoors in summer. Showroom open
mid-May–mid-Oct., daily 10–6; other
times by appointment.

Folkheart (802-453-4101), 18 Main
St., Bristol. Open daily 10–5, Sun.
11–4. Papier-mâché artist and shop
owner Pamela Smith lives in Nepal
half of the year and paints. When she
returns to Vermont, she brings
Nepalese folk art with her. This colorful shop displays it, along with her

papier-mâché masks, and folk art from
Vietnam, Mexico, and elsewhere.

Lincoln Pottery (802-453-2073), 220
W. River Rd., Lincoln. Open daily
noon–5. Judith Bryant creates wheel-
thrown stoneware. Her studio and
showroom are located in an old dairy
barn.

Brandon Artists Guild (802-247-
4956; www.brandonartistsguild.org),
7 Center St., Brandon. A nonprofit
gallery representing crafts and fine
artists in the Brandon area.00

SPECIAL SHOPS **Gourmet Provence** (802-247-3002), 37 Center St.,
Brandon. A good place to pick up a
cup of coffee and a fresh-baked croissant. The shop, a spin-off of Robert
and Line Barral's Café Provence bistro
up the street, also stocks wines, gourmet foods, and kitchen stuff. Bakery
and take-out.

Daily Chocolate (802-877-0087), 7
Green St., Vergennes. Open weekdays
11–6, Sat. 10–3. A recent addition to
Vergennes's culinary renaissance is
this artisanal chocolate shop opposite
the town's best food shop, **The Fat
Hen**. Chris White makes every lus-
cious caramel by hand, and packs
them into sumptuous gift boxes.

Wood Ware (802-388-6297), Rt. 7
south of Middlebury, is the home of
good values in furniture, beds, lamps,
solid butternut door harps, and
dozens of other items. Interesting gift
items as well. Open daily (closed Sun.
in winter).

Kennedy Brothers Marketplace
(802-877-2975), 11 N. Main St.
(Rt. 22A), Vergennes, no longer produces its own oak and pine woodenware, but a Factory Marketplace
serves as cooperative space for many

woodworkers and craftspeople. Open daily 9:30–5:30.

Maple Landmark Woodcraft (1-800-421-4223; www.maplelandmark.com), 1297 Exchange St., Middlebury, manufactures games and giftware, including the well-known "Name Trains" and "Montgomery Schoolhouse" lines. Weekdays 9–5, Sat. 9–4.

Vermont HoneyLights (802-453-3952; 1-800-322-2660; www.vermont honeylights.com), 9 Main St., Bristol. Unusual assortments of hand-poured and rolled beeswax candles are produced in this small building. These are not the same candles you see in every gift store between here and Los Angeles. Worth a look.

Beau Ties Ltd. (802-388-0108; 1-800-488-8437; www.beautiesltd.com), 69 Industrial Ave., Middlebury. Bow ties from every fabric imaginable. The retail store features the current catalog choices plus vintage ties, accessories, and gifts. The store is open weekdays 10–4:30 (see also "Factory Tours.")

✳ Special Events

Late February: **Middlebury College Winter Carnival** (802-388-4356)—ice show, concerts, snow sculpture.

Mid-March: **The Pig Race** winds up with a fine pork barbecue. Information from Blueberry Hill Inn, Goshen.

Memorial Day weekend: Middlebury's **Memorial Day parade** is a popular annual event featuring lots of school marching bands, Scouts, Little Leaguers, politicians, floats, and fire trucks. It starts at 9 AM (not sharp), but you can catch the same parade 2 hours later in **Vergennes** if you prefer to sleep in.

Early June: **Annual Ladies Car Rally** (802-877-6737). This is a special—and very popular—fund-raiser for the Vergennes Opera House. If you happen to have a wonderful antique car (the driver must be female, but the navigator needn't be), you could call ahead to register. If not, come catch the finish of the rally with festivities on the Vergennes green.

July 4: Bristol hosts one of the most colorful **Independence Day parades** around with its comic Outhouse Race, crafts fair, and parade. Brandon's parade is the day before.

Early July: A 6-day **Festival on the Green**, Middlebury, features individual performers and groups such as the Bread & Puppet Theater as well as a potpourri of music from folk to jazz to exotic international talent. No charge for admission. Rokeby Museum's **Annual Pie and Ice Cream Social** with music and house tours; 802-877-3406.

Early August: **Addison County Field Days** (802-545-2257), New Haven—livestock and produce fair, horse pull, tractor pull, lumberjacks, demolition derby, and other events. There's also a **Taste of Vermont** dinner one night that requires reservations, but the food is worth the small effort.

Early October: **Dead Creek Wildlife Day** (802-241-3700)—wildlife demonstrations, nature walks, crafts, and food. **Vergennes Fiddlers' Contest** at the Vergennes Opera House (802-877-6737).

Mid-December: **Holiday Open House at the Henry Sheldon Museum** (802-388-2117), Park St., Middlebury. Come take a look at Christmas as it used to be with holiday traditions, activities, and decorations.

BURLINGTON REGION

Superbly sited on a slope overlooking Lake Champlain and the Adirondack Mountains, Burlington is Vermont's financial, educational, medical, and cultural center. While its fringes continue to spread over recent farmland (the core population hovers around 40,000, but the metro count is now more than 150,000), its heart beats ever faster. Few American cities this size offer as lively a downtown, as many interesting shops and affordable, varied restaurants, or as easy an access to boats, bike paths, and ski trails.

"Downtown Vermont" may sound like a contradiction, but that's just what Burlington is. Vermont is known for mountains, white-steepled churches, and cows, for rural beauty and independent-spirited residents. Its only real city is backed by and overlooks mountains, has more steeples than high-rises, and offers plenty of green space (more about the cows later). Burlington actually pushes the possibilities of the sophisticated, urban good life—the ecological, healthy, responsible good life, that is.

The community was chartered in 1763, 4 years after the French were evicted from the Champlain Valley. Ethan Allen, his three brothers, and a cousin were awarded large grants of choice lots along the Onion (now Winooski) River. In 1791 Ira Allen secured the legislative charter for the University of Vermont (UVM), from which the first class, of four, was graduated in 1804. UVM now enrolls more than 9,000 and is the largest of the city's three colleges.

Ethan and Ira would have little trouble finding their way around the city today. Main streets run much as they did in the 1780s—from the waterfront uphill past shops to the school Ira founded and on to Winooski Falls, site of Ira's own grist- and sawmills.

Along the waterfront, Federal-style commercial buildings house shops, businesses, and restaurants. The ferry terminal and neighboring Union Station, built during the city's late-19th-century boom period as a lumbering port—when the lakeside trains connected with myriad steamers and barges—are now the summer venue for excursion trains, ferries, and cruise boats. The neo-Victorian Burlington Boathouse is everyone's window on Lake Champlain, a place to rent a row- or sailboat, to sit sipping a morning coffee or sunset aperitif, or to lunch or dine on the water. The adjacent Waterfront Park and promenade are linked by bike paths to a series of other lakeside parks (bike and in-line skate rentals abound), which include swimmable beaches.

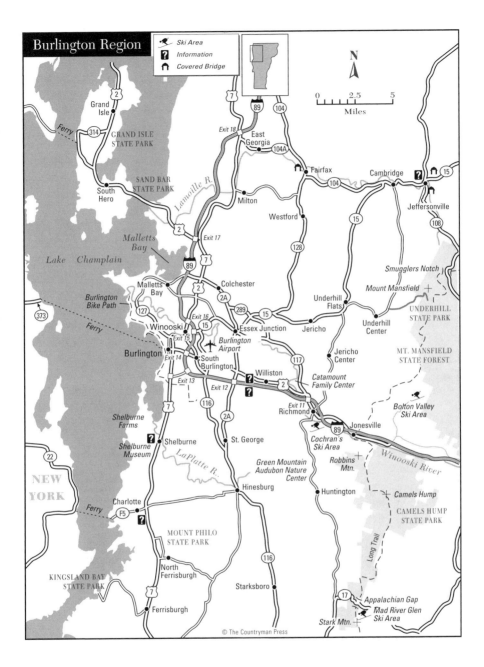

Halfway up the hill, the graceful Unitarian Church, designed in 1815 by Peter Banner, stands at the head of Church Street—now a bricked, traffic-free marketplace for four long blocks, a promenade that's become a 21st-century-style common, the place everyone comes to graze.

Theater and music are constants, but Burlington is best when winter winds soften to cool breezes. The city celebrates summer with an exuberance literally trumpeted from the rooftops in its opening salvo to summer: the Discover Jazz

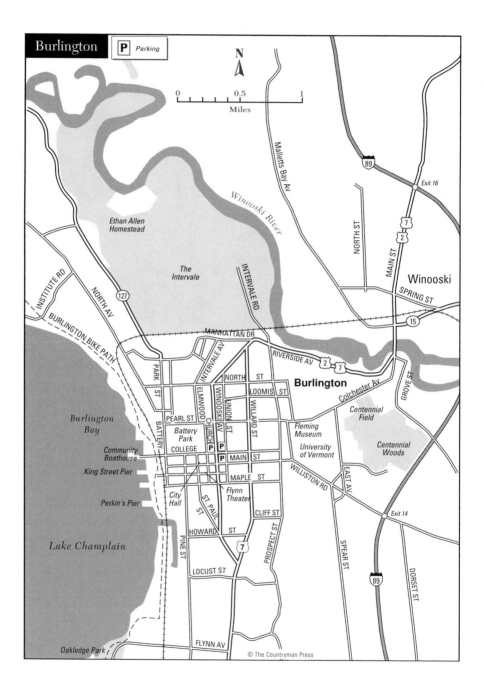

Burlington

P Parking

N

0   0.5   1
Miles

Mallets Bay Av

89

Exit 16

Ethan Allen
Homestead

Winooski River

North Av

127

Institute Rd

Burlington Bike Path

The
Intervale

Intervale Rd

North St

Main St

7
2

Winooski

Spring St

15

Manhattan Dr

Riverside Av

2
7

Colchester Av

Grove St

Burlington

Park St

Intervale Av

Elmwood Av

Winooski Av

Church St

North   St

Union St

Loomis   St

Willard St

Fleming
Museum

Centennial
Field

Centennial
Woods

Battery

Pearl St

Battery
Park

College

P
P

Main   St

Maple   St

University
of Vermont

Williston Rd

East Av

Burlington
Bay

Community
Boathouse

King Street Pier

Perkin's Pier

City
Hall

St Paul   St

Flynn
Theater

Cliff St

Prospect St

Exit 14

Spear St

Lake Champlain

Pine St

Howard   St

7

Locust St

Dorset St

89

Oakledge Park

Flynn Av

© The Countryman Press

Festival. The weeklong celebration includes some 200 performances. Stars perform at the Flynn Center for the Performing Arts, but jazz venues include buses and ferries, street corners, parks, rooftops, and restaurants. This festival is followed by the Mozart Festival (also in varied venues) and a variety of music, both indoor and out, all summer.

Burlington in the 1950s and '60s was a different place. Docks and waterside railyards had become privately owned wastelands, littered with high grass and rusting debris. The few public beaches were closed due to pollution, and the solution was seen as "urban renewal." In the '70s some 300 homes and 40 small businesses were demolished, and large luxury condo/retail development was planned. Then in 1981, Burlington elected as mayor Bernie Sanders, who had campaigned on the slogan "The Waterfront Is Not for Sale."

The present waterfront includes several new parks, such as Oakledge (formerly a General Electric property) just south of downtown, and Leddy (site of a former rendering plant) in the North End; the waterside green space is linked by an 8-mile recreational path that now extends across the Winooski River into Colchester and will soon extend across Lake Champlain to the Champlain Islands on the bed of the old Rutland Railroad.

Downtown lodging options are mysteriously limited, though expanding. Still, it is possible to walk from one high-rise hotel and several pleasant B&Bs to sights and water excursions, dining and shopping. Of course it's also appealing to bed down in the real countryside that's still within minutes of the city, so we have included B&Bs in nearby Jericho, Williston, Richmond, and Shelburne.

A couple of decades ago the Shelburne Museum, 6 miles south of the city, was the big sight-to-see in the area, although in recent years this "collection of collections" has been upstaged by Burlington itself. The museum's treasures range from a vintage Champlain Lake steamer to outstanding art and folk art. At neighboring Shelburne Farms—New England's most fabulous estate—there are plenty of prizewinning cows (and cheese), miles of lakeside walks, and a mansion in which you should dine, sleep, or at least breakfast.

GUIDANCE **The Lake Champlain Regional Chamber of Commerce** (802-863-3489; 1-877-686-5253; www.vermont.org), 60 Main St., Burlington 05401. Request brochure guides. Open Mon.–Fri. 8:30–5 year-round, also weekends 10–2 Memorial Day–Labor Day. Not the most obvious place for an information center (it's housed in the former motor vehicles building, halfway between Church St. and the waterfront), this one is augmented by a staffed information booth at the airport. This is also the regional marketing organization.

Newspapers: The daily *Burlington Free Press.* For current entertainment happenings, pick up *Seven Days*, a fat, free weekly published Wed. and stacked in the entryways of many shops and cafés.

GETTING THERE *Note:* Burlington is Vermont's single most car-free destination, accessible by bus from Boston and Montreal and by train from New York City and Montreal, blessed with good local public transport and little need to use it.

By air: **Burlington International Airport** (802-863-2874; 802-863-1889) is just 3 miles from downtown, served by Continental Express, United Airlines, US Airways, and Delta Connection (Comair). JetBlue, Northwest, and Independence are the new airlines serving Burlington; JetBlue has led the way in discounting ticket prices, so there are good deals to be had (www.jetblue.com). Half a dozen auto rental firms are at the airport.

By bus: **Vermont Transit Lines** (1-800-552-8737; www.vermonttransit.com), headquartered in Burlington, offers service to Albany, Boston, New York City, Montreal, Portland, and many points between. Buses depart from 345 Pine St., south of the downtown area; plenty of parking.

By car: I-89, Rts. 7 and 2.

By ferry: **The Lake Champlain Transportation Company** (802-864-9804; www.ferries.com), King St. Dock, Burlington. Descended from the world's oldest steamboat company, LCTC offers three local car-ferry services. Between mid-May and mid-October the car ferries make the 75-minute crossing between Burlington and Port Kent, N.Y. Apr.–early Jan. they also ply between Charlotte, just south of Burlington, and Essex, N.Y. Year-round service is offered on the 15-minute run between Grand Isle (see "The Northwest Corner") and Plattsburgh, N.Y.

By train: **Amtrak** (1-800-872-7245; in Canada: 1-800-4-AMTRAK; www.amtrak .com). The Vermonter (Washington to St. Albans via New York and Springfield, Ma.) stops at Essex Junction, 5 miles north of Burlington. (The station is served by two cab companies and by Burlington CCTA buses; see *Getting Around.*) Faster, more scenic service from New York City is available via the Adirondack to Port Kent, N.Y., which connects with the ferry to Burlington, and its free bus up Main Street.

GETTING AROUND *By bus:* **Chittenden County Transportation Authority** (802-864-0211; www.CCTAride.org). CCTA bus routes radiate from the corner of Cherry and Church streets. (hub of the Church Street Marketplace), serving the Shelburne Museum, the airport, the ferry, and the Champlain Mill in Winooski as well as all the colleges and shopping areas. The fare is $1.25 (60¢ for ages 5–17, 60 and over, and the disabled,). Transfers are free. Buses run daily, 6 AM–9 PM, though not on Sun. except for airport runs. The CCTA also operates the College Street Shuttle, a free trolley on wheels that runs up and down the length of College St. four times per hour, from the medical complex and UVM at the top of the hill to Union Station and the ferry dock on the lake (daily in summer, weekdays in winter).

MEDICAL EMERGENCY Emergency service is available by calling **911**.

Fletcher Allen Health Care (802-847-2434; www.fahc.org) on the UVM campus, 111 Colchester Ave., Burlington, has a 24-hour emergency room.

✴ Nearby Villages

Jericho. Northeast of Burlington, Jericho is best known for the **Old Red Mill** (Jericho Historical Society: 802-899-3225), on Rt. 15 at Jericho Corners (open

Mon.–Sat. 10–5, Sun. 1–5—except Jan.–Mar., when it's open only Wed., Sat., and Sun.). This tower-topped, 1800s red mill set above a gorge is one of the most photographed buildings in Vermont and appropriately houses prints and mementos relating to one of the state's most famous photographers, Wilson A. "Snowflake" Bentley. A Jericho farmer who was the first person in the world to photograph individual snowflakes, Bentley collected more than 5,000 micro-photos. A basement museum also tells the story of the many mills that once lined six sets of falls. Sales from the crafts store benefit the preservation of the building, which is owned by the Jericho Historical Society. A 20-acre park behind the mill, along the river, offers picnic tables and hiking trails. Ask directions to nearby Jericho Center, with its oval village common and **Jericho Center General Store** (802-899-3313), a genuine, old-fashioned market that's been operating since 1807. Linda St. Amour and her family carry the usual fresh, frozen, and canned produce, plus socks, mittens, gloves, boots, and so on. The syrup and beans (which, we can attest, bake up nicely) are local. While you're in the neighborhood, stop at **Snowflake Chocolates** (802-899-3373) at 81A Rt. 15 to experience the indescribable smell of warm, handmade chocolates.

Richmond. East of Burlington on Rt. 2 (I-89, Exit 11) and the Winooski River, Richmond was badly damaged in the flood of 1927 but still has a brief, architecturally interesting downtown. Turn down Bridge St. and drive by the old Blue Seal grain store (now a restaurant; see *Dining Out*) and the library (a former church) to the **Old Round Church**. This 16-sided building, one of the most unusual in the state, was constructed in 1812–13 as a community meetinghouse to serve five denominations; in winter its illuminated windows are a vision of Christmas past (open daily July 4–Labor Day 10–4, also weekends in spring and fall).

Shelburne. Beyond the commercial sprawl of Shelburne Rd. (Rt. 7 south from Burlington) lie two of Vermont's greatest treasures, both the legacy of 19th-century railroad heirs William Seward and Lila Vanderbilt Webb. In the 1880s the couple hired Frederick Law Olmsted to landscape their 4,000-acre lakeside model farm, and in 1946 their daughter-in-law founded a major museum of Americana. Today 1,400 acres of the estate—**Shelburne Farms**—survive as a combination inn and demonstration farm, complementing the exhibits in no fewer than 39 buildings in the nearby **Shelburne Museum**. Inevitably shops and attractions continue to multiply along Rt. 7; the latest, the **Vermont Teddy Bear Company** Factory and Museum, threatens to draw more visitors than either Shelburne Farms or the Shelburne Museum. (See *To See* for details about all three.)

Winooski is just across the 32-foot Winooski Falls from Burlington. Ira Allen was the first to harness the

OLD ROUND CHURCH IN RICHMOND
Joe Citro

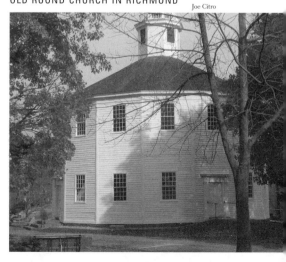

water that subsequently powered several mammoth, brick, 19th-century mills, attracting the workers from Ireland, Canada, and Eastern Europe who settled in the cottages that line its streets. The waterfall, with its art deco bridge, and the common, framed by the vintage-1867 Winooski Block and the handsome Champlain Mill (now a shopping/dining complex), still form the center of town, which underwent a major redesign in 2005. St. Michael's College, with its Playhouse (presenting a variety of stage performances) and art gallery (802-654-2535), is just up Allen St. (Rt. 15).

✳ To See

MUSEUMS AND ATTRACTIONS ♂ ♿ **Shelburne Museum** (802-985-3344; www.shelburnemuseum.org), Rt. 7, Shelburne (6 miles south of Burlington), is open late May–late Oct., daily 10–5. $18 adults, $13 students over 10, $9 ages 6–10. Family cap $48. Tickets are good for 2 consecutive days, and parking is free. This fascinating "collection of collections" features American folk art but also includes paintings by Rembrandt, Degas, Monet, and Manet. More than three dozen buildings, many of them historic transplants from around New England, each house a different collection. They are set in 45 landscaped acres that include flower and herb gardens, an apple orchard, and more than 90 varieties of lilacs (the annual Lilac Festival is usually the third weekend in May).

An adequate description of the collections (more than 80,000 objects) would fill a separate chapter. Highlights include a 1915 steam locomotive and a vintage-1890 private Palace Car; the side-wheeler *Ticonderoga*, in her basin near the Colchester Reef Lighthouse; the amazing folk art in the Stagecoach Inn (weather vanes, cigar-store figures, trade signs, and figureheads); the American paintings (by Fitz Hugh Lane, Winslow Homer, and many other lesser-known but superb 19th-century New England painters); the Webb Memorial Building, with its elegant rooms (originally in a New York penthouse) hung with impressionist paintings (including a portrait of the museum's founder, Electra Havemeyer Webb, by Mary Cassatt); and the heirloom quilts (the collection includes some 900 American quilts). There are also the Horseshoe Barn's marvelous carriages; the Castleton Slate Jail; Shaker Shed; Dorset House and its decoys, Audubon game bird prints, and fowling pieces; a general store; an up-and-down sawmill; an old-fashioned carousel; and much more. The ticket is good for 2 days because you may well want to allow time to absorb it all.

Acquisitions continue, but this is still substantially the collection of one woman, gathered at a time when few people were interested in Americana. Electra Havemeyer was 18 in 1910 when she bought her first cigar-store figure. Three years later she married James Watson Webb of Shelburne (son of the wealthy couple who had built Shelburne Farms; see below). Over the next 30 years she raised five children, traveled widely, and managed homes on Long Island and in Manhattan and a 50,000-acre "camp" in the Adirondacks, as well as the Shelburne estate. Gradually she filled all her holdings (even her indoor tennis court) with her treasures, founding the museum in 1947 when her husband retired to Shelburne. Both died in 1960, but their vision for the museum was fulfilled by their son, the late J. Watson Webb Jr. The **Owl Cottage Family Activity Cen-**

ter gives kids some hands-on time; a number of displays, such as a model circus parade, are also geared to children. There's a museum shop and cafeteria, picnic areas, and small buses for the disabled or just footsore. The visitors center is a rare round barn. Inquire about gallery talks, classes in traditional crafts, and frequent special events.

✔ **Shelburne Farms** (802-985-8686; www.shelburnefarms.org), 1611 Harbor Rd., Shelburne, just east of Rt. 7. The Farm Store and Visitors Center (802-985-8442), with an exceptional introductory film, are open year-round, daily 9–5 (10–5 in the off-season). Mid-May–late Oct., general admission for the walking trails, children's farmyard, and cheesemaking operation on the 1,400-acre lakeside property costs $6 adults, $5 seniors, $4 ages 3–14; full 1½-hour open-wagon tours are offered four times daily mid-May–mid-Oct. Guided tours cost $9 adults, $8 seniors, $7 ages 3–17. Nov.–Apr., no charge for the walking trails. Inquire about inn and garden tours, afternoon tea on the South Porch, Breeding Barn tours, and special events. This grand 1880s lakeside estate is now a non-profit experimental farm and educational and cultural center. Comprising 3,800 acres at its zenith, this rural masterpiece was landscaped by Frederick Law Olmsted (who also designed Central Park) and America's pioneer forester Gifford Pinchot. It was designed for William Seward Webb and Lila Vanderbilt Webb (their daughter-in-law Electra Havemeyer Webb founded Shelburne Museum), to include a model farm with magnificent Norman-style barns and a 110-room summer "cottage" on a bluff overlooking Lake Champlain.

The mansion is now the Inn at Shelburne Farms (open mid-May–mid-Oct.; see *Lodging* and *Dining Out*). The immense, four-story, Queen Anne/shingle-style 416-foot **Farm Barn** (housing pigs, chickens, and other farm animals) is now a place for children to collect eggs, learn to milk a cow, or enjoy a hayride. It also houses the cheesemaking facility. The **Coach Barn**, once occupied by locally bred hackneys, now houses changing art exhibits and frequent workshops. The most recent addition to the holdings is the massive 418-foot-long **Breeding Barn** (open only through scheduled tours), where the hackneys were bred. The farm's

INN AT SHELBURNE FARMS

Diane E. Foulds

prizewinning cheddar cheese, made from its own herd of Brown Swiss cows, is sold, along with other Vermont products, in the Farm Store. A walking trail winds from the visitors center about 1 mile to the top of Lone Tree Hill for sweeping views of Lake Champlain and the Adirondacks. Inquire about naturalist-led bird walks and special events.

Tip: The Inn at Shelburne Farms is open to the public by reservation for breakfast as well as dinner. (No admission fee.) Enjoy the most elegant breakfast in New England, get a glimpse of the spectacular library and living room, then stroll the lakeside perennial, herb, and rose gardens.

Burlington waterfront (www.enjoyburlington.com). As noted in the chapter introduction, Burlington's revived waterfront affords dramatic views and is accessible to the public. The handsome (vintage-1915) **Union Station** at the base of Main Street is now public space (changing art exhibits), and the King Street Dock remains home to the **Lake Champlain Transportation Company** (LCTC), established in 1826. At the base of College Street, at the College Street Pier, the (1991) **Community Boathouse** echoes the design of the Lake Champlain Yacht Club built on this site in 1889. The new waterfront draws **ECHO at the Leahy Center for Lake Champlain** (802-864-1848; www.echovermont .org), 1 College St., operated by the Champlain Basin Science Program. ECHO, which stands for "ecology, culture, history, and opportunity," is both a science center and a world-class lake aquarium that is irresistible to kids. ECHO is open to the public year-round, daily 10–5, Thu. to 8 PM. Closed only Thanksgiving, Christmas Eve, and Christmas Day. $9 adults, $8 seniors and students, $6 ages 3–17 (ask about annual passes and group rates). The 7.6-mile **Burlington Bike Path** links these sites with the nearby **Waterfront Park** to the north (which includes a boardwalk promenade) and with **Perkin's Pier** (parking, boat launch, picnic area, canal boat exhibit, and waterfront benches) just to the south. Farther south is **Oakledge Park** with two picnic shelters, a beach, and a wheelchair-accessible tree house. Several more beaches and parks stretch in both directions. Not surprisingly, shops and restaurants have proliferated along neighboring Battery Street; **Battery Park** is the visually majestic setting for free summer concerts Thu. and Sun. and for frequent special events.

BURLINGTON'S CHURCH STREET MARKETPLACE

Kim Grant

Church Street Marketplace. The city's shopping and dining hub, the Church Street Marketplace extends four car-free blocks, from the graceful Unitarian Church, designed in 1815 by Peter Banner, to City Hall at the corner of Main St. A fanciful fountain plays at its head, and the bricked promenade is spotted with benches and boulders from different parts of the state. The marketplace buildings themselves, a mix of 19th-century and art deco styles, house more than 100 shops and an ever-increasing number of restaurants. Walk through a storefront at 49 Church St. and you are in the **Burlington Town Center**, a multilevel (stepped into the hillside), multishop complex resembling many in Montreal but few in New England. Unlike Boston's Quincy Market, Church Street is a public thoroughfare, open daily and geared as much to residents as to tourists.

&. **Robert Hull Fleming Museum** (802-656-0750; www.uvm.edu/~fleming), Colchester Ave., on the University of Vermont campus. Open weekdays 9–4 (summer months noon–4), Sat. and Sun. 1–5; closed Mon. Limited parking. $5 adults, $3 students and seniors, $10 per family. Vermont's largest collection of international treasures. Varied collections of early to postmodern art, natural history, archaeology, and geology. Holdings include ancient primitive art from several cultures and continents, a collection of American portraits and landscapes (from the 18th century to contemporary works), and frequent special exhibits showcasing everything from Picasso to teacups. Gift shop. The building was designed by the renowned firm of McKim, Mead & White, which also designed UVM's Ira Allen Chapel (1927) and Burlington's City Hall.

Fire House Gallery (802-865-7165), 135 Church St., Burlington, next to City Hall. Open Wed.–Sun. noon–6, but noon–8 on Fri. A nonprofit community space showcasing work by top Vermont artists. Inquire about First Friday Art Trolley Tours, a free tour of local art galleries the first Friday of every month, Apr.–Nov. (5–7 PM).

The Ethan Allen Homestead (802-865-4556; www.ethanallenhomestead.org), off Rt. 127 just north of the downtown Burlington waterfront (take the North Avenue Beaches exit off Rt. 127, the Northern Connector). Open all year, daily May–Oct., Mon.–Sat. 10–4, Sun. 1–4. Vermont's godfather is memorialized here in the timber farmhouse in which he lived out the last years of his turbulent life; he died in 1789. The visitors center offers interesting descriptive and multimedia exhibits, and the setting is a working garden and an extensive park with some 4 miles of walking trails along the Winooski River. $5 adults, $4 seniors, $3 ages 5–17; under 5 free; family rate $15.

Heritage Winooski Mill Museum (802-655-9477), Champlain Mill, Winooski. Mon.–Sat. 10–9, Sun. noon–5. No admission charge. Gallery and hall exhibits on life and work in the woolen mills at Winooski Falls circa 1835 through 1956.

FOR FAMILIES ♂ **Vermont Teddy Bear Company Factory and Museum** (802-985-3001; 1-800-829-BEAR; www.vermontteddybear.com), 6655 Shelburne Rd., Rt. 7 at the south end of Shelburne Village. Open daily 9–5, till 6 in summer months. A phenomenon in its own right, the huge, fanciful new birthplace of well over 100,000 teddy bears a year now includes a museum depicting teddy bear history; visitors are also invited to make their own teddy bear ($19–24) and to take the highly entertaining tour ($2 adults, free for children under 12.). There is, of course, a huge teddy bear store.

♂ **National Museum of the Morgan Horse** (802-985-8665; www.morgan museum.org), 122 Bostwick Rd. near Rt. 7, Shelburne, next to the Shelburne Museum. Open weekdays (except Wed.) 9–4, Sat. 10–2. Closed Sun. The history of the Morgan horse in America is depicted, with changing exhibits. Guided tours can be arranged with advance notice. Admission by donation.

✍ **Lake Champlain Chocolates Factory Tour** (802-864-1807; www.lake champlainchocolates.com), 750 Pine St., Burlington. The factory itself is chocolate colored, and inside you learn the whole truffle-making process. Afterward you can sample the goods for free, stock up on seconds, or sit down at the café for chocolate ice cream or cocoa. Guided factory tours are offered weekdays 9–2 on the hour.

✳ To Do

ARTS VACATIONS Shelburne Art Center (802-985-3648; www.shelburneart center.org), P.O. Box 52, 64 Harbor Rd., Shelburne, 05482. This small, nonprofit complex, the former Shelburne Craft School, has been holding classes for children and adults for 60 years. It offers year-round workshops of varying length in pottery, woodworking, fiber, metal, stained glass, and all the fine arts, and shows local work in the on-site gallery. Summer camp programs for children. Classes and summer programs are also offered at the **Firehouse Center for the Visual Arts** (802-865-7166; www.burlingtoncityarts.com/classes) in Burlington at 149 Church St.

BALLOONING One of the best ways to get an eyeful of the entire Champlain Valley is to soar overhead in a hot-air balloon. Jeff Snyder's outfit, **Above Reality, Inc.**, will take you up any time of year at sunrise or sunset (802-899-4007; 1-877-386-7473; www.balloonvermont.com), P.O. Box 75, Jericho 05465.

BICYCLING The **Burlington Bike Path** (www.enjoyburlington.com) runs for 8 miles along the waterfront, connecting eight different parks, beginning with Oakledge Park in the south. A ferry will shuttle you across the Winooski River to the continuation of the path in Colchester and on up to the Champlain Islands. Fun side trips include Ethan Allen Park, the Ethan Allen Homestead, Intervale Community Farms, and the Salmon Hole Fishing Area off Riverside Ave. **Rental bikes** (including tandems, trailers, and trail-a-bikes) and in-line skate rentals are available from the **SkiRack** (802-658-3313), 85 Main St. This path is used for walking, running, and in-line skating as well as biking. Note that CCTA buses have bicycle racks. For serious bicyclists, we recommend the *Greater Burlington Hiking and Biking Map*, published by Map Adventures (www.map adventures.com), which details several Burlington area loops and longer tours on both sides of Lake Champlain, using ferries. You can also download a free Burlington biking map at www.localmotionvt.org.

Mountain bikers should check out the 450-acre **Catamount Family Center** (802-879-6001; www.catamountoutdoor.com), Governor Chittenden Rd., Williston: a 40 km trail system, also rentals and food in the 1796 house built by Vermont's first governor as well as the three-guest-room **Catamount's B&B** (802-878-2180) nearby at 592 Governor Chittenden Rd.

✍ **Sleepy Hollow Ski and Bike Center** (802-434-2283; www.skisleepyhollow .com) 1805 Sherman Hollow Rd., Huntington, features over 10 miles of single-track plus another 20 miles of converted ski trails linking to the Catamount Family Center Mountain Bike Trail. The bike shop rents equipment, and you can take a dip in the on-site pond. Adults $6 per day, children $4, kids 6 and under, free. Open daily, late May–late Oct.

There is also the **Essex Transportation Trail**, a 3-mile rail-trail from the Essex Police Station to Rt. 15 (Lang Farm); the **Shelburne Recreation Trail**, from Bay Rd. through Shelburne Bay Park to Harbor Rd.; the unpaved **Intervale Bikepath**, from Gardener's Supply on Intervale Ave. to the Ethan Allen Homestead; and **Causeway Park** in Colchester, a packed-gravel trail that follows an old railroad bed out into Lake Champlain. **Bolton Valley** also offers mountain biking on its cross-country and alpine trails.

BIRDING ✿ **The Birds of Vermont Museum** (802-434-2167; www.birdsof vermont.org), adjacent to the Green Mountain Audubon Center at 900 Sherman Hollow Rd., Huntington. Open May–Oct., daily 10–4; by appointment in winter. Carvings of more than 200 species of birds by Robert Spear Jr.; also nature trails, recorded birdsongs. $5 adults, $4 seniors, $2.50 ages 3–17.

BOATING *Note:* The regular LCTC 75-minute ferry crossing from Burlington to Port Kent, N.Y., is a great ride and a bargain.

Burlington Community Boathouse (802-865-3377), foot of College St., Burlington. Rowboats, Rhodes and Laser sailboat rentals, captained day sails, sailing lessons, fishing charters, June–Oct. *Winds of Ireland* (802-863-5090; www.windsofireland.net), based here, offers day and sunset sails, bareboat charters, and instruction.

Spirit of Ethan Allen III (802-862-8300; www.soea.com). Seasonal, daily scenic cruises as well as dinner cruises aboard a triple-deck, 500-passenger excursion boat, departing from the Burlington Community Boathouse (see above) mid-May–mid-Oct. Narrated sightseeing, plus sunset cruises, dinner, lunch and brunch cruises, murder mystery, and '50s night cruises. Specialty cruises include a lobster fest, a night of big-band music, and an Elvis show on the lake. Sightseeing cruise$11.99 adults, $5.99 ages 3–11.

Lake Champlain Cruises (802-864-9669; www.ferries.com/cruise), King Street Dock, Burlington. The *Adirondack*, the *Champlain*, and now a third cruise boat, the *Northern Lights*, regularly sail the waters of Lake Champlain, offering brunch, lunch, dinner, scenic, and entertainment cruises of all sorts. The caterer runs two local seafood restaurants. The supper club and special entertainment cruises cost about $35 per person, less for the daytime outings.

✿ **Lake Champlain Community Sailing Center** (802-864-2499; www.lccsc .org), located along the Burlington Bike Path, is a nonprofit, public access sailing center with a host of learn-to-sail and learn-to-canoe programs for kids, adults, and families, as well as rentals. Keel boat rentals cost $50 per hour ($310 for 8 hours) on weekends, less on weekdays. LCCSC also offers adaptive programs for the disabled.

✿ **Whistling Man Schooner Co.** (802-598-6504, www.whistlingman.com), boarding behind the ECHO Center for Lake Champlain at the foot of College

Diane E. Foulds

ONE OF THE TWO YURTS AT MAPLE WIND
FARM IN HUNTINGTON

St. in Burlington. Captain Glen Find-holt can accommodate up to 12 passengers on his 43-foot sloop, the *Friend Ship*, for blissful 2-hour sails, three times a day. Don't forget sunscreen (bring a sweater if sailing after sunset).

Waterfront Boat Rentals (802-864-4858; 1-877-964-4858; www.water frontboatrentals.com), Perkins Pier, at the bottom of Maple St., Burlington. Open daily, 10 AM–sunset. The place to rent canoes, kayaks, rowboats, and a variety of speedboats, life jackets and safety equipment included. By the hour. Bring a picture ID and be prepared to pay a security deposit.

Also note: Day sails and local marinas are listed with the Lake Champlain Regional Chamber of Commerce (see *Guidance*).

CAMPING 🐾 🐾 **On The Loose** (802-434-7257; 1-800-688-1481; www.otloose .com), 1035 Carse Rd., Huntington 05462. Beth Whiting and Bruce Hennessey rent two canvas-sided, Mongolian-style yurts year-round on their 150-acre hilltop **Maple Wind Farm** in Huntington, about 35 miles southeast of Burlington. Inside are bunks sleeping 10, a table and chairs, a propane stove, kitchen equipment, and a woodstove. Outside is firewood, miles of nature and hiking trails, and an outhouse. $135 per night buys exclusive use.

DIVING **Lake Champlain Historic Underwater Preserves** (802-457-2022). The Vermont Division for Historic Preservation (www.historicvermont.org) maintains seven shipwrecks, identified by Coast Guard–approved buoys, at various points on Lake Champlain; all are open to scuba divers. The *Horse Ferry*, the *Coal Barge*, the *O. J. Walker* canal boat, and the *General Butler* are off Burlington. The *Phoenix* and the *Diamond Island Stone Boat* are in Colchester and Vergennes, respectively, and the *Champlain II*, a passenger ship, lies on the New York side across from Basin Harbor. **Waterfront Diving Center** (802-865-2771; www.waterfrontdiving.com), 214 Battery St., Burlington, provides equipment rentals and repair, and instruction in snorkeling, underwater archaeology, photography, scuba, and charters to historic preserved shipwrecks.

See also *Boating*.

FISHING **Champ Charters** (802-864-3790), 78 Main St., Burlington; Paul Boileau offers fishing charters. **Schirmer's Fly Shop** (802-863-6105), 34 Mills Ave., South Burlington, specializing in Ed Schirmer's own flies, tackle, accessories, trips, and instruction. For a fishing guide, contact the Vermont Outdoor Guide Association (1-800-425-8747; www.voga.org). The **Salmon Hole fishing area** off Riverside Ave., just beyond Tortilla Flats Mexican Restaurant, is a popular local spot, as is the **Fishing Pier** on the Burlington waterfront behind the Water Department building next to the Coast Guard station.

GOLF **Vermont National Country Club** (802-864-7770; www.vnccgolf.com), 1227 Dorset St., South Burlington, an 18-hole, Jack Nicklaus–designed championship course; **Marble Island Resort** (802-864-6800), Marble Island Rd., Malletts Bay, Colchester, 9 holes; **Rocky Ridge Golf Club** (802-482-2191), St. George (5 miles south on Rt. 2A from Exit 12 off I-89), 18 holes; **Kwiniaska** (802-985-3672; www.kwiniaska.com), 5531 Spear St., Shelburne, 18 holes, Vermont's longest course; **Williston Golf Course** (802-878-3747), 424 Golf Course Rd., Williston, 18 holes; **Essex Country Club** (802-879-3232), 332 Old Stage Rd., Essex Junction, 18 holes; **Cedar Knoll Country Club** (802-482-3186), 13020 Rt. 116, Hinesburg, 27 holes; **Links at the Lang Farm** (802-878-0298; www.linksatlangfarm.com), 39 Essex Way, Essex, 18 holes.

HIKING See Camels Hump State Park and Mount Philo State Park under *Green Space*.

HORSEBACK RIDING **Auclair Riding Ranch** (802-238-6964), Hinesburg Rd., South Burlington. Hour-long trail rides, $30 for adults, Apr.–Oct.

KAYAKING **Champlain Kayak Club** (www.ckayak.com) and the **Lake Champlain Maritime Museum** (www.lcmm.org) are both excellent sources of information.

True North Kayak Tours (802-860-1910; www.vermontkayak.com). Jane and David Yagoda offer instruction and guided tours from a variety of locations on Lake Champlain. Inquire about multiday paddles through the Champlain Islands with B&B lodging.

PaddleWays (802-238-0674; www.paddleways.com). Burlington-based Kevin and Michele Rose offer 3-hour tours, instructional classes, full-day and multiday tours on Lake Champlain.

Umiak Outfitters (802-865-6777; www.umiak.com). Based in Stowe, Umiak offers guided kayaking on Lake Champlain plus rentals and instruction at its waterfront location at Burlington's North Beach. Kayak and canoe rentals also are available from **Waterfront Boat Rentals** (802-864-4858; 1-877-964-4858; www.waterfront boatrentals.com) at Perkin's Pier, at the bottom of King St. in Burlington.

SPECTATOR SPORTS ✔ **The Vermont Lake Monsters** (802-655-4200). Formerly known as the Expos, Burlington's minor-league baseball team plays at Centennial Field (off Colchester Ave.) all summer. You can park at UVM and take a shuttle bus to the game. The season is mid-June–Sep. 1, tickets are cheap, the park is lovely, the concession food is pretty good, and there's a giant Day-Glo dancing Champ mascot for the

SUNSET AT PERKIN'S PIER IN BURLINGTON
Kim Grant

kids. All in all, a great time—and the baseball isn't bad. The Monsters operate a souvenir store in the Champlain Mill (802-655-9477), Winooski.

SWIMMING **North Beach** (802-862-0942), off North Ave. at 60 Institute Rd., Burlington (turn at the high school), provides tent and trailer sites, picnic tables, a snack bar, a changing room, and swimming from a long, sandy beach, late May–early Sep.; vehicle charge, pedestrians and bicyclists free. (Just before the park is the entrance to Rock Point, where the Episcopal Diocese of Vermont maintains Bishop Hopkins' Hall School, the bishop's residence, a conference center, and an outdoor chapel.)

Other beaches: **Leddy Park**, a more secluded, tree-lined beach with picnic areas, grills, and tables (farther off North Ave., turn left before the shopping mall onto Leddy Park Rd. and drive to the end). **Oakledge Park** (802-865-7247), a tiny yet cozy beach with a rocky spit, plus sheltered picnic area and numerous open-air picnic tables with grills, three tennis courts, a two softball fields, volleyball courts, and walking trails. At the southern end of the bike path off Rt. 7, at the end of Flynn Ave. Fee for vehicles, pedestrians and bicyclists free. **Red Rocks Park** (802-864-4108), Lyons Rd., South Burlington's small but serviceable public beach, is valued mostly for its forested hiking trails, with a few picnic tables overlooking the lake. Open mid-June–late Aug. Fee.

✳ Winter Sports

CROSS-COUNTRY SKIING *Northern Vermont Nordic Skiing and Snowshoe*, a weatherproof map ($6.95) detailing cross-country and snowshoeing trails throughout the region, is available at local outlets and from Map Adventures (www.mapadventures.com).

Bolton Valley (802-434-3444; www.boltonvalley.com), Bolton. Ranging in elevation from 1,600 to 3,200 feet, this 100 km network is Vermont's highest cross-country system, with snow that usually lasts well into April. About 35 km are machine groomed. There is a wide and gently sloping 3.6-mile Broadway and a few short trails for beginners, but most of the terrain is backwoods, much of it splendidly high wilderness country. You can take an alpine lift to the peak of Ricker Mountain and ski Old Turnpike, then keep going on cross-country trails for a total of 7 miles. There's a ski school, rentals are available in the cross-country center, and experienced skiers are welcome to stay in the area's high huts by reservation. Telemarking is a specialty here, along with guided tours. Trail fee.

The legendary 12-mile **Bolton-to-Trapp trail** originates here (this is by far the preferred direction to ski it), but requires spotting a car at the other end or on Moscow Rd. Inquire about the exciting new telemark/backcountry trail beginning at the top of Bolton's Wilderness Chair and meandering down into Little River State Park in Waterbury–Stowe. Again, a car needs to be spotted at the other end.

⋆ **Catamount Outdoor Family Center** (802-879-6001; www.catamount outdoor.com), 421 Governor Chittenden Rd., Williston. The 35 km of groomed trails at this nonprofit, family-owned recreation area include a 3 km loop that is lit up for night skiing. All of it radiates over rolling terrain, both wooded and open. Geared to all abilities. Guided tours, rentals, instruction, warming hut. Trail fee.

✆ **Sleepy Hollow Ski and Bike Center** (802-434-2283; www.skisleepyhollow .com), 1805 Sherman Hollow Rd., Huntington. Dave, Sandy, Molly, and Eli Enman offer over 40 km of well-groomed cross-country ski trails that weave through an 870-acre tract up to the elevated Butternut Cabin (which can be rented all year) with its gorgeous views of Camels Hump. Another 20 km are good for snowshoeing, and there are rentals, lessons, and a warm-up lodge with accommodations. Popular with the locals, Sleepy Hollow also offers night skiing on a 2 km loop each Mon., Wed., and Fri., sunset–9 PM.

Note: See *Green Space* for more about local parks with trails that lend themselves to cross-country skiing.

DOWNHILL SKIING **Bolton Valley Resort** (802-434-3444; 1-877-926-5866; www.boltonvalley.com), Bolton. This mountain is smaller and less commercial than the state's better-known ski areas, but has advantages the others lack. For one thing, it has the second highest base elevation of any winter resort in New England, meaning lots of natural snow. The mini village is cozy and Alp-like, keeping everything within walking distance. A fitness center furnishes muscle-building (and muscle-soothing) facilities, including a sauna, pool, multiperson Jacuzzi, massages, and more, while 62 trails cover 165 skiable acres, about half of them geared to intermediate-level skiers (a quarter cater to beginners; a quarter to experts). At night the lights go on over 12 trails and 3 lifts, making Bolton the state's largest night-skiing destination. There's something for everyone: snowshoeing, lots of Nordic trails, and an illuminated 5-acre snowboard and ski park with jumps and a groomed half-pipe. Since Bob Fries and his partners took over in 2002, some $2.3 million has been invested to polish things up. Bolton has a new wood-fired pizzeria, a spiffied-up restaurant called **Bailey's at the Valley** (see *Eating Out*), new glades and backcountry trails for the more adventuresome, and a brand-new quad chairlift that runs from the base lodge to Vista Mountain's 3,150-foot summit, the most ambitious improvements in 20 years.

Set atop a winding, 6-mile road that is blissfully free of the fast-food and chain-hotel establishments that plague other ski areas, the spot is refreshingly scenic while still being accessible to Richmond, a 10-minute drive, and to the Burlington airport some 20 miles away. Prices are another attraction. Lift tickets are considerably lower than in southern Vermont, with plenty of enticements: a reduced rate for women on Wed., deals for the locals, and ski packages that include overnights and breakfast at the

SNOWBOARD INSTRUCTION AT BOLTON VALLEY

Anthony Marnora

resort's ski-in, ski-out hotel. In summer the trails fill with hikers and mountain bikers, and the lift runs for downhill mountain bikers on weekends. Residents of the 200 private condos have the mountain largely to themselves much of the time, though vacationers are gradually discovering the Adventure Center, with its tennis courts, fitness room, pool, and 18-hole disk golf course, along with an outdoor ropes course, zipline, and high wire, plus kayaking, rappelling, caving, and bike races. Owner Fries is developing more activities for summer visitors. Until then, the resort will remain an unspoiled natural area teeming with wildlife and terrific alpine views. With its steep access road veering off a lonely stretch of Rt. 2 between Montpelier and Burlington, this is a genuinely self-contained resort whose atmosphere is guaranteed to make you want to stay put for a while.

Vertical drop: 1,704 feet.

Trails: 64.

Lifts: 7: 2 quads, 4 double chairlifts, 1 surface.

Base elevation: 2,100 feet.

Snowmaking: 60 percent.

Rates: Full season, half-day, night-skiing, and package ticket options are available.

✍ **Cochran Ski Area** (802-434-2479; www.cochranskiarea.com), Cochran Rd., Richmond 05477. When Mickey and Ginny Cochran bought this hillside farm in 1961, little did they know that in 1998 it would become the nation's first nonprofit ski area and the incubator of Olympic champions. Two generations of Cochrans have joined the U.S. Ski Team, and two have won top trophies. What started in 1961 as a single backyard slope with a 400-foot rope tow has stretched into a good-sized racing mountain with six trails and four surface lifts, including two rope tows, a T-bar, and a handle. This is the state's best children's and instructional spot. Olympic gold medalist Barbara Ann Cochran runs Ski Tots, teaching parents to instruct their own 3- to 5-year-olds. The lodge serves hot snacks and rents equipment, there's a ski school, and free Lollipop Races are held each Sunday; winners receive lollipops. Open on weekends and during holiday weeks 9–4; otherwise Tue., Thu., and Fri. 2:30–5. Full-season family pass $300 if purchased before Dec., $400 thereafter. Day passes $18 adults, $12 for students and half days.

Note: See also **Smugglers' Notch Resort** in "North of the Notch and the Lemoille Valley," "Stowe and Waterbury," and "Sugarbush/Mad River Valley." Five major alpine areas are within easy striking distance of Burlington.

ICE SKATING **Leddy Arena** (802-864-0123), a modern, indoor rink at Leddy Park, Burlington. Rentals. The **Catamount Outdoor Family Center** (802-879-6001; www.catamountoutdoor.com) floods a 250-meter skating oval, which is illuminated at night. And skating on Lake Champlain from **Waterfront Park** is a special rite of winter on those ever-rarer occasions when the lake freezes over; flags indicate ice safety.

SLEIGH RIDES **Shelburne Farms** (802-985-8442; www.shelburnefarms.org) offers rides in 10-passenger sleighs through a 19th-century-esque landscape of

Joe Citro

OAKLEDGE PARK IN BURLINGTON

sculpted forests and snow-covered fields, with visions of opulent barns in the distance. For more on the farm, see *Museums and Attractions*. Daily late Dec.–Jan. 1, then weekends through Feb. $7 adults, $5 ages 3–17.

✳ Green Space

Burlington Parks and Recreation (802-865-7247; www.enjoyburlington.com). Request a copy of the Burlington *Bike Paths & Parks* map or pick it up at the chamber of commerce. Burlington's lakeside parks are superb.

& **Oakledge Park** (take Flynn Ave. off Pine St. or Rt. 7) offers swimming and picnicking and sports a wheelchair-accessible tree house (parking fee, but you can bike or walk in). **Red Rocks Park** just south, occupying the peninsula that divides Burlington from South Burlington (take Queen City Pkwy. off Rt. 7), offers walking and cross-country ski trails (no bikes allowed) as well as a beach. **Ethan Allen Park** (North Ave.) is a 67-acre preserve, once part of Ethan's farm (it's near the Homestead) and webbed with trails that climb to the Pinnacle and to a Norman-style stone tower built on Indian Rock in 1905 (open Memorial Day–Labor Day, Wed.–Sun. noon–8); both high points offer panoramic views of Lake Champlain.

Winooski Valley Park District (802-863-5744; www.wvpd.org) consists of 17 parks, one a wetlands, one landlocked, and most maintained as nature preserves. A few contain canoe launches and bike paths. **The Intervale** (entrance on Riverside Ave. and N. Prospect St.) along the Winooski River offers walking as well as bike trails and includes Intervale Community Farms (802-660-3508), Gardener's Supply (retail and catalog outlet), and a seasonal organic farm stand. Also along the Winooski: a children's discovery garden and walking trails in the 67-acre park around the Ethan Allen Homestead (park headquarters), at **Macrea Farm Park**, and **Half Moon Cove Park**. **Delta Park** at the mouth of the Winooski River is a magical place with a sandy trail traversing woods to a wetland observation platform. **Centennial Woods** offers nature trails; access is from East Ave.

Bayside Park (802-655-0811), off Blakely Rd. in Colchester. The site of a 1920s resort, the park now offers sports facilities, a beach, and walking trails. In winter this is also a popular spot for ice fishing, sailboarding, and ice skating.

For **Sand Bar State Park** and other green space to the north, see "The Northwest Corner."

To the east

Underhill State Park (802-899-3022; www.vtstateparks.com)—on the western edge of 4,300 feet Mount Mansfield, the state's highest peak—lies within the 34,000-acre Mount Mansfield State Forest. Camping mid-May–mid-Oct., a Civilian Conservation Corps log picnic pavilion, and four trails to the summit ridge of Mount Mansfield. It's accessed from Pleasant Valley Rd. west of Underhill Center.

The Green Mountain Audubon Nature Center (802-434-3068, http://vt.audubon.org/centers.html), Huntington. (Turn right at Round Church in Richmond; go 5 miles south to Sherman Hollow Rd.) Trails wind through 230 acres of representative habitats (beaver ponds, orchards, and woodlands). Interpretive classes offered. Groups are welcome to watch (and help in) the wood-fired sugaring conducted each year. Open all year, but call ahead to confirm.

Camels Hump State Park. Vermont's most distinctive and third highest mountain (4,083 feet) is best accessed from Huntington via East St., then East St. to Camels Hump Rd. Request a free map and permission for primitive camping (at lower elevations) from the Vermont State Parks in Waterbury (802-241-3655; 1-800-VERMONT; www.vtstateparks.com). The **Green Mountain Club** (802-244-7037; www.greenmountainclub.org), 4711 Waterbury–Stowe Rd. (Rt. 100), Waterbury Center, also has maps and maintains shelters, lodging, and the Hump Brook Tenting Area. Camping facilities are available on the reservoir in nearby Little River State Park. The name "Camel's Rump" was used on Ira Allen's map in 1798, but by 1830 it was known as "Camel's Hump." *Note:* All trails and roads within the park are closed during mud season, which can occur anytime from mid-March to early May.

VIEW OF CAMELS HUMP

Joe Citro

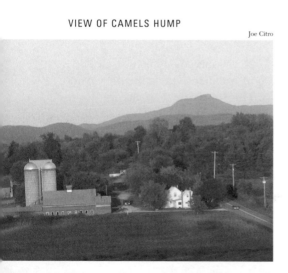

To the south

LaPlatte River Marsh Natural Area, Shelburne; parking on Bay Rd. Managed by The Nature Conservancy of Vermont, this 211-acre preserve at the mouth of the LaPlatte River is rich in bird life. It is traversed by an easy trail (45 minutes round-trip).

Shelburne Bay Park, Shelburne. (Park on Bay Rd., across from the entrance to the Shelburne Farms visitors center.) The Shelburne Recreation Department maintains a blue-blazed trail along the bay through mixed woods.

Shelburne Farms. Five miles of easy trails on 1,400 acres landscaped by Frederick Law Olmsted, who designed New York's Central Park.

H. Lawrence Achilles Natural Area, Shelburne, access off Pond Rd. A short hiking trail leads to Shelburne Pond.

Mount Philo State Park (802-425-2390; 802-372-5060), Charlotte. Founded in 1924, Vermont's oldest state park has a small, intimate, mountaintop picnic area and campground, with spectacular views of the valley, lake, and Adirondacks. A short but steep ascent off Rt. 7 (not recommended for trailers or large RVs); 15 campsites; $2.50 adults, $2 ages 16 and under.

Kingsland Bay State Park (802-877-3445), Ferrisburgh. West from Rt. 7 on Little Chicago Rd., about 1.5 miles north onto Slang Rd., 3 miles to Lake Champlain. Picnic areas and tennis courts on 130 acres.

✻ Lodging

In Burlington 05401
HOTELS ✐ ᕦ **Wyndham Burlington** (802-658-6500; 1-800-658-6504; www.wyndhamburlington.com), 60 Battery St. Formerly the Radisson-Burlington, this 257-room hotel has one of the best lake views in town, plus a glassed-in restaurant and bar, **Seasons on the Lake**, that makes for nice sunset-watching; the **Oak Street Café** (802-658-6500) serves three meals daily (portions are large). Most rooms contain the standard two double beds, though lakeside rooms on the sixth and seventh floors furnish robes, and five rooms open onto the indoor pool and 25-foot Jacuzzi. There are 15 meeting rooms ranging from small to large, a fitness center, and an airport shuttle. $99–219. Six rooms are wheelchair accessible.

🐾 ✐ ᕦ **The Sheraton-Burlington** (802-865-6600; 1-800-325-3535; www.sheraton.com), 870 Williston Rd. With 309 rooms, this is Vermont's largest hotel and the city's convention and trade center. It's set on campus-like grounds in South Burlington at the top of the hill by the UVM campus and the medical center, near the I-89 (Exit 14W) and Rt. 2 interchange

with easy bus access to downtown. Pool, fitness center, conference rooms, restaurant, pub, and 24 wheelchair-accessible rooms. $139–259 per room, depending on season. Small pets okay.

BED & BREAKFASTS **Willard Street Inn** (802-651-8710; 1-800-577-8712; www.willardstreetinn.com), 349 S. Willard St. Burlington's most elegant inn, this 1881 brick mansion built grandly in the upscale hill section (a few blocks from Champlain College) offers 14 guest rooms, all with private bath. Guests enter an elaborate cherry-paneled foyer and are drawn to the many-windowed, palm-filled solarium with its black-and-white marble floor. The spacious living room has a grand piano and hearth, and the dining room is the site for breakfast with its long, formal table. Guest rooms are decorated individually and range in size and detailing from the master bedroom to former maids' rooms on the third floor; all are tastefully done and equipped with phone, TV, and air-conditioning. Top dollar gets you a canopy bed, lake view, and private bath (but lake views can also be enjoyed for less). The home was built by

Charles Woodhouse, a state senator and prospering merchant whose portrait graces the walls; nowadays the Davis family are your hosts. $125–225 includes a full breakfast.

& **Lang House** (802-652-2500; 1-877-919-9799; www.langhouse.com), 360 Main St. Innkeeper Kim Borsavage offers 11 rooms with private bath in this lovely restored 1881 Eastlake Victorian, done in period furnishings, lush fabrics, and antiques. Two come with working fireplace, one is accessibly on the ground floor, the third-floor rooms have lake views, and the former carriage house out back houses a suite with a queen and a double futon. Our favorites are the Van Ness Room with its turret and lake vista, and the Captain Lyon Room with its pineapple four-poster, flax-tinted walls, hidden TV, and a turret nook with a table and chairs. Common areas include a comfortable living room, a sunroom, and a breakfast area with its historic photos of Burlington as it looked a century ago. Everything is close by; rooms on the lower level have kitchen facilities for those seeking long-term stays. $145–215 includes full breakfast; off-season specials. Dog in residence.

✎ **Howard Street Guest House** (802-864-4668; www.howardstreet guesthouse.com), 153 Howard St. A beautiful space on the second floor of a detached carriage barn: a sunny, open living room, dining area, and kitchen with skylights and gorgeous birch floors, all furnished with flair, including a queen bed and a pullout sofa. Air-conditioning and Internet access. Andrea Gray's house is in a quiet residential area, about a 15-minute walk from the waterfront and Church Street Marketplace. Good for a romantic getaway or a business-person needing space to spread out. $150 per night. Discounts for longer-term stays.

Sunset House (802-864-3790; www .sunsethousebb.com), 78 Main St. Paul and Nancy Boileau have thoroughly renovated this 1854 Queen Anne–style home, a former boardinghouse two short blocks from the waterfront. The four air-conditioned guest rooms share two baths and are decorated with family antiques; there's a kitchen nook upstairs for visitors' use. The living room has easy chairs, puzzles, games, and a TV. $99–139 includes continental breakfast.

Beyond Burlington
RESORTS ⊙ ✎ & **Bolton Valley Resort** (802-434-3444; 1-877-9BOLTON; www.boltonvalley.com), Bolton Valley 05477. A high mountain valley with a cluster of restaurants, shops, condominiums, and an indoor sports center, the Bolton resort is set on 5,000 wooded acres that abound with birds and wildlife. In winter it's snow-minded with slope-side lodging and night skiing; in summer the focus is on tennis, hiking, mountain biking, and adventure ropes. Facilities include a five-floor, 60-room hotel, 70 suites, and condominium rentals. Some rooms come with fireplace and kitchenette; most have kings or multiple doubles and balconies with mountain views. The sports center houses an exercise room, pool, tennis courts, game room, and snack bar. Rooms range $79–149 with continental breakfast; condos are higher, depending on size.

⊙ 🐾 ✎ & **The Inn at Essex** (802-878-1100; 1-800-727-4295; www .vtculinaryresort.com), 70 Essex Way (Rt. 15 east), Essex Junction 05452. Set on 18 acres in a suburban area

10 miles northeast of downtown Burlington (handy to IBM), this contemporary, neo-Colonial resort has undergone a makeover by Vermont designer Susan Sargent, who has brightened its 120 rooms and suites with boldly colored wallpapers and fabrics. Several rooms come with working fireplace, a few with whirlpool bath or kitchen facilities. But what sets the inn apart is its partnership with the New England Culinary Institute, whose 190 white-clad chefs and students staff both of its restaurants. Cooking classes and demonstrations abound; fresh herbs grow in the landscaped gardens. You can choose between the formal dining room, Butler's, and the more casual NECI Commons café, both educational laboratories swarming with cooks (see *Dining Out* and *Eating Out*). Besides the first-rate food, the complex boasts a conference and fitness center, a menu of spa services, a golf course, and an outdoor heated pool; the Essex Outlet shopping mall is right around the corner. $99–499 includes continental breakfast; no charge for children under 10 or the airport shuttle, but pets cost $25 per night. Inquire about special packages.

INNS ✎ ♿ **Inn at Shelburne Farms** (802-985-8498; www.shelburnefarms .org), Shelburne 05482. Open mid-May–mid-Oct. Guests are treated to a peerless taste of Edwardian grandeur in this 45-room, Queen Anne–style mansion built by William Seward and Lila Vanderbilt Webb on a spectacular bluff overlooking Lake Champlain. Completed in 1899, the house is the centerpiece of a 1,400-acre estate (see *Museums*). Perhaps because its transition from mansion to inn in 1987 entailed a $1.6 million restoration but no sale (the Webb family has turned the estate into a nonprofit environmental education organization), there is a rare sense of a time as well as place here. Turn-of-the-20th-century furnishings predominate (most are original), and you feel like an invited rather than a paying guest. You can play billiards in the richly paneled game room, leaf through one of the 6,000 leatherbound books, or play the piano in the library. Common space includes the Main Hall, a magnificent room divided into sitting areas with fireplaces and dominated by a very grand staircase. There's also an elegant tearoom (tea is served daily) and the Marble Room, a formal dining room with silk damask wall coverings, a marble floor, and long windows overlooking the formal gardens and lake. Don't miss the third-floor playroom, with its dollhouses. Guest rooms vary in size and elegance—from the second-floor master bedroom, to servants' quarters, to the two secluded cottages and three-bedroom house—which means room prices also vary. The Green Room, in which we slept, was painstakingly but far from fussily decorated; its wallpaper was specially made to echo the mauve-and-green fabric in a splashy '20s screen. With its alcove desk, freestanding old mirror, fresh flowers, luxurious turn-of-the-20th-century bath, and water view, there was a sense of comfort and space. Guests have access to tennis, boating, a swimming beach, sumptuous gardens, and walking trails. Rates for the 24 luxurious, individualized bedrooms (17 with private bath) run $105–390, including a 15 percent service charge. There is a 2-night minimum stay on weekends. Breakfast and dinner are extra, and memorable.

ꝏ ❄ ✔ **Black Bear Inn** (802-434-2126; 1-800-395-6335; www.blkbear inn.com), 4010 Bolton Access Rd., Bolton 05477. Built in the '60s as a ski lodge, this is now very much a hilltop country inn. Owners Jill and Brian Drinkwater offer 26 rooms, all with bath and 11 with private outdoor hot tub. The quaint lobby is dominated by a roaring stone hearth. There's a gift shop, and common areas are festooned with bears, both of the teddy and taxidermied variety. Rooms range from bare-bones basic to luxuriously appointed chalets, and gas fireplaces abound. An overnight entails free access to the indoor pool at Bolton Valley a mile up the hill, ski-in, ski-out proximity to trails, a discount on ski tickets, and a full breakfast in the skylight-ceilinged dining room. This is a favorite place for groups: one extended family has been coming for 30 years, at which time the dining room is full. A standard room is $104 for two with breakfast in spring and summer, $164 for two with breakfast and dinner. Better rooms are higher. Pets are invited to stay at the Bone & Biscuit Inn—an unheated outdoor kennel—or in the room for a $20 nightly fee.

BED & BREAKFASTS Willow Pond Farm (802-985-8505; www.virtual cities.com/vt/willow.htm), 133 Cheesefactory Lane, Shelburne 05482. If we had special sections for birders and gardeners, Sawyer and Zita Lee's elegant home would top both lists. Zita inherited the 200-acre farm, and in 1990 the couple designed and built this exceptional house, a blending of old lines and modern spaces. Windows let in the view of vast rose and perennial gardens with many bird feeders, a willow pond, and a lotus pond whose spectacular blossoms open in August. The living and dining rooms overlook the gardens and ponds and convey a sense of light and space. A full breakfast and the Lees' special cappuccino blend are served at an oval table in the dining area. The upstairs master bedroom overlooks the Adirondacks and contains a cozy built-in sleeping loft for kids (12 or older only). That and the two smaller rooms are furnished in exquisite antiques, Oriental carpets, and handmade quilts made for the king- and queen-sized bed. All have private bath. $95–135 with breakfast. There is a 2-night minimum.

ꝏ ❦ ❄ ✔ **Homeplace B&B** (802-899-4694; www.homeplacebandb .com), P.O. Box 96, 90 Old Pump Rd. (1.5 miles off Rt. 15), Jericho 05465. This intriguing, H-shaped house is secluded in a 100-acre wood at the end of a 0.5-mile driveway. The interior is a maze of hidden nooks and corners filled with scholarly books and European antiques. There's a big, secluded swimming pond in the rear, a duck pond in the front, a screened-in terrace with bucolic views, and a bevy of animals: chickens, horses, sheep, dogs, a donkey, and a cat. The plant-filled living room is artful and eclectically furnished with marble floors, a wood-burning fireplace, walls of books, and interesting knickknacks. There are six guest rooms, four with private bath and two with shared. Our favorite, the "attic," has two twin beds and a wondrous double that is built into a picture window, with curtains that draw shut on both sides. Depending on the season, you might wake up to lilacs, changing foliage, or birds hovering from a feeder on the adjacent apple tree. Innkeeper Mariot

Huessy serves up eggs from the hens in the hexagonal barn, Vermont-roasted coffee, fresh fruit, delicious flapjacks or muffins, and fascinating conversation. $80–90 single, $90–100 double, including breakfast. Extended stays, pets, and children possible by prearrangement. No credit cards.

∞ **Hidden Gardens B&B** (802-482-2118; www.thehiddengardens.com), 693 Lewis Creek Rd., Hinesburg, 05461. This delightful post-and-beam house is surrounded by 250 acres of land trust forest and bordered with exceptional, seemingly tropical gardens that cascade down the side of a hill to a trout-stocked pond and continue the length of a small field. Driving in through the trees, you would never dream that such a botanical paradise awaits. A sunken garden by the house is filled with water lilies, orchids, and large, exotic blossoms, and the grounds are laced with waterfalls, trails, and benches, like a Japanese garden. The two air-conditioned guest rooms, one a double and one a king, feature elegant linens and share a bath (if both are occupied). The common rooms are spacious and sunny with vaulted ceilings, book nooks, fine art, a granite-countered kitchen, ubiquitous windows, and a golden retriever. Guests can build a bonfire by the pond, fish, swim, stay in the rustic pond-side cabin, or hike wooded trails. The gardens are ideal for weddings and civil unions, and light winter meals are available with advance notice. Marcia Pierce's breakfasts are scrumptious. $80–145. Kids 8 and over; no pets.

& **Heart of the Village Inn** (802-985-2800; 1-877-808-1834; www.heartofthevillage.com), 5347 Shelburne Rd. (Rt. 7), P.O. Box 953, Shelburne 05482-0953. A handsome 1886 home that truly is in the heart of town, just steps from the Shelburne Museum. The two living rooms, dining room, and 10 guest rooms (5 in the inn, 5 in the carriage house) are all carefully, comfortably decorated. All have air-conditioning, fine linens, and in-room phone and cable TV, as well as private bath. The most deluxe are in the carriage house: the two-room honeymoon or Webb Suite, for example, has two skylights, sofas, and a two-person whirlpool bath. The Barstow Room has wheelchair access. Rates are $130–245, with breakfast and afternoon refreshments included.

∞ & **Sinclair Inn Bed & Breakfast** (802-899-2234; 1-800-433-4658; www.sinclairinnbb.com), 389 Rt. 15, Jericho 05465. This fully restored 1890 Queen Anne "painted lady" is located in a village setting within easy driving distance of Richmond and Burlington. All six rooms have private bath and air-conditioning, and one is fully handicapped accessible. The lawns overflow with perennials and water lilies. Sally Gilbert-Smith is your hostess. $90–160 per couple includes a full breakfast and afternoon tea. Children over 10 welcome.

∞ ✒ **The Richmond Victorian Inn** (802-434-4410; 1-888-242-3362; www.richmondvictorianinn.com), 191 E. Main St., P.O. Box 652, Richmond 05477. On Rt. 2 in the village of Richmond (2 miles off I-89), this exceptionally clean and classy house has five comfortable guest rooms, all with private bath, all individually decorated with antiques and equipped with down comforters, bathrobes, and good reading lights. The Hummingbird Room has both a single and double bed, and a ground-floor room has its own Jacuzzi. Scottish-born Frank Stewart, a former chef and caterer, runs the place with his American wife, Joyce, serving up fresh homemade breads each morning. Rates $95–150 for a double include a full gourmet breakfast. Children over 6 welcome.

🍁 **Maple Grove Farm B&B** (802-878-4875; maplebnb@aol.com), 3517 Oak Hill Rd., Williston 05495. Open year-round. Ginger and David Isham are the fourth generation of the Isham family to operate this 108-acre farm, one of the last four in this historic town just east of Burlington. While they have sold their dairy herd, the vintage-1852 Gothic Revival farmhouse retains its surrounding pastures and sugarhouse. Guests are comfortably bedded in the Blue Room with its queen-sized bed and private bath. Common space includes a big living room and a den with piano, and breakfast is a full, fun affair. $50–75; discounts for more than 2 nights.

∞ ✆ **Elliot House** (802-985-2727; 1-800-860-4405; www.elliothouse.com), 5779 Dorset St., Shelburne 05482. This updated 1865 Greek Revival farmhouse adjoins 400 acres of Nature Conservancy land with hiking and cross-country ski trails and mountain views both east and west. Anne and George Voland offer three graciously furnished guest rooms, all with private bath. Common areas include a library and sitting room with piano. Guests can wander the extensive gardens, relax on the patio, or take a dip in the secluded swimming pool. $90 per night, with homemade breakfast.

✆ **Inn at Charlotte** (802-425-2934; 1-800-425-2934; www.innatcharlotte .com), 32 State Park Rd., Charlotte 05445. A contemporary home on the Rt. 7 turnoff to Mount Philo. Duker

and Josefina Bower host guests in four air-conditioned rooms, all with bath, private entrance, and TV. Two have king-sized bed and cathedral ceilings and open out onto an oval pool. The Family Room comes with a queen, two singles, and a mini fridge, and a separate cottage contains a double brass bed and Mexican-tiled floor. There are tennis courts and leather-sofa-filled common areas; breakfast is served family-style. Burlington is a 12-mile drive. Duker's mesmerizing portraits, sculptures, and surrealistic paintings are displayed in the adjacent **Mt. Philo Gallery**. $105–130 rates include full breakfast.

✆ **By the Old Mill Stream** (802-482-3613; www.bythestream.com), 84 Richmond Rd., Hinesburg 05461. An 1860s farmhouse with wide, wooden floorboards, tin ceilings, and central air-conditioning. Kids will appreciate the pool table in the front hall and the hot tub seating eight. The upstairs guest room has a sitting area, the downstairs a queen-sized bed; both have private bath. The grounds include gardens that border a waterfall (it powered the mill for Isaiah Dow, who built the house). $125 includes a full breakfast.

∞ 🍁 ✆ **Windekind Farm** (802-434-4455; www.windekindfarms.com), 1425 Bert White Rd., Huntington 05462. Hidden away in a 160-acre upland valley that's seen little development since it was last farmed around 1935, this is a sensational spot, expansive and remote with distant views and total quiet but for a gurgling brook. Camels Hump State Park spreads for miles, providing space for an extensive network of upland trails. Mark Smith and his Dutch-born wife, Marijke, live in a restored farmhouse and accommodate guests in two contemporary, comfortable, centrally heated cottages. Both are fully equipped with firewood, dishes, pots and pans, laundry, and linens. Guests bring groceries and cook their own meals. The Studio, perfect for two, is a 600-square-foot upstairs apartment that is bright and airy with a queen-sized bed, satellite TV, and mountain views. The Forge is a 1,000-square-foot, two-floor converted post-and-beam blacksmith shop with a cupola, woodstove, and high-ceilinged living room, accommodating four. Outside are numerous gardens and ponds, plus ducks, heifers, friendly dogs, endless hiking and cross-country skiing potential, and Mark's shop, where he builds historically accurate miniature steam locomotives that haul firewood, curious adults, and ecstatic children. The grounds are ideal for weddings and tented receptions. The Studio rents for $250–275 per weekend, $550–675 per week. The Forge is $950 per week for two, $1,100 for four.

MOTOR INNS 🐾 ✒ ⚕ **Hawthorn Suites** (802-860-1212; 1-800-527-1133; www.hawthornsuitesburlington .com), 401 Dorset St. (just off Rt. 2), South Burlington 05403. Opened in 1998 by Chuck and Ralph DesLauriers, with an open-timbered lobby, featuring suites with separate living rooms (containing foldout couches) and bedrooms: 104 one-bedroom suites and 8 two-bedroom; some rooms include fireplace and jet tub. Facilities include an indoor pool, a spa/Jacuzzi, and fitness machines. While it's located in the heart of South Burlington's strip malls, it's just minutes from downtown Burlington, and there's a complimentary airport shuttle. $99–359 (depending on length of stay)

includes a breakfast buffet. Pets are welcome for $5 per night.

✒ ⚕ **Marriott Courtyard** (802-879-0100; 1-800-321-2211), 177 Hurricane Lane, Williston 05495. At Exit 12 off I-89, this Marriott Courtyard is a known quantity with a laundry, in-room refrigerator and work desk, HBO, a whirlpool, and an exercise room. Both rooms and suites are available. Rates begin at $119 for a room with two double beds.

∞ 🐾 ✒ ⚕ **Hampton Inn and Conference Center** (802-655-6177; 1-800-HAMPTON; www.hamptoninn burlington.com), 42 Lower Mountain View Dr. (Rt. 7 north), Colchester 05446, Exit 16 off I-89. North of Burlington, the inn offers 187 well-furnished rooms, indoor pool, whirlpool, fitness facilities, free airport shuttle, and hot breakfast buffet. Kids stay free with adults. Rates begin at $99.

🌸 ✒ **G. G. T. Tibet Inn** (802-863-7110; www.ggttibetinn.com), 1860 Shelburne Rd., South Burlington 05403. At least a dozen 1960s-era motels line Burlington's periphery, but this one stands out. Owner Kalsang G. G. T. (the initials stand for "Gangjong Gesar Tsang"), a Tibetan refugee, arrived here in 1993. He worked multiple jobs, lived frugally, and bought this two-story lodge. In 1995 the Dalai Lama gave Kalsang's innkeeping aspirations his blessing. The 20 air-conditioned rooms are clean and comfortable, with cable TV, microwave, fridge, and use of the outdoor pool. Prices are low, with discounts for seniors and families. $39–49. For meals, Pauline's is right next door (see *Dining Out*).

CAMPING See *To Do*.

✳ Where to Eat

Note: Burlington offers the best choice of restaurants and cafés between Boston and Montreal, but the best are not all downtown.

DINING OUT ✍ ♿ **Inn at Shelburne Farms** (802-985-8498; www.shelburnefarms.org), Shelburne. Open for dinner (and breakfast) by reservation, mid-May–late Oct. This turn-of-the-20th-century manor offers imaginative cuisine in a magnificent setting: walls covered in fin-de-siècle silk damask from Spain, a black-and-white marble floor, and a stunning sunset view of Lake Champlain and the Adirondacks. You might begin with chilled Amish peach and sparkling wine soup, then dine on naturally raised beef tenderloin with sweet corn and Swiss chard polenta ($29), or pan-roasted chicken with a ragout of beets, fingerling potato, fava beans, *haricots verts*, and roasted pepper tapenade ($21). Dessert might be a chocolate truffle cake with peppermint ice cream, mixed berry napoleon with sweet mascarpone cream, or Vermont-made cheeses with poached figs and crostini. Smokers can have coffee served on the terrace. Breakfast, open to the public by reservation, is also an event: granola pancakes, brioche French toast, eggplant and cheddar frittata, or poached eggs with herbed hollandaise and home fries.

Café Shelburne (802-985-3939; www.cafeshelburne.com), 5573 Shelburne Rd. (Rt. 7), Shelburne. Open for dinner from 5:30 daily, except Sun. and Mon. Located across from the Shelburne Museum, this chef-owned and -operated, authentically French bistro serves up European atmosphere and fabulous food. Lobster potpie, pan-roasted Vermont quail in a white wine sauce, and pan-sautéed tenderloin of venison in a chestnut ragout with red wine sauce are examples of the overall superb menu. Chef Patrick Grangien, who studied chocolate making in Lyon, also sells his own exemplary truffles wrapped up in golden gift boxes. The dessert list is long and masterful, making this unquestionably one of the best restaurants in the state. Entrées are in the $20–25 range.

Butler's (802-764-1413; www.necidining.com), the Inn at Essex, 70 Essex Way (off Rt. 15), Essex Junction. Open daily for all three meals (though closed for Sunday dinner Nov.–Apr.). In the deft hands of the New England Culinary Institute, the cuisine in this elegantly informal room with high-backed, upholstered chairs is a visual as well as gustatory treat, and the service is top-notch. Menus change daily, but a typical dinner might start with asparagus leek soup ($3.75) and Chef Jacques's rich country pâté ($5.75); proceed to grilled breast of duck with fig chutney ($16), crisp-skin salmon with fennel risotto ($17), or grilled rack of lamb with polenta and broccoli rabe ($21). Elaborate desserts might include a caramelized phyllo napoleon with cranberry compote.

Starry Night Café (802-877-6316), 5359 Rt. 7, Ferrisburgh. Dinner seatings are 5–9:30 daily except Tue. Chef-owner David Hugo is a Culinary Institute of America grad who has introduced playfully experimental Euro-Asian fare using local ingredients. Entrées range from grilled mahimahi in a smoked tomato and mussel beurre blanc ($20), to a goat cheese ravioli with spinach, tomato, and basil sauce ($15). Desserts are all $5.50. Call ahead, because it's a full 25-minute drive south of Burlington.

A Single Pebble (802-865-5200; www.asinglepebble.com), 133 Bank St., Burlington. Open nightly for dinner, weekdays for lunch. This is a rare find: a Chinese restaurant that serves the real thing. Chef-owner Steve Bogart trained in China and returns each year for inspiration. No fried rice, egg rolls, or MSG here. Instead you get authentic Beijing fare: Chop Your Head Off Soup, for example, a savory blend of ground pork, shredded cabbage, and rice cake noodles, or Ants Climbing a Tree, a smoky-tasting blend of cellophane noodles, ground pork, black mushrooms, scallions, and tree ear fungus. All is served banquet-style on fine china with the strains of classical Chinese music in the air, and sharing is encouraged. There are numerous small dishes to choose from, like dumplings and mock eel. Entrées $16–18. Reservations essential.

L'Amante (802-863-5200; www.lamante.com), 126 College St., Burlington, open for dinner daily except Sunday. Truly superior northern Italian cuisine in a spare, low-lit, urban decor of hardwood floors, cream-colored walls, modern art, and fresh flowers. You might start with a caramelized onion tart and proceed to grilled flatiron steak with a potato shallot tart and roasted tomatoes in red wine sauce, or roasted chicken with truffled mashed potatoes, grilled leeks, and rosemary jus. Entrées $21–23.

The Kitchen Table (802-434-8686; www.thekitchentablebistro.com), 1840 W. Main St., Richmond. Dinner nightly. Steve and Lara Atkins, both biology majors, met at the New England Culinary Institute and cut their teeth working at restaurants in California's Napa Valley. Now they operate this superlative bistro in a home that once belonged to Vermont's first governor. The offerings are fresh and healthy, the decor brick-walled and tasteful.

Vermont Fresh Network (802-229-4706; www.vermontfresh.net), 116 State St., Montpelier, 05620. Vermont's better restaurants share more than an interest in fine cuisine. Increasingly, they display a distinctive green sign flaunting their affiliation to an exclusive club: Vermont Fresh Network, a nonprofit that partners chefs with local farmers. The idea came to Pam Knights in 1994, while she was public relations director at the New England Culinary Institute. Such a network, she felt, would not only provide restaurateurs with the freshest ingredients—from venison to just-picked berries—but also keep local producers in business, which in turn would help preserve Vermont's rural landscape. With the help of Roger Clapp, then deputy commissioner of agricultural development, Knights founded VFN in 1996. Today Vermont's finest dining establishments are members, and the little green sign has come to be regarded as a prestigious badge of culinary savvy.

You're likely to find Vermont rabbit pâté, free-range chicken, wild mushrooms with sautéed sweetbreads, wild king salmon, artisan cheeses, and locally raised beef. Entrées $10–28.

Pauline's Café & Restaurant (802-862-1081; www.paulinescafe.com), 1834 Shelburne Rd. (Rt. 7 south), South Burlington. Open daily for lunch, dinner, and Sunday brunch. It is worth braving the strip development traffic for the elegant simplicity of this downstairs café or the more formal upstairs dining rooms. The subtle cuisine often features wild and local edibles, such as mushrooms, cattail shoots, sea beans, and fresh black and white truffles, all artfully presented in sensible portions. Entrées might be Shelburne Farms chicken breasts sautéed in herbs, scallions, cream, and Shelburne Farms cheddar cheese, or domestic lamb rack with lemon herb crust, served with Madeira sauce and Vermont chèvre medallions. Café prices $11–15, upstairs $16–26.

Smokejacks (802-658-1119; www.smokejacks.com), 156 Church St., Burlington. Open weekdays for lunch, daily for dinner; brunch served Sat. and Sun. Owner Leslie Myers is tight with local farmers and artisan cheesemakers, and the menu proves it. It offers 14 different cheeses, entrées that brim with locally produced fare, and an impressive martini selection. Located on the corner of Church St. and Main, this postmodern bistro is in the center of everything, and though servings are not large, they're generally excellent. Full bar and good wine list. Entrées $16–23.

Taste of Burlington (802-658-4844; www.tasteofburlington.com), 112 Lake St. Open weekdays for lunch, nightly for dinner. Chef-owner Rick

Benson, a devoted Phish fan, named this spiffy eatery for one of their songs, and was delighted when the now-disbanded rock group gave him a 200-gallon tank full of their tropical marine life. Now it's part of the decor. The walls are penny colored, the abstract art his own doing, and the food just as creative: flatiron steak with olive demiglaze, fresh seafood over saffron lemon risotto, spinach and artichoke strudel, and honey and coriander glazed salmon, just for starters. Oodles of pasta dishes, wonderful desserts, and drinks with fresh-squeezed tropical fruits. $14–29.

🌂 **Blue Seal Restaurant** (802-434-5949), Bridge St., Richmond. Open Tue.–Sat. 5:30–9:30. Reservations suggested. Housed in a vintage-1854 feed store, chef-owner Debra Weinstein's casual restaurant may not look—or charge—the part, but it's right up there with the Burlington area's finest. The menu is American food with southwestern flavors. You might begin with the vegetarian soup of the day or a warm spinach salad with nuggets of bacon and goat cheese ($5–7.50), then dine on pan-roasted salmon with roasted garlic mashed potatoes, herb oil, and salsa. A favorite dessert is double-layered devil's food cake with coffee swirl ice cream. Entrées $10.50–19.

EATING OUT *Note:* Thanks to Burlington's huge student population, many of the following restaurants offer "dining-out" quality at "eating-out" prices.

In Burlington
Daily Planet (802-862-9647), 15 Center St. Open daily. Dinner and lighter bar menu nightly. The atmosphere is light and airy in this solarium-

style bistro on a tiny side street next to the main downtown pedestrian area. The All Natural Planet Burger is a favorite, and the vegetarian offerings are numerous, including wild mushroom pasta and eggplant manicotti. The menu often changes, but is always imaginative. Moderately priced.

Leunig's Bistro (802-863-3759), 115 Church St. (near College St.). Open daily for brunch, lunch, and dinner. In classic bistro style, Leunig's has dark wood, gleaming coffee machines, romantic lighting, and streetside tables for people-watching, all of which makes it one of Church Street's most sought-after lunch spots. The food is fresh and good, though somewhat pricey. Frequent live entertainment.

Five Spice Café (802-864-4045; www.fivespicecafe.com), 175 Church St. Open daily for brunch, lunch, dinner. Dim sum plus stellar offerings from a variety of Asian countries—Thailand, Vietnam, Indonesia, India, and China—and the spices are as hot as you care to take them. The dining rooms (on two levels) are small and intimate, the prices moderate. Try the ginger-tangerine cheesecake.

Souza's Churrascaria (802-864-2433), 55 Main St. Open nightly (except Mon.) for dinner, and Sunday brunch. A parade of grilled meats and salads (vegetables for non-meat-eaters) comes your way at this prix fixe all-you-can-eat Brazilian restaurant, a relative newcomer and totally unlike any other place in town. $29.95 per person usually includes at least 11 meats and five desserts. The $15.95 Sunday brunch is a miniature version of dinner.

Trattoria Delia (802-864-5253; www .trattoriadelia.com), 152 St. Paul St. Open daily 5–10. Exposed wooden beams, a roaring fire, and Italian pottery make this one of Burlington's most romantic restaurants. For over 10 years, owners Thomas and Lori Delia have refined the menu to the point that it is as authentically Italian as possible this far from Europe, introducing such things as deep-fried baby squid, wood-smoked handmade mozzarella, and herb-marinated olives from Puglia. Entrées range from $12.50 for spaghetti *con polpette* (with veal meatballs) to $26 for *filetto al barbera d'alba* (filet mignon with white truffle butter). Reservations.

Three Tomatoes (802-660-9533), 83 Church St., in the cellar of the old Howard Opera House at the marketplace. A busy, low-lit place with an excellent southern Italian menu, plus top-drawer, wood-fired pizzas. You might lunch on the pasta of the day, or dine on fusilli sautéed with wood-smoked chicken, sweet peas, mushrooms, plum tomatoes, black pepper, rosemary, and light cream. Bad acoustics, but good atmosphere. Outdoor tables in summer. Italian mineral water and wines, moderate prices.

Sakura (802-863-1988), 2 Church St. Lunch and dinner every day. Vermont's first (but no longer its only) Japanese restaurant is a resounding success. At lunch its soothing ambience is an oasis of calm and an appropriate setting for savoring sushi and sashimi dishes or simply deep-fried salmon served with a tangy sauce. Vegetarians will appreciate dishes like avocado, bean curd, boiled spinach, vegetable tempura, and hijiki (cooked seaweed). Lone diners appreciate the seats lining the long sushi bar.

Sweetwater's (802-864-9800), 118 Church St. (corner of College St.). Open 7 days, 11:30 AM–midnight.

Housed in a former and splendidly restored 1920s bank building, this is a deservedly popular spot. One of the house specialties is bison. You might lunch on a bison burger, a Thai peanut chicken cake, or a choice of daily specials. The square bar is one of Burlington's prime schmoozing spots, and the streetside tables are glassed in so you can people-watch year-round. Moderate.

❦ Parima Restaurant (802-864-7917; www.parimathai.com), 185 Pearl St. Open daily for lunch and dinner. The peerless polished wood and ornate glass lamps—the legacy of a previous incarnation, Déjà Vu,—have survived to make this the city's most beautiful dining decor. Parima's owners have adapted it into their own private, low-lit sanctuary serving an exhaustive selection of Thai and American dishes, with a small outdoor patio in summer. Live music on Friday nights. Entrées $13–25.

American Flatbread, Burlington Hearth (802-861-2999; www.american flatbread.com), 115 St. Paul St. Open daily for lunch and dinner. In the dead of winter, the wood-fired oven emanates blissful heat, though this spacious spot is popular year-round. The mostly organic pizzas are made to order in as many varieties as the beers on tap, and are priced $8.50–19.75.

Halvorson's Upstreet Cafe (802-658-0278), 16 Church St. Open daily for lunch, dinner, and brunch. An old landmark that's expanded its basic all-American menu and added beer, wine, and nightly specials. Summer court-yard in back, and streetside seats in the front. Moderate.

❦ Pacific Rim (802-651-3000), 111 St. Paul St. Open daily except Sun. for lunch and dinner, this café is pan-Asian with an innovative twist. There's a big choice of hot and cold noodles, plus Korean shrimp cakes, orange chicken stir-fry, dumplings, salads, and desserts, like ginger cheesecake. Order and pick up at the counter; everything is fresh, made to order, and delicious, and the price is right.

Red Square Bar and Grill (802-859-8909; www.redsquarevt.com), 136 Church St. Open afternoons for people-watching and for dinner, music till 2 AM. Jack O'Brien's attractive space features a copper bar, iconoclastic local art, dark nooks and crannies to hide in, and music 6 nights a week.

Stone Soup (802-862-7616), 211 College St. Open daily, except Sun., for all three meals. A hugely popular storefront cafeteria specializing in vegan and vegetarian dishes; great soups, salads, and breads. Inexpensive.

Cobblestone Deli & Market (802-865-3354; www.cobblestonevt.com), 152 Battery St. Open daily, weekdays 7–7, Sat. 8–6, Sun. 8–5. A self-serve café and deli located next to the last patch of cobblestone from the days when this part of town was the city's commercial core. Pick up a sandwich to take on the bike path or to picnic by the lake.

Henry's Diner (802-862-9010) 155 Bank St. Closed Mon. A long-established diner around the corner from the Church Street Marketplace. Here you can get the meat loaf and thick gravy you've been hankering for. Diner fans should also check out the meat-loaf-shaped **Oasis Diner** (802-864-5308) at 189 Bank St. for more classic Americana.

Nectar's (802-658-4771), 188 Main St. A basic meat-and-potatoes eatery for breakfast and lunch, noteworthy for its french fries with gravy and its association with the music band Phish; the dance floor upstairs was where the group got its start.

♣ ✐ **Bove's Cafe** (802-864-6651), 68 Pearl St. Dinner nightly, lunch on Sat. Closed Sun. and Mon. Burlington's oldest restaurant, started by an Italian American family after the war and still going strong. Narrow booths, Elvis songs on the Wurlitzer, and heaping plates of steaming spaghetti, plus fresh bread, terrific antipasto salads, and some of the lowest prices in town. You won't go hungry here. Full bar.

The Vermont Pub and Brewery (802-865-0500; www.vermontbrewery .com), 144 College St. Open daily 11:30 AM–1 AM. Despite the modern building, there's an old beer-hall atmosphere (tile floor, huge bar, brass), specializing in ales, lagers, and fine ginger ale brewed on the premises. The huge menu includes Cornish pasties, cock-a-leekie pie, bratwurst, and fish-and-chips. Prices run the gamut.

India House (802-862-7800), 207 Colchester Ave. Lunch and dinner daily. This warm, reliable restaurant serves traditional curries, tandoori chicken, and the like, plus puffy poori bread, in an out-of-the-way spot near Centennial Park and the University of Vermont campus. Moderate.

Penny Cluse Cafe (802-651-8834; www.pennycluse.com), 169 Cherry St. Innovative, healthy, hearty breakfasts and lunches in an atmosphere of art and natural wood. Famous for black beans, polenta, great biscuits. One of the best breakfast spots in Burlington—but come early or stand in line.

Four Corners of the Earth (802-657-3869), 310 Pine St. Open for lunch daily except Sun. This deli in the basement of a 19th-century mill conjures the city's best sandwiches, hands down. Ladislav Pancisin draws on his world travels to create the best combinations of flavors, Jamaican to Cuban.

✐ **The Hot Dog Lady**. Lois Bodoky has her imitators, but she was the first and she's still the most reasonably priced and all-around best. Look for her cart at noon every day at the Church Street Marketplace: $1 hot dog with kraut.

On the waterfront

✐ **The Ice House** (802-864-1800), 171 Battery St. Open for lunch and dinner daily, with seasonal open-air decks overlooking the ferry slip and marina. This was a pioneer of the city's upscale restaurant scene, a 19th-century icehouse with massive stone walls and timbers. American regional dishes feature steak, seafood, and Vermont lamb. Kids' menu; brunch served Mother's Day–mid-Oct.

Seasons Bistro (802-859-5013; www .wyndhamburlington.com). Looking west from its perch on an upper floor of the Wyndham Hotel at 60 Battery St., this classy, relatively pricey bistro is three-tiered so everyone can enjoy the view. The sunken bar serves free tapas.

✐ **Shanty on the Shore** (802-864-0238), 181 Battery St. Open daily 11–11. Handy to the ferry with spectacular lake views both inside and out; this is a good place for burgers and sandwiches as well as seafood platters, crabcakes, and seasonal specials. Children's menu and exotic drinks.

Breakwater Cafe & Grill (802-864-9804), King Street Dock. Part of the LCTC ferry complex, an informal dockside space serving sandwiches, fried baskets, soups, and salads all day and evening in summer; frequent live (and loud) music.

Whitecaps (802-862-1240), at the Boathouse. Open Memorial Day–Labor Day, 7:30 AM–sunset. A relaxing, casual spot; sandwiches and salads on dockside tables with umbrellas.

In Winooski

🐾 🍴 **Papa Frank's** (802-655-2433), 13 W. Center St. (A block west of Main St.: Heading north over the Winooski River, take your first left, first right, and park.) Open for lunch and dinner daily. A red-sauce Italian neighborhood restaurant that caters to families as well as students. Good for pizza, calzones, and classic dishes. The vegetables are fresh, and garlic bread comes with your order.

Sneakers (802-655-9081; www.sneakersbistro.com), 36 Main St. Open daily 7–3. This little bistro serves such a great Sunday brunch that the line winds out the door. The eggs Benedict is delectable, the pancakes huge and fluffy, lots of fresh fruit, and the orange juice freshly squeezed.

In Essex Junction and Colchester

Libby's Blue Line Diner (802-655-0343), 1 Roosevelt Ave., Rt. 77, Colchester, with its tile floor, marble counters, and great views, attracts itinerant diner buffs and area fans for breakfast, lunch, and dinner daily. Try the banana bread French toast.

NECI Commons (802-764-1489), 70 Essex Way, Essex Junction, at the Inn at Essex. Open daily for lunch and dinner. Until 2005 this up-and-coming American bistro operated from Burlington's Church Street Marketplace. But it proved so popular that the NECI (New England Culinary Institute) students who staffed it were too exhausted to study. The school

moved it next to its other learning lab, Butler's, replacing what used to be The Tavern. The food is still terrific, the service great, and the decor new and upbeat. Moderate.

Vietnam Restaurant (802-872-9998), 137 Rt. 15. Lunch and dinner daily (except Sun.). Though the decor is spare at best, this simple, family-run spot is a revelation, serving authentic, fresh Vietnamese fare, from cilantro-packed spring rolls and jack fruit milk shakes to steaming noodle-filled broths. Friendly, laid-back, inexpensive, delicious.

Williston Road to Richmond

Silver Palace (802-864-0125), 1216 Williston Rd., South Burlington. Open daily for lunch and dinner (dinner only on Sun.). Hidden behind Burger King in the commercial sprawl that is Williston Road, this Chinese restaurant is a cut above the rest. The Asian cuisine is artfully prepared, served on white tablecloths with fine glassware by a doting owner. More pricey than other Chinese eateries, but worth it.

🍴 ♿ **Old Brick Café** (802-872-9599; www.oldbrickcafe.com), 7921 Williston Rd. (Rt. 2), in the center of Williston Village. Serves breakfast and lunch daily, and abundant weekend brunches. Closed Mon. Soups, sandwiches, cappuccino, and fresh-baked pastries in a renovated brick home with a sunny interior. Outdoor deck in summer.

Bailey's at the Valley (802-434-6821; www.boltonvalley.com/baileys), 4302 Bolton Access Rd., Bolton Valley. Open for dinner Wed.–Sat. With its copper bar, moose antler chandeliers, and mountain views, this intimate place is special even without the top-notch fare of New England Culinary Institute grad Andrew LeHaye. Try the Gorgonzola-crusted New York strip steak ($20), the roasted portobello and goat cheese strudel ($16), or the toasted cavatelli and duck confit with caramelized onions, Vermont goat cheese, and fresh thyme ($8). There's a children's menu, a bar menu, and numerous local microbrews to choose from. In summer you can sit out on the deck.

Toscana Café/Bistro (802-434-3148), 27 Bridge St., Richmond. Open daily except Mon. for lunch and dinner, Sunday brunch. Chef-owners Jon and Lucie Fath have created an Old World, Mediterranean feel in a small Vermont village, serving crabcakes, crispy artichokes, and wild mushroom ravioli. For dinner, try the grilled salmon with ginger citrus beurre blanc, wasabi mashed potatoes, and snap peas ($15.95), or the beef tenderloin with peppercorn demiglaze and fresh asparagus ($23.95).

Al's French Frys (802-862-9203; www.alsfrenchfrys.com), 1251 Williston Rd., South Burlington. Really, that's how it's spelled. Open daily 10:30 AM–midnight. Burlington's own (amazingly fast) fast-food joint, a long-enduring classic that is spanking clean in its art-deco-inspired, neon-splashed digs. Fries, burgers, dogs, and shakes, with a playground out back, picnic tables, and ice cream cones, sundaes, and creemees dispensed from a side window as long as weather permits.

Parkway Diner (802-658-1883), 1696 Williston Rd., South Burlington. Open daily for breakfast, lunch, and dinner. A cozy 1955 chrome- and wood-filled diner car that buzzes all day with warmth and activity. Sit at the counter or snag a booth for lovingly prepared American, Italian, and Greek classics.

On Shelburne Road (Route 7 south)

Koto Japanese Steakhouse (802-660-8976), 792 Shelburne Rd. (Rt. 7). Open daily for lunch and dinner. A traditional hibachi house with knife-juggling waiters, sushi bar, goldfish swimming in an aisle-side aquarium, and delicious lunches served in partitioned Japanese boxes. Expensive.

Tuscan Kitchen (802-862-1300; www.reelhospitality.com), 1080 Shelburne Rd. Open nightly at 4 PM. The former Perry's Fish House has reinvented itself as a warm, cavernous Italian pizza and pasta spot with open hearths, stucco walls, and rustic stone accents. The menu includes seafood, steaks, and salads along with crusty bread, roasted garlic in olive oil, and Puccini in the background. Full bar, moderate prices.

Sauce (802-985-2830), 97 Falls Rd., in the Shelburne Shopping Center east of Rt. 7. Open daily for lunch and dinner, Sunday for brunch. Fresh, abundant, tasty fare in a contemporary ambience of celadon-hued walls and natural wood booths. Recent offerings included grilled whole quail on a corn galette with chipotle and fig glaze, mushroom fettuccine with oyster sauce, and pan-seared duck breast with mushroom and barley risotto and a sauce of black mission figs, rosemary, and port. Entrées $14–16.

Harrington's (802-985-2000), Shelburne. Across from the Shelburne Museum, a good bet if you can snag one of the few tables and don't mind the Styrofoam at the excellent deli here. Specialties include the "World's Best Ham Sandwich" (Harrington's is known for its corn-smoked ham); also smoked turkey, quiche, homemade soups, sausage chili made with

Harrington's own pork sausages, and chocolate mousse.

In Hinesburg

🦞 🍷 ♿ **Papa Nick's** (802-482-6050), 10997 Rt. 116, midtown. Open daily, all meals. A friendly, affordable family restaurant with a diverse menu and Greek accents, including daily specials like moussaka and chicken souvlaki. Homemade pies, ice cream, and creemees to go in summer. Kids' menu.

🍷 **Good Times Café** (802-482-4444), Rt. 116, Hinesburg, where the road takes a sharp left. Lunch and dinner Tue.–Sun. 11–9, including everything from Cajun to East Indian. Live music on Wed. night (tickets sometimes required). The homemade pizza here is great ($8.50 and up), as are the soups, stews, salads, lasagnas, and chana masala. Daily dinner specials. This is a find.

CAFFEINE/SNACKS

In Burlington

Dobra Tea (802-951-2424; www .dobratea.com), 80 Church St. (entrance on Bank St.). Open 11–10 weekdays, noon–10 weekends. The first North American branch of a Czech chain, Burlington's sole teahouse offers 60 varieties from 10 countries, each served as it would be in its native land. Savor Ilati, a rich, black tea from Nepal poured into square ceramic cups; or Tung Ting from Taiwan in small, shallow cups. Each pot is freshly brewed at the precise temperature and time required. In the back you can shed your shoes and lounge on pillows the way a tea drinker would in Uzbekistan.

Mirabelle's (802-658-3074; www .mirabellescafe.com), 198 Main St.

A delightful bakery and lunch spot featuring special teas, coffees, mouthwatering pastries, made-to-order sandwiches, soups, salads, and light fare. Try the ploughman's lunch, a bit of everything with a dab of fresh fruit. Open daily except Sun. 7 AM–6 PM, Sat. 8–5.

Muddy Waters (802-658-0466), 184 Main St., just up from Church St., open every day, all day. Excellent coffee, homemade desserts, vegan specials, smoothies, beer, and wine by the glass in a dimly lit, brick-walled den with sofas, lots of reading material, and earnest conversation. Bring a book.

Uncommon Grounds (802-865-6227), 42 Church St. They roast their own here, offering the largest selection in town along with teas and Italian syrup-based drinks. Down a piece of chocolate cake while perusing the day's papers, which are laid out on wooden holders. Outside seating in summer.

Speeder and Earl's. A slim counter and coffee bar downstairs at 104 Church St. (802-860-6630), and a zany shop at 412 Pine St. (802-658-6016), same complex as the Fresh Market, featuring their own blends and assorted pastries. Try the popular "Clockwork Orange"—mocha with orange zest and almonds.

Euro Gourmet Market & Café (802-859-3467), 61 Main St. Open daily. Vladimir and Anita Selec are the owners of this sidewalk café near the waterfront. With its umbrella-topped tables, this is the place for handmade Turkish coffee, Bosnian pastries, fresh panini sandwiches, and Balkan specialties that fill the shelves in the back. The large windows make people-watching irresistible.

The Wine Bar at Wineworks (802-951-9463; www.wineworks.net), 133 St. Paul St., open every day except Sun. at 4. The city's sole wine bar, offering several varieties by the glass, plus a full liquor bar, light fare, and comfortable seating. The adjacent store offers wine appreciation workshops.

Ben & Jerry's (802-862-9620), 36 Church St. This scoop shop isn't the original location, but the world's legendary ice cream makers did get their start a few blocks away (on the corner of St. Paul and College Sts.).

✳ Entertainment

Note: For current arts and entertainment in Burlington, call the **Burlington City Arts line** at 802-865-7166, or check *Seven Days* (www.sevendays vt.com), a free weekly publication that's available everywhere around town.

MUSIC Vermont Mozart Festival performances (802-862-7352; www .vtmozart.com), 125 College St., Burlington 05401. Summer concerts in various settings—on ferries, at the Shelburne Museum and/or Shelburne Farms, at the Basin Harbor Club, in churches. Winter chamber series.

Vermont Symphony Orchestra (802-864-5741; 1-800-VSO-9293; www.vso.org), 2 Church St., Suite 19, Burlington. One of the country's first statewide philharmonics presents a five-concert Chittenden County series at the Flynn Center; outdoor summer pops at Shelburne Farms and elsewhere.

St. Michael's College concerts (802-655-2000), in Colchester, feature jazz, pop, and classical productions.

Burlington Choral Society (802-878-5919). A volunteer, 100-voice choir presents several concerts a year.

The Discover Jazz Festival (Flynn box office: 802-86-FLYNN; www .discoverjazz.com), Burlington, 10 days in early June, a jazz extravaganza that fills city parks, clubs, restaurants, ferries.

Battery Park Summer Concert Series, Burlington, Thu. and Sun. nights.

THEATER Flynn Center for the Performing Arts (802-86-FLYNN; www.flynncenter.org), 153 Main St., Burlington. The city's prime stage for music and live performance is a refurbished art deco movie house, now home to plays, musical comedies, jazz concerts, and lectures, in addition to movies. Constantly evolving, it has an art gallery and several smaller performances spaces as well.

Royall Tyler Theater (802-656-2094; www.uvmtheater.org), University Place, on the University of Vermont campus, Burlington, stages an eclectic, top-notch seasonal repertory of classic and contemporary plays.

Waterfront Theatre (802-862-7469; www.waterfronttheatre.org), 60 Lake St., Burlington. The newest addition to the city's cultural scene is this non-profit, independently run complex that acts as a forum for local production groups. The neo-Victorian brick complex facing the waterfront houses a 136-seat theater and a film presentation room, and plans are afoot to open a café.

St. Michael's College Theater Department (802-654-2000; www .smcvt.edu), Winooski, presents two major productions, fall and spring; also an excellent summer playhouse series (802-654-2281).

Lane Series (802-656-4455; www .uvm.edu/laneseries) sponsors major musical and theatrical performances around Burlington fall through spring.

DRIVE-IN ♪ **Sunset Drive-In** (802-862-1800; www.sunsetdrivein.com), Porter's Point Rd., Rt. 127 off North Ave., Colchester. It's for real: three screens, a snack bar, mini golf, and a kiddie playground.

MUSICAL VENUES For jazz, blues, rock, and dance clubs, check out these nightspots, all in Burlington: **Nectar's** (802-658-4771), 188 Main St., and above it, **Club Metronome** (802-865-4563), **135 Pearl St.** (802-863-2343), is the area's only gay and lesbian rallying point; dance floor and cabaret theater downstairs, bar and dining room up. **Red Square Bar and Grill** (802-859-8909) offers frequent nightly music. **Ri Ra** (802-860-9401), an Irish bar at 123 Church St., has live bands Thu. and Sat., karaoke on Mon., and the **Thai Bar at Parima** (802-864-7917) has music Thu.–Sat. **Higher Ground** (802-654-8888), 1214 Williston Rd., South Burlington, is the place to hit the dance floor.

✳ Selective Shopping

DOWNTOWN MARKETPLACES **The Church Street Marketplace**. Nearly 100 stores, restaurants, and services line four blocks of Church St., nicely paved, landscaped, closed to traffic, and enlivened by seasonal arts shows, weekend festivals, sidewalk cafés, and wandering entertainers. Park at a city-owned garage for a 2-hour discount. Parking is free all day Sunday at the Burlington Town Center garage, accessible from Pine and Bank Sts. or from Cherry St.

Pine Street area. There's a small yet interesting cluster of businesses on Pine St. between Flynn Ave. and Kilburn St., just south of the Vermont Transit terminal. Parking is never a problem. Highlights include Four Corners of the Earth lunch deli, Fresh Market/Cheese Outlet deli and café, Burlington Futon Co., Great Harvest Bread Company, Speeder and Earl's Coffee Roastery and Espresso Bar, Café Piccolo, and Lake Champlain Chocolates Factory and café. A number of small crafts businesses are tucked behind Speeder and Earl's, and there are two lighting shops, The Lamp Shop and Conant Custom Brass, with its delightful selection of unusual chandeliers, lights, thermometers, and brass objects.

Burlington Town Center. This vast, mostly underground indoor agora is linked to a parking garage and Filene's (which is changing its name to Macy's in fall of 2006); its 80 mostly upscale stores stock just about everything, starting with a minuscule Starbucks café and a few food stands.

ART GALLERIES **Fire House Art Gallery** (802-865-7166; www.burling toncityarts.com/firehousegallery), 149 Church St., Burlington, open daily except Mon. noon–5. Pick up a copy of the *First Friday Art Trolley Tours* pamphlet guide. The trolley runs only first Fridays of each summer month, but the map is a good gallery locator any day. Be sure to check out the iconoclastic exhibits at the **Amy Tarrant Gallery**, by the Flynn Center for the Performing Arts at 153 Main St., and down the hill, the **Katharine**

Montstream Studio and Gallery

(802-862-8752; www.kmmstudio
.com), in Union Station at 1 Main St.
Perhaps more than any other, the
work of this native-born watercolorist
and oil painter perfectly depicts the
lake and mountain landscapes of the
Burlington waterfront and downtown
area in greeting cards, prints, and
paintings. Open daily except Sun.
Another favorite is outsider artist
Dug Nap (802-860-1386; www
.dugnap.com), whose animals and
locals evoke a dark humor reminiscent of Gary Larsen's *The Far Side*.
Nap shows his work by appointment
at his studio, which is only a block
south of City Hall at 184 Church St.

**ANTIQUES SHOPS Ethan Allen
Antique Shop** (802-863-3764), 1625
Williston Rd., Rt. 2 east of Burlington,
has a large stock of early American
and country furniture and accessories.
Open daily; Sun. by appointment.

Authentica (802-310-0096) in Charlotte (call for directions). Thu.–Sat.
2–6 PM. Lydia Clemmons sells
museum-quality African antiques
and crafts drawn from every corner
of the continent, ranging from baskets
to calabashes, jewelry, woodenware,
sculpture, fabrics, drums, and masks.

Architectural Salvage Warehouse
(802-658-5011), 53 Main St., Burlington, sells marvelous artifacts from
old houses and buildings, like marble
sinks, crystal doorknobs, and claw-
foot tubs.

**Deforge Brothers Fine Furniture
and Antique Center** (802-985-
4911), 3093 Shelburne Rd., south of
Burlington. Open 10–5 daily year-
round, Sun. 12–5. Quality furniture
and antiques in every size and shape
from more than 35 dealers.

Champlain Valley Antique Center
(802-985-8116), 4067 Shelburne Rd.,
Shelburne, offers the wares of 25
dealers.

☀ ✍ **Upstairs Antiques** (802-859-
8966), 207 Flynn Ave., Burlington.
Open daily 10–6. A hodgepodge of
collectibles from furniture to books to
housewares.

Whistle Stop Antiques (802-951-
9189), 208 Flynn Ave., Burlington,
opposite Upstairs Antiques, by the
railroad tracks. Also open daily 10–5.
An assortment of china, silver, furniture, clothes, tools, and every type of
houseware imaginable.

BOOKSTORES

In Burlington

The minuscule **Everyday Book
Shop** (802-862-5191) at 194 College
St. is the lone surviving independent
bookstore in the downtown area.
Barnes & Noble (802-864-8001),
102 Dorset St., is a two-story book
department store in South Burlington,
and **Borders Books** (802-865-2711)
is at 29 Church St. **Crow Bookshop**
(802-862-4397) at 14 Church St. has a
good selection of discounted books,
and **North Country Books** (802-
862-1463) is a basement with over
50,000 used and rare titles, plus cards,
antique maps, prints, and ephemera,
downstairs at 2 Church St.

Elsewhere

✍ **Flying Pig Children's Books**
(802-425-2600; www.flyingpigbooks
.com). Former teachers Josie Leavitt
and Elizabeth Bluemle have created
Vermont's largest children's bookstore,
with close to 40,000 titles catering to
the under-12 set, and a good selection
for adults. Housed in a former post
office at 86 Ferry Rd. just off Rt. 7 in

Charlotte. **The Book Rack and Children's Pages** (802-872-2627), another great spot for kids, is located in the Essex Outlet Center in Essex.

CRAFTS SHOPS

In Burlington
Frog Hollow on the Marketplace (802-863-6458), 86 Church St., is a branch of the Vermont State Craft Center of Middlebury, a showcase for fine things crafted in the state, from furniture and art glass to handwoven scarves, sheepskin hats, photography, woodenware, and jewelry of every sort.

Jane Koplewitz Collection (802-658-3347; www.janekoplewitz.com), 28 Church St. Beautifully crafted handmade jewelry.

Bennington Potters North (1-800-205-8033; www.benningtonpotters .com), 127 College St., sells kitchenware, home furnishings, glass, woodenware, and Bennington Pottery at "factory prices."

Church and Maple Glass Studio (802-863-3880; www.churchand maple.com), 225 Church St. Closed Sun. Bud Shriner, a former emergency room physician, bought the old Yellow Cab garage several years ago and has transformed it into a glass-blowing studio with a reasonably priced array of colorful wares.

Outside Burlington
The Vermont Gift Barn (802-658-7684; www.vermontgiftbarn.com), 1087 Williston Rd., South Burlington. Open daily 9–8, Sun. 10–5. An overview of Vermont-made products, from specialty foods and weavings to jewelry, Bennington Pottery, furniture, fine art prints, and Simon Pearce glass.

George Scatchard Lamps (1-800-643-5267; www.gslamps.com), P.O. Box 71, Underhill 05489. Located between Underhill Flats and Cambridge on Rt. 15. Open June–Dec., weekdays 8:30–4:30, Sat. 9:30–4:30. George Scatchard has been making pottery for over 40 years out of a converted barn, now a contemporary, weatherworn showroom for his simple but multiple-shaped, natural-colored lamps. Seconds at reduced prices.

Vermont Folk Rocker (802-453-2483; www.vermontfolkrocker.com), 3820 Rt. 116, Starksboro. Open daily, but call ahead to be sure someone's there. Jim Geier's handmade hardwood rocking chairs have won a reputation for their fine workmanship, body-molding comfort, and durability.

FARMS AND WINERIES Vermont Wildflower Farm (802-425-3641, Rt. 7, Charlotte (5 miles south of the Shelburne Museum). Open Apr.–Oct., daily 10–5. Paths lead through 6 acres of wildflowers in fields and woodland settings; flowers and trees labeled; a large gift shop; and "the largest wildflower seed center in the East."

Charlotte Village Winery (802-425-4599; www.charlottevillagewinery .com), 3968 Greenbush Rd., Charlotte (from Rt. 7 go west on Ferry Rd. to the Charlotte village store, then left onto Greenbush Rd.). A newly hatched winemaking operation with a viewing deck overlooking acres of pick-your-own blueberry fields. Free wine tastings daily in summer, 11–5.

FOOD AND DRINK Almost Home Market (802-453-5775; www.almost homemarket.com), 28 North St., Bristol. Open weekdays 7:30–6:30, Sat.

8–5. Closed Sun. What used to be a local mom-and-pop store has transformed itself into this inspired gourmet shop where you can eat in or pick up and go. Roasted Provençal chicken, lemon chipotle hummus, fresh-baked breads and pastries, and Vermont Coffee Company beans roasted right in Bristol are among the attractions.

Lake Champlain Chocolates (802-864-1807; www.lakechamplain chocolates.com), 750 Pine St., Burlington. Open 7 days. The home of the American Truffle and other pricey delectables offers discounts on some of its premium chocolates. Tours available weekdays from 9–2, on the hour. There's also a café with flavored coffees, hot chocolate drinks, chocolate ice creams, and the like; it's open daily 9–6, Sun. noon–5. Or indulge at the **factory store** and café at 63 Church St. (802-862-5185).

Snowflake Chocolates (802-899-3373), 81 Rt. 15A, Jericho Corners. Bob and Martha Pollak's handcrafted chocolates are so good. Try the dark, liqueur-laced truffles. Their downtown shop is at 150 Dorset St. in the Blue Mall in South Burlington (802-863-8306). Open daily 10–5.

Fresh Market (802-863-3968; 1-800-447-1205), 400 Pine St., Burlington. Open daily 8–7, Sun. 10–5. Formerly the Cheese Outlet, this is the best deli in town. The shelves groan with local and imported cheeses, gourmet jams and chocolates, foodie magazines, wines, fresh-baked pies and pastries, beautiful produce, and a case loaded with scrumptious olive and mozzarella combinations, freshly made gourmet salads and roast meats, and other tempting concoctions. A dining area provides a self-serve café

with hot drinks and made-to-order sandwiches so you can down your purchases on the spot.

The Great Harvest Bread Company, next door at 382 Pine St. (802-660-2733) also provides a sandwich-ordering and -eating area for its peerless hearty loaves and fruit-filled pastries. Try the Hi-5 fiber with flax, oat bran, millet, and other healthy grains. Open weekdays 7–6, Sat. 8–5; closed Sun.

Magic Hat Brewing Company (802-658-BREW; www.magichat.net), 5 Bartlett Bay Rd., South Burlington (turn off Rt. 7 at the Jiffy Lube). A microbrewery offering free tours and samples in summer, 10–6 daily, Sun. noon–5. Retail store on site.

Note: The **Saturday Farmer's Market** in City Hall Park (8:30–2:30 summer through fall) is a wonderful place to stroll with the kiddies past artful pies, plants, fruits, cheeses, breads, dumplings, and veggies, as well as crafts, jewelry, clothes, and art.

SPORTS STORES **Burton Snowboards** (802-660-3200; www.burton .com), 80 Industrial Pkwy. (near Oakledge Park), Burlington. Open Mon.–Fri. 9–8, Sun. 11–6. The factory's retail and factory outlet for Vermont's name-brand snow- and skateboards and gear.

The Outdoor Gear Exchange (802-860-0190; www.gearx.com), 152 Cherry St., Burlington. Used and new outdoor sporting equipment: cross-country skiing, snowshoeing, rock climbing, hiking, camping and backpacking gear. It's rock-climbing central.

The Downhill Edge and Ski Rack (802-658-3313), 85 Main St., Burlington. This combined store features high-performance sailboards, gives lessons, and offers rentals. It's also a major source of cycling, running, in-line skate, and ski gear and wear, plus camping equipment.

Climb High (802-985-5055; www .climbhigh.com), 2438 Shelburne Rd., Shelburne. Hiking, biking, rock climbing, cross-country skiing—you name it, this store has the gear for it, plus quick and reasonable repairs. The best part is that you don't have to drive into downtown Burlington.

North Star Sports (802-864-5310, northstarsports.net), 100 Main St., Burlington. Sells, rents, and repairs bikes of all sorts, plus skis, snowshoes, and other sporting equipment.

VINTAGE CLOTHING AND FURNISH-INGS Old Gold (802-864-7786), 180 Main St., is a fun and funky store. **Battery St. Jeans** (802-865-6223), 7 Marble Ave., offers more grungy but cool clothing. **Recycle North** (appli-ances, furniture, books) at 266 Pine St. and its salvaged building supplies department across the street (have someone direct you) is a nonprofit with a huge supply of recycled house-wares that also provides job training in appliance repair. All are in Burling-ton. At **The Exchange** (802-878-3848), 167 Pearl St. (Rt. 15), Essex Junction, you're apt to find Donna Karan and Ralph Lauren. This used-clothing shop, probably the best in the state, has fabulous stuff, but it's also higher priced.

MORE SPECIAL STORES

In Burlington
Peace and Justice Store (802-863-8326; www.pjcvt.org), 21 Church St., run by the city's active Peace and Jus-tice Center, a source of alternative

publications and third-world-crafted items—jewelry, cards, clothing—all purchased from wholesalers commit-ted to nonexploitation and social jus-tice. The bulletin board is also worth checking. Open daily 10–6 (later on weekends), Sun. noon–5.

Gardener's Supply (802-660-3505), 128 Intervale Rd. (there's also an out-let at Taft's Corners in Williston). One of the largest catalog seed and garden suppliers in New England, with a retail store and nursery adjacent to demon-stration gardens along the Winooski River in Burlington's Intervale.

Apple Mountain (802-658-6452; www.applemountain.net), 30 Church St., is a Vermont products gift and food shop; on the touristy side, but fun. Socks, ceramics, jewelry, scents, books, and more. Open daily 9–9, Sun. 10–6.

Purple Shutter Herbs (802-865-HERB; 1-888-865-HERB; www .purpleshutter.com), 100 Main St. Laura Brown's emporium is the local source for culinary, medicinal, and cos-metic herbs and tinctures, plus gifts, teas, books, cosmetics, and cards with a botanical theme. Ask about classes.

Anichini (802-868-0171; www.anichini .com), 210 College St. Fabulous im-ported bed linens, silks, cashmere blankets, and Italian glassware, all dis-counted in this company store, one of three in New England (the others are in Manchester, Vt., and West Leba-non, N.H.). The Vermont-based pur-veyor sells most of its line to swanky hotel chains.

In the Charlotte–Shelburne area
Dakin Farm (802-425-3971), Rt. 7, Ferrisburgh (and 100 Dorset St. in South Burlington), is one of the princi-pal purveyors of cob-smoked hams and bacon. This roadside store also stocks a

variety of other Vermont food products and gifts. Try the maple soft serve.

Shelburne Farm Store and Visitors Center (802-985-8442), open daily year-round 9–5 (10–5 in the off-season; see a full description of what this place is about under *Museums*). The store features the prizewinning cheddar cheeses made from the milk of the estate's own Brown Swiss herd. A variety of Vermont products is also stocked.

Harrington's, Rt. 7, across from the Shelburne Museum, Shelburne, has been known for years for its delectable (and expensive) corncob-smoked hams, bacon, turkey, pork chops, and other goodies. The shop also displays cheeses, maple products, griddlecake mixes, jams, fruit butters, relishes, baked goods, wines, and coffees. Harrington's headquarters (Rt. 2, Richmond) include a smaller store.

The Shelburne Country Store, Rt. 7, Shelburne, encloses several gift galleries under the same roof—a sweets shop, cards, foods, housewares, lamp shades, et cetera.

🐾 **The Vermont Teddy Bear Factory Store** (802-985-3001; 1-800-829-BEAR), 6655 Shelburne Rd. (Rt. 7), Shelburne (see *For Families*), is immense.

In Winooski
The Champlain Mill (802-655-9477), 1 Main St., is a creatively converted woolen mill that houses historical displays and features a variety of shops.

Also in Greater Burlington
University Mall (802-863-1066), Dorset St., off Williston Rd. (I-89, Exit 14E), South Burlington. Your basic shopping mall with 70 stores; Kohl's, Bonton, and JCPenney are the anchors. The **Essex Outlet Fair**

(802-657-2777), Rts. 15 and 289 in Essex, includes Polo Ralph Lauren, Jones New York, Levi's, Jockey, and Bali, plus a new cinema complex.

✳ Special Events

February: **Burlington Winter Festival**, at Waterfront Park—dogsled rides, snow and ice sculptures (802-864-0123). **Penguin Plunge**—hundreds dive into the waterfront's icy waves to raise money for Special Olympics Vermont.

Saturday before Lent: **Magic Hat Mardi Gras**—a parade and block party at the Church Street Marketplace.

March: **Vermont Flower Show** at the Sheraton in South Burlington—3 days of color and fragrance mark the end of winter.

May: **Lilac Sunday** at Shelburne Museum (802-985-3346)—a festival of 19th-century food and games when the museum's many lilac bushes are in peak bloom.

Early June: **Arts Alive Festival**, a showcase of Vermont artists. **Vintage auto rally** at the Shelburne Museum (802-985-3346). **Discover Jazz Festival**—for 9 days, the entire city of Burlington becomes a stage for more than 200 musicians (see *Entertainment*). **Lake Champlain International Fishing Derby**—for details about registration and prizes, check with the chamber of commerce.

Late June: **Green Mountain Chew Chew**, Burlington—a 3-day food festival featuring more than 50 restaurants; continuous family entertainment at Waterfront Park. **Showcase of Agriculture** at the American Morgan Horse Association (802-985-4944), adjacent to the Shelburne Museum.

LAKE CHAMPLAIN FROM SOUTH BURLINGTON

Early July: Gala **Independence Day celebrations** on the Burlington waterfront—fireworks over the lake with live bands in Battery Park, children's entertainment, a parade of boats, and blessing of the fleet. **Vermont Brewer's Festival**—local microbreweries ply their stuff under tents at Waterfront Park. **Ferrari Street Fest**—the Italian sports cars take up position on Church St. for passerbys to admire.

Mid-July–mid-August: **Vermont Mozart Festival** performances in various locations, including Lake Champlain ferries.

Late July, early August: **Vermont Quilters Festival**, New England's largest, at the Champlain Valley Fair Exposition grounds in Essex Junction (www.vqf.org; 802-485-7092).

Mid-August: **The Shelburne Craft Fair** at Shelburne Farms features dozens of exhibitors. **Latino Festival** on the Burlington waterfront, a weekend of Latin musical events.

Late August: **Champlain Valley Exposition**, Essex Junction Fairgrounds—a big, busy, traditional county fair with livestock and produce exhibits, trotting races, midway, rides, spun-sugar candy—the works.

September: **Burlington Literary Festival**, 3 days of readings, lectures, workshops, book signings, and events, organized by Burlington City Arts.

Mid-September: **Annual Harvest Festival**, Shelburne Farms (802-985-8686). **Fools-A-Float**—a parade of land and sea craft, downtown Burlington. **Art Hop**—open-studio weekend in Burlington.

Early October: **Marketfest** celebrates Burlington's cultural diversity. Two hundred dealers convene for the **Champlain Valley Antiques Festival** at the Champlain Valley Exposition in Essex Junction.

Mid-October: **Vermont International Film Festival**, a weekend of short and long flicks focusing on the environment, war and peace, and justice, scattered at theaters around town (www.vtiff.org).

Late October: **Annual Halloween Costume Parade and Festival**, at noon, on Church St., Burlington.

Early December: **Christmas Weekend** at the Shelburne Museum—a 19th-century festival; call 802-985-3344 for dates and details. **Vermont International Festival** (802-863-6713), food, crafts, dance, and music from 40 countries, at the Champlain Valley Exposition fairgrounds on Rt. 15 in Essex Junction.

December 31: **First Night** (802-863-6005), the end-of-the-year gala—parades, fireworks, music, mimes, and myriad performances that transform downtown Burlington into an alcohol-free "happening."

THE NORTHWEST CORNER

INCLUDING THE ISLANDS, ST. ALBANS, AND SWANTON

I nterstate 89 is the quickest but not the most rewarding route from Burlington to the Canadian border. At the very least, motorists should detour for a meal in St. Albans and a sense of the farm country around Swanton. We strongly recommend allowing a few extra hours—or days—for the route up through the Champlain Islands, Vermont's Martha's Vineyard but as yet unspoiled.

THE ISLANDS

The cows and silos, hay fields and mountain views couldn't be more Vermont. But what about those beaches and sailboats? They're part of the picture, too, in this land chain composed of the Alburg peninsula and three islands—Isle La Motte, North Hero, and South Hero.

The Champlain Islands straggle 30 miles south from the Canadian border. Thin and flat, they offer some of the most spectacular views in New England: east to the highest of the Green Mountains and west to the Adirondacks. They also divide the northern reach of the largest lake in the East into two long, skinny arms, freckled with smaller outer islands. It's a waterscape well known to fishermen and sailors.

This is Grand Isle County, Vermont's smallest, with a small but steadily growing year-round population. It was homesteaded by Ebenezer Allen in 1783 and has been a quiet summer retreat since the 1870s.

In the 19th century visitors arrived by lake steamer to stay at farms. Around the turn of the 20th century a railway spawned several hotels, and with the advent of automobiles and Prohibition, Rt. 2—the high road down the spine of the islands—became one of the most popular roads to Montreal, a status it maintained until I-89 opened in the 1960s.

Happily, the 1960s, as well as the '70s, '80s, and '90s, like the interstate, seem to have passed these islands by. The selection of North Hero as summer home of the Royal Lipizzan Stallions in the 1990s is the biggest thing that's happened here since Theodore Roosevelt's visit in 1901. (It was here at Lieutenant Governor

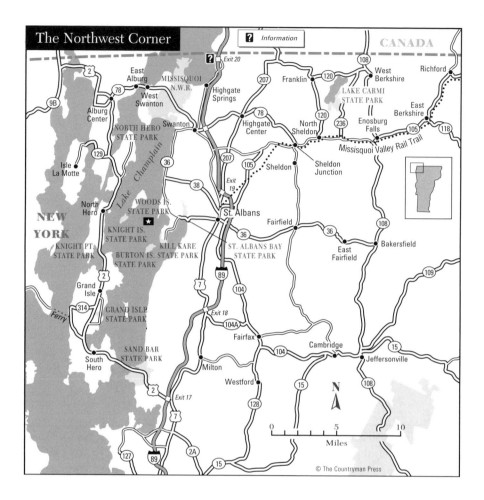

Nelson Fisk's estate that Vice President Theodore Roosevelt, who was attending a Vermont Fish and Game League banquet, learned that President William McKinley, also a visitor here in 1897, had been shot in Buffalo, New York.)

Isle La Motte is the smallest and quietest of the islands, and it's crossed and circled by narrow roads beloved by bicyclists. St. Anne's Shrine near the northern tip marks the site of a 17th-century French fort, and a rocky, tree-topped hump in the middle of a cow pasture at the southern end of the island is said to be the oldest coral reef in the world. Other evidence of the island's geological distinction can be seen in the fossils embedded in its stone houses, as well as in the marble facades of New York's Radio City Music Hall and the U.S. Capitol building. A quarry for the unique black Isle La Motte limestone marble is now a protected preserve.

The rural, laid-back beauty of these islands is fragile. Their waterside farms and orchards are threatened, not by tourism, but by quiet, steady suburbanization. Burlington is only half an hour south of Grand Isle, and Montreal is just 60 miles north.

Viewed primarily as a summer destination, this is a great place to visit in September and October when its many apple orchards are being harvested and bicycling is at its best. Roads are little trafficked, mysteriously overlooked by mainstream leaf-peepers.

GUIDANCE **Lake Champlain Islands Chamber of Commerce** (802-372-8400; 1-800-262-5226; info@champlainislands.com; www.champlainislands.com), P.O. Box 213, North Hero 05474, next door to the Hero's Welcome General Store, maintains a year-round office and publishes a list of accommodations, restaurants, marinas, campgrounds, and trailer parks. **The Franklin County Regional Chamber of Commerce** (802-524-2444; www.islandsandfarms.com) maintains an information center on the green in downtown Swanton.

GETTING THERE *By car:* From New York State and Montreal, Rt. 2 from Rouses Point, and from Vermont, Rt. 78 from Swanton (an exit off I-89). From Vermont on the south, I-89 Exit 17 to Rt. 2, which runs the length of the islands.

By ferry: **Lake Champlain Transportation Company** (802-864-9804; www.ferries.com) offers year-round, 15-minute ferry crossings between Gordon's Landing, Grand Isle, and Cumberland Head, New York.

MEDICAL EMERGENCY Emergency service is available by calling **911**.

Marine emergencies: Call 802-372-5590.

✴ Must-See

St. Anne's Shrine (802-928-3362; 802-928-3385), Isle La Motte, Rt. 129. Open mid-May–mid-Oct., free admission. An open-sided Victorian chapel on the shore marks the site of Vermont's first settlement, a French fort built in 1666. There are daily outdoor Masses in summer and Sunday services as long as weather permits. The shrine is a pleasant and peaceful place with a public beach, a cafeteria, and a picnic area in a large pine grove, presumably descended from what Samuel de Champlain described as "the most beautiful pines as I have ever seen" near this spot. Champlain himself is honored here with a massive granite statue, which was carved in Vermont's Pavilion at Montreal's 1967 Expo. Don't miss the History Room inside under the snack bar; its cases contain historical artifacts that have washed ashore over the years, among them a tomahawk blade, an old ax head, the remains of pewter cups, and ancient pottery shards. The complex, maintained by

ST. ANNE'S SHRINE ON ISLE LA MOTTE
VDT

ISLE LA MOTTE'S MARBLE MAGNATE

The Fisk Marble Quarries, the oldest in the state, were first used by the French in 1664 to make a kiln for Fort St. Anne, Vermont's first colonial settlement. The Fisk family acquired them in the 1780s, working them over four generations. In 1884 the quarries passed to Nelson W. Fisk, who recognized their potential, as a construction boom was under way in America's cities. When polished, this black marble was magnificent, a coveted building material for churches, courthouses, libraries, and bridges. From the spacious company dock, Nelson soon developed a thriving freight business, shipping boatloads of apples, lumber, even ice to markets farther south. His marble found its way into the U.S. Capitol, New York's Radio City Music Hall, the Vermont State House in Montpelier, and other important landmarks. With wealth came opportunity: Fisk was elected first to the Vermont House, then the Senate. He became a trustee at three state colleges, a delegate to two Republican national conventions, and in 1892 was appointed postmaster at an officially created Fisk Post Office set up at his own company.

By 1897 he was lieutenant governor, hosting President William McKinley at the family mansion, an 1802 stone affair by the lake. While Vice President Teddy Roosevelt was visiting in 1901, McKinley was shot, and it fell upon Fisk to break the news. It was a dark omen; Fisk's shipping fortunes soon dwindled, and he himself would die unexpectedly in 1923. Within 6 weeks, an inferno leveled the family estate. Today all five of the island's once thriving quarries lie still, and little remains of the Fisk fortune but a few surviving outbuildings and an overgrown ruin.

THE FISK QUARRY PRESERVE IN ISLE LA MOTTE

Joe Citro

the Edmundites, the Roman Catholic order that runs St. Michael's College in Colchester, includes a gift shop with books on the site's history.

✳ Also See

Hyde Log Cabin, Rt. 2, Grand Isle. Open July–Labor Day, Wed.–Sun. 11–5. Admission $1. Built by Jedediah Hyde in 1783 when the area was a wilderness accessible only by water,

Diane E. Foulds

HYDE LOG CABIN IN NORTH HERO

the cedar log cabin was restored by the Vermont Board of Historic Sites in 1956 and leased to the Grand Isle Historical Society, which has furnished it with a bounty of 18th-century artifacts—furniture, kitchenware, toys, tools, clothing, and atmosphere. At age 14 Hyde had enlisted in the Revolutionary War. From the spoils, he received a surveyor's compass and theodolite, which he later used to survey Grand Isle and other parts of the state. Ira and Ethan Allen had named the islands "The Two Heroes" in their own honor, and parceled out grants to their fellow Green Mountain Boys. Most of them sold their grants, and Hyde purchased several on what would later become known as Grand Isle. This cabin housed 150 years' worth of Hydes at a spot about 2 miles southwest of where it stands today.

Isle La Motte Historical Society. Open July–Aug., Sat. 1–4. This old stone school building and blacksmith shop is on Rt. 129, 4 miles south of the bridge. Displays include a sculpture of local stone that's been partially polished, graphically illustrating that the stone used in many local buildings is marble. It also displays the cane chair used by President McKinley and Vice President Theodore Roosevelt during their stays at the Fisk mansion, and the industrial looms of weaving entrepreneur Elizabeth Fisk, who, with her prominent husband, acted as their hosts. The Chazy Reef (see below) lies underfoot.

The Chazy Reef, Isle La Motte. Buried under the entire southern third of the island, this 450-million-year-old limestone-embedded coral reef is probably the world's oldest, evidence that Vermont was once contained within a tropical sea. Coral can harden into limestone that, over millennia, can morph into marble. Two sites can be visited by the public. One is the Fisk Quarry Preserve, which adjoins Fisk Farm (see *Lodging*). A pedestrian footpath leads to a viewing area where ancient, spiral-shaped reef-building organisms can be spotted in the quarry walls. Parking is 60 feet to the south of the path. The second site is on Goodsell Ridge. Driving south on the island's main road, turn left onto Quarry Rd. by the historical society and left again at the next T; the viewing area is on your left. Both sites are maintained by the Isle La Motte Preservation Trust (802-928-3364), which asks that visitors park only in designated areas and not along the road.

Fish Culture Station (802-372-3171), Bell Hill Rd., Grand Isle. Just beyond the Plattsburgh, N.Y., ferry on Rt. 314, look for the large hatchery (it's precisely 2 miles up Rt. 314 from Rt. 2), open 8–4 daily. Fish are brought to the facility as freshly spawned eggs (up to 2.2 million eggs at any one time), incubated, then transferred to a series of tanks; well worth checking out.

✳ To Do

BICYCLING With its flat roads (little trafficked once you are off Rt. 2) and splendid views, the islands are popular biking country. Isle La Motte is especially well suited to bicycling. There are five interpretive theme loops that roam through the gently rolling terrain, easily followed with the help of a map available at the chamber of commerce. Still in the planning stage is a rail-trail that links South Hero with Colchester by following the railbed of the old Rutland Railroad. The trip takes you on a magnificent journey across Lake Champlain. Lake views don't get any better than this, and it's flat to boot.

Rental bikes: Check with **Hero's Welcome General Store** (802-372-4161), North Hero Village; **Loon's Landing Watercraft & Bike Rentals** (802-372-8951), North Hero; **Grand Isle Canoe, Bike & Kayak** (802-782-ISLE) at 300 Rt. 2; or **Bike Shed Rentals** (802-928-3440), 1071 West Shore Rd., Isle La Motte, a mile south of St. Anne's Shrine. Both Ruthcliffe Lodge and Terry Lodge (see *Lodging*) offer bikes to their guests. **Mountain Lake Expeditions** (802-777-7646, 1340 Lockhouse Point, North Hero) has instituted a very helpful delivery service that deposits bicycles, kayaks, or canoes right at your front door.

BIRDING Located on one of the major flyways, the islands are particularly rich in bird life: Herons, eagles, ospreys, cormorants, among others, migrate through the area. Prime birding sites include the **South Hero Swamp** and **Mud Creek** in Alburg and the **Sand Bar Wildlife Refuge** across from Sand Bar State Park. See also Knight's Island Sate Park under *Green Space*.

BOAT EXCURSIONS **Driftwood Tours** (802-373-0022), North Hero, offers several daytime, sunset, and moonlight cruises in a boat that seats a maximum of six passengers. Captain Holly Poulin offers nature and fishing tours and also does dinner cruises in conjunction with the North Hero House. The trips take 2 hours and leave from the North Hero House Pier.

Ferry Cruise (802-864-9804), Rt. 314, Grand Isle. If you don't get out on the water any other way, be sure to take the 15-minute ferry to Plattsburgh, New York, and back.

BOATING Rental boats are available in North Hero from **Anchor Island Marina** (802-372-5131), **Charlie's Northland Lodge** (802-372-8822), and **Hero's Welcome** (802-372-4161; kayaks and canoes only). In South Hero, **Apple Tree Bay** (802-372-3922) offers canoes, sailboats, and pontoon boats. **Tudhope Sailing Center and Marina** (802-372-5320), at the bridge in Grand Isle, also offers sailboats, powerboats, boat slips, sailing instruction, and charters. **Mountain Lake Expeditions** (see *Bicycling*) will bring kayaks and canoes right to your door.

FISHING Lake Champlain is considered one of the finest freshwater fisheries in America. With the right bait and a little luck, you can catch trout, salmon, smelt, walleye, bass, pike, muskellunge, and perch. Don't expect area fishermen to give away their favorite spots, but you can find hints, maps, equipment, bait, and advice from local fishing pundit Charlie North at **Charlie's Northland** in North

Hero (802-372-8822) or from Chas Salmon at **Raven Ridge Guide Service** in
Richford (1-888-933-4616; www.ravenridge.net).

GOLF AND MINI GOLF **Alburg Country Club** (802-796-3586), Rt. 129, 3 miles
west of South Alburg; 18 lakeside holes, gentle, shady terrain, snack bar.

Barcomb Hill Country Club at Apple Tree Bay (802-372-5398), Rt. 2, South
Hero. Open May–late Oct. A nine-hole, par-3 executive golf course. Rental carts
and clubs.

Wilcox Golf Course (802-372-8343), Grand Isle, offers nine lakeside holes, golf
carts, pro shop, rentals.

✔ **Beaver Creek Mini Golf** (802-372-5811), Rt. 2, North Hero. Open Memorial
Day–Labor Day. An 18-hole miniature golf course.

✳ Green Space

✔ **Alburg Dunes State Park** (802-796-4170), Alburg. This little-trammeled
area features the longest sandy beach on Lake Champlain, and its shallowness
makes it excellent for swimming with young ones; rare flora and fauna; limited
day use only. Call for directions or ask locally.

✔ **North Hero State Park** (802-372-8727) has 99 wooded tent or trailer sites
and 18 lean-to sites arranged in three loops, each with a restroom and hot showers (no hookups); mostly in lowland forests with access to open fields, a beach,
boat launch, boat rentals, and picnic and children's play areas.

Grand Isle State Park (802-372-4300). Vermont's second largest (and most
visited) state park has 155 campsites, including 33 lean-tos (no hookups) on 226
acres, with a beach, playground, nature trail, and recreation building.

Knight's Island State Park by way of Burton Island State Park (802-524-6353).
The *Island Runner* (802-524-6353), a ferry operated by the state, crosses the
water to Knight's Island every couple of hours between Memorial Day and
Labor Day. There's even an optional gear delivery service. The seven campsites
at Knight's Island are primitive (there are no facilities)—even clothing is optional! To maximize privacy, campsites are hidden from public view. Not to be
missed is the brochure-guided "Walk of Change" that explores island ecology.

✔ **Knight Point State Park** (802-372-8389), located on the southern tip of North
Hero, is the best place to swim, especially for children. A former farm facing The
Gut, a quiet, almost landlocked bay, its grounds include a fine brick house and a
nature trail that loops around the point. From the sandy beach you can watch
boats pass through the drawbridge between the islands. Canoes and rowboats are
available for rent, and there are picnic tables with grills.

Sand Bar State Park (802-893-2825) fills to capacity on sunny weekends in summer, but this oasis with its shallow, sandy beach and adjacent 1,000-acre wildlife
refuge is a fine place to relax on weekdays. Picnic tables, sailboarding school.

See also *Green Space* in "St. Albans and Swanton" (page 495) for more islands
and the Missisquoi National Wildlife Refuge. The complete rundown on state
parks is at www.vtstateparks.com (1-888-409-7579).

✳ Lodging

Note: See *Green Space* for information on campgrounds in North Hero and Grand Isle State Parks. Families who don't camp tend to rent cottages for a week or more. The chamber of commerce can furnish details about numerous old-fashioned lakeside cottage clusters.

INNS AND BED & BREAKFASTS

Thomas Mott B&B (802-796-4402; 1-800-348-0843), 63 Blue Rock Rd., Alburg 05440. This 1838 English country cottage with a splendid view of the Green Mountains is a real find. Hosts Susan and Bob Cogley keep a fridge full of complimentary Ben & Jerry's ice cream pops. There are four guest rooms, each with private bath. Guests are welcome to use the canoe and the swimming/fishing dock. Cross-country skiers and snowmobilers are at home here in winter (local rentals available), with 40 miles of dedicated trails adjacent. $115 includes a great breakfast. Children over 12 welcome.

North Hero House (802-372-4732; 1-888-525-3644; www.northhero house.com), Rt. 2, North Hero 05474. Open May–Nov. This century-old summer hotel has become a popular spot for boaters, bikers, and travelers of all sorts. All the rooms—9 upstairs and 17 more across Rt. 2—have private bath. The inn offers a comfortable sitting area, an inviting pub, and a large public dining room beyond (see *Dining Out*). Facilities include a long, grassy dock at which Champlain steamers once moored; canoes, kayaks, power- and pedal boats are available. Our favorite (alas, the most expensive) rooms are in the three buildings that face, even extend out over, the lake—Homestead, South-wind, and Cove House—so that you fall asleep to lapping water. In summer $95–295 per couple B&B, $14.95 per child. The many specialty weekends include murder mysteries and musical events. Check the web site for packages.

Fisk Farm (802-928-3364; www.fiskfarm.com), 3849 West Shore Rd., Isle La Motte 05463. Owner Linda Fitch offers two lovely guest cottages on the former site of the Fisk family estate. The Ice House, built of wood and stone next to the main house, is a beauty, a place we would like to reserve for a special occasion, but only in warm weather (it has a fireplace but no other heating). There is a rustic Shore Cottage, said to have been built as a playhouse in North Hero and brought across the ice. The ruins of the gray stone Fisk mansion have been preserved in the front garden, currently the scene of Sunday-afternoon teas, and the horse and carriage barn has been preserved as an art gallery. The mansion burned in 1924, but thanks to Fitch, who has dedicated years to restoring the property, it's an exceptionally tranquil place that offers a window into not only the history of Vermont but also the earth. Rates begin at $100 for the Shore Cottage and $125 for the Ice House (both of which have their own kitchens) but vary according to the length of time reserved and the season. Grills are available, and guests may help themselves to the herb garden.

Ruthcliffe Lodge & Restaurant (802-928-3200; 1-800-769-8162; www .ruthcliffe.com), 1002 Quarry Rd., Isle La Motte 05463, open Mother's Day–Columbus Day. Way out at the end of Old Quarry Rd., this lakeside compound includes a small motel and lodge with a total of six rooms, all with private bath and many featuring lakeside panoramas. Mark and Kathy Infante are warm hosts, and the food is well known and highly rated (see *Dining Out*); three meals a day are served. There's a 40-foot water's-edge patio for dining, as well as the cozy knotty-pine dining room in the lodge. Swimming and fishing are out the front door; rental boats and bikes are available. Rates range from $119 for a room with a full bath to $159 for a two-room adjoining unit with a bath and a half, including a full country breakfast.

The Ransom Bay Inn (802-796-3393; 1-800-729-3393), 4 Center Bay Rd., Alburg 05440. A stone house built beautifully in the 1790s, originally a stagecoach stop, set back from Rt. 2 within walking distance of a small beach. On the Vermont Register of Historic Places. Plenty of common space, with three working fireplaces, an exposed-beam living room area opening onto a patio, a more formal parlor, and a resident cat. Guests are accommodated in two large airy and 2 smaller rooms, all nicely furnished with period antiques and private bath. $70–95 year-round includes a choice of breakfast entrées and homemade jams, and dinner is available ($22 per person) with advance notice.

Paradise Bay Bed & Breakfast (802-372-5393), 50 Light House Rd., South Hero 05486. This is a very gracious new house in a secluded setting with plenty of deck space overlooking the lake. The two large, nicely furnished guest rooms share a bath in a separate wing. $89–125 per couple.

Charlie's Northland Lodge (802-372-8822; 802-372-3829; www.charliesnorthlandlodge.com), 3829 Rt. 2, North Hero 05474, in the heart of the village. Built by Charlie's grandparents early in the 19th century, this year-round lodge contains three guest rooms furnished in country antiques, two with air-conditioning and private bath; all have private entrance, and a guest parlor. The lodge is part of a nifty little complex that includes a private beach, a sporting and gift shop, boat and motor rentals, fishing licenses, bait, and tackle. $90–125 includes continental breakfast. Housekeeping cottages available.

Terry Lodge (802-928-3264; www.geocities.com/terry_lodge), 2925 West Shore Rd., Isle La Motte 05463. Open May 15–Oct. 15. A friendly, family kind of place in a superb location: on a quiet road not far from St. Anne's Shrine, across a narrow road from the lake with a fine lakeside deck and swim raft. Most of the seven rooms in the lodge have lake views. Breakfast and dinner (family-style) are served. There's also a four-unit motel ($95–125), a housekeeping cottage ($500 per week), and a housekeeping apartment ($475 per week) in the rear. Bike rentals and golf are available nearby. Lodge rooms are $80 with breakfast, $115 per couple MAP. Request one of the front rooms with a lake view.

RUTHCLIFFE LODGE IN ISLE LA MOTTE

Joe Citro

Kim Grant

OVERLOOKING LAKE CHAMPLAIN IN NORTH HERO

🍎 **Allenholm Orchards Bed & Breakfast** (802-372-5566; 1-888-721-5666; www.allenholm.com), 150 South St., South Hero 05486. Pam and Ray Allen offer a guest suite—a bedroom furnished in family antiques, including a queen-sized canopy bed, and a large living room with a TV, VCR, board games, and full-sized pool table, plus a full private bath, patio, rose garden, and private airport. A country breakfast is served upstairs in the dining room or, if preferred, on your patio. The suite is on the lower level of the Allens' modern home; it opens onto more than 100 acres of apples, billed as Vermont's oldest commercial orchard. Established in the 1870s, it's now owned and operated by the sixth generation of Allens. $98 per couple for the bedroom, $165 for the entire suite.

∞ 🍎 **Ferry Watch Inn** (802-372-3935), 121 West Shore Rd., Grand Isle 05458. This wonderfully restored lakefront home, originally built in 1800, overlooks the broad lake with spectacular views of the Adirondacks and the most wonderful sunsets. Janet and Troy Wert offer three guest rooms (two with shared bath; one with private bath) with antique double beds

renowned for their comfort. The property is within walking distance of a nine-hole golf course. $95 per room with shared bath or $115 with private bath includes full country breakfast. Ask about weekly rates.

Crescent Bay Farm (802-372-4807; www.crescentbaybb.com), South Hero 05486. This restored 1820s farmhouse is a working farm with three guest rooms, two with private bath ($105 includes breakfast). Dave and Julie Lane have 20 llamas, plus cats, dogs, and Black Angus beef at a country location with flower gardens, lake views, and one of the many miniature stone castles scattered around the Champlain Islands.

🐾 🍎 **Heron's Way B&B** (802-372-8352; www.heronsway.com), 424 Rt. 2, South Hero 05486. Private sandy beach and dockage. The king bedroom has a private bath and balcony overlooking the lake, and the queen suite has a private bath and sitting room. Both rent for $115, and come with air-conditioning, heat, a TV/VCR, and a lavish breakfast.

Sampler House Bed & Breakfast (802-893-2724; www.samplerhouse.com), 22 Main St., Milton 05468. Off Rt. 7, about halfway between Burlington and St. Albans. Peter and Deborah Martin have restored their 1830 brick Cape on Milton's main avenue, offering guests three comfortable air-conditioned rooms, each with private bath and wireless Internet. The bright, dual-level suite in the rear is suited for lengthier stays with its full kitchen, sofa, and satellite TV. $75–95 includes breakfast.

OTHER LODGING ∞ 🐾 🍎 **Shore Acres Inn & Restaurant** (802-372-8722; www.shoreacres.com), 237

Shore Acres Dr., North Hero 05474. Motel rooms open May–early Oct. This pleasant motel commands one of the most spectacular views of any lodging place in Vermont. Set in sweeping, peaceful, beautifully groomed grounds, 23 comfortable rooms face the lake and the Green Mountains. There's a bar-lounge; breakfast and dinner are served (see *Dining Out*). Four of the guest rooms are in the garden house, away from the lake. Susan and Mike Tranby have worked hard to make this an exceptionally friendly as well as comfortable place. Amenities include lawn chairs, two clay tennis courts, a driving range, lawn games, and 0.5 mile of private shore for swimming. All rooms have either a queen, king, two twins, or two doubles, TV, and ceiling fan or air conditioner when lake breezes fail. $90–190 per room. Pets accommodated for $15 the first night, $5 each night thereafter.

❀ **Wilcox Cove Cottages & Golf Course** (802-372-8343 in summer; 802-453-3779 in winter), Rt. 314, mailing address: 3 Camp Court, Grand Isle 05458. Open June–mid-Sep. This homey, lakeside cottage colony and nine-hole public golf course, less than a mile from the ferry, is a real find. Each of the seven cottages has a living room, dining area, fully equipped kitchen, one bedroom with twin beds, bathroom with shower, and one or two screened porches. They are completely furnished except for sheets, pillowcases, and bath and kitchen towels, and can be rented for $550 a week including greens fees. Golf is $13 per day, and pets are welcome. Occupancy is limited to two adults unless arrangements are made in advance.

✳ Where to Eat

DINING OUT **Sand Bar Inn** (802-372-6911; www.appleislandresort .com), 59 Rt. 2, South Hero. A fine-dining restaurant with a casual atmosphere right on the lake, this place is not what you would expect when seen from Rt. 2. Among the offerings are a duck breast in blackberry sauce served with ginger polenta and duck confit, several fish and shellfish dishes, and grilled pesto lamb chops. Reservations are suggested. In-season, the restaurant is open daily 5–9. The chef also does private parties. On the expensive side.

Shore Acres Inn & Restaurant (802-372-8722), Rt. 2, North Hero. Reservations for dinner are a must much of the time. Also open for breakfast June–Aug. and for lunch in July and Aug.; dinner is served weekends until New Year's as well. The dining room's large windows command a sweeping view of the lake, with Mount Mansfield and its flanking peaks in the distance. It's a very attractive room with a large fieldstone hearth. You might begin with coconut-beer-battered shrimp ($6.95) or grilled homemade polenta ($4.95), then dine on Apple Island chicken or roast rack of lamb. Entrées ($12.95–26.95) come with home-baked bread, a salad, and seasonal vegetables. The chocolate pie is famous. Early-bird special Mon.–Thu.

Ruthcliffe Lodge & Restaurant (802-928-3200; www.ruthcliffe.com), 1002 Quarry Rd., Isle La Motte. Open mid-May–Columbus Day for dinner, July and Aug. for lunch, weekends for dinner over winter. Overnight moorings available for dinner guests. Be sure to reserve for dinner before you drive out to this rustic building, way off the main drag and overlooking the lake. Dine in the pine-paneled dining room or outside on the deck. Owner-chef Mark Infante specializes in Italian dishes like chicken Marsala and veal Sorrentina, but the menu might also include shrimp scampi Ruthcliffe ($19.95) or pecan-crusted halibut in a tomato, anchovy, and lemon sauce ($21.95). Entrée prices include soup, salad, and vegetables, and a 15 percent gratuity is automatically added to the check.

⊙⊙ **North Hero House** (802-372-4732; 1-888-525-3644), Rt. 2, North Hero. Open May–Nov., this historic old inn is famous for its Friday lobster buffet. Dining on the glassed-in veranda is popular with its lake views, or better still, at one of the umbrella-covered tables on the lawn; the main dining room adjoins a solarium that's used for private parties. Menu selections might include sautéed and confited Weston Farm rabbit with Vermont goat cheese beignets, turned Yukon gold potatoes, and summer vegetables ($24.25), grilled venison with savory sweet potato pie, port sauce, braised greens, and herbed butter basted vegetables ($23.50), or filet mignon with chili onion rings and roasted baby potatoes with Vermont

GRAND ISLE LAKE HOUSE

Joe Citro

blue cheese sauce ($27.75). Entrées range $17–28, and the pub has its own casual fare.

WEDDING RECEPTIONS ⊙⊙ **Grand Isle Lake House**, East Shore Rd., Grand Isle. For details and reservations, contact Bev Watson at 802-865-2522 or go to www.grandislelakehouse.com. Built on Robinson's Point as the Island Villa Hotel in 1903, this is a classic mansard-roofed 25-room summer hotel with a wraparound porch, set in 55 acres of lawn that sweep to the lake. From 1957 until 1993 it was a summer girls camp run by the Sisters of Mercy. Since 1997 it has been owned by the Preservation Trust of Vermont, which has restored the upstairs rooms beautifully, as it has the lobby, kitchen, and dining rooms. It is currently available as a site for conferences and wedding receptions (80 can sit down in the dining room and another 125 guests on the porch; tents on the lawn can accommodate 250 guests).

EATING OUT Blue Paddle Bistro (802-372-4814; www.bluepaddlebistro.com). Open for dinner Tue.–Sat., lunch Thu.–Sat., and Sunday brunch. South Hero's newest buzz is this cheerful place at 316 Rt. 2 with a water sculpture behind the bar and a crafts gallery upstairs. To get it off the ground, owners Mandy Hotchkiss and Phoebe Bright gave paddles to investors. Now the paddles cover the walls, and the café hums with activity year-round. Fresh breads, salads, and sandwiches for lunch, full bar, and dinner entrées ($8.95–15.95) such as Gorgonzola-stuffed meat loaf, bourbon-marinated flank steak, and miso-encrusted salmon with shiitake mushrooms and leek risotto. Outdoor deck in summer.

Hero's Welcome (802-372-4161; www.heroswelcome.com), Rt. 2, North Hero Village. Open daily year-round, an upscale general store with a good deli, a bakery, and a café with waterside seating. "Heroic" sandwiches— think Thomas Jefferson and Gentleman Johnny Burgoyne— and freshly made soups.

North Hero Marina (802-372-5953; www.northhero.com), 2253 Pelot's Point Rd., North Hero. You eat on the porch, no more than 10 people at a time, and the pool next door invites you in to pass the time between courses. The eating arrangements make it very seasonal. The house specialty is fish of all sorts.

🍴 **Margo's Café and Bakery** (802-372-6112), Rt. 2, Grand Isle. Open mid-May–mid-Oct., closed Mon. and Tue. Behind this simple facade lies a cozy, popular bakery-café serving continental breakfast and light lunches indoors, outdoors, or to go, and featuring the work of local artists. Margo serves dinner (BYOB) Thu.–Sun., which might be sole stuffed with asparagus, carrots, and scallions in a lemon verbena sauce, or prosciutto purses in white wine and purple basil sauce. Inexpensive.

Tuddy's (802-796-4114), 99 Rt. 2, Alburg. Open daily except Mon. for breakfast, lunch, and dinner, Sun. 8–3. Catherine Tudhope serves up classic backcountry fare at reasonable prices.

🍴 & **Grand Isle Ferry Dock Snack Bar** (802-372-5042), Grand Isle. Breakfast 7–11 AM; open in summer till 8 PM, winter till 3. Don't miss the french fries or the bread that Roy and Marcia Lamphere make for sandwiches. Tables inside and picnic tables outside.

Links on the Lake (802-796-4248), 230 Rt. 129, Alburg. Lunch daily except Mon., dinner Fri. and Sat. 5–9. Good food and reasonable prices in a pretty setting at the Alburg Country Club. There's a good seafood pasta, and the house special is Hungarian goulash. Moderate.

Sun Burger's Snack Bar along Rt. 2 in Grand Isle is a grand place to stop for homemade ice cream or the eponymous burgers.

Note: See also Fisk Farm under *Lodging* and inquire about Tea Garden Art Shows with music on summer Sundays, 1–5.

✳ Entertainment

🎵 **Royal Lipizzan Stallions** (802-372-8400; www.hermannslipizzans .com), mid-July through Aug., performing Thu.–Sun. at a new arena in Knight Point State Park in North Hero, just north of the drawbridge from Grand Isle. Tickets through the chamber of commerce. Visitors welcome every day on the grounds of the Islands Center for Arts & Recreation (www.icarvt.org). These elegant and unusually strong white horses bred in the 16th century for battle and show are known for their intricate maneuvers, many executed midair. Only a few hundred representatives of the breed survive. Colonel Herrmann's family have been training Lipizzans since 1618, when their ancestors received some as a gift from Hapsburg Austrian Emperor Ferdinand II. The Herrmanns winter in Florida and come to North Hero for 6 weeks each summer. Tickets $10–17.

Music at Snow Farm Vineyard (802-372-9463), West Shore Rd., South Hero. If you fancy meeting the locals, a popular event is the Thursday summer music series beginning at 6:30 PM on the vineyard's lawn. The music ranges, over the course of the season, from classical to rock. It's free, and all you need to bring is a picnic and a chair (bug spray wouldn't be a bad idea, either). You can buy your wine on site.

✳ Selective Shopping

ANTIQUES Pick up a current copy of the pamphlet guide *Antique the Champlain Islands* at Hero's Welcome General Store. The usual count is half a dozen shops, but they are all seasonal and tend to close as one thing, open as another. Standbys include **Blue Heron Antiques**, 288 Rt. 2, South Hero, the **Back Chamber Antiques Store**, North Hero Village, and **Tinker's Barn**, gifts and antiques at 479 Rt. 2, South Hero. Also check with **Alburg Auction House**, Lake St., Alburg, open Sat. 2–6 and 7–midnight.

CRAFTS **McGuire Family Furniture Makers** (802-928-4190; www .mcguirefamilyfurnituremakers.com), 239 Main St., Isle La Motte. Open year-round, but call. Two generations of this talented family are involved in the day-to-day production of stunning antique reproduction furniture in spare, heirloom, Shaker, and 18th-century designs: four-poster beds, peg-leg tables, grandfather clocks, dressers—anything you want designed, and some surprisingly affordable.

Island Craft Shop (802-863-5723), a cooperative located behind the chamber of commerce and open daily mid-May–mid-Oct. Works of local and area artisans.

The Upstairs Gallery, above the Blue Paddle Bistro, stocks Harry Wicks's fine wood bowls, jewelry, stained glass, and more.

ORCHARDS ✿ **Allenholm Farm** (802-372-5566; www.allenholm.com), 111 South St., P.O. Box 300, South Hero 05486. Open July–Dec. 24, 9–5. A sixth-generation, 100-acre apple orchard, Vermont's oldest, with a farmstead selling Vermont cheese, honey and maple syrup, jams and jellies, and Papa Ray's famous home-made pies. There's also a petting paddock with rabbits, chickens, goats, horses, a camel, and a donkey. See also *Special Events* (the Allens are the power behind the October Apple Fest).

Hall's Orchard (802-928-3418; 802-928-3226), 4461 Main St., Isle La Motte 05463. The 1820s brick house sits across from the orchard that has been in the same family since the house was built. The apples we bought here on a crisp October morning are the best we can remember finding anywhere.

✿ **Hackett's Orchard** (802-372-4848), 86 South St., South Hero 05486. Perennials, maple syrup, fruits, berries, and fresh-picked vegetables in summer; apples, cider, and pumpkins in fall. The farm stand has a family picnic and play area. Fresh cider doughnuts are a specialty, as are the homemade fruit pies.

SPECIAL STORES **Hero's Welcome General Store** (1-800-372-HERO; www.heroswelcome.com), Rt. 2, North Hero. Former Pier 1 CEO Bob Camp and his wife, Bev, have transformed this 19th-century landmark into a bright, smart, multilevel emporium: café and bakery, gift shop, art gallery, grocery, Vermont gourmet food products, sports clothes, outdoor toys and sporting goods, wine shop, and bookstore, retaining its flavor as a community gathering spot. They offer canoe, kayak, and bike rentals as well as boat launch, and plans are afoot for even more.

Vermont Nut Free Chocolates (802-372-4654; 1-800-468-8373; www .vermontnutfree.com), 316 Rt. 2, South Hero, in the center of town. Watch chocolates being handmade at this minuscule clapboard factory, then descend upon the store. Open daily except Sunday, 9–5.

Charlie's Northland Sporting and Gift Shop. A serious fishing-gear source, but also assorted sportswear and gifts.

WINERY **Snow Farm Vineyard** (802-372-9463; www.snowfarm.com), 190 West Shore Rd. (follow signs from Rt. 2 or Rt. 314), South Hero 05486. Open Memorial Day–Oct., 10–4:30. Vineyard tours are offered daily at 11 and 2. This pioneering Lake Champlain vineyard is the fruition of several years' hard work by lawyers Molly and Harrison Lebowitz. Visitors enter a barnlike building that is the winery-showroom with a tasting counter. There they learn that this is still a relatively new operation (opened in 1997). Initially it processed and bottled wine from grapes grown in New York's Finger Lakes, gradually mixing these with the harvest from vines on Snow Farm's 10 acres. The farm's Blanc de Noirs was awarded a bronze medal at the 1998 Eastern International Wine Competition. (See also *Entertainment*.)

✳ Special Events

Note: Check with the chamber of commerce about weekly events. See Fisk Farm under *Lodging*; inquire about Tea Garden Art Shows with music, summer Sundays.

June: **Taste of the Islands: Food & Wine** (*second weekend*), South Hero—local food purveyors show off their culinary creations, accompanied by Snow Farm Vineyard wines. **Celebrate Champlain! Islands Festival** (*third weekend*), Grand Isle—classes and demos on sailboarding, kayaking, sailing, and canoeing; music and BBQ.

July 4: **Parades** and **barbecues** in South Hero and Alburg, and **Island House and Garden Tour** in Grand Isle.

Mid-July–mid-August: **Lipizzan Stallions** (see *Entertainment*).

August: **Grand Isle County Art Show & Sale** (*first weekend*). **Northumbrian Pipers Convention Community Dance and Concert** (*last weekend*), North Hero Town Hall. **Lake Champlain Bluegrass Festival** in Alburg.

Early September: **Teddy Roosevelt Toast**, Isle La Motte, at the Fisk Farm—a presentation pays tribute to a person or group that has furthered TR's mission with respect to our natural resources and cultural heritage.

Columbus Day weekend: **Apple Fest**—crafts fair, a "press-off," plenty of food and fun (802-372-5566).

ST. ALBANS AND SWANTON

Once an important railroad center and still the Franklin County seat, St. Albans (population: 7,549), on Rt. 7, is showing signs of revitalization. Its firm place in the history books was assured on October 19, 1864, when 22 armed Confederate soldiers, who had infiltrated the town in mufti, held up the three banks, stole horses, and escaped back to Canada with $208,000, making this the northernmost engagement of the Civil War. One of the raiders was wounded and eventually died, as did Elinus J. Morrison, a visiting builder who was shot by the bandits. The surviving Confederates were arrested in Montreal, tried, but never extradited; their leader, Lieutenant Bennett H. Young, rose to the rank of general. When he visited Montreal again in 1911, a group of St. Albans dignitaries paid him a courtesy call at the Ritz-Carlton!

Swanton (population: 6,423) occupies a flat area circled by farmland and intersected by the Missisquoi River. Archaeological digs have unearthed evidence that Algonquian tribes lived here as far back as 8000 BC. The French settled the area about 1748, naming it 15 years later for Thomas Swanton, a British officer in the French and Indian Wars. Due to its proximity to the Canadian border (only 6 miles north), Swanton witnessed a fair bit of smuggling in the 19th century and during Prohibition. During World War I the long-abandoned Robin Hood–Remington Arms plant produced millions of rounds of ammunition for the Allied armies. Today an estimated 20 percent of the population is of Abenaki origin, and the Abenaki Tribal Council and museum is based here. The idyllic village green is home to a pair of swans, a tradition since 1963, when England's Queen Elizabeth II sent the town a pair for its bicentenary, thinking its name had something to do with swans.

GUIDANCE Franklin County Regional Chamber of Commerce (802-524-2444; www.stalbanschamber.com), 2 N. Main St., St. Albans 05478, provides brochures and general information.

The Swanton Chamber of Commerce (802-868-7200), Merchants Row, Swanton 05488, has an information booth at the north end of the village green. Open occasionally.

MEDICAL EMERGENCY Emergency service is available by calling **911**.
Northwestern Medical Center (802-524-5911; 1-800-696-0321), St. Albans.

✳ To See and Do

St. Albans Historical Museum (802-527-7933), at 9 Church St. (facing Taylor Park), open mid-June–early Oct., weekdays 1–4, or by appointment. This artifact-rich museum was established by the St. Albans Historical Society in 1971 in a three-story brick schoolhouse erected in 1861. Exhibits include a fascinating old-time country doctor's office, Civil War artifacts, period costumes, and Central Vermont Railroad memorabilia. A diorama of the town uses lights and narration to demonstrate how a group of Confederate soldiers held up three local banks in 1864, making off with $208,000 in loot before setting off makeshift bombs and

Kim Grant

MUSEUMS AND PUBLIC BUILDINGS FLANK THE TOWN GREEN IN ST. ALBANS.

galloping to Canada. Samples of the stolen bills are on display. $4 adults; ages 14 and under are free.

Chester A. Arthur Birthplace (802-828-3051; www.dhca.state.vt.us/Historic Sites/html/arthur.html), North Fairfield. A replica of the little house where the 21st (and usually underrated) president was born can be found 10 miles east on Rt. 36 to Fairfield (open June–mid-Oct., Wed.–Sun. 11–5). In the visitors center, exhibits examine the controversy over the actual site of Arthur's birth, which had an impact on the question of his eligibility to serve as president. Arthur's conduct as president in light of his reputation as a leading New York State political boss is also examined.

Abenaki Tribal Museum and Cultural Center (802-868-2559; www.abenaki nation.org), 100 Grand Ave., Swanton. Usually open 9–4 Mon.–Fri. (call ahead to confirm), the center offers an intriguing overview of historic Abenaki life, from clothing to tools and crafts, with a time line explaining the fur trade and transportation. The stars of this exhibit are the ceremonial headdresses, the birch-bark and dugout canoes, and the intricate handwoven baskets.

Site of former Abenaki Christian mission, on Monument Rd., about a mile north of Swanton off Rt. 7. It's easy to envision a thriving Indian settlement at this riverside spot opening onto Lake Champlain. A granite marker and totem pole commemorate the location of Vermont's first Jesuit mission, established about 1700, and the St. Francis (Abenaki) Indian village that grew up around it. Unmarked Abenaki burial grounds span the length of Monument Rd.

& **Railroad Depot Museum** (802-868-4744; www.swantonhistoricalsociety.org), 58 S. River St., Swanton. Open May–Oct., Tue.–Sat. 11–3. The first passenger train arrived here in 1863, and by the time this depot was built in 1875, the town was a transportation hub. Note the separate ladies' and men's waiting rooms and the scores of historical photos and artifacts. Put out of commission in 1968, it was the Abenaki tribal headquarters for a brief period, then slated for demolition.

But the town saved it, and it opened as a museum in 2002. Now it houses the local historical society and tells the story of the railroad's impact on the area.

🐾 ✿ ♿ **Enosburg Falls Opera House** (802-933-6171; www.enosburgopera house.org), 123 Depot St., Enosburg Falls. An 1892 structure that fell into decades of disuse until the community mustered the funds to restore it, the intimate stage is the site for year-round events, including Vermont Symphony Orchestra concerts, plays, musicals, and the annual Miss Vermont Pageant. Tickets and schedules online.

BIKING **Missisquoi Valley Rail Trail** (802-524-5958), 140 S. Main St., St. Albans. The Northwest Regional Planning Commission supervises this 26.5-mile-long trail, converted from the abandoned Central Vermont Railroad bed into a path for cross-country skiing, bike riding, hiking, snowmobiling, dogsledding, snowshoeing, and just plain strolling, but not for ATVs or dirt bikes. It leads from St. Albans to Sheldon Junction, from there to Enosburg Falls, and winds up in Richford, at the Canadian border. You can stop along the trail at **The Abbey** restaurant for lunch (or breakfast if you're a real early bird). A free map/guide shows trailside facilities.

Porter's Bike Shop (802-868-7417), 110 Grand Ave., Swanton, is a find for out-of-luck bicyclists. Pauline Porter carries an impressive array of bike parts and can salvage a doomed trek when something on the bike gets broken.

First Trax Skis, Bikes, and Boards (802-326-3073; www.firsttrax.net), Main St., Montgomery Center. Road and mountain bikes, gear, repairs, and guided tours. Ask about trail networks. Open daily (closed Tue. in summer).

CANOEING AND FISHING **Raven Ridge Canoe Rental and Guide Service** (802-933-4616; 1-888-933-4616; www.ravenridge.net), 222 Raven Ridge, Richford. Chas Salmon and Olga Lermontov provide fishing guides for bass, trout, northern pike, and walleye on Lake Champlain, and for native brook trout in mountain streams and beaver ponds. They rent kayaks and canoes (with life jackets) and shuttle you to and from the river. They also take families and groups on wildlife-viewing and photographic expeditions.

FARMS AND ORCHARDS TO VISIT 🐾 ✿ **Carman Brook Maple & Dairy Farm** (802-868-2347; 1-888-84-MAPLE; www.cbmaplefarm.com), 1275 Fortin Rd., Swanton. Daniel and Karen Fortin run a modern dairy operation that welcomes curious vacationers. Depending on the season, you can tour the cutting-edge barn, watch maple syrup being made, taste a variety of maple products, or take the 5-minute hike past the barn to the Abenaki Medicine Caves, known among the locals as the mystical spot where generations of Abenaki gathered medicinal herbs and sought cures. Gift shop, daily tours (call ahead).

West Swanton Orchards and Cider Mill (802-868-7851), Rt. 78 west, West Swanton. Open June–Nov., daily 10–5. A family-owned orchard with 11 varieties of apples, a cider mill, and a gift shop featuring Vermont products and home-made baked goods. Take a walk on the nature trail that winds through the 62 acres of trees.

GOLF Champlain Country Club (802-527-1187; www.champlaincountryclub .com), Rt. 7, 3 miles north of St. Albans. A nine-hole course built in 1915, some holes terraced. Restaurant.

Richford Country Club (802-848-3527), Golf Course Rd., Richford. A hilly, scenic nine holes, just 0.5 mile from the Canadian border. Established 1930.

Enosburg Falls Country Club (802-933-2296), Rts. 105 and 108, N. Main St., Enosburg Falls. A hilly, reasonably priced nine-hole course with friendly staff and good views from the restaurant.

✳ Green Space

St. Albans Bay State Park, 4 miles west on Rt. 36, is a good place for picnics, with several tables and grills stretched out along the waterfront, but the water is too shallow and weedy for decent swimming.

Kamp Kill Kare State Park (802-524-6021), once a fashionable summer hotel site and then, for years, a famous boys summer camp; on Point Rd. off Rt. 36, St. Albans Bay. Surrounded on three sides by the lake, it affords beautiful views and can therefore be crowded on weekends, but it's usually blissfully quiet other days; swim beach, playgrounds, boat rentals, and boat access (fee) to Burton Island.

Burton Island State Park (802-524-6353), a lovely, 250-acre island reached from Kill Kare by park boat or by your own. Facilities include 17 tent sites, 22 lean-tos, and a 100-slip marina with electrical hookups and 15 moorings. Campers' gear is transported to campsites by park vehicle. Fishing off this beautiful haven is usually excellent. Also accessible for day use; nature center, swim beach, food concession, hiking trails, boat rentals.

Lake Carmi State Park (802-527-8383), at 460 Marsh Farm Rd., Enosburg Falls. Take Exit 19 off I-89 and drive 2 miles on Rt. 104; 1.5 miles north on Rt. 105; 3 miles north on Rt. 108. Set in rolling farmlands, the 482-acre park has 177 campsites, making it the largest camping area in the state. Facilities include two cabins and 35 lean-tos, some on the beach of this sizable lake; nature trails; boat ramp and rentals. Lake Carmi is the state's fourth largest.

Woods Island State Park (802-524-6353), 2 miles north of Burton Island. Primitive camping is available on this mile-long, 0.25-mile-wide island of 125 acres. Five widely spaced campsites with no facilities are linked by a trail. The island is unstaffed, although there are daily ranger patrols; reservations for campsites must be made through Burton Island State Park (see above). There is no public transportation to the island; the best boat access is from Kill Kare.

BURTON ISLAND STATE PARK

Joe Citro

The Missisquoi National Wildlife Refuge (802-868-4781; www.fws.gov), at 371 N. River St. On the river's delta, this spectacular 6,592-acre waterfowl area lies 2 miles west of Swanton on Rt. 78 to East Alburg and the islands. Habitats are about equally divided among brushland, timberland, and marsh, through which wind Black Creek and Maquam Creek Trails, adding up to about 1.5 miles or a 2-hour ramble; both are appropriately marked for the flora and fauna represented. Hawks, marsh birds, songbirds, and great blue herons are frequent visitors, and migratory birds stop over on their voyage from northern breeding areas to wintering areas in the south. There's a boat launch (though some areas are closed to boating to protect habitat), fishing from the Missisquoi River, and blueberry picking in the bog off Tabor Rd. in July and Aug. The walking trails convert to cross-country ski use in winter; for details, get a copy of the free brochure published by the U.S. Fish and Wildlife Service. Open most of the time, but call ahead to confirm; dress in light colors and bring insect repellent if you're visiting in the hotter months.

✳ Lodging

RESORT ✎ ♿ **The Tyler Place Family Resort** (802-868-4000; 802-868-3301; www.tylerplace.com), Box 901, Rt. 7, Old Dock Rd., Highgate Springs 05460. Open late May–mid-Sep. One of the country's oldest and most popular family resorts continues to thrive on 165 acres of woods, meadows, and a mile of undeveloped lakeshore. At the height of the season it's rather like a jolly, crowded cruise ship with a lively crew. Faithful partisans have been returning year after year for three generations of the Tyler family's management. They provide just about every conceivable form of recreation for adults and children 2–17 years of age, with separate programs and dining for each group (special arrangements for infants). The children's recreation centers are exceptional. There are heated indoor and outdoor swimming and wading pools, six tennis courts, and equipment for kayaking, fishing, sailboarding, and more. Accommodations vary: You'll find the contemporary inn, plus 27 cottages, a farm, and a guest house, for a total of 66 cottages and family suites, over 40

with fireplace. Each unit has two or more bedrooms, air-conditioning, and a pantry or kitchen. The inn has a spacious dining room with good food, and a big lounge with bar. Rates are per adult: $96–299 per day for most of the season, with some packages available at either end.

FARM VACATION 🐾 ✎ **Berkson Farms** (802-933-2522; www.berkson farms.com), 1205 W. Berkshire Rd. (Rt. 108 north), Enosburg Falls 05450. A mile north of the village, this 670-acre working dairy farm along the Canadian border welcomes families year-round. The renovated, nicely maintained century-old farmhouse, managed by Sam and Lisa Hogaboom, can accommodate 8 to 10 people in four bedrooms, one of which has a private bath. There's a spacious living room and a library as well as a comfy family and game room with TV and VCR. But the main attractions, especially for kids, are the cows, ducks, sheep, goats, rabbits, and donkey, along with sugaring in-season. Cross-country skiing can be enjoyed, along with hayrides and local swimming holes, and there's golf at the nearby 18-hole Enosburg Falls Country Club. Rates are $55–75 per couple, including a full breakfast, or stay an entire week: a mere $330 ($180 for kids 2–12) includes 6 nights, and three meals a day. Well-behaved pets accepted.

BED & BREAKFASTS ∞ 🐾 ⚘ **Back Inn Time** (802-527-5116; www.back inntime.us), 68 Fairfield St., St. Albans 05478. A gorgeously furnished Victorian with sloping lawns, exquisite gardens, and four outdoor porches. Pauline Cray and Paul Ralston have spent 3 years restoring its interior to look the way it might have in the 1860s. The living room, chandeliered dining room, and library are done in sumptuous mauves, russets, and burgundies, with flowing drapes, Oriental carpets, and shining hardwood floors. Antiques abound, as do fine details, like the dark fireplace marble and intricate tiling. There are oil portraits on the walls, and British chef Cathy Crommack serves high tea in the rear tearoom with scones and clotted cream. The six guest rooms include four small ones with full-sized bed, all with shared bath, and two master bedrooms with fireplace, one with private bath. (There is also a four-bedroom lakeside cottage available June–Oct. for $950 per week, $174 per day.) Built by Victor Atwood, a railroad magnate during the Civil War, the house is only minutes from the town center. $85–150 includes a full breakfast. Candlelit dinners available with advance notice; ask about the many packages. The whole building can be rented out for weddings.

∞ ⚘ **Grey Gables Mansion** (802-848-3625; 1-800-299-2117; www .greygablesmansion.com), 122 River St., Richford 05476. A stunning, turreted mansion built around 1890 by local lumber baron Sheldon Boright, this Queen Anne Victorian is the most beautiful structure in town, with hardwood floors, period wallpapers, stained glass, beautiful gardens, a wraparound porch, and a widow's walk. Guests enter past the carved walnut-and-mahogany staircase, and can linger in the fireplaced living room or in the library. Tim and Debby Green (and their pet collie) offer five antiques-filled guest rooms, all with full bath, cable TV, and wireless Internet. Hot meals are available at the downstairs pub, and candlelit dinners are available by prearrangement. This is a terrific place for weddings or civil unions, and bikers will be interested in the Missisquoi Valley Rail Trail connecting to St. Albans. The VAST snowmobile trail passes right outside, and there are numerous packages. $99–139 includes a full breakfast.

⚘ **Country Essence B&B** (802-868-4247; http://mysite.verizon.net/ clmessier), 641 Rt. 7, Box 95, Swanton 05488, 1.5 miles north of the village on Rt. 7. Armand and Cheryl Messier provide two pretty rooms with private bath, reached by a private staircase entrance in their 1850s homestead on 12 groomed acres. There's an in-ground swimming pool and a large outdoor playground for kids. $75 per room double occupancy with country breakfast. French is spoken.

Bayview B&B (802-524-5609), 860 Hathaway Point Rd., St. Albans 05478. Located on Hathaway Point amid the colony of bayside cottages, this simple remodeled farmhouse with a nice screened-in porch has three rooms with shared bath at $55–75 per room. Continental breakfast. Weekly rates.

🐾 🏡 🦮 **Buck Hollow Farm** (802-849-2400; 1-800-849-7985; www .buckhollow.com), 2150 Buck Hollow Rd., Fairfax 05454, off Rt. 104, occupies a renovated 1790s carriage house on 400 spectacular acres. Brad Schwartz has decorated each of the four rooms (with two shared baths) with antiques, queen-sized four-poster, and TV. Guests are encouraged to use the four-person outdoor hot tub and the heated pool or browse the antiques shop; children have a play area and can ride the pony. $68–109 per room, including full country breakfast.

Tetreault's Hillside View Farm (802-827-4480), 143 South Rd., Fairfield 05455, is a warm, hospitable home in a quiet village. There's a fireplace in the family room, antiques, and braided rugs. French spoken. $60–65 per double. No pets; kids over 9 welcome.

Parent Farmhouse B&B (802-524-4201; 1-888-603-7135), 854 Pattee Hill Rd., Georgia 05468. Lucy and Roger Parent offer three rooms with shared bath at the rate of $85 for a double, $55 for a single. The 19th-century brick farmhouse is near Lake Champlain with plenty of walking and biking opportunities. No credit cards.

OTHER LODGING **Comfort Inn & Suites** (802-524-3300; 1-800-228-5150; www.vtcomfortinn.com), 813 Fairfax Rd., Rt. 104, at Exit 19 off I-89, St. Albans 05478. This new branch of the well-known chain has

81 guest rooms—several of which are suites—complimentary continental breakfast, indoor pool, and fitness room, at $89–159 with special rates for families, seniors, and business groups.

The Cadillac Motel (802-524-2191), 213 S. Main St., St. Albans 05478, is a pleasant cluster of 54 units surrounding a swimming pool, with mini golf and a coffee shop in summer. $65–80 double.

♿ **Econo Lodge** (802-524-5956; 1-800-55-ECONO; www.econolodge .com), 287 S. Main St., St. Albans 05478, has a AAA rating and the look of a B&B. $56–115 per night, with "senior-friendly" rooms available.

CAMPGROUNDS See Burton Island State Park, Lake Carmi State Park, and Woods Island State Park under *Green Space*.

Homestead Campground (802-524-2356), 864 Ethan Allen Hwy., Exit 18 off I-89 in Georgia, offers 160 shaded campsites with water and electric hookups, laundry facilities, hot showers, cabin and camper rentals, a playground, and two swimming pools. The season is May 1–Oct. 15.

✳ **Where to Eat**

Chow!Bella (802-524-1405; www .chowbella.us), 28 N. Main St., St. Albans. Open daily (except Sun.) for lunch and dinner. This intimate, sophisticated wine bar has recently doubled in size, expanding into an adjacent space and bringing its Mediterranean style and freshly prepared food along with it. The sleek, brick-walled Encore room features a long bar, low-lit booths, and extra tables. Emphasis is on steaks, pasta, and flatbread pizza baked in an open hearth. Entrées range from simple $7 pastas and pizzas to grilled portobello mushrooms stuffed with feta cheese and Middle Eastern grains ($11) or a $24 beef tenderloin filet mignon. Full bar; frequent live music.

Jeff's Maine Seafood (802-524-6135), 65 N. Main St., St. Albans, obviously began as a fish shop and deli and has expanded into an attractive restaurant with specialties like pecan-crusted salmon ($17.95) and a New York strip steak au poivre with red wine demiglaze ($21.95). A fish case displays the daily catch, which you can eat here or take out. One of the top chowder houses in the state, Jeff's is housed in a Civil War–era building with a striped awning and views on the adjacent park. Live music Sat. nights. Open daily (except Sun.) for lunch, Tue.–Sat. for dinner (daily during peak season).

♦ ⑤ **The Old Foundry Restaurant** (802-524-9665), 3 Federal St., St. Albans. Open for dinner daily except Sun. Housed in one of the city's few 1840s buildings to have escaped the town's big 1895 fire, this antique foundry is a great setting for traditional fare like charbroiled rib steak and filet mignon, fried seafood, and charbroiled salmon fillet. There's an outdoor deck in summer and a full bar.

♦ **Bayside Pavilion** (802-524-0909), 15 Georgia Shore Rd., St. Albans. A popular steak house that hums in summer, when dining moves to the outside deck with views on St. Albans Bay. Full bar, moderate prices, kids' menu, live music on Fri.

Park Cafe (802-527-0669), 84 N. Main St., St. Albans. Cappuccino, sandwiches, and baked goods, with specialty salads, signature breakfast

wraps, and pancakes. Open daily except Sun., 7–3.

♦ **McGuel's Irish Burro** (802-527-1276), 18 Lake St., St. Albans. The owners are Irish, and the food is Mexican. Prices are very reasonable: Combo platters run $8–11. Fajitas are a house specialty. The restaurant is open 11:30 AM–8 or 10 PM, depending on the day. The same menu is available in the pub.

Sweet Nothings (802-527-5118), 94 Main St., St. Albans. Open daily. Julie Ludko and Linda Carrol sell Vermont-made chocolate and candy by the pound in this gift shop and soda fountain. In the back is an ice cream parlor where you can snag a sundae, float, milk shake, or more traditional sweets, like homemade cookies, pies, and cake.

Kartula's Café & Bagel Bakery (802-524-0800), 32 S. Main St., St. Albans. Open for breakfast and lunch; closed Sun. Freshly made New York–style bagels in a sunny location, with sandwiches made to order from a long blackboard menu that includes French bread and fresh greens. Fresh pies, cakes, and specialty breads to boot. A popular local lunch spot.

Foothills Bakery (802-849-6601), 1123 Main St., Fairfax. Open daily except Sun. for breakfast and lunch. This bakery, housed in the old post office and much beloved by a local clientele, serves freshly baked muffins, scones, Danishes, cinnamon buns, and frittatas early on, then sandwiches on fat slices of homemade bread.

🍴 ♦ ⑤ **K. J.'s Diner** (802-527-7340), 51 S. Main St., St. Albans. Open daily 6 AM–9 PM. Americana in tasty, generous portions in an air-conditioned diner serving breakfast all day, plus lunch and dinner. Great salads, pasta, wraps, and BBQ. Kids' menu.

🍴 ✐ **My-T-Fine Creamery Restaurant** (802-868-4616), 159 Rt. 7, Swanton. Open daily for home-style breakfast, lunch, and dinner.

✳ Selective Shopping

As the Crow Flies (802-524-2800; www.asthecrowfliesvt.com), 58 N. Main St., St. Albans. Open weekdays and Sat., plus Sun. noon–4. A spiffy new kitchen shop in a former hardware store, with specialty foods, wines, cookbooks, gourmet-related gifts, gadgets, housewares, and sundries.

Better Planet Books, Toys & Hobbies (802-524-6835), 44 N. Main St., St. Albans, is a bright place for books, toys, games, puzzles, hobby kits, and art supplies.

The Eloquent Page (802-527-PAGE), 23 Catherine St., a block west of Rt. 7 in downtown St. Albans. Donna Howard stocks over 35,000 used and collectible books, with a big section on Vermont and a wide variety of doll, dollhouse, and children's titles.

BEC Enterprises (802-849-2706), 148 Main St. (Rt. 104), Fairfax. Open May–Oct., 10–4:30, Sun. noon–5. A huge 1850 barn loaded with vintage kitchenware, dishes, glassware, and everything imaginable. Upstairs, Bridget Morgan presides over a surprisingly good collection of vintage books, academic and otherwise, at terrific prices, though a bit musty (the barn is not heated in winter).

Richford Antique and Craft Center (802-848-3836), 66 Main St., Richford. Open daily 10–5. Twenty rooms filled with antiques, crafts, and collectibles, plus Vermont folk art and vintage clothing.

✳ Special Events

✐ *Late April:* **Maple Festival**, St. Albans (802-524-5800; www.vt maplefestival.org). For 3 days the town turns into a nearly nonstop "sugarin' off" party, courtesy of the local maple producers, augmented by a parade, crafts and antiques shows, a pancake breakfast, specialty food show and sale, footrace, and other events.

Late May: **Abenaki Heritage Celebration** (802-868-2559), on the green, Swanton—a powwow with costumed dancing, Native music, foods, books, and crafts.

✐ *First weekend in June:* **Vermont Dairy Festival** (802-933-8891), Enosburg Falls. Milking contest, baking contest, midway rides, cow plop contest, crafts fair, horse pulling, animal barn, and more.

✐ *Early August:* **Franklin County Field Days** (802-868-2514), Airport Rd., Highgate. Classic old-time country fair with cattle exhibits, crafts fair, games, rides, musical entertainment, tractor and horse pulls, cattle judging, draft horse show, and ox pulling.

Mid-September: **Civil War Days** (802-524-2444), St. Albans. A lively weekend of encampments at Taylor Park, a tour of an Underground Railroad home, echoes of the 1864 Confederate Raid, parade, barbecue, music, and a crafts show.

Stowe Area and North of the Notch

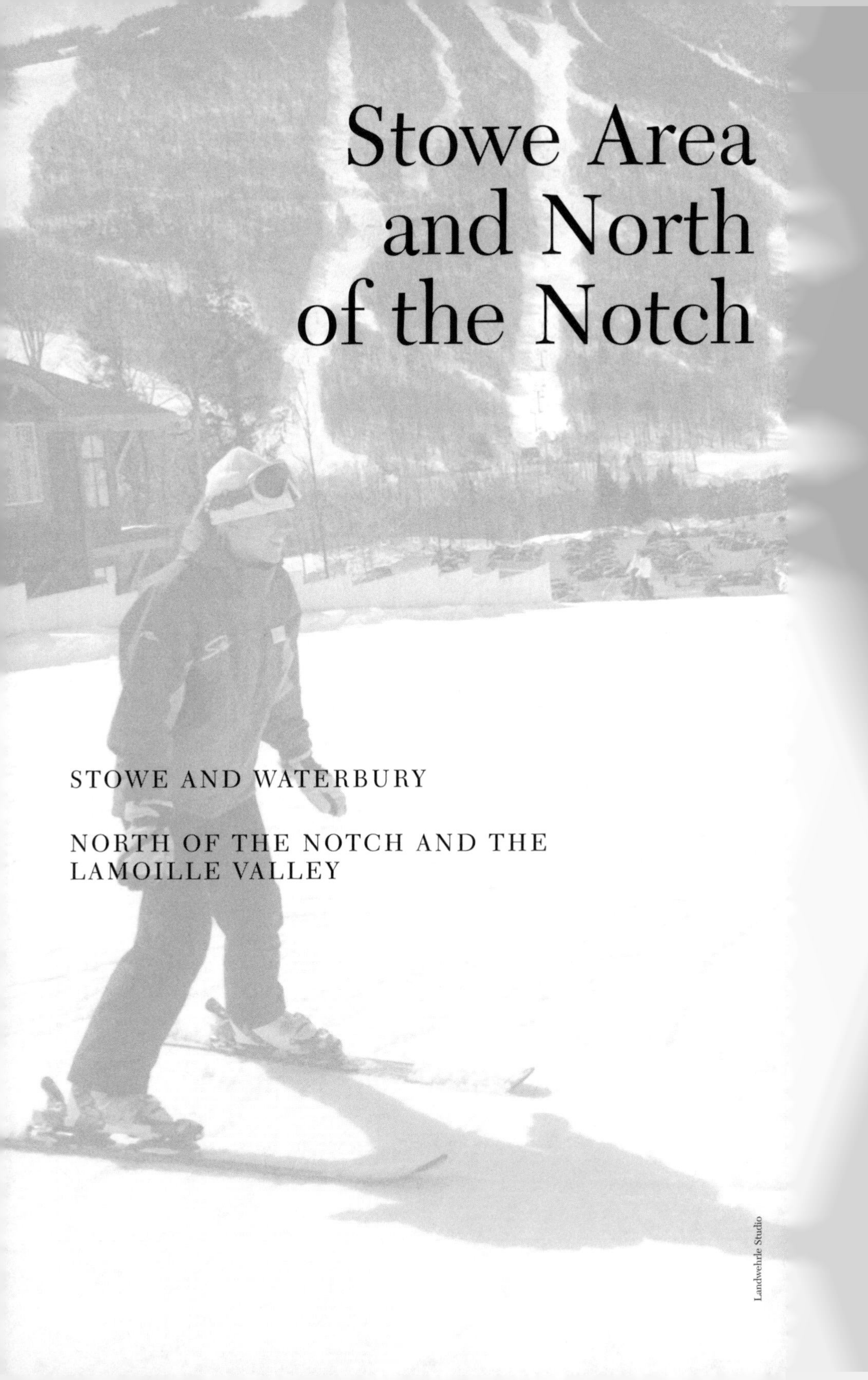

STOWE AND WATERBURY

NORTH OF THE NOTCH AND THE
LAMOILLE VALLEY

Landwehrle Studio

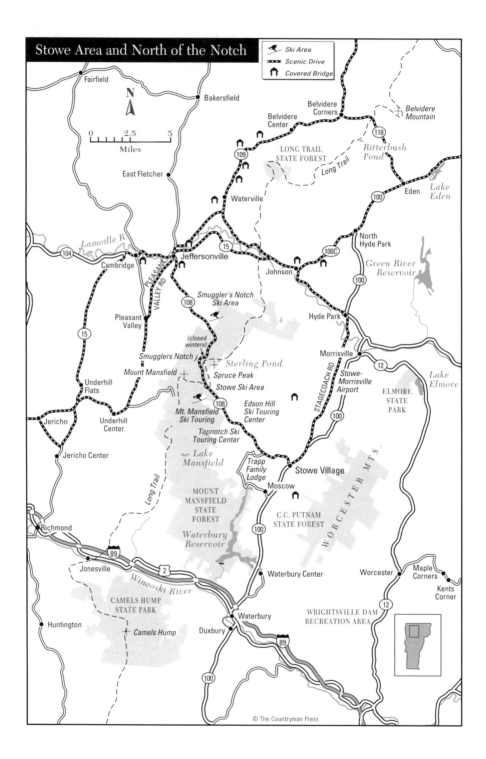

Stowe Area and North of the Notch

Legend:
- Ski Area
- Scenic Drive
- Covered Bridge

N

0 — 2.5 — 5
Miles

Fairfield

Bakersfield

Belvidere Corners

Belvidere Center

Belvidere Mountain

118

East Fletcher

LONG TRAIL STATE FOREST

Long Trail

Ritterbush Pond

Waterville

109

100

Eden

Lake Eden

Lamoille R.

104

Cambridge

Jeffersonville

15

Johnson

100C

North Hyde Park

100

Green River Reservoir

PLEASANT VALLEY RD

Pleasant Valley

108

Smuggler's Notch Ski Area

Hyde Park

15

(closed winters)

Sterling Pond

Morrisville

12

Lake Elmore

Underhill Flats

Smugglers Notch

Mount Mansfield

Spruce Peak

Stowe Ski Area

Stowe-Morrisville Airport

ELMORE STATE PARK

Jericho

Underhill Center

108

Mt. Mansfield Ski Touring

Edson Hill Ski Touring Center

STAGECOACH RD

100

Jericho Center

Topnotch Ski Touring Center

Lake Mansfield

Long Trail

Trapp Family Lodge

Stowe Village

Moscow

W O R C E S T E R   M T S.

MOUNT MANSFIELD STATE FOREST

C.C. PUTNAM STATE FOREST

Richmond

89

Waterbury Reservoir

100

Jonesville

2

Winooski River

Waterbury Center

Worcester

Maple Corners

Kents Corner

12

CAMELS HUMP STATE PARK

WRIGHTSVILLE DAM RECREATION AREA

Huntington

Camels Hump

Duxbury

Waterbury

89

100

STOWE AND WATERBURY

K nown as the "ski capital of the East," Stowe is the state's premier summer resort as well. A 200-year-old village that looks like a classic Vermont village should look, it's set against the massive backdrop of Mount Mansfield, which looks just like Vermont's highest mountain should look.

By the mid–19th century, men were already taxing their imaginations and funds to entice visitors up onto the heights of Mount Mansfield—which bears an uncanny resemblance to the upturned profile of a rather jowly man. In 1858 an inn was built under the Nose, a project that entailed constructing a 100-yard log trestle above a chasm and several miles of corduroy road made from hemlock. In Stowe Village at that time, a hotel, the Mansfield House, accommodated 600 guests.

Swedish families moved into Stowe in 1912 and began using their skis to get around. Then, in 1914, the Dartmouth College librarian skied down the Toll Road. Serious skiing, however, didn't begin until 1933, when the Civilian Conservation Corps cut a 4-mile-plus trail for just that purpose. The following year the town formed its own Mount Mansfield Ski Club, setting up basic lodging near the bottom of the ski trail in a former logging camp. By 1937 a rope tow had been rigged from the camp to the top of the trail, powered by a Cadillac engine. Lift tickets cost 50¢ per day, $5 per season.

While its name keeps changing, the Stowe Mountain Resort Company is still the same outfit formed in 1951 from the various small concerns that had evolved in the 1930s and '40s to serve skiers, and it's still owned by the same insurance company, AIG (American International Group). The good news is continuity and an immense sense of pride and history. Sometimes slow to respond to the demands of this quickly changing industry, the company has become much more aggressive over the past decade with its building and expansion plans.

What the "Mountain Company" does, it always does first-class. Just as it was a Cadillac engine (not the Ford used in Woodstock) that first hauled Stowe skiers, the eight-passenger gondola, installed in 1991, is one of the world's fastest, and the Cliff House in the summit Octagon offers meals with spectacular alpine views. On the other hand, a small '50s base lodge, expanded and renovated a couple of times, still serves the mountain's primary trail network—although not for long.

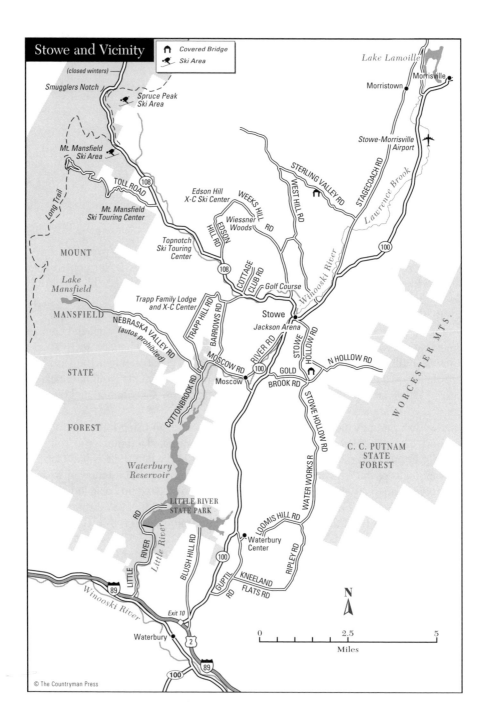

Stowe and Vicinity

Covered Bridge
Ski Area

Lake Lamoille

Morrisville

Morristown

(closed winters)

Smugglers Notch

Spruce Peak
Ski Area

Stowe-Morrisville
Airport

Mt. Mansfield
Ski Area

STERLING VALLEY RD

STAGECOACH RD

Long Trail

TOLL ROAD

108

Edson Hill
X-C Ski Center

WEEKS HILL RD

WEST HILL RD

Lawrence Brook

100

Mt. Mansfield
Ski Touring Center

Wiessner
Woods

EDSON HILL RD

MOUNT

Topnotch
Ski Touring
Center

108

COTTAGE CLUB RD

Golf Course

Winooski River

*Lake
Mansfield*

MANSFIELD

Trapp Family Lodge
and X-C Center

TRAPP HILL RD

BARROWS RD

Stowe

Jackson Arena

RIVER RD

NEBRASKA VALLEY RD
(autos prohibited)

STOWE HOLLOW RD

N HOLLOW RD

STATE

MOSCOW RD

100

GOLD BROOK RD

W O R C E S T E R   M T S.

Moscow

COTTONBROOK RD

FOREST

WATER WORKS R.

STOWE HOLLOW RD

C. C. PUTNAM
STATE
FOREST

*Waterbury
Reservoir*

LITTLE RIVER
STATE PARK

RD

LOOMIS HILL RD

Little River

BLUSH HILL RD

Waterbury
Center

RIPLEY RD

LITTLE RIVER RD

100

GUPTIL RD

KNEELAND FLATS RD

N

Winooski River

89

Exit 10

0   2.5   5

Miles

Waterbury

2

100   89

© The Countryman Press

The Mountain Company in recent years has been focusing on its most basic need: water. In the '90s it became painfully clear that natural snow in northern New England is too fickle a base for the huge business that skiing has become. Ski operators and skiers alike are not about to invest big bucks unless they can depend on snow, and to make snow, you need water.

So Stowe has come up with a Master Plan. It involves digging special ponds for snowmaking, and creating a 35-acre slope-side village at Spruce Peak, a smaller mountain just across Rt. 108 from Mount Mansfield. Some 440 housing units are slated to go in, as well as a new Spruce base lodge, an 18-hole golf course, a conference center, and a hotel, all with a spiffier, more upscale image. The 10-year, $300 million project even envisions an aerial transfer lift that skiers can take (starting in 2007) between Mansfield and Spruce without having to remove their skis. Skiing at Spruce Peak has already improved with a newly installed high-speed lift to the summit, the widening of the top-to-bottom Main Street trail, and a newly automated snowmaking system. Also in the works are plans to expand the Mansfield base lodge, add two new lifts, and enlarge the Inn at the Mountain. All is to be accomplished by 2014.

In the meantime the quality of alpine skiing and snowboarding at Stowe continues to be outstanding. The cross-country ski network of more than 150 km is the largest in the East, popular in large part because of its elevation: Many trails meander off the high walls of the cul-de-sac in which the resort nestles, and you can usually count on snow on many miles of trail through April.

Stowe actually now attracts more visitors in summer and fall than it does in winter. From June through mid-October it offers a superb golf course, tennis courts, theater, an alpine slide, and gondola rides to the top of the mountain, as well as hiking, biking, fishing, and special events every week of summer and fall. Year-round it boasts more than 2,200 rooms, accommodating a total of 7,500 visitors on any given night. There are also more than 50 restaurants and 100 or so shops.

What's most amazing about Stowe is the way it has managed to keep its commercial side low-key and tasteful, a sideshow to the natural beauty of the place. Even in nonskiing months, most visitors are lured from their cars and onto their feet and bicycles, thanks to the 5.5-mile Stowe Recreation Path, which parallels the Mountain Road from the village (albeit at a more forgiving grade) to Mount Mansfield, through cornfields, wildflowers, and raspberry patches.

In warm-weather months Stowe is also an excellent pivot from which to explore northern Vermont: 30 miles from Burlington, just over the Notch from the little-touristed Lamoille Valley, and a short drive from both Montpelier and Barre on the one hand and the Northeast Kingdom on the other. Lodging options range from funky to fabulous, including a number of self-contained resorts as well as inns, lodges, motels, and condominiums. The Stowe Area Association has been in business since 1936, matching visitors with lodgings they can afford and enjoy.

Most Stowe-bound visitors know Waterbury, 10 miles down Rt. 100, simply as an I-89 exit; they know the strip just to the north as the home of Ben & Jerry's ice cream factory, one of the state's most popular attractions. The old town itself lies along a southward bend in the Winooski River, and several interesting shops and restaurants are housed in the brief downtown between the traffic light and the railroad station. Waterbury Reservoir, accessible from Waterbury Center, is the obvious place in this area to swim and paddle a canoe or kayak.

GUIDANCE **The Stowe Area Association** (802-253-7321; 1-877-247-8693; www .gostowe.com), Box 1320, 51 Main St., Stowe 05672. Open daily Nov.–Mar., 9–8; the rest of the year 9–5. This service, housed in its own building in the middle of Stowe Village, provides information on more than 60 local lodging places and will make reservations; it also publishes seasonal guides listing most things in the area and is a walk-in source of advice about what's going on.

GETTING THERE *By bus:* **Vermont Transit/Greyhound** (1-800-552-8737) stops in Montpelier with connections from Boston, New York, and points south.

By train: **Amtrak** from Washington, DC; New York City; and Springfield, Mass., stops in Waterbury.

By plane: The **Stowe-Morrisville Airport**, 7 miles north, provides private plane services and charters. **Burlington International Airport**, 34 miles away, is served by major carriers (see "Burlington Region").

By taxi: **Peg's Pickup/Stowe Taxi** (1-800-370-9490).

By car: From most points, I-89 Exit 10, and 15 minutes north on Rt. 100.

GETTING AROUND During winter season the municipally owned **Stowe Trolley** (802-253-9200; www.gmtaride.org) circles the 7 miles between the village and the mountain every 30 minutes, 8 AM–10 PM. Pick up a schedule. Trolley tokens are $1, and 1-week passes cost $10. Tue. and Thu. shopping runs to Morrisville are also offered; in summer trolley tours run every day, leaving the town office at 11 AM and lasting 75 minutes. **Mountain View Tours** (802-635-2022; 1-888-564-7111) offers private, personalized excursions of the area for any size group.

MEDICAL EMERGENCY Emergency service is available by calling **911**.

Copley Hospital (802-888-4231), Morrisville.

✳ To See

Mount Mansfield (802-253-3500), the highest point in Vermont—4,395 feet (it gained 2 feet when it was remeasured in 1998) at the Chin—yields a truly spectacular view, accessible primarily in summer, unless you can clamber up to the summit from the Cliff House restaurant at the top of the gondola over ice and snow. In summer there are two easy ways up: the Toll Road and an eight-passenger gondola.

The Toll Road (802-253-3000) begins 7 miles up Rt. 108 from the village of Stowe; look for the sign on your left just before the Inn at the Mountain. Open late May–mid-Oct., weather permitting, 10–5. $20 per car in 2006, raised annually. Motorcycles are no longer permitted; bikes and hikers are free. First laid in the mid–19th century, this steep, winding road led to a hotel that served the public until 1957. (It was demolished in the mid-1960s.) The road also serves as a ski trail in winter. It terminates at the Mount Mansfield Summit Station, just below the Nose (4,062 feet). A 0.5-mile Tundra Trail follows the Long Trail (red-and-white blazes on the rocks) north to Drift Rock (the trek should take 20 minutes); another mile along the trail brings you to the summit of Mount Mansfield (round-trip: 2 hours).

The gondola (802-253-3000) at Stowe operates mid-June–mid-Oct. at Mount Mansfield, weather permitting, 10–5. $17 adults, $9 ages 6–12, $12 ages 65 and older; $39 for a family of four round-trip. The eight-passenger gondola runs from Midway Lodge to the Cliff House; a half hour's trek brings you up to the Chin. However you get there, the view from the summit (the Chin) is spectacular on a clear day: west across 20 miles of farmland to Lake Champlain; east to the Worcester Range across the Stowe Valley; north to Jay Peak (35 miles distant) across the Lamoille Valley; and south, back along the Green Mountains, to Camels Hump. Mount Washington is visible to the east, Whiteface to the west. Be sure to catch the 5 PM gondola unless you fancy a long walk down.

Stowe Village. A classic, early-19th-century Vermont village with a spired white meetinghouse at one end of Main Street and a brick stagecoach inn at the other, Stowe offers a satisfying variety of stores and restaurants all within an easy stroll. The former wooden high school (one block up School St. from Main) is now the **Helen Day Art Center** (802-253-8358; www.helenday.com), open in summer daily noon–5 except Mon., closed Sun. too in winter. The changing art exhibits are frequently well worth checking out ($3 per adult, $1 seniors, and 50¢ students). The mid-19th-century Bloody Brook Schoolhouse museum next door is open on request in summer months.

Smugglers Notch is the high (elevation: 2,162 feet), extremely winding and narrow stretch of Rt. 108 just north of Mount Mansfield, with 1,000-foot cliffs towering on either side. The first carriage road through this pass wasn't opened until 1894, but the name reflects its heavy use as a route to smuggle cattle down from Canada during the War of 1812, not to mention hooch during Prohibition. One of two formally designated State Scenic Roads in Vermont, Smugglers Notch is known for rock formations: Smugglers Head, Elephant Head, the Hunter and His Dog, the Big Spring, Smugglers Cave, and the Natural Refrigerator. The Notch is closed in winter, inviting cross-country skiing and snowshoeing. See also *To See* in "North of the Notch."

Vermont Ski Museum (802-253-9911; www.vermontskimuseum.org), Old Town Hall, 1 S. Main St., Stowe. See the actual lifts that carried the first skiers up the Vermont mountains and the ski equipment they used to come down. Discover how dozens of tiny ski areas grew into the handful of mega resorts that dominate the industry today. Watch old ski movies and vintage ski footage on a giant plasma screen. The museum shop sells ski-related gifts. Closed Tue. except during holidays. Admission by donation.

Ben & Jerry's Ice Cream Factory Tours (802-882-1260; 1-866-BJ-TOURS; www.benjerry.com), Rt. 100 (take Exit 10 off I-89 and go north 1 mile), Waterbury. No American ice cream has a story, let alone a taste, to match that of the totally Vermont-made sweet and creamy stuff concocted by high school buddies Ben

Cohen and Jerry Greenfield, whose personalities linger though they have sold the company to Unilever. More than two decades ago they began churning out Dastardly Mash and Heath Bar Crunch in a Burlington garage; they have now outgrown this seemingly mammoth plant, which has outstripped the Shelburne Museum as Vermont's number one attraction. A half-hour tour of the plant is offered all year, daily 10–5 (9–8 in July and Aug.). The gift store, selling an amazing number of things relating to cows and Vermont, is open 10–6, as is the Scoop Shop. The tour includes a multimedia show, a look (from an observation platform) at the production room, and a free sample of one of the many "euphoric flavors." The grounds include picnic facilities and some sample black-and-white cows. $3 adults, $2 seniors, ages 12 and under free.

COVERED BRIDGES The **Gold Brook Bridge** in Stowe Hollow, also known as Emily's Bridge because Emily is said to have hanged herself from it (due, so the story goes, to unrequited love), remains the most haunted structure in the state (take School St. about 8 miles to Covered Bridge Rd.). There is another picturesque bridge spanning Sterling Brook off Stagecoach Rd., north of the village.

SCENIC DRIVES Not only is Stowe pleasantly situated for touring in all directions, but it is also organized to offer visitors well-researched printed tours. Pick up a copy of *Roads and Tours* from the **Stowe Area Association** (see *Guidance*). A summer drive through Smugglers Notch is a must.

✳ To Do

AIR RIDES For **hot-air ballooning**, inquire at Stoweflake Mountain Resort and Spa (802-253-7355; www.stoweflake.com). Whitcomb Aviation's Stowe Soaring, based at the Stowe-Morrisville State Airport (802-888-7845; 1-800-898-7845), offers **glider rides**, instruction, and rentals.

ALPINE SLIDE **Stowe's alpine slide** (802-253-3000) is accessed from the Spruce Peak Base Lodge, Mountain Rd., Stowe. Open late June–early Sep., 10–5, then on weekends through Columbus Day. $14 adults, $10 juniors and seniors; discounts for multiple-ride packages.

BIKING The equipage here is a mountain bike, and the rental sources are **AJ's Ski & Sports** (802-253-4593; 1-800-226-6257; www.ajsports.com), **Pinnacle Ski & Sports** (802-253-7222; 1-800-458-9996; www.pinnacleskisports.com), **Boots 'N Boards** (802-253-4225), the **Nordic Barn** (802-253-6433), and **Skier Shop** (802-253-7919; 1-800-996-8398; www.skiershop.com) in Stowe. Neophytes usually head for the 5.5-mile **Stowe Recreation Path** (see *Hiking and Walking*); next there's a 10-mile loop through part of the Mount Mansfield State Forest and into the Cottonbrook Basin. **Green Mountain Bike Tours** (802-279-1619) and the **Inn at Turner Mill** (802-253-2062), on Mountain Rd., offer mountain biking tours. Pick up a copy of *Northern Vermont—Mountain Biking* published by Map Adventures of Portland, Maine (207-879-4777; www.mapadventures .com); it maps and describes over 30 local mountain bike trail and road rides.

BOATING Canoes and kayaks can be rented from **AJ's Ski & Sports** (802-253-4593; www.ajsports.com) and **Umiak Outfitters** (802-253-2317; www.umiak .com), Stowe. Umiak also offers river trips, lessons, and guided trips on the Winooski and Lamoille Rivers, on Lake Champlain, and throughout the state.

CAMPING **Little River Camping Areas** (802-244-7103; 1-800-658-6934 off-season reservations), 3444 Little River Rd., Waterbury 05676. Six miles north of Waterbury on the 830-acre Waterbury Reservoir: 81 tent and trailer campsites, including 20 lean-tos, plus swimming beaches, playgrounds, boat launch, boat rentals, ball field, nature museum, hiking, and snowmobile trails in Little River State Park.

See also *Green Space* for information on camping in Smugglers Notch and Elmore State Parks.

CARRIAGE RIDES **Edson Hill Manor**, **Golden Eagle Resort**, and **Stowehof Inn** in Stowe all offer carriage rides. **Gentle Giants Sleigh, Carriage, and Wagon Rides at Topnotch** (802-253-2216) in Stowe offers carriage and wagon rides, as does the **Trapp Family Lodge** (802-353-5813).

FISHING The Little River in Stowe is a favorite for brook trout, along with Sterling Pond on top of Spruce Peak and Sterling Brook. Contact **Reel Vermont** (802-223-1869; www.reelvt.com), geared to guiding everyone (families included) from neophytes to pros. **Catamount Fishing Adventures** (802-253-8500; www .catamountfishing.com), run by Willy Dietrich, is located in Stowe. It offers year-round guide service, including ice fishing. **Fly Fish Vermont** (802-253-3964; 1-800-535-9763; www.flyrodshop.com) is another Stowe resource.

The **Fly Rod Shop** (802-253-7346; www.flyrodshop.com), 2703 Waterbury Rd. (Rt. 100), Stowe, carries a full line of gear and offers full- and half-day guided tours.

FLEA MARKETS **The Waterbury Flea Market** (802-244-5916), the biggest in northern Vermont, rolls out its tables every weekend May–Oct., 7–7 (weather permitting), on a grassy, 10-acre roadside spot on Rt. 2 just north of the village (Exit 10W off I-89). Concession stand. The **Charlotte Flea Market** (802-425-2844) is smaller but equally interesting; on weekends, 6 AM–5 PM, Apr.–Oct. The **Stowe Farmers' Market** sells fresh produce and local wares all summer next to the Red Barn Shops on Mountain Rd., weekends 11–3.

GOLF **Stowe Country Club** (802-253-4893; www.stowe.com), an 18-hole course with a 40-acre driving range, putting green, restaurant, bar, pro shop, and school. **Stoweflake Mountain Resort and Spa** (802-253-7355; www.stoweflake.com), adjacent to the Stowe Country Club, also offers instruction. The **Farm Resort** (802-888-3525; 1-866-888-5810; www.farmresortlodging.com), Rt. 100, 6 miles north of Stowe in Morrisville, offers nine holes, a driving range, putting green, rentals, and snack bar. **The Players Club** (802-253-2800) at 4000 Mountain Rd. is a year-round golf and indoor training facility.

Blush Hill Country Club (802-244-8974), a nine-hole course in Waterbury, has marvelous views.

Country Club of Vermont (802-244-1800), Waterbury. This 18-hole course gets rave reviews.

HIKING AND WALKING Green Mountain Club (GMC) (802-244-7037; www .greenmountainclub.org), a few miles south of Stowe Village on Rt. 100 in Waterbury Center, maintains a Hiker's Center stocked with hiking maps, guides, and gear. Inquire about workshops and special events.

Stowe Recreation Path is a 5.5-mile paved path that begins in Stowe Village behind the Community Church, winds up through cornfields, wildflowers, and raspberry patches, and parallels Mountain Rd. (but at a more forgiving pitch). It's open to walkers, joggers, bicyclists, and more. Note the **Quiet Path** along the Mayo River, a mile loop off the main path (it begins across from the Golden Eagle) reserved for walkers (no mountain bikers or in-line skaters).

Mount Mansfield. See the introduction to this section and *To See* for a general description of Vermont's highest mountain. For walkers (as opposed to hikers), it's best to take the Toll Road or gondola up and follow the Tundra Trail. Serious hikers should at least purchase the weatherproof map of the Mount Mansfield region and can profit from the *Long Trail Guide*, both published by the Green Mountain Club. A naturalist is on hand May–Nov. along the heavily traveled, 2.5-mile section of the Long Trail between the Forehead and the Chin; the Green Mountain Club maintains Butler Lodge, 0.5 mile south of the Forehead, and Taft Lodge, below the Chin, as shelters for hikers.

Smugglers Notch. The Long Trail North, clearly marked, provides an easy, mile-plus hike to Sterling Pond, a beautiful spot at 3,000 feet, and fish-stocked, too. Elephant Head can be reached from the state picnic area on Rt. 108; a 2-mile trail leads to this landmark—from which you can also continue on to Sterling Pond and thence out to Rt. 108 only a couple of miles above the picnic area. No one should drive through Smugglers Notch without stopping to see the Smugglers Cave and to clamber around on the rocks.

Other local hikes are detailed in *Day Hiker's Guide to Vermont*, which is published by the Green Mountain Club and available from the Stowe Area Association: **Stowe Pinnacle** is a popular 2.8-mile climb; **Mount Hunger** (4 miles) is the highest peak in the Worcester Range; **Taft Lodge** (3.4 miles) is steep but takes you to the oldest lodge on the Long Trail; **Belvidere Mountain** in Eden is a 3½-hour trek yielding good views in all directions; **Ritterbush Pond** and **Devil's Gulch**, also in Eden, are about 2½ hours round-trip; and **Elmore Mountain** in Elmore State Park is a 2- to 3-hour hike with spectacular views.

Camels Hump, from Waterbury. See "Burlington Region" for details. This trail is also detailed in *50 Hikes in Vermont* (Backcountry Publications). One trail starts from Crouching Lion Farm in Duxbury; it's a 6½-hour round-trip hike to the unspoiled summit of Vermont's third highest mountain. Pick up a map at the GMC Hiker's Center (see above).

Little River Trail System, Mount Mansfield State Forest, Waterbury. There are seven beautiful trails through the Ricker Basin and Cotton Brook area, once a settlement for 50 families who left behind cellar holes, stone fences, cemeteries, lilacs, and apple trees. Accessible from both Stowe and Waterbury. Pick up the self-guiding booklet from the Vermont State Department of Forests, Parks and Recreation in Waterbury (802-241-3678).

See also "Barre/Montpelier Area" for hiking in the Worcester Range.

Note: Northern Vermont—Hiking Trails, published by Map Adventures of Portland, Maine (207-879-4777; www.mapadventures.com), is worth picking up.

HORSEBACK RIDING **Nordic Barn Riding Stables** (802-253-6433) and **Topnotch Resort** (802-253-8585), Mountain Rd., Stowe, offer trail rides and lessons. **Edson Hill Manor Stables** (802-253-8954), Stowe, gives guided trail rides. Also **Peterson Brook Farm** (802-253-9052), in Stowe. **Windy Willows Farm** (802-635-7300) and **Vermont Icelandic Horse Farm** (802-496-7141) offer trail rides all year long.

IN-LINE SKATING **Stowe-in-Line Skate Park** (802-253-3000) at the base of Spruce Peak was the nation's first, and includes a speed oval, a half-pipe, freestyle ramps, and a timed downhill slalom course. Rentals available.

ROCK CLIMBING Check with **Umiak Outfitters** (802-253-2317) in Stowe for instruction and ropes course.

SWIMMING **Waterbury Reservoir**, the best local beach, is accessible from Little River State Park (see *Camping*). **Forest Pool** on Notchbrook Rd., **Sterling Falls**, and the swimming holes in **Ranch Valley** are all worth checking; ask locally for directions. The nonprofit community pool is **The Swimming Hole** (802-253-9119), featuring a competition-sized pool in a barn with a toddler and child swimming area. Many lodging places also have their own pools that nonguests may use for a fee.

TENNIS **The Topnotch Tennis Center** (802-253-9649), Stowe. Four indoor and six outdoor courts, pro shop, instruction, ball machines, videotape, round robins; open daily (hours vary).

Inn at the Mountain Tennis Club at the **Stowe Mountain Resort** (802-253-7311), six well-maintained clay courts adjacent to the Inn at the Mountain, 8–6, available by the hour (dress: whites required).

Free public courts can be found at the town recreation area off School St. A number of inns have courts available to the public; inquire at the Stowe Area Association (802-253-7321).

✸ Winter Sports

CROSS-COUNTRY SKIING A 150 km network of trails that connects ski centers in this area adds up to some of the best ski touring in New England. Given the high elevation of much of this terrain, the trails tend to have snow when few other areas do, and on windy, icy days, cross-country can be better in Stowe than downhill. All four touring centers (in Stowe) honor the others' trail tickets (if you ski, not drive, from one to the next).

Trapp Family Lodge Cross-Country Ski Center (802-253-8511). Located on Trapp Hill Rd., off by itself in the upper reaches of the valley, this is one of the oldest and most beautiful commercial trail systems—40 km of set trails and a total of 85 km of trails at elevations of 1,100–3,000 feet. The basic route here is up and up to a cabin in the woods, a source of homemade soups and chili. Start early enough in the day and you can continue along ridge trails or connect with the Mount Mansfield system. Lessons, equipment rental and sales, and outstanding pastries are all available, as well as guided tours.

Stowe Mountain Resort Cross-Country Center (802-253-3688), Mountain Rd. Located near the Inn at the Mountain, this center offers 35 km of set trails, plus 45 km of backcountry trails, at elevations of 1,200–2,800 feet. Trail fees are $16 adults, $9 for juniors and seniors. It's possible to take the Toll House lift partway up the Toll Road and ski down (a good place to practice telemarking). You can also take the quad close enough to the summit to enable you to climb to the very top (via the Toll Road) for a spectacular view out across Lake Champlain; the descent via the Toll Road is relatively easy. Another beautiful trail circles Sterling Pond high in the saddle between Spruce and Madonna Mountains (accessible via chairlift). Connecting trails link this system with the Trapp Family Lodge trails (see above) along some of Stowe's oldest ski trails, such as Ranch Camp and Steeple, dating to the 1920s, as well as new backcountry trails winding along the curved inner face of the mountain.

Edson Hill Ski Touring Center (802-253-7371), Edson Hill Rd. Relatively uncrowded on the uplands north of the Mountain Rd., the area offers 30 miles of set trails, 25 more on outlying trails at elevations between 1,200 and 2,150 feet; instruction, rental, sales, full lunches, and guided tours available.

Topnotch Touring Center (802-253-8585), Mountain Rd., Stowe. Novice to expert, a total of 20 km of groomed trails on 120 private acres; instruction, equipment rental, café, and restaurant available, also changing rooms.

Backcountry tours are offered by the **Stowe Mountain Resort** (802-253-3688) and **Trapp Family Lodge** (802-253-8511).

Remember: Backcountry skiing is best done with a guide if you don't know the area.

DOWNHILL SKIING ♂ **Stowe Mountain Resort** (1-800-253-4SKI; www.stowe .com for information, snow reports, and slope-side lodging). Big changes are afoot on the mountain. A 2005 makeover has brought long-awaited improvements to Stowe's two neighboring peaks. Mount Mansfield, whose famous Front Four trails plunge almost vertically down its legendary face, has a quad and double to get you to the top (wear a neck warmer, goggles, and sunscreen). Under the Octagon Café, these expert slopes feature tree-shaded glades and some of the longest trails in the East, though you also have the option of half a dozen intermediate trails that snake down at more forgiving angles. It's an easy traverse from this side of the mountain to the trails served by the eight-person, high-speed gondola to the elevated Cliff House, from which long, ego-building runs like Perry Merrill sweep to the valley floor. The daredevil set gravitates to the Mansfield Triple, with its two new terrain parks, superpipe, and freestyle. Those seeking something tamer can head for the southern-facing Toll House, a double chair with a slow, easy descent through tranquil hardwoods.

Stowe regulars ski Mount Mansfield in the morning, switching after lunch to south-facing Spruce Peak across Rt. 108. It's there, at what the resort calls Mount Mansfield's "mellow sister," that the biggest changes are under way. Spruce Peak has gained a high-speed quad, a new beginner slope, and New England's first fully automated snowmaking system to keep the slopes dusted top to bottom. Extensive trail work has opened up little-explored backcountry stretches, while the central Main Street trail has been widened and contoured for easier navigation. The Children's Adventure Center, connected by free shuttles every 10 minutes, serves as home to the Ski and Snowboard School and children's programs, and lifts access extensive novice trails. All told, about a fifth of Stowe's nearly 50 (predominantly intermediate-level) trails have been refurbished. A $300 million revitalization will soon transform Spruce's base area into a modern, self-contained community, Spruce Peak at Stowe. A decade in the planning, it will include a posh lodge, an 18-hole golf course, a performing arts center, a skating rink, a five-star hotel and spa, a sprinkling of upscale restaurants and shops, and a slew of private homes and condos, many of which are already sold.

With more people on the slopes year-round, expect more activity here in summer months. Besides the golf course and tennis courts, you can ride the lift to the top of Spruce Peak and climb into the alpine slide, a concrete channel that whisks you 2,300 feet down the mountainside. The new Stowe Climbing Wall offers challenges to a variety of expertise levels, and Bungee Trampolines harness you up for a spectacular bounce. But don't leave without taking a gondola ride; the whole area—peaks, valleys, and fields—opens up before you. Alternatively, you can drive your own car up the 4.5-mile Toll Road, park, and clamber around the summit; hiking paths connect to the Long Trail.

Lifts: 8-passenger gondola, 3 high-speed quad chairlifts, 4 double and 2 triple chairlifts, 2 surface.

Trails: 48, also glade skiing; 25 percent expert, 59 percent intermediate, 16 percent beginner.

Vertical drop: 2,360 feet on Mount Mansfield, 1,550 feet on Spruce Peak.

Snowmaking: Covers 80 percent of the terrain trails served by all of the 12 lifts.

Facilities: 8 restaurants, including those in the Inn at the Mountain, 3 base lodges, plus the Octagon Café & Gallery (you can send free e-mail postcards) and the newly renovated Cliff House at the top of the busiest lifts; cafeterias, rentals, ski shops, shuttle bus.

Ski school: 200 instructors; a lift especially designed for beginners at Spruce Peak, where novices learn to make the transition from easy to intermediate trails.

Night skiing: More than 20 acres on Mount Mansfield are lighted Thu.–Sat. nights 5–9.

For children: Day care from 6 weeks in Cubs Infant Daycare. The Children's Learning Center offers day care or a combo of care and lessons at Spruce Peak.

Rates: Go to www.stowe.com for current ticket prices.

(*Note:* For downhill skiing at **Smugglers' Notch**, see "North of the Notch"; it is possible to ski back and forth between the two areas when the Spruce Chair is operating.)

ICE CLIMBING The **Inn at Turner Mill** (802-253-2062) offers information about ice-climbing expeditions, and the owner himself is an avid climber. Smugglers Notch is a favorite ice-climbing spot.

Landwehrle Studio

SKIING AT THE MAIN MOUNTAIN, STOWE

ICE SKATING Ice skating is available at the Olympic-sized **Jackson Arena** (802-253-6148) in the village. Call for public skating times. There's also skating on the pond at **Commodores Inn** (802-253-7131). The town of Waterbury has a large new skating arena called the **Ice Center** (802-244-4040).

SLEIGH RIDES In Stowe sleigh rides are found at **Stoweflake Resort** (802-253-7355), **Edson Hill Manor** (802-253-7371, not Tue. or Thu.), and **Trapp Family Lodge** (802-253-5813).

SNOWBOARD RENTALS **Misty Mountain Snowboards** (802-253-3040), top of the Mountain Rd., Stowe, advertises "the fastest snowboard rentals in town." Two newer shops are **Cherry-Bone Snowboard & Skate Shop** (802-253-2900) and **Dark Side Snowboards** (1-877-422-3275).

SNOWMOBILING **Stowe Snowmobile Tours** (802-253-6221; www.stowesnow mobiletours.com) offers rentals and tours of the Mount Mansfield State Forest, and is also a source of information about local trails. **Smugglers' Notch Snowmobile Tours** (1-800-451-8752) provides guided daytime and evening tours.

SNOWSHOEING Tubbs, New England's leading snowshoe manufacturer, is located in Stowe but does not sell shoes directly. On the other hand, **Umiak Outdoor Outfitters** (802-253-2317) offers guided moonlit snowshoe tours, fondue and gourmet dinner tours, even a package tour at the Ben & Jerry's Factory in Waterbury so you can snowshoe before you eat the ice cream. **Trapp Family Lodge Cross-Country Ski Center** has designated more than 15 km of its trails as snowshoe-only. The **Stowe Mountain Resort Cross-Country Center** has cut 5 km of dedicated trails and permits snowshoers on all 80 km of its cross-country trails. **Topnotch at Stowe Resort** has also designated some snowshoe-recommended routes, and permits snowshoes on all 20 km of its trails.

The obvious place to go is, of course, up the unplowed stretch of Rt. 108 into Smugglers Notch, and the more adventurous can also access more than 40 miles of hiking terrain on and around Mount Mansfield, but it's best to check with the **Green Mountain Club** (see *Hiking and Walking*), which also sponsors a February Snowshoe Festival. Local rental sources are plentiful. Pick up a copy of

throughout the region. It's available at Umiak and other local stores in Stowe.

HEALTH SPAS **The Spa at Topnotch** (802-253-8585) and **Golden Eagle Resort** (802-253-4811) are both available for day visits. **Trapp Family Lodge** (802-253-8511) and the **Green Mountain Inn** (802-253-7301) offer massage services. The **Stowe Gym** (802-253-2176) on Mountain Rd. has state-of-the-art machines, aerobics and Spinning classes, and more. The **Stoweflake Spa & Sports Club** (802-253-7355) has a spanking-new facility that includes a hair-and-nail salon, treatment and fitness rooms galore, whirlpools, saunas, steam rooms, a waterfall, and lots of staff to pamper you. The **Swimming Hole** (802-253-9229) on Weeks Hill Rd. has a lap pool and fitness center, aqua aerobics, personal training, swimming instruction, a children's pool, and a waterslide.

✳ Green Space

For fees and reservation rules, see *Campgrounds* in "What's Where."

Mount Mansfield State Forest. The largest state forest in Vermont—27,436 acres—much of which lies on the other (western) flank of the mountain. The 10-mile Cottonbrook Trail starts at Cottonbrook Rd. off Nebraska Valley Rd. in Stowe. Follow the blazes.

Smugglers Notch State Park (802-253-4014), Stowe 05672; 10 miles up Mountain Rd. (Rt. 108) from Stowe Village, open mid-May–mid-Oct. Thirty-eight campsites, including 14 lean-tos. A few miles beyond the camping area, just beyond the highest point on this high, winding road—open only late May–early Oct., weather permitting—is a turnoff with parking, toilet, and an information center.

Elmore State Park (802-888-2982), Lake Elmore 05657. Open late May–mid-Oct., 14 miles north of Stowe on Rt. 100, then east to Morrisville, south 5 miles on Rt. 12; 709 acres with a beach, bathhouse, rental boats, 45 sites for tents and trailers including 15 lean-tos, picnicking, hiking trail up Elmore Mountain.

Wiessner Woods (802-253-7221; www.stowelandtrust.org). An 80-acre preserve with nature trails maintained by the Stowe Land Trust. The entrance is on Edson Hill Rd., the next right after the entrance to Stowehof Inn.

✳ Lodging

Most accommodations are found either in Stowe Village or along—or just off—the 7.2-mile Mountain Rd. (Rt. 108), which connects the village with the ski slopes. Unless otherwise noted, all are in Stowe 05672.

RESORTS ⏴ ♿ **The Trapp Family Lodge** (802-253-8511; 1-800-826-7000; www.trappfamily.com), 700 Trapp Hill Rd., is an alpine-modern version of the fabled Austrian schloss once owned by the family of *Sound of Music* fame. Johannes von Trapp lives nearby and remains involved in the property's day-to-day operations. The 73-room lodge with its 17-room luxury wing offers ample common space: a charming greenhouse sitting room, three common rooms with fireplaces, and a library, cocktail lounge, large dining room, and conference facilities. Twenty more rooms are in the motel-style Lower Lodge, and over 100 guest house time-share units (inquire about vacancies) are ranged in tiers on the slope below, commanding sweeping views of the Worcester Range. The inn's 2,700 acres are webbed with cross-country ski trails, also good for splendid walks. There are tennis courts and a spring-fed pool as well as an indoor pool, a sauna, and a workout room in the Sports Center. Come in late March (when the sugarhouse is operating and the sun is warm but there is still snow on the high and wooded trails) or in early December (when there is sometimes snow), and you can pay half as much as you would in foliage season. A 2- or 3-day minimum is mandatory in peak periods like foliage and Christmas. Inquire about family packages (children 16 and under stay free), and about nature walks, snowshoeing, sleigh rides, and children's, exercise, and cross-country ski programs. $245–485 in summer; $285–520 in fall, excluding the Columbus Day weekend. For Columbus Day, Thanksgiving, and Christmas, the rates run $505–735 and include a five-course dinner and full breakfast.

🍸 🐾 **The Stowe Inn** (802-253-4030; 1-800-546-4030; www.stoweinn.com), 123 Mountain Rd. This inn has changed hands several times in recent years, but the new owners, Jed and Annika Lipsky, have set about renovating and refurbishing the place with a sense of purpose and good taste. The 17th-century landmark building overlooks Stowe's Little River. It offers 17 comfortable bedrooms with private bath as well as bright, spacious

common areas with fireplaces in the main building and another 20 rooms in the Carriage House, which is more in the motel style (a maximum of two pets can stay in this section for a $15 fee). The dining room, leased to a well-respected local chef, opened in late 2003. Rates in summer and winter range from $89 for a double room in the Carriage House midweek to $189 for a deluxe room in the main inn on the weekend. All rates include continental breakfast.

🐾 ✏ ♿ **Edson Hill Manor** (802-253-7371; 1-800-621-0284; www.edsonhill manor.com), 1500 Edson Hill Rd. Set on 225 cultivated acres on a high slope, the manor was built in the 1940s with brick from the old Sherwood Hotel of Burlington. Most of the living room beams were hewn for Ira and Ethan Allen's barn, which stood in North Burlington for more than a century. In the inn itself the nine guest rooms are each very individual, most with wood-burning fireplace and hand-painted mural in the bath. The honeymoon suite with a view over the gardens is Room 3, and Room 5 has gables, a canopy bed, and the same view. Four carriage houses, each with three or four units, are ranged in tiers behind the main house; these have knotty-pine walls, wing chairs and reproduction antiques, fireplaces, books, and a spacious, in-the-woods feel. Under the ownership of William O'Neil and family, the small dining room has acquired an enviable reputation (see *Dining Out*). Living rooms are furnished in antiques, hung with exceptional art. Facilities include a stable and trails for horseback riding, outdoor pool, stocked trout pond, and 40 km of cross-country trails. $159–219 per couple B&B or $50 more with dinner; multiday packages available.

☀ ♿ **Green Mountain Inn** (802-253-7301; 1-800-253-7302; www.green mountaininn.com), 18 S. Main St. Lowell Thomas, President Chester Arthur, and President Gerald Ford were guests in this brick-and-clapboard landmark, which dates back to 1833, when it was built as a private home. In the 1850s it became a hotel, and it last changed ownership in 1982, when it was acquired by a Canadian, Marvin Gameroff, who has since tastefully renovated the rooms in the inn itself, outfitting them with country furniture especially made for the inn, adding niceties like salt-glaze stoneware lamps and appealing art. The 107 antiques-filled rooms and suites, all with private bath, air-conditioning, queen canopy beds, cable TV, and telephone, are located in the Main Inn, Annex, Clubhouse, Mill House, Depot Building, Sanborn House, and, most recently, the Mansfield House with special perks such as fireside double Jacuzzi, DVD player with surround sound, marble bath, and original artwork. The dining options: a formal **Main Street Dining Room**, and the downstairs Whip Bar & Grill, which offers a poolside patio in summer and a fire in colder months (see *Eating Out*). Afternoon tea and cookies are served in the living room. $149–479 per room in winter and summer (2-night minimum stay on weekends); less in the off-season. The suites and efficiencies are more. Guests enjoy complimentary use of Athletic Club facilities, located just on the other side of the pool.

♪ **Inn at the Mountain and Condominiums** (802-253-3656; 1-800-253-4754; www.stowe.com), 5781 Mountain Rd. The Mount Mansfield Company's luxurious 26-room lodge, as well as a number of town houses and 30 truly luxurious one-, two-, and three-bedroom Mountain Club condominiums, are currently the closest lodging to the lifts. Facilities include **H. H. Bingham's** restaurant, clay tennis courts, swimming pools, and the **Toll House Health Spa**. From $109–389 EP per room or suite in low season to $169–999 in high season. Some condos sleep up to eight people comfortably (children under 12 stay free). A 10 percent service charge is added to the bill; discounts available through numerous packages.

∞ ♪ ♿ **Stowehof Inn** (802-253-9722; 1-800-932-7136; www.stowehof inn.com), 0.5 mile off Rt. 108 on the road to Edson Hill. This Swiss-chalet-style structure was built in 1950 to be an inn, but an AIG executive quickly grabbed it up as a corporate retreat. Now it's back to being an inn, and it's a good thing, because the place transports you into a fantasy world from the moment you step through its sod-roofed porte cochère entrance, perched as it is on two tree trunks. The Grimes family has done a major renovation over the past 5 years to keep it modern yet still quaint. No two of the 46 guest rooms are alike (some are suites; a few are fireplaced demisuites with optional kitchenette), but all come with private bath and balcony with superlative views. Room 45 is an example of a "classic" with a king-sized four-poster bed and miles of alpine scenery. The main floor is furnished like the inside of a castle, with meandering hallways, fireplaced nooks and libraries, a conference room shaped like a covered bridge, and mementos like the divining rod

STOWEHOF INN

Joe Citro

that located the water source for the building. Windows everywhere let in the view. Facilities include a lower-level pub and game room, fine dining (see *Dining Out*), tennis courts, a triangular pool with mountain views, an indoor pool, a sauna, fitness room, Jacuzzi, tennis courts, and cross-country ski trails connecting with the larger network. Rates start at $99 in winter midweek and climb to $500 for the best rooms on a holiday weekend, with minimum stays required. Some lodging packages include breakfast and some don't, so ask.

Topnotch Resort and Spa (802-253-8585; 1-800-451-8686; www.topnotch-resort.com), 4000 Mountain Rd. The lap of luxury: uncommonly comfortable rooms, lounging areas with a polo club ambience, professional-quality gardens, and for meals, the convivial **Buttertub Bistro** or the stately, glass-sided, highly rated main dining room at **Maxwell's**. This upscale health-and-fitness spa, Vermont's most famous, offers everything from standard hotel accommodations to sumptuous resort homes. The spa provides over 120 fragrant treatments in 34 treatment rooms as well as spacious showers,

whirlpools, steam rooms, saunas, and leather-chaired fireplace lounges in superb new facilities, including a 60-foot-long indoor pool with skylights and a throbbing waterfall. The Ledges, recently added family units, come with two or three bedrooms and all the bells and whistles. Contemporary sculpture abounds, and at the outdoor swimming pool you can snack cabana-style, with formally clad waiters serving you at your poolside table. A red barn down across Mountain Road serves as a cross-country ski center in winter (50 km of groomed trails connect with other trail systems in Stowe); you'll also find a riding stable, a tennis academy, and a handy skating rink. Rates begin at $275 and run to $785 in low season, $335–885 in high, and include use of the pool and Jacuzzi; the exercise program is extra. A MAP plan is offered; inquire about spa packages. Pets welcome in some rooms ($50 onetime fee).

Golden Eagle Resort Motor Inn (802-253-4811; 1-800-626-1010; www.goldeneagleresort .com), 511 Mountain Rd. The 12-unit motel that Herb and Ann Hillman bought in 1963 has evolved through two generations into an amazing 80-acre complex with 94 units. Accommodations range from standard hotel rooms to mini suites and one-bedroom suites. Two-bedroom apartments and a full house are available for larger families. Family geared as well as owned, it offers a lot for children. In summer there's a formal hiking and crafts program on selected days for 3- to 12-year-olds, and on certain nights, year-round, there are movies with popcorn and pizza. Amenities include a playground as well as an attractive health spa with indoor pool, large whirlpool, sauna, exercise equipment, and massage services. There are also outdoor heated pools (swimming lessons are offered); a clay tennis court; fish-stocked ponds; shuffleboard, badminton, lawn games, and game rooms; and a coffee shop and restaurant. Throughout, you have the sense of a well-run resort. A 50-acre wildlife area with walking trails adjoins the property. $99–275 per room; fully handicapped-accessible rooms available.

⌀ ♪ ♿ **Stoweflake Mountain Resort & Spa** (802-253-7355; 1-800-253-2232; www.stoweflake.com), 1746 Mountain Rd. The small ski lodge that the Baraw family opened more than 30 years ago has mushroomed into New England's largest spa plus a full-facility, 116-room resort (including 9 luxury suites and 60 town houses of various sizes). There are bright, comfortable, inn-style rooms in the original lodge and many nicely furnished motel rooms in the garden wing (besides its own motel wing, the resort includes the former Nordic Motor Inn). All rooms have cable TV, phone, and private bath; common space includes a library and lobby with fireplaces and sitting area, along with a large living room with a sunken fireplace. The Spa & Sports Club includes a Cybex circuit, racquetball/squash court, indoor pool, Jacuzzis, saunas, 30 treatment rooms, and a glass-roofed Aqua Solarium containing a Hungarian mineral pool and a heated jet-filled "pond" with a 15-foot waterfall made to replicate Stowe's moss-covered Bingham Falls. Separate ladies' and men's lounges feature steam and massage rooms. There are also tennis courts, badminton, volleyball, croquet, horseshoes, a putting green, and a brand-new nine-hole

executive par-3 golf course, not to mention the Stowe Country Club right next door. Dining options include **Winfield's Bistro** and the pubby **Charlie B's**. $144–510 per room or suite; $234–1,015 for townhouse units; MAP rates and many packages.

INNS AND BED & BREAKFASTS 🐾 ♪

♿ **The Gables Inn** (802-253-7730; 1-800-GABLES-1; www.gablesinn.com), 1457 Mountain Rd. Randy Stern and Annette Monachelli are warm, personable hosts who have created one of Stowe's most relaxing and welcoming inns. Common rooms include a comfortable living room with fireplace, a solarium, and a downstairs game room/lounge (BYOB). There's a swimming pool on the landscaped grounds, which angle off from Mountain Rd., across from an open stretch of the Stowe Recreation Path. The hot tub is steps from the front door, the better to hop into in winter. Each of the 16 rooms (all with private bath) in the main house is different. Those in the Carriage House (handicapped accessible) feature whirlpool and fireplace; the two river-view suites in the neighboring house across the brook have fridge, microwave, and coffeemaker, as well as fireplace and double Jacuzzi. Pets are fine in some rooms for a $10 nightly charge. The famously good breakfasts are also open to the public and generally considered the best in town (see *Eating Out*). $80–235 B&B in high season, $78–165 in low season.

Stone Hill Inn (802-253-6282; www.stonehillinn.com), 89 Houston Farm Rd. (off Rt. 108). A luxury bed & breakfast run by Amy and Hap Jordan. Nine guest rooms all have two-person fireside Jacuzzi with comfy king-sized bed. Hap cooks breakfast, which is taken in a sunny, window-lined room overlooking woods and fields. Guests can use the toboggan, snowshoes, video library, and pool table, and hors d'oeuvres are spread out every evening at 5. $265–390 per room, depending on the season. Ask about specials.

⌬ ✎ **Fiddler's Green Inn** (802-253-8124; 1-800-882-5346; www.fiddlers greeninn.com), 4859 Mountain Rd., 5 miles from the village toward the mountain. Less than a mile from the lifts, this pleasant yellow 1820s farmhouse can sleep no more than 18 guests (making it great for small groups) in six comfortable guest rooms tucked under the eaves. Guests gather around the fieldstone hearth in the living room and at the long table off the sunny kitchen. BYOB. Hammocking or hiking and skiing, depending on the season, are close by. In summer and winter longtime owners Bud and Carol McKeon cater to bicyclists and cross-country skiers. $60–125 B&B; dinner possible on request. Families welcome.

🐾 ✎ **The Inn at Turner Mill** (802-253-2062; 1-800-992-0016; www .turnermill.com), 56 Turner Mill Lane. Sequestered in the pines by Notch Brook, off Mountain Rd. just a mile from the lifts, this complex was splendidly built in the 1930s by an eccentric woman doctor. Its 10 wooded acres include a mountain stream and "refreshing" swimming hole; there's also an outdoor pool. The two guest rooms are nicely decorated with handcrafted log furniture and have cable TV and private bath. There are also two chaletlike, fully equipped apartments. Greg and Mitzi Speer are

friendly hosts who can find a babysitter and help with transfers from Burlington or Waterbury. Snowshoe rentals are available, and guests get half a day free. They can also ski their way from the quad to the back of the inn. This used to be as high as a car could drive up Mountain Rd.; the Civilian Conservation Corps ski trails (now cross-country ski trails) are within easy striking distance. $75–110 per room, more for apartments. No meals.

⌬ 🐾 🐾 ✎ **Ski Inn** (802-253-4050; http://ski-inn.com), 5037 Mountain Rd. Harriet Heyer has been welcoming guests to Stowe's oldest ski lodge—one of the handiest places to the lifts—since Pearl Harbor Day, and she specializes in solo travelers. Designed as a ski lodge, the inn is set back from Mountain Rd. amid hemlocks and evergreens. The 10 guest rooms are bright and meticulously clean, each with both a double and a single bed, some with several; shared and private baths. There is a pine-paneled BYOB bar and attractive sitting and dining rooms, and you pay no gratuities. Stowe's cross-country network can be accessed from the back door. $55–65 per person MAP (dinners are hearty) in winter; $55–65 per room with continental breakfast in summer. Pets and children welcome on certain conditions.

⌬ **Brass Lantern Inn** (802-253-2229; 1-800-729-2980; www.brass lanterninn.com), 717 Maple St. (Rt. 100), is a welcoming B&B at the northern edge of the village. Your host is Andy Aldrich, a Vermonter raised on a Richmond dairy farm, who was named Vermont B&B Innkeeper of the Year for 2001. His work as a homebuilder is evident in this nicely renovated 1800s building, with its planked floors and comfortable common rooms. The nine stenciled and papered guest rooms are furnished with antiques and hand-stitched quilts; all have private bath, and six have whirlpool tub and gas-burning fireplace. There's a separate two-bedroom cottage, and the small pub and porch are for guests only. Guests enjoy gym privileges at the Stowe Gym. Breakfast is a serious affair, maybe sourdough French toast, apple crêpes, or broccoli and mushroom quiche. $95–135 in low season, $95–175 in regular, and $115–225 per couple in high season. Small weddings are a specialty.

⊙ ❦ ✍ **Auberge de Stowe** (802-253-7787; 1-800-387-8789; www .aubergedestowe.com), 692 S. Main St. This 18th-century brick farmhouse and converted carriage house (formerly called the Bittersweet Inn) is a find. Shawn and Chantal Kerivan offer six rooms, including a pair of two-bedroom suites, all with private bath. The house is right on Rt. 100 along the river, but there is a view and a sense of space in the back. Amenities include a comfortable living room, a BYOB bar, a good-sized swimming pool, a large lawn, and a hot tub. $59–98 includes a substantial continental breakfast with homemade pastries. A 6 percent service charge is added. The owners speak both German and French.

& **Ten Acres Lodge** (802-253-7638; 1-800-327-7357; www.tenacreslodge .com), 14 Barrows Rd. This 1840s red-clapboard inn has a luxurious feel and a reputation for fine dining. We recommend the suites with fireplace, sitting area, and a balcony in Hill House Suite, a newish complex up behind the old inn. Many of the rooms have been completely refur-

bished. The two cottages, one with two and the other with three bedrooms, and with kitchen and fireplace, are also exceptional. The grounds include a pool, tennis court, and hot tub. Doubles are $79–325 and include a full breakfast.

⊙ ❦ & **Ye Olde England Inn** (802-253-7558; 1-800-477-3771; www .englandinn.com), 433 Mountain Rd. Anglophiles can revel in the English accent, decor, and menu. The rooms are unabashedly luxurious, from the 17 Laura Ashley–style rooms in the inn to the 3 two-bedroom English "cottages" beside the swimming pool (each with fireplace, Jacuzzi, and kitchen). There are 10 suites on a rise behind the inn, each with a four-poster bed, Jacuzzi, deck, and lounge with a fireplace, wet bar, fridge, and microwave. A full English breakfast and tea are included in $119–369 rates, except in the cottages. Mr. Pickwick's Pub & Restaurant serves lunch and dinner (see *Eating Out*). The extravagant breakfasts are served in **Copperfield's**, the inn's other dining room.

Foxfire Inn (802-253-4887; www .foxfireinn.com), 1606 Pucker St. (Rt. 100) north of Stowe Village. This early-19th-century farmhouse is set on 70 wooded hillside acres. The five guest rooms have wide-board floors (several have exposed beams) and are furnished with antiques, each with private bath. There's also a four-bedroom house available for short-term rental. Downstairs there is plenty of space for guests away from the large, public dining room, well respected for its Italian fare (see *Dining Out*). $130 per double room in high season, $85 in low season, includes a full breakfast served in the garden room.

⊙ 🐾 🐟 ♿ **Commodores Inn** (802-253-7131; 1-800-447-8693; www .commodoresinn.com), 823 S. Main St., P.O. Box 970, Rt. 100 south. Carrie Nourjian runs this establishment with 72 large rooms, all with private bath (request one in the back, overlooking the lake). There's a living room with a fireplace; also three Jacuzzis and saunas and an indoor and outdoor pool. The **Stowe Yacht Club Dining Room** (a popular watering hole and spot for an evening burger) overlooks a 3-acre lake on which model sailboat races are regularly held, not to mention canoeing and kayaking. $98–198, breakfast included, service charges extra. Children 12 and under stay free, and pets are welcome for $10 per stay.

🐾 **Inky Dinky Oink, Ink** (802-253-3046; www.oinkink.com), 117 Adams Mill Rd., Moscow 05672. The playful name reflects the artwork of innkeeper Liz Le Serviget, who houses guests in two air-conditioned rooms in this renovated 1840s farmhouse, which a previous owner transported here from

Nebraska. One room has two single beds that can be joined together, the other a double bed with a two-tiered outdoor deck, private entrance, and private bath with Jacuzzi. Art and books are everywhere, and the breakfasts are fresh, imaginative, and largely organic. $95–135. Pets okay (with restrictions).

In Waterbury 05676

🐾 🐟 **The Old Stagecoach Inn** (802-244-5056; 1-800-262-2206; www.old stagecoach.com), 18 N. Main St. A classic stagecoach inn built in 1826 with a triple-tiered porch but substantially altered in the 1880s, when a millionaire from Ohio added oak woodwork, ornate fireplaces, and stained glass. Renovated in 1987, the inn is run by John and Jack Barwick. There are eight guest rooms and three efficiency suites, all tastefully furnished but varying widely—from a queen-bedded room with a sitting area, fireplace, and private bath to small rooms with a shared bath. Two efficiency suites are studios; the other has two bedrooms and a sitting area. Many of the rooms are large enough to accommodate families. Coco, the African gray parrot, sits by the fireplace in the living room adjoining the library, with its fully licensed bar. Regular-season rates are $65–120 per room; foliage-season and winter holidays $75–180. A full breakfast, including a selection of hot dishes, is included. Pets allowed in some rooms.

⊙ 🐾 🐟 **Grünberg Haus** (802-244-7726; 1-800-800-7760; www.grunberg haus.com), 94 Pine St., Rt. 100 south of Waterbury. This secluded, Tyrolean-style chalet with carved balconies has 11 guest rooms, 8 with private bath, and three cottages (open Memorial Day–Oct.) where pets are

STAGECOACH INN, WATERBURY

Joe Citro

allowed for $5 per night. Many of the rooms have wood-beamed ceilings. Innkeepers Jeff and Linda Connor serve a full breakfast of homemade breads and baked goods, a fresh fruit creation, and a main dish such as ricotta-stuffed French toast. Facilities include a garden deck and self-serve pub and game room. Hiking and snowshoe trails behind the inn feed into a 20 km cross-country trail system. The dark-wood-beamed common rooms include a large fieldstone fireplace. In winter the inn offers discounts at Stowe, Sugarbush, Bolton, and Mad River Glen (all within easy striking distance). Children must be over age 5. Dog in residence.

∞ ✎ **Moose Meadow Lodge** (802-244-5378; www.moosemeadowlodge .com), 607 Crossett Hill. Greg Trulson and Willie Docto have created an enchanting mountain sanctuary with Adirondack touches in this cedar log inn, the only one we've encountered in Vermont. The spirit is Ernest Hemingway with panache: mounted trophies, exposed wood walls, a wraparound deck with mountain views, a large stone fireplace, and exotica (trophies include a water buffalo from Uganda and a 155-pound black bear). The four guest rooms are rustically luxurious with private bath; one has a two-person steam bath, and the basement hot tub seats five. The 86 acres are blissfully secluded, with a trout-stocked swimming pond, a tree-surrounded bonfire area, and countless trails. Snowshoes are available at no charge. You may choose to tackle the 25-minute uphill hike to the Sky Loft, a glass-enclosed mountaintop gazebo with 360-degree views. Rates of $129–169 include an imaginative gourmet breakfast.

&. **Thatcher Brook Inn** (802-244-5911; 1-800-292-5911; www.thatcher brook.com), Exit 10 off I-89, then take Rt. 100 north. Twenty-two guest rooms in this restored Victorian country inn, once the home of a lumber baron, all have private bath, and many have a whirlpool and/or fireplace. $79–350 (plus $5 daily service charge) includes breakfast.

In Waterbury Center 05677

&. **The Birds Nest Inn** (802-244-7490; 1-800-366-5592; www.birds nestinn.com), 5088 Waterbury–Stowe Rd. (Rt. 100). This 1832 three-gabled home, formerly known as the Black Locust Inn, has six rooms with private bath, polished wood floors, and stained-glass transoms. One king-bedded room is handicapped accessible. Len, Nancy, and Valerie Vignola (assisted by golden retriever Lady) get great reviews for hospitality. $135–195 ($20–30 more for deluxe rooms) includes three-course breakfasts and afternoon appetizers. Closed Apr. and Nov.

May Farm B&B (802-244-7306; 1-800-729-9093; www.mayfarm.com), 4706 Waterbury–Stowe Rd. The farm, built in 1790, offers down comforters, stained glass, Oriental carpets, and a hot tub under the stars. Breakfast is served in three courses, and if that doesn't hold you, there's a late-afternoon beverage service with hors d'oeuvres. Rates $80–150.

MOTELS

In Stowe 05672

Arbor Inn (802-253-4772; 1-800-543-1293; www.arborinnstowe.com), 3214 Mountain Rd. This is the former home of Olympian Billy Kidd. The owners offer 12 rooms and suites, all with private bath, recently renovated and furnished in antiques, equipped with TV and a small fridge. Two rooms have fully equipped kitchen; four have a fireplace, and two come with two-person whirlpool tub. Common space includes a game room, pool table, and outdoor pool and Jacuzzi. Amenities include two fieldstone fireplaces, spectacular views of Mount Mansfield, and English gardens in summer. $85–265 per room (service charges extra) with full breakfast.

♣ ✄ **Alpenrose** (802-253-7277; 1-800-962-7002), 2619 Mountain Rd. A pleasant, small motel with just five rooms, four of which are efficiencies with kitchenettes; direct access to a cross-country network and the Stowe Recreation Path. $65–80 per room in winter, $55–65 in low season, no meals included.

In Waterbury 05676

✄ ♿ **Best Western Waterbury-Stowe** (802-244-7822; 1-800-621-7822), 45 Blush Hill Rd., Exit 10 north, I-89. There are 79 rooms with private bath and a restaurant for casual dining. A few luxury suites have whirlpool bath and fireplace. Amenities include a large indoor pool with a glass roof, and a full-sized fitness center with high-end weight and aerobic equipment, hot tub, and sauna. Positioned just off the interstate, this is a popular way stop with family-geared rates and access to Sugarbush as well as Stowe. $139–199 per couple in high season, $79–129 in low; many family-sized rooms.

CONDOMINIUMS **Stowe Country Rentals** (802-253-8132; 1-800-639-1990; www.stowecountryrentals.com) handles condos and houses. **Country Village Rentals** (802-253-8777;

1-800-320-8777; www.cvrandr.com) specializes in upscale homes, both old and new. **All Seasons Rentals** (802-253-7353; 1-800-54-STOWE; www.stowerentals.com) and **Rentals at Stowe** (802-253-9786; 1-800-848-9120, ext. 624; www.rentalsatstowe.com) also rent homes and condos.

The Village Green at Stowe (802-253-9705; 1-800-451-3297; www.vgasstowe.com), 1003 Cape Cod Rd., Stowe 05672. Seven nicely designed buildings set on 40 acres (surrounded by the Stowe Country Club links) contain 73 two- and three-bedroom town houses, all brightly furnished. A recreation building has a heated indoor pool, Jacuzzi, sauna, game and changing rooms; also an outdoor pool and two tennis courts. Winter rates excluding holidays begin at $200–300 per night for a two-bedroom; $250–335 per night in summer, more for three-bedroom units; weekly rates.

♟ **Notch Brook Condominiums** (802-253-4882; 1-800-253-4882), 1229 Notch Brook Rd., Stowe 05672. In the shadow of Spruce Peak with a spectacular view of Mount Mansfield, an unusually well-built (though no one seems to know why Vermont architect Robert Burley designed them with flat roofs) complex of 36 rooms and 35 condominiums ranging from doubles through three-bedroom town houses. Most rooms are available by the day and week. Amenities include saunas, tennis, an outdoor pool that's heated for winter use, and complimentary continental breakfast. $150–550 per unit in winter, less in summer; more in peak holiday periods.

1836 Cabins (802-244-8533; www.1836cabins.com), P.O. Box 128, Waterbury Center 05677, are tucked into a pine forest whose logging roads become cross-country ski and snow-shoeing trails in winter. Completely furnished one- and two-bedroom units with kitchen and TV. Rates $99 for two, standard; $139 for deluxe (two bedrooms, gas fireplaces); about $20 more over holidays.

DORMS ⚘ **Round Hearth at Stowe** (802-253-7223; 1-800-344-1546; www .roundhearth.com), 39 Edson Hill Rd., Stowe 05672. A dormitory-style operation, complete with chaperones and all sorts of amenities for teen groups, such as DJ dances on Saturday night, outdoor hot tubs, and large-screen TVs. Merry and Grady Vigneau do everything from winter ski trips to summer sports camps and basket-making workshops. They also own and operate the **Red Fox Alpine Lodge at Smugglers Notch**. Call for group rates.

CAMPGROUNDS See *Camping* and *Green Space* for information on campgrounds in the area.

✳ Where to Eat

DINING OUT **Blue Moon Cafe** (802-253-7006; www.bluemoonstowe.com), 35 School St., Stowe. Open for dinner daily. A very small, candlelit bistro with a huge reputation. Owner Jim Barton serves "contemporary American" dishes. The menu changes weekly, but a typical appetizer might include a chanterelle tart ($8.25) or venison carpaccio ($10.25), followed by dill potato crusted Arctic char with Pinot Noir sauce ($20) or tenderloin of beef with Brie and caramelized balsamic red onions ($32). Dinner for two with wine is about $95.

Edson Hill Manor (802-253-7371; www.edsonhillmanor.com), 1500 Edson Hill Rd., Stowe. Open for din-

ner nightly in-season; reservations required. The small, gracious dining room at this low-key resort has soared to the top of local restaurant ratings. The menu changes daily. The appetizer menu ($9–11) might feature house-cured gravlax with Brie turnover and vodka rémoulade. Entrées ($19–24) might be bacon-roasted Chilean sea bass, seared rare tuna loin, or roast rack of New Zealand lamb with Madeira reduction.

Mes Amis (802-253-8669), 311 Mountain Rd., Stowe. Closed Mon. Mes Amis is the premier French restaurant in Stowe. The food is French-bistro-style and very well done. There are a number of small rooms, which creates an intimate dining atmosphere. You might begin with oysters on the half shell and move on to duck breast, clams Angelique, or an excellent rabbit stew. Entrées $21–40.

Red Basil (802-253-4478), 294 Mountain Rd., Stowe. The hottest Thai restaurant in town, open daily for lunch and dinner. Appetizers include an array of sushi, plus fried crab wontons and Thai ravioli (both $5.95); house specials are pattaya ($19.95), which is seafood in green curry sauce, or a dish called swimming ($19.95)— soft-shell crab and duck with tamarind sauce and red curry sauce. They also make a mean martini.

Foxfire Inn and Italian Restaurant (802-253-4887), Rt. 100, north of Stowe Village. Dinner nightly. Favored by local residents for a predictably good night out. The setting is a 1850s country farmhouse, and the menu is large. You might begin with rolled eggplant (baked with ricotta and prosciutto, mozzarella, and Romano cheese) ($7.25), then dine on veal saltimbocca ($21.95) or chicken stuffed with Gorgonzola cheese, pancetta, and figs sautéed in a creamy Marsala wine sauce ($17.95).

Emily's at Stowehof Inn (802-253-9722), secluded on a hillside 0.5 mile off Rt. 108, Stowe. Innovative American cuisine in a small, romantic dining room. Appetizers range $6–13 and include quail and pheasant with an orange vinaigrette sauce and truffle oil drizzle, beef carpaccio, and poached shrimp with cocktail sauce and Absolut citron. The entrées might include smoked pork loin in an apple bourbon sauce, mushroom ravioli in a Madeira mushroom cream sauce, or venison tenderloin with a red wine cherry demi sauce. $50 for two entrées and a bottle of wine. **Coslin's Pub** downstairs offers less formal fare, complimentary appetizers during ski season, and live jazz on Friday night.

Trapp Family Dining Room (802-253-8511), Trapp Hill Rd., Stowe. Open daily. Austrian chef Juergen Spagolla offers noteworthy formal dining (often to the strains of live harp music) with a three-course ($38) and five-course ($45) prix fixe menu; always includes Austrian specialties, like Wiener schnitzel with spaetzle, but also varied fare, like smoked pork chop with Gewürztraminer-apricot compote, Vermont cheddar mashed potatoes, and asparagus. Lighter meals are served in the lounge and in the **Austrian Tea Room**, which serves lunch and afternoon tea, specializing in tortes, strudels, and wursts.

Trattoria La Festa (802-253-8480; www.trattorialafesta.com), 4080 Upper Mountain Rd., Stowe (next to Topnotch Resort). Dinner served daily except Sun. (open on long weekends). On the upper reaches of the Mountain Rd. with terrace dining in summer, a pleasant spot owned by three experienced chefs, two of them brothers born and raised in Aprilia, a small coastal town not far from Rome. True to the nature of an Italian trattoria, the food is varied. Reliably delicious antipasti, such as carpaccio di carne (thin slices of filet mignon with onions, capers, extra-virgin olive oil; $8.50); specialty pastas like penne Michelangelo (penne sautéed with fresh vegetables and grilled shrimp in a garlic wine sauce; $14.50), and four-course, family-style dinners that can be preordered.

EATING OUT

In Stowe

Cliff House (1-800-253-4SKI, www.stowe.com), in the Octagon at Mount Mansfield's summit. Recent renovations have doubled the floor-to-ceiling window seating, broadening the panoramic view so diners can take in Mount Mansfield, the Worcester Range, even Mount Washington on clear days. The decor is brighter and more upscale, and dinners are back, at least on Fri. and Sat. evening. The menu changes each week, but is resolutely focused on local ingredients, from artisanal cheeses to Vermont breads, brews, and produce, all combined to make meals as memorable as this rarefied spot at 3,625 feet, accessible only by gondola. Some examples of the fare are Atlantic lobster bisque, baked Brie in pastry, lamb stew, and shepherd's pie. Lunch is served daily 11–3, and reservations are essential. Pricey.

Gracie's Restaurant (802-253-6888; www.gracies.com), 1652 Mountain Rd., Stowe. Open 11:30 AM–10 PM (later on weekends). Sue and Paul Archdeacon have moved their popular dog-themed pub and gift shop from the center of town to this larger spot on Mountain Rd., and it's still a great place to eat when you pull into town late. You can dine on one of Gracie's outstanding "dog-gone" burgers, or on Gracie's scampi or crabcakes. At lunch we recommend Gracie's famous chicken sandwich served with bacon, mayo, and guacamole ($7.95) or the vegetable flatbread ($6.95). Gracie, an Airdale whom the Archdeacons rescued from the pound (his picture hangs at the bottom of the stairs), was a fixture at the Shed all those years Paul worked there as bartender. Dinner entrées average $12.95–24.95.

✐ **McCarthy's Restaurant** (802-253-8626), Mountain Rd. next to the Stowe Cinema. Open 6:30–2:30 daily. The local gathering place: quick, cheerful service, an open black-and-white-checked kitchen, oilcloths on the tables, wood skis on the walls, and deep wooden booths. Daily specials for breakfast and lunch, plus a big breakfast menu and a wide selection of soups and sandwiches on homemade breads. Kids' menu, boxed lunches to go. Great all around.

✐ **Restaurant Swisspot** (802-253-4622), 128 Main St., Stowe Village. An old reliable, open nightly for lunch and dinner. Soups, quiche, and fondue are lovingly prepared. For lunch, there are tempting burgers with Swiss cheese, and a wide variety of sandwiches. Fondues are a specialty of the house; try the Swiss cheese fondue ($17 for one, $27 for two) or beef fondue Bourguignonne for two ($33). Other options: raclette ($7), Wiener schnitzel with spaetzle ($18), and garlic shrimp sauté ($17). Children's menu. Try the Matterhorn sundae with hot Tobler sauce ($5).

✐ **The Gables Inn** (802-253-7730; 1-800-GABLES-1; www.gablesinn.com), 1457 Mountain Rd. Breakfast served 8–10:30 daily, Sunday and holiday brunch until 12:30. Breakfast is an event, served on the enclosed front porch and in the cheerful dining room. The daily blackboard breakfast specials might include French toast stuffed with cream cheese, walnuts, and molasses ($6.50); a Vermont cheddar cheese omelet with mushrooms, peppers, onions, and garden herbs ($7.50); or portobello mushroom Benedict ($8.95). Mimosas, scrumptious coffee cakes, and mounds of fresh fruit.

✐ **The Shed Restaurant and Brewery** (802-253-4364), Mountain Rd., open daily for lunch and dinner, also Sunday buffet brunch and a late-night menu (10–midnight). Ken and Kathy Strong's old landmark pub has expanded over the years into a complex that includes a microbrewery as well as a large, greenhouse-style dining room. The varied menu (with equally varied prices) includes salads, tacos, baked onion soup, zucchini boats, barbecued ribs, seafood strudel, and, of course, Shed burgers. Children's menu.

Whip Bar & Grill (802-253-7301; www.thewhip.com), Main St. at the Green Mountain Inn. Open daily 11:30–9:30; Sunday brunch is a specialty. For charm and good food at palatable prices, the Whip is hard to beat. The antique buggy whips, brass dumbwaiter, and vintage photos recall the tavern's status. It boasts Stowe's first liquor license, from 1833. In summer there's patio dining and a view of lawns and the pool; in winter the focus is on a roaring hearth. There is a blackboard menu, always a choice of grilled meats or fish, a raw bar, and specials ranging from pan-blackened fish to Montreal smoked meat with hot mustard. Dinner specials include roast Quebec duckling with blackberry gastrique and sesame-seared yellowfin tuna with citrus-soy reduction. Prices range $8.50–26.95.

✍ **Miguel's Stowe-Away Lodge and Restaurant** (802-253-7574), 3148 Mountain Rd. This snug old farmhouse, the original Miguel's, is a reliably good bet featuring innovative Mexican fare like *camarones chipotle* (Gulf shrimp in an orange chipotle cream sauce), as well as the usual Tex-Mex "especiales" and a gringo and full children's menu. This is the place for margaritas. Entrées $10.95–19.95.

Mr. Pickwick's Pub & Restaurant at Ye Olde England Inn (802-253-7558), 433 Mountain Rd. Open for lunch, dinner, and Sunday brunch. "A Dickens of a place" offers English-style fish-and-chips ($18.95) or steak-and-kidney pie ($17.95), but also more esoteric fare, like tamarind-glazed ostrich steak served with sweet potato ($24.95) and Vermont pheasant breast with artichokes, cremini mushrooms, and spinach gnocchi ($25.95). There is a vast collection of beers, single-malt whiskeys, vintage ports, and a martini bar.

Moscow Tea House (802-253-2955), 147 Adams Mill Rd., Moscow. Open year-round, Thu.–Sat. noon–5. This flower-rich sanctuary is the quiet doing of Jayne Stearns, an herbalist and horticulturist. The tearoom is in an old farmhouse off a dirt road, which is heated by a woodstove in winter. The homemade pastries and savories contain garden-fresh ingredi-

ents and are served with herbal and regular teas on the front porch and in the combination tearoom/gift shop with dried herbs and flowers hanging from the rafters. Tea $3, plates $7. Call ahead for directions and reservations. No credit cards.

✍ **Dutch Pancake Cafe** (802-253-5330), 900 Mountain Rd. at the Grey Fox Inn. Open daily 8–11, for brunch until 12:30 on winter weekends and holidays, and for dinner 5:30–8:30. There are about as many types of pancakes (more than 80) served here as you could think of, and then some, ranging from blueberry and cream to shredded potato onion and cheese ($7.95–9.75), all in a decor with Delft tile touches. Dinner could be flatbread pizzas, hearty sandwiches, or . . . pancakes. Kid's menu.

✍ **Depot Street Malt Shoppe** (802-253-4269), 57 Depot St., Stowe Village. Open daily for lunch and dinner. A fun, '50s decor with a reasonably priced diner-style menu to match, a great lunch stop with old-style fountain treats like malted frappes, egg creams, and banana splits.

In Waterbury
Michael's on the Hill (802-244-7476; www.michaelsonthehill.com), Rt. 100 between Waterbury and Stowe. Michael's is fine Italian fare with a little something extra. You might dine on hand-rolled lasagna with hearts of palm, Asiago, and truffle foam; roasted organic Scottish salmon with crisp artichoke hearts and Merlot reduction; or grilled shrimp with heirloom beet and pear salad and kaffir lime leaf vinaigrette. In general, entrée prices run $18–35, with the menu adapted frequently to seasonal foods. Piano music is offered on Fri. and Sat. nights. Dinner 5–9; closed Tue.

Arvad's Grill & Pub (802-244-8973; www.arvads.com), 3 S. Main St. Open daily 11:30–11:30. A wildly popular (read: crowded) way stop (just off I-89, Exit 10) with attractive brick-walls-and-hanging-plants decor, varied lunch and dinner menus, a full bar, and an outdoor veranda in summer. Dine on pasta primavera ($12) or chicken, beef, pork, or shrimp stir-fry ($13). Nightly specials; try the Cabot fries (made with the local cheddar).

Tanglewoods (802-244-7855), 179 Guptil Rd. (going north on Rt. 100, the first right turn after Ben & Jerry's), Waterbury Center. A huge red barn miraculously transformed into a charming, intimate eatery. Chef-owners Carl and Diane Huber whip up a fusion of American favorites, from sesame coriander crusted tuna steak in scallion-ginger sauce with wasabi ($19.95) to seared breast of duck with chipotle demi-glaze and papaya relish. There are handmade pastas, innovative starters, and a café menu ranging $7–13.

Marsala Salsa (802-244-1150), 13–15 Stowe St. Open Mon.–Sat. 5–9:30, Tue.–Sat. in summer months. An anomaly in these parts: authentic Caribbean fare in an old Vermont storefront. Born in Trinidad and reared on Indian cuisine, chef-owner Jan Chotalal blends those flavors with Mexican for such specialties as shrimp pillows, pot stickers, Baja rellenos, curried chicken, and grilled Island shrimp. On the spicy side. Live music on Fridays; kids' menu. Entrées $10.50–15.95.

✳ Entertainment

Stowe Cinema (802-253-4678), at the Stowe Center, Rt. 108. Standard seats as well as a bar viewing area for first-run films.

The Lamoille County Players (802-888-4507; www.lamoillecounty players.com) stage plays at the Hyde Park Opera House, Hyde Park.

Stowe Theater Guild (802-253-3961; www.stowetheater.com), staged upstairs at the Akeley Memorial Building in Stowe Village, offers a series of summer musicals and Broadway favorites.

Stowe Performing Arts (802-253-7792; www.stowearts.com) presents a series of three summer Sunday-evening concerts followed by three **Vermont Mozart Festival** concerts held in the natural amphitheater of the Trapp Family Meadow. Patrons are invited to bring a preconcert picnic. The setting is spectacular, with the sun sinking over Nebraska Notch.

APRÈS-SKI There are reputedly 50 bars in Stowe. Along Mountain Rd., look for après-ski action at the **Matterhorn** (802-253-8198), with live music every weekend during ski season. **Charlie B's**, at Stoweflake, is also usually lively, as is **Mr. Pickwick's Pub**, source of one of Vermont's largest selections of beers (the better to wash down its steak-and-kidney pie). In Waterbury check out **The Alchemist** (802-244-4120; www .alchemistbeer.com) at 23 S. Main St.: chocolate-colored walls, black tables and ceiling, good bar fare.

✳ Selective Shopping

ARTISANS **Stowe Craft Gallery & Design Center** (802-253-4693; 1-877-456-8388; www.stowecraft .com), 55 Mountain Rd., Stowe. Open 10–6 daily. Outstanding crafts from throughout the country including contemporary glass, furniture, jewelry, and ceramics. The interior design showroom on Main Street features lighting, rugs, hardware, and furniture.

Little River Hotglass Studio & Gallery (802-253-0889; www.little riverhotglass.com), 593 Moscow Rd., Moscow. Open to the public daily except Tue. 10–5, noon–5 on Sun. We are kicking ourselves for not stocking up on the lovely, reasonably priced glass Christmas balls that Michael Trimpol creates in this small and very attractive studio just off Rt. 100. The specialty is exquisite colored glass creations: weights, bowls, balls, and perfume bottles.

Ziemke Glass Blowing Studio (802-244-6126; www.zglassblowing.com), 3033 Rt. 100, Waterbury Center. Studio and showroom open daily 10–6. Glass is usually blown Thu.–Sun.

Stowe Gems (802-253-7000; www .stowegems.com), in the village near the Helen Day Art Center at 70 Pond St. Open daily 10–5. Barry Tricker polishes and sets exquisite stones, including tanzanite, tourmaline, Tahitian pearls, and freshwater pearls.

West Branch Gallery & Sculpture Park (802-253-8943), 17 Towne Farm Lane, Stowe, 1 mile up Mountain Rd., behind the Rusty Nail. Open daily 11–6. Contemporary sculpture in glass, oil, steel, stone, and mixed media.

Cotswold Furniture Makers (802-253-3710; www.cotswoldfurniture .com), 132 Mountain Rd. Open daily 10–6. John Lomas, a graduate of the London College of Furniture, creates classic Shaker and Arts and Crafts furniture by hand, selling it along with Tibetan rugs, Simon Pearce glass, and decorative objects.

Moriarty Hat & Sweater Shop (802-253-4052; www.moriartyhat .com), Stowe. Many long years ago Mrs. Moriarty began knitting caps for Stowe skiers, and her distinctive style caught on. It is now widely imitated, but the originals remain a Stowe tradition.

FOOD AND DRINK Cabot Annex Store (802-244-6334; 1-800-881-6334; www.cabotcheese.com/annex .html), 2653 Waterbury–Stowe Rd. (Rt. 100), Waterbury, 1.4 miles north of Ben & Jerry's, in the same complex as Lake Champlain Chocolates (see below). Open year-round, daily 9–6. While the prizewinning cheese isn't made here, this is its major showcase, displaying a full line of dairy products (plenty of samples), along with other Vermont specialty foods and crafts. Also in the annex store are **Green Mountain Coffee Roasters** (1-888-879-4627), **Lake Champlain Chocolates** (802-241-4150), the chocolate maker that started out in Burlington, and the **Vermont Teddy Bear Co.**, makers of those gift bears.

Cold Hollow Cider Mill (802-244-8771; 1-800-3-APPLES; www.cold hollow.com), 3600 Rt. 100, Waterbury, is one of New England's largest producers of fresh apple cider; visitors can watch it being pressed and sample the varieties. The retail stores in this big red barn complex stock every conceivable kind of apple jelly, butters, sauces, natural fruit preserves, honey, pancake mixes, pickles, and mustards, plus Vermont books and other gifts. Try the rhubarb wine at the **Grandview Winery** next door. Open year-round, daily 8–6.

In Waterbury Village follow your nose to the java at the headquarters of **Green Mountain Coffee Roasters** (802-882-2134; www.greenmountain coffee.com), whose company store features freshly made cappuccino and free samples of coffees from around the world. Open weekdays 6:30–5, Sat. 8–1, at 40 Foundry St.

OTHER **Bear Pond Books** (802-253-8236; www.stowebooks.com), Depot Building, Stowe Village. Open daily. An excellent family-owned, independent bookstore; calendars, cassettes, the town's best selection of cards, and an entire section devoted to Vermont books.

Brick House Book Shop (802-888-4300), 632 Morristown Corners Rd., Morrisville. Open Tue.–Sat. 2–5, Sun. and Mon. by appointment. Proprietor Alexandra Heller has amassed 70,000 old books, fiction and nonfiction, hardcover and paperback. She also offers a search and mail service.

Shaw's General Store (802-253-4040), 54 Main St., Stowe Village. Established in 1895 and still a family business, a source of shoelaces and cheap socks as well as expensive ski togs and Vermont souvenirs.

Lackey's Variety Store (802-253-7624), Main St., Stowe Village, open 8:30–8:30 daily. An 1840s building that has housed many enterprises and is now "just a variety store," according to Frank Lackey, its owner of more than 48 years. An anomaly in this resort village, it still stocks nail clippers, india ink, shoe polish, scissors, not to mention patent medicine and magazines. The walls are hung with posters for 1930s ocean liners and long-vanished local movie houses and lined with antique bottles, boxes, and other fascinating ephemera.

Stafford's Country Store and Pharmacy (802-253-7361), Main St., Stowe Village. The village's full-service pharmacy (parking in the rear), also a selection of European music boxes, toys, books, and Vermont products.

Stowe St. Emporium (802-244-5321), 23 Stowe St., Waterbury. A large, eclectic selection of clothing and gifts.

Fly Rod Shop (802-253-7346; www.flyrodshop.com), 2703 Waterbury Rd. (Rt. 100), Stowe, carries a full line of name-brand fishing gear. Full- and half-day instructional tours.

Straw Corner Mercantile (802-253-3700), Mountain Rd., Stowe. Folk art, Americana gifts, and decorative accessories. Shaker boxes, Nantucket baskets, cards, calendars, boxes, and earthenware.

Misty Meadows Herb and Perennial Farm (802-253-8247), 785 Stagecoach Rd., Stowe. Open mid-May through fall, 9–5 daily. Display gardens feature herbs and perennials in a farm setting; also potpourri, everlasting wreaths, seasonings, and herbs. Certified organic.

Nebraska Knoll Sugar Farm (802-253-4655), 256 Falls Brook Lane, Stowe. Lewis and Audrey Coty's sugarhouse is open in-season, and syrup and maple cream are available year-round. We advise calling before, especially in winter when the steep back road (especially if you come via Trapp's) is four-wheel-drive only (we chickened out three-fourths of the way there).

See also the Johnson Woolen Mills in "North of the Notch"; the short and scenic drive there is certainly worth the effort.

✳ Special Events

Mid-January: **Winter Carnival** is one of the oldest and most gala village winter carnivals in the country—a week of snow sculptures, sled dog races, ski races, public feeds.

Last weekend of February: **Stowe Derby**, the country's oldest downhill/cross-country race—a 10-mile race from the summit of Mount Mansfield to Stowe Village, which usually attracts about 300 entrants.

Easter: **Easter parade** at Spruce Peak; **Easter egg hunt**.

May: Lamoille County Players present **musicals** at the Hyde Park Opera House.

Late June: **Stowe Garden Festival** (1-800-247-8693)—garden tours, crafts show, speakers.

July 3: **Stowe Independence Day Celebration** (802-253-7321) starting at 11 AM midtown—parade, food, games, performers, fireworks. Separate festivities in the village of Moscow, too small for its own band, so they parade to the music of radios.

Mid-July: **Stoweflake Hot-Air Balloon Festival** (1-800-253-2232; www.stoweflake.com)—annual balloon launch and tethers with live music, food, a beer garden, and kids' activity corner.

Late July: **Mutt Strutt** (802-888-5065)—a dog festival with contests, food, and prizes at Jackson Arena. **International Food and Wine Festival**, Stoweflake Resort Field. **Stowe Performing Arts Summer Festival**—a week of concerts ranging from chamber to symphony music, including bands and choral groups, presented in a number of places. **Lamoille County Field Days**, a

weekend agricultural fair in Morrisville—tractor pulling, crafts, children's rides.

Mid-August: **Antique & Classic Car Show** (802-253-7321). Over 800 models on display, 3 days, 8–5. Parade, car auction, corral, fashion-judging contest, auto-related flea market. Nichols Field on Rt. 100 south.

Late August: Lamoille County Players stage a **musical** in the Hyde Park Opera House.

September: **Exposed! Outdoor Sculpture Exhibition** (802-253-8358), Helen Day Art Center, tours with the sculptors. Maps available.

Mid-September: **Annual British Invasion** (802-253-5320; www.british invasion.com). North America's largest all-British sports car show—contests, food, displays at Mayo Farm Events Field, Weeks Hill Rd., Stowe. **Oktoberfest** (802-253-7321), Jackson Arena—a 2-day fest with oompah bands, parade, Bavarian food, microbrews, and children's tent.

Second weekend of October: **Stowe Foliage Art & Craft Festival** (802-253-7321), Stowe Events Field. Three days of juried art and fine crafts from 160 exhibitors, wine tasting, music, magicians, and a special "off the grid" section.

Pre-Halloween: **Lantern Tours**. Carry a candlelit lantern while taking a "ghost walk" through Stowe, hearing tales of the village's resident ghosts. Tue.–Thu. and Sat. nights at 8, Sep. 13–Nov. 1. Walks begin at the visitors center on Main St. (802-253-7321).

NORTH OF THE NOTCH AND THE LAMOILLE VALLEY

Vermont's most dramatic road winds up and up from Stowe through narrow, 2,162-foot-high Smugglers Notch, then down and around cliffs and boulders. Just as it straightens and drops through woodland, motorists are startled by the apparition of a condominium town rising out of nowhere (Smugglers' Notch Resort, a self-contained, family-geared village that accommodates some 2,000 people). However, as Rt. 108 continues to descend and finally levels into Jeffersonville on the valley floor, it's clear that this is a totally different place from the tourist-trod turf south of the Notch. This is the Lamoille Valley.

Smugglers Notch, as well as the village of Jeffersonville, is in Cambridge, one of several towns worth exploring along the Lamoille River. Jeffersonville has been a gathering place for artists since the 1930s, and Johnson, 9 miles west along Rt. 15, is also now an art center. It's easy to see why artists like this luminous landscape: open, gently rolling farm country. The Lamoille River itself is beloved by fishermen and canoeists, and bicyclists enthuse about the little-trafficked roads.

While Smugglers Notch is the more dramatic approach, the prime access to the Lamoille Valley region is Rt. 100, the main road north from Stowe, which joins Rt. 15 (the major east–west road) at Morrisville, the commercial center for north-central Vermont. Just west on Rt. 15 is Hyde Park, the picturesque county seat, famed for its year-round theater.

North of the Lamoille Valley is the even less-trafficked Missisquoi River Valley, and between the two lies some beautiful, very Vermont country.

GUIDANCE **Stowe–Smugglers Notch Regional Marketing Organization** (1-877-247-8693; www.stowesmugglers.org), Morrisville, is a source of information for the entire region.

Lamoille Valley Chamber of Commerce (802-888-7607), P.O. Box 445, 43 Portland St., Morrisville 05661. The office in the Tegu Building in Morrisville is open year-round. A summer information booth is at the junction of Rts. 15 and 100 at the Morrisville Mobil station; open May–Oct.

GETTING THERE *By air:* See "Burlington Region." Given 48 hours' notice, Smugglers' Notch Resort arranges transfers for guests.

By train: **Amtrak** stops at Essex Junction (1-800-872-7245).

By car: When the Notch is closed in winter, the route from Stowe via Morrisville is 26 miles, but in summer via Rt. 108 it's 18 miles from Stowe.

MEDICAL EMERGENCY Emergency service is available by calling **911**.

Copley Hospital (802-888-4231), Morrisville.

Diane E. Foulds

ENTRANCE TO SMUGGLERS' NOTCH RESORT

✳ To See

Smugglers Notch. During the War of 1812, Vermonters hid cattle and other supplies in the Notch prior to smuggling them into Canada to feed the British army—which was fighting the U.S. Army at the time. A path through the high pass existed centuries before European settlement, but it wasn't until 1910 that the present road was built, which, with its 18 percent grade, is as steep as many ski trails and more winding than most. Realizing that drivers are too engrossed with the challenge of the road to admire the wild and wonderful scenery, the state's Department of Forests and Parks has thoughtfully provided a turnoff just beyond the height-of-land. An information booth here is staffed in warm-weather months; this is a restful spot by a mountain brook where you can picnic, even grill hot dogs. The Big Spring is here, and you can ask about hiking distances to the other local landmarks: the Elephant Head, King Rock, the Hunter and His Dog (an outstanding rock formation), Singing Bird, the Smugglers Cave, Smugglers Face, and the natural reservoir. See the "Stowe and Waterbury" chapter for details about the easy trail to Sterling Pond and about the trail to the Elephant Head.

COVERED BRIDGES *In and around Jeffersonville:* Look for the **Scott Bridge** on Canyon Rd. across the Brewster River near the old mill; the 84-foot-long bridge is 0.1 mile down the road. To find the **Poland Bridge** (1887) from the junction of Rts. 108 and 15, drive north and turn onto Rt. 109, angling off onto the road along the river; the bridge is in 0.2 mile. Heading west on Rt. 15 toward Cambridge Village, look for Lower Valley Rd.; the **Gates Farm Bridge** (1897) is a few hundred feet from where the present road crosses the river.

In Waterville and Belvidere: Back on Rt. 109, continue north to Waterville and, at Waterville Town Hall (on your right), turn left; the **Church Street Bridge** (1877) is in 0.1 mile. Back on Rt. 109, continue north; the **Montgomery Bridge** (1887) is east of the highway, 1.2 miles north of town hall. Go another 0.5 mile north on Rt. 109 and turn right; the **Kissin' Bridge** (1877) is in 0.1 mile. Continue north on Rt. 109, and 1.5 miles from the Waterville Elementary School (just after the bridge over the North Branch), turn left and go 0.5 mile to the **Mill Bridge** (1895)) in Belvidere. Back on Rt. 109, continue north 0.9 mile and turn left to find the **Morgan Bridge** (1887). See the "Jay Peak Area" chapter for a description of six more covered bridges another dozen miles north in Montgomery.

In Johnson: Take Rt. 100C north from its junction with Rt. 15 for 2.6 miles and turn right; the **Scribner Bridge** (around 1919) is 0.3 mile on your right.

Note: For detailed descriptions of all these sites, see *Covered Bridges of Vermont* by Ed Barna (The Countryman Press).

GALLERIES **Mary Bryan Memorial Art Gallery** (802-644-5100; www.bryan memorialgallery.org), 180 Main St., Jeffersonville. Open daily 11–5 June–Oct., otherwise Thu.–Sun. 10–4. Built by Alden Bryan in memory of his wife and fellow artist, Mary Bryan, this mini museum has changing exhibits featuring artists who have worked in Jeffersonville.

Vermont Studio Center (802-635-2727; www.vermontstudiocenter.org), Johnson. Over the past 16 years this nonprofit center has absorbed 20 buildings in the village of Johnson. The lecture hall is a former meetinghouse, and the gallery, exhibiting the work of artists in residence, is in a former grain mill one street back from Main, down by the river. Some 50 professional artists and writers from throughout the country are usually here at any given time. They come to take advantage of the studio space and the chance to learn from each other through lectures and critiques. Inquire about gallery openings and evening slide shows and lectures.

Dibden Center for the Arts (802-635-1476; www.johnsonstatecollege.edu/ resources/138.html), Johnson State College, Johnson. Open weekdays during the academic year, noon–6. Changing solo and group shows.

SCENIC DRIVES Four loop routes are especially appealing from Jeffersonville:

Stowe/Hyde Park (44-mile loop). Take Rt. 108 through Smugglers Notch to Stowe Village, drive up the old Stagecoach Rd. to Hyde Park (be sure to see the old Opera House), and head back through Johnson.

Belvidere/Eden (40-mile loop). From Jeffersonville, Rt. 109 follows the North Branch of the Lamoille River north to Belvidere Corners; here take Rt. 118, which soon crosses the Long Trail and continues to the village of Eden. Lake Eden, 1 mile north on Rt. 100, is good for swimming and boating; return on Rts. 100, 100C, and 15 via Johnson.

Jericho/Cambridge (38-mile loop). From Jeffersonville, drive southwest on Pleasant Valley Rd., a magnificent drive with the Green Mountains rising abruptly on your left. Go through Underhill Center to the junction with Rt. 15. At Rt. 15, either turn right to head back to Cambridge or continue south on Jericho Center Rd.; return via Jericho and Rt. 15 to Cambridge Village, then drive back along Rt. 15 to Jeffersonville.

Jeffersonville/Johnson (18-mile loop). From the junction of Rts. 15 and 108, head north on Rt. 108, but turn onto Rt. 109 (note the Poland Covered Bridge on your right). Take your first right, Hogback Rd., which shadows the north bank of the Lamoille River most of the way into Johnson. Return via Rt. 15.

HISTORIC HOUSE The Noyes House Museum (802-888-7617), Rt. 100, 1 Main St., Morrisville. Open mid-June until Sep., Wed.–Sat. Guided tours 1–5 or by appointment. Admission by donation. Carlos Noyes was a 19th-century banker who spent much of his fortune expanding this 1820 Federal-style homestead. Its 18 rooms and carriage barn contain one of the state's best collections of Vermont memorabilia, including an 1,800-piece Cheney pitcher and Toby jug collection, and Indian Joe's canoe.

✳ To Do

BICYCLING *Rentals:* Mountain bike rentals are available in Jeffersonville at **Foot of the Notch Bicycles** (802-644-8182) and in Jeffersonville at **Pinnacle Ski & Sports** (1-877-445-1280), Rt. 108 at Smugglers' Notch.

Bicycle touring: **Smugglers Notch Inn** (802-644-6607). The owners can help with local bike routes.

The **Cambridge Greenway** recreation path runs 1.3 miles along the Lamoille River from Jeffersonville east.

Missisquoi Valley Rail Trail, a 26-mile-long recreation path, traverses the northern tier of this region, following the Missisquoi River from Enosburg Falls to Richford. For a map, call the Northwest Regional Planning Commission (802-524-5958; www.nrpcvt.com).

CANOEING AND KAYAKING The **Lamoille River** from Jeffersonville to Cambridge is considered good for novices in spring and early summer; two small sets of rapids.

Bert's Boats (802-644-8189; www.bertsboats.com), at 73 Smugglers View Rd. in Jeffersonville, rents canoes and kayaks and offers shuttle service. Paddles are all flat and Class I water.

Green River Canoe & Kayaks (802-644-8336) operates from 155 Junction Hill Rd. in Jeffersonville. Guided canoe and kayaking trips, especially ecotours led by trained naturalists; also instruction and rentals.

See also Sterling Ridge Resort under *Lodging.*

A MID-RIDE NOSH AT 158 MAIN RESTAURANT & BAKERY, JEFFERSONVILLE

Diane E. Foulds

FISHING The stretch of the Lamoille River between Cambridge and Johnson reputedly offers great fly- and spin-fishing for brown trout.

Green Mountain Troutfitters (802-644-2214; www.gmtrout.com), 233 Mill St. (Rt. 108S), Jeffersonville. Fishing gear, clinics, and guided tours.

Smugglers' Notch Resort (1-800-451-8752) offers frequent fly-casting clinics, fly-fishing stream tours, and smallmouth bass fishing in-season.

T. J.'s Outdoors (802-888-6210), 81 Bridge St., Morrisville, offers year-round fishing, archery, and muzzle-loader supplies, and fishing guide service May–Sep.

Pleasant Valley Fly Fishing Guides (802-644-2813; www.pleasantvalleyfly fishing.com). Lawton Weber specializes in dry-fly wild trout fishing in his half- and full-day excursions. All expertise levels welcome; all equipment provided.

GOLF **Copley Country Club** (802-888-3013), Country Club Rd., Morrisville, is a nine-hole course open May–Oct.

HIKING **Prospect Rock**, Johnson. An easy hike yields an exceptional view of the Lamoille River Valley and the high mountains to the south. Look for a steel bridge to the Ithiel Falls Camp Meeting Ground. Hike north on the white-blazed Long Trail 0.7 mile to the summit.

Belvidere Mountain–Ritterbush Pond and **Devil's Gulch**. These are basically two stretches of the Long Trail; one heads north (3½ hours round-trip) to the summit of Belvidere Mountain, the other heads south (2¾ hours round-trip) to a gulch filled with rocks and ferns. Both are described in the Green Mountain Club's *Long Trail Guide*.

HORSEBACK RIDING ♂ **Brewster River Horse Center** (802-644-8051), 480 Edwards Rd. off Rt. 108, Jeffersonville, 1.3 miles from Smugglers' Notch Resort, offers guided trail rides and pony rides for kids June–mid-Oct.

LaJoie Stables (802-644-5347; www.lajoiestables.com), 992 Pollander Rd. in Jeffersonville. Horseback riding offered all year, including trail rides, pony rides, and overnight treks.

LLAMA TREKS **Northern Vermont Llama Co.** (802-644-2257), 766 Lapland Rd., Waterville. Treks depart from the Smugglers' Notch Resort and head into the backcountry. Geoff and Lindsay Chandler offer half- and full-day treks, depending on the season. Snacks are provided with half-day treks, picnic and snack for full-day outings. Call for rates and to reserve. Family rates available.

Applecheek Farm (802-888-4482; www.applecheekfarm.com), 567 McFarlane Rd., Hyde Park. Trek on "wilderness trails," picnic and farm tour included.

PICNICKING There are several outstanding roadside picnic areas: On Rt. 108, 0.2 mile north of the junction with Rt. 15 at Jeffersonville, four picnic tables (one covered) on the bank of the Lamoille; on Rt. 108 south of Jeffersonville Vil- lage on the east side of the highway; on Rt. 108 in Smugglers Notch itself (see *To See*); on Rt. 15, just 1.5 miles east of the Cambridge–Johnson line.

SWIMMING **Brewster River Gorge**, accessible from Rt. 108 south of Jefferson- ville (turn off at the covered bridge).

Smugglers' Notch Resort (802-644-8851; 1-800-451-8752) features an elabo- rate water park with eight heated pools and four waterslides in summer, plus a winter pool.

Green River Reservoir State Park (802-888-1349) is an undeveloped, 653-acre reservoir with about 19 miles of shoreline. One of the largest unsullied ponds in Vermont. Access is from the south off Green River Dam Rd.

TENNIS Courts at **Smugglers' Notch Resort** (1-800-451-8752), and a summer program of clinics for adults and children and daily instruction at the TenPro Tennis School.

WALKING The **Cambridge Greenway** recreation path runs 1.3 miles along the Lamoille River from Jeffersonville east.

Lamoille County Nature Center (802-888-4965), Cole Hill Rd., Morrisville. Two nature trails offer easy walking and the chance to see deer, bear, and a variety of birds, also lady's slippers in early summer. Inquire about programs offered in the outdoor amphitheater.

✳ Winter Sports

CROSS-COUNTRY SKIING **Nordic Ski and Snowshoe Adventure Center** (802-644-8851), Smugglers' Notch Resort. Narrow trails wind up and down through the trees, then climb meadows away from the resort complex, for a total of 27 km of cross-country trails and 20 km of snowshoe trails; rentals; also telemark, skate skiing, and snowshoe rentals; lessons and tours; repairs in the warming hut, where there is cocoa by the woodstove.

Smugglers Notch. The steep, rocky stretch of Rt. 108 that is closed to traffic for snow season is open to cross-country skiers. Guided tours are offered by the Nordic Adventure Center (see above).

DOWNHILL SKIING ✍ **Smugglers' Notch Resort** (1-800-451-8752; www .smuggs.com), Jeffersonville. In 1956 a group of local residents organized Smugglers' Notch Ski Ways on Sterling Mountain, a western shoulder of 3,640-foot-high Madonna. In 1963 a high-powered group headed by IBM board chairman Tom Watson gained a controlling interest and began developing the area as Madonna Mountain, a self-contained, Aspen-style resort. Only two owners later, with 600 condominiums, Smugglers' is a major ski destination poised over a natural snow bowl with a satisfying variety of terrain spread over three interconnected mountains: beginner trails on Morse Mountain (2,250 feet), intermediate runs on midsized Sterling Mountain (3,010 feet), and expert and glade skiing on Madonna, the highest of the three, with its spectacular long-distance views. (A shuttle links the base areas eight times per hour.) You're greeted by a huge, muddy parking lot, but don't be put off: This is one of New England's best-run vacation spots, summer and winter both. Warm-up huts serve hot meals atop the two highest peaks, and a full range of restaurants lies at the base.

It soon becomes clear why many Vermont skiers bypass Stowe for "Smuggs": The crowds are thinner, the prices lower, and the trails more challenging. After all, this is the site of the only triple-black-diamond run in the East, a sheer drop halfway down Madonna known as The Black Hole. One trail goes 3.5 miles, making it northern Vermont's largest vertical descent, a whopping 2,610 feet. But you also find the opposite extreme: Sir Henry's Learning and Fun Park at the base of Morse Mountain is a mini slope with a half-speed chairlift, a great place for toddlers (and older beginners) to cut their teeth. Two attendants wait on each end to catch you; there's also a Magic Carpet lift on an electric conveyer belt that inches you along like a moving sidewalk.

Throughout, the atmosphere feels carefree and fun, like being in a big summer camp with endless things to do. In winter everyone trudges around pink-cheeked in oversized ski boots; in summer they're barefoot and towel-swathed, lapping ice cream while still dripping from one of the many pools. You can leave your "good" clothes at home, as there's no formality here, unless you dress up for the resort's best restaurant, the romantic Hearth & Candle (see *Dining Out*). But you don't need to, and few bother. Even if you choose not to ski, there is plenty to keep you occupied: an impressive child care center amuses the wee ones while their parents lose themselves in art or herbal workshops, an array of spa indulgences, or invigorating snowshoe treks. There's also an excellent cross-country network. The condo units run the gamut in upkeep and decor, and though they're rarely luxurious, all are clean and comfortable. After all, you come here to be outside, not in. Being so far north, snow lingers long past mid-season, and there's plenty of snowmaking just to be sure. One of the best times to come is early March, when it's relatively warm, and midweek, when it's empty. For that matter, a 5-day ski week, which automatically includes lessons for all family members, is usually the best option.

Midsummer is the bonus: Smugglers' has hands-down the largest and best-organized summer family program in New England. The ski-centered resort miraculously transforms itself into a children's paradise. Upward of 400 kids ages 3–17 participate in four camps, and the fun never stops. Six different play-grounds, a nature center, a Ping-Pong and arcade room for rainy days, and waterslides like the Little Smugglers Lagoon—a faux cave with a waterfall, foun-tains, spouts, and a shallow "river" that propels inner-tubed youngsters around one end of the pool. Supervising them are 180 college-aged counselors who have a knack for engaging kids. We were especially tickled by the shuttle service, six-person canopied golf carts that pick you up and taxi you wherever you want to go, free of charge. Most packages last 5–7 days and include everything but meals so that parents can go off and do their own thing without worrying, be it tennis lessons, golf, guided mountain hikes, day trips to Montreal, art or yoga classes, facials, cooking demonstrations, or wine tastings. Thursday is country fair day, with games, face painting, sack races, and pony rides. There is mini golf, a teen center with interactive video games, evening bonfires and fireworks, and Rum Runner's Hideaway, a pristine, 8-acre lake high up the mountain with canoes, paddleboats, and a water trampoline.

Lifts: 6 double chairlifts, 2 surface.

Trails: 78, including two 3.5-mile trails; 25 percent expert, 56 percent intermediate, 19 percent beginner.

Vertical drop: 2,610 feet.

Snowmaking: 61 percent.

Facilities: Mountain Lodge, base lodge with ski shop, rentals, cafeteria, pub. The reception center/ski shop at Morse Mountain has a Village Center, source of rentals and tickets; the complex also includes a ski shop, deli, country store, and restaurant/snack bar. Top of the Notch warming hut is at the Sterling chair terminal. Snowboarding.

Ski school: Group and private lessons at Morse and Madonna, beginners at Morse. Children's ski and snowboarding camp.

For children: Day care for kids 6 weeks–3 years. Discovery Dynamos Ski Camp for 3- to 5-year-olds—all day with hot lunch and two lessons, games, and races. Adventure Rangers Ski and Snowboard Camps for 6- to 10-year-olds: all day with hot lunch and two lessons; games and races. The Notch Squad is for kids 11–14. Mountain Explorers Ski Program for 15- to 17-year-olds begins at noon daily; lesson and evening activities; two teen centers.

Rates: $56 for a 1-day, 3-mountain adult lift ticket; $40 ages 6–18. Kids 5 and under ski free.

Note: Lodging packages greatly reduce ski-week rates.

ICE SKATING **Smugglers' Notch Resort** rink (flooded tennis courts) is lighted at night as part of its FunZone.

Crew Arena (802-888-0166; www.crewarena.org), 704 Bridge St., Morrisville. A year-round indoor skating rink iced over June–Feb. Call for public skating schedule.

SLEIGH RIDES *♂* **Applecheek Farm** (802-888-4482; www.applecheekfarm .com), 567 McFarlane Rd., Hyde Park. John and Judy Clark's gentle Belgians, Sparky and Sam, take you through the woods by day or night. Hot beverage and farm tour included.

LaJoie Stables (802-644-5347), on Pollander Rd. in Cambridge. Sleigh rides offered all winter.

Charlie Horse Sleigh Rides (802-888-2220; www.charliehorserides.com), 421 N. Hyde Park Rd., Hyde Park, 13 miles from Stowe Village on Rt. 100. Anthony Godin offers 20- to 25-minute rides through the woods daily 10–6.

SNOWMOBILING **Smugglers' Notch Snowmobile Tours** (1-800-347-8266), Junction Hill Rd., Jefferson. Evening 1-hour tours through Smugglers Notch. Customized day tours from 2 to 4 hours. Ride on new Polaris machines.

✳ Lodging

RESORT *♂* &. **Smugglers' Notch Resort** (802-644-8851; 1-800-451-8752 U.S. and Canada; 0800-169-8219 UK), 4323 Rt. 108 south, Smugglers' Notch 05464. More than 600 condominium units in a variety of shapes accommodate a total of 2,600 people. Geared to families, clubs, and reunions, the resort offers a year-round combination of good things: skiing, swimming, tennis, and a varied program of summer activities, including a supervised children's schedule of fishing, movies, family activities, nature and hiking, games, music and dance, arts and crafts in an all-day camp format, disk golf, mini golf, and more. Summer tennis and other packages are also available. The resort excels at catering to children, with a variety of very distinct facilities and programs geared to different ages. Treasures, the nursery for newborns and tots, is particularly impressive, as is the program for teens. In winter a Club Smugglers' 5-day ski week includes lodging, lift tickets, ski or snowboard camp for ages 3–5, lessons for youth–age 17, and learn-to-ski lessons for adults, plus use of the Fun-Zone, pool, tubing, and other extras from $99 per adult per day, and from $79 per youth (17 and under). In summer a comparable program, including FamilyFest Camp Programs for youngsters, begins at $1,569 per week for a two-child family. Add 14.5 percent for combined state tax and service charge. *Note:* Condominium units are all individually owned and vary from studios, to five-bedroom suites (all recently upgraded), to luxury units with TV as well as Jacuzzi in the bath. Some condos are wheelchair accessible. Units also vary widely in location, from roadside to slope-side to up in the woods.

INNS AND BED & BREAKFASTS

∞ ✍ **Smugglers Notch Inn** (802-644-6607; 1-866-644-6607; www.smugsinn.com), 55 Church St., P.O. Box 280, Jeffersonville 05464. Dating in part from the 18th century, this is a comfortable village inn that's been gentrified without losing its old-fashioned appeal. The living room retains its decorative tin ceiling as well as its brick fireplace, and remains a casual,

inviting space with plenty of books and games. A fully licensed, half-circular bar with a copper footrail fills a corner on the way to the columned dining room, which is hung with paintings by artists who have stayed here over the years, a good place for weddings and reunions. The 11 guest rooms all have private bath and country quilts; the room we slept comfortably in was warmed by a gas fireplace. Facilities include an outdoor hot tub. Dining is as simple as walking downstairs to the restaurant or Village Tavern (see *Dining Out*). Innkeepers Patrick and Lisa Martin will hand out maps of good local bike routes. $89–129 per room includes a full breakfast. Extra service charges added.

∞ ✍ **Sterling Ridge Resort** (802-644-8265; 1-800-347-8266; www.sterlingridgeresort.com), 155 Sterling Ridge Dr., Jeffersonville 05464. Sterling Ridge is a secluded log cabin village with a variety of attractively furnished accommodations scattered among fields, ponds, and flower beds. Pond House is a four-bedroom farmhouse that's great for families ($140–250 per night). The main inn, built in 1988, has been divided into three- and four-bedroom suites ($120–225 per night). Back beyond the pond, Scott and Susan Peterson have built 18 one- and two-bedroom log cabins ($80–195 per night, with a 2-night minimum stay), each nicely designed with a fireplace, cathedral ceiling, fully equipped kitchen, and outdoor grill. The inn's 80 acres are webbed with 20 km of trails; facilities include a hot tub and outdoor pool. Mountain bikes, boats, and snowshoes are available.

∞ **Donomar Inn** (802-644-2937; www.donomar.com), 916 Rt. 108 south, Jeffersonville 05464. The most popular spot in this handsome country home is the solarium, a tiled, sun-filled dining area off the kitchen with gorgeous mountain views. There's also a cozy library with a fireplace and Oriental carpets, a fieldstone fireplace in the great room, a six-person outdoor hot tub (bring your swimsuit), and a common room with a TV/VCR/DVD player. Mary Bouvier and Moira Donovan, both educators, provide guests with snowshoes for treks over their 8 acres of adjacent fields. Guests have their choice of six air-conditioned rooms, four with private bath, some with fireplace and Jacuzzi. Rates range $80–175 per room double occupancy, which includes a full breakfast of fresh fruit, homemade breads, a hot entrée, and imported teas. Resident dog and cat.

✎ **Fitch Hill Inn** (802-888-3834; 1-800-639-2903; www.fitchhillinn.com), 258 Fitch Hill Rd., Hyde Park 05655. Handy to many parts of the North Country, this 18th-century hilltop house owned by Julie and John Rohleder is elegantly maintained. There are six air-conditioned guest rooms, each with private bath and most named for a state (our favorite is

THE GOVERNOR'S HOUSE IN HYDE PARK

Diane E. Foulds

Vermont), all nicely furnished and equipped with ceiling fans; two are able to accommodate more than two people. Two rooms, New Hampshire and Green Mountains, come with small kitchen, two-person whirlpool tub, and fireplace. There is ample common room, an outdoor hot tub, two covered porches for guest use, and an impressive library of videos for the VCR. $135–205 in high season, $85–155 in low, includes a full hot breakfast and afternoon snack.

Three Mountain Lodge (802-644-5736; www.threemountainlodge.com), Rt. 108, Smugglers' Notch Rd., Jeffersonville 05464. Built in 1966 to house the University of Vermont outing club, the lodge was later used to put up the UVM and Johnson State College ski teams. Smugglers' Notch Resort was using it as a ski dorm until Steve and Colleen Blood came along in 1984. It's now primarily a restaurant (see *Eating Out*), but a guest cottage adjacent to the lodge is available for travelers looking for comfortable private accommodations. Nightly rates for the cottage range $65–85 ($400–570 per week) with a maximum occupancy of four.

∞ ⅊ **The Governor's House in Hyde Park** (802-888-6888; 1-866-800-6888; www.onehundredmain .com), 100 Main St., Hyde Park 05655. Suzanne Boden has completely restored this sumptuous mansion to reflect the periods of 1893—when the house was erected—and 1759 when the Longfellow House, after which it was designed, was built in Cambridge, Ma. There are eight guest rooms, six with private bath and one fully handicapped accessible, as is the entire first floor of the inn. Boden serves an elegant afternoon tea in the library on Thu. and Sun. and alfresco suppers when there is a production at Hyde Park Opera House across the street. Guests are invited to arrive early for lemonade and croquet on the expansive lawns, or simply to sit on the back portico and enjoy hors d'oeuvres (BYOB) as the sun sets behind the mountains. $110–245 (singles $95) includes three-course breakfast, and tea.

Village Victorian (802-888-8850; 1-866-266-4672; www.villagevictorian .com), 107 Union St., Morrisville 05661. Ellen and Philip Wolff are your hosts in an 1890s Victorian in the village of Morrisville, just 7 miles from Stowe. All five guest rooms have queen bed and private bath, with a TV/VCR combo and air conditioner in each. The Wolffs also offer a fully furnished, winterized lake cottage on Shadow Lake, about 30 miles northeast. $100–200 includes full breakfast. Discounts for longer stays.

Also see Berkson Farms in "The Northwest Corner."

Nye's Green Valley Farm Bed & Breakfast (802-644-1984; www .nyesgreenvalleyfarm.com), 8976 Rt. 15 west, Jeffersonville 05464. A brick Colonial about 4 miles east of Jeffersonville on Rt. 15. As a child, Marsha Nye Lane played in this 1810 former stagecoach tavern that her great-grandfather had bought in 1867, that her uncle had farmed, and that her father was born in. It passed through several owners; when she learned that the bank had foreclosed on the property, she and her husband, David, bought and restored the farmhouse to look the way she remembered it. Now it accommodates guests

Diane E. Foulds

NYE'S GREEN VALLEY FARM BED & BREAKFAST, JEFFERSONVILLE

in three air-conditioned rooms, one with private bath. All of them are light and cozy with quilts and comfy chairs. Breakfast, served family-style, includes freshly baked breads, fresh fruit, and two or three choices of entrées. Common rooms are beautifully furnished with rare antiques, including a collection of handblown inkwells. There's a steep, narrow staircase in the kitchen, and you notice square-headed nails in the floors and ceilings. Outdoors is a pond, the scene of summer campfires, a thriving garden with the tallest bee balm we've ever seen, and the Lanes' antiques shop, one of eight nearby. $75–95 includes breakfast.

TOWN HOUSES Notch Glen Rentals (802-644-5985; www.notch glenrentals.com), 150 Chez Lane, Jeffersonville 05464. Tastefully appointed townhouse units with panoramic views of Smugglers Notch and Mount Mansfield. Available as one-, two-, or three-bedroom units equipped with a full kitchen, dining and living room, and satellite and/or cable TV. One bedroom is available as a separate efficiency with full bath, king-sized bed, and kitchenette, or included as a third bedroom, and there's also a 19th-century post-and-beam barn. Located on Rt. 108 south just 3 miles from Smugglers' Notch Resort, Notch Glen is convenient to antique barns, fine art studios, and several gift shops. Rates by the week, the month, or the year.

MOTEL 🐾 🧺 ♿ **Sunset Motor Inn** (802-888-4956; 1-800-544-2347; www .sunsetmotorinn.com), 160 Rt. 15 west, at the junction of Rts. 100 and 15, Morrisville 05661. Fifty-five comfortable units, some with whirlpool bath and refrigerator, several that are fully wheelchair accessible. Therre are three fully equipped three-bedroom houses, with easy access to several ski areas and an outdoor pool. The family-friendly **Sam's Charlmont Restaurant** (see *Eating Out*) is right next door. Rates $58–163, houses $140–275. Kids 12 and under stay free.

CAMPGROUND **Brewster River Campground** (802-644-2126; www .brewsterrivercampground.com), 110 Campground Dr., off Rt. 108, Jeffersonville 05464. Just 20 "low-tech" tent sites, a tepee, and several lean-tos on 20 secluded acres with a 40-foot waterfall and a river where you can pan for gold. There's a fire pit, picnic tables, and a modern bathhouse (free hot showers); no pets (but there's a local kennel). Tent sites are $20 per night, hookups $25; a lean-to is $30. Not suitable for large vehicles with internal plumbing.

✳ Where to Eat

DINING OUT **Hearth & Candle** (802-644-1260), Smugglers' Notch Resort, Jeffersonville. Open daily 4:30–9. One of the first structures built in the condo village, this well-respected dining spot in an old New England–style homestead is the most formal place in town. The atmosphere is upscale English pub. Moderate.

Smugglers Notch Inn and Restaurant (802-644-6607; www.smuggsinn .com), at the Smugglers Notch Inn, 55 Church St. (Rt. 108 between Jeffersonville and Smugglers). Open daily for lunch and dinner. Formerly known as The Hungry Lion, this country eatery does a full menu of seafood, poultry, pasta, beef, and vegetarian dishes, plus salads and sandwiches, a light menu, and selections for kids. Entrées range $10.95–24.95 (for twin rock lobster tails). Try the lamb and Guinness stew. The dining room shares space with The Village Bakery.

See also 158 Main, below.

EATING OUT 🐾 ♿ **Persico's Plum & Main** (802-635-7596), middle of Main St., Johnson. Open 6 AM–8 PM weekdays, until 9 Fri. and Sat., 8 AM–1 PM Sun. Closed Mon. Culinary Institute of America graduate Pat Persico could be writing his own ticket in Stowe, but this Vermont native would rather serve local folks along with the stray skier and leaf-peeper. The breakfast specials might include apple cinnamon griddlecakes with home fries and syrup, or a bacon, cheddar, and onion omelet. The lunch menu covers the basics, but the ingredients are fresh and locally grown, and the soup homemade. The dinner menu changes nightly but could include baked fresh haddock with a spinach seafood stuffing, or prime rib of beef. BYOB. Inquire about specialty nights, like roast turkey or Italian. Pat's wife, Laurel, bakes the desserts, like coconut cream and maple oat nut pie. Entrées range $10.95–19.95.

158 Main (802-644-8100), 158 Main St., Jeffersonville. Serving breakfast, lunch, and dinner daily except Mon. Jack Foley has introduced a menu of "innovative traditionalism" featuring organic vegetables from local farms, seafood chowders, big, fresh salads, and the usual steaks, seafood, and pizza. The high-ceilinged, hardwood-floored dining room, formerly a dry goods store, shares space with a bakery selling fudge-covered brownies, cookies, Italian- and French-style baguettes, and whole wheat loaves fresh from the oven. The lunch and dinner menus cover the basics, but the ingredients are fresh and locally grown and the soup homemade. Breakfast could be French toast made with baguettes and Grand Marnier, Florentine eggs Benedict with spinach, or a shrimp and Gorgonzola salad. BYOB. Dinner entrées run $11–18.

Sam's Charlmont Restaurant (802-888-4242; 1-800-781-4626), 116 Rt. 100, Morrisville, at the junction of Rts. 100 and 15. Open daily, all three meals. This family restaurant has been around for 40 years and remains a fixture in Morrisville, hosting local banquets and special events and generally keeping its many faithful customers happy. Owner Sam Jadallah has improved upon the winning menu: meat loaf, lasagna, strawberry waffles, and large portions. Air-conditioned booths, pine tables. Reasonable.

Melben's Restaurant (802-888-3009), 10 Railroad St., Morrisville, down the street from the Bijoux Cinema. Moderately priced Italian specialties and fresh seafood. Open daily for lunch and dinner, Sunday for brunch.

Hilary's (802-888-5352), Rt. 100, Northgate Plaza, Morrisville. Breakfast, lunch, dinner, and Sunday brunch are all served daily in this pleasant place that's good for everything from sandwiches to seafood, from vegetarian dishes to steak. Fully licensed.

Three Mountain Lodge (802-644-5736), Rt. 108, Smugglers' Notch Rd., Jeffersonville. Open 4–9 PM; closed Mon. in peak season, Mon. and Tue. in low season. The restaurant attached to the Three Mountain Lodge features fresh New England seafood, Black Angus beef, vegetarian entrées, homemade pasta, and homemade ice cream. Daily and seasonal specials. Shrimp scampi is $15.95, veal St. Pierre is $21.95, and the Three Mountain Steak, smothered in mushrooms, is $27.95.

The Bee's Knees (802-888-7889; www.thebeesknees-vt.com), 82 Lower Main St., Morrisville. Open Tue.–Fri., 6:30 AM–10 PM, Sat. and Sun., 8 AM–10 PM. Sharon Deitz's Caribbean- and African-accented bistro serves up stunning surprises in such a northern clime: quinoa feta soup with scallions, for example, along with curried tofu salad sandwiches, ginger-laced drinks, and the cool, spicy cucumber soup we had on a muggy day in June. The tables are mismatched, the decor artsy, the clientele laid-back, and children welcome to play with the toys. Fair-trade coffee, organic wine. Live music nearly every night.

Edelweiss Bakery and Kaffee Shop (802-635-7946), 325 Lower Main St. west, Johnson. Breakfast, lunch, Sunday brunch. Closed Mon. The bakery is downstairs, the café up in this converted Victorian just outside town. The European-style fare includes croissants, baguettes, whole-grain breads, and delectable fruit tarts. Lunches include fresh salads from the new salad bar, unusual sandwich combinations, and delicious soups.

Bad Girls Café (802-635-7423), 38 Main St., Johnson. Open weekdays 7–7, Sat. and Sun. 8–6. Laid-back student hangout with art on the walls and fresh-brewed java, plus frozen frapuccinos, veggie salads, paninis, and fresh-baked sweets. You order in the kitchen of this 19th-century house and sit down in the mango-colored living room or in the former dining room, where online computers are available by the hour.

✳ Entertainment

Lamoille County Players (802-888-4507); call for summer schedule of productions.

The Cambridge Arts Council stages theater, concerts, and coffee-houses in Jeffersonville. Check local bulletin boards.

Vermont Studio Center Lecture and Reading Series, Johnson. For a schedule of the frequent presentations by artists and writers, call the center (802-635-2727).

Bijoux Cineplex 4 (802-888-3293), Portland St. (Rt. 100), Morrisville. All shows $4 on Tue. and Thu.

BAD GIRLS CAFÉ IN JOHNSON

Diane E. Foulds

✳ Selective Shopping

ANTIQUES 1829 Antique Center (802-644-2912), 8147 Rt. 15, Jeffersonville (2.5 miles east of the village). Open year-round daily except Sunday. Carolyn and Richard Hover's great old barn is filled on three floors with a wide assortment of country furniture and furnishings representing 40 dealers.

Green Apple Antique Center (802-644-2989), 60 Main St., Jeffersonville. Daily 9–5, Sun. 11–4. Located in the old Noble Pearl Building, this center represents more than 30 dealers and consigners.

Smugglers' Notch Antiques (802-644-2100; www.smugglersnotch antiques.com), Rt. 108 south. Daily May–Oct., 10–5; Nov.–Apr., open Fri.–Sun. This dairy-barn-turned-antiques-center with 40 dealer booths specializes in custom-made and antique furniture.

The Buggyman Antiques Shop (802-635-2110), Rt. 15, Johnson. Open daily 10–5. A big old barn and 18th-century farmhouse filled with antiques, including wagons, buggies, and sleighs.

Victorian House Antiques (802-635-9549), Johnson. A multidealer and consignment shop.

Antiques By Vermont Hands (802-635-7664; www.byvermont hands.com), Rt. 15, Johnson (1 mile west of the village), carries fine European and early American antiques and some locally made furniture. Open daily except Tue. 10–5, or by appointment.

Nye's Green Valley Farm Antiques (802-644-1984), Rt. 15 between Jeffersonville and Johnson. Open daily 10–5:30. Old Vermont farmhouse furnishings and a wide selection of American pressed glass.

ART AND CRAFTS GALLERIES Quilts by Elaine (802-644-6635; www.quilts byelaine.com), 127 Main St., Jeffersonville. Open 9–5 daily except Wed. Elaine Van Dusen makes great quilts from crib to king sized as well as wall hangings.

Vermont Rug Makers (802-635-2434), Rt. 100C east of Johnson, and Main St. in Stowe. Open 10–5 except Sunday. Handmade rugs from around the world.

Milk Room Gallery (802-644-5122; www.milkroomgallery.com), 105 Main St., Jeffersonville, open year-round. A collection that started in the milk room of a nearby farm has blossomed into this midvillage gallery featuring Vermont landscapes through the eyes of New England artists, plus sculpture, pottery, rugs, and framing.

Boyden Farm, intersection of Rts. 15 and 104, just west of Cambridge Village. The second story of this shop/winery (see below) is filled with exquisite Quebec- and Vermont-made antique reproduction furniture and furnishings. Local crafts and artisanal foods are displayed downstairs.

Tegu Gallery (802-888-1261; www.riverartsvt.org), Portland St., Morrisville. Open Mon.–Fri. 8–4:30. A new gallery run by River Arts, the Tegu Gallery exhibits the work of regional artists as well as that created by participants in River Arts' workshops.

FARMS AND A WINERY Boyden Valley Winery (802-644-8151), 64 Rt. 104, at the intersection of Rts. 15 and 104, just west of Cambridge Village. Open June–Dec., Tue.–Sun. 10–5; otherwise Fri.–Sun. 10–5. At

this fifth-generation working cattle farm bordering the Lamoille River, David Boyden has turned an 1878 carriage barn into a microwinery producing over a dozen fruit and grape wines. Wine tours and tastings are offered at 11:30 and 1, and the apple wine we brought home was excellent. Maple syrup and Vermont products and country antique furniture reproductions (see above) are also sold. Try the French cheese plate with wine for $14.95. Farm tours.

Applecheek Farm (802-888-4482; www.applecheekfarm.com), 567 McFarlane Rd., Hyde Park. Call before coming. A dairy farm with a maple sugaring operation; other farm animals include llamas, emus, draft horses, and miniature horses. Llama treks with picnic, barbecue with horse and wagon rides.

SPECIALTY STORES Johnson Woolen Mills (802-635-7185; 1-877-635-WOOL; www.johnsonwoolen mills.com), 51 Lower Main St., Johnson. Open year-round, daily except Sun. 9–5; June–Jan., open Sun. 10–4. Although wool is no longer loomed in this picturesque mill, the fine line of clothing for which Johnson Woolen Mills has long been known is made on the premises. This mill's label can still be found in shops throughout the country, and its famous, heavy green wool work pants, a uniform of Vermont farmers, are especially popular in Alaska. Although there are few discounts at the factory store, the selection of wool jackets and pants—for men, women, and children—is exceptional. The mail-order catalog is replete with sweaters, wool ties, hunting jackets, blankets, and other staples available in the shop.

Three Mountain Outfitters (802-644-8563). Located at Smugglers' Notch Resort. Seasonal sports clothes for all ages as well as toys, shoes and boots, T-shirts, and accessories.

Marvin's Butternut Country Store (802-635-2329), 31 Main St., Johnson, is open Mon.–Sat. 9–5:30, Sun. 11–4. This is the retail outlet for the Marvin family's maple products, plus a variety of specialty foods and Vermont gifts.

The Studio Store (802-635-2203; 1-800-887-2203), Pearl St., Johnson, adjacent to the Vermont Studio Center. Open Wed.–Sat. 10–6, Sun. noon–5. A fully stocked artist's supply store, independently owned.

🐾 ♿ **Arthur's Department Store** (802-888-3125), 63 Main St., Morrisville. Arthur and Theresa Breault and their daughter, Adrienne, do their buying in New York, Boston, Dallas, and Las Vegas; they have created an unexpectedly fine and friendly source of clothing, and footwear for men, women, juniors, and children. Genuine bargains in the basement.

Vermont Maple Outlet (802-644-5482), 3929 Rt. 15 between Jefferson and Cambridge. A nice selection of cheese, syrup, handmade jams, and gift boxes. Open daily 9–5.

Forget-Me-Not Shop (802-635-2335), Rt. 15, 1.5 miles west of Johnson. This eclectic store carries international military surplus clothing and gear, gift items of all sorts, jewelry, and famous-label clothing at discounted prices. Open daily 9–9.

✳ Special Events

Last weekend of January: **Winterfest**—a primitive biathlon with muzzle loaders and snowshoes.

March: **Marchfest**. Four weeks of special events at Smugglers' Notch Resort—Nordic, alpine races, broomball tournaments, crafts shows, folk dances, snow sculpture, fireworks, ball.

First weekend of June: **Vermont Dairy Festival**—arts and crafts, horse pulling, stage shows, 2-hour Saturday parade, country-and-western jamboree Sunday.

July 4: **Celebration**, Jeffersonville—an outstanding small-town parade at 10 AM followed by a chicken barbecue, games, crafts, cow-flop bingo, and a frog-jumping contest on the green behind the elementary school. Evening music and fireworks at Smugglers' Notch Resort, food.

Late July: **Lamoille County Field Days** (802-635-7113), Rt. 100C, Johnson—a classic small-town fair with family entertainment. Wheelchair accessible. **Morristown Community Festival** (802-888-1261)—art, food, music, sidewalk sale along Main Street in Morrisville.

Early August: **Blueberry Festival** (802-456-7012), Grand View Winery, Cambridge—pies, jams, wines, and plain old berries; live music; free.

Labor Day weekend: **Festivities** in Cambridge—barbecue on the green, flea market, family road run (3.1 miles) from Jeffersonville to Cambridge along back roads.

The Northeast Kingdom

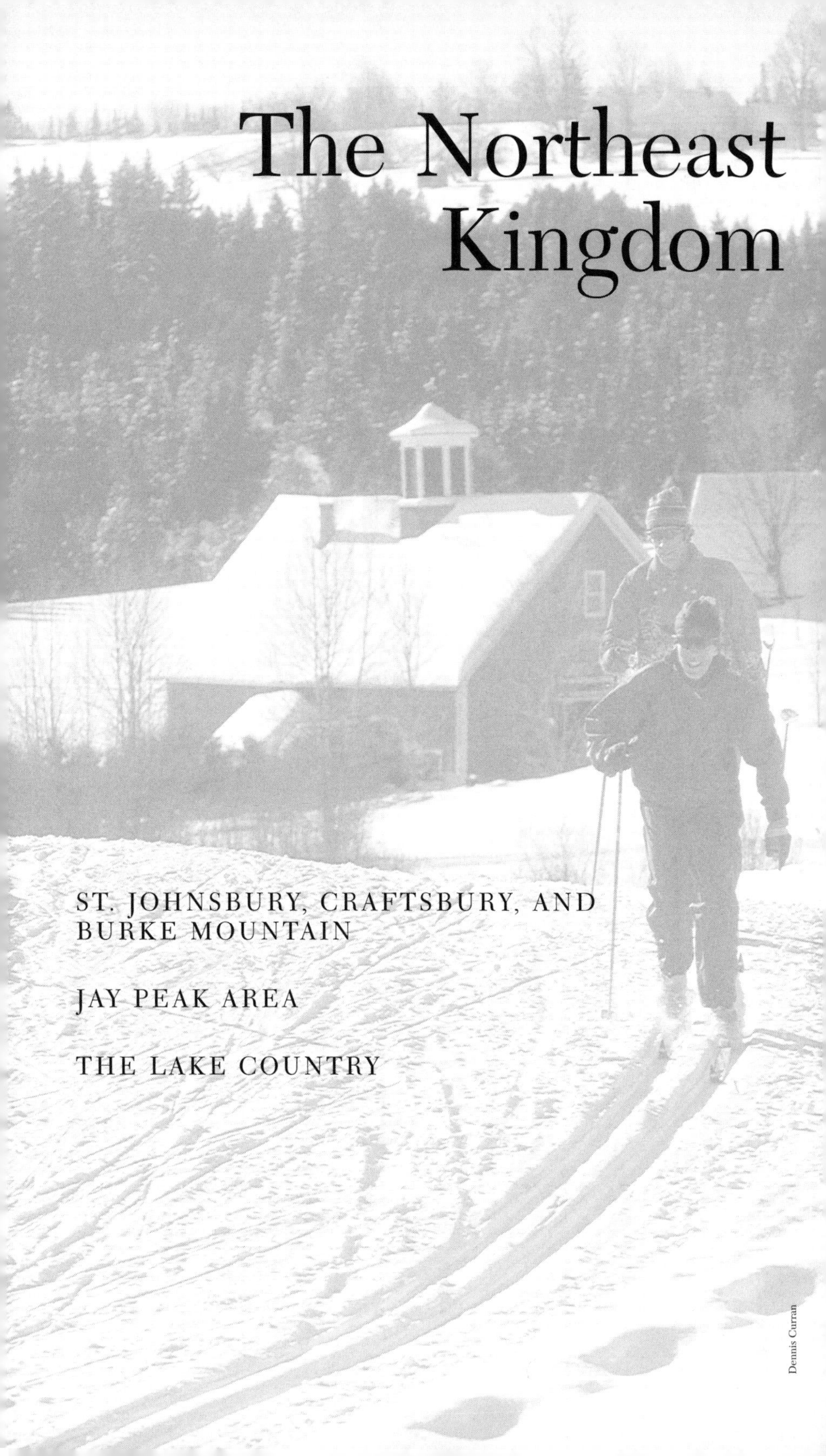

ST. JOHNSBURY, CRAFTSBURY, AND
BURKE MOUNTAIN

JAY PEAK AREA

THE LAKE COUNTRY

Dennis Curran

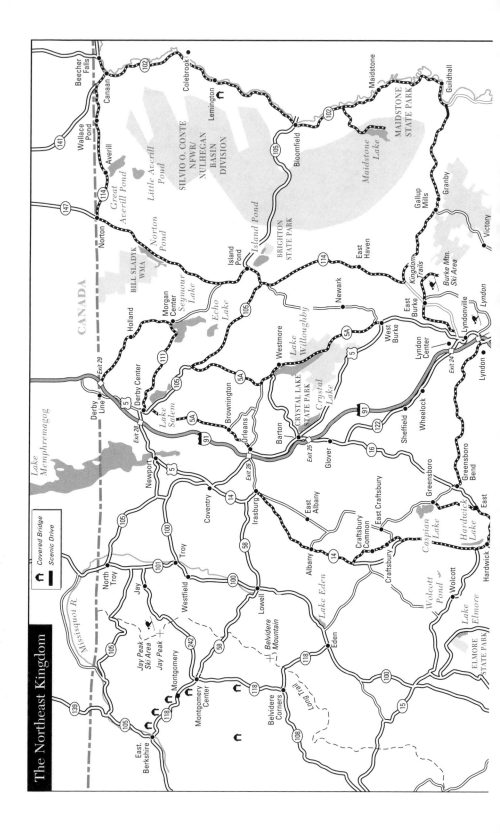

The Northeast Kingdom

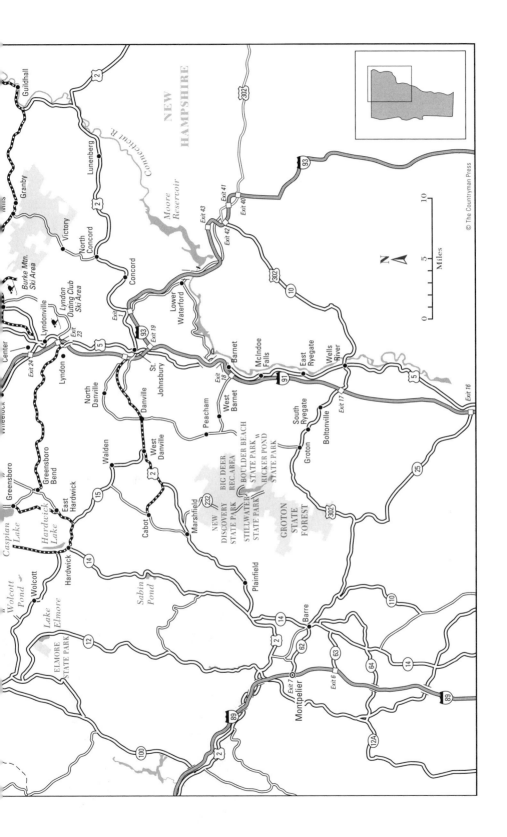

© The Countryman Press

INTRODUCTION

> *You know, this is such beautiful country up here. It ought to be called the Northeast Kingdom of Vermont.*

It was in 1949 that Senator George Aiken made this remark to a group in Lyndonville. The name he coined has since stuck to Vermont's three northeastern counties: Orleans, Caledonia, and Essex.

This is the state's most rural and lake-spotted corner, encompassing more than 2,000 square miles, including 37,575 acres of public lakes and ponds and 3,540 miles of rivers. Aside from a few dramatic elevations, such as Jay Peak on its northwestern fringe and Burke Mountain at its heart, this is a predominantly high, open, glacially carved plateau of humped hills and rolling farmland, with some lonely timber country along the northern reaches of the Connecticut River.

Until now neither Burke Mountain nor Jay Peak has had much impact on surrounding communities in summer and fall. That, however, may soon change. Burke's new owners plan major developments, including an 18-hole golf course such as the one Jay Peak is slated to open this summer.

At present the area attracts no more summer visitors than it did in the era of trains and steamboats, when large hotels clustered on Lakes Memphremagog and Willoughby. Foliage season, which begins early here and is frequently over by Columbus Day, draws relatively few leaf-peepers, perhaps because of the way the roads run. I-93 puts St. Johnsbury within a 3-hour drive of Boston but farther from New York than most of Vermont.

Lodging options range from elegant country inns and full resorts to ski lodges and condominiums, summer cottages and working farms. All the amenities are here: golf, tennis,

GEORGE AIKEN

and horseback riding as well as plenty of hiking, fishing, canoeing, and kayaking. Winter sports include ice fishing, tracking and snowshoeing, some of New England's best snowmobiling, and cross-country as well as downhill skiing.

The key to this Kingdom is following farm roads and—in the process of finding an isolated B&B or craftsperson, a maple producer or swimming hole—stumbling on breathtaking views and memorable people. Frequently you come across traces of the Kingdom's oldest thoroughfare, the 48-mile Bayley-Hazen Military Road, which runs diagonally across the region. It was begun at Wells River on the Connecticut River in 1776 by General Jacob Bayley, and continued in 1778–79 by General Moses Hazen as far as Hazen's Notch (a plaque on Rt. 58 tells the story). It was a flop as the invasion route but served settlers well after the Revolution when it came time to establish towns in this area. Many communities here boomed in the mid– and late 19th century with the advent of railroads.

The Northeast Kingdom has a story to tell. Listen at a lunch counter, in a general store, at a church supper, at a county fair, or during the peerless Northeast Kingdom Foliage Festival. Admittedly it's fading, but you can sharpen your ear with Howard Frank Mosher's beautifully written books—*Northern Borders*, *Where the Rivers Flow North*, and *A Stranger in the Kingdom*. Kingdom-based filmmaker and arts activist Jay Craven has turned two of these into films.

Unfortunately, while this is the single most distinctive corner of the entire state, 2,000 square miles is too large an area to describe without dividing it in three. If you have a particular passion such as canoeing, cross-country skiing, fishing, hiking, or mountain biking, check *To Do* under all three.

GUIDANCE **The Northeast Kingdom Travel and Tourism Association** (802-626-8511; 1-888-884-8001; www.travelthekingdom.com), a nonprofit umbrella organization promoting the area, publishes the useful *Travel Planner* and *Cultural Heritage Tour Map*. Also excellent hiking and biking guides to the region.

GETTING THERE *By car:* I-93 makes the Northeast Kingdom far more accessible from the southeast than is still generally realized: Bostonians can be in St. Johnsbury in 3 hours. Note that I-91 works like a fireman's pole, a quick way to move north–south through the Kingdom. In snow, beware the high, open, 16-mile stretch of highway between Lyndon Center and Barton known as Sheffield Heights.

MEDICAL EMERGENCY Emergency service is available by calling **911**.

Northeastern Vermont Regional Hospital (802-748-8141), 1315 Hospital Dr., St. Johnsbury. **North Country Hospital** (802-334-7331), 189 Prouty Dr., Newport.

ST. JOHNSBURY, CRAFTSBURY, AND BURKE MOUNTAIN

With a population of less than 7,600, St. Johnsbury is the largest community in the Northeast Kingdom. Thanks to members of the Fairbanks family, who began manufacturing their world-famous scale here in the 1830s, it is graced with an outstanding museum of natural and local history, a handsome athenaeum, and an outstanding academy. The general late-19th-century affluence that St. J (as it is affectionately known) enjoyed as an active rail junction and industrial center has been commemorated in ornate brick along Railroad Street and sloping Eastern Avenue and in the fine mansions along Main Street, set high above the commercial downtown. In the 1960s, when Fairbanks became a division of a conglomerate—which threatened to move the scaleworks south—townspeople themselves raised the money to subsidize a new plant. The point is that this is a spirited community boasting one of the country's oldest town bands (performing Monday nights all summer in Courthouse Park), a busy calendar of concerts, lectures, and plays, and all the shops and services needed by residents of the picturesque villages along the Connecticut River to the south, the rolling hills to the southwest and northwest, and the lonely woodlands to the east. Less than a dozen miles north, the wide main street of Lyndonville is also lined with useful shops. Burke Mountain, a short way up Rt. 114, is accessible by car as well as by foot in summer and draws skiers from throughout the Northeast in winter.

As Rt. 2 climbs steeply west from St. J to Danville, a spectacular panorama of the White Mountains unfolds to the east. The village of Danville itself is a beauty, and the back roads running south to Peacham and north to Walden follow ridges with long views. Continue on through Hardwick and north to Craftsbury, where fields roll away like waves to the mountains in the distance.

Craftsbury is a composite of scattered villages, most of which you drive through in a trice. It's Craftsbury Common, with its magnificent common surrounded by white homes, academy, and church, that compels you to stop. Get lost in the surrounding web of well-maintained dirt roads. Eventually you hit a paved, numbered road, and in the meantime you find some of Vermont's most breathtaking farmscape, spotted with small lakes and large ponds. Don't miss Greensboro, an early-20th-century summer compound on Caspian Lake.

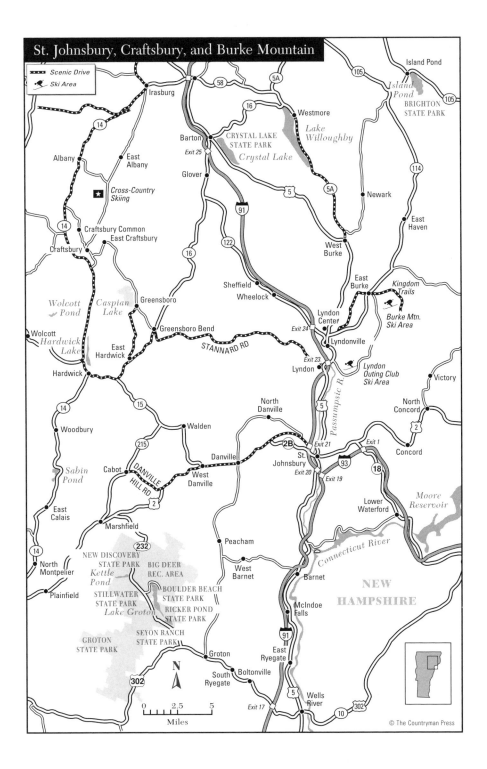

St. Johnsbury, Craftsbury, and Burke Mountain

Scenic Drive
Ski Area

Island Pond

105

105

Island
Pond
BRIGHTON
STATE PARK

114

58

Irasburg

16

Westmore

Lake
Willoughby

14

Albany

East
Albany

Barton

Exit 25

CRYSTAL LAKE
STATE PARK

Crystal Lake

Glover

5

5A

Newark

East
Haven

Cross-Country
Skiing

91

14

Craftsbury Common

East Craftsbury

122

West
Burke

Craftsbury

16

East
Burke

Kingdom
Trails

Wolcott
Pond

Caspian
Lake

Greensboro

Sheffield

Wheelock

Burke Mtn.
Ski Area

Wolcott

Hardwick
Lake

Greensboro Bend

STANNARD RD

Lyndon
Center

Exit 24

Lyndonville

East
Hardwick

Hardwick

Exit 23

Lyndon

Lyndon
Outing Club
Ski Area

Victory

14

15

North
Danville

5

North
Concord

Woodbury

Walden

2

215

Danville

2B

Sabin
Pond

Cabot

DANVILLE

HILL RD

West
Danville

St.
Johnsbury

Exit 21

Exit 1

Concord

2

Exit 20

93

Exit 19

18

East
Calais

Marshfield

Lower
Waterford

Moore
Reservoir

14

North
Montpelier

NEW DISCOVERY
STATE PARK
Kettle
Pond

232

BIG DEER
REC. AREA

Peacham

West
Barnet

Barnet

Connecticut River

NEW

Plainfield

STILLWATER
STATE PARK

BOULDER BEACH
STATE PARK

RICKER POND

Lake Groton
STATE PARK

HAMPSHIRE

McIndoe
Falls

GROTON
STATE PARK

SEYON RANCH
STATE PARK

N

Groton

East
Ryegate

302

South
Ryegate

Boltonville

5

Wells
River

91

0   2.5   5

Miles

Exit 17

10

302

© The Countryman Press

GUIDANCE Northeast Kingdom Chamber of Commerce (802-748-3678; 1-800-639-6379; www.nekchamber.com), Suite 3, 51 Depot Square, St. Johnsbury 05819. The chamber maintains an outstanding year-round welcome center in its vintage railroad station, open in summer and fall Mon.–Thu. 9–6, Fri. and Sat. 9–8, Sun. 11–2; in winter Mon.–Fri. 8:30–5, Sat. 10–5, and Sun. 11–2. A source for lodging, dining, and general information for the region.

✴ Towns and Villages

Barnet (population: 1,690). An old Scots settlement encompassing the villages of McIndoe Falls as well as East and West Barnet and Barnet Center. The village of Barnet itself is on a curve of the Connecticut River, almost lost today in a curious intertwining of I-91 and Rt. 5. **Goodwillie House** (802-633-2563) in Barnet Center, built in 1790 by a Scottish pastor, served as a stop on the Underground Railroad and now houses the collections of the Barnet Historical Society; unfortunately it's only open by request and on Fall Foliage Day. Drive to West Barnet to find **Harvey's Lake** (good for both fishing and swimming); along the way stop by the 1870s **Ben Thresher's Mill** (open Sat. 10–2 July–Sep., and daily during foliage season). The beautiful round red **Moore Barn** sits above the Passumpsic River in East Barnet (north on Rt. 5 from Barnet). Also see the **Karmê Chöling Shambhala Meditation Center** (www.karmecholing.org) under *Lodging*.

Burke (population 1,571; 802-626-4124 chamber of commerce; www.burke vermont.com). The town includes Burke Hollow and West Burke, but it's the village of East Burke that offers attractive shops, restaurants, and lodging. That's because it's home to Burke Mountain alpine and cross-country ski areas and Burke Mountain Academy as well as Kingdom Trails, best known for mountain biking but also good for hiking and cross-country skiing. Add to all this separate trails for snowmobiling. The library and historical society building (802-626-9823), with its paintings and historical collection, is open Mon., Tue., and Thu. 2–5, also by appointment.

Cabot (population: 1,090). Known during the War of 1812 for its distilleries (the whiskey was sold to Canadians), this distinctly upcountry village is now famed for its cheese. The Cabot Farmers Co-op Creamery is Vermont's major producer, and its visitors center is a popular attraction. Cabot is called the mother of the Winooski because the river rises in four of its ponds.

Concord (population: 1,205). Six miles east of St. Johnsbury on Rt. 2, Concord is a proudly built village with an unusual number of columned houses. The **Concord Museum** (802-695-330) is found upstairs in the tower-topped town hall; there's a picture of St. Johnsbury's Railroad Street, painted in the 1940s, on its stage curtain. A plaque declares this to be the site of the country's first "Normal School" (to train teachers) in 1823, founded by the Reverend Samuel R. Hall, who is also credited with inventing the blackboard. Photos of Concord in the 1890s line the walls in the Mooselook Restaurant east of the village on Rt. 2. A short way farther along, the 400-acre Miles Pond offers boat access, as does Shadow Lake in Concord Center.

Kim Grant

CRAFTSBURY COMMON

Craftsbury (population: 994). Few places convey such a sense of tranquility and order as the village of Craftsbury Common. In summer, petunias bloom in the post office window boxes, and the green of the grass contrasts crisply with the white fence. In winter, the general whitewash of this scene contrasts with the blue of the sky. Throughout the year there are nearby places to stay and books to check out at the desk in the new Craftsbury Public Library with its imposing portraits of Ebenezer and Samuel Crafts. Unlike most North Country pioneers, Ebenezer was university educated (Yale, class of 1740). Forced to sell his tavern in Sturbridge, Ma. (the still-popular Publick House), due to war debts, he made his way here over the Bayley-Hazen Military Road, eventually bringing his family and 150 of his Sturbridge neighbors this way on sleds. Ebenezer was quick to establish a school here. His son Samuel, a Harvard graduate who served two terms as Vermont's governor, founded the Academy, which still serves as the public high school for the town. The **Sterling College** campus adds to the variety. In East Craftsbury the **John Woodruff Memorial Library** (802-586-9692) preserves the look of the general store (vintage 1840s) while offering its stock of 20,000 books, including many children's titles, to visitors as well as residents. Open Wed. and Sat. 9–noon, 2–5, and 7–9:30; also 12:15–1:30 on Sun. Many farmers welcome visitors to their sugarhouses during sugaring season in late March and early April and sell syrup from their farmhouses year-round. Inns and B&Bs offer year-round lodging, and **Craftsbury Outdoor Center** offers one of the most

JOHN WOODRUFF MEMORIAL LIBRARY, EAST CRAFTSBURY

Christina Tree

extensive and dependable cross-country ski networks in New England; its summer sculling program is also nationally recognized. The extensive web of well-surfaced dirt roads meandering in all directions is beloved by bicyclists and horseback riders.

Danville (population 2,211; www.danvillevt.com). Until 1855, Danville was the shire town of Caledonia County. Its village is exceptionally beautiful, set high on a plateau, with a large green complete with bandstand and Civil War monument. The imposing town hall was built as the county courthouse, and the small, square Passumpsic Savings Bank is one of the safest strongholds around, thanks to devices installed after it was last held up, in 1935. Danville is headquarters for the American Society of Dowsers. **Dowser's Hall** (802-684-3417) is open weekdays 9–5; note the summer concerts on the green (see *Entertainment*) and the Danville Fair (see *Special Events*). **West Danville** is a crossroads (Rts. 15 and 2) village with Hastings Store, a great, old-fashioned general-store-cum-post-office, at its center. One of the world's smallest libraries sits across the road at Joe's Pond (named for a Native American beloved by early settlers), which features a public beach with picnic and sanitary facilities. The water from Joe's Pond is said to empty, eventually, into Long Island Sound, while that from Molly's Pond (a mile south, named for Joe's wife) presumably winds up in the Gulf of St. Lawrence.

Greensboro (population: 770). Shaped like an hourglass, Caspian Lake has a century-old following. The unusual purity of its water is checked three times weekly in-season by its association of cottage owners—who include noted authors, educators, and socialites—all of whom mingle in Willey's Store in the center of Greensboro. You'll also find a public beach and resort facilities maintained by Highland Lodge, also open in winter for cross-country skiing. Greensboro claims Vermont's oldest (nine-hole) golf course.

Hardwick (population: 3,174; 802-472-3397 chamber of commerce) is a small trading center for the southwestern corner of the Kingdom. Main Street is unexpectedly Victorian, a reminder of the town's heyday as one of the world's largest granite processors. The granite was actually in Woodbury, 5 miles south, whence it arrived by rail. Thousands of skilled European craftsmen moved to town beginning in the 1870s and continuing into the 1920s; a number of French Canadians remain. The Lamoille River runs through town, good for fly-fishing. East Hardwick is also worth finding. **The Hardwick Historical Society** (802-563-2508), housed in the former Hardwick Depot, is open May–Sep., Mon., Wed., and Fri. 10–2. The **Hardwick Town House** (802-472-8800), noted for its hand-painted stage curtains, is a venue for film and live performances, open Wed.–Sat. 10–3.

Lyndon (population: 5,448). An up-and-down roll of land encompasses the villages of Lyndonville, Lyndon Center, Lyndon Corner, Red Village, and East Lyndon, and the neighborhoods of Vail Hill, Pudding Hill, Darling Hill, and Squabble Hollow. Lyndon isn't a tourist town, but it offers real, down-home hospitality and **five covered bridges**. The village of Lyndonville was developed by the Passumpsic River Railroad Co. in the 1860s. Besides a handsome (long gone)

PEACHAM

Christina Tree

station and a number of brick rail shops, the company laid out broad streets, planted elm trees, and landscaped Bandstand Park. **Lyndon State College** is on Vail Hill (T. N. Vail was the first president of AT&T; he came here to buy a horse and ended up buying a farm, which eventually turned into 20 farms, much of which is now occupied by the campus). Lyndonville's famous product is Bag Balm. Band concerts are held Wednesday evenings during summer months in Bandstand Park. The Caledonia County Fairgrounds are the site of frequent events; the Caledonia County Fair itself runs for 5 days in early August. **Lyndon Area Chamber of Commerce** (802-626-9696) maintains www.lyndonvermont.com and an information center in the **Historic Lyndon Freight House** (see *Eating Out*), which also showcases the town's railroading history.

Peacham (population: 635). High on a ridge overlooking the White Mountains, this is a tiny but aristocratic village settled just after the Revolution, with a fine new library at the four-corners. Peacham's handsome homes and setting have attracted retired professors, literati, artistic luminaries, and ambassadors. All three Peachams (South, East, and Center) are worth exploring, as are the roads between. The **Historical House**, an 1820s school, is open July–early Oct., Sun. and Mon. 2–4, also on July 4 and Foliage Day. The latter is when the 1820s blacksmith shop operates and "Ghost Walks," with current residents impersonating long-deceased counterparts, are offered in the hilltop cemetery—which tells its own story and offers one of the best views in the Kingdom any day.

✳ To See

LOCAL ATTRACTIONS **The American Society of Dowsers** (802-684-3417; www.dowsers.org) is headquartered in Dowser's Hall (open weekdays 9–5), Brainerd St., just off the common in Danville; the **American Society of Dowsers Bookstore** (1-800-711-9497), also here, is open Wed.–Sat. 9–6, selling books about dowsing, also books and tapes on healing, and dowsing equipment. The ancient art of dowsing is the knack of finding water through the use of a forked stick, a pair of angle rods, or a pendulum. The society has thousands of members throughout the world; its annual convention is held in June at Lyndon State College. It happens to be headquartered here because in the fall of 1958 some 50 people from different parts of the country congregated in Danville to demonstrate dowsing techniques as part of the Northeast Kingdom Foliage Festival. The founding of the society in 1961 was an outgrowth of these annual demonstrations. Weekend workshops are also offered.

MUSEUMS ✐ **The Fairbanks Museum and Planetarium** (802-748-2372; www.fairbanksmuseum.org), 1302 Main, St. Johnsbury. Open year-round, Mon.–Sat. 9–5, Sun. 1–5 (closed Mon., mid-Oct.–mid-Apr.). $5 adults, $4 seniors and ages 5–17; $3 for planetarium shows, which are Sat. and Sun. at 1:30 year-round, 11 and 1:30 daily in July and Aug. A wonderfully Victorian-style "Cabinet of Curiosities," said to be the oldest science education museum in the nation and the state's only public planetarium, the Fairbanks is much more as well.

"I wish the museum to be the people's school . . . to teach the village the meaning of nature and religion," explained Franklin Fairbanks at the museum's 1891 dedication.

The main hall is capped by a 30-foot-high, barrel-vaulted ceiling, its floor lined with Victorian-style cabinets displaying thousands of stuffed animals: from mice to moose, from bats to bears (including a superb polar bear), birds galore (from hummingbirds to passenger pigeons), reptiles and fish, insect nests. Founder Franklin Fairbanks was passionate about nature, and the collection represents most native species of mammals and birds as well as many gathered from around the world, a total of 3,000 specimens. The Vermont State Geologic Collection is also displayed, along with an extensive herbarium of New England plants. The balcony, which circles the entire hall level, is lined with historical displays depicting local 19th-century life (including the Civil War) and "ethnological" exhibits drawn from a 5,000-piece collection representing most of the world's far corners. Altogether the museum displays 160,000 objects.

In the planetarium, which seats just 50 people, you learn about the night sky as it appears in the Northeast Kingdom. The museum is also a U.S. weather observation station, and its daily "Eye on the Sky" forecasts are a fixture of Vermont Public Radio (VPR). The weather station is in the basement, worth a visit to see exhibits telling the story of the Fairbanks family and their scales and an interactive kids-geared exhibit. There is a fine little gift shop. The museum archives include a resource library for studies and information about the Northeast Kingdom. Ambitious exhibits in the main gallery change seasonally. The annual Fairbanks Festival of

THE FAIRBANKS MUSEUM

Courtesy of the Fairbanks Museum

Traditional Crafts (late Sep.) features demonstrations of the Kingdom's traditional home industries.

St. Johnsbury Athenaeum and Art Gallery (802-748-8291; www.stjathenaeum.org), 1171 Main St., St. Johnsbury. Open

HORACE AND FRANKLIN FAIRBANKS

St. Johnsbury Anethaeum

Mon. and Wed. 10–8, Tue., Thu., Fri., 10–5:30, Sat. 8:30–4, closed Sun. Donation appreciated. Completed in 1871, the athenaeum was conceived and carefully created (not just donated) by Horace Fairbanks, who personally selected the paintings and leather-bound collection of 7,000 books. The art gallery, the big attraction, is said to be the oldest unaltered gallery in the country and has a distinctly 19th-century feel. Smaller canvases and sculptures are grouped around the outsized painting *Domes of the Yosemite*, by Albert Bierstadt. Natural light through an arched skylight enhances the effect of looking into the Yosemite Valley. The gallery is at the rear of this fascinating public library, a National Historic Landmark, which has recently reopened after extensive renovations that included adding 18 feet to the former lecture hall (now open stacks), uncovering arched windows, subtly inserting an elevator, and generally restoring the 1870s look of the galleried reading rooms.

INSIDE THE ST. JOHNSBURY ANETHAEUM

Christina Tree

Bag Balm (802-626-3610; www
.bagbalm.com), Rt. 5, Lyndonville.
Developed in 1899 as an antiseptic
ointment for cattle, Bag Balm proved
particularly effective for chapped
udders and is still used by Vermont
farmers. In recent years its campy,
old-fashioned green tins have begun
to appear in Madison Avenue pharmacies and ski resort boutiques, at three
or four times the price they fetch
locally. The factory is at 184 Williams
St. (across the RR tracks and up the
hill from the info center in the middle
of the village). Tours are offered
weekdays, 1–2:30. The company,
which has been owned by the same
family since it opened its doors, still
employs just four workers "on the
floor." Bag Balm is sold here, but it's
cheaper in Russell's Drugstore, May
Store, or Lyndonville Hardware.

**DAIRY
ASSOCIATION
COMPANY, INC.**

MAKERS OF

Bag Balm
SINCE 1899

✿ **Cabot Creamery Visitors Center** (802-563-2231; 1-800-837-4261; www
.cabotcheese.com), Cabot Village (no way can you miss it). Open year-round:
June–Oct., daily 9–5; the rest of the year, Mon.–Sat. 9–4, from 10 in Jan. Cabot
has been judged "best cheddar in the world" at the industry's olympics. Cooperatively owned by dairy farmers since 1919, the center showcases its history
with a video and offers a half-hour tour of "Cheddar hall" to view the cheesemaking (token fee per person over age 12 includes samples). The store features
all of Cabot's many dairy products, along with other Vermont products. Call
ahead to check when cheese is being made and inquire about the week's
specials.

Maple Grove Farms of Vermont (802-748-5141; www.maplegrove.com), 1052
Portland St. (Rt. 2 east), St. Johnsbury. May through Oct., guided tours offered
daily 8–4:30 of "the world's oldest and largest maple candy factory." In business
since 1915, this is an old-fashioned factory in which maple candy is made from
molds. A film in the adjacent museum depicts maple production and displays
tools of the trade. A large, neighboring gift store stocks many things besides
maple.

Also see *Gardens* under *Selective Shopping*.

COVERED BRIDGES All five within northern Caledonia County are in Lyndonville—one 120-foot, 1865 bridge across the Passumpsic, 3 miles north of
town off Rt. 114; one as you enter town, a genuine 1869 bridge moved from its
original site; two in Lyndon Corner (one dating from 1879, the other from 1881,
both west off Rt. 5); the fifth in Lyndon Center on Rt. 122.

ᕗ **The Great Vermont Corn Maze** (802-748-1399; www.vermontcornmaze
.com), Patterson Farm, Wheelock Rd., North Danville. Open Aug. and Sep.,
10–5; Oct., 10–4 (until the second to last Sunday). It takes from 40 minutes to
2 hours to thread the miles of pathways between walls of corn. "Cheater Poles"
along the way permit a quick exit. A barnyard nature center, gardens, and
"Miney's Korny Kid Korn Maze" are geared to younger children. Call first if
the weather is questionable. Everyone we've talked to who has found this place
has been enthusiastic, but we've also spoken to several people who never did
find it. Begin at the blinking light on Rt. 2 in Danville and head north; it's best
to download the map on the web site. $9 over age 15, $7 ages 4–14 and 62-plus.

🐾 *ᕗ* **Stephen Huneck's Dog Chapel and Gallery** (802-748-5593; www
.huneck.com), 1356 Spaulding Rd., marked from Rt. 2 east of St. Johnsbury.
Open Mon.–Sat. 10–5, Sun. 11–4. The full-scale wooden chapel "welcomes all
creeds and breeds. No dogma allowed." Seven surrounding acres on "Dog
Mountain" are planted in wildflowers, and visitors are welcome to bring (or e-
mail) photos of their beloved animals to grace the chapel walls. The gallery, of
course, showcases nationally known Huneck's stylish, carved wooden animals and
bold, fanciful furniture, panels and jewelry, and his children's books, featuring
his black Lab Sally. Dogs welcome.

SCENIC DRIVES **Route 2 west from St. Johnsbury to Danville**. As the road
climbs steadily, the White Mountains rise like a white wall in the distance. This
actually works better if you are driving east from Danville. Either way, be sure to
pull off (there's an eastbound pullout) to appreciate the panorama.

Danville Hill Road. Continue west on Rt. 2 from West Danville to East Cabot;
after Molly's Pond, take the right-hand turn—Danville Hill Rd., marked for
Cabot. This is a high road with long mountain views; note the Cabot Creamery
Visitors Center in Cabot.

Burke Mountain. A 2.5-mile auto road to the summit of Burke Mountain
(3,267 feet) commands a sweeping view of the North Country; picnic areas are
provided halfway and at the summit. This preserve was formerly the 10,000-acre
Darling State Forest, donated to the state in 1933. The road was constructed by
the Civilian Conservation Corps. The toll road and campsites in the campground
are open May 25–Oct. 15.

Darling Hill Road from Rt. 114 in East Burke, 5 miles south to Rt. 114 in
Lyndonville, follows a ridge past a magnificent former estate that once encompassed many old homesteads and still offers great views. The bright yellow
38-room mansion, on a private drive, has been beautifully restored.

Greensboro Village to East Hardwick. The road passes through Hardwick
Street (that's the name of the hamlet) and a fine collection of Federal and Greek
Revival houses; from Greensboro Village to Hardwick it makes a beeline through
high and open farm country; and from Craftsbury Common north to Rt. 14
through Albany and Irasburg, it follows the rich farmland of the Black River
Valley.

Lyndon to Greensboro Bend. An old ridge road with splendid views, 17-mile **Stannard Mountain Road** is unpaved but usually well graveled most of the way, best traveled in summer and fall. Check locally, though, because there are occasional washouts. The views are best driving west.

✳ To Do

BIKING **Kingdom Trails Association** (802-626-0737; www.kingdomtrails.org). The East Burke area is webbed by roughly 100 miles of trails, a composite of systems on Darling Hill, around the village, and on Burke Mountain itself, as well as the Burke cross-country trails, maintained by a conservation organization that includes more than 40 landlords. Pick up a map and a day pass ($7 adults, $5 ages 8–15 or $25 per person, $75 per family for a "Green Season" pass) at the association office in the rear of Bailey & Burke's General Store. Trails include snowmobile and fire roads, but the core is a 25 km singletrack system with some glorious views. Rentals of bikes and extensive equipment are available from **East Burke Sports** (802-626-3215; www.eastburkesports.com) and from the **Village Sports Shop** (802-626-8448), 511 Broad St. (Rt. 5) in Lyndonville.

Craftsbury Outdoor Center (802-586-7767; www.craftsbury.com), Craftsbury Common, rents 21-speed fat-tire bikes and offers instruction and guide service on 200 miles of dirt roads and cross-country ski trails.

The **Northeast Kingdom Development Association** web site (www.nvda.net) offers bike touring suggestions and downloadable maps.

FISHING Fishing is huge here. The Kingdom is pocked with glacial lakes and laced with streams. For regulations, check under Fish & Game at www.nek chamber.com. Check out **Harvey's Lake** in West Barnet, the **Moore Reservoir**, **Shadow Lake**, and **Miles Pond** in Concord, **Ricker** and **Levi Ponds** in Groton State Forest, **Lake Eligo** and **Caspian Lake** in Greensboro, and **Little** and **Great Hosmer Ponds** in Craftsbury, as well as the **Lamoille**, **Passumpsic**, **Moose**, and **Connecticut Rivers**. Local lakes are also good for salmon, lake and rainbow trout, and perch. There are trout in the streams, too. A handicapped-accessible fishing platform has been constructed in **Passumpsic Village** on the Passumpsic River. The **Lamoille River** in Hardwick is good for trout and perch.

At **Seyon Ranch** in Groton State Park (see *Lodging*) there is squaretail trout fishing, with flies only, from boats rented at the site. George Willy at the **Village Inn in East Burke** (again, see *Lodging*) offers guiding and driftboats. Under *Camping* see also **Harvey's Lake Cabins and Campground**; also see **Quimby Country** and **Seymour Lake Lodge**, and *Fishing* in "The Lake Country."

Northeast Kingdom Outfitters (802-754-9471; www.northeastkingdomout fitters.com) offers fly-fishing schools as well as driftboat fishing trips and guide service on local lakes and ponds.

FITNESS CENTER **The Club at Old Mill** (802-748-5313), Perkins St., St. Johnsbury. Indoor tennis, racquetball, aerobics, Nautilus, free weights, sauna, Jacuzzi. $10 day passes.

GOLF St. Johnsbury Country Club (802-748-9894; 1-800-748-8899), off Rt. 5 north, open daily mid-May–Oct. This is an outstanding PGA-rated, 18-hole course, truly one of the Kingdom's gems. The original nine holes were designed in 1923; nine more were added by Geoffrey Cornish. Amenities include cart rentals and **GreenSideRestaurant**, all newly renovated in 2005.

Mountain View Country Club (802-533-9294), Greensboro, nine holes. Established 1898; open to nonmembers midweek only. Use of carts permitted only for health reasons.

Kirby Country Club (802-748-9200), 5 miles east of St. Johnsbury on Rt. 2 in Kirby. Open daily Apr.–Nov. Marc Poulin's evolving, challenging nine-hole course and clubhouse offer great views. Reasonably priced.

HIKING AND WALKING TRAILS *Note:* See Craftsbury Outdoor Center and Kingdom Trails Association under *Biking*.

Groton State Forest Trail System (802-584-3829). Off Rt. 232 (which runs north–south, connecting Rts. 2 and 302), this 25,623-acre forest is primarily known for camping facilities but also offers an extensive year-round trail system accessing major points of interest. Favorite hikes include the Peacham Bog Natural Area and two trails to the summit of Owls Head Mountain (there's a summer road as well as a trail), where a handsome old CCC wood-and-stone watchtower commands spectacular views. See *Green Space* for an overall description of the forest.

HORSEBACK RIDING DND Stables (802-626-8237) in East Burke. Debby Newland guides riders 12 and older (unless they are experienced) of all abilities on trails that extend from her farm to local snowmobile and cross-country trails, as well as the Kingdom Trails system. Younger children are welcome to ride in the ring. Rides are tailored to the rider (maximum of four) and can be as long as desired.

PADDLING East of St. Johnsbury, the **Moore** and **Comerford Reservoirs**, created by dams, are good for canoeing (there are two boat launches in Lower Waterford)—as we found out one evening, listening to birdcalls and watching a baby beaver swim steadily toward a beaver lodge beneath the pines. Below the Comerford Dam, the stretch of the **Connecticut River** south to McIndoe Falls (now the McIndoe Dam) is excellent, and the portage around the dam isn't difficult. Other rivers that invite canoeing are the **Passumpsic** and **Moose**, which join the Sleeper at St. Johnsbury. A boat launch on the Moose River can be accessed from Concord Avenue in St. J, and look for a boat launch on the Passumpsic in Passumpsic Village, 5 miles south of St. Johnsbury. Canoe and kayak rentals are available from **East Burke Sports** (802-626-3215; www.eastburke sports.com) in East Burke and from **Village Sport Shop** (802-626-8448), 511 Broad St., Lyndonville. **Craftsbury Outdoor Center** (see *Sculling*) rents canoes and kayaks for use on Great and Little Hosmer Ponds and on the Black River. **Highland Lodge** has canoes and kayaks for use on Caspian Lake by its guests. Boat rentals are available from **Injun Joe Court** (802-684-3430;

Amy Wilton, Laughing Dog Photography

SCULLING AT CRAFTSBURY OUTDOOR
CENTER

www.injunjoecourt.net), Rt. 2, West Danville, and **Harvey's Lake Campground** (802-633-2213), West Barnet. This area is pocked with lakes, and launches are shown on the state map. Also see *Camping*.

RUNNING Craftsbury Outdoor Center (802-586-7767; www.craftsbury.com), Craftsbury Common, offers 5-, 6-, and 7-day camps late June through July; different sessions focus on training for triathlons, marathons, road racing, Masters running, and just plain fun and fitness. Camps are open to all ages and abilities; the reasonably priced all-inclusive price covers coaching, lodging, and three daily meals.

SCULLING Craftsbury Outdoor Center (802-586-7767; www.craftsbury.com), Craftsbury Common, has offered nationally acclaimed summer sculling programs for 30 years. Weekend, 4-day, and weeklong sessions run late May–mid-Sep. Open to all ages and ski levels. Sessions include tailored coaching, video analysis, demo equipment, and access to the swim beach, massage, nature trails, and mountain biking with lodging and three daily meals.

SWIMMING There are public beaches on **Harvey's Lake** in West Barnet; **Caspian Lake** near Greensboro Village; **Joe's Pond** in West Danville; **Molly's Pond** in Marshfield; **Shadow Lake Beach** (in Glover marked from Rt. 16); **Miles Pond** in Concord; and within **Groton State Forest**, notably at **Boulder Beach State Park** (802-584-3823; www.vtstateparks.com). If you can find it also check out **Ticklenaked Pond** in Ryegate (off Rt. 302 west of Wells River). There are also public pools in St. Johnsbury and in Lyndonville.

✳ Winter Sports

CROSS-COUNTRY SKIING AND SNOWSHOEING Two of New England's outstanding cross-country trail systems are found in this area. Unfortunately, you have to settle on one or the other—given the way the roads run, they're an hour's drive apart.

In the Craftsbury area
Craftsbury Outdoor Center Nordic Ski Center (802-586-7767; www.craftsbury.com), Craftsbury Common, grooms 85 km of its 130 km marked and maintained trail system; it offers rentals, instruction, and lodging packages. The system connects with **Highland Lodge** (see *Lodging*) in Greensboro, which offers a total of 60 km of trails, 15 of them well groomed. The only major New England cross-country system that's nowhere near an alpine ski hill, the Craftsbury Outdoor Center/Highland Lodge trails web the kind of red-barn-spotted farmscape that's equated with, but increasingly rare in, Vermont. They traverse

rolling fields, woods, and maple and evergreen groves, with stunning views of the distant Green Mountains. Thanks to their elevation and Craftsbury's exceptional grooming, they also represent some of the most dependable cross-country skiing in the Northeast and usually remain skiable well into March and sugaring season. Home to the late-January Bankworth Craftsbury Ski Marathon, one of Vermont's standout winter events. Daily trail passes available.

In East Burke

Burke Cross-Country Ski Area (802-535-7722; www.burkexc.com). Groomed trails begin at 1,300 feet and wind through woods that yield to panoramic views. Rentals, lessons, guided tours; an 80 km system that connects with the **Kingdom Trails** network (see *Biking*). Some 50 more km of trails wind through the village and loop along Darling Hill with spectacular views (best accessed from the Wildflower Inn and the Inn at Mountain View Farm). Trail fees required.

&. **Seyon Ranch State Park** (802-584-3829; www.vtstateparks.com). This isolated 1890s hunting/fishing lodge deep in Groton State Forest has been winterized and caters to cross-country skiers with 5 miles of groomed trails. See *Lodging*. See also **Hazen's Notch** in "Jay Peak Area."

DOGSLED TOURS **Hardscrabble Dogsled Tours** (802-626-9895), based in Sheffield, offers tours ranging in length from 1 to 6 hours, also guided snowshoeing.

DOWNHILL SKIING AND SNOWBOARDING **Burke Mountain** (802-626-3322; www.skiburke.com), East Burke. "The Vermonter's Mountain" is a big peak with a respectable vertical, known for excellent terrain and reasonable prices. After many ups and downs, it has been acquired by Ginn Company, a Florida-based development firm with plans to develop an on-mountain village and an 18-hole golf course. Home of Burke Mountain Academy, a prep school for aspiring racers, known for the number of graduates who become Olympic contenders. In recent years snowmaking coverage (abetting a 250-inch annual snowfall) and glade skiing terrain have been substantially increased.

Lifts: 2 quad chairlifts, 2 surface lifts.

Trails and slopes: 34 trails, 9 glades (100 acres).

Elevation: 3,267 feet.

Vertical drop: 2,000 feet.

Snowmaking: 80 percent.

Snowboarding: 4 terrain parks, season-long freestyle program.

Facilities: Sherburne Base Lodge includes glass-walled Tamarack Grill as well as a cafeteria; a midslope lodge serves the upper mountain. Trailside lodging is offered in dozens of privately owned condos (Burke Vacation Rentals: 802-626-1161; Mountainside Property Rentals: 802-626-3548). Also check with the Burke Area Chamber of Commerce (www.burkevermont.com), the best way to compare local lifts and lodging packages, including local motels and B&Bs.

Programs: Cub Den Day Care, open weekends and holiday periods; ski school, rentals.

Rates: Weekends $52 adults, $39 seniors and juniors; weekdays $42 adults, $36 seniors and juniors—but substantially less with lodging.

SLEIGH RIDES Wildflower Inn (see *Lodging*) arranges sleigh rides for guests and will accommodate nonguests when possible.

SNOWMOBILING Given the extent of the trail system, accessibility to the trail from local lodging places, and dependable snow cover, this area is becoming as well known among snowmobilers as it is to cross-country skiers. The trail systems, however, seldom cross. **The Northeast Kingdom Chamber of Commerce** (802-748-3678; 1-800-639-6379; www.nekchamber.com) publishes a map listing what's required to sled here and a list of the local clubs from which you must purchase a VAST membership in order to use the trails. Rentals are available from **All Around Power Equipment** (802-748-1413), Rt. 5 north, St. Johnsbury. Echo Ledge Farm Inn in East St. Johnsbury offers snowmobile storage as well as trail access. Also see *Snowmobiling* in "The Lake Country."

✳ Green Space

Barr Hill Nature Preserve, Greensboro. Turn right at the town hall and go about 0.5 mile to Barr Hill Rd. (another left). The trails at Barr Hill, managed by The Vermont Nature Conservancy, overlook Caspian Lake. Don't miss the view from the top. In winter ski and snowshoe trails are maintained by Highland Lodge.

Groton State Forest (www.vtstateparks.com). This 25,600-plus-acre forest is the second largest contiguous landholding by the state of Vermont. It's a scenic and rugged place, best known for its five separate campgrounds (see *Camping*) and fishing, but it also harbors Lake Groton and both Osmore and Ricker Ponds. There's an extensive year-round trail system. The area was intensively logged, beginning in 1873 with the opening of the Montpelier & Wells Railroad that ran through the forest, ending in the 1920s when most of the timber had been cut. Subsequent fires further altered the landscape from evergreens to mostly maple and birch. The naturalist-staffed **Groton Nature Center** (802-584-3823) in **Boulder Beach State Park** (a day-use area featuring a swim beach on Lake Groton), marked from Rt. 232, is open June–early Sep. and serves as the information source for the forest and the trailhead for the 2.5-mile trail to Peacham Bog. Seyon Ranch State Park (see *Lodging*) is on Noyes Pond in another part of the forest, catering to groups, fishermen, and cross-country skiers.

Hardwick Trails, Hazen Union School, Hardwick. Six miles of nonmotorized nature and recreational trails wind through the woods behind the high school in the middle of the village.

Victory Basin, alias Victory Bog. This 4,970-acre preserve administered by the Vermont Fish and Wildlife Department includes a 25-acre boreal bog with rare plant life, 1,800 acres of wetlands, 1,084 acres of hardwoods, and 71 acres of clearings and old fields. The dirt road access is via Victory; there are three parking areas: Mitchell's Landing, Lee Hill, and Damons Crossing.

Waterford Dam at Moore Reservoir. New England Power offers guided tours of the huge complex of turbines. There are also picnic sites and a boat launch here. The approach is from the New Hampshire side of the Connecticut River, just below Lower Waterford, Vt., off Rt. 135.

In St. Johnsbury

Fred Mold Park, near the confluence of the Passumpsic and Moose Rivers, is a great picnic spot by a waterfall and old mill. **The Arlington Preserve**, accessible from Waterman Circle, is a 33-acre nature preserve with woods, meadows, and rock outcroppings.

See also *Biking*, *Hiking and Walking Trails*, and *Camping*.

✳ Lodging

In the St. Johnsbury area

& **Rabbit Hill Inn** (802-748-5168; 1-800-76-BUNNY; www.rabbithill.com), Rt. 18, Lower Waterford 05848. Brian and Leslie Mulcahy welcome you to this pillared landmark, an inn since 1795. All 19 rooms and suites are romantic confections, with canopy beds, antiques, and "indulging" bathrooms. Many have working fireplace, Jacuzzi for two, and private porch. All have been painstakingly furnished, complete with a "room diary." Summer swimming and fishing in a freshwater pond, canoeing, and golf privileges; winter cross-country skiing and snowshoeing. $275–435 per couple includes breakfast, afternoon tea, and five-course, candlelit dinner.

🐾 ☀ **Broadview Farm B&B** (802-748-9902), 2627 McDowell Rd., North Danville 05828. Open Memorial Day–Oct. This shingle-style country mansion has been in Molly Newell's family since 1901. It's set on 300 acres with a panoramic view of mountains, on a farm road in North Danville that, Molly assures us, was once the Boston–Montreal Rd. In the late 19th century, before its shingles and gables, this old farmhouse took in summer boarders, advertising its 2,000-foot elevation as a sure escape from malaria and hay fever. Today the elevation suggests dependable cross-country skiing. Molly has thoroughly renovated the old place, removing 4,000 pounds of radiators, replacing windows, and gutting and redesigning the kitchen, while preserving the fine woodwork, detailing, and maple floors throughout the house. The three guest rooms are furnished with family antiques (check out the great oak set in the Yellow Room). Baths are private or shared; $90–120 double includes a full breakfast. Dogs $5 per night.

🐾 **The Albro Nichols House** (802-751-8434; www.nekchamber.com/albronicholshouse), 53 Boynton Ave., St. Johnsbury 05819. This 1840s Federal-style house sits up behind Arnold Park at the head of Main

BROADVIEW B&B, NORTH DANVILLE

Christina Tree

Street, a flowery, quiet setting that's still within strolling distance of St. Johnsbury's museums, galleries, theaters, shops, and restaurants. Margaret Ryan is a former prep school dean and a high school theater director who clues in guests to the Kingdom's cultural scene. The pleasant, square Rose Room with private bath ($90) is on the ground floor; the upstairs rooms (both $70), one with twin beds, the other with a double (this would be a delightful room for a single person, too), share a book-lined sitting room and a bath. Common rooms feature plenty of books and interesting art; a full breakfast is included. *Note:* Rates don't change during foliage season.

Emergo Farm B&B (802-684-2215; 1-888-383-1185; www.emergofarm .com), 261 Webster Hill, Danville 05828. Just north of the village, this strikingly handsome farm is a prizewinning, sixth-generation working dairy farm. The upstairs apartment has two bedrooms, full kitchen, sitting room (with a pullout) , and bath. Older children only, please. Rooms are also available individually with private bath. The farm's 230 acres include a hilltop with panoramic views of much of the Kingdom. Historical and present-day farm tours are offered, and livestock includes Nigerian dwarf goats as well as 125 head of cattle (90 milking cows). Lori Webster charges $90–150 per room including a full breakfast, served downstairs in the dining room.

♣ Echo Ledge Farm Inn (802-748-4750; www.echoledgefarm.com), P.O. Box 75, East St. Johnsbury 05838. Ruth Neborsky and her family are your hosts at this bed & breakfast on a farm established in 1793. The five comfortable bedrooms have private baths and are nicely, comfortably furnished. Guests have a wing of the old farmhouse to themselves, a dining area with fridge as well as the living room. Afternoon tea, plenty of books, local menus, and a full breakfast are included in the $95 rate, less for a twin-bedded room without bath. Wine and beer are available. In winter snowmobilers can easily access the VAST Corridor Trail; snowmobile storage is offered (inquire about rentals). The adjacent 200-year-old barn houses antiques and gifts. Paths lead down to the Moose River across Rt. 2.

The Old Homestead (802-633-4016; 1-877-OLD-HOME; www.theold homestead.com), P.O. Box 150, Barnet 05821. Gail Warnaar plays the oboe and bassoon, sells music for double-reed instruments, and offers five rooms in her 1850s village home, which faces Rt. 5 and backs on gardens and meadow. Two second-floor rooms (private baths) feature porches overlooking the grounds, while a small first-floor single room with a spool bed (shared bath) is appealing. Common space is comfortable, and musical groups will find rehearsal space. $69–135 includes a breakfast of fruit and fresh-baked bread; reduced rates for weekdays and longer stays.

The Gardeners Rest B&B (802-748-9388; www.gardenersrest.com), 682 Daniels Farm Rd., Waterford 05819. Brits Margaret and Keith Rowlett are passionate gardeners who are transforming the acres around their vintage-1854 farmhouse into a model English garden, the kind that blazes with color spring through fall and encompasses a shady lane, carefully orchestrated views, pergolas, and

⊙ ✐ ⟨ **The Wildflower Inn** (802-626-8310; 1-800-627-8310; www.wildflower inn.com), 2059 Darling Hill Rd., Lyndonville 05851. One of Vermont's best family-geared resorts clusters around a 19th-century farmhouse set high on a ridge with a spectacular view across

Christina Tree

THE VIEW FROM WILDFLOWER INN, LYNDONVILLE

surrounding hills and valleys. It's surrounded by its own 500 acres, with extensive flower gardens and trails maintained for hiking, mountain biking, and cross-country skiing. Jim and Mary O'Reilly have eight children (five boys, three girls), and have fitted rooms and condo-style suites with child-geared amenities, such as small rockers and diaper-changing tables, but no TVs. The idea is to get children out of their rooms and let them find one another in the playroom, the outdoor play structures, the petting barn, the pool (there's one for toddlers), or the Playbarn—hub of supervised morning art, crafts, and summer nature programs for ages 3–11. For older children a sports complex offers basketball, a batting cage, tennis court, playing field, and (also a big appeal for parents) the beckoning system of the Kingdom Trails (see *Biking*). For cross-country skiers, Burke Mountain's trails are minutes away. Adult spaces include a sauna and outdoor hot tub, an attractive parlor and library—stocked with games and the kind of books you really want to read. The landscaped pool commands a spectacular view of rolling hills, and there are also lawn games and walking trails. Dinner is in Juniper's (see *Dining Out*), but for children, there's the option of parent-free dining at Daisy's Diner, a 5:30–9:30 dinner and activity program (summer only). Breakfast is a three-course production, and tea is also served.

Upstairs in the main house, two family suites have great views. A total of 24 units (10 rooms and 14 suites), some with and some without views, include a romantic hideaway with whirlpool bath in the old schoolhouse (with view) and Grand Meadow ($399), a two-bedroom retreat sleeping 8 with two baths (a Jacuzzi in one), full kitchen, dining and lounging area, and view. $99–189 for rooms, $129–219 for one-room suites, $169–299 for two-room suites, $169–389 for three-room suites. Rates are per couple B&B plus $25 per child over age 3; free for ages 3 and under. Singles pay $20–25 less. Inquire about special packages.

a couple of ponds. The 16 acres includes meadows and a brook. The house sits 0.5 mile off hardtop but just 5 miles from St. J and I-93. There's one downstairs guest room and two upstairs rooms with garden views and sloping ceilings, all with private bath. $85–115 includes a full breakfast with homemade granola and a hot "savory" or sweet. Not appropriate for children under age 14.

🐾 🎐 **The Inn at Maplemont Farm** (802-633-4880; 1-800-230-1617; www .maplemont.com), Rt. 5, Barnet 05821. Tom and Sherry Tolle's well-kept, large yellow farmhouse sits in a bucolic 43 acres across the road from the Connecticut River. The three guest rooms are pleasant, all with private bath; South Peacham, the ground-floor twin, is particularly attractive. Pet and livestock accommodations are available if you arrange in advance. $90–120 per night includes a hearty breakfast.

🌾 🎐 **Long Meadow Inn** (802-757-2538; 1-800-394-2538), 1886 Ryegate Rd. (Rt. 5), Wells River 05081. This stately brick Federal farmhouse, standing all alone by the river in East Ryegate, once a stagecoach stop, is now nicely restored by Roy and Ellen Canlon. There are five pretty guest rooms, two with private bath. There's a private dock, also swimming in nearby Tickle Naked Pond. From $45 for a single, shared bath, to $65–80 for a double room with private bath, full breakfast included.

In the Burke Mountain–Lyndonville area

∞ 🐾 ♿ **The Inn at Mountain View Farm** (802-626-9924; www.innmtn view.com), 3383 Darling Hill Rd., East Burke 05832. Like the Wildflower Inn, this is part of a onetime 9,000-acre hilltop estate owned by Elmer Darling, a Burke native, who built the brick creamery in 1890 to supply dairy products to his Fifth Avenue Hotel (it used to churn out 600 pounds of butter a month and 70 pounds of cheese per day). The inn also includes the neighboring "Farm House" and the magnificent red barns and other outbuildings. It's backed by 440 acres that spread across a high ridge and are laced with paths, part of the Kingdom Trails network (see *To Do*) maintained for walking, mountain biking, and cross-country skiing. Marilyn Pastore has tastefully decorated the 14 guest rooms (private baths), which are divided between the Creamery and the Farm House with its three "luxury suites," each with fireplace and Jacuzzi. A sauna is accessible to all guests. The centrally air-conditioned Creamery, however, houses the inn's common space: a sitting room with a big old painting of Lake Willoughby, a signboard for the lake's long-defunct dance hall, and a restaurant serving breakfast to guests and open to the public 5 nights a week (see *Dining Out*), featuring seasonal tables on the patio set in the perennial gardens and gourmet backpacker lunches for those who wish. Inquire about donkey walkabouts with two miniature Sicilian donkeys, Molly and Emmy. The inn is a favorite for weddings and reunions, given its renovated Morgan barn. $155–265 includes a full breakfast and tea. Horses can be boarded in the barn. Inquire about special packages.

🌾 🐾 **The Village Inn of East Burke** (802-626-3161; 802-793-4517; www.villageinnofeastburke.com), Box 186, East Burke 05832. This comfortable, affordable B&B offers many rarely found amenities, like a fully equipped guest kitchen; a truly inviting living room with a fireplace, books, games, and satellite TV; an outdoor Jacuzzi; gardens; and a streamside picnic area. All five rooms have private bath, and some are large enough to accommodate families. Innkeeper George Willy is also a fishing guide who offers driftboat tours, while Lorraine Willy raises bees and maintains a large organic garden. Both are plugged into all the sporting possibilities of the area. $85 includes breakfast. Inquire about reasonably priced "stay and play" packages for fishing, skiing, and biking.

🐾 Branch Brook Bed & Breakfast (802-626-8316; 1-800-572-7712; bbbb@together.net), P.O. Box 217, Lyndon 05849. This is an exceptional house with long, graceful parlor windows, built in the 1850s, beautifully converted to a B&B by Ted and Ann Tolman. The room with a pencil-post canopy bed, locally crafted from cherrywood, is worthy of brides; two rooms are tucked under exposed beams, furnished with antiques. All but two of the five have private bath. Prices are $80–100 per couple with a hearty breakfast; Ann Tolman has a food-service background and prides herself on breakfasts prepared on her English Aga Cooker. Two of Lyndon's five covered bridges are within walking distance.

Moonlight Inn Vermont (802-626-0780; moonlightinnvt@aol.com), P.O. Box 1325, 801 Center St., Lyndonville 05851. Shirley Banks welcomes visitors with genuine western friendliness, while Dick Banks is the quiet, capable Vermonter. Their spacious Victorian house on a quiet side street offers comfortable common space and three second-floor guest rooms, one with twins, all with private bath. A serious quilter, Shirley offers lessons and quilting weekends. $95 includes a full breakfast.

In the Craftsbury area
◯ 🐾 ✦ Inn on the Common (802-586-9619; 1-800-521-2233; www.innonthecommon.com), Craftsbury Common 05827. One of the Kingdom's crown jewels is now owned by well-known Vermont innkeepers Jim and Judi Lamberti. They've lightened and freshened the 15 guest rooms, removing heavy draperies, retaining the mix of well-chosen wallpapers, fabrics, antiques, and original art; five rooms have a woodstove or wood-burning fireplace, and one has a Jacuzzi. Rooms are divided among three Federal-style buildings, two facing each other and the third a short walk away, by the village's magnificent common. The main inn also houses an attractive library and one of the region's best restaurants (see *Dining Out*). In summer you can take advantage of the solar-heated pool, the perennial gardens, lawn croquet, and the tennis court. Nearby Craftsbury Outdoor Center is a destination for mountain biking, running, and sculling, and offers some of New England's best cross-country skiing. $189–299 per couple (low season $135–255) includes a four-course dinner and full breakfast. Pets are $25 by prior reservation. Children are welcome but the inn is really appropriate only for those over age 9.

✦ Highland Lodge (802-533-2647; www.highlandlodge.com), Greensboro 05841. Open Memorial Day weekend–mid-Oct. and Christmas week–mid-Mar. A rambling Victorian-era inn, set in 120 acres on the shore of Caspian Lake, that manages to be both airy in warm weather and cozy in winter, now managed by the second generation of Smiths (David and Wilhelmina)—hosts whose warmth is reflected in the atmosphere. Common rooms include a comfortable library with desks and armchairs, a game room, a living room with fireplace, and a sitting room with baby grand piano. Upstairs are 11 rooms, all with private bath. There are also 11 cottages (4 remain open in winter). In summer, facilities include tennis courts and a pleasant beach with bathhouse and canoes, kayaks and a small sailboat, along with the nature trails on the property and in the adjacent Barr Hill Nature Preserve; in winter the draw is cross-country skiing on the extensive trail network radiating from the inn's touring center, rising to unusual elevations with superb views. Inside, there is an unusual amount of relaxing space. Outside, rockers line the expansive porch. For children, there's an organized summer program (ages 4–9) in the Play Barn with an outstanding art program; resulting artwork is tacked to nearby pine trees, a truly astonishing "Gallery in the Woods." $240–310 per couple, $35–75 per child depending on age, includes dinner as well as breakfast; inquire about family rates. Less in May and weekdays in June, Sep., Oct., Jan., and Mar.

✒ **Craftsbury Inn** (802-586-2848; 1-800-336-2848; www.craftsburyinn .com), Rt. 14, Craftsbury 05826, across from a classic general store in Craftsbury Village. Closed in early Nov. and in Apr. Bill and Kathy Maire are your hosts at this handsome 1850 Greek Revival–style inn, built as a private residence in the 1850s with a second-story wraparound porch. There are attractive living and game rooms. Upstairs, the 10 guest rooms (6 with private bath) are also nicely decorated, with beds ranging from canopy through twins to a kids' bunk room. This is a working fiber farm, with llamas, sheep, goats, and rabbits. Kathy spins the yarn, which is hand dyed, and the couple make handcrafted knitting needles. $140–180 per couple MAP, $90–130 B&B; midweek packages and single rates are available.

Whetstone Brook Bed & Breakfast (802-586-6916), 1037 South Craftsbury Rd., Craftsbury 05826-4220. An 1826 Vermont classic Cape that, with additions, has been home to six generations of the Wilson family is now Audrey and Bryce Wilson's retirement project, a pleasant B&B. There's a piano in the living room and an Aga stove in the kitchen; the small round tables in the dining room are positioned to view the meadow through the French doors. An upstairs room with a double and single has a private bath, while two more rooms share; the ground-floor Apple Blossom Room has a queen bed and private bath. $79–109 includes a full breakfast.

❀ **The Kimball House** (802-472-6228; www.kimballhouse.com), 173 Glenside Ave., Hardwick 05843. Sue and Todd Holmes have lived in this big, handsome 1890s "painted lady" since 1979 but have only recently (with their four children grown) converted it to a B&B. All three guest rooms are upstairs (one has twin iron beds) and share two full baths, one upstairs and one down. There's plenty of common space, plus a big wraparound porch and backyard. $79 per couple includes a full breakfast, maybe eggs Benedict.

MOTOR LODGES 🐾 ✍ **Fairbanks Inn** (802-748-5666; www.stjay.com), 401 Western Ave. (Rt. 2 east), St. Johnsbury 05819. This three-story, 45-unit, surprisingly luxurious motel on the outskirts of town has central air-conditioning, cable, dataports, outdoor heated pool, and fitness center privileges. $79–169 single or double per standard room, more triple and quad and for mini suites; the honeymoon suite is $179–259. Pets accepted in ground-level rooms. Many kinds of packages; children under age 18 stay free. Inquire about the manager's special.

✍ **Comfort Inn & Suites** (802-748-1500; www.vtcomfortinnsuites.com), off I-91, Exit 20, Rt. 5 south. A 107-unit high-rise motel with an indoor heated pool, a fitness center, a video arcade, cable, dataports, direct VAST trail access. $119–159 (depending on date) for standard rooms, suites $159–299.

🐾 ✍ **Colonnade Inn** (802-626-9316; 1-877-435-5688), 28 Back Center Rd., Lyndonville 05851. A two-story, 40-unit motel just off I-91, Exit 23. Standard motel rooms, cable TV and phone, continental breakfast. $55 double, $65 for a two-bedded room ($5 per additional person), more during foliage. Children stay free.

RENEWAL CENTERS FOR BODY AND SPIRIT **Karmê Chöling Shambhala Meditation Center** (802-633-2384; www.karmecholing.org), 369 Patneaude Lane, Barnet 05821. Receptionist: 9–5 weekdays, 1:30–5 weekends. The oldest (founded in 1970) and probably still the best of New England's Buddhist meditation centers, Karmê Chöling follows the Tibetan Buddhist path of understanding one's own mind through meditation. What began as a small center in an old farmhouse now includes 540 wooded, path-webbed acres, six meditation halls, a practice pavilion, an *azuchi* (Zen archery range), a large organic garden, private guest rooms, and dining facilities. The centerpiece remains the original, now expanded farmhouse with its beautiful Main Shrine Room. Casual visitors are welcome (call beforehand), but this is all about 1- to 7-day retreats (many are geared to weekends) on a variety of themes but with the practice of "mindfulness meditation" at their heart. The daily routine begins with a 6:30 wake-up call and continues until 10:30 lights-out. Space to sleep in the Main Shrine is included in the cost of a program.

♨ 🏠 **Craftsbury Outdoor Center** (802-586-7767; 1-800-729-7751; www.craftsbury.com), P.O. Box 31, 535 Lost Nation Rd., Craftsbury Common 05827. Recreational facilities are the big attractions here, with accommodations for 90 guests divided between two rustic lodges: 35 rooms sharing lavatory-style hall bathrooms, 7 with private bath, 2 efficiency apartments, and 4 housekeeping cottages sleeping four to eight. Three meals are served, buffet-style, in the dining hall. Guests come for the programs offered: running, sculling, walking, mountain biking, and cross-country skiing, along with winter Elder Hostel programs; or they stay and enjoy the outdoors at their own pace. Facilities include swimming at Lake Hosmer, exercise rooms, sauna, tennis courts, and 320 acres. From $86–175 per person / $140–273 per couple, including three plentiful meals with vegetarian options; family and multiday rates are available. Pets are allowed in two lakeside cottages ($50 cleaning fee). (See also *Biking, Sculling, Running,* and *Cross-Country Skiing.*)

OTHER LODGING &. **Seyon Ranch State Park** (802-584-3829; www .vtstateparks.com). This isolated 1890s hunting/fishing lodge on Noyes Pond, deep in Groton State Forest, is staffed and open year-round, catering to fishermen and cross-country skiers, snowshoers, and snowmobilers in-season, offering retreats and courting groups in between. There's a living room with fireplace, a dining room, and a meeting space. Six rooms have double and queen beds, and there are bunk rooms with shared baths, accommodating a total of 16, and serving up to 50 for meals. Inquire about special programs like quilting and cooking. Managers Cory and Shana Drew offer three meals daily. $69 per room, meals extra.

CAMPING **Groton State Forest** (802-584-3829; www.vtstateparks .com) in Marshfield and Groton. This 25,623-acre preserve offers five separate campgrounds, each an individual state park, all accessed from Rt. 232. **New Discovery Campground** (802-584-3042) has a total of 47 campsites, 14 of them lean-tos; beach privileges and hiking trails; primitive camping. **Stillwater Campground** (802-584-3822), on the west side of Lake Groton, has a total of 63 tent sites, 16 lean-tos; campers' beach and boat launch; rental boats, dump station. **Ricker Pond Campground** (802-584-3821) has a total of 33 campsites, 22 of them lean-tos, on the south side of Ricker Pond; campers' beach, rental boats, nature trail, dump station. **Big Deer State Park** (802-584-3822) has 28 tent/trailer sites (no hookups) near Boulder Beach and Groton Nature Center with many miles of trails. **Kettle Pond** (802-426-3042), on the south side of the pond, has walk-in fishing, group camping, hiking, and snowmobiling. For an overview of Groton State Forest see *Green Space.*

Burke Mountain Campground (802-626-1390; 802-626-3322), a small campground on Burke Mountain with five lean-tos and room for 21 tents, is geared to hikers and bikers. See the Summertime at Burke section of www.skiburke.com.

Harvey's Lake Cabins and Campground (802-633-2213; www.harveys lakecabins.com), 190 Camper's Lane, Box 26, West Barnet 05821. One of Vermont's oldest public campgrounds, with 10 lakefront, furnished (antique funk decor) cabins with kitchen, bath, living area, loft bedrooms ($585–750 per week with daily rentals in off-seasons) and 53 wooded sites for RVs and pop-up tents on 35 acres. Paddle boats, swimming, and fishing; also bicycle rentals.

✳ Where to Eat

DINING OUT

In the St. Johnsbury area
Elements (802-748-8400; www .elementsfood.com), 98 Mill St. (off Railroad St.), St. Johnsbury. Open for dinner Tue.–Sat. 5–9:30, for lunch Memorial Day–Columbus Day 11:30–1. Reservations advised. A former water-powered woodworking mill with all its wheels and belts still intact makes a great space for this hip new hideaway just off the main drag. A long bar backed by blocks of glass divides the space into two distinct

dining areas (we prefer the bar side); in summer a deck overhangs the Passumpsic River. Chef Ryan O'Malley and his wife, sous-chef Allyson O'Malley, combine local ingredients wherever possible in novel and delicious ways. A summer menu might range from vegetable strudel in a feathery phyllo pasty with sautéed chard and carrot ginger sauce, to filet mignon, to apricot-glazed ham. "Small plates," including house pâté and summer trout cakes, are also offered. For dessert, try the corn bread pudding with dried cranberries, crème Anglaise, and homemade caramel. Dinner entrées $14–24. The list of wines by the glass, as well as by the bottle, is extensive.

Rabbit Hill Inn (802-748-5168; 1-800-76-BUNNY; www.rabbithill.com), Rt. 18 in Lower Waterford. Open to outside guests by reservation, space permitting. The elegant dining room holds just 15 tables, and both food and atmosphere are carefully orchestrated. There's candlelight, and music many nights, to complement three-course dinners with a $43 prix fixe. First courses in an early-winter menu included smoked duck breast with a fava bean puree and beet salad. A choice of five entrées included a vegetable napoleon baked with manchego cheese, served with mixed greens and roast tenderloin of herbed, marinated beef. The half dozen desserts range from a cheese plate to bittersweet flourless chocolate cake. Add 18 percent service.

Creamery Restaurant (802-684-3616), Danville. Open Tue.–Fri. for lunch and dinner, Sat. for dinner only. A former creamery with a blackboard menu featuring homemade soups, curries, and pad Thais, along with salads, pies, and a choice of meat and seafood dishes. Breads and soups are homemade, and salad comes with all dinners. Marion Beattie has been owner-manager for 30 years. Entrées $14–20; there's a less expensive pub menu.

In the Lyndonville–Burke area
River Garden Café (802-626-3514; www.rivergardencafe.com), Rt. 114, East Burke Village. Open Wed.–Sun. for lunch and dinner; Sunday brunch is 11–2. Reservations advised. A popular place with an attractive decor and wide-ranging menu. Lunch is a varied choice of sandwiches, wraps, and salads. Dinner entrées might include pepper-crusted lamb loin, roast salmon served with artichoke hearts, olives, and tomatoes on couscous, or Jamaican jerk chicken with eggplant Parmesan. A café burger or steak sandwich is also available at night. Entrées generally run $12.95–23.95, and the wine list is a point of pride. Breads and desserts are homemade. The café atmosphere is casually elegant, with a year-round back porch and summer patio dining within earshot of the river. The "just for kids" menu begins at $1.95 for a PB&J sandwich.

The Inn at Mountain View Farm (802-626-9924; www.innmtview.com), Darling Hill Rd., East Burke. Open for dinner to outside guests by reservation, Wed.–Sun. This brick-walled room, once the heart of a working creamery, is an attractive, candlelit dining room with a varied menu. A choice of seven entrées might include roasted tofu and red peppers with a spicy peanut sauce; seared scallops with sautéed snow peas and carrots, cilantro, lime, and chili garlic sauce; and roast leg of lamb with a garlic and rosemary crust. Entrées $14.95–23.95. Specials vary each night, as do the featured wines.

❧ **Juniper's at The Wildflower Inn** (802-626-8310; www.wildflowerinn .com), between Lyndonville and East Burke on Darling Hill Rd. Open (except Nov. and Apr.) Mon.–Sat. 5:30–9. Reservations advised if you want a table on the sunporch, over-looking a spread of hills and valleys. You can dine on filet mignon ($25), but entrées on an extensive menu average $15 and tend toward comfort foods like "slow cooked shepherd's pie," roast all-natural pork, and Vermont-raised lemon-herb chicken. "Junior Juniper" plates begin at $4 for grilled Vermont cheese with fries. Entrées come with warm rolls and salad. Sandwiches and burgers are also available. Much of the beef served is from all-natural belted Gal-loway cattle raised here on Darling Hill. Salads and sandwiches are also served. Vermont beer featured.

In the Craftsbury area

Inn on the Common (802-586-9619; 1-800-521-2233; www.innonthe common.com), Craftsbury Common. Open to the public by reservation Wed.–Sun. evenings. The inn dining room has the feel of an elegant res-taurant. The à la carte menu changes seasonally and offers several choices per course. On a summer evening you might begin with a lobster bisque, then dine on wild salmon with wild rice or beef tenderloin with béarnaise sauce. Dessert might be Vermont Green Mountain cheesecake or key lime pie. Innkeeper Jim Lamberti prides himself on the wine list; selec-tions are available with each course. Entrées $21.50–25.50, plus 15 per-cent gratuity.

Highland Lodge (802-533-2647; www.highlandlodge.com), Greens-boro. The inn is open late May–mid-Oct. and Christmas week–mid-Mar. Nonguests are welcome for breakfast, lunch, and dinner (by reser-vation); in winter lunch is served Thu.–Sun. The inn's old-fashioned dining room is attractive, and in sum-mer there's also service (weather per-mitting) on the wraparound front porch. The dinner menu, featuring local produce, changes daily and usu-ally includes five entrées. At this writ-ing choices range from linguine with saffron cream and julienne vegetables to roulade of pork tenderloin with shi-itake sauce ($18–24). Dessert might be a walnut torte with chocolate ganache ($5.50). You can also choose from a lighter burger, sandwich, and salad menu ($10.50–13.50). All beef served is Black Angus. There's a respectable wine list.

EATING OUT

In and around St. Johnsbury

Black Bear Tavern & Grille (802-748-1428; www.blackbeartavern grille.com), 205 Hastings Hill Rd. Open for lunch and dinner. Just north of downtown, adjacent to the Holiday Motel but its own place, locally popu-lar with a gracious, friendly atmos-phere and an upscale sports bar. Steaks, seafood, burgers, and sand-wiches, all reasonably priced.

❧ **Surf & Sirloin** (802-748-5412), 264 Portland St. (Rt. 2 east). Open for breakfast, lunch, and dinner, 6 AM–9 PM daily. This local standby is east of the bridge into town. Chef-owner Calvin Belknap had served as execu-tive chef at the Mount Washington Hotel and other prestigious inns, but this longtime local favorite is home.

As a native son, Calvin is more interested in perpetuating the reputation of a local institution than offering upscale, high-end cuisine.

Piccolo's (802-751-6116), 378 Railroad St., Open Mon.–Wed. 8–4, Thu.–Sat. 8 AM–10 PM, Sun. 10–3. New in 2005, this "American bistro" fills the need for a downtown espresso bar; also serving sandwiches, burgers, hot sandwiches, and panini. The reasonably priced dinner menu includes pastas and vegetarian shepherd's pie, some interesting soups (Cajun blackened corn, roasted red pepper, and crab chowder) and entrées such as scallion pancakes with hoisin pork, Brazilian orange pork and black beans, and coquilles Saint-Jacques.

Danville Restaurant (802-684-3484), 86 Rt. 2 west, Danville Village. Open for breakfast Tue.–Sat. 7–11, lunch Tue.–Fri. 11–1:30, dinner Fri. and Sat. Housed in a village inn, this family restaurant is good for all three meals at reasonable prices in a friendly atmosphere, from hamburgers to full-course meals; daily specials.

Good Fellas Tavern & Restaurant (802-748-4249), 59 Parker Rd., just off Rt. 2, Danville. Open daily (except Tue.) in summer and fall, 4–9; Sun. 11:30–8. Known for homemade soups, seafood, and pasta. The tavern features three TVs.

  Anthony's Restaurant (802-748-3613), 321 Railroad St. Open 6:30 AM–8 PM weekdays, until 9 Fri., from 7 Sun. Anthony and Judy Proia have run this cheerful family-geared diner since 1979, remodeling it several times to make it handicapped accessible and give it a homier feel. Regulars still gather around the counter, and there are booths as well. Breakfast is big: specialty omelets and

about everything else you can think of. "Specials" at all three meals. The fries are homemade, along with the soups; pies are a point of pride.

Mooselook Restaurant (802-695-2950), Rt. 2, east of Concord. Open 6 AM–8 PM, closed Mon. and at 7 PM in winter. This is a better-than-average North Country kind of place: "Most" soups are homemade, and specialties include country-fried steak and Vermont-fried chicken; all meals include soup and choice of potato and vegetable. This is also "home of the slugger," a 7-ounce burger with all the fixings. For visitors the additive is what's on the walls: dozens of vintage photos of what this area was all about more than a century ago.

Kham Thai Cuisine (802-751-8424), 1112 Memorial Dr. (Rt. 5 north). Open daily 11–9, until 10 Fri. and Sat. A great addition to local dining options, reasonably priced, reliable.

Upper Valley Grill (802-584-3101), junction of Rts. 302 and 232, Groton. Open 6 AM–9 PM daily. At the junction of two lonely stretches of road, this is a welcome oasis: a general store with a friendly, U-shaped counter in back, good for homemade soups, apple pie, and daily specials.

In the Lyndonville–Burke area
  The Historic Lyndon Freight House (802-626-1174), 1000 Broad St., Lyndonville. Open daily 6:30–9:30. Local dairy farmers Eric and Cathy Paris have salvaged and restored this middle-of-town former freight station (1868), transforming it into a combination restaurant/railroad museum, information center, and ice cream parlor. The food is fabulous: local meats, fresh greens and veggies, fresh-baked breads, and the fluffiest

Christina Tree

FAMILY AT FREIGHT HOUSE, LYNDONVILLE

of omelets plus Carmen's wildly popular ice cream (64 flavors). There's more: Starbucks coffee and a crafts gallery. This is one of 2 buildings left from the 22 built here by the Boston & Maine. This village sprang into existence with the 1860s arrival of the railroad and remained an important rail yard for the B&M until the 20th century. Most local families have railroad ties, and memorabilia has come pouring in. Note the original freight scale in the dining room and glass tabletops showcasing some of the 3,000 freight bills and letters found stashed in the walls during the renovations. Walls are hung with early-1900s photos. There's much more upstairs in the Iron Horse Gallery (extra seating), where a model train circles an evolving diorama of a 1940s Lyndonville, complete with the brick depot that once stood next door (demolished in the 1970s). Occasionally, too—as it did to the delight of our small grandson—a real train still comes rumbling by.

Miss Lyndonville Diner (802-626-9890), Rt. 5 south, Lyndonville. Open from 6 AM until supper, famed for strawberry pancakes with whipped cream for breakfast, pie, homemade French toast, and jumbo eggs. This is

one of the famous railroad diners, along with Miss Newport and Miss Bellows Falls, that made their way to Vermont years ago. When they came, they brought with them the best of classic diner fare.

⚓ The Pub Outback (802-626-1188; www.thepuboutback.com), East Burke, out back of the Bailey's & Burke General Store. Open daily 4–9, later Fri. and Sat. This former cow barn is now a cheerful pub with a full menu, from soups to pitas, veggies, burgers, sandwiches, steaks, pastas, the works. Children's menu. Full bar.

Café Sweet Basil (626-9713), 60 Depot St., Lyndonville. Open for lunch Wed.–Fri.11:30–2, for dinner Wed.–Sat. 5:30–9:30, live jazz Wed. night. This is an appealing-looking café with an interesting menu. We lunched on a grilled tomato soup and quesadilla—good, but service was painfully slow. Still, we would like to give it a try for dinner. Entrées $14.95–16.95.

In the Craftsbury area
House of Pizza (802-472-3380), Wolcott St. (Rt. 115, north of the village), Hardwick. Open daily 10–9, until 10 Fri. and Sat. This can be a crucial road-food stop if you are heading up to Craftsbury on a snowy evening. The pizzas are good, also salads, lasagna, calzones, grinders.

Beyond the Garden Café (802-586-9970), 2778 N. Craftsbury Rd., just north of the common. Open June–Nov. 1, Tue.–Fri. 11:30–2:30, Sun. brunch 10–2:30. Dinner Thu.–Sat. by reservation. Also open during peak winter periods. In this house, literally beyond the garden—handy to Craftsbury Outdoor Center—Penny Strong offers an exceptional vegetarian menu featuring local organic produce. Dinner is a seven-course set menu ($29.95), including nonalcoholic wine. Specialties are eggplant torte and sesame seitan.

Craftsbury General Store (802-586-2811), 118 S. Craftsbury Rd., Craftsbury Village. Open 5 AM–7:45 PM; closing Sun. at 6. A good deli, plus pies, pizzas, wraps, burgers, salads, and dozens of entrées like roast pork tenderloin with sautéed apples and shallots, sides of roasted root vegetables and risotto with sun-dried tomatoes and slivered almonds, and bakery items like pumpkin cream rolls—to go.

Buffalo Mountain Coop and Café (802-472-8800), upstairs in the co-op, Main St., Hardwick. Open Mon.–Sat. 9–6, Sun. 10–4. Soups, coffees, light food, grilled cheese with avocado.

For **Warners Gallery**, **Happy Hours Restaurant**, and **P&H Truck Stop** in Wells River, see "Lower Cohase."

BREWS **The Brick House and Perennial Pleasures Nursery** (802-472-5104), East Hardwick (posted from Rt. 16). Open Memorial Day–Labor Day, noon–4; closed Mon. English-born Judith Kane serves a traditional "Cream Tea" (cucumber sandwiches, scones, and fresh cream) and offers an assortment of teas, cold drinks, and pastries. Reservations suggested, but patrons "are welcome to pop in." Many come just for the gift shop, known for its splendid summer hats as well as jewelry, clothing, books, gardening tools, and more. The 3 acres of perennial gardens (www.perennialpleasures.net, open 10–5) represent more than 900 varieties of plants, featuring heirloom flowers—lemon lilies, golden glow— and medicinal plants.

Trout River Brewing Company (802-616-9396; www.troutriver brewing.com), Rt. 5, Lyndonville. Fri. and Sat. 5–8:30, open for hand-tossed pizzas as well as the selection of ales and other draft brews, made on the premises. The three signature beers here are Rainbow Red (medium bodied), Scottish Ale, and Hoppin' Mad Trout; also seasonal specials. Inquire about tours and tastings.

✳ Entertainment

Catamount Arts (802-748-2600; 1-888-757-5559; www.catamountarts .com), 139 Eastern Ave., St. Johnsbury. The Catamount Arts Center (the former St. Johnsbury Post Office) is the venue for a film series that includes nightly film screenings (7 PM) also Sun. matinees Nov.–Apr. The 100-seat auditorium also hosts more than 30 live Showcase Presentations annually and the biweekly jazz on a Sunday series. Regional artists are featured in the gallery here, and some 3,000 video rentals are available in the lobby. Catamount Arts was established in 1975 as a nonprofit cultural organization serving the region.

Star Theater (802-748-4900; 802-748-9511), 18 Eastern Ave., St. Johnsbury. Cinemas 1-2-3; first-run movies.

Craftsbury Chamber Players (1-800-639-3443; www.craftsbury chamberplayers.org) has brought chamber music to northern Vermont for 40 years. The series runs mid-July–mid-Aug. Check the current schedule for performances at the Hardwick Town House, the Presbyterian Church in East Craftsbury, and Fellowship Hall in Greensboro. Most performers are faculty members at the Juilliard School of Music in New York City.

Hardwick Town House (802-472-8800), 127 Church St., Hardwick, an 1860 schoolhouse, has been the anchor venue for the Craftsbury Chamber Players and also now hosts a variety of programs: film, drama, music, and other live performances. The stage features a vintage hand-painted curtain.

♪ **Vermont Children's Theater** (summer only: 802-626-5358), Darling Hill Rd., Lyndonville. Sited next to the Wildflower Inn, this is a genuine theater in a former hay barn. Local youngsters (some 120 are usually involved) perform amazingly well. Performances in July are by thespians ages 7–18. Tickets: $8 adult, $4–6 for youngsters.

♪ **Circus Smirkus** (802-533-7443; 1-800-532-7443; www.smirkus.org), performances at Sterling College, Craftsbury Common, June–mid-Aug. Over the past 20 years, this has evolved into a nationally recognized program cultivating acrobatic and other circus skills for children— ranging from a "smirking weekend" for 6- to 8-year-olds to advanced sessions focused on performances here and on the road.

Band concerts: **St. Johnsbury Town Band concerts**, weekly all summer at the bandstand in Town Hall Park, Mon. 8 PM. **Lyndonville Town Band concerts**, every Wednesday in summer at 8 PM. **Danville** concerts on the green, Sundays at 7 in July and Aug. **Craftsbury band concerts** at the band shell on the common, Sundays at 7 in July and Aug. In **Greensboro**, concerts on the dock at Caspian Lake are sponsored by the Greensboro Association, summer Sundays at 7:30.

✳ **Selective Shopping**

ANTIQUES SHOPS Route 5
Antiques & Collectibles (802-626-5430), Rt. 5, Lyndonville. Open daily, except Tue., 10–5. A multidealer and consignment shop.

Antiques & Emporium (802-626-3500), 182 S. Wheelock Rd., Lyndonville. Open daily 10–5, except Tue. Housed in a former grade school, a multigroup shop with everything from rugs and clocks to furniture, pottery, and prints.

BOOKSTORES Boxcar & Caboose Bookshop (802-748-3551; 1-800-754-9830; www.boxcarandcaboosee.com), 394 Railroad St., St. Johnsbury. Opened in 2005 by St. Johnsbury Academy history teacher Scott Beck and wife Joelle, filling the void left by the town's previously beloved bookstore when it closed. This is a bright, well-stocked store with a large children's section and café (coffees, bagels).

The Galaxy Bookshop (802-472-5533; www.galaxybookshop.com), 7 Mill St., Hardwick. Since Linda Ramsdell moved her shop into a vintage-1910 bank building, she's offered not only ample space for her stock but also probably the only drive-through book and rental audiotape (call ahead) service in the country. Audiotapes? Local farmers listen while driving tractors and doing chores. This is a full-service bookstore specializing in Vermont writers and unusual titles; armchairs invite lingering. The satellite **Stardust Books** (802-586-2200) in the former library on Craftsbury Common is open Sat. 10–1 (coinciding with the farmer's market) and Wed. 3–6; its café is also open weekdays 7:30–9:30 AM. Inquire about frequent author readings and other special events.

Green Mountain Books & Prints
(802-626-5051), 1055 Broad St.,
Lyndonville (Rt. 5 on the corner of
the common). Open Mon.–Sat. 9–5.
Ellen Doyle is the second generation
of her family to preside over this book
lover's heaven: an unusual mix of new
and used books; many new, discounted titles and rare books. Doyle seems
to know something about every book
in the place. Vermontiana, Native
American, and children's books are
specialties, but the range is wide and
patrons are welcome to sit in a corner
for as long as they wish. Bigger than it
looks at first: There are separate children's and fiction rooms.

Antiquarian Muse (802-472-3536),
144 Main St., Hardwick. Open weekdays 10–3. A brick house filled with
5,000 used and collectible books for
adults and children.

Lilac Cottage Books (802-525-
4482), Shields Lane, Glover. Open
May 30–Oct. 30 on an honor system.
Sherry Urie offers four rooms filled
with new and used books.

CHEESE For the **Cabot Creamery
Visitors Center**, see *To See*.

Bonnie View Sheep Farm (802-755-
6878), 2228 South Albany Rd., Craftsbury Common. Neil Urie produces his
award-wining cheeses—blue, Camembert, and feta, as well as a hard Vermont Shepherd–style cheese—on the
470-acre farm that's been in the family
since 1890. He's not really set up for
visitors but not averse to those who
drop by, no easy feat given the maze
of dirt roads leading to his farm. It's
sublime backcountry, however, and

5 PM is the best time to come. The
cheese is sold at local stores.

Jasper Hill Farm (802-533-2566),
Garvin Hill Rd., Greensboro. Mateo
and Andy Kehler make Winnemere
cheese (cloth-bound hard cheddar
that needs to age for a year), Bayley-
Hazen Blue, and Constant Bliss
(named for a Union scout from
Greensboro killed in the Civil War),
all soft, washed-rind cheese, available
at Willey's.

Up-A-Creek Cheese (802-755-
6723), Albany. This delicious, prizewinning raw sheep's-milk Belgian
Abby–style cheese, made locally by
Frankie and Marybeth Whittin, is
available by phone or from Highland
Lodge in Greensboro.

CRAFTS SHOPS

In the St. Johnsbury area
**Northeast Kingdom Artisans
Guild** (802-748-0158), 430 Railroad
St. Open Mon.–Sat.; closed Mon. off-
season. This cooperative of more than
60 Vermont artists showcases some
magnificent work in many media.

Uniquity (802-748-1912), 443 Railroad St. Open daily 9:30–5:30, Sun.
11–4. Locally made quilts, baskets,
paintings, candles, household accessories, and gifts, plus a frame shop.

Peacham Corner Guild (802-
592-3332), 643 Bayley-Hazen Rd.,
Peacham Corner. Open June–mid-
Oct.; closed Tue., but otherwise 10–5,
Sun. 11–5. A cooperative selling
handcrafted gifts and small antiques.

Songbird Pottery (802-563-2330),
3764 Mack Mountain Rd., West
Danville. Open daily 1–4, but call
before. Harley and Patricia Strader
make functional and decorative glazed

stoneware from local materials. Lead-free and dishwasher-safe.

In the Craftsbury–Greensboro area

Mill Village Pottery (802-586-9971), 6 Mill Village Rd. (on the way to Craftsbury Outdoor Center), Craftsbury Common. Open summer and fall 10–5 daily; usually open off-season, too, but call ahead. Lynn Flory specializes in one-of-a-kind vessels and unusual functional ware such as the "Yunan steamer," a lidded ceramic pot with a conical chimney in its center, designed to retain vitamins and minerals.

The Miller's Thumb (802-533-2960; www.themillersthumb.com), Greensboro Village. Open Memorial Day–Oct., daily 10–5:30. A former gristmill built in 1792 with a view of Greensboro Brook churning down falls below, through a window in the floor. Owners Anne and Rob Brigham have a great eye for selecting art, crafts, home furnishings, and gift items, many made locally; check out the furniture and clothing upstairs.

Caspian Hot Glass Studio (802-533-7129; www.caspianglass.com), top of Breezy Ave., Greensboro. Open May–Jan., daily 10–5. Glassblowers Jacob Barron and Lucas Lonegren work in their sugarhouse-shaped studio and display their original glass lighting and tableware—also ornaments and art glass—in the attached gallery.

FARMS **Brigid's Farm** (802-592-3062), 123 Slack St., Peacham. Call ahead. A small farm with sheep, Angora goats, and dairy goats with a weaving studio and mittens, hand-spun yarns, spinning wheels, natural dye extracts, and supplies sold.

Snowshoe Farm (802-592-3153; www.snowshoefarm.com), 520 The Great Rd., Peacham. Open year-round, but call. Ron and Terry Miller breed alpacas and process their fiber, selling it along with hand-knit or woven alpaca products.

Stillmeadow Farm (802-755-6713), 158 Urie Rd., South Albany. In the greenhouses at this handsome farm that's been in the same family since the 1830s, Elizabeth Urie sells a variety of vegetable plants and flowers; hanging baskets are a specialty. Open May–July.

Randall Stick Park (802-748-6203; www.randallstickparkplacealpacas.com), 521 Morrill Rd., Danville. Year-round, but call before coming. Huacaya alpacas are bred, also pet alpacas for sale.

GALLERIES *Note:* St. Johnsbury's most famous art gallery is the St. Johnsbury Athenaeum (see *To See*).

GRACE Gallery (802-472-6857), 13 Mill St., Hardwick. Open Tue.–Thu. 10–3. *GRACE* stands for "Grassroots Art and Community Effort," a 25-year-old program that offers art workshops and displays the rotating exhibits in the old firehouse.

GARDENS **Vermont Daylilies** (802-533-2438), behind Lakeview Inn, Main St., Greensboro. Over 500 varieties of daylilies with display gardens; also potted daylilies, hostas, and garden perennials on sale. The gardens are always open, while the store is open May–Sep. 10–5.

Perennial Pleasures Nursery (802-472-5104; www.perennialpleasures.net), East Hardwick. Open May–Sep. Sited at the Brick House (see *Brews*) and run by Rachel Kane, this unusual nursery specializes in authentic 17th-, 18th-, and 19th-century restoration gardens. There are 3 acres of flowering perennial and herb gardens, grassy walks, and arbors; more than 375 varieties of plants are available.

GENERAL STORES **Hastings Store** (802-684-3398), West Danville. See West Danville under *Towns and Villages*.

Willey's Store (802-533-2621), Greensboro Village. One of the biggest and best general stores in the state, in business over 100 years; an extensive grocery, produce, and meat section, local dairy products (check out Constant Bliss Cheese, made in Greensboro), hardware, toys, and just about everything else you should have brought for a vacation but forgot. Don't miss the upstairs with its selection of everything from flannel shirts and buttons through yard cloth and boots. Helpful staff will help you find what you are looking for.

Bailey's & Burke General Store (802-626-9250; www.baileysand burke.com), Rt. 114, East Burke. Open weekdays 8–7, Sun. 8–8. This classic old general store has been nicely fancied up by longtime local residents Jody Fried and Bill Turner. The second-floor gallery has been restored and displays work by local craftsmen. Downstairs are breads, pies, cookies, and coffee cakes baked daily right here; also a gourmet deli featuring specialty pizzas, cheeses, cold cuts, soups, and salads with café tables to eat them at. A selection of wines, coffees, and teas.

Peacham Store (802-592-3310), Peacham Village. Open spring–New Year's. Crafts, collectibles, and specialty foods. Gourmet food to take out.

Christina Tree

THE FARMER'S DAUGHTER

See *Eating Out* for the **Craftsbury General Store**.

SPECIAL SHOPS **The Farmer's Daughter** (802-748-3994), Rt. 2 east of St. Johnsbury. Open mid-Apr.–mid-Nov., daily 8–8. Billed as the country's oldest "Gift Barn"—not just because the barn is 180 years old but also because it's been under the same ownership for 43 years. A lot of stuff, much of it hokey but fun.

Moose River Lake and Lodge Store (802-748-2423), 370 Railroad St., St. Johnsbury. Open except Sun. 10–5; in summer Sun., too (11–4). Antiques, rustic furniture, and accessories for the home, camp, or cabin: taxidermy specialties, deer antlers and skulls, prints, pack baskets, fishing creels and snowshoes, folk art, an extensive wine collection, and more.

Peter Glenn of Vermont (802-748-3433; www.peterglenn.com), 452 Railroad St., St. Johnsbury. A full four-season sports shop, top quality at good prices.

Caplan's Army Store Work & Sportswear (802-748-3236), 457 Railroad St., St. Johnsbury. Established in 1922 and still in the same family, a serious source of quilted jackets, skiwear, Woolrich sweaters, hunting boots, and such; good value and friendly service.

Samadhi Store and Workshop (802-633-4440), 30 Church St., Barnet. Open Mon.–Fri. 9–5, Sat.10–4. An offshoot of nearby Karmê Chöling, selling singing bowls and gongs, Japanese yukata robes, teas, Vermont-made raku incense bowls, lacquerware from Japan and Korea, locally made meditation benches and tables, and meditation cushions and yoga mats made on site.

Diamond Hill Store (802-684-9797), Rt. 2, Danville on the green. This former general store is now a sleek emporium specializing in handmade chocolates, wine, and gifts.

Through the Woods (802-748-5369), 397 Railroad St., St. Johnsbury. Specializes in crafts and collectibles for the home. An interesting shop with lots of unusual items.

Natural To a Tee (802-626-3568; www.hempvt.com), 37 Depot St., Lyndonville. "Why Hemp?" Linda Leete-Laviletta has plenty of answers and a varied sampling—from socks, shirts, and dog collars to lotions and jewelry made from this environmentally friendly and health-inducing substance.

SUGARHOUSES **Rowell Sugarhouse** (802-563-2756), 4962 Rt. 15, Walden. Visitors are welcome year-round, 9–5. Maple cream and candy as well as sugar; also Vermont honey and sheepskins, crafts, paintings.

Gebbie's Mapleburst Farm (802-533-2984), 2183 Gebbie Rd., Greensboro. A major local maple producer that's been welcoming visitors for generations.

Goodrich's Sugarhouse (802-563-9917; www.goodrichmaplefarm.com), just off Rt. 2 by Molly's Pond in East Cabot. A family tradition for seven generations, open to visitors Mar.–Dec. with a full line of award-winning maple products.

Goss's Sugar House (802-633-4743), 101 Maple Lane, Barnet. Gordon and Pat Goss have won a blue ribbon for their syrup at the Caledonia County Fair. They welcome visitors, sell year-round, and will ship.

High Meadow Farm (802-467-3621), East Burke. The sugarhouse is open in-season. Call for directions.

Martin Calderwood (802-586-2297), South Albany Rd., Craftsbury. A major producer. Sugar parties arranged on request.

✳ Special Events

February: **Snowflake Festival Winter Carnival**, Lyndonville–Burke. Events include a crafts show, snow sculpture, ski races for all ages and abilities, sleigh rides, music, and art.

March: **Open sugarhouses** (*last weekend*; www.vtmaple.org).

May: In East Burke the **Annual White-Water Canoe Race** on the Passumpsic River, May 1. **Hardwick Spring Festival** (*last weekend*) includes a parade, crafts fair, and chicken BBQ. **Annual Vermont Open Studio Weekend** (www.vermontcrafts.com) on Memorial Day weekend.

June: **Lumberman's Day** at Burke Mountain in Lyndonville. **Dowsers National Convention** (802-684-3410), held at Lyndon State College.

June–October: **Farmer's markets**, in downtown St. Johnsbury Sat. 9–1; in

September–October:
Northeast Kingdom Fall Foliage Festival, the last week in September or first one in October. Seven towns take turns hosting visitors, feeding them breakfast, lunch, and dinner, and guiding them to beauty spots and points of interest within their borders.

Christina Tree

NORTHEAST KINGDOM FALL FOLIAGE FESTIVAL

In Walden the specialty is Christmas wreath making; in Cabot there's a tour of the cheese factory; in Plainfield, farm tours; in Peacham, a Ghost Walk and crafts fair; in Barnet the exceptional historical society house is open, and guided tours of back roads are outstanding. The finale comes in St. Johnsbury, with a farmer's market and art and crafts fair. For details, contact the Northeast Kingdom Chamber (see *Guidance*).

Craftsbury Sat. 10–1; in Danville Wed. 9–1; in Hardwick Fri. 3–6.

July: The **July 4 parade** in Cabot is the best around (802-563-2279). **Peacham Independence Day festivities** include a Ghost Walk in the cemetery, with past residents impersonated. **Burklyn Arts Council Summer Craft Fair** (*Saturday closest to July 4*) in Bandstand Park, Lyndonville. **Antiques and Uniques Fair** in Craftsbury Common. **Stars and Stripes Pageant**, Lyndonville (*last weekend*)—big auction, parade featuring Bread and Puppet Uncle Sam, barbecue. The **Irasburg Church Fair** is the third Saturday.

July–August: **Circus Smirkus** (802-533-7443), Greensboro. A children's circus camp stages frequent performances.

August: **Old Home Days**, Craftsbury Common—parade, games, crafts

(802-586-7766). **Danville Fair** (*first weekend*) on the green features a parade with floats, more than 75 years of traditions. **Caledonia County Fair** (*third week*), Mountain View Park, Lyndonville—horse, pony, and ox pulling; cattle, sheep, alpaca, rabbit, and swine shows; midway, rides, demolition derby, music.

First weekend of October: **Fall Foliage Craft Fair** in Hardwick.

Saturday after Thanksgiving: **Kirby Quilters Craft Fair** (www.kirby quilters.com)—huge (fills two gyms at Lyndon State College).

December: **Burklyn Christmas Crafts Market** (*first weekend*)—a major gathering of North Country craftspeople and artists in the Lyndon Town School.

New Year's Eve: **First Night** celebration in St. Johnsbury.

JAY PEAK AREA

Jay Peak towers like a sentinel above a wide valley in which the state of Vermont and the province of Quebec meet at three border crossings and mingle in the waters of Lake Memphremagog—and in general ambience. The sentinel itself has fallen to the French. The face of Vermont's northernmost peak is owned by Mont-Saint-Saveur International, and more than half of the patrons at Jay Peak ski area hail from across the border. Montreal is less than 2 hours away.

In summer and fall as well as in winter, a 60-passenger aerial tram hoists visitors to the 3,861-foot summit of Jay Peak. The view sweeps from Mount Washington to Montreal, back across the lake, down the spine of the Green Mountains, and southwest across Lake Champlain to the Adirondacks. The year 2006 is slated to see the opening, after 15 years of planning and permitting, of an 18-hole golf course at the resort—a phenomenon that will undoubtedly affect the quiet (some called it dead) of summer and fall in this region.

In winter, storms sweep down from Canada or roll in from Lake Champlain, showering the clutch of mountains around Jay with dependable quantities of snow. Admittedly, given its exposed position, Jay can be windy and frigid in January and February (we try to visit in March), the reason—along with spectacular snowfall—that regulars are drawn by "off-piste" skiing through glades and into the backcountry beyond. In nearby Hazen's Notch cross-country skiers also find some of the most dependably snowy and beautiful trails in New England.

Walk the length of the border between New England and Canada and you will not find a more distinctive stretch than this western fringe of the Northeast Kingdom. This is big-sky farm and logging country with isolated mountains and unexpectedly high passes. It has a haunting quality. Jay Village is a crossroads with a gas station and general store from which Rt. 242 climbs steeply 4 miles to the Jay Peak access road, then dips steeply 9 miles down to Montgomery Center. Montgomery, known for its six covered bridges, is 2 more miles to the west, and the Hazen's Notch angles back east over a high woods pass and down through fields into Lowell. An inviting drive in summer, it's open only for the first 4 miles in winter, just far enough to access magnificent snowshoeing and cross-country ski trails.

In contrast with most ski resort areas, the innkeepers, restaurateurs, and shopkeepers here are a mix of self-sufficient natives and the interesting kind of people who tend to gather in the world's beautiful back-and-behind places.

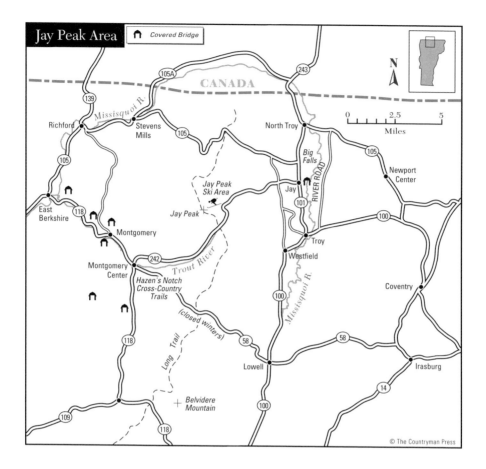

Jay Peak Area · Covered Bridge

CANADA

N

Richford · Stevens Mills · North Troy · Big Falls · Newport Center · Jay Peak Ski Area · Jay · RIVER ROAD · East Berkshire · Montgomery · Troy · Westfield · Montgomery Center · Hazen's Notch Cross-Country Trails · Coventry · Long Trail · (closed winters) · Lowell · Irasburg · Belvidere Mountain

0   2.5   5
Miles

© The Countryman Press

GUIDANCE

The **Jay Peak Area Association** (www.jaypeakvermont.org) offers an overview of area activities as well as lodging and dining.

Jay Peak Resort (802-988-2611; outside Vermont: 1-800-451-4449; www.jay peakresort.com) also offers information about area lodging/dining.

GETTING THERE *By air:* **Burlington International Airport** (802-863-1889; www.burlingtonintlairport.com) is a 1½-hour drive.

By train: **Amtrak** (1-800-872-7245; www.amtrak.com) service stops in St. Albans.

By car: From points south take I-91, Exit 26, at Orleans and follow Rt. 5 north for 4 miles to Coventry. Head north on Rt. 14 and then south on Rt. 100, 11 miles to Troy. Travel 3 miles north on Rt. 101 to the turnoff for Jay (Rt. 242). Believe it or not, this is shorter and less confusing than exiting in Newport.

WHEN TO GO Foliage and winter seasons both begin early here: By the last week in September color is substantial but the inns are empty. The area fills only on winter weekends, when buses from Montreal augment the crowds on the slopes. Midweek is relatively empty all season except during Canadian school vacations (check), but during Presidents' Week (public school vacation in New England) it's the one major mountain that isn't crowded. Given the windchill factor, we like to ski here in March, which can be glorious. For cross-country it's great all winter. July through October has been very quiet—but in 2006 (see the chapter introduction) that may change.

MEDICAL EMERGENCY Emergency service is available by calling **911**.

North Country Hospital & Medical Center (802-334-7331), Prouty Dr., Newport.

✳ To See

Jay Peak summit. The spectacular view from the top is accessible via the 60-person tram at Jay Peak Resort (802-966-2611), Rt. 242, Jay. It operates daily during ski season and from the last weekend in June through Labor Day, then in foliage season, mid-Sep.–Columbus Day, 10–5, weather permitting. $10 adults, $7 ages 14 and under, $30 family pass.

Hazen's Notch. From Montgomery Center, an unpromising narrow road, Rt. 58, climbs steeply east, quickly changing to dirt. In winter it's open only for the first 4 miles and is the site of a popular ski-touring spot. In summer it's a beautiful road, dappled with sunlight through the thick foliage. Look for a picnic spot near the height-of-land, close to a clear roadside spring. A historic site plaque says the road through the high pass was built by General Moses Hazen in 1778–79, commissioned by George Washington himself. The road was begun in 1776, 48 miles to the southeast at the town of Wells River on the Connecticut River, and was intended to reach St. John, Quebec. It was abandoned on this spot in April 1779 when the news that British patrols might use it as an invasion route (it was meant to work the other way) reached the camp at Hazen's Notch.

Montgomery and its covered bridges. Montgomery boasts a grand total of six Town lattice covered

> **BIG FALLS OF THE MISSISQUOI**
> River Rd. hugs the river, paralleling Rt. 101 between Troy and North Troy. You can access the falls from either town or from Vielleux Rd. off Rt. 101 at its junction with Rt. 105. This last is the prettiest route, through farmland and through the covered bridge south of the falls. Look for the unmarked pull-off in a grove of pine trees. The falls, thundering through a deep gorge, are awe-inspiringly magnificent.

BIG FALLS IN THE NORTH TROY AREA

Christina Tree

bridges: one right in Montgomery Village over Black Falls Creek; one south on Rt. 118; another nearby but 3 miles off Rt. 118 on West Hill on an abandoned side road over a waterfall; another northwest on Rt. 118 over the Trout River; and two in Montgomery Center, both a mile west of Rt. 118 over the Trout River (see our area map). Montgomery Village itself is picturesque. It began as a lumbering center and was for a long time one of the world's major producers of timothy grass seed culture. The Montgomery Historical Society's collection is housed in an 1835 wooden church, open June–Sep. at stated hours; the society also sponsors Saturday-evening concerts on the common in July and Aug.

St. Benoit du Lac (819-843-4080; http://st-benoit-du-lac.com), Austin, Quebec. Open daily. This French Benedictine monastery, founded in 1912, is sited on the west shore of Lake Memphremagog. It's an impressive building, and the resident monks welcome visitors for daily Mass and for vespers (usually 5 PM)), at which Gregorian chant is sung. The shop sells monastery products such as cheese and hard cider, as well as recordings of Gregorian chant, vestments, and religious articles. The easiest route from Newport is via the North Troy border crossing, then through Mansonville, South Bolton, and Austin. The shop is open Mon.– Sat. 9–10:45 and 11:45–4:30; until 6 in July and Aug.

✳ To Do

BICYCLE TOURING A time-honored and -tested 22.6- or 33.7-mile ride begins at the Black Lantern Inn (see *Lodging*) in Montgomery Village, passes two covered bridges along Rt. 118 north, and takes you to East Berkshire; you can simply continue to Enosburg Falls, where Lake Carmi offers camping and swimming, or turn onto the Richford Rd., looping back to Montgomery or up into Canada.

The **Missisquoi Valley Rail Trail** begins in Richford and runs 26.4 miles west to St. Albans.

MOUNTAIN BIKING **Jay Peak** (802-988-2611; 1-800-451-4449) maintains a network of trails for experienced mountain bikers via its aerial tramway, which will transport them and their bikes to the 3,861-foot summit from which several routes descend: 20 miles of alpine and 15 miles of cross-country.

CANOEING The 86-mile-long **Missisquoi River** makes a complete loop around Jay, passes briefly through Quebec, and continues across Vermont to empty into Lake Champlain. The upper half of the river near Jay offers fast water in spring, and the lower reaches are gentle and broad, good spring and summer ground for beginners and those who enjoy traversing outstanding rural landscape. For canoes and boat rentals, contact the **Missisquoi Riverbend B&B** (802-744-9991), Rt. 100, Troy.

FISHING The **Trout River** deserves its name. Brook trout can also be found in the **Missisquoi**, and **Lake Memphremagog** harbors smallmouth bass and salmon, among other species. See "The Lake Country" for boat rentals.

GOLF The long-promised 18-hole golf course at **Jay Peak Championship Golf Course** at Jay Peak Resort (www.jaypeakresort.com), Rt. 242, Jay, is slated to open in the summer of 2006. Designed by Graham Cooke and persistently planned and permitted over the past 15 years by Jay Peak president (and enthusiastic golfer) Bill Stenger, it emphasizes natural features and offers some memorable views.

Also see the Newport and Orleans golf clubs in "The Lake Country."

HIKING The **Long Trail** terminates its 262-mile route at the Canadian border, 10 miles north of Jay Peak, but the trek up Jay itself is what most hikers look for here. The most popular ascent is from Rt. 242, 1.2 miles west of the entrance to the ski area; the round-trip hike takes 3 hours. For details on this and the section of the trail between Hazen's Notch and Rt. 242, also for the final, fairly flat leg to the border, see the *Long Trail Guide*, published by the Green Mountain Club, which maintains the trail and four shelters in this area.

✿ **Hazen's Notch Association** (802-326-4799; www.hazensnotch.org), 1421 Hazen's Notch Rd. (Rt. 58), Montgomery Center. Open May 15–Nov. 15. No trail fee, but contributions appreciated. Twenty miles of this network are maintained for hiking, winding through 2,500 acres of privately owned woods and meadows; it's 15 minutes to Bear Paw Pond. The 2-mile-long Burnt Mountain Trail ascends to the 2,700-foot summit of Burnt Mountain, an open summit with 360-degree views that include Hazen's Notch, the Jay Mountains, Mount Mansfield, and Lake Champlain. Stop by the welcome center on Rt. 58. Dogs must be leashed. Inquire about frequent nature walks, fly-fishing workshops, and other special events. Sharon and Rolf Anderson offer nature and ecology day camps for children 6–9, Adventure Day and Overnight Camps for those 10–15.

HORSEBACK RIDING Missisquoi Riverbend B&B (802-744-9991), Rt. 100 in Troy Village, offers trail rides.

SWIMMING A number of inns have their own pools. The most popular local swimming hole is at Jay Four Corners, downstream from the Rt. 101 bridge.

TENNIS ✿ **Jay Peak Resort** (802-988-2611) maintains tennis courts in warm-weather months.

✳ Winter Sports

CROSS-COUNTRY SKIING Hazen's Notch Cross-Country Ski and Snow-shoeing Center (802-326-4708; www.hazensnotch.org), Rt. 58, Montgomery Center. This outstanding touring center offers 45 km of meticulously tracked trails, some with fine views of Jay and the Cold Hollow Mountains, connecting with the Catamount Trail. In business since 1978, when Val Schadinger and Rolf Anderson first laid out the trails, Hazen's Notch offers a rustic, noncommercial atmosphere that has attracted a loyal following. Early and late in the season, this tends to be one of half a dozen cross-country networks in New England that have snow (elevation: 900–2,800 feet). Ten miles of dedicated snowshoe trails include the path up Burnt Mountain. Lessons and rentals, also moonlight tours.

DOWNHILL SKIING ✿ **Jay Peak** (information and reservations: 802-988-2611; 1-800-451-4449 including Canada; snow conditions: 802-988-9601; www.jaypeak

resort.com). While there's an easy-intermediate trail (Northway) off the summit, Jay Peak regulars duck into glades right off the top. Jay's 20 glades and extreme chutes are what draw many of its regulars, who like to strike out into 150 acres of backcountry terrain. Unlike regular runs, wooded trails ("glades") cannot be covered by human-made snow and so require a lot of the natural stuff, which is what Jay Peak has in spades: an average of 330 inches annually. That's twice the snow many New England areas receive.

The original trails here are stateside, on a shoulder of Jay Peak. Still considered some of the toughest runs in Vermont, they were carved 30 years ago by local residents. An enterprising Kiwanis group (it included the parish priest) convinced the Vermont Legislature to reroute existing roads up over the high ridge from which Jay's access road rises, thus linking it to northwestern Vermont as well as to the Northeast Kingdom. They imported an Austrian skimeister to create a true trail system and ski school. In the early 1960s Weyerhaeuser Corporation acquired the ski area and installed a Swiss-built tramway to Jay's Peak, which it topped with a Sky Haus tram station, a building that emphasizes the crest of the summit and gives it a distinctly Matterhorn-like cap. Weyerhaeuser also built the large, sturdy, Tyrolean-style base complex that still stands and includes a 48-room hotel.

Since 1978 the resort has been owned by the Montreal-based owners of Saint-Saveur, a lucrative Laurentian ski area. The original trams have been replaced with sleek cars, lifts have been improved, and condominiums have been proliferating. Weekends can be mobbed by Montrealers, but midweek is frequently wide open, and spring skiing is superb.

Lifts: 60-passenger aerial tramway; 3 quad chairs, 1 triple, 1 double; 1 T-bar.

Vertical drop: 2,153 feet.

Trails and slopes: 76 trails, glades, and chutes totaling more than 50 miles of skiing, spread over 2 peaks, connected by a ridgeline; 100+ acres of gladed terrain.

Off-piste skiing: 200 acres.

Snowboarding: 4 terrain parks; board demo center, rentals, instruction.

Snowmaking: 80 percent of the total 385 acres.

Snowshoeing: Weekly snowshoeing walks led by a naturalist.

Facilities: Austria Haus and Tram Haus base lodges with cafeteria, pub, and ski and rental shop. Sky Haus cafeteria at the summit. Nursery and day care facilities. Rentals. A lighted skating rink and skate rentals. Van service is offered from Burlington International Airport (80 miles away) and from the Amtrak station in St. Albans (a 45-minute drive).

Ski school: U.S.- and Canadian-certified instructors, adult and junior racing clinics, American Teaching Method (ATM). Telemarking instruction and rentals offered.

For children: Mountain Explorers for both skiing and snowboarding for 5- to 12-year-old group, kinderschool for ages 2–5. Day care for ages 2–7.

Rates: $58 adult, $42 junior (14 and under), but far cheaper for multidays and with lodging packages.

SLEIGH RIDES Phil & Karen's Sleigh/Hayrides (802-744-9928), 143 Kennison Rd., Westfield. Old-fashioned sleigh- or hayrides are offered through meadows and along a quiet road, drawn by Belgians Charlie and Duke.

Missisquoi Riverbend B&B (802-744-9991) offers sleigh rides.

SNOWMOBILING The area is webbed with **Vermont Association of Snow Travelers** (VAST) trails; check with the local inns.

✳ Lodging

On-mountain

Jay Peak Resort (1-800-451-4449; www.jaypeakresort.com).

✎ **Hotel Jay** (1-800-451-4449), Rt. 242, Jay 05859. Located right at the lifts, an adequate but tired lodge with 48 big rooms, some with double beds, some queen and some twin beds, color TV, phone, and private bath; a pleasant public dining room, a game room, family room, sauna and Jacuzzi, outdoor pool (summer only). In winter a 2-day package including lift, lodging, two breakfasts, and one dinner is $333 per person (except over the holidays). Kids 14 and under stay and ski free; you're charged only for meals. Way less off-season.

Condominiums: **Jay Peak Condominiums**. A total of 217 condos and town houses, 85 percent in the rental pool, have been constructed in clusters over the years and vary widely in look and size, studios to five-bedrooms; all have fireplace, living room, and fully equipped kitchen. Not all are trailside. From $385 per person including lifts for 2 nights during ski season.

Off-mountain

INNS ◎ **Black Lantern Inn** (802-326-4507; 1-800-255-8661; www.blacklantern.com), Montgomery 05470. A white-pillared brick inn built in 1803 as the Montgomery Village stage stop, this is the area's most appealing place to stay. Innkeepers Deb and Dr. Bob Winders offer eight attractive rooms (private baths) and seven suites (one with three bedrooms) divided between the main inn and neighboring Burdette House with its back deck (Adirondack chairs are also positioned behind the inn) with a spectacular view of Hazen's Notch. Some have fireplace or wood-burning stove and steam shower or whirlpool bath. The inn itself also offers a small reading/talking area, warmed by a soapstone stove off a cozy taproom; there's a low-beamed, charming dining room (see *Dining Out*). This is not a place for children. Beyond the porch is the village with its six covered bridges, and from the back there is a hot tub under the gazebo with a view of Hazen's Notch, a venue for small weddings. Summer is low season: $104 per room, $141–219 per suite B&B. Ski season: $116 for rooms, from $153 for suites.

Jay Village Inn (802-988-2306; www.stayatjay.com), 1078 Rt. 141, Jay 05859. Three miles downhill in Jay Four Corners, this classic ski lodge offers recently refurbished rooms, family suites (sleeping 4–5), and apartments (sleeping 6–12). There's plenty of atmosphere: a massive fireplace, an informal pub and restaurant serving flatbread pizza, burgers, and a full menu that (once more) has a good

Christina Tree

VIEW FROM BLACK LANTERN INN

rep. In summer there's a heated pool. In ski season $59–119 per room, $199–199 per family suite, and from $150 per apartment.

The Lodge at Jay (802-988-4459; 1-877-204-7039; www.thelodgeatjay .com), Rt. 242, Jay Four Corners 05859. This well-built lodge has been recently renovated. Facilities include a restaurant and pub and an evolving spa that at present includes a steam room, sauna, and exercise room with massage available on request. There's also an entertainment room with a wide-screen TV. Winter rates from $98 midweek, $119 on weekends in ski season, including tax and continental breakfast, more for family suites; under 14 free with parents. Inquire about ski-and-stay packages.

BED & BREAKFASTS

Phineas Swann B&B (802-326-4306; www.phineasswann.com), Box 43, Main St., Montgomery Center 05471. John Perkins and Jay Kerch have brought considerable skill, resources, and energy to this delightful village B&B. Jay, a former NYC interior decorator, has created three rooms, four attractive suites, and two separate one-bedroom apartments with kitchens in the River House Annex right on the Trout River (out back). Two more suites are due for completion in 2006. John, recently returned from 20 years overseas

working for an international bank, is an enthusiastic chef. "One-bedrooms" (with a sitting are) are $165–195; two-bedroom suites with a living room and sleep sofa are $195–295; B&B in the main inn is $99–195, depending on the room and size; and apartments are $150 per day (3-day minimum), $625 weekly. Dogs are very welcome (hosted by two resident Scotties).

Missisquoi Riverbend B&B (802-744-9991; www.riverbendvt.com), 6198 Rt. 100, Troy 05868. A Victorian farmhouse on the edge of the village offers 15 acres on the Missisquoi River. Innkeepers Paul Becker and Jim McKimm enjoy introducing guests to the delights of paddling (canoes available) and a pedal boat. The house offers two guest rooms with shared bath and two suites with private bath. This is a comfortable, casual place with fireplaces in the dining room and library. Birders are particularly welcome; horseback riding and sleigh rides are offered. $80–95 in low season and $90–110 high includes a full breakfast.

Woodshed Lodge (802-988-4444; 1-800-495-4445; www.wood shedlodge.com), Rt. 242, Jay 05459. Just 3 miles from Jay Peak, this landmark old lodge is maintained by John and Chris Engler, who cater to families. Three of the seven rooms have private bath (one with whirlpool tub), while four share two baths. There's a sitting room upstairs and a library/TV lounge downstairs. $50–70 per couple in summer, $75–100 in winter includes breakfast; $10 per extra person, $5 per child. Inquire about weekend specials, including one dinner.

Idyllwild East Bed & Breakfast (802-988-9830; www.idyllwildeast .com), 1387 Rt. 101, Troy 05859.

Proncell and Dortha Johnson's contemporary house is remarkably roomy. The three attractive guest rooms (two with shared bath) are off a big entry-level family room with a wood-burning stove and TV. On the second floor is a larger, brighter "great room" with a dining area and eat-in kitchen. Common space also includes a back deck and more than 3 landscaped acres. $95 double with breakfast; family and meal plan rates available.

Couture's Maple Shop and Bed & Breakfast (802-744-2733; 1-800-845-2733; www.maplesyrupvermont.com), 560 Rt. 100, Westfield 05874-9197. Pauline and Jacques Couture raised six children in this 1892 farmhouse while also maintaining a dairy farm and sizable maple syrup business. Three guest rooms with queen-sized bed and pullout couch share a bath. The cow barn is out the back door, and the sugarhouse is just up the hill. $85 per couple ($20 per extra person) includes a full breakfast served in the newly renovated farm kitchen.

Rose Apple Acres Farm (802-988-4300; 1-877-879-9135; www.roseapple acres.com), 721 East Hill Rd., North Troy 05859. Closed in winter. Jay and Camilla Meads's comfortable house sits on 52 acres, with lovely views. It's a real farm with sheep, goats, and horses. Located 10 miles from Jay Peak, near a covered bridge on the Missisquoi River; good for fishing and canoeing. There are two guest rooms, one with private bath. Camilla makes porcelain dolls in her studio (see *Selective Shopping*). The Meads cater to Long Trail hikers with a special rate of $35 per person; they will shuttle hikers to and from the trailhead or bus. Otherwise, $80 includes breakfast.

✳ Where to Eat

DINING OUT Black Lantern Inn (802-326-4507), Montgomery Village. Dinner is served nightly in-season, less often in spring and summer. Phone to reserve. The low-beamed dining room of this delightful old inn is the most romantic setting in the area for candle-lit dinners. While the menu changes nightly, you might begin with spinach- or sausage-stuffed button mushrooms followed by Black Angus filet mignon stuffed with Green Mountain Blue Cheese and roasted garlic, or corn-crusted shrimp with sweet and hot onions, with roasted strawberries Amaretto or bittersweet chocolate Chambord for dessert. Entrées range from $13.50 for a vegetarian dish to $30 for a full rack of lamb (which can be shared for a plate fee) with pomegranate glaze and fresh mint.

North Troy Village Restaurant (802-988-4063), Main St., North Troy. Open at 5 PM daily except Tue.; Thu.–Sun. off-season. Irene McDermott and chef Gary Birchard ("The Bear") have an enthusiastic following. The attractive dining room in this 1890s village hotel is the scene of memorable meals. The menu is extensive and features seafood, pastas, prime rib specials, and dinners for two such as rack of lamb and broiled seafood specialty dishes. There's a kids' menu and "mini-meals," like a 5-ounce tournedo (why don't others do this?) as well as a burger. Warning: The "Little Bear Cut" is enormous. Kids menu. Entrées $9.95 (pastas)–25.95 for rack of lamb. All come with soup and salad, homemade bread, and veggies.

Paddington's (802-326-3232), Rt. 242 between the Jay Peak access road and Montgomery Center. Open Thu.–Sun. 5–9:30. We have only breakfasted here, but chef-owners Gary and Mary Jane Bouchard-Pike both hold culinary school degrees and spent their lives in the restaurant business. Specialties include prime rib with Yorkshire pudding, and Cornish pasty (golden flaky crust filled with Vermont cheddar, a blend of fresh herbs, and veggies). Entrées $12.95–21.95, including house salad, vegetables, starch, and fresh-baked bread. Children's menu available.

Hidden Country Restaurant (802-744-6149), Rt. 100, Lowell. Open Mon.–Sat. 4:30–9 PM, Sun. 8:30–11:30 AM. Begun in 1988 by Joe St. Onge, this restaurant draws diners from throughout the Kingdom. Plenty of atmosphere (must be seen to be appreciated) and the specialty is prime rib ($19.95 for 24 ounces, $15.95 for 14 ounces). Rolls and desserts are homemade, and the specialty cocktails and Friday fish fry are famous. There's a trout pond for paid fishing and an eight-hole chip-and-putt golf course.

EATING OUT *The Belfry* (802-326-4400), Rt. 242, between Montgomery Center and the Jay Peak access road. Open nightly 4–late. No reservations, and during ski season you'd better get here early if you want a booth. Built in 1902 as a schoolhouse, this is the area's most popular pub, and the food's good, thanks to longtime manager Chantal Pothier who now owns it, along with Marty Lumbra, who drives the local school bus. If you've been here a day or two, chances are you will recognize someone in the crowd around the mirrored oak-and-marble back bar. The soup is homemade, and the blackboard lists daily specials, like pan-blackened fish and grilled lamb chops. The set menu features "Belfry

Steak" ("price depends on the chef's mood"), salads, burgers, and deep-fried mushrooms. Wednesday is Italian night. Inquire about music.

Bernie's Café (802-326-4682), Main St., Montgomery Center. Open 6:30 AM–10 PM, later on weekends. The best place around for lunch, and not bad for dinner, either. Bigger than it looks from its greenhouse-style front, this is a genuine gathering spot for the area. Breakfast options include bagels, smoked salmon, and eggs any style, and the breads (including wheat onion, six-grain, and herb) are baked daily, for sale separately as well as used in sandwiches. Soups are a luncheon specialty, and at dinner the menu ranges from sautéed scampi through pastas. Fully licensed with a pub in back. John Boucher frequently presides behind the counter.

Junction 101 Restaurant (802-744-2700), 4278 Rt. 100, Troy. Open daily 5 AM–9 PM, until 10 Sat., Sun. 7 AM–9 PM. Tina Farrell, chef-owner, offers good "affordable family dining": steak, seafood, and nightly specials, full-service bar.

Jay Village Inn (802-988-2306; www.stayatjay.com), 1078 Rt. 242, Jay. A warm, informal lodge atmosphere, reasonably priced nightly specials—shrimp, scallops, lamb, served with bread and salad, kids' menu, full-service bar.

Inglenook Lodge (802-988-2880), Rt. 202, Jay. The menu changes frequently but this big, cheerful lodge dining room is always a good deal, specializing in complete dinners with a soup and salad bar.

The Lodge at Jay Restaurant and Pub (802-988-4459), Rt. 202, Jay Four Corners. A popular lodge restaurant specializing in steak, pasta, burgers, and ribs with nightly specials. **Squidwards Nightclub and Bar** downstairs features a wide choice of beers on tap and weekend entertainment during ski season.

Trout River Traders (802-326-3058; www.troutrivertraders.com), Montgomery Center. Open 9–5 daily. This is a great lunch stop, good for soups from scratch, good chili, overstuffed sandwiches such as chicken with dill. All meats are roasted on the premises, and bread is fresh baked. Cappuccino, lattes, and espresso are served at the soda fountain, along with New York egg creams and Italian cream sodas. Some tables, overstuffed chairs, a woodstove in winter.

The Old Bobbin Mill Restaurant & Pub (802-744-2233), Rt. 100, Westfield. Open daily except Mon. 7 AM– 8 PM, later Fri. and Sat.; closing at 7 PM Sun. Local fiddlers gather for Wednesday breakfast. This is a genuine old lumber turned bobbin mill, turned crafts shop, turned pub and restaurant. Menus and servings are large and prices low. Dinner choices include chicken with biscuits and Montreal-style chicken kebabs, with fries and salad. Beer and wine served. Thursday is Mexican night.

Jay Country Store (802-988-4040), Jay Village. Open daily 6:30 AM–9 PM, Sun. 7:30–8. Sandwiches at the counter and in the sunny solarium reflect the quality of the store's deli.

✳ Selective Shopping

Trout River Traders (802-326-3058; www.troutrivertraders.com), Montgomery Center. Michael Savel and Mark Cellucci have reestablished this photogenic old country store as the village gathering place. Relax with a latte in an easy chair by the fire or on the back deck and browse the shelves for local crafts and products, gifts, antiques, specialty foods, and locally spun yarn and locally made hats and scarves.

Jay Country Store (802-988-4040), Jay Village. Open daily. The center of Jay Village, selling papers, gas, food, and wine basics, also a deli (see *Eating Out*), plus an interesting assortment of gift items and cards.

Couture's Maple Shop (802-744-733; 1-800-845-2733), 560 Rt. 100, Westfield. Open year-round, Mon.–Sat. 8–6. A long-established maple producer: maple candy, cream, granulated sugar, pancake mix, and salad dressing, as well as syrup; will ship anywhere.

Jed's Maple Products (802-744-2095; www.jedsmaple.com), 475 Carter Rd., Westfield. Syrup, candy, and frosted nuts. Inquire about the annual Mud Season Sugar On Snow Party.

Rose Apple Acres Dolls (802-988-4300), East Hill Rd., North Troy. Modern porcelain figures and restoration.

✳ Special Events

Last Sunday of January: **Hazen's Notch Ski Race**.

Mid-February: **Winter Festival**— varied events including a race from the summit of Jay Peak to Jay Village.

July–August: **Concerts on the common**, presented by the Montgomery Historical Society on Saturday evening (802-326-4404). **Harvest Day**, Montgomery.

September: **Concerts on the common** in the Montgomery Village church.

October: **Octoberfest**, Columbus Day weekend, Jay Peak—big annual art and crafts fair.

THE LAKE COUNTRY

INCLUDING NEWPORT, BARTON, AND ISLAND POND

The northeast corner of the Northeast Kingdom is spotted with some of the most beautiful lakes in New England. The largest of these is Memphrema-gog and the most dramatic, Lake Willoughby. There are many more, however, especially in Essex County, the easternmost and loneliest corner of Vermont, in which publicly owned land has recently increased substantially.

At the height of railroad passenger service, large wooden hotels rose on the shores of several of these lakes. In Newport, at the southern tip of Lake Mem-phremagog (which stretches more than 30 miles north into Canada), the 400-room Memphremagog House stood next to the railroad station, Newport House was across the street, and the New City Hotel was nearby. Guests came by train from Boston and Philadelphia. Lindbergh came with his *Spirit of Saint Louis*, and there was a racetrack and a paddle-wheeler. The city's past splendor is recalled in archival photos mounted by the Memphremagog Historical Society of Newport in the State Office Building, where there's also a display on northern Vermont Abenaki people, from Paleolithic through current times. Recently the city has reclaimed its lakefront with a marina and outstanding walkway.

Less than a dozen miles northeast of Newport is the split-nationality commu-nity of Derby Line, Vt., and Stanstead, Quebec. This is a major border crossing (I-91 continues north as Highway 55), linking with the major east–west highway between Montreal and Quebec City. The international line runs right through the Haskell Opera House in Derby Line—the audience in America attends con-certs in Canada. We have included two outstanding inns in East Hatley, Quebec Province, because they are, in fact, the best-known places to stay in this area.

West of Derby Center you are quickly in little-trafficked lake country: Lakes Derby and Salem, Seymour and Echo all have good fishing, and dozens of smaller ponds have boat launches. Island Pond is a town as well as a lake, and for travel-ers it looms large on the map because you have to pass through it to get to the empty (of people, but teeming with moose, black bear, and other wildlife), lake-pocked land surrounding the town in every direction. It's the obvious place to stop for lunch or dinner. There's good fishing around Averill where Quimby Country, the region's oldest and most unusual resort, is squirreled away. Beyond,

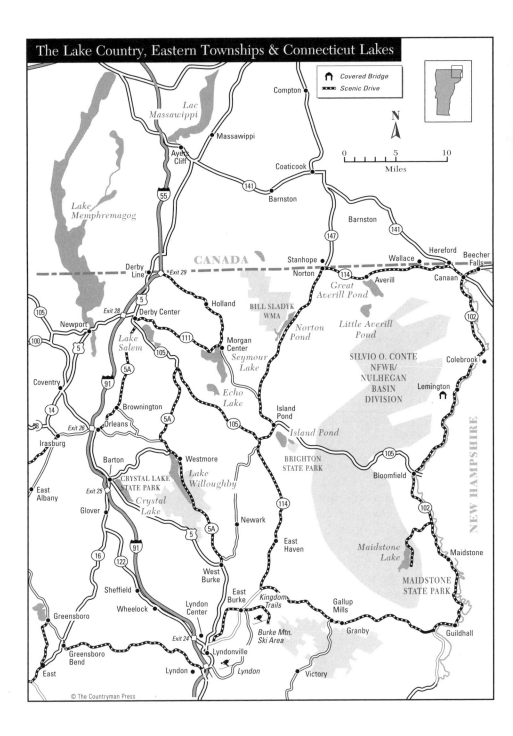

The Lake Country, Eastern Townships & Connecticut Lakes

Covered Bridge
Scenic Drive

N

0   5   10
Miles

Compton

*Lac
Massawippi*

Massawippi

Ayers
Cliff

Coaticook

55

141

Barnston

Barnston

147

141

*Lake
Memphremagog*

CANADA

Derby
Line

Exit 29

Stanhope

Norton

114

Averill

Wallace

Hereford

Beecher
Falls

Canaan

*Great
Averill Pond*

102

5

Holland

BILL SLADYK
WMA

*Norton
Pond*

*Little Averill
Pond*

105

Newport

Exit 28

Derby Center

111

Morgan
Center

*Seymour
Lake*

Colebrook

100

5

*Lake
Salem*

105

SILVIO O. CONTE
NFWR/
NULHEGAN
BASIN
DIVISION

Coventry

5A

91

*Echo
Lake*

Island
Pond

Lemington

14

Brownington

5A

Island Pond

NEW HAMPSHIRE

28

Exit 26

Orleans

105

BRIGHTON
STATE PARK

Bloomfield

105

Irasburg

Barton

CRYSTAL LAKE
STATE PARK

Westmore

*Lake
Willoughby*

102

East
Albany

Exit 25

*Crystal
Lake*

Glover

5

5A

Newark

*Maidstone
Lake*

Maidstone

16

91

122

East
Haven

MAIDSTONE
STATE PARK

Sheffield

West
Burke

Greensboro

Wheelock

Lyndon
Center

East
Burke

*Kingdom
Trails*

Gallup
Mills

Granby

Guildhall

Exit 24

*Burke Mtn.
Ski Area*

Greensboro
Bend

Lyndonville

East

Lyndon

Lyndon

Victory

© The Countryman Press

this lonely stretch of the Connecticut River dwindles into a stream, and then widens into the Connecticut Lakes.

Lake Willoughby, west of Barton, is one of Vermont's most hauntingly beautiful lakes. Mounts Hor and Pisgah, which rise abruptly from opposite shores, create a fjordlike effect when viewed from the public beach in Westmore at the northern end or from the southern tip of the lake. Mostly undeveloped, Willoughby is surrounded for much of its length by state forest, and the water is stocked with salmon and rainbow trout. A well-known resort area in the days of grand hotels and steamboats, it now has a limited, loyal following of sailors, sailboarders (there is always a breeze here), and year-round fishermen.

Barton, this area's southernmost commercial center, also obviously boomed in the late 19th century, when six passenger trains a day stopped in summer, bringing guests to fill the town's big hotels (long gone) or the gingerbread "camps" (still there) on Crystal Lake. Its shops serve the communities of Brownington to the east, Irasburg and Glover to the west, plus the beautiful web of farm roads between West Glover and Albany.

GUIDANCE Vermont North Country Chamber of Commerce (802-334-7782; www.vtnorthcountry.org) maintains a walk-in visitors center on the Causeway in Newport, theoretically open daily year-round but volunteer operated.

The Derby Line Welcome Center (802-873-3311) on I-91 south, with restrooms, at the border serves arriving Canadians.

Barton Area Chamber of Commerce (802-525-1137; www.bartonarea chamber.com), P.O. Box 403, Barton 05822, serves the southern part of this region and has listings of summer lakeside cottages.

Island Pond Chamber of Commerce (802-723-6300; www.islandpond chamber.org).

GETTING AROUND Two pieces of advice: (1) Avoid driving lonely stretches after dark and if you must, do so slowly, watching for moose, which are difficult to spot at night and deadly if you collide at high speed. (2) Gas up. Pumps are few and far between, and tempting woods roads abound.

WHEN TO COME Snowmobilers converge on Island Pond and ice fishers come to many of the lakes in winter; fishermen come in spring, hunters in fall. Otherwise this is summer and fall foliage country.

✳ Villages

Barton Village (population: 742). The hotels are gone, but Crystal Lake remains beautiful, with a clifflike promontory on one side and public beaches at its northern rim. There is golf here, and the town of Barton itself packs an astounding number of services into its small downtown. The Crystal Lake Falls Historical Association maintains the **Pierce House Museum** (802-525-6251) on Water St., next to the old-fashioned office of the *Barton Chronicle*, an excellent little weekly covering much of Orleans and Essex Counties.

Christina Tree

THE NEWPORT WATERFRONT

Brownington Village is a crossroads full of outstanding, early-19th-century buildings, the core of a once proud hill town long since eclipsed by such valley centers as Barton, Orleans, and Newport. There are 19th-century flower and heirloom herb gardens behind the Eaton House and a spectacular panorama from the wooden observatory set up in a meadow behind the church. A descriptive walking tour booklet is available at the **Old Stone House Museum**, the big attraction in the village.

Island Pond (population: 1,260). The crossroads of Vermont's lonely, northeasternmost corner, Island Pond has the look and feel of an outpost.

A sign in front of the city-sized depot reads, PIONEER RAILROAD PLANNER JOHN A. POOR'S DREAM OF AN INTERNATIONAL RAILROAD CONNECTING MONTREAL, CANADA, WITH THE ICE-FREE HARBOR OF PORTLAND, MAINE, BECAME A REALITY ON JULY 18, 1854, WHEN THE FIRST THROUGH TRAINS MET AT THIS GREAT HALFWAY POINT ON THE GRAND TRUNK RAILWAY. During the late 19th century and into the 20th, Island Pond hummed with the business of servicing frequent passenger trains and freight trains transporting logs and wood pulp. No longer. Today it's a funky village on a pond with an island in its center. The Twelve Tribes, a religious community, has rooted here, buying and restoring many of the Victorian houses and operating the town's one big specialty store. Winter is now the season here. Island Pond is the region's snowmobiling capital.

❋ To See

Bread and Puppet Theater Museum (802-525-3031; www.theaterofmemory .com), Rt. 122, Glover. Open mid-May–Oct., 10–5. The internationally known Bread and Puppet Theater tours in winter, but much of the year the weathered, vintage-1863 dairy barn is open to anyone who stops (free, but donations welcome). It houses one of the biggest collections and some of the biggest puppets in the world: huge and haunting puppet dwarfs, giants, devils, and other fantastic figures of good and evil, the artistic expressions of German-born Peter Schumann who founded the Bread and Puppet Theater in 1962 and moved it to Glover in

The Old Stone House Museum (802-754-2022; www.oldstonehousemuseum.org), off Rt. 58 east of Orleans in Brownington. Open May 15–Oct. 15, Wed.–Sun. 11–5. $5 adults, $4 county residents, $2 students. This striking, four-story, 30-room granite building with a clerestory, completed in 1836 as a dormitory for the Orleans County Grammar School, houses the collections of the Orleans County Historical Society Museum. The building is all the more dramatic, set among the village's scattering of early-19th-century houses and the surrounding 55 acres of farmland. Its story is compelling. The

Old Stone House Museum

ALEXANDER TWILIGHT

school's headmaster and the building's architect was Alexander Twilight (1795–1875), the first person of African parentage to attend an American college (Middlebury, 1823) or serve in a state legislature (Vermont House of Representatives, 1836). The museum includes a visitors center in the circa-1839 Alexander Twilight House, from which guided tours depart to view the Old Stone House. Here, some rooms have been restored while others showcase special exhibits and historical collections from towns throughout Orleans County (including tools, paintings, furniture, and decorative arts). The Lawrence Barn features an exhibit titled A Hard Row to Hoe: Two Centuries of Farming in Orleans County. Inquire about special, year-round workshops. **Old Stone House Day**, second Sunday in August, represents one of the Kingdom's biggest annual events with a farmer's market, picnic, kids' activities, live music, crafts demonstrations, and more. Any day, pick up the walking tour guide to the Brownington Historic District— and don't miss the view from the observatory tower on Prospect Hill. This is one of the most magical places in Vermont.

OLD STONE HOUSE

Old Stone House Museum

1974. Inquire about tours, but usually visitors wander and wonder. Publications and postcards are sold in the shop. Sat. and Sun. in July and Aug., performances are staged in the outdoor arena in the neighboring field; inquire about Friday-night performances in the timber-frame theater.

LAKES Lake Memphremagog, Newport. Vermont's second largest lake at 33 miles long—only 5 miles of which are within the United States—Memphrema-gog stretches north from Newport. See St. Benoit du Lac in "Jay Peak Area" as well as listings under *Boating*, *Fishing*, and *Swimming*.

Lake Willoughby, Westmore. Vermont's most dramatic lake, nearly 5 miles long and more than 300 feet deep, shaped like a stocking with a foot toward the north and Mount Pisgah and Mount Hor rising to more than 2,500 feet on opposite sides at the southern end. See *Boating*, *Fishing*, *Swimming*, and *Lodging*.

Seymour Lake. There is a public beach in the tiny village of Morgan Center, also the spot to rent boats for fishing for landlocked salmon. In winter this lake is peppered with fishing shanties, and there is a system of cross-country trails (ungroomed).

Echo Lake. Much smaller than Seymour Lake and adjoining it on the south, this lake is circled by a dirt road and gently rolling hills. There is also public boat access. Good fishing for trout and landlocked salmon.

Island Pond is actually a small lake with a 20-acre island off the sandy beach and a wooded campground in Brighton State Park. Boating and fishing are both easily accessible.

Crystal Lake, Barton. Roughly 3 miles long and about 1 mile wide, in places more than 100 feet deep, this glacial lake is beautifully sited between rough-hewn mountains. Crystal Lake State Park (see *Swimming*) is justly popular; summer rental cottages can be found through the Barton Area Chamber of Commerce. Also see *Fishing*.

Maidstone Lake, Guildhall. One of Vermont's cleanest, clearest, most remote lakes was designated a state park in 1938. This was wilderness, but the Civilian Conservation Corps built fireplaces for camping, along with the lodge and picnic shelter that are still in use (see *Green Space*). The lake offers good trout fishing but is best known as a loon nesting area.

LAKE WILLOUGHBY

Christina Tree

The town of Glover also harbors three, small fish-stocked lakes: **Daniels Pond**, **Shadow Lake**, and **Lake Parker**.

SCENIC DRIVES

West Burke to Westmore. The stretch of Rt. 5A along Lake Willoughby is one of the most breathtaking anywhere.

Island Pond–Lake Willoughby shortcut. An easy route to navigate from Westmore on Lake Willoughby: Turn north in the middle of the village on Hinton Ridge Rd. and follow it through high, rolling farmland and forest (never mind name changes) until it reaches a T intersection. Turn right and right again onto Rt. 105 into Island Pond. The reverse direction is even more beautiful but tricky at the beginning (left onto Hudson Rd. off Rt. 105 and then your second left onto Westmore Rd.).

✳ To Do

BIKING While the region's formal mountain biking meccas are described in the St. Johnsbury chapter, this pristine area offers hundreds of miles of dirt and logging roads. Request the excellent bike map for the Kingdom from the **Northeast Kingdom Travel and Tourism Association** (1-800-884-8001).

BIRDING The most famous birds in the Kingdom are the peregrine falcons that nest on Mount Pisgah on Willoughby Lake. Falcons return in spring, nest during summer, and leave by August. Early morning and late afternoon are the best times to see them from the north end of the west-facing cliff.

Over 100 species of birds have been spotted around Lake Willoughby alone. Maidstone Lake is famed as a nesting area for loons, and the Nulhegan Basin is an important breeding habitat for migratory birds and nesting thrushes and warblers. Boreal forests in the basin support rare species such as spruce grouse, gray jay, Wilson's warbler, olive-sided flycatcher, rusty blackbird, black-backed woodpecker, and three-toed woodpecker. A splendid, free *Connecticut River Birding Trail/Northern Section* map/guide is available locally; also see www.birdtrail.org.

BOATING With thousands of miles of rivers and streams and the lion's share of the Kingdom's more than 37,000 acres of lakes and ponds, this area offers some of the best paddling in the Northeast. The DeLorme *Vermont Atlas and Gazetteer* shows put-ins.

North Woods Stewardship Center (802-723-6551; www.northwoodscenter .org), 10 Mile Square Rd., East Charleston (5 miles west of Island Pond), offers rental canoes on the Clyde River, also guided canoe expeditions on a variety of waters. **White Caps Campgrounds** (802-467-3345) at the southern end of Lake Willoughby rents canoes and kayaks. Aluminum boats (14 feet) with small motors, also pontoons and sailboats, may be rented at **Newport Marine** (802-334-5911) at Eastside Restaurant Docks, Farrants Point, on Lake Memphremagog in Newport. Boats are also available at **Brighton State Park** in Island Pond (see *Green Space*), **Anglin' Boat Rentals** on Crystal Lake in Barton (802-525-3904), and **Nulhegan Guiding** (802-895-4328) in Island Pond.

On the Connecticut River, Canaan is a good place to put in, but there are several rapids at the start. Canoeing is also good below Colebrook, N.H., for 3 miles but then rather fast for an equal distance. (See also *Fishing*.)

FISHING This is a fly-fishing mecca, drawing serious fishermen to wilderness brooks and ponds as well as rivers and lakes. Most general stores sell 3-day

ISLAND POND LOOP This 66-mile loop circles the northeastern corner of Vermont, beginning in Island Pond and heading north on Rt. 114. The Canadian National Railway's Grand Trunk line from Montreal to Portland, Maine, hugs the highway the full 16 miles to Norton. This railway was once Montreal's winter lifeline to Europe, as goods could not be shipped into or out of the frozen port of Montreal during the coldest months. About halfway to **Norton**, near the south end of long and slender **Norton Pond** (there's a boat launch on Rt. 114), a gravel road to the left leads into the Bill Sladyk Wildlife Management Area, frequented by hunters, fishermen, and loggers. Just before you reach the tiny village of Norton (opposite slightly larger Stanhope, Quebec), the forest thins out and farmland reappears. Norton is the site of the notorious Earth People's Park, a 1960s-style, loosely governed hippie commune that has survived but has dwindled from hundreds to perhaps two dozen residents. The road passes several farms, a school, and the **Norton Country Store** (open daily 7 AM–9 PM), then swings abruptly eastward to avoid the imposing Canadian port-of-entry.

Continuing eastward along the border, Rt. 114 reenters the forest, passing a series of lakes, most of which are dotted with hunting and fishing camps. The largest of the lakes is Great Averill Pond. For directions to the boat launch, stop by the **Lakeview Store** (open daily 8–7), where owner Priscilla Roy sells the wool that she spins, also weaving supplies and locally handcrafted items. East of the store a road leads to **Quimby Country**, one of Vermont's oldest and most interesting resorts (see the boxed description in *Lodging*). Shortly after passing Big Averill, you leave the St. Lawrence watershed and begin a rapid descent into the Connecticut River Valley. Halfway from Averill to Canaan, the road skirts the south shore of sizable Wallace Pond, almost entirely within the province of Quebec.

Canaan, 14 miles east of Norton, is a pleasant pocket of civilization with a handsome green, Fletcher Park, that features a lovely Greek Revival building in its far corner. Built as a tavern in 1846 and said to have served for a while as the northernmost U.S. stop on the Underground Railroad, this is now the **Alice M. Ward Memorial Library** (802-266-7135), worth a stop to see the Canaan Historical Society's changing exhibits upstairs.

In **Bessie's Diner** (see *Eating Out*), across from the green on Rt. 114, a framed tintype depicts Canaan as the village was when a covered bridge spanned the Connecticut River here, connecting it with West Stewartstown, N.H. Today you barely notice the river, here just a fledgling stream spanned by a brief bridge. Turn north along this stream if you want to see the village of Beecher Falls, 2 miles north. The small, sagging village is dominated by the huge Ethan Allen Furniture plant (closed at this writing) and is a Canadian border crossing. Across another brief bridge is Stewartstown, N.H.

In reality these far corners of Vermont and N.H. form a region of their own, a fishing, snowmobiling, and moose-watching mecca known by various names but most accurately as the **Connecticut Lakes**. You might want to detour north on Rt. 3 in New Hampshire (Vermont ends at Beecher Falls). A state-operated

Great North Woods Welcome Center, open daily 9–7, weekends 8–8 (with restrooms), south of Pittsburg orients visitors to the series of four lakes strung along the 22 semi-wilderness miles north of town (www.greatnorthwoods.org). This stretch of Rt. 3 is known as "Moose Alley" for reasons easy to grasp if you drive it on a summer evening. Fishing lodges and rental camps, salted away around these lakes, far outnumber lodging options contained in the entire vast area of Vermont covered by this chapter, but you see few from the road. Die-hard Connecticut River buffs may want to hike in to its source, a small pond accessible via a path beside the Rt. 3 border station (restrooms).

From Canaan the loop turns south on Rt. 102, through river-bottom farmland, through Lemington, and past the impressively long **Columbia covered bridge,** which demands a photo stop. This stretch of the river valley alternately narrows and widens, and the road tunnels through forest, broken occasionally by farms, fields, and glimpses of impressive mountains. In Bloomfield (the store may or may not be open) the Grand Trunk railroad line angles east across the road, heading for Portland. Here our route turns west on Rt. 105 (it's 16 miles back to Island Pond).

For another rewarding detour, however, continue at least the mile down Rt. 102 to the wooded path (on the left) into **Brunswick Springs**, once the site of a mineral springs resort. At this sacred Abenaki site, the resort's buildings repeatedly burned; only their foundations and an eerie cement stairway leading down to the riverbank remain. Please be respectful of the property, now owned by a local Abenaki group. Water from the sulfur springs still runs from spigots. Park next to the white wooden former town hall (on your left, heading south). The road in is usually chained off. It's roughly a 15-minute walk in.

Another 4 miles south on Rt. 102 (and 5 miles in on a dirt road) brings you to **Maidstone State Park**, offering camping and swimming as well as fishing. The Connecticut River widens noticeably the farther south you drive on Rt. 102, and views of the White Mountains are increasingly dramatic. If you continue another 7 miles south to Guildhall, you are informed by a billboard-sized sign that the town was "discovered" in 1754, chartered in 1761, and settled in 1764, making it the oldest town in northeastern Vermont (by contrast, Norton was not settled until 1860). An attractive, square green is flanked by historically interesting buildings: a tiny courthouse, church, town hall (the Guild Hall, 1798), and an ornate 1909 Classical Revival library with stained-glass windows. An unassuming white-clapboard house serves as a county lockup.

Two miles downriver from Guildhall, a town road marked GRANBY runs west off Rt. 102, beginning as a paved road but becoming gravel well before reaching the tiny hamlets of Granby and Gallup Mills, about 8 miles from Rt. 102. This is wild, wooded, and boggy country, good for spotting moose and bear. Lumber camps and sawmills once peppered this area, and there was even a steam railway. The road finally descends about 8 miles west of Granby to reach Rt. 114, joining it a couple of miles north of East Burke. Take Rt. 114 some 12 miles north through rolling, mixed farm- and forestland to its junction with Rt. 105, 2 miles west of Island Pond.

fishing licenses (see *Fishing* in "What's Where" for fishing regulations). Check in the *Vermont Atlas and Gazetteer* for local access points to ponds. Rental boats, bait, and tackle are available at the sites listed under *Boating*. The pamphlet *Vermont Guide to Fishing*, prepared by the Vermont Fish and Wildlife Department, available locally, tells where to find what. **Northeast Kingdom Outfitters** (802-754-9471; www.northeastkingdomoutfitters.com), based in Lyndonville, offers fly-fishing schools as well as driftboat fishing trips and guide service on local lakes and ponds and on the Connecticut River. **Osprey Fishing Adventures** (603-922-3800; www.ospreyfishingadventures.com). Biologist Ken Hastings of Colebrook, N.H., is the fishing guru for this stretch of the river, offering, 1- and 3-day fly-fishing trips on his driftboat. Guides can also be found through the **Vermont Outdoor Guide Association** (1-800-425-8747; www.voga.org), and through local fishing-geared lodging, listed below.

In May head for the **Willoughby Falls Wildlife Management Area**. From Orleans drive east on Rt. 58 for 0.2 mile. At the BROWNINGTON sign bear left and drive 0.1 mile to the Vermont Fish and Wildlife parking area. Between the last week in April and the second week in May, wild rainbow trout climb the falls here, jumping high to clear the whitewater to reach their spawning ground. **Willoughby** is known as the prime fishing lake; check out the **Clyde River** for brook trout and landlocked salmon, the **Barton River** for trout and perch. **Lake Memphremagog** is good for smelt, smallmouth bass, and walleye, in addition to salmon and trout, but also has plenty of milfoil. **Seymour Lake** is (at this writing) milfoil-free and known for bass and lake trout. **Holland Pond** and **Echo Lake** are known for rainbow trout, and **Norton Pond** is known for fighting pike. Ice fishing is particularly popular on Memphremagog and Seymour Lake. There is a state fish hatchery in Newark; **Newark Pond** has an access and is good for yellow perch along with trout. The **Willoughby River** is known, especially in early spring, for rainbow trout, as are the **Barton** and **Black Rivers**. The **Clyde River**, acclaimed as the first river in the country to have a dam removed for environmental reasons, is known for landlocked Atlantic salmon. Lodging geared to fishermen includes **Seymour Lake Lodge** in Morgan, which offers advice and free boats to its guests, and **Quimby Country**, a self-contained resort that includes 70-acre Forest Lake, 0.5 mile from 1,200-acre Great Averill Pond, both lonely and remote but good for trout and salmon; rowboats can be rented here by the day. Also see the **Village Inn** of East Burke in the "St. Johnsbury, Craftsbury, and Burke Mountain" chapter, and check out *Green Space* as well.

GOLF **Newport Country Club** (802-334-2391), off Mount Vernon St., overlooking the lake. Eighteen holes, rentals, instruction, restaurant; Apr.–Nov.

Dufferin Heights Golf Club (819-876-2113), Stanstead, Quebec. May–Nov. Nine holes, cart rentals, restaurant.

Orleans Country Club (802-754-2333), Rt. 58, near Lake Willoughby. Apr.–Nov.; 18 holes, rentals, instruction.

Barton Golf Course (802-525-1126), Telfer Hill Rd., Barton. Apr.–Sep., 18 holes, cart rentals, low fees.

Grandad's Invitational, Newark. This nine-hole course is a local legend. Ask around for directions and leave your fee in the mailbox.

HIKING AND WALKING **Mount Pisgah** and **Mount Hor**, Lake Willoughby. Named respectively for the place where the Lord sent Moses to view the Promised Land and for the place Moses' brother Aaron died after the Lord commanded him to go there, these twin mountains, separated by a narrow stretch of lake, form Willoughby Gap. Both are within the 7,000-acre Willoughby State Forest and offer well-maintained hiking trails. Mount Pisgah (2,751 feet) on the east side of the lake (access marked from Rt. 5A) has fairly short climbs yielding spectacular views of the White Mountains; trails up Mount Hor (2,648 feet) begin on the Civilian Conservation Corps road, 1.8 miles west of its junction with Rt. 5A, and also offer panoramic views of the Green Mountains to the west. For details, consult *50 Hikes in Vermont* (Backcountry Guides) and *Day Hiker's Guide to Vermont* (Green Mountain Club).

Wheeler Mountain. The trail begins on Wheeler Mountain Rd., which leaves the north side of Rt. 5, 8.3 miles north of West Burke and 5 miles south of Barton Village. From the highway, the unpaved road climbs 1.9 miles to the trailhead.

Bald Mountain. There are excellent views from the newly restored fire tower at the summit of this, the tallest peak in the Willoughby Lake area. Trails ascend to the summit from both the north (Lookout's Trail, 2.8 miles) and the south (Long Pond Trail, 2.1 miles). From the north side of Bald Mountain, you can hike on trails and wilderness roads all the way to the summit of Mount Hor; Haystack Mountain (a side trip) has excellent views and two trails. Details can be found in *Day Hiker's Guide to Vermont* (see *Hiking and Walking* in "What's Where").

Bluff Mountain (elevation: 2,380 feet) looms over Island Pond to the north. It's a popular climb, with spectacular views. The trail starts from Rt. 114, north of the village. Inquire locally for directions.

Monadnock Mountain (elevation: 3,140 feet), in Lemington, towers over the Connecticut River and Colebrook, N.H. A trail runs west, beginning as a driveway off Rt. 102 near the bridge to Colebrook. An abandoned fire tower crowns the summit.

HORSEBACK RIDING **Perry Farm** (802-754-2396) in Brownington offers hourlong trail rides at $25 per person.

Galloping Acres Riding Stable (802-754-2337), Ticehurst Rd., Brownington. Open year-round, 10–dusk. Horseback riding through woods and fields on back roads, also wagon pulled by Belgians.

SWIMMING In Newport try **Prouty Beach**, a public facility on Lake Memphremagog. On Seymour Lake there is a public beach in Morgan Center. There are state facilities at **Brighton State Park** (802-723-9702) in Island Pond, a large beach that is sandy and shallow for quite a way out, great for children. **Crystal Lake State Beach** (802-525-6205), 90 Bellwater Ave., Barton (just east of the village off Rt. 15), is open daily late May–Sep., with lifeguard, bathhouse (built of stones quarried on the lake and built in the late 1930s by the CCC), and picnic facilities; and **Pageant Park**, a mile farther east on Rt. 16, is a town-owned park open daily until 10 PM, also with a bathhouse and camping (primarily tenting). **May Pond**, also along Rt. 16 in Barton, is a great spot for swimming, canoeing, and kayaking. **Lake Willoughby** has small public beaches at both its northern and southern tips. **Boulder Beach Day Use Area** (802-584-3820) in Groton State Forest has a public beach, picnic area, snack bar, and bathhouse.

✳ Winter Sports

CROSS-COUNTRY SKIING **North Woods Stewardship Center** (802-723-6551; www.northwoodscenter.org), 10 Mile Square Rd., East Charleston (5 miles west of Island Pond), is a 1,700-acre preserve with 40 km of groomed skiing and snowshoeing trails. Rentals and guided tours are offered.

Sugarmill Farm (1-800-688-7978), Rt. 16, Barton. Eleven km of marked trails meander through the farm; 800- to 1,400-foot elevations.

DOWNHILL SKIING See Burke Mountain and Jay Peak in their respective chapters.

SLEIGH RIDES **Perry Farm** (802-754-2396) in Brownington offers hay- and sleigh rides for groups of up to 10 people. At **Galloping Acres** (802-754-2337), Brownington Center, wagon and sleigh rides are offered.

SNOWMOBILING *Northeast Kingdom Snowmobile Map* is free from the Northeast Kingdom Chamber of Commerce (1-800-639-6379). Island Pond is the snowmobiling capital of the Kingdom, from which groomed VAST (Vermont Association of Snow Travelers: 802-229-0005) trails radiate in all directions. The local Brighton Snowmobile Club maintains a snow phone: 802-723-4316. **Kingdom Cat Corp.** (802-723-9702; www.kingdomcat.com) on Cross St. in Island Pond is the snowmobile rental operation in the area, and offers guided tours.

✳ Green Space

Note: For more information on Vermont state parks, visit www.vtstateparks.com.

Brighton State Park (802-723-4360), Island Pond, 2 miles east on Rt. 105 to State Park Rd. Open mid-May–mid-Oct. Campsites are nestled in a stand of white birch trees on Spectacle Pond: 63 tent/trailer sites, 21 lean-tos, and a rental cabin. The park includes frontage on the south shore of Island Pond, where there's a day-use area that features a sandy beach (check to make sure it's open), a bathhouse with restrooms, and rental boats. Hiking trails include a leisurely trek to Indian Point and wildlife. Watch for moose and loons.

Maidstone State Park (802-676-3930), RR 1, Box 388, Brunswick 05905. Open Memorial Day–Labor Day. Five miles south of Bloomfield on Rt. 102, then 5 miles on dirt road, this is the most remote Vermont state park and retains much of its wilderness forest of maple, beech, and hemlock. The park's camping and day-use facilities are on Maidstone Lake, one of the most pristine lakes in Vermont. It's home to lake trout, rainbow trout, and brookies. Moose sightings and the call of the loon are common. There's a beach, picnic area, picnic shelter, hiking trails, 45 tent/trailer sites, and 37 lean-tos.

NorthWoods Stewardship Center (802-723-6551; www.northwoodscenter.org), 10 Mile Square Rd., East Charleston (5 miles west of Island Pond), is a 1,700-acre preserve with 40 km of walking/skiing and snowshoeing trails. Aside from its formal nature hikes, guided canoeing, and frequent outreach programs, the center also serves as an informal clearinghouse for local canoe, fishing, tracking, and nature guides.

Bill Sladyk Wildlife Management Area, off Rt. 114, south of Norton Pond: 9,500 forested acres, also accessible via a gravel road past Holland Pond from Holland Village, 11 miles east of Derby. A detailed map is available from the Fish and Wildlife Department in Waterbury (802-241-3700).

♿ **Silvio O. Conte National Fish and Wildlife Refuge, Nulhegan Basin Division** (802-962-5240; www.nulhegan.com), 5360 Rt. 105, Brunswick. Mailing address: P.O. Box 2127, Island Pond 05846. In 1999 when the Champion International Corporation announced plans to sell its holdings in Essex County, the U.S. Fish and Wildlife Service purchased this 26,000-acre tract (roughly 10 miles in diameter) that's home to rare animals and migratory birds. The Vermont Agency of Natural Resources acquired some 22,000 adjoining acres to form the West Mountain Wildlife Management Area; another 84,000 acres surrounding these preserves continue to be logged but with easements to protect their development. Over 100 species of birds nest in the Nulhegan Basin, which is home to moose, black bear, beaver, fisher, white-tailed deer, and coyote. The Nulhegan River and its tributaries harbor brook trout, bullhead, chain pickerel, chub, and more. The refuge is open to hunting, fishing, trapping, bird-watching, and hiking. It includes 40 miles of gravel roads, 17 miles of wooded pathways, and the Mollie Beattie Bog interpretive boardwalk (handicapped accessible). No biking. Request a map.

✳ Lodging

In Newport/Derby Line
Water's Edge B&B (802-334-7726; www.watersedgebnb.com), 324 Wishing Well Ave., Newport 05855. Several miles north of downtown Newport, Pat Bryan's contemporary house sits right on the edge of Lake Memphremagog. Common space is tasteful and includes a deck. The three guest rooms include a queen room with a lake view ($75), a splendid corner queen with two windows on the lake ($90), and a suite with a sitting area and gas stove ($125). All rooms have private bath and TV. In summer guests have use of the canoe, rowboat, and dock; in winter there's snowmobile and ice-fishing access right out the front door. Bird-watching year-round. Rates include a full breakfast. Residents include two big, gentle dogs, and Shadow, a small black cat.

Garden of Edie bed & Breakfast (802-766-8116; www.gardenofedie.com), 2005 Herrick Rd., Derby 05819. High on a ridge that seems to define the border between Vermont and Quebec, with 90- to 100-mile views. This is a contemporary house with three comfortable rooms (request one with a view), shared baths, and an ebullient host who includes full breakfasts, perhaps Swedish pancakes, and afternoon specialty cakes (she is a baker) in rates of $115–120 per couple.

The Post Inn Beam Bed and Breakfast (802-766-8845; www.post innbeam.com), 1422 Herrick Rd., Derby 05819. Built as an elegant retirement retreat with an open kitchen, cathedral ceilings, and plenty of glass, southerner Margaret Ann Kerr's home is set in meadows and maples, on the edge of a working sugarbush with long views off across the Kingdom. Two upstairs guest rooms with private bath—one with a king and another with a queen—are $115 per couple; and a third, a delightful children's room, is $57 as a companion's room. A full gourmet breakfast is included.

Cliff Haven Farm Bed & Breakfast (802-334-2401; www.cliffhavenfarm bedandbreakfast.com), 5463 Lake Rd., Newport Center 05857. Jacques and Mini LeBlanc's 19th-century post-and-beam farmhouse, set in their 300 acres, overlooks Lake Memphremagog. All three guest rooms have private bath with whirlpool tub; they're also fitted with gas fireplace, antiques, TV/VCR, microwave, and small fridge. $135–175 includes a full breakfast and afternoon tea.

The Birchwood B&B (802-873-9104; www.together.net/~birchwd), 502 Main St., Derby Line 05830. Betty and Dick Fletcher's handsome 1920s village house has three spacious, antiques-furnished (the couple owns an antiques store), immaculate bedrooms with private bath: the Double Bed Chamber (antique pineapple bed), the blue-and-white Queen Canopy Chamber, and the green-and-pink Twin Bed Room. The fireplace in the formally furnished living room is frequently lit, and guests gather around the long formal dining table for full, candlelit breakfasts. $105–110 includes breakfast.

In the Barton area

Maple Manor B&B (802-525-9591; www.maple-manor.com), 77 Maple Lane, West Glover 05875. This elaborate mansion with more than a touch of fantasy is an anomaly in the surrounding farmscape, a 250-acre estate specializing in elaborate weddings. The original farmhouse has been expanded and fitted with French doors, a conservatory, and many large windows through which the light streams. Both the common rooms and three guest rooms are exuberantly decorated. $125–225 per night includes a three-course candlelit breakfast served at the formally set dining room table, overlooking the flower gardens and pool. The top floor of the equestrian barn can accommodate groups of up to 200 for wedding receptions. Sleigh rides are offered in winter.

☙ **Rodgers Country Inn** (802-525-6677; 1-800-729-1704; www.virtual vermont.com/rodgers), 582 Rodgers Rd., West Glover 05875. Not far from Shadow Lake, this 350-acre farm has been in Jim Rodgers's family since the 1800s. The farmhouse has five guest rooms sharing three baths. Common space includes an enclosed porch, living rooms, and a game room with a TV and VCR. Nancy Rodgers serves meals family-style in the large kitchen/dining area. $45 per adult, $22.50 per child under 12 ($250/$135 per week), includes an ample breakfast and dinner. B&B rates available. Snowmobilers welcome. Inquire about a rental cottage, $400 per week.

☕ ♿ **Angie's Haven** (802-754-6182; www.angies-havenbb.com), 2587 Schoolhouse Rd., Brownington 05860. This renovated 1890s farmhouse with a contemporary addition is sited on a back road, surrounded by rolling fields. Louise Evens offers three rooms, one on the ground floor that's handicapped accessible (including the bath) with twin beds and a view of Willoughby Gap ($110 double). Upstairs a suite with twin beds (which can be a king) offers this same view and has a sitting area and Jacuzzi tub ($120–130). A smaller room with a double bed also has a private bath (with shower, $90). Add $25 for a third person. Rates include a full breakfast.

On Lake Willoughby

♿ **WilloughVale Inn on Lake Willoughby** (802-525-4123; 1-800-594-9102; www.willoughvale.com), RR 2, Box 403, Westmore 05860. This special lakeside inn just keeps getting better and better. The original farmhouse/restaurant here has been replaced by a new inn, tastefully built along traditional lines with windows that maximize the spectacular lake view. It is now owned and operated by the Gameroff family, who also own the Green Mountain Inn in Stowe. Recently the size of its restaurant (see *Dining Out*) has been reduced to increase common space and add luxury suites with lake views. Guest rooms in the inn itself include three "luxury suites" with fireside Jacuzzi and private porch, one with a living/dining room and kitchen, and seven attrac-

tive rooms with private bath, phone, and TV (one handicapped accessible). There are four housekeeping cottages (one and two bedrooms) with fireplaces across the road, right on the lake. A taproom and light dinners are available; breakfast is also available for guests. Standard rooms with queen beds in the main inn begin at $85 midweek in winter and spring and $135 in summer and fall; the Lupine Room, with four-poster and Jacuzzi, ranges $129–189; weekly rates are offered. The Pisgah Cottage with a Jacuzzi, living room with fireplace, pullout sofa bed, and eat-in kitchen as well as deck and private dock is $169 midweek in low season, $229–249 in high. The other cottages are the same or slightly less, with weekly rentals in summer $1,398–1,542. Canoe, bicycle, and snowshoe rentals are available on the premises. Inquire about packages with meals and lodging, also lifts and lodging (with nearby Burke).

In Irasburg/Albany

Brick House B&B (802-754-2108), 4862 Rt. 14, Irasburg 05845. Roger and Jo Sweatt welcome you to their 1875 brick house just off the common in this small, very Vermont village. There are three guest rooms, one twin bedded (or king) with private bath, and two (one with a lace-topped canopy bed and the other with a brass bed) sharing a bath. A breakfast, which might include Jo's crustless mushroom quiche, is included in $70–80 double.

Village House Inn (802-755-6722), P.O. Box 228, Rt. 14, Albany 05820. This fine Victorian village house with a wraparound porch is a full-service inn with eight crisply decorated bedrooms (private baths) just minutes from Craftsbury Common and adjacent to the Catamount cross-country ski trail. Kate Fletcher serves a full breakfast, included in $89 per couple. Dinner is available on request (depending on the number) to guests in winter; the dining room is open to the public by reservation in summer (see *Dining Out*). Handy to VAST trails and to Craftsbury cross-country trails.

In the North Country

🐾 ❀ ✿ ♿ **Seymour Lake Lodge** (802-895-2752; www.seymourlake lodge.com), Rt. 111, Morgan 05853. Brian and Joan Du Moulin both grew up right around here (on opposite sides of the border) and maintain a casual, rustic lodge geared to fishermen and hunters. They offer nine rooms (two with private bath). A two-bedroom suite with laundry facilities, phone, TV, and fridge is handicapped accessible. Guests also have access to the kitchen (fridge, freezer, stove, microwave) and the BBQ so they can cook their own lunch and dinner. The Du Moulins also operate an antiques shop on the premises. The inn is open for winter ice fishing and snowmobiling (it's on the VAST trail). Use of canoes, kayaks, and a sailboat is free to guests, and there's a swim beach across the road. Small rental boats for fishing are available. The game room includes a TV and VCR, a Ping-Pong table, and darts, and a computer jack is available. $65–90 per couple, $10 less single and $10 per extra person, includes a continental self-serve breakfast. An apartment with wood-burning stove, sleeping up to five, is $80 single, $10 for each extra person. Children and pets welcome

Lakefront Inn & Motel (802-723-6507; www.thelakefrontinn.com),

Cross St., Island Pond 05846. A two-story motel and a main building housing the lobby and suites with one or two bedrooms (some with fireplace) in the center of the village overlooking the pond. Six of the 20 units have built-in kitchenette. A floating dock is reserved for motel guests, and a heated multibay garage is available for guests to work on servicing their snowmobiles in winter. Just across the way are public tennis courts, a beach, a picnic area, a boat launch, a lighted ice hockey rink, and a children's playground. Robert and Sharon Dexter charge $79–300 for two people in winter (high season), $10 per extra person.

Lake Salem Inn (802-766-5560; www.lakesaleminn.com), 1273 Rt. 105, Derby 05829. This attractive inn with its columned porch is set on 7 acres overlooking Lake Salem. Joe and Mo Profera offer four guest rooms, all with private bath. The spacious first-floor "library" ($125) has a queen-sized sleigh bed and a sitting area, the "Zen Room" ($115) is airy and tranquil, and both the Wyoming Room and the Hideaway have lake views and private decks ($155). Common space includes a TV, books, and games; there's a back deck and boat dock. Rates include a full breakfast, and dinner (Joe used to own an Italian restaurant) is available on request. No children, please.

In the Eastern Townships of Quebec

Some 20 miles north of Derby Line (I-93 continues in Canada as I-55) lies the village of North Hatley on Lake Massawippi. Founded in the 1770s by loyalists who moved north from New England during the Revolution, it became a fashionable resort for

☀ ♨ **Quimby Country** (802-822-5533; www.quimbycountry.com), P.O. Box 20, Averill 05901. This is one of Vermont's most historic, unusual, and appealing resorts. About as north (less than 3 miles from Canada) and as east (10 miles from New Hampshire) as you can get in the Kingdom, Quimby's first opened as a fishing lodge in 1894. Set in literally thousands of acres of woodland, it's currently a grouping of 20 cottages with woodstoves in their living rooms, each different and named for a fishing fly, plus the original

Christina Tree

QUIMBY COUNTRY

lodge with the big hearth and many of its original Adirondack-style furnishings in its book-lined common room, a, spacious old-fashioned dining room with polished wood tables, and a rocker-lined porch, all overlooking 70-acre Forest Lake. A woods path leads to 1,200-acre Great Averill Pond.

Under the management of Hortense Quimby (daughter of the founder), this evolved into a family-oriented resort, attracting an elite following so fiercely loyal that on Miss Quimby's death in the1960s, a number of regulars formed a corporation to buy it and perpetuate its special ambience. Thanks to innkeeper Joanie Binns, who has been at Quimby's one way or another for 30 years, newcomers quickly feel as welcome as multigenerationers. When the place is in full operation, late June–late Aug., the staff top two dozen and guests are limited to 70. All three meals are served. There's a supervised children's program for ages 6–15, as well as a full program of family-inclusive happenings such as picnics on a remote beach and sunset cookouts and music at "The Rocks" on Big Averill. Amenities include kayaks, cameos and sailboats, a tennis court, playground, and rec hall. Rates are $145–167 per adult, $65–96 per child depending on age

and week, including all three meals and the kids' program which offers swimming, hiking, overnight camping, and rainy-day activities. Reasonable rates during spring fishing season (May 10–June 27), and again Aug. 30–foliage season, when cottages are available on a housekeeping basis and it's quiet enough to hear the leaves fall. This is a great place for birders, walkers, good conversation, and family reunions.

Christina Tree

wealthy (American) southerners, who sold their summer homes in "Yankee-land" after the Civil War. In 1900 there were 15 summer hotels here, one with 365 rooms. The village with its lakeside shops, cafés, and walk-way, is charming, but the real draw presently consists of two competing inns, both built as private mansions and among the most highly rated in Canada. Both are dining destinations revered for their French haute cui-sine and extensive wine cellars. If you can't stay the night, come for lunch (but reserve), driving through a rolling, pastoral landscape that's simi-lar to yet distinctly different from Ver-mont. We recommend the drive from the Norton or Beecher Falls cross-ings, via rural roads. Given the Cana-dian exchange rate, a meal or night here represents outstanding value. In winter the region is known for both alpine and cross-country skiing. Tourism Quebec offers detailed infor-mation about the Eastern Townships at www.easterntownships.org.

Hovey Manor (819-842-2421; 1-800-661-2412; www.hoveymanor.com), 575 Hovey Rd., North Hatley, Quebec, Canada J0B 2C0. A pillared southern-style lakeside mansion built in 1900 by the president of Georgia Power, set in 25 acres with lovely English gardens. The Stafford family have owned and operated it as an inn since 1979. The 40 guest rooms—divided among the original mansion, icehouse, pump house, electric house, and care-taker's residence—vary in size and decor, but most have lake views, many with fireplace, Jacuzzi, and balcony. Amenities include two beaches, a lakeside pool, access to kayaks and sailboats, and cross-country ski trails. Dining is central here. In addition to

the formal dining room, a fireside pub is the venue for lunch, served in-sea-son on the lakeside terrace. $290–610 MAP per couple (Canadian). Winter packages from $125 U.S. per person.

Auberge Hatley (819-842-2451; 1-800-336-2451; www.aubergehatley .com), 325 Chemin Virgin, North Hat-ley, Quebec, Canada J0B 2C0. The feel in this much-expanded vintage-1903 mansion (25 guest rooms when we stayed here in 2005; an additional 18 were planned) is more formal than that of its rival. It's set way up a hill-side with a pool and stunning views down the lake from the dining room and terrace, but a less easy access to its private beach. A member of Relais & Châteaux; the focus is on serious gastronomy; a vineyard is planned. Request a room with a view. $340–640 per couple MAP in winter, $430–690 in summer (Canadian). Winter pack-ages from $125 U.S. per person.

Note: Summer rental cottages are listed with the Newport and Barton Chambers of Commerce. See *Guidance.*

CAMPGROUNDS See **Brighton State Park** and **Maidstone State Park** in *Green Space.*

✳ Where to Eat

DINING OUT *Note:* Canada's Hovey Manor and Auberge Hatley (see *Lodging*) represent this area's destina-tion dining. Check their web sites for current menus.

Lago Trattoria (802-334-8222; www .lagotrattoria.com), 95 Main St., New-port. Open Tue.–Sun. from 5 PM. Chef-owner Frank Richardi claims not to fry anything except calamari, a departure for downtown Newport, as is the sophisticated modern Italian decor. The menu includes pastas and staples like chicken Marsala and cacciatore. Try the semi-boned, slowly roasted duck with apricot glaze, served with butternut squash ravioli, maple-roasted root vegetables, and marinated beans. Pizzas from $9, otherwise entrées $14.25–19.50. Also see *Eating Out* for Lago Express.

◈ **Eastside** (802-334-2340), 47 Landing St., Newport. Open for lunch and dinner weekdays, breakfast too on weekends. A large old landmark with a seasonal outdoor deck and dock. The reasonably priced lunch menu might include lamb stew and biscuits or grilled chicken salad. The night's special might be marinated center-cut pork chop, deep-fried oysters, or Yankee pot roast. The salad bar can be a meal in itself. Many locals come just for dessert (try the pecan ribbon). Live entertainment Fri. and Sat. Dinner entrées $13.95–19.95. Children's menu.

WilloughVale Inn (802-525-2123; www.willoughvale.com), Rt. 5A, Westmore. Open nightly in July and Aug. and Labor Day–Columbus Day; Thu.–Sat. during the Christmas and ice-fishing seasons, but call to check. The Willoughby Room and less formal Tap Room both overlook Lake Willoughby, and the food is fine. Begin with New England crabcakes and dine on apple and cheddar stuffed chicken, eggplant parmigiana with wild mushroom ravioli, or filet mignon wrapped in bacon. Entrées $15.95–22.95. You can always also get a burger or turkey sandwich.

◈ **Quimby Country** (802-822-5533; www.quimbycountry.com), off Rt. 114, Averill (see *Lodging*). Open by reservation to nonguests, last week of

June–last week in Aug., serving a very full breakfast ($10) and a generous, delicious dinner (BYOB) featuring fresh, local produce, on-premises daily baking, and a limited menu as well as weekly lobster bakes ($30). Children's menu.

The Village House Inn & Restaurant (802-755-6722), Rt. 14, Albany. Open late June–Aug. by reservation. Kate Fletcher offers a limited but dependable and reasonably priced menu. You might begin with butternut squash soup, then dine on pork escallops sautéed with lemon, capers, and white wine.

EATING OUT

In and around Newport
Lago Express (802-334-8649; www.lagotrattoria.com), 95 Main St., Newport. Open weekdays 10–5, Sat. 10–4. A new extension of the area's most popular restaurant (see *Dining Out*), this café and gourmet market has an extensive sandwich and (hot and cold) deli menu, featuring homemade eggplant topped with mozzarella and tomato sauce, sweet stuffed peppers, Italian sausage, lasagna layered with six kinds of imported cheese, veggie ravioli, and the like. Café sidewalk seating, weather permitting.

The Brown Cow (802-334-7887), 900 East Main St., Newport, open daily 6 AM–2 PM except Sunday. This is a nice spot to linger over breakfast (served all day); sandwich and salad lunches, reasonably priced dinners. Homemade ice cream on homemade pie.

Newport Natural Foods Café (802-334-2626), 194 Main St., Newport. Open Mon.–Sat. 9–5 (until 6 Fri.), Sun. 10–4. This vegetarian's oasis is hidden in the rear of an extensive health food store, good for smoked tempeh, chickenless chicken salad, cream cheese wraps, and a variety of soups, also a good salad bar and wholesome baked goods.

Derby Cow Palace (802-766-4724), Main St. (Rt. 5), Derby. Open at noon on weekends, from 3 PM weekdays. This is the most recent venture for Doug Nelson, owner of the largest local dairy operation and of Cow Town Elk Ranch. Needless to say, the pleasant log restaurant specializes in beef, from burgers to prime rib. Fully licensed, with a bar menu.

La Vielle Douane (819-876-2776), 232 Dufferin, Stanstead, Quebec. Literally "the old customs" house, steps across the border from Derby Line, this is your standard Greek eatery featuring souvlaki and pizza, but it has a full family restaurant menu and it's fun to order "truite arc-en-ciel" instead of rainbow trout. Fully licensed.

Morgan Country Store (802-895-2726), Rt. 111, Morgan Center. A genuine general store with a pay phone (few cell phones work around here), post office, live bait, and an extensive breakfast, lunch (burgers, sandwiches, salads), and pizza menu.

Martha's Diner (802-754-6800), Rts. 5/14, Coventry. Open Mon.–Fri. 5 AM–2 PM, Sat. 5–1, Sun. 6–noon. A classic chrome diner with classic diner food.

In Island Pond and beyond

🍴 ♪ **Jennifer's Restaurant** (802-723-6135), Cross St. Open daily for breakfast, lunch, and dinner, with a children's menu. The town's gathering spot, a cheery restaurant known for good food, especially seafood. Hearty

breakfast sandwiches; roast turkey and surf and turf for dinner. Beer and wine served.

Friendly Pizza (802-723-4616), 31 Derby St. (Rt. 105). Closed Mon., otherwise open from 11 until at least 9 PM. John Koxarakis offers a wide variety of pizzas, also steaks, spaghetti, sandwiches, grinders, and Greek salad, in his small eatery on the southern fringe of the village.

DeBanville's General Store (802-962-3311), 47 Rt. 105, Bloomfield. Open Sun.–Wed. 8–8, Thu.–Sat. 8–9. A glorious big, new general store in this lonely junction (just above Brunswick Springs) is a source of subs, wraps, and deli items.

In Canaan

🍴 ♪ **Bessie's Diner** (802-266-3310), 166 Gale St. Open weekdays except Mon. from 6, Sat. from 7, and Sun. from 8; closes at 8 every night. Admittedly we're suckers for cheap and friendly, but Vernon and Bonnie Crawford's place is so pleasant and wholesome—ditto for the food—that we can't rave enough. On our last visit we went for the "gobbler": turkey, cream cheese, cranberry, and lettuce. The menu includes burgers, 30 different kinds of sandwiches, open-faced bagel-wiches (try the Grump-Fish), subs, and wraps. Poutines (Quebec-style french fries with gravy and cheese curds) are a specialty, and a wide and reasonably priced choice is available at dinner. Service is fast and friendly. Wine and beer.

Cow Licks, an ice cream window, operates summers.

In Lake Willoughby

Kingdom Cookin' Restaurant and Mr. Bear's Bar (802-525-4347), 280 Rt. A, Westmore. Open Tue.–Fri.

11–3 and 5–9, later Sat. Lunch sandwiches and soups, full dinner menu. Specialties include sausage, peppers, mushrooms, and onions in a homemade bread bowl, maple pecan pork chops, and buttermilk fried chicken.

Northern Exposure (802-525-3789), Rt. 5A, Westmore on Lake Willoughby. Open Mon.–Sat. 6 AM–9 PM, Sun. 8–8; in winter, weekdays 6–6, Sat. 7–6, Sun. 8–6. A general store with a deli good for grinders, steak-and-cheese, chili, and soup of the day. In summer the ice cream shop features Hershey's.

In the Barton area

Candlepin Restaurant (802-525-6513), Rt. 5 north of Barton. Open daily for all three meals. Just minutes off I-91, a big, friendly place with booths, known for seafood specialties and staples like Vermont roast turkey and homemade pie; beer and wine served.

✳ Entertainment

&. **Haskell Opera House** (819-873-3020), Derby Line. This splendid vintage-1904 theater has perfect acoustics, three antique sets, a rare roll-up curtain depicting scenes of Venice, and a rococo interior. Its season runs late Apr.–mid-Oct. and includes performances by a resident theater company, opera, and dance, and a variety of outstanding concerts.

QNEK Productions (802-334-8145), the summer resident theater company at the Haskell, offers reasonably priced evening and matinee productions of musicals and other stock Broadway hits. Tickets for opera house performances are also available at the Woodknot Bookshop, Newport (802-334-6720).

Bread and Puppet Theater Museum (802-525-3031), Rt. 122, Glover. The internationally known Bread and Puppet Theater with its huge and haunting puppet dwarfs, giants, and devils performs Sundays in July and Aug. at 3 PM outdoors; inquire about Friday-night performances in the timber-frame theater. Also see *To See.*

Waterfront Cinemas (802-334-6572), 137 Waterfront Plaza, Newport. First-run films on three screens.

✳ Selective Shopping

Bogner Factory Outlet (802-334-0135), 150 Main St., Newport. Looking more like a boutique than the outlet it is—for the nationally known ski- and sportswear partially made in town.

Woodknot Books (802-334-6720), 137 Main St., Newport. Open 9–5 except Sun., Fri. until 6. A good selection of books and magazines.

The Great Outdoors (802-334-2851), 177 Main St., Newport. In summer the store features an extensive array of fishing gear and sells fishing licenses; four-season sporting goods. Rental bikes, kayaks, and canoes, also rental in-line skates, snowshoes, cross-country skis, and snowboards.

Country Thyme (802-766-2852; 1-800-334-7905; www.countrythyme vermont.com), 60 Rt. 111, Derby (near the junction of Rts. 111 and 5). Every inch of the ground floor in Kay Courson's house is crammed with gifts, toys, specialty foods, Christmas decorations, and more.

In Island Pond

Simon the Tanner (802-723-4452), Cross and Main Sts. Open daily except Sat., closing at 3 on Fri.,

STEVE STACEY'S "CHISEL & SAW"
CREATIONS, ISLAND POND

Christina Tree

otherwise 9–5, until 8 on Thu. This is an unlikely spot for such a huge shoe store, but here it is selling a wide variety of name-brand shoes—Birkenstock and Clarks sandals, Dansko and Stegmann clogs, Doc Martens, work boots, winter boots, Tubbs snowshoes, and a big selection of athletic shoes, all at below-usual prices. There's also a bargain basement. Candles, specialty food, wrought iron, natural soaps, and body care products made by the Twelve Tribes, an international sect that rooted in Island Pond several decades ago, restoring a number of houses and winning the respect of the community.

Chisel & Saw (802-723-4915), Rt. 114, Island Pond. Steve Stacey's colorful chain-saw carvings fill his roadside garden. The dancing bears, Buddhas, and Merlins are all for sale; visitors welcome.

In the Barton–Glover–Irasburg area

Currier's Quality Market (802-525-8822), Glover. Open year-round daily, Mon.–Sat. 6–9, Sun. 9–6. James and

Gloria Currier's general store is a must-stop if just to see the 948-pound (stuffed) moose and variety of formerly live animals lurking in the aisles and festooned from the rafters in this old-style emporium. In addition to staples and a good deli counter with hot specials, this is a major sporting goods store, selling fishing and hunting licenses and stocking extensive gear.

Evansville Trading Post (802-754-6305), Rt. 58 between Orleans and Lake Willoughby. Open early May–Oct. A crafts cooperative for Clan of the Hawk, the local Abenaki Indian band. The 39-acre tribal grounds are the scene of a big powwow the first weekend in August and a crafts show the last week in July.

Steffi's Studio (802-754-6012), Irasburg green. Steffi Huess crafts gold and silver jewelry, and sells it along with other local arts and crafts right from the front room in her home.

Labour of Love Gardens (802-525-6695), Rt. 16, Glover Village. An acre of public gardens is behind the house, on the Barton River, mid-May until frost, plus antiques and crafts.

Lake Parker Country Store (802-525-6985; 1-800-893-6985), Main St., West Glover. By Lake Parker. Good for basics plus sandwiches and baked goods. This is a prime outlet for prizewinning Bonnie View Farm sheep cheese, made in nearby South Albany.

Sugarmill Farm Maple Museum (802-525-3701), Rt. 16 south of Barton Village. Mid-Mar.–mid-Nov. The Auger family sells their own syrup; sugar-on-snow in-season.

Sugarwoods Farm (802-525-3718), 2287) Rt. 16, Glover. Open May–Sep., 8–4:30; Feb.–Apr., Sat. 8–1. A major outlet for maple syrup, candy, and sugaring equipment.

In Averill

Lakeview Store (802-822-5570), Rt. 114, Averill. Open daily 8–7. A no-nonsense general store except for the fabulous wools and some handcrafted items: bowls, sweaters, baskets, also weaving supplies. Pick a fleece at nearby Swanson Oldfarm and the store's owner, Priscilla Roy, will spin it.

✳ Special Events

February: **Newport Winter Carnival**. **Island Pond Snowmobile Races**.

March: **Sugaring** throughout the region.

June: **Antique Gas/Steam Engine Show** at the Old Stone House Museum in Brownington (www.oldstone housemuseum.org).

July: **Memphremagog International Aquafest**—a swim race from Newport to Magog in Canada (32 miles), also a waterskiing tournament, parade, public suppers, and more.

August: **Orleans County Arts and Crafts Fair** (*first Saturday*) in Barton (802-334-7325); **International Car Show** in Newport (802-334-6079); **Orleans County Fair** (*last week*; 802-525-555) in Barton, an old-fashioned event at the extensive fairground—horse, pony, and ox pulling, harness racing, stage shows, demo derby, tractor pull, arts, crafts, and agricultural exhibits. **Clan of the Hawk Pow Wow** at the Evansville Trading Post (see *Selective Shopping*). **Old Stone House Day**—open house, picnic lunch, crafts demonstrations at the museum in Brownington Village (www.oldstonehousemuseum .org). **North Country Moose Festival** (*last week*)—based in Colebrook, N.H., a series of colorful events on both sides of the Connecticut River.

CURRIER'S GENERAL STORE, GLOVER

Christina Tree

INDEX

W

Continued on next page

Continued from previous page